Contents

Colour section 1

Introduction 6
Where to go 8
When to go 12
Things not to miss 15

Basics 25

Getting there 27
Getting around 32
Accommodation 37
Food and drink 40
The media 43
Festivals 44
Outdoor activities 46
Spectator sports 49
Travel essentials 51

Guide 59

1. Toronto 61
2. Ontario 105
3. Montréal and Southwest Québec 209
4. Québec City and Northern Québec 267
5. The Maritime Provinces..... 355
6. Newfoundland and Labrador 445
7. The Prairie Provinces .... 50[illegible]
8. The Canadian Rockies 603
9. The BC Interior.................. 697
10. Vancouver and Vancouver Island 743
11. The North.......................... 863

Contexts 947

History 949
The natural environment 962
Books 970

Language 977

Québecois French.................. 979

Travel store 987

Small print & Index 991

Wild Canada colour section following p.408

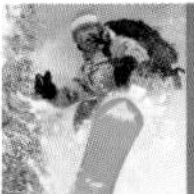

Skiing and snow-boarding colour section following p.728

◀◀ The Art Gallery of Ontario, Toronto ◀ Jasper National Park, Alberta

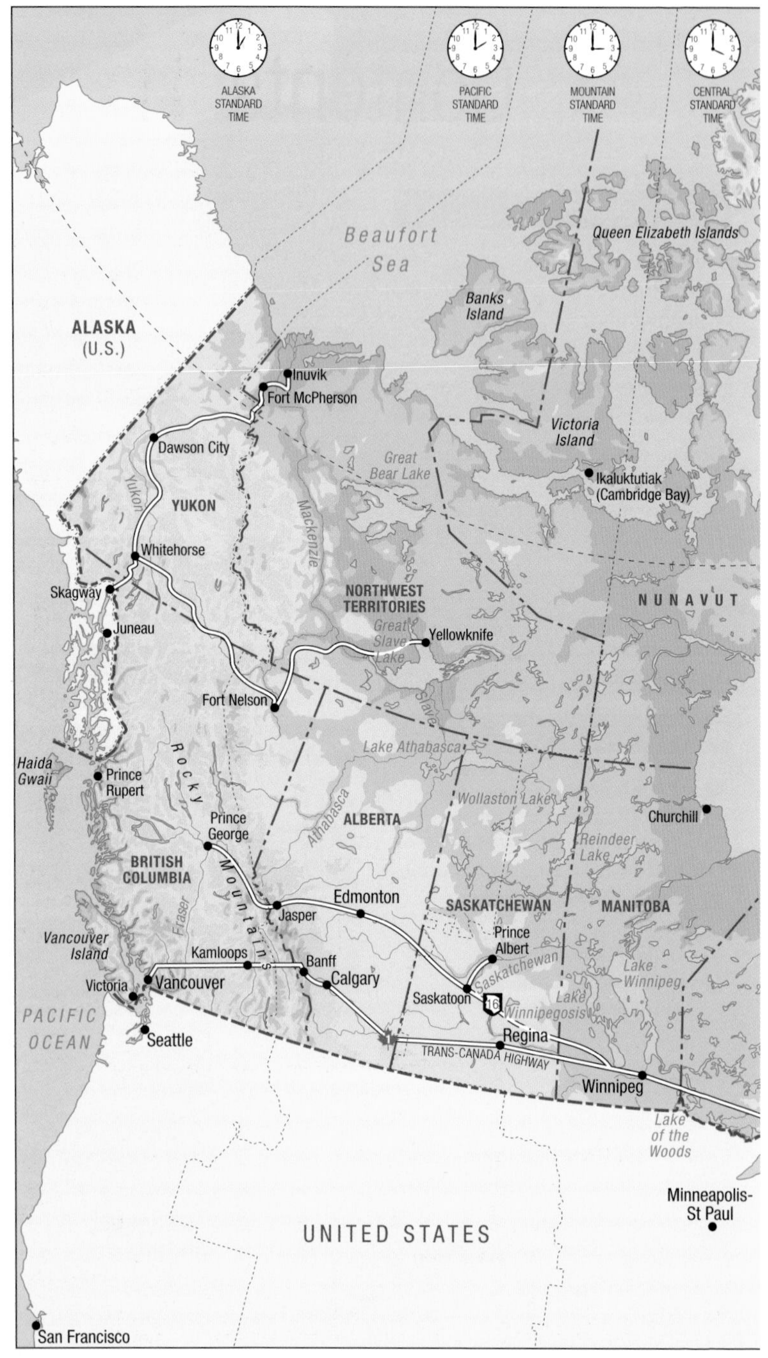
ALASKA STANDARD TIME
PACIFIC STANDARD TIME
MOUNTAIN STANDARD TIME
CENTRAL STANDARD TIME
Beaufort Sea
Queen Elizabeth Islands
Banks Island
ALASKA (U.S.)
Inuvik
Fort McPherson
Victoria Island
Dawson City
Great Bear Lake
Ikaluktutiak (Cambridge Bay)
Yukon
YUKON
Mackenzie
Whitehorse
Skagway
NORTHWEST TERRITORIES
NUNAVUT
Juneau
Great Slave Lake
Yellowknife
Fort Nelson
Slave
Lake Athabasca
Haida Gwaii
Prince Rupert
Rocky Mountains
Wollaston Lake
Churchill
Prince George
Athabasca
ALBERTA
Reindeer Lake
BRITISH COLUMBIA
Edmonton
SASKATCHEWAN
MANITOBA
Jasper
Fraser
Vancouver Island
Prince Albert
Kamloops
Banff
Saskatchewan
Lake Winnipeg
Calgary
Victoria
Vancouver
Saskatoon
16
Lake Winnipegosis
PACIFIC OCEAN
Seattle
1
Regina
TRANS-CANADA HIGHWAY
Winnipeg
Lake of the Woods
Minneapolis-St Paul
UNITED STATES
San Francisco

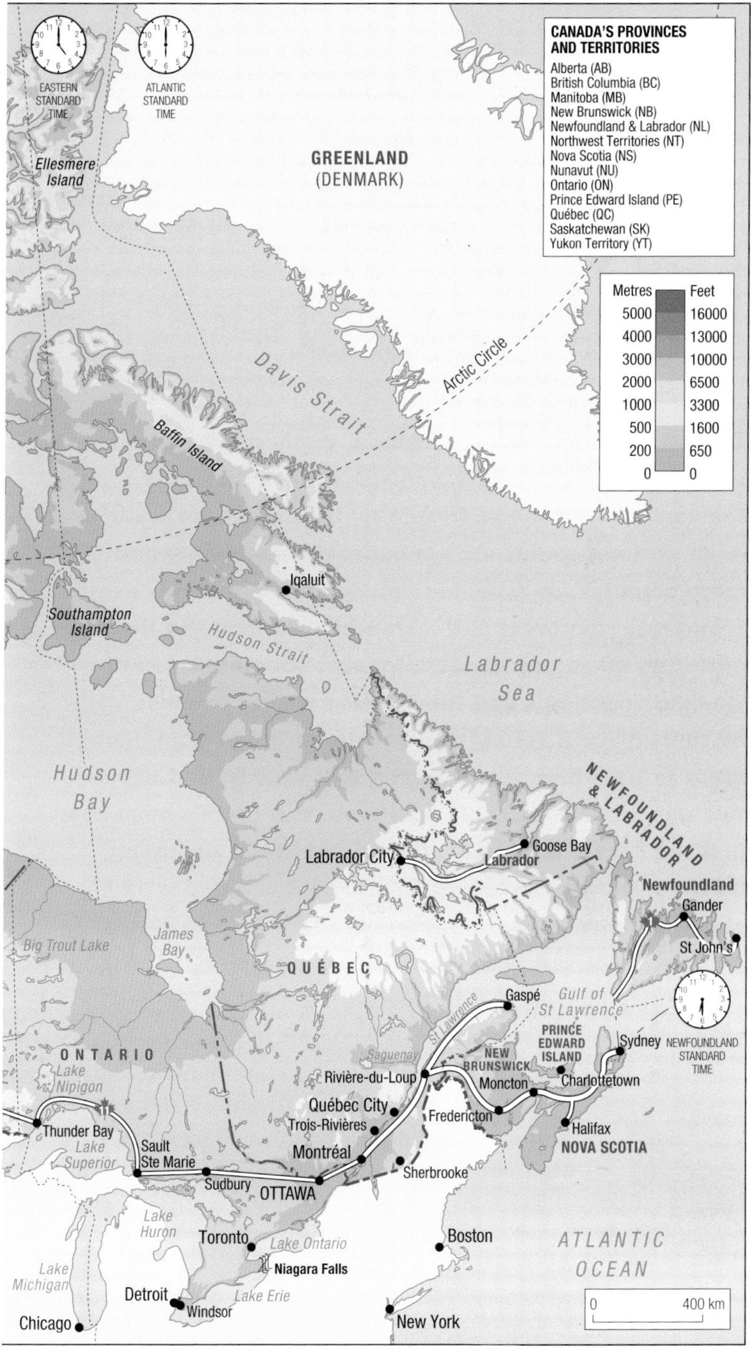

EASTERN STANDARD TIME
ATLANTIC STANDARD TIME
CANADA'S PROVINCES AND TERRITORIES
Alberta (AB)
British Columbia (BC)
Manitoba (MB)
New Brunswick (NB)
Newfoundland & Labrador (NL)
Northwest Territories (NT)
Nova Scotia (NS)
Nunavut (NU)
Ontario (ON)
Prince Edward Island (PE)
Québec (QC)
Saskatchewan (SK)
Yukon Territory (YT)
Metres
Feet
5000
16000
4000
13000
3000
10000
2000
6500
1000
3300
500
1600
200
650
0
0
GREENLAND
(DENMARK)
Ellesmere Island
Davis Strait
Arctic Circle
Baffin Island
Iqaluit
Southampton Island
Hudson Strait
Labrador Sea
Hudson Bay
NEWFOUNDLAND & LABRADOR
Labrador City
Goose Bay
Labrador
Newfoundland
Gander
St John's
Big Trout Lake
James Bay
QUÉBEC
Gaspé
Gulf of St Lawrence
St Lawrence
NEWFOUNDLAND STANDARD TIME
Sydney
PRINCE EDWARD ISLAND
NEW BRUNSWICK
Charlottetown
Moncton
ONTARIO
Lake Nipigon
Saguenay
Rivière-du-Loup
Québec City
Trois-Rivières
Fredericton
Halifax
NOVA SCOTIA
Thunder Bay
Lake Superior
Sault Ste Marie
Montréal
Sherbrooke
Sudbury
OTTAWA
Lake Huron
Toronto
Lake Ontario
Boston
ATLANTIC OCEAN
Niagara Falls
Lake Michigan
Detroit
Windsor
Lake Erie
New York
Chicago
0
400 km

Introduction to Canada

The home of ice hockey, caribou, lumberjacks, igloos and maple syrup, right? Well, yes – but that's just scratching the surface of Canada. In reality, it's one of the world's most striking countries, a mixture of raw beauty and more complex, unexpected landscapes including desert, temperate rainforest and lush orchards. Add the Rockies' glittering lakes and majestic peaks, spectacular fjord-slashed coastlines and the rippling prairie expanse with all the sky for a ceiling and you've got more than enough room to truly lose yourself (and the crowds) and explore this almost unimaginably vast land. But there's more than just the "great outdoors". Canada's cities – charming Québec, trendy Vancouver, cosmopolitan Toronto and stylish Montréal among them – are rich with historical and cultural treasures and populated by a diverse, friendly and engagingly modest mix of people.

Bounded by the Atlantic and Pacific oceans on its east and west, Canada stretches from a southern latitude similar to Rome's up to the northern reaches of the Arctic Ocean – an area the United Kingdom could fit into 41 times over. Much of this expanse is sparsely inhabited and the majority of Canadians live in its southern half, relatively close to the border with the US. Like its neighbour to the south, Canada is a spectrum of cultures, a hotchpotch of immigrant groups who supplanted the continent's many aboriginal peoples. But whereas citizens of the US are encouraged to perceive themselves as Americans above all else,

Canada's official policy of multiculturalism has fostered an ethnic mosaic where, alongside the majorities of British and French descent, Chinese, Ukrainian, Indian, Haitian, Italian, Greek, Ethiopian and many other communities maintain the traditions of their homelands.

For the visitor, the mix that results from this mostly exemplary tolerance is an exhilarating experience, offering such widely differing cultural, artistic and culinary experiences as Vancouver's huge Chinatown, the Inuit heartlands of the far north, the austere religious enclaves of Manitoba or the Celtic-tinged warmth of the Maritimes.

Yet some Canadians are often troubled by the lack of a clear self-image, tending to emphasize the ways in which their country is different from the US as a means of self-description. The

Fact file

- Canada, the second-largest country in the world, covers almost ten million square kilometers, a quarter of which is the Inuit homeland of Nunavut.
- Canada extends across six time zones and shares a border of 8900km with the US. The highest point is Mount Logan (5959m).
- The population is almost 33 million, with an average life expectancy at birth of 80 years. Almost a half claim British ancestry, a quarter French ancestry and just under a million (3.3 percent) claim aboriginal ancestry.
- Canada is a confederation comprising ten provinces and three territories. It has been self-governing since 1867, but retains ties to Britain: the Canadian head of state is Queen Elizabeth II.
- Canada's colossal natural resources help put it among the world's top-ten richest countries. Almost two-thirds of its power is hydroelectric, and it's one of the few developed nations that is a net exporter of energy.

▲ Cove Island, Fathom Five National Marine Park, Ontario

question "What is a Canadian?" continues to linger, with the on-again, off-again and always acrimonious debate over Québec's secession, but ultimately there can be no simple characterization of a people whose country is not so much a single nation as it is a committee on a continental scale. Pierre Berton, one of Canada's finest writers, wisely ducked the issue: A Canadian, he quipped, is "someone who knows how to make love in a canoe".

Despite this balancing act, one thing is clear: Canadians have an overwhelming sense of pride in their history, their culture and the awe-inspiring beauty of their land. Indeed, Canada embraces all this – as well as its own clichés – with an energy that's irresistible.

Where to go

The time and expense involved in covering Canada's immense distances means most visitors confine their trips to the area around one of the main cities – usually Toronto, Montréal, Vancouver or Calgary for arrivals by air. These centres are all culturally rich but still vary widely in what they offer; the one thing they have in common, along with all other Canadian cities, is that they are within easy reach of the great outdoors.

Canada's most southerly region, south **Ontario**, contains not only the country's manufacturing heart and its largest city, **Toronto**, but also **Niagara Falls**, the premier tourist sight. North of Toronto there's the far less packaged scenic attraction of **Georgian Bay**, a beautiful waterscape of pine-studded islets set against crystal-blue waters. Like the forested Algonquin park, the bay is also accessible from the Canadian capital, **Ottawa** – not as dynamic a city as Toronto, but still well worth a stay for its galleries, museums and handful of superb restaurants.

▲ The National Gallery of Canada, Ottawa

Québec, set apart by the depth of its French tradition, focuses on its biggest city, **Montréal**, which is for many

▲ Legendary music venue Les Foufones Electriques, Montréal

people the most vibrant place in the country, a fascinating mix of old-world style and commercial dynamism.

The pace of life is more relaxed in the historic provincial capital **Québec City**, and more easygoing still in the villages dotted along the St Lawrence lowlands, where glittering spires attest to the enduring influence of the Catholic Church.

For something more bracing, you could continue north to **Tadoussac**, where whales can be seen near the mouth of the splendid **Saguenay Fjord** – and if you're really prepared for the wilds, forge on to **Labrador**, as inhospitable a zone as you'll find in the east.

Across the mouth of the St Lawrence River, the pastoral **Gaspé Peninsula** – the easternmost part of Québec – borders **New Brunswick**, a mild-mannered introduction to the three **Maritime Provinces**, whose people have long been dependent on timber and the sea for their livelihood. Here, the tapering **Bay of Fundy** boasts amazing tides – rising and falling by nine metres or more – and superb maritime landscapes, while the region's tiny fishing villages are at their most beguiling near **Halifax**, the busy capital of **Nova Scotia** and a fascinating meeting place of former British and French cultures. Perhaps even prettier, and certainly more austere, are the land and seascapes of **Cape Breton Island**, whose rugged topography anticipates that of the island of **Newfoundland** to the north. Newfoundland's isolation has spawned a distinctive culture that's at its most lively in **St John's**, where the local folk-music scene is Canada's best. The island also boasts some of the Atlantic seaboard's finest landscapes, particularly the flat-topped peaks and glacier-gouged lakes of Gros Morne National Park.

Back on the mainland, separating Ontario from Alberta and the Rockies, the prairie provinces of **Manitoba** and **Saskatchewan** have a reputation for dullness that's unfair: even in the flat southern parts there's the diversion of **Winnipeg**, whose traces of its early days make it a good place to break a trans-Canadian journey. Numerous lakes and gigantic forests offer magnificent canoeing and hiking and in the far north, beside Hudson Bay, **Churchill** – remote, but accessible by train – is famous for its polar bears, beluga whales and easy viewing of the Northern Lights.

Moving west, the wheatfields of **Alberta** ripple into ranching country on the approach to the **Canadian Rockies**, whose reputation for natural drama is more than borne out by the reality. The province's two main cities,

Aboriginal peoples

The British and French were latecomers to Canada, a country that for thousands of years was home to a vast aboriginal population. Today, almost a million Canadians claim descent from these first peoples, from the so-called "Indians" of the central and western heartlands, to the Inuit, inhabitants of the great sweep of Canada's north. A third group, the Métis – descendants of mixed unions of white and aboriginal people – also have a distinct identity, part of a rich cultural, social and artistic mosaic that provides a beguiling complement to the mainstream. You'll find evidence of Canada's former aboriginal life in many museums and galleries, and plenty of areas nurturing living aboriginal cultures, though there's no escaping the fact that many aboriginal people are among the most marginalized of Canadians.

Hoodoos in Drumheller, Alberta

Edmonton and **Calgary**, have both grown fat on the region's oil and gas fields, and provide useful springboards for trips into the mountains – most popularly to the resorts of **Banff**, **Lake Louise** and **Jasper**. Calgary also offers access to one of Canada's most fascinating – and seemingly incongruous – landscapes, the hoodoo-ridden Badlands.

Further west **British Columbia** embodies the popular picture of Canada to perfection: a land of snow-capped summits, rivers and forests, pioneer villages, gold-rush ghost towns, and some of the greatest hiking, skiing, fishing and canoeing in the world. Its urban focus, **Vancouver**, is the country's third largest city, known for its spectacular natural setting, fabulous food and a laidback West Coast hedonism. Off the coast lies **Vancouver Island**, a microcosm of the province's immense natural riches and home to **Victoria**, a devotedly anglophile little city. It's also well worth journeying over to the island's west coast to take in the rugged beauty of Pacific Rim National Park's **Long Beach** and **Clayoquot Sound**.

North of British Columbia, wedged alongside Alaska, is the **Yukon Territory**, half grandiose mountains, half sub-arctic tundra, and full of evocative echoes of the Klondike gold rush. **Whitehorse**, its capital, and **Dawson City**, a gold-rush relic, are the major towns here, each accessed by dramatic frontier highways. The **Northwest Territories** and **Nunavut**, covering the Canadian Arctic, are an immensity of forest, lakes, tundra and ice, the realm of Dene and Inuit aboriginal peoples, whose traditional way of life is being threatened as oil and gas exploration reaches ever-northwards. Roads are virtually non-existent in the deep north, and only the frontier city of **Yellowknife**, plus a handful of ramshackle villages, offer the air links and resources necessary to explore this wilderness.

When to go

Canada's climate is hugely varied, but it's a safe generalization to say the areas near the coast or the Great Lakes have milder winters and cooler summers than the interior. **July and August** are reliably warm throughout the country, even in the far north, making these the busiest months to visit. **November to March** is an ordeal of sub-zero temperatures almost everywhere except on the west coast, though winter days in many areas are clear and dry, and all large Canadian towns are geared to the challenge of cold conditions, with covered walkways and indoor malls protecting their inhabitants from the worst of the weather.

The **Maritime Provinces** and **eastern Canada** have four distinct seasons: chill, snowy winters; short, mild springs; warm summers (which are shorter and colder in northern and inland regions); and long, crisp autumns. Summer is the key season in the resorts, though late September and October, particularly in New Brunswick, are also popular for the autumn colours. Coasts year-round can be blanketed in mist or fog.

In **Ontario** and **Québec** the seasons are also marked and the extremes intense, with cold, damp and grey winters in southern Ontario (drier and colder in Québec) and a long temperate spring from about April to June.

Long Beach, Pacific Rim National Park, British Columbia

Summers can be hot, but often uncomfortably humid, with the cities often empty of locals but full of visitors. The long autumn can be the best time to visit, with equable temperatures and few crowds.

The central provinces of **Manitoba**, **Saskatchewan** and **Alberta** experience the country's wildest climatic extremes, suffering the longest, harshest winters but also some of the finest, clearest summers, punctuated by fierce thunderstorms. Winter skiing brings a lot of people to the **Rockies**, but summer is still the busiest time, when July and August offer the best walking weather and the least chance of rain – though this often falls in heavy downpours, the mirror of winter's raging blizzards.

The southwestern parts of **British Columbia** enjoy some of Canada's best weather: the extremes are less marked and the overall temperatures generally milder than elsewhere. Much of the province, though, bears the brunt of Pacific depressions, so this is one of the country's damper regions: visiting between late spring and early autumn offers the best chance of missing the rain.

Across the **Yukon**, the **Northwest Territories** and **Nunavut** winters are bitterly cold, with temperatures rarely above freezing for months on end, though precipitation year-round

Epic journeys

A country the size of Canada lends itself to epic journeys. Travelling by car or bus, you can enjoy some of the world's greatest wilderness drives, from the Icefields Parkway through the heart of the Rockies to routes that push some of North America's last frontiers: the Alaska and Cassiar highways in British Columbia, for example, or the Dempster Highway in the Yukon, the only public road on the continent to cross the Arctic Circle. Trains also offer superlative rides, whether it's the northbound route to Churchill or the classic transcontinental odyssey from Toronto to Vancouver. At sea, ferries also ply routes that provide a dramatic window on glorious scenery, none more so than the boats running up the Inside Passage from Vancouver Island towards Alaska.

◄ Cold-weather fun at Québec City's Winter Carnival

is among the country's lowest. Summers are short but surprisingly warm. Spring – though late – can produce outstanding displays of wild flowers across the tundra.

Average temperatures and snowfall

	Jan	Feb	Mar	Apr	May	Jun	Jul	Aug	Sep	Oct	Nov	Dec
Calgary, AB												
Max/min °C	-3/-16	-1/-12	3/-8	11/-2	17/3	21/7	23/9	23/9	17/4	13/-1	3/-9	-2/-14
Max/min °F	26/4	31/10	38/17	51/28	62/37	69/45	74/49	73/48	63/39	55/30	37/16	28/6
Precipitation (mm)	13	10	15	25	53	76	71	48	48	15	13	13
Halifax, NS												
Max/min °C	-1/-9	-1/-9	3/-5	8/-1	13/4	18/9	22/13	22/13	18/10	13/5	8/1	2/-6
Max/min °F	31/16	30/15	37/23	46/31	55/39	65/48	71/55	71/56	65/50	55/41	46/33	36/21
Precipitation (mm)	130	107	112	109	104	104	99	102	91	122	140	150
Montréal/Ottawa, ON												
Max/min °C	-7/-16	-5/-14	2/-7	11/1	18/7	23/12	26/15	24/14	19/9	13/3	4/-2	-4/-11
Max/min °F	20/4	23/6	35/19	51/33	65/45	74/54	79/59	76/57	67/49	55/38	40/28	25/12
Precipitation (mm)	51	51	56	66	76	84	86	89	84	74	81	74
Toronto, ON												
Max/min °C	-3/-11	-2/-11	3/-6	11/1	18/6	23/11	27/14	25/13	21/9	14/3	7/-1	0/-8
Max/min °F	27/12	29/12	38/22	52/33	65/43	74/52	80/57	77/56	69/48	57/38	45/30	32/18
Precipitation (mm)	46	46	56	64	66	69	76	84	74	64	71	66
Vancouver, BC												
Max/min °C	6/0	8/1	9/2	12/4	16/8	19/11	22/12	22/13	18/10	13/6	9/3	6/1
Max/min °F	42/32	46/34	49/36	54/40	61/46	66/51	71/54	71/55	65/50	56/43	48/37	43/33
Precipitation (mm)	150	125	109	76	61	46	36	38	64	114	170	178

things not to miss

It's not possible to see everything that Canada has to offer in one trip – and we don't suggest you try. What follows, in no particular order, is a selective and subjective taste of the country's highlights: beautiful landscapes, alluring cities, great activities and spectacular events. They're arranged in five colour-coded categories to help you find the very best things to see, do and experience. All entries have a page reference to take you straight into the guide, where you can find out more.

01 Montréal's Just For Laughs Page **218** • Catching some of the thousands of acts at the world's largest comedy festival is just one of the ways to enjoy this city's many delights.

02 Snowboarding in Whistler Page **791** & ***Skiing and snowboarding* colour section** • Hit the same slopes where Olympians triumphed at North America's largest ski resort, with hundreds of acres of mind-blowing terrain.

03 Watch polar bears in Churchill Page **597** • Bleak and solitary, this northern town bills itself as the "polar bear capital of the world" – with justification.

04 Ottawa's Parliament buildings Page **174** • The impressive seat of government and centrepiece of Canada's agreeable capital.

05 Sea kayaking in Nova Scotia Page **380** & **395–396** • Paddle your way along the province's beautiful sheltered bays, coves and inlets.

06 Dawson City Page **909** • Take a step back into history in once-thriving Dawson City, the centre of the great 1898 Klondike gold rush.

07 Stanley Park, Vancouver Page **765** • A huge part of Vancouver's appeal is Stanley Park, a peaceful retreat in this equally relaxed and attractive city.

08 Calgary Stampede Page **555** • Let your inner cowboy (or girl) loose at this annual bonanza of all things rodeo and Western.

09 Live music in the Maritimes Pages **369** & **459** • Halifax and St John's are east coast enclaves of live music excellence, with everything from rock to jazz and folk to traditional Celtic.

10 Wildlife Page **963** • Wildlife encounters are virtually assured in all of Canada's national parks and wilderness areas.

11 The art of the Group of Seven Page **88** • Some of Canada's best-known artists – including Tom Thomson – were a part of this collective, whose work celebrates the country's landscape.

12 Jasper Page **658** • Ice-climbing is just one of the activities possible in the Canadian Rockies' largest national park – where hiking, biking and skiing trails can take you deep into the backcountry.

13 See a glacier up close Page **655** • The largest collection of snow and ice in the Canadian Rockies is at the Columbia Icefield, home of the famed Athabasca Glacier.

14 Explore Vieux-Québec Page **270** • With its clutch of fine old buildings, handsome location and great restaurant scene, Québec City's historic old town feels more European than Canadian.

15 St John's Page **450** • The dramatic approach to St John's old sea port is through a slender channel called The Narrows, but this thriving, fun city is hard to beat for scenery and a night on the town.

16 The Laurentians Page **255** • Some of the finest and most diverse scenery in Québec, from rolling farmland to a vast coniferous forest.

17 Canoe in Algonquin Provincial Park Page **161** • The wild tracts of this enormous park – the largest in Ontario – are best explored by canoe.

18 Haida Gwaii Page **878** • Explore this magical west-coast archipelago of 200 islets for its vibrant aboriginal culture, unique fauna and deep, mossy forests.

19 **Bay of Fundy** Page **400** • These rugged New Brunswick sea cliffs and sheltered coves experience the highest tides in the world.

20 **Drive the Icefields Parkway** Page **652** • Taking in the dramatic Rockies for over 200km, this is one of the world's most beautiful drives.

21 **Aurora borealis** Page **870** • Swirling sheets of iridescent colour, the disconcertingly beautiful Northern Lights can often be seen all across Canada's north.

22 **Niagara Falls** Page **114** • Millions come to see the falls – two great sheets of water thundering over a 50m precipice.

23 **Lunenburg** Page **374** • Of all the old fishing towns along the Nova Scotian coast, Lunenburg is the prettiest.

24 Taking in the coast at Pacific Rim National Park Page **835** • The majestic centrepiece of Vancouver Island is a beguiling mix of islets, rainforests and mountains.

25 Eat your way across the nation Pages **98, 242** & **775** • From PEI lobster and Montréal's famous smoked meat (below) to Alberta's succulent beef and Toronto or Vancouver's mind-boggling array of excellent restaurants, Canada is more than ever a foodie's dream destination.

26 Whale-watching Pages **335, 812–813** & **836** • On both the east and west coasts, venturing out to view whales – from orcas to humpbacks and minke to belugas – at close quarters is a popular and unforgettable experience.

27 Prince Edward Island Page **428** • The reddish sands of PEI's National Park band the island's northern shore, and are perfect for strolling, swimming or sunning.

28 **Hiking in Banff** Page **622** • Countless trails make it easy to escape the crowds and explore the great outdoors around the Rockies' bustling summer capital.

29 **Afternoon tea in Victoria** Page **814** • High tea at the venerable Empress Hotel (the best-known landmark in this genteel west-coast city) is an experience to remember.

30 **Mount Robson** Page **671** • The highest peak in the Canadian Rockies, set amid stunning scenery on the Alberta/BC border.

Basics

Basics

Getting there 27

Getting around 32

Accommodation 37

Food and drink 40

The media 43

Festivals 44

Outdoor activities 46

Spectator sports 49

Travel essentials 51

Getting there

Most US travellers visit Canada by car, but there are plenty of flights, buses, ferries and trains that cross the border. Other travellers, including those from the UK, Australia, New Zealand and South Africa, have little choice but to fly.

Airfares from the UK, Australia and New Zealand to Canada tend to be highest around mid-June to early September, the peak tourist season. You'll get the best prices during the low season, mid-November through April (excluding Christmas and New Year, when seats are at a premium).

Flights from the UK and Ireland

Most nonstop scheduled flights **from Britain** to Canada depart from London Heathrow or Gatwick with a handful of departures from airports around Britain supplemented by holiday charter flights. The main gateways are Montréal, Toronto and Vancouver, but there are also nonstop scheduled flights to Calgary, Edmonton, Ottawa, Halifax and St John's. Connecting flights from these airports delve into every corner of the country.

A standard return from London to Toronto with Air Canada can cost anywhere between £350 and £650 (low/high season), and a little more to Vancouver. Most airlines also offer good-value **open-jaw** deals that enable you to fly into one Canadian city and back from another – useful if you want to make your own way across the country.

From Ireland, the only daily nonstop flights are in the summer (mid-April to mid-Oct) with Air Canada from Dublin to Toronto; on all other flights you will have to change planes, usually either in the UK or US. Typical **return fares** on direct Dublin–Toronto flights (7hr) are around €600, and €1000 with connections to Vancouver.

Flights from the US

From the US to Canada there are plenty of nonstop **flights** on Air Canada and most US airlines, though prices, especially on east coast routes, are relatively expensive. WestJet offers flights primarily from the American West, and with the exception of Las Vegas routes, most of these are seasonal. Toronto is generally the cheapest destination for the major airlines. Fares change drastically depending on season and when you purchase: in summer, expect to pay around US$250 for New York to Toronto; US$400 for New York to Montréal; US$350 for New York to Halifax; at least US$500 from Chicago to most of the big cities; US$350 for LA to Calgary; and US$300 for LA to Vancouver. WestJet flights between Las Vegas and Toronto can be as low as US$125 one-way, even in summer.

Because **domestic flights** wholly within the US or Canada can cost less than flights between the two countries, you could save by crossing the border before or after your flight. This is especially true of long-haul flights: a transcontinental flight from New York to Vancouver can be considerably more expensive than a similar flight to Seattle (which lies only a hundred miles south of Vancouver).

Flying north/south is reasonably quick: New York to Montréal takes around 1hr 15min; New York to Toronto 1hr 30min; New York to Halifax 1hr 50min; LA to Vancouver 2hr 45min; and LA to Calgary 3hr. Flying east/west between countries usually involves a stopover or onward connection, so New York–Vancouver can take 7–8hr.

Flights from Australia, New Zealand and South Africa

The Air Canada and Air Zealand services from Sydney to Vancouver are the only nonstop connections between Canada and Australia – high season rates are around A$2200 return. If you're heading to other parts of Canada, airlines tend to quote you fares via LA or Vancouver to your chosen destination; you'll often get cheaper rates flying through LA via airlines like Delta, which charge under A$2000 return from Sydney to Toronto, even in summer (with two stops), and United, which flies through San Francisco (flights to Calgary and Montréal on these carriers won't cost much more). Flights from other cities in **Australia route through** Sydney.

There are no direct flights **from New Zealand** to Canada, and you'll usually end up changing planes in LA: you can get flights from Auckland to Vancouver from NZ$2000 return via Qantas and Alaska Airlines, while Air Canada, Air New Zealand and United also fly via LA for slightly more. Flights to Toronto also pass through LA – expect to pay around NZ$2700 in peak season.

South Africa has no nonstop flights to Canada, and your cheapest options are usually to fly on KLM via Amsterdam to Toronto (R10,000 in high season) or via London (BA) and Frankfurt (Lufthansa) to Vancouver (around R15,000). South Africa Airways offers services to Toronto and Vancouver via London or Washington, D.C. from around R15,000 and R24,000 respectively, in high season.

By car

The **US highway** system leads into Canada at thirteen points along the border. The busiest corridors are from Blaine, WA to White Rock, BC; from Detroit, MI to Windsor, ON; from Buffalo, NY to Fort Erie, ON; and at Niagara Falls. You may encounter traffic jams at the border, particularly at weekends, in the summer and on US or Canadian holidays, but given that most border posts are open 24hr, you can usually beat the lines by starting early. From New York to Montréal (383 miles) reckon on eight hours' driving; from San Francisco to Vancouver (954 miles), around nineteen hours. Mapmaker Rand

Six steps to a better kind of travel

At Rough Guides we are passionately committed to travel. We feel strongly that only through travelling do we truly come to understand the world we live in and the people we share it with – plus tourism has brought a great deal of **benefit** to developing economies around the world over the last few decades. But the extraordinary growth in tourism has also damaged some places irreparably, and of course **climate change** is exacerbated by most forms of transport, especially flying. This means that now more than ever it's important to **travel thoughtfully** and **responsibly**, with respect for the cultures you're visiting – not only to derive the most benefit from your trip but also to preserve the best bits of the planet for everyone to enjoy. At Rough Guides we feel there are six main areas in which you can make a difference:

- Consider what you're contributing to the **local economy**, and how much the services you use do the same, whether it's through employing local workers and guides or sourcing locally grown produce and local services.
- Consider the **environment** on holiday as well as at home. Water is scarce in many developing destinations, and the biodiversity of local flora and fauna can be adversely affected by tourism. Try to patronize businesses that take account of this.
- Travel with a purpose, not just to tick off experiences. Consider **spending longer** in a place, and getting to know it and its people.
- Give thought to how often you **fly**. Try to avoid short hops by air and more harmful night flights.
- Consider **alternatives to flying**, travelling instead by bus, train, boat and even by bike or on foot where possible.
- Make your trips "**climate neutral**" via a reputable carbon offset scheme. All Rough Guide flights are offset, and every year we donate money to a variety of charities devoted to combating the effects of climate change.

McNally's website (Ⓦwww.randmcnally.com) has a good road-trip tool, with routes and mileage charts.

Vehicle insurance is compulsory and it's also advisable to obtain a yellow Non-Resident Inter-Province Motor Vehicle Liability Card from your insurance company before you go. Make sure you have documents establishing proof of insurance and proof of vehicle ownership with you at all times while driving in Canada. If renting a car in the US fill up before going – US prices are still less than in Canada. See p.52 for general entry requirements.

By bus

The Greyhound bus network extends into Canada from several points on the US East Coast and one each from the West and Midwest; prices below are for cheap **14-day advance tickets**. Some bus passes (see p.35) are valid in the US and Canada.

Travelling overland from San Diego to Montréal, say, is easy: it's an epic, three-day journey (with at least three bus changes), but if you're on a tight budget, the US$162 fare is a bargain – though be sure to factor in three days worth of food and drink. Greyhound and Trailways buses compete on the busy runs **from New York** to Montréal and Toronto, offering half a dozen trips per day. Fares for the eight-hour journey to Montréal are around US$140 return; the 12hr marathon to Toronto is around the same price for advance tickets. Trips **from Boston** to Montréal start at US$52 one-way and the journey takes around seven hours.

Other cross-border connections include **from Burlington**, VT to Montréal (4 daily; 2hr 30min–3hr; US$20 one-way); **from Seattle** to Vancouver (5 daily; 4hr; US$19 one-way); and **from Fargo, ND** to Winnipeg (1 daily; 4hr 45min; US$35 one-way).

For real bargains, check out Mega Bus, which runs between New York and Toronto (fares can be as low as US$40 one-way). Acadian offers links to the Maritimes from Bangor, Maine (Saint John US$48, Halifax US$90), which is part of the Greyhound network – Boston is about 5hr and U$30 away.

By train

For specific journeys, the **train** is usually more expensive than the bus (and often the plane), though special deals, especially in off-peak periods, can bring the round-trip cost down considerably.

Two routes on **Amtrak** from the north-eastern US have direct connections with **VIA Rail**, Canada's national rail company: the "Maple Leaf" from New York to Toronto via Buffalo and Niagara Falls (1 daily; 12hr; from US$97 one-way); and the "Adirondack" from New York to Montréal via Albany and Plattsburgh (1 daily; 10hr 50min; from US$62 one-way). In the Northwest, the "Amtrak Cascades" runs from Seattle to Vancouver (1 daily; 4hr; from US$47 one-way). All these fares are for travel in economy class, where pillows are provided for overnight journeys.

Reserve as far as possible in advance, as it is compulsory to have a seat and some of the eastern-seaboard trains in particular get completely booked. Some rail passes for the US network are also valid as far as a Canadian gateway like Vancouver or Montréal. For more on these, and train travel within Canada, see p.36.

By ferry

With the cancellation of the Yarmouth to Maine ferries in late 2009, there are now just three US-Canada ferry routes, all on the West Coast. Apart from the enjoyment of the ride, the boats can save you hours of driving. Always **book ahead**.

On the **West Coast**, the *Victoria Clipper* catamaran for foot passengers runs between Seattle and Victoria on Vancouver Island, three times daily from late June to August, twice daily in May, June and September and once daily for the rest of the year (2hr 45min; from US$85 one-way). The most useful West Coast ferry is the Washington State Ferries service from Anacortes to Sidney, on Vancouver Island. The ferry travels twice daily in summer, and once daily in winter via the San Juan archipelago (average-sized vehicle with driver $42.95 each way, extra adult passengers $16 each; 3hr). Further north, Alaska Marine Hwy ferries link several Alaskan towns with Prince Rupert.

In December 2009 the Yarmouth to Portland and Bar Harbor ferry service was cancelled after Nova Scotia suspended financial support.

Airlines, agents and operators

Airlines

Air Canada Ⓦwww.aircanada.com.
Air New Zealand Ⓦwww.airnewzealand.co.nz.
Air North Ⓦwww.flyairnorth.com.
Air Transat Ⓦwww.airtransat.com.
American Airlines Ⓦwww.aa.com.
bmi Ⓦwww.flybmi.com.
British Airways Ⓦwww.ba.com.
Cathay Pacific Ⓦwww.cathaypacific.com.
Continental Airlines Ⓦwww.continental.com.
Delta Ⓦwww.delta.com.
Frontier Airlines Ⓦwww.frontierairlines.com.
KLM Ⓦwww.klm.com.
Lufthansa Ⓦwww.lufthansa.com.
Qantas Airways Ⓦwww.qantas.com.au.
South African Airways Ⓦwww.flysaa.com.
United Airlines Ⓦwww.united.com.
US Airways Ⓦwww.usairways.com.
WestJet Ⓦwww.westjet.com.

Agents and operators

American Holidays Northern Ireland Ⓣ028/9051 1800, Republic of Ireland Ⓣ01/673 3840; Ⓦwww.american-holidays.com. Offers tour packages from Ireland to the US and Canada.

Backroads US Ⓣ510/527-1555 or 800/462-2848, Ⓦwww.backroads.com. Cycling, hiking and multi-sport tours in the Rockies, Québec and Nova Scotia.

Canada's Best Canada Ⓣ01502/565-648, Ⓦwww.best-in-travel.com. Canada specialist offering a wide range of holiday options. Deals in cottages, resorts and inns, as well as hotels. Package and tailor-made holidays.

Cosmos US Ⓣ1-800/276-1241, Ⓦwww.cosmos.com. Planned vacation packages with an independent focus.

ebookers UK Ⓣ0871/223 5000, Republic of Ireland Ⓣ01/431 1311; Ⓦwww.ebookers.com. Low fares on an extensive selection of scheduled flights and package deals.

Ecosummer Expeditions Canada & US Ⓣ1-800/465-8884, International 1-250/674-0102, Ⓦwww.ecosummer.com. Wilderness expeditions and ecotourism focusing on BC, especially the Gulf and Haida Gwaii.

Exodus UK 1-800/843-4272, Ⓦwww.exodus.co.uk. Adventure and action-oriented vacation packages focused on low-impact tourism, mostly in Western Canada.

Explore Holidays Australia Ⓣ1300/731 000, Ⓦwww.exploreholidays.com.au. Accommodation and package tours to Canada.

Frontier Ski UK ⓣ020/8776 8709, ⓦwww.frontier-ski.co.uk. Leading Canadian ski holiday specialist, with trips to the Rockies and Québec.
Gap Adventures Real Traveller US ⓣ1-800/708-7761, UK ⓣ0870/999 0144, Australia ⓣ1300/853 325, New Zealand ⓣ0800/333 307; ⓦwww.gapadventures.com. Adventure company taking small groups on specialist programmes that include walking, biking, overlanding, adventure and cultural trips. Québec, the Rockies and BC-focused.
Go Fishing Worldwide UK ⓣ020/8742 1566, ⓦwww.gofishingworldwide.co.uk. Fishing trips to Labrador, New Brunswick, Québec, the Yukon, Alberta, BC, Ontario and NWT.
Great Rail Journeys UK ⓣ01904/521 936, ⓦwww.greatrailuk.com. Canada coast-to-coast by train.
Kuoni Travel ⓣ01306/747 002, ⓦwww.kuoni.co.uk. Major tour operator running long-haul package holidays. Especially good deals for families.
Moose Travel Network Canada ⓣ1-888/816 6673, ⓦwww.moosenetwork.com. Outfit that runs hop-on and hop-off backpacker mini-coach tours in BC, Alberta, New Brunswick, Nova Scotia, Ontario and Québec. See p.36 for more details.
North America Travel Service UK ⓣ020/7569 6710, ⓦwww.northamericatravelservice.co.uk. Various itineraries cater to city breaks, cruises, spa vacations, guided tours and more.
North South Travel UK ⓣ01245/608 291, ⓦwww.northsouthtravel.co.uk. Friendly, competitive travel agency, offering discounted fares worldwide. Profits are used to support projects in the developing world, especially the promotion of sustainable tourism.
Rod and Reel Adventures ⓣ1-800/356-6982, ⓦwww.rodreeladventures.com. Fishing holidays.
Ski Independence ⓣ0845/310 3030, ⓦwww.ski-i.com. Wide range of ski packages, mostly to the Rockies.
Ski Safari ⓣ01273/224 060, ⓦwww.skisafari.com. Sixteen Canadian resorts in the Rockies and Québec.
STA Travel US ⓣ1-800/781-4040, UK ⓣ0871/230 0040, Australia ⓣ134/782, New Zealand ⓣ0800/474 400, SA ⓣ0861/781 781; ⓦwww.statravel.com. Worldwide specialists in independent travel; also student IDs, travel insurance, car rental, rail passes and more. Good discounts for students and under-26s.
Trailfinders UK ⓣ0845/058 5858, Republic of Ireland ⓣ01/677 7888, ⓦwww.trailfinders.com. Australia ⓣ1300/780 212, ⓦwww.trailfinders.com.au. One of the best-informed and most efficient agents for independent travellers.
Travel Cuts US ⓣ1-800/592-2887, Canada ⓣ1-888/246-9762; ⓦwww.travelcuts.com. Popular, long-established student-travel organization.
travel.com.au Australia ⓣ1300/130 482, ⓦwww.travel.com.au. Itineraries, accommodation and car hire, as well as ski trips, adventure travel and family vacations.
Travelplan Australia ⓣ1300/130 754, ⓦwww.travelplan.com.au. Holidays in the snow worldwide, plus extreme heli-skiing trips.
Travelsphere UK ⓣ0800/567 7372, ⓦwww.travelsphere.co.uk. Wide range of options includes cruises, activity-based vacations and short trips.
TrekAmerica UK ⓣ0845/313 2614, ⓦwww.trekamerica.co.uk. Offers small-group adventure vacations.
Wildlife Worldwide UK ⓣ0845/130 6982, Ireland ⓣ01/440 7477, ⓦwww.wildlifeworldwide.com. Trips for wildlife and wilderness enthusiasts, including whale and polar-bear watching packages.

Rail contacts

Amtrak US ⓣ1-800/872-7245, ⓦwww.amtrak.com.
VIA Rail ⓣ1-888/842-7245, ⓦwww.viarail.ca.

Bus contacts

US-based bus companies

Greyhound US ⓣ1-800/231-2222, ⓦwww.greyhound.com.
Mega Bus US and Canada ⓣ877/462-6342, ⓦwww.megabus.com.
Trailways US ⓣ1-800/776-7548, ⓦwww.trailwaysny.com.

Canadian bus companies

Acadian ⓣ1-800/567-5151, ⓦwww.acadianbus.com. The only significant bus company in the Maritime Provinces.
Coach Canada ⓣ1-800/461-7661, ⓦwww.coachcanada.com. Assorted services in Ontario and Québec.
DRL Coachlines ⓣ709/263-2171 or 1-888/263-1854, ⓦwww.drlgroup.com. Newfoundland's only long-distance bus company.
Greyhound Canada ⓣ1-800/661-8747, ⓦwww.greyhound.ca. Long-distance buses in Québec, Ontario, central and western Canada.
Ontario Northland ⓣ1-800/461-8558, ⓦwww.ontarionorthland.ca. Long-distance bus (and train) services in Ontario.
Orléans Express ⓣ1-888/999-3977, ⓦwww.orleansexpress.com. Long-distance bus services in Québec.
Red Arrow ⓣ1-800/232-1958, ⓦwww.redarrow.ca. Services to and from Calgary, Edmonton, Banff and Lake Louise.

Saskatchewan Transportation ⓣ1-800/663-7181, ⓦwww.stcbus.com. Services across Saskatchewan.

Ferry contacts

Alaska Marine Hwy US ⓣ1-800/382-9229, International 907/235-7099; ⓦwww.akferry.org.
Black Ball Ferries ⓣ360/457-4491, ⓦwww.cohoferry.com.
Victoria Clipper US ⓣ1-800/888-2535, ⓦwww.clippervacations.com/ferry.
Victoria Express US ⓣ250/361/9144, ⓦwww.victoriaexpress.com.
Washington State Ferries US ⓣ206/464-6400 or 1-888/808-7977, ⓦwww.wsdot.wa.gov/ferries/.

Getting around

Beyond the cities, getting around Canada by public transport can be tough: train services are limited to a light scattering of routes, and although buses are much more plentiful and cheap, bus stations and stops can be miles from the nearest hotel or campsite. Flying is far more expensive, and the vast bulk of visitors rent a car and drive.

By plane

Canada has a comprehensive network of **domestic flights** that covers every corner of the country. The big carriers are **WestJet** (ⓣ1-888/937-8538, ⓦwww.westjet.com) and **Air Canada** (ⓣ1-888/247-2262, ⓦwww.aircanada.com) and its subsidiary airlines, although there are a number of smaller airlines operating regionally. Throughout the *Guide*, we have given details of the most useful services.

Prices remain generally high: a one-way fare from Toronto to Winnipeg with Air Canada can cost $225–250, and about the same on WestJet. Standard fares to the more remote settlements in the north can become prohibitively expensive for casual travellers: single flights from Toronto to Goose Bay can be $800, and well-over $1000 to Iqaluit. One way around this particular cost is **Canada's Arctic Circle Air Pass** (ⓣ1-800/661-0407 ext 223, ⓦwww.canadasarcticcircleairpass.com), which allows you to fly return from Vancouver, Calgary or Edmonton to five destinations in the Yukon or Northwest Territories, starting from $879. For a way to cut costs outside of the north, think about an **Air Canada Flight Pass**. There are endless permutations, but the principle is that you buy sets of coupons, each of which is valid for an internal flight; the larger the area covered by the pass, the more expensive it is. For example, the Explore Canada Pass offers four to eight coupons valid over the summer, starting at $700 (4 flights) for Atlantic Canada.

By car

Travelling by **car** is the best way to see Canada. Any US, UK, Australian or New Zealand national over 21 with a full driving licence is allowed to drive in Canada, though rental companies may refuse to rent to a driver who has held a full licence for less than one year, and under-25s almost invariably get lumbered with a higher insurance premium. Car-rental companies will expect you to have a credit card; if you don't, they may refuse to rent to you.

Gas (petrol)

Most of Canada's vehicles – and almost every rental car – run on **unleaded fuel**, which is sold by the litre. Gas stations thin out markedly in the more remote regions, where you should fill up where you can. Gas is heavily taxed in Canada and is usually thirty percent more expensive than the US (though still cheaper than the UK). Prices can vary widely throughout the country: Ontario gas is often 20–30¢ cheaper (per litre) than Newfoundland and the Northern Territories.

Roads and hazards

Canada has a superb road network and although **multi-lane highways** radiate from every city, the bulk of the system is comprised of (lightly used) **two-lane highways**. Exits on multi-lane highways are numbered by the kilometre distance from the beginning of the highway, not sequentially – thus exit 55 is 10km after exit 45. In the north and off the beaten track, highways may be entirely of **gravel**. After rain, gravel and dirt roads are especially treacherous; if you're planning a lot of dirt-road driving, you'd be well advised to rent a four-wheel-drive.

Rural road hazards include moose and other large animals trundling into the road – particularly in the summer at dawn and dusk, when the beasts crash through the undergrowth onto the highway to escape the flies, and in winter, when they want to lick the road salt. Warning signs are posted in the more hazardous areas. Headlights can dazzle wild animals and render them temporarily immobile.

Parking

In cities, parking meters are commonplace, charging 25¢–$1.50 or more per hour. Car parks charge up to $30 a day. If you park in the wrong place (such as within 5m of a fire hydrant) your car may be towed away – if this happens, the police will tell you where your car is impounded and then charge you upwards of $350 to hand it back. When parking, ensure you park in the same direction as the traffic flow.

Rules of the road

Canadians drive on the **right-hand side** of the road. In most urban areas, streets are arranged on a grid system, with traffic lights at most intersections; at **junctions without traffic lights** there will be either yellow triangular "Yield" signs or red octagonal "Stop" signs ("Arrêt" in Québec) at all four corners. In the latter case, priority is given to the first car to arrive, and to the car on the right if two or more cars arrive at the same time. Except in Québec, you can **turn right on a red light** if there is no traffic approaching from the left. Traffic in **both directions** must stop if a **yellow school bus** is stationary with its flashing lights on, as this means children are getting on or off.

Driving laws are made at provincial level, with the maximum speed limit ranging 100–110kmph on major hwys, 80kmph on rural hwys and 50kmph or less in built-up areas. On-the-spot fines are standard for speeding violations, for failing to carry your licence with you and for having anyone who isn't wearing a seat belt.

Canadian law requires that any **alcohol** be carried unopened in the boot of the car. On the road, **spot checks** are frequently carried out, particularly at the entrances and exits to towns, and the police do not need an excuse to stop you.

Renting a car or RV

The least expensive way to **rent a car** is usually to take a fly-drive package or book in advance with a major rental company (see opposite). Competition is fierce and special deals are more commonplace in the shoulder and low seasons.

In Canada itself, expect to pay from around $300 a week for a two-door economy saloon in low season to $450 in high season, though throughout the year special promotions are offered by the major companies, which can get rates down to as low as $200 per week. Provincial **taxes** and GST or HST (see p.51) are not included in the rates, but the biggest hidden surcharge is often the **drop-off charge**, levied when you intend to leave your car in a different place from where you picked it up. Check if **unlimited mileage** is offered – an important consideration in a country where towns are so widely dispersed. The usual free quota, if you don't get unlimited mileage, is 150–200km per day, woefully inadequate if you're contemplating some serious touring – after which an extra charge of around 13-20¢ per kilometre is standard. You should also check your **insurance policy** for the excess applied to claims and ensure that, in general terms, it provides adequate levels of financial cover. Additionally, the **Loss Damage Waiver (LDW)**, a form of insurance that isn't included in the initial rental charge, is well worth the expense. At around $25 per day, it can add substantially to the total cost, but without it you're liable for every scratch to the car – even if it wasn't your fault.

A **recreational vehicle (RV)** can be rented through most travel agents specializing in Canadian holidays. It's best to arrange rental before getting to Canada, as RV-rental outlets are not too common. You can rent a huge variety of RVs right up to giant mobile homes with two bedrooms, showers and fully fitted kitchens. A price of around $1300 in low season, $2200 in high season, for a five-berth van for one week is fairly typical. On top of that you have to take into account the **cost of fuel** (some RVs do less than 25km to the litre), extra kilometre charges, drop-off charges, and the cost of spending the night at designated RV parks. Canada also has strict regulations on the size of vehicle allowed; in Ontario the maximum length for a trailer is 48 feet, 75 feet for trailer plus car – if you are coming from the US check that your RV isn't over the limit.

Car rental agencies

Alamo Ⓦ www.alamo.com.
Avis Ⓦ www.avis.com.
Budget Ⓦ www.budget.com.

Driving distances in kilometres

The figures shown on this chart represent the total distances **in kilometres** between selected cities in the Canada and the US. They are calculated on the shortest

	Calgary	Chicago	Edmonton	Halifax	Montréal	New York	Ottawa
Calgary							
Chicago	2760						
Edmonton	299	2750					
Halifax	4973	2603	5013				
Montréal	3743	1362	3764	1249			
New York	4294	1280	4315	1270	610		
Ottawa	3553	1220	3574	1439	190	772	
Regina	764	2000	785	4225	2979	3534	2789
St John's	6334	3950	6767	1503	2602	2619	2792
Seattle	1204	3200	1352	5828	4585	4478	4334
Toronto	3434	825	3455	1788	539	880	399
Vancouver	977	3808	1164	5970	4921	5382	4531
Whitehorse	2385	4854	2086	7099	5850	6427	5660
Winnipeg	1336	1432	1357	3456	2408	2966	2218
Yellowknife	1828	4240	1524	6537	5268	5800	5098

Dollar ⓦwww.dollar.com.
Hertz ⓦwww.hertz.com.
Holiday Autos ⓦwww.holidayautos.co.uk.
National ⓦwww.nationalcar.com.
Skycars ⓦwww.skycars.com.
Thrifty ⓦwww.thrifty.com.

Driveaways

A variation on car rental is a **driveaway**, where you deliver a car from one place to another on behalf of the owner. The same rules apply as for renting – but look the car over beforehand as you'll be lumbered with any repair costs and a large fuel bill if it's a gas guzzler. Most driveaway companies (such as ⓦwww.canadadriveaway.com) will want a personal reference as well as a deposit of up to $500. The most common routes are Toronto or Montréal to Vancouver or Florida and Arizona/New Mexico in the autumn and winter. Not a lot of leeway is given – around eight days is the time allowed for driving from Toronto to Vancouver.

By bus

Greyhound Canada runs most of the long-distance **buses** west of Toronto, including a service along the Trans-Canada Hwy from Toronto to Vancouver, and is well represented in the east of the country, though here a network of smaller companies rules the roost (see the *Guide* for details). Long-distance buses run on a fairly full timetable (at least during the day), stopping only for meal breaks and driver changeovers.

Fares are pretty standard from company to company: for example, Toronto to Winnipeg, a distance of 2100km, costs around $140 one-way (cheaper in advance), while Montréal to Toronto, an eight-and-a-half hour (540km) ride, costs around $65 one-way. See "Getting There" (p.29) for a list of **Canadian bus companies**.

Bus passes

If you're intending to explore Canada by bus, but Salty Bear and the **Moose Travel Network** don't appeal (see p.36), you may be able to save money by buying a **bus pass**. The most comprehensive – and popular – is the **Greyhound Discovery Pass**, covering almost all of Canada and most of the USA. The pass is valid for seven, fifteen, thirty or sixty days at $199/299/399/499 respectively. Passengers with travel starting in the US can purchase passes (US$199–499) online up to two hours before travel, and the passes will be available at the relevant terminal; if starting in Canada, Canadian travellers must buy the pass online at least 14 days in advance, others at least 21 days ahead (you can buy any pass in person up to the day of travel). You can also obtain hefty discounts by buying

available route by road, rather than straight lines drawn on a map. For conversion, the figure **in miles** is roughly two-thirds of that given in kilometres: 8km equals 5 miles.

Regina							
5581	St John's						
1963	7200	Seattle					
2670	3141	4050	Toronto				
1742	7323	230	4412	Vancouver			
2871	8452	2796	5528	2697	Whitehorse		
571	5010	2548	2099	2152	3524	Winnipeg	
2309	7891	2500	4979	2620	1927	2681	Yellowknife

Moose Travel and Salty Bear

Aimed at backpackers, both the **Moose Travel Network** (eastern office ⓣ416/504-7514 or 1-888/816-6673, western office 604/777-9905 or 1-888/244-6673, ⓦwww.moosenetwork.com) and **Salty Bear Adventure Travel** (Toronto ⓣ1-866/377-3077, Halifax ⓣ1-888/425-2327, ⓦwww.saltybear.ca), provide a completely different experience from regular buses. Their mini-coaches (seating 15– 21 people) hit the major destinations on the travellers' circuit in both western and eastern Canada (but not the centre) between May and mid-October; there are some additional winter packages, and also links with VIA Rail.

Moose's jump-on, jump-off services stop three days a week in the major cities and interesting smaller towns, and you don't need to book your own accommodation, since Moose ensures that a hostel dorm bed is available for every passenger at all major stopovers. There's no time limit, so you can take as long as you like to complete a circuit, and you get picked up and dropped off at the door of your hostel. There's also no age limit, although most travellers tend to be in the 19–34 age bracket; to match this, there's an array of adventure activities offered as add-ons. Moose has a range of **bus passes** with their Big West Pass costing around $579 and their Big East Pass $604; the Mega Moose Pass, covering east and west, will run you about $1134.

Salty Bear offers a similar service, primarily in the Maritimes, ranging from day-trips from Halifax ($79) to the Island Hopper Pass (from $489), which covers Cape Breton and PEI.

normal tickets twenty-one or fourteen days in advance.

By ferry

You'll likely make the most use of Canadian ferries in BC, travelling between Vancouver, Vancouver Island, the Gulf Islands and north up the Inside Passage as far as Prince Rupert. BC Ferries (ⓣ250/386-3431, ⓦwww.bcferries.com) run all these services and fares are reasonable. To go from Vancouver to Victoria, for example, costs $13.50 per passenger, plus another $45 with car.

On the east coast, you might take a ferry between Caribou, Nova Scotia and Prince Edward Island (ⓣ1-877/635-7245, ⓦwww.peiferry.com; see p.389), which costs $16, plus another $63 with car. Yet the more useful route would be from Sydney, Nova Scotia to points in Newfoundland (ⓣ1-800/341-7981, ⓦwww.marine-atlantic.ca; see p.398). For example, a trip to Channel-Port aux Basques, Newfoundland from Sydney costs $29, plus another $82 with car.

By rail

Canadian **passenger trains** are now few and far between, though at least the national carrier, **VIA Rail** (ⓣ1-888/842-7245, ⓦwww.viarail.ca), runs speedy and efficient services between Montréal and Toronto. VIA also runs several prestige routes through some of Canada's finest scenery, the long, thrice weekly haul between Toronto and Vancouver, the two-day journey from Jasper to Prince Rupert, and the excursion round Québec's Gaspé peninsula being the prime examples.

There's always a choice of **ticket** on these flagship routes. The most basic entitles passengers to a reclining seat and access to a public lounge and dome car, but not much else. Top-of-the-range tickets include meals in the restaurant car, access to comfortable lounges, hot showers and accommodation in either a bunk-bedded sleeper, a "roomette" for one, or a bedroom for two. For more information, check with VIA or consult ⓦwww.seat61.com. To give an idea of peak-season **fares**, Toronto to Vancouver tickets cost anywhere between $521 (super-saver economy), $1390 (upper berth) and $2000 for a single cabin; expect to pay about 25 percent less for off-peak travel.

VIA sells a number of **rail passes**, which can reduce costs considerably. Perhaps the most tempting is the **Canrailpass** (June to mid-Oct $923; rest of year $576), which allows unlimited travel for twelve days within a thirty-day period at the basic class.

Other, smaller companies offer **scenic rail trips**: **Rocky Mountaineer** trains (ⓣ604/606-7245 or 1-877/460-3200, ⓦwww.rockymountaineer.com) run from Vancouver to several western destinations, including Jasper, Kamloops, Banff and Calgary; Ontario Northland's **Polar Bear Express** (ⓣ1-800/461-8558, ⓦwww.northlander.ca) goes from Cochrane to Moosonee, with connections on the **Northlander** train from Toronto to Cochrane; **Algoma Central Railway** (ⓣ705/946-7300 or 1-800/242-9287, ⓦwww.agawacanyontourtrain.com) has excursions through the Agawa Canyon (see p.198); the **White Pass & Yukon Railroad** trains (ⓣ907/983-2217 or 1-800/343-7373 ⓦwww.wpyr.com) runs from Fraser to Skagway (see p.896); and the epic **Québec North Shore & Labrador Railway** (ⓦwww.tshiuetin.net) travels between Sept-Îles in Québec and Emeril Junction in Labrador, now operated by Tshiuetin Rail Transportation (see p.486).

By bike

City cyclists are reasonably well catered for in Canada: most cities have cycling lanes and produce special maps, and long-distance buses, ferries and trains will allow you to transport your bike either free or at a minimal charge. An interesting on-going project is the development of a **coast-to-coat recreational path**, the 21,500km Trans Canada Trail (ⓦwww.tctrail.ca), sections of which are already open to cyclists. The Canadian Cycling Association (CCA; ⓣ613/248-1353, ⓦwww.canadian-cycling.com) has information on cycling and publishes several books, including the *Complete Guide to Cycling in Canada*. Standard bike-rental costs start at around $15–20 per day, plus a sizeable cash sum or a credit card as deposit; outlets are listed throughout the guide.

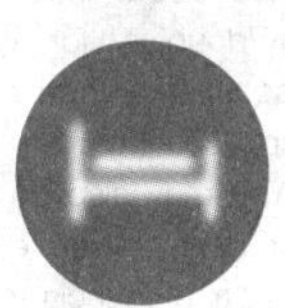

Accommodation

Given the vast size of the country, it's no surprise that the price of accommodation in Canada varies widely. The least expensive options are camping and dormitory beds in hostels, where prices start at around $25. Prices for hotels and motels are less predictable, though you'll be lucky to get a double room for less than $100 in high season wherever you are.

If you're heading into remote parts of the country, check the availability of accommodation before setting off. Places that look large on the map often have few facilities at all, and US visitors will find motels far scarcer than in similar regions back home.

It's best to try to **book a room** before you arrive, particularly in summer. Also look out for local events and festivals such as the Calgary Stampede, when accommodation is always at a premium. Most places have a 24-hour-notice cancellation policy, but in places like Banff it can be as much as three days. **Room taxes** can add as much as seventeen percent to the quoted price; the highest rates tend to be in the Maritime Provinces (fifteen–seventeen percent), the lowest in Alberta (nine percent). For more on taxes, see p.51.

Local **tourist information offices** will invariably help out with accommodation if you get stuck: most offer free advice and will book a place free of charge, but few are willing to commit themselves to specific recommendations.

Accommodation price codes

Throughout this book, **accommodation prices** have been graded with the **codes** below, corresponding to the cost of the cheapest double room in high season. However, with the exception of the budget motels and lowliest hotels, there's rarely such a thing as a set rate for a room. A basic motel in a seaside or mountain resort may double its prices according to the season, while a big-city hotel in Québec or Vancouver that charges $200 per room during the week will often slash its tariff at the weekend when all the business visitors have gone home. The high and low seasons for tourists vary widely across the country, but as a general rule **high season** refers to July and August, **shoulder season** is May, June, September and October, and **low season** refers to the rest of the year. Only where we explicitly say so do the room rates we've indicated include local **taxes**; everywhere else, they exclude taxes.

- ❶ $40 and under
- ❷ $41–60
- ❸ $61–80
- ❹ $81–100
- ❺ $101–125
- ❻ $126–175
- ❼ $176–240
- ❽ $241 and over

Hotels

Canadian **hotels** tend to fall into one of three categories: high-class establishments, plain downtown places and roadside motels (see below). In the cities, the emphasis is on the business traveller rather than the tourist. **Top-notch** hotels charge anywhere between $150 and $500, though $250 would get you a fairly luxurious double in most places.

Mid-price hotels are often part of a chain, such as *Holiday Inn* or *Best Western*, and usually offer a touch more comfort than middling motels. You should be able to find a high-season double in such places from around $110; more if you're in a well-known resort or the downtown area of a major city.

Bottom-bracket hotels – those costing anything from $65–80 – are mostly hangovers from the days when liquor laws made it difficult to run a bar without an adjoining restaurant or hotel. Found in most medium- and small-sized towns, they usually have the advantage of being extremely central but the disadvantage is that the rooms are mostly an afterthought.

Motels

Motels may be called inns, lodges, resorts or motor hotels, but they all amount to much the same thing: driver-friendly, reasonably priced and reliable places on the main highways almost always on the edge of town. The simplest rooms start at around $60, with the **average price** nearer $75 – though in resorts and more remote areas it's not unusual to find well over $100 being charged for what are fairly basic rooms. Prices usually drop in the larger centres the further you move from downtown. Many offer **off-season rates**, usually between October and April, some have triple- or quadruple-bedded rooms, and most are fairly relaxed about introducing an extra bed into "doubles" for a nominal charge. Many also offer a **family plan**, whereby youngsters sharing their parents' room stay free. You may also be able to negotiate cheaper deals if you're staying more than one night, and especially if you're staying a week – many places advertise weekly rates.

Bed-and-breakfasts

In recent years, there has been a dramatic increase in the number of **B&Bs** – or **Gîtes du Passant** – both in the big cities and in the towns and villages of the more popular resort areas. **Standards** are generally very high, and prices are around $85 and upwards per couple including breakfast. There are no real savings over cheaper hotels and motels – B&Bs in Canada are more like their posh American counterparts than the budget European version – but you'll often wind up with a wonderful room in a heritage building in a great location, with the chance to meet Canadians on closer terms.

Hostels, Ys and student accommodation

Canada has around 56 **Hostelling International (HI)** hostels and around 150 non-affiliated hostels, with almost all of the latter members of the Backpackers Hostels Canada network – these can range from small, typical dormitory-type hostels to summer student accommodation and budget guest houses with private rooms. Many un-affiliated hostels still give discounts for HI members or students. Quality varies considerably, but most of the hostels listed on the websites below should be of a reasonably high standard, and we've described the best ones in this guide. Dorm beds usually range $20–25, with basic private rooms starting at $35.

Both the **YMCA** and **YWCA** also offer hotel accommodation in many Canadian cities. Some of them, such as the Banff Y Mountain Lodge and YWCA Hotel in Vancouver are part of the Backpackers Hostels network, while others – like the Montreal Y Hotel – are more like smart, private hotels. Most Ys in Canada are focused on providing community activities and affordable housing for locals – tourist accommodation, where offered, is usually a related but separate business.

In Canada's university cities it's usually possible to stay in **student accommodation** during the summer vacation. The accommodation is adequate and functional, if soulless, and you'll have access to the campus's sports facilities; on the downside, most places are a good distance from city centres. Prices for single and double rooms start at around $35. It's a good idea to call well ahead to be sure of a room – many places are part of the Backpackers Hostels network (see website below).

Youth hostel and Y associations

Backpackers Hostels Canada ⓣ1-888/920-0044, ⓦwww.backpackers.ca.
Hostelling International Canada ⓣ1-800/663-5777, ⓦwww.hihostels.ca.
YMCA Canada ⓣ416/967-9622, ⓦwww.ymca.ca.
YWCA Canada ⓣ416/962-8881, ⓦwww.ywcacanada.ca.

Farm vacations

Farm vacations, where you spend time as a paying guest on a working farm, give you the chance to eat well, sleep cheaply – and even work (if you want) – as well as mingle with your hosts. Ontario has a range of farm-based B&Bs with reasonably priced accommodation. In western Canada, it's possible to stay on a ranch and work as a ranch-hand. Due to the isolation of these places prices are usually for full board and include riding (from £75 per day). For further details, consult tourist offices and provincial accommodation guides. The UK-based **Independent Traveller** (ⓣ01509/618 800, ⓦwww.itiscanada.co.uk) offers ranching holidays.

Camping

Few countries offer as much scope for **camping** as Canada. Many urban areas have a campground (in Canada the convention is to term the whole site a "campground" and individual pitches as "campsites"); all national parks and the majority of provincial parks have government-run sites, and in most wilderness areas and in the vast domain of Canada's federally owned Crown Lands you can camp rough more or less where you please. If you're travelling with a **tent**, check a campground's small print for the number of **unserviced** (tent) campsites, as many places cater chiefly to **RVs**, providing them with full or partial hook-ups for water and electricity.

During July and August campgrounds can become as busy as all other types of accommodation in cities, and particularly near mountain, lake or river resorts. Either aim to arrive early in the morning or book ahead. Generally reservations can only be made with ease at **private campgrounds**, not – crucially – at national park or provincial park campgrounds, where access is often, but certainly not always, on a first-come, first-served basis (you can make reservations at some national parks; check ⓦwww.pccamping.ca for more details). Finally, check that your chosen site is open: many only open seasonally, usually from May to October.

Types of campground

At the bottom of the camping pile are **municipal campgrounds**, usually basic affairs with few facilities, which are either free or cost only a few dollars – typically $5 per tent, $10 per RV. **Private campgrounds** run the gamut: some are as basic as their municipal cousins, others are like huge outdoor pleasure complexes with shops, restaurants, laundries, swimming pools and tennis courts. Private campgrounds have several ways of **charging** – some do so by the vehicle, others per couple and comparatively few on a tent or per-person basis. Two people sharing a tent might pay anything between $2.50 and $25 each, though an average price would be nearer $15.

Campgrounds **in national and provincial parks** are run respectively by Parks Canada and individual provincial governments. All are immaculately turned out and most, in theory, are open only between May and September. In practice, most are available year-round, though key facilities are offered and fees collected only in the advertised period: off season you may be expected to leave fees in an **honesty box**. You'll usually find at least one site serviced for **winter camping** in the bigger national parks, particularly in the Rockies. **Prices** vary from about $21.50–38.20 per tent for full amenities (electricity, sewage, water and showers), depending on location and the time of year, and $15.70–17.60 for basic pitches (wood, water and pit toilets). Most parks also have basic **backcountry sites** usually providing only fire pits and firewood (see below). If you want to use an official backcountry campground or just camp rough in parks, you must obtain an overnight permit from the park centre ($9.80).

Primitive camping

Though commonplace in all the larger national and provincial parks, **primitive camping** (or backcountry/wilderness camping as it's known in Canada) has certain rules that must be followed. In particular, check that fires are permitted: in large parts of Canada they aren't allowed in summer because of the risk of forest fire. If they are permitted, use a fire pit (if provided), or a stove in preference to local materials. In wilderness areas, try to camp on previously used sites. Be especially aware of the precautions needed when in **bear** country (see p.625). Where there are no toilets, bury human waste at least 10cm into the ground and 30m from the nearest water supply and campsite. Canadian parks ask for all rubbish to be carried away; elsewhere burn rubbish, and what you can't burn, carry away. **Never drink** from rivers and streams, however clear and inviting they may look. If you have to drink **water** that isn't from taps, you should boil it for at least ten minutes, or cleanse it with an iodine-based purifier or a Giardia-rated filter, available from camping or sports shops.

Food and drink

The sheer number of restaurants, bars, cafés and fast-food joints in Canada is staggering, though at first sight there's little to distinguish mainstream Canadian urban cuisine from that of any American metropolis: the shopping malls, main streets and highways are lined with pan-American food chains, trying to outdo each other with their bargains and special offers.

However, it's easy to leave the chain restaurants behind for more interesting options, as the standard of **Canadian cuisine** has improved dramatically in the last few years. In the big cities there's a plethora of ethnic and speciality restaurants; on either seaboard the availability of fresh fish and shellfish enlivens many menus, and even out in the country – once the domain of unappetizing diners – there's a liberal supply of first-rate, family-run cafés and restaurants, especially in the more touristy areas. Almost every café and restaurant has a **no-smoking** policy.

Breakfast

Breakfast is taken very seriously all over Canada, and with prices averaging between $5 and $15 it's often the best-value and most filling meal of the day. Whether you go to a café, coffee shop or hotel snack bar, the breakfast menu, on offer until around 11am, is a fairly standard fry-up: eggs in various guises, ham or bacon. Whatever you order, you nearly always receive a dollop of fried potatoes, called **hash browns** or, sometimes, home fries. Other favourite breakfast options include English muffins or, in posher places, bran muffins, a glutinous fruitcake made with bran and sugar, and waffles or pancakes, swamped in butter with lashings of maple syrup. Also, because the breakfast/lunch division is never hard and fast, mountainous meaty sandwiches are common too.

In the big cities, look out also for specialist **coffee shops**, where the range of offerings verges on the bewildering. As a matter of course, coffee comes with cream or half-and-half (half-cream, half-milk) unless you specifically ask for skimmed milk. **Tea**, with either lemon or milk, is also drunk at breakfast.

Lunch

Between about 11.30am and 2.30pm, many big-city restaurants offer special **set menus** that are generally excellent value. In Chinese and Vietnamese establishments, for example, you'll frequently find rice and noodles, or buffets for $8–12, and many Japanese restaurants give you a chance to eat sushi very reasonably for under $20. Pizza is also widely available, from larger chains to family-owned restaurants and pavement stalls. Favourites with white-collar workers are café-restaurants featuring wholefoods and vegetarian meals, though few are nutritionally dogmatic, serving traditional meat dishes and sandwiches too; most have an excellent selection of daily lunch specials for under $10.

Dinner

If you're in a large city or town, choosing where to eat **dinner** is really just a matter of whatever takes your fancy – and is within your budget. Outside these areas, you're more likely to end up at smaller, family-owned restaurants, cafés or bistros, where prices might be cheaper but the quality of the food is often no less impressive than what you'd find in a big city. Pubs and bars aren't a bad place to grab a meal either, and if what they offer is not overly inventive (chicken wings, variations of burger, fish and chips) you can bet it will be filling.

You can find pretty much any type of cuisine in Canada's larger cities, with Montréal, Toronto and Vancouver especially standing out for their choice of **ethnic** restaurants. Most run a dinner service starting anywhere between 5–7pm and ending between 10–11pm, if not later. Expect to pay anywhere from $12–40 for a main dish at most places, and considerably more at fancier establishments. The average cost of a dinner for two, with wine, would be roughly $60–80. See "Regional Dishes", below, for more on what to expect menu-wise.

Regional dishes

Largely swamped by the more fashionable regional European and ethnic cuisines,

Tipping

Almost everywhere you eat or drink, the service will be fast and friendly – thanks to the institution of **tipping**. Waiters and bartenders depend on tips for the bulk of their earnings and, unless the service is dreadful, you should top up your bill by fifteen percent or more. A refusal to tip is considered rude and mean in equal measure. If you're paying by credit card, there's a space on the payment slip where you can add the appropriate gratuity.

traditional Canadian cooking relies mainly on local game and fish, with less emphasis on vegetables and salads. In terms of price, decent meals for two without wine average between $30 and $50.

Newfoundland and Labrador

Newfoundland's staple food has traditionally been the cod, usually in the form of fish and chips, though with supplies dwindling, this is becoming more of a luxury. More common are salmon, halibut and hake, supplemented by more bizarre dishes like cod tongues (cheeks), "jiggs dinner" (salted beef and vegetables), fish and brewis (salt cod with hard bread, softened by pork fat and molasses) and seal flipper pie. The island's restaurants rarely serve seal or moose (hunters can only sell cooked moose meat to restaurants, thereby making it almost impossible for them to serve it fresh), but many islanders join in the annual licensed shoot and, if you befriend a hunter, you may end up across the table from a hunk of either animal. Caribou meat from Labrador is far more common, often turning up in burgers, and local bakeapples (cloudberries) and partridgeberries (loganberries) are used in jams, desserts and sauces.

The Maritimes

In the Maritimes, lobster is excellent everywhere, as are oysters, clams, scallops and herring, either on their own or in a fish stew or clam chowder; best value are the lobster suppers, especially on Prince Edward Island, where you'll get mountains of seafood for $25–30. Nova Scotia is famous for its blueberries, Annapolis Valley apple pie, fat archies (a Cape Breton molasses cookie) and rappie pie (an Acadian dish of meat or fish and potatoes). New Brunswick is known for its fiddleheads (fern shoots) and dulse (edible seaweed).

Québec

Québec is renowned for its outstanding French-style cuisine, and pork forms a major part of the **local** diet, both as a spicy pâté known as *creton*, and in *tourtière*, a minced pork pie. There are also splendid thick pea and cabbage soups, beef pies (*cipâte*), and all sorts of ways to soak up maple syrup – *trempette* is bread drenched with it and topped with fresh cream. For quicker **snacks** there's smoked meat sandwiches (the best of which can be had in Montréal), bagels and *poutine*, fries covered in melted mozzarella cheese or cheese curds and gravy.

Ontario

Fish is Ontario's most distinctive offering, though the pollution of the Great Lakes has badly affected the freshwater catch. Try the whitefish, lake trout, pike and smelt, but bear in mind that these are easier to come by in the north of the province than in the south.

The west and far north

Northern Saskatchewan and **Manitoba** are the places to try fish like the goldeye, pickerel and Arctic char, as well as pemmican (a mixture of dried meat, berries and fat) and fruit pies containing the Saskatoon berry. The **Arctic** regions feature caribou steak, and **Alberta** is also noted for its beef. **BC** features Pacific fish and shellfish of many different types, from cod, haddock and salmon to king crab, oysters and shrimp. Here and there, there's also the odd **aboriginal peoples'** restaurant, most conspicuously at the Wanuskewin Heritage Park in Saskatoon, Saskatchewan, where the restaurant serves venison, buffalo and black-husked wild rice. **Vancouver** is also one of the best places in North America for Chinese and Japanese food; other ethnic cuisines are also well represented.

Drinking

Canadian **bars** are mostly long and dimly lit counters with a few customers perched on stools or the surrounding tables and booths. Yet, despite the similarity of layout, bars vary enormously, from the male-dominated, rough-edged drinking holes concentrated in the blue-collar parts of the cities and the mining and oil towns of the north, to more fashionable city establishments that provide food, live entertainment and an inspiring range of cocktails.

The **legal drinking age** is 18 in Alberta, Manitoba, Saskatchewan, Québec, Northwest Territories, Nunavut and the Yukon, and 19 in the rest of the country, though it's rare for anyone to have to show ID, except at the government-run liquor stores (closed Sun), which exercise a virtual monopoly on the sale of alcoholic beverages of all kinds direct to the public; the main exception is Québec, where beer and wine are sold at retail grocery stores.

Beer and wine

By and large, Canadian **beers** are unremarkable, designed to quench your thirst rather than satisfy your palate. Everywhere they're served ice-cold, and light, fizzy concoctions rule the roost. The three largest Canadian brewers, **Molson**, **Sleeman** and **Labatts**, market a remarkably similar brew under all sorts of names. In the 1990s these companies pioneered the gimmicky **ice beer** concept: by lowering the temperature of beer to just below the freezing point of water and skimming the resulting layer of ice off the top, they created a brew with a higher alcohol content.

The slightly tastier beers of **Great Western Brewing**, one of the country's largest regional brewers, are produced in Saskatoon, Saskatchewan, while the heavily marketed **Moosehead** beer is produced in Saint John, New Brunswick. A welcome trend is the proliferation of independent **microbreweries**, whose products are sold either in a pub on the brewery premises or are available in local restaurants, bars and pubs – these remain pretty much confined to the bigger cities.

Canadian wines are fast developing an excellent reputation, particularly those from Ontario's Niagara-on-the-Lake region and BC's Okanagan Valley. Imported wines from a wide range of countries are also readily available and not too pricey.

The media

Despite the all-pervasive influence of the US media, Canada's vibrant free press, local radio and – to a lesser extent – national TV stations demonstrate a high degree of independence from their southern neighbour, retaining an often subtle but distinctive voice.

Newspapers and magazines

Canada's only national daily **newspapers** are the *National Post* and the outstanding *Globe and Mail*, whose coverage of domestic politics and contemporary issues is superb. Every major city has at least one daily newspaper and standards are generally high – the *Toronto Star* and *Calgary Herald* being two cases in point. In Québec, the tabloid *Journal de Montréal* is the bestselling French-language paper in North America, competing with the more high-brow *La Presse* and the intellectual (and separatist) *Le Devoir*.

Most of Canada's major cities also have **free weekly listings papers**, often with news and features with an alternative slant. The small-c conservative *Maclean's* and French-language *L'actualité* are the most popular weekly news magazines, while *The Walrus* – a high-brow, Canadian equivalent of *The New Yorker* – is also a good read.

TV and radio

The Canadian Broadcasting Corporation (CBC) is the primary national and regional **TV** provider. The main commercial station is the Canadian Television Corporation (**CTV**), a mix of Canadian, American and regional output. Most US stations can also be picked up in every part of Canada thanks to cable and satellite.

The majority of Canadian **radio stations** stick to a bland commercial format. Most display little originality – though they can be good sources of local nightlife and entertainment news, and road and weather reports. On the other hand, the state-subsidized CBC channels provide diverse, listenable and well-informed programmes. Driving through rural areas can be frustrating, as for hundreds of kilometres you might only be able to receive one or two very dull stations, if anything at all.

Festivals

Every province chips in with its share of festivals, from pageants and parades celebrating local events, through to more prestigious theatrical seasons and film festivals. For further details of the festivals listed below, including more precise dates, see the relevant account in the Guide. The provincial tourist offices listed on p.56 can provide free festival and events calendars for each region.

January

Polar Bear Swim Vancouver, BC. A New Year's Day swim in the freezing waters of English Bay Beach – said to bring good luck for the year (if you survive).

Banff/Lake Louise Ice Magic Festival Banff and Lake Louise, AB. Ski races, skating parties and the incredible International Ice Sculpture Competition on the shores of Lake Louise.

February

Winterlude Ottawa, ON. Winter-warming activities like ice sculpting, snowshoe races, ice boating and skating for all on the canal.

Winter Carnival Québec City, QC (Ⓦwww.carnaval.qc.ca). Two-week festival of winter-sports competitions, ice-sculpture contests and parades. Includes the Canadian ski marathon when skiers race between Lachute and Gatineau.

Montréal Highlights Festival Montréal, QC (Ⓦwww.montrealenlumiere.com). Festival that, like Québec City's, tries to make the most of winter with a multitude of shows and food events.

March

Pacific Rim Whale Festival Tofino and Ucluelet, Vancouver Island, BC (Ⓦwww.pacificrimwhalefestival.com). Celebrating the spring migration of grey whales with lots of whale-spotting expeditions as well as music and dance events.

April

Shaw Festival Niagara-on-the-Lake, ON (Ⓦwww.shawfest.com). Highly regarded theatre festival featuring the work of George Bernard Shaw and his contemporaries. Performances from April to late Oct.

May

Apple Blossom Festival Annapolis Valley, NS (Ⓦwww.appleblossom.com). Community-oriented festival held in the small towns and villages of this apple-producing valley in Nova Scotia.

Banff Summer Arts Festival Banff, AB (Ⓦwww.banffcentre.ca/bsaf). Young-artist showcase: music, opera, dance, drama, comedy and visual arts, from May to Aug.

Stratford Festival Stratford, ON (Ⓦwww.stratfordfestival.ca). Stratford is well known for its first-class Shakespeare Festival. Runs from May to early Nov.

Canadian Tulip Festival Ottawa, ON (Ⓦwww.tulipfestival.ca). Three million tulips in a riot of colour all over the city.

June

Edmonton International Jazz Festival Edmonton, AB (Ⓦwww.edmontonjazz.com). Ten days of jazz concerts, free outdoor events and workshops.

Pride Week Toronto, ON (Ⓦwww.pridetoronto.com). Gigantic celebration of gay culture, with huge parades and street parties that attract a million spectators.

Great Atlantic Blues Festival Halifax, NS (Ⓦ www.atlanticbluesfest.com). Big musical event showcasing the best of US and Maritime blues – cancelled in 2009, but hopes to be on again in 2010.
Festival International de Jazz de Montréal Montréal, QC (Ⓦ www.montrealjazzfest.com). The world's largest jazz festival (ten days) features over five hundred shows, including the world's top names; most outdoor performances are free, but note that over two million people attend.

July

Canada Day Ottawa, ON, and nationwide. Fireworks, parades and a day off for patriotic shenanigans every July 1.
Pow-wows Nationwide (Ⓦ www.powwows.com). Traditional native Canadian celebrations that take place on reserves across the country in July and August.
Calgary Stampede Calgary, AB (Ⓦ calgarystampede.com). One of the biggest rodeos in the world: all the usual cowboy trappings, plus chuck-wagon rides, craft exhibitions, aboriginal dancing and much more.
Capital Ex Edmonton, AB (Ⓦ www.capitalex.ca). Family-targeted festival featuring theme park and fairground games, a food festival, parades, live music shows and the replica Chilkoot Gold Mine.
Loyalist City Festival Saint John, NB. Celebration of the city's loyalist heritage with parades in period costume.
Antigonish Highland Games Antigonish, NS (Ⓦ www.antigonishhighlandgames.ca). All sorts of traditional Scottish sports and activities recall the settlement of the area by Highlanders.
Atlantic Jazz Festival Halifax, NS. (Ⓦ jazzeast.com). First-class jazz festival pulling in big names from round the world.
Caribana Festival Toronto, ON (Ⓦ www.caribanafestival.com). Large-scale six-week West Indian carnival with music, dance and a flamboyant parade.
Festival d'Été Québec City, QC (Ⓦ www.infofestival.com). Arts performances, live bands and other shows on and off the streets and parks of Québec City.
Glengarry Highland Games Maxville, ON (Ⓦ www.glengarryhighlandgames.com). Tucked away in the corner of eastern Ontario, you'll find the North American Pipe Band Championships, Highland dancing, Gaelic sport competitions and an overall rollicking good time. Usually the last weekend in July.
Juste Pour Rire (Just for Laughs) Montréal, QC and Toronto, ON (Ⓦ www.hahaha.com). Internationally acclaimed comic get-together with comedians from around the world performing in theatres and outdoor stages.

August

Fringe Theatre Festival Edmonton, AB. One of North America's most prestigious alternative-theatre festivals.
Montréal Pride Montréal, QC (Ⓦ www.fiertemontrealpride.com). Québec's turn to celebrate gay pride, with another huge parade and street parties.
Squamish Days Loggers Sports Festival Squamish, BC (Ⓦ www.squamishdays.ca). The continent's biggest lumberjacks' convention with impressive logging competitions.
Festival Acadian Caraquet, NB (Ⓦ www.festivalacadien.ca). Celebration of Acadian culture in the northeast of New Brunswick.
Miramichi Folk Song Festival Newcastle, NB (Ⓦ www.miramichifolksongfestival.com). New Brunswick's prestigious folk festival, featuring many of the finest fiddlers in the Maritimes.

September

Toronto International Film Festival Toronto, ON (Ⓦ www.tiff.net). Internationally acclaimed film festival spread over ten days, inundated with Hollywood stars.

October

Vancouver International Film Festival Vancouver, BC (Ⓦ www.viff.org). Another of Canada's highly rated film fests.
Okanagan Fall Wine Festival Okanagan, BC (Ⓦ www.owfs.com). One of the many wine events in this vine-growing region.
Oktoberfest Kitchener-Waterloo, ON (Ⓦ www.oktoberfest.ca). Alcohol and cultural events in honour of the twin towns' roots.
Black and Blue Montréal, QC (Ⓦ www.bbcm.org). Major gay arts festival in Montréal.

November

Canadian Finals Rodeo Edmonton, AB (Ⓦ www.canadianfinalsrodeo.com). Pure Canuck rodeo.

December

Carol Ships Vancouver, BC (Ⓦ www.carolships.org). When carol singers sail around Vancouver harbour in sparkly boats.
New Year's Eve Nationwide, but celebrated in style in St John's, Newfoundland, where everyone heads from the pub to the waterfront for a raucous midnight party.

Outdoor activities

Canada's mountains, lakes, rivers and forests offer the opportunity to indulge in a vast range of outdoor pursuits. We've concentrated on fishing, hiking, skiing and canoeing – four of Canada's most popular activities – and on the national parks, which have been established to preserve and make accessible the best of the Canadian landscape.

Other popular activities such as whale-watching, riding and rafting are covered in some detail in the main text. Once in Canada you can rely on finding outfitters, equipment rental, charters, tours and guides to help you in most areas; tourist offices invariably carry full details or contact numbers.

The national parks

Canada's 42 **national parks** are administered by Parks Canada (Ⓦwww.pc.gc.ca), and local staff based at **park information centres**. Visit these to pick up special **permits** if you intend to fish or camp in the backcountry, and for information and audiovisual displays on flora, fauna and outdoor activities. Many offer talks and nature walks presented by park naturalists, as well as reports on snow, weather and recent bear sightings. The national parks system also administers 166 **National Historic Sites** – important historical sites dotted around the country.

Supplementing the national parks is a network of **provincial parks** in every province in the country. Entry to these parks is sometimes free, though often you'll have to pay a small fee of around $5 for three days' use. You'll also have to pay for fishing and hunting permits as well as campgrounds on top of this; specifics vary from province to province.

National park permits

All those entering Canada's national sites and parks require a **park permit**, regardless of their mode of transport, though permits are most commonly sold to cover all those entering in a particular vehicle from a roadside booth on the park boundary. This costs around $7.80 to $9.80 per person per day with concessions for the young and old. If you intend to visit a number of national parks and sites, it might be worth investing in an annual national pass, which provides one adult admission to 27 parks for $67.70; and to an additional 78 National Historic Sites – called the "Discovery Package" – for $84.40; family or group passes, covering a whole car-load of people, cost around double.

Additional permits are also required to fish (see p.48) and backcountry camp in national parks: both are generally available from park information centres.

Hiking

Canada boasts some of North America's finest **hiking**, and whatever your ability or ambition you'll find a walk to suit almost anywhere in the country. All the national and many provincial parks have well-marked and well-maintained trails, and a visit to any park centre or local tourist office will furnish you with adequate **maps** of the usually very well-marked local paths. If you're venturing into the backcountry try to obtain the appropriate 1:50,000 sheet from the Canadian Topographical Series. For key hiking areas we've given a brief summary of the best trails in the appropriate parts of the guide, though with over 1500km of paths in Banff National Park alone, these recommendations only scratch the surface. Park staff can advise on other good walks, and detailed trail guides are widely available for most popular regions.

Before setting off on anything more than a short stroll be properly informed of local conditions and be **properly equipped**. Hiking at lower elevations should present few problems, though swarms of **mosquitoes** near water can drive you crazy; anything containing DEET should be fairly reliable repellents. For more on specific health problems, see p.625.

Main hiking areas

The most extensive and rewarding hiking trail networks are in the **Rockies national parks** of Alberta and BC. Thousands of kilometres of well-kept and well-tramped paths crisscross the four main parks – Banff, Jasper, Yoho and Kootenay – as well as the smaller enclaves of Glacier, Revelstoke and Waterton Lakes. Scope for hiking of all descriptions is almost limitless. More modest areas dotted all over **BC** boast walking possibilities out of all proportion to their size: we pay less attention to these, but by most relative standards hiking here is still among the best in North America.

In **Manitoba**, the Riding Mountain National Park offers about thirty hiking trails, but though there's plenty of upland walking to be had in the prairie provinces, you have to move east to **Québec**'s Mauricie, Forillon and Gatineau parks for a taste of mountains comparable to the western provinces. In **Ontario**, Lake Superior Provincial Park and Algonquin Park are the most challenging terrains. **New Brunswick**'s Fundy National Park offers coastal walks, while **Newfoundland**'s hiking centres on its two national parks: Terra Nova on the east coast, and the high plateau and fjords of the west coast's Gros Morne. For the truly bold, however, nothing can match the **Arctic** extremes of Baffin Island, whose principal trail lies over an icecap that never melts.

Long-distance footpaths

In areas with highly developed trail networks, seasoned backpackers can blaze their own **long-distance footpaths** by stringing together several longer trails. Recognized long-haul paths are relatively rare, though more are being designated yearly. One of the best is the **Chilkoot Trail** from Dyea in Alaska to Bennett in BC, a 53-kilometre hike that closely follows the path of prospectors en route to the Yukon during the 1898 gold rush (see p.896). The most popular is probably Vancouver Island's demanding **West Coast Trail**, which runs for 80km along the edge of the Pacific Rim National Park (see p.847).

More far-reaching walks include the Rideau Trail, which follows paths and minor roads for 386km from Kingston to Ottawa; the 690-kilometre Bruce Trail from Queenston, on the Niagara River, to Tobermory on the Bruce Peninsula; and the Voyageur Trail along the north shores of lakes Superior and Huron, which is the longest and most rugged route in the province. In the Maritimes, the Confederation Trail (p.431) cuts a bucolic path across PEI, while the Fundy Trail (p.419) in New Brunswick and, in particular, the **East Coast Trail** (p.460) in Newfoundland offer a more rugged experience.

Bears, cougars and snakes

Hiking in the Canadian wilderness is far safer than wandering around most cities, but make no mistake, **bears** are potentially very dangerous, and most people blow a whistle while walking in bear country to warn them off. If confronted don't run, make loud noises or sudden movements, all of which are likely to provoke an attack.

Cougars pose a somewhat lesser threat, with most attacks occurring in BC – unlike bears, the best strategy with cougars is to try and fight them off (they usually avoid groups altogether).

Snake bites are more common in some parts of Canada (there are rattlesnakes in Georgian Bay Islands National Park for example), but even then only a handful are reported each year and fatalities are rare – wear proper boots and if you do disturb a snake back away so that it has room to move freely. Even the most venomous bites can be treated successfully if you receive immediate medical attention (call ⓣ911 or notify park staff).

Realistically, your biggest irritations while hiking are likely to be mosquitoes, flies and black flies, but for more information on **wildlife dangers**, see p.625

Skiing

Wherever there's good hiking in Canada, there's also usually **skiing**. The increasingly popular resorts of the Rockies and BC are the main areas and the country's leading resorts are at Whistler, Banff and Lake Louise. But there's also great skiing in Québec, and a few good runs at the minor day resorts that dot the other provinces. Most cities are also close to excellent cross-country trail networks.

Canadian ski packages are available from travel agents worldwide, but it's perfectly feasible to organize your own trips, as long as you book well ahead if you're hoping to stay in some of the better-known resorts. **Costs** for food, accommodation and ski passes are still fairly modest by US and European standards: expect to pay $50–75 per day (depending on the quality and popularity of the resort) for lift tickets, plus another $30 or more per day to rent equipment.

Fishing

Canada is **fishing** nirvana. While each region has its specialities, from the Arctic char of the Northwest Territories to the Pacific salmon of BC, excellent fishing can be found in most of the country's abundant lakes, rivers and coastal waters. Many towns have a fishing shop for equipment, and any spot with fishing possibilities is likely to have companies running boats and charters. Most provinces publish detailed booklets on everything that swims within the area of their jurisdiction.

Fishing is governed by a range of **regulations** that vary between provinces and are usually baffling at first glance, but usually boil down to the need for a non-resident permit for freshwater fishing, and another for saltwater fishing. These are increasingly available online (search the provincial government websites) or from most local fishing or sports shops for $60 and up, and are valid for a year. Short-term (one- or six-day) licences are also available in some provinces ($15–30). A licence to fish in Ontario consists of an Outdoors Card for $9, plus a one-year fishing licence tag for $68 – one day tags are $18.25; call ⓣ1-800/387-7011). Alberta fishing licences are $70.90 (one year) and $26.63 (one day), Northwest Territories charges $40 per year and $30 per day, while BC charges a whopping $80 annually ($20 for one day). Additional permits are required to fish in national parks; available from park administration centres, these cost around $34.30 annually or $9.80 daily. There may well be quotas on the types and numbers of fish you can catch, which you can find out when you buy a permit.

Canoeing

Opportunities for **canoeing** are limited only by problems of access and expertise: some of the rapids and portages on the country's more challenging routes are for real pros only. The most straightforward regions to canoe are in **Ontario**, with its estimated 250,000 lakes and 35,000km of waterways, some 25,000km of which have been documented as practical canoe routes. The key areas are the Algonquin, Killarney and Quetico provincial parks, though the single most popular run is the 190-kilometre Rideau Canal, a tame run from Kingston to Ottawa.

The rivers of **BC** offer generally more demanding whitewater routes, though the lake canoeing – in Wells Gray Provincial Park, for example – is among the country's most beautiful. One of the province's other recognized classics is the 120-kilometre trip near Barkerville on the Cariboo River and the lakes of the Bowron Lakes Provincial Park. More challenging still are the immense backcountry lakes and rivers of the Mackenzie River system and the barrenlands of the **Northwest Territories**, where you can find one of the continent's ultimate river challenges – the 300-kilometre stretch of the South Nahanni River near Fort Simpson. Growing in popularity, partly because of improved road access, are trips on and around the **Yukon** River system, particularly the South Macmillan River east of Pelly Crossing. Other areas that will test the resources of any canoeist are to be found in **Manitoba** and **Labrador** – all detailed in this guide.

Once you've decided on an area, provincial tourist offices can provide full lists of **outfitters** (see p.56). These will rent out equipment, organize boat and plane drop-offs, and arrange provisions for longer trips. **Costs** range from $150 to $250 for weekly canoe rental.

Spectator sports

Canadians are sports-mad – so much so that they have two national sports: ice hockey in winter and lacrosse in summer. But it's the former that's the real national obsession; in 2004, CBC's "Greatest Canadian" top ten included two retired hockey players: Don Cherry (best known for his irascible sports commentary) and Wayne Gretzky (aka "The Great One"), regarded as the best player of all-time and afforded god-like status in Canada. Dropping in on a hockey game can give visitors an unforgettable insight into a city and its people.

Ice hockey

With players hurtling around and the puck clocking speeds of over 160kph, ice hockey would be a high-adrenaline sport even without its relaxed attitude to combat on the rink (as an old Canadian adage has it: "I went to see a fight and an ice-hockey game broke out"). The National Hockey League (Ⓦwww.nhl.com) currently consists of thirty teams, six of which are from Canada (though Canadians usually make up over half the players in the league). Each team plays over eighty games a season, which lasts from October to May. **Tickets** start at around $50 for ordinary games, rise to well over $200 for play-offs and nearly always need to be bought in advance. The Montréal Canadiens are the most successful team, with 24 Stanley Cup championships, and were the last Canadian winner, back in the 1992–93 season. Regardless of who makes it to the final, don't expect to get much done the night of a Stanley Cup match – most of Canada shuts down to watch the games.

Canadian football

Professional Canadian football (similar to the American variety) – played under the aegis of the Canadian Football League (Ⓦwww.cfl.ca) – is largely overshadowed by the National Football League in the US, chiefly because the best home-grown talent moves south in search of better money while NFL castoffs move north to fill the ranks. The two countries' games vary slightly – Canada's uses a longer, wider field, has fewer "downs" and uses bigger balls – but the Canadian version is faster-paced, higher-scoring and more exciting. The season lasts from June to November, each team playing a match a

Canada's major-league professional sports teams

Specific details for the most important teams in all the sports are given in the various city accounts. They can also be found through the major league websites:

Ice Hockey – NHL

Calgary Flames ⓣ403/777-2177, ⓦwww.calgaryflames.com.
Edmonton Oilers ⓣ780/414-4000, ⓦwww.edmontonoilers.com.
Montréal Canadiens ⓣ514/790-1245, ⓦwww.canadiens.com.
Ottawa Senators ⓣ613/599-0250, ⓦwww.ottawasenators.com.
Toronto Maple Leafs ⓣ416/815-5500, ⓦwww.mapleleafs.nhl.com.
Vancouver Canucks ⓣ604/899-4600, ⓦwww.canucks.com.

Canadian Football – CFL

BC Lions ⓣ604/589-ROAR, ⓦwww.bclions.com.
Calgary Stampeders ⓣ403/289-0258, ⓦwww.stampeders.com.
Edmonton Eskimos ⓣ403/448-1525, ⓦwww.esks.com.
Hamilton Tiger Cats ⓣ905/547-2287, ⓦwww.ticats.ca.
Montréal Alouettes ⓣ514/871-2255, ⓦwww.montrealalouettes.com.
Saskatchewan Roughriders ⓣ306/569-2323, ⓦwww.riderville.com.
Toronto Argonauts ⓣ416/341-2700, ⓦwww.argonauts.ca.
Winnipeg Blue Bombers ⓣ204/784-2583, ⓦwww.bluebombers.com.

Baseball – MLB

Toronto Blue Jays ⓣ416/341-1000, ⓦwww.bluejays.ca.

Basketball – NBA

Toronto Raptors ⓣ416/366-DUNK, ⓦwww.nba.com/raptors.

week. The play-offs at the end of the season culminate with the hotly contested Grey Cup. **Tickets** are fairly easy to come by and start at around $37.

Baseball

The Toronto Blue Jays are the only Canadian team to play in the major North America's **Major League Baseball** (ⓦwww.mlb.com). Even if you don't understand the rules, visiting a game can be a pleasant day out, drinking beer and eating burgers and popcorn in the sun, among a friendly, family-oriented crowd. There are over eighty home games each season, played from April to late September, with play-offs continuing through October. Blue Jays tickets can be hard to come by so it might be worth watching one of the minor league teams, which play in most major cities including Vancouver, Edmonton, Calgary and Winnipeg.

Basketball

Basketball was invented in Springfield, Massachusetts by Canadian Dr James A. Naismith in 1891, but since then Canadian interest has been fairly low with teams coming and going and national leagues foundering. Canada does have one team – the Toronto Raptors – in the US National Basketball Association (ⓦwww.nba.com). Despite making the play-offs in 2007 and 2008, the team has yet to win a major championship. The season lasts from November to April and **tickets** cost from $20 to well over $200.

Lacrosse

Canada has three teams in the National Lacrosse League, or NLL (ⓦwww.nll.com) – the Toronto Rock, the Calgary Roughnecks and the Edmonton Rush. This is the indoor version of the game and (perhaps because of its level of speed and activity matches that of ice hockey) all three teams draw good crowds. **Tickets** aren't hard to get in any of the three cities, with the cheapest ranging from $18–27.

Rodeo

Professional **Canadian rodeo tournaments** are as big as their US counterparts, and just as much fun. If you're looking for an alternative to big league professional sports, this is a good option – and something you're not likely to see matched if coming from Europe. Rodeos generally take place in the western provinces (Alberta, BC and Saskatchewan), and are organized by the Canadian Professional Rodeo Association (T 403/250-7440, W www.rodeocanada.com). The season starts in March and ends in November. Prices can be as low as $10 in some venues, rising to well over $100 for the finals.

Travel essentials

Costs

By western European standards, most of Canada is **reasonably priced**, with basic items – from maps through to food and clothing – costing less than back home. US residents, Australians and New Zealanders, on the other hand, will find prices higher, but usually not by much (gas and car rental is invariably more pricey than in the US). The exceptions are usually remote areas, like Labrador and the far north, where everything starts to get significantly more expensive – travel here is much harder on a budget. Accommodation, almost certainly your major outlay, can be very pricey in the country's cities and towns – especially if you're after a degree of comfort – but there are plenty of bargains to be had, not least in the burgeoning hostel and B&B market.

On **average**, if you're prepared to buy your own picnic lunch, stay in hostels and stick to the least expensive bars and restaurants, you could get by on around £36/US$58/C$60 a day. Staying in a good B&B, eating out in medium-range restaurants most nights and drinking regularly in bars, you'll get through at least £90/US$145/C$150 a day, with the main variable being the cost of your room. On £150/US$240/C$250 a day, you'll be limited only by your energy reserves – though if you're planning to stay in the best hotels and make every night a big night out, this still won't be enough.

Taxes

Virtually all prices in Canada for everything from bubble gum to hotel rooms are quoted **without tax**, which means the price you see quoted is not the price you'll end up paying. With the exception of Alberta, the Yukon, Nunavut and NWT, each province levies a **Provincial Sales Tax** (**PST**) of between five (Saskatchewan) and ten percent (PEI) on most goods and services, including hotel and restaurant bills, and this is supplemented by the **Goods and Services Tax** (**GST**), a five percent levy applied nationwide. In New Brunswick, Nova Scotia and Newfoundland and Labrador, the two taxes are amalgamated into the so-called **Harmonized Sales Tax** (**HST**) at a rate of thirteen percent; Ontario and BC are expected to apply this flat HST rate in 2010.

All this means Alberta has the lowest total sales tax of just five percent (though hotels are slapped with an additional four percent), while PEI has the highest, at 15.5 percent.

Canada's Foreign Convention and Tour Incentive Program provides some GST/HST tax relief for non-residents, though the rules remain rather complicated and individuals receive far less benefit. Essentially, rebates are only available on eligible tour packages – if you qualify you can expect to claim back fiftey percent of tax paid on the package. Eligible tour packages must include "either short-term and/or camping accommodation in Canada" and at least one service (transportation services or guide or interpreter services). If you think you qualify, visit ⓦwww.cra-arc.gc.ca and prepare for a long read.

Crime and personal safety

Canada is one of the safest countries in the world and although there are a few crime hot-spots, these are confined to the peripheries of the country's three big cities – Toronto, Montréal and Vancouver. Few Canadian citizens carry **arms**, muggings are uncommon, and even in the cities, street crime is infrequent. Canadian officials are notorious for coming down hard if you're found with **drugs**, especially on non-Canadians. Stiff penalties are imposed, even when only traces of any illegal substance are found. Police are also diligent in enforcing **traffic laws**.

Electricity

Electricity in Canada is supplied at an alternating current of 110 volts and at a frequency of 60Hz, the same as in the US. Other foreign visitors will usually need transformers for appliances like shavers and hair dryers – most phones, laptops and mp3 players can usually handle both 220/240 and 110 volt currents. For all appliances, you'll need a plug converter for Canada's two-pin sockets.

Entry requirements

Most citizens of the EU, Norway, Iceland and most Commonwealth countries, including the UK, Australia and New Zealand, only need a **valid passport** to enter Canada – passport holders from Bulgaria, the Czech Republic, Poland (holders of non-biometric passports only), Romania and South Africa must still apply for visas.

As of June 2009, US citizens need a passport or approved alternative to enter Canada. Alternatives include passport cards, new enhanced driver's licences and "Trusted Traveller" cards, such as NEXUS, SENTRI and FAST – passport cards can only be used at land borders. US Citizens can stay in Canada for up to six months without a visa.

All visitors to Canada by air and sea have to complete the **Welcome to Canada** customs declaration form, which you'll be given on the plane or at the port of arrival.

Canadian high commissions, embassies and consulates abroad

Australia
Commonwealth Avenue, Canberra, ⓣ02/6270 4000, ⓦwww.australia.gc.ca. Consulates in Melbourne, Perth and Sydney.

Germany
Leipziger Platz 17, 10117 Berlin ⓣ030/203120, ⓦwww.germany.gc.ca. Consulates in Düsseldorf, Munich and Stuttgart.

Ireland
7-8 Wilton Terrace, Dublin 2 ⓣ01/234 4000 ⓦwww.ireland.gc.ca.

New Zealand
Level 11, 125 The Terrace, Wellington ⓣ04/473 9577, ⓦwww.newzealand.gc.ca. Consulate in Auckland.

South Africa
1103 Arcadia St, Hatfield, Pretoria ⓣ012/422-3000. Consulate in Durban.

UK
Macdonald House, 1 Grosvenor Sq ⓣ020/7258 6600, ⓦwww.canada.org.uk. Honorary consulates in Belfast, Cardiff & Edinburgh.

USA
501 Pennsylvania Ave NW, Washington DC 20001 ⓣ202/682-1740, ⓦwww.washington.gc.ca. Consulate Generals in Atlanta, Boston, Buffalo, Chicago, Dallas, Denver, Detroit, Los Angeles, Miami, Minneapolis, New York, San Francisco and Seattle; consulates in Anchorage, Houston, Raleigh, Philadelphia, Phoenix and San Diego.

The **immigration officer** decides the **length of stay permitted** – usually not more than three months. The officers rarely refuse entry, but they may delve deep, asking you for details of your schedule and enquiring as to how much money you have and what job you do; they may also ask to see a return or onward ticket. Non-Americans that cross into Canada by land and intend to return to the US should keep their US I-94W form – you can use it again when re-entering the US (only by land), and you won't need to fill in the Canadian entry form.

For visits of more than six months, study trips and stints of (temporary) employment, contact the nearest Canadian embassy, consulate or high commission for authorization prior to departure. Once inside Canada, if you need an extension of your stay or want to change the basis on which you were admitted, you must apply to the nearest Canada Immigration Centre at least thirty days before the expiry of the authorized visit.

For **duty-free**, the standard allowance is 1.5 litres of wine or 1.14 litres of liquor or 24 355ml bottles/cans of beer, plus two hundred cigarettes, fifty cigars or cigarillos, and 200g of tobacco.

Health

Canada has an excellent **health service**, but non-residents are not entitled to **free** health care, and medical costs can be astronomical – get insurance before you go (see p.54). If you have an accident, medical services will get to you quickly and charge you later. If you are carrying medicine prescribed by your doctor, also bring a copy of the prescription – first, to avoid problems at customs and immigration and, second, for renewing medication with Canadian doctors, if needed. Most larger towns and cities should have a 24 hour or late-opening pharmacy. For general information on public health, and a list of **travel clinics** across Canada, the Public Health Agency of Canada is a good resource (ⓦwww.phac-aspc.gc.ca).

You are unlikely to face any special health issues in Canada, though there are certain dangers in the **backcountry**. Tap water is generally safe to drink, but at campgrounds water is sometimes good for washing only. You should **always boil backcountry water** for at least ten minutes to protect against the **Giardia** parasite, which thrives in warm water, so be equally careful about swimming in hot springs – if possible, keep nose, eyes and mouth above water. Symptoms are intestinal cramps, flatulence, fatigue, weight loss and vomiting, all of which can appear up to a week after infection. If left untreated, more unpleasant complications can arise.

Blackflies and **mosquitoes** are notorious for the problems they cause walkers and campers, and are especially bad in areas near standing water and throughout most of northern Canada. Late April to June is the blackfly season, and the mosquito season is from June until about October. If you're planning an expedition into the wilderness, take three times the recommended daily dosage of vitamin B complex for two weeks before you go, and to take the recommended dosage while you're in Canada; this cuts down bites by up to 75 percent.

Once you're there, **repellent creams and sprays** may help: the best are those containing DEET. Don't go anywhere near an area marked as a blackfly mating ground – although it's very rare, people have died from bites sustained when the creatures are in heat. Also dangerous is **West Nile virus**, a mosquito-born affliction with life-threatening properties; the virus has infected people as far west as Alberta and has killed almost fifty since 1999, so pay attention to local advice.

If you develop a large rash and flu-like symptoms, you may have been bitten by a tick carrying lyme borreliosis, or **lyme disease**. This is easily curable, but if left untreated can lead to nasty complications. It's spreading in Canada, especially in the more southerly and wooded parts of the country, so you should check on its prevalence with the local tourist authority. It also may be advisable to buy a strong tick repellent and to wear long socks, trousers and sleeved shirts when walking.

In a medical **emergency**, call ⓣ911.

In backcountry areas, look out for **poison ivy**, which grows in most places, but particularly in a belt across southern Ontario and Québec. If you're likely to be walking in affected areas, ask at tourist offices for tips on where it is and how to recognize it. The ivy causes itchy open blisters and lumpy sores up to ten days after contact. If you do come into contact with it, wash your body and clothes as soon as possible, smother yourself in calamine lotion and try not to scratch. In serious cases, hospital emergency rooms can give antihistamine or adrenalin jabs. For dangers posed by **wild animals**, see p.47.

Insurance

Prior to travelling, you should take out an **insurance policy** to cover against theft, loss and illness or injury. You'll probably want to contact a **specialist travel insurance company**, or consider the travel insurance deal we offer (see box, below). Most policies exclude so-called **dangerous sports** unless an extra premium is paid: in Canada this can mean whitewater rafting, mountain climbing and so on. If you need to make a claim, keep **receipts** for medicines and medical treatment. In the event you have anything stolen, you must obtain a **crime report** statement or number from the police.

Internet

Internet access is commonplace at Canadian hotels, hostels and even B&Bs and there are also oodles of internet cafés in cities and towns. Free internet access is available at all major libraries. The site Ⓦwww.wi-fihotspotlist.com/browse/ca carries a useful province-by-province list of hundreds of wi-fi hotspots across the country.

Mail

Every Canadian city, town and village of any significant size has its own **post office**, operated by **Canada Post** (Ⓦwww.canadapost.ca). Opening hours are usually Monday to Friday 8.30am–5.30pm, though a few places open on Saturday from 9am–noon. Much more numerous are Canada Post **service counters** inside larger stores, especially pharmacies, and here opening hours vary considerably, though core hours are the same as those of the post offices. To check for the nearest postal outlet, call Ⓣ1-800/267-1177, or consult the website. Apart from Canada Post outlets, **stamps** can be purchased from automatic vending machines, the lobbies of larger hotels, airports, train stations, bus terminals and many retail outlets and newsstands. Current **postal charges** are 57¢ for letters and postcards up to 30g within Canada, $1 for the same weight to the US and $1.70 for international mail (also up to 30g).

Maps

In addition to the maps in this guide, the **free maps** issued by each provincial tourist office (see p.56) are excellent for general driving and route planning, especially as they provide the broad details of ferry connections. The best of the **commercially produced maps** are those published by Rand McNally (Ⓦwww.randmcnally.com) and MapArt (Ⓦwww.mapart.com).

Rough Guides travel insurance

Rough Guides has teamed up with WorldNomads.com to offer great **travel insurance** deals. Policies are available to residents of over 150 countries, with cover for a wide range of **adventure sports**, 24hr emergency assistance, high levels of medical and evacuation cover and a stream of **travel safety information**. Roughguides.com users can take advantage of their policies online 24/7, from anywhere in the world – even if you're already travelling. And since plans often change when you're on the road, you can extend your policy and even claim online. Roughguides.com users who buy travel insurance with WorldNomads.com can also leave a positive footprint and donate to a community development project. For more information go to Ⓦ**www.roughguides.com/shop**.

Metric conversions

All figures are approximate:

1 centimetre = 0.39 inches;	1 inch = 2.5cm;	1 foot = 30cm.
1 metre (100cm) = 1.1 yards or 39 inches;	1 yard = 0.9m.	
1 kilometre (1000m) = 0.6 miles;	1 mile = 1.6km;	8km = 5 miles.
1 hectare (10,000sq m) = 2.5 acres;	1 acre = 0.4ha.	
1 litre = 2.1 US pints;	1 US pint = 0.5 litres;	1 US quart = 0.9 litres.
1 litre = 0.3 US gallons;	1 US gallon = 3.8 litres.	
1 litre = 1.8 UK pints;	1 UK pint = 0.6 litres.	
1 litre = 0.2 UK gallons;	1 UK gallon = 4.5 litres.	
1 kilogram or kilo (1000g) = 2.2lb;	1lb = 45g/0.45kg;	1oz = 28g.

Temperatures

°C	-10	-5	0	5	10	15	20	25	30	35
°F	14	23	32	41	50	59	68	77	86	95

Measurements

Canada uses the **metric system**, though many people still use the imperial system. Distances are in kilometres, temperatures in degrees Celsius, and foodstuffs, petrol and drink are sold in grams, kilograms or litres.

Money

Canadian currency is the **Canadian dollar** ($), made up of 100 cents (¢). Coins come as 1¢ (penny), 5¢ (nickel), 10¢ (dime), 25¢ (quarter), $1 and $2. The $1 coin is known as a "loonie", after the bird on one face; the $2 coin is known as a "toonie". There are notes of $5, $10, $20, $50 and $100. **US dollars** are widely accepted, but generally – banks, etc apart – on a one-for-one basis. It's not a good deal as the US dollar is (usually) worth more than its Canadian counterpart. For up-to-date **exchange rates**, check Ⓦwww.xe.com.

Banking hours are a minimum of Monday to Friday 10am to 3pm, but many have late opening – till 6pm – on one night a week, others are open on Saturday mornings.

ATMs are commonplace. Most accept a host of **debit cards**, including all those carrying the Cirrus coding. All major credit and charge cards are widely accepted.

Phones

When **dialling** any Canadian number, either local or long-distance, you must include the area code. Long-distance calls – to numbers beyond the area code of the telephone from which you are making the call – must be prefixed with "1".

Most **mobile** providers in Canada (Bell, Telus, SaskTel & MTS) use CDMA technology compatible with their US counterparts, so US mobile users should have no problems using their phones; you should still check whether international charges apply. Rogers Wireless and several other providers use GSM850 and GSM1900, which means that mobiles bought in the UK and **Europe** can also be used in Canada (assuming you have a roaming option and your phone is compatible with GSM 850/1900) – in this case you'll definitely be charged international rates for incoming calls that originate from home. UK providers that have roaming agreements with Rogers include Orange, T-Mobile, Vodafone and 3. In Canada, **mobile networks** cover every city and town, but in rural areas you'll struggle to get a signal.

Useful phone numbers

Police, fire, ambulance Ⓣ911.
Operator Ⓣ0.
Information Within North America Ⓣ411; international, call the operator Ⓣ0.

Time

Canada has six **time zones**, but only four-and-a-half hours separate the eastern extremities of the country from the western.

Calling home from abroad

Note that the initial zero is omitted from the area code when dialling the UK, Ireland, Australia and New Zealand from abroad.

Australia international access code + 61

New Zealand international access code + 64

UK international access code + 44

US and Canada international access code + 1

Ireland international access code + 353

South Africa international access code + 27

Newfoundland is on **Newfoundland time** (3hr 30min behind the UK and 1hr 30min ahead of the eastern US).

The Maritimes and Labrador are on **Atlantic** (4hr behind the UK and 1hr ahead of the eastern US), though southeastern Labrador follows Newfoundland time.

Québec and most of Ontario are on **Eastern** (5hr behind the UK) – the same zone as New York and the eastern US.

Manitoba, the northwest corner of Ontario, and Saskatchewan are on **Central** (6hr behind the UK; same as US Central).

Alberta, the Northwest Territories and a slice of northeast BC are on **Mountain** (7hr behind the UK – same as US Mountain).

In the west, the Yukon and the remainder of BC are on **Pacific** (8hr behind the UK and 1hr ahead of Alaska – same as US Pacific).

Nunavut spans a number of time zones, from Mountain to Atlantic.

For **daylight savings** (used in all regions except Saskatchewan, parts of Québec and northeast BC), clocks go forward one hour on the first Sunday of April, and back one hour on the last Sunday in October.

Tourist information

All of Canada's provinces have their own tourist **website** and these, along with those run by **Parks Canada**, covering the country's national parks and historic sites, and **Travel Canada**'s generic website (ⓦwww.travelcanada.ca), are the most useful source of information before you set out. Each province and territory operates a **toll-free visitor information line** for use within mainland North America. In Canada itself, there are **provincial and territorial tourist information centres** along the main hwys, especially at provincial boundaries and along the US border; **information centres** at every national and many provincial parks, selling fishing and backcountry permits and giving help on the specifics of hiking, canoeing, wildlife watching and so forth; and **tourist offices** in every city and town.

Provincial toll-free information numbers and websites

Alberta Within North America toll-free ⓣ1-800/252-3782, from elsewhere 780/427-4321, ⓦwww1.travelalberta.com.

British Columbia ⓣ1-800/435-5622, ⓦwww.hellobc.com.

Manitoba ⓣ1-800/665-0040 or 204/927-7800, ⓦwww.travelmanitoba.com.

New Brunswick ⓣ1-800/561-0123, ⓦwww.tourismnewbrunswick.ca.

Newfoundland and Labrador ⓣ1-800/563-6353, ⓦwww.newfoundlandandlabradortourism.com.

Northwest Territories Within North America toll-free ⓣ1-800/661-0788 or 867/873-5007, ⓦwww.spectacularnwt.com.

Nova Scotia Within North America toll-free ⓣ1-800/565-0000, from elsewhere 902/425-5781, ⓦwww.novascotia.com.

Nunavut ⓣ1-866/686-2888, ⓦwww.nunavuttourism.com.

Ontario ⓣ1-800/668-2746, ⓦwww.ontariotravel.net.

Prince Edward Island Within North America toll-free ⓣ1-800/463-4734, from elsewhere 902/368-4444, ⓦwww.tourismpei.com.

Québec Within North America toll-free ⓣ1-877/266-5687 and from the UK toll-free ⓣ0800/051-7055, from elsewhere 514/873-2015, ⓦwww.bonjourquebec.com.

Saskatchewan Within North America toll-free Ⓣ1-877/237-2273, or Ⓣ306/787-9600, Ⓦwww.sasktourism.com.
Yukon Ⓣ1-800/661-0494, Ⓦtravelyukon.com.

Government websites

Australian Department of Foreign Affairs Ⓦwww.dfat.gov.au, Ⓦwww.smartraveller.gov.au.
British Foreign & Commonwealth Office Ⓦwww.fco.gov.uk.
Canadian Department of Foreign Affairs Ⓦwww.international.gc.ca.
Irish Department of Foreign Affairs Ⓦwww.foreignaffairs.gov.ie.
New Zealand Ministry of Foreign Affairs Ⓦwww.mft.govt.nz.
South African Department of Foreign Affairs Ⓦwww.dfa.gov.za
US State Department Ⓦwww.travel.state.gov.

Other useful websites

Assembly of First Nations Ⓦwww.afn.ca. Lobbying organization of Canada's native peoples, with plenty to get you briefed on the latest situation.
Canadian Ice Hockey Ⓦwww.hockeycanada.ca. The official site of the amateur governing body for the national obsession.

Public holidays

National holidays

New Year's Day Jan 1
Good Friday Varies; March/April
Easter Sunday Varies; March/April
Easter Monday Varies; March/April (widely observed, but not an official public holiday).
Victoria Day Third Mon in May
Canada Day July 1
Labour Day First Mon in Sept
Thanksgiving Second Mon in Oct
Remembrance Day Nov 11 (only a partial holiday; government offices and banks are closed, but most businesses are open).
Christmas Day Dec 25
Boxing Day Dec 26

Provincial holidays

Alberta Third Mon in Feb (Alberta Family Day); first Mon in Aug (Heritage Day).
British Columbia First Mon in Aug (British Columbia Day).
Manitoba First Mon in Aug (Civic Holiday).
New Brunswick First Mon in Aug (New Brunswick Day).
Newfoundland and Labrador March 17 (St Patrick's Day); third Mon in April (St George's Day); third Mon in June (Discovery Day); first Mon in July (Memorial Day); third Mon in July (Orangeman's Day).
Northwest Territories First Mon in Aug (Civic Holiday).
Nova Scotia First Mon in Aug (Civic Holiday).
Nunavut April 1 (Nunavut Day).
Ontario First Mon in Aug (Civic Holiday).
Québec Jan 6 (Epiphany); Ash Wednesday; Ascension (forty days after Easter); June 24 (Saint-Jean-Baptiste Day); Nov 1 (All Saint's Day); Dec 8 (Immaculate Conception).
Saskatchewan First Mon in Aug (Civic Holiday).
Yukon Third Mon in Aug (Discovery Day).

The Globe and Mail Ⓦwww.theglobeandmail.com. Canada's premier newspaper online.
National Atlas of Canada Online Ⓦwww.atlas.nrcan.gc.ca. Maps, stats and plenty of details on Canada's geographic features.
National Library of Canada Ⓦwww.collectionscanada.gc.ca. Information on all things Canadian, ordered by subject. Includes Canadian arts, literature, history.
Parks Canada Ⓦwww.pc.gc.ca. Excellent website with detailed information on all of Canada's national parks and national historic sites. Reserve space at some national parks at Ⓦwww.pccamping.ca.

Travellers with disabilities

At least in its cities and towns, Canada is one of the best places in the world to travel if you have limited mobility or other **physical disabilities**. All public buildings are required to be wheelchair-accessible and provide suitable toilet facilities, almost all street corners have dropped kerbs and public phones are specially equipped for hearing-aid users. Wheelchair users may encounter problems when travelling on urban public transport, but this is changing rapidly. Out in the wilds, things are inevitably more problematic, but almost all the national parks have accessible visitor and information centres and many have specially designed, accessible trails. In addition, VIA Rail offers a good range of services for travellers with disabilities – and the larger **car-rental companies** (see p.34) can provide vehicles with hand controls at no extra charge, though these are usually only available on their most expensive models; book one as far in advance as you can. Provincial tourist offices (see p.56) are the prime source of information on accessible hotels, motels and sights. To obtain a parking privilege permit, drivers with disabilities must apply to a provincial authority, though the permit itself, once issued, is valid across Canada.

Guide

Guide

1 Toronto ... 61

2 Ontario ... 105

3 Montréal and Southwest Québec ... 209

4 Québec City and Northern Québec ... 267

5 The Maritime Provinces ... 355

6 Newfoundland and Labrador ... 445

7 The Prairie Provinces ... 501

8 The Canadian Rockies ... 603

9 The BC Interior ... 697

10 Vancouver and Vancouver Island ... 743

11 The North ... 863

1

Toronto

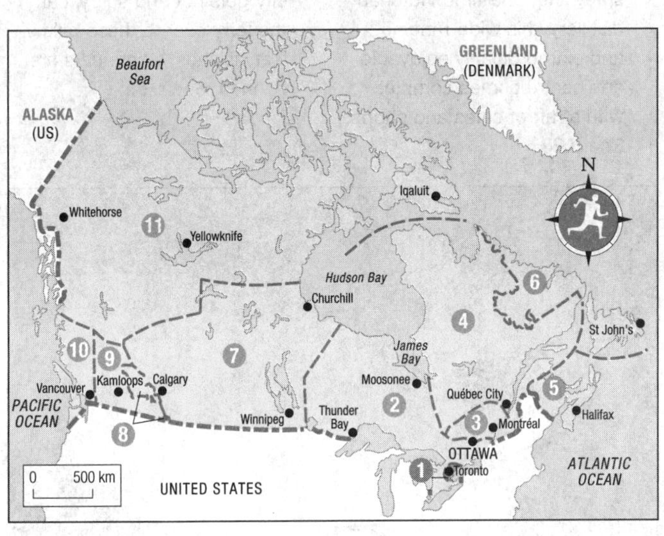
Beaufort Sea
GREENLAND (DENMARK)
ALASKA (US)
N
Iqaluit
Whitehorse
Yellowknife
Hudson Bay
Churchill
St John's
James Bay
Vancouver
Kamloops
Calgary
Moosonee
Québec City
PACIFIC OCEAN
Winnipeg
Thunder Bay
Montréal
Halifax
OTTAWA
Toronto
ATLANTIC OCEAN
0 500 km
UNITED STATES
1
2
3
4
5
6
7
8
9
10
11

CHAPTER 1

Highlights

* **Toronto International Film Festival** North America's largest film festival, a star-studded ten-day affair held in September. See p.67
* **Queen Street West** Groove away in the hippest part of the city, awash with cafés, restaurants and idiosyncratic shops. See p.76
* **Distillery District** In a sprawling, one-time Victorian distillery, this wide-ranging and extraordinarily enjoyable arts centre comes complete with a raft of cafés and shops. See p.83
* **The Art Gallery of Ontario** A superb collection of Canadian art with the Group of Seven very much to the fore. See p.86
* **Gardiner Museum** A connoisseur's collection of ceramic art drawn from every corner of the globe. See p.93
* **Toronto Islands** When the city gets hot and sultry, catch the ferry over to these balmy, leafy islands, where cars are banned. See p.96

▲ A ferry returns to the city from the Toronto Islands

1

Toronto

The economic and cultural focus of English-speaking Canada, **TORONTO** is the country's largest metropolis with a population of around five and a half million souls. It sprawls along the northern shore of Lake Ontario, its vibrant, appealing centre encased by a jangle of satellite townships and industrial zones that cover – as the **Greater Toronto Area** (GTA) – no less than one hundred square kilometres. For decades, Toronto was saddled with unflattering sobriquets ("Toronto the Good", "Hogtown") that reflected a largely deserved reputation for complacent mediocrity, but those dull days are long gone. In recent years, successive city administrations and a raft of wealthy benefactors have lavished millions of dollars on glitzy architecture, slick museums, an excellent public-transport system and the reclamation and development of the lakefront. As a result, Toronto has become one of North America's most likeable cities, an eminently liveable place whose citizens keep a wary eye on both their politicians and the developers.

Though some of the gloss has worn thin during the recent recession, huge shopping malls and high-rise office blocks reflect the many economic successes of the last decades, a boom that has attracted **immigrants** from all over the world, transforming an overwhelmingly Anglophone city into a cosmopolitan one of some sixty significant minorities. Indeed, getting the feel for Toronto's diversity is one of the city's great pleasures. Nowhere is this better experienced than in its myriad **cafés** and **restaurants**, where standards are high and prices are characteristically low. Toronto also boasts a pulsating **club scene**, not to mention a classy programme of **performing arts**, from dance to theatre and beyond.

The city has its share of attention-grabbing sights and the majority are conveniently clustered in the city centre. The most celebrated of them is the **CN Tower**, until recently the world's tallest freestanding structure, which stands next to the modern hump of the **SkyDome** stadium, now the Rogers Centre. The city's other prestige attractions kick off with the **Art Gallery of Ontario**, which possesses a first-rate selection of Canadian painting, and the **Royal Ontario Museum**, where pride of place goes to the Chinese and aboriginal peoples collections. Yet it's the pick of Toronto's smaller galleries that really add to the city's charm. There is a superb collection of ceramics at the **Gardiner Museum**, a fascinating range of footwear at the **Bata Shoe Museum** and the small but eclectic **Gallery of Inuit Art** owned by the Toronto Dominion Bank. There are fascinating period homes too, most memorably the mock-Gothic extravagances of **Casa Loma** and the Victorian gentility of **Spadina House**, not to mention the replica colonial fortress of **Fort York**, where Toronto began. Spare time also for

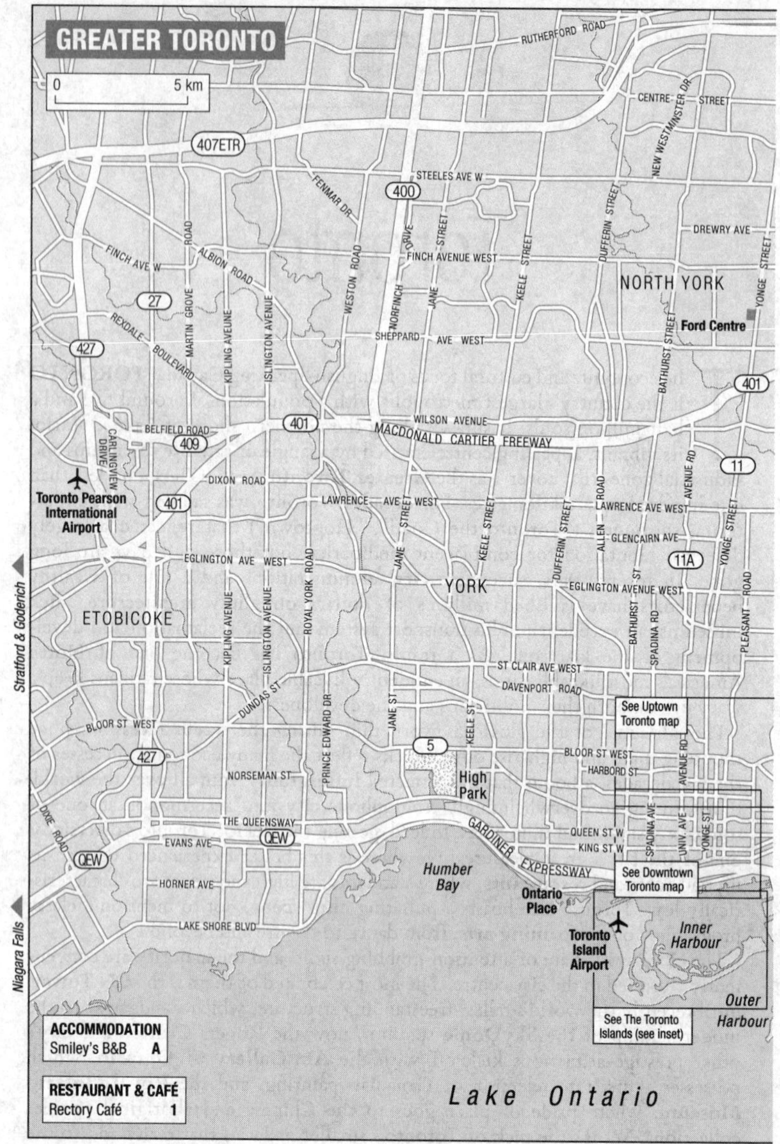

the good-looking buildings of the lively **St Lawrence** neighbourhood and the **Distillery District**, Toronto's brightest arts and entertainments complex, sited in a capacious former distillery.

Toronto's sights illustrate different facets of the city, but in no way do they crystallize its **identity**. The city remains opaque, too big and diverse to allow for a defining personality and this, of course, adds an enticing air of excitement and unpredictability to the place.

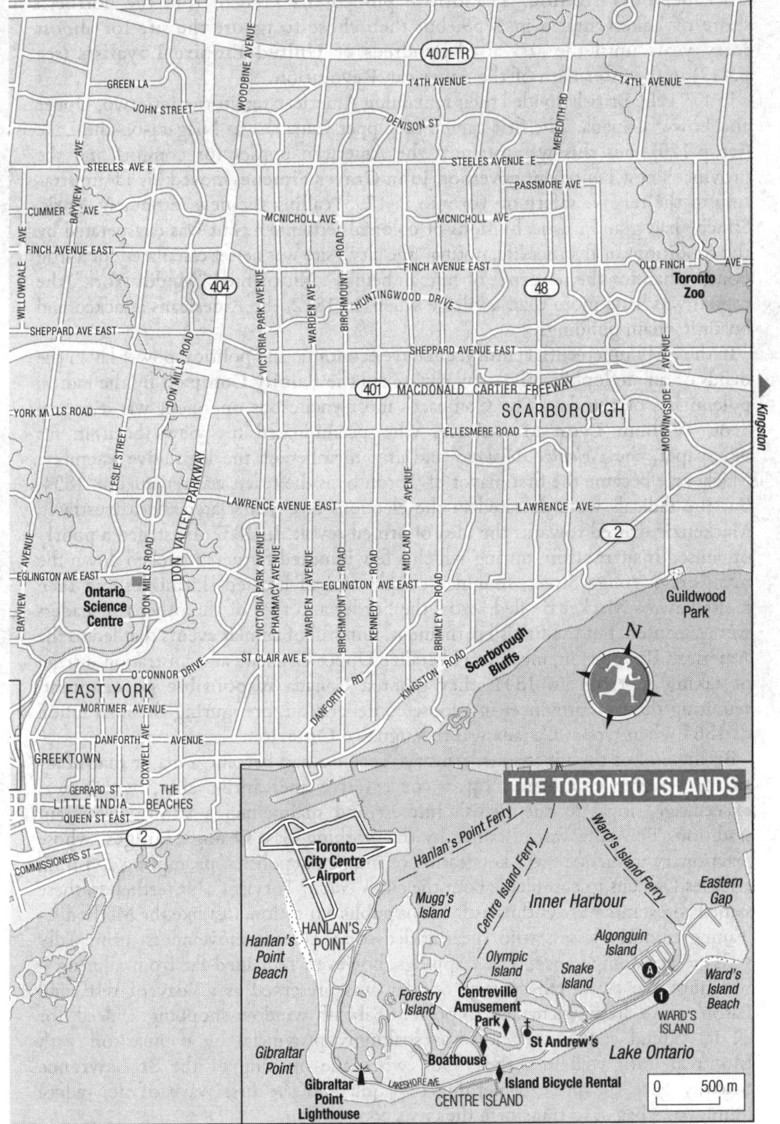

A brief history of Toronto

Situated on the slab of land separating Lake Ontario and Georgian Bay, **Toronto** was on one of the early portage routes into the interior, its name taken from the Huron for "place of meeting". The first European to visit the district was the French explorer Étienne Brûlé in 1615, but it wasn't until the middle of the eighteenth century that the French made a serious effort to control Lake Ontario with the development of a simple settlement and stockade, **Fort Rouillé**. The British pushed the French from the northern shore of Lake Ontario in 1759, but then chose to ignore the site for almost forty years until the arrival of hundreds of **United Empire Loyalists** (see p.417) in the aftermath of the American Revolution.

In 1791 the British divided their remaining American territories into two, Upper and Lower Canada. The first capital of Upper Canada was Niagara-on-the-Lake (see p.120), but this was too near the American border for comfort and the province's new lieutenant governor, **John Graves Simcoe**, moved his administration to the relative safety of Toronto in 1793, calling the new settlement **York**. Simcoe had grand classical visions of colonial settlement, but was exasperated by the conditions of frontier life, noting "the city's site was better calculated for a frog pond…than for the residence of human beings". Nicknamed "Muddy York", the capital was little more than a village when, in 1812, the Americans attacked and burnt its main buildings.

In the early nineteenth century, effective economic and political power lay in the hands of an anglophilic oligarchy christened the **Family Compact** by the radical polemicists of the day. The Compact's most vociferous opponent was a radical Scot, **William Lyon Mackenzie**, who promulgated his views both in his newspaper, the *Colonial Advocate*, and as a member of the legislative assembly. Mackenzie became the first mayor of Toronto, as the town was renamed in 1834, but the radicals were defeated in the elections two years later and a frustrated Mackenzie drifted towards the idea of armed revolt. In 1837, he staged a poorly organised **insurrection**, during which a few hundred farmers marched down the main drag, Yonge Street, fought a couple of half-hearted skirmishes and then melted away. Mackenzie fled across the border and two of the other ringleaders were executed, but the British parliament, mindful of similar events that led to the American Revolution, moved to liberalize Upper Canada's administration instead of taking reprisals. In 1841, they granted Canada **responsible government**, reuniting the two provinces in a loose confederation, prefiguring the final union of 1867 when Upper Canada was redesignated **Ontario**.

By the end of the nineteenth century, Toronto had become a major **manufacturing centre** dominated by a conservative mercantile elite, which was exceedingly loyal to the British interest and maintained a strong Protestant tradition. This elite was sustained by the working-class **Orange Lodges**, whose reactionary influence was a key feature of municipal politics, prompting a visiting Charles Dickens to complain about the city's "rabid Toryism". Nevertheless, these same Protestants were enthusiastic about public education, just like the Methodist-leaning middle classes, who spearheaded social reform movements, principally suffrage and temperance. The trappings, however, remained far from alluring – well into the twentieth century Sunday was preserved as a "day of rest" and Eaton's store drew its curtains to prevent Sabbath window-shopping. Indeed, for all its capital status, the city was strikingly provincial by comparison with Montréal until well into the 1950s, when the opening of the **St Lawrence Seaway** gave the place something of a jolt and the first wave of non-white immigrants began to transform the city's complexion.

In the 1960s, the economy exploded, and the city's appearance was transformed by the construction of a series of mighty, modernistic **skyscrapers**. This helter-skelter development was further boosted by the troubles in Québec, where the clamour for fair treatment by the francophones prompted many of Montréal's anglophone-dominated financial institutions and big businesses to transfer to Toronto.

In the last thirty years, Toronto's economy has followed the cycles of boom and retrenchment common to the rest of the country. In the mid-1990s, the **Progressive**

Toronto's leading festivals

The **Toronto International Film Festival** or **TIFF** (Ⓦwww.tiffg.ca) is one of the most respected festivals in the world – and the largest in North America. A ten-day affair, the festival begins on the first Thursday in September and lines to get into the films can be fearsome. Single, same-day **tickets** are available from the Film Festival's box offices (or as **rush tickets** immediately before screenings), but regular TIFF attendees mostly buy **books of tickets in advance** – a somewhat more economical method – or opt for one of several **passes**, which can be purchased from the TIFF website. In all cases, book well ahead.

In late June, there's the outstanding **Toronto Jazz Festival** (Ⓦwww.tojazz.com), which usually overlaps with the week-long **Gay & Lesbian Pride** (Ⓦwww.pridetoronto.com), culminating in a whopping Pride Day Parade. Late July sees **Caribana** (Ⓦwww.caribana.com), a West Indian carnival with a fantastic parade plus music and dance, as well as the **Beaches International Jazz Festival** (Ⓦwww.beachesjazz.com).

Conservatives took control of Ontario, and their hard-nosed leader, Mike Harris, pushed through a major governmental reorganization, combining the city of Toronto with its surrounding suburbs to create the "Mega City" of today. The change was deeply unpopular in Toronto itself, but Harris still managed to get himself re-elected in 2000 with the large-scale support of small-town and suburban Ontario. A hated figure amongst the province's liberals and socialists, Harris's conservative social policies were often blamed for a dramatic increase in the number of homeless people on the city's streets. In 2003, the Progressive Conservatives lost the provincial election to the Liberals, heralding a move towards more moderate, consensual politics; the Liberals remain in power at time of writing.

Arrival

Toronto Pearson International Airport, some 25km northwest of the city centre, is linked to almost every important city in the world as well as every major Canadian town and city. The vast majority of visitors to Toronto arrive by plane.

Toronto's **bus** and **train stations** are conveniently located downtown and they link Toronto to a wide range of Canadian and American cities. Those arriving by **car** will find the city encircled by motorways, a straightforward drive except during rush hour when traffic congestion can be a real pain.

By air

Arriving by **air**, you'll almost certainly land at the city's main airport, **Toronto Pearson International** (Ⓦwww.gtaa.com). There are two passenger terminals (Terminals 1 and 3), both with the usual full range of facilities, including currency exchange offices, ATMs and free hotel hotlines; the two terminals are connected by the free, 24hr **LINK Train**.

There are several ways to get downtown from the airport, but the least expensive is to catch the **Airport Rocket** (#192; daily every 20–30min, 5.30am–1.30am; $2.75 one-way), which takes about 25 minutes to reach **Kipling subway station**, at the west end of the subway network; from there, it takes another 30 minutes by subway to get downtown. The TTC (Toronto Transit Commission, see p.69) operates the Rocket, which stops outside both terminals.

The **Airport Express bus** (daily every 20–30min, 5am–12.30am; $20 one-way, $33 round-trip; ⓣ905/564-3232, ⓦwww.torontoairportexpress.com), which also picks up passengers outside both terminals, takes forty to sixty minutes to reach downtown, though heavy traffic can make the journey longer. The bus drops passengers at the coach station (see below) and a number of Toronto's hotels; if you're the last on the drop-off list, add another twenty minutes to the journey time. You can buy **tickets** either at the Airport Express bus kiosks at the airport or from the driver.

A **taxi** from the airport to the city centre is about $50, a few dollars less if you take the airport **limo service** (a shared taxi system). Unlike taxis, the price of a limo is fixed, an important consideration if you arrive (or leave) during rush hour; the disadvantage is that they usually only leave when they're full.

The much smaller **Toronto City Centre Airport** (ⓦwww.torontoport.com) is close to downtown on Hanlan's Point, one of the Toronto Islands (see p.96). There are flights to the airport from a number of other Canadian cities and the sole carrier is **Porter Airlines** (ⓣ416/619-8622 or 1-888/619-8622, ⓦwww.flyporter.com). From the airport, there's a **minibus** to the *Royal York* hotel, on the corner of Front Street West and York Street.

By Bus

Well connected to most of the major towns of eastern and central Canada, Toronto's **coach terminal** is conveniently located downtown at 610 Bay St, metres from Dundas Street West and a five-minute walk from the subway station at the corner of Yonge and Dundas. The two main carriers are Greyhound (ⓦwww.greyhound.ca) and Coach Canada (ⓦwww.coachcanada.com); for routes to and from the city, see 'Travel details', p.103. If you're arriving late at night, note that the bus station's immediate environs are unsavoury. It only takes a couple of minutes to reach more reassuring parts of downtown, but if you're travelling alone it's probably sound advice to take a taxi.

By rail

All incoming and outgoing trains use **Union Railway Station**, at the corner of Bay Street and Front Street West. Most long-distance trains are provided by VIA Rail (ⓣ1-888/842-7245, ⓦwww.viarail.ca), though Ontario Northland (ⓣ1-800/461-8558, ⓦwww.northlander.ca) chips in with the epic Northlander train to and from Cochrane (for Moosonee; see p.194). The Union station complex is the hub of the city's public transportation system, incorporating both a subway station and the main **GO** train terminal (see p.70).

By car

From Niagara Falls and points west along Lake Ontario, most traffic arrives via the Queen Elizabeth Way (**QEW**), which funnels into the **Gardiner Expressway**, an elevated motorway (notorious for delays) that cuts across the southern side of downtown, just south of Front Street. From the east, most drivers opt for the equally busy **Hwy 401**, which sweeps along Lake Ontario before veering off to slice through the city's suburbs north of downtown. Driving in from the north, take **Hwy 400**, which intersects with **Hwy 401** northwest of the centre, or **Hwy 404**, which meets **Hwy 401** northeast of the centre. On all routes you can expect delays during rush hours (roughly 7.30–9.30am and 4.30–6.30pm).

To relieve congestion on Hwy 401, an alternative motorway, **Hwy 407 ETR** (ⓦwww.407etr.com), has been built further north on the city's outskirts. It was

North America's first all-electronic toll highway: instead of tollbooths, each vehicle is identified by an electronic tag, and the invoice is posted later. Toll charges are fixed but vary – at peak times vehicles are charged 21.35¢ per kilometre – and there's also a small supplementary charge per trip for any vehicle without a transponder; these vehicles are identified by licence plate photos. If you rent a car, know that rental companies add an extra administration charge (around $15) if you take their vehicles on this road.

Information

The Ontario Tourism travel **information centre** (Mon–Sat 10am–6pm & Sun 11am–5pm; ⓣ1-800/ONTARIO, or within Toronto ⓣ416/314-5899) is street level inside the Atrium on Bay mall, 20 Dundas St West, at Yonge and stocks a comprehensive range of information on all the major attractions in Toronto and throughout Ontario. Most of it is free, including reasonably good-quality city maps, the Ride Guide to the city's transport system and entertainment details in the monthly magazine *Where* (ⓦwww.where.ca). Ontario Tourism will also book hotel accommodation on your behalf both in Toronto and across all of Ontario. They also operate ⓦwww.ontariotravel.net, which is particularly strong on practical information.

Tourism Toronto (Mon–Fri 8.30am–6pm; ⓣ1-800/499-2514 or 416/203-2500; ⓦwww.seetorontonow.com), the city's official visitor and convention bureau, does not have an information office, but does run a telephone information line, whose operators can handle most city queries and will make hotel reservations on your behalf. You can also scour bags of information and book accommodation on their website.

City transport

The Toronto Transit Commission, or **TTC** (ⓣ416/393-4636 helpline, ⓦwww.ttc.ca), operates the city's public transportation, which is fast, frequent and efficient, with an integrated network of subways, buses and streetcars serving virtually every corner of the city. With the exception of downtown, where all the major sights are within easy walking distance of each other, your best option is to use public transport to hop between attractions – especially in the cold of winter or the sultry summer. The TTC has gone to great lengths to assure the safety of its passengers: all subway stations have designated waiting areas (DWAs), which are well lit, have an intercom connection with TTC staff and are monitored by closed-circuit TV. TTC buses also operate a **Request Stop Program**, which allows women travelling alone late at night (9pm–5am) to get off buses wherever they want, and not just at regular TTC stops. A similarly positive approach has been adopted for passengers with **disabilities**, who can use a dedicated service, Wheel-Trans (ⓣ416/393-4222).

Tickets, tokens and passes

On every part of the TTC system a single journey **costs** $2.75. Adults (non-concessionary passengers) are only issued with metallic **tokens**, everyone else (seniors, students and children) can opt to receive either the metallic tokens or **tickets**. Both tickets and tokens are available at all subway stations and from

Orientation and street numbers

Yonge Street is Toronto's principal north–south artery. Main drags perpendicular to Yonge use this intersection to change from west to east – Queen Street West, for example, becomes Queen Street East when it crosses Yonge. Therefore, 1000 Queen Street West is, for example, a long way from 1000 Queen Street East.

bus and streetcar drivers. A batch of five tickets or tokens cost $11.25 (ten for $22.50) at any station and at many convenience stores and newsstands. Each ticket or token entitles passengers to one complete journey of any length on the TTC system. If this involves more than one type of transport, it is necessary to get a **paper transfer** at your point of entry. Streetcar and bus drivers issue transfers, as do the automatic machines located at every subway station. A **day pass** costs $9 and provides one adult with unlimited TTC travel on any day of the week. At weekends, the same pass can also be used as a family ticket, covering up to six people with a maximum of two adults. Day passes can be purchased at any subway station.

The subway

Toronto's **subway**, the core of the city's public transportation network, is a simple, three-line system. There are two main lines: one cuts east to west along Bloor Street and Danforth Avenue, while the other forms a loop with Union Station at its head; north of Union, one part of this subway line runs along University Avenue, the other along Yonge Street. **Transferring** between the two subway lines is possible at three stations only: Spadina, St George and Bloor-Yonge. The subway operates Mon–Sat 6am–1.00am & Sun 9am–1.00am.

Buses and streetcars

The **bus** and **streetcar** network couldn't be simpler, as a bus and/or streetcar station adjoins every major subway stop. Hours of operation vary with the route, but are comparable with subway times; there is also a limited network of **night buses** running along key routes roughly hourly between 1am and 6am.

Commuter lines

GO trains (Ⓣ416/869-3200, Ⓦwww.gotransit.com) arrive and depart from Union Station, linking the city centre with various suburbs and satellite towns. There are no free transfers from the TTC system to GO train lines, though these are primarily used by commuters and are little used by tourists based in the city.

Taxis

Taxis cruise the city in numbers. Give the driver your destination and ask the approximate price before you start. **Fares** are generally reasonable and are based on a fixed tariff of $3 per kilometre plus a small pick-up charge. As an example, a ride from Union Station to the corner of Bloor and Yonge streets should cost around $10. Taxis can also be reserved in advance. Of the multitude of companies to choose from, two of the most dependable are Co-op Cabs (Ⓣ416/504-2667) and Diamond Taxicab (Ⓣ416/366-6868). Toronto taxi drivers anticipate a tip of ten to fifteen percent on the total fare.

Accommodation

As Toronto's popularity as a tourist destination has increased, so the availability of **hotel** accommodation, especially in the mid-price range, has shrunk. During peak season (late June–Aug) and throughout most of the city's big festivals, booking in advance is essential. Most of the city's hotels occupy modern skyscrapers, though the opening of a string of **boutique hotels** has livened things up considerably. Prices fluctuate depending on when and for how long you stay; in general, a clean, centrally located hotel double room starts at $140. **Bed and breakfast** accommodation tends to be less expensive and although most of these establishments are not as central as the city's hotels, they often take you out into Toronto's quainter neighbourhoods. Budget-conscious travellers might want to consider one of the city's **hostels** or opt instead for a **student room** in one of the university's halls of residence, available – with some variation – from the second week in May to late August. The Ontario Tourism travel information centre (see p.69) will help in **finding a hotel room**, as will Tourism Toronto (see p.69).

Hotels

Bond Place 65 Dundas St East; Subway: Dundas ⓣ416/362-6061 or 1-800/268-9390, ⓦwww.bondplace.ca. This straightforward, tower-block hotel is popular with package-tour operators and handily located, just a couple of minutes' walk from the Eaton Centre. It has simple, unassuming doubles and there are often weekend reductions. ❻

Delta Chelsea Inn 33 Gerrard St West, at Yonge; Subway: Dundas ⓣ416/595-1975 or 1-800/243-5732, ⓦwww.deltachelsea.com. Near the Eaton Centre, this whopping hotel has excellent leisure facilities, including swimming pool, gym, sauna and childcare. The comfortable, attractively furnished rooms are a comparative bargain, with substantial weekend discounts. ❻

Drake Hotel 1150 Queen St West, at Beaconsfield ⓣ416/531-5042 or 1-866/372-5386, ⓦwww.thedrakehotel.ca. Part night club, restaurant, bar and art venue, the *Drake* is one of the most fashionable places in town. The hotel section (which can be noisy) has just nineteen rooms, a mixture of ultra luxurious and kitsch/bizarre, from the handcrafted furniture and big beds through to the peculiar dolls left on the pillows. It's west of the centre – to get there take the Queen St streetcar (#501). ❼

Fairmont Royal York 100 Front St West; Subway: Union ⓣ416/368-2511 or 1-866/540-4489, ⓦwww.fairmont.com/royalyork. When it was completed in 1927, the *Royal York* was the largest hotel in the British Empire and it still retains much of its original grandeur, especially in the sprawling lobby, which is decked out with mosaic floors, coffered ceilings and massive chandeliers. Still, the rooms aren't as pricey (or as stylish) as you might expect and there are substantial off-season and weekend discounts. ❼

Gladstone Hotel 1214 Queen St West, at Gladstone ⓣ416/531-4635, ⓦwww.gladstonehotel.com. Continuously open since 1889, the *Gladstone* follows the dictum "new ideas in old buildings". All the uber-cool rooms have been designed by different local artists, right down to the wallpaper, and communal areas serve as art galleries. The splendid hand-operated cage elevator is still working, operated by Hank Young, the "Gladstone Cowboy". It's west of the centre, two blocks from the *Drake* (see opposite) – to get there take the Queen St streetcar (#501) ❻

Le Germain 30 Mercer St; Subway: St Andrew ⓣ416/345-9500 or 1-866/345-9501, ⓦwww.germaintoronto.com. Immaculate boutique hotel kitted out in the full flourish of modern style, from the handsome foyer, with its soaring ceiling, open fire and acres of glass, through to the stylish, well-appointed guest rooms. A five- to ten-minute walk west from the subway. ❽

Le Méridien King Edward 37 King St East; Subway: King ⓣ416/863-9700, ⓦwww.starwoodhotels.com. Designed by E.J. Lennox (see p.83) in 1903 and with a long list of famous guests – from Mark Twain to John and Yoko – this distinguished old hotel has recently been restored to its Beaux Arts best. Rooms range from chic minimalism to faux Edwardian. ❽

Novotel Toronto Centre 45 The Esplanade; Subway: Union ⓣ416/367-8900, ⓦwww.novotel.com. Located in a splendidly converted old building, with an elegant arcaded facade and other Art Deco flourishes, this chain hotel offers excellent service at moderate prices. Its relative affordability

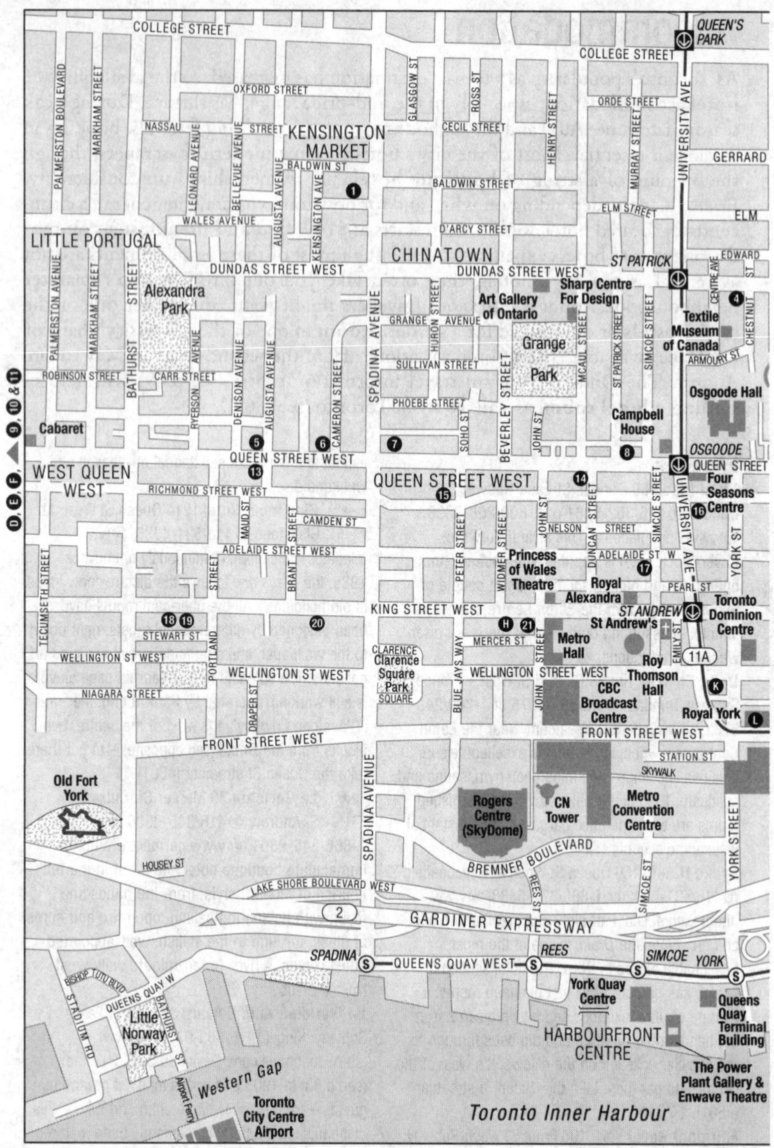

may be linked to its noisy location – it abuts the railway – but otherwise, the location is excellent, close to the downtown core and the Distillery District. 6

Strathcona 60 York St; Subway: Union ⓣ416/363-3321 or 1-800/268-8304, ⓦwww.thestrathconahotel.com. A great location for this recently revamped hotel, whose well-equipped guest rooms are kitted out in unfussy, modern style. 6

Victoria 56 Yonge St; Subway: King ⓣ416/363-1666 or 1-800/363-8228, ⓦwww.hotelvictoria-toronto.com. This pleasant hotel occupies a dignified old building in the heart of downtown. The

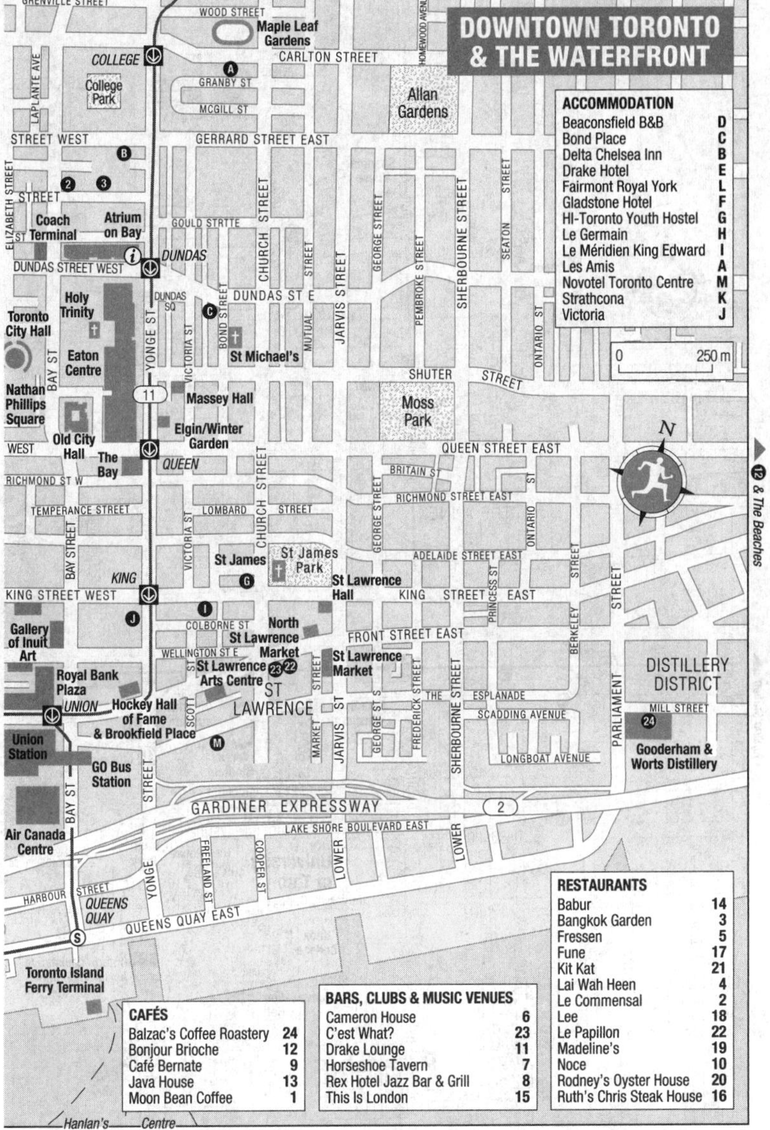

fifty-odd rooms are clean and crisply furnished, if a tad cramped. 6

Windsor Arms 18 St Thomas St; Subway: Bay ⓣ416/971-9666 or 1-877/999-2767, ⓦwww.windsorarmshotel.com. One of the city's most distinctive hotels, the *Windsor* occupies an immaculate brick-and-stone-trimmed neo-Gothic building that is actually a replica of the original 1911 edifice that was burnt down in the 1990s. Open fires, columns, stained-glass windows and Georgian-style furniture characterize the interior. What's new are the condominiums on top, plus the no-expense-spared spa; the service is also top notch. 8

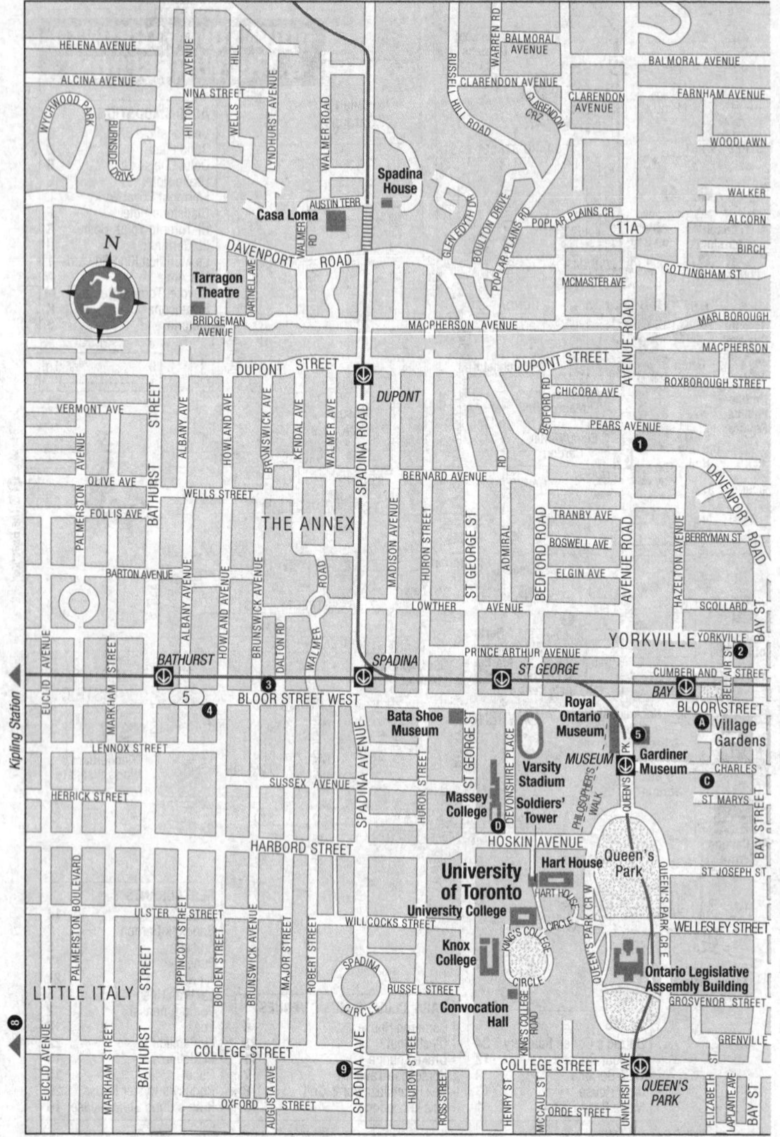

B&Bs

Au Petit Paris 3 Selby St; Subway: Sherbourne ⓣ416/928-1348, ⓦwww.bbtoronto.com/aupetitparis. Cosy B&B in an attractively renovated Victorian terrace house. Each of the guest rooms is decorated in modern style, with hardwood floors and pastel-painted walls, and comes complete with a queen-size bed and en-suite facilities. Vegetarian breakfasts are the house speciality, prepared by the French-speaking owners, and the breakfast room has a lovely little balcony. ❻

Beaconsfield B&B 38 Beaconsfield Ave ⓣ416/535-3338, ⓦwww.bbcanada.com/771.html.

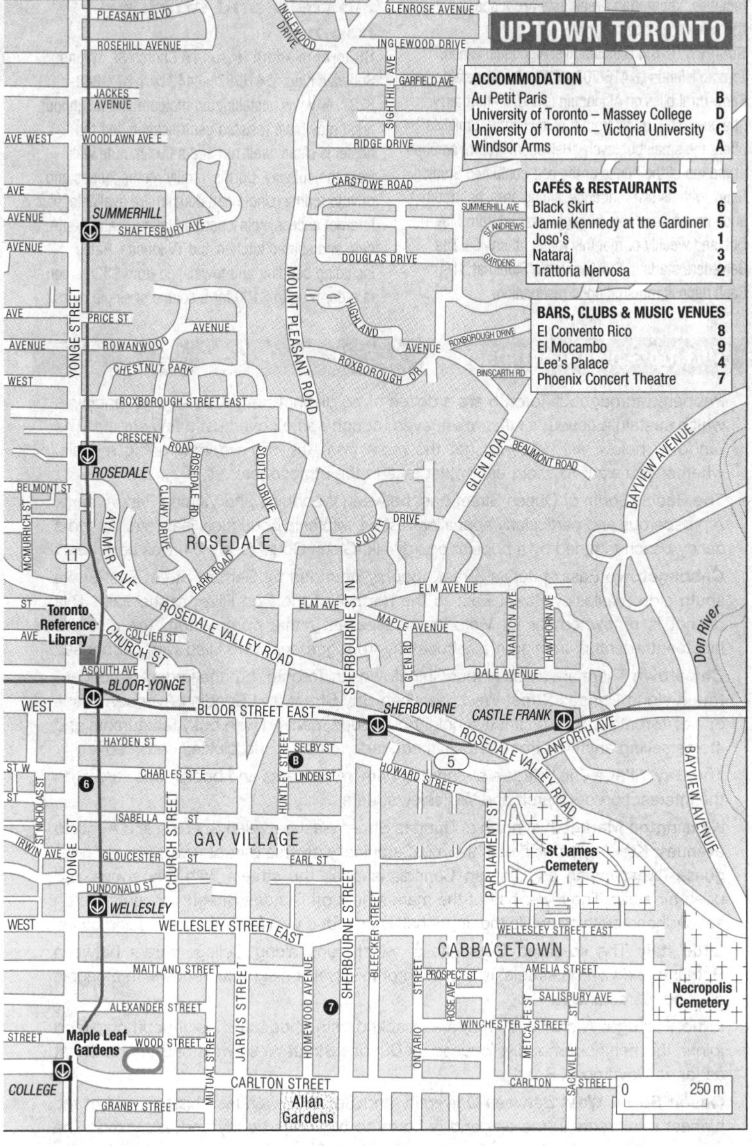

This substantial 1880s mansion with its pillared porch is situated in the fashionable Queen St West neighbourhood to the west of the centre. It offers three guest rooms (two en suite; ⑥), each of which is decorated in a lively, colourful style, as are the public areas. Outside deck too. Open May–Oct; minimum two-night stay. To get there take the Queen St streetcar (#501). Room with shared facilities ④

Les Amis 31 Granby St; Subway: College ⓣ416/591-0635, ⓦwww.bbtoronto.com. Downtown B&B located a short stroll from the Eaton Centre and holding a handful of pleasantly furnished rooms, some en suite, others with shared facilities. Vegetarian breakfasts are a speciality – the crêpes go down a treat. ❺

Smiley's B&B 4 Dacotah Ave, Algonquin Island, Toronto Islands ⓣ416/203-8599, ⓦwww.erelda.ca. Semi-rural bliss on Algonquin Island, a short ferry ride (see p.96) away from the city centre. Smiley's offers the small but lovely "Belvedere" room, perched at the top of the house or the self-contained Studio Suite, with its own entrance, sitting area, bathroom and kitchen, available for nightly rental from May–Oct, and weekly or monthly rental otherwise. The Belvedere starts at $80/night; the Studio at $180. Cash deposit required upon reservation.

Hostels and student rooms

HI-Toronto Youth Hostel 76 Church St, at King; Subway: King ⓣ416/971-4440 or 1-877-848-8737, ⓦwww.hostellingtoronto.com.The neighbourhood may have resisted gentrification, but the hostel is clean, well-run and a five-minute walk from the subway. Dorms, family rooms, quads and private rooms (single and double) are available, plus internet access, coin-operated laundry, an on-site café and shared kitchen and TV lounge. Rates, including bedding and towels, go from $32/person in a dorm up to $100 for a double or single room.

Toronto's neighbourhoods

Peppered throughout Toronto are a dozen or so distinct **neighbourhoods**, enclaves which sustain a flavour all their own, even though some cover just a few streets. The rundown below will help you get the most from the city's demographic mosaic, whether you want to shop, eat or just take in the atmosphere.

The Beach South of Queen Street East between Woodbine and Victoria Park Avenue. A prosperous and particularly appealing district with chic boutiques, leafy streets and a sandy beach trimmed by a popular boardwalk. Glenn Gould (see p.84) was born here.

Cabbagetown East of Jarvis Street, roughly bounded by Gerrard Street East on its south side, Wellesley Street East to the north and the Don River to the east. This district is renowned for its Victorian houses. Its name comes from the district's nineteenth-century immigrants, whose tiny front gardens were filled with cabbages.

Chinatown There are actually four Chinatowns in Toronto, but the largest is concentrated along Dundas Street West, between Bay Street and Spadina Avenue. This is one of Toronto's most distinctive neighbourhoods, packed with busy restaurants and stores selling anything from porcelain and jade to herbs and pickled seaweed.

The Gay Village The Village's plethora of bars, restaurants and bookshops zero in on the intersection of Church and Wellesley streets.

Kensington Market Just north of Dundas Street West between Spadina and Augusta avenues, Kensington Market is the most ethnically diverse part of town, where Portuguese, West Indian and Jewish Canadians pack the streets with tiny shops and open-air stalls. The lower half of the market, just off Dundas Street, concentrates on secondhand clothing, while the upper half is crowded with fresh-food stalls and cafés.

Little Italy The so-called Corso Italia, which runs along College Street between Bathurst and Clinton streets, is one of Toronto's livelist neighbourhoods with a gaggle of good restaurants.

Little Portugal A crowded, vital area packed with shops and neighbourhood food joints, this neighbourhood is focused on Dundas Street West, west of Bathurst Street as far as Dovercourt Road.

Queen Street West Between University and Spadina avenues, this has one of the highest retail rents in the city and is home to all things trendy and expensive. The students and punks who once hung around here have, however, moved on to what is known as **West Queen West**, between Bathurst Street and Ossington Avenue.

Yorkville Just above Bloor Street West between Bay Street and Avenue Road, Yorkville was "alternative" in the 1960s, with appearances by figureheads of the counterculture like Gordon Lightfoot and Joni Mitchell. Today, the alternative vibe of the place is long gone, and the district holds some of Toronto's most chi-chi clothing shops and art galleries, as well as several good bars and restaurants.

University of Toronto: Massey College 4 Devonshire Place; Subway: St George ⓣ416/946-7843, ⓦwww.utoronto.ca/massey. The one-time stomping ground of author Robertson Davies, this old and distinguished college reportedly also boasts the presence of at least one ghost. Simple singles and doubles are available, with breakfast included on weekdays, from May–early Aug. Singles $50, doubles $100.

University of Toronto: Victoria University 140 Charles St West; Subway: Museum ⓣ416/813-4098, ⓦwww.vicu.utoronto.ca. Victoria University's sprawling campus, spreading south from Charles St, offers single and double rooms (with breakfast) in several of its halls of residence from mid-May to late Aug. Single room $60, doubles $80.

The City

Toronto has evolved from a lakeside settlement, but its growth has been sporadic and mostly unplanned, resulting in a cityscape that can strike the visitor as a particularly random mix of the run-down, the old and the new. This apparent disarray, when combined with the city's muggy summers, means most visitors spend their time hopping from sight to sight on the transit rather than walking. Yet if you've the time and determination to get under the skin of the city, take to your feet and Toronto will slowly reveal itself. The logical place to start an exploration is **Downtown Toronto** at the **CN Tower**, whose observation platforms provide panoramic views over the city and its immediate surroundings. From here, it's a brief stroll to the handsome symmetries of **Union Station**, which stands on the edge of the **Banking District**, whose striking skyscrapers march north up Yonge Street as far as Adelaide Street. Beyond Adelaide Street lies the main shopping area, revolving around the enormous **Eaton Centre**, which is itself a stone's throw from the neo-Gothic intricacies of the old **City Hall** and the modernism of **Nathan Philips Square**. From the square, it's another short haul to the **Art Gallery of Ontario**, holding the city's finest collection of paintings, and another, slightly longer trek west to **Fort York**, an accurate and intriguing reconstruction of the British outpost established here in 1793.

Moving on into **Uptown Toronto**, the northerly reaches of **University Avenue** are framed by a string of bristling, monochromatic office blocks that stomp up to the imposing stonework of the **Ontario Legislative Assembly Building**. This marks the start of what amounts to a museum district, comprising the delightful ceramics of the **Gardiner Museum**, the rambling applied arts collections of the vast **Royal Ontario Museum** and the fascinating **Bata Shoe Museum**. A pair of contrasting Victorian mansions – grandiose **Casa Loma** and genteel **Spadina House** – are a short subway ride away. Finally, save time for the redeveloped **Harbourfront** south of Union Station, which offers flashy shops and galleries as well as the jetty from where passenger **ferries** make the short hop over to the bucolic **Toronto Islands**.

The CN Tower

To the dismay of many Torontonians, the **CN Tower** (daily 9am–10pm, sometimes later; observation deck & glass floor $22, Sky Pod $5 extra; ⓦwww.cntower.ca), at 301 Front St West, has become the city's symbol. It's touted on much of the city's promotional literature, features on thousands of postcards and holiday snaps and has become the obligatory start to most tourist itineraries. From anywhere in the city, it's impossible to miss its slender form poking high above the skyline, reminding some of French novelist Guy de Maupassant's quip about another famous tower: "I like to lunch at the Eiffel Tower because that's the only place in Paris I can't see it."

Unlikely as it may seem, the celebrity status of the CN Tower was entirely unforeseen, its origins plain and utilitarian. In the 1960s, the Canadian Broadcasting Corporation (CBC) teamed up with the railway conglomerate Canadian National (CN) to propose the construction of a bigger and better transmission antenna. The CBC eventually withdrew from the project, but CN, who owned the land, forged ahead. To the company's surprise, they found the undertaking stirred intense public interest – so much so that long before the tower was completed, in 1975, it was clear its potential as a tourist sight would be huge: today, broadcasting only accounts for about twenty percent of the tower's income, with the rest provided by the two million tourists who throng here annually. Come early (especially on school holidays) to avoid the crowds.

Though recently pipped to the post by the Burj Khalifa, in Dubai, the CN Tower was for several decades the **tallest freestanding structure in the world**, its sleek and elegant tower tapering to a minaret-thin point 553m (1815ft) above the city centre. Details of its construction are provided in a series of photographs and touch-screen displays on the mezzanine level, just beyond the main access ramp and security check-in. The background information is extremely interesting, revealing all sorts of odd facts and figures, though it's hardly reassuring to know the tower is hit by lightning between sixty and eighty times a year.

From the foot of the tower, **glass-fronted elevators** whisk you up the outside of the building to the indoor and outdoor **Look Out level** at 346m. The circular galleries here provide views over the whole of the city, which appears flattened and without much perspective – though markers help by pointing out the most conspicuous sights. This is also where you'll find *360 The Restaurant* (which slowly revolves around the tower, taking 72 minutes to make one revolution), and the reinforced **glass floor** – a vertigo shock that goes some way to justifying the tower's pricey admittance fee. You are, however, still 100m from the top of the tower, with a separate set of lifts to carry visitors up to the **Sky Pod**, a confined little gallery that doesn't really justify the extra expense.

The Rogers Centre (SkyDome)

Next door to the CN Tower stands the **Rogers Centre**, formerly the **SkyDome**, which is home to two major Toronto sports teams – the Blue Jays baseball team and the Argonauts, of Canadian Football League fame. The stadium seats 53,000 and is used for special events and concerts as well as sports. Opened in 1989, it was the first stadium in the world to have a fully retractable roof, an impressive feat of engineering with four gigantic roof panels mounted on rail tracks taking just twenty minutes to cover the stadium's eight acres of turf and terrace. The SkyDome was much touted by the city at the time, but the end result is really rather ugly and when the roof is closed the stadium looks like a giant armadillo. **Guided tours** (call for schedule ⓣ416/341-2771, ⓦwww.rogerscentre.com; $13.75), worth it only if you're sticking around for a sporting event, last an hour and begin with a fifteen-minute film about the stadium's construction. The ensuing walking tour takes in a dressing room and a stroll on the playing field.

Union Station

The **Skywalk** is a sheltered walkway leading from the Rogers Centre to **Union Station**, at Front Street West and Bay Street, a distinguished Beaux Arts structure designed in 1907 and completed in 1927. The station's exterior is imposing, with its long row of Neoclassical columns, but the interior is the real highlight, the vast **main hall** boasting a coffered and tiled ceiling of graceful design. Like other North American railway stations of the period, Union Station has the flavour of a medieval cathedral, with muffled sounds echoing through its stone cloisters and daylight filtering through its high-arched windows. The station's grandiose quality was quite deliberate; in the days when the steam train was the most popular form of transport, architects were keen to glorify the train station, and, in this case, to conjure up images of Canada's vastness – a frieze bearing the names of all the Canadian cities reachable by rail at the time of construction runs around the hall.

The Banking District: the Royal Bank Plaza and the Toronto Dominion Centre

Opposite the east end of Union Station, the **Banking District,** which extends north as far as Queen Street, kicks off with the **Royal Bank Plaza**, at 200 Bay St, where the two massive towers were designed by local architect Boris Zerafa. Each tower is coated with a thin layer of gold, and despite Zerafa's assertion that the gold simply added texture to his creation, it's hard not to believe the Royal Bank wanted to show off a bit.

To the left of the Royal Bank – and to the right of the *Royal York* hotel – a gated **stone stairway** climbs up from Front Street West to a tiny plaza overseen by a phalanx of skyscrapers. It's a delightful spot, in a heart-of-the-city sort of way, and **Catherine Widgery**'s *City People*, a folksy set of life-size aluminium figures attached to the stairway's walls, adds a touch of decorative élan. The walkway continues down to Wellington Street West, just a few metres from the southern tower – now the Waterhouse Tower – of the **Toronto Dominion Centre,** whose four reflective black blocks straddle Wellington Street between Bay and York streets. Arguably the most appealing of the city's modern skyscrapers, the four towers are without decoration, but as an ensemble they achieve an austere beauty that can't help but impress.

The Toronto Dominion Gallery of Inuit Art

The **Toronto Dominion Gallery of Inuit Art** (Mon–Fri 8am–6pm, Sat & Sun 10am–4pm; free), in the South – or Waterhouse – Tower of the Toronto Dominion Centre, boasts an outstanding collection of over a hundred pieces of

Selling air

In one of the city's stranger ordinances, Toronto's buildings were once decreed to have a **"notional maximum altitude"**. Owners of historic properties were not allowed to extend their buildings upwards, but they were permitted to sell the empty space between their roofs and the notional maximum to builders of new structures. Consequently, developers literally bought empty space and added it on to the maximum height they were already allowed for their buildings, thus creating the skyscrapers that the original ordinance seemed to forbid.

The arrangement enhanced neither the old nor the new, and was quickly followed up by an even stranger agreement. By the late 1980s, preservationists had convinced the city that no more of the city's old buildings should be demolished. Yet developers still wanted to build new downtown buildings, and several deals emerged where a new complex would incorporate or literally engulf the old – the most extreme example being Brookfield Place at the corner of Yonge and Front streets (see p.82).

Inuit sculpture. Spread over two levels, the collection is owned by the Toronto Dominion Bank, who commissioned a panel of experts to celebrate Canada's Centennial in 1965 by collecting the best of postwar Inuit art. The gallery contains examples of all the favourite themes of Inuit sculpture, primarily animal and human studies, supplemented by a smattering of metamorphic figures, in which an Inuit adopts the form of an animal, either in full or in part. Other sculptures depict deities, particularly Sedna, the sea goddess. Inuit religious belief was short on theology, but its encyclopedic animism populated the Arctic with spirits and gods, the subject of all manner of Inuit folk tales. Most of the pieces are in soapstone, but there are bone, ivory and caribou-antler pieces too. The only problem is the almost total lack of labelling, though a free introductory booklet, available from the rack at the start of the gallery, does provide some assistance.

St Andrew's Presbyterian Church and Roy Thomson Hall

Crossing over Wellington Street, and walking between the other three towers of the Toronto Dominion Centre, you soon pass **Joe Fafard**'s herd of grazing cows – seven extraordinarily realistic **bronze statues** that have proved immensely popular with the city's office workers. From here, it's a short detour west along King Street to **St Andrew's Presbyterian Church** (daily 9am–4pm; free) at 75 Simcoe St. Marooned among the city's skyscrapers, this handsome sandstone church is a reminder of an older Toronto, and its Romanesque Revival towers and gables have a distinctly Norman appearance. Built in 1876 for a predominantly Scottish congregation, the church has a delightful interior, its cherrywood pews and balcony sloping down towards the chancel with dappled light streaming in through the stained glass windows.

Across Simcoe Street from St Andrew's, **Roy Thomson Hall**, the home of the Toronto Symphony Orchestra (see p.102), was completed in 1982 to a design by Canada's own Arthur Erickson. The hall looks like an upturned soup bowl by day, but at night its appearance is transformed, its glass-panelled walls radiating a skein of filtered light high into the sky.

The CBC Centre

From Thomson Hall, it's a brief walk southwest to the **CBC Broadcasting Centre**, at 250 Front St West, a ten-storey edifice whose painted gridiron beams make the building aesthetically bearable, but not much more. Since its foundation in 1936, the **CBC** – the Canadian Broadcasting Corporation – has built up an international reputation for the impartiality of its radio and television news and, although it carries commercials unlike the UK's BBC, it remains in public ownership. The CBC used to offer guided tours of the Broadcasting Centre, but these have been discontinued, at least for the moment. You can still visit the CBC museum (Mon–Fri 9am–5pm; free; Ⓦwww.cbc.ca/museum), where, among a series of modest exhibits, vintage CBC TV shows are shown in a mini-theatre. In addition, three sets of push-buttons – one set each for public affairs, news and kids' programmes – access about forty brief programme clips, from perceptive comments on the US war in Vietnam to a particularly potty piece of 1969 social scaremongering in which the reporter claims – among much else – that the assorted drug-addled hippies of Toronto's Yorkville (see p.76) would "make love to anyone".

From the CBC Broadcasting Centre, it's a twenty–minute hoof **west** to Fort York, and half that **east** to the Hockey Hall of Fame and the St Lawrence district (see p.82).

Fort York

Modern-day Toronto traces its origins to **Fort York** (mid-May to Aug daily 10am–5pm; Sept to mid-May Mon–Fri 10am–4pm, Sat & Sun 10am–5pm; $9; ⓣ416/392-6907, ⓦwww.fortyork.ca), a colonial stockade built in 1793 on the shores of Lake Ontario to bolster British control of the Great Lakes. Since then, landfill has pushed the lakeshore southwards and marooned the fort, which was reconstructed in the 1930s, under the shadow of the (elevated) Gardiner Expressway just to the west of Bathurst Street. There are **two entrances** to the fort: a well-signed main entrance off Lakeshore Boulevard West, and a pedestrians' back entrance via a path off Bathurst Street. To get to the latter, head west along Front Street from the CBC Broadcasting Centre, turn left onto Bathurst Street, walk over the bridge and the path is on the right. To shorten the walk, take the King Street tram west to King and Bathurst streets. To reach the front entrance by public transport, take streetcar #509 from Union Station and get off on Fleet Street, from where it's a ten-minute walk via Fort York Boulevard or Garrison Road.

Fort York was initially a half-hearted, poorly fortified affair, partly because of a lack of funds, but mainly because it was too remote to command much attention – never mind that the township of York was the capital of Upper Canada. Yet in 1811 a deterioration in Anglo-American relations put it on full alert. There was a sudden flurry of activity as the fort's ramparts and gun emplacements were strengthened, but it was still too weak to rebuff the American army that marched on York in 1813, destroying the fort in the process. After the war, the fort was rebuilt and its garrison made a considerable contribution to the development of Toronto, as York was renamed in 1834. The British army moved out in 1870 and their Canadian replacements stayed for another sixty years; the fort was opened as a **museum** in 1934. Throughout the summer, costumed guides give the low-down on colonial life and free plans of the fort are issued at reception.

The fort

The fort's carefully restored earth and stone **ramparts** are low-lying, thick and constructed in a zigzag pattern, both to mitigate against enemy artillery and to provide complementary lines of fire. They enclose a haphazard sequence of log, stone and brick buildings, notably a couple of well-preserved **blockhouses**, complete with heavy timbers and snipers' loopholes. In one of them – **Building No.5** on the plan – an introductory video outlines the history of the fort and an exhibit explores the various military crises that afflicted Canada from the 1780s to the 1880s, especially the War of 1812.

Moving on, **Building No.6** started out as a magazine but ended up as a storehouse. Its ground floor now holds a modest display on the role of black soldiers and settlers in the early history of Ontario. Above, an archeological section displays the various bits and pieces unearthed at the fort, including buckles, brooches, plates, clay pipes and tunic buttons. Across the fort, **Building No.4**, the Blue Barracks, is a 1930s reconstruction of the junior officers' quarters, while **Building No.3** is the former officers' quarters and mess. The latter boasts several period rooms and two original money vaults, hidden away in the cellar. Opposite is **Building No.8**, the stone and brick powder magazine, which has 2m-thick walls and spark-proof copper and brass fixtures.

The Hockey Hall of Fame

From the CBC Broadcasting Centre (see opposite), it's a short haul east to the **Hockey Hall of Fame** (Mon–Fri 10am–5pm, Sat 9.30am–6pm & Sun 10.30am–5pm; $15, children 4–13 years old & the over-65s $10; Ⓦwww.hhof.com), 30 Yonge St at Front Street West, a highly commercialized, ultra-modern tribute to Canada's national obsession – though you wouldn't think so from the outside: the only part of the Hall visible from the street is the old **Bank of Montréal** building, a Neoclassical edifice dating back to 1885. The **entrance** to the Hockey Hall of Fame is below ground in the adjacent Brookfield Place, a large, glass-roofed retail complex on the west side of Yonge Street that entirely encloses the old bank building. Inside the Hall are a series of exhibition areas, featuring a replica of the Montréal Canadiens' locker room, a mini **ice-rink,** copious biographical details of the sport's great names, descriptions of the various National Hockey League teams, and, in the trophy room, the very first Stanley Cup, donated by Lord Stanley, the Governor General of Canada, in 1893.

The St Lawrence District

The **St Lawrence district**, lying just to the east of Yonge Street, between The Esplanade, Adelaide Street East and Frederick Street, is one of the city's oldest neighbourhoods, enjoying its first period of rapid growth after the War of 1812. In Victorian times, St Lawrence became one of the most fashionable parts of the city, and although it hit the skids thereafter, it was revamped and partly gentrified in the late 1990s. The best approach is along Front Street East, heading east from Yonge Street. From this direction, you'll soon reach **St Lawrence Market** (Tues–Thurs 8am–6pm, Fri 8am–7pm & Sat 5am–5pm; Ⓦwww.stlawrencemarket.com), at Front and Market streets, a capacious red-brick building of 1844 that holds the city's best food and drink market. Spread out across the main and lower levels are stalls selling everything from fish and freshly baked bread to international foodstuffs, all sorts of organic edibles and Ontario specialities, including cheese, jellies, jams and fern fiddleheads. The market is at its busiest on Saturday, which also means you can drop by the **North St Lawrence Market**, an authentic farmers' market (Sat 5am–4pm) housed in the long brick building opposite, on the north side of Front Street.

St Lawrence Hall

Behind North St Lawrence Market, just along Jarvis Street, stands **St Lawrence Hall**, one of Toronto's most attractive Victorian buildings, a palatial edifice whose columns, pilasters and pediments are surmounted by a dinky little cupola. Dating from 1850, the hall was built as the city's main meeting place, with oodles of space for balls, public lectures and concerts. Some performances were eminently genteel, others decidedly mawkish – it was here that the "Swedish songbird" **Jenny Lind** made one of her Canadian appearances – and yet others more urgent, like the anti-slavery rallies of the 1850s. The bad taste award goes to the American showman and circus proprietor **P.T. Barnum**, one-time mayor of his hometown of Bridgeport, Connecticut, and author of the bizarre *The Humbugs of the World*. It was Barnum who saw the potential of his fellow Bridgeportonian, the diminutive (60cm) Charles Sherwood Stratton, aka **Tom Thumb**, exhibiting him as a curiosity here in St Lawrence Hall as well as anywhere else that would pay.

St James Anglican Cathedral

On the other side of King Street, a couple of hundred metres west from St Lawrence Hall, rises the graceful bulk of **St James Anglican Cathedral**, whose yellowish stone is fetchingly offset by copper-green roofs and a slender spire. An excellent example of the neo-Gothic style once popular in every corner of the

British Empire, the cathedral boasts scores of pointed-arch windows and acres of sturdy buttressing. Inside, the nave is supported by elegant high-arched pillars and flanked by an ambitious set of **stained glass windows** that attempts to trace the path by which Christianity reached Canada from Palestine via England. It's all a little confusing, but broadly speaking, the less inventive windows depict Biblical scenes, whereas those that focus on English history are the more ingenious.

The Distillery District

The **Distillery District** (Ⓦwww.thedistillerydistrict.com) is home to Toronto's newest arts and entertainment complex, sited in the former **Gooderham and Worts Distillery**, an extremely appealing industrial "village" on Mill Street, near the foot of Parliament Street. This rambling network of over forty brick buildings once constituted the largest distillery in the British Empire. In operation as such until 1990 it was founded in 1832, when ships could sail into its own jetty, though landfill subsequently marooned it in the lee of the railway lines and the tail end of the Gardiner Expressway.

Since its demise, the distillery has been sympathetically redeveloped by a small group of entrepreneurs, who chose to integrate many of the original features into the revamp – including its quirky walkways and bottle runways – and, with refreshing integrity, to exclude all multinational chains. One of the architectural highlights is the **Pure Spirits** building, which features French doors and a fancy wrought-iron balcony. Among much else, the complex holds art galleries and artists' studios, designers, a chocolatier, bakeries, shops, a microbrewery and a couple of performance venues. Most of the galleries and shops **open** daily at 9am or 10am and close at 6pm; the cafés and bars stay open later.

To get to the Distillery District by public transport, take the King Street streetcar (#504) east to Parliament Street; it's a five-minute walk from there.

Nathan Phillips Square

Back in the city centre, on Queen Street West, **Nathan Phillips Square** is one of Toronto's most distinctive landmarks, the whole caboodle designed in the 1960s by a Finnish architect, the determined functionalist **Viljo Revell**. The square is framed by an elevated walkway and focuses on a reflecting pool, which becomes a skating rink in winter. Toronto's modernist **City Hall** overlooks the square, its curved glass-and-concrete towers fronted by *The Archer*, a Henry Moore sculpture that resembles nothing so much as a giant propeller. Revell won all sorts of awards for this project, which was then considered the last word in urban design, though today its rain-stained blocks look rather dejected. Had Revell's grand scheme been fully implemented, the city would have bulldozed the **Old City Hall**, a flamboyant pseudo-Romanesque building on the east side of the square. Completed in 1899, it was designed by **Edward J. Lennox**, who developed a fractious relationship with his city council paymasters. They had a point: the original cost of the building had been estimated at $1.77m, but Lennox spent an extra $750,000 and took eight years to finish it. Lennox had the last laugh, carving gargoyle-like representations of the city fathers on the arches at the top of the front steps and placing his name on each side of the building – something the city council had expressly forbidden him to do.

The Eaton Centre

Beginning on the north side of Queen Street West, the **Eaton Centre** (Mon–Fri 10am–9pm, Sat 9.30am–7pm & Sun 11am–6pm; Ⓦwww.torontoeatoncentre.com)

Glenn Gould

In the 1970s, anyone passing the Eaton's department store around 9pm on any day of the year might have seen the door unlocked for a distracted-looking figure swaddled in overcoat, scarves, gloves and hat. This character, making his way to a recording studio set up for his exclusive use inside the store, was perhaps the most famous citizen of Toronto and certainly the most charismatic pianist in the world – **Glenn Gould**.

Not the least remarkable thing about Gould was that very few people outside the CBS recording crew would ever hear him play live. In 1964, aged just 32, he retired from the concert platform, partly out of a distaste for the accidental qualities of any live performance, partly out of hatred for the cult of the virtuoso. Yet no pianist ever provided more material for the mythologizers. He possessed a memory so prodigious that none of his acquaintances was ever able to find a piece of music he could not instantly play perfectly, but he loathed much of the standard piano repertoire, dismissing romantic composers such as Chopin, Liszt and Rachmaninoff as little more than showmen. Dauntingly cerebral in his tastes and playing style, he was nonetheless an ardent fan of Barbra Streisand – an esteem that was fully reciprocated – and once wrote an essay titled "**In Search of Petula Clark**". He lived at night and kept in touch by phoning his friends in the small hours of the morning, talking for so long that his monthly phone bill ran into thousands of dollars. Detesting all blood sports (a category in which he placed concert performances), he would terrorize anglers on Ontario's Lake Simcoe by buzzing them in his motorboat. He travelled everywhere with bags full of medicines and would never allow anyone to shake his hand, yet soaked his arms in almost scalding water before playing in order to get his circulation going. At the keyboard, he sang loudly to himself, swaying back and forth on a creaky little chair made for him by his father – all other pianists sat too high, he insisted. And even in a heatwave he was always dressed as if a blizzard were imminent. To many of his colleagues, Gould's eccentricities were maddening, but what mattered was that nobody could play like Glenn Gould. As one exasperated conductor put it, "the nut's a genius".

Gould's **first recording**, Bach's *Goldberg Variations*, was released in 1956, and became the bestselling classical record of that year. Soon after, he became the first Western musician to play in the Soviet Union, where his reputation spread so quickly that for his final recital more than a thousand people were allowed to stand in the aisles of the Leningrad hall. On his debut in Berlin, a leading German critic described him as "a young man in a strange sort of trance" whose "technical ability borders on the fabulous". The technique always dazzled, but Gould's fiercely wayward intelligence made his interpretations controversial, as can be gauged from an announcement by **Leonard Bernstein**, who, when he was conducting Gould on one occasion, informed the audience that what they were about to hear was the pianist's responsibility, not his. Most notoriously of all, he had a very low opinion of Mozart's abilities – and went so far as to record the **Mozart** sonatas in order to demonstrate the legendary composer died too late rather than too soon. Gould himself **died** suddenly in 1982 at the age of 50 – the age at which he had said he would give up playing the piano entirely.

Gould's **legacy of recordings** is not confined to music. He made a trilogy of radio documentaries on the theme of solitude: *The Quiet in the Land*, about Canada's Mennonites; *The Latecomers*, about the inhabitants of Newfoundland; and *The Idea of North*, for which he taped interviews with people who, like himself, spent much of their time amid Canada's harshest landscapes. Just as Gould's musical interpretations sounded like nobody else's, these were documentaries like no others, each a complex weave of voices that are overtly musical in construction. Gould's **eighty-odd piano recordings** are the basis of his enduring popularity, and nearly all of them have been reissued on CD and DVD. One of the most poignant is his second version of the *Goldberg Variations*, the last record issued before his death.

is a three-storey assortment of shops and restaurants spreading out underneath a glass-and-steel arched roof. By shopping-mall standards, the design is appealing and the flock of fibreglass Canada geese suspended from the ceiling adds a touch of decorative flair. Maps of the shopping mall are displayed on every floor, but the general rule is the higher the floor, the more expensive the shop. The centre takes its name from **Timothy Eaton**, an Ulster immigrant who opened his first store here in 1869. His cash-only, fixed-price, money-back-guarantee trading revolutionized the Canadian market and made him a fortune. Soon a Canadian institution, Eaton kept a grip on the pioneer settlements in the west through his mail-order catalogue, known as the "homesteader's bible" – or the "wish book" among native peoples – while Eaton department stores sprang up in all of Canada's big cities. In recent years, the company has struggled to maintain its profitability and the branch in the Eaton Centre has been taken over by Sears.

Elgin Theatre and Winter Garden

Across from the Eaton Centre, just north of Queen Street at 189 Yonge, the **Elgin and Winter Garden Theatre** (guided tours only, Thurs at 5pm & Sat at 11am; $10; 90min; ⓣ416/314-2871, ⓦwww.heritagetrust.on.ca) is one of the city's most unusual attractions. The first part of the guided tour covers the **Elgin**, an old vaudeville theatre, whose ornate furnishings and fittings have been restored after years of neglect. The Elgin was turned into a cinema in the 1930s and, remarkably enough, its accompaniment, the top-floor **Winter Garden**, also a vaudeville theatre, was sealed off. Such double-decker theatres were first introduced in New York in the late nineteenth century and soon became popular along the east coast, but only a handful have survived. Even better, when this one was unsealed, its original decor was found to be intact, the ceiling hung with thousands of preserved and painted beech leaves illuminated by coloured lanterns. In the event, much of the decor had to be replaced, but the restoration work was painstakingly thorough and the end result is delightful.

West to the Campbell House

Immediately to the west of Nathan Phillips Square, along Queen Street West, stands **Osgoode Hall**, an attractive Neoclassical pile built for the Law Society of Upper Canada early in the nineteenth century. Looking like a cross between a Greek temple and an English country house, it's protected by a wrought-iron **fence** designed to keep cows and horses off its immaculate lawn. Across Queen Street, at the corner of University Avenue, rises the glittering Four Seasons Centre for the Performing Arts, which is home to both the Canadian Opera Company (see p.102) and the National Ballet of Canada (see p.102). Close by, on the west side of University Avenue, is **Campbell House** (Tues–Fri 9.30am–4.30pm, Sat noon–4.30pm; plus May–early Oct Sun noon–4.30pm; $6; ⓦwww.campbellhousemuseum.ca), originally built on Adelaide Street for Sir William Campbell, Chief Justice and Speaker of the Legislative Assembly – and transported here in 1972. There are

Vintage fashion

Toronto has a number of excellent **secondhand** and **vintage fashion** shops and there's a concentration of them down along Queen Street West. **Cabaret**, 672 Queen St W (Mon–Wed & Sat 11am–6pm, Thurs & Fri 11am–7pm & Sun 1–5pm ⓣ416/504-7126, ⓦwww.cabaretvintage.com), is one of the best – especially for knock-em-down 1940s hats à la Barbara Stanwyck.

regular guided tours of the period interior and these provide a well-researched overview of early nineteenth-century Toronto. At the time, Campbell was a leading – and surprisingly progressive – figure among the ruling elite, eschewing the death penalty whenever possible, and even awarding the radical William Lyon Mackenzie (see p.66) damages when a mob of Tories wrecked his printing press in 1826.

The Art Gallery of Ontario

Located just west of University Avenue along Dundas Street West, the **Art Gallery of Ontario** (Tues–Sun 10am–5.30pm, Wed till 8.30pm; $18, but free Wed 6–8.30pm; Ⓦwww.ago.net; St Patrick subway), or AGO, is celebrated both for its wide-ranging collection of foreign and domestic art and its excellent temporary exhibitions. It has also just emerged from a thorough revamp in which the architect Frank Gehry (perhaps most famous for Bilbao's Guggenheim Museum), has transformed its appearance with a startling glass and wood north facade on Dundas Street, and a new, four-storey titanium and glass wing overlooking Grange Park to the south. The remodelling has added acres of extra gallery space and the AGO's permanent collection – plus the temporary exhibitions – are now exhibited on **six floors**: the Concourse Level is used for the clumsily named 'Inuit Visible Storage display' of Inuit art; Level 1 is largely devoted to European art; Level 2 holds a wonderful collection of Canadian paintings as well as a battery of Henry Moore sculptures; Level 3 has hospitality suites; Level 4 has a regularly rotated selection of contemporary art, as does Level 5. There is a café, a restaurant, a large gift and bookshop, and a first-rate programme of guided tours free with admission.

▲ A streetcar passes the Art Gallery of Ontario

Cornelius Krieghoff and Paul Kane

Two of nineteenth-century Canada's best known artists are Cornelius Krieghoff and Paul Kane. Each artists' work explored – naturally, for the time – Canada's outdoors, with Krieghoff's ouevre focusing largely on eastern Canada (especially Québec), and Kane's more on the west.

Born in Amsterdam, Cornelius Krieghoff trained as an artist in Düsseldorf before emigrating to New York in 1836, where, at 21, he joined the US army, serving in the Second Seminole War in Florida. Discharged in 1840, Krieghoff immediately re-enlisted, claimed three months' advance pay and then deserted, hot-footing it to Montréal with the French-Canadian woman he had met and married in New York. In Montréal, he picked up his brushes again, but without any commercial success. In 1852 Krieghoff moved to **Québec City** and found a ready market for his paintings among the well-heeled British officers, who liked his folksy renditions of Québec rural life. This was the start of Krieghoff's most productive period. Over the next eight years he churned out dozens of souvenir pictures – finely detailed, anecdotal scenes that are his best work. Yet in the early 1860s – for reasons that remain obscure – he temporarily stopped painting, returning to Europe for five years before another stint in Québec City; with the officer corps gone though, he failed to sell his work. In 1871, he went to live with his daughter in **Chicago** and died there in 1872.

Irish-born, Paul Kane emigrated to Toronto in the early 1820s. In 1840, he returned to Europe and was so impressed by a touring exhibition of paintings of the American Indian that he promptly decided to return to Canada. In 1846, he wrangled a spot on a westward-bound **fur-trading expedition**, travelling from Thunder Bay to Edmonton by canoe and crossing the Rockies by horse before returning to Toronto in 1848. During his trip, Kane made some seven hundred sketches, which he then painted onto canvas, paper and cardboard. Like many early Canadian artists, Kane's paintings often displayed a conflict in subject (North American) and style (European); indeed, it wasn't until the Group of Seven (see p.88) that a true Canadian aesthetic emerged.

In 1859, Kane published *Wanderings of an Artist among the Indian Tribes of North America*, the story of his long travels. It includes this account of **Christmas dinner** at Fort Edmonton: "At the head, before Mr Harriett, was a large dish of boiled buffalo hump; at the foot smoked a boiled buffalo calf...one of the most esteemed dishes among the epicures of the interior. My pleasing duty was to help a dish of mouffle, or dried moose nose, [while] the worthy priest helped the buffalo tongue and Mr Randall cut up the beaver's tails."

Level 1: the European collection

The AGO possesses an eclectic sample of European fine and applied art, including ivory and alabaster pieces, illuminated manuscripts, exquisite cameos and fine porcelain, much of it the gift of newspaper tycoon, Kenneth Thomson, aka Lord Thomson of Fleet (1923–2006). Early **paintings** include some rather pedestrian Italian altarpieces, Pieter Brueghel the Younger's incident-packed *Peasant Wedding* and a strong showing for Dutch painters of the Golden Age, including Rembrandt, Van Dyck, Frans Hals and Goyen. Look out also for **Rubens**' exquisite *Massacre of the Innocents*, a typically stirring canvas, whose writhing, muscular figures date to the middle of his career.

Level 2: Canadian eighteenth- and nineteenth-century painting

Distributed among forty numbered galleries on Level 2, the AGO has the finest collection of **Canadian paintings** in the world (the galleries are not organised chronologically, which can be rather frustrating). From the **eighteenth century**, one noteworthy canvas is a curiously unflattering *Portrait of Joseph Brant* by William

Berczy. A Mohawk chief, Brant (see p.126) is shown in a mix of European and native gear, an apt reflection of his twin loyalties. Notable among the early to mid-nineteenth-century Canadian paintings is the cheery *Passenger Pigeon Hunt* by Antoine Plamondon. From the same period comes the work of John O'Brien, who is well represented by *The Ocean Bride leaving Halifax Harbour*. O'Brien specialized in maritime scenes, turning out dozens of brightly coloured pictures of sailing ships and coastal settings. Equally interesting is the work – and life – of the prolific Cornelius Krieghoff (see p.87). The AGO owns a large sample of Krieghoff's paintings, including characteristic winter scenes like his *Settler's Log House* and *The Portage Aux Titres*. Look out also for the canvases of one of the era's most fascinating figures, Irish-born Paul Kane (see p.87), notably his *Landscape in the Foothills with Buffalo Resting* and *At Buffalo Pound*, where bison are pictured in what looks more like a placid German valley than a North American prairie.

Folksy and/or romanticized country scenes and landscapes ruled the Canadian artistic roost from the 1850s through to the early twentieth century. By and large this was pretty routine stuff, but Homer Watson's glossy Ontario landscapes, with their vigorous paintwork and dynamic compositions, made him a popular and much acclaimed artist – Queen Victoria even purchased one of his paintings, and Oscar Wilde dubbed him "the Canadian Constable". The AGO possesses several Watson paintings, including the two handsome and well-composed canvases, *The Old Mill* and *The Passing Storm*, but his *Death of Elaine* – inspired by a Tennyson

The Group of Seven

In the autumn of 1912, a commercial artist by the name of **Tom Thomson** returned from an extended trip to the Mississauga country, north of Georgian Bay (see p.156), with a bag full of sketches that were to add new momentum to Canadian art. His friends, many of whom were fellow employees of the art firm of Grip Ltd in Toronto, saw Thomson's naturalistic approach to indigenous subject matter as a pointer away from the influence of Europe, declaring the "northland" as the true Canadian "painter's country". World War I and the death of Thomson – who drowned in 1917 – delayed these artists' ambitions, but in 1920 they formed the **Group of Seven**. Initially, the group was comprised of Franklin H. Carmichael, Lawren Harris, A.Y. Jackson, Arthur Lismer, J.E.H. MacDonald, F.H. Varley and Frank Johnston; later, they were joined by A.J. Casson, L.L. Fitzgerald and Edwin Holgate. Working under the unofficial leadership of **Harris**, they explored the wilds of Algoma in Northern Ontario, travelling around in a converted freight car, and later foraged even further afield, from Newfoundland and Baffin Island to British Columbia.

They were immediately **successful**, staging forty shows in eleven years, a triumph due in large part to Harris's many influential contacts. Yet there was also a genuine popular response to the intrepid frontiersman element of their aesthetic. Art was a matter of "taking to the road" and "risking all for the glory of a great adventure", as they wrote in 1922, while "nature was the measure of a man's stature", according to Lismer. Symbolic of struggle against the elements, the Group's favourite symbol was the lone pine set against the sky, an image whose authenticity was confirmed by reference to the "manly" poetry of Walt Whitman.

The **legacy** of the Group of Seven was – and perhaps still is – double-edged. On the one hand, they established the autonomy of Canadian art, but on the other their contribution was soon institutionalized, and well into the 1950s it was difficult for Canadian painters to establish an identity that didn't conform to the group's precepts. Among many later painters the Group was very unpopular, but the Ontario artist Graham Coughtry was, for one, very generous: "They are the closest we've ever come to having some kind of romantic heroes in Canadian painting".

poem – is a bizarrely unsuccessful venture into ancient legend, the eponymous maiden looking something like a stick insect.

Level 2: Canada's Group of Seven

One of the most distinctive artists of the **Group of Seven** (see opposite) was Lawren Harris, whose 1924 *Above Lake Superior* is a pivotal work, its clarity of conception, with bare birch stumps framing a dark mountain beneath Art Deco clouds, quite exceptional. Equally stirring is his surreal *Lake Superior*, one of an army of paintings inspired by the wild, cold landscapes of the lake's north shore. Harris was also partial to urban street scenes and the AGO has several – including two of Toronto – each painted in a careful pointillist style very different from his wilderness works.

The *West Wind* by Tom Thomson is another seminal work, an iconic rendering of the northern wilderness that is perhaps the most famous of all Canadian paintings. Thomson was the first to approach the wilderness with the determination of an explorer and a sense that it could encapsulate a specifically Canadian identity. A substantial sample of his less familiar (but no less powerful) works are part of the AGO collection, including the moody *A Northern Lake*, the Cubist-influenced *Autumn Foliage 1915*, the sticky dabs of colour of *Maple Springs*, and his *Autumn's Garland*. There is also a whole battery of preparatory sketches of lakes and canyons, waterfalls and forests, each small panel displaying the vibrant, blotchy colours that characterize Thomson's work.

A contemporary of the Group – but not a member – the gifted Emily Carr focused on the Canadian west coast in general, and its dense forests and native villages in particular, as in her dark and haunting *Thunderbird* and the deep green foliage of both *Indian Church* and *Western Forest*.

Level 2: the Henry Moore Sculpture Centre

The AGO owns the world's largest collection of sculptures by Henry Moore, with the emphasis firmly on his plaster casts, alongside a few of his bronzes. Given a whole gallery, the sheer size and volume of Moore's output is impressive, but actually it was something of an accident his work ended up here at all. In the 1960s, Moore thought London's Tate Gallery was going to build a special wing for his work. When the Tate declined, Moore negotiated with the AGO instead, after being persuaded to do so by the gallery's British representative, Anthony Blunt – the art expert who was famously uncovered as a Soviet spy in 1979.

Levels 4 and 5: Contemporary art

Spread over two levels, the AGO's collection of contemporary art showcases work by European, British and American artists from 1960 onwards. Around two hundred pieces are exhibited and they cover a wide range of media, from painting, sculpture and photography through to film and installation. The displays are changed fairly regularly, but prime pieces you can expect to see include Andy Warhol's *Elvis I* and *II*, Mark Rothko's *No.1 White and Red* and Claes Oldenburg's *Giant Hamburger*.

South of the AGO: The Sharp Centre for Design

Although not part of the AGO itself, immediately to the south of it, along McCaul Street, is the Ontario College of Art & Design. It once occupied a plain brick building until the extraordinary **Sharp Centre for Design** was added to it in 2004. Created by the English architect Will Alsop – his first building in North America – the centre comprises a giant black-and-white-panelled rectangular "table-top", perched high up at roof level and supported by mammoth multi-coloured steel legs; it holds art studios, theatres and so forth and has variously been described as "adventurous" and "ludicrous". Regardless, it certainly is big.

Chinatown and Kensington Market

Back on Dundas Street, the AGO is fringed by **Chinatown**, a bustling and immensely appealing neighbourhood cluttered with shops, restaurants and street stalls. The boundaries of Chinatown are somewhat blurred, but its focus, since the 1960s, when the original Chinatown was demolished to make way for the new City Hall, has been Dundas Street West between Beverley Street and Spadina Avenue. The first Chinese to migrate to Canada arrived in the mid-nineteenth century to work in BC's gold fields. Subsequently, a portion of this population migrated east, and a sizeable Chinese community sprang up in Toronto in the early 1900s. Several more waves of migration – the last influx following the handing over of Hong Kong to mainland China by the British in 1997 – have greatly increased the number of Toronto's Chinese, bringing the population to approximately 280,000.

Next door to Chinatown, just north of Dundas Street West, between Spadina and Augusta avenues, lies Toronto's most ethnically diverse neighbourhood, pocket-sized **Kensington Market**. It was here, at the beginning of the twentieth century, that Eastern European immigrants squeezed into a patchwork of modest little brick and timber houses that survive to this day. On Kensington Avenue they established a lively **open-air street market** and this has been the main feature of the neighbourhood ever since. The lower half of the market, just off Dundas Street, concentrates on secondhand clothes, while the upper half is crowded with cafés and fresh-food stalls.

The Ontario Legislative Assembly

Peering north down University Avenue from College Street, you'll see the pink sandstone mass of the **Ontario Legislative Assembly** (frequent 30min guided tours: late May to Aug daily 9am–4pm; Sept to late May Mon–Fri 10am–4pm; free; ⓣ416/325-7500, ⓦwww.ontla.on.ca), which dates to the 1890s. Elegant it certainly isn't, but although the building is heavy and solid, its ponderous symmetries do have a certain appeal, with block upon block of roughly dressed stone assembled in the full flourish of the Romanesque Revival style. Seen from close up, the design is even more engaging, its intricacies a pleasant surprise: above the chunky columns of the main entrance is a sinuous filigree of carved stone, adorned by mythological creatures and gargoyle-like faces. The main facade also sports a Neoclassical frieze in which the Great Seal of Ontario is flanked by allegorical figures representing art, music and agriculture. Inside, the foyer leads to the wide, thickly carpeted **Grand Staircase**, whose massive timbers are supported by gilded iron pillars. Beyond, among the long corridors and arcaded galleries, is the **Legislative Chamber**, where the formality of the mahogany and sycamore panels is offset by a series of whimsical little **carvings**: look for the owl overlooking the doings of the government and the hawk overseeing the opposition benches. Under the Speaker's gallery, righteous **inscriptions** have been carved into the pillars, which is a bit of a hoot considering the behaviour of the building's architect, Richard Waite. Waite was chairman of the committee responsible for selecting an architect; and, as chairman, he selected himself.

The provincial assembly typically sits from late September to late June, with breaks at Christmas and Easter, and although guided tours avoid the chamber when the body is in session, the **visitors' gallery** is open to the public during its deliberations; call for further details and times.

The University of Toronto

From the Ontario Legislative Assembly, it's a short walk west to the various faculties of the **University of Toronto**, opened in 1843 and the province's most prestigious academic institution. The university's older buildings, with their quadrangles, ivy-covered walls and Gothic interiors, deliberately evoke Oxford and Cambridge with **Hart House**, at the west end of Wellesley Street on **Hart House Circle**, being the prime example. Hart House is attached to the **Soldier's Tower**, a neo-Gothic memorial erected in 1924 to honour those students who had died in World War I. It adjoins an arcaded **gallery**, which is inscribed with a list of those university students killed in World War I along with Canadian **John McCrae**'s *In Flanders Fields*, arguably the war's most famous poem. Optimistically, the builders of the memorial didn't leave any space to commemorate the dead of any further war – so the names of the students killed in World War II had to be inscribed on the walls at the foot of the tower.

The Royal Ontario Museum

From both the Legislative Assembly and Hart House, it's a short hop north to the **Royal Ontario Museum** (daily 10am–5.30pm, Fri till 9.30pm; $22, free after 4.30pm on Wed; Ⓦwww.rom.on.ca; Museum subway), or ROM, at 100 Queen's Park. This is Canada's largest and most diverse museum, holding a vast hoard of fine and applied art drawn from every corner of the globe, and supplementing the permanent collection is an ambitious programme of temporary exhibitions. The ROM has recently been revamped and expanded; the original building, a substantial and serious-minded stone structure facing Queen's Park, is now overshadowed by a large and flashy extension, known as the **Michael Lee-Chin Crystal**, whose six crystal-shaped, aluminium-and-glass cubes march along Bloor Street West. Lee-Chin, a wealthy businessman, footed the bill, but the design was actually the brainchild of Daniel Libeskind, a Polish-born American architect. The museum spreads over **five main floors**: Level B2 is used for temporary exhibitions; Level 1 holds a superb collection of aboriginal Canadian artefacts plus several galleries devoted to east Asia, particularly China; Level 2 is a mix of geology and natural history, with the dinosaurs the star turn; Level 3 is more ethnographic, with pride of place being the ancient Egyptian collection; and Level 4 is devoted to textiles and costumes.

Level 1: The Canadian galleries

The Sigmund Samuel Gallery on Level 1 displays much of the ROM's **early** Canadian collection, which is strong on furniture, silverware, ceramics and glass. There's an intriguing collection of late eighteenth- and early nineteenth-century trade silver here too, with examples of the assorted knick-knacks – including axe heads, musket balls, scissors and metal armbands – European traders swapped with natives for furs. Here also is the iconic *Death of Wolfe* by Benjamin West. The British general James Wolfe inflicted a crushing defeat on the French outside Québec City in 1759, but was killed during the battle. West's painting transformed this grubby colonial conflict into a romantic extravagance, with the dying general in a Christ-like pose, a pale figure held tenderly by his subordinates. West presented the first version of his painting to the Royal Academy of Arts in 1771 and it proved so popular that he spent much of the next decade painting copies.

The adjoining **First Peoples** gallery is outstanding. Its large glass cabinets examine each and every one of Canada's major native groupings, the exhibits supported by clear and concise descriptions and apposite quotations. Particular highlights include a rare buffalo war robe, recording the owner's bellicosity on the Canadian prairie; some wonderful west coast masks and ceremonial headdresses; a dozen paintings by the artist-explorer Paul Kane (see p.87); and, most remarkable of all, the war bonnet and war shirt of **Sitting Bull**, who fled over the border into Saskatchewan shortly after defeating General Custer at the Battle of the Little Bighorn in 1876; during his exile Sitting Bull gave his bonnet and shirt to a Mountie – hence its appearance here.

Level 1: the old ROM entrance hall

The domed and vaulted old entrance hall of the original ROM building is an extravagant affair, whose ceiling is decorated with a brilliant mosaic of imported Venetian glass. Bolted into the adjacent stairwells are four colossal and stunningly beautiful aboriginal peoples crest poles (commonly but erroneously referred to as totem poles). Dating from the 1880s, and the work of craftsmen from the Haida and Nisga'a peoples of the west coast, these poles – the tallest is 24.5m – are decorated with stylized carvings representing the supernatural animals and birds associated with particular clans.

Level 1: The Chinese collection

The ROM's world-class **Chinese collection** spans six millennia, from 4500 BC to 1900 AD. Key parts of it are devoted to **Chinese Temple Art**, including three large and extraordinarily beautiful Daoist and Buddhist wall paintings dating from around 1300 AD. Other key exhibits in the Chinese section include a remarkable collection of tomb and temple figurines, comprising a couple of hundred ceramic pieces representing funerary processions of soldiers, musicians, carts and attendants. There is also a fabulous cabinet of snuff bottles, some carved from glass and rock crystal, others from more exotic materials, such as amber, ivory, bamboo and even tangerine skin. The most popular component of the Chinese collection is its Ming Tomb. The aristocracy of the Ming Dynasty (1368–1644 AD) evolved an elaborate style of monumental funerary sculpture, and the ROM holds the only example outside of China, though it is actually a composite tomb drawn from several sources rather than an intact, original whole.

Level 2: The Age of Dinosaurs

Among the assorted natural history galleries on Level 2, the highlight is the Age of Dinosaurs section, which holds the ROM's splendid collection of fossil-skeletons, the pick being those retrieved from the Alberta Badlands, near Calgary in western Canada. The Badlands are the richest source of dinosaur fossils in the world, having yielded over three hundred complete skeletons and 35 dinosaur species – ten percent of all those known today. Among the accumulated beasties, look out for the pig-sized, super-armoured armadillo and the rampant herd of Albertosaurus, a Jurassic-period carnivore of large proportions and ferocious appearance.

Level 3: The Egyptian collection

The ROM is strong when it comes to Ancient Egypt, owning several finely preserved mummies, including the richly decorated sarcophagus of Djedmaatesankh, a court musician who died around 850 BC. Even more unusual is the assortment of mummified animals, including a crocodile, a hawk and a weird-looking cat. There is also the intriguing Punt Wall, a 1905 plaster cast of the original in Queen Hatshepsut's temple in Deir el-Bahri, Egypt. The events depicted on the wall occurred in the year 1482 BC, and represent a military expedition to Punt, which lay south of Egypt near present-day Somalia.

The Gardiner Museum

The **Gardiner Museum** (Mon–Thurs 10am–6pm, Fri 10am–9pm, Sat & Sun 10am–5pm; $12, free Fri after 4pm; Ⓦwww.gardinermuseum.com), just across the street from the ROM at 111 Queen's Park, holds a superb collection of **ceramics**. Spread over three small floors, the museum's exhibits are beautifully presented, and key pieces are well labelled and explained.

On the main floor, the **pre-Columbian** section, composed of over three hundred pieces from regions stretching from Mexico to Peru, is one of the most comprehensive collections of its kind in North America, providing an intriguing insight into the lifestyles and beliefs of the Mayan, Incan and Aztec peoples. The sculptures are all the more remarkable because the potter's wheel was unknown in pre-Columbian America, meaning everything on display was hand-modelled. On this floor also is an exquisite sample of fifteenth- and sixteenth-century tin-glazed **Italian majolica**, mostly dishes, plates and jars depicting classical and Biblical themes designed by Renaissance artists. The most splendid pieces are perhaps those from the city – and pottery centre – of Urbino, including one wonderful plate portraying the fall of Jericho.

The second floor has Japanese and Chinese porcelain, plus an especially fine sample of eighteenth-century **European porcelain**, most notably hard-paste wares (fired at very high temperatures) from Meissen, Germany. This floor also holds a charming collection of Italian *commedia dell'arte* figurines, doll-sized representations of theatrical characters popular across Europe from the middle of the sixteenth to the late eighteenth century. The predecessor of pantomime, the *commedia dell'arte* featured stock characters in improvised settings, but with a consistent theme of seduction, age and beauty: the centrepiece was always an elderly, rich merchant and his beautiful young wife.

Bata Shoe Museum

Within easy walking distance of the Gardiner, the **Bata Shoe Museum** (Mon–Sat 10am–5pm, Thurs until 8pm, & Sun noon–5pm; $12; Ⓦwww.batashoemuseum.ca), 327 Bloor St West at St George Street, was built for Sonja Bata, of the Bata shoe manufacturing family, to display the extraordinary assortment of footwear she has spent a lifetime collecting. The museum begins on **Level B1** with an introductory section entitled "All About Shoes", which presents an overview on the evolution of footwear. Among the more interesting exhibits in this section are pointed shoes from medieval Europe, where different social classes were allowed different lengths of toe, and tiny Chinese silk shoes used by women whose feet had been bound. A small adjoining section is devoted to **specialist footwear**, most memorably French chestnut-crushing clogs from the nineteenth century and a pair of Dutch smugglers' clogs with the heel and sole reversed to leave a footprint intended to hoodwink any following customs officials.

Level G features a large glass cabinet showcasing all sorts of celebrity footwear. The exhibits are rotated regularly, but look out for Buddy Holly's loafers, Marilyn Monroe's stilettos, Princess Diana's red court shoes, Nureyev's ballet shoes and Elton John's ridiculous platforms. Level 2 and Level 3 are used for temporary exhibitions that draw extensively on the museum's permanent collection – there isn't enough room to show everything at once.

Casa Loma

From Dupont subway station, it's a five-minute walk north up the slope of Spadina Road to Davenport Road and the flight of steps leading to Toronto's most bizarre attraction, **Casa Loma** (daily 9.30am–5pm, last admission 4pm; $18, parking $3/hour; Ⓦwww.casaloma.org), at 1 Austin Terrace. A folly to outdo almost any other, Casa Loma is an enormous towered and turreted mansion built for Sir Henry Pellatt between 1911 and 1914. Every inch the self-made man, Pellatt made a fortune by pioneering the use of hydroelectricity, harnessing the power of Niagara Falls to light Ontario's expanding cities. Determined to construct a house no one could ignore, Pellatt gathered furnishings from all over the world and even imported Scottish stonemasons to build the wall around his six-acre property. He spent more than $3m fulfilling his dream, but business misfortunes and the rising cost of servants forced him to move out in 1923, earning him the nickname "Pellatt the Plunger". His legacy is a strange mixture of medieval fantasy and early twentieth-century technology: secret passageways, an elevator and claustrophobic wood-panelled rooms baffled by gargantuan pipes and plumbing.

The ground floor

A clearly numbered route goes up one side of the house and down the other. It begins on the ground floor in the **great hall**, a pseudo-Gothic extravaganza with an 18m-high cross-beamed ceiling, a Wurlitzer organ and enough floor space to accommodate several hundred guests. Hung with flags, heavy-duty chandeliers and suits of armour, it's a remarkably cheerless place, but in a touch worthy of an Errol Flynn movie, the hall is overlooked by a balcony at the end of Pellatt's second-floor bedroom: presumably he could, like some medieval baron, welcome his guests from on high.

Next is the **library**, followed by the walnut-panelled **dining room**, which leads to the **conservatory**, an elegant and spacious room with a marble floor and side-panels set beneath a handsome Tiffany domed glass ceiling. This is perhaps the mansion's most appealing room, its flowerbeds kept warm even in winter by the original network of steam pipes. The nearby **study** was Pellatt's favourite room, a serious affair engulfed by mahogany panelling and equipped with two secret passageways – one leading to the wine cellar, the other to his wife's rooms.

The second and third floors

On the second floor, **Sir Henry's suite** has oodles of walnut and mahogany panelling, which stands in odd contrast to the 1910s white-marble, high-tech bathroom, featuring an elaborate multi-nozzle shower. **Lady Pellatt's Suite** wasn't left behind in the ablutions department either – her bathroom had a bidet, a real novelty in George V's Canada.

The third floor holds a mildly diverting display on Pellatt's one-time regiment, the **Queen's Own Rifles**, tracing their involvement in various campaigns from the 1885 suppression of the Métis rebellion in western Canada (see p.578) through to World War I and beyond. From the third floor, wooden staircases clamber up to two of the house's **towers**, from where there are pleasing views over the house and gardens.

The Lower Level and the gardens

On the ground floor, stairs lead down to the **lower level**, which was where Pellatt's money ran out and his plans ground to a halt. Work never started on the bowling alleys and shooting range he'd designed, and the swimming pool only got as far as the rough concrete basin that survives today. Pellatt did manage to complete the 250m-long **tunnel** running from the house and pool to the **carriage**

room and **stables**, where his thoroughbred horses were allegedly better-treated than his servants, chomping away at their oats and hay in splendid iron and mahogany stalls. The stables are a dead-end, so you'll have to double back along the tunnel to reach the house and the exit.

Before you leave, spare time for the **terraced gardens** (May–Oct daily 9.30am–4pm), which tumble down the ridge at the back of the house. They are parcelled up into several different sections and easily explored along a network of footpaths, beginning on the terrace behind the great hall.

Spadina House

Quite what the occupants of **Spadina House** (guided tours: Jan–March Sat & Sun noon–5pm; April–Aug Tues–Sun noon–5pm; Sept–Dec Tues–Fri noon–4pm, Sat & Sun noon–5pm; $8; Ⓦwww.toronto.ca) must have thought when Casa Loma went up next door can only be imagined, but there must have been an awful lot of curtain-twitching. The two houses are a study in contrasts: Casa Loma a grandiose pile, Spadina an elegant Victorian property of genteel appearance dating from 1866. Spadina was built by James Austin, a wealthy banker of Irish extraction whose descendants lived here until 1983, when the house was bequeathed to the city. The Austins' long and uninterrupted occupation means the house's furnishings are nearly all genuine family artefacts, and they provide an intriguing insight into their changing tastes and interests.

Particular highlights of the **guided tour** include the conservatory trap door that allowed the gardeners to come and go unseen by their employers, an assortment of period chairs designed to accommodate the largest of bustles, the original gas chandeliers and a couple of canvases by Cornelius Krieghoff (see p.87). Pride of place goes to the **Billiard Room**, which comes complete with an inventive Art Nouveau decorative frieze, and the **Library**, equipped with a sturdy oak bureau and a swivel armchair.

The waterfront and the Toronto Islands

There is much to enjoy on the north shore of **Lake Ontario**, despite its industrial blotches and the heavy concrete brow of the Gardiner Expressway. Footpaths and cycling trails now nudge along a fair slice of the **waterfront** and the **Harbourfront Centre** offers a year-round schedule of activities. Even better are the **Toronto Islands**, whose breezy tranquillity attracts droves of city-dwellers during the city's humid summers. It only takes fifteen minutes to reach them by municipal ferry (see p.96), but the contrast between the city and the islands could hardly be more marked, not least because the islands are almost entirely **vehicle-free**.

The Harbourfront Centre

Toronto's grimy docks once disfigured the shoreline nearest the city centre, a swathe of warehouses and factories that was unattractive and smelly in equal measure. Today it's another story: the port and its facilities have been concentrated further east, beyond the foot of Parliament Street, while the **waterfront** west of Yonge Street has been redeveloped in grand style, sprouting luxury condominium blocks, jogging and cycling trails, offices, shops and marinas. The focus of all this activity is the **Harbourfront Centre**, stretching west from the foot of York Street, whose various facilities include an open-air performance area and the **Power Plant Contemporary Art Gallery** (Tues–Sun noon–6pm, Wed till 8pm; $6, free Wed after 5pm; Ⓦwww.thepowerplant.org). Every year, the gallery presents about a dozen exhibitions of contemporary art, often featuring emerging Canadian artists. It's mostly cutting-edge stuff; indecipherable to some, exciting to others.

To reach the Harbourfront Centre by **public transport**, take streetcar #509 or #510 from Union Station and get off at Queens Quay Terminal, the second stop.

The Toronto Islands

Originally a sandbar peninsula, the **Toronto Islands**, which arch around the city's harbour, were cut adrift from the mainland by a violent storm in 1858. First used as a summer retreat by the Mississauga Indians, the islands went through various incarnations during the twentieth century: they once hosted a baseball stadium, where slugger Babe Ruth hit his first professional home run, saw fun fairs featuring horses diving from the pier and even served as a training base for the Norwegian Air Force during World War II. Today, this archipelago, roughly 6km long and totalling around 800 acres, seems worlds away from the bustle of downtown, a perfect spot to relax and unwind – and a place where visitors' cars are **banned**; many locals use wheelbarrows or golf buggies to move their tackle, while others walk or cycle.

The city side of the archipelago is broken into a dozen tiny islets dotted with cottages, leisure facilities, verdant gardens and clumps of wild woodland. By comparison, the other side of the archipelago is a tad wilder and more windswept, consisting of one long sliver of land, which is somewhat arbitrarily divided into three "islands". From the east these are: **Ward's Island**, a quiet residential area with parkland and wilderness; **Centre Island**, the busiest and most developed of the three; and **Hanlan's Point**, which leads round to Toronto's City Centre Airport (see p.68). Hanlan's Point also holds the city's best **sandy beach** – though, as Lake Ontario is generally regarded as being too polluted for swimming, most visitors stick to sunbathing.

Arrival and information

Passenger ferries bound for the Toronto Islands depart from the mainland **ferry terminal**, located behind the conspicuous *Westin Harbour Castle* hotel, between the foot of Yonge and Bay streets. To get to the ferry terminal from Union Station, take the #509 or #510 streetcar and get off at the first stop, Queen's Quay. The islands have three **ferry docks** – one each on Ward's Island, Centre Island and Hanlan's Point. The ferries to Ward's Island and Hanlan's Point run year-round, while the ferry to Centre Island only operates from spring to fall. During peak season (May to early Sept), ferries to all three islands depart at regular intervals, either every half-hour, every 45 minutes or every hour; at other times of the year, it's usually hourly. Ferries begin running between 6.30am and 9am and finish between 9pm and 11.30pm, depending on the service and the season. For schedule details, call Ⓣ416/392-8193 or check Ⓦwww.toronto.ca/parks. Regardless of the time of year, a return **fare** for adults is $6.50. Cyclists are allowed to take their **bikes** with them unless the ferry is jam-packed and in-line skates are permitted, but must be removed while on board.

Practicalities

From May to September, **bike rental** is available on Centre Island from Island Bicycle Rental (Ⓣ416/203-0009), located a five-to ten-minute walk from the

Centre Island ferry dock at the foot of the pier. They open daily at around 10.30am and stock ordinary bicycles, tandems and even quadracycles; they don't take reservations except for groups of ten or more. Canoe and paddleboat rental is available on Centre Island, from the **Boat House**, a five-to ten-minute walk from the Centre Island ferry dock. Renting a boat allows you to paddle round the islands' network of mini-lagoons and reach a couple of tiny wooded islets that are otherwise inaccessible. Aside from walking, cycling and rowing, the other means of conveyance is a free and fairly frequent **trackless train** that runs across the islands throughout the summer; you can board the train at any point along its circuitous route. For **eating** and **drinking**, it's all fast–food except for the **Rectory Café** (ring for hours, ⓣ416/203-2152), on Ward's Island, where they serve tasty snacks and light meals. Several hours are needed to explore the islands by bike, a full day if you are on foot, or you can overnight at an island B&B (see p.76).

The suburbs

The satellite **suburbs** and industrial areas that make up most of Toronto are of little appeal, a string of formless settlements sprawling over a largely flat and dreary landscape, which extends from Scarborough in the east to Mississauga in the west and north beyond Steeles Avenue. Nevertheless, the region is home to several prestige attractions, most notably the **Ontario Science Centre**, which showcases dozens of interactive science displays, and the **Toronto Zoo**.

Ontario Science Centre

Featuring over eight hundred exhibits on science and technology, the **Ontario Science Centre** (daily 10am–5pm; $18, seniors & children aged 13–17 $13.50, aged 4–12 $11; ⓣ416/696-1000, ⓦwww.ontariosciencecentre.ca), at 770 Don Mills Rd, draws over one million visitors per year, with children to the fore. One of the most popular exhibits is **The Human Body**, where visitors can discern the inner workings of human biology through life-sized three-dimensional displays and various quizzes and games. There's also easily understood information on complex medical advances, including bioengineering, DNA fingerprinting and immunology. Another big pull is the **OMNIMAX Theatre**, which boasts a 24-metre-high wraparound screen with digital sound. Admission to the OMNIMAX shows is an extra $9-12. To reach the Science Centre **by car** from downtown Toronto, take the Don Valley Parkway and follow the signs from the Don Mills Road North exit. By **public transport**, take the Yonge Street subway line north to Eglington station and transfer to the Eglington Avenue East bus; get off at the Don Mills Road stop.

Toronto Zoo

Set on the hilly edge of the Rouge Valley, **Toronto Zoo** (daily: March–May & Sept 9am–6pm; June–Aug 9am–7.30pm; Oct–Feb 9.30am–4.30pm; $21, children 4–12 $13; ⓦwww.torontozoo.com) encompasses a 710-acre site that does its best to place animals in their own environments; **six pavilions** representing different geographic regions are filled with indigenous plants and more than five thousand animals. Hardy species live outside in large paddocks, and an open train, the **Zoomobile**, zips around between the pavilions. The zoo also has an extensive breeding, recovery and reintroduction programme.

Arriving by **car**, take Hwy 401 to Scarborough (exit 389) and drive north on Meadowvale Road, following the signs for the zoo. Via **public transport** – which takes about fifty minutes from downtown – catch the Sheppard East #85B bus from the Sheppard subway station. Fast-food chains mostly dominate the **eating** options, but there are picnic areas.

Eating and drinking

Toronto heaves with **cafés and restaurants**, with everything from smart and expensive designer places to informal neighbourhood joints. Some of the best emphasize their use of Canadian ingredients – fish and wild animal meat, particularly – but there's no real distinctive local cuisine. **Prices** range from fancier restaurants, where a meal will set you back upwards of $60, to bargain-basement cafés, where a decent-sized snack or sandwich works out at just a few dollars. The majority of places fall somewhere in between – a $25 bill per person for a two-course meal, excluding drinks, is a reasonable average in a restaurant, a tad less in a café.

For **drinking**, many of Toronto's traditional **bars** are rough-and-ready places that look and feel like beer halls. Until the 1980s, it was common for them to have one entrance for men accompanied by women, the other for men only, and although these formalities have been stripped away, many of the city's bars remain firmly blue collar; others – and these are the pick – have morphed into clubs or at least bar-lounges (see p.100).

Cafés

Balzac's Coffee Roastery 55 Mill St, Bvd 60; Streetcar: King (#504) ⓣ416/207-1709, ⓦwww.balzacscoffee.com. *Balzac's* has a relaxed, arty feel and occupies the old pump room of the Gooderham & Worts Distillery, at the heart of the Distillery District. It churns out nicely presented espresso-type coffees, plus matching cakes and light bites. Daily 9am–8pm.

Bonjour Brioche 812 Queen St East, at DeGrassi; Streetcar: Queen (#501) ⓣ416/406-1250. This patisserie-café draws hordes from all over the city on account of its fruit tarts, buttery croissants, puffy brioche and delectable *pissaladiere*, a variation on pizza from Provence. The sit-down menu is a blackboard full of soups, sandwiches, omelettes and quiche. There's always a queue for Sunday brunch, and almost everything has gone by 2pm, so come early. Tues–Fri 8am–5pm, Sat 8am–4pm & Sun 8am–3pm.

Café Bernate 1024 Queen St West; Streetcar: Queen (#501) ⓣ416/535-2835. The steam machine is in full swing at this neighbourhood spot, and the sunny yellow walls are hung with local artists' work. The menu offers some plump sandwiches and coffee drinkers get free refills. Mon–Sat 11am–4pm.

Jamie Kennedy at the Gardiner 111 Queen's Park; Subway: Museum ⓣ416/362-1957, ⓦwww.jamiekennedy.ca. Jamie Kennedy, a big-name chef hereabouts, has taken over the running of the café-restaurant at the Gardiner Museum (see p.93). A creative lunch menu features local, seasonal ingredients amid spick-and-span minimalist decor. Mains average about $9, much more in the evening. Daily 11.30am–3.00pm & Fri 6–8.30pm.

Java House 537 Queen St West, at Augusta; Streetcar: Queen (#501) ⓣ416/504-3025. Boho meets Bauhaus at this alternative/eccentric café with its alternative/eccentric clientele. Serves up inexpensive sandwiches, salads and snacks. Daily 8am–midnight.

Moon Bean Coffee 30 St Andrew's St; Streetcar: Spadina (#510) ⓣ416/595-0327, ⓦwww.moonbeancoffee.com. One of a dwindling band of cafés that still roast their own beans, this is a Kensington Market institution, its patio a perfect spot to watch the world go by while sampling the delicious soups, sandwiches and pastries.

Trattoria Nervosa 75 Yorkville Ave; Subway: Bay ⓣ416/961-4642, ⓦwww.eatnervosa.com. One of the few reasonably priced café-restaurants left in Yorkville, this establishment is strong on Italian-style salads, pastas and pizzas. Antipasti start at around $10. Daily11am–10pm.

Restaurants

Babur 273 Queen St W; Subway: Osgoode ⓣ416/599-7720, ⓦwww.babur.ca. Rich, buttery sauces, delicately spiced stews and fluffy naan and pori breads, all delivered to your linen-cloth table by helpful waiters at this large, smart and modern Indian restaurant. Daily 11am–10pm. Mains average around $13.

Bangkok Paradise 506 Queen St West, at Denison; Streetcar: Queen (#501) ⓣ416/504-3210, ⓦwww.bangkokparadise.ca. Informal and usually packed, the menu of this funky spot has all the satay, noodle and curry classics you'd expect, plus a wide range of Thai vegetarian options. Mon–Fri 10.30am–11pm, Sat & Sun noon–11pm. Mains from $9.

Black Skirt 3 Charles St East, at Yonge; Subway: Bloor-Yonge ⓣ416/935-0240. This much-praised restaurant, with its wide-ranging and very authentic southern Italian menu, has been kitted out in adventurous/atmospheric style, a mix of brown-leather benches, wood floors and shades of cream and brown. Attentive service helps make for a fine night out. Mains average $25. Mon–Sat 11am–11pm.

Fressen 478 Queen St West, at Augusta; Streetcar: Queen (#501) ⓣ416/504-5127, ⓦwww.fressenrestaurant.com. Ultra cool vegetarian restaurant, where regulars ignore the pastas and pizzas and head straight for the entrees. A full meal can also be made of the excellent appetizers, and the juice/smoothie list is extensive. Main courses average $15. Daily 5.30–10pm, plus Sat & Sun 10am–3pm.

Fune 100 Simcoe St; Subway: St Andrew ⓣ416/599-3868, ⓦwww.fune.sites.toronto.com. The star turn at this neat and trim Japanese restaurant is the sushi bar – very Tokyo-style with little boats floating by along a channel from the sushi chefs to you and everyone else. The seafood couldn't be fresher and prices are reasonable. Mon–Fri 11.30am–2.30pm & 5–10.30pm; Sat 5–11.30pm & Sun 5–10pm.

Joso's 202 Davenport Rd ⓣ416/925-1903, ⓦwww.josos.com. This celebrated restaurant, described at length by Margaret Atwood in her novel *The Robber Bride*, is famous for two things: its squid-ink risotto and the plethora of breasts and buttocks in owner Joso Spralja's paintings and statues. Reservations are essential and mains cost around $25. It's a fifteen-minute walk north of Bloor St West along Avenue Rd; take a taxi. Mon–Fri 11.30am–3pm & 5.30–11pm; Sat 5.30–11pm.

Kit Kat 297 King St West, at John; Subway: St Andrew ⓣ416/977-4461, ⓦwww.kitkattoronto.com. Antipasti, pastas, steaks and seafood dominate the uncomplicated menu of this busy, attractively decorated bar and grill, where the cuisine is firmly southern Italian. Mains from $23. Mon–Fri 11.30am–11.30pm, Sat 4–12pm & Sun 4–11.30pm.

Lai Wah Heen At the *Metropolitan* hotel, 108 Chestnut St; Subway: St Patrick ⓣ416/977-9899, ⓦwww.metropolitan.com/lwh. The name means "elegant meeting place", which this Chinese restaurant most certainly is. The high-end dining room atmosphere is matched by the complex menu, best described as Hong Kong modern, with dishes including Lustrous Peacock – a salad of barbecued duck, chicken and jellyfish on slivered melons garnished with eggs. It's also noted for its dim sum (lunch only). Main courses range from $20–45. Daily 11.30am–3pm & 5.30–10.30pm.

Le Commensal 655 Bay St; Subway: Dundas ⓣ416/596-9364, ⓦwww.commensal.ca. The cafeteria-style set-up of this large, airy vegetarian restaurant is its only drawback. Otherwise, the variety of offerings is excellent: soups, great salads, hearty pot-pies, stews, casseroles and baked goods are clearly marked for vegans or vegetarians. There's also a large dessert counter, plus takeout. Lunch or dinner for two costs $16–30. Entrance is on Elm St. Mon–Fri 11.30am–9.30pm, Sat noon–10pm & Sun noon–9.30pm.

Le Papillon on Front 69 Front St East; Subway: Union ⓣ416/367-0303, ⓦwww.lepapillonfront.com. Attractive, French-cum-Québécois restaurant where the house speciality is crêpes (sweet or savoury), though the bistro-style menu covers all the French classics with style. Mains average $18, less at lunch, crêpes $16. Tues–Fri noon–2.30pm & 5–10.30pm; Sat & Sun 11am–3pm for brunch & 5pm–11pm.

Lee 603 King St West, at Portland; Streetcar: King (#504) ⓣ416/504-7867, ⓦwww.susur.com/lee. This is super chef Susur Lee's most recent venture, a high-octane restaurant-cum-bar with dappled lighting and lots of room. The menu is Asian fusion with bells on – try the sashimi of charred scallop with salted plum, wasabi and toasted nori seaweed. Pick and mix several dishes all together is the way to go. Mains from $16. Reservations advised. Mon–Sat 5–11pm.

Madeline's 601 King St West, at Portland; Streetcar: King (#504) ⓣ416/603-2205, ⓦwww.susur.com/madelines. Next door to – and owned by the same man as – *Lee* (see above), this classy restaurant is kitted out in a flamboyant version of fin-de-siècle style. The extensive menu covers many bases, from Cornish hen with gorgonzola cheese to *carpaccio* of bison. Mains from $16. Reservations advised. Mon–Sat 6–11pm.

Nataraj 394 Bloor St West, at Brunswick; Subway: Spadina ⓣ416/928-2925, ⓦwww.nataraj.ca. It's Delhi-specific dishes with a tandoori twist at this excellent Indian restaurant, where the tandoori oven is on view through a window into the kitchen. Try the spicy stews and shrimp *pakoras*. Mains from $9. Daily 5–10.30pm.

Noce 875 Queen St West, at Walnut; Streetcar: Queen (#501) ⓣ416/504-3463, ⓦwww.nocerestaurant.com. This little house (the 'nut' name comes from the cross street) has become an exceptional Italian restaurant. The pasta is rolled by hand, the beef *carpaccio* melts on the tongue and the meat tumbles right off the bone. Mains from $12. Reservations advised. Mon–Fri noon–2.30pm & 6–11pm, Sat & Sun 6–11pm.

Rodney's Oyster House 469 King St West, at Spadina; Streetcar: King (#504) ⓣ416/363-8105, ⓦwww.rodneysoysterhouse.com. Toronto's favourite oyster bar, ensconced in a handsomely modernized old basement, serves up tons of the slippery delicacies, plus scallops, mussels, crab and shrimp. The only regular fish is salmon and trout. Main courses average around $22. Mon–Sat 11.30am–1am.

Ruth's Chris Steak House At the *Hilton* hotel, 145 Richmond St West, at University; Subway: Osgoode ⓣ416/955-1455, ⓦwww.ruthschris.com. The decor may be a tad too traditional for some tastes – sombre and really rather utilitarian – but the steaks, served on piping hot plates – are the best in town. Mains from $40. Daily 4.30–10pm, Fri & Sat till 10.45pm.

Nightlife and entertainment

Toronto has its fair share of **live music venues**. The city's **jazz** scene is strong, with several first-rate joints in and around the city centre. The **club scene** is also strong, if not exactly earth-shattering, but there's more than enough to keep anyone going for days (and nights) on end. For **listings**, consult *NOW* (ⓦwww.nowtoronto.com), which emphasizes live music, *TRIBE* (ⓦwww.tribemagazine.com), which specializes in dance/rave/house discos, and *Eye* (ⓦwww.eyeweekly.com), which carries a bit of both; all three are free weeklies widely available around town.

For **performing arts**, Toronto sustains a wide-ranging programme of theatre, opera, ballet and classical music. Its particular strength is its **theatre scene**, the third-largest in the English-speaking world, after London and New York. For film, Toronto's mainstream **cinemas** show Hollywood releases before they reach Europe and there are several art-house places – as befits a city that hosts what is generally regarded as one of the world's best film events, the renowned **Toronto International Film Festival** (see p.67).

Bars, clubs and music venues

Cameron House 408 Queen St West; Streetcar: Queen (#501) ⓣ416/703-0811, ⓦwww.thecameron.com. A line of huge metal ants march up the side of this legendary place, just west of Spadina Ave at the foot of Cameron St, and the front is subject to ever-changing murals of women's faces – you can't miss it. The interior is a clash of Beaux Arts boudoir and honky-tonk bar, and the stage at the back of the room has provided a showcase for emerging talent of every genre.

C'est What? 67 Front St East, at Church; Subway: Union Station ⓣ416/867-9499, ⓦwww.cestwhat.com. Located in a dark, low-ceilinged basement in the St Lawrence district, *C'est What* has over thirty micro brews on tap plus an impressive selection of single malt scotches and hearty pub food. The performance space here has seen the likes of Bare Naked Ladies and Jeff Buckley. Daily 11.30am–2am.

Drake Lounge At the *Drake* hotel (see p.71) Streetcar: Queen (#501). ⓣ416/531-5042, ⓦwww.thedrakehotel.ca. This smooth lounge-bar has been a hit since it opened in 2004. A wet bar serving house tipples like the Dorothy Parker cocktail (vodka, cranberry juice and Chambord) and a sushi bar keep the crowd satisfied as they sprawl on fat sofas, club chairs or loungers. Over the fireplace, a huge flat-screen TV projects live or taped shows held in the basement performance space.

El Convento Rico 750 College St, between Bathurst and Ossington; Streetcar: College

▲ Queen Street West

(#506) ⓣ416/588-7800, ⓦwww.elconventorico.com. Walking into this lively joint, replete with red velvet, flocked wallpaper and baroque spot welding, makes you feel like you've stumbled on the best party in town. The crowd ranges from earnest suburbanites to dishy Latino drag queens, and the DJs spin Latin and disco classics. Mon–Sat until 4am (Sun until 10pm).

El Mocambo 464 Spadina Ave, at College; Streetcar: College (#506) ⓣ416/777-1777, ⓦwww.elmocambo.ca. The stuff of legends insofar as live acts are concerned, having had visits from luminaries like the Rolling Stones, B.B. King, Blondie and hometown favourites like Nash the Slash. The tables are sticky and the carpet is scary, but the bands are (usually) great.

Horseshoe Tavern 370 Queen St West; Streetcar: Queen (#501) ⓣ416/598-4226, ⓦwww.horseshoetavern.com. Many Toronto bands got their start here, and it's still a favourite place for the newly-famous to play a set or one-off concert. The interior is relentlessly unglamorous, but the low cover charge is a major compensation.

Lee's Palace 529 Bloor St West; Subway: Bathurst ⓣ416/532-1598, ⓦwww.leespalace.com. *Lee's* continued popularity has nothing to do with the decor, the food or even the draft beer. Its reputation is entirely based on the outrageous bands it consistently books. Patrons can also check out the DJ dance action upstairs at the aptly named Dance Cave.

Phoenix Concert Theatre 410 Sherbourne St, just north of Carlton; Streetcar: Dundas (#505) ⓣ416/323-1251, ⓦwww.libertygroup.com. This flashy, five-bar, three-venue concert emporium specializes in booking big-name acts longing for intimate gigs. Everyone from Mtisyahu to Richard Thompson, Cesaria Evora and the Misfits has performed here.

The Rex Jazz & Blues Bar 194 Queen St West, at St Patrick; Subway: Osgoode. ⓣ416/598-2475, ⓦwww.therex.ca. In arguments about which is the best jazz club in town, this one is consistently near the top of the list. A well-primped crowd lounges in the spiffed-up interior, but any reservations about pretensions evaporate once the music – which is always top-notch – begins.

This Is London 364 Richmond St West, at Spadina; Streetcar: Queen (#501) ⓣ416/351-1100, ⓦwww.thisislondonclub.com. Entry is off an alleyway and up a flight of stairs. Clubbers like the stylish interior, DJ selections of disco, soul and good old Top 40, but the real buzz is the women's washrooms: they take up the whole top floor, and hairdressers and make-up artists are on hand for touch-ups.

Theatre

Princess of Wales Theatre 300 King St West, at John; Subway: St Andrew ⓣ416/872-1212, ⓦwww.mirvish.com. Built to accommodate the helicopter in *Miss Saigon*, this addition to Toronto's more traditional playhouses manages to have a surprisingly intimate feel, despite its 2,000 seats.
Royal Alexandra Theatre 260 King St West, at Simcoe; Subway: St Andrew ⓣ416/872-1212, ⓦwww.mirvish.com. Built in 1906, the "Royal Alex" is a charming Edwardian theatre that has been fully restored to its original, gilt-edged glory. It puts on everything from classical theatre to exuberant musicals, such as *Mamma Mia*.
St Lawrence Centre for the Arts 27 Front St East, at Scott; Subway: Union ⓣ416/366-7723, wwww.stlc.com. Home to the Canadian Stage Company, the centre contains two stages: the Bluma Appel Theatre, the facility's main stage, where primarily new works by contemporary artists are shown, and the upstairs, studio-sized Jane Mallett Theatre, which presents experimental and workshop productions.
Soulpepper Theatre 55 Mill St, Distillery District; Streetcar: King (#504) ⓣ416/203-6264, ⓦwww.soulpepper.ca. This youthful theatre company, which performs a classical repertory, has lured leading talents from the likes of the Stratford festival (see p.130). The Young Centre for the Performing Arts, also in the Distillery District (see p.83), is the troupe's home.

Classical music

Glenn Gould Studio 250 Front St West, at John; Streetcar: King (#504) ⓣ416/205-5000, ⓦwww.glenngouldstudio.cbc.ca. Named after the great pianist himself (see p.84), this small, boxy hall located downtown in the Canadian Broadcasting Centre (see p.80) is so sprung for sound that enthusiastic performances leave audiences literally vibrating. The programming is first-rate, generally showcasing Canadian talent.
Massey Hall 178 Victoria St, at Yonge; Subway: Dundas ⓣ416/872-4255, ⓦwww.masseyhall.com. Built in the late 1800s, this recital hall boasts great acoustics and has hosted a wide variety of performers – everyone from Maria Callas to Jarvis Cocker.
Roy Thomson Hall 60 Simcoe St; Subway: St Andrew ⓣ416/872-4255, ⓦwww.roythomson.com. Home to the Toronto Symphony Orchestra (ⓣ416/593-4828, ⓦwww.tso.on.ca), this modern hall looks like an upturned soup bowl during the day, but at night the place is transformed, its glass-panelled walls casting light into the sky and over the reflecting ponds outside. Inside, the circular hall has excellent sightlines, and its acoustics have been tweaked to rave reviews.

Opera and ballet

Canadian Opera Company Four Seasons Centre for the Performing Arts, 145 Queen St West; Subway: Osgoode ⓣ416/363-8231, ⓦwww.coc.ca. Canada's national opera troupe has impressed international audiences for years with its ambitious productions and devotion to young talent. Seats are often scarce, particularly for the eagerly anticipated season premieres, so reserve as far in advance as possible; ticket prices begin at $60.
National Ballet Company Same address as Canadian Opera Company ⓣ416/345-9686, ⓦwww.national.ballet.ca. The NBC's prima ballerinas are much admired, as is the company itself, performing classical ballet and contemporary dance with equal artistry; tickets $40–200.

Cinemas

Cinémathèque Jackman Hall, Art Gallery of Ontario, 317 Dundas St West, at McCaul; Streetcar: Dundas (#505) ⓣ416/968-3456, ⓦwww.cinemathequeontario.ca. Cinémathèque is a year-round extension of the Toronto International Film

Spectator sports in Toronto

Baseball The Blue Jays (ⓦwww.bluejays.com), of Major League Baseball's American League division, play at the Rogers Centre (see p.78).

Canadian football The Argonauts (ⓦwww.argonauts.on.ca), of the Canadian Football League, also play at the Rogers Centre.

Ice hockey The Maple Leafs (ⓦwww.mapleleafs.nhl.com), of the National Hockey League, play home fixtures in the Air Canada Centre, behind Union Station.

Festival (see p.67) with an imaginative and far-reaching programme.
Cineplex Odeon Varsity 55 Bloor St West, at Balmuto; Subway: Bloor-Yonge ⓣ416/961-6304, ⓦwww.cineplex.com. Eleven-screen behemoth with good sightlines, great sound and comfortable seats.
Scotiabank Theatre 259 Richmond St West, at John; Streetcar: Queen (#501) ⓣ416/368-5600, ⓦwww.cineplex.com. Perfect venue for those who want to feel like extras in *Blade Runner*. Half the spectacle is in the theatre itself, with a mammoth, outdoor pixel-board cube showing film clips, an almost vertical ride up the escalator to the cinemas and a sound system that will blast you out of your seat.

Listings

Bookshops World's Biggest Bookstore, 20 Edward St, just north of Dundas St between Yonge St and University Ave (Mon–Sat 9am–10pm, Sun 11am–8pm; ⓣ416/977-7009), is huge and has a strong Canadian section. Indigo has several branches in Toronto, including in the Eaton Centre (ⓣ416/591-3622, ⓦwww.chapters.indigo.ca).
Car rental Discount, 134 Jarvis St (ⓣ416/864-0632); National, Union Station, 65 Front St West (ⓣ416/364-4191); Enterprise, Simcoe Place, 200 Front St West (ⓣ416/751-1342).
Consulates Australia, 175 Bloor St East ⓣ416/323-1155; Ireland, 20 Toronto St ⓣ416/366-9300; New Zealand, 965 Bay St, ⓣ416/947-9696; UK, 777 Bay St ⓣ416/593-1290; USA, 225 Simcoe St ⓣ416/595-6506.
Internet Most city hotels provide internet access for their guests either free or at minimal charge. The Toronto Reference Library (see below) also provides free access.
Laundry The Laundry Lounge, 527 Yonge St, north of College (ⓣ416/975-4747).
Left luggage Union Station, Front St at Bay, has lockers, as does the Toronto Coach Terminal, 610 Bay St at Dundas.
Library The main library is the Toronto Reference Library, 789 Yonge St, one block north of Bloor (Mon–Thurs 9.30am–8.30pm, Fri 9.30am–5.30pm, Sat 9am–5pm, Sun Sept–June 1.30–5pm; ⓣ416/395-5577, ⓦwww.torontopubliuclibrary.ca).
Pharmacies Shopper's Drug Mart, 66 Wellington St West (ⓣ416/365-0927) and 728 Yonge St (ⓣ416/920-0098). For a holistic pharmacy, including herbal and traditional treatments, try the Big Carrot Wholistic Dispensary, 348 Danforth Ave ⓣ416/466-8432.
Post offices Canada Post operates branches in scores of locations, including in pharmacies and stationery stores. One handy location is downtown inside the Royal Bank Plaza, 200 Bay St, at Front.
Shopping The Eaton Centre (see p.83) should service the need of most shoppers; those looking for a non-mall environment should visit Queen St West (see p.76) for second-hand and vintage clothes. If you're looking for outdoor gear or clothing, try Mountain Equipment Co-op, 400 King St West at Peter (Mon–Wed 10am–7pm, Thurs 10am–9pm, Fri & Sat 10am–6pm, Sun 11am–3pm; ⓣ604/876-6221, ⓦwww.mec.ca), which has the city's widest selection of outdoor equipment and also does rentals.

Travel details

Trains

Ontario Northland (ⓣ1-800/461-8558, ⓦwww.northlander.ca)
Toronto to: Cobalt (6 weekly; 7hr 40min); Cochrane (6 weekly; 11hr); Gravenhurst (6 weekly; 2hr); Huntsville (6 weekly; 3hr); North Bay (6 weekly; 5hr); Temagami (6 weekly; 7hr).
VIA Rail (ⓣ1-888/842-7245, ⓦwww.viarail.ca)
Toronto to: Kingston (2–3 daily; 2hr 30min); London (4 daily; 2hr); Montréal (2–3 daily; 4hr 30min); Niagara Falls (2 daily; 2hr); Ottawa (3–5 daily; 4hr 15min); Parry Sound (3 weekly; 4hr); Stratford (2 daily; 2hr 10min); Sudbury Junction (3 weekly; 8hr); Windsor (4 daily; 4hr); Winnipeg (3 weekly; 28hr 45min).

Buses

Coach Canada (ⓣ1-800/461-7661, ⓦwww.coachcanada.com)
Toronto to: Brockville (3 daily; 4hr 15min); Kingston (8 daily; 3hr); Montréal (8 daily; 7hr); Niagara Falls (hourly; 1hr 30min–2hr).
Greyhound (ⓣ1-800/661-8747, ⓦwww.greyhound.ca)
Toronto to: Hamilton (4 daily; 1hr); Kitchener (every 30min–1hr; 1hr 45min); London (13 daily; 2hr 30min–3hr); Midland (2 daily; 2hr 30min, change at Barrie); Montréal (8 daily; 7hr 30min–9hr); Niagara Falls (hourly; 1hr 30min–2hr); Ottawa (9 daily; 5–6hr); Owen Sound (3 daily; 4hr); Penetanguishene (2 daily; 2hr 45min, change at Barrie); Sault Ste Marie (3 daily; 10hr 50min); Thunder Bay (3 daily; 21hr); Wawa (4 daily; 14hr); Windsor (5 daily; 4–5hr); Winnipeg (3 daily; 30hr 30min).
Ontario Northland (ⓣ1-800/461-8558, ⓦwww.northlander.ca)
Toronto to: Bracebridge (4 daily; 2hr 45min); Gravenhurst (4 daily; 2hr 30min); Huntsville (4 daily; 3hr); North Bay (4–5 daily; 6hr); Orillia (1 daily; 2hr); Parry Sound (3 daily; 3hr 15min); Port Severn (3 daily; 2hr 45min); Sudbury (3 daily; 6hr).

2

Ontario

Ontario, Canada's second-largest province, stretches all the way from the St Lawrence River and the Great Lakes to the frozen shores of Hudson Bay. Some two-thirds of this territory – all of the north and most of the centre – is occupied by the forests and rocky outcrops of the **Canadian Shield**, whose ancient Precambrian rocks were brought to the surface by the glaciers that gouged the continent during the last ice age. The glaciers produced a flattened landscape studded with thousands of lakes and it was the local Iroquois who first coined the name "Ontario", literally "glittering waters". The **Iroquois** – as well as their **Algonquin** neighbours to the north – hunted and fished the Canadian Shield, but their agricultural activities were confined to the more fertile and hospitable parts of southern Ontario, in which the vast majority of the province's ten million people are now concentrated.

Spread along the north shore of **Lake Ontario** is Canada's biggest city, **Toronto** (see Chapter 1), with a population of around five and a half million. To either side of this giant metropolis are sprawling suburbs and ugly industrial townships. Among them, the gritty steel city of **Hamilton** has one or two interesting historic sights, and there's also Canada's premier tourist spot, **Niagara Falls** – best visited on a day-trip from Toronto or from chi-chi **Niagara-on-the-Lake** nearby. Most of the rest of **southwest Ontario** is deeply rural, a vast tract of farmland sandwiched between lakes Huron and Erie. Highlights here include **Goderich** and **Bayfield**, two charming little towns tucked against the bluffs of the Lake Huron shoreline, and **Stratford**, with its much-vaunted theatre festival. For landscape, the most attractive regions of southwest Ontario are the **Bruce Peninsula** and the adjacent **Georgian Bay**, whose **Severn Sound** is the location of the beautiful **Georgian Bay Islands National Park** as well as a pair of top-notch historical reconstructions, **Discovery Harbour** and **Sainte-Marie among the Hurons**.

In central Ontario, inland from the coastal strip bordering Georgian Bay, are the myriad Muskoka Lakes, the epicentre of what Canadians call "cottage country". Every summer, the province's city folk arrive here in their thousands to fish, go boating and swim, hunkering down in their lakeside cottages – though "cottages" is something of a misnomer as these second homes range from humble timber chalets to vast mansions; many locals swear this mass retreat into the semi-wilderness is the quintessential Canadian experience. With the notable exception of several superb hotels, there is nowhere in particular to aim for and the main towns – primarily **Gravenhurst** and **Bracebridge** – are far from inspiring. Your best bet if you're after the great outdoors is to keep going north to **Algonquin Provincial Park**, a vast

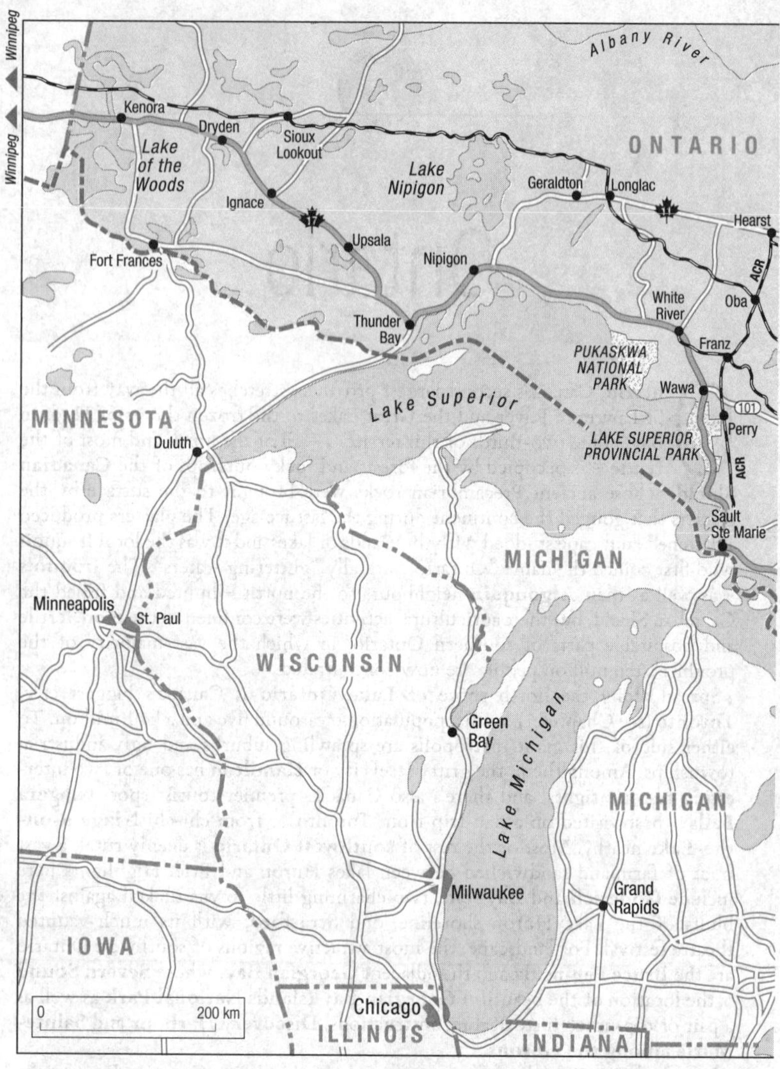

wilderness where beavers and black bears roam and you can canoe for days without seeing a soul. Alternatively head east for the towns bordering the St Lawrence River, primarily **Kingston**, a handsome university town with a clutch of fine limestone buildings. North of here, within easy striking distance, is **Ottawa**, the nation's capital, a surprisingly small city of top-rank museums and galleries, plus – and this may be something of a surprise if you're familiar with the city's bureaucratic image – a lively restaurant and bar scene.

Northern Ontario offers a natural environment stunning in its extremes, but the travelling can be hard and the specific sights too widely separated for comfort. Two main roads cross this sparsely inhabited region, **Hwy 11** in the north

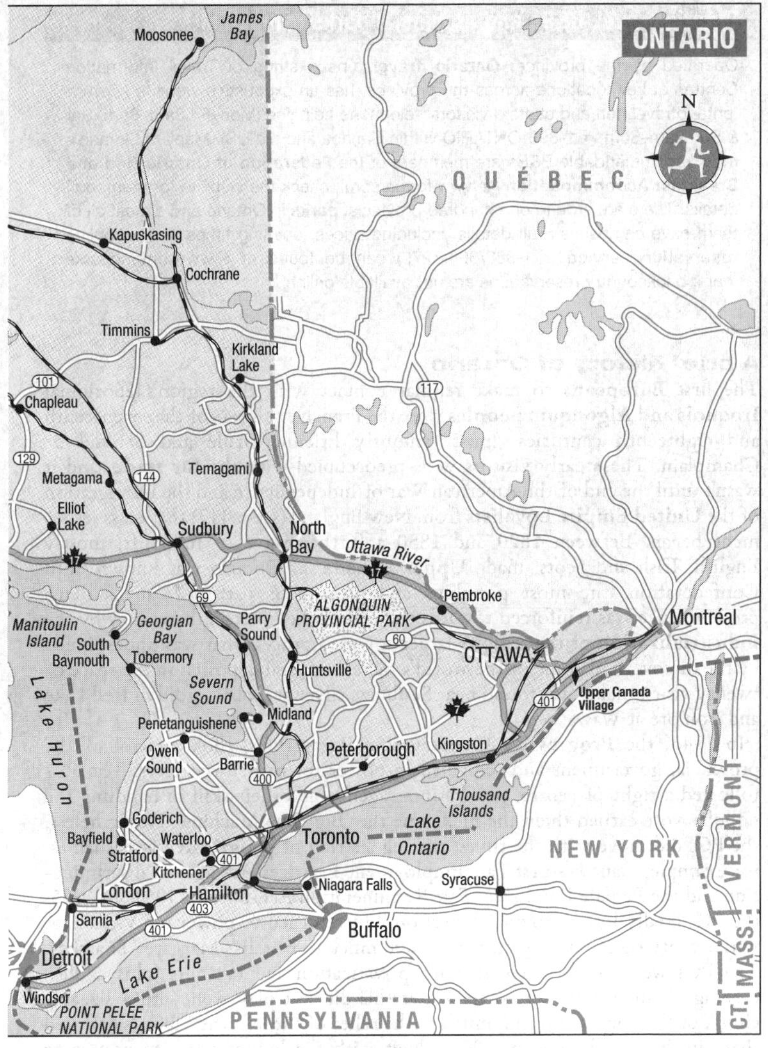

and **Hwy 17** to the south. The former links a series of mining towns and has little to offer, while the latter passes near – or cuts through – a string of parks, including the extravagantly wild **Lake Superior Provincial Park**. Hwy 17 also visits **Sault Ste Marie** – terminus of the **Agawa Canyon** train, which affords a glimpse of the otherwise impenetrable hinterland – plus the grain port of **Thunder Bay**, an ideal stopping point on the long journey west (or east). North of Hwy 11 lies a brutal country where hunters are the only regular visitors, though the passing tourist can get a taste of the terrain on board the Polar Bear Express train, which links **Cochrane**, on Hwy 11, with **Moosonee** on the shores of James Bay.

Ontario Travel, B&Bs and provincial parks campsites

Operated by the province, **Ontario Travel** runs a string of Travel Information Centres at key locations across the province, has an exhaustive website (ⓦwww.ontariotravel.net) and staffs a visitors' telephone help line (Mon–Fri 8am–8pm, Sat & Sun 9am–6pm; ⓣ1-800-ONTARIO within Canada and the US). Many of Ontario's most recommendable B&Bs are members of the **Federation of Ontario Bed and Breakfast Accommodation** (ⓦwww.fobba.com); check the website for members' details. There are around one hundred provincial **parks** in Ontario and almost all of them have campsites. Full details, including prices, opening times and an online **reservation service** (ⓣ1-888/668-7275) can be found at ⓦwww.ontarioparks.com; backcountry reservations are not available online).

A brief history of Ontario

The first **Europeans** to make regular contact with the region's aboriginal **Iroquois and Algonquin peoples** were the French explorers of the seventeenth and eighteenth centuries, most famously Étienne Brûlé and Samuel de Champlain. These early visitors were preoccupied with the **fur trade**, and it wasn't until the end of the American War of Independence and the immigration of the **United Empire Loyalists** from New England (see p.417) that mass settlement began. Between 1820 and 1850 a further wave of migrants, mostly English, Irish and Scots, made **Upper Canada**, as Ontario was known until Confederation, the most populous and prosperous part of Canada. This pre-eminence was reinforced towards the end of the nineteenth century by the **industrialization** of the region's larger towns, a process that was underpinned by the discovery of some of the world's richest mineral deposits: in the space of twenty years, nickel was found near Sudbury, silver at Cobalt, gold in Red Lake and iron ore at Wawa.

In 1943, the **Progressive Conservative Party** (PCs) took control of the provincial government and remained in power for over forty years. The PCs followed a right-of-centre, pro-business agenda and their skill in handling the popular vote earned them the nickname the 'Big Blue Machine'. Nevertheless, the PCs did move with the times, passing a string of **progressive acts** such as, for example, Canada's first Fair Employment Practices Act against discrimination and the Female Employees Fair Remuneration Act, both in 1951. In 1985, the PCs finally lost a provincial election, but returned to power ten years later with a flinty right-wing agenda that owed much to Britain's Margaret Thatcher. The PCs were much taken up with privatization and tax cuts (plus endless carping about welfare scroungers), but this did not play well with a sizeable chunk of the population and, much to the relief of the left, the Liberals defeated them in 2003 and again in 2007, albeit with the lowest voter turnout ever recorded in the province (52.6 percent).

Economically, Ontario's timber and mining industries, massive hydroelectric schemes and myriad factories long kept the province at the top of the economic ladder, though the 2008–09 recession did hit manufacturing very hard. The province's industrial success has also created massive **environmental problems**, most noticeable in the wounded landscapes around Sudbury and the polluted waters of lakes Erie and Ontario – problems which the provincial government has started to tackle, albeit somewhat tardily.

Southwest Ontario

The chain of towns to the east and west of Toronto, stretching 120km along the edge of Lake Ontario from Oshawa to Hamilton, is often called the **Golden Horseshoe**, a misleadingly evocative name that refers solely to the area's geographic shape and economic success. This is Ontario's manufacturing

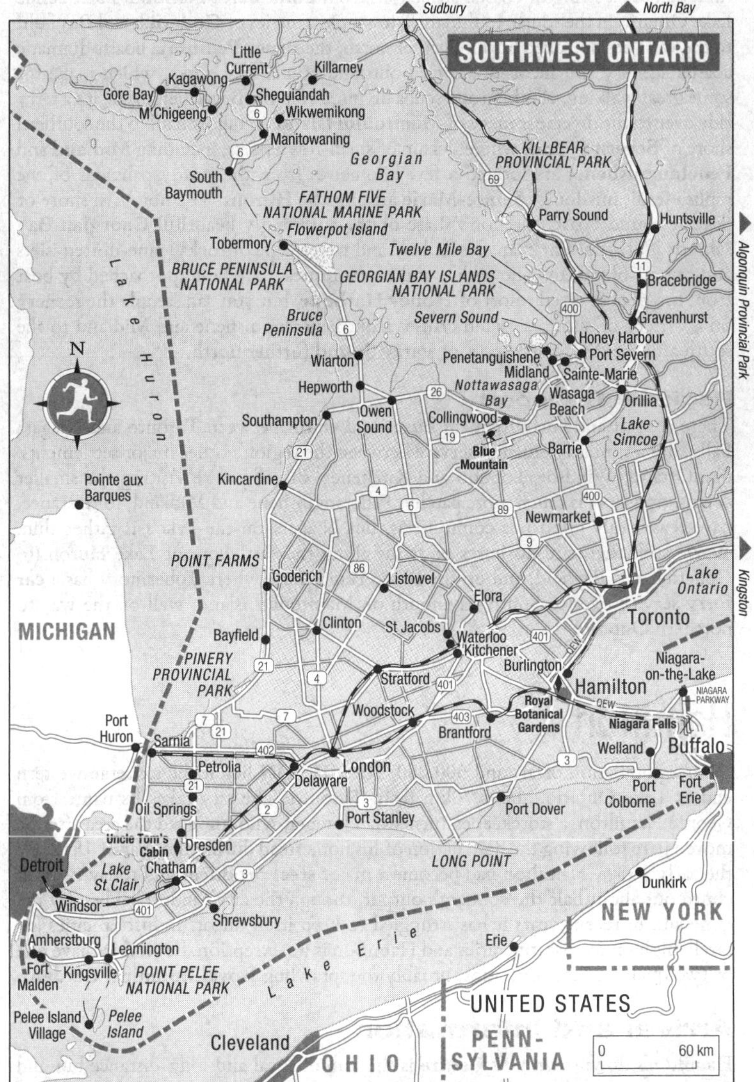

heartland, a densely populated and frequently ugly strip whose most notable attraction is the **Royal Botanical Gardens**, close to Hamilton. Further round the lake are the famous **Niagara Falls**, though the adjoining town of Niagara Falls is of little appeal; you're much better off exploring the Niagara region from **Niagara-on-the-Lake**, just a few kilometres downstream from the falls.

West of the Golden Horseshoe, much of southwest Ontario remains profoundly rural, a lightly populated region of rolling fields intercepted by a light scattering of family farmsteads. Yet there are towns here, most memorably **Stratford**, and **London**, a busy kind of place with an amenable, leafy centre. Beyond this agricultural belt are a string of coastal attractions from **Point Pelee National Park** beside Lake Ontario in the south, to the small-town pleasantries of **Goderich** and **Bayfield** to the west beside Lake Huron. Further north, the **Bruce Peninsula** boasts dramatic coastal scenery and incorporates two outstanding national parks, which make for some great walking, climbing and scuba diving. From the Bruce Peninsula, it's a ferry ride over to the diverse scenery of **Manitoulin Island** or a short haul to the southern shore of **Severn Sound**, where a chain of small-town ports, including **Midland** and **Penetanguishene**, are located a few kilometres from the sturdy palisades of the replica Jesuit mission of **Sainte-Marie among the Hurons**. The northern shore of Severn Sound boasts the lion's share of the stunningly beautiful **Georgian Bay Islands National Park**, an elegiac land and waterscape of rocky, pine-dotted islets and crystal-blue lake. The park – and its campsites – are best approached by boat from the pocket-sized resort of **Honey Harbour**, but you can sample the scenery on a variety of summer island cruises from Penetanguishene and Midland to the south and the dinky little port of **Parry Sound** further north.

Regional Transport

There are fast and fairly frequent **buses and trains** between Toronto and Niagara Falls, and a similarly efficient service between the region's other major settlements, like Ottawa, Windsor, London and Kitchener. But if you're visiting the smaller towns, transport is much more patchy: Penetanguishene and Midland, for instance, have reasonably good bus connections, but Niagara-on-the-Lake's is rather thin. Worse still, there are no buses or trains along the east shore of Lake Huron (to Goderich and Bayfield) and up the Bruce Peninsula – where Tobermory has a **car ferry** service over to South Baymouth on Manitoulin Island, well on the way to northern Ontario.

Hamilton

With a population of around 500,000, **HAMILTON** lies at the extreme western end of Lake Ontario, about 70km from Toronto. The city takes its name from George Hamilton, a storekeeper-turned-landowner, who surveyed the area after he moved here following the destruction of his homestead during the War of 1812. By the early 1900s, Hamilton had become a major **steel producer** and today its mills churn out about half the country's output, though the city's industrial heyday has gone and in recent years it has struggled to keep itself afloat. Industrial cities are rarely high on tourist itineraries and Hamilton is no exception, but it does have one or two quality attractions, most notably the sprawling **Royal Botanical Gardens**.

Arrival and information

Hamilton's downtown **GO Centre** is the hub of local and long-distance bus and train services; it's located at 36 Hunter St East and James St South, a couple of blocks south of Main Street. The **tourist information office** is in between Main and King streets at 34 James St South (Mon–Fri 8.30am–4.30pm; ⓣ905/546-2666 or 1-800/263-8590, ⓦwww.tourismhamilton.com). They can supply you with brochures on the city and its surroundings, plus restaurant and hotel lists.

The City

Hamilton is a large and sprawling city (with a confusing one-way street system), but its **downtown core** is surprisingly compact, running east to west parallel to the lakeshore along King Street West and Main Street West - between Bay Street North and James Street North. Here, just one block south of Main Street West at 41 Jackson St West, is **Whitehern** (July–Aug Tues–Sun 11am–4pm; Sept–June Tues–Sun 1–4pm; $6; ⓦwww.hamilton.ca/cultureandrecreation), an excellent example of Victorian architecture, its good-looking, columned portico set against the precise symmetries of the house's shuttered windows and imposing stonework. The interior holds an eccentric mix of styles, ranging from a splendid mid-nineteenth-century circular stairway to a dingy wood-panelled 1930s basement – all the garbled legacy of the McQuesten family, who lived here from 1852 until the 1960s.

Close by, also in the city centre, is the **Art Gallery of Hamilton** (Tues & Wed noon–7pm, Thurs & Fri noon–9pm, Sat & Sun noon–5pm; $10; ⓦwww.artgalleryofhamilton.on.ca), which occupies a brutally modern building at 123 King St West. The gallery displays a representative sample of Canadian painting drawn from its permanent collection, including a good selection of works by the Group of Seven (see p.88), and offers a lively programme of temporary exhibitions.

Dundurn Castle

From the Art Gallery, it's about twenty minutes' walk north along James Street North and then west along York Boulevard to the entertaining **Dundurn Castle** (July–Aug daily 10am–4pm; Sept–June Tues–Sun noon–4pm; $10; ⓦwww.tourismhamilton.com). A handsome villa, it was built in the 1830s for Sir Allan Napier MacNab, a soldier, lawyer and land speculator, who became one of the leading conservative politicians of the day: he was knighted for his loyalty to the Crown during the Upper Canada Rebellion of 1837, when he employed bands of armed Indians to round up supposed rebels and loot their property. Carefully renovated, Dundurn is an impressive building with an interior that easily divides into upstairs and downstairs, the former filled with fine contemporaneous furnishings, the latter a warren of poorly ventilated rooms for the dozens of servants. Nearby, the gatekeeper's cottage has been turned into a small **Military Museum** (July–Aug daily 11am–5pm; Sept–June Tues–Sun 1–5pm; $3, but free with admission to the castle), detailing local involvement in the War of 1812 and in the Fenian (Irish-American) cross-border raids of the 1860s.

The Royal Botanical Gardens

Heading northwest from Dundurn Castle, York Boulevard clips over the western reaches of Hamilton harbour bound for the neighbouring city of Burlington. The **Royal Botanical Gardens** (daily 10am–dusk ⓣ905/527-1158, ⓦwww.rbg.ca; $10), at 680 Plains Rd West, cover some 3000 acres on the far side of the harbour, their several sections spread over 15km of wooded shoreline. The flower displays here are simply gorgeous with highlights including the Hendrie Park Rose Garden (best June–Oct) and the neighbouring Laking Garden with its irises and peonies (May & June). These two gardens adjoin the main **RBG visitor centre** (daily 10am–dusk), where there's a shop, café and several inside areas featuring forced bulbs, orchids and cacti. Wilder parts of the RBG are round to the west with the 800-hectare Cootes Paradise Sanctuary latticed with hiking trails.

Most Hamilton-Burlington **buses** stop outside the RBG visitor centre and from here a **shuttle bus** (May–Aug, every 45min; free) visits all the main sections of the RBG. At other times of the year, you'll need a car.

Practicalities

Most of what you'll want to see in Hamilton can be seen in a day, so there's likely no need for you to **stay** overnight. Yet if you do find yourself in need of a room, there's no shortage. Most of the major hotel chains have branches here, with double rooms starting from around $100; one of the most comfortable is the centrally located *Sheraton Hamilton*, 116 King St West (Ⓣ905/529-5515, Ⓦwww.starwoodhotels.com; ⑥). Tourism Hamilton (Ⓣ 905/546-2666 or 1-800-263-8590, Ⓦwww.tourismhamilton.com) has a full listing of hotels, motels and B&B options.

Niagara Falls and the Niagara River

In 1860, thousands watched as **Charles Blondin** walked a tightrope across **Niagara Falls** for the third time. Midway, he paused to cook an omelette on a portable grill, and then had a marksman shoot a hole through his hat from the *Maid of the Mist* boat, fifty metres below. As attested by Blondin - and the innumerable lunatics and publicity seekers who have gone over the falls in every craft imaginable – the falls simply can't be beat as a theatrical setting. Yet, in truth, the stupendous first impression doesn't last long and to prevent the thirteen million visitors who arrive each year from getting bored by the sight of a load of water crashing over a 52-metre cliff, the Niagarans have ensured that the falls can be seen from every angle imaginable – from boats, viewing towers, helicopters, cable cars and even tunnels in the rock face behind the cascade. The **tunnels** and the **boats** are the most exciting, with the entrance to the former right next to the falls and the latter leaving from the foot of the cliff at the end of Clifton Hill, 1100m downriver. Both give a real sense of the extraordinary force of the waterfall, a perpetual white-crested thundering pile-up that had Mahler bawling "At last, fortissimo" over the din.

Both the **Niagara Parkway** road and the **Niagara River Recreation Trail** (see p.119), a jogging and cycle path, stretch the length of the Niagara River from Fort Erie, 32km upstream from the falls, to Niagara-on-the-Lake.

Arrival

Trains and buses from Toronto and most of southern Ontario's larger towns serve the town of **NIAGARA FALLS**, 3km to the north of the watery action.There are fast and frequent **Coach Canada buses** (Ⓣ1-800/461-7661, Ⓦwww.coachcanada.com) to the bus station in Niagara Falls town from both Toronto and Buffalo. There is also a twice daily VIA **train** service (Ⓣ1-888/842-7245, Ⓦwww.viarail.ca) to Niagara Falls from Toronto. By train or bus, the journey time from Toronto is about two hours. From Toronto, the train is the more scenic way to travel, but delays on the return leg – on which the evening train mostly originates in New York – can be a real pain. If you're travelling by **car**, a day is more than enough time to see the falls and squeeze in a visit to Niagara-on-the-Lake.

The **train station** is on Bridge Street at Erie Avenue, 3km north of the falls themselves. The **bus station** is across the street. For those **driving**, parking

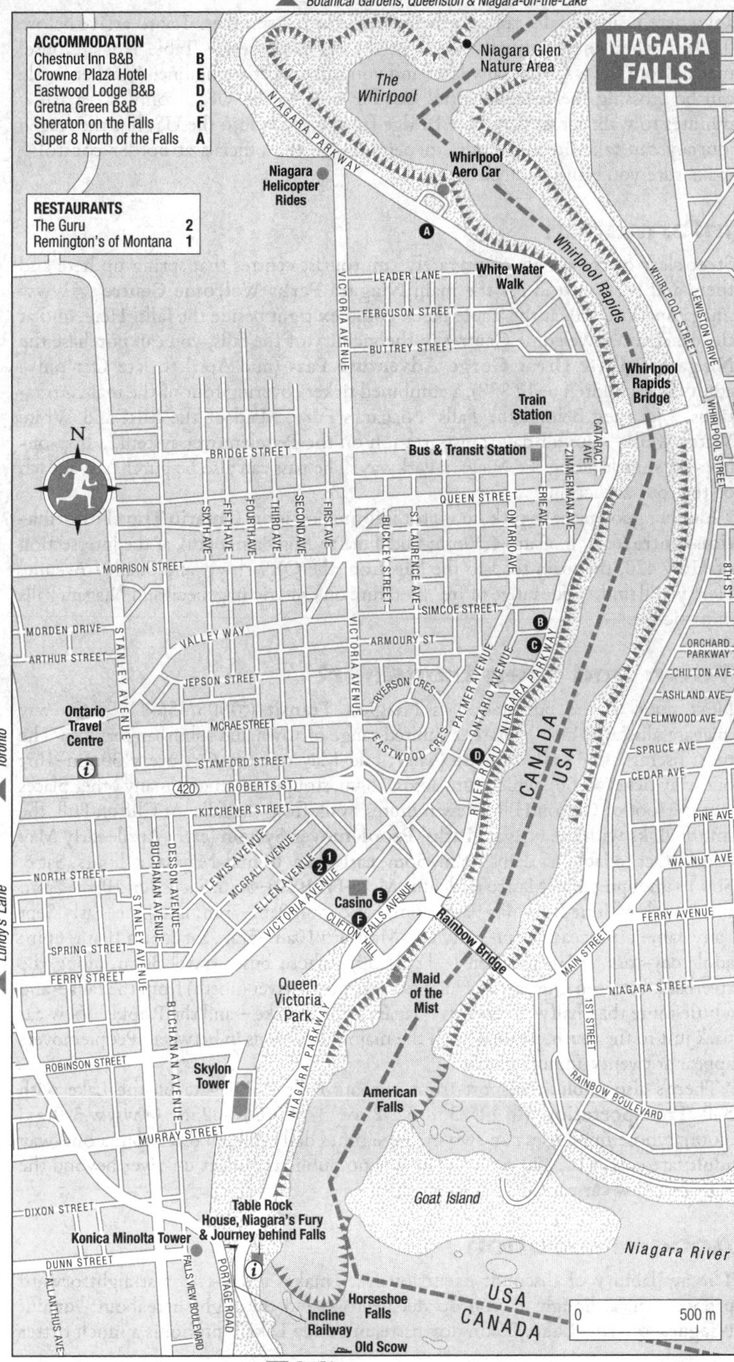

Botanical Gardens, Queenston & Niagara-on-the-Lake
NIAGARA FALLS
ACCOMMODATION
Chestnut Inn B&B B
Crowne Plaza Hotel E
Eastwood Lodge B&B D
Gretna Green B&B C
Sheraton on the Falls F
Super 8 North of the Falls A
RESTAURANTS
The Guru 2
Remington's of Montana 1
Niagara Glen Nature Area
The Whirlpool
NIAGARA PARKWAY
Whirlpool Aero Car
Niagara Helicopter Rides
Whirlpool Rapids
White Water Walk
LEADER LANE
FERGUSON STREET
BUTTREY STREET
VICTORIA AVENUE
Whirlpool Rapids Bridge
WHIRLPOOL STREET
LEWISTON DRIVE
Train Station
Bus & Transit Station
BRIDGE STREET
CATARACT AVE
ZIMMERMAN AVE
ERIE AVE
QUEEN STREET
SIXTH AVE
FIFTH AVE
FOURTH AVE
THIRD AVE
SECOND AVE
FIRST AVE
BUCKLEY STREET
ST LAURENCE AVE
ONTARIO AVE
MORRISON STREET
8TH ST
SIMCOE STREET
MORDEN DRIVE
VALLEY WAY
ARMOURY ST
ORCHARD PARKWAY
CHILTON AVE
ARTHUR STREET
STANLEY AVENUE
JEPSON STREET
RYERSON CRES
PALMER AVENUE
ONTARIO AVENUE
RIVER ROAD / NIAGARA PARKWAY
ASHLAND AVE
ELMWOOD AVE
Ontario Travel Centre
MCRAE STREET
EASTWOOD CRES
CANADA
USA
SPRUCE AVE
CEDAR AVE
Toronto
STAMFORD STREET
420
(ROBERTS ST)
KITCHENER STREET
PINE AVE
LEWIS AVENUE
MCGRALL AVENUE
DESSON AVENUE
BUCHANAN AVENUE
NORTH STREET
ELLEN AVENUE
VICTORIA AVENUE
WALNUT AVE
Casino
CLIFTON HILL
FALLS AVENUE
Rainbow Bridge
FERRY AVENUE
Lundy's Lane
SPRING STREET
MAIN STREET
FERRY STREET
Maid of the Mist
NIAGARA STREET
Queen Victoria Park
1ST STREET
ROBINSON STREET
Skylon Tower
RAINBOW BOULEVARD
American Falls
MURRAY STREET
Goat Island
DIXON STREET
Table Rock House, Niagara's Fury & Journey behind Falls
Konica Minolta Tower
Niagara River
DUNN STREET
ALLANTHUS AVE
FALLS VIEW BOULEVARD
PORTAGE ROAD
Horseshoe Falls
Incline Railway
USA
CANADA
0 500 m
Old Scow
Fort Erie

anywhere near the falls can be a major hassle in the summer. Try to arrive before 9.30am when there's usually space in the car park beside Table Rock House, metres from the waterfall; any later and you can expect a long line. Another hassle can be crossing the **international border** over to the US; it only takes a few minutes to walk across Rainbow Bridge from Canada into the US, but the return journey can take literally hours, depending on the officials at border control – make sure you bring your **passport**.

Information

Steer clear of the gaggle of privately run tourist centres that spring up here and there and head instead for the main **Niagara Parks Welcome Centre** (Ⓦwww.niagaraparks.com), at the Table Rock complex right beside the falls. Here, and at the other three Welcome Centres in the vicinity of the falls, you can purchase the **Niagara Falls & Great Gorge Adventure Pass** (mid-April to late Oct only; adults $40, children 6–12 $28), a combined ticket covering four of the main attractions – Journey Behind the Falls, Niagara's Fury, Maid of the Mist and White Water Walk – plus all-day transportation on the Peoplemover system, a hop-on-hop-off shuttle along the Niagara Parkway. The pass can also be purchased at each of the four attractions.

Another good place to pick up visitor information is the **Ontario Travel information centre** (daily 8.30am–4.30pm; mid-June to Aug 8am–8pm), at the intersection of Hwy 420, the main road to the falls from the QEW hwy, and Stanley Avenue. Here you'll find a wide range of free literature on Ontario in general and Niagara Falls in particular.

Town and area transport

Next door to the bus station is **Niagara Transit** (Ⓣ905/356-1179, Ⓦwww.niagarafalls.ca), which operates a limited range of town and suburban services. The most useful is the **Falls Shuttle** (daily: mid-May to early Oct every 30min–1hr; one-way ticket $3.50), which runs across town, stopping – among many other places – at the foot of Clifton Hill, a few minutes' walk from the falls. At Clifton Hill, the shuttle links with the Niagara Parks' **Peoplemover System** (early April–early May & mid-Oct to late Oct daily 10am–5pm; early May to mid-May same hours, Sat & Sun 10am–6pm; mid-May to mid-June Mon–Fri 10am–6pm, Sat & Sun 10am–7pm; third week of June Mon–Fri 9am–6pm, Sat & Sun 9am–7pm; late June–early Sept daily 9am–11pm; early Sept–early Oct Mon–Fri 10am–5pm, Sat & Sun 10am–6pm; adult day-pass $7.50, children 6–12 $4.50), whose buses travel 30km along the riverbank between Queenston Heights Park, down-river (north) from the falls – and a little more than halfway towards Niagara-on-the-Lake – and the Rapids' View car park just to the south, pausing at all the major attractions in between. Peoplemovers appear at twenty-minute intervals.

There's also public transport from Niagara Falls to Niagara-on-the-Lake with **5-0 Transportation** (Ⓣ905/358-3232 or 1-800/667-0256, Ⓦwww.5-0taxi.com), whose minibuses run two or three times daily in each direction; a one-way adult fare costs $10, $20 return. There is no public transport up-river beyond the Rapids' View car park.

Accommodation

The availability of discount excursion fares makes a day-trip a straightforward proposition, although, if you do decide to spend the night hereabouts, quaint **Niagara-on-the-Lake**, 26km downstream beside Lake Ontario, is a much better option than the crassly commercialized town of Niagara Falls itself. But Niagra-on-the-Lake gets very crowded in high season; try to to book at least a couple of days in advance.

Niagara Falls is billed as the "Honeymoon Capital of the World", which means many of its **motels and hotels** have an odd mix of cheap, basic rooms and gaudy suites with heart-shaped bathtubs, waterbeds and the like. In summer, hotel and motel rooms fill up fast, so book ahead, but out of season it's a buyer's market so haggling can often bring the price way down. The least expensive choices are either out along **Lundy's Lane**, a dispiriting motel strip that extends west of the falls for several kilometres, or in the run-down town centre near the bus and train stations. You're much better off spending a little more to stay on leafy **River Road**, running down-river from the foot of Clifton Hill, where there are several good **B&Bs**. If you want a room with a decent **view of the falls**, you'll be paying premium rates. The premier hotels on **Falls Avenue**, beside Clifton Hill, and **Fallsview Boulevard**, on top of the ridge directly above the falls, offer the best views but you should always check the room first: descriptions can be fairly elastic and some rooms claiming to be in sight of the falls require minor gymnastics for a glimpse.

Hotels

Crowne Plaza Hotel 5685 Falls Ave ⓣ905/374-4447 or 1-800/263-7135, ⓦwww.niagarafallscrowneplazahotel.com. Just metres from the foot of Clifton Hill, this is one of Niagara's older and most attractive hotels, a tidy tower block with Art Deco flourishes whose upper storeys (and more expensive rooms) have splendid views over the American Falls. Marilyn Monroe stayed here in Room #801 while filming *Niagara* – and you can stay there too for no extra charge. 7

Sheraton on the Falls 5875 Falls Ave ⓣ905/374-4445 or 1-888/229-9961, ⓦwww.sheratononthefalls.com. Walloping skyrise, whose upper floors have wondrous views of the American Falls. Large and well-appointed rooms with supremely comfortable beds. 7

Super 8 North of the Falls 4009 River Rd ⓣ905/356-0131, ⓦwww.super8.com. Routine-verging-on-the-ugly motel in a pleasant location, flanked by parkland near the Aero Car (see p.119) about 1.5km from the falls. Bike rental, free parking and complimentary shuttle service to Clifton Hill. Doubles from 3, but depending on demand prices can soar to 6 – but the rooms aren't worth that price.

B&Bs

Chestnut Inn B&B 4983 River Rd ⓣ905/374-7623, ⓦwww.chestnutinnbb.com. Expansive, nineteenth-century house a short drive from Clifton Hill holding four ornately decorated, period-style en-suite rooms. The owners can help arrange transport to the bus and rail stations, if required. 6

Eastwood Lodge B&B 5359 River Rd ⓣ905/354-8686, ⓦwww.theeastwood.com. Five commodious, a/c en-suite bedrooms in a rambling old villa with wide balconies and attractive garden. 6

Gretna Green B&B 5077 River Rd ⓣ905/357-2081 or 1-888/504-3565, ⓦwww.gretnagreenniagara.com. Pleasant and well-tended B&B in an attractive older house with four, en-suite guest rooms decorated in vibrant pastel shades. 6

The Falls

Even if you've seen all the postcards and watched all the films, nothing quite prepares you for your first glimpse of the **falls**, a fearsome white arc shrouded in clouds of dense spray with the river boats struggling down below, mere specks against the surging cauldron. There are actually two cataracts, as tiny **Goat Island** divides the accelerating water into two channels: on the far side, across the frontier, the river slips over the precipice of the **American Falls**, 320m wide but still only half the width of the **Horseshoe Falls** on the Canadian side. The spectacle is even more extraordinary in winter, when snow-covered trees edge a jagged armoury of freezing mist and heaped ice blocks.

All this may look like a scene of untrammelled nature, but it isn't. Since the early twentieth century, hydroelectric schemes have greatly reduced the water flow, and all sorts of tinkering has spread what's left of the river more evenly over the crest line. As a result, the process of erosion, which has moved the falls some 11km upstream in 12,000 years, has slowed down from one metre per year to just 30cm. This obviously has advantages for the tourist industry, but the environmental consequences of harnessing the river in such a way are still unclear. More positively, the cardsharps and charlatans who overran the riverside in Blondin's day are long gone with the **Niagara Parks Commission** (ⓦwww.niagaraparks.com), which controls the area along the Canadian side of the river and beside the falls, ensuring the immaculately tended tree-lined gardens and parkland remain precisely so.

Table Rock House

At **Table Rock House**, you can get disarmingly close to the crest line of the Horseshoe Falls at a free **observation platform** and from here you can also spot the rusting remains of the **Old Scow**, stuck against the rocks in the middle of the river just upstream. In 1918, this flat-bottomed barge was being towed across the Niagara River when the lines snapped and the boat – along with the two-man crew – hurtled towards the falls. There must have been an awful lot of praying going on, because – just 750m from the precipice – the barge caught against the rocks, and it's stayed there ever since.

Inside Table Rock House, elevators travel to the base of the cliff, where the tunnels for the **Journey Behind the Falls** (daily 9am–dusk, sometimes later; $12.50, children 6–12 $7.50) lead to points directly behind the cascade. It's a stupendous sight, which is probably more than can be said for Table Rock's other attraction, **Niagara's Fury** (daily 9am–dusk, sometimes later; $15, children aged 6–12 years $9), a self-billed "4-D experience" that aims to recreate the creation of the falls.

At the back of Table Rock House, a footbridge leads over to a pocket-sized **Incline Railway** ($2), which travels up to the assorted tower blocks of Fallsview Boulevard. Here, the Ramada Plaza Hotel incorporates the **Konica Minolta Tower** (daily: June–Sept 9am–11pm; Oct–May 9am–10pm; $5, children 6–12 years $2.50; ⓦwww.niagaratower.com), which has its own elevated observation decks.

Maid of the Mist boats and Clifton Hill

From Table Rock House, a wide path leads north along the edge of the river gorge, with the manicured lawns of **Queen Victoria Park** to the left and views over to the American Falls to the right. At the end of the park is Clifton Hill, the main drag linking the riverside with the town of Niagara Falls. From the jetty below Clifton Hill, **Maid of the Mist boats** (daily: April to late June 9.45am–5.45pm; late June to early Sept 9am–7pm; early Sept to late Oct 9.45am–4.45pm; boats leave every 15min in high season, otherwise every 30min; $15, children 6–12 $9, including waterproofs; ⓦwww.maidofthemist.com) edge out into the river and push up towards the falls, an exhilarating trip no one should miss.

Clifton Hill itself is a fantastically tawdry collection of fast-food joints and bizarre attractions, from the innocuous House of Frankenstein to the eminently missable Ripley's Believe It or Not! Close by, near the Rainbow Bridge off Victoria Avenue, is one of the town's two 24hr **casinos**, a bristlingly modern structure where kids can watch their parents fritter away their inheritance; the other is up on Fallsview Boulevard. If you're keen to avoid all this commercialization, then stick to the well-kept **riverside** area. There are a string of attractions further downstream, beginning with the White Water Walk, 3km away (see p.119).

▲ The Maid of the Mist at Niagara Falls

Eating and drinking

The restaurant scene in Niagara Falls is hardly pulsating and there are dozens of cheap chain **restaurants** and fast-food joints along and around Clifton Hill. For something rather more distinctive you'll have to venture a little further afield – to **Victoria Avenue** at the top of Clifton Hill, though even here pickings are thin. *The Guru* (Ⓣ905/354-3444; daily noon–11pm)), at 5705 Victoria Ave, is a modest little place, with tasty and reasonably priced Indian food. Vegetarians are particularly well catered for and main courses average around $13. *Remington's of Montana* (Ⓣ905/356 4410; daily 4–11pm), at 5657 Victoria Ave, is an attractively decorated place – all subdued lighting, wood panelling and Wild West statuettes – serving tasty and well-prepared steaks, its speciality, from $24.

Downstream from the falls

The **Niagara River Recreation Trail** is a combined bicycle and walking track that travels the entire length of the Niagara River from Lake Erie down to Lake Ontario; for most of its 58km it runs parallel to the main road, the scenic **Niagara Parkway**. Downstream from the falls, trail and parkway cut across the foot of Clifton Hill (see p.118) before continuing north for a further 3km to reach the **White Water Walk** (daily April to mid-May 9am–4.30pm; mid-May to mid-June 9am–6pm; mid-June to early Sept 9am–7pm; early Sept to late Nov 9am–5pm; $9). This comprises an elevator and then a tunnel, which leads to a boardwalk overlooking the Whirlpool Rapids, where the river seethes and fizzes as it makes an abrupt turn to the east.

From here, it's a further 1km along the parkway to the brightly painted **Whirlpool Aero Car** (daily: early March to late June 9am–4.45pm; late June to early Sept 9am–7.45pm; early Sept to mid-Nov 9am–4.45pm; $11.50, children 6–12 $6.80), a cable-car ride across the gorge that's as near as you'll come to emulating Blondin's tightrope antics. Another 500m brings you to **Niagara Helicopter Rides**, 3731 Victoria Ave (Ⓣ905/357-5672, Ⓦwww.niagarahelicopters.com), who offer a breathtaking twelve-minute excursion over the falls for $120 per person; costs can often be reduced if you are in a group and no bookings are required.

Niagara Glen to the Butterfly Conservatory

Pushing on, it's another short hop of 2.5km to the **Niagara Glen Nature Area** (daily dawn to dusk; free), where paths lead down from the clifftop to the bottom of the gorge. It's a hot and sticky trek in the height of the summer, and strenuous at any time of the year, but rewarding for all that – here at least (and at last) you get a sense of what the region was like before the tourist hullabaloo.

Nearby, about 800m further downstream along the parkway, lies the Niagara Parks Commission's pride and joy, the immensely popular **Niagara Parks Botanical Gardens** (daily dawn to dusk; free), whose various themed gardens – including rose, bog and parterre – flank the huge, climate-controlled **Butterfly Conservatory** (daily: early March to mid-June 9am–6pm; mid-June to early Sept 9am–9pm; early Sept to early Oct 9am–6pm; early Oct to early March 9am–5pm; $11.50), which houses over 2000 exotic butterflies in a tropical rainforest setting.

Queenston Heights Park

About 3km further on, **Queenston Heights Park** marks the original location of the falls, before the force of the water – as it adjusts to the hundred-metre differential between lakes Erie and Ontario – eroded the riverbed to its present point, 12km upstream. A pleasant expanse of greenery, the park's cardinal feature is a grandiloquent monument to **Sir Isaac Brock**, the Guernsey-born general who was killed here in the War of 1812, leading a head-on charge against the invading Americans.

Queenston

From beside the park, the Niagara Parkway begins a curving descent down to the little village of **QUEENSTON**, whose importance as a transit centre disappeared in 1829 when the falls were bypassed by the Welland Canal, which runs a few kilometres to the west of the river between lakes Erie and Ontario.

In the village, on Partition Street at Queenston Street, the **Laura Secord Homestead** (guided tours: early May to June Mon–Fri 9.30am–1.30pm, Sat & Sun 11am–5pm; July to early Sept daily 11am–5pm; rest of Sept Wed-Sun noon-4pm; $5) is a reconstruction of the substantial timber-frame house of Massachusetts-born **Laura Ingersoll Secord**. It was from here, during the War of 1812, that Secord proved her dedication to the imperial interest by walking 30km through the woods to warn a British platoon of a surprise attack planned by the Americans. As a result, the British and their native allies laid an ambush and captured over five hundred Americans at the Battle of Beaver Dams. Secord had good reason to loathe the Americans – during the war they looted her house and her husband was badly wounded at the battle of Queenston Heights – but in the years following her dramatic escapade she kept a low profile, possibly fearing reprisals in what was then a wild, frontier area. The tour provides an intriguing introduction to Secord's life and times and the house itself is of elegant proportions with a full crop of period furnishings and fittings.

From Queenston, it's about 11km to Niagara-on-the-Lake.

Niagara-on-the-Lake

Boasting elegant clapboard houses and verdant, mature gardens, all spread along tree-lined streets, **NIAGARA-ON-THE-LAKE**, 26km downstream from the falls, is one of Ontario's most charming little towns, much of it dating from the early nineteenth century. The town was originally known as Newark and became the first capital of Upper Canada in 1792, but four years later it lost this distinction to York (Toronto) because it was deemed too close to the American frontier, and therefore vulnerable to attack. The US army did, in fact, cross the river in 1813,

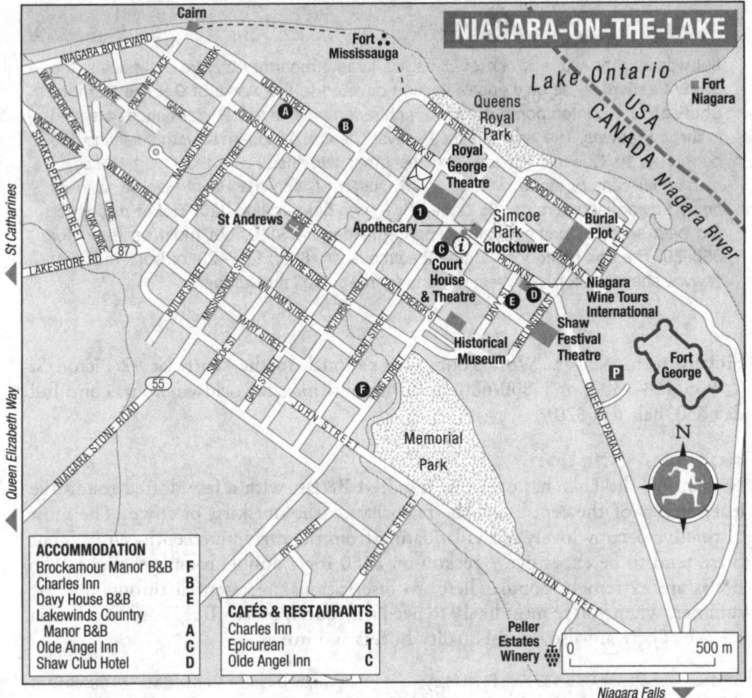

destroying the town, but it was quickly rebuilt and renamed. It has managed to avoid all but the most sympathetic of modifications ever since, except just away from the centre down on Melville Street, where a rash of new development and a marina add nothing to the appeal of the place.

Niagara-on-the-Lake attracts too many day-trippers for its own good, but the crowds stick religiously to the souvenir and knick-knack shops of the main street and melt away by 5 or 6pm. The town is also popular as the location of one of Canada's most acclaimed theatre festivals, the **Shaw Festival**, which celebrates the works of George Bernard Shaw with performances from April to late October, and it is also surrounded by **wineries**, many of which encourage visitors (see p.124).

Arrival and information

5-0 Transportation (see p.116) provides a reliable **minibus service** linking Niagara Falls and Niagara-on-the-Lake. They pick up passengers at several locations in Niagara Falls, including the *Sheraton on the Falls* hotel, and drop them off just behind the Court House Theatre, metres from the **tourist office**, in the basement of the Court House (daily: May to mid-Oct 10am–7.30pm; mid-Oct to April 10am–5pm; Ⓣ905/468-1950, Ⓦwww.niagaraonthelake.com). The office issues town maps and operates a free **room reservation service**, which can be a great help in the summer when the town's hotels and B&Bs – of which there are dozens – get very busy.

It only takes a few minutes to stroll from one end of town to the other, but to venture further afield – especially to the falls – you might consider renting a

The Shaw Festival

Showcasing the work of one of Canada's largest repertory theatre companies, the **Shaw Festival** is the only one of its kind devoted to the works of **George Bernard Shaw** and his contemporaries – and a rich repertoire it is too. Performances are held in **three theatres**. The largest is the Festival Theatre, a modern structure seating 850 people at 10 Queen's Parade, and the other two theatres – the Court House, a nineteenth-century stone building at 26 Queen St, and the Royal George, with its fancy Edwardian interior at 85 Queen St – both hold around 320. **Ticket prices** for the best seats at prime weekend performances hit $110, but most seats go for $50–70. The box office for all three theatres is ⓣ1-800/511-7429, or book online at ⓦwww.shawfest.com. The festival runs from April to late October.

bicycle from Niagara Wine Tours International, in the centre at 92 Picton St (ⓣ905/468-1300, or 1-800/680-7006, ⓦwww.niagaraworldwinetours.com; full day $30, half day $20).

Accommodation

Niagara-on-the-Lake has over one hundred **B&Bs**, with a few dotted round the leafy streets of the centre and the majority on the outskirts of town. The most distinctive occupy lovely old villas dating from the early nineteenth century, but these tend to be expensive – reckon on $150 for a double room per night. The B&Bs are extremely popular here, so reservations are essential throughout the summer, when you're most likely to need the tourist office's free room reservation service. There are also several quality **hotels** and **inns**.

Brockamour Manor B&B 433 King St, at Mary ⓣ905/468-5527, ⓦwww.brockamour.com. This elegant B&B has six en-suite guest rooms ranging from the commodious Sir Brock's Bedchamber to the two smaller rooms in the old servants' quarters. With its high gables and wide veranda, the house itself is a splendid affair dating from 1812 and it's surrounded by an attractive wooded garden. ❼

Charles Inn 209 Queen St ⓣ905/468-4588 or 1-866/556-8883, ⓦwww.charlesinn.ca. This charming old inn, dating from the 1830s, has all sorts of idiosyncratic features, from the most splendid of verandas to old cast-iron fireplaces. There are twelve guest rooms, each decorated in a fetching version of period style and the beds are super-comfortable. Unlike many of its rivals, the inn has not been overly spruced up, which gives it real character – but at a price. ❼

Davy House B&B 230 Davy St ⓣ905/468-5307, or 1-888/314-9046, ⓦwww.davyhouse.com. Cosy, two-storey clapboard house with a particularly pleasant veranda. Each of the bedrooms is decorated in a modern version of retro style. Within easy strolling distance of the town centre. ❻

Lakewinds Country Manor B&B 328 Queen St at Dorchester ⓣ905/468-1888 or 1-866/338-1888, ⓦwww.lakewinds.ca. Expansive Victorian mansion with six a/c guest rooms and suites, each of which is decorated in a particular style – Florentine or Singaporean, for example. The house possesses a handsome veranda and is surrounded by a well-kept garden and comes complete with an outdoor heated pool. ❼

Olde Angel Inn 224 Regent St , off Queen ⓣ905/468-3411, ⓦwww.angel-inn.com. Dating from the 1820s, this is the oldest inn in town. Offers a handful of simple but perfectly adequate rooms in the main building and a couple of annexe-cottages too. ❺

Shaw Club Hotel 92 Picton St ⓣ905/468-5711 or 1-800/511-7070, ⓦwww.shawclub.com. This hotel may be owned by the same people who run the *Charles Inn* but the two are chalk and cheese, with the *Shaw* being a sharply decorated, ultra-modern place, from the tropical fish tank in the foyer to the minimalist guest rooms – with plasma screen TVs – and beyond; the nicest rooms have balconies. The hotel is linked to the deluxe Shaw Spa next door. ❼

The Town

It's the general flavour of Niagara-on-the-Lake that appeals rather than any specific sight, but **Queen Street**, the main drag, does hold a dinky brick **clock tower** as well as the old **Court House**, a good-looking, Neoclassical stone structure of 1847. Close by also is the **Apothecary** (mid-May to Aug daily noon–6pm, Sept to mid-Oct Sat & Sun noon-6pm; free), a museum restoration of an 1869 pharmacy. It's worth a peep for its beautifully carved walnut and butternut cabinets, crystal gasoliers and porcelain jars.

From Queen Street, it's a five- to ten-minute walk to the town's finest building, **St Andrews Church**, at Simcoe and Gage streets, a splendid illustration of the Greek Revival style dating to the 1830s. It has a beautifully proportioned portico and the interior retains the original high pulpit and box pews. From here, it's a brief stroll to the **Niagara Historical Museum** (daily: May–Oct 10am–5pm; Nov–April 1–5pm; $5; ⓦwww.niagarahistorical.museum), at 43 Castlereagh St, one of the province's more enjoyable community museums with a lively programme of temporary exhibitions. Highlights of the permanent collection include a potpourri of military artefacts and an entertaining selection of old photographs.

Also of interest is the fenced **burial plot** at the east end of Simcoe Park, at Wellington and Byron streets, which is where you'll find the earthly remains of 25 Polish soldiers who died during the great influenza epidemic of 1918–19 (see below). Walk northwest from here, to the edge of the town grid at Simcoe and Front streets, and you'll reach the start of the **footpath** that leads across the golf course to the earthen ramparts of what was once **Fort Mississauga**, pushed tight against Lake Ontario. It's a pleasant and easy 1km-long stroll to the fort – allow an hour or so.

Fort George

There is more military stuff not too far away at the one-time British outpost of **Fort George** (May–Oct daily 10am–5pm; $11.70; ⓦwww.pc.gc.ca), 600m southeast of the town centre via Picton Street.

Built in the 1790s as one of a line of stockades that was slung across the Great Lakes to protect Canada from the US, the original Fort George was destroyed during the War of 1812, but the site was thoroughly excavated and the fort reconstructed in splendid style in the 1930s. Today the palisaded **compound** with its protective bastions holds about a dozen buildings, among them the officers' quarters and two log **blockhouses**, which doubled as soldiers' barracks. The difference between the quarters and the barracks is striking. The former are comparatively

Polish soldiers in Niagara-on-the-Lake

In the later stages of World War I, over twenty thousand **Poles** mustered in the US to form a Polish brigade. It was a delicate situation, as the Allies needed the soldiers but the Poles were committed to the creation of an independent Poland at a time when their country was ruled by Russia, an ally of the US. In the event, policy differences with the US government prompted the Poles to move over the border to Niagara-on-the-Lake, where they established a base camp. Paid and equipped by France, the Poles were trained by Canadian officers and then shipped off in batches to fight on the Western front, thereby deferring their attempts to create an independent Poland. At the end of the war, with the Tsar gone and the Bolsheviks in control of Russia, the Polish brigade – or "Blue Army" as it was called from the colour of their uniform – crossed Germany to return to their homeland, where they played a key role in the foundation of an independent Poland. The graves of the 25 Polish soldiers in Niagara-on-the-Lake recall these historical complexities, and a shrine has been erected in their honour.

spacious and were once – as recorded on shipping lists – furnished with fancy knick-knacks, while the latter housed the men and some of their wives (six wives out of every hundred were allowed to join the garrison) in the meanest of conditions. A tunnel links the main part of the fort with one of the exterior bastions, or ravelins, which is itself the site of a third, even stronger blockhouse. The only original building is the **powder magazine** of 1796, its interior equipped with wood and copper fittings to reduce the chances of an accidental explosion; as an added precaution, the soldiers working here went barefoot. There are also ninety-minute lantern-light **ghost tours** of the fort – good fun with or without an apparition (May–June Sun 8.30pm; July–Aug Sun, Mon, Wed, Thurs & Fri 8.30pm; Sept Sun 7.30pm; $10; ⓣ905/468-6621, ⓦwww.niagaraghosts.com). Tours begin at the car park in front of the fort; **tickets** can be purchased either in advance at the fort's gift shop, or from the guide thirty minutes before the start of the tour.

Eating and drinking

By sheer weight of numbers, the day-trippers set the gastronomic tone in town, but one or two good **cafés and restaurants** have survived the flood to offer tasty meals and snacks.

Charles Inn 209 Queen St ⓣ905/468-4588. Attracting an older clientele, this smart and mildly formal restaurant, in one of the ground-floor rooms of the *Charles Inn* (see p.122), has a carefully crafted menu: try the hen with field mushrooms and asparagus in a cabernet jus. Mains average $27. Open daily. Reservations recommended.

Ontario wines

Until the 1980s, **Canadian wine** was something of a joke. The industry's most popular product was a sticky, fizzy concoction called "Baby Duck", and other varieties were commonly called "block-and-tackle" wines, after a widely reported witticism of a member of the Ontario legislature: "If you drink a bottle and walk a block, you can tackle anyone." This state of affairs was transformed by the **Vintners Quality Alliance** (VQA; ⓦwww.vqaontario.com), who have, since 1989, come to exercise tight control over wine production in Ontario, which produces around eighty percent of Canadian wine. The VQA's appellation system distinguishes between – and supervises the quality control of – two broad types of wine. Those wines carrying the **Provincial Designation** on their labels must be made from one hundred percent Ontario-grown grapes from an approved list of European grape varieties and selected hybrids; those bearing the **Geographic Designation** (eg Niagara Peninsula, Pelee Island), can only use *Vitis vinifera*, the classic European grape varieties, such as Riesling, Chardonnay and Cabernet Sauvignon. As you might expect from a developing wine area, the results are rather inconsistent, but the **Rieslings** have a refreshingly crisp, almost tart flavour with a mellow, warming aftertaste – and are perhaps the best of the present range, white or red.

More than twenty **wineries** are clustered in the vicinity of **Niagara-on-the-Lake.** Most of them have showrooms, others offer guided tours and just about all of them have tastings. The town's tourist office carries a full list with opening times, but the handiest is the **Peller Estates Winery**, whose vineyards and large modern showroom are on the edge of town, 2.5km from Queen Street, at 290 John St East (Sun–Thurs 10am–7pm, Fri & Sat 10am–9pm; ⓣ905/468-4678, ⓦwww.peller.com). Peller has produced a clutch of much-praised vintages and they do a good line in one of Canada's specialities, **ice wine**, a sweet dessert wine made from grapes that are left on the vine till December or January, when they are hand-picked at night while frozen. The picking and the crushing of the frozen grapes is a time-consuming business and this is reflected in the price – from about $25 per 375ml bottle of either sparkling or regular.

Epicurean 84 Queen St ☎905/468-3408, Ⓦwww.epicurean.ca. A pleasant café in the day and an amenable bistro at night. The menu is strong on local ingredients and offers vegetarians a good range of options. Bistro main courses (including Ontario rabbit) are around $20. Daily 9am–11pm.

Olde Angel Inn 224 Regent St, in the eponymous inn (see p.122). With its low-beamed ceilings and flagstone floors, this is the town's most atmospheric pub, serving a first-rate range of draught imported and domestic beers. Also offers filling and very affordable bar food – Guinness steak-and-kidney pies from $12 – and has an à la carte restaurant at the back. Daily 11am–1am.

Upstream from Niagara Falls to Fort Erie

Heading upstream from the falls past the **Old Scow** (see p.118), both the **Niagara Parkway** and the **Niagara River Recreation Trail** stay close to the river giving pleasant views over to the US. Nonetheless, this portion of the river is much less appealing than the stretch to the north of the falls – especially so beyond humdrum **CHIPPAWA**, which is where America's Grand Island divides the river into two drowsy channels. Further up-river, just 26km from the falls, the Niagara Parkway peters out at **FORT ERIE**, a small industrial town that also marks the end of the Queen Elizabeth Way linking Toronto with the American city of Buffalo. The one noteworthy site here is **Old Fort Erie** (early May to June daily 10am–5pm; July & Aug daily 10am–6pm; Sept to early Oct Wed–Sun 11am–4pm; $9.25, children 6–12 $5.15; Ⓦwww.niagaraparks.com), which overlooks Lake Erie from the mouth of the Niagara River just 2km south of town. The Americans razed the original fort in 1814, but it was painstakingly rebuilt in the 1930s as a Depression make-work scheme. The layout is similar to that of Fort George (see p.123) with a dry ditch, earth-and-stone ramparts and protruding bastions encircling a central compound, though here the outer gate is much more imposing, comprising a pair of huge double doors strengthened by iron studs. The central compound holds the usual spread of army buildings, including officers' quarters, barracks and a powder magazine, plus a modest museum that explores the fort's history.

Brantford

BRANTFORD, a quick 40km west of Hamilton on Hwy 403, takes its name from **Joseph Brant**, an Iroquois chieftain who was one of the most intriguing figures of colonial Canada (see p.126). Brant helped the British during the American War of Independence and, after their defeat, he and his followers were obliged to make a hasty exit from New York State before the Americans could take their revenge. Brant was ceded a large tract of land beside the Grand River on the site of what is today Brantford in 1784. European settlers reached the area in numbers in the 1850s and subsequently Brantford developed as a manufacturing centre churning out agricultural equipment by the wagon load. By the 1980s, the town was in decline as many of its factories and foundries went bust or relocated. Brantford still bears the scars of this de-industrialization, but a concerted effort has been made to breathe new life into the centre and, for the most part, this has been a success with a batch of new leisure facilities and shopping centres. For Canadians, Brantford is most famous as the home town of **Wayne Gretzky**, probably the greatest ice hockey player of all time; for everyone else, the town is best known as being the one-time home of the inventor of the telephone, **Alexander Graham Bell**.

Arrival and information

There are **buses and trains** to Brantford from several neighbouring cities, but to see the town's key sights you'll need a car. **Buses** to downtown Brantford pull in on Darling Street, one block north of Dalhousie. The **train station** is a short walk north of the centre on Wadsworth Street, just off Market Street.

The **tourist office** is on Wayne Gretzky Parkway, just off (and signposted from) Hwy 403 (mid-May to Oct Mon-Fri 9am–8pm, Sat 9am–9pm & Sun 9am–5pm; Nov to mid-May Mon–Fri 9am–7pm, Sat 10am–8pm & Sun 10am–4pm; ⓣ519/751-9900 or 1-800/265-6299, ⓦwww.visitbrantford.ca). They supply free city maps, which are extremely useful as Brantford can be a little difficult to negotiate, and have a complete list of local **accommodation**, including half a dozen B&Bs, though there's no compelling reason to actually stay here.

The Town

Brantford's modest **town centre** fans out from Dalhousie and Colborne streets, which run parallel to each other for about a kilometre and a half. There are no real highlights here, though the **Sanderson Centre for the Performing Arts** (ⓦwww.sandersoncentre.ca), at 88 Dalhousie St, does occupy a creatively recycled old vaudeville and silent-movie house dating back to 1919.

From Colborne Street, take Murray and then Mohawk streets for the 2km-drive southeast to the **Woodland Cultural Centre** (Mon–Fri 9am–4pm, Sat & Sun 10am–5pm; $7; ⓦwww.woodland-centre.on.ca), one of the most comprehensive First Nations' museums in Ontario. Acting as a sort of historical primer, the museum

Trouble in the colonies – the life and times of Joseph Brant

Born in modern-day Ohio, **Joseph Brant** (1742–1807) – or **Thayendanega** – was a Mohawk leader, whose stepfather had close ties with the British. This connection was reinforced when Joseph's sister, **Molly**, married the British Superintendent for Indian Affairs, William Johnson, who subsequently sponsored Brant's college education. Brant learnt to read and write English, took to wearing European clothes and even became an Anglican and Freemason, but he had another life too, odd-jobbing as a member of Mohawk war parties. By the mid-1760s, Brant had established himself as a farmer in New York State and was so well regarded by the British that, in 1776, they took him to London, where he was presented to King George III and became something of a celebrity, the subject of a string of official portraits. In each of them, Brant is shown in a mix of European and native gear – typically, he carries a tomahawk and has a Mohawk hairdo, but wears a dress coat with a sash – an apt reflection of his twin loyalties. Duly impressed by the power and wealth of the imperial capital, Brant remained loyal to the British during the **American War of Independence**, his repeated, large-scale raids – and alleged savagery – earning him the soubriquet "**Monster Brant**" among the colonials.

After the war, when neither the British nor the Americans felt militarily secure, both sides tried to woo Brant, who became adept at playing the whites off against each other; despite his blood-curling reputation, he was even invited to Philadelphia to meet President Washington in 1792. From the British, Brant secured a sizeable chunk of land beside the **Grand River** in modern-day Brantford, where his followers moved in 1784, but he was unable to protect his native allies from further American encroachment. Sensing failure, Brant withdrew to Burlington, near Hamilton, to live the life of a gentleman farmer (complete with servants and slaves) and it was here he died. In 1850, Mohawks carried Brant's **coffin** the 55km from Burlington to Brantford's Royal Chapel of the Mohawks (see p.127).

concentrates on the Six Nations of the Grand River, **Mohawks** who started out in New York State as members of the Iroquois League before retreating north at the end of the American War of Independence. The collection is displayed chronologically, beginning with an assortment of trade goods, plus several wampum belts recording treaties between the British and the Mohawks. There's also a portrait of Joseph Brant (see p.126) in native gear and an incisive section on racist representations of Native Americans in popular culture from the nineteenth century onwards.

Her Majesty's Royal Chapel of the Mohawks

From the Woodland Centre, it's a further 700m along Mohawk Street to **Her Majesty's Royal Chapel of the Mohawks** (May–June & Sept–Oct Wed–Sun 10.30am–5pm; July & Aug daily 10.30am–5pm; free), a spindly clapboard structure that dates back to 1785, making it the first Protestant church in Ontario. The church was built both to celebrate the Mohawk–British alliance and to replace the original chapel in New York, which the Mohawks were forced to abandon when they moved north. They did, however, retrieve the inscribed **plaques** that now stand behind the altar, religious inscriptions of the Lord's Prayer and the Creed written in a phonetic (and technically inaccurate) version of Iroquois. The stained glass **windows** depicting events in the history of the Six Nations were added in the 1950s. Behind the church is the tombstone of Joseph Brant, though his coffin was only moved here (from Burlington, Ontario) in 1850.

The Bell Homestead

Brantford's most popular attraction, the **Bell Homestead National Historic Site**, 94 Tutela Heights Rd (Tues–Sun 9.30am–4.30pm; $5; Ⓦwww.bellhomestead.ca), is located about 4km south of the centre, among the low wooded hills overlooking the Grand River. Soon after his arrival from Edinburgh in 1870, **Alexander Graham Bell** took a job as a teacher of the deaf, motivated by his mother's loss of hearing and, in his efforts to discover a way to reproduce sounds visibly, he stumbled across the potential of transmitting sound along an electrified wire. The consequence was the first long-distance call, made in 1876 from Brantford to the neighbouring village of Paris. The Bell Homestead consists of two simple, clapboard buildings. The first, moved here from Brantford in 1969, housed Canada's original Bell company office and features a series of modest displays on the history of the telephone. The second, the cosy family home, fronts a second small exhibition area devoted to Bell's life and research. There's no **public transport** from Brantford to the homestead.

Kitchener, St Jacobs and Elora

The industrial city of **Kitchener**, about 40km north of Brantford, is southern Ontario at its most prosaic, but amid the prevailing architectural gloom there are a couple of sights that are worth an hour or so, and you can also drop by **St Jacobs**, a centre of Mennonite settlement. In marked contrast, **Elora**, 30km north of Kitchener, is a pleasant little village of old stone houses and mills on the periphery of the **Elora Gorge**, a narrow limestone ravine that's a popular spot for a day's walk and picnic.

Kitchener

KITCHENER, just off Hwy 401 about 100km west of downtown Toronto, lies at the centre of an industrial belt whose economy has traditionally been based on rubber, textiles, leather and furniture. The town was founded as Sand Hills in 1799 by groups of **Mennonites**, a tightly knit Protestant sect who came here from the US, where their pacifist beliefs had incurred the wrath of their neighbours during the American Revolution. Soon after, German farmers began to arrive in the area. The new settlers had Sand Hills renamed Berlin in 1826, but during World War I it was thought prudent to change the name yet again and to prove their patriotism they chose "Kitchener" after the British field marshal. Today around sixty percent of Kitchener's inhabitants are descendants of German immigrants, a heritage celebrated every year during **Oktoberfest** (Ⓦwww.oktoberfest.ca), nine days of alcoholic stupefaction when even the most reticent of men can be seen wandering the streets in lederhosen.

The Mennonites have drifted out of Kitchener itself, and are concentrated in the villages north and west of **Waterloo**, Kitchener's glum northerly neighbour, with a particular concentration in **St Jacobs**.

Arrival and information

Kitchener's **bus station** is at 15 Charles St West, one block west of the main street, King, and the town centre. The **train station** is at Victoria and Weber Street West, from where it's a ten-minute walk south to downtown.

The downtown Kitchener **tourist office** is at 200 King St West (June–Aug Mon–Fri 10am–5pm, Sat 10am–4pm & Sun noon–4pm; Sept–May Mon 10am–4pm, Tues–Thurs 9am–5pm, Fri 10am–5pm & Sat noon–4pm; Ⓣ519/745-3536 or 1-800/265-6959, Ⓦwww.explorewaterlooregion.com). They issue free city maps and supply a full list of local **accommodation**, although it's not likley you'll want or need to stop over night here.

The Town

At the heart of Kitchener, on King Street East, is the much-lauded **Farmers' Market** (Sat 7am–2pm, year-round; Ⓦwww.kitchenermarket.ca), where you should be sure to sample the delicious German sausages. The **Mennonite** traders are unmistakable, with the men wearing traditional black suits and broad-brimmed hats, or deep-blue shirts and braces, the women ankle-length dresses and matching bonnets. Yet the Ontario Mennonites are far from an homogeneous sect – over twenty different groups are affiliated to the **Mennonite Central Committee** (MCC). They all share certain religious beliefs reflecting their Anabaptist origins – the sole validity of adult baptism being crucial – but precise practices and dress codes vary from group to group. Members of the traditional wing of the Mennonite movement, sometimes called **Amish**, own property communally and shun all modern machinery, travelling to the market and around the back lanes on horse-drawn buggies. To explain their history and faith, the MCC runs 'The Mennonite Story' in the neighbouring village of St Jacobs.

Kitchener's only other tourist sight of any real note is **Woodside**, the boyhood home of prime minister William Lyon Mackenzie King (1874–1950), about 1km northeast of the centre at 528 Wellington St North (mid-May to mid-Dec daily 1–5pm; $3.90, Ⓦwww.pc.gc.ca). Set in a pretty little park, the house has been restored to its late-Victorian appearance and has an interesting display in the basement on King's life and times, though it doesn't give too much away about his eccentricities. A dog lover and spiritualist, he amalgamated the two obsessions by believing his pets were mediums.

St Jacobs

The village of **ST JACOBS**, just north of Waterloo via Hwy 85, is home to a popular Mennonite craft shop and **The Mennonite Story**, 1408 King St North

(April to mid-Dec Mon–Sat 11am–5pm & Sun 1.30–5pm; Jan–March Sat 11am–4.30pm & Sun 2–4.30pm; ⓣ519/664-3518; $4), a small but intriguing tourist-office-cum-interpretation-centre that gives the historical low-down on the Mennonites.

Elora

Sloping up from the craggy banks of the Grand River, **ELORA** was founded in the 1830s by settlers who harnessed the river's waters to power their mills. Some of the original limestone cottages have survived, along with a large grist mill, the main landmark, which has been converted into the *Elora Mill Inn*, a clever adaptation of what has long been the most important building in town. Most visitors come here to gaze at the **waterfalls** beside the inn – even though they're only a few metres high – and then stroll on to viewpoints overlooking the neighbouring, 3km-long **Elora Gorge**, a forested ravine with limestone cliffs; the more adventurous have a bash at **tubing** – basically floating down the river on an inner tube; see ⓦwww.grandriver.ca for further details.

Practicalities

Elora, just ten-minutes' walk from end to end, is most pleasantly approached from the southwest – along Route 21 – across a narrow bridge that leads into the main street, Metcalfe, which cuts across tiny Mill Street, adjoining the falls. Elora is well equipped with **B&Bs**. One of the best is *Drew House*, 120 Mill St East (ⓣ519/846-2226 ⓦwww.drewhouse.com; ❺), in an attractively maintained, nineteenth-century house and former stables on the south side of the village; the property has large, leafy gardens and there are eleven guest rooms, some en suite others with shared facilities. There's only one **hotel**, the enjoyable *Elora Mill Inn*, on Mill Street (ⓣ519/846-9118 or 1-866/713-5672, ⓦwww.eloramill.com; ❼), which boasts thirty guest rooms decorated in a modern version of period style, some with log fires and beamed ceilings. The hotel also has a first-rate **restaurant**.

Stratford

STRATFORD, some 50km west of Kitchener, is a likeable country town of thirty thousand people, which rises head and shoulders above its neighbours as the host of the **Stratford Festival** (see p.130), originating in 1953 and now one of the most prestigious theatrical occasions in North America, attracting no fewer than half a million visitors every year. It only takes an hour or so to work out what is where in Stratford, beginning with the town's **downtown** core, on and around the junction of Ontario and Downie streets, where a handsome set of nineteenth-century brick facades reach an idiosyncratic hiatus in the grandiose **city hall**, a brown-brick fiesta of cupolas, towers and limestone trimmings. The town is also bisected by the meandering **Avon River**, whose leafy banks are lined with immaculately maintained footpaths and overlooked by the largest of the town's four theatres, the opulent **Festival Theatre**.

Arrival and information

From Stratford's **train station**, on Shakespeare Street, it's a fifteen-minute stroll north via Downie Street to the town's **main crossroads**, where Downie, Ontario and Erie streets meet. Greyhound **buses** pull in an inconvenient 2.5km east of these crossroads at the end of Burritt Street, a turning off Ontario Street. From the

The Stratford Festival

Each year, North America's largest classical repertory company puts on the **Stratford Festival** (Ⓣ519/273-1600 or 1-800/567-1600, Ⓦwww.stratfordfestival.ca), featuring two of Shakespeare's tragedies and one of his comedies; this programme is augmented by other classical staples – Molière, Chekhov, Jonson and so forth – as well as by the best of modern and musical theatre. The festival also hosts a lecture series, various tours (of backstage and a costume warehouse, for example), music concerts, an author reading series and meet-and-greet sessions with the actors. The festival runs from mid-April to early November and there are performances in four downtown theatres – the Festival, the Tom Patterson, the Avon and the Studio. Regular **tickets** cost between $30 and $90 depending on the performance and seat category, though there are all sorts of discount deals for students, seniors, same-day performances and previews; many plays are sold out months in advance. Call or check the website to book.

town crossroads, it's also the briefest of strolls down the slope to both the Avon River and a seasonal **visitor information centre** on York Street (June–Sept daily 10am–6pm; Ⓣ519/271-5140 or 1-800/561-7926, Ⓦwww.welcometostratford.com). Out of season, head for the other visitor information centre, downtown at 47 Downie St (Jan–Sept Mon–Fri 8.30am–4.30pm, Sat & Sun 8am–6pm; Oct Mon–Fri 8.30am–4.30pm, Sat & Sun 10am–6pm; Nov–Dec Mon–Fri 8.30am–4.30pm & Sat 10am–2pm; same numbers & website). Both offices issue free town maps and a visitors' guide, which carries accommodation listings and has details of the Stratford Festival.

Accommodation

Stratford has over 200 guesthouses and B&Bs plus around a dozen hotels and motels, but **vacant rooms** can still be hard to find during the festival's busiest weekends, when the tourist offices' **accommodation booking service** is particularly useful.

Acrylic Dreams B&B 66 Bay St Ⓣ519/271-7874, Ⓦwww.acrylicdreams.com. Handily located a ten-minute walk from the main crossroads, this cottage-style, timber house, which dates from the 1870s, has four intimate guest rooms decorated in pastel browns and creams. The owners serve up home-made breakfasts with the vegetarian in mind, plus offer yoga and reflexology sessions. 5

Avonview Manor B&B 63 Avon St Ⓣ519/273-4603, Ⓦwww.bbcanada.com/4708.html. There are three lushly decorated, mostly en-suite rooms in this expansive Edwardian villa on a quiet residential street on the north side of the River Avon, about 800m from the main crossroads. It also has an outside pool in the garden. 6

Deacon House B&B Inn 101 Brunswick St Ⓣ519/273-2052, Ⓦwww.bbcanada.com/1152.html. Six cosy, period guest rooms (four en suite) are on offer in this appealing high-gabled house just a few minutes' walk from the town crossroads. There's also a wide veranda for guests to relax on. 5

Eating and drinking

Stratford's theatre goers support a hatful of excellent **cafés and restaurants** and several of the best are but a stone's throw from the town's main crossroads, at the junction of Downie, Ontario and Erie streets.

Balzac's Coffee Roastery 149 Ontario St Ⓣ519/273-7909, Ⓦwww.balzacscoffee.com. First-rate range of Fairtrade coffees plus pastries and cakes are to be had at this branch of a small, Ontario chain that also has outlets in Toronto and Niagara Falls. Daily 8am–9pm.

Down The Street 30 Ontario St ⓣ519/273-5886, ⓦwww.downthestreet.ca. There is a touch of the Parisian café to this plushly decorated bar and restaurant, with its chandeliers and deep reds and browns, just metres from the main town crossroads. The menu is perhaps a little too wide-ranging for its own good, but there's lots of choice – from cod to noodles and beyond. Mains average $24 at night, less at lunch. Reservations recommended. Tues–Sat 11.30am–1am, kitchen till 9.30pm, but restricted hours in winter.

Fellinis 107 Ontario St ⓣ519/271-3333, ⓦwww.fellinisstratford.com. Large Italian/Mediterranean restaurant offering a delicious range of fresh pizzas and pastas from $10. Daily 11am–9pm.

York Street Kitchen 41 York St ⓣ519/273-7041, ⓦwww.yorkstreetkitchen.com. Funkily decorated café-restaurant in the basement of what was once a warehouse, just opposite the riverside information centre. The wide-ranging menu covers everything from cabbage rolls to quiche and meatloaf and every effort is made to source ingredients locally. The sandwiches are a particular speciality – 'double-fisted, two-napkin' affairs that only cost a few dollars; there's also a takeout counter. Daily 8am-8pm.

London

The citizens of **LONDON**, 60km southwest of Stratford, are proud of their clean streets, efficient transport system and neat suburbs, but to the outsider the main attractions of this university town are the leafiness of the centre and two **music festivals** – the four-day Sunfest of World Music (ⓦwww.sunfest.on.ca) and the three-day Home County Folk Music Festival (ⓦwww.homecounty.ca), both held in July.

London owes its existence to a one-time governor of Upper Canada, **John Graves Simcoe**, who arrived in 1792 determined to develop the wilderness far to the west of Lake Ontario. Because of its river connections, he chose the site of London as his new colonial capital and promptly renamed its river the Thames. Simcoe's headlong approach to his new job irritated his superior, Governor Dorchester, who vetoed his choice with the wry comment 'I presume the approach to be by hot-air balloon'. When York (present-day Toronto) was chosen as the capital instead, Simcoe's chosen site lay empty until 1826, yet by the 1880s London was firmly established as the economic and administrative centre of a prosperous agricultural area. With a population of some 455,000, it remains so today – despite the lightning: London has more lightning strikes than anywhere else in Canada, running at 30-40 per year.

Arrival and information

London's **train station** is centrally situated at York and Richmond streets, a couple of minutes' walk from the **bus depot** at York and Talbot streets. London is a fairly easy place to get your bearings – the **downtown core** is laid out as a grid to either side of its main east–west thoroughfare, Dundas Street.

The main **tourist office** (Mon–Fri 8.30am–4.30pm & Sat 10am–5pm; also April–Oct Sun noon–5pm; ⓣ519/661-5000, ⓦwww.londontourism.ca) is at 391 Wellington St, at Dundas.

Accommodation

The cheapest **accommodation** in town is to be found in the hotels in the vicinity of the bus station, but these are little more than flop-houses and are best avoided. A better bet is to make for the *Idlewyld Inn*, the most appealing place in town, a twenty-minute walk to the south of the centre at 36 Grand Ave (ⓣ519/433-2891 or 1-877/435-3466, ⓦwww.idlewyldinn.com; ❻). The inn occupies a rambling Victorian mansion that retains many of its original fittings and its graceful public

rooms come complete with open fireplaces. Each of the 23 en-suite guest rooms is pleasantly furnished in a modern rendition of period style and all are very comfortable. A less expensive second choice is the *Rosneath B&B*, on the north side of the centre at 779 Waterloo St (ⓣ519/438-7822, ⓦwww.rosneathbedbreakfast.on.ca; ④). There are two guest rooms (one en suite) in this extensively modernized house dating back to the 1890s.

The Town

At the west end of Dundas Street, close to the river, is the chunkily modernist **Museum London**, 421 Ridout St North (June–Aug Tues–Sun 11am–5pm, Thurs till 9pm; Sept–May Tues–Sun noon–5pm, Thurs till 9pm; donation; ⓦwww.museumlondon.ca). Designed by famed Canadian architect Raymond Moriyama – whose work is often characterized by a preference for contorted curves and circles rather than straight lines – the museum looks a bit like a giant bicycle shed. The gallery's permanent collection features a somewhat indeterminate mix of lesser eighteenth- and nineteenth-century Canadian painters, but there's an interesting section devoted to contemporary photography and the temporary modern art exhibitions – some of which come here straight from Toronto – are usually excellent.

London's oldest residence, the **Eldon House** (Jan–April Sat & Sun noon–5pm; May & Oct–Dec Wed–Sun noon–5pm; June–Sept Tues–Sun noon–5pm; donation; ⓦwww.eldonhouse.ca) is a couple of minutes' walk north from the museum at

481 Ridout St North. Built in the 1830s by John Harris, a retired Royal Navy captain, the house is a graceful clapboard dwelling, whose interior has been returned to its mid-nineteenth-century appearance. The British influence is also easy to pick out in the nearby **St Paul's Anglican Cathedral**. A simple red-brick structure built in the English Gothic Revival style in 1846, it's in marked contrast to the rival **St Peter's Catholic Cathedral**, just to the north at Dufferin and Richmond streets, a flamboyant, high-towered, pink-stone edifice typical of the French Gothic style popular among Ontario's Catholics in the late nineteenth century.

Eating and drinking

Cafés, restaurants, diners and snack bars line up along **Richmond Street**, where the competition - plus the town's many university students – keeps prices down. The best **deli** sandwiches, coffees and cakes are sold at *Café One*, at 551 Richmond St (Ⓣ519/642-2331, Ⓦwww.cafeonerestaurants.com; daily 10am–11pm). One of the most tempting **restaurants** here is *Garlic's* (Ⓣ519/432-4092, Ⓦwww.garlicsoflondon.com; daily 11.30am–11pm), at 481 Richmond St, a smart and modern Italian place with a macrobiotic slant to their dishes; main courses are in the mid-$20s. Away from Richmond Street, but also in the centre, is *Budapest* (Ⓣ519/439-3431; Mon–Sat 11am–3pm & 4–10pm; Sun 3–10pm), at 348 Dundas St at Waterloo Street, a family-run establishment offering first-rate Hungarian food – the goulash is a treat – with mains from $20.

London's **bar and music** scene is concentrated on and around Richmond Street. The coolest spot is *Up on Carling*, 153 Carling St (Thurs–Sat from 9pm; Ⓣ519/434-6600, Ⓦwww.uponcarling.ca); Carling Street is a short side street off Richmond Street just north of Dundas Street. There are four different bars and visiting DJs ramp it up most weekends. A dress code is in effect.

Windsor and around

"I'm going to Detroit, Michigan, to work the Cadillac line" growls the old blues number, but if the singer had crossed the river from Detroit he'd have been equally at home amongst the car plants of **WINDSOR**, 190km southwest of London. The factories were established as subsidiaries of the American auto industry and for

London to Windsor on Highway 3

The 190km-long yomp along **Hwy 401** from London to Windsor is fast but really rather dull, whereas the much prettier **Hwy 3** cuts a parallel if slightly slower route through the rural heart of the region. The most enjoyable part of Hwy 3 is the 90km section between London and **Shrewsbury**, where you can turn inland to rejoin Hwy 401, though Hwy 3 does continue west almost as far as Point Pelee National Park (see p.137). Between London and Shrewsbury, Hwy 3 slips through a string of one-horse villages, passing pioneer graveyards, overgrown wooded dells, antique timber farmhouses and wheat fields that stretch as far as the eye can see. It's a handsome, very relaxing drive, but you won't see much of **Lake Erie**, which is hidden from view by a long, rolling bluff. If you're keen to get to the lakeshore, the most agreeable township hereabouts is **PORT STANLEY**, whose tiny centre straddles a slow-moving creek as it nears Lake Erie about 40km south of London – and 20km or so from Hwy 3. The *Kettle Creek Inn* is a good place to stay here; it's an immaculately maintained nineteenth-century building at 216 Joseph St (Ⓣ519/782-3388 or 1-866/414-0417, Ⓦwww.kettlecreekinn.com; ⑧ including dinner).

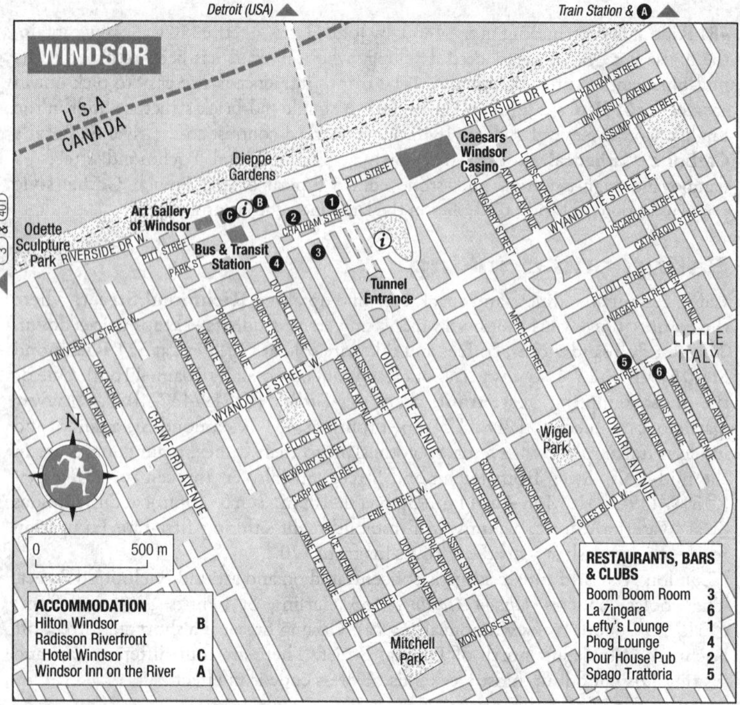

many years the forceful Canadian Automobile Workers Union made sure there were thousands of well-paid jobs. In recent years, the trials and tribulations of the American auto companies have cast a long and destructive shadow over Windsor, whose prospects look far from rosy unless the city can diversify. Despite these woes, there's no doubt living opposite Detroit still makes the "Windsors" feel good: they read about Detroit's problems – the crime and the crack – and shake their heads in disbelief for this robustly working-class city still has a firm sense of community.

For the visitor, Windsor has a certain appeal as a border town with both an attractive riverside setting and a surprisingly compact downtown core. It has a clutch of good restaurants and a lively if somewhat rough-at-the-edges bar scene, plus it's a useful base for popping out to two nearby attractions, the remains of the British **Fort Malden** in Amherstburg, 25km to the south, and **Point Pelee National Park**, about 70km away to the southeast.

Arrival and information

Home to Greyhound, Windsor **bus station** is located right in the centre of town on Church Street at Pitt Street, a couple of minutes' walk from the main downtown drag, Ouellette Avenue. Also at the bus station is **Transit Windsor** (Ⓣ519/944-4111), which operates a shuttle bus service (1–3 hourly) over to downtown Detroit via a **tunnel** whose entrance is also in the city centre at Goyeau and Park streets; vehicles bypassing Windsor en route to Detroit use the Ambassador Bridge, on Hwy 3. Windsor's shack-like **train station** is 3km east of the city centre along the riverfront at 298 Walker Rd and Riverside Drive East; to get into the centre, take a taxi ($8).

The Windsor **Convention and Visitors' Bureau** is across the street from the bus station at 333 Riverside Drive West (Mon–Fri 8.30am–4.30pm; ⓣ519/255-6530 or 1-800/265-3633, ⓦwww.visitwindsor.com). There's also an **Ontario Travel information centre** beside the Detroit tunnel at 110 Park St East, at Goyeau (mid-May to Aug daily 8am–8pm; Sept to mid-May daily 8.30am–5pm; ⓣ519/973-1338).

Accommodation

The best **hotel** rooms in Windsor are in the tower blocks along the riverfront in full view of the Detroit skyline. Options here include the massive *Radisson Riverfront Hotel Windsor*, 333 Riverside Drive West (ⓣ519/977-9777 or 1-800/395-7046, ⓦwww.radisson.com/windsorca; ⓻), where the rooms are large and extremely comfortable or the comparable *Hilton Windsor*, 277 Riverside Drive West (ⓣ519/973-5555, ⓦwww.hilton.com; ⓻). More distinctive is the *Windsor Inn on the River*, in a substantial, two-storey, late nineteenth-century house about 4km east of Ouellette Avenue at 3857 Riverside Drive East (ⓣ519/945-2110 or 1-866/635-0055, ⓦwindsorinnontheriver.com; ⓺). The inn, flanked on either side by modern apartment blocks, has wide views over the river and each of its en-suite guest rooms is decorated in an attractive version of period style; the breakfasts are outstanding.

The City

Most of the downtown core action is focused on Ouellette Avenue between the river and Wyandotte Street, but there are no particularly worthy sights to be seen here. **Dieppe Gardens**, stretching along the waterfront from the foot of Ouellette Avenue – and part of a longer riverside park – is a fine spot to view the audacious Detroit skyline. Here also, just to the east of Ouellette Avenue at the bottom of McDougall Street, is the fantastically popular and ultra-glitzy **Caesars Windsor casino**, open 24hr a day, 365 days of the year. The casino's boosters claim it has played a leading role in the rejuvenation of downtown Windsor, but many others aren't convinced. Rather more uplifting, and also on the riverfront, this time to the west of Ouellette Avenue, is the **Art Gallery of Windsor**, which is housed in a flashy modern building at 401 Riverside Drive West (Wed 11am–5pm, Thurs & Fri 11am–9pm, Sat & Sun 11am–5pm; $5, free on Wed; ⓦwww.artgalleryofwindsor.com). The gallery has a well-deserved reputation for the excellence of its temporary exhibitions, while the permanent collection is noted for its late nineteenth- and early twentieth-century Canadian paintings. In particular, look out for the striking canvases of the Group of Seven (see p.88). There's more art at the open-air, open-access **Odette Sculpture Park**, a whimsical assortment of over thirty modern sculptures dotted along the riverfront park between Church Street and the Ambassador Bridge, about 3.5km west of Ouellette Avenue.

Eating and drinking

For **food**, head for Windsor's **Little Italy**, where a string of restaurants line up along Erie Street East, between Howard and Lincoln streets, about 1.5km southeast of the city centre. Among others, it's here you'll find *Spago Trattoria*, 614 Erie St East (daily 11.30am–10.30pm; ⓣ519/252-9099), an informal place that serves excellent and very authentic pizzas ($15), plus all the Italian classics (with mains averaging $20). Close by, at 769 Erie St East, is *La Zingara* (daily except Sat 11.30am–2.30pm & daily 5–10pm; ⓣ519/258-7555, ⓦwww.lazingaratrattoria.com), a smooth and polished restaurant where the sauces are rather more subtle, the menu more inventive – try the linguine with fresh clams; main courses average $23.

For **drinking**, there are a number of popular downtown **bars** dotted on and around Ouellette Avenue. Options include *Lefty's Lounge*, a gritty bar with an outside terrace at 34 Chatham St East, and the *Pour House Pub*, a deep and dark tavern at 46 Chatham St West. Windsor also has a lively **club and live music** scene with two good bets being the *Boom Boom Room*, 315 Ouellette Ave (Ⓦwww.boomboomroom.ca), a raucously groovy spot with lots of house music and star DJs, and the *Phog Lounge*, a similarly vibrant spot at 157 University Ave West Ⓣ519/253 1605, Ⓦwww.clubzone.com); both places are popular with university students.

South of Windsor: Amherstburg and Fort Malden

Highway 20 runs south from Windsor, slicing through the industrial region that flanks the Detroit River, whose murky waters form the border with the US. The one-time enmity of the Americans prompted the British to build a fort here, close to the mouth of the Detroit River at **AMHERSTBURG** in 1796, but it proved difficult to supply and they were forced to abandon it during the War of 1812. Reoccupied after the war, the British made half-hearted attempts to strengthen the fort, but most likely it would have been abandoned had it not been for the Rebellion of 1837. In a panic, the colonial powers rebuilt what was now called **Fort Malden** and garrisoned it with four hundred soldiers, stationed here to counter the efforts of the insurgents and their American sympathizers. The last troops left in 1859 and the fort was handed over to the provincial government, who promptly turned it into a lunatic asylum.

Fort Malden

Now renovated and restored, the early nineteenth-century ditches and bastions of **Fort Malden National Historic Site** (May–Aug daily 10am–5pm; Sept & Oct Mon–Fri 1–5pm, Sat–Sun 10am–5pm; $3.90; Ⓦwww.pc.gc.ca), beside the Detroit River in Amherstburg, comprise a sequence of grassy defensive lines that surround the excavated foundations of several buildings and a single-storey brick **barracks** of 1819. The interior of the barracks, complete with British army uniforms, is deceptively neat and trim for, as the guides explain, conditions were appallingly squalid. Across from the barracks, the asylum's old laundry and bakery has been turned into an **interpretive centre** with intriguing accounts of the various episodes of the fort's history, including the War of 1812 and the Rebellion of 1837. Original artefacts are few and far between, but you'll spy the powder horn of the **Shawnee** chief and staunch British ally, **Tecumseh**, one of the most formidable and renowned of the region's leaders. Born in what is now Ohio in 1769, Tecumseh spent the better part of his life struggling to keep American settlers from spreading west into Shawnee territory. To this end he allied himself with the British, who he felt were less of a territorial threat than the colonials. By the sheer force of his personality, he managed to hold together an aboriginal army of some size. He was killed in the War of 1812 and his army promptly faded away.

Southeast of Windsor: Leamington and Pelee Island

Heading southeast from Windsor on Hwy 3, it's about 60km to **LEAMINGTON**, a dreary agricultural town that bills itself as the "Tomato capital of Canada" – with a massive Heinz factory to prove the point. More importantly, Leamington is also just 8km or so from **Point Pelee National Park** (see p.137) and from the

Ferries to Pelee Island

Car ferries linking the mainland with Pelee Island are operated by Ontario Ferries (ⓣ519/724-2115 or 1-800/661-2220, ⓦwww.ontarioferries.com) and there are two **departure ports**, Leamington and neighbouring Kingsville, about 10km to the west. There are sailings between April and mid-December (1–3 daily) and the journey time is about one hour and thirty minutes. **Prices** are the same whichever port you use with one-way fares costing $7.50 per person, bicycles $3.75 and cars $16.50.

town docks **car ferries** (see above) sally out across Lake Erie to **Pelee Island**, whose quiet country roads are flanked by orchards and vineyards. Some 15km long and 6km wide, the island possesses a pair of nature reserves – Lighthouse Point and Fish Point – at its northern and southern extremities and one significant settlement, **PELEE ISLAND village**, where the boat docks, but it's the rural atmosphere that is of most appeal.

Point Pelee National Park

Occupying the southernmost tip of Canada's mainland – and at the same latitude as Rome and Barcelona – **Point Pelee National Park** (daily: April to mid-Oct 6am–10pm; mid-Oct to March 7am–7pm; April to mid-Oct $7.80, otherwise free; no camping) occupies the southern half of a twenty-kilometre sandspit. The park boasts a variety of habitats rarely matched in Canada, including marshlands and open fields, but most remarkably it is one of the few places where the ancient **deciduous forest** of eastern North America has survived. One-third of the park is covered by this jungle-like forest, packed with a staggering variety of trees, from hackberry, red cedar, black walnut and blue ash to vine-covered sassafras. The park's mild climate and its mix of vegetation attract thousands of **birds** on their spring and autumn migrations. In September, the sandspit also funnels thousands of southward-moving **monarch butterflies** across the park, their orange and black wings a splash of colour against the greens and browns of the undergrowth.

From the **park entrance** it's a three-kilometre drive down behind the shore to the start of the Marsh Boardwalk nature trail, where there's bike and canoe rental during the summer. It's a further 4km to the **visitor centre** (April–Oct daily 10am–5pm; Nov–March Sat & Sun only 10am–5pm; ⓣ519/322-2365), at the beginning of the Tilden Wood and Woodland trails. From April to early October propane-powered "trains" shuttle the last 2km from the visitor centre to the start of the short footpath leading to the tip of the peninsula. The tip itself is merely a slender wedge of coarse brown sand that can't help but seem a tad anticlimactic – unless, that is, a storm has piled the beach with driftwood.

Practicalities

Given the flatness of the terrain, the best way to explore the island is by **bike**; these can be rented from Comfortech (ⓣ519/724-2828; advance booking required), metres from the dock. Ferry schedules usually make it easy to visit the island on a day-trip, but there are several **places to stay**: the pick is the *Wandering Pheasant Inn*, in a pretty, two-storey house in the southeast corner of the island at 1060 East West Rd (ⓣ519/724-2270, ⓦwww.thewanderingpheasantinn.com; ⑤). There are twelve well-appointed rooms here, most en-suite, each decorated in a bright and breezy manner. The inn is also a brief walk from the beach and there's an outdoor jacuzzi. For Pelee Island **maps** and further **information**, check out ⓦwww.pelee.org.

Highway 21: Dresden to Sarnia

The large chunk of farmland rolling 100km west from **London** (see p.131) to the inconsequential border town of **Sarnia** is one of the less absorbing parts of the province. It was also one of the last parts of southern Ontario to be cleared and settled, its heavy clay soil being difficult to plough and becoming almost impassable in rain. The district is bisected by **Highway 21**, which serves as a handy short cut between both Windsor (see p.133) and Point Pelee National Park (see p.137) and the good-looking towns of the Lake Huron shoreline, primarily Bayfield and Goderich (see p.140). Fortunately, Hwy 21 also passes by the area's three points of interest. These are – from south to north – **Uncle Tom's Cabin Historic Site**, where a group of escaped US slaves found refuge in the 1830s; the **Oil Museum of Canada**, recalling the local oil boom of the middle of the nineteenth century; and small-town **Petrolia**, also a result of the oil rush. You'll need a car for Hwy 21 as there are **no buses**.

Uncle Tom's Cabin

Highway 401 trucks east from Windsor to intersect with **Hwy 21** after about 100km. Turn north onto Hwy 21 and it's a further 30km to the agricultural town of **DRESDEN**, which is itself just 2km from **Uncle Tom's Cabin Historic Site** (late May to June & Sept to late Oct Tues–Sat 10am–4pm, Sun noon–4pm; July & Aug daily 10am–4pm; $6.25; Ⓦ www.uncletomscabin.org), comprising a handful of old wooden buildings, most notably a plain and simple church.

Here also is the clapboard house that was once the home of the **Reverend Josiah Henson**, a slave who fled from Maryland to Canada in 1830 by means of the Underground Railroad, or UGRR (see below). Henson and a group of abolitionist sympathizers subsequently bought 200 acres of farmland round Dresden and founded a vocational school for runaway slaves known as the British American Institute. Unable to write, Henson dictated his life experiences and in 1849 these narrations were published as *The Life of Josiah Henson – Formerly a Slave*. It's a powerful tract, unassuming and almost matter of fact in the way it describes the routine savagery of slavery – and it was immediately popular. One of its readers was **Harriet Beecher Stowe**, who met Henson and went on to write the most influential abolitionist text of the day, *Uncle Tom's Cabin* (1852), basing her main character on Henson's accounts. Most of the Dresden refugees returned to the US

The Underground Railroad

The **Underground Railroad** (UGRR) started in the 1820s as a loose and secretive association of abolitionists dedicated to smuggling slaves from the southern states of America to Canada. By the 1840s, the UGRR had become a well-organized network of routes and safe houses, but its real importance lay not so much in the number of slaves rescued – the total was small – but rather in the psychological effect it had on those involved in the smuggling. The movement of a runaway usually involved very few people, but many more, particularly neighbours and friends, knew what was happening and therefore were complicit in the breaking of the law. To the extent that white Americans could be persuaded to accept even the most minor role in the UGRR, the inclination to compromise with institutional slavery was undermined, though the psychology of racism remained intact: like Beecher Stowe's Uncle Tom, the freed negroes were supposed to be humble and grateful, simulating childlike responses to please their white parent-protectors.

after the Civil War, but Henson stayed on, accumulating imperial honours that must have surprised him greatly. He was even presented to Queen Victoria and, in commemoration of this royal connection, a crown surmounts his tombstone, which stands outside the complex; he died in 1883. Henson's book is hard to get hold of, but copies are sold here at the **interpretive centre**, where there's also a small museum on slavery and the UGRR plus an intriguing video giving more details on Henson's life and times.

Oil Springs

Some 25km north of Dresden, Hwy 21 scuttles past the Oil Museum of Canada just before it reaches tiny **OIL SPRINGS**, which once formed the nucleus of a rough-and-ready frontier district whose flat fields were packed with hundreds of eager oil-seekers and their hangers-on.

The first prospectors were attracted to the area by the patches of black and sticky oil that had seeped to the surface through narrow fissures in the rock. These **gum beds** had long been used by local native peoples for medicinal and ritual purposes. In 1858 James Miller Williams dug North America's **first commercial oil well**, and in 1862 a certain Hugh Shaw drilled deeper than anyone else and, at 49m, struck the first **gusher**. The shock of seeing the oil fly up into the trees prompted Shaw, a religious man, to use the words of his Bible – "And the rock poured me out rivers of oil" (Job 29:6). Shaw became rich, but his luck ran out just one year later when the gas and sulphur fumes of his own well suffocated him. At the height of the boom, the oilfields produced about thirty thousand barrels of crude a day, most of it destined for Sarnia, transported by stagecoach and wagon along a specially built plank road.

The **Oil Museum of Canada** (May–Oct daily 10am–5pm; Nov–April Mon–Fri 10am–5pm; $5; Ⓦwww.lambtononline.com/oil_museum) has been built next to the site of James Williams' original well 1km south of Oil Springs. Highlights of the open-air display area include a nineteenth-century blacksmith's shop, with some fascinating old sepia photos taken during the oil boom, and an area of gum bed. The inside of the museum has a motley collection of oil-industry artefacts and background geological information. Oil is still produced in the fields around the museum, drawn to the surface and pushed on into an underground system of pipes by some seven hundred low-lying pump jacks.

Petrolia

The grand stone-and-brick buildings of tiny **PETROLIA**, just off Hwy 21 about 10km north of Oil Springs, speak volumes about the sudden rush of wealth that followed the discovery of the region's oil. This was Canada's first oil town and as the proceeds rolled in, so the Victorian mansions and expansive public buildings followed. Several have survived, dotted along and around the main drag, Petrolia Line. Three prime examples are the **Municipal Offices**, at Petrolia Line and Greenfield Street; **Nemo Hall**, an impressive brick building decorated by splendid wrought-iron trimmings at 419 King St and Victoria Street; and **St Andrew's Presbyterian church**, close by at Petrolia Line and Queen Street, which is awash with neo-Gothic gables and towers. To emphasize the town's origins, its street-lamps are cast in the shape of oil derricks, but once you've admired the architecture there's no reason to stay on.

From Petrolia, it's about 12km along Hwy 21 to **Highway 402**, the motorway linking London to the east and **Sarnia** away to the west, and a further 80km to Lake Huron's Bayfield.

Bayfield and Goderich

A popular holiday spot, the southern section of the **Lake Huron shoreline** is trimmed by sandy beaches and a steep bluff, which is interrupted by the occasional river valley. The water is much less polluted than Lake Ontario, the sunsets are fabulously beautiful, and in **Bayfield** and **Goderich** the lakeshore possesses two of the most appealing places in the whole of the province. You will need your own transport to get to either: there are no **buses** at all.

Bayfield

Beguiling **BAYFIELD** is a wealthy and good-looking village whose handsome timber villas nestle among well-tended gardens beneath a canopy of ancient trees – all about 90km north of London. The locals have kept modern development at arm's length – there's barely a neon sign in sight, never mind a concrete apartment block – and almost every old house has been beautifully maintained: look out for the scrolled woodwork, the fanlights and the graceful verandas. Historical plaques give the low-down on the older buildings that line Bayfield's short **Main Street**, and pint-sized **Pioneer Park** on the bluff overlooking the lake at the west end of Main Street is a fine spot to take in the sunset. If you have the time, venture down to the **harbour** on the north side of the village and from there ramble up along the banks of the Bayfield River where, in season, you can pick wild mushrooms and fiddleheads. In winter there's also ice fishing and skating here.

Arrival and information

The **tourist office** (May–Sept daily 10am–6pm; ⓣ519/565-2499 or 1-866/565-2499, ⓦwww.villageofbayfield.com), in the booth by Hwy 21 just north of the Bayfield River bridge, has a full list of local **accommodation** and staff will help you find a room, though their assistance is only really necessary in July and August when most places – including the B&Bs – are heavily booked. At other times of the year, it's easy enough to find a place yourself.

Practicalities

The best **hotel** around is the outstanding *Little Inn of Bayfield*, 26 Main St North (ⓣ519/565-2611 or 1-800/565-1832, ⓦwww.littleinn.com; ❼), a tastefully modernized early nineteenth-century timber-and-brick building with a handsome second-floor veranda and delightfully furnished rooms, most of which have jacuzzis; there's an annexe across the street with equally pleasant rooms. The village also possesses several charming **B&Bs**, including the appealing *Clair on the Square*, in a handsome, renovated old house beside the village green at 12 The Square (ⓣ519/565-2135, ⓦwww.claironthesquare.ca; ❻). There's also **camping** at Pinery Provincial Park (reservations on ⓣ1-888/668-7275, ⓦwww.pinerypark.on.ca), a popular chunk of forested sand dune between Lake Huron and Hwy 21 about 40km south of Bayfield.

Bayfield has several great places to **eat**, but it's hard to beat the smart and chic restaurant of the *Little Inn of Bayfield*, which is the best place to sample fish from Lake Huron – perch, white fish, pickerel or steelhead; mains here average around $30. Less expensive is the *Albion Hotel*, nearby and also on Main Street, where they serve filling bar food and meals from around $12 for a main course.

Goderich

GODERICH, at the mouth of the Maitland River just 20km north of Bayfield, is a delightful country town, whose postcard prettiness is balanced by a working harbour. It began life in 1825, when the British-owned Canada Company bought two and a half million acres of southern Ontario – the **Huron Tract** – from the government at the ridiculously low rate of twelve cents an acre, amid rumours of bribery and corruption. Eager to profit on their investment, the company pushed the **Huron Road** through from Stratford in the east to Goderich in the west, an extraordinary effort through wild terrain. Completed in 1828, the road attracted the settlers the company needed. Within thirty years, the Huron Tract had two flourishing towns, Stratford (see p.129) and Goderich, and was producing large surpluses of grain for export, as it continues to do today.

Arrival and information

Goderich **tourist office** sits beside Hwy 21 at the intersection of Nelson and Hamilton, a couple of minutes' walk to the northeast of the central circle (mid-May to Sept daily 9am–6pm; Oct to mid-May Mon–Fri 9am–4.30pm; ⓣ519/524-6600 or 1-800/280-7637, ⓦwww.goderich.ca). They issue free town maps and have a comprehensive list of local **accommodation**, which includes around fifteen B&Bs.

Accommodation

One of the most appealing B&Bs in town is the *Colborne B&B* (ⓣ519/524-7400 or 1-800/390-4612, ⓦwww.colbornebandb.com; ④), 72 Colborne St, a large, brick building located just to the west of the central circus. It has four guest rooms, all en suite, each simply decorated. Also near the centre is the equally tempting *Twin Porches B&B* (ⓣ519/524-5505, ⓦwww.bbcanada.com/3694.html; ②; May–Oct), 55 Nelson St East, in an immaculate Victorian house with fine gingerbread scroll-work; the period decor in the public rooms is splendid and there are three air-conditioned guest rooms, with a shared bathroom.

The **hotel** scene is less varied, the cream of the local crop being the plush *Benmiller Inn & Spa* (ⓣ519/524-2191 or 1-800/265-1711, ⓦwww.benmiller.on.ca; ⑥), which occupies a handsomely converted 1830s wool mill in an attractive wooded dell to the east of Goderich. To get there, take Hwy 8 out of town and watch for the sign after about 6km. There's **camping** near Goderich at Point Farms Provincial Park (mid-May to early Oct; ⓣ519/524-7124, ⓦwww.ontarioparks.com; reservations ⓣ1-888/668-7275), just 7km north along the lakeshore.

The Town

The wide, tree-lined avenues of Goderich's geometrical centre radiate out from a grand octagonal central circle dominated by the town's white-stone Courthouse. From here, the four main streets follow the points of the compass with North Street leading in a couple of minutes to the **Huron County Museum** (May–Dec Mon–Sat 10am–4.30pm & Sun 1–4.30pm; Jan–April Mon–Fri 10am–4.30pm & Sat 1–4.30pm; $5, $7.50 with Huron Gaol; ⓦwww.huroncounty.ca/museum), which concentrates on the district's pioneers. Highlights include lots of old sepia photos and a fantastic array of farm implements.

Huron Historic Gaol

At the far end of North Street, turn right along Gloucester Terrace and you'll soon reach the high stone walls of the **Huron Historic Gaol** (May–Aug Mon–Sat 10am–4.30pm, Sun 1–4.30pm; Sept to late Oct Mon–Fri 1–4pm, Sat 10am–4.30pm & Sun 1–4.30pm; $5, $7.50 with Huron County Museum) at 181 Victoria St North.

One of the province's most intriguing attractions, the gaol was constructed as a combined courthouse and jail between 1839 and 1842. Visits begin on the

third floor of the main block, whose claustrophobic courtroom and council chamber were originally situated next to a couple of holding cells. There were two problems: the design was most unpopular with local judges, who felt threatened by the proximity of those they were sentencing; the other was the odour emanating from the privies in the exercise yard below. In 1856, the administration finally gave way and built a new courthouse in the town centre, separating the jail and the judiciary once and for all. The jail's **second and first floors** hold the original jailer's apartment and a string of well-preserved prison cells, reflecting various changes in design between 1841 and 1972, when the prison was finally closed. The worst is the leg-iron cell for "troublesome" prisoners, where unfortunates were chained to the wall with neither bed nor blanket. End your tour at the **Governor's House**, with its attractively restored late Victorian interior.

West Street and the lakeshore

Back in the centre, West Street leads the 1km through a cutting in the bluffs to the **Lake Huron shoreline** at the south end of the harbour and salt works. A footpath leads northeast round the harbour, passing the grain elevators on its way to the Menesetung Bridge, the old CPR railway bridge that now serves as a pedestrian walkway across the Maitland River. On the north side of the river you can pick up the **Maitland Trail** for the brief but enjoyable jaunt along the river's north shore. In the opposite direction – south from the harbour – some 1.5km of shoreline has been tidied up to create a picnic area, but although the sunsets are spectacular the sandy **beach**, right at the end, is scrawny.

Eating and drinking

Goderich is no gourmet's paradise, but *Bailey's*, right in the centre of town at 120 Court House Square (Mon–Sat 11.30am–2pm & Tues–Sat 5.30–8.30pm; ⓣ519/524-5166), does much to fill the gaps, offering a wide and well-presented menu from English-style fish and chips ($17) through to chicken breast stuffed with spinach ($25). The *Park House Tavern & Eatery*, 168 West St, is the town's liveliest bar and offers wide views over Lake Huron (daily 11.30am–11.30pm).

The Bruce Peninsula and Nottawasaga Bay

Separating the main body of Lake Huron from Georgian Bay, the **Bruce Peninsula** holds two of Ontario's national parks. The more distinctive is the **Fathom Five National Marine Park**, at the northern tip of the peninsula, which provides wonderful sport for divers. The second is the **Bruce Peninsula National Park**, comprising two slabs of forested wilderness on either side of Hwy 6, its northern portion offering magnificent coastal hiking on a small section of the Bruce Trail (see p.144). There's camping at both parks and a reasonable choice of hotel and motel accommodation at lively **Tobermory**, from where you catch the ferry to **Manitoulin Island**. Spare time also for a quick zip round the interesting old port of **Owen Sound** at the base of the peninsula.

East of Owen Sound the southern curve of Georgian Bay forms **Nottawasaga Bay**, one of the province's most popular holiday areas. In summer the focus of attention is the crowded resort of **Wasaga Beach**, where a seemingly endless string of chalets and cottages fringe the several kilometres of protected sand that make up **Wasaga Beach Provincial Park**. To the west of Wasaga Beach, inland from the gritty port of **Collingwood**, is the **Blue Mountain ski area**.

Public transport is reliable and frequent to the major towns, but the Bruce peninsula has no bus services at all. **Greyhound** (Ⓣ1-800/661-8747, Ⓦwww.greyhound.ca) operates buses from Toronto to Owen Sound (2–3 daily) and Collingwood (1–2 daily).

Owen Sound

OWEN SOUND, just under 200km northwest of Toronto, occupies the ravine around the mouth of the Sydenham River, at the foot of the Bruce Peninsula. In its heyday, Owen Sound was a rough and violent port packed with brothels and bars, prompting the Americans to establish a consulate whose main function was to bail out drunk and disorderly sailors. For the majority it was an unpleasant place to live, and the violence spawned an especially active branch of the Women's Christian Temperance Organization, whose success was such that an alcohol ban was imposed in 1906 and only lifted in 1972. The town was in decline long before the return of the bars, its port facilities undercut by the railways from the 1920s, but it's managed to reinvent itself and is now an amiable sort of place well worth at least a pit stop.

Arrival and information

The **bus station** is on 3rd Avenue East at 10th Street East, ten minutes' walk from the **tourist office**, which is next door to the Marine-Rail Museum at 1155 1st Ave West (Mon–Thurs 9am–5pm, Fri 9am–6pm, Sat 10am–5pm, Sun 10am–4pm; Ⓣ519/371-9833 or 1-888/675-5555, Ⓦwww.owensoundtourism .com). They have a list of local accommodation, including details of a dozen **B&Bs**.

The **orientation** of Owen Sound's streets can be a little confusing, but there is a logic: avenues run north-south and streets east-west, while the river, which bisects the compact town centre, separates avenues and streets East from those marked West.

The Town

There are three central sights of interest, kicking off with the **Marine-Rail Museum**, overlooking the harbour in the old railway station at 1155 1st Ave West (June–Aug Mon–Sat 10am–5pm, Sun noon–5pm; Sept to early Oct Tues–Fri noon–4pm, Sat 11.30am–3.30pm; early Oct to May Tues–Fri noon–4pm; $4; Ⓦwww.marinerail.com). The museum has photos and scale models of old trains and ships and there is an old log tug and a caboose outside.

Perhaps more diverting are the **Tom Thomson Art Gallery**, 840 1st Ave West (late May to early Oct Mon–Sat 10am–5pm & Sun noon–5pm; early Oct to late May Tues–Fri 11am–5pm, Sat & Sun noon–5pm; $5; Ⓦwww.tomthomson.org), which features temporary exhibitions by Canadian artists and a clutch of Thomson's less familiar paintings; and the **Billy Bishop Museum**, 948 3rd Ave West (late May to Aug Mon–Sat 10am–5pm, Sun noon–5pm; Sept–Dec & April to late May Tues–Sun 11am–4pm; Feb–March Tues–Fri noon–4pm; $4; Ⓦwww.billybishop.org), concentrating on the military exploits of Canada's Victoria Cross-winning air ace.

Practicalities

For accommodation, one of the handiest **B&Bs** is the *Brae Briar*, at 980 3rd Ave West (Ⓣ519/371-0025, Ⓦwww.bbcanada.com/622.html; ❹), just off 10th Street downtown, which occupies a pleasant, two-storey, detached house with three old-fashioned guest rooms. More upmarket – but worth every cent – is *The Highland Manor*, at 867 4th Ave West (Ⓣ519/372-269, Ⓦwww.highlandmanor.ca; ❻) featuring five period rooms in a striking 1872 mansion with high ceilings and a handsome garden veranda. **Advance** booking is strongly recommended at the height of the season (mid-July to mid-Aug).

For downtown **food**, two options really stand out: *Jazzmyns Tapas & Taps*, 261 9th St East (Ⓣ519/371-7736, Ⓦwww.jazzmyns.com), which serves up excellent, inexpensive meals – anything from tapas to pizzas and burgers; and the *Rocky Raccoon Café*, 941 2nd Ave East (Ⓣ519/374-0500, Ⓦwww.rockyraccooncafe.com), where the Nepalese chef/owner has injected some Asian spice into standard Canadian food, creating such marvels as the delicious Indian Maple Spice Bread.

The Bruce Peninsula National Park

Heading northwest from Owen Sound, **Highway 6** scoots up the middle of the Bruce Peninsula to reach – after about 100km – the turning for the **Bruce Peninsula National Park** at **Cyprus Lake**. The park is a mixture of limestone cliff, rocky beach, wetland and forest that's best visited in June when the wild flowers are in bloom and it's not too crowded. At Cyprus Lake are the park's headquarters and all-year **campsites,** which operate on a first-come, first-served basis in winter, by reservation from May to September (Ⓣ1-877/737-3783, Ⓦwww.pccamping.ca). Four hiking trails start at the northern edge of Cyprus Lake and three of them connect with one of the most dramatic portions of the **Bruce Trail**, a long-distance footpath which follows the route of the Niagara Escarpment as it weaves its way across Ontario from Queenston (see p.120) to Tobermory (see below).

Tobermory

Just 11km or so beyond the Cyprus Lake turning, Hwy 6 slips into **TOBERMORY**, a bustling fishing village and holiday resort at the northern tip of the peninsula. There are no sights as such, but it's a pleasant spot with Tobermory's tiny centre focused on a slender inlet, **Little Tub harbour**. Here, **car ferries** (see p.147) leave for South Baymouth on Manitoulin Island (see p.146) and **passenger boats** shuttle out to Fathom Five National Marine Park (see p.145).

The **National Park office**, complete with theatre, exhibition space and adjacent lookout tower, is located a five-minute walk south of town at 120 Chi sin tib dek Rd (May & Sept–Oct Sun–Fri 10am–5pm; June–Aug Sun–Thurs 8am–8pm, Fri 8am–10pm, Sat 8am–9pm; Nov–April Wed–Sat noon–4pm; Ⓣ519/596-2233, Ⓦwww.pc.gc.ca) and covers both of the national parks, issuing maps and free brochures. There's also a village **tourist office** (May-June & Sept to mid-Oct daily 9am-5pm; July-Aug daily 9am-9pm; Ⓣ519/596-2452; Ⓦwww.tobermory.org), down by the harbour, and they have a complete list of local accommodation.

Practicalities

There are a dozen or so **hotels and motels** in and around Tobermory, mostly brisk, modern affairs that are comfortable without being especially distinctive. One good choice is the *Grandview Motel* (Ⓣ519/596-2220, Ⓦwww.grandview-tobermory.com; ❻), with eighteen spick-and-span rooms on the east side of the harbour at the junction of Bay and Earl streets. A second recommendation, also on the east side of the harbour, is the two-storey, balconied *Blue Bay Motel*, 32 Bay St (Ⓣ519/596-2392, Ⓦwww.bluebay-motel.com; ❺).

The *Grandview Motel* has the town's best **restaurant** with views out across the harbour and tasty, reasonably priced dishes with seafood a speciality – try the whitefish and ocean perch. There are also several lively **bars** and **cafés** beside the harbour – the *Crow's Nest* is as good as any with regular live music.

Around Tobermory: Fathom Five National Marine Park

Fathom Five National Marine Park (Ⓦwww.pc.gc.ca) comprises nineteen uninhabited islands and the waters that surround them at the end of the Bruce Peninsula, offshore from Tobermory.

To protect the natural habitat, only **Flowerpot Island**, 4km from the mainland, has any amenities, with limited space for **camping** – six sites only – and a couple of short hiking trails that explore its eastern reaches. A delightful spot, Flowerpot takes its name from two pink-and-grey rock pillars that have been eroded away from its eastern shore – and these are readily seen on the islet's hiking trails. From May to mid-October, Flowerpot Island is easily reached by **boat** from Tobermory. Several operators run regular boats out to the island, either dropping passengers off and then collecting them later or pausing at Flowerpot as part of a longer excursion – just stroll along Little Tub harbour until you find the service that suits. One reliable company is Blue Heron (Ⓣ519/596-2999, Ⓦwww.blueheronco.com). The

▲ The pillars of Flowerpot Island, near Tobermory

Diving in Fathom Five National Marine Park

The park is known across Canada for the excellence of its **diving**; the waters are clear, there are extraordinary rock formations and around twenty shipwrecks. Prospective divers must register in person at the **registration office**, also housed in the park office. Diving gear can be rented down by the harbour at G&S Watersports (ⓣ519/596-2200, ⓦwww.gswatersports.com), who also offer diving lessons and kayak rental.

return fare from Tobermory to Flowerpot is $30–40, depending whether you're getting off at the island or staying on board. Prospective campers need to make reservations at and get permits from the park office (see p.144). Both hikers and campers need to pack their own food and drink.

Manitoulin Island

The **Ojibwa** believed that when Gitchi Manitou (the Great Spirit) created the world he reserved the best bits for himself and created **Manitoulin** (God's Island) – the world's largest freshwater island (at over 2700 square kilometres) – as his home. Divine intervention or not, Manitoulin is strikingly different from the harsh grey rocks of the Canadian Shield that surrounds it, its white cliffs, wide lakes, gentle woodland and stretches of open, prairie-like farmland presenting an altogether more welcoming aspect. This rural idyll has long attracted hundreds of summer **sailors**, who ply the lakes that punctuate the island, and has proved increasingly popular with motorized city folk, who arrive here in numbers on the car ferry from Tobermory (see p.147). Yet it's easy enough to escape the crowds, either by driving along the **northeast shore**, arguably the prettiest part of the island, or by hunkering down in one of Manitoulin's secluded **resorts**.

A brief history of Manitoulin Island

About a quarter of the island's twelve thousand inhabitants are aboriginals, descendants of groups believed to have arrived here over ten thousand years ago. Archeologists have uncovered evidence of these Paleo-Indians at **Sheguiandah**, on the east coast, and the small display of artefacts at the museum here contains some of the oldest human traces found in Ontario. Much later, in 1836, the island's aboriginal peoples – primarily, Ojibwa and Odawa – reluctantly signed a treaty that turned Manitoulin into a refuge for several Georgian Bay bands who had been dispossessed by white settlers. Few of them came, which was just as well because the whites soon revised their position and wanted the island all for themselves. In 1862, this pressure culminated in a second treaty that gave most of the island to the newcomers. It was all particularly shabby and, to their credit, the Ojibwa band living on the eastern tip of the island at **Wikwemikong** refused to sign. Their descendants still live on this so-called "unceded reserve" and, during the third weekend in August, hold the largest **powwow** in the country.

East Manitoulin

Heading north from the South Baymouth ferry dock, Hwy 6 cuts inland before veering east to reach – after 30km – the lakeshore hamlet of **MANITOWANING**, where the treaty of 1836 was signed. There's nothing much to detain you here, though you might drop by the modest **Assiginack Museum** (June–Sept daily 10am–5pm; $3; ⓣ705/859-3905), whose pioneer bygones are mostly housed within the sturdy limestone building that once served as the local jail.

From Manitowaning, a side road runs east to the village of **WIKWEMIKONG**, on Smith Bay, some 14km from Hwy 6 – and the focus of the eponymous Indian Reserve. Canada's foremost native theatre group, **De-Ba-Jeh-Mu-Jig** (meaning 'story teller') is based here and holds regular bilingual (English & Ojibway) performances of native legends and contemporary plays by native playwrights during the summer (July & Aug; call for dates, venues and reservations, ⓣ705/859-2317, ⓦwww.debaj.ca).

Back at Manitowaning, Hwy 6 pushes north cutting across rolling farmland en route to **SHEGUIANDAH**, where the **Centennial Museum of Sheguiandah** (early May to late Sept daily 10.30am–4.30pm, Thurs till 8pm; early April to early May & late Sept to mid-Oct Wed–Sun 12.30–4.30pm; ⓦwww.manitoulin-island.com/museums; $4;) is mainly concerned with the pioneer families who first farmed and traded here. Named photographs tell you who was who – and who was related to whom – in what was once an extremely isolated and tightly knit community, where the inhabitants were called "Haweaters" by outsiders after their liking for the scarlet fruit of the hawthorn tree. It was in this wooded bayshore setting that archeologists found the remains of a Paleo-Indian settlement around 10,000 years old. It was a remarkable find but most of the artefacts were carted off to big museums elsewhere, leaving this museum with a display case of crudely fashioned quartzite tools – a weak display for something so important.

Little Current

From Sheguiandah, it's a short hop to **LITTLE CURRENT**, Manitoulin's largest settlement with a population of just 3000. The town is the site of the island's main **tourist office** (early May to June and Sept to early Oct daily 10am–4pm; July & Aug daily 8am–8pm; early Oct to early May Wed–Sat 10am–4pm; ⓣ705/368-3021, ⓦwww.manitoulintourism.com), located beside the swing bridge from where Hwy 6 continues north to the mainland over a series of inter-island causeways.

Little Current also has one of the least expensive places to **stay** on the island, the *Anchor Inn*, 1 Water St (ⓣ705/368-2023, ⓦwww.anchorgrill.com; ❷), which offers very basic but perfectly adequate rooms above a bar and restaurant – though you might need ear plugs when the karaoke gets going. The *Anchor Grill* is the most convenient place to **eat**, with whitefish its speciality (for around $18). A few doors up at 7 Water St, *Loco Beanz* (ⓣ705/368-2261) serves a stiff espresso, bagels and freshly baked cookies.

North Manitoulin

Heading west from Little Current, Hwy 540 ducks and weaves its way right along the northern edge of Manitoulin, giving long, lingering views over the North Channel and slipping past the trailheads of several popular hiking routes. After around 30km, the road passes through **M'CHIGEENG**, where the **Great Spirit Circle Trail** (Mon–Fri 9am–4.30pm; ⓣ705/377-4404, ⓦwww.circletrail.com)

Getting to Manitoulin Island

From the south, Manitoulin can be reached by **car ferry** from Tobermory (May to mid-Oct 2–4 daily; $15.95 one-way, cars $34.70; 2hr; ⓣ1-800/265-3163, ⓦwww.ontarioferries.com). Ferries arrive on the island's south coast, docking at South Baymouth. From the north, the island is accessible by **road** (and bridge) from Hwy 17 to the west of Sudbury (see p.195). There are no bus or train services to or around the island.

offers information on Manitoulin's native traditions and heritage, as well as organizing workshops on everything from baking bannock to hand-drum singing.

KAGAWONG, about 15km from M'chigeeng, is arguably the best-looking settlement along the north shore, comprising an attractive ensemble of old timber houses draped around a wide, sheltered bay. It also possesses the **Bridal Veil Falls**, a great spot for cool dips on hot days. From here, it's a further 18km on Hwy 540 to **GORE BAY**, which zeroes in on its busy marina and is home to the *Gore Bay Queens Inn B&B*, 19 Water St (ⓣ705/282-0665, ⓦwww.thequeensinn.ca; mid-May to late Oct; ⑤), a large old house with eight elegantly furnished rooms, oodles of atmosphere and a large communal veranda offering stunning views over the bay.

Collingwood and Blue Mountain

The small-time port of **COLLINGWOOD**, 65km east of Owen Sound on **Nottawasaga Bay**, has a clutch of fine early twentieth-century buildings dotted along its main street, Hurontario. More importantly, the town is also the gateway to the **Blue Mountain**, a segment of the Niagara Escarpment whose steepish slopes are now a major winter sports area, mainly for **alpine skiing** though several cross-country trails have also been developed. To get there from Collingwood, take the **Blue Mountain Road** (Hwy 19) which reaches – after about 10km – the **downhill ski slopes** at the *Blue Mountain Resort* (ⓣ705/445-0231 or 1-877/445-0231, ⓦwww.bluemountain.ca; ⑤), a large and modern sprawl comprising three hotels and an inn that is the centre of wintertime activity with shops, restaurants and cafés. In total, the Blue Mountain ski area has 34 downhill ski slopes of varying difficulty with a maximum vertical drop of 219m. The prime season is from mid-December to mid-March. Both the town of Collingwood and the Blue Mountain Resort also host the annual four-day **Elvis Festival** (ⓦwww.collingwoodelvisfestival.com), held in late July and featuring more than 120 tribute artists and a whole lot of shakin' going on.

Wasaga Beach

With its amusement parks and fast-food joints, there's nothing subtle about **WASAGA BEACH**, 20km east along the bayshore from Collingwood, but the beach itself is of fine golden sand, the swimming is excellent and you can rent all manner of watercraft from jet skis to canoes.

There's also one historical curiosity at the **Nancy Island Historic Site** (late May to mid-June Sat & Sun 10am–6pm; mid-June to early Sept daily 10am–6pm; early Sept to mid-Oct Sat & Sun 11am–5pm; free, but paid parking), on the main drag – Mosley Street – behind Beach Area 2. In the War of 1812, the Americans managed to polish off the few British ships stationed in the upper Great Lakes without too much difficulty and the last Royal Navy vessel, the supply ship *Nancy*, hid out here just off the bay at the mouth of the Nottawasaga River. The Americans tracked down and sunk the *Nancy*, but silt subsequently collected round the sunken hull to create Nancy Island. In 1927, the hull was raised from the silt and today it forms the main exhibit of the island's museum, whose imaginative design resembles the sails of a schooner.

If you decide to stay the night there are lots of reasonably priced **motels** as well as cottages and campsites; just drive along Mosley Street until a place takes your fancy; the local Chamber of Commerce's year-round **information centre** at 550 River Rd West, in Beach Area 1 (Mon–Sat 9am–5pm, Sun 10am–4pm; ⓣ705/429-2247 or 1-866/292-7242, ⓦwww .wasagainfo.com), can also help you find somewhere. There's also a seasonal information centre at 1816 Mosley St (early

May to June & Sept–Oct Mon–Fri 10am–5pm, Sat & Sun 10am–4pm; July & Aug daily 10am–5pm).

Severn Sound

Severn Sound, the southeastern inlet of Georgian Bay, is one of the most beautiful parts of Ontario. The bay's sheltered southern shore is lined with tiny ports and its deep-blue waters are studded by the outcrops of the **Georgian Bay Islands National Park**, whose glacier-smoothed rocks and wispy pines were celebrated by the Group of Seven painters. In **Discovery Harbour**, on the edge of **Penetanguishene**, and **Sainte-Marie among the Hurons**, outside **Midland**, Severn Sound also possesses two of the province's finest historical reconstructions – the first a British naval base, the second a Jesuit mission. There's more lovely Canadian Shield scenery on the road north to **Parry Sound**, an agreeable little port that also serves as a convenient stopping point on the long road north to Sudbury and Northern Ontario. You can also head southeast from Severn Sound to **Orillia**, home of the Stephen Leacock Museum – and just 120km from Toronto on hwys 11 and 400.

There's a frequent Greyhound **bus** (ⓣ1-800/661-8747, ⓦwww.greyhound.ca) service from Toronto to Orillia and the same company also links Toronto with Midland and Penetanguishene, though you do have to change at Barrie. Ontario Northland buses (ⓣ 1-800/461-8558, ⓦwww.ontarionorthland.ca) connect Toronto with Orillia (for North Bay and points north) as well as Port Severn and Parry Sound (for Sudbury and points north).

Penetanguishene and around

The most westerly town on Severn Sound, amenable **PENETANGUISHENE** – "place of the rolling white sands" in Ojibwa – was the site of one of Ontario's first European settlements, a Jesuit mission founded in 1639, then abandoned in 1649 following the burning of Sainte-Marie (see p.153). Europeans returned some 150 years later to establish a trading station, where local Ojibwa exchanged pelts for food and metal tools, but the settlement remained insignificant until just after the War of 1812, when the British built a naval dockyard that attracted a bevy of French and British shopkeepers and suppliers. Today Penetanguishene is one of the few places in southern Ontario that maintains a bilingual (French-English) tradition.

Arrival and information

Greyhound's daily **bus** service from Toronto to Penetanguishene (via Barrie, where you change buses, and Midland) pauses at the bus stop on Robert Street East at Peel, immediately to the east of Main Street. From here, it's a five- to ten-minute walk down Main Street to the harbour, where the **tourist office** (mid-May to June & Sept to early Oct Wed-Sun 10am-6pm, July-Aug daily 10am-8pm; ⓣ705/549–2232, ⓦwww.penetanguishene.ca) has details on local accommodation. If you decide to use Penetanguishene as a base, you can zip off to other local attractions with Union Taxi, 2 Robert St East (ⓣ705/549–7666).

The Town

Main Street is a pleasant place for a stroll, its shops and bars installed behind sturdy red-brick facades. It's the general atmosphere that appeals rather than any particular sight, but the **Centennial Museum** (Mon–Sat 9am–4.30pm, Sun

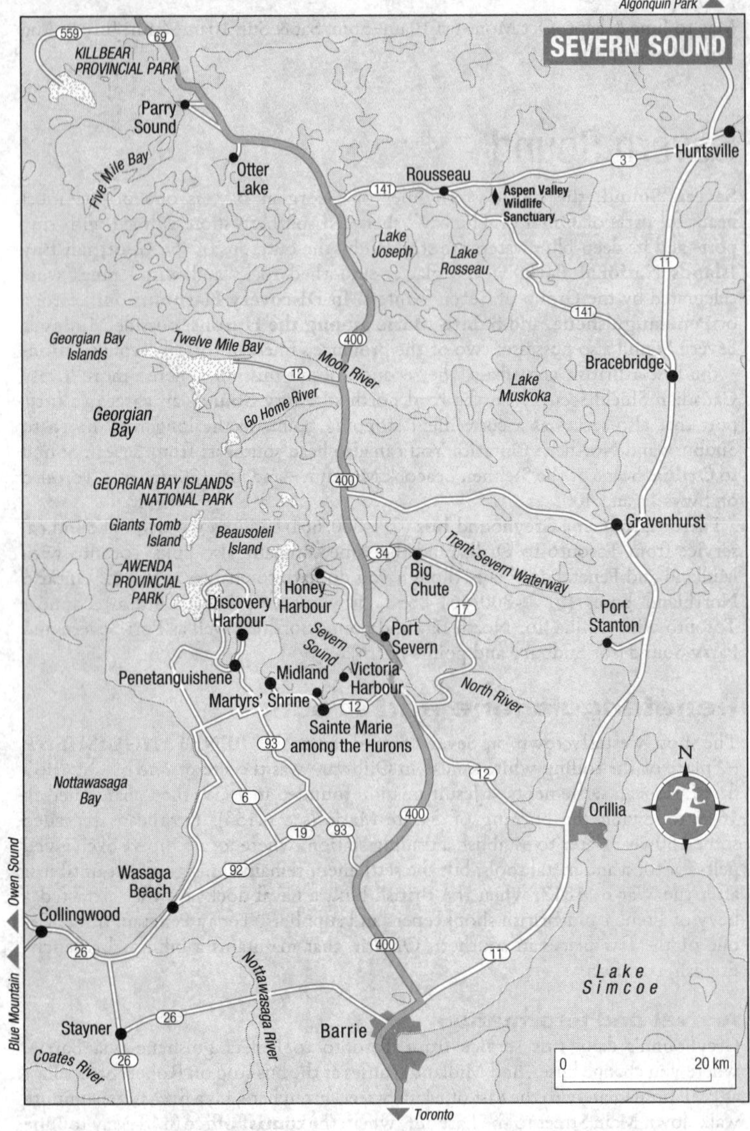

noon–4.30pm; $4.50; Ⓦ www.pencenmuseum.com), at 13 Burke St, just east of Main Street along Beck Boulevard, is worth a quick visit. The museum occupies the old general store and offices of the Beck lumber company, whose yards once stretched right along the town's waterfront. The company was founded in 1865 by Charles Beck, a German immigrant who made himself immensely unpopular by paying his men half their wages in tokens that were only redeemable at his stores. The museum has several displays on the Beck lumber company, including examples of these "Beck dollars".

Doubling back from the museum, it's a short walk to the jetty at the north end of Main Street, from where there are enjoyable **cruises** of the southern stretches of Georgian Bay and its myriad islands – known collectively as the **Thirty Thousand Islands** (mid-June to Aug 1–2 cruises daily; May & early June, Sept & early Oct occasional sailings; $18–25 depending on duration; ⓣ705/549-7795 or 1-800/363-7447, ⓦwww.georgianbaycruises.com).

Discovery Harbour

Penetanguishene's prime tourist attraction, **Discovery Harbour** (late May to June Mon–Fri 10am–5pm; July & Aug daily 10am–5pm; $6.50; ⓦwww.discoveryharbour.on.ca), situated about 5km north of the town centre, is an ambitious reconstruction of the important British naval base that was established here in 1817. The principal purpose of the base was to keep an eye on American movements on the Great Lakes following the War of 1812, and between 1820 and 1834 up to twenty Royal Navy vessels were stationed here. Ships from the base also supplied the British outposts further to the west and, to make navigation safer, the Admiralty decided to chart the Great Lakes. This monumental task fell to **Lieutenant Henry Bayfield**, whose charts remained in use for decades. The naval station was more short-lived. By 1834, relations with the US were sufficiently cordial for the Navy to withdraw, and the base was turned over to the Army, who maintained a small garrison here until 1856.

Now staffed by enthusiastic costumed guides, the sprawling site spreads along a hillside above a tranquil inlet, its green slopes scattered with accurate reconstructions of everything from a sailors' barracks to several period houses, the prettiest of which is the **Keating House**, named after the base's longest-serving adjutant, Frank Keating. Only one of the original buildings survives – the dour limestone **Officers' Quarters**, dating from the 1840s. However, pride of place goes to the working harbour-cum-dockyard, where a brace of fully rigged **sailing ships**, the *HMS Bee* and *HMS Tecumseth*, have been rebuilt to their original nineteenth-century specifications. Discovery Harbour also accommodates the **King's Wharf Theatre** (ⓣ705/549-5555 or 1-888/449-4463, ⓦwww.kingswharftheatre.com), which offers a season of plays, concerts and musicals from mid-June to August.

Practicalities

For **accommodation**, the pick of the town's B&Bs is the *Georgian Terrace Guest House* (ⓣ705/549-2440, ⓦwww.georgianterrace.ca; ❻), 14 Water St, a handsome 1860s mansion which was built for the first mayor of Penetanguishene. The three large and well-appointed suites are decorated in period style with all the modern trimmings and the splendid veranda is the perfect place to snuggle up with a glass of wine and enjoy the stunning view over the bay. There's also the delightful *No.1 Jury Drive B&B*, 1 Jury Drive (ⓣ705/549-6851, ⓦwww.jurydrbb.huronia.com; ❺), whose five comfortable en-suite guest rooms occupy an attractive modern house near Discovery Harbour; the leafy suburban setting is very relaxing and the breakfasts are superb – especially the home-made carrot muffins.

For **food**, the *Blue Sky Family Restaurant*, 32 Main St (daily 6am-9pm, except Tues 6am-2pm; ⓣ705/549-8611), is an agreeable small-town diner offering good-quality snacks and meals at very affordable prices.

Awenda Provincial Park

Awenda Provincial Park (ⓣ705/549-2231, ⓦwww.ontarioparks.com), just 11km northwest of Penetanguishene, is one of Ontario's larger parks, its delightful mainland portion dominated by a dense deciduous forest that spreads south from the Nipissing Bluff on the edge of Georgian Bay. The other section,

Giants Tomb Island, lies offshore, but you need your own boat to get there. Awenda has a few small rock-and-pebble beaches, four good **campsites** (mid-May to early Oct), and a handful of hiking trails starting near the park office, which issues trail guides and maps.

Midland

MIDLAND, just to the east of Penetanguishene, lost its engineering plants in the 1930s, its shipyards in 1957 and much of its flour-mill capacity in 1967. Yet it has bounced back, shrugging off these setbacks with the help of provincial and federal grants, and nowadays the town has a sprightly air, its main drag – King Street – an amenable parade of shops and cafés with the occasional mural to brighten up the sturdy brick buildings.

Arrival and information

Greyhound buses from Toronto to Midland via Barrie pull in at the bus depot, which they share with Central Taxi (Ⓣ705/526-2218), at 207 King St. From here, it's a short walk to the waterfront and the **tourist office**, at the foot of King Street (May–June daily 9am-5pm, July & Aug daily 8am–8pm, Sept–April Mon–Fri 9am–5pm; Ⓣ705/526–7884, Ⓦwww.southerngeorgianbay.on.ca). They have the details on local accommodation.

The Town

Efforts to cash in on the tourist industry have included the construction of a marina and the redevelopment of the harbourfront, where sightseeing **cruises of the Thirty Thousand Islands** that necklace Georgian Bay leave from mid-May to mid-October (1–3 daily; $24; 2–3hr; reservations on Ⓣ705/549-3388 or 1-888/833-2628, Ⓦwww.midlandtours.com).

The **Huronia Museum & Huron–Ouendat Village** (May–Oct daily 9am–5pm, Nov–April Mon–Fri 9am–5pm; $7; Ⓦwww.huroniamuseum.com), a twenty-minute walk south of the harbour via King Street on Little Lake Park Road, is a worthwhile stop. Highlights include a large number of Huron artefacts and a series of photos tracing the pioneer settlement of Midland. The adjacent **village,** which is just being put to rights after a bad fire, is a replica of a sixteenth-century Huron settlement, its high palisade encircling storage pits, drying racks, a sweat bath, a medicine man's lodge and two long houses. These long houses are characteristic Huron constructions, their bark-covered walls of cedar poles bent to form a protective arch. They hold tiers of rough wooden bunks, draped with furs, while up above herbs, fish, skins and tobacco hang from the roof to dry. It's all very interesting and feels surprisingly authentic, though it still lags behind the comparable section of the nearby Sainte-Marie among the Hurons (see opposite).

Practicalities

For **accommodation**, one perfectly adequate and fairly central option is the *Victorian Inn B&B* (Ⓣ705/526-4441 or 1-877/450-7660, Ⓦwww.victorianinn.on.ca; ❺), a good-looking Victorian house with wraparound veranda at 670 Hugel Ave and 6th. The unusual and rather engaging *Little Lake Inn B&B* (Ⓣ705/526-2750 or 1-888/297-6130, Ⓦwww.littlelakeinn.com; ❻), at 669 Yonge St at 5th, is also good, with four well-appointed en-suite guest rooms. The modern front part of the house leads to an older section at the back with high-beamed ceilings and park views.

For **food**, try *The Explorers Café* (Ⓣ705/527-9199), a busy little place tucked away in a back alley just off 345 King St. The New Zealand chef serves up mouth-watering creations such as maple salmon and savoury pie for around $18.

Alternatively, the *Rye Café*, at 292 King St, serves first-class deli-style sandwiches and has good, inexpensive breakfasts.

Sainte-Marie among the Hurons

One of the province's most arresting historical attractions is **Sainte-Marie among the Hurons** (late April to mid-May & mid- to late Oct Mon–Fri 10am–5pm; mid-May to mid-Oct daily 10am–5pm; Ⓦ www.saintemarieamongthehurons.on.ca; $12), the carefully researched and beautifully maintained site of a crucial episode in Canadian history. It's located 5km east of Midland beside Hwy 12; there are no buses, but a taxi from Midland is only $10 or so.

Some history

In 1608, the French explorer and trader **Samuel de Champlain** returned to Canada believing that the only way to make the fur trade profitable was by developing alliances with native hunters. The **Huron** were the obvious choice, as they already acted as go-betweens in the exchange of corn, tobacco and hemp from the native bands to the south and west of their territory, for the pelts collected to the north. In 1611, having participated in Huron attacks on the Iroquois, Champlain cemented the alliance by a formal exchange of presents. Yet his decision to champion one tribe against another – and particularly his gifts of firearms to his allies – disrupted the balance of power among the native societies of the St Lawrence and Great Lakes area and set the stage for the destruction of Sainte-Marie almost forty years later.

Meanwhile, the **Jesuits**, who established their centre of operations at Sainte-Marie in 1639, had begun to undermine social cohesion within the Huron community by turning a substantial minority Christian. The Hurons had also been enfeebled by the arrival of three European sicknesses – measles, smallpox and influenza. Then, in 1648, the Dutch on the Hudson River began to sell firearms to the **Iroquois**, who launched a full-scale invasion of Huronia in March 1649, slaughtering their enemies as they moved in on Sainte-Marie. Fearing for their lives, the Jesuits of Sainte-Marie burnt their settlement and fled. Eight thousand Hurons went with them; most starved to death on Christian Island, in Georgian Bay, but a few made it to Québec. During the campaign two Jesuit priests, fathers **Brébeuf and Lalemant**, were captured at the outpost of Saint-Louis, near present-day Victoria Harbour, where they were bound to the stake and tortured, as per standard Iroquois practice. The image of Catholic bravery and Indian cruelty lingered in the minds of French-Canadians long after the sufferings of the Hurons had been forgotten.

The mission site

A visit to Sainte-Marie starts in the reception centre with an audiovisual show that provides some background information before the screen lifts dramatically away to reveal the painstakingly restored mission site. There are 25 wooden buildings here, divided into two sections: the Jesuit area with its watchtowers, chapel, forge, living quarters, well-stocked garden and farm buildings, stocked with pigs, cows and hens; and the native area, including a hospital and a pair of bark-covered long houses – one for Christian converts, the other for "heathens". Costumed guides act out the parts of Hurons and Europeans with great gusto, answering questions and demonstrating crafts and skills, though they show a certain reluctance to eat what was once the staple food of the region, **sagamite**, a porridge of cornmeal seasoned with rotten fish. The grave in the simple wooden **church of St Joseph** between the Christian and native areas is the place where the (remaining) flesh of Brébeuf and Lalemant was interred after the Jesuits had removed the bones for future use as reliquaries.

The museum

A path leads from the site to the excellent **museum**, which traces the story of the early exploration of Canada with maps and displays on such subjects as fishing and the fur trade, seen in the context of contemporary European history. This leads into a section on the history of the missionaries in New France, with particular reference to Sainte-Marie. Information on the archeology of the site follows: the mission's whereabouts were always known even though Victorian settlers helped themselves to every chunk of stone – from what was known locally as "the old Catholic fort" – because the Jesuits had deposited the necessary documentation in Rome. Excavations began on the site in the 1940s and work is still in progress.

The Martyrs' Shrine and Wye Marsh

The eight Jesuits who were killed in Huronia between 1642 and 1649 are commemorated by the **Martyrs' Shrine** (mid-May to mid-Oct daily 8.30am–9pm; $3; Ⓦwww.martyrs-shrine.com), a twin-spired, 1920s church which overlooks Sainte-Marie from the other side of Hwy 12. Blessed by Pope John Paul II in 1984 the church, along with the assorted shrines and altars in its grounds, is massively popular with pilgrims. Inside, the transepts hold a number of saintly reliquaries, most notably the skull of Brébeuf, and a stack of crutches discarded by healed pilgrims. Back across Hwy 12 and next door to Sainte-Marie is the **Wye Marsh Wildlife Centre** (daily 9am–5pm; $11; Ⓦwww.wyemarsh .com), whose footpaths explore a patch of wetland and woodland.

Orillia

If you're heading south from Severn Sound towards Toronto, you might consider a brief detour to **ORILLIA**, a small town set beside Lake Couchiching, which is itself separated from the much larger Lake Simcoe by a short and narrow promontory; the town is also on Hwy 11, the road to Algonquin Provincial Park (see p.161). Orillia lies just to the west of the narrow channel – **The Narrows** – that connects the two lakes, a waterway that was once a centre of Huron settlement. Today Orillia is a trim little town of 27,000 citizens – part lakeside resort, part farming centre.

Arrival and information

Buses arrive and depart from Orillia **bus station**, sited in the former railway station at the southern end of the town centre on Front Street South. The main **tourist office** is also here (Mon–Fri 9am–5pm; Ⓣ705/326-4424, Ⓦwww.orillia .com); the Leacock Museum is 2km away to the south.

The Town

Orillia's humdrum **town centre** spreads out on either side of the main drag, **Mississaga Street**, which runs east from Hwy 11 to Lake Couchiching. At the foot of Mississaga, **Centennial Park** incorporates a marina, a harbour and a boardwalk that runs north to **Couchiching Beach Park**, complete with an Edwardian bandstand and a bronze statue of Champlain, who landed here in 1615.

The town's principal attraction, the **Stephen Leacock Museum** (mid-May to mid-Oct daily 9am–5pm; $5; Ⓦwww.leacockmuseum.com), is located some 3km southeast of the centre along the lakeshore – just follow the signs. Built in 1928, this was the summer home of the humorist and academic Stephen Leacock until his death in 1944. His most famous book, *Sunshine Sketches of a Little Town*, gently mocks the hypocrisies and vanities of the people of Mariposa, an imaginary town so clearly based on Orillia that it caused great local offence. Some of the rooms contain furnishings and fittings familiar to Leacock, others shed light on his career, interests and attitudes. Indeed, although the books may be engagingly whimsical, you can't help but wonder about a man who had concealed spyholes in his library so that he could watch his guests and, perhaps worse, carefully positioned his favourite living-room chair so that he could keep an eye on his servants in the pantry via the dining-room mirror. After you've explored the house, take a few minutes for the easy stroll out along the adjacent wooded headland and drop by the giftshop, which sells almost all of his works.

Port Severn and around

Sitting on the northern shore of Severn Sound at the mouth of the Severn River, minuscule **PORT SEVERN** is the gateway to the **Trent–Severn Waterway**, a 400km canalized route connecting Georgian Bay with Lake Ontario. With a maximum depth of only 2m, it's of little commercial importance today, but until the late nineteenth century this was one of the region's principal cargo routes.

Arrival and information

The Ontario Northland **bus** service from Toronto to Parry Sound and Sudbury drops passengers at the gas station on Hwy 400 on the edge of Port Severn; there are no connections on to Honey Harbour.

If you have the inclination for a serious **boating trip,** check with Parks Canada (Ⓣ1-888/773-8888, Ⓦwww.pc.gc.ca), whose website provides detailed information on fees, lock times and other nautical-related regulations. It's open from the middle of May to the middle of October and takes about a week to travel from one end to the other. Taster **cruises** (late Sept to mid-Oct 1 daily; $26; Ⓣ1-888/833-2628, Ⓦwww.midlandtours.com) lasting 2hr 30min, leave from Lock #45 in Port Severn, travelling as far as the **Big Chute Marine Railway**, where boats are lifted over the eighteen-metre drop between the upper and lower levels of the river. The Big Chute is something of a yawn, but it certainly attracts its share of visitors, most of whom drive here – just follow the signs off Hwy 400 (Exit 162) north of Port Severn.

Practicalities

If you're planning to **stay**, the smart and briskly modern *Inn at Christie's Mill* (Ⓣ705/538-2354 or 1-800/465-9966, Ⓦwww.christiesmill.com; ⑥), 263 Port Severn Rd North, is a sound choice. It also has the district's best **restaurant** with views out across the river. The menu has a seasonal and local bent with mains averaging around $25; Sunday brunch is especially popular, an all-you-can-eat extravaganza for $15.95. Reservations are advised and the restaurant operates restricted hours out of season. Even better is the delightful *Severn Lodge* (Ⓣ705/756-2722 or 1-800/461-5817, Ⓦwww.severnlodge.on.ca; ⑦), 116 Gloucester Trail, which has a wonderful solitary location among dense forests overlooking a wide and quiet section of the Trent–Severn Waterway. The main lodge and chalets have all the facilities of a mini-resort, including canoe and motorboat rental, an artificial beach, a restaurant and an outdoor swimming pool. To get there, leave Hwy 400 at Exit 162 (also the turning for the Big Chute Marine Railway – see above); the lodge is 7km along Route 34.

Honey Harbour

It's 13km northwest from Port Severn across the mouth of the river and along Route 5 to **HONEY HARBOUR**, the nearest port to the Georgian Bay Islands National Park. Little more than a couple of shops, a liquor store and a few self-contained hotel resorts, the village achieved some notoriety in the 1970s when the bar of the *Delawana Inn* was the site of violent confrontations between Toronto's Hell's Angels and local Ojibwa; the feud ended with the Angels walking home after their bikes had been dynamited.

Things are much more civil today, but Honey Harbour is still a lively place in summer, with motorboats whizzing in and out as cottagers drop by to collect supplies. If you decide to stay here – eschewing the offshore campsites of the national park (see below) – the best place is the lakeside *Delawana Inn* (Ⓣ705/756-2424 or 1-888/335-2926, Ⓦwww.delawana.com; ❽ for bed and breakfast in high season, with discounts on package deals; mid-May to mid-Oct), an extensive resort complex with spacious chalet cabins dotted round its pine-forested grounds and its own little island patterned with hiking trails. Guests have use of the resort's canoes, kayaks and windsurfing boards.

Georgian Bay Islands National Park

A beautiful area to cruise, the **Georgian Bay Islands National Park** (Ⓦwww.pc.gc.ca) consists of a scattering of about sixty islands spread between Honey Harbour and Twelve Mile Bay, about 50km to the north. The park's two distinct landscapes – the glacier-scraped rock of the Canadian Shield and the hardwood forests and thicker soils of the south – meet at the northern end of the largest and most scenic island, **Beausoleil**, a forty-minute boat ride west of Honey Harbour.

Arrival and information

The Parks Canada **visitor centre** is located at Lock #45 in Port Severn (mid-May to June Mon–Thurs 9am–4pm, Fri–Sun 9am–6pm; July & Aug daily 9am–7pm; Sept to mid-Oct Mon–Fri 9am–3.30pm, Sat & Sun 9am–5pm; Ⓣ705/538-0559). They provide a full range of information on walking trails and flora and fauna. In winter, it's sometimes possible to reach the park on the ice, but an advance call to the park office is essential to get advice on local conditions.

Several Honey Harbour operators run a **water taxi** service over to three of the park's islands – Beausoleil ($50–60 one-way), Centennial Island ($55–65) and Island 95 ($50–60). **Honey Harbour Boat Club** (Ⓣ705/756-2411), at the marina at the end of Route 5, is as good as any. Water taxi prices are fixed – the park office has the list – but times are negotiable; be sure to arrange an agreed pick-up time before you get dropped off. If you want to head southwest, a one-way water-taxi trip to Midland (see p.152) costs around $120. The park also organizes its own boat trips to Beausoleil, a fifteen-minute journey each way (and around four hours on the island) with the **Georgian Bay Islands Day Tripper** (July & Aug Thurs–Mon 3 daily; $15.70 return, $5.80 park admission included; Ⓣ705/526-8907). Reservations are essential for both the day-trip and the water taxis.

Park accommodation

There are eleven **campsites** on **Beausoleil Island**, costing $15.70 a night and all of them operate on a self-registration, first-come, first-served basis. The exception is Cedar Spring ($25.50), where the visitor centre (Ⓣ705/756-8907) takes reservations on half the 87 sites for bookings between May and September; there is an additional $10 fee for this service. For everywhere else, ask about availability at the Port Severn park office before you set out – and don't forget the insect repellent.

Hiking in the park

Beausoleil has twelve short **hiking trails**, including two that start at the **Cedar Spring landing stage**, on the southeastern shore. These are the Treasure Trail

> **The Massasauga rattlesnake**
>
> The endangered **Massasauga rattlesnake** is the only venomous snake in eastern Canada and a small population hangs around the Georgian Bay Islands National Park. Tan-coloured with dark brown blotches, an adult specimen is 50 to 70cm long with a heavy body and triangular head. In the unlikely event you stumble across one, give it a wide berth. The snake prefers marsh and mixed forest, so if you are hiking in this kind of habitat, be sure to pick up one of the advisory leaflets at the park office.

(3.8km), which heads north behind the marshes along the edge of the island, and the Christian Trail (1.5km), which cuts through beech and maple stands to the balsam and hemlock groves overlooking the rocky beaches of the western shoreline. At the northern end of Beausoleil, within comfortable walking distance of several other **jetties**, are the Cambrian (2km) and Fairy (2.5km) trails, two delightful routes through the harsher scenery of the Canadian Shield. Nearby, just to the west, is the Dossyonshing Trail (2.5km), which tracks through a mixed area of wetland, forest and bare granite in the transitional zone between the two main landscapes.

Parry Sound

A cheerful little place, **PARRY SOUND** sits beside an inlet of Georgian Bay some 70km north of Port Severn. It takes its name from the Arctic explorer Sir William Edward Parry, but it earned the nickname "Parry Hoot" on account of the water-bound log-drivers hereabouts, who chose this as the place to get drunk in. Things are more genteel today and the town is now popular with tourists for the **boat cruises** that leave the harbour bound for the **Thirty Thousand Islands** out in the bay.

Arrival and information

Parry Sound is on the Ontario Northland (Ⓣ1-800/461-8558, Ⓦwww.ontarionorthland.ca) **bus** route from Toronto to Sudbury. Buses pull into *Richard's Coffee House*, 119 Bowes St, 1km or so to the east of the town centre. To get downtown from here, call Parry Sound Taxi (Ⓣ705/746-1221). The main **tourist office** is in the former railway station at 70 Church St (Mon–Fri 9am–5pm; Ⓣ705/746-4213 or 1-800/461-4261, Ⓦwww.gbcountry.com). From here, it's 800m south along Church Street to the centre and 300m more to Government Wharf, just below the centre of town at the end of Bay Street, which is also the location of a second **seasonal tourist office** (June–Sept daily 9am–8pm) next to the jetty of the Island Queen cruise boat. Both tourist offices have details on local accommodation.

Cruises and trips from town

Parry Sound proper is short of specific sights, though its pocket-sized harbour is overshadowed by a splendid Edwardian railway **trestle bridge** and the few blocks that make up the commercial centre – along and around **James Street** – are dotted with good-looking, old brick and stone buildings.

Parry Sound is best known as being the home port of the **Island Queen** (June to mid-Oct 1 daily at 1pm; July & Aug also at 10am; 3hr for $32, 2hr $24; Ⓣ705/746-2311 or 1-800/506-2628, Ⓦwww.island-queen.com), which squeezes through these islands in a spectacular **cruise** of either two or three hours' duration. The two-hour morning cruise heads north to weave its way through the inner islands, which are dotted with summer cottages, while the afternoon cruise sails south to the more remote islands of Georgian Bay, thereby providing a better chance of spotting wildlife. Both cruises pass through the **Hole in the Wall**, a narrow channel barely able to accommodate the boat. If you're short on time, you might consider flying over the islands in a **floatplane** with Georgian Bay Airways (May to mid-Oct; $100–$125; ⓣ705/774-9884 or 1-888/786-1704, ⓦwww.georgianbayairways.com). The jetty for both the Island Queen and the floatplanes is at Government Wharf.

Practicalities

If you're **staying** the night, an enticing option is the *Bayside Inn* (ⓣ705/746-7720, ⓦwww.psbaysideinn.com; ⑥), which occupies an 1880s building close to the jetty at 10 Gibson St. Its ten guest rooms have all recently been renovated in warm shades, giving it a homely feel. A good alternative is the *Victoria Manor B&B*, in the centre at 43 Church St and Rosetta (ⓣ705/746-5399, ⓦwww.solutionsforu.com /victoria; ⑤). Occupying a handsome 1907 house, this B&B comes complete with turrets, a grand portico and immaculate gardens; there are five guest rooms (one en suite) each kitted out in pleasant period style.

For **food**, *The Country Gourmet* (Mon–Fri 7.30am–4pm & Sat 8am–4pm; ⓣ705/746-5907), in the centre at 65 James St, is a smashing deli and bakery selling the tastiest of meals and snacks. In the evening, try the *Bay St Café* (ⓣ705/746-2882), 22 Bay St by Government Wharf, where the menu runs from fish and chips to tuna steak and salads.

Killbear Provincial Park

The wild and rugged Georgian Bay shoreline, formed by glaciers that scoured the rock and dumped mighty boulders onto its long beaches, is seen to fine advantage in **Killbear Provincial Park**, reached by driving 18km north from Parry Sound on Hwy 69 then 20km southwest on Route 559.

The park occupies a tapering peninsula, with spindly cedars and black spruce clinging precariously to a shoreline of pink-granite outcrops, the classic Canadian Shield scenery so beloved by Tom Thomson (see p.88). The best of the park's three short **hiking trails** is the easy 3.5km loop of the **Lookout Point Trail**, which slips through the maple, beech and yellow birch forest of the park's rugged interior to reach a lookout across Parry Sound; allow a couple of hours. Killbear has seven **campsites** (mid-May to early Oct; reservations on ⓣ519/826-5290 or 1-888/668-7275, ⓦwww .ontarioparks.com; $33–40), some by the water, others in the forest, some with showers, others not.

From Killbear, it's about 180km north to Sudbury (see p.195) along Hwy 69.

Central Ontario

Lying between Lake Ontario's northern shore and the Ottawa River Valley, **central Ontario** is largely defined by the **Canadian Shield**, whose endless forests, myriad lakes and thin soils dip down from the north in a giant wedge. This hostile terrain has kept settlement down to a minimum, though latterly the very wildness of the land has attracted lots of Canadian holidaymakers, who come here to hunker down in their lakeside cottages. The centre of all this holiday activity is the

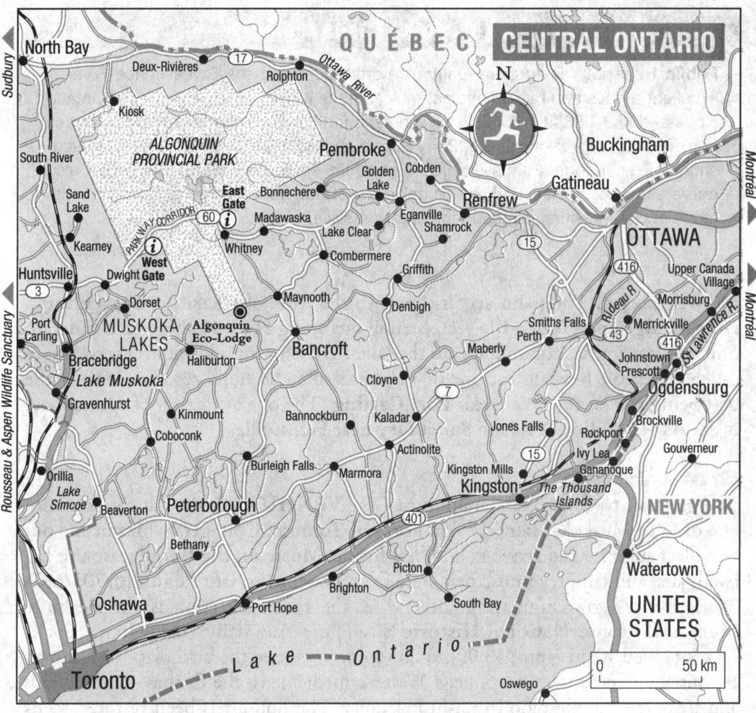

Muskoka Lakes, a skein of narrow lakes and rivers, and their main supply towns, **Gravenhurst** and **Bracebridge**. Staying in a cottage or a resort is the one sure-fire way of appreciating the beauty of the area, but if you're after wilderness head further north to the wondrous expanse of **Algonquin Provincial Park** with its abundant wildlife and extraordinarily large network of canoe routes. The implacability of the Shield breaks up as it approaches the **St Lawrence River** at the east end of Lake Ontario and it's here you'll find a string of historic towns and villages. The pick is **Kingston**, founded by United Empire Loyalists (see p.417) and renowned for its fine limestone buildings, not to mention its good restaurants and quality B&Bs. Kingston is also useful as a stepping stone on the road east to either Montréal (see p.215) or **Ottawa**, Canada's engaging capital city, which boasts some of the country's finest museums and a first-rate restaurant and bar scene.

The Muskoka Lakes

The main route from Toronto to Algonquin Provincial Park passes through the **Muskoka Lakes**, a region of more than 1500 lakes and hundreds of **cottage** retreats. Named after an Ojibwa chief, Mesqua-Ukee, who settled here with his people after aiding the British during the War of 1812, the area was opened to tourism in 1860, when two hikers made the two-day trek from Toronto to a small Ojibwa settlement at what is now the town of Gravenhurst. By the 1890s, the lakes had become the haunt of wealthy families from southern Ontario and although things are more democratic today, this is still primarily the preserve of

Public transport in the Muskoka Lakes region

Public transport along Lake Ontario's north shore and the St Lawrence River is excellent by bus and rail. Things get trickier in the Muskoka Lakes area, but Ontario Northland (ⓣ1-800/461-8558, ⓦwww.ontarionorthland.ca) operates two bus routes from Toronto, one linking Orillia, Parry Sound and Sudbury, the other Orillia, Gravenhurst, Bracebridge, Huntsville (for **Algonquin Park**) and North Bay; they also operate the Northlander **train** (once daily except Sat) from Toronto to Cochrane with stops at Gravenshurst, Bracebridge and Huntsville.

the well heeled. The main access towns to the Muskoka Lakes – **Gravenhurst**, **Bracebridge** and **Huntsville** – are strung out along Hwy 11. None has much to offer the passing visitor and nor do the lakes. Driving round is pointless so you're much better off heading for one of the area's splendid hotel resorts – one of the best being the *Sherwood Inn* near **Port Carling**. The one attraction of special note is the **Aspen Valley Wildlife Sanctuary** near Huntsville.

Gravenhurst

The gateway to Muskoka is humdrum **GRAVENHURST**, sited at the southern end of Lake Muskoka, some 170km north of Toronto. Cottagers whizz in and out to collect supplies and arrive in numbers for the **Music on the Barge** season of big band, jazz and country music held here from late June to late August (ⓣ705/687-3412, ⓦwww.gravenhurst.ca). Otherwise, the main attraction is the **Bethune Memorial House National Historic Site** (June–Aug daily 10am–4pm; Sept & Oct Sat–Wed 10am–4pm; $3.90), at 235 John St North, the birthplace of Norman Bethune, a doctor who introduced Western medicine to the Chinese in the 1930s and invented mobile blood-transfusion units. The house has been restored to its appearance in 1890 and has displays on Bethune's considerable accomplishments – he was even praised by Chairman Mao – all detailed in English, French and Chinese.

For **food**, head for *The Muskoka Café* (Mon–Sat 10am–3pm), an amenable little place on the main street, 125 Muskoka Rd South, selling wraps, soups and a particularly delicious blueberry pie.

Bracebridge and Port Carling

BRACEBRIDGE, 20km north of Gravenhurst, prides itself on being "Halfway to the North Pole" – and on that basis bills itself as the summer home of Santa Claus, who hangs out among the theme-park rides of **Santa's Village** just southwest of town (late June to Aug daily 10am–6pm; adults and children over 5 $27, 2–4s $22, under 2s free; ⓦwww.santasvillage.ca). There's not much else, though the short main drag, **Manitoba Street**, is lined with a pleasant ensemble of Victorian red-bricks, worth at least a few minutes.

Driving west from Bracebridge along Hwy 118, it's about 25km to the lakeside hamlet of **PORT CARLING**, the nearest settlement to one of the region's finest hotel–resorts, the *Delta Sherwood Inn*, 1090 Sherwood Rd (ⓣ705/765-3131 or 1-866/844-2228, ⓦwww.deltahotels.com; ⑧ all inclusive), a handsome complex of luxurious chalet-villas set deep in the Muskoka woods – call for directions. Each of the guest rooms is kitted out in smart modern style and the food is first-rate – try the rack of lamb with apple mint chutney.

Huntsville

Workaday **HUNTSVILLE**, 35km beyond Bracebridge on Hwy 11, is as near as the buses and trains get to Algonquin Park and partly as a result it has become a bustling little town as compared to its nearest neighbours. Ontario Northland **buses** pull into the bus depot, on the north side of town at 377 Centre St North, and their **Northlander train** pauses at the train station about 600m away to the south (and across the river) at 2 Centre St South.

For moving on to **Algonquin Park** by public transport, your only option is Hammond Transportation's thrice weekly minibus service, which operates from July to late August (for more details, see p.162). If you find yourself marooned here, head for the main **tourist office,** just off Main Street at 8 West St North (Mon–Fri 9am–5pm, Sat 10am–4pm; ⓣ705/789-4771, ⓦwww.huntsvilleadventures.com), which can help with local accommodation. For somewhere to **eat**, your best bet is *Soul Sistas Wellness Kitchen*, 79 Main St East (ⓣ705/789-6655), where they specialize in organic food such as salads, soups and smoothies.

Aspen Valley Wildlife Sanctuary

The fascinating **Aspen Valley Wildlife Sanctuary** (May–Oct Wed & Sun 1–4pm; donation; ⓣ705/732-6368, ⓦwww.aspenvalleywildlifesanctuary.com) gives you a chance to see many of Canada's wild species in a natural habitat. Audrey Tournay founded the sanctuary over thirty years ago and it's now the largest **black bear rehabilitation centre** in the world. Spread over a thousand acres, the sanctuary houses orphaned bear cubs – often rescued in the hunting season – nursing them until they're strong enough to be released back into the wild. You won't get up close and personal with the bear cubs, as they need to be kept shy of humans, but the permanent residents (animals unfit ever to be released) more than compensate. Look out for the Arctic wolves, raccoons, birds of prey, a North American black bear which was used for training dogs in dog-bear fights and an African lion which was rescued from a seventeen-year old who kept it as a pet. To get to the sanctuary from Huntsville, follow the Aspdin Road (County Road #3) until you get to the signed turning a couple of kilometres short of **Rosseau,** a journey of about 35km.

Algonquin Provincial Park

Created in 1893 at the behest of logging companies keen to keep the farmers out, **Algonquin Provincial Park** (ⓦwww.algonquinpark.on.ca) is Ontario's oldest and largest provincial park and for many it comprises the quintessential Canadian landscape. Located on the southern edge of the Canadian Shield, the park straddles a **transitional zone**, with the hilly two-thirds to the west covered in a hardwood forest of sugar maple, beech and yellow birch, while in the drier eastern part jack pines, white pines and red pines predominate. Throughout the park, the lakes and rocky rounded hills are interspersed with black spruce bogs, a type of vegetation typical of areas far further north. **Canoeing** is very popular here and with an astounding 1600km of routes there's a good chance of avoiding all contact for days on end. **Wildlife** is as varied as the flora – any trip to Algonquin is characterized by the echo of birdsong, from the loons' ghostly call to the screech of ravens. Beavers, moose, black bears and raccoons are all resident, as are white-tailed deer, whose population thrives on the young shoots that replace the trees felled by the park's loggers. Public "howling parties" – which can attract up to two thousand people – set off into the wilderness during August in search of **timber wolves**, or rather their howls: many of the rangers are so good at howling that they can get the animals to reply.

▲ A moose makes its way across the road near Algonquin Park

Arrival and information

If you're reliant on **public transport**, there are trains and buses to Huntsville (see p.161), from where Hammond Transportation (☎705/645-5431, Ⓦwww.hammondtransportation.com) run an **Algonquin Park shuttle** to points along the Parkway Corridor from July to late August (3 weekly; $36 each way). **Access** to the park is via either the **West Gate**, 45km from Huntsville on Hwy 60, or – if you're arriving from Ottawa and points east – the **East Gate**. A day-pass costs $15 per vehicle. The two gates are linked by the 56km-long **Parkway Corridor** – also known as the Frank McDougall Parkway – the park's only road. Away from the corridor, walking and canoeing are the only means of transport.

The well-signposted main **visitor centre** is 43km inside the park from the West Gate (late April to mid-May & mid-Oct to late Oct daily 10am–5pm; late May to June & Sept to mid-Oct daily 10am–6pm; July & Aug daily 9am–9pm; Nov to late April Sat & Sun 10am–4pm; ☎705/633-5572). Besides the inevitable gift shop, it holds a series of dioramas explaining the park's general and natural history. The visitor centre also has a comprehensive range of literature describing every aspect of the park, from maps and detailed hiking trail and canoeing route guides through to booklets on native folklore. The **park offices** at both the West and East gates have trail descriptions and other park information, but there's not so wide a range; individual trail guides are also available at most trailheads.

If you're heading for the **backcountry**, pick up food and water before you get here as outlets in the park are few and far between. In all cases, backcountry **camping** requires a permit. These are available at both the West and East gates and at the visitor centre ($11 per person per night). For campsites, see p.164.

Guided tours and public transport

For **all-in tours**, Call of the Wild, 23 Edward St in Markham, a suburb of Toronto (☎905/471-9453 or 1-800/776-9453, Ⓦwww.callofthewild.ca), runs personalized and relaxed adventure canoe trips in the park (three/four/five days:

$365/485/610) with experienced guides. Prices include all meals, permits and equipment. Return transport from Toronto is an extra optional $140 and it's essential to book in advance.

The Parkway Corridor

Heading into Algonquin Park from Huntsville along the Parkway Corridor, the location of trailheads and campsites is indicated by distances from the West Gate. Fourteen **day-hikes** begin beside the road and of these the 2km **Beaver Pond Trail** (Km45) is a rugged but easy trail that takes you past huge beaver dams, while the equally short but somewhat steeper **Lookout Trail** (Km39) offers fine views. For a longer trail with greater chances of spotting wildlife, the 11km **Mizzy Lake Trail** (Km15) is recommended. Spare time also for both the **Algonquin Art Centre** (Km20; daily: late June to mid-Oct 10am–5pm; donation; Ⓦwww.algonquinartcentre.com), which has regularly rotated exhibitions on the park's flora and fauna, and the **Algonquin Logging Museum** (late May to early Oct daily 9am–5pm; free with park day-pass), near the East Gate at Km54.5. Here, an easy 1.3km loop trail threads past some fascinating old logging leftovers, including a tugboat, a locomotive, sawlog camp and sleighs.

The beaver

The **beaver** is Canada's national animal: it appeared on the first postage stamp issued by the colony in 1851, and now features on the back of the 5¢ piece. There was nothing sentimental about this choice – beaver pelts kick-started the colonial economy – and only recently has the beaver been treated with restraint and protected from being indiscriminately bumped off.

Beavers are aquatic rodents, growing to around 75cm long and weighing about 35kg. Aboriginal peoples hunted the beaver for its thick, soft **pelt**, composed of long guard hairs and a dense undercoat, to use for clothing. European fur traders soon realized the value of beaver pelts, particularly in the manufacture of the all-weather, all-purpose **hat** worn by every man of any substance. To keep up with demand the beaver was extensively trapped, and the French *voyageurs* pushed further and further west along the lake and river systems in pursuit of the animal, thereby opening up much of the interior. The beaver was hunted to the point of extinction in much of eastern Canada, but had a reprieve when the beaver hat went out of fashion in the late nineteenth century; today beavers are comparatively commonplace.

Beavers start to build their **dams**, which can be up to 700m wide, by strategically felling one tree across a stream. This catches silt and driftwood and the beaver then reinforces the barrier with sticks and stones plus grass and mud, which is laboriously smoothed in as a binding element. The **lodge** is constructed simultaneously; sometimes it forms part of the dam and sometimes it is fixed to the shore or an island in the pond. It is about 2m in diameter and has two entrances – one accessible from land and one from underwater – both for its own convenience and to be able to escape its predators in any emergency, along with a lot of tail slapping to give the alarm. Lodges are topped with grass thatch and a good layer of mud, which freezes in winter, making them virtually impenetrable. During the autumn, the beaver stocks its **pond** with the soft-bark trees and saplings that make up its diet. It drags them below the water line and anchors them to the mud at the bottom before retiring to the lodge for the winter, only emerging to get food from the pond or repair the dam. Beaver lakes are not the tree-fringed paradises portrayed by some nature-film makers; nearer the mark is a mud-banked pond, surrounded by untidily felled trees and with a bedraggled-looking domed heap of sticks and sludge somewhere along its banks.

Campsites, cabins and lodges

Strung along the Parkway Corridor are eight park **campsites**. The less crowded sites tend to be those that prohibit motorboats, namely Canisbay Lake (Km23; mid-May to early Oct); Mew Lake (Km30; all year); Pog Lake (Km37; early June to early Sept); Kearney Lake (Km37; early June to early Sept); and Coon Lake (Km40; mid-June to Aug). Mew Lake is the only campsite open year-round. The cost of a pitch, covering a car and up to six people, is $26–40; **reservations** are essential (ⓣ519/826-5290 or 1-888/668-7275, ⓦwww.ontarioparks.com). Rangers who roamed the park in its early years built dozens of backcountry **log cabins**, some of which have survived and are now rented out for $55–85 per person per night; check the park website for details.

Also lining the Parkway Corridor are several privately owned **lodges and mini-resorts**, ranging from the simple and unaffected to the comparatively lavish. One of the best is *Killarney Lodge* (ⓣ705/633-5551, ⓦwww.killarneylodge.com; ⑧ including meals; early May to mid-Oct), whose cosy log cabins dot a spindly promontory that hooks out into the Lake of Two Rivers (Km 32). A second good option is *Bartlett Lodge* (ⓣ705/633-5543 or 1-866/614-5355, ⓦwww.bartlettlodge.com; ⑧ including meals; mid-May to mid-Oct), comprising a scattering of eco-friendly cabins overlooking Cache Lake at Km 23. Here, you can also opt for one of two tents, which come complete with comfortable king-size beds and private deck (⑦ breakfast included). The lodge can only be reached by boat; pick up the marked phone at the jetty and someone will come to get you. If you're after a bit more wilderness, head for the lakeside *Algonquin Eco-Lodge* (ⓣ905/471-9453 or 1-800/776-9453, ⓦwww.algonquinecolodge.com; ⑧ including meals), which is well off the beaten track at the southern tip of the park. It's perfect for canoeing and hiking, but access is convoluted: leave the park via the East Gate, turn right onto Hwy 127 after **Whitney** and carry on until you reach **Maynooth**. At Maynooth, turn right onto Hwy 62 and shortly afterwards turn right again onto **County Road 10** (Peterson Rd) and watch for the lodge sign after 18km. The total distance from the East Gate to the lodge is about 70km.

Canoeing and hiking

The park interior is best explored by **canoe**, and there are several **outfitters** dotted along the Parkway Corridor. One of the best is the Portage Store at Canoe Lake (Km14; summer ⓣ705/633-5622, winter 705/789-3645, ⓦwww.portagestore.com). **Rates** vary enormously depending on the sort of canoe you rent, but the simplest models cost about $27 per day, $23 per day for five days and more. The Portage Store also rents tents, life vests and all the associated canoeist's tackle, and organizes guided canoe trips; in all cases, reservations are essential. Given Algonquin's immense popularity, canoeing is best avoided at holiday weekends: horror stories abound of three-hour jams of canoeists waiting their turn to tackle the portages between some of the more accessible lakes. Incidentally, Canoe Lake was where the artist **Tom Thomson** (see p.88) drowned in 1917 – and there's a monument to him about forty-minutes' canoe paddle from the Portage Store.

The interior can also be experienced on one of two main long-distance hiking trails. These are the **Western Uplands Backpacking Trail** (Km3), which is composed of a series of loops that allow you to construct a hike of between 32km and 88km; and the **Highland Backpacking Trail** (Km29; 19km or 35km).

Kingston

Birthplace of the rock singer Bryan Adams but prouder of its handsome limestone buildings, the city of **KINGSTON**, a fast 260km east of Toronto along Hwy 401, is the largest and most enticing of the communities along the northern shore of Lake Ontario. The town occupies an attractive and strategically important position where the lake narrows into the St Lawrence River, its potential first recognized by the French who built a fortified fur-trading post, **Fort Frontenac**, here in 1673. It was not a success, but struggled on until 1758 when it fell to a combined force of British, Americans and Iroquois, a victory soon followed by an influx of United Empire Loyalists (see p.417), who promptly developed Kingston – as they renamed it – into a major shipbuilding centre and naval base. The money rolled in and the future looked rosy when the completion of the Rideau Canal (see p.171), linking Kingston with Ottawa in 1832, opened up its hinterland. Kingston became Canada's **capital** in 1841 and although it lost this distinction just three years later it remained the region's most important town until the end of the nineteenth century. In recent years, Kingston – and its 150,000 inhabitants – has had as many economic downs as ups, but it does benefit from the presence of **Queen's University**, one of Canada's most prestigious academic institutions, and of the **Royal Military College**, the country's answer to Sandhurst and West Point.

Central Kingston's medley of old buildings displays every architectural foible admired by the Victorians, from neo-Gothic mansions with high gables and perky dormer windows to elegant Italianate villas. The cream of the stylistic crop are the city's Neoclassical limestone buildings, especially **City Hall** and the **Cathedral of St George**. Kingston also holds the first-rate **Agnes Etherington Art Centre** gallery and **Bellevue House**, once the home of Prime Minister Sir John A. Macdonald. Add to this several superb B&Bs, a cluster of good restaurants and scenic **boat trips** round the **Thousand Islands** just offshore, and you have a city that is well worth a couple of days.

Arrival and information

Trains from Toronto (4–6 daily; 2hr 30min) pull into the **train station** just off John Counter Boulevard (and near Hwy 2), an inconvenient 7km northwest of the city centre. Taxi fare from the station to downtown is about $15 or you can catch

Guided tours by land and river

Kingston offers a full complement of guided tours. Top of the list are **cruises** out amongst the **Thousand Islands** (see box, p.172) from the dock at the foot of Brock Street. The islands, which speckle the St Lawrence River as it leaves Lake Ontario, range from tiny hunks of rock to much larger islets with thick forest and lavish second homes. It's a pretty cruise at any time of the year, but especially so in autumn when the leaves turn. Several companies offer cruises, but the benchmark is set by Kingston 1000 Islands Cruises (Ⓣ613/549-5544, Ⓦwww.1000islandscruises.ca), whose three-hour sightseeing excursions are as good as any (mid-May to mid-Oct 1–3 daily; $29). Another enjoyable outing is the **Haunted Walk of Kingston**, a ninety-minute narrated stroll through the older parts of town beginning in the centre at the Prince George Hotel opposite the tourist office (May to mid-Oct 1–2 daily; $13; Ⓣ613/549-6366, Ⓦwww.hauntedwalk.com).

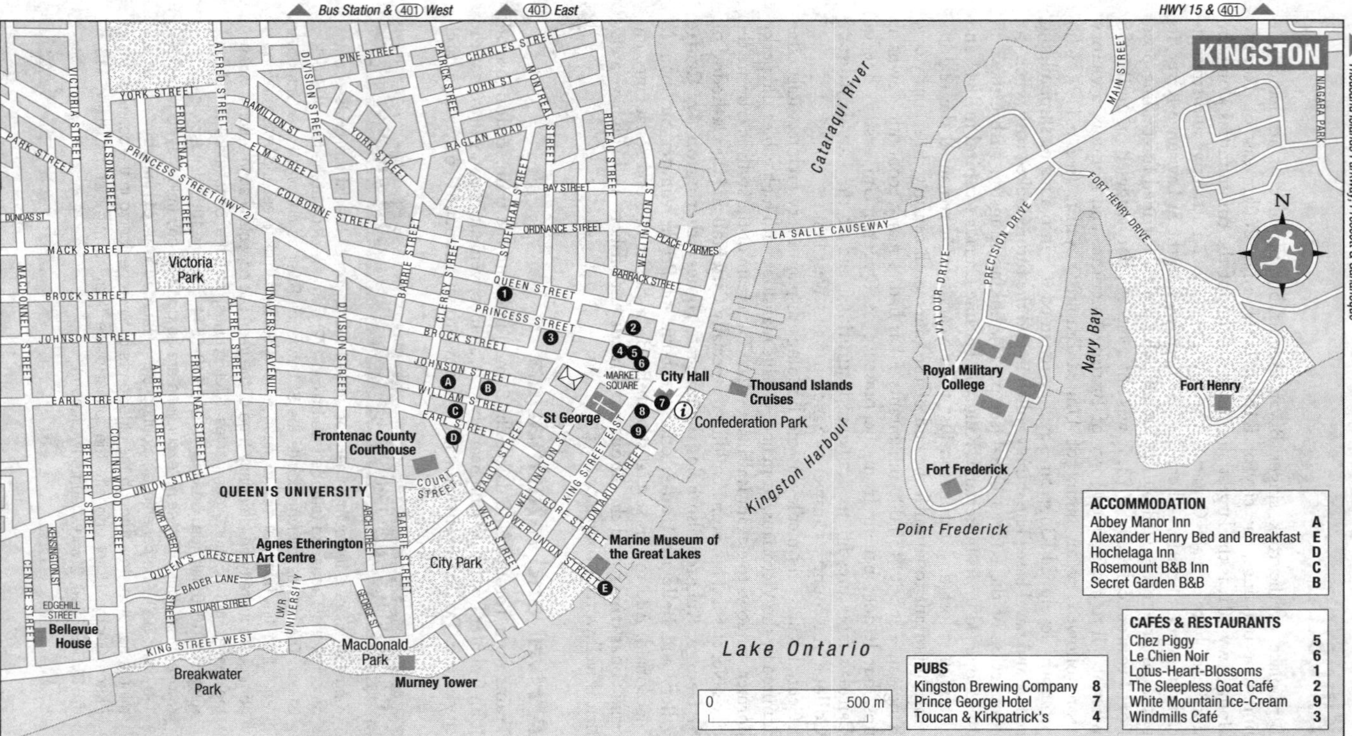
KINGSTON
Bus Station & 401 West
401 East
HWY 15 & 401
Thousand Islands Parkway, Prescott & Gananoque
Train Station & 401
Penitentiary Museum
ACCOMMODATION
Abbey Manor Inn A
Alexander Henry Bed and Breakfast E
Hochelaga Inn D
Rosemount B&B Inn C
Secret Garden B&B B
CAFÉS & RESTAURANTS
Chez Piggy 5
Le Chien Noir 6
Lotus-Heart-Blossoms 1
The Sleepless Goat Café 2
White Mountain Ice-Cream 9
Windmills Café 3
PUBS
Kingston Brewing Company 8
Prince George Hotel 7
Toucan & Kirkpatrick's 4
0 500 m
Lake Ontario
Kingston Harbour
Cataraqui River
Navy Bay
Point Frederick
Fort Frederick
Royal Military College
Fort Henry
Thousand Islands Cruises
Confederation Park
City Hall
Market Square
St George
Frontenac County Courthouse
Queen's University
Agnes Etherington Art Centre
City Park
Marine Museum of the Great Lakes
MacDonald Park
Murney Tower
Breakwater Park
Bellevue House
Victoria Park
La Salle Causeway
Fort Henry Drive
Main Street
Niagara Park
Precision Drive
Valour Drive
Place d'Armes
Barrack Street
Queen Street
Princess Street
Brock Street
Johnson Street
William Street
Earl Street
King Street East
Ontario Street
Wellington St
Gore Street
Lower Union Street
West Street
Bagot Street
Court Street
Barrie Street
Arch Street
George St
Lwr University
Queen's Crescent
Bader Lane
Stuart Street
King Street West
Union Street
Division Street
University Avenue
Alfred Street
Frontenac Street
Albert Street
Collingwood Street
Beverley Street
Kensington St
Edgehill Street
Centre Street
Macdonnell Street
Dundas St
Mack Street
Victoria Street
Nelson Street
Park Street
Princess Street (Hwy 2)
York Street
Hamilton St
Elm Street
Colborne Street
Raglan Road
Pine Street
Charles Street
John St
Patrick Street
Clergy Street
Sydenham Street
Montreal Street
Bay Street
Ordnance Street
Rideau Street
Wellington St
Lwr Albert

Kingston Transit bus C (Mon–Fri every 30min, Sat & Sun hourly). The long-distance **bus station** for both Greyhound (Ⓣ1-800/661-8747, Ⓦwww.greyhound.ca) and Coach Canada (Ⓣ1-800/461-7661, Ⓦwww.coachcanada.com) services is also on John Counter Boulevard, just west of Division Street, about 5km to the north of the city centre. Taxi fare from the bus station to downtown is about $12 or take Kingston Transit bus C (see above for times). Kingston Transit's bus information line is Ⓣ613/546-0000.

Kingston's **tourist office** is in the centre of the city, on the harbourfront at 209 Ontario St (June–Aug daily 9am–6pm; May & Sept–April daily 9am–5pm; Ⓣ613/548-4415 or 1-888/855-4555, Ⓦwww.kingstoncanada.com). It has a wide range of local and regional information and operates a free room reservation service.

Accommodation

Kingston has an excellent range of **accommodation**, much of it in or near the city centre. The best places are those inns and B&Bs which occupy grand old buildings, but there are less expensive options, most distinctively beds/berths in a decommissioned **coastguard ship**. At the top end of the market, reservations are advised in July and August.

Abbey Manor Inn 181 William St Ⓣ613/545-0422 or 1-866/723-1872, Ⓦwww.abbeymanorinn.com. This appealing, three-storey Victorian redbrick, with its inviting porch, has seven well-maintained guest rooms, all en suite and in a central location. ❻

Alexander Henry B&B 55 Ontario St Ⓣ613/542-2261, Ⓦwww.marmuseum.ca. Kingston's most unusual lodgings are in this former coastguard ice-breaker, moored downtown next to the Marine Museum. Berths vary from a bunk in a tiny cabin to more comfortable quarters in a two-berth cabin. The ship itself dates from the 1950s and is a sturdy affair with narrow stairways and corridors, all to the salty taste of the sea. Open mid-May to early Oct. ❹–❻

Hochelaga Inn 24 Sydenham St South Ⓣ613/549-5534 or 1-877/933-9433, Ⓦwww.hochelagainn.com. This sprawling inn, located in a residential area within easy walking distance of the centre, occupies a good-looking Victorian mansion with a playful central tower, bay windows and wraparound veranda. There are 21 guest rooms, all en suite, and although the furnishings and fittings are rather pedestrian, each is very comfortable. ❻

Rosemount B&B Inn 46 Sydenham St South Ⓣ613/531-8844 or 1-888/871-8844, Ⓦwww.rosemountinn.com. An eminently appealing B&B, which occupies a strikingly handsome, distinctively Italianate old limestone villa – one of Kingston's finest buildings. The *Rosemount* has ten guest rooms, all en suite, decorated in attractive period style. The breakfasts are delicious and there's an on-site "vinotherapy" spa, which uses wine-based products. ❻

Secret Garden B&B 73 Sydenham St South Ⓣ613/531-8884 or 1-888/871-8844, Ⓦwww.thesecretgardeninn.com. One of Kingston's most enjoyable B&Bs, with seven extremely comfortable rooms, all en suite and each decorated in charming antique style. The house is a fetching Victorian building of timber and brick with verandas and porches and a splendid bay-windowed tower. ❻

The City

The obvious place to start a visit is **City Hall** (guided tours: June–Sept Mon–Fri 10am–4pm, plus Sat & Sun in July & Aug 11am–3pm; 30min; free), a copper-domed, stone extravagance which, with its imposing Neoclassical columns and portico, dominates the waterfront as was intended – a suitably grand structure for what was scheduled to be the Canadian Parliament. By the time the building was completed in 1844, Kingston had lost its capital status and – faced with colossal bills – the city council had to make some quick adjustments, filling the empty corridors with shops and stalls and even a saloon. Things are more sedate today, with municipal offices occupying most of the space, but the tour does provide a fascinating insight into the development of the city and includes a trip up the **clock tower**.

Outside, the **Market Square**, at the back of City Hall, is home to an excellent open-air **market** (Mon–Sat); on summer Sundays the square is given over to craft and antiques stalls. In front of City Hall is the site of the original French outpost and this is now marked by the pocket-sized **Confederation Park**, whose manicured lawns run behind the harbour with its marina and squat, nineteenth-century Martello tower. Here also, from the dock at the foot of Brock Street, there are regular **cruises** out to and among the Thousand Islands (see p.172).

Anglican Cathedral and Marine Museum

It's a five-minute walk west from Confederation Park to Kingston's finest limestone building, the **Anglican Cathedral of St George**, at King and Johnson streets. Dating from the 1820s, the stirring lines of the cathedral, with its Neoclassical portico and dainty domes, are deceptively uniform, for the church was remodelled on several occasions, notably after severe fire damage in 1899. The capacious interior holds some delightful Tiffany stained glass windows and, attached to the wall of the nave, is a plain **memorial** to Molly Brant (1736–97), a Mohawk leader and sister of Joseph Brant (see p.126). From the cathedral, it's a brief stroll to the main commercial drag, **Princess Street**, whose assorted shops, offices and cafés stretch up from the lakeshore. Alternatively, it's a short hop back to the waterfront and the **Marine Museum of the Great Lakes** (March to late May Wed–Fri 10am–4pm & Sat noon–4pm; late May to Sept daily 10am–4pm; $8.50), at 55 Ontario St, a somewhat dowdy accumulation of maritime bygones, where the shipbuilders' gallery is of some mild interest. Moored alongside is the unusual *Alexander Henry B&B* (see p.167).

Murney Tower

From the Marine Museum, it's a five- to ten-minute stroll west to **Murney Tower** (mid-May to Aug daily 10am–5pm; $3), by the lake at the foot of Barrie Street. The most impressive of four such towers built in Kingston to defend the dockyards against an anticipated US attack during the Oregon Crisis of 1846–47, this one is packed with military memorabilia including old weapons, uniforms and recreated nineteenth-century living quarters. The design of the tower, built as a combined barracks, battery and storehouse, was copied from a Corsican tower (at Martello Point) that had proved particularly troublesome to the British navy. A self-contained, semi-self-sufficient defensive structure with thick walls and a protected entrance, the Martello design proved so successful that towers like this were built throughout the empire, only becoming obsolete in the 1870s with advances in artillery technology. Incidentally, on Christmas Day 1885, members of the Royal Canadian Rifles regiment set out to skid around the frozen lake equipped with their field **hockey sticks** and a **lacrosse ball**, thereby inventing (or at least so Kingstonians assert) the sport that has become a national passion – ice hockey.

Queen's University and the Agnes Etherington Art Centre

Striking inland up Barrie Street, with City Park on the right, it's a ten-minute walk to the top of the park, where the **Frontenac County Courthouse** of 1858 is another grand limestone pile whose whopping Neoclassical portico is fronted by a fanciful water fountain and surmounted by a copper dome. Head west from here, along Union Street, and you'll soon be in the midst of the **Queen's University campus**, whose various college buildings fan out in all directions. The place to aim for here is the first-rate **Agnes Etherington Art Centre** (Tues–Fri 10am–4.30pm,

Sat & Sun 1–5pm; $4; Ⓦwww.aeac.ca), on the corner of University Avenue and Bader Lane. The gallery has an excellent reputation for its temporary exhibitions, so the paintings are regularly rotated, but the first two rooms usually kick off in dramatic style with a vivid selection of Canadian Abstract paintings. Beyond, a healthy slice of gallery space is mostly devoted to the **Group of Seven**, with two highlights being a striking *Evening Solitude* by **Lawren Harris** and the carpet-like, rolling fields of **Arthur Lismer**'s *Québec Village*, while **Tom Thomson** chips in with his studied *Autumn, Algonquin Park*. Other exhibits to look out for are the **Inuit** prints of Kenojuak and Pitseolak – two of the best-known Inuit artists of modern times; a satisfying collection of Dutch seventeenth-century paintings, including two Rembrandts; heritage **quilts** from eastern Ontario; and the work of **Jack Bush**, who began painting in the style of the Group of Seven, but graduated into forceful, strongly coloured abstracts.

West of the centre: Bellevue House

Born in Glasgow, **Sir John Alexander Macdonald** (1815–91) emigrated to Canada in his youth, settling in Kingston, where he became a successful corporate lawyer, an MP – representing the town for nearly forty years – and ultimately prime minister (1867–73 and 1887–91). A shrewd and forceful man, Macdonald played a leading role in Canada's Confederation, with a little arm-twisting here and a little charming there, to ensure the grand plan went through. In the 1840s, Macdonald rented **Bellevue House** (daily: April–May & Sept–Oct 10am–5pm; June–Aug 9am–6pm; $3.90; Ⓦwww.pc.gc.ca), a bizarrely asymmetrical, pagoda-shaped building located about 2km west of the city centre, beyond the university campus, at 35 Centre St. The idea was that the country air would improve the health of Macdonald's wife, Isabella, whose tuberculosis was made worse by the treatment – laudanum. Isabella never returned to good health and died after years as an invalid, leaving Macdonald alone (with the bottle). Both the house and gardens have been restored to the period of the late 1840s, when the Macdonalds lived here.

The Penitentiary Museum

From Bellevue House, it's another 1km west along King Street West to the intriguing **Penitentiary Museum** (May–Oct Mon–Fri 9am–4pm, Sat & Sun 10am–4pm; donation; Ⓦwww.penitentiarymuseum.ca), which occupies the former prison warden's house dating from the 1870s – today's penitentiary is just across the street. The house was built by the prisoners and seven of its rooms now hold a fascinating assortment of exhibits, from examples of inmate arts and crafts to contraband the prisoners smuggled in and escape devices by which means they intended to get out – and no wonder they did: the "Punishment and Restraint" section has examples of the sort of fate awaiting them, from a simple wooden easel to which prisoners were tied for a good old flogging through to the large and cumbersome contraption for a touch of water-boarding.

East of the centre: Fort Frederick and Old Fort Henry

The twin headlands over the **La Salle Causeway** to the east of downtown Kingston have long been used by the military. The first is home to the **Royal Military College**, the training academy for officers of all three services, and the **Royal Military College Museum** (July & Aug daily 10am–5pm; donation; Ⓦwww.rmc.ca), housed in the old Martello tower at **Fort Frederick** and stuffed with military bric-a-brac. The second headland holds **Fort Henry** (late May to Sept daily 10am–5pm; $11.50; Ⓣ613/542-7388, Ⓦwww.forthenry.com), a large and imposing fortress built to keep the Americans at bay after the War of 1812.

The fort's thick stone-and-earth ramparts are flush with the lie of the land to protect against artillery bombardment, but as it turned out it was all a waste of time and money. Anglo-American relations improved and the fort never saw a shot fired in anger, so when the last garrison departed at the end of the nineteenth century, the fortress fell into disrepair. Restored in 1938, the fort's focus is now the large **parade ground**, where volunteers periodically dress up in military gear and fill the fort with the smoke of muskets and cannons and the racket of bugles, drums and fifes. These enactments are firmly aimed at families, and there's lots for kids to do, from joining in on drill parades and helping with the gun salute, to participating in lessons in a Victorian schoolroom. You can also explore the ramparts, with views over the St Lawrence River, and examine the fort's magazines, kitchens and officers' quarters.

Eating and drinking

Kingston has a good supply of quality **restaurants** and a wide range of inexpensive **cafés**, many of which prosper from its large student population. The city also has several lively British- and Irish-style **pubs** and a modest live music scene: for **listings**, see the bi-monthly freebie *Key to Kingston*, available from major hotels, B&Bs, restaurants and the tourist office.

Cafés and restaurants

Chez Piggy 68R Princess St ☎613/549-7673, Ⓦwww.chezpiggy.com. Something of a Kingston institution, where locals bring their kith and kin to celebrate, this large, split-level restaurant is housed in restored stables dating from 1810. The patio is packed in summer and the attractive interior has kept its rough stone walls. The wide-ranging menu features all manner of main courses served in bountiful helpings, from Thai and Vietnamese through to South American and standard North American dishes. Mains average around $23. Mon–Sat 11.30am–11.30pm, Sun 11am–10pm.

Le Chien Noir 69 Brock St ☎613/549-5635, Ⓦwww.lechiennoir.com. Spirited bar-cum-bistro with smart, modern decor and a first-rate menu featuring local, seasonal ingredients in creative combinations; try the free-range chicken with cheddar grits and asparagus. Mains average around $28. Daily 11am–10pm.

Lotus-Heart-Blossoms 185 Sydenham St ☎613/549-7777, Ⓦwww.lotus-heart-blossoms.com. Warm and modern, this vegetarian café does a good line in salads, veggie burgers and wraps. As you'll judge from their "eastern" gear, the serving staff are on the mystical hot line – with Sri Chinmoy – but they don't push it. Mains are about $9. Mon–Sat 11.30am–9pm & Sun 11am–8pm.

The Sleepless Goat Café 91 Princess St ☎613/545-9646, Ⓦwww.thesleeplessgoat.ca. Relaxed bakery-cum-café serving good sandwiches, delicious breads and rolls, great desserts and Fairtrade coffee, all at affordable prices. Mon–Fri 7am–11pm, Sat & Sun 8am–11pm.

White Mountain Ice-Cream 176 Ontario St. Seriously rich home-made ice cream and waffle cones. Try the White Mountain special: vanilla dotted with chocolate, pecan and maple brittle.

Windmills Café 184 Princess St ☎613/544-3948, Ⓦwww.windmills-cafe.com. There are good cakes and a wide-ranging menu at this agreeable café-restaurant, which serves up everything from salads and noodles to burgers and steaks. Mains average $25. Daily 7.30am–11pm.

Pubs

Kingston Brewing Company 34 Clarence St ☎613/542-4978, Ⓦwww.kingstonbrewing.ca. The best pub in town, serving natural ales and lagers brewed on the cosy premises, as well as filling bar food. The patio is a great place to park yourself and enjoy a brew in summer.

Prince George Hotel 200 Ontario St. Opposite the tourist office, the ground floor of this old inn is subdivided into two bars. There's *Tir Nan Óg* (Ⓦwww.kingston.tirnanogpubs.com), an Irish pub, and the English-style *Old Speckled Hen*.

The Toucan & Kirkpatrick's 76 Princess St ☎613/544-1966, Ⓦwww.thetoucan.ca. Two ersatz Irish bars in one building offering a wide range of domestic and imported beers, plus live gigs and DJ nights. Open until 2am nightly.

Kingston to Ottawa via the Rideau Canal

If you're travelling on **from Kingston to Ottawa**, the obvious route is east along Hwy 401 and then north up Hwy 416, a journey of 175km. With more time, it's worth considering taking **Hwy 15** and then, at Smiths Falls, **Hwy 43** (and ultimately hwys 2, 5, 13 and 73) inland from Kingston as these minor roads follow much of the route of the **Rideau Canal** (open for boats mid-May to mid-Oct; ⓦwww.pc.gc.ca). Completed in 1832 after a mere six years' work, the 202km canal – and its 24 lock stations – cuts through the slab of coniferous and deciduous forest, bogs, limestone plains and granite ridges separating Ottawa and Kingston. It was intended to provide safe inland transport at a time of poor Anglo-American relations, but after the political situation improved it developed as an important route for regional commerce. The canal's construction led to the development of **Bytown**, renamed Ottawa in 1855, but in the second half of the nineteenth century the railways made it obsolete. Today, it is plied by holiday traffic and motorists visit its **locks**. The two most interesting are **Kingston Mills** (Locks 46–49), 12km inland from Kingston on Hwy 15, and **Jones Falls** (Locks 39–42), about 50km from Kingston. At the latter, the complex includes four locks, a dam, a former blacksmith's forge and a defensible lockmaster's house.

To break the journey, aim for the pleasant little canalside town of **MERRICKVILLE** (Locks 21–23), 100km or so from Kingston. A popular tourist spot, there are several places to stay here, including around a dozen B&Bs as well as *Sam Jakes Inn*, whose modernized interior is lodged within an attractive Victorian building at 118 Main St East (ⓣ613/269-3711 or 1-800/567-4667, ⓦwww.samjakesinn.com; ⑧). More affordable is the five-room *Millisle B&B*, in an expansive Victorian house with a smashing veranda overlooking the lock at 205 Mill St (ⓣ613/269-3627, ⓦwww.bbcanada.com/millislebb; ⑥). It takes five days – and $1700 – to get from Kingston to Ottawa **by boat** on the Rideau Canal with Ontario Waterways (ⓣ705/327-5767 or 1-800/561-5767, ⓦwww.ontariowaterwaycruises.com); there are between three and six cruises monthly from mid-May to mid-October; reservations are essential.

The upper St Lawrence River

East of Kingston, Hwy 401 and the calmer, prettier Hwy 2 follow the northern shore of the **St Lawrence River**, whose island-studded waters were tricky going until the 1950s when the US and Canadian governments created the **St Lawrence Seaway**. An extraordinarily ambitious project, the Seaway extends 3790km inland from the Atlantic by means of lakes, rivers and locks to the west end of Lake Superior. Fifteen locks were installed on the St Lawrence River alone, each big enough to handle massive ocean-going freighters, while a string of dams harnessed the river's hydroelectric potential. But it all came at a price, as the Seaway necessitated the relocation of many riverside towns. There were also long-term **environmental** costs, with ships transporting species previously unknown here on their hulls and in their bilge. Use of the Seaway has declined somewhat, as shipping has been overtaken by the move towards road and air.

Leaving Kingston, **Hwy 2** begins by cutting across rolling farmland and offering fleeting views of the region's scenic highlight, the **Thousand Islands**, a confetti of lightly forested granite islands poking out of the river for the 80km between Kingston and Brockville. The islands are best seen on a **cruise**, available at most riverside towns, including Kingston (see p.165), though those from **Gananoque** and **Rockport** are generally rated the best. The towns dotting the river are not especially enthralling – the pick is low-key **Prescott** – largely because the varied charms of Ottawa (see p.174) are only 175km from Kingston. The most scenic part

The Thousand Islands

Geologically, the **Thousand Islands** form part of the Frontenac axis, a ridge of million-year-old rock that stretches down into New York State. Aboriginal peoples called the islands *Manitouana* – the "Garden of the Great Spirit" – in the belief they were created when petals of heavenly flowers were scattered on the river; more prosaically, the islands later gave their name to a salad dressing. The **Thousand Islands** first hit the national headlines in the late 1830s, when they were the haunt of an irascible Canadian pirate, William Johnston, whose irritation with the British prompted him and his gang to spend several years harrying British shipping and Canadian farmers until he retired (with his booty) to New York State. Thereafter, the islands became a popular retreat for the rich and famous – including Irving Berlin and Jack Dempsey – but it was **George Boldt**, the owner of New York's *Waldorf Astoria*, who outdid himself. In 1899, he bought one of the islands and reshaped it into a heart as a tribute to his wife – hence the name **Heart Island**. He then plonked a whopping – and whoppingly expensive – ersatz medieval castle on top of the island, but promptly abandoned **Boldt Castle** (daily: mid-May to June & Sept 10am–6.30pm; July & Aug 10am–7.30pm; early Oct 10am–5.30pm; US$4; ⓦwww.boldtcastle.com) when his wife died, taking his new salad-dressing recipe back with him back to New York.

For **cruises** out into the Thousand Islands, you're spoiled for choice, but one obvious place to aim for is **GANANOQUE**, 30km east of Kingston, where the main **cruise boat** operator is the **Gananoque Boat Line** (1hr trip, late May to mid-Oct 4–6 daily, $17; 3hr trip May to mid-Oct 2–5 daily $25; ⓣ613/382-2144 or 1-888/717-4837, ⓦwww.ganboatline.com). Highlights of the longer cruise include a good look at Just Room Enough Island, with its single tiny home, and, at the other extreme, Millionaire's Row on much larger Wellesley Island. The same company also does five-hour cruises (mid-May to late Sept 1 daily; $30, but castle extra), which include a two-hour stop at Boldt Castle; the castle is in US waters, so bring your **passport**.

From Gananoque, it's about 25km east to tiny **ROCKPORT**, the nearest Canadian dock to Boldt Castle. The **Rockport Boat Line**, 23 Front St (ⓣ613/659-3402 or 1-800/563-8687, ⓦwww.rockportcruises.com), offers a range of one- and two-hour cruises ($18/26), plus up to four trips a day over to Boldt Castle ($20).

of the drive is along the **Thousand Islands Parkway**, a 40km stretch of Hwy 2 beginning just to the east of Gananoque where the road is shadowed by a combined cycle and footpath.

There are frequent Greyhound (ⓣ1-800/661-8747, ⓦwww.greyhound.ca) and Coach Canada buses (ⓣ1-800/461-7661, ⓦwww.coachcanada.com) along Hwy 401 and VIA trains (ⓣ1-888/842-7245, ⓦwww.viarail.ca) link Kingston with Montréal or Ottawa via Brockville.

Brockville

From Kingston it's 30km east to **Gananoque**, from where there are regular boat trips out into the Thousand Islands (see above). Just beyond Gananoque, the **Thousand Islands Parkway** loops off Hwy 2 to slip along the north bank of the river, passing the hamlet of Rockport, where there are also Thousand Islands' boat trips (see above), on its scenic 40km-long route. The Parkway ends a few kilometres short of **BROCKVILLE**, a substantial little town that takes its name from the Canadian general Isaac Brock, who was killed near Niagara Falls during the War of 1812. Today the town centre is somewhat careworn, but the harbourfront is pleasant enough and the **main square** remains suitably commanding, fanning out from an ambitious war memorial. The square is flanked by sturdy stone buildings, notably the neo-Romanesque pinkish former post office and, at the top, the rambling Neoclassical County Courthouse to either side of which are no less than three good-looking Victorian churches.

Prescott and around

Pocket-sized **PRESCOTT**, 20km east of Brockville along the river, was rendered almost obsolete by the St Lawrence Seaway, but previously it had been important as a deep-water port and trans-shipment centre. Beside Hwy 2 on the east side of town, the crumbling, partly-submerged dark-black **timbers** of the old town jetty recall busier days, as does the imposing bulk of **Fort Wellington** (mid-May to Sept daily 10am–5pm; $4; Ⓦwww.pc.gc.ca). Work started on the fort in 1812 during the Anglo-American war, but by the time it was finished the war was over. The military moved out in 1869 and, after years of neglect, the fort has been returned to its 1830s appearance, complete with a two-storey blockhouse-cum-barracks, an officers' quarters, powder magazine and a cookhouse.

Prescott has one excellent **place to stay**, the *Blue Heron Inn B&B*, just west of the handful of shops that make up the town centre, at 1648 Hwy 2 (Ⓣ613/925 0562, Ⓦwww.bbcanada.com/blueheroninn; ⑤). Occupying an attractively revamped old stone house, the inn has an outdoor pool and three well-appointed en-suite guest rooms; the breakfasts are first rate.

The Battle of the Windmill

The Americans never attacked Fort Wellington, but it did serve as the muster station for the militia in the lead-up to the **Battle of the Windmill** in 1838. In the aftermath of the shambolic Rebellion of 1837, hundreds of refugee rebels took off into the Ontario bush or fled to the US. One of the larger groups hunkered down in the Thousand Islands and, together with their American sympathizers, planned an attack on Canada, hoping this would stir a general rebellion. Two hundred of them landed beside a stone windmill 2km east of Prescott, but there was no widespread uprising and the invaders ended up occupying the windmill instead. The militia surrounded them and, after a dogged fight, they were forced to surrender: eleven were executed and most of the rest were transported to Australia. The **windmill** – now a lighthouse – has survived and makes for a pleasantly brief excursion and is signed from Hwy 2.

Johnstown and the Upper Canada Village

East of Prescott, it's just 5km to **JOHNSTOWN**, where there's a **choice of routes** with Hwy 416 cutting north to Ottawa and Hwy 401 continuing along the St Lawrence River bound for Montréal. About 40km east of Prescott, Hwy 401 passes **Upper Canada Village** (mid-May to mid-Oct daily 9.30am–5pm; $19; Ⓦwww.uppercanadavillage.com), one of the region's most popular attractions. In the 1950s, the construction of the St Lawrence Seaway raised the river level, threatening many of the old buildings along the river bank. The best were painstakingly relocated to this purpose-built, sixty-acre complex, which recreates 1860s rural Ontario life with a wide range of buildings, from farmhouses and farm outhouses to a bakery, a parsonage, a church, a wool factory, a saw mill and a blacksmiths. It is all very well done and the staff dress up in period gear to demonstrate traditional skills, producing cheeses, quilts, brooms, bread and cloth in exactly the same way as their pioneer ancestors. In the adjacent riverside park is the **Battlefield Monument**, which – along with a visitor centre – commemorates the Battle of Crysler Farm in 1813, when a small force of British and Canadian soldiers drove off American invaders; Crysler Farm was itself submerged by the Seaway. From the Village, it's a 90-minute drive to Ottawa.

Ottawa

OTTAWA may be the capital of the second-biggest country on the planet, but it wrestles with its reputation as a bureaucratic labyrinth of little charm and character. The problem is that many Canadians who aren't federal employees – and even some who are – blame Ottawa for all the country's woes. All too aware of this, the Canadian government has spent big to turn Ottawa into "a city of urban grace in which all Canadians can take pride" (so the promotional literature runs) and despite the undoubted success of the policy, this very investment is itself often resented. The innate hostility is deeply rooted, dating back as far as 1857 when **Queen Victoria** declared Ottawa the capital, leaving Montréal and Toronto smarting at their rebuff.

In truth, Ottawa is neither grandiose nor tedious, but a lively cosmopolitan city of around one million, with a clutch of outstanding **national museums**, a pleasant riverside setting and superb cultural facilities like the National Arts Centre. Throw in acres of parks and gardens, miles of bicycle and jogging paths – many of them along the **Ottawa River** – lots of good hotels and B&Bs and a busy café-bar and restaurant scene and you have enough to keep the most diligent sightseer going for a day or three, maybe more. It's also here that Canada's bilingual laws really make sense: French-speaking **Gatineau**, just across the river in Québec, is commonly lumped together with Ontario's Ottawa as the "Capital Region", and on the streets of Ottawa you'll hear as much French as English.

Ottawa's festivals

Federal funding ensures national holidays – especially Canada Day on July 1 (☎613/239-5000, Ⓦwww.canadaday.gc.ca) – are celebrated in style, while seasonal **festivals** like the Winterlude and the Canadian Tulip Festival are as lavish as any in the country. Ethnic festivals embracing the city's diverse population are smaller but equally entertaining and there's a wide variety of musical festivals. The tourist office (see opposite) has the full calendar of events or check out Ⓦwww.ottawafestivals.ca. The selection below is arranged chronologically.

Winterlude ☎613/239-5000, Ⓦwww.canadascapital.gc.ca. A snow-and-ice extravaganza spread over most of the weekends in February. Concentrated around the frozen Rideau Canal, it includes ice sculptures at Confederation Park – renamed the Crystal Garden for the duration – and snow sculptures around Dows Lake. Other events include speed skating, bed- and dog-sled races.

Tulip Festival ☎613/567-5757 or 1-800/66TULIP, Ⓦwww.tulipfestival.ca. Held over three weeks from early May, this is the oldest of Ottawa's festivals. It began in 1945 when the Dutch sent 100,000 tulip bulbs to the city both to honour Canadian soldiers who had liberated the Netherlands and as a thank you for sheltering Queen Juliana, who had taken refuge in Ottawa during the war. The bulbs are planted around Parliament, along the canal and around Dows Lake, a gigantic splash of colour accompanied by concerts, parades, fireworks and a huge craft show. The major events take place in Major's Hill Park and Dows Lake – but few are free, and the festival now has a reputation for being rather touristy.

Ottawa International Jazz Festival ☎613/241-2633 or 1-888/226-4495, Ⓦwww.ottawajazzfestival.com. Ten days in late June/early July. One of Ottawa's most popular festivals, showcasing more than four hundred musicians. The main stage is in Confederation Park with concerts several times daily. In addition, local bands play around Byward Market and at city clubs.

Bluesfest ☎613/247-1188 or 1-866/258-3748, Ⓦwww.ottawabluesfest.ca. Held over ten days in July, this is Canada's largest festival of blues and gospel with concerts held in various venues and free shows in Confederation Park.

Some history

The one-time hunting ground of the Algonkian-speaking Outaouais, **Ottawa** received its first recorded European visitor in 1613 in the shape of Samuel de Champlain. The French explorer pitched up, paused to watch his aboriginal guides make offerings of tobacco to the misty falls (which now lie submerged beneath the river), and then took off in search of more appealing pastures. Later, the **Ottawa River** became a major transportation route, but the Ottawa area remained no more than a camping spot until 1800, when **Philemon Wright** snowshoed up here along the frozen Ottawa River from Massachusetts. Wright founded a small settlement, which he called Wrightstown and subsequently **Hull** (now **Gatineau**) after his parents' birthplace in England. Hull flourished but nothing much happened on the other (Ottawa) side of the river until 1826, when the completion of the **Rideau Canal** (see p.171) linked the site of present-day Ottawa to Kingston and the St Lawrence River. The canal builders were under the command of **Lieutenant-Colonel John By** and it was he who gave his name to the new settlement, **Bytown**, which soon became a hard-edged lumber town characterized by drunken brawls and broken bones.

In 1855 Bytown re-christened itself **Ottawa** in a bid to become the capital of the Province of Canada, hoping a change of name would relieve the town of its tawdry reputation. As part of their pitch, the community stressed the town's location on the border of Upper and Lower Canada and its industrial prosperity. **Queen Victoria** granted their request in 1857, though this had little to do with their efforts and much more to do with her artistic tastes: the Queen had been looking at some romantic landscape paintings of the Ottawa area and decided this was the perfect spot for a new capital. Few approved and Canada's politicians fumed at the inconvenience – former prime minister Sir Wilfred Laurier found it "hard to say anything good" about the place.

Give or take some federal buildings – including the splendid trio of neo-Gothic buildings that make up today's Parliament – Ottawa remained a workaday town until the late 1940s, when the Paris city planner **Jacques Greber** was commissioned to beautify the city with a profusion of parks, wide avenues and tree-lined pathways. The scheme transformed the city, defining much of its current appearance, and today Greber's green and open spaces confine a city centre that is a fetching mix of Victorian architecture and modern concrete-and-glass office blocks.

Arrival and information

Ottawa International Airport (Ⓦwww.ottawa-airport.ca) is located about 15km south of the city centre. From the airport, the **YOW Airporter** (daily every 30min 5am–11pm; $15 one-way, $25 return; Ⓣ613/260-2359, Ⓦwww.yowshuttle.com) runs to over twenty downtown hotels, either on its standard route or by request. City bus #97 (daily every 20–30min 5am–2am), operated by OC Transpo (Ⓦwww.octranspo.com), makes the same journey at a fraction of the cost and will drop you downtown at several stops. A **taxi** from the airport to downtown costs $30.

Ottawa's **train station** (Ⓣ1-888/842-7245, Ⓦwww.viarail.ca) is on the south-eastern outskirts of the city, about 4km from the centre, off the Queensway (Hwy 417) at 200 Tremblay Rd. There are direct services to and from Kingston, Montréal and Toronto. OC Transpo buses #94 and #95 go downtown from the train station; the same journey by taxi costs about $15. **Long-distance buses**, including Greyhound (Ⓣ1-800/661-8747, Ⓦwww.greyhound.ca), use the **bus station**, 1.5km south of the city centre at 265 Catherine St, at Kent, just off the Queensway. Take OC Transpo bus #4 to get downtown.

The **Capital Infocentre**, 90 Wellington St at Metcalfe (daily: mid-May to Aug 9am–9pm; Sept to mid-May 9am–5pm; Ⓣ613/239-5000 or 1-800/465-1867,

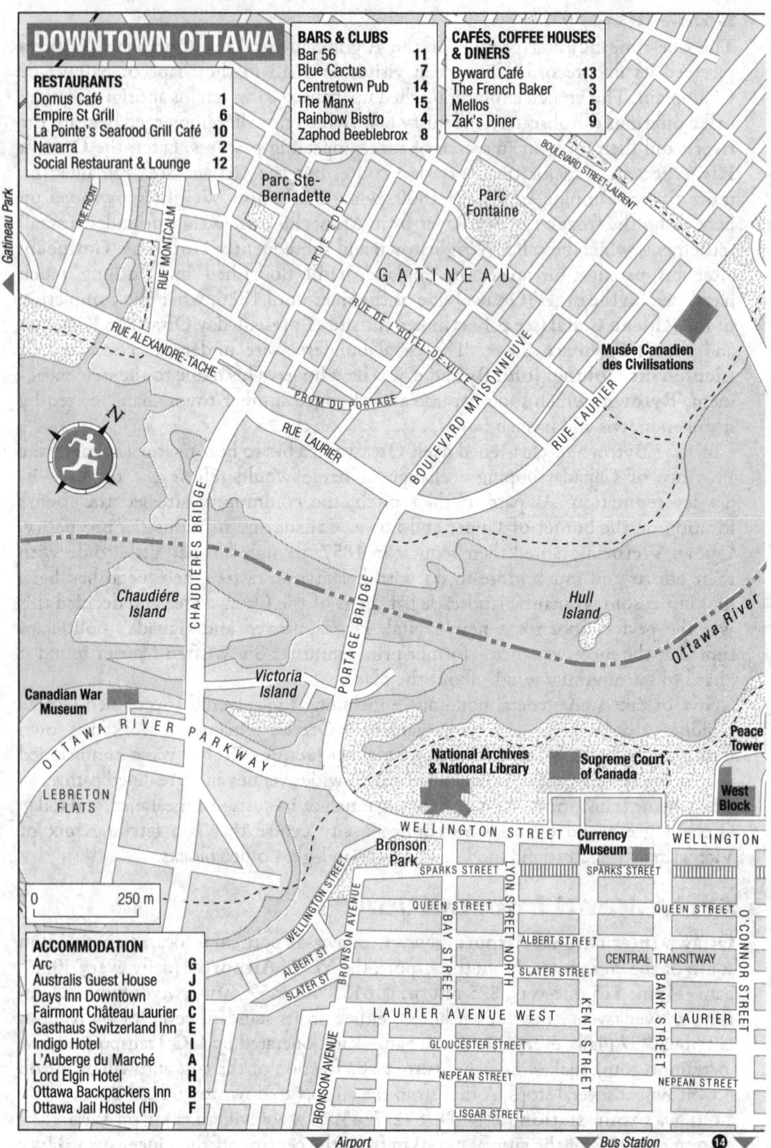

ⓦ www.canadascapital.gc.ca), is located opposite the Parliament Buildings. It's a busy place, so don't be surprised if you have to queue. It has racks of free leaflets, including a useful *Visitor Guide*, and the staff issue free public transport maps and will help you find accommodation. They also sell the **Capital Museums Passport**, which is valid for seven days and allows the bearer free admission into Ottawa and Gatineau's nine leading museums. The cost is $30 ($75 per family of up to five), so you have to be fairly diligent to make it pay. The passport is also on sale at participating museums.

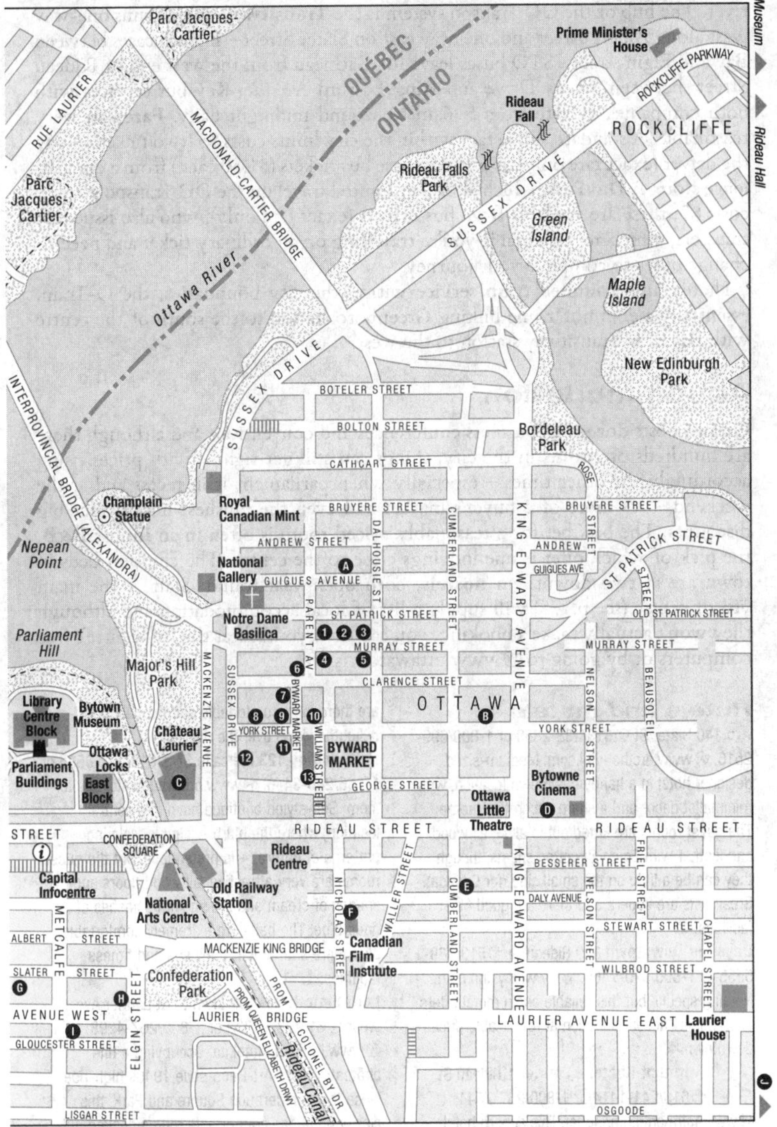

City transport

Most of Ottawa's key attractions – as well as most of its better restaurants, bars and hotels – are clustered in the downtown area within comfortable walking distance of Confederation Square. If you're venturing further afield, you may need to catch a **bus**. **OC Transpo** (Ⓣ613/741-4390, Ⓦwww.octranspo.com) provides a comprehensive network of bus services across Ottawa and its suburbs, while **STO buses** (Ⓣ819/770-3242, Ⓦwww.sto.ca) cover Gatineau and the north side of the river. The hub of the OC Transpo system is the **Transitway**, which runs one-way west along Albert Street and one-way east on Slater Street – in both cases between Bay and Elgin streets. STO buses leave for Gatineau from the west end of Rideau Street, between Sussex Drive and King Edward Avenue. Key bus services with both companies operate from 5–6am to around midnight daily. **Fares** are very reasonable. A standard single fare within the city limits costs $3 (two tickets) – pay the driver (exact fare only) or pre-purchase bus tickets ($1.50 each) from a convenience store. A **DayPass**, which allows unlimited travel on the OC Transpo system, costs $7; these are available from bus drivers (exact fare only), who also issue free transfers, which are essential if you're travelling on an ordinary ticket and need to change buses to complete your journey.

There's also a limited **train** service within the city boundaries, the O-Train, essentially a commuter line linking Greenboro station to the south of the centre with Bayview Transitway station to the west.

Accommodation

Ottawa hosts dozens of business conferences and conventions and although there are hundreds of **rooms** in the city, things can still get tight – with prices rising accordingly. At other times – especially when parliament is in recess and at the weekend – it's more of a buyer's market and even the plushest hotels offer big discounts. The best bet for a reasonably priced room is often in an **inn** or **B&B**, the pick of which offer prime lodgings close to the centre. The cheapest beds in town are at two downtown **hostels**, both open year-round. Staff at the main visitor centre (see p.175) will supply a list of local accommodation and although they won't actually make a booking, you can do it yourself at the Infocentre's free computers or by going to Ⓦwww.ottawatourism.ca.

Hotels and motels

Arc 140 Slater St Ⓣ613/238-2888 or 1-800/699-2516, Ⓦwww.arcthehotel.com. Medium-sized designer hotel in a handy downtown location, with minimalist decor and a sharp decorative theme. The guest rooms are kitted out in style, all wood and leather with Egyptian cotton sheets, though they can be a little on the small side (for Canada). Breakfasts are superb and there are good fitness facilities. ⑥

Days Inn Downtown 319 Rideau St Ⓣ613/789-5555 or 1-800/329-7466, Ⓦwww.daysinn.com. Nothing special but this reliable chain motel offers good quality accommodation at reasonable prices downtown. ④

Fairmont Château Laurier 1 Rideau St Ⓣ613/241-1414 or 1-800/257-7544, Ⓦwww.fairmont.com/laurier. This superb hotel, Ottawa's finest, has pretty much everything. It was opened in 1912 as a prestige railway hotel for the Grand Trunk Pacific Railway. A fine example of the French Renaissance – or château – style, the exterior is a forest of copper-clad turrets, spires and towers. Inside, the public areas boast marble floors, high ceilings, chandeliers and soaring columns, plus extravagantly embossed lifts. The rooms themselves are not quite as grand, but they are thoroughly comfortable and the best offer delightful views over the river. ⑥

Hotel Indigo 123 Metcalfe St Ⓣ613/231-6555 or 1-866/246-3446, Ⓦwww.ottawadowntownhotel.com. Self-styled boutique hotel in a central location, where the blurb – 'simple, calming patterns of nature' – is pretentious, but the guest rooms are very attractive, all wood floors and shades of cream and brown with splashes of deep blue. The beds are extremely comfortable, plus there's an indoor pool, spa and fitness facilities. ⑦

Lord Elgin Hotel 100 Elgin St at Laurier Ave West Ⓣ613/235-3333 or 1-800/267-4298, Ⓦwww.lordelginhotel.ca. Occupying a fine château-meets-Art-Deco-style 1940s high-rise close to Confederation Square and Park, this classy hotel has comfortable rooms decked out with crisp, modern furnishings. The prices are reasonable, with discounts on the weekend. ⑦

Inns and B&Bs

Australis Guest House 89 Goulburn Ave Ⓣ613/235-8461, Ⓦwww.bbcanada.com/1463.html. Self-billed as "A touch of Australia", this cosy B&B is in a straightforward terrace house a couple of kilometres east of the Rideau Canal, just off –

and to the south of – Laurier Ave East. It has just two guest rooms (one en suite), both decorated in a folksy style. ④

Gasthaus Switzerland Inn 89 Daly Ave at Cumberland ⓣ613/237-0335 or 1-888/663-0000, ⓦwww.ottawainn.com. There are 22, pleasant en-suite rooms in this long-established, three-storey stone inn, which dates from the 1870s. Some of the rooms are kitted out in modern style, others are distinctly retro. The inn prides itself on its breakfasts, especially its (Swiss-style) muesli. The central location is great, but the streets nearby are a tad seedy. ⑤

L'Auberge du Marché 87 Guigues Ave ⓣ613/241-6610 or 1-800/465-0079, ⓦwww.aubergedumarche.ca. In the heart of Byward Market, this extremely appealing B&B occupies an unassuming, two-storey, nineteenth-century brick house, whose interior has been renovated in sympathetic style. There are four a/c bedrooms (one en suite) and the breakfasts are first-rate. It's a popular spot, so reservations are recommended. ③

Hostels

Ottawa Backpackers Inn 203 York St ⓣ613/241-3402 or 1-888/394-0334, ⓦwww.ottawahostel.com. Spartan, informal, medium-sized hostel in a chalet-like building on a very ordinary sidestreet close to the Byward Market. Self-catering facilities, internet access and linen supplied (free). Forty-five beds in dorms of up to ten bunk-beds. $25 per person per night, doubles cost $70. ③

Ottawa Jail Hostel 75 Nicholas St at Daly ⓣ613/235-2595 or 1-866/299-1478, ⓦwww.hihostels.ca/ottawa. At Ottawa's old prison, which has been converted into an HI hostel, visitors sleep in former cells, complete with bars on the windows. The old admissions area is now a kitchen, the former chapel a TV and games lounge. There are six- or eight-bed dorms ($33/29, non-members $38/34), a more private and family-suited "warden's quarters" ($120, non-members $150), a twin cell ($40, non-members $45), a private cell ($55, non-members $60) or double rooms ($77, non-members $87); rates for all rooms (except the warden's quarters) drop slightly from Oct–early May. There's also a laundry, free bedding, internet access and free wi-fi. It's handily located downtown, just south of Rideau Street's Rideau Shopping Centre. Reservations recommended.

The City

Almost all of Ottawa's major sights are clustered on or near the south bank of the Ottawa River to either side of the Rideau Canal. It's here you'll find the monumental Victorian architecture of **Parliament Hill**, the outstanding art collection of the **National Gallery** and the **Byward Market**, the hub of the restaurant and bar scene. Many visitors only cover these, but there are a clutch of other attractions, most memorably the fascinating **Canadian War Museum**, housed in a striking building a couple of kilometres to the west of the centre, and **Laurier House**, packed with the possessions of the former prime minister William Lyon Mackenzie King and located 1.5km southeast of downtown. There is also some minor attractions to the east of the centre, on the far side of the Rideau River, principally the governor-general's mansion, **Rideau Hall**, and the **Canada Aviation Museum**.

Parliament Hill

Perched high above the Ottawa River, on the limestone bluff that is **Parliament Hill**, Canada's postcard-pretty **Parliament Buildings** (ⓦwww.parl.gc.ca/vis) have a distinctly ecclesiastical air, their spires, pointed windows and soaring clock tower amounting to "a stupendous splodge of Victoriana" as travel writer Jan Morris expressed it. Begun in 1859 and seventy years in the making, the complex comprises a trio of sturdy neo-Gothic structures, whose architectural certainties were both a statement of intent for the emergent country and a demonstration of the long reach of the British Empire. The Parliament Buildings were designed to be both imperial and imperious, but they certainly didn't overawe the original workmen, who urinated on the copper roof to speed up the oxidization process.

Tickets for Centre Block

In the summer, tickets for guided tours of Centre Block are available at the **Info-Tent** (mid-May to late June daily 9am–5pm; late June–Aug Mon–Fri 9am–8pm, Sat & Sun 9am–5pm), which is erected behind West Block and to the left of Centre Block every year. From early September to mid-May, head instead for the Visitor Welcome Centre at the base of the Peace Tower.

Two popular events are staged on Parliament Hill: the **Changing of the Guard**, when the Governor General's Foot Guards march onto the Hill dressed in full ceremonial uniform of bright-red tunics and bearskin hats – if it's hot enough, you might even see some of them topple over in a faint (daily: late June to late Aug 10–10.30am); and a free summer-evening **sound and light show** (early July to mid-Sept), illustrating Canada's history with alternate French and English performances nightly.

Centre Block

Dominating architectural proceedings is **Centre Block** (guided tours when parliament in session: weekday mornings and some afternoons, plus Sat & Sun 9am–3.20pm; when parliament not in session: daily 9am–3.20pm; free; ⓣ613/992-4793), home of the Senate and the House of Commons and in fact a replacement for the original building, which was destroyed by fire in 1916. This second structure was supposed to be the same as its predecessor, but it ended up about twice the size. The **Peace Tower**, rising from the middle of the facade, was added in 1927 as a memorial to Canadians who served in World War I. The Peace Tower can be visited independently (same times; free) and is not part of the **guided tour**, whose (changeable) itinerary includes a quick gambol round the **House of Commons**, where the Speaker's chair is partly made of English oak from Nelson's flagship *Victory*, and the red-carpeted **Senate** with its murals of scenes from World War I surmounted by a beautiful gilded ceiling. At the back of the Centre Block is the **Library**, the only part of the building to have survived the fire of 1916; the circular design and the intricately carved wooden galleries make it the most charming part of the building.

The **debates** in both the House of Commons and the Senate are open to the public, who can observe proceedings from the public galleries. Most of the gallery seats are pre-booked, but a small number are allocated on the day, on a first-come, first-served basis: ask for further information on arrival. To check what is being debated and when, consult the website. Parliament's liveliest debates are usually during **Question Period**, when the Opposition interrogates the Prime Minister.

West Block, East Block and the grounds

Flanking Centre Block are **West Block** (no public access) and **East Block** (July & Aug daily 10am–5pm; free), where the guided tour pops into four Confederation-era rooms, most memorably the original governor general's office and the Privy Council Chamber. Costumed guides provide the history. The manicured lawns surrounding the Parliament Buildings are dotted with **statues**, two of the more interesting occupying a tiny hillock just to the west of Centre Block. Here, **Queen Victoria** has been stuck on a plinth guarded by a lion and offered laurels from below, while **Lester Pearson** (Prime Minister 1963–68) lounges in an armchair, the epitome of the self-confident statesman. Round the back of Centre Block there are pleasant views across the Ottawa River to Gatineau (see p.186) with the low green hills of Québec rolling away into the distance.

Confederation Square and the Rideau Canal

Triangular **Confederation Square**, a brief stroll from Parliament Hill, is a breezy open space dominated by the magnificent **National War Memorial**, in which a soaring stone arch is surmounted by representations of liberty and peace. Down below, a swirling, finely executed bronze depicts returning service men and women passing through the arch – from war to peace – and manages to convey both their exultation and sorrow. To the square's west, across Elgin Street, is **Sparks Street**, a pedestrianized strip of shops and restaurants, but probably most notable as the site of Canada's only **political assassination** at the federal level: a suspected Fenian sympathizer shot Thomas D'Arcy McGee, a father of confederation, here in 1868; a decent pub on the corner of Sparks and Elgin streets now bears McGee's name. On the southeast side of the square is the complex of low concrete buildings that houses the **National Arts Centre** (see p.188), which clunks down to the **Rideau Canal**, a narrow sliver of water that becomes the **world's longest skating rink** in winter. Opposite, across the canal, rise the stirring lines of Ottawa's former **railway station**, now – rather sadly – a conference centre.

Following the west side of the Rideau Canal north towards the Ottawa River, it only takes a minute or two to reach the pretty flight of **locks** connecting the canal and river, with Parliament Hill rising on one side, the *Fairmont Château Laurier* on the other. Beside the foot of the locks is the **Bytown Museum** (daily mid-May to mid-Oct 10am–5pm; mid-Oct to mid-May Tues–Sun 11am–4pm; $6; Ⓦwww.bytownmuseum.com), Ottawa's oldest building, where military supplies were stored during the construction of the canal. Here, a short film explores the history of the waterway and the difficulties involved in its construction; afterwards you can take a peek at a scattering of bygones from the city's earliest days. During the summer, **canal boat trips** leave from the top of the locks, **river trips** from the bottom. The main operator is Paul's Boat Lines (Ⓣ613/225-6781, Ⓦwww.paulsboatcruises.com), who charge $16 for an hour-long canal cruise, $18 for the river. There are no more than seven and no less than three river and canal departures from May to October; reservations are advised.

Major's Hill Park and Nepean Point

Doubling back from the Bytown Museum, climb up the steps to the **bridge** abutting Confederation Square and it's a short walk east to **Sussex Drive**, whose southern section holds some of Ottawa's oldest buildings, mostly stone houses that now accommodate a battery of chi-chi shops and restaurants. Nearby, **Major's Hill Park** rolls across a small hill above the Ottawa River. This was where Colonel By decided to build his house and the extant foundations bear a plaque attesting to its history. Major's Hill Park slopes down towards **Nepean Point**, a pint-sized headland that nudges out into the river bisected by the main road – and bridge – to Gatineau (see p.186). On the far side of the road a path climbs up the headland to an outside theatre and, at the tip, a statue of Champlain, from where there are wide river views. The statue is actually a cock-up dating back to 1915: Champlain is shown holding his astrolabe – his navigational aid – aloft, but it is in fact upside down.

National Gallery of Canada

Across the road from Major's Hill Park, the **National Gallery of Canada** (daily May–Sept 10am–5pm, Thurs till 8pm; Oct–April Tues–Sun 10am–5pm, Thurs till 8pm; $9, free Thurs after 5pm; Ⓦwww.national.gallery.ca) occupies a cleverly conceived building whose acres of glass reflect the turrets and pinnacles of Parliament Hill. The collection was founded in 1880 by the then-governor general, the Marquis of Lorne, who persuaded each member of the Royal Canadian Academy to donate a painting or two. Over the next century artworks were gathered from all over the world, resulting in a permanent collection now numbering more than 25,000 pieces. The exhibits are rotated, so although the paintings mentioned below will probably be on display, there are no guarantees; the gallery also holds world-class **temporary exhibitions**. The collection spreads over two main levels and free plans are issued at the reception desk; the gallery shop sells guides to both the permanent collection and the exhibitions.

The Canadian galleries: 1750 to 1880

The **Canadian galleries**, laid out in roughly chronological order on **Level 1**, are the finest in the building, following the history of Canadian painting from the mid-eighteenth century to modern times. They begin with religious art from Québec, including a flashy gilded high altar of basswood and butternut by **Paul Jourdain**. A further section is devoted to the emergence of secular art in early-nineteenth-century Québec, with paintings by immigrant artists trained in Europe. The most notable of these was **Joseph Légaré**, a painter, politician and nationalist; his *Cholera Plague, Québec* is a typical example of his fastidiously romantic work. For popularity, none could match **Cornelius Krieghoff**, who could turn his hand to anything requested by his middle class patrons – as illustrated by his *Winter Landscape* and *White Horse Inn by Moonlight*; for more on **Krieghoff**, see p.87. Close by, just off the main concourse, is one of the gallery's more unusual exhibits, the **Rideau Street Chapel**, rebuilt piece by piece after it was threatened with demolition in 1972. Designed in the 1880s by the architect and priest Canon Georges Bouillon for a local convent school, it has slender cast-iron columns supporting a fan-vaulted ceiling – one of the few extant examples of its kind in North America.

Back on the main gallery concourse, a small collection of early nineteenth-century paintings from the Maritimes and Ontario occupies Room A104. The highlight here is the unique **Croscup Room** from Nova Scotia. Once the living room of a shipping family, it's altogether a peculiar affair, its bright and cheerful murals juxtaposing an apparently haphazard mix of images from mid-nineteenth-century North America and Europe – portraits of Micmac Indians next to bagpipe-playing Scots and so forth. Here also, look out for the evocative frontier scenes of **Paul Kane**, Canada's first artist-explorer; for more on Kane, see p.87.

The Canadian galleries: 1880s to 1920s

In the second half of the nineteenth century Canadians were still in thrall to European masters – the Royal Canadian Academy of Arts sent its students to Paris to complete their training – and this state of affairs continued into the twentieth century. The soberly romantic rural scenes of **Homer Watson** illustrate the point, their inspiration derived from contemporary Dutch landscape painters.

It was to be the **Group of Seven** (see p.88) who developed a Canadian aesthetic in a style that aimed to capture the spirit and vastness of the northern landscape, rather than rendering it into a tamer European version and vision. The two rooms devoted to the Group's canvases feature the seminal paintings of **Tom Thomson**, whose startling *Jack Pine* was in effect the Group's clarion call – trees, often windswept or dead, are a constant symbol in the Group's landscape paintings. Using rapid, brash and often brutal brushstrokes, the Group's works are faithful less to the landscape itself than to the emotions they evoked – **Lawren Harris**'s *North Shore, Lake Superior*, A.Y. Jackson's *Red Maple* and J.E.H. Macdonald's *The Solemn Land* are all memorable examples.

The Canadian galleries: 1930s to 1960s

After Macdonald's death in 1932, the Group of Seven formed the **Canadian Group of Painters**, embracing all Canadian artists of the time whatever their style. Landscape remained the dominant genre in this period, but the effects of the Depression forced politics to the fore; *Ontario Farm House* by **Carl Schaefer**, which turns a landscape into a social statement, is a first-rate example.

Following the **Canadian Group of Painters** is a selection of **abstract paintings** produced in Montréal from the 1940s to the 1970s. In Canada, it was the **Montréal Automatistes** who first explored abstraction, though the **Platiciens**, who hit the artistic big-time in the 1950s, rejected their emphasis on the expressive qualities of colour, choosing geometrical and analytical forms instead. Elsewhere in Canada, other painters chose a very different route, most strikingly **Alex Colville**, whose magic realism is seen to good advantage in his *To Prince Edward Island*, an acrylic emulsion on masonite work from 1965.

The contemporary art collection

Beginning with the 1960s, the **Contemporary Art collection** is spread over Levels 1 and 2. The highlights here are almost exclusively the work of American artists, most notably **Andy Warhol**'s *Brillo Soap Pads Boxes*, his serigraphs of Chairman Mao and George Segal's life-size assemblage *The Gas Station*. Canadians pop up here and there, but they almost always seem to take the lead from foreigners – witness the shadow of New York's Abstract Expressionists falling over Charles Gagnon's *Cassation/Open/Ouvert*.

The Inuit collection

The gallery's small but eclectic collection of **Inuit art and sculpture** is displayed in the basement. The kernel of the Inuit material is its soapstone sculptures, but there are whale bone and ivory pieces, as well as brightly coloured drawings. Two particular sculptors to look out for are **Charlie Inukpuk**, who carved the elemental *Woman who Killed a Bear with a Mitten*, and **Jackoposie Oopakak**, whose superb *Nunali* is a representation of the whole Arctic world delicately carved onto a set of caribou antlers.

The European galleries

On Level 2, the **European galleries** begin with a medley of medieval Gothic and Renaissance paintings and panel-paintings from Northern Europe, though it's the collection of works from **seventeenth-century** Europe that is most impressive. There's Bernini's sculpture of his patron Pope Urban VIII, Claude Lorrain's *Landscape with a Temple of Bacchus*, an *Entombment* by Rubens, Rembrandt's sumptuous *Heroine from the Old Testament* and Van Dyck's *Suffer the Little Children to Come Unto Me*.

From Britain in the **eighteenth century** there are portraits by Reynolds and Gainsborough plus the iconic *Death of General Wolfe* by **Benjamin West**, an American who became George III's official painter. West depicts Wolfe in a Christ-like pose, lying wounded and surrounded by his adjutants – and the painting made Wolfe a British hero. The **nineteenth-century** selection is basically a show of minor paintings by great artists, but Turner's *Mercury and Argus* is of interest, its shimmering sunset anticipating the exquisite qualities of his later works.

The final European galleries feature **twentieth century** works, featuring a diverse and top-quality range of paintings and sculptures, including works by Klimt, Matisse, Picasso and Dali.

The Abstract Expressionists

One room on Level 2 is devoted to **American Abstract Expressionists**. This is where you'll usually find **Barnet Newman**'s *Voice of Fire*, the very mention of which causes some Canadians to froth at the mouth – not because of its artistic significance but because it cost a cool $1.76m. The artist intended the 5.5-metre-high piece to give the viewer a "feeling of his own totality, of his own separateness, of his own individuality, and at the same time of his connection to others, who are also separate". Such blandishments did not satisfy everyone; one Tory MP ranted that it looked like "…two cans of paint and two rollers and about 10 minutes would do the trick" – and indeed it really is just three parallel lines, two blue and one red in the middle. The same room also contains lesser works by Jackson Pollock and Mark Rothko.

Notre Dame and the Royal Canadian Mint

The twin silver spires of the capital's Catholic cathedral, the **Notre Dame Basilica** (Mon 11.30am–6pm, Tues–Sat 9am–6pm & Sun 8am–8pm; free), poke high into the sky across the street from the National Gallery. Completed in 1890, the neo-Gothic cathedral has a long and gaudily decorated nave reaching a sort of ecclesiastical crescendo in a massive high altar piece, which is flanked by a herd of pious wooden sculptures, many of which were carved by the carpenters and masons who worked on the Parliament Buildings.

From the basilica, it's a brief stroll north along Sussex Drive to the **Royal Canadian Mint** (guided tours: mid-May to Aug Mon–Fri 9am–6pm, Sat & Sun 9am–4.30pm; Sept to mid-May daily 9am–4pm; $5, $3.50 on weekends; Ⓦwww.mint.ca), where you can view different aspects of currency production and design – though the printing and minting is now done in Winnipeg.

West of the centre: the Canadian War Museum

The exemplary **Canadian War Museum** (daily May–June & Sept–early Oct 9.30am–5pm, Thurs till 8pm; daily July–Aug 9.30am–6pm, Thurs & Fri till 8pm; mid-Oct to April Tues–Sun 9.30am–5pm, Thurs till 8pm; $12; free on Thurs after 4pm; Ⓦwww.warmuseum.ca) is housed in a striking modern building at 1 Vimy Place, on Lebreton Flats, a parcel of land beside the Ottawa River about 2km west of Confederation Square. The museum is divided into four main display areas, which work their way through Canada's military history with an accompanying text and quotations. The first gallery, the 'Battleground: Wars on Our Soil, earliest times to 1885', features a good selection of Native Canadian weaponry – tomahawks, muskets and so forth – plus a curious suit of West Coast 'armour', made of leather and Chinese coins. The museum really gets into its stride when it reaches **World War I**. There are lots of fascinating photographs in this section, but it's the incidental detail that impresses most: Canada was keen for its soldiers to use a Canadian rifle, but the end product – the Ross Rifle – often jammed, while the rum ration came in barrels labelled "SRD" (Service Regimental Depot), which the troops re-branded as "Seldom Reaches Destination". The section on World War II is similarly intriguing and there's good stuff on the Cold War – including details of the strange case of the Russian defector **Igor Gouzenko**, who was so scared of retribution that he was often interviewed with a bag over his head. Next door to the fourth gallery is the **Lebreton Gallery**, a large hangar packed with all sorts of military hardwear, such as tanks, armoured cars and artillery pieces.

Southeast of the centre: Laurier House

The **Laurier House**, about 1km east of the Laurier Bridge at 335 Laurier Ave East (April to mid-May Mon–Fri 9am–5pm; daily mid-May to early Oct 9am–5pm; $3.90; Ⓦwww.pc.gc.ca), is the former home of prime ministers Sir Wilfred Laurier and William Lyon Mackenzie King. **Laurier**, Canada's first French-speaking prime

▲ The Canadian War Museum, Ottawa

minister, served from 1896 to 1911, while **Mackenzie King**, his self-proclaimed "spiritual son", was Canada's longest-serving – from 1921 to 1930 and 1935 to 1948. Notoriously pragmatic, King enveloped his listeners in a fog of words through which his political intentions were barely discernible. The perfect illustration – and his most famous line – was "Not necessarily conscription, but conscription if necessary", supposedly a clarification of his plans at the onset of World War II. Even more famous than his obfuscating rhetoric was his personal eccentricity. His fear that future generations would view him simply as the heir of his grandfather William Lyon Mackenzie – who led the Upper Canada rebellions of the 1830s (see p.66) – eventually led him into spiritualism. He held regular séances to tap the advice of great dead Canadians, including Laurier, who allegedly communicated to him through his pet dog.

King's possessions dominate the **house**; look for his crystal ball and a portrait of his obsessively adored mother, in front of which he placed a red rose every day. The house also contains a reconstruction of a study belonging to Prime Minister **Lester B. Pearson**, who was awarded the Nobel peace prize for his role in the 1956 Arab–Israeli dispute.

East of the centre: Rideau Falls, Rideau Hall and beyond

Take Sussex Drive out of the city centre and you soon reach **Rideau Falls**, at the mouth of the Rideau River, where the twin cataracts are separated by Green Island. It's a pleasant spot and you can stroll out into the **Rideau Falls Park** or follow the **Rockcliffe Parkway**, which sticks close to the river bank on its way to the Aviation Museum. En route, you'll pass the riverside **Prime Minister's Residence**, a stately stone mansion barely visible through the trees at 24 Sussex Drive, and then the Neoclassical **Rideau Hall** (free guided tours, call Ⓣ 1-866/842-4422, Ⓦ www.gg.ca for schedule), home of Canada's governors general since Confederation. The hall's **gardens** of maples and fountains are usually open from 8am to one hour before sunset; call ahead to be certain.

Canada Aviation Museum

At the east end of the Rockcliffe Parkway, 5km from downtown, is the huge hangar of the **Canada Aviation Museum** (daily May–Aug 9am–5pm; Sept–April Wed–Sun 10am–5pm; $9; Ⓦ www.aviation.technomuses.ca). Highlights include a replica of the *Silver Dart*, which made the first powered flight in Canada in 1909; it flew for a full nine minutes, a major achievement for a contraption that seems to be made out of spare parts and old sheets. There are also bombers and fighters from both world wars and later, including a British Harrier jet.

Gatineau

Though firmly incorporated within the Capital Region, **GATINEAU** (formerly **Hull**), lying just across the river from Ottawa in the province of Québec, remains quite distinct and predominantly francophone. For years it served mainly as Ottawa's nightspot as its bars were open two hours longer than those in the capital, but with this alcoholic advantage now gone – and its paper mills relegated to minor importance – Gatineau struggles to compete with its neighbour. It does have one major museum, the **Musée Canadien des Civilisations**, and it also edges the handsome scenery of **Gatineau Park**, whose assorted lakes and forested hills cover no less than 360 square kilometres and is a prime spot for **hiking, mountain biking** and **cross-country skiing**.

STO **buses** (Ⓣ819/770-3242, Ⓦwww.sto.ca) operate a frequent service from the west end of Rideau Street to the Musée Canadien des Civilisations or you can walk – it only takes ten minutes to get there from the National Gallery. There are no buses to Gatineau Park.

Musée Canadien des Civilisations

Standing on the far side of the Alexandra Bridge from the National Gallery is Gatineau's pride and joy, the whopping **Musée Canadien des Civilisations** (daily: Sept to early Oct, Thurs until 8pm, Thurs 8pm; early Oct–April Tues–Sun 9.30am–5pm, Thurs until 8pm; $12; Ⓦwww.civilization.ca), whose distinctive, curvy limestone contours are supposed to represent the rocky sweep of the Canadian Shield; the best view is from the Ottawa side of the river.

The museum spreads over four floors and the entrance, where you can pick up a free plan, is on Level 2. Also on Level 2 is a mixed bag of attractions, including a Children's Museum and an IMAX screen showing nature and adventure films (for a supplementary fee). Upstairs, Level 3 holds **Canada Hall**, which tracks through Canada's history from the Viking colony on Newfoundland (see p.482) to the 1970s. It's an ambitious affair, featuring life-size reconstructions of historical environments, including among others an Acadian settlement and a fur-trading post, a Métis camp, a frontier farm, a Maritime shipyard and an Ontarian Main Street circa 1900. Level 4 holds temporary exhibitions and then it's down to Level 1 for the **Grand Hall**, easily the largest room in the museum and perfectly designed to display a magnificent collection of around twenty Pacific Coast **totem poles**. The main line of poles stands outside six native "houses" which explore Pacific Coast native culture, including displays on trade, religious beliefs, tribal gatherings and art.

Gatineau Park

Long popular with the capital's hikers and cyclists, the forested hills and lakes of **Gatineau Park** (Ⓦwww.canadascapital.gc.ca/gatineau) begin just 3km to the west of the Musée Canadien des Civilisations – just follow the signs. The park was founded in 1934 when the government snapped up the land to stop its deforestation for firewood during the hard years of the Depression and it's now latticed with **hiking trails**, many of which are readily reached along the park's most scenic road, the **Champlain Parkway**, which is a turning off the park's main road, the **Gatineau Parkway**. The Champlain Parkway meanders its way

Byward Market

Since the 1840s, the **Byward Market** neighbourhood (known simply as "The Market" to locals), just east of Sussex Drive and north of Rideau Street, has been a centre for the sale of farm produce, but it's now also Ottawa's hippest, hottest district. At its heart, the 1920s **Byward Market building** (mid-May to mid-Oct daily 6am–6pm, mid-Oct to mid-May daily 8am–5pm; Ⓦwww.byward-market.com) is home to cafés and delis, specialist food and fresh fruit and vegetables stalls and these merge with the street stalls outside. Many of Ottawa's best restaurants and bars are located here and at night the area buzzes until the early hours.

across the southeastern reaches of the park before reaching its conclusion at the **Champlain Lookout**, 24km from the park's southern entrance. There's a grand view of a distinctive landscape from here, with the granite outcroppings of the Canadian Shield transitioning down to the rich green fields of the St Lawrence lowlands.

Plans of the park are available at all the region's tourist offices and there are two **information centres** in the park itself, one at the southern entrance near Gatineau (June to mid-Oct daily 9am–5pm), the other off the Gatineau Parkway beyond the Champlain Parkway turning (daily 9am–5pm; Ⓣ819/827-2020); trail leaflets and park maps are available at both.

Eating and drinking

Ottawa has a good range of **restaurants**, some geared firmly to the expense account, but the majority informal, reasonably priced affairs where a main course should rarely cost more than $25. Ethnic restaurants are commonplace, (including some excellent places in **Chinatown** on Somerset Street West, roughly between Percy and Rochester streets) and there are a few decent bars and restaurants south of Confederation Square along **Elgin Street**. But the pick of the city's restaurants are in the **Byward Market area** (see above), which is also where you'll find lots of popular **cafés** and a boisterous **bar and pub** scene. Most of the establishments we have listed below are in or very near the market.

The market is home to the city's best **delicatessens** and fresh produce stalls, while **fast-food** vans provide sustenance at night. These are something of an Ottawa institution, mainly on account of their *poutine* – fries covered in gravy and cheese curds. Another municipal institution is **Beavertails**, a flat, deep-fried dough sprinkled with all sorts of sweet toppings, and on sale at Canadian Beavertails, in the Byward Market at the junction of George and William streets.

Bakeries, cafés and diners

Byward Café 55 Byward Market Square Ⓣ613-241-5555. Straightforward café inside Byward Market (at the south end) selling a wide range of snacks and light meals – sandwiches, pastas, salads and so forth – at very reasonable prices. Open daily 8am–7pm, later in summer.

The French Baker/Le Boulanger Français 119 Murray St Ⓣ613/789-794, Ⓦwww.frenchbaker.ca. Much-praised bakery, with a handful of seats for in-house eating, that does a great line in French bread and sell what many local thinks are the best croissants in town. Open daily 7am–5.30pm.

Mellos 290 Dalhousie St. Old-fashioned, diner-style café, where they serve all the local favourites, including *poutine* (see above). Open from early in the morning till late at night.

Zak's Diner 14 Byward Market Square Ⓣ613/241-2401, Ⓦwww.zaksdiner.com. A 1950s-style time warp with chrome decor, rock-'n'-roll blaring from the jukebox and (pretty average) all-American food, though the shakes will take your breath away. Burgers from $9. Open 24hr, seven days a week.

Restaurants

Domus Café 87 Murray St ⓣ613/241-6007, ⓦwww.domuscafe.ca. This delightful restaurant – more properly called *John Taylor at the Domus* to distinguish itself from the Domus houseware store next door – is strong on local, organic and seasonal produce. They excel with their fruit and vegetables, which are simply wonderful, converting them into splendidly creative concoctions like *prosciutto* wrapped hen with potatoes, mushrooms and tomato chutney in a red wine jus. The premises are delightful, the decor reminiscent of a country store. Mains from $28, $20 at lunch. Reservations recommended. Mon–Sat 11.30am–2pm & 5.30–9pm, plus Sun 11.30am–2pm.

Empire Grill 47 Clarence St ⓣ613/241-1343, ⓦwww.empiregrill.com. Smart and polished restaurant, with first-rate steaks and an extensive wine list. The bar, chic and appealing, offers smooth background music, with jazz the particular favourite. Mains from $20. Open daily 11.30am–1am.

La Pointe's Seafood Grill Café 55 York St ⓣ613/241-6221, ⓦwww.lapointefish.ca. Atmospheric, long-established Byward Market restaurant serving quality seafood at reasonable prices in informal, basement premises. Open daily 11am–9.30pm.

Navarra 93 Murray St ⓣ613/241-5500, ⓦwww.navarrarestaurant.com. Small and intimate Spanish restaurant that has garnered all sorts of rave reviews. The well-crafted menu features some real delights: try the roasted pig cheeks and garlic prawn. Mains from $22. Open Tues–Fri & Sun 11.30am–2pm & Mon–Sat 5.30–10pm.

Social Restaurant & Lounge 537 Sussex Drive ⓣ613/789-7355, ⓦwww.social.ca. Plush restaurant-cum-lounge bar decorated in creams and browns with splashes of deep red, plus modern art on the walls. The menu focuses on Canadian ingredients – from BC halibut to Alberta lamb – though the mains, which average around $30, do tend to the minimal. Open daily 7pm–midnight, bar till 2am Thurs–Sat.

Nightlife and entertainment

Ottawa has become a major port of call for big-name rock and pop acts, most of whom appear at **Scotiabank Place**, about 15km west of downtown at 1000 Palladium Drive, Kanata (ⓦwww.scotiabankplace.com). Otherwise, downtown is home to a number of busy **bars** and several good **clubs**, featuring both live music and DJs. For **listings**, consult the *Xpress* (ⓦwww.ottawaxpress.ca), a weekly freebie widely available across town.

Ottawa's cultural focus is the **National Arts Centre**, 53 Elgin St (ⓣ613/947-7000, ⓦwww.nac-cna.ca), which presents plays by its resident **theatre** company as well as touring groups, **concerts** by its resident orchestra and **operas** and **dance** from (among others) the National Ballet of Canada and the Royal Winnipeg Ballet; the acoustics are outstanding. Quality **theatre** is also on offer from the Great Canadian Theatre Company, who perform at the Irving Greenberg Theatre Centre, 1233 Wellington St West (ⓣ613/236-5196, ⓦwww.gctc.ca), and the Ottawa Little Theatre, 400 King Edward Ave (ⓣ613/233-8948, ⓦwww.ottawalittletheatre.com).

Cinema options include the Bytowne Cinema, 325 Rideau St (ⓣ613/789-3456, ⓦwww.bytowne.ca), the capital's most popular repertory cinema, and the Canadian Film Institute, 2 Daly Ave (ⓣ613/232-6727, ⓦwww.cfi-icf.ca), which shows art-house and mainstream films usually arranged by theme.

Bars, pubs and clubs

Bar 56 56 Byward Market ⓦwww.collectionbar56.com. Big loft, above *The Collection* bar, with great martinis and vinyl couches. House, hop and techno with DJs from all over Canada along with weird and wacky live acts. Open daily 5pm-2am.

Blue Cactus Bar & Grill 2 Byward Market ⓣ613/241-7061, ⓦwww.bluecactusbarandgrill.com. Hectic bar with a good line in cocktails and stylish modern decor. It's not a bad place to stop for a meal, with a southwestern, TexMex sort of menu.

Centretown Pub 340 Somerset St West ⓣ613/594-0233. Popular gay bar, ten minutes' walk south of Laurier Ave West along O'Connor St.

The Manx 370 Elgin St. A twenty-minute walk south of Byward Market, this basement pub packs the locals in tight and the youngish crew have an energetic bash at all the twenty-odd beers on draught.

Rainbow Bistro 76 Murray St ⓣ613/241-5123, ⓦwww.therainbow.ca. Atmospheric blues and jazz club with regular jam sessions and good side lines in reggae, funk, rock and ska. Open nightly and sometimes during lunch.

Zaphod Beeblebrox 27 York St at Byward Market ⓣ613/562-1010, ⓦwww.zaphodbeeblebrox.com. The whole spectrum of live bands appear at this groovy Byward Market joint, with everything from country and western to alternative, plus featured DJ slots. Open nightly.

Listings

Airport ⓣ613/248-2000, ⓦwww.ottawa-airport.ca.
Bike rental Rent-A-Bike, East Arch, Plaza Bridge, 2 Rideau St (mid-April to Oct daily 9am–5pm; ⓣ613/241-4140, ⓦwww.rentabike.ca).
Bookshops Chapters, 47 Rideau St at Sussex Drive, has a large and first-rate selection of Canadian literature and non-fiction.
Car rental Discount, 1749 Bank St (ⓣ613/667-9393); Hertz, 30 York St, Byward Market (ⓣ613/241-7681 and airport 613/521-3332); National, at the airport (ⓣ613/737-7023).
Embassies Australia, 50 O'Connor St (ⓣ613/236-0841); Ireland, 130 Albert St (ⓣ613/233-6281); New Zealand, 99 Bank St (ⓣ613/238-5991); UK, 80 Elgin St (ⓣ613/237-2008); US, 490 Sussex Drive (ⓣ613/238-5335).
Gay & lesbian Gayline Ottawa ⓣ613/238-1717.
Ice hockey From Sept to April, the Ottawa Senators play NHL games at Scotiabank Place, 1000 Palladium Drive, Kanata, Ottawa (ⓣ613/599-3267, ⓦhttp://senators.nhl.com), about 15km west of downtown. Tickets are sometimes available for as cheap as $14, but you can pay up to $130.
Internet access Most hotels, B&Bs and cafés provide internet access for their guests either free or at minimal rates. Internet cafés are also numerous, especially along Bank St.
Laundry Rideau Coinwash, 436 Rideau St (ⓣ613/789-4400).
Outdoor equipment The Expedition Shoppe, 43 York St (ⓣ613/241-8397, ⓦwww.expeditionshoppe.com), carries a good – if pricey – range of outdoor gear; Mountain Equipment Co-Op, 366 Richmond Rd, west of the centre (ⓣ613/729-2700, ⓦwww.mec.ca), has a huge selection of all sorts of outdoor gear and does equipment rental.
Pharmacy Rideau Pharmacy, 390 Rideau St (Mon–Fri 9am–9pm, Sat 9am–6pm, Sun noon–6pm; ⓣ613/789-4444); Shoppers Drug Mart, 702 Bank St (8am–midnight; ⓣ613/233-3202).
Post office 59 Sparks St, corner of Confederation Square.
Taxis Blue Line ⓣ613/238-1111; Capital Taxi ⓣ613/744-3333.
Whitewater rafting Owl Rafting (ⓣ1-800/461-7238, ⓦwww.owl-mkc.ca) offers an excellent programme of whitewater rafting on the Ottawa River, near Pembroke, about 170km northwest of Ottawa. A one-day excursion costs $110–130 with rental of all the necessary tackle and a buffet lunch included.

Northern Ontario

Stretching north from the shores of Lake Huron and Lake Superior to the frozen reaches of Hudson Bay, **northern Ontario** is a land of sparse population and colossal distances. Give or take the odd ridge and chasm, the landscape is almost entirely flat, an endless expanse of forest and lake pouring over the mineral-rich rocks of the **Canadian Shield**. To the anglophile elite of the south, the region was (and still is) seen as somewhat rough and crude, a region populated by backwoodsmen. Such disdain ignores the economic facts. The north once produced the furs that launched Canada's economy and its raw materials – gold, silver, nickel, timber – continue to pay for Toronto's gleaming skyscrapers. The extractive nature of the northern economy and the harshness of the climate have

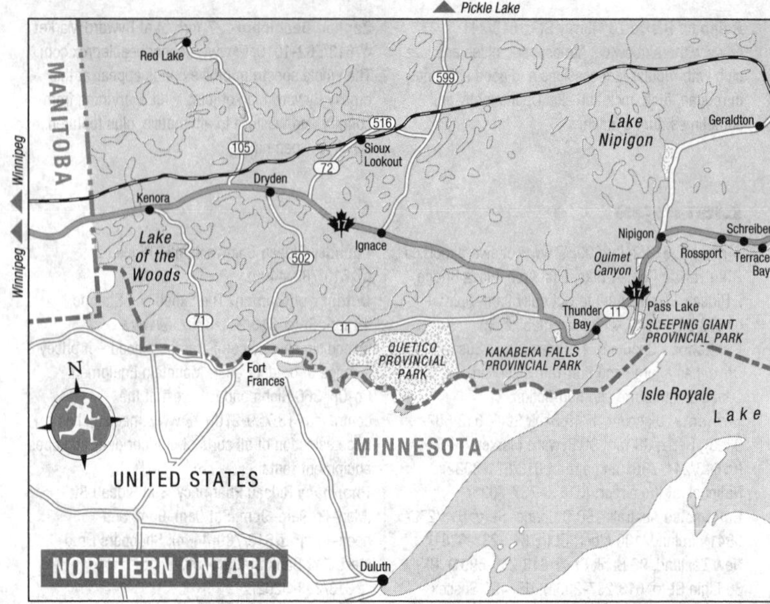

defined the locals' attitude to their surroundings: **hunting and fishing** are the big deals here – and most visitors who come here join in. Summer is a more pleasant time to visit, but watch out for the mosquitoes and **blackflies** that often make life absolutely miserable: pack repellent and the proper gear; the best time to go hiking is either at the start of spring or in the autumn.

Because of the huge distances involved, it's important to plan an itinerary carefully. Northern Ontario is traversed by two main highways, Hwy 11 and the much more interesting Hwy 17. **Highway 11** begins by slicing through **North Bay**, 345km north of Toronto, before pushing on to the hunting and fishing resort of **Temagami**. From here, it's a manageable hop onto **Cochrane**, notable as the starting point for the rail line that strikes north beyond the road network to **Moosonee**. This line, plied by Ontario Northland's **Polar Bear Express** train, makes for one of the most unusual excursions in the province and is a comfortable if long-winded way of seeing something of Ontario's immense northland. From Cochrane, Hwy 11 leads west to a series of mining towns, but there's little along this route besides vast emptiness.

There are two obvious ways to join **Highway 17**. The faster route comes up from Parry Sound (see p.157), meeting Hwy 17 at **Sudbury**, or you can join Hwy 17 just west of Sudbury along Hwy 6 from **Manitoulin Island** (see p.146). Whichever route you choose, your first stop on Hwy 17 should be **Sault Ste Marie**. This industrial town is only of middling interest, but it is the terminus for a splendid wilderness train trip on the **Algoma Central Railway**. From Sault Ste Marie, Hwy 17 begins its long haul round **Lake Superior** passing by, or through, a string of parks, notably **Lake Superior Provincial Park** and **Pukaskwa National Park**, both of which have dramatic lakeshore hiking trails and campsites. Beyond lies the inland port of **Thunder Bay**, the last place of much appeal before Winnipeg (see p.507), a further 680km to the west.

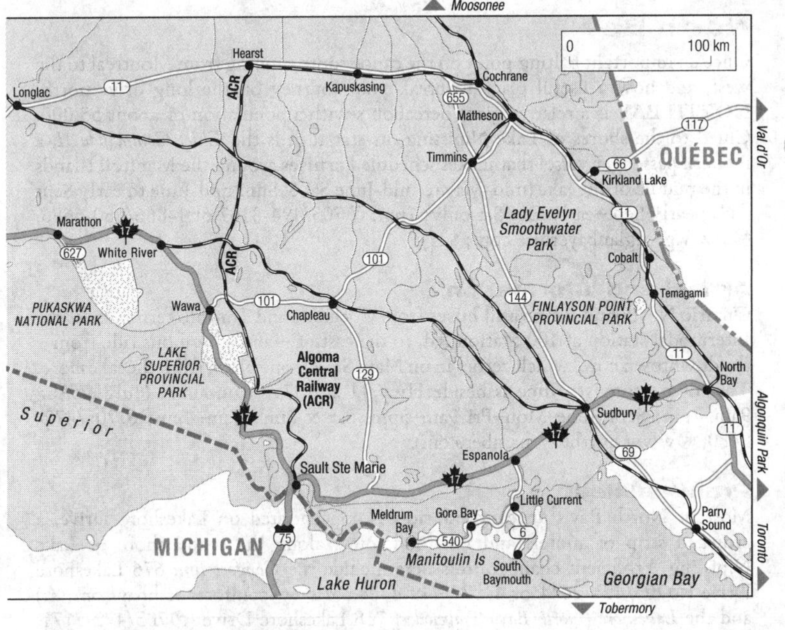

Regional transport

Public transport is sketchy across northern Ontario, but Ontario Northland (Ⓣ 1-800/461-8558, Ⓦ www.ontarionorthland.ca) does operate regular **buses** and the Northlander **train** from Toronto to North Bay and points north to Cochrane. At Cochrane, passengers can change for the same company's Polar Bear Express (see p.194) to Moosonee on James Bay. Greyhound **buses** (Ⓣ 1-800/661-8747, Ⓦ www.greyhound.ca) also service the region, with their busiest route being along the Trans-Canada Hwy between Toronto and Winnipeg, while **VIA Rail** (Ⓣ 1-888/842-7245, Ⓦ www.viarail.ca) links Toronto with Sudbury Junction and points west to Winnipeg. If you're heading for a particular park, hotel, motel or campsite, you should check to see how near you'll get by bus or train – towns and even villages in northern Ontario can sprawl over several kilometres. Hardy souls who visit in winter should be aware that driving on both Hwy 11 and Hwy 17 can be perilous.

North Bay and north to Moosonee

Hwy 11 cuts a 1000km-long arc through the remoter reaches of northern Ontario before meeting up with Hwy 17 as it approaches Thunder Bay. The first 380km of the highway, from the small lakeshore town of **North Bay** to **Cochrane**, are relatively tractable, but thereafter you really need a four-wheel drive and endless patience: the gritty resource towns beyond Cochrane are widely dispersed and of very limited interest. Cochrane is also the starting point for the train ride to **Moosonee**, beyond the road network and close to the shores of James Bay. Ontario Northland **trains** and **buses** run in this region (see above) but you really need a car to be sure of getting where you want, when you want.

North Bay

Once an important halting point on the canoe route running from Montréal to the west, and now a useful place to break your journey on the long drive north, **NORTH BAY** is a relative giant hereabouts with a population of about 55,000. Glued to the shores of Lake Nipissing, its star turn is the *Chief Commanda II*, a modern passenger vessel that makes scheduled **cruises** around the Manitou Islands in the middle of the lake (mid-May to mid-June Sat & Sun; mid-June to early Sept daily; early Sept–early Oct Sat only; 1pm; ⓣ705/494-8167 or 1-866/660-6686, ⓦwww.georgianbaycruise.com; $21).

Arrival and information

Ontario Northland **trains and buses** from Cochrane and Toronto terminate at the Intermodal station at 100 Station Rd, to the east of – and a local bus ride from – the downtown core, which zeroes in on Main Street, one block from the lakeshore. The town's **tourist office** is beside Hwy 11 at 1375 Seymour St (July & Aug 9am–7pm; Sept–June Mon–Fri 9am–5pm, Sat & Sun 10am–4pm; ⓣ705/472-8480, ⓦwww.northbaychamber.com).

Practicalities

Most of North Bay's **accommodation** is concentrated on Lakeshore Drive, a crowded strip of motels and fast-food joints along the sandy shore of Lake Nipissing. Proficient chain **motels** here include the *Comfort Inn*, 676 Lakeshore Drive (ⓣ705/494-9444 or 1-877/449-4484, ⓦwww.comfortnorthbay.com; ⑤) and the *Lakeshore (North Bay) Travelodge*, 718 Lakeshore Drive (ⓣ705/472-7171, ⓦwww.travelodge.com; ⑤).

For **food**, try *Café Chicago* (ⓣ705/472-9510; ⓦwww.chicagocafe.ca; closed Mon), 167 Main St, which specializes in Asian fusion dishes, with mains from $20. There's a good Japanese restaurant, *Kabuki House* (ⓣ705/495-0999), at 349 Main St West, that serves excellent *teppanyaki*. The town's best café is the *Urban Café* (Mon-Fri 8am–4pm; ⓣ705/472-0032; ⓦwww.urbancafenorthbay.com), at 101-B Worthington St East.

Temagami

Surrounded by lakes and forests, the pleasant resort-village of **TEMAGAMI**, 100km beyond North Bay on Hwy 11, has been attracting tourists since the early 1900s, when it was the site of the region's first grand hotel. It now serves as a base for extended forays into the wilderness – mostly hunters and fishermen travelling by floatplane and/or canoe. To get a view of this wilderness, climb the 30-metre-high **Temagami Tower** ($4) just before you hit town.

Ontario Northland **trains** and **buses** pull in at the station on Hwy 11 close to the **information centre**, at 7 Lakeshore Drive (May–Oct Mon–Fri 9am–6pm, Sat & Sun 10am–6pm; ⓣ705/569-3344 or 1-800/661-7609, ⓦwww.temagamiinformation.com). Just across the street in a bright red building is the Temagami Outfitting Company (May–Sept; ⓣ705/569-2595, ⓦwww.icanoe.ca), which will set you up for a **canoe trip** including all gear, food and the necessary permits for $85 a day.

For **accommodation**, the *Smoothwater Wilderness Ecolodge* (ⓣ705/569-3539 or 1-800/569-4539, ⓦwww.smoothwater.com; ④), provides bed and breakfast and camping pitches in a secluded spot beside James Lake, about 14km north of town off Hwy 11. There's more **camping** at **Finlayson Point Provincial Park** (mid-May to late Sept; ⓣ705/569-3205, ⓦwww.ontarioparks.com; $33–40), beside Lake Temagami, just south of town.

Grey Owl: the great con artist?

Temagami was once home to one of Canada's most colourful characters, Wah-Sha-Quon-Asin, aka **Grey Owl**. An early conservationist, Grey Owl travelled Canada, Britain and the US spreading the message of respect for the wilderness, publishing articles in such magazines as *Country Life*, and publishing books that became bestsellers. Yet it was only when he died in 1938 at the age of 50 that his true life story slowly emerged.

Grey Owl was actually born **Archie Belaney** in Hastings, England. He emigrated to Canada at the age of 17 to escape an authoritarian aunt and, after spending time in Toronto, made his way to the silver mine in Cobalt. On a whim, he got off the train at Temagami, where he worked as a guide in the tourist camps and became fascinated by the stories and customs of the local Ojibwa. Unusually for the time, Belaney married a young Ojibwa named **Angele** and they had a daughter, but Belaney was prone to drinking and rowdiness and was run out of town after a brawl. He moved to **Biscotasing**, a railway stop and Hudson Bay trading post north of Sudbury, where he became a forest ranger, but his arrest warrant caught up with him and he had to leave town again – though not before making **Marie Girard**, another native woman, pregnant.

During World War I, Belaney fought with the Canadian army in Flanders, where he was wounded in the foot. During his convalescence in England, he married his nurse, thereby adding bigamy to his many accomplishments. In the event, however, the call of the Canadian wilderness proved his marriage's undoing and Belaney returned to Biscotasing, stopping en route to see Angele for four days, during which another child was conceived. Back in Biscotasing, Belaney became the town drunk, living an anarchic life of fighting, drinking and trapping under his Grey Owl persona. For reasons that remain obscure, Belaney then had a change of heart, returning to Temagami to live with Angele and their two children in 1925, but he was off again after he met Anahereo, a 19-year-old Iroquois woman. Belaney and Anahereo moved to a hut in northern Québec, where their only companions were two beavers; it was these two animals (and a third that followed) that inspired much of Belaney's **writing** and prompted him to start a **beaver colony**. To raise money for the project he began writing and lecturing about his (fictional) life, a publicity campaign that secured him the post of **warden** of Riding Mountain National Park and later Prince Albert National Park in Manitoba.

Belaney's long absences and the days spent writing led to the collapse of his relationship with Anahereo, but it didn't take long for him to meet and marry a replacement, a French-Canadian who adopted the Indian name **Silver Moon**. Grey Owl made a lecture tour of Britain and the US in 1938, which included an audience with King George and the princesses Elizabeth and Margaret, but it left him so exhausted he died later the same year. Only then did his wives, friends and family find out the full truth.

Cobalt

Local legend has it that the silver boom at **COBALT**, just off Hwy 11 some 50km north of Temagami, started when a blacksmith named Fred La Rose threw a hammer at a fox and hit a rock instead, breaking off a great hunk of silver in the process. Whatever the truth, mining began here in earnest in 1903, but the high times ended with the Great Depression and Cobalt struggled on until the last mine closed in 1990. Cobalt today is designated a national historic site but it's hardly compulsive viewing. The best you'll do is Canada's oldest **Mining Museum** (daily: June–Sept 9am–5pm; Oct–May 1-4pm; $3.25), which includes a collection of luminous stones. There is more information about Cobalt's mining past in the

visitor centre (May–Sept daily 9am–5pm, Oct–April weekdays only; ⓣ705/679-5191, ⓦwww.historiccobalt.com) at 1 Station St.

North to Cochrane

Some 100km north of Cobalt, Hwy 11 passes over the **Arctic Watershed**, a slight elevation in the Canadian Shield that divides Ontario's water flow: to the north, all water flows to Hudson Bay, to the south it meanders down to the Great Lakes and the St Lawrence. Beyond, it's a tedious haul on Hwy 11 to **COCHRANE**, 280km from Temagami. Cochrane, hometown of Tim Horton – one-time hockey player and founder of the ubiquitous coffee and doughnut chain – is a modest place that grew up as a repair and turntable station for the railroad companies serving the far north. Most of the workshops have closed down, but Cochrane is still the departure point for Ontario Northland's Polar Bear Express train (see below), which ventures north beyond the road network to Moosonee, on James Bay.

Repeating the polar bear theme is the oversized **Polar Bear statue** on the way into town. It marks the entrance to the **information centre** (July–Aug Mon–Fri 8am–6pm, Sat & Sun 10am–2pm; Sept–June Mon–Fri 9am–4.30pm; ⓣ705/272-4926, ⓦwww.town.cochrane.on.ca), at 4 3rd Ave. The most convenient place to stay in Cochrane is the *Station Inn* (ⓣ705/272-3500 or 1-800/265-2356, ⓦwww.ontarionorthland.ca; ⑤) right above the train station, but for more character head to the *North Adventure Inn* (ⓣ705/272-6683, ⓦwww.northadventureinn.ca; ③), just west of town on Hwy 11, which has four fibre-glass igloos, each with bathroom and kitchenette.

Moosonee and Moose Factory Island

The Crees have been hunting and fishing Hudson Bay for several thousand years and they make up the majority of the population of **MOOSONEE**, which was founded in 1903 by a French fur-trading company, Révillon Frères. The **Révillon Frères Museum** (closed at the time of writing), in one of the original company buildings, traces the history of the settlement and its largely unsuccessful attempt to challenge the local monopoly of the **Hudson's Bay Company**. The latter had established the trading post of **Moose Factory Island**, just offshore from Moosonee, in 1673, which makes it the oldest English-speaking community in Ontario. **Water taxis** ($9 one-way) zip travellers from the jetty at Moosonee to the island, where the **Moose Factory Centennial Museum Park** (late June to early Sept; free) holds the original blacksmith's shop, graveyard, powder magazine (the island's only stone building) and a tepee where the locals sell bannock (freshly baked bread). South of here, **St Thomas Anglican Church**, built in 1860, has an

Cochrane to Moosonee by train

A popular excursion, Ontario Northland's **Polar Bear Express** (July & Aug Mon to Fri & Sun; Sept–June Mon–Fri 1 daily; ⓣ1-800/461-8558, ⓦwww.ontarionorthland.ca) cuts across 300km of desolate backwoods on its way from Cochrane to Moosonee, on the Moose River as it empties into James Bay. This is as far north as anyone can easily (or reasonably) go in Ontario – but, despite the name, you won't see any polar bears. In July and August, the train departs Cochrane at 9am and arrives in Moosonee at 1.50pm, departing Moosonee 6pm and arriving back in Cochrane at 10.45pm. The return fare is $104.90 and **reservations** are compulsory. In July and August, there's live entertainment, a restaurant and snack bar, but the rest of the year it's more authentic – and quiet.

▲ Traditional aboriginal homes at the Cree Cultural Interpretive Centre, Moose Factory Island

altar cloth of beaded moose hide, prayer books written in Cree and removable floor plugs to prevent the church floating away in floods. The **Cree Cultural Interpretive Centre** (daily late June–late Aug 10am-5pm; ⓣ705/658-2733; ⓦwww.moosecree.com; $10), at the other end of the island, is run by locals and has several exhibits about native life on the island including a replica campground.

Practicalities

One interesting **place to stay** is Moose Factory Island's *Cree Village Ecolodge* (ⓣ705/658-6400, ⓦwww.creevillage.com; ➐), which occupies an attractive wood and glass structure and has light and spacious rooms with fabulous views of the river. Its restaurant offers a mix of contemporary and native cuisine including baked trout and caribou. In Moosonee, the *Polar Bear Lodge* (ⓣ416/244-1495, ⓦwww.polarbearlodge.com; ➎) is opposite the public jetty, but its rooms are as bland as its exterior.

Sudbury

The economic centre of northeastern Ontario, sprawling **SUDBURY**, some 165km north of Parry Sound (see p.157) and 130km northeast of Little Current on Manitoulin Island (see p.146), is parked on the edge of the **Sudbury Basin**, a pit created either by a volcano or, the preferred theory, by a giant **meteor**. Whatever did the damage, the effect was to throw one of the world's richest deposits of **nickel and copper** towards the surface. It was the nickel – used to temper steel – that made Sudbury's fortune, but its by-products caused acute environmental degradation. Most of the damage was done by a smelting method known as heap roasting, used until the 1920s, which spread clouds of sulphurous fumes over forests already ravaged by lumber firms and mineral prospectors, who often started fires to reveal the traces of metal in the bare rocks below. Likened to Hell and Hiroshima, the bleak landscape had only one advantage: in 1968 it enabled Buzz Aldrin and Neil Armstrong to practise their great leap for mankind in a ready-made lunar environment. Having continued to produce sulphur-laden smoke from the stacks of their nickel smelters, the mining companies were finally forced to take action when a whole community of workers from **Happy Valley**, just northeast of Sudbury (and now ringed off by a large steel fence), were evacuated in the 1970s because of the number of sulphur-induced illnesses. Since then, pollutants have been greatly reduced and the city has implemented an ambitious re-greening programme, which has been widely acclaimed by environmentalists.

Arrival and information

Sudbury's principal **train station** – Sudbury Junction – is about 10km northeast of the town centre on Lasalle Boulevard, with services south to Toronto and west to Winnipeg. There are no buses into town: you have to take a taxi (Ⓣ705/673-9999). The Greyhound **bus** depot is at 854 Notre Dame, about 3km north of the centre. The **tourist office** (June–Aug daily 8.30am–6.30pm; Sept–May Mon–Fri 8.30am–4.30pm; Ⓣ1-877/304-8222, Ⓦwww.sudburytourism.ca or www.rainbowcountry.com) is 10km south of downtown beside Hwy 69; there's a seasonal office (May–Aug daily 10am–6pm) downtown at the local train station on Elgin Street.

Accommodation

Sudbury has a number of proficient chain **motels** with one of the more encouraging being the central *Best Western Downtown Sudbury*, 151 Larch St (Ⓣ705/673-7801, Ⓦwww.bestwestern.com; ⑤). A much more intimate option is the *Boulangerie du Village* (Ⓣ705/675-7732 or 1-888/675-7732, Ⓦwww.aubergesudbury.com; ⑥), at 104 Durham St in the centre of town, with two fully equipped suites – complete with fireplace – decorated in an elegant antique style. The smell of freshly baked bread will tell you when breakfast is ready, served downstairs in the bakery-cum-deli.

The Town

Sudbury's key attractions are located to the south and west of the **downtown core**, which is focused on Elm Street between Notre Dame Avenue and Durham Street. Making the most of the city's unusual geology, **Science North** (daily: April–June & Sept–Dec 10am–4pm; July & Aug 9am–6pm, Ⓣ705/523-4629 or 1-800/461-4898; $19 for Science Centre, $35 for all attractions; Ⓦwww.sciencenorth.ca), a huge snowflake-shaped structure south of the centre on Ramsey Lake Road, is installed in a cavern blasted into the rock of the Canadian Shield. The hands-on displays enable you to simulate a miniature hurricane, gauge your fitness, lie on a bed of nails, learn to lip-read, call up amateur radio hams worldwide and tune in to weather-tracking stations, all under the guidance of students from the city's university. The museum also has a collection of insects and animals, some of which can be handled, an IMAX Theatre, various virtual-reality rides and a planetarium.

The town's symbol, a nine-metre-high steel replica of a five-cent piece, known as the **Big Nickel**, stands by the Trans-Canada Hwy on the western approach to town. The nickel marks the entrance to **Dynamic Earth** (daily: April–June & Sept to mid-Oct 10am–4pm; July & Aug 9am–6pm; Ⓣ705/523-4629 or 1-800/461-4898, Ⓦwww.dynamicearth.ca; $19), where an imaginative range of attractions has been located in an old nickel mine, from multimedia features on the world's cultures through to an exploration of old mine shafts and stories exploring Sudbury's history.

Eating and drinking

For **food**, the absolute hit is *Respect is Burning* (Mon & Sat 5–10pm, Tues–Fri 11.30am–2.30pm & 5–10pm; ⓣ705/675-5777, ⓦhttp://ribsupperclub.com), at 82 Durham St, a large and funky warehouse-style lounge serving mainly Italian food, with mains from around $16; try the fettuccine with shrimp and scallops. As an alternative, *The Red Lobster*, 1600 Lasalle Blvd (ⓣ705/560-9825), does a good line in local pickerel as does the more expensive *Teklenburg's* (ⓣ705/560-2662; closed Sun & Mon), just down the street at no. 1893. A good option for a **drink** is the *Laughing Buddha*, 194 Elgin St (ⓣ705/673-2112), where they serve over ninety beers as well as pizzas, sandwiches and snacks; the folksy interior matches the idiosyncratic clientele.

Sault Ste Marie

Strategically situated beside St Mary's River, the tortuous link between lakes Superior and Huron, industrial **SAULT STE MARIE** – more popularly **The Soo** – sits opposite the Michigan town of the same name and sees constant two-way traffic, with two sets of tourists keen to see how the other lot lives. The Soo, 300km from Sudbury, is northern Ontario's oldest community, originally settled by Ojibwa fishing parties. The French called these Ojibwa *Saulteux* ("people of the falls") and the Jesuit missionaries who followed added the Christian sobriquet to give the town its present name. Initially, The Soo flourished as a gateway to the fur-rich regions inland, but it was the construction of a **lock and canal** in the nineteenth century that launched its career as a Great Lakes port and industrial centre, churning out pulp, paper and steel. Too industrial to be pretty, The Soo has a reasonable range of attractions and motels, but its real appeal is as the starting point for a splendid wilderness train ride on the **Algoma Central Railway**.

Arrival and information

The Soo's Greyhound **bus station** is at 73 Brock St, between Queen Street East and the waterfront. Local and provincial information is available at the **Ontario Travel Centre** (daily: mid-May to June 8am–6pm; July to early Sept 8am–8pm; early Sept to mid-May 8.30am–4.30pm; ⓣ705/945-6941 or 1-800/668-2746, ⓦwww.ontariotravel.net), at 261 Queen St West, a ten-minute walk west from the bus station along Queen Street.

The City

Some 2km long and three blocks wide, The Soo's **downtown** runs parallel to the waterfront to either side of the main drag, Queen Street East. All the principal sights are here, beginning with the enjoyable **Ermatinger Old Stone House** (April–May & mid-Oct to early Dec Mon–Fri 9.30am–4.30pm; June to mid-Oct daily 9.30am–4.30pm; ⓣ705/759-5443; $7), right at the east end of the town centre at 831 Queen St East. Built in 1814, the house was originally home to the fur trader Charles Ermatinger and his Ojibwa wife Manonowe and their thirteen children. Since then the building has served as a hotel, the sheriff's house and a social club. Restoration has returned the house to early nineteenth-century appearance and the period-costumed staff bake tasty cakes in the summer.

The waterfront

The spruced-up section of The Soo's elongated **waterfront** begins just five minutes' walk away to the west of Ermatinger House, at the foot of East Street. First up is the **Art Gallery of Algoma** (Wed–Sun 11am–6pm; ⓣ705/949-9067, ⓦwww.artgalleryofalgoma.on.ca; $3), at 10 East St, whose temporary exhibitions usually feature local artists. From here, it's a couple of minutes' walk to the **Museum Ship Norgoma** (daily: June–Aug noon–8pm; ⓣ705/256-7447, ⓦwww.norgoma.org; $6), an old Great Lakes' passenger ferry that has ended up moored here, and the **Roberta Bondar Pavilion**, a prominent tent-like permanent structure named after Canada's first woman astronaut, a Soo local; the pavilion is used for concerts and exhibitions. Nearby is the **Station Mall**, a sprawling shopping centre that has sucked the commercial heart out of downtown; in front of the mall is the Algoma Central Railway station (see below).

The Algoma Central Railway

The 476km-long **Algoma Central Railway** (ACR) was constructed in 1901 to link The Soo's timber plants with the forests of the interior. The first recreational users were members of the Group of Seven, who shunted up and down the track in a converted boxcar, stopping to paint whenever the mood took them. The ACR's timber days are long gone, but today the railway offers one of Ontario's finest excursions, with the train snaking through a wonderful wilderness of deep ravines, secluded lakes and plunging gorges. To see it all, sit on the left-hand side – otherwise you'll end up looking at an awful lot of rock. There are **three tours** to choose from, all departing from the Algoma Central Railway Terminal, in downtown Soo at 129 Bay St and Dennis (ⓣ705/946-7300 or 1-800/242-9287, ⓦwww.agawacanyontourtrain.com).

The **Agawa Canyon Tour Train** takes a day to cover the first 200km of track and back (late June to mid-Oct departs daily at 8am, returns 6pm; $70; $90 in the fall). **Reservations** are strongly advised and essential in the autumn, when the leaves turn. A two-hour stop within the canyon's 180-metre-high walls allows for a **lunch break** and a wander around the well-marked nature trails, which include a lookout post from where the rail line appears as a thin silver thread far below. Unless you are properly equipped don't miss the train back – the canyon gets very cold at night, even during the summer, and the blackflies are merciless. During the winter, the **Snow Train** (late Jan to mid-March Sat only; departs 8am, returns 5pm; $70) travels a little further north. It passes right through the canyon to the dramatic exit, where the walls are only 15m apart, before returning to The Soo. The third and longest trip is the **Tour of the Line** (Nov to early May Wed, Fri & Sun departs 9am, arrives Hearst 6.40pm; early May to Oct Thurs, Sat & Mon departs 9.20am, arrives Hearst 7pm; $202 return, excluding accommodation), a return trip that takes two days with an overnight stay in **Hearst**, the ACR's northern terminus. This is the weakest of the three excursions, as the scenery north of the canyon is dreary pine forest and Hearst isn't riveting. Passengers are responsible for arranging their own accommodation in Hearst; ring the Hearst Chamber of Commerce (ⓣ1-800/655-5769) in advance for details of availability; or contact the *Companion Hotel*, 930 Front St, Hearst (ⓣ705/362-4304 or 1-888/468-9888, ⓦwww.companion-hotel-motel.ca; $88; ❹).

The ACR also runs a regular **passenger train** from The Soo to Hearst four times weekly from early May to October, three times weekly in winter. Passengers on this train (commonly called the "moose meat special" on account of its popularity with hunters and trappers) get off and on at various points along the line, paying as little as $19 for a short journey or up to $136 for the trip to Hearst. Schedule details are available from the ACR, which also has information about renting **boxcars** and details of the several **outback lodges** that dot the line.

A good twenty-minute walk west of Station Mall, Canal Drive crosses one of the river's narrow channels to reach St Mary's Island, home to the **Sault Ste Marie Canal National Historic Site** (open access; free). Here, you can stroll along the lock and investigate the old stone buildings that surround it with the help of a series of explanatory plaques.

Practicalities

Among the town's many **motels and hotels**, the *Comfort Inn* (Ⓣ705/759-8000, Ⓦwww.choicehotels.ca; ❺), at 333 Great Northern Rd, has plain but modern rooms. More character can be found downtown at *Brockwell Chambers B&B* (Ⓣ705/949-1076, Ⓦwww.brockwell.biz; ❹), at 183 Brock St, with four stylish rooms, all en suite.

The Soo's gastronomic speciality is **pizza** – which is apparently quite unlike pizza anywhere else. The most popular place is *Mrs. B's* (Ⓣ705/942-9999), at 76 East St, where large pizzas begin at $15. The finest downtown restaurant is *A Thymely Manner* (Ⓣ705/759-3262; Tues–Sat), at 531 Albert St, which is well known for its local lamb (from nearby St Joseph's Island) and its great Caesar salad; reservations are a must. Along the Great Northern Road, at no. 357, *The Steamy Bean Café* (Ⓣ705/253-9690) serves up coffee and cakes in a relaxed setting with sofas and internet terminals.

Lake Superior's north shore

With a vast surface area of no less than 82,000 square kilometres, **Lake Superior** is the largest freshwater lake in the world, and one of the wildest. Its northern shore between Sault Ste Marie and **Thunder Bay** is a windswept, rugged region formed by volcanoes, earthquakes and glaciers, its steep, forested valleys often overhung by a steely canopy of grey sky. The native Ojibwa lived in fear of the storms that would suddenly break on the lake they knew as Gitche Gumee, the Big-Sea-Water, and white sailors were inordinately suspicious of a lake whose icy waters caused its victims to sink like stones: Lake Superior never gives up its dead. For the most part, Hwy 17 sticks close to the north shore of Lake Superior between Sault Ste Marie and Thunder Bay, but a screen of trees almost always keeps the lake out of view. This stretch of road is 690km long, so unless you're up for a gruelling thrash or have to reach Thunder Bay (see p.203) quickly it's much better to dawdle and dally. Along the way are two magnificent parks, **Lake Superior Provincial Park** and **Pukaskwa National Park**, where there's camping and hiking – though the insects can be unbearable from May to August, sometimes longer. The small towns dotted along the highway mostly fail to inspire, but low-key **Wawa**, about a third of the way along, has several good places to stay, while diminutive **Rossport**, a further 300km west, is easily the prettiest settlement hereabouts.

Greyhound **buses** regularly travel Hwy 17 between Toronto and Winnipeg, but don't expect them to drop you exactly where you want: if you are aiming for a specific motel or campsite, check how far you'll have to walk.

Lake Superior Provincial Park

Heading north from Sault Ste Marie on Hwy 17, it's about 120km to the southern perimeter of **Lake Superior Provincial Park** (April–Oct; day-use fee $13; Ⓦwww.lakesuperiorpark.ca), which offers ready access to Lake Superior's granite

Lake Superior Provincial Park's Coastal Trail

The finest of the park's many trails, the **Coastal Trail** begins some 140km from Sault Ste Marie at Sinclair Cove and runs north to Chalfant Cove. It comprises a challenging 48km-long route of high cliffs, sand and cobbled beaches, sheltered coves and exposed granite ledges. There are numerous designated backcountry campsites on the trail and the burnt-out fires on the beaches indicate where most people choose to pitch. The entire trek takes about five to seven days but access points enable you to do shorter sections; the southern part of the trail is not as demanding, with fewer climbs and easier going on sand rather than cobbled beach. Maps and trail guides are available at the park office and the visitor centre (see below).

shoreline and its immediate hinterland. Autumn is the best time to visit, when the blackflies have abated and the forests of sugar maples and yellow birch flash with colour, but the scenery and wildlife are enthralling year-round. Moose, chipmunks and beavers are the most common, sharing their habitat with the more elusive white-tailed deer, woodland caribou, coyote, timber wolves and black bears, as well as myriad migratory and resident birds.

Practicalities

Hwy 17 cuts through the park for around 100km, passing, after about 10km, the **visitor centre** (daily: May–June & Sept–early Oct 9am–5pm, July & Aug 9am–8pm; ⓣ705/882-2026), located at the Agawa Bay campground. Both the visitor centre and the main **park office** (daily May–Oct 8am–4.30pm; ⓣ705/856-2284), a further 60km away to the north, sell hiking and canoe route maps as well as backcountry camping permits ($9.50), which are compulsory if you're heading off into the wilderness. Both also have information on vacancies at the park's three major **campsites**. These are the basic **Crescent Lake** (mid-June to mid-Sept; $25.50) on the park's southern boundary; popular **Agawa Bay** (May to mid-Oct; $31.75–36.75), 8km further north and right on Lake Superior; and **Rabbit Blanket Lake** (May to late Oct; $31.75–36.75) just north of the park office and ideal for forays into the interior. The latter two campsites have electrical hook-ups, showers and laundry facilities. The rangers will warn you if weather conditions look perilous, but always expect the worst – the park receives more rain and snow than any other park in Ontario. There are no park services of any kind from November to April, when service roads (but not Hwy 17) are barred and gated.

Wawa

The unassuming, former iron-mining town of **WAWA**, 14km north of the park, was named after the Ojibwa word for wild goose – and to hammer home the point there's a great big steel model of the bird at the entrance to town, outside the **visitor centre** (daily: late May to early Sept 8am–8pm; early Sept to mid-Oct 9am–5pm; ⓣ1-800/367-9292, ⓦwww.wawa.cc). The model has helped to make Wawa a busy stopping point on the Trans-Canada Hwy (Hwy 17), which was just the idea. In the 1960s, much to the chagrin of local businessfolk, the hwy was routed a couple of kilometres to the west of town – hence the goose to pull passing motorists in.

Practicalities

Modern **motels** line up along Wawa's main street, Mission Road, including the workaday *Wawa Motor Inn* (ⓣ705/856-2278 or 1-800/561-2278, ⓦwww.wawamotorinn.com; ④). Much more distinctive is the secluded *Rock Island*

Lodge (Ⓣ705/856-2939 or 1-800/203-9092; Ⓦwww.rockislandlodge.ca; ④), 10km from Wawa; take the Trans-Canada Hwy south from town and turn right (west) after 5km along Michipicoten River Village Road; the lodge is on a sandy beach, its wooden patio literally hanging over Lake Superior. The four guest rooms have no phones and no TV, but it's a popular spot and reservations are advised. They also offer kayaking trips and teepee-camping.

A stay in Wawa isn't complete without eating at the *Kinniwabi Pines Restaurant*, Hwy 17 South (May–Oct daily 8am–10pm; Ⓣ705/856-7226; dinner from $20), which is famous hereabouts for its Caribbean cuisine, a speciality of the Trinidadian chef.

White River

Beyond Wawa, it's 90km of forest until you reach the next settlement of any interest, **WHITE RIVER**. There's nothing much to it, but it does have two claims to fame. First, in 1935 the temperature here dropped to a mind-boggling -57°C (-72°F), the lowest ever recorded in the whole of Canada – and hence the whopping thermometer hanging by Hwy 17. Second, this was the home of a small bear cub named Winnipeg who was exported to London Zoo in 1914 and became the inspiration for **Winnie-the-Pooh**. To emphasize the connection, you'll spot a fibreglass Winnie up a tree beside the highway.

Pukaskwa National Park

From White River, Hwy 17 turns west, heading back towards the Lake Superior shoreline. After about 85km, just short of the little lakeshore town of **Marathon**, Hwy 17 clips past Hwy 627, the 15km-long sideroad that provides the only access to **Pukaskwa National Park** (open year-round, limited services in winter; Ⓦwww.pc.gc.ca; $5.80), a chunk of hilly boreal forest interspersed by muskeg and loch that fills out an enormous headland with a stunning coastline. Hwy 627 goes to **Hattie Cove**, the site of the park's only **campsite** ($25.50 unserviced, $29.40 serviced), three sandy beaches and a **visitor centre** (late June to mid-Sept daily 9am–5pm; Ⓣ807/229-0801), which sells trail guides and backcountry camping permits ($9.80 per night). From Hattie Cove, the **Coastal Hiking Trail** travels 60km south through the boreal forest and over the ridges and cliffs of the Canadian Shield. It is not an easy hike, but it is magnificent and there are regular backcountry campsites on the way. In the summer, McCuaig Marine Services (Ⓣ807/229-0193) offers a water taxi service to the head of the trail at Swallow River, so you can just hike one-way back to Hattie Cove. Far less arduous are the

Terry Fox

West of Nipigon, highways 17 and 11 merge to become the Terry Fox Courage Highway, named after **Terrance Stanley Fox** (1958–81), one of modern Canada's most remarkable figures and heroes. At the age of 18, Fox developed cancer and had to have his right leg amputated. Determined to advance the search for a cure, he nevertheless planned a money-raising run from coast to coast and on April 12, 1980, he set out from St John's, Newfoundland. For 143 days he ran 26 painful miles a day, covering five provinces by June and raising $34m. In September, at mile 3339, just outside Thunder Bay, lung cancer forced Terry to abandon his run; he returned home to Port Coqitlam, BC, where he died the following summer. More than $85m has now been raised for cancer research in his name and in his honour the **Terry Fox Monument**, a finely crafted bronze statue, has been placed on top of a ridge in a little park above the highway just to the east of Thunder Bay.

short trails departing from or near the visitor centre. Of these, the rocky **Southern Headland Trail** (2.2km) offers superb views over Lake Superior before hitting Horseshoe Beach where you can continue on the **Beach Trail** (1.5km) leading you back to the campsite.

Rossport

Some 130km from the Pukaskwa turning, Hwy 17 passes close to **ROSSPORT**, a pretty little village draped around a tiny, sheltered bay. Originally a Hudson's Bay Company trading post, the settlement prospered as a fishing port until the 1960s, when a combination of over-fishing and a sea-lamprey attack on the lake trout led to the industry's decline. Today Rossport is the quietest of villages and one that makes for a perfect overnight **stay** on the long trek north. The *Rossport Inn* (ⓣ807/824-3213 or 1-877/824-4032, ⓦwww.rossportinn.on.ca; ❸) occupies a fine lakeside setting, with seven bedrooms in the main house and ten wooden cabins, all with double beds, in the garden; the only thing spoiling your nightly rest is the noise of the freight train. The inn has a good restaurant, but the place to **eat** is the *Serendipity Café* (ⓣ807/824-2890, ⓦwww.serendipitygardens.ca; closes 9pm), a surprisingly sophisticated spot where, if available, you can sample locally caught lake trout, among other tasty dishes. You can also **stay** here, in one of four stylish self-catering studios with views of the lake (❺; breakfast box included).

Ouimet Canyon and Sleeping Giant Provincial parks

From Rossport, it's 80km to **NIPIGON**, where Hwy 11 finishes its mammoth trek across northern Ontario to merge with Hwy 17. After a further 35km or so, Hwy 17 reaches the 11km-long turning that leads north away from the lake to one of the region's more spectacular sights in **Ouimet Canyon Provincial Park** (daily mid-May to early-Oct, daylight hours; ⓣ807/977-2526, ⓦwww.ontarioparks.com; $2). The canyon was formed during the last ice age, when a sheet of ice 2km thick crept southward, bulldozing a fissure 3km long, 150m wide and 150m deep. Nearly always deserted, the canyon has two lookout points that hang over the terrifyingly sheer sides with the permanently dark base lurking below – an anomalous frozen habitat whose perpetual snow supports some very rare arctic plants.

Back on Hwy 17, it's about another 25km west to Hwy 587, which branches south down to Sibley Peninsula, almost all of which is taken up by **Sleeping Giant Provincial Park**. Although the park is dramatically scenic, it's a bit of a pain to get to and there's not much to do once you're there, bar some rather tough and longish trails. The whole thing is really best seen from Hwy 17, where you

Amethysts

Amethyst, a purple-coloured variety of quartz, was first discovered near the shores of Lake Superior between the Ouimet Canyon and Thunder Bay in the middle of the nineteenth century. It is still mined hereabouts and particular deposits have been turned into well-signposted tourist attractions; Hwy 17 whizzes past a string of them. One of the best is **Blue Points Amethyst Mine** (mid-May to mid-Oct daily), about 58km east of Thunder Bay. Tours of the open-pit mine are free, but you can pick up a bucket and digging tool to gather as many lumps of rock as you want, and pay a minimal amount for your booty on the way out. Amethysts can be polished with baking soda.

can get a fine view of the four flat-topped mountains that resemble a recumbent giant and which gave the park its name.

Thunder Bay

The Lake Superior port of **THUNDER BAY**, some 110km from Nipigon, is much closer to Winnipeg than to any other city in Ontario, and consequently its 120,000 inhabitants are prone to see themselves as westerners. Economics as well as geography define this self-image, for this was until recently a booming grain-handling port – grain harvested in the Prairies. Some grain still arrives here by rail

▲ Skating on Lake Superior, near Thunder Bay

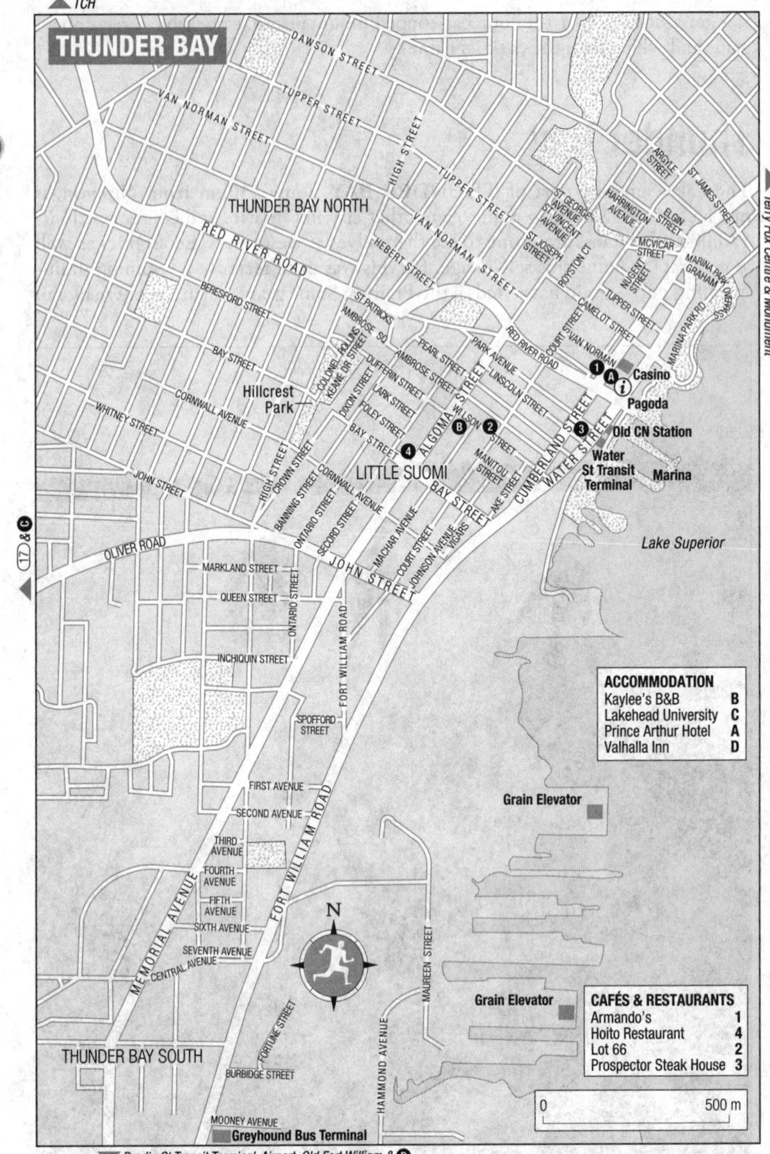

to be stored in the town's gigantic grain elevators on its way to the Atlantic, but since the 1990s the economics of the trade have favoured Canada's Pacific ports and many of the elevators that dominate the harbourfront are now literally rotting away.

Scarred by industrial complexes and crisscrossed by rail lines, Thunder Bay is not immediately enticing, but it does have enough of interest to make a pleasant stopover on the long journey to or from Winnipeg. The most agreeable part of town is the few blocks stretching inland from behind the marina in **Thunder Bay North**, north of Central Avenue, where you'll also find several good cafés and restaurants. **Thunder Bay South** is much less appealing, but on its outskirts is the city's star turn, the replica fur-trading post of **Old Fort William**.

Some history

Thunder Bay was created in 1970 when the two existing towns of Fort William and Port Arthur were brought together under one municipal roof. **Fort William** was the older of the two, established in 1789 as a fur-trading post and subsequently becoming the upcountry headquarters of the North West Company. It lost its pre-eminent position when the North West and Hudson's Bay companies merged, but it remained a fur-trading post until the end of the nineteenth century. In the middle of the nineteenth century, rumours of a huge **silver** lode brought prospectors to the Lake Superior shoreline just north of Fort William, where **Port Arthur** was established. The silver didn't last and the Port Arthur, Duluth and Western railway (PD&W), which had laid the lines to the mines, was soon nicknamed "the Poverty, Distress and Welfare". The Canadian Northern Railway, which took over the abandoned PD&W lines, did much to rescue the local economy, but did not bring Fort William and Port Arthur closer together. Rudyard Kipling noted that, "The twin cities hate each other with the pure, passionate, poisonous hatred that makes cities grow. If Providence wiped out one of them, the other would pine away and die." The 1970 amalgamation bypassed Kipling's prediction and nowadays these parochial rivalries have all but vanished.

Arrival and information

Thunder Bay Airport (Ⓦwww.tbairport.on.ca) is on the southwest edge of the city, about 13km from Thunder Bay North, which is where you want to head. To get from one to the other, take local **bus #3 Airport** (every 30min) to the Brodie Street transit terminal in Thunder Bay South and then either change or stay on the bus (depending on the service) for onward transportation to Thunder Bay North, where buses pull into the Water Street terminal behind the marina. Thunder Bay Transit (Ⓣ807/684-3744, Ⓦwww.thunderbay.ca/transit) operates local **buses**. The flat fare is $2.50; ask for a transfer if you need more than one bus to complete your journey. With services to and from Sault Ste Marie and Winnipeg, the long-distance **Greyhound bus station** (Ⓣ807/345-2194) is located about 3km south of Thunder Bay North at 815 Fort William Rd; there are no **trains**.

There are two **tourist offices** in Thunder Bay. One is downtown in the landmark Pagoda building on Water Street at the foot of Red River Road (mid-June to early Sept, Tues–Sat 10am–6pm; Ⓣ807/684-3670 or 1-800/667-8386, Ⓦwww.thunderbay.ca); the other is in the Terry Fox Centre by the Terry Fox Monument (daily: mid-June to early Sept 8.30am–7.30pm; Sept to mid-June 9am–5pm; Ⓣ807/983-2041), on Hwy 17 just north of town.

Accommodation

Thunder Bay has a healthy supply of reasonably priced **motel and hotel** accommodation, as well as lodgings in **student rooms** on Lakehead University's campus.

Kaylee's B&B 2 Machar Ave Ⓣ807/345-6813, Ⓦwww.bbcanada.com/3719.html. Centrally located just one block from the Hoito canteen (see p.207), this long-standing B&B has three rooms with shared facilites and provides a shuttle service from the airport/bus terminal. ③

Lakehead University Lakehead University Ⓣ807/343-8485, Ⓦwww.conferenceservices.lakeheadu.ca. With its manicured lawns and miniature lake – students call it Lake Inferior – the campus is a pleasant spot. Single ($35) and double ($40) rooms, as well as townhouses or apartments

($100 for a basic version, $140 for fully equipped) are available from May–Aug. Access to the university's sports facilities is an extra $6 per day. The campus is located about 4km southwest of the Pagoda; the #2 Crosstown bus from the Water St terminal by the marina goes right past it.

Prince Arthur Hotel 17 Cumberland St North ⓣ807/345-5411 or 1-800/267-2675, ⓦwww.princearthur.on.ca. Built by the CNR in 1908, this imposing stone-and-brick block is bang in the centre of town. Inside, there are flashes of its original Edwardian elegance, but most of the furnishings are modern and the rooms are similar, as well as being large and comfortable. ④

Valhalla Inn 1 Valhalla Inn Rd ⓣ807/577-1121 or 1-800/964-1121, ⓦwww.valhallainn.com. Perhaps the best-looking of the city's hotels, this modern, brick-and-timber hotel offers over two hundred spacious and well-equipped rooms. ⑤

The Town

Thunder Bay's 5km-long **waterfront** is home to a string of **grain elevators**, whose striking architecture – all modernist lines and pure functionalism – can't fail to impress. In the middle of the industrial jangle is the **marina** and behind it the old CN **railway station**, whose distinctive high-pitched gables, turrets and dormer windows were built to resemble a French château. The station was erected in 1906 and three years later CN dipped into their pockets again to create the **Pagoda**, a fanciful bandstand just across the street that now houses a tourist office (see p.205).

Thunder Bay North's most appealing enclave is the Finnish district of **Little Suomi**, focused on the Bay and Algoma streets intersection, about ten minutes' walk southwest from the Pagoda. There are over forty ethnic groups in Thunder Bay and several of them maintain their own institutions, but none more so than the Finnish. Arriving in the 1870s, the first Finns to get here were left-wing refugees escaping the Tsar, whereas those who arrived after 1917 were right-wing opponents (plus the odd anarchist) of the Bolsheviks, leading to a political divide within the community that still echoes today. Little Suomi's architecture is resolutely suburban, but the town's most atmospheric restaurants are here (see opposite). Head west along Bay Street from Algoma Street and you'll soon reach **Hillcrest Park**, perched on a low ridge, offering great views out across the lake.

Southwest of Thunder Bay: Old Fort William

Thunder Bay's tour de force is the reconstructed fur-trading post of **Old Fort William** (daily mid-May to mid-Oct 10am–5pm; ⓦwww.fwhp.ca; $14), in a loop of the Kaministiquia River about 15km southwest of the town centre, 13km upriver from its original site. At the entrance is a **visitor centre**, where a first-rate film traces the history of the fort and explains its workings. From here, it's a quick stroll or bus ride to the fort, a large palisaded compound which has been restored to its appearance in 1815, when it was the inland headquarters of the North West Company and their major trans-shipment base. Impeccably researched and staffed by students dressed in period gear, the forty-odd buildings that fill out the compound illuminate the fort's original purpose with everything from simple storehouses to the capacious Great Hall. Look out for the **fur warehouse**, festooned with the pelts of beaver, lynx and arctic fox, and the **canoe workshop**, where exquisite birch-bark canoes are made to traditional designs for museums all over Canada. There are demonstrations of contemporary trades and crafts, a working kitchen, kitchen garden and a farm complete with sheep, pigs and cows.

West from Thunder Bay to Winnipeg

Heading west from Thunder Bay, it's almost 700km to **Winnipeg** in Manitoba (see p.507). The logical place to break your journey is **Kenora**, almost 500km away along Hwy 17, through the interminable pine forests of the Canadian Shield. First choice for **accommodation** here is the landmark, eleven-storey *Best Western Lakeside Inn*, 470 1st Ave South (Ⓣ807/468-5521, Ⓦwww.bestwestern.com; ⑥), from where there are panoramic views over the town and its surroundings. Remember to put your watch back one hour when you cross into the **Central time zone**, about 60km west of Thunder Bay.

Eating and drinking

Thunder Bay's choicest places to **eat** are in Little Suomi, on Cumberland Street, just up from the Pagoda, and around the marina near the old CN station.

Armando 28 Cumberland St North Ⓣ807/344-5833. Trim Italian restaurant offering good pizzas, pastas and a baritone performance at your table with your order. Closed on Sun.

Hoito Restaurant 314 Bay St Ⓣ807/345-6323. Established in 1918, Thunder Bay's best-known Finnish café-cum-canteen is always full and the specials on the board should not be missed. The salt fish, potatoes and *viili* (buttermilk) are delicious. Breakfasts start at $5, dinners at $12. Open Mon–Fri 7am–8pm, Sat & Sun 8am–8pm.

Lot 66 66 South Court St Ⓣ807/683-7708. Delicious king crab, Indian shrimps, tapas and tasting platters are what to go for in this dark and cosy restaurant, which has become the town's newest hot-spot. The wine bible is a must for connoisseurs, with bottles ranging from $23 to a whopping $400. Open Tues–Sat from 4pm.

Prospector Steak House 27 South Cumberland St Ⓣ807/345-5833. A local favourite, the *Prospector* has pictures of old-time Thunder Bay on the walls and serves chowder from brass prospector's vats, along with such dishes as ribs and locally caught fish, all from $20. Open daily from 4pm.

Travel details

Trains

Ontario Northland Ⓣ1-800/461-8558, Ⓦwww.ontarionorthland.ca.

Cochrane to: Moosonee on the Polar Bear Express (July & Aug 1 daily except Sat; 4hr 20min; Sept–June 1 daily Mon–Fri; 5hr).

VIA Rail Ⓣ1-888/842-7245, Ⓦwww.viarail.ca.

Kingston to: Montréal (4–5 daily; 2hr 45min); Ottawa (3–5 daily; 2hr); Toronto (4–5 daily; 2hr 30min).

London to: Stratford (2–3 daily; 1hr)

Ottawa to: Gananoque (1 daily; 1hr 35min); Kingston (4–5 daily; 2hr); Montréal (4–6 daily; 2hr); Toronto (3–5 daily; 4hr 15min).

Buses

(For buses from Toronto, see p.104)

Greyhound Ⓣ1-800/661-8747, Ⓦwww.greyhound.ca.

Kenora to: Winnipeg (2 daily; 2hr 30min).

Kingston to: Montréal (2–3 daily; 5hr 20min); Ottawa (2–3 daily; 2hr 45min).

London to: Hamilton (4–5 daily; 2hr); Kitchener (6–10 daily; 2hr); Owen Sound (1 daily; 4hr 30min, including 2 changes); Stratford (2 daily; 1hr 20min); Windsor (4–5 daily; 2hr 40min).

North Bay to: Ottawa (3 daily; 5hr); Sudbury (3 daily; 2hr).

Ottawa to: Kingston (2–3 daily; 2hr 45min); Montréal (hourly; 2hr 30min); North Bay (3 daily; 5hr); Sudbury (3 daily; 7hr 30min); Toronto (8–10 daily; 5–6hr).

Sault Ste Marie to: Kenora (2 daily; 16hr); Thunder Bay (2 daily; 9–10hr); Toronto (3 daily; 10hr 30min); Wawa (2 daily; 3hr); White River (1 daily; 4hr 15min); Winnipeg (2 daily; 20hr).

Sudbury to: Montréal (3 daily; 11hr); North Bay (3 daily; 2hr); Ottawa (3 daily; 7hr 30min); Sault Ste Marie (3 daily; 4hr 30min).; Thunder Bay (2 daily; 15hr).

Thunder Bay to: Kenora (2 daily; 6hr 30min); Sault Ste Marie (2 daily; 9–10hr); Sudbury (2 daily; 15hr); **Toronto** (2 daily; 21hr); Winnipeg (2 daily; 9hr).

Ontario Northland ⓣ1-800/461-8558, ⓦwww.ontarionorthland.ca.

North Bay to: Bracebridge (4 daily; 2hr); Cobalt (2 daily; 1hr 45min); Cochrane (2 daily; 6hr 15min); Gravenhurst (4 daily; 2hr 10min); Huntsville (4 daily; 1hr 40min); Orillia (4 daily; 3hr 15min); Temagami (2 daily; 1hr 10min); Toronto (4 daily; 5hr 30 min).

Sudbury to: Cochrane (1 daily; 6hr 45min); Hearst (1 daily; 9hr); Parry Sound (2 daily; 2hr); Port Severn (3 daily; 3hr 15min); Toronto (2 daily; 6hr).

Coach Canada (ⓣ1-800/461-7661, ⓦwww.coachcanada.com)

Kingston to: Montréal (8 daily; 3hr 20min); Toronto (9 daily; 3hr).

3

Montréal and Southwest Québec

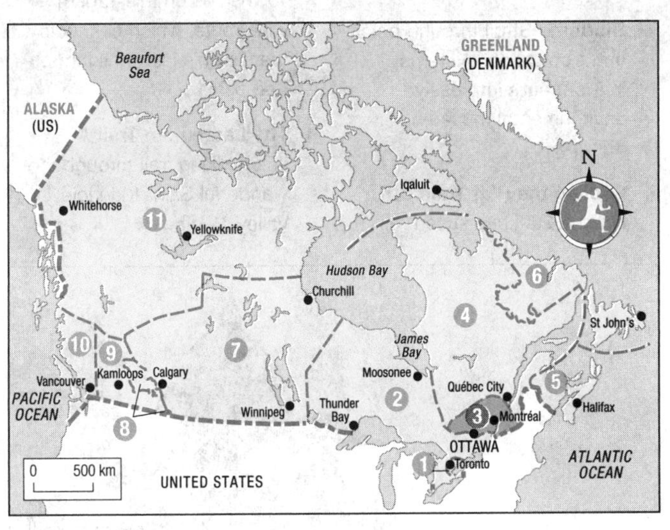

CHAPTER 3

Highlights

* **Montréal Jazz Festival** From late June, crowds gather for free outdoor shows of both big-name performers and newcomers.See p.218

* **Vieux-Montréal** Wander around narrow streets lined with centuries-old buildings and monuments. See p.224

* **Plateau Mont-Royal** Montréal's cultural melting pot has cosy cafés, wild nightlife and restaurants for all tastes. See p.237

* **Biodôme** Stroll through polar and tropical ecosystems in Montréal's impressive environmental museum. See p.240

* **Cycling the P'tit Train du Nord** A 200km disused rail bed converted into a scenic bicycle trail. See p.257

* **Mont-Tremblant** Eastern Canada's premier ski resort is a great spot year-round for outdoor pursuits. See p.257

* **Knowlton** Relax at this leafy, lakeside village, where you can browse art galleries and sample the region's deservedly famous duck. See p.260

* **La Route des Vins** Sip your way across the Eastern Townships on this 120km wine route, which connects the region's lush vineyards. See p.261

* **The Laurentian Trail** A 75km hiking trail through the wonderful Saint-Mauricie Valley. See p.265

▲ Saint Joseph's Oratory, Mont-Royal

3

Montréal and Southwest Québec

As home to the only French-speaking society in North America, Québec is totally distinct from the rest of the continent – so distinct, in fact, that its political elite have been obsessed with the politics of secession for decades. The province was ceded to the British after the conquest of the French in 1759 and yet more than two hundred years later the legacy of 'New France' is as tangible as ever. After the colony was transferred to British rule, the Québécois were allowed to maintain their language and Catholic religion, which ensured large families and a prevalence of French-speakers throughout the following generations – a political move termed the *revanche du berceau* ("revenge of the cradle"). Centuries later, the result is a unique blend of North American and European influence and a province with an interesting dual-personality. Nowhere is this more evident than in **Montréal and Southwest Québec**. Within striking distance of Ottawa, and pressed hard against the US border with Vermont, New Hampshire and Maine, this one tiny corner of the province has led both the economic and political resurgence of French-speaking Canada throughout the last century.

Home to over a third of all Québécois, the island metropolis of **Montréal** is fiercely proud of both its European heritage and its reputation as a truly international city. There can be few places in the world where people on the street flit so easily between two or more languages – sometimes within the same sentence – or whose cafés and bars ooze such a cosmopolitan feel.

From downtown Montréal the mirrored skyscrapers that vie for space between colony-era cathedrals and historic buildings have a view across to the St Lawrence River and the wilderness beyond that was once the source of the city's wealth and power. These days the vast wilds of Southwest Québec are admired for their natural beauty rather than their promise of furs and minerals and there are several

Information and hotel reservations

Fédération des Agricotours Ⓦwww.agricotours.qc.ca. An excellent service listing quality-inspected bed and breakfasts throughout Québec.

Tourisme Québec Ⓣ1-877/266-5687, Ⓦwww.bonjourquebec.com. Information and a province-wide accommodation booking facility.

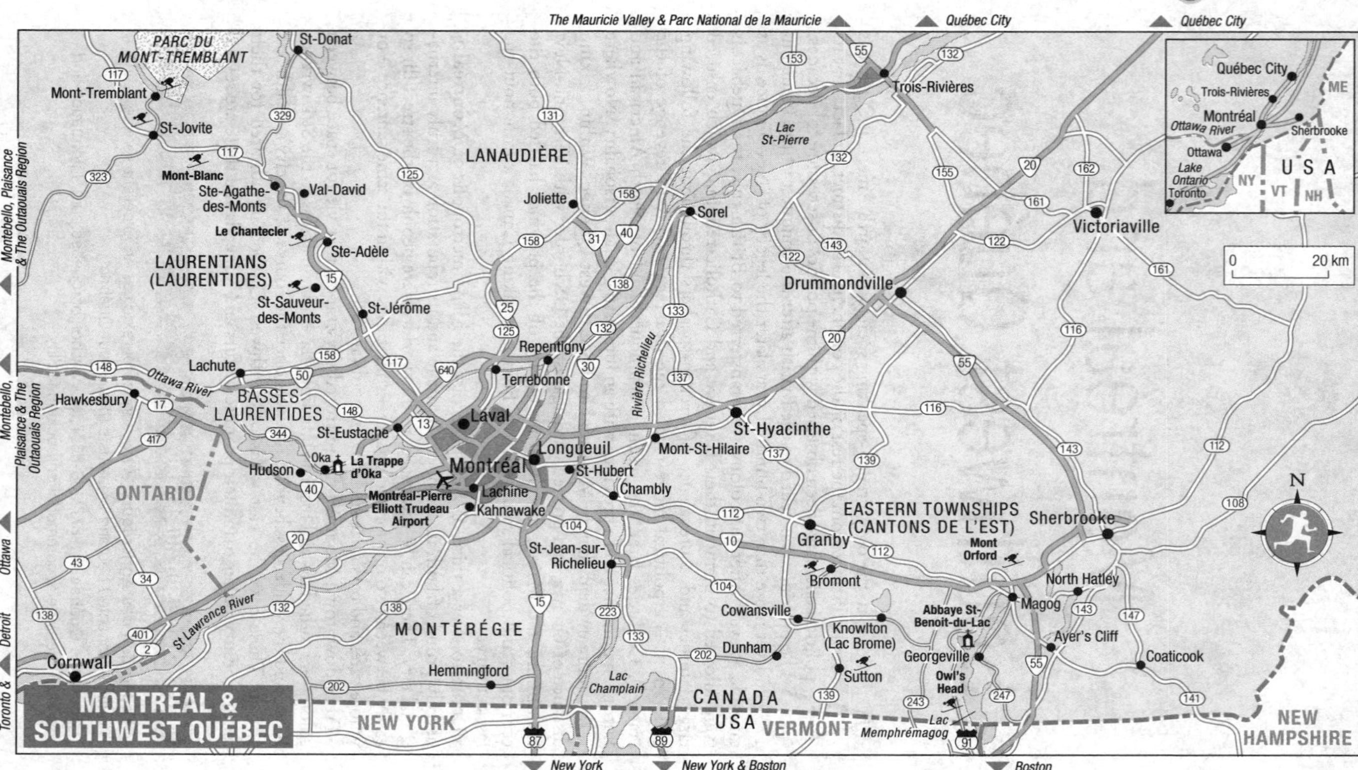
The Mauricie Valley & Parc National de la Mauricie
Québec City
Québec City
Montebello, Plaisance & The Outaouais Region
Montebello, Plaisance & The Outaouais Region
Ottawa
Detroit
Toronto &
New York
New York & Boston
Boston
PARC DU MONT-TREMBLANT
St-Donat
Mont-Tremblant
St-Jovite
Mont-Blanc
Ste-Agathe-des-Monts
Val-David
Le Chantecler
Ste-Adèle
LAURENTIANS (LAURENTIDES)
St-Sauveur-des-Monts
St-Jérôme
LANAUDIÈRE
Joliette
Trois-Rivières
Lac St-Pierre
Sorel
Victoriaville
Drummondville
Lachute
Ottawa River
Hawkesbury
BASSES LAURENTIDES
St-Eustache
Repentigny
Terrebonne
Laval
Rivière Richelieu
St-Hyacinthe
Mont-St-Hilaire
Longueuil
Montréal
St-Hubert
Chambly
Oka
La Trappe d'Oka
Hudson
Lachine
Montréal-Pierre Elliott Trudeau Airport
Kahnawake
ONTARIO
EASTERN TOWNSHIPS (CANTONS DE L'EST)
Sherbrooke
Granby
Mont Orford
Bromont
St-Jean-sur-Richelieu
St Lawrence River
MONTÉRÉGIE
Cowansville
Knowlton (Lac Brome)
Abbaye St-Benoit-du-Lac
Magog
North Hatley
Ayer's Cliff
Coaticook
Dunham
Sutton
Georgeville
Owl's Head
Cornwall
Hemmingford
Lac Champlain
CANADA
USA
NEW YORK
VERMONT
Lac Memphrémagog
NEW HAMPSHIRE
Québec City
Trois-Rivières
Montréal
Ottawa River
Sherbrooke
Ottawa
Lake Ontario
Toronto
USA
ME
NY
VT
NH
0
20 km
N
MONTRÉAL & SOUTHWEST QUÉBEC

carefully groomed rural getaways just an hours drive out of the city. To the north, the hilly and forested **Laurentians** offer outdoor activities year- round, including over 500km of dedicated cycling, hiking and horseriding trails in the summer and eight downhill ski centres and 2000km of prepared cross-country ski routes in the winter. To the south of Montréal, the **Eastern Townships (Cantons-de-l'Est)**, which spread across the foothills of the Appalachian mountains, lure city dwellers into the country with a more opulent approach to the outdoors. Originally a place of refuge for Americans wanting to stay loyal to the British Crown during and after the American War of Independence in 1775–1783, within two generations the majority of the area's population were French Canadian. Today, although the townships maintain an anglophone veneer (and very British-sounding names), they are 94 percent francophone. The Gallic ancestry of most Townshippers is clear in their attitude towards hedonistic pleasures: surrounding themselves with specialized restaurants, vineyards and expert cheese makers, they eat and drink in a style that combines the simplicity of the first Norman settlers with the rich tastes of the contemporary French. The flawless country inns and dreamy spas flaunting impeccable gardens and unbelievable views are a plus, too.

Train services within the region run from Montréal to Ontario, New Brunswick and into the US as well as connecting Québec City and the north of Québec. For most destinations, **buses** are your best bet for getting around, with the major places connected by regular services, supplemented by a network of smaller local lines.

A brief history of Québec

Although various **First Nations** have lived in pockets of the province for millennia and there had been sporadic European contact to the east, Québec's history really begins with Jacques Cartier's 1535 voyage. He sailed up the St Lawrence stopping at Stadacona and Hochelaga – present-day Québec City and Montréal, respectively. The early days of the colony revolved around the fur trade and attempts to convert the natives to **Christianity**. The priests' tasks were made more difficult by the fact that the French had aligned with the Algonquin and Huron nations to gain access to their **fur-trading networks**, while those groups' traditional enemies, the Iroquois Confederacy, had formed alliances with the Dutch and then the British. Louis XIV made **New France** a royal province in 1663 dispatching troops and, subsequently, unmarried Frenchwomen, the so-called **filles du roi**. Periodic skirmishes between the French and British and their native allies continued to be a destabilizing factor, stunting the growth of the colony. Matters were resolved somewhat when twelve hundred colonists met with an even greater number of natives from across eastern North America at Pointe-à-Callière in Montréal to sign **La Grande Paix**, the Great Peace treaty of 1701.

It wasn't until mid-century that further serious conflict broke out, with the British and French again at odds in the **Seven Years' War** (also known as the French and Indian War). The turning point took place in 1759 with the Battle of the Plains of Abraham (see p.288). The British consolidated their hold with the 1774 Québec Act (see p.953), a pre-emptive move that helped resist American attempts to take over the colony. After the Americans won independence from Britain, a flood of **United Empire Loyalists** fled across the Canadian border, settling primarily in the Eastern Townships and present-day Ontario.

The creation of Lower and Upper Canada in 1791 emphasized the inequalities between anglophones and francophones and later led to rebellion (see p.253). Investigating its causes, Lord Durham concluded that English and French relations were akin to "two nations warring within the bosom of a single state". His prescription for peace was immersing French-Canadians in the English culture of

Aboriginal peoples in Québec

Francophone–anglophone relations may be the principal concern of most Québécois – eighty percent of them have French as their mother tongue – but the province's population also includes eleven nations of **aboriginal** peoples, the majority of whom live on reservations. Aboriginal grievances are particularly acute in Québec as most of the province's tribes are English-oriented – the **Mohawks** near Montréal even fought on the side of the British during the conquest. Still, relations are even bad between the authorities and French-speaking groups. The **Hurons** (see p.952) near Québec City battled in courts for eight years to retain their hunting rights, while around James Bay the **Cree** fought and won the right to block the expansion of Québec's hydroelectric network which, had it been completed as planned, would have covered an area the size of Germany. Begun in 1971, the project nonetheless resulted in the displacement of Cree and **Inuit**.

Aboriginal peoples have categorically voted against separation and have used mostly peaceful methods to register their land claims, which amount to 85 percent of the province's area. There was violence at the Mohawk uprising at Oka near Montréal in 1990 (see p.254), which, though condemned by most Canadians and aboriginals, drew attention to the concerns of aboriginal Canadians.

North America; the subsequent 1840 Act of Union joining Lower and Upper Canada can be seen as a deliberate attempt to marginalize francophone opinion within an English-speaking state.

French-Canadians remained insulated from the economic mainstream until nineteenth-century **industrialization**, financed and run by the better-educated anglophones, led to a mass francophone migration to the cities. By the mid-twentieth century, a French-speaking middle class had begun to articulate the grievances of the workforce and to criticize the suffocating effect the Church was having on francophone opportunity. The shake-up of Québec society finally came about with the so-called **Quiet Revolution** in the 1960s, spurred by the provincial government under the leadership of Jean Lesage and his Liberal Party of Québec. The provincial government took control of welfare, health and education from the Church and, under the slogan *Maîtres chez-nous* ("Masters of our own house"), established state-owned industries that reversed anglophone financial domination.

In order to implement these fiscal policies, Québec needed to administer its own taxes, and the provincial Liberals, despite being staunchly federalist, were constantly at loggerheads with Ottawa. Encouraged and influenced by other nationalist struggles, Québécois' desire for recognition and power reached a violent peak in 1970, when the terrorist **Front de Libération du Québec** (FLQ) kidnapped a provincial government minister and a British diplomat in Montréal (see p.959). Six years later a massive reaction against the ruling provincial Liberals brought the separatist **Parti Québécois** (PQ) to power. Led by René Lévesque, the PQ accelerated the process of social change, particularly with unilingual language law **Bill 101** and held a referendum on sovereignty that 6.5 million people voted 60:40 against (see p.960).

In 1993, Québec's displeasure with federalism was evident in the election of the Bloc Québécois – a federal party commited to shattering federalism – to the ironic status of Her Majesty's Loyal Opposition in Ottawa. The separatist cause received added support in 1994 when the PQ was returned to provincial power after vowing to hold another **referendum** on separation from Canada. The 1995 vote was so close – Québec opted to remain within Canada by a margin of less than one percent – that calls immediately arose for a third referendum (prompting pundits to refer to the process as the "neverendum").

The PQ lost power to the Liberals in 2003, and today little hope remains of achieving the dream of a sovereign Québec in the near future – if ever – and yet, 'The National Question' rumbles on. The current political climate suggests that Québécois would now rather see a new deal that keeps them in Canada and view the threat of sovereignty as a way to strengthen their position in federal matters.

Montréal

MONTRÉAL, Canada's second-largest city, is geographically as close to the European coast as to Vancouver, and in look, taste and feel it combines some of the finest aspects of the two continents. Its North American skyline of glass and concrete rises above churches and monuments in a melange of European styles as varied as Montréal's social mix. This is also the world's third-largest French-speaking metropolis after Paris and Kinshasa, but only two-thirds of the city's three and a half million people are of French extraction, the other third being a cosmopolitan mishmash of *les autres* ("the others"), including British, Eastern Europeans, Chinese, Italians, Greeks, Jews, Latin Americans and Caribbeans. The memorable result is a truly multidimensional city, with a global variety of restaurants, bars and clubs, matched by a calendar of festivals that makes this the most vibrant place in Canada.

It is also here that the two main linguistic groups – anglophones and francophones – come into greatest contact with one another. In the wake of the "francization" of

▲ Café Santropole, in Montréal's Plateau district

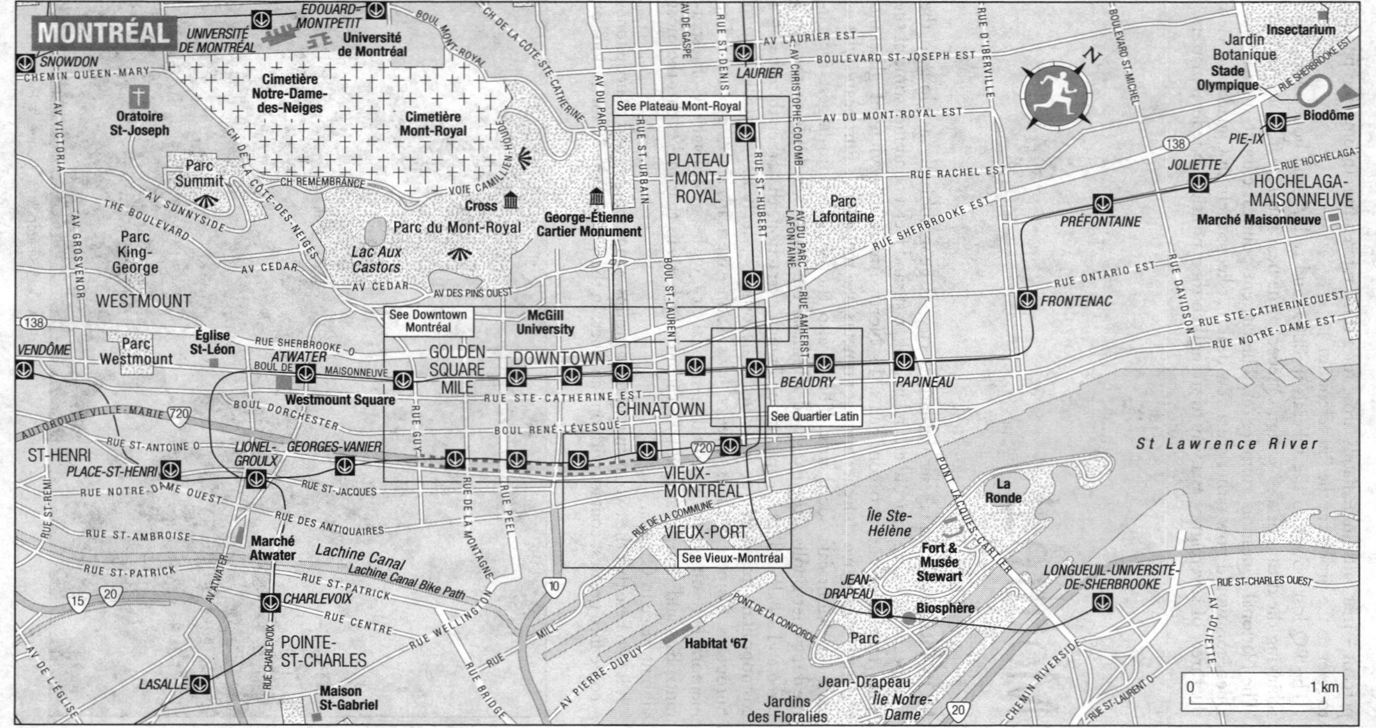
MONTRÉAL
Snowdon
Université de Montréal
Edouard-Montpetit
Université de Montréal
Cimetière Notre-Dame-des-Neiges
Cimetière Mont-Royal
Oratoire St-Joseph
Parc Summit
Parc du Mont-Royal
Lac Aux Castors
Cross
George-Étienne Cartier Monument
Parc King-George
Westmount
Parc Westmount
Église St-Léon
Vendôme
Atwater
Westmount Square
See Downtown Montréal
McGill University
Golden Square Mile
Downtown
Chinatown
See Plateau Mont-Royal
Plateau Mont-Royal
Laurier
Parc Lafontaine
See Quartier Latin
Beaudry
Papineau
Frontenac
Préfontaine
Joliette
Pie-IX
Biodôme
Stade Olympique
Jardin Botanique
Insectarium
Hochelaga-Maisonneuve
Marché Maisonneuve
St Lawrence River
St-Henri
Place-St-Henri
Lionel-Groulx
Georges-Vanier
Vieux-Montréal
Vieux-Port
See Vieux-Montréal
Marché Atwater
Lachine Canal
Lachine Canal Bike Path
Charlevoix
Pointe-St-Charles
Lasalle
Maison St-Gabriel
Habitat '67
Parc Jean-Drapeau
Jean-Drapeau
Biosphère
Fort & Musée Stewart
Île Ste-Hélène
La Ronde
Jardins des Floralies
Île Notre-Dame
Longueuil-Université-de-Sherbrooke
Chemin Queen-Mary
Av Victoria
Av Grosvenor
The Boulevard
Av Sunnyside
Ch de la Côte-des-Neiges
Ch Remembrance
Voie Camillien-Houde
Boul Mont-Royal
Ch de la Côte-Ste-Catherine
Av Cedar
Av des Pins Ouest
Av du Parc
Rue St-Urbain
Boul St-Laurent
Av de Gaspé
Rue St-Denis
Rue St-Hubert
Av Christophe-Colomb
Av du Parc Lafontaine
Rue Amherst
Av Laurier Est
Boulevard St-Joseph Est
Av du Mont-Royal Est
Rue Rachel Est
Rue Sherbrooke Est
Rue D'Iberville
Boulevard St-Michel
Rue Hochelaga
Rue Ontario Est
Rue Davidson
Rue Ste-Catherine Ouest
Rue Notre-Dame Est
Rue Sherbrooke O
Boul de Maisonneuve
Rue Ste-Catherine Est
Boul René-Lévesque
Boul Dorchester
Autoroute Ville-Marie
Rue Guy
Rue de la Montagne
Rue Peel
Rue St-Antoine O
Rue St-Jacques
Rue Notre-Dame Ouest
Rue St-Rémi
Rue St-Ambroise
Rue des Antiquaires
Rue St-Patrick
Av Atwater
Rue Charlevoix
Rue Centre
Rue Wellington
Rue Bridge
Av de l'Église
Rue de la Commune
Rue Mill
Av Pierre-Dupuy
Pont de la Concorde
Pont Jacques-Cartier
Chemin Riverside
Rue St-Laurent O
Rue St-Charles Ouest
Av Joliette
138
720
10
15
20
0
1 km

Québec, English-Canadians hit Hwy 401 in droves, tipping the nation's economic supremacy from Montréal to Toronto. Though written off by Canada's English-speaking majority, the city did not sink into oblivion. Instead, it has undergone an incredible resurgence, becoming one of the driving forces behind the high-tech industries helping transform Canada's economy.

Everywhere you look there are the signs of civic pride and prosperity. In the historic quarter of **Vieux-Montréal**, on the banks of the St Lawrence River, the streets and squares are flanked by well-tended buildings, from the mammoth **Basilique Notre-Dame** and steepled **Chapelle de Notre-Dame-de-Bon-Secours**, to chic boutique hotels. Old houses have been converted into lively restaurants and shops, abandoned warehouses into condos and the disused **Vieux-Port** into a summer playground with landscaped parklands facing onto the St Lawrence. Beneath the forested rise of **Mont Royal**, the boulevards and leafy squares of **downtown** are alive from the morning rush hour right through to the wee hours, when clubbers return from the establishments of **rue Ste-Catherine** and the diverse bars and lounges of the nearby **Plateau** and **Quartier Latin** districts. Below ground are the walkways of the **Underground City** and the outstanding **Métro** system, while towards the eastern outskirts the **Stade Olympique**'s leaning tower overshadows the vast **Jardin Botanique**, second in international status only to London's Kew Gardens.

The city also boasts some excellent museums. The **Centre Canadien d'Architecture** has one of the continent's most impressive specialist collections, focusing on the role of architecture in society, innovative design practice and the history of ideas. The **Musée d'Art Contemporain** is Canada's only museum devoted entirely to contemporary art and the **Musée des Beaux-Arts** is the oldest fine-arts museum in the country. Equally outstanding are the museums devoted to Montréal and Canadian history; of these, the **Musée McCord** has a mint collection of native artefacts, while the **Musée d'Archéologie et d'Histoire de Montréal** delivers a state-of-the-art presentation of archeological findings at the site of Montréal's founding in 1642.

Some history

The island of Montréal was first occupied by the St Lawrence **Iroquois,** whose small village of Hochelaga ("Place of the Beaver") was situated at the base of Mont Royal. The first European contact occurred in 1535 when Jacques Cartier was led here while searching for a northwest route to Asia. A permanent European presence was not established until 1611; the French settlement was little more than a small garrison, and it wasn't until 1642 that the colony of Ville-Marie was founded. Bloody conflict with the Iroquois, fanned by the European fur-trade alliances with the Algonquins and Hurons, was constant until the **Great Peace treaty** of 1701 prompted the growth of Montréal into the main embarkation point for the fur and lumber trade. When Québec City fell to the British in 1759, Montréal briefly served as the capital of New France. The ensuing **British occupation** saw a flood of Irish and Scottish immigrants who soon made Montréal North America's second-largest city.

With the creation of the **Dominion of Canada** in 1867, Montréal emerged as the nation's premier port, railroad nexus, banking centre and industrial producer. Its population reached half a million in 1911 and doubled in the next two decades with an influx of émigrés from Europe. It was also during this period that Montréal acquired its reputation as Canada's "sin city". During Prohibition in the US, Québec became the main alcohol supplier to the entire continent: the Molsons and their ilk made their fortunes here, while prostitution and gambling thrived under the protection of the authorities. Only in the wake of World War II and the subsequent economic boom did a major anti-corruption operation begin, tied in with rapid architectural growth. The most glamorous episode in the city's face-lift came with **Expo '67**, the World's Fair that attracted fifty million visitors to Montréal. Yet it was the city's anglophones who were benefiting from the prosperity, and beneath the smooth surface francophone frustrations were reaching dangerous levels. These reached an apex with the 1970 FLQ crisis, the reverberations of which shook the nation (see p.959).

The combination of the PQ's election in 1976, the consequent Bill 101 language laws they introduced and the threat of sovereignty prompted an anglophone exodus in the tens of thousands from the city, chiefly to Toronto.

A Canada-wide economic recession in the mid-1990s saw Québec lag behind the rest of the country in economic growth. After the 1995 referendum a tacit truce was made on the issue of separation and the boarded-up shops that lined rue Ste-Catherine gradually reopened, while the derelict pockets on the edges of downtown and Vieux-Montréal were renovated. But perhaps the most enduring change is that the gaps left by departing anglophones have been filled by young **bilingual** francophones, who feel in charge of their own culture and economy. At the same time, many anglophones that stayed have also become bilingual, and these days it's perfectly normal to hear the two languages intermingling wherever you may be.

Arrival and information

Montréal's main international **airport** is the Aéroport International Pierre-Elliott-Trudeau de Montréal (occasionally referred to by its old name of **Dorval**), or just **Montréal-Trudeau** for short (code YUL; ⓣ514/394-7377 or 1-800/465-1213, ⓦwww.admtl.com), located 22km southwest of the city. The Aérobus 24h airport shuttle service (departures every 30min, every hour in early morning and late-night; takes 35–45min; $16 one-way, ⓣ514/631-1856, ⓦwww.autobus.qc.ca) links to the Station Centrale d'Autobus Montréal, on the eastern edge of the Quartier Latin. From here you can take the metro or a taxi. Several local buses run from the airport to downtown but they take ages. A taxi downtown is around $35–45.

Montréal's festivals and events

Montréal has a different festival every week throughout the summer months (pick up the quarterly *What to do in Montréal* guide at the tourist office for a comprehensive list or visit ⓦwww.tourism-montreal.org). Most event **tickets** can be purchased through Admission (ⓣ514/790-1245 or 1-800/361-4595, ⓦwww.admission.com).

The **Festival International de Jazz de Montréal** (ⓦwww.montrealjazzfest.com) is North America's largest, with more than four hundred shows in late June and early July, most of them free at huge open-air stages surrounding Place des Arts. The lively, mid-June **First Peoples' Festival** (ⓦwww.nativelynx.qc.ca) celebrates aboriginal peoples history, featuring traditional activities, from throat-singing to stonecutting, and culminating in the summer solstice and National Aboriginal Day (June 21). The mid-July **Juste pour Rire** ("Just For Laughs"; ⓦwww.hahaha.com) is the world's largest comedy festival, with past headliners including Tim Allen, Rowan Atkinson, Jim Carrey, John Candy, Lily Tomlin and Whoopi Goldberg. Just afterwards, the **Francofolies** (ⓦwww.francofolies.com) brings French musicians from around the world to various downtown stages. The most visually spectacular of the city's shindigs is

Montréal's main **train station**, Gare Centrale, is below the *Queen Elizabeth Hotel* on the corner of boul René-Lévesque and rue Mansfield, and is entered at 895 rue de la Gauchetière ouest. The station is the major terminus for Canada's VIA Rail trains from Halifax, Toronto, Ottawa, Québec and the Gaspé, as well as US Amtrak trains from Washington and New York. The Underground City links it to Bonaventure Métro station and the rest of downtown. Long-distance **buses** use the Station Centrale d'Autobus Montréal, at 505 boul de Maisonneuve est (Ⓣ514/842-2281 for info on all bus lines). The Berri-UQAM Métro station is beneath it. A number of bus lines – including Orléans Express (Ⓣ1-888/999-3977, Ⓦwww.orleansexpress.com), Québec's main coach company – serve various destinations.

Montréal's main information centre, **Infotouriste** (daily: late-June to Aug 9am–7pm; Sept–Oct & Mar to mid-June 9am–6pm; Nov–Feb 9am–5pm; Ⓣ514/873-2015 or 1-877/266-5687, Ⓦwww.bonjourquebec.com) is at 1001 rue du Square-Dorchester on the corner of rue Metcalfe. The nearest Métro is Peel: walk south on rue Peel past rue Ste-Catherine. It has masses of useful free information and offers an accommodation service, which will make any number of free calls to find you vacancies. The **Tourist Information Centre of Old Montréal**, on the northwest corner of Place Jacques-Cartier at 174 rue Notre-Dame est (April–June & Sep–Oct daily 9am–5pm; Jun–Aug daily 9am–7pm; Nov–March Wed–Sun 9am–5pm; Ⓦwww.tourism-montreal.org) provides information on the city only.

City transport

The **public transport** system links the 65-station **Métro** to 150 bus routes, all run by the STM (Société de transport de Montréal; Ⓣ514/288-6287, Ⓦwww.stm.info). The clean, speedy, reliable and cheap Métro system has four colour-coded lines; the major interconnecting stations are **Berri-UQAM** (which links the orange, green and yellow lines), **Lionel-Groulx** (green and orange), and **Snowdon** and **Jean-Talon** (blue and orange). Coloured signs indicate the direction of each line by showing the name of the end-station. A **correspondance**, available from machines beyond the turnstiles at the Métro stations, allows you to complete your journey by bus at no extra cost, but you must get one at the beginning of your

the **International Fireworks Competition** late in July, with breathtaking, music-coordinated pyrotechnics. The action takes place at the La Ronde amusement park and tickets are around $40 (including ride pass), but across the water and on the Jacques-Cartier Bridge the spectacle is free. In late July, sounds of African beats fill the city with the **Festival International Nuits d'Afrique** (Ⓦwww.festivalnuitsdafrique.com). There are many food-tasting events and, in some cases, boozy ones, like the June **Mondial de la Bière** (Ⓦwww.festivalmondialbiere.qc.ca) in the Gare Windsor, which offers the opportunity to sample more than 250 brands of beer from around the world. In late January, Île Ste-Hélène hosts ice-sculpting and general carousing with the **Fête des Neiges de Montréal** (Ⓦwww.fetedesneiges.com). Of the many film festivals, the most notable is the **Montréal World Film Festival** in late August (Ⓦwww.ffm-montreal.org). The late-April **Vues d'Afrique** (Ⓦwww.vuesdafrique.org) is gaining prominence for bringing African and Caribbean films to Montréal. Finally, the world-renowned **Cirque du Soleil** (Ⓦwww.cirquedusoleil.com) has a big-top season in its home city every other year.

Bixi: Pedal your way across Montréal

Montréal's new public bike system – the first in North America – features over three thousand self-service bikes available 24 hour across the city, from May to October. Montréal researched similar bike programmes in other cities, including Paris and Barcelona, to emerge with the well-oiled, wonderfully accessible Bixi (Ⓦwww.bixi.com; the name comes from "bike" plus "taxi"). Hiring a bike is simple: At a Bixi stand (which are all solar-powered, and liberally scattered across the city), swipe your credit card and ride off. To encourage short trips, the first half-hour is free; beyond that, it's $5 per 24 hours. They also offer 30-day ($28) and one-year ($78) subscriptions.

journey, not as you depart the Métro. The transfer system also works in reverse, from buses to Métro: ask the driver for one as you board. Most **buses** stop running at 12.30am, shortly before the Métro, though some run all night.

A one-way **fare** on either Métro or bus is $2.75 (exact change on the bus); you can also get six trips for $12.75 or ten trips for $20. The STM has a **tourist pass** that allows unlimited travel in a day for $9 (or $17 for three consecutive days); it's available from the information centres, Berri-UQAM, Bonaventure and Peel Métro stations and, from late April to late October, at all downtown Métro stations. OPUS cards, with a reloadable smart chip, were phased in during 2009 and replaced most old STM cards. Opus cards (which are to last for four years) cost a one-time fee of $3.50, which is to go up to $7 in 2010. You can buy and recharge your card at all Métro stations from fare vending machines or fare collectors.

It is rarely necessary to take a **taxi**. Taxi Diamond (Ⓣ514/273-6331) and Taxi Co-op (Ⓣ514/725-9885) are two reliable services.

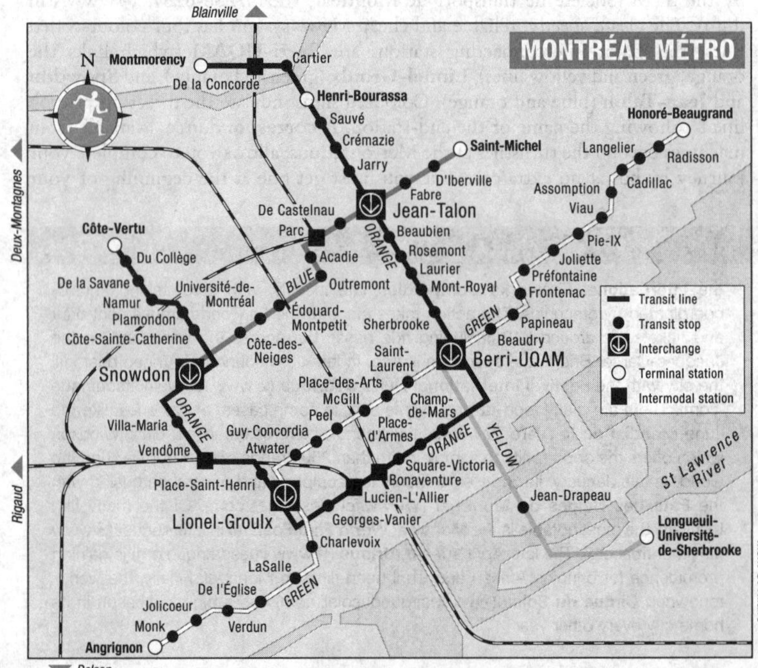

Accommodation

Plenty of Montréal's **accommodation** is geared towards expense-account travellers. Fortunately for visitors, there are a growing number of boutique hotels in Vieux-Montréal offering more atmosphere at generally lower prices. Moderately priced hotel rooms are concentrated around the lively St-Denis area, with even cheaper options in the rundown section along rue St-Hubert east of the bus terminal. An alternative is to stay in one of the city's many **B&Bs,** often located in interesting neighbourhoods like the Plateau. Rock-bottom prices are charged in the city's **hostels** and **university residences.**

Hotels

Abri du Voyageur 9 rue Ste-Catherine ouest; Métro: St-Laurent ⓣ514/849-2922 or 1-866/302-2922, ⓦwww.abri-voyageur.ca. While the location could be better – it is smack in the middle of the red-light district – the rooms are clean, several have exposed brick walls and hardwood floors, and it is just steps away from Chinatown and Vieux-Montréal. They also offer studios with kitchenettes. ❷

Anne ma Soeur Anne 4119 rue St-Denis; Métro: Mont-Royal ⓣ514/281-3187, ⓦwww.annemasoeuranne.com. On a prime stretch of rue St-Denis, this stylish seventeen-room hotel is a great find. The sunny, yellow rooms (all with wi-fi) feature kitchenettes, large bathrooms and some have large private terraces. Croissants are delivered to the room every morning. ❺

Auberge Bonaparte 447 rue St-François-Xavier; Métro: Place–d'Armes ⓣ514/844-1448, ⓦwww.bonaparte.com. A handsome upscale inn, steps from the Basilique Notre-Dame, built in 1886 and shaded by smart burgundy awnings. Inside, the quarters are decked out with wrought-iron headboards, hardwood floors, French dormer windows and some have view of the Basilique's gardens. Breakfast included. ❻

Auberge Casa de Mateo 440 rue St Francois-Xavier; Métro: Place d'Armes. ⓣ514/286-9589, ⓦwww.casademateo.com. Offering bright, spacious and clean rooms, the best thing about this auberge is undoubtedly its location – right in the heart of Vieux-Montréal. Breakfast included. ❹

Auberge Les Passants du Sans Soucy 171 rue St-Paul ouest; Métro: Place-d'Armes ⓣ514/842-2634, ⓦwww.lesanssoucy.com. Brass beds and hardwood floors contribute to the romantic atmosphere at this charming inn, and some rooms have wooden beams and stone walls. Breakfast, served in a skylit nook, is included. The lobby doubles as an art gallery with works by Québécois artists. ❻

Castel Saint-Denis 2099 rue St-Denis; Métro: Berri-UQAM or Sherbrooke ⓣ514/842-9719, ⓦwww.castelsaintdenis.qc.ca. One of the better small hotels in Montréal, it's right in the trendy St-Denis area, but quiet. Wi-fi available, and a continental breakfast included. ❸

Château de l'Argoat 524 rue Sherbrooke est; Métro: Sherbrooke ⓣ514/842-2046, ⓦwww.hotel-chateau-argoat.qc.ca. A fanciful cream-coloured fortress offering 25 spacious and attractive rooms with high ceilings, quaint chandeliers and private bath, some with a whirlpool tub. Breakfast and parking included. ❹

Château Versailles 1659 rue Sherbrooke ouest; Métro: Guy-Concordia ⓣ514/933-8111 or 1-888/933-8111, ⓦwww.versailleshotels.com. A unique, beautifully furnished hotel located in four stone buildings on the northwestern edge of downtown. Book well in advance, as it is one of the city's most popular hotels; cheap winter weekend rates also available. ❼

Hôtel Gault 449 rue Ste-Hélène; Métro: Square-Victoria ⓣ514/904-1616 or 1-866/904-1616, ⓦwww.hotelgault.com. One of the more glamorous boutique hotels, this is the place to stay – if you can afford it. The thirty individually designed loft-style rooms in this 1871 warehouse are a design-junkie's dream, with Arne Jacobsen fixtures, white-oak panelling and custom-made linens. Luxury amenities include an in-room "jet lag" massage. ❽

Manoir des Alpes 1245 rue St-André; Métro: Berri-UQAM ⓣ514/845-9803 or 1-800/465-2929, ⓦwww.hotelmanoirdesalpes.qc.ca. This Victorian building near the bus station is a three-star hotel with Swiss overtones and dark-wood furnishings. Rates include buffet breakfast and parking. ❸

Opus Montréal 10 Sherbrooke Ouest; Métro: St-Laurent ⓣ514/843-6000 or 1-866/744-6346, ⓦwww.opushotel.com/montreal. Designer chic meets history at this cool-toned hotel housed in an avant-garde 1914 building that's been artfully modernized. If you're in Montréal for the nightlife, this is the spot: It sits within strolling distance of the Plateau and club-crammed boul St-Laurent. Or, sip a cocktail at *Koko Bar*'s chill outdoor lounge. 7

Hôtel de Paris 901 rue Sherbrooke est; Métro: Sherbrooke ⓣ514/522-6861 or 1-800/567-7217, ⓦwww.hotel-montreal.com. An old mansion near rue St-Denis with a balcony café to hang out in, with other rooms in nearby properties. The cheaply furnished rooms have tiny beds but all are en suite with TVs, telephone and most have a/c. 4

Hôtel St-Paul 355 rue McGill; Métro: Square-Victoria ⓣ514/380-2222 or 1-866/380-2202, ⓦwww.hotelstpaul.com. Housed in a former bank, this most minimalist of Vieux-Montréal's boutique hotels has white walls and linens that contrast nicely with the dark-wood floors and elegantly simple furnishings of the rooms and suites. The *Vauvert* restaurant serves tasty French and Québécois dishes. 7

Le Saint-Sulpice Hôtel 414 rue St-Sulpice; Métro: Place-d'Armes ⓣ514/288-1000 or 1-877/785-7423, ⓦwww.lesaintsulpice.com. It would be hard to find a better-placed hotel in Vieux Montréal. The lovely boutique property sits on a cobblestoned street, in the shadow of the Basilique Notre-Dame. The hotel is all suites, each with a fireplace and kitchenette, and some with an ample terrace. *S Le Restaurant* serves French food with Middle Eastern touches, including superb seafood, in a leafy courtyard that overlooks the neighbouring Sulpician Seminary gardens. 6–7

B&Bs

Boulanger Bassin B&B 4293 rue de Brébeuf; Métro: Mont-Royal ⓣ514/525-0854, ⓦwww.bbassin.com. Wake up to an extravagant breakfast – from smoothies to eggs Benedict - at this friendly B&B north of Parc Lafontaine. The three bright and colourful rooms are simple but nicely furnished and all have private bath. Kids under 6 stay free, and weekend discounts in low season. 5

La Maison du Patriote 169 rue St-Paul est; Métro: Champ-de-Mars ⓣ514/397-0855, ⓦwww.lamaisondupatriote.ca. Unbeatable location, just around the corner from Place Jacques-Cartier, and friendly student ambience with free wi-fi. Rooms are simple but clean, but dorms can feel crowded and have air mattresses rather than beds. 3

Le Petit Prince Bed and Breakfast 1384 Overdale; Métro: Lucien-L'Allier. ⓣ514/938-2277 or 1-877/938-9750, ⓦwww.montrealbandb.com. If you are searching for a place to romance your sweetheart in downtown Montréal, this is it. Each individually decorated room has its own double whirlpool bath and either a functioning fireplace or a private balcony. 7

Petite Auberge les Bons Matins 1401 av Argyle Métro: Lucien-l'Allier ⓣ514/931-9167 or 1-800/588-5280, ⓦwww.bonsmatins.com. Located on a tree-lined street near downtown and busy rue Crescent, this well-appointed B&B-style inn has spacious rooms and suites as well as six apartments (7), each with special architectural features (archways, exposed brick, fireplace), large windows and private bathroom. 5

Aux Portes de la Nuit 3496 av Laval; Métro: Sherbrooke ⓣ514/848-0833, ⓦwww.auxportesdelanuit.com. Well situated on one of the Plateau's most attractive streets, this Victorian house has five rooms, all with private bath, and one with a private balcony. 4

Hostels

Auberge Alternative 358 rue St-Pierre; Métro: Square-Victoria ⓣ514/282-8069, ⓦwww.auberge-alternative.qc.ca. Montréal's finest hostel is located in a refurbished 1875 Vieux-Montréal warehouse. Rooms for six to twenty people and one double. You don't need to be a member to stay here. The hostel celebrates the local art community, with a small gallery and occasional art classes. Has free Fairtrade coffee and tea, and a breakfast of organic breads and cereals ($5). 1–2

Auberge Chez Jean 4136 av Henri-Julien; Métro: Mont-Royal ⓣ514/843-8279, ⓦwww.aubergechezjean.com. You'll either love or hate this very unofficial hostel. Guests bunk down all over the common rooms on its three floors, making it a great place to make new friends quickly, but forget about privacy unless you take one of the few closed rooms. Free breakfast and internet (including wi-fi). 1

Auberge de Jeunesse Internationale de Montréal (HI) 1030 rue Mackay; Métro: Lucien-L'Allier ⓣ514/843-3317 or 1-866/843-3317, ⓦwww.hostellingmontreal.com. With 250 beds, this is a large, well-located hostel with single, family or shared rooms (all rather sombrely coloured) that all have a/c and their own showers. Staff are friendly and helpful, and offer fun activities like bar tours. Free wi-fi also available. Book ahead from June–Sept. 1–2

Gîte Plateau Mont-Royal 185 rue Sherbrooke est; Métro: Sherbrooke ⓣ514/284-1276 or 1-877/350-4483, ⓦwww.hostelmontreal.com. Bright six- to eight-bed dorms and private rooms (with shared bath), an extremely chilled-out common room and great Plateau location make this one of the city's best backpacker options. Continental breakfast included. ❶–❸

Le Sous-bois 431 rue St-Vincent; Métro: Berri-UQAM. ⓣ514/879-1394, ⓦwww.lesousbois.com. Bunk down on air matresses in the main dorm or go for the private wooden cabins in the courtyard (❷). Cosy, friendly and good value for its Vieux-Montréal location. Includes free internet, phone calls, tea, coffee, breakfast, linen and towels. ❶

Hôtel Y des Femmes (YWCA) 1355 boul René-Lévesque ouest; Métro: Lucien-L'Allier or Guy-Concordia ⓣ514/866-9942, ⓦwww.ydesfemmesmtl.org. Single, double and triple rooms for men and women in this rather pricey downtown YWCA, but only women have access to the pool and gym facilities. Kitchen and laundry facilities and internet access also available. ❷–❸

Student rooms

McGill University Residences 3935 rue University; Métro: McGill ⓣ514/398-5200, ⓦwww.residences.mcgill.ca/summer.html. Popular residences for visiting anglophones and consequently often full. Four of the buildings are on the slopes of Mont Royal but Royal Victoria College is on the edge of downtown. Good weekly rates. Mid-May to mid-Aug only. ❶–❷

McGill University New Residence Hall 3625 av du Parc; Métro: Place-des-Arts ⓣ514-398-3471, ⓦwww.mcgill.ca/nrh. This former upscale hotel has been converted into a residence hall, and the result is comfortable rooms (with a kitchenette on each floor), as well as ample suites, each with their own kitchenette. Rates include breakfast. Open mid-May to mid-Aug. ❺

Les Résidences Universitaires UQAM 303 boul René-Lévesque est; Métro: Berri-UQAM ⓣ514/987-6669, ⓦwww.residences-uqam.qc.ca. Over a hundred clean and simply furnished studios with double bed, kitchenette and private bath, as well as apartments, in this Quartier Latin student residence. Open mid-May to mid-Aug. ❷

The City

Though Montréal island is large (51km by 16km), the heart of the city itself is very manageable. It's divided into Vieux-Montréal along the St Lawrence River, a downtown high-rise business core on the south side of the hill of Mont Royal and the lively Plateau and Quartier Latin neighbourhoods to the east. The main east–west arteries are rue Sherbrooke, boulevard de Maisonneuve, rue Ste-Catherine and boulevard René-Lévesque, all divided into east (*est*) and west (*ouest*) sections by the north–south **boulevard St-Laurent**, known locally as "The Main". North–south street numbers increase as you progress north from the St Lawrence River.

You're most likely to start by sampling the old-world charm of **Vieux-Montréal**. The narrow streets, alleys and squares are perfect for strolling, and every corner reveals an architectural gem, from monumental public edifices to the city's early steep-roofed homes. Close by, the parklands of the **Vieux-Port** adjoin a child-friendly science centre and departure points for getting onto the water. To the northwest, in the compact **downtown** area, the glass frontages of the office blocks reflect Victorian terraces and the spires of numerous churches, underlain by the passages of the **Underground City**, which link hotels,

Museum passes

The **Carte Musées Montréal** (Montréal Museums Pass $45; including transport $50; ⓦwww.museesmontreal.org) grants free admission to 34 museums in the city for three consecutive days at a significant discount; buy it at tourist offices or participating museums.

shopping centres and offices with the Métro. Rising above downtown, the city's landmark, **Mont Royal** – which the residents simply call "The Mountain" – is best accessed from the easterly Plateau Mont-Royal. This is the spot where the city's pulse beats fastest, as the cafés, restaurants and bars of **The Main** and rue St-Denis throng with people day and night. Further out to the east, the enormous **Stade Olympique** complex and the vast green space of the **Jardin Botanique** are the main pull. The islands facing the Vieux-Port that make up Parc Jean-Drapeau and the westerly Lachine Canal offer all manner of activities, many of them family-friendly.

Vieux-Montréal

Severed from downtown by the Autoroute Ville-Marie, the gracious district of **Vieux-Montréal** was left to decay until the early 1960s, when developers started to step in with generally tasteful renovations that brought colour and vitality back to the area. North America's greatest concentration of seventeenth-, eighteenth- and nineteenth-century buildings has its fair share of tourists, but it's popular with Montréalers, too – formerly as a symbolic place to air francophone grievances; more recently as a spot to wander around, check out the buskers on Place Jacques-Cartier, take in the historic monuments and roam the port's waterfront. Place d'Armes is the most central Métro station, although Square-Victoria or Champ-de-Mars are handier for the western and eastern ends of the district.

Place d'Armes and around

The focal point of Vieux-Montréal is **Place d'Armes**, its centre occupied by a century-old statue of Maisonneuve, whose missionary zeal raised the wrath of the displaced Iroquois. The mutt among the luminaries represents the animal who warned the French of an impending attack in 1644; legend says the ensuing battle ended when the supposedly unarmed Maisonneuve killed the Iroquois chief on this very spot.

Basilique Notre Dame

Despite a skyscraper on its west side, Place d'Armes is still dominated by the twin-towered, neo-Gothic **Basilique Notre-Dame** (Mon–Fri 8am–4.30pm, Sat 8am–4pm, Sun 12:30–4pm; $5, light show $10; Ⓦ www.basiliquenddm.org; Métro: Place-d'Armes), the cathedral of the Catholic faithful since 1829. Its architect, the Protestant Irish-American James O'Donnell, was so inspired by his creation he converted to Catholicism in order to be buried under the church. The western tower, named Temperance, holds the ten-tonne Jean-Baptiste bell, whose booming could once be heard 25km away. The breathtaking gilt and sky-blue interior, flooded with light from three rose windows unusually set in the ceiling, and flickering with multicoloured votive candles, was designed by Montréal architect Victor Bourgeau. Most notable of the detailed furnishings are Louis-Philippe Hébert's fine wooden carvings of the prophets on the pulpit and the awe-inspiring main altar by French sculptor Bouriché. Imported from Limoges in France, the stained-glass windows depict the founding of Ville-Marie. Behind the main altar is the **Chapelle Sacré-Coeur**, destroyed by a serious fire in 1978 but rebuilt with an impressive modern bronze reredos by Charles Daudelin. Time your visit for the "And then there was light" *son et lumière* show for a history lesson and a chance to see the architectural details artfully lit up; otherwise take advantage of one of the twenty-minute guided tours (half-hourly, Mon–Fri 9am–4pm, Sat 9am–3:30pm, Sun 12:30–3:30pm; included in entry).

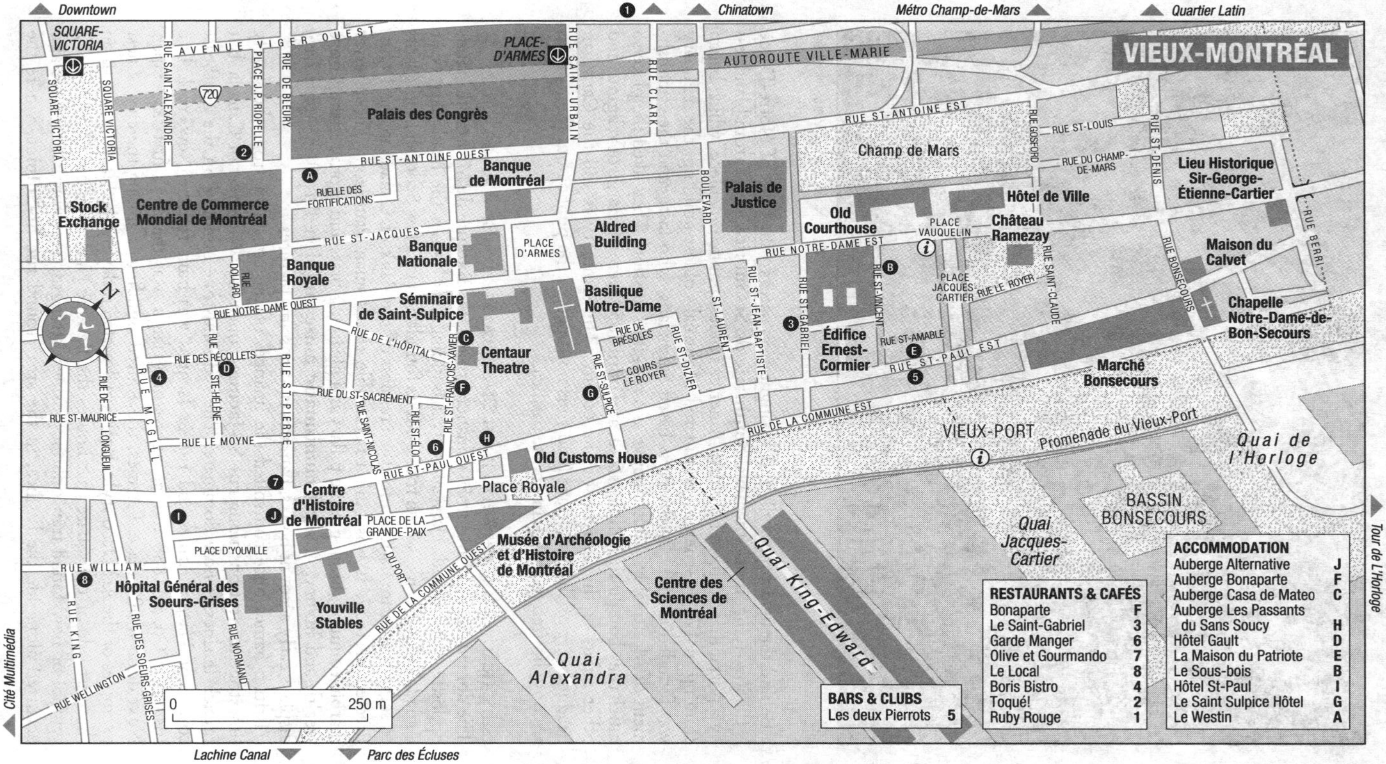

VIEUX-MONTRÉAL

Downtown
Chinatown
Métro Champ-de-Mars
Quartier Latin
Tour de L'Horloge
Lachine Canal
Parc des Écluses
Cité Multimédia

SQUARE-VICTORIA
PLACE-D'ARMES
Palais des Congrès
Stock Exchange
Centre de Commerce Mondial de Montréal
Banque de Montréal
Banque Nationale
Banque Royale
PLACE D'ARMES
Aldred Building
Basilique Notre-Dame
Séminaire de Saint-Sulpice
Centaur Theatre
Old Customs House
Place Royale
Centre d'Histoire de Montréal
Musée d'Archéologie et d'Histoire de Montréal
Youville Stables
Hôpital Général des Soeurs-Grises
Palais de Justice
Champ de Mars
Old Courthouse
PLACE VAUQUELIN
Hôtel de Ville
Château Ramezay
PLACE JACQUES-CARTIER
Édifice Ernest-Cormier
Marché Bonsecours
Lieu Historique Sir-George-Étienne-Cartier
Maison du Calvet
Chapelle Notre-Dame-de-Bon-Secours
VIEUX-PORT
Promenade du Vieux-Port
Quai de l'Horloge
BASSIN BONSECOURS
Quai Jacques-Cartier
Quai King-Edward
Centre des Sciences de Montréal
Quai Alexandra

AVENUE VIGER OUEST
AUTOROUTE VILLE-MARIE
RUE ST-ANTOINE OUEST
RUE ST-ANTOINE EST
RUE ST-JACQUES
RUE NOTRE-DAME OUEST
RUE NOTRE-DAME EST
RUE ST-PAUL OUEST
RUE ST-PAUL EST
RUE DE LA COMMUNE OUEST
RUE DE LA COMMUNE EST
SQUARE VICTORIA
RUE SAINT-ALEXANDRE
PLACE J.P. RIOPELLE
RUE DE BLEURY
RUE SAINT-URBAIN
RUE CLARK
BOULEVARD ST-LAURENT
RUE ST-JEAN-BAPTISTE
RUE ST-GABRIEL
RUE ST-VINCENT
RUE ST-AMABLE
RUE GOSFORD
RUE ST-LOUIS
RUE DU CHAMP-DE-MARS
RUE SAINT-CLAUDE
RUE LE ROYER
RUE ST-DENIS
RUE BONSECOURS
RUE BERRI
RUELLE DES FORTIFICATIONS
RUE DOLLARD
RUE DES RÉCOLLETS
RUE STE-HÉLÈNE
RUE DE L'HÔPITAL
RUE ST-FRANÇOIS-XAVIER
RUE DU ST-SACRÉMENT
RUE SAINT-NICOLAS
RUE ST-ÉLOI
RUE ST-SULPICE
RUE DE BRÉSOLES
COURS LE ROYER
RUE ST-DIZIER
RUE ST-PIERRE
RUE MCGILL
RUE LE MOYNE
RUE ST-MAURICE
RUE DE LONGUEUIL
RUE WILLIAM
RUE KING
RUE WELLINGTON
RUE DES SOEURS-GRISES
RUE NORMAND
PLACE D'YOUVILLE
PLACE DE LA GRANDE-PAIX
DU PORT
720

0 250 m

ACCOMMODATION

Auberge Alternative	J
Auberge Bonaparte	F
Auberge Casa de Mateo	C
Auberge Les Passants du Sans Soucy	H
Hôtel Gault	D
La Maison du Patriote	E
Le Sous-bois	B
Hôtel St-Paul	I
Le Saint Sulpice Hôtel	G
Le Westin	A

RESTAURANTS & CAFÉS

Bonaparte	F
Le Saint-Gabriel	3
Garde Manger	6
Olive et Gourmando	7
Le Local	8
Boris Bistro	4
Toqué!	2
Ruby Rouge	1

BARS & CLUBS

Les deux Pierrots	5

▲ Interior of the Basilique Notre-Dame, Vieux-Montréal

Behind the fieldstone walls and wrought-iron gates to the right of Notre-Dame is the low-lying, mock-medieval **Séminaire de St-Sulpice**, saved from blandness by a portal that's topped by North America's oldest public timepiece, which began chiming in 1701. Generally considered Montréal's oldest building, the seminary was founded in 1685 by the Paris-based Sulpicians, who instigated the establishment of Montréal by Maisonneuve as a religious mission. They liked the place so much they bought the whole island, and until 1859 were in charge of religious and other affairs as the *seigneurs* of the colony. The seminary is still the Canadian headquarters of the Sulpicians (and thus not open to the public), but their duties are now limited to maintaining the basilica.

Banque de Montréal and rues St-Jacques and St-Sulpice

The domed shrine of Montréal's financial rulers, the **Banque de Montréal**, stands opposite. This grand, classical-revival building still houses the headquarters of Canada's oldest bank, which rose from its foundation by a few Scottish immigrants to serve the entire nation until the creation of the Bank of Canada in the 1930s. Erected in 1837, it was built to resemble the Roman Pantheon. The interior marble counters, black granite pillars and gleaming brass and bronze fittings ooze wealth and luxury. A small **numismatic museum** (Mon–Fri 10am–4pm; free) displays early account books, banknotes, coins and pictures.

British names once controlled the finances of the continent from the stately limestone institutions along **rue St-Jacques**, once the Wall Street of Canada, but French businesses now dominate. The red-sandstone building on the northeast corner of Place d'Armes and rue St-Jacques was built for the New York Life Insurance Co. in 1888 and, at eight storeys high, was the city's first skyscraper. Next door at 501 Place d'Armes, the Aldred Building is among the city's finest examples of the Art Deco style. Both are dwarfed today by the black monolith on the west side of the square that houses the Banque Nationale, built in 1967 as a symbol of new-found francophone business strength. Transformations have also occurred alongside the basilica, in the area around **rue St-Sulpice**, where the warehouses constructed in the Victorian era to cope with the growing trade of Montréal's harbour have been converted into luxurious flats and offices, as well as a couple of boutique hotels.

Along rue Notre-Dame

The city's first street, **rue Notre-Dame**, was laid out in 1672 and runs east–west across Vieux-Montréal. Other than the financial buildings of rue St-Jacques, there is little of particular interest to the west of Place d'Armes; it's more rewarding to head east along Notre-Dame from the top of rue St-Sulpice, past the black glass behemoth of the **Palais de Justice** on the corner of boulevard St-Laurent. It overshadows its forerunner, the imposing **Old Courthouse**, erected by the British to impress upon the French population the importance of abiding by their laws; today it serves as municipal offices. Criminal trials took place across the street, at 100 rue Notre-Dame est, in the **Édifice Ernest Cormier**, built in 1925, and now used as an appellate court.

Further along, the 1800 Maison de La Sauvegarde at no. 160, with its rough-hewn limestone facade, high chimneys and steeply pitched roof and dormers, was among the last homes to be built in the local French vernacular. Opposite, on the eastern side of the Old Courthouse, **Place Vauquelin**, centred on a pretty fountain and statue of the naval commander Jean Vauquelin, gives views of the **Champ de Mars** to the north. Excavations to build a car park here hit rock, which turned out to be the original city walls; they were excavated, restored and the area was made into a pleasant grassy space instead of a car park.

East of Place Vauquelin, the ornate **Hôtel de Ville** (City Hall) was built in the 1870s and is a typical example of the area's civic buildings of the time when French-speaking architects looked to the mother country for inspiration. On a visit to Expo '67, General de Gaulle chose its second-floor balcony to make his "Vive le Québec libre!" speech, which left the city's anglophones reeling at the thought that Québec was on its way to independent status and infused francophones with a political fervour that ended in the October Crisis (see p.959).

Place Jacques-Cartier

The cobbled **Place Jacques-Cartier** opposite City Hall slopes down towards the river and offers spectacular views of the Vieux-Port, but is overrun with buskers, street artists and caricaturists throughout the summer. The city-run **tourist office** (see p.219) occupies a stone building at the northwest corner. Restaurants and cafés surrounding the square hustle for business, while the narrow **rue St-Amable** to the west is dotted with artists selling quaint watercolours and tinted photos of Montréal scenery alongside tacky caricatures. Your best bet for souvenirs here is the small courtyard market tucked away from the street, where jewellery stalls offer some decent artisan-crafted pieces. A few buildings on the square – Maison Vandelac, Maison del Vecchio and the Maison Cartier – show the features typical of Montréal architecture in the 1800s, with pitched roofs designed to shed heavy snowfall and small dormer windows to defend against the cold.

At the top of the square itself, the controversial **Nelson Monument** stands above the few stalls that serve as the only reminders that this was once Montréal's main marketplace. The city's oldest monument – the column is a third the height of its more famous London counterpart, but predates it by a few years – was funded by anglophone Montréalers delighted with Nelson's 1805 defeat of the French at Trafalgar. Québec separatists adopted it as a rallying point in the 1970s. Ironically, the anglophones never liked the monument much either, because it faced away from the water.

Château Ramezay Museum

East of Place Jacques-Cartier, the long and low fieldstone manor of the **Château Ramezay Museum** (June to mid-Oct daily 10am–6pm; mid-Oct to May Tues–Sun 10am–4.30pm; $9; ⓣ514/861-3708, ⓦwww.chateauramezay.qc.ca; Métro Champ-de-Mars), set in lovely gardens, looks much as it did in 1705 when it was built for Montréal's eleventh governor, Claude de Ramezay. It later served as the North American headquarters for the Compagnie des Indes, before passing into the hands of the British in 1760. During the fleeting American invasion fifteen years later, Benjamin Franklin stayed here in an attempt to persuade Montréalers to join the United States, but he lost public and church support by not promising the supremacy of the French language in what would have been the fourteenth state. Its collection of oil paintings, domestic artefacts, tools, costumes and furniture from the eighteenth and nineteenth centuries is thorough and informative. The most impressive room is a reconstruction of the *Salle des Nantes*, complete with 18th-century mahogany walls and woodwork imported from the Compagnie des Indes headquarters in France. In the whitewashed stone vaults below, the exhibits take on more of an educational slant, recreating domestic scenes of the early European settlers that include a kitchen with a dog-powered roasting spit.

Lieu historique national de Sir-George-Étienne-Cartier

At the intersection of rues Notre-Dame and Berri, a five-minute walk east, the **Lieu historique national de Sir-George-Étienne-Cartier** (late April to late June & mid-Sept to late-Dec Wed–Sun 10am–noon & 1–5pm; late June to mid-Sept 10am–5:30pm; $3.90; ⓣ514/283-2822; ⓦwww.pc.gc.ca/cartier; Métro: Champ-de-Mars) comprises two adjoining houses inhabited by the Cartier family from 1848 to 1871. The cocky Sir George-Étienne Cartier was one of the fathers of Confederation, persuading the French-Canadians to join the Dominion of Canada by declaring: "We are of different races, not for strife but to work together for the common welfare." Today, leaders of French-Canadian nationalism decry Cartier as a collaborator, and the displays in the east house diplomatically skirt over the issue of whether he was right or wrong and emphasize instead his role in the construction of Canada's railways. This collection is decidedly bizarre, with Muppet-like figures representing the founding fathers on the main floor, while eight white-painted papier-mâché models of Cartier himself sit at a round, glass-domed table upstairs. The stuffily decorated rooms in the west house are more interesting, furnished with more than a thousand original artefacts to evoke the period when Cartier lived here.

Rue St-Paul

A block south of rue Notre-Dame, **rue St-Paul**, one of Montréal's most attractive thoroughfares, is lined with nineteenth-century commercial buildings and Victorian lampposts, the buildings little changed from when Charles Dickens stayed here, although they now house restaurants, art galleries and specialist shops selling everything from Inuit crafts to kites.

Chapelle Notre-Dame-de-Bon-Secours

Mark Twain noted that, in Montréal, "you couldn't throw a brick without hitting a church", and near rue St-Paul's eastern end is Montréal's favourite: the delicate and profusely steepled **Chapelle Notre-Dame-de-Bon-Secours** (Tues–Sun: May–Oct 10am–5.30pm; mid-March to April & Nov to mid-Jan 11am–3.30pm; free), or the Sailors' Church. The outstretched arms of the Virgin on the tower became a landmark for ships on the St Lawrence and, once safely landed, the mariners would endow the chapel with wooden votive lamps in the shape of ships, many of which are still here. The chapel dates back to the earliest days of the colony, when Maisonneuve helped cut the wood for what was Ville-Marie's first church, under the instigation of Marguerite Bourgeoys, who had been summoned to Ville-Marie to teach the settlement's children. The devout Bourgeoys also founded the nation's first religious order and was in charge of the *filles du Roi* – orphaned French girls sent to marry bachelor settlers and multiply the colony's population. She was canonized in 1982, becoming Canada's first saint. Today's chapel contains a small **museum** devoted to her life (same hours; $8; ⓣ514/282-8670, ⓦwww.marguerite-bourgeoys.com; Métro: Champ-de-Mars). The entry price is worth it mainly for the chance to climb the narrow stairs leading to the summit of the tower above the apse, where the "aerial chapel" affords excellent views over the port and the old town.

Maison du Calvet

Opposite the chapel is the three-storey, high-chimneyed **Maison du Calvet**, built in 1725 and one of Montréal's best examples of French domestic architecture. Photographed, painted and admired more than any other house in the district, it was the home of a Huguenot draper and justice of the peace called Pierre Calvet, a notorious turncoat who changed his allegiances from the French to the British and then to the Americans. Today it houses a pricey inn and restaurant (*La Maison Pierre du Calvet*; 405 rue Bonsecours; ⓣ514/282-1725, 1-866/544-1725 ⓦwww.pierreducalvet.ca; ⑧ including breakfast).

Rue Bonsecours

Rue Bonsecours, which links rue St-Paul to rue Notre-Dame, is another typical Vieux-Montréal street. The grey-painted, many-dormered **Maison Papineau** at no. 440 was home to four generations of the Papineau family, including Louis-Joseph who, as Speaker of the Assembly, championed the *habitants* of the St Lawrence farmlands against the senior Catholic clergy, the British government and Montréal's business class. Calling for democratic election of the executive officers of church and government, he fuelled the rage of the *Patriotes* – the leaders of Lower Canada reform – but deserted the scene as the 1837 rebellion reached a bloody climax (see p.253). The house remains a private residence, but renovations have significantly altered its exterior facade from the days when the Papineaus lived here.

The silver-domed **Marché Bonsecours** (Jan to early May & early Nov to Dec daily 10am–6pm; early May to late June Sun–Thurs 10am–6pm & Fri–Sat 10am–9pm; late June to early Sept 10am–9pm; early Sept to early Nov Sun–Wed 10am–6pm, Thurs–Fri 10am–9pm & Sat 10am–7pm; ⓣ514/872-7730, ⓦwww.marchebonsecours.qc.ca) extends beyond the intersection of rue Bonsecours and rue St-Paul. For years this elegant building was used for municipal offices, but for the city's 350th birthday in 1992 it was restored and transformed to house restaurants, boutiques, a number of shops specializing in Québécois crafts, expensive artworks and exhibitions.

Vieux-Port

The south side of the Marché Bonsecours faces onto the **Vieux-Port de Montréal**, once the import and export conduit of the continent. When the main shipyards shifted east in the 1970s they left a lot of vacant space, which has since been renovated for public use, with biking, cross-country skiing and jogging paths and exhibitions in the quayside hangars.

At the Vieux-Port's easternmost point, the **Tour de l'Horloge** on the Quai de l'Horloge rises 51m above sea level. The clock tower was built in 1922 to

Boat trips in and around Montréal

The Vieux-Port is the major departure point for various **boat trips**. The best by far is the **jet boat** run by Saute-Moutons, departing every two hours from the Quai de l'Horloge (June–Sept daily 10am–6pm; $65; ⓣ514/284-9607, ⓦwww.jetboatingmontreal.com; check website for discount coupons). Scooting through the Lachine Rapids, the trip will leave you wet, exhilarated and terrified. They also offer speed boat trips for $25. Meandering Bâteau Mouche **cruises** leave from the Quai Jacques-Quartier (mid-May to mid-Oct 4 daily; $20.46; ⓣ514/849-9952 or 1-800/361-9952, ⓦwww.bateau-mouche.ca). The glass-topped boats offer lovely views of the surrounding islands and the river. Most tours last around two hours, though there are longer dinner cruises. A more unique way to see the area is the **Amphi-bus** (June–Sept hourly departures 10am–10pm, May & Oct 4 daily; $32; ⓣ514/849-5181, ⓦwww.montreal-amphibus-tour.com), which leaves from the corner of rue de la Commune and boulevard St-Laurent, or the Centre Infotouriste downtown.

commemorate the men of the Merchant Fleet who died in World War I; ships were recorded as having entered the harbour as soon as they had passed it. The 192 steps leading up to the observatory, will reward you with excellent views of the harbour, the St Lawrence Seaway, Vieux-Montréal, the islands and Mont Royal. Westward, across the pedalboat-filled Bassin Bonsecours, there's a seasonal information centre (ⓦwww.quaysoftheoldport.com for seasonal opening times) located at the northwest corner of the **Quai Jacques-Cartier**, which is a good place to find out about weekend activities and performances portside.

The main events of the Vieux-Port are clustered in and around the next hangar westward, the **Quai King-Edward**. There's an IMAX cinema here (English screening times vary), which is part of the **Centre des Sciences de Montréal** (Mon–Sat 10am–9pm, Sun 10am–5pm; exhibit or film $12, both $20; ⓣ514/496-4629 or 1-877/496-4724, ⓦwww.montrealsciencecentre.com; Métro: Place-d'Armes), an interactive science and entertainment complex. Divided into three exhibition halls, focusing on themes of life, information and matter, the massive rooms contain little that will keep you occupied, but most kids will enjoy some of the hands-on exhibits. At the end of the pier itself there is a **lookout point** up a few flights of stairs, with explanatory panels showcasing a panorama of Vieux-Montréal and the islands.

Place Royale and Place d'Youville

Once the site of duels, whippings and public hangings amidst the peddlers and hawkers who sold wares from the incoming ships, **Place Royale** is dominated by the neat classical facade of the Old Customs House and a fine museum. Close by is the charming public square of **Place d'Youville**, which includes the Founder's Obelisk, a monument to the city founders. The square's eastern portion was renamed **Place de la Grande-Paix** in 2001, to mark the tercentennial of the Great Peace of Montréal, a treaty signed here in 1701 to end the conflict between the Natives and French settlers.

Musée d'Archéologie et d'Histoire de Montréal

At the nearby **Pointe-à-Callière**, now landlocked after the changes in the Vieux-Port, is the **Musée d'Archéologie et d'Histoire de Montréal** (late June to early Sept Mon–Fri 10am–6pm, Sat & Sun 11am–6pm; rest of year Tues–Fri 10am–5pm, Sat & Sun 11am–5pm; $14; ⓣ514/872-9150, ⓦwww.pacmuseum.qc.ca; Métro: Square-Victoria), at 350 Place Royale.

The museum occupies the striking modern Éperon building on the Pointe, visible across the parkland from the Quai King-Edward. The $27m centre, which spreads underground below Place Royale as far as the Old Customs House, focuses on the development of Montréal as a meeting and trading place, as told through the archeological remains excavated here at the oldest part of the city. The high-tech audiovisual presentation gives an excellent introduction to the museum, to archeology generally, and to that of Montréal in particular. Early remnants of the city include the city's first Catholic cemetery, eighteenth-century water conduits and sewage systems and walls dating from different centuries. The underground sections emerge into the Old Customs House, which holds a gift shop. Be sure to leave time for the generally excellent temporary shows, all with an archeological theme, on the Éperon building's upper floors. The museum offers free guided tours at different times; in the summer, tours are generally run four times daily on weekdays, and three times on the weekends – check the website for current times.

Centre d'Histoire de Montréal and Youville Stables

Halfway along Place d'Youville, a century-old red-brick fire station has been converted into the **Centre d'Histoire de Montréal** (Tues–Sun 10am–5pm; $6; ⓣ514/872-3207, ⓦwww.ville.montreal.qc.ca/chm; Métro: Square-Victoria). The multimedia exhibits of the city's history aren't terribly in-depth, but are fine for a sketchy overview. The competing soundtracks of films shown in the warren of rooms upstairs (including a factory cloakroom and a kitchen circa 1950) attempt to capture daily life in Montréal. Temporary exhibitions are usually quite stimulating, including photographic essays on the city's diverse ethnic and cultural communities. The barren car park covering the western half of Place d'Youville gives no indication that this was once a marketplace, which also served as the Parliament of United Canada from 1844 until it was torched by Tory rioters in 1849.

On the south side of the square is **Youville Stables**, whose shady courtyard, gardens, restaurants and offices was one of the first of the area's old buildings to be gentrified. (The complex was once a warehouse; the stables were next door.) Dating from 1825, the courtyard layout is a throwback to a design used by the earliest Montréal inhabitants as a protection against Iroquois hostilities.

Square Victoria and around

To reach downtown (in a roundabout fashion), head back towards the archeology museum and detour up rue St-François-Xavier to find the **Centaur Theatre**. Located at no. 453, and housed in the former Montréal Stock Exchange – Canada's first – it is the main English-language theatre in Montréal today. Continue north to reach rue St-Jacques, where to the east, at no. 362, you'll pass the sumptuous **Banque de Montréal** (formerly the Molson Bank) and to the west, at no. 362, the **Royal Bank**. When it was built in 1866, the latter was the tallest building in the British Empire, at 23 storeys.

At the northwestern end of Vieux-Montréal, the entire block of rue St-Jacques between rue St-Pierre and Square Victoria is taken up by the **Centre de Commerce Mondial de Montréal**, an architectural gem and prominent business address. Inaugurated in 1991 with the hope of reviving the former business district, the structure incorporates the facades of the centuries-old buildings that formerly stood there. Inside, the **ruelle des Fortifications**, so named because the former alley marked the location of the city's stone walls, was transformed into a lofty interior arcade adorned with boutiques, restaurants, a soothing fountain and a statue of Amphitrite, Poseidon's wife. At its easternmost end is a chunk of the Berlin Wall.

Across the street, renovations to **Square Victoria** have made it a more welcoming space, but it's still a far cry from its heyday when it was surrounded by buildings and bustling with activity from the city's haymarket. The imposing skyscraper bracketing the west side of the square used to be the digs of the **Montréal Stock Exchange**, but futures are traded there now instead of shares. Also of note is the **Art Nouveau grill** adorning the Métro station entranceway – which once graced a station on the Paris Métro – donated to the city for Expo '67.

Downtown Montréal

Montréal's **downtown** lies roughly between rue Sherbrooke and rue St-Antoine to the north and south, towards rue St-Denis in the east and overlapping with an area known as the Golden Square Mile (see p.236) as it stretches west beyond rue Guy. Of the main streets, **rue Ste-Catherine** offers the most in the way of **shopping**, dining and entertainment, while **boulevard de Maisonneuve** is more business-oriented. A number of Métro stations on the green and orange lines provide easy access to downtown's attractions – most are linked to the so-called Underground City (see p.234). The area is also dotted with old churches, museums and public squares filled with activity from buskers, artists and market vendors.

Square Dorchester and around

Formerly a Catholic cemetery, **Square Dorchester** is a leafy spot right in the centre of downtown that is as good a place as any to get your bearings – the Art

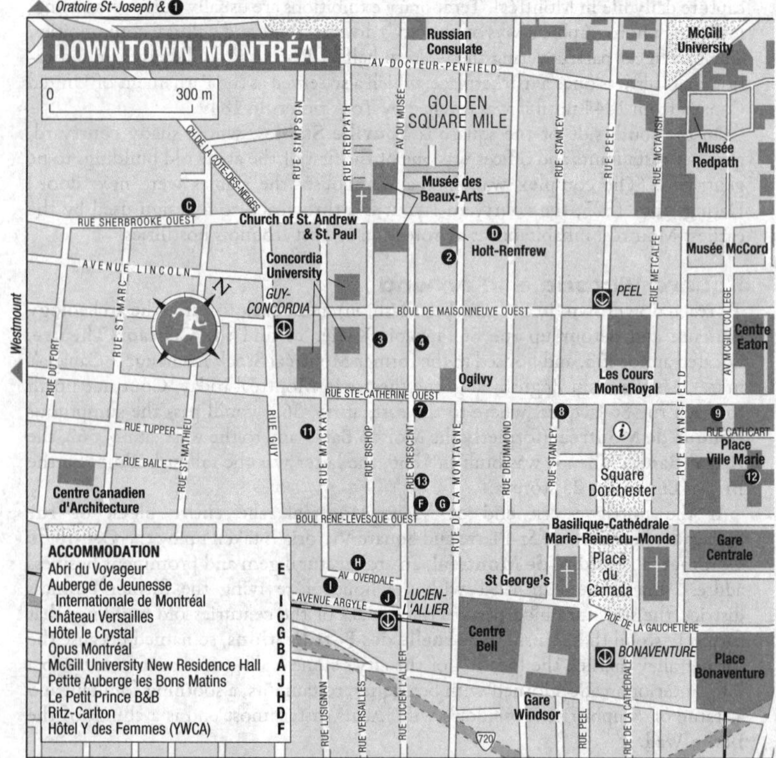

ACCOMMODATION	
Abri du Voyageur	E
Auberge de Jeunesse Internationale de Montréal	I
Château Versailles	C
Hôtel le Crystal	G
Opus Montréal	B
McGill University New Residence Hall	A
Petite Auberge les Bons Matins	J
Le Petit Prince B&B	H
Ritz-Carlton	D
Hôtel Y des Femmes (YWCA)	F

Deco-inspired Dominion Square Building on the north side of the square is the site of the Infotouriste office (see p.219) and the starting point for guided bus tours; there are also occasional lunchtime concerts here in summer. The southern half of the square is partitioned off as **Place du Canada**, which commemorates the 1967 centennial. Along its west side, the area's oldest building is the Victorian **St George's Anglican Church** (Tues–Sun 9am–4pm; ⓣ514/866-7113, ⓦwww.st-georges.org). Its solid neo-Gothic exterior gives way to a lofty interior, where trusses that rise in a series of arches support the gabled roof.

The city's legendary ice-hockey team, the **Montréal Canadiens**, known as "the Habs", short for "Habitants", play in the 21,000-seat **Centre Bell** (ⓦwww.centrebell.ca; ⓣ514/932-2582), at 1260 rue de la Gauchetière ouest, two blocks west of the Place du Canada. The centre is also the venue for rock concerts, classical-music performances and family entertainment. English guided tours take place daily at 11.15am and 2.45pm ($8). If you fancy a puck or a hockey jersey, head inside to the Canadiens' Souvenir Boutique (Mon–Wed 9.30am–6pm, Thurs & Fri until 9pm, Sat & Sun until 5pm).

Basilique-Cathédrale Marie-Reine-du-Monde

Dwarfed by its high-rise neighbours, the **Basilique-Cathédrale Marie-Reine-du-Monde** (Mon–Fri 7am–7.30pm, Sat 7.30am–8.30pm, Sun 8.30am–7.30pm, ⓦwww.cathedralecatholiquedemontreal.org; Métro: Bonaventure) was commissioned by Bishop Ignace Bourget in 1875 as a reminder that Catholicism still

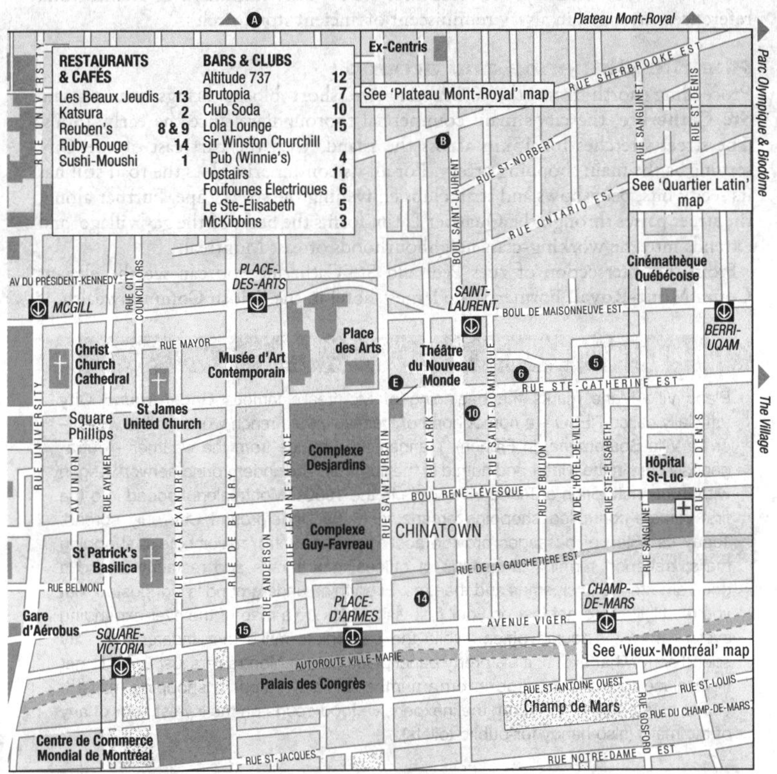

dominated the largest city in the new Dominion of Canada. Impressed by St Peter's while visiting Rome, Bourget created a scaled-down replica of the famous church. While the statues crowning St Peter's facade are of the Apostles, the thirteen statues atop its smaller cousin represent the patron saints of the parishes that donated them. The inside is not as opulent as you might expect, though the high altar of marble, onyx and ivory is surmounted by a gilded copper reproduction of Bernini's baldachin over the altar in St Peter's. To your left on entering is the Chapelle des Souvenirs, which contains various relics, including the wax-encased remains of St Zoticus, a patron saint of the poor.

Centre Canadien d'Architecture

A few blocks west of the Centre Bell, the **Centre Canadien d'Architecture** (CCA), 1920 rue Baile (Wed–Sun 10am–5pm, Thurs to 9pm and free after 5.30pm; ⓣ514/939-7026, ⓦwww.cca.qc.ca; Métro: Guy-Concordia) inhabits a wonderfully sleek building with a curiously windowless facade and vast glass doors. The design incorporates the beautifully restored Shaughnessy Mansion (the former residence of a president of the Canadian Pacific Railway) and its Art Nouveau conservatory, while the light-filled galleries display the museum's vast collection of prints, drawings and books in exhibitions ranging from individual masters to whole movements from all cultures and periods. Behind the museum on the south side of boulevard René-Lévesque are the whimsical **CCA Sculpture Gardens** (daily 6am–midnight; free). Designed by prominent Montréal artist and architect Melvin Charney, the sculptures are a wacky mishmash of architectural references, arranged in a way reminiscent of ancient stone circles.

Rue Ste-Catherine and around

Proceeding north from the CCA for two short blocks brings you to **rue Ste-Catherine**, the city's main commercial thoroughfare since the early 1900s. The street stretches for 15km across the island, with the part east of rue Guy serving as the main shopping artery. For all its consumerist gloss the road still has its seedy bits, peepshows and strip clubs enlivening the streetscape. Further along, the street passes through the Quartier Latin, forms the heart of the gay village, and extends into the working-class neighbourhoods of east Montréal.

From the intersection of rues Peel and Ste-Catherine you can see the elegant **Cours Mont-Royal**. Formerly the largest hotel in the British Commonwealth, it

The Underground City

Place Ville Marie marks the beginning of Montréal's famous **Underground City** (officially called RÉSO – a homophone of "réseau", the French word for "network" – or La Ville Souterraine, in French), planned as a refuge from the weather – outrageously cold in the winter and humid in the summer. The underground network began with the construction of Place Ville Marie in the 1960s. Montréalers flooded into the first climate-controlled shopping arcade, and the Underground City duly spread. Today its 33km of passages provide access to the Métro, major hotels, shopping malls, transport termini, thousands of offices, apartments and restaurants and a good smattering of cinemas and theatres. Everything underground is signposted, but you're still likely to get lost on your first visit – pick up a map of the ever-expanding system from the tourist office. While the pamphlets make the Underground City sound somewhat exotic, it's a pretty banal place – most Montréalers just use it to get from place to place, or drop in on a number of fairly standard shopping malls. If you're on a budget, check out the inexpensive food courts on the lowest floor of any of the malls (also handy for public toilets).

now contains four floors of shops (including those of expensive designers), topped by apartments and offices. Peek inside and gawk up at the fourteen-storey-high atria and chandeliers preserved from the hotel. One of these hangs from the coffered ceiling over a permanent catwalk – a testament to the fashion aspirations of the shopping centre. Standing out amongst the skyscrapers and malls, the cross-shaped, 46-storey **Place Ville Marie** has been a Montréal landmark since the 1960s, its rooftop searchlight visible for miles around, while below ground its shopping mall was one of the main catalysts of the Underground City. It marks one end of **avenue McGill College**, a broad boulevard lined with skyscrapers that frame a view of McGill University and the mountain beyond.

Christ Church Cathedral

A block or so further east of Place Ville Marie the grounds of the 1859 Anglican **Christ Church Cathedral** (daily 10am–6pm; ⓣ514/843-6577, ⓦwww.montreal.anglican.org/cathedral; Métro: McGill), 635 rue Ste-Catherine ouest and Square Phillips, opposite, provide a break in the commercial strip. By 1927, the church's slender stone spire was threatening to crash through the wooden roof and was replaced with the peculiar aluminium replica. Inside, the soaring Gothic arches are decorated with heads of angels and the evangelists, but the most poignant feature is the Coventry Cross, made from nails salvaged from England's Coventry Cathedral, which was destroyed by bombing during World War II. With the decline in its congregation, the cathedral authorities' desperation for money led them to lease all the land around and beneath the church. For nearly a year, Christ Church was known as "the floating church" – it was supported on concrete struts while the developers tunnelled out the glitzy Promenades de la Cathédrale, a boutique-lined part of the Underground City.

Place des Arts and Musée d'Art Contemporain de Montréal

A couple of blocks east of Square Phillips, Ste-Catherine slopes down towards **Place des Arts**, Montréal's leading performing-arts centre and the site of major festivals throughout the summer. The layout tends to throw newcomers: the entrances to all the performance halls are via an underground concourse. Atop that is a large plaza, with a series of gardens and fountains. This part of town, called the **Quartier des Spectacles**, is undergoing a major, long-term renewal as Montréal's entertainment district; it will include theatres, cultural centres and galleries, and will also incorporate the Place des Arts.

Occupying the west side of the Place des Arts plaza, the **Musée d'Art Contemporain de Montréal** (Tues–Sun 11am–6pm, Wed till 9pm; $8, free Wed evenings 6–9pm; ⓣ514/847-6226, ⓦwww.macm.org; Métro: Place-des-Arts) is Canada's first museum devoted entirely to contemporary art. The city's foremost showcase for work by Québécois artists, such as Paul-Émile Borduas and Jean-Paul Riopelle, the museum also has works by other Canadian and international artists. One wing is devoted to the permanent collection; the other stages temporary exhibitions. There's also a small sculpture garden – though difficult to find, it holds a Henry Moore sculpture amid the greenery. On the first Friday night of the month (except Jan and Aug), the museum features live music, cocktails and tours of exhibits (regular admission).

Rue Sherbrooke and around

Rue Sherbrooke crosses half of the island of Montréal but, other than the Stade Olympique far out east, its most interesting part is the few blocks from McGill University to rue Guy, an elite stretch of private galleries, exclusive hotels and **boutiques**, including Yves Saint-Laurent, Ralph Lauren and Giorgio Armani.

The Ritz-Carlton and around

At the corner of rue Drummond is the **Ritz-Carlton**, Montréal's most ornate hotel; Elizabeth Taylor married Richard Burton here. Inside, the small **Claude Lafitte Art Gallery** (Mon–Sat 10.30am–5pm, Sun noon–5pm; ⓣ514/842-1270, ⓦwww.lafitte.com) has works by Picasso, Miró, Chagall and Canadian artists Riopelle, Fortin, Lemieux, Borduas and Pellan. The hotel remains a symbol of what was once known as the **Golden Square Mile**; although downtown has encroached upon its southern precincts, the area between rue Sherbrooke, chemin de la Côte-des-Neiges, the mountain and McGill University retains many of the sumptuous mansions (though many now do duty as commercial or university buildings). From the late nineteenth century to World War II, about seventy percent of Canada's wealth was owned by a few hundred people who lived here. Known as the Caesars of the Wilderness, the majority were Scottish immigrants who made their fortunes in brewing, fur trading and banking, and who financed the railways and steamships that contributed to Montréal's industrial growth.

Musée des Beaux-Arts

West of the Ritz, at the corner of rue Crescent – a lively street filled with boutiques and bars – stands Canada's oldest museum, the **Musée des Beaux-Arts** (Tues–Fri 11am–5pm, Sat & Sun 10am–5pm, occasional special exhibits Wed until 9pm; $15, half price on Wed after 5pm; ⓣ514/285-2000 or 1-800/899-6873, ⓦwww.mmfa.qc.ca; Métro: Guy-Concordia), with a pavilion on either side of rue Sherbrooke at nos. 1379 and 1380. The Canadian art collection is one of the country's most impressive, covering the spectrum from the devotional works of New France, through paintings of the local landscape by, among others, James Wilson Morrice, Maurice Cullen and Clarence Gagnon, to the more radical canvases by the Automatistes – Paul-Émile Borduas and Jean-Paul Riopelle – who transformed Montréal's art scene in the 1940s. The **Group of Seven** get a showing too, but the most accomplished paintings are in the European section, with canvases by such masters as El Greco, Rembrandt and Memling.

Just west of the museum, at the intersection of rues Sherbrooke and Redpath, is another reminder of the Scottish roots of this neighbourhood – the **Church of St Andrew and St Paul**, the regimental church of the Black Watch, the Highland Regiment of Canada. Though the Gothic Revival building is not particularly impressive, the stained glass windows are worth a quick peek.

McGill University

Further west is the city's most prestigious university, **McGill**, entered through a Neoclassical stone gate at the top of avenue McGill College, a principal boulevard with wide pavements adorned with sculptures, most notably Raymond Mason's *The Illuminated Crowd*, portraying a mass of larger-than-life people – generally faced by an equally large crowd of tourists. The university was founded in 1813 from the bequest of James McGill, a Glaswegian immigrant fur trader, and the university is now world-famous for its medical and engineering schools. The ornate limestone buildings and their modern extensions are perfect for relaxing or for a walk above the street level of downtown. A boulder on the campus near Sherbrooke marks the spot where the original Iroquois village of Hochelaga stood before European penetration. In the middle of the campus is the **Musée Redpath** (Mon–Fri 9am–5pm, Sun 1–5pm, closed Sat all year; free; ⓣ514/398-4086, ⓦwww.mcgill.ca/redpath; Métro: McGill), the first custom-built Canadian museum, with an eclectic anthropological collection of musical instruments, dinosaur bones and two Egyptian mummies.

Musée McCord d'Histoire Canadienne

Facing the McGill campus, in the handsome early twentieth-century McGill Union building at 690 rue Sherbrooke ouest, is the **Musée McCord d'Histoire Canadienne** (Tues–Fri 10am–6pm, Sat–Mon 10am–5pm; winter closed Mon; $13, free first Sat of the month before noon; ⓣ514/398-7100, ⓦwww.mccord-museum.qc.ca; Métro: McGill), an extensive museum of Canadian history. The main part of the collection was amassed by the Scots-Irish McCord family over an eighty-year period from the mid-nineteenth century and represents a highly personal vision of the development of Canada, which they saw as a fusion of colonial and declining native elements. The museum is particularly strong on native artefacts; highlights include First Nations items such as furs, ivory carvings and superb beadwork. Nearby, ornate jewellery and other memorabilia from elite Montréal families contrast with the gritty floor-to-ceiling black-and-white pictures of the city famed photographer William Notman took in the mid-1800s.

Mont Royal and the Plateau

Boulevard St-Laurent – **The Main** – leads all the way up from Vieux-Montréal to the northern extremities of the city. North of rue Sherbrooke is the absorbing **Plateau Mont-Royal** district, where Montréal's cosmopolitan diversity is evident in distinct enclaves of immigrant neighbourhoods. Running parallel to **rue St-Denis**, the Plateau's other main artery and, at its southern end, the heart of the upbeat studenty **Quartier Latin**, this zone is where the most fun can be had in Montréal, with a huge array of ethnic food outlets and bars. If the party atmosphere is too much, you can head for the landscaped expanse of **Mont Royal** or the reverent hush of the **Oratoire St-Joseph** on the mountain's northwest flank.

Plateau Mont-Royal and the Quartier Latin

Traditionally, **boulevard St-Laurent** divided the English in the west from the French in the east of the city. Montréal's immigrants, first Russian Jews, then Greeks, Portuguese, Italians, East Europeans and, more recently, Latin Americans, settled in the middle and, though many prospered enough to move on, the area around The Main is still a cultural mix where neither of the two official languages dominates. Delis, bars, nightclubs, hardware stores, bookshops and an increasing number of trendy boutiques provide the perfect background to a wonderful jumble of sights, sounds and smells.

Wandering north from rue Sherbrooke on The Main, you'll pass through the strip's flashiest block, filled with see-and-be-seen restaurants and clubs, before arriving at one of Montréal's few pedestrianized streets, **rue Prince-Arthur**, thronged with buskers and caricaturists in the summer. Its eastern end leads to the beautiful fountained and statued **Square St-Louis**, the city's finest public square. Designed in 1876, the square was originally the domain of bourgeois Montréalers, and the magnificent houses were subsequently occupied by artists, poets and writers. The east side of the square divides the lower and upper areas of **rue St-Denis**. The part of rue St-Denis leading south from rue Sherbrooke to rue Ste-Catherine – the **Quartier Latin** – has long had a rather grubby reputation, but continues to be colonized by terrace cafés and bars crammed with students from the nearby Université du Québec à Montréal (UQAM) well into the early hours. By contrast, the Plateau stretch of rue St-Denis north of the square is the stamping ground of the francophone intellectual set, where a different yet equally heady atmosphere pervades the sidewalks. Here you'll find some of the city's most upscale boutiques and restaurants.

ACCOMMODATION

Anne ma Soeur Anne	C
Auberge Chez Jean	B
Boulanger Bassin B&B	A
Château de l'Argoat	F
Gîte Plateau Mont-Royal	G
Hôtel de Paris	E
Aux Portes de la Nuit	D

RESTAURANTS & CAFÉS

A L'os	1
Amelio's	34
Bagel Bagel	8
Beauty's	3
La Binerie Mont-Royal	4
Brulerie St-Denis	14
Chu Chai	12
Euro Deli	27
Fonduementale	9
La Iguana	20
La Jardin de Panos	15
Laloux	23
Maestro SVP	28
Moishe's	18
Pintxo	22
Pizzédélic	33
Red Thai	31
Café Santropol	16
Schwartz's	19
Senzala	2
Shed Café	32
Thai Express	25

Mont Royal

Little more than a hill to most tourists but a mountain to Montréalers, **Mont Royal** reaches just 233m but its two square kilometres of greenery are visible from almost anywhere in the city. Mont Royal holds a special place in the history of the city – it was here that the Iroquois established their settlement and that Maisonneuve declared the island to be French – but for centuries the mountain was privately owned. Then, during an especially bitter winter, one of the inhabitants cut down his trees for extra firewood. Montréalers were outraged at the desecration, and in 1875 the city bought the land for the impressive sum of $1 million. Frederick Law Olmsted, designer of New York's Central Park and San Francisco's Golden Gate Park, was hired to landscape the hill, which now provides 56km of jogging paths and 20km of skiing trails to keep city inhabitants happy year-round. The city has steadfastly refused any commercial developments on this lucrative site, the only construction being **Lac aux Castors**, built in the 1930s as a work-creation scheme for the unemployed; it now serves as a skating rink in the winter and pedal-boat playground in the summer. In the 1950s, protection of the mountain reached a puritanical extreme when a local journalist revealed young couples were using the area for amatory pursuits and, even worse, that people were openly drinking alcohol. Consequently all of the underbrush was uprooted, which only succeeded in killing off much of the ash, birch, maple, oak and pine trees. Within five years Mont Royal was dubbed "Bald Mountain" and a replanting campaign had to be instigated.

Walks up Mont Royal

There are various access points for a walk up the mountain but the most popular starting point is at the **George-Étienne Cartier monument** along avenue du Parc, most easily accessed by following rue Rachel westward from boulevard St-Laurent. You can also take the Métro to Mont-Royal station, walk west along avenue du Mont-Royal and turn left on avenue du Parc, or get off the Métro at Place-des-Arts and take bus #80, disembarking halfway along the park. However you get there, the angel-topped monument is hard to miss on summer Sundays, when buskers and people of all ages congregate until the sun goes down. From here, several paths lead towards the summit and the illuminated cross that commemorates Maisonneuve placing a wooden cross here in 1642. The gentlest slope is along chemin Olmsted, a carriage trail that winds lazily up from the monument, past the top of rue Peel (the easiest access from downtown), and along the summit. In addition to the aforementioned Lac aux Castors, chemin Olmsted provides access to the **Maison Smith** (daily 9am–5pm; free; ⓣ514/843-8240, ⓦwww.lemontroyal.com), which houses an information centre and exhibition on the mountain, and proceeds to the Chalet, fronted by a **lookout point** offering fine views of downtown and the St Lawrence beyond.

Oratoire St-Joseph

On the northwest side of the mountain the awesome **Oratoire St-Joseph** (Basilica: May–Oct 7am–9pm, Nov–April 7am–5.30pm; Museum: Daily 10am–5pm; ⓦwww.saint-joseph.org) rises from its green surroundings near Montréal's highest point. In 1904, Brother André – who was canonised as Québéc's **first saint** in early 2010 – built a small chapel here to honour St Joseph, Canada's patron saint. Before long, Brother André's ability to heal people had earned him the sobriquet "The Miracle Man of Montréal", and huge numbers of patients took to climbing the outside stairs on their knees to receive his grace. Satisfied clients donated so much money that in 1924 he could afford to begin work on this immense granite edifice, which was completed in 1967, thirty years after his death. It is topped by a dome second in size only to St Peter's in Rome.

The interior does not live up to the splendour of the Italianate exterior, though the chapel in the apse is richly decorated with green marble columns and a gold-leaf ceiling. In the adjoining anteroom, thousands of votive candles burn along the walls, and proof of Brother André's curative powers hang everywhere: crutches, canes and braces are crammed into every available space. The roof terrace, above the portico, has excellent views of the city and provides access to the gardens. A small upstairs museum displays items relating to Brother André's life, including the room in which he died, which was shifted here from a local hospice. Brother André's heart is enclosed in a glass case; the devout believe it quivers occasionally. Outside, the **Way of the Cross** has some particularly beautiful sculptures in smooth, white Carrara marble and Indiana buff stone by Montréal artist Louis Parent – a tranquil site used as a setting for the Denys Arcand film *Jésus de Montréal*. You can also visit the small building a few metres away from the Oratory that contains the original chapel and Brother André's tiny room.

If you don't want to walk across the summit to get there, the nearest Métro is Côte-des-Neiges, from where the way to the oratory is signposted; buses #51, #165, #166 and #535 also stop nearby.

Parc Olympique and around

It's best to take the Métro to Pie-IX (pronounced "pee-nuhf") station in order to view Montréal's most infamous architectural construction, the **Parc Olympique**. The main attraction, the **Stade Olympique**, is known by Montréalers as the "Big O" for three reasons: its name, its circular shape and the fact that it took the city 30 years to pay for it. The main facilities for the 1976 Summer Olympics were designed by Roger Taillibert, who was told money was no object. The complex ended up costing $1.4 billion (over $2 billion with subsequent interest and maintenance) – and it was not even completed in time for the games. It's now used sporadically, and in a continuing attempt to pay the debts, the schedule features a range of events, from monster truck races to the occasional CFL football play-off game to trade shows. Daily **guided tours** are available (Ⓣ514/252-4737 or 1-877/997-0919 for schedule, Ⓦwww.rio.gouv.qc.ca; $8). The stadium's 175-metre **tower** is a major engineering feat – the highest inclined tower in the world. Its main function was to hold a retractable 65-tonne roof, but the 45-minute retraction process never really worked properly, and today sections of the roof are prone to falling in. The attraction is the **funicular** that takes you up the tower to an observation deck with sixty-kilometre views and an exhibition of historic photos of Montréal (daily mid-June to early Sept 9am–7pm; otherwise 9am–5pm; $15). Near the Stade Olympique sits the snazzy **Saputo Stadium**, home to the city's professional soccer team, the Montréal Impact.

The Biodôme

Also in the stadium's shadow is the **Biodôme** (late Feb–early Sept daily 9am–5pm, otherwise Tues–Sun only; $12.75; Ⓣ514/868-3000, Ⓦwww.biodome.qc.ca; Métro: Viau), housed in a building shaped like a bicycle helmet that started life as the Olympic velodrome. Now it is a stunning environmental museum comprising four ecosystems: tropical, Laurentian forest, St Lawrence maritime and polar. You can wander freely through the different zones, which are planted with appropriate flourishing vegetation and inhabited by the relevant birds, animals and marine life. It's all highly educational and good fun, but try to avoid visiting on Sundays, when it seems like the entire population of Québec and their children head there.

Jardin Botanique

Just north of the stadium and linked by a free shuttle bus (mid-May to mid-Sept daily every 30min 11am–5pm) is the **Jardin Botanique de Montréal**, 4101 rue Sherbrooke est (mid-May to Nov daily 9am–6pm; rest of the year Tues–Sun 9am–5pm, guided tours daily 10am and 1.30pm; $12.75 May–Oct, $9.75 rest of year; ⓣ514/872-1400, ⓦwww.ville.montreal.qc.ca/jardin; Métro: Pie-IX). The grounds and greenhouses contain some thirty types of gardens from medicinal herbs to orchids. Highlights include a Japanese garden, its ponds of water lilies bordered by greenish sculptured stone and crossed by delicate bridges. The nearby Chinese garden is especially resplendent during the autumn lantern festival. Other attractions include the Insectarium (same hours and ticket), a bug-shaped building containing insects of every shape and size.

Parc Jean-Drapeau

The former Parc des Îles, renamed **Parc Jean-Drapeau** following the death in 1999 of the long-time mayor, comprises **Île Ste-Hélène** and the artificial **Île Notre-Dame**, constructed from fill dredged from the river and from the construction of the Métro (whose yellow line includes the Jean-Drapeau stop, located on Île Ste-Hélène). Île Notre-Dame, with its beach, canals and gardens, seems quieter than its neighbour – unless you venture here during one of the big motorsports weekends, when cars tear their way along the Circuit Gilles-Villeneuve, which rings the island. Bus #167 links the Métro with the attractions on both islands.

The Biosphère

Not far from the Métro station hovers the **Biosphère** (late June to mid-Sept daily 10am–6pm; mid-Sept to late June Mon–Fri noon–5pm, Sat & Sun 10am–5pm; $8.50; joint ticket with Musée Stewart $15; ⓣ514/283-5000, ⓦwww.biosphere.ec.gc.ca), a giant sphere of interlocking aluminium triangles designed by Buckminster Fuller for Expo '67. Today, it's an interactive museum focusing on the St Lawrence Seaway and the Great Lakes. The exhibits change yearly and there are lots to amuse children, from interactive touch-screens to skill-testing games, movies and multimedia displays. On the fourth floor, a stupendous lookout point takes in the St Lawrence River and the city, foregrounded by the giant Alexander Calder stabile, *Man* – one of many pieces of public art dotted about the island.

Musée Stewart

A twenty-minute walk from the Biosphère around the winding chemin du Tour de l'Île will get you to the grounds of Montréal's only **fort**, a U-shaped building situated close to the river's edge. Built by the British between 1820 and 1824 as a defence against the threat of American invasion – which never came – it played a number of roles, including a World War II prison camp, before opening as the **Musée Stewart** (daily 10am–5pm; $10, joint ticket with Biosphère $15; ⓦwww.stewart-museum.org). In the fortified arsenal commissioned by the Duke of Wellington, the museum contains a collection of weapons and assorted domestic and scientific artefacts. The fort is also the summer venue for the re-enactment of seventeenth- and eighteenth-century military manoeuvres by actors dressed as the Fraser Highlanders and Compagnie Franche de la Marine.

La Ronde

The shrieking sounds that can be heard all over the island's eastern point, beyond the Jacques-Cartier bridge, emanate from **La Ronde** (mid-June to Sept daily 10am–10.30pm, otherwise see website for schedule; rides $36, grounds only $22.60; ⓣ514/397-2000, ⓦwww.laronde.com). The city's amusement park is the venue for various celebrations throughout the year, including the annual Fireworks Competition from June to July.

Eating

Montréal's ethnic diversity is amply displayed by the variety of **cuisines** available – everything from the rich meat dishes of traditional Québécois cuisine, to creatively prepared Japanese *maki* to earthy Portuguese nosh. The city has its own **Chinatown** just north of Vieux-Montréal, a **Little Italy** around Jean-Talon Métro (near the excellent **Jean-Talon market**; Ⓦwww.marchespublics-mtl.com) and a **Greek** community whose cheaper restaurants are concentrated along Prince Arthur; for more traditional Greek cuisine head further north along avenue du Parc.

Most prominent of the ethnic restaurants are the **Eastern European** establishments dotted around the city. Opened by Jewish immigrants who came to work in the garment factories, their speciality is **smoked meat**, which has become a Montréal obsession, served between huge chunks of rye bread with pickles on the side. Another Montréal speciality is **poutine**, fries smothered in gravy and cheese curds, which is generally served in diners and snack joints. Incidentally, Montréal comes a close second to New York as the **bagel** capital of the world; they're sold everywhere from grimy outlets to stylish cafés.

Masses of restaurants also line the area around rue Ste-Catherine downtown, while Vieux-Montréal has an ever-expanding number of places to eat, but many are touristy and slightly overpriced. The best for food – and upbeat atmosphere – is in the more French area of the metropolis, around **the Plateau** and **Quartier Latin**. Montréal has long embraced the concept of *apportez votre vin* ("bring your own wine"), and you'll find plenty of "BYOW" establishments on rue Prince Arthur and avenue Duluth, many of which serve good ethnic cuisine.

Cafés, bakeries and delis

Bagel Etc. 4320 boul St-Laurent; Métro: Mont-Royal or bus #55. Trendy New York-type diner. Excellent bagels from the simple cream cheese to caviar, and lavish breakfasts. Daily 8am–5pm.

Beauty's 93 av du Mont-Royal ouest; Métro: Mont-Royal or bus #55. A brunch institution with wonderful 1950s decor – and delicious breakfasts, from fat omelettes to fresh fruit. Be prepared to get up early on the weekend to avoid the queue.

La Binerie Mont-Royal 367 av du Mont-Royal est; Métro: Mont-Royal. Four tables and a chrome counter seat the hundreds of people who visit this well-known café daily. The menu consists of beans, beans and more beans with ketchup, vinegar or maple syrup. Also served is pork, beef, *tourtière* (a minced pork pie) and *pouding chômeur* ("unemployed pudding"), a variation on bread pudding.

Brulerie St-Denis 1587 rue St Denis; Métro: Berri-UQAM. A nirvana for those that obsess over their coffee beans. Hundreds of varieties, roasted and ground on site, with plenty of tables on the terrace to sit and savour the perfect caffeine hit.

Café Santropol 3990 rue St-Urbain; bus #55 or Métro: Sherbrooke or Mont-Royal, or bus #55. Mostly vegetarian café on the corner of av Duluth. Spectacular during the summer when its blooming back terrace is a welcome oasis from the busy streets, Santropol still retains its charm in winter thanks to its cosy atrium. Huge sandwiches, quiches, salads and home-made vegetarian chilli are offered as well as various herbal teas and excellent organic Fairtrade coffees.

Le Club Sandwich 1560 rue Ste-Catherine est; Métro: Beaudry. Boasting over sixty varieties of sandwiches, this relaxed 24hr diner also serves all-day breakfasts and is famous for its coleslaw. Brunch from $14.

Euro Deli 3619 boul St-Laurent; Métro: Sherbrooke or bus #55. Busy deli where you can stuff yourself for under $10 on sandwiches, calzone, pasta and veggie food – and top it off with a potent espresso.

Fairmount Bagel Bakery 74 av Fairmount ouest; Métro: Laurier or bus #55. Possibly the best bagel outlet in Montréal, offering a huge variety of bagels. There is nowhere to sit, but arm yourself with a bag of bagels, a pot of cream cheese and some smoked salmon (lox), perch on the nearest curb and you'll soon be in bagel heaven. Open daily 24hr.

▲ Jean-Talon market, north Montréal

Kilo 5206 boul St-Laurent; Métro: Laurier or bus #55. Creating the most divine cakes, particularly the cheesecake, this patisserie is expensive but worth every cent. Open late on weekends.

Olive et Gourmando 351 rue St-Paul; Métro: Square-Victoria. The smell of fresh baguettes greets you at this warm, delightful café-bakery. Cosy up at a wooden table and enjoy a fig scone with a dash of orange zest, sandwiches like the "Viva Las Vegan", heaped with marinated tofu and crushed olives, and smoked trout with sundried tomato. Open Tues–Sat 8am–6pm.

La Paryse 302 rue Ontario est; Métro: Berri-UQAM. Lesbian-owned retro diner with an extraordinary and exotic range of burger fillings, including tasty veggie-burgers.

Reuben's Deli 1116 rue Ste-Catherine ouest; Métro: McGill or Peel. An excellent deli with a wealth of smoked meats, tasty fries, a frantic atmosphere and friendly service. A favourite with local business types, and thus packed at lunch. A second outlet, a couple of blocks east at no. 888, is cheaper as it's in a (cosy) basement.

Schwartz's 3895 boul St-Laurent; bus #55 or Métro: Sherbrooke. A Montréal institution: a small, narrow deli serving up colossal smoked-meat sandwiches, with surly service thrown in as part of the package. Line-up out the door at weekends.

Senzala 177 rue Bernard ouest; Métro: Outremont. If your taste buds need a wake-up call in the morning head to this Brazilian café in Mile End for brunch and sample creative concoctions such as poached eggs in avocado and tomato sauce. Or, come later and ease into the evening over a *caipirinha* (or three).

Wilensky's Light Lunch 34 av Fairmount ouest; Métro: Laurier or bus #55. Used for countless film sets because the decor hasn't changed since 1932 – and that includes the till, grill and drinks machine. The Wilensky Special includes bologna and three types of salami and costs around $3. Mon–Fri 9am–4pm.

Restaurants

Asian

Azuma 5263 boul St-Laurent; Métro: Laurier or bus #55 ☎514/271-5263. A popular Japanese restaurant that looks a little run-down from the outside but there's nothing shabby about the food. Creatively prepared traditional dishes, and good *soba* noodles.

Bato Thai 1310 rue Ste-Catherine est; Métro: Beaudry ⓣ514/524-6705. An elegant, nautical themed Thai restaurant in The Village, but with slow service. There are cheap lunch deals from $14 during the week and make sure you don't leave without trying the spectacular fried ice-cream.

Chu Chai 4088 rue St-Denis; Métro: Mont-Royal or Sherbrooke ⓣ514/843-4194, ⓦwww.chuchai.com. Excellent, fresh vegetarian Thai food with lunch menus and dinner from around $25.

Katsura 2170 rue de la Montagne; Métro: Peel ⓣ514/849-1172. Large and popular downtown Japanese restaurant. Fairly expensive but they serve cheaper *bento* boxes and the like for weekday lunch.

Red Thai 3550 boul St-Laurent; Métro: Sherbrooke or St-Laurent ⓣ514/289-0998. This restaurant serves up exquisite Thai in a dodgy decor straight out of *Anna and the King*. Most dishes around $17.

Ruby Rouge 1008 rue Clark; Métro: Place-d'Armes ⓣ514/390-8828, ⓦwww.restaurantrubyrouge.com. Montréal's vast temple to dim sum, right in the heart of Chinatown. At around $4 a serving it's well-priced but not dirt-cheap. There are often long queues so get there early.

Sushi-Moushi 3193 boul Decarie; Métro: Plamondon ⓣ514/369-8860, ⓦwww.sushimoushi.ca. In a town where sushi is an obsession, *Sushi-moushi* is a locals' favourite. Specializes in decorative, well-priced *maki*.

Soy 5258 boul St-Laurent; bus #55 ⓣ514/499-9399. Deliciously prepared light dishes from the Orient. *Soy* is especially good for lunch, when a three-course meal costs under $15.

Thai Express 3710 boul St-Laurent; Métro: Sherbrooke ⓣ514/287-9957. The name says it all: speedy Thai at low prices – for under $10, you'll get a seriously hearty serving of curries and stir-fries with wonderfully aromatic spices.

French

Les Beaux Jeudis 1449 rue Crescent; Métro: Guy-Concordia ⓣ514/288-5656. Classy, but unpretentious, Parisian-style bistro with a flower-decked terrace in summer. Great value all-you-can-eat weekday specials.

Bonaparte 443 rue St-François-Xavier; Métro: Place-d'Armes ⓣ514/844-4368, ⓦwww.bonaparte.com. Part of the eponymous auberge at no. 447 (see p.221), this moderately priced, well-situated French restaurant in Vieux-Montréal serves excellent fresh fish and seafood – including a tasty lobster stew flavoured with vanilla – and there are tables on the breezy balconies. Evening table d'hôte $28–$40.

Boris Bistro 495 rue McGill; Métro: Square-Victoria ⓣ514/848-9575, ⓦwww.borisbistro.com. Locals flock to this large, bustling outdoor terrace – one of the most inviting in Vieux-Montréal. The menu ranges from braised rabbit and duck confit to grilled trout, along with a fine list of wines.

Fonduementale 4325 rue St-Denis; Métro: Mont-Royal ⓣ514/499-1446, ⓦwww.fonduementale.com. Set in a historic two-storey house with a warm fireplace in winter and a blooming outdoor terrace in summer. The fondue, starting at just $19, is divine and the meals are long and languid. Generous table d'hôte menus from $29.

Garde Manger 408 rue St-Francois-Xavier; Métro: Square-Victoria ⓣ514/678-5044. A festive, familial atmosphere fills this popular restaurant helmed by an enthusiastic young chef. Seafood is the specialty – try the signature massive wooden trough spilling over with fresh shellfish – but equal care is given to the superb steak frites. Rock tunes, a bustling bar and a cocktail-fuelled crowd make for one of the liveliest dining spots in Vieux-Montréal.

Joe Beef 2491 rue Notre-Dame ouest; Métro: Lionel-Groulx ⓣ514/931-3999. The daily changing specials are scrawled on a blackboard at this casual Lachine Canal bistro named after Charles "Joe-Beef" McKiernan, a 19th-century innkeeper and a Montréal "working class hero". The chefs take advantage of the nearby Atwater Market to compose their simple but inspired dishes, from pasta with sweet hunks of lobster to a juicy steak with bone marrow.

Laloux 250 av des Pins est; Métro: Sherbrooke ⓣ514/287-9127, ⓦwww.laloux.com. This Parisian-style bistro serves pricey *nouvelle cuisine* – like trout with eggplant caviar – but most people come simply to enjoy the refined wood-panel and polished-brass decor. Expect to pay around $55 for lunch and up to $150 for dinner with a bottle of wine.

Le Local 740 rue William; Métro: Square-Victoria ⓣ514/397-7737, ⓦwww.resto-lelocal.com. This lively restaurant appears to have all the right ingredients: A creative, pedigreed chef; an eye-catching rustic-industrial interior, with artfully angled glass and steel; and a menu that hinges on fresh, often locally sourced ingredients. Beet salad with crisp bacon is enriched with truffle oil, and braised octopus is mixed with chorizo and pecans.

A L'Os 5207 boul St-Laurent; Métro: Laurier ⓣ514/270-7055. This stylish, inviting restaurant with an open kitchen lives up to its name "On the Bone," with excellent meaty dishes, including a succulent filet mignon with bone marrow, sweetbreads with smoked paprika and chorizo and braised rabbit. Bring your own wine. Closed Mon.

Au Petit Extra 1690 rue Ontario est; Métro: Papineau ⓣ514/527-5552. Large, lively and affordable bistro (set lunch menu from $13 and dinner around $35) with great food and authentic French feel, but it's a bit of a hike east.

Le Saint-Gabriel 426 rue St-Gabriel; Métro: Place-d'Armes ⓣ514/878-3561, ⓦwww.lesaint-gabriel.com. This historic, romantic restaurant – said to be where the first North American liquor licensce was issued, in 1754 – is popular for date nights. In the summer, dine under the stars on the outdoor terrace and enjoy classic – though relatively pricey – French cuisine from lamb with polenta to garlic-infused veal, and a tasty crème brûlée.

Toqué! 900 Place Jean-Paul-Riopelle; Métro: Square-Victoria ⓣ514/499-2084, ⓦwww.restaurant-toque.com. Renowned chef Normand Laprise holds court here and the dining experience is ultra chic, high-end and unforgettable – if you can get a seat and afford the price tag. Reservations are essential and dinner starts at $91.

Mediterranean

Amelio's 201 rue Milton; Métro: Place-des-Arts or bus #24 ⓣ514/845-8396, ⓦwww.ameliospizza.com. Basic and hearty pasta, pizza and meatball subs from $9 in a tiny half-basement restaurant in the heart of the McGill University student ghetto. The prices are excellent and the service friendly. Bring your own wine.

Arahova Souvlaki 256 rue St-Viateur ouest; bus #80 ⓣ514/274-7828. Superb, authentic Greek cuisine for under $10, including an excellent tzatziki. Popular with the after-clubbing crowd.

Bottega 67 rue St-Zotique est; Métro: Laurier ⓣ514/277-8104, ⓦwww.bottega.ca. Dominated by the huge authentic pizza oven, this back-to-basics pizza place is run by a master baker who trained in Naples. The results are divine, all for $10–15. Start off with *sfizis*, Neapolitan small plates of fried calamari and rice croquettes stuffed with mozzarella. Reservations essential.

Le Jardin de Panos 521 av Duluth est; Métro: Sherbrooke or Mont-Royal ⓣ514/521-4206. Beats out the numerous cheap Greek *brochetteries* on rue Prince Arthur in taste and has a garden to boot. An average meal will cost $15–30. Bring your own wine.

Maestro SVP 3615 boul St-Laurent; Métro: Sherbrooke or bus #55 ⓣ514/842-6447. When oysters are in season, this is the place to get them, served in myriad ways for $30 per dozen. Try one in a shooter with vodka and horseradish sauce for a quick kick.

Milos 5357 av du-Parc; bus #80 ⓣ514/272-3522, ⓦwww.milos.ca. Expensive, but the finest Greek restaurant in the city, especially notable for its fresh seafood. Early-bird and Sunday dinners are cheaper at $35.

Piccolo Diavolo 1336 rue Ste-Catherine est; Métro: Beaudry ⓣ514/526-1336. Devilishly hip place to eat Italian; dimly lit with plenty of hell-themed touches. Pizzas, pastas and meatier dishes, including good veal *osso buco*. Dinner for around $20.

Pintxo 256 rue Roy; Métro: Sherbrooke ⓣ514/844-0222, ⓦwww.pintxo.ca. Mediterranean flair heats up this corner of the Plateau. A cheery yellow façade gives way to an inviting interior of exposed brick, wooden floors and colourful paintings. Delectable *pintxos*, or small plates, include octopus carpaccio drizzled with a cava vinaigrette and hot, grilled chorizo. Wet the lips with one of the excellent Spanish wines.

Pizzédélic 3467 boul St-Laurent; Métro: St-Laurent or bus #55 ⓣ514/845-0404, ⓦwww.pizzedelic.net. Tasty and experimental square pizzas for under $16 cemented the reputation of this place and spawned a second location at 39 rue Notre-Dame ouest in Vieux-Montréal. The daily lunch special is a bargain at $6.99.

Pizzeria Napoletana 189 rue Dante; bus #55 ⓣ514/276-8226. Authentic Little Italy pizzeria where nothing is over $15; take your own alcohol and expect to queue at the weekend.

North American

La Iguana 51 rue Roy est; Métro: Sherbrooke ⓣ514/844-0893, ⓦwww.restaurant-laiguana.com. Traditional Mexican food in sumptuous surroundings for $10–25. Try the giant shrimp drizzled in a citrus sauce and the steak fajitas.

Laurier BBQ 381 av Laurier ouest; bus #80 ⓣ514/273-3671. Great hunks of Québec-style barbecued chicken and huge salads; a Montréal favourite for half a century.

Moishe's 3961 boul St-Laurent; Sherbrooke or bus #55 ⓣ514/845-3509, ⓦwww.moishes.ca. Favourite haunt of Montréal's business community. Excellent (and huge) steaks, upwards of $30, with notoriously bad-tempered service. Reservations recommended.

Patati Patata 4177 boul St-Laurent; bus #55 ⓣ514/844-0216. With only enough room for a dozen people this is a tiny place with excellent and cheap home-made food. The *poutine* – supposedly the best in Montréal – is well worth a try.

Le Resto du Village 1310 rue Wolfe; Métro: Beaudry. Just off rue Ste-Catherine, this small diner serves filling comfort food such as pâté chinois (shepherd's pie) and *poutine* for less than $15 to a largely gay crowd. Open 24hr.

Le Saloon 1333 rue Ste-Catherine; Métro: Beaudry ⓣ514/522-1333, ⓦwww.lesaloon.ca. Amiable bistro with steaks, seafood, salad and fruity cocktails served to tunes spun by DJs. Great weekend brunch.

Shed Café 3515 boul St-Laurent; Métro: St-Laurent or Sherbrooke ⓣ514/842-0220. Hamburger, salad and sandwich joint ($10–15) with sumptuous cheesecakes, where trendy Montréalers come to see and be seen. Avant-garde, wacky interior, well-stocked bar and a DJ after 8pm. Open until 1am (weekends 3am).

Nightlife and entertainment

Montréal well deserves its "party central" title: The city's **nightlife** keeps going strong into the small hours of the morning – **bars** are generally open until 3am. One of the liveliest after-dark areas is the bar-packed **Plateau**. Cutting a wide swath through the Plateau – and into the adjacent neighborhood of Mile-End, which seems to get more popular by the minute – is **Boulevard St-Laurent**, lined on both sides with an eclectic array of places, from sleek lounges to dive bars. **Downtown**, the action centres on rue Crescent, while Vieux-Montréal is increasingly buzzing with new hotel lounges and restaurant-bars. Also popular are the student-packed **Quartier Latin** bars and the nearby **Village**, heart of the gay scene (see p.248).

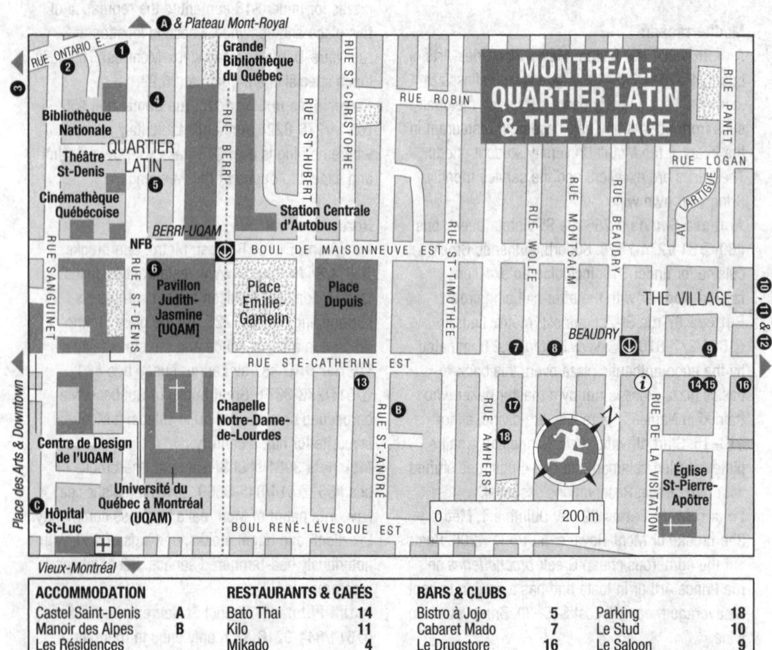

Many bars have regular music nights, with **jazz** being especially popular. Otherwise, there are numerous venues in the city, with top-name touring bands playing at the Centre Bell and other large venues. For **information**, the *Mirror* (Ⓦ www.montrealmirror.com) and *Hour* (Ⓦ www.hour.ca) are free English weekly newspapers with excellent listings sections. The English-language daily *Montréal Gazette* also carries comprehensive listings, especially on Fridays.

Bars

Bar Fly 4062 boul St-Laurent; Métro: Saint Laurent. This bar revels in live music, featuring local bands – from punk to blues – nearly every night of the week. Unpretentious and deliciously sleazy, it's popular with tattooed and pierced teens and twentysomethings.

Le Bifteck 3702 boul St-Laurent; Métro: Sherbrooke or bus #55. Perennially popular studenty, cheap beer bar with taped music from grunge to hip-hop that overflows onto two floors at the weekend and outside in the summer.

Bily Kun 354 av du Mont-Royal est; Métro: Mont-Royal Ⓦ www.bilykun.com. Packed brasserie-pub, with stuffed ostrich heads on the minimalist walls overlooking tables and booths. DJ's and occasional live bands, from jazz to funk.

Blizzarts 3956a boul St-Laurent; bus #55. Funked-out lounge-bar with retro furnishings, Sputnik-lighting and a tiny dance floor. Draws a late-twentysomething Plateau crowd.

Brutopia 1219 Crescent St; Métro: Lucien L'Allier Ⓦ www.brutopia.net. A welcoming pub spread over three floors with a terrace and balcony that has a huge range of exotic beers brewed on site in the copper drums behind the bar. Live bands most nights of the week as well as lively open mic and trivia nights.

Else's 156 rue Roy East; Métro: Sherbrooke. Casual, good-natured, come-as-you-are neighbourhood watering hole, where locals knock back beer, hang out and play board games. Excellent cider on tap – and surprisingly tasty bar nibbles.

L'Île Noire 342 rue Ontario est; Métro: Berri-UQAM. A homage to the Scottish pub complete with mahogany bar stools and traditional pint glasses. Popular with British ex-pats, it stocks over 140 types of whisky from $5 to $500 a shot.

Jello Bar 151 rue Ontario est; Métro: St-Laurent. Enjoy live jazz and blues at this bar furnished with 1960s and 1970s novelties – kitsch but irresistibly slinky. Martini cocktails are the house speciality.

Laïka 4040 boul St-Laurent; bus #55 Ⓦ www.laikamontreal.com. Café by day, lounge by night, heaven-sent haven by early morning, *Laïka*'s sleek, cool-toned decor attracts a casually chic crowd at any time of day, though the service can be a bit spotty.

Lola Lounge 1023 rue de Bleury; Métro: Square-Victoria. With plenty of sofas to sink into and specialist DJs creating chilled-out vibes every night of the week, this is a place to sit, chat with friends and soak up the atmosphere.

McKibbins 1426 rue Bishop; Métro: Guy-Concordia Ⓦ www.mckibbinsirishpub.com. Spot-on Irish pub, with a chatty, amiable crowd; tasty pub grub; great Guinness; and live local bands on Fri and Sat.

Sir Winston Churchill Pub 1459 rue Crescent; Métro: Peel or Guy-Concordia. Known locally as *Winnie's*, this large English-style pub is part of a complex of nine bars that attracts an older crowd of local and visiting anglophone professionals. Pool tables and a small dance floor. Prime pick-up joint.

Le Ste-Élisabeth 1412 rue Ste-Élisabeth; Métro: Berri-UQAM Ⓦ www.ste-elisabeth.com. Don't miss the secluded tree-shaded outdoor courtyard with ivy-covered walls lit by stained glass lamps or the glass terrace upstairs. This is a bar that seems to transport you far away from the city, perfect for an intimate drink – from chilled champagne to local brews – with friends.

Sofa 451 rue Rachel est; Métro: Mont-Royal. A sophisticated bar-lounge where well-dressed twenty and thirtysomethings smoke cigars and drink port while appreciating groovy music from acid jazz to house.

Whisky Café 5800 boul St-Laurent; Métro: Outremont or bus #55 Ⓦ www.whiskycafe.ca. Sleek lounge where the top-shelf liquor – including over 150 scotch whiskeys – are matched by the upscale crowd. The next-door cigar lounge is one of the few spots where you can light up. The designer interior extends to the bathrooms, which may be the most stylish in all of Montréal.

Clubs and music venues

Altitude 737 1 Place Ville Marie; Métro: McGill or Bonaventure Ⓦ www.altitude737.com. Popular with the financial district crowd, the main selling point of this club on the top three floors of Montréal's tallest building is the stunning panoramic view of the city, not the meat-market atmosphere. The swank restaurant serves French and European fare.

Le Balattou 4372 boul St-Laurent; bus #55 wwww.balattou.com. This popular world music club is resolutely dark, smoky, crowded, hot and loud, but also friendly. Live acts every night; closed Mon.

Bistro à Jojo 1627 rue St-Denis; Métro: Berri-UQAM ⓦwww.bistroajojo.com. Low ceilings and stone walls give this unpretentious blues cave an intimate feel. Shows nightly from around 10pm.

Café Campus 57 rue Prince-Arthur est; Métro: Sherbrooke. Notorious as a place that knows how to party, Café Campus has live acts every night. Particularly recommended is Retro Tuesday (which attracts a young crowd) and Blues Wednesday. Francophone Sundays are free.

Casa del Popolo 4873 boul St-Laurent; or bus #55 Métro: Laurier or bus #55 ⓣ514/284-3804. "The House of the People" is a sofa-strewn, low-key Plateau spot where high-calibre spoken-word evenings and folk and other bands perform. They also have lively DJ nights and by day, serve soups and salads, making it a mingle-worthy spot any time from noon until 3am.

Club Soda 1225 boul St-Laurent; Métro: St-Laurent ⓦwww.clubsoda.ca. Large live-music venue that attracts all the best acts and has reached almost legendary status in Montréal. Cover charge of around $25.

Les Deux Pierrots 104 rue St-Paul est; Métro: Champ-de-Mars ⓦwww.lespierrots.com. Québécois folk singers are the mainstay of this club and everyone sings along. There's usually a good crowded atmosphere but don't expect to understand a word unless your French is excellent. Outside terrace in the summer.

Les Foufounes Électriques 87 rue Ste-Catherine est; Métro: St-Laurent ⓦwww.foufounes.qc.ca. A bizarre name ("The Electric Ass") for a bizarre and wonderful bar-club venue. Known as *Foufs*, it's the best place in Québec for alternative bands, attracting a young crowd from ravers to punks. Huge outside terrace perfect for summer evenings. Tickets for bands $5–15, club nights free–$10; admission to the bar is free and pitchers of beer are cheap.

Macaroni 4448 St-Laurent; Métro: Mont-Royal ⓦwww.macaronibar.ca. This snazzy resto-club serves Italian food – and a good array of potent cocktails. Come nightfall, DJs spin booming club tunes and the massive outdoor terrace fills with Euro-stylish partiers flirting under the stars.

La Mouche 1284 St-Denis; Métro: Berri-UQAM ⓦwww.lamouche.ca. The popular *La Mouche* rocks out with pounding club tunes, while overhead beams of light are trained on the

Gay Montréal

Montréal has an excellent **gay** scene, with the action concentrated in the area known as **The Village** – roughly located on rue Ste-Catherine est between rue Amherst and the Papineau Métro station. There's a **tourist information kiosk** at 1311 rue Ste-Catherine est (late June to early Sept Mon–Thurs 11am–6pm, Fri–Sun 10am–8pm; ⓣ514/522-1885 or 1-888/595-8110), in front of **Priape**, a popular sex shop and clothing store that also sells books and tickets to events.

Phone services and websites offer support, referrals and events information. **CAEO Quebec** (ⓣ514/866-5090 daily 7–11pm, ⓦwww.caeoquebec.org) runs Gay Line (English); Gai Écoute (ⓣ514/866-0103, ⓦwww.gaiecoute.org) is in French. *Fugues* (ⓦwww.fugues.com) is the city's monthly French gay and lesbian magazine (there's usually a small English section among the ads and pictures).

In early August, **Divers Cité** (ⓦwww.diverscite.org), the gay and lesbian pride parade, is the event of the year; also popular are the Fall **image + nation** film festival (ⓦwww.image-nation.org) and the week of events leading up to the massive **Black & Blue** circuit party (ⓦwww.bbcm.org) around Thanksgiving weekend. Various clubs also throw gay nights, like the lively **Mec Plus Ultra** gay "tea dance" (generally last Sun of the month, 5pm–3am; $6) at *Le Belmont*, 4483 Boul St-Laurent (ⓦwww.lebelmont.com).

Most of the **restaurants** and hangouts in The Village cater to a lesbian, bisexual and gay crowd in the evening, but are more mixed during the day. Unless noted otherwise, Métro Beaudry is the nearest station for the places listed below.

Bars, clubs and discos

Cabaret Mado 1115 rue Ste-Catherine est ⓦwww.mado.qc.ca. Local drag celebrity packed, sweaty dance floor. Cool off with chilled cocktails in the low-lit lounge. Open Fri–Sat from 10pm.

Orchid 3556 boul St-Laurent; Métro: Sherbrooke or bus #55. Playing mostly house with a mix of soul, salsa and R&B this popular club is just big enough to strut your stuff without getting lost in the crowd. Dress beautiful to get in. Fri night drink specials for the ladies. Cover charge $10.

Tokyo Bar 3709 boul St-Laurent; Métro: St-Laurent, Sherbrooke or bus #55. Whether you choose to groove on the dance floor or sip martinis on the rooftop terrace, *Tokyo* delivers. The swank Asian decor, sultry lighting and resident DJs who spin crowd favourites make for a great night out.

Upstairs 1254 rue MacKay; Métro: Guy-Concordia ⓦwww.upstairsjazz.com. Upstairs is actually downstairs in a cosy half-basement with fresh jazz and blues on tap nightly in a wonderfully attitude-free atmosphere. Predominantly thirtysomething crowd. Cover charge varies.

The performing arts and cinema

Montréal's most prestigious centre for the **performing arts** is the Place des Arts, 175 rue Ste-Catherine ouest (ⓦwww.pdarts.com), a five-hall complex with a comprehensive year-round programme of dance, music and theatre. It forms part of the newly formed **Quartier des Spectacles**, an entertainment district that will include theatres and cultural centres.

Theatre and opera

The Théâtre de Verdure in Parc Lafontaine is an outdoor theatre with a summer-long programme of free plays, ballets and concerts. Another eclectic venue is the Théâtre St-Denis, 1594 rue St-Denis (ⓦwww.theatrestdenis.com), which presents blockbuster musicals and other shows. The city's foremost French-language **theatre** is the Théâtre du Rideau Vert, 4664 rue St-Denis

Mado and her cohorts camp it up for a mixed, fun-loving clientele, who inevitably end the evening on the huge dancefloor partying the night away.

Le Complexe Sky 1474 rue Ste-Catherine est ⓦwww.lecomplexesky.com. Choose between the café bar on the first floor, the male strip club on the second floor or the unfailingly pounding dancefloor and cabaret on the third floor. Attracts the beautiful-people set after work during the week.

Le Drugstore 1366 rue Ste-Catherine est. An extravagant six-floor bar complex complete with pool lounge, rooftop terrace and even a popcorn machine. With homely 1960's decor it is busiest before 11pm and popular with both lesbians and gay men.

Parking 1296 rue Amherst ⓣ514/282-1199, ⓦwww.parkingbar.com. One of the city's most popular gay clubs, with several dancefloors and lounges catering to all genres and tastes. Call ahead or check website as they're due to move to the Olympia Theatre. Men-only on Fri and Sat nights. Cover charge $3–5.

Stereo 858 rue Ste-Catherine est ⓦwww.stereo-nightclub.com. Stereo rocks as an after-hours club – and the stereo system in question kicks techno, house and drum'n'bass from 2am until whenever. Fri & Sat only. Cover charge $25–30.

Le Stud 1812 rue Ste-Catherine est ⓦwww.studbar.com. Popular "leather and Levis" bar, with pool tables and generously flowing beer.

Unity 1171 rue Ste-Catherine est ⓦwww.clubunitymontreal.com A young, mixed and outgoing crowd fill the large dancefloor here, though the *Bamboo Bar* upstairs tends to get more packed and sweaty – head to the rooftop terrace to cool off and take in an unforgettable view of the city.

Spectator sports in Montréal

Canadian football The Montréal Alouettes (Ⓦwww.montrealalouettes.com) represent the city in the Canadian Football League (CFL). Home games are at McGill University's Percival Molson Stadium, 475 av des Pins ouest. Tickets cost $25–125.

Ice hockey The Montréal Canadiens (Ⓦwww.canadiens.com), play at the Centre Bell, 1250 rue de la Gauchetière ouest (Métro: Lucien-L'Allier or Bonaventure). Tickets start at $28.

Soccer Montréal Impact (Ⓣ514/328-3669, Ⓦwww.montrealimpact.com), the city's professional soccer team, play at the Saputo Stadium, 4750 Sherbrooke est (Métro: Viau). Tickets start at $10.

(Ⓦwww.rideauvert.qc.ca), which gives prominence to Québec playwrights, while the Théâtre du Nouveau Monde, 84 rue Ste-Catherine ouest (Ⓦwww.tnm.qc.ca), presents a mix of contemporary and classic plays in French. Montréal's main English-language theatre is the Centaur Theatre, 453 rue St-François-Xavier (Ⓦwww.centaurtheatre.com). The Segal Centre for Performing Arts at The Saidye, 5170 chemin de la Côte-Ste-Catherine (Ⓦwww.saidyebronfman.org), contains an exhibition centre and a three-hundred-seat venue for English (and Yiddish) music, dance, film and theatre.

The Orchestre Symphonique de Montréal (Ⓦwww.osm.ca) and Orchestre Métropolitain (Ⓦwww.orchestremetropolitain.com) stage regular **concerts** at Place des Arts and the Basilique Notre-Dame. The city also has a programme of free summer concerts in various city parks. L'Opéra de Montréal (Ⓦwww.operademontreal.com) produces around five bilingually subtitled productions a year at Place des Arts.

Dance

Montréal has more than ten excellent **dance** troupes, from Les Grands Ballets Canadiens (Ⓦwww.grandsballets.qc.ca) and Les Ballets Jazz de Montréal (Ⓦwww.balletsdemontreal.com) to the avant-garde La La La Human Steps and O Vertigo, who perform at various times at the Place des Arts, Théâtre de Verdure and during the festivals.

Film

The main repertory **cinema** in English is the NFB's (National Film Board) CineRobotheque, 1564 rue St-Denis (Ⓦwww.nfb.ca). The Cinémathèque Québécoise, 335 boul de Maisonneuve est (Ⓦwww.cinematheque.qc.ca), has excellent screening and exhibition programmes; Ex-Centris, 3536 boul St-Laurent (Ⓦwww.ex-centris.com), has a penchant for alternative French film and experimental digital works. Check online (Ⓦwww.cinemamontreal.com), in the *Montréal Gazette* or the free weeklies for show times; verify the English film you want to see is playing in **v.o.** (*version originale*), not v.f. (*version français*); the latter means it's dubbed.

Listings

Bike rental The cheapest way to pedal around Montréal is on the public bike programme, Bixi (see p.220). Cycle Pop, near Parc Lafontaine at 1000 rue Rachel est (Ⓣ514/526-2525, Ⓦwww.cyclepop.ca), rents from $25 per day. In the Vieux-Port is Ça Roule, 27 rue de la Commune est, facing Quai King-Edward (Ⓣ514/866-0633, Ⓦwww.caroulemontreal.com); both offer lessons and excellent guided tours. The Maison des Cyclistes, 1251 rue Rachel est (Ⓣ514/521-8356, Ⓦwww.velo.qc.ca), is a superb resource for cycling information and organized tours out of the city.

Books and maps Paragraphe, 2220 av McGill College (Ⓦwww.paragraphbooks.com) is one of the best bookstores in town. Travel books in English and French are also available at Librairie du Voyage Ulysse, 4176 rue St-Denis and 560 av du President-Kennedy (Ⓦwww.ulyssesguides.com).

Camping equipment You can rent or buy all you need for the outdoors at Altitude Sports Plein-Air, 4140 rue St-Denis (Ⓣ514/847-1515 or 1-800/729-0322, Ⓦwww.altitude-sports.com; Métro: Mont-Royal).

Car rental Avis, 1225 rue Metcalfe (Ⓣ514/866-7906); Budget, 1240 rue Guy (Ⓣ514/938-1000); Discount, 607 boul de Maisonneuve ouest (Ⓣ514/286-1554); Hertz, 1073 rue Drummond (Ⓣ514/938-1717); and Thrifty, 845 rue Ste-Catherine est (Ⓣ514/845-5954).

Consulates UK, 1000 rue de la Gauchetière ouest (Ⓣ514/866-5863); US, 1155 rue St-Alexandre (Ⓣ514/398-9695); Germany, 1250 boul René-Lévesque ouest, Suite 4315 (Ⓣ514/931-2277); for Australia, Ireland, New Zealand and South Africa, contact the embassy in Ottawa (see p.189).

Currency exchange American Express, 1141 boul de Maisonneuve ouest (Ⓣ514/284-3300); Bureau de Change du Vieux-Montréal, 230 rue St-Jacques (Ⓣ514/284-8686); Calforex, 1250 rue Peel (Ⓣ514/392-9100); Thomas Cook, Centre Eaton, 705 rue Ste-Catherine ouest (Ⓣ514/284-7388). You can withdraw money at ATMs throughout the city if your card is Cirrus or Plus compatible.

Internet access The 24h Café Depot, on boul St-Laurent at rue Prince-Arthur est, offers free wi-fi – and decent coffee. There are several internet cafes along boul St-Laurent in the Plateau and in the university neighbourhoods of UQAM and McGill. Larger post offices have free access (15min limit).

Medical emergencies Central English-language hospitals that are part of the McGill University Health Centre "superhospital" (Ⓣ514/934-1934) are the Montréal General Hospital, 1650 av Cedar, on the mountain's slope northwest of downtown, and Royal Victoria Hospital, 687 av des Pins ouest, up the hill from McGill University. Centre Dentaire, 3546 av Van-Horne (Ⓣ514/342-4444) is a 24hr dental clinic. There's a walk-in dental clinic on the third floor of Montréal General Hospital (Mon–Fri 8am–noon & 1–4pm, but go early; after-hour emergencies call Ⓣ514/934-8075).

Pharmacies Most downtown outlets of Jean Coutu and Pharmaprix are open until 11pm and midnight, respectively. The Pharmaprix near the Oratory, at 5122 chemin de la Côte-des-Neiges, is open 24hr (Ⓣ514/738-8464).

Post office 1250 rue University (Mon–Fri 8am–5.45pm).

Taxis Co-op Ⓣ514/725-9885; Diamond Ⓣ514/273-6331.

Weather and road conditions Environment Canada (Ⓣ514/283-3010, Ⓦwww.weatheroffice.gc.ca) for weather and winter road conditions; Transports Québec (Ⓣ514/284-2363, Ⓦwww.mtq.gouv.qc.ca) for roadworks. Traffic reports are also on radio stations such as CJAD (800 AM). Skiers can check snow conditions at Ⓦwww.maneige.com.

Southwest Québec

Beyond the city limits, Montréalers are blessed with superb holiday regions, most within an hour or two of the metropolis. The lake-dotted countryside of **Southwest Québec** offers a range of recuperative pleasures for the city-dweller or visitor: relaxing country drives and nosing about historic sites, cycling and hiking in summer and a plethora of ski hills to choose from come winter.

Just across the river to the northwest of Montréal, along the fertile banks of the St Lawrence, the **Basses Laurentides** (Lower Laurentians) are dotted with white-washed farm cottages, stone chapels, a monastery and a provincial park that all make an easy day-trip from Montréal. Continue along to the largely wilderness stretch of the **Outaouais** region beginning around 130km west of Montréal and extending

Tourism information for Southwest Québec

Eastern Townships ⓣ819/820-2020 or 1-800/355-5755, ⓦwww.easterntownships.org.
Laurentides ⓣ450/436-8532 or 1-800/561-6673, ⓦwww.laurentides.com.
Mauricie ⓣ819/536-3334 or 1-800/567-7603, ⓦwww.tourismemauricie.com.
Outaouais ⓣ819/778-2222 or 1-800/265-7822, ⓦwww.outaouais-tourism.ca.

along the north side of the Rivière Outaouais (Ottawa River). Once the domain of Algonquin tribes, the region was not developed until the 1800s, when it became an important centre for the lumber industry. While the bulk of the activities in the region are of an outdoorsy nature – hiking, snowmobiling, cycling and cross-country skiing – it's worth stopping in **Montebello** for its historical heritage.

Extending along the north side of the St Lawrence from the Ottawa River to the Saguenay River are the **Laurentians** – one of the world's oldest ranges – where five hundred million years of erosion have moulded a rippling landscape of undulating hills and valleys. The most accessible stretch lies north of Montréal but, unlike the more historic Basses Laurentides, settlement in the upper Laurentians did not begin until the 1830s, when the construction of the P'tit Train du Nord railway tracks let in the mining and lumber industries. When the decline in both industries left the area in a depression, salvation came in the form of the recreational demands of the growing populace of Montréal. The region is now one of North America's largest ski areas, and the train tracks have been replaced by a terrific cycling trail.

Along the US border to the east of Montréal, the charm of the **Cantons-de-l'Est** (Eastern Townships) lies in the lush farmlands, vineyards, maple woods, lakeshore villages and luxurious country inns along with art galleries and antique shops. The region is popular with city dwellers in search of quiet weekends punctuated by active pursuits on the lakes and trails.

Along the north shore of the St Lawrence, the rather dull drive to Québec City (see p.270) provides access to a couple of worthwhile distractions. The **Mauricie** valley, home to the province's smallest national park, has a web of waterways and lakes set amid a landscape of mountainous forest. Spanning the mouths of the Rivière Mauricie, **Trois-Rivières** is a seemingly unprepossessing town unless you detour to its historic centre.

The Lower Laurentians (Les Basses Laurentides)

Once the domain of various aboriginal groups, the **Lower Laurentians** (Basses Laurentides) were granted by Ville-Marie's governors to the colony's first seigneurs, who, using a modified version of the feudal land system of the motherland, oversaw the development of the land by their tenants, or *habitants*. As the rivers were the lifeline of the colony, these tenant farms were laid out perpendicular to the water in long, narrow, rectangular seigneuries that shaped life under the long regime.

St-Eustache

The first town of note in the region is **ST-EUSTACHE**, about forty minutes' drive through the suburbs northwest of Montréal by Hwy 13 or 15, then southwest on Hwy 640; the main tourist office is en route, just off exit 14 from Hwy 640 (summer: daily 9am–5pm; rest of year 9am–4pm; ⓣ450/491-4444, ⓦwww.basseslaurentides.com).

Most of the town is a monotonous sprawl, except for the riverside historic centre, **Vieux St-Eustache**, where the frustrations of the *habitants* with the British occupancy met a tragic end in the 1837 uprising. About thirty buildings survived the battle that put down the rebellious *Patriotes* led by Louis-Joseph Papineau (see below) and these are located along two narrow streets in Vieux St-Eustache. Most are simply marked with heritage signs, and inaccessible to the public, but the **church**, at 123 rue St-Louis, still bears a few scars and offers free guided tours (late June to late Aug Tues–Fri 9.30am–4.30pm, Sun noon–4.30pm). The cross street, rue St-Eustache, has two sights worth visiting, the most impressive being the wedding-cake Manoir Globensky at no. 235 (May–Oct daily 10am–noon & 1–4pm; ⓦwww.moulinlegare.com, ⓣ450/974-5170; $5 including entrance to the Moulin Légaré; call ahead to confirm hours), which doubles as the **Musée de St-Eustache et des Patriotes** and includes displays, films and temporary exhibitions on local history. Opposite, the eighteenth-century **Moulin Légaré**, at no. 232, is the oldest water-powered flour mill in continuous operation in North America; guided tours are available but you can get a glimpse of the works from the bakery shop in front.

Oka

About 20km southwest of St-Eustache on Hwy 344 lies the small lakeside town of **OKA**. Although associated with the armed stand-off between the Mohawks and police (see p.254), there isn't much to see in the town itself, though worth a visit is the **Abbaye Cistercienne d'Oka**, 1600 chemin d'Oka (Mon–Sat 4am–7:30pm; ⓣ450/479-8361, ⓦwww.abbayeoka.com), one of North America's oldest monasteries. Commanding a spectacular site just outside town, its century-old bell tower rises from the hills. The Trappists arrived here from France in 1880, their life in Canada beginning in a miller's house now overshadowed by the rest of the complex and the landscaped gardens of the abbey. The nearby monastery shop (closed Sun) sells organic Trappist products, from maple syrup and chocolates to variations on the delicious Oka cheese.

Between the town and monastery, the **Calvaire d'Oka** with its seven mid-eighteenth-century stone chapels is best visited on September 14, when native pilgrims hold the Feast of the Holy Cross along the banks of Lac des Deux Montagnes. The

The rebellion of 1837

In the early 1800s, British immigrants to Lower Canada were offered **townships** (*cantons*), while francophones were not allowed to expand their holdings, exacerbating the resentment caused by the favouritism extended to English-speaking businesses in Montréal. The situation was worsened by high taxes on British imports and a savage economic depression in 1837. Wearing Canadian-made garments of *étoffe du pays* as a protest against British imports, the leaders of Lower Canada reform – known as **the Patriotes** – rallied francophones to rebel in Montréal. As Louis-Joseph Papineau, the Outaouais region seigneur whose speeches in the Assembly had encouraged the rebellions, fled the city, fearful that his presence would incite more rioting, the government sent military detachments to the countryside, the hotbed of the *Patriotes*. Two hundred *Patriotes* took refuge in St-Eustache's church, where eighty of them were killed by British troops, who went on to raze much of the town.

The Oka Mohawk standoff

In the summer of 1990, Oka became the stage for a confrontation between **Mohawk** warriors from Kanesatake and the provincial government. The crisis began when Oka's town council decided to expand its golf course onto a sacred burial ground, a provocation to which the Mohawks responded by arming themselves and staking out the territory. Québec's public security minister sent in the provincial police to storm the barricades; in the ensuing fracas a policeman was killed – no one knows by whom, but the autopsy established it was not by a police bullet. Hostilities reached a new pitch and the two sides became ever more polarized. As sympathetic Mohawks from the Kahnawake reserve south of Montréal set up barricades across the Mercier Bridge, groups of white Québécois attacked them with stones, while other aboriginal peoples throughout Canada and the US showed solidarity with the Mohawks. The crisis lasted 78 days, until 350 Canadian soldiers encircled a core of fifty Mohawks, forcing them to give up. Some believe the natives went too far at Oka, and the existing distrust between aboriginal peoples and other Canadians seems to have deepened. As Georges Erasmus, former national chief of the Assembly of First Nations, said: "Our demands are ignored when we kick up a fuss – but they are also ignored if we do not."

Calvaire is reached by a 5.5km trail up the Colline d'Oka, a hill that gives views of the region, and is set within the **Parc National d'Oka** (year-round; $3.50; ⓣ450/479-8365 or 1-888/727-2652, ⓦwww.parcsquebec.com), a verdant provincial park with 45km of hiking and cycling trails and a long stretch of sandy beach. There are serviced campsites (starting at $32) and more rustic spots to pitch a tent.

Montebello and around

The drive from Montréal to Gatineau (see p.186) on scenic Hwy 148 takes in a few riverside villages that used to be thriving logging towns. The first stop en route, 135km west of Montréal, is **MONTEBELLO**, a picturesque village named after seigneur, politician and Rebellion leader Louis-Joseph Papineau's estate.

The town is one of the Outaouais' main attractions thanks to a resort-friendly atmosphere that includes horseriding, boating, upscale boutiques and the inimitable *Fairmont Le Château Montebello*, 392 rue Notre-Dame (ⓣ819/423-6341 or 1-800/441-1414, ⓦwww.fairmont.com/montebello; ⑧), the world's largest log building. Built by the Seigneury Club in 1930 in ninety days, the original three buildings are made up of ten thousand red-cedar logs. Even if you don't stay, check out the six-hearthed fireplace in the massive hexagonal lobby – and, for a relaxing splurge, enjoy a riverside lunch.

The *Château* abuts the **Site historique national du Manoir Papineau** (mid-May to mid-June Wed–Sun 10am–5pm, mid-June to early Sept daily 10am–5pm, mid-Sept to mid-Oct Sat & Sun only; site free; house tour $7.80; ⓣ819/423-6965, ⓦwww.pc.gc.ca/papineau), Papineau's tranquil estate comprising his manor house, chapel and granary over a sizeable tract of land. The ticket office is on the main road at 500 rue Notre-Dame in an old train station shared with the **tourist information centre** (late-June to early Sept daily 9am–6pm; rest of year Tues–Sat; 9am–4pm; ⓣ819/423-5602; ⓦwww.tourismeoutaouais.com). Voyageur **buses** drop passengers off twice daily down the street at no. 535. For reasonable **accommodation**, try *Le Clos des Cèdres*, 227 rue St-Joseph (ⓣ819/423-1265, ⓦwww.leclosdescedres.ca; ⑤) or

Motel l'Anse de la Lanterne, 646 rue Notre-Dame (☎819/423-5280; ③), which has a good restaurant. Most **restaurants** are on the main drag; *Le Zouk*, at 530 Notre-Dame, has a pub-bistro menu and sunny terrace.

The only other stop of interest between Montréal and Gatineau is **PLAISANCE**, 15km west of Montebello (and 30km east of Gatineau). Once the region's main lumber centre, the main draw today is the **Parc National de Plaisance** (late April to mid-Oct; $3.50; ☎819/427-5334 or 1-800/665-6527, Ⓦwww.sepaq.com), a tiny provincial park made up of three *presqu'îles* with hiking and cycling trails. In the spring, you can enjoy the spectacle of thousands of Canadian geese as they pass through the park on their northern migration.

If you're not going any further west, follow **Highway 323** northeast from Montebello to Mont-Tremblant (see p.257) and return to Montréal via the Laurentians. It's a pleasant trip – a flat valley laced with rivers gives way to rising terrain where the road twists through forested hills – and the sandy beach of Lac-des-Plages is half-way along.

The Laurentians (Les Laurentides)

The slopes of the **Laurentians**, a vast sweep of coniferous forest dotted with hundreds of tranquil lakes and scored with rivers, was once Montréal's "wilderness back yard". Winter sports have done away with the region's former tranquility as thousands of Québécois take to the slopes at more than 25 ski resorts, causing huge traffic jams. Still, much of the land has remained relatively untouched – like the **Parc National du Mont Tremblant** – and the area is a must-see when autumn colours arrive. The Laurentians really cater to families on a week's sporty vacation, and much of the **accommodation** is pricey, as it includes gyms, tennis courts, golf courses and the like. A smattering of B&Bs and numerous motels offer an alternative to those on a tight budget, as do the hostels in Val-David and Mont-Tremblant itself.

Two **roads** lead from Montréal to this area of the Laurentians: the Autoroute des Laurentides (Hwy 15) and the slower Hwy 117; choose the latter if you want to go antique hunting, as there are a number of large shops around Piedmont. Limocar Laurentides (☎514/842-2281 or 1-866/692-8899, Ⓦwww.limocar.ca) offers a regular **bus** service from the Station Centrale d'Autobus de Montréal to most of the towns. Other than Tremblant – which costs a small fortune – rates for **ski passes** are around $45 a day in the decent areas, a few dollars more at weekends.

Saint-Sauveur-des-Monts

The ski resorts start 60km from Montréal and can be visited easily as day-trips. The first is **SAINT-SAUVEUR-DES-MONTS**, with over 35 pistes in the immediate vicinity. Its resident population of seven thousand is boosted to a peak-season maximum of thirty thousand, and the main drag, rue Principale, reflects the influx with restaurants of all stripes, as well as shops and boutiques. Come nightfall, skiers take to the numerous glitzy clubs and discos.

Information on shopping and skiing is available from the Bureau Touristique, 605 chemin des Frênes near exit 60 from Hwy 15 (Mon–Fri 9am–5pm; ☎450/227-3417 or 1-800/898-2127, Ⓦwww.saint-sauveur.net or Ⓦwww.tourismepdh.org); there's also a kiosk near the church on rue Principale in the warmer months.

Hotels cater to a resort crowd who expect all the amenities: The classy *Le Relais St-Denis*, 61 rue St-Denis (☎450/227-4766 or 1-888/997-4766, Ⓦwww.relaisstdenis.com; ⑥) with well-appointed rooms and a pool. For cosy

Laurentians information and hotel reservations

The Laurentians has a free **accommodation booking service** for the region (ⓣ1-800/561-6673, ⓦwww.laurentides.com). You can pick up information on the resorts at the helpful regional **tourist office** (late June to Aug daily 8.30am–8.30pm; rest of year Sat–Thurs 8.30am–5pm, Fri 8.30am–6pm; ⓣ450/224-7007, ⓣ1-800/561-6673), located at exit 51 off Hwy 15. During the ski season, you can get information on snow conditions at ⓦwww.quebecskisurf.com, as well as on the radio and in the local newspapers.

comforts, the B&B *Couette et Fourchette*, at 342 rue Principale (ⓣ450/227-6116, ⓦwww.couetteetfourchette.com; ❸–❹), has comfortable rooms.

If you're **eating** on a budget, you can fill up at a branch of the Montréal outfit *Pizzédélic*, 16 rue de la Gare, and relax over a strong cup of coffee at *Brûlerie des Monts*, 197 rue Principale. Mid-price local spots include *La Bohème*, 251 rue Principale (ⓣ450/227-6644), which serves French food, or the lively Italian restaurant *Papa Luigi*, 155 rue Principale (ⓣ450/227-5311) with Italian and seafood dishes from $25.

Val-David

Further north along Hwy 117, **VAL-DAVID** is the bohemian resort of the Laurentians, favoured by artists and craftspeople; the main street, rue de l'Église, has galleries and shops, many run by the artisans themselves. The village thrums with artistic energy during the popular midsummer festival 1001 Pots (ⓦwww.1001pots.com), which features ceramic workshops, creative classes for kids and plenty of crafts shopping. The town also has some non-ski-related activities come summertime, with plenty of hiking trails and rock climbing faces in the area and the P'tit Train du Nord bicycle path (see box, p.257).

The **tourist office** is at 2525 rue de l'Église (daily 9am–5pm; ⓣ819/322-3104 or 1-888/322-7030, ⓦwww.valdavid.com).

Accommodation

Le Chalet Beaumont 1451 rue Beaumont ⓣ819/322-1972, ⓦwww.chaletbeaumont.com. Val-David's excellent but noisy hostel is a massive chalet with roaring fires in the winter and great views year-round. It's a twenty-minute walk from the bus station, but offers a pick-up service. Dorms $25; ❷

La Maison de Bavière 1470 chemin de la Rivière ⓣ819/322-3528, ⓦwww.maisondebaviere.com. You can watch the river rapids from the fireplace-warmed sitting room in the winter or sit outside on the terrace and sip away on a glass of wine in the summer at this pleasant, four-room Bavarian-themed B&B. It also has two studio apartments, with kitchen, for those interested in longer stays (starting at $150 per night and dropping $10 with each subsequent night). ❹

Gite Café Plumard 1641 chemin de la Rivière ⓣ819/322-2182, ⓦwww.gitecafeplumard.com. Wake up to a three-course breakfast (including gourmet pancakes) at this comfortable B&B, whose three rooms all come with a private bathroom and shower, wi-fi access, TV and DVD player. Two private cabins also available for rental. ❹

Auberge Prema Shanti 1005 Tour du Lac ⓣ819/322-2345 or 1-877/622-2345, ⓦwww.premashanti.ca. African and Oriental influences combine to create a tropical-tinged getaway, which offers yoga, meditation and handsome rooms in a peaceful lakeside setting. All rooms have a kitchenette and private bath. Also offers dorm-style room for groups. ❹

La Sapinière 1244 chemin de la Sapinière ⓣ819/322-2020 or 1-800/567-6635, ⓦwww.sapiniere.com. With a vast wine cellar, excellent restaurant, spa and a gorgeous lakeside setting, this lodge by Mont Alta is the swishest place to stay in town. Choose from regular rooms, junior or executive suites or a private three-room chalet. ❽

Eating and drinking

Rue de l'Église has decent, well-priced **restaurants**, including *Le Grand Pa*, at no. 2481 (Ⓣ819/322-3104), which serves simple French food for around $10 and has live music at weekends. Enjoy fresh, artisanal baked breads at *La Vagabonde*, 1262 chemin de la Rivière (Ⓣ819/322-3953; closed Mon & Tues), while for tasty Québécois food, try *Au Petit Poucet*, just south of the village at 1030 Hwy 117 (Ⓣ819/322-2246).

Mont-Tremblant

Situated 130km north of Montréal, **MONT-TREMBLANT** is the Laurentians' oldest and most renowned ski area (Ⓦwww.tremblant.ca) focused on the range's highest peak, **Mont Tremblant** (960m), so called because the native population believed it was the home of spirits that could move the mountain. In the late 1990s, the company that developed British Columbia's ski resort of Whistler (see p.791) pumped large amounts of money into Tremblant, and the resulting European-style ski village has made it a premier ski destination. The 95 runs are for all levels, with a maximum vertical drop of more than 640m and the longest ski run in Québec. One-day **ski passes** cost $70.35.

Mont-Tremblant comprises the resort itself plus the merged town of **St-Jovite**, the area's commercial centre, and tiny **Mont-Tremblant Village**, 10km north. The resort also includes a glitzy casino (Sun–Wed 11am–1am, Thurs–Sat 11am–3am; Ⓦwww.casinosduquebec.com/mont-tremblant) which you can reach by an aerial gondola or daily shuttle.

The **Parc National du Mont Tremblant**, a large wilderness area spreading northwards from the villages, is a favourite with Québécois. Skiing, snowmobiling and snowshoeing are favoured winter sports; in summer the park attracts campers, canoeists, hunters and hikers – in remote areas you may see bears, deer and moose. The park's three lakeside **campsites** must be reserved in advance (Ⓣ819/688-2281 or 1-800/665-6527, Ⓦwww.sepaq.com; park entry $3.50, sites $22 and up).

The main **tourist information** office for Mont-Tremblant is just off Hwy 117 as you enter St-Jovite, at 48 chemin de Brébeuf (June–Sept Sun–Thurs 9am–7pm,

The P'tit Train du Nord bicycle trail

The bed of **Le P'tit Train du Nord**, a disused railway line that once ferried Montréalers to the Laurentians' resorts, now sees brisk business as a major **bicycle trail**; every summer, thousands of cyclists pedal its 200km, running north from St-Jérôme to Mont-Laurier, taking in the mountain views along the way. The former rail stations have been renovated and now often house tourist information centres, some with facilities such as showers and snack bars. In winter, the snow-covered route is equally in demand by **cross-country skiers** who can explore numerous side-trails branching off into the hills between St-Jérôme and Val-David, and to **snowmobilers** – the Ste-Agathe to Mont-Laurier stretch is part of the network of thousands of kilometres of trails that crisscross the province. **Information**, as well as a guide with maps and list of services (including cycle repair, baggage transport and accommodation) along the route, is available from the Association Touristique des Laurentides (see p.256).

Pause Plein Air (1381 rue De la Sapinière, Val-David Ⓣ819/322-6880 or 1-877/422-6880, Ⓦwww.pausepleinair.com) offers gentle, four-hour return trips by canoe or kayak down the North River between Val-David and Mont Rolland; they also rent bikes, canoes and kayaks.

▲ Le P'tit Train du Nord bike path

Fri & Sat 9am–8pm; Oct–May daily 9am–5pm; ⓣ819/425-3300 or 1-800/322-2932, ⓦwww.tourismemonttremblant.com); a second tourist office is located further north at 5080 montée Ryan (ⓣ819/425-2434).

Accommodation

Auberge de Jeunesse International du Mont-Tremblant 2213 chemin du Village, Mont-Tremblant village ⓣ819/425-6008 or 1-866/425-6008, ⓦwww.hostellingtremblant.com. An excellently-kitted out hostel with all the usual amenities you'd expect to find, plus a café and bar, snowshoe and bike rental, volleyball court, free wi-fi and free parking. Dorms for $29, private or family rooms (double or single occupancy) ❸

Ermitage du Lac 150 chemin du Cure-Deslauriers, Mont-Tremblant resort ⓣ819/681-2222 or 800/461-8711, ⓦwww.tremblant.ca. One of the many options available in the resort itself, this pleasant hotel has 69 spacious rooms and suites, each equipped with a kitchenette; some rooms also have a fireplace and balcony. ❻

Fairmont Tremblant 3045 chemin de la Chapelle, Mont-Tremblant resort ⓣ819/681-7000 or 1-800/441-1414, ⓦwww.fairmont.com/tremblant. One of the more glamourous choices in the area, situated by Lac Tremblant and facing the base of the mountain. Has a heated indoor and outdoor pool, two outdoor whirlpools, a fitness centre, ski rental, an excellent restaurant and a ski-in, ski-out lounge. ❽

Hôtel Mont Tremblant 1900 chemin du Village, Mont-Tremblant village ⓣ819/425-3232 or 1-888/887-1111, ⓦwww.hotelmonttremblant.com. Less pricey than its Fairmont competition, but set right where the P'tit Train du Nord bike path (see p.257) passes Lac Mercier, so ideally suited for cyclists. Has an "authentic" Irish pub, a restaurant serving French cuisine and a café. Also offers free shuttle service to the slopes in winter. Price includes breakfast. ❹

Tremblant Onwego Inn 112 chemin Plouffe, Mont-Tremblant Village ⓣ819/429-5522 or 1-866/429-5522, ⓦwww.tremblantonwego.com. Also set on Lac Mercier's shores and close to the bike trail, this inn has thematically-decorated (Boat, Egyptian, African and Circus) as well as standard rooms and suites with kitchenettes, some with lake views. The private beach is an excellent place to make use of the inn's free canoes, kayaks and pedal boats in the summer. Wi-fi available in each unit. ❺

Eating, drinking and nightlife

For **eating**, there are plenty of options in all price brackets at the Tremblant resort. In the St-Jovite sector, the lively *Antipasto*, 855 rue Ouimet (ⓣ819/425-7580) turns out hearty servings of Italian pastas. *Chez Roger*, 444 rue St-Georges (ⓣ819/429-6991), offers rich French cuisine at slightly elevated prices. For a coffee, settle into the decently priced café-bar, *Le Bistro Brunch Café*, at no. 814 rue

Ouimet. The best **party scene** is at the resort's *après-ski* spots, which are ideally suited to stilletos and slick, party garb. The top spot is the perennially popular *Le P'tit Caribou*, 125 Chemin Kandahar (Ⓣ819/681-4500), where a cocktail-fuelled crowd hangs out until the wee hours. Or, ease into the evening at *Le Saint Georges*, a relaxed pub with a terrace at 890 rue de St-Jovite.

The Eastern Townships (Cantons-de-l'Est)

Beginning about 80km east of Montréal and extending to the US border, the **Eastern Townships** were once Québec's best-kept secret, but the nineteenth-century villages – many spruced up with luxury amenities - have since become a preferred getaway for Montréalers, and a growing ski industry – concentrated around Mont Sutton, just north of the Vermont border – is making its mark on the land. Yet the region's agricultural roots are still evident, especially in spring, when the maple trees are tapped for syrup. At this time of year, remote *cabanes à sucre* offer sleigh rides and traditional Québécois treats such as maple taffy – strips of maple syrup frozen in the snow.

The land, once the domain of scattered groups of aboriginal peoples, was later settled by United Empire Loyalists hounded out of the US after the American Revolution. Their loyalty to the crown resulted in freehold land grants from the British, and townships with very English names like **Sherbrooke** and **Granby** were founded. In the mid-nineteenth century the townships opened up to industry, which attracted an influx of French-Canadians seeking work: today, nearly 95 percent of the 400,000 population are francophone. For the most part, relations between the linguistic groups have been amicable, though pockets like the towns and villages around **Knowlton** and **North Hatley** remain staunchly tied to their anglophone heritage.

You can reach the region from Montréal by the Autoroute des Cantons-de-l'Est (Hwy 10), which has a useful **information centre** for the whole region at exit 68, southwest of Granby (daily June–Sept 8am–7pm; Oct–May 8am–4pm; Ⓣ450/375-8774 or 1-866-472-6292, Ⓦwww.easterntownships.org). Slower Hwy 112 wends through small villages and past forests and lakes; if you've got plenty of time, detour south onto the secondary roads nearer the US border that pass rustic barns, duck under covered bridges and wind through the province's fledgling vineyards. A dozen or so Limocar **buses** a day from Montréal (Ⓣ514/842-2281 or 1-866/700-8899, Ⓦwww.transdev.ca) stop in Magog and Sherbrooke; less often in Granby (4 daily) and Bromont (2 daily).

Granby and Bromont

Approached from Montréal, the Cantons-de-l'Est begins at the drab city of **GRANBY**. The **Zoo de Granby** (late June to late Aug daily 10am–7pm, Sept–Oct Sat & Sun 10am–5pm; Ⓦwww.zoodegranby.com; $32.99) is Québec's best-known zoo. It shares the site with the **Parc Aquatique Amazoo** (same schedule and entry price) a popular water park with pools and slides. Granby's **information centre** is at 650 rue Principale (daily June to early Sept 8am–6pm; rest of year 9am–5pm; Ⓣ450/372-7056, Ⓦwww.granbybromont.com).

Just south of Granby, **BROMONT** is focused on the 405m ski and snowboarding hill at its centre, **Ski Bromont** (Ⓣ450/534-2200 or 1-866/276-6668, Ⓦwww.skibromont.com; day ticket $59). In summer, the hill metamorphoses into a hiking and mountain biking centre and watery playground at the slides and pools of the **Bromont Aquatic Park** (early to late June daily 10am–5pm; late June to mid-Aug daily 10am–6.30pm; mid-Aug to late Aug 10am–5pm; Ⓦwww.skibromont.com; $35). Less energetic options include the tiny **Musée du Chocolat**, 679 rue Shefford (Mon–Fri 8.30am–6pm, Sat & Sun 8am–5.30pm; Ⓣ450/534-3893, Ⓦwww.museeduchocolatdebromont.ca; free), where you can learn about chocolate-making while nibbling on some fine specimens from the attached candy store. Across the street is the 1889 **Église St-Francois-Xavier**, with a delicate tin-clad tiered steeple and a vault decorated in minty pastels.

Practicalities

Among the assortment of good **B&Bs** in the area is the cosy *La Maison aux Pignons Verts*, 129 rue D'Adamsville in the village of Adamsville, 10km southwest of Bromont (Ⓣ450/260-1129, Ⓦwww.lamaisonauxpignonsverts.com; ❹). In Bromont, *Auberge Nuits de St-Georges*, 792 rue Shefford (Ⓣ450/534-0705 or 1-888/534-0708, Ⓦwww.aubergenuitsdestgeorges.com; ❺), is a handsome red-brick house with six suites.

For **eating**, *L'Âme du Pain*, 702 rue Shefford, Bromont, is a bakery serving good sandwiches and salads on a shady terrace; pizza and more substantial dishes are available later on. Just up the road is *Auberge Le Madrigal*, 46 boul de Bromont (Ⓣ450/534-3588), which serves local cuisine, including duck and salmon in an apricot chutney.

Knowlton

The serene, leafy township of Lac Brome, named after the lovely lake in its centre, encompasses several hamlets, the most inviting of which is the petite **Knowlton**, known for its Loyalist history. The county museum, the **Société Historique du Comté du Brome**, at 130 chemin Lakeside (mid-May to mid-Sept 10am–4.30pm, Sun 11am–4.30pm; $5; Ⓣ450/243-6782), features several floors crammed with regional cultural artefacts as well as the star piece, a Fokker DVII airplane.

Knowlton's real draw is the chance to spend a peaceful weekend just milling about, sipping coffee and perusing antique shops and art galleries, which you'll find on the two main thoroughfares, chemins Lakeside and Knowlton. *Galerie Bistrot Carpe Diem* (61 chemin Lakeside), housed in a restored tannery, features modern sculptures as well as a sunny upstairs deck overlooking the river.

Knowlton also buzzes with performing arts thanks to **Theatre Lac Brome**, at 9 chemin Mont Écho (Ⓣ450/242-2270, Ⓦwww.theatrelacbrome.ca), which showcases English-language plays, often comedies, in July and August. Bed down at the *Auberge Knowlton* (Ⓣ450/242-6886, Ⓦwww.aubergeknowlton.ca; ❺) and enjoy lunch at the inn's *Relais* restaurant, where you can try Lac Brome's deservedly famous duck. The friendly owners are also a great source of information on the area, and can provide walking maps of town. Among the many lively festivals are the late-September Lac Brome duck festival, and the early August Letters from Knowlton (Ⓦwww.lescorrespondances.ca/knowlton), a literary festival featuring local authors; the French version has been running for several years in the nearby town of Eastman.

Magog and around

The summer resort town of **MAGOG**, about 40km east of Bromont, gets its name from a corruption of an aboriginal word meaning "great expanse of water" – now known as **Lac Memphrémagog**, one of the township's largest lakes, on which it borders. A strange beast known as Memphré supposedly lurks in its waters (the subject of various fishy tales since 1798).

La Route des Vins (The Wine Route)

Sip your way through the Eastern Townships on the 120km **La Route des Vins** (Ⓦwww.laroutedesvins.ca) which connects the region's lush vineyards, many of which are notable for their ice wines. The tourist office (see below) and the route website have an easy-to-follow map. The wine route snakes across the southwest wedge of the townships, and along the way you can indulge in Québécois wines at sixteen vineyards. The friendly **Vignoble L'Orpailleur** (Daily: May to Oct 9am–6pm; Nov to Dec 9am–5pm; Jan to April 10am–5pm; guided tours (French only) mid-June to Oct four times daily; Ⓣ450/295-2763, Ⓦwww.orpailleur.ca), southwest of Knowlton near the village of Dunham, is well primed for visitors, with a small museum and sunny restaurant. **Domaine Les Brome** (May to Oct daily 11am–6pm, Nov to April Sat & Sun 11am–6pm; Ⓣ450/242-2665, Ⓦwww.domainelesbrome.com), west of Lac Brome, in Ville de Lac-Brome, features a superb array of wines – and a gorgeous view of vineyards with the lake shimmering in the distance.

Magog itself is a lively spot fairly teeming with bars and restaurants along its main street, rue Principale. One quirky diversion is at the **Labyrinthe Memphrémagog** on the westernmost of the beaches fronting the lake – you can navigate a maze on in-line skates or on foot (mid-June to early Sept daily 10am–dusk, May to mid-June & early Sept to mid-Oct Fri–Mon 10am–dusk; Ⓣ819/868-4188, Ⓦwww.labyrinthemagog.ca; $10). You can also explore the area on numerous well-kept bike trails; Ski-Vélo Vincent Renaud, set back from the main drag at 395 rue Principale ouest (Ⓣ819/843-4277, Ⓦwww.skivelo.com), rents bicycles for about $20 a day.

Otherwise, you could fill your time by going on one of the various boat cruises that ply the river in the summer, or opt for a day-long cruise south over the border to Newport, Vermont (June–Sept; $55; Ⓣ819/843-8068 or 1-888/842-8068, Ⓦwww.croisiere-memphremagog.com; passport needed). Check with the **information centre** (June to mid-Oct daily 8.30am–8pm; mid-Oct to May daily 9am–5pm, Fri until 7pm; Ⓣ1-800/267-2744, Ⓦwww.tourisme-memphremagog.com), midway between the town and the labyrinth at 55 rue Cabana, accessed by Hwy 112, for information.

Practicalities

There are many places to **stay** in Magog. Among the B&Bs are a few century-old houses clustered together: At *Ô Bois Dormant*, 205 rue Abbot (Ⓣ819/843-0450, Ⓦwww.oboisdormant.qc.ca; ⑤), the inviting rooms have fireplaces; and *Au Coeur de Magog*, 120 rue Merry Nord (Ⓣ819/868-2511, Ⓦwww.aucoeurdemagog.com; ③), is a fine old house with pink shutters and floral bedspreads in the cosy rooms. *L'Auberge du Grand Lac*, 40 rue Merry Sud (Ⓣ819/847-4039 or 1-800/267-4039, Ⓦwww.grandlac.com; ⑤–⑦) is a central hotel with a rooftop terrace.

Several **bars** and **restaurants** lie along rue Principale ouest: *Le Panier à Pain*, at no. 382, serves up healthy sandwiches and soups, while *Le Martimbeault*, at no. 341 (Ⓣ819/843-3182), offers dinners of rich French food. *La Memphré*, 12 rue Merry Sud, is a pleasant bar with views of the lake from the veranda where they serve quality pub food and a tasty local beer. For a taste of countrified Québec, enjoy farm-fresh regional food at the inn *Aux Jardins Champêtre* northwest of Magog at 1575 chemin des Pères (Ⓣ819/868-0665, Ⓦwww.auxjardinschampetres.com), including produce from local markets, pungent cheeses from the nearby Benedictine Abbaye (see p.262) and duck from Lac Brome.

Abbaye Saint-Benoît-du-Lac

About 25km southwest of Magog via Hwy 245 along the lakeshore is the **Abbaye Saint-Benoît-du-Lac**, its presence signalled by white-granite turrets. It's occupied by some sixty Benedictine monks, renowned for their Gregorian chants (daily 7 & 11am; also Mon–Wed & Fri–Sun 5pm, Thurs 7pm) and their Ermite blue cheese (shop open late June to Oct Mon–Sat 9am–6pm, Sun noon–6pm). The abbey's doors are open to anyone who needs a retreat for spiritual reflection. Food and **accommodation** are free, though a donation of $50 is expected (ⓣ819/843-4080 men or 843-2340 women; appropriate clothing required; ⓦwww.st-benoit-du-lac.com). There is no public transport to the abbey; a taxi costs about $30 from Magog.

Mont Orford

A mature sugar maple forest blankets three-quarters of the small **Parc National du Mont-Orford** (ⓦwww.sepaq.com/pq/mor/en/), 10km north of Magog via Hwy 141. Ski on Mont Orford (859m) in winter or hike in the summer: the chair-lift operates year-round. There's not much to see in the tiny town of **ORFORD** itself, but the well-run **hostel** on Hwy 141, *Auberge du Centre d'Arts Orford*, 3165 chemin du Parc (ⓣ819/843-3981 or 1-800/567-6155, ⓦwww.arts-orford.org; ❶–❸), is a great base for exploring the park, and offers both dorm and private rooms. You can also **camp** at one of the park's sites or off in the woods (ⓣ819/843-9855 or 1-800/655-6527, ⓦwww.sepaq.com; $16–38). Other accommodation options are more upscale in price and service: *Auberge de la Tour*, 1837 Alfred-Desrochers (ⓣ819/868-0763, ⓦwww.auberge-de-la-tour.com; ❹), is a charming country inn. For **dining**, *Tonnerre de Brest*, 2197 chemin du Parc (ⓣ819/847-1234), serves up crêpes, mussels and fries.

North Hatley

The region east of Magog holds its Loyalist connections dear, and this is one of the few areas in Québec where you'll encounter vestiges of the snobbish anglophone attitudes that once pervaded the whole province. **NORTH HATLEY**,

▲ North Hatley, Eastern Townships

a thirty-minute drive east from Magog along Hwy 108, is an anglophone bastion, with boutiques selling Lipton teas and tweeds; the resident population steadfastly refuses to change the town's name to "Hatley Nord". The village is also home to the lively theatre company The Piggery (Ⓣ819/842-2431, Ⓦwww.piggery.com), which puts on an eclectic array of shows, from musicals to bluegrass, throughout the summer. Several art galleries and antique shops are clustered along the waterfront.

Practicalities

North Hatley boasts one of Québec's classiest **inns**: the romantic *Manoir Hovey* (Ⓣ819/842-2421 or 1-800/661-2421, Ⓦwww.manoirhovey.com; ⑧), at 575 chemin Hovey, nestled along the lake with its private beach and boats. Cheaper and in the village itself, *Serendipity Bed & Breakfast*, 340 chemin de la Rivière (Ⓣ819/842-2970, Ⓦwww.serendipitybb.qc.ca; ④), is a century-old house. The comfy *Auberge le Coeur d'Or*, 85 rue School (Ⓣ819/842-4363, Ⓦwww.aubergelecoeurdor.com) has cosy rooms (③–⑤) and fully equipped cottages (⑥–⑦).

For fresh bread, sandwiches and hearty salads, stop in at the inviting café *Saveurs et Gourmandises*, 39 rue Main (Ⓣ819/842-3131). The English-style gastro-pub *Le Pilsen*, 55 rue Principale, serves up locally brewed Massiwippi ales – and the food to go with it, like juicy burgers, mussels and fries. The expensive but exquisite *Café Massiwippi*, 3050 chemin Capelton (Ⓣ819/842-4528; open evenings only, and sometimes for lunch in the summer) serves creative dishes, from smoked trout with yellow beets to duck foie gras. Expect to pay over $30 for a main dish.

Sherbrooke

The 100,000-strong university town of **SHERBROOKE**, 147km east of Montréal, revels in the title "Queen of the Eastern Townships", a strange accolade for a town that's no great shakes and has just a few minor attractions, clustered in Vieux-Sherbrooke around the 1.5km gorge carved by the Rivière Magog. The **tourist office** is at 785 rue King ouest (mid-June to mid-Aug daily 9am–7pm; rest of year Mon–Sat 9am–5pm, Sun 9am–3pm; Ⓣ819/821-1919 or 1-800/561-8331).

The city's two main museums are modest in scope. The **Musée des Beaux Arts de Sherbrooke**, 241 rue Dufferin (Tues–Sun noon–5pm; $7.50; Ⓣ819/821-2115, Ⓦwww.mbas.qc.ca) displays nineteenth- and twentieth-century pieces by Québécois artists and visiting collections of good quality. The hands-on exhibits at the **Musée de la Nature et des Sciences**, 225 rue Frontenac (Wed–Sun 10am–5pm; $7.50; Ⓣ819/564-3200, Ⓦwww.mnes.qc.ca) explore Québec's seasonal flora and fauna, with both live and stuffed animals and videos. The **Centre d'interprétation de l'histoire de Sherbrooke**, 275 rue Dufferin (end June to early Sept Tues–Fri 9am–5pm, Sat & Sun 10am–5pm; rest of the year Tues–Fri 9am–noon & 1–5pm, Sat & Sun 1–5pm; $6; Ⓣ819/821-5406, Ⓦwww.shs.ville.sherbrooke.qc.ca) delves into the town's history.

Practicalities

You'll find plenty of **accommodation** in the modern motels along the main drag of rue King ouest. For more charm, head to *Marquis de Montcalm* (Ⓣ819/823-7773, Ⓦwww.marquisdemontcalm.com; ④), a friendly B&B near the gorge. For **dining** downtown, *Le Petit Parisien*, 243 rue Alexandre (Ⓣ819/822-4678), is an ambient bring-your-own-wine restaurant where fine grilled meats will set you back $20–30.

Montréal to Québec City

Two **autoroutes** cover the 270km between Montréal and Québec City, though plenty of VIA Rail **trains** and Voyageur **buses** also trawl the route: the boring Hwy 20 cuts along the south shore of the St Lawrence, and the even more banal Hwy 40 takes to the north side with very few rest-stops en route, so fill up before leaving Montréal.

Hwy 138, the old chemin du Roi (King's Highway), also meanders along the north shore but gives a closer look at rural Québec and farms left over from the seigneurial regime, like the **Seigneurie de Terrebonne** (May to early Sept Wed–Sat 10am–9pm, Sun 10am–5pm, early Sept to late Dec Thurs & Fri 1–9pm, Sat & Sun 10am–5pm, rest of the year weekends only; free, guided tours $5; Ⓦwww.ile-des-moulins.qc.ca), on the Île des Moulins about thirty minutes northeast of downtown Montréal via Hwy 25 (exit 22 est). A seigneury from 1673 to 1883, the restored nineteenth-century buildings – including the manor house of the area's last seigneur and Canada's first francophone millionaire, Joseph Masson – powerfully evoke life under the old regime.

Trois-Rivières

The major town between Montréal and Québec City is **TROIS-RIVIÈRES**, located midway between the two, at the point where the Rivière St-Maurice splits into three channels – hence the name "Three Rivers" – before meeting the St Lawrence. The European settlement dates from 1634, when the town established itself as an embarkation point for the French explorers of the continent and as an iron-ore centre. Lumber followed, and today Trois-Rivières is one of the world's largest producers of paper, the delta chock-full of logs to be pulped. It's often dismissed as an industrial city and little else, but its shady streets of historic buildings – neither as twee as Québec City, nor as monumental as Vieux-Montréal – are worth a wander, and the town is a good starting point for exploring the Mauricie Valley.

The **information centre**, at 1457 rue Notre Dame (late June to early Sept daily 9am–8pm; early Sept to mid-Oct & mid-May to late June Mon–Fri 9am–5pm, Sat & Sun 10am–4pm, mid-Oct to mid-May Mon–Fri 9am–5pm; Ⓣ819/375-1122 or 1-800/313-1123, Ⓦwww.tourismetroisrivieres.com), has maps and an accommodation service.

Accommodation

The cheapest option is downtown at the clean and comfortable **hostel**, *La Flottille*, 497 rue Radisson (Ⓣ819/378-8010, Ⓦwww.hihostels.ca; dorms $22, room ❶). A number of attractive **B&Bs** are situated in heritage homes in Vieux Trois-Rivières: *Le Fleurvil* at no. 635 rue des Ursulines, has five rooms in a low-lying house (Ⓣ819/372-5195 or 1-877/375-5190, Ⓦwww.fleurvil.qc.ca; ❸); and the gorgeous *Manoir DeBlois*, 197 rue Bonaventure, an 1828 stone house with original wood floors and an antique-strewn salon (Ⓣ819/373-1090 or 1-800/397-5184, Ⓦwww.manoirdeblois.com; ❹–❻).

The Town

Trois-Rivières' compact downtown core branches off from the small square of **Parc du Champlain** and extends south down to the waterfront. Facing the park to the east, at 363 rue Bonaventure, the **Cathédrale de l'Assomption** (Mon–Fri 7–11.30am & 1.30–5.45pm, Sat 7am–8pm, Sun 9.30am–noon & 2–5.45pm; free), is notable for its stained glass windows by Guido Nincheri and massive Gothic Revival style reminiscent of Westminster Abbey.

Head south, past the pretty **Manoir de Niverville** at no. 168, one of the town's oldest buildings and the home of the local seigneur, until the water is in sight. Take a left turn to reach the narrow and ancient rue des Ursulines, the city's most attractive thoroughfare; two art galleries, at nos. 802 and 864, are especially worth a visit for contemporary printmaking during the Biennale Internationale d'Estampe Contemporain (odd-numbered years, mid-June to Aug). Further along is the **Musée des Ursulines**, whose slender, silver dome dominates the street. A former convent established by a small group of Ursuline nuns who arrived from Québec City in 1697, it includes a chapel with attractive frescoes and gilt sculptures. The nunnery's treasures are displayed in a little museum in the old hospital quarters (May–Nov Tues–Sun 10am–5pm; March & April Wed–Sun 1–5pm; Nov–Feb by appointment only; $3.50 including chapel visit; ⓦwww.musee-ursulines.qc.ca).

Just east of the cathedral, the **Musée Québécois de Culture Populaire**, 200 rue Laviolette (late June to early Sept daily 10am–6pm; rest of year Tues–Sun 10am–5pm; museum or prison $9, both $14; ⓦwww.culturepop.qc.ca) has folk and pop culture exhibitions but the real highlight is the old **prison** that adjoins it. Dating from 1822, it housed up to eighty inmates at a time until 1980, and while the decades of graffiti tell a story, it's nothing compared to the tales of the guides – most of them once served time here.

Across the river east of downtown is the **Sanctuaire Notre-Dame-de-Cap**, 626 rue Notre-Dame (free; ⓦwww.sanctuaire-ndc.ca; bus #2), in the merged town of Cap-de-la-Madeleine, accessible from Hwy 40 (exit 205); a few of the Québec–Montréal buses also stop here. Adjacent to a pleasant park marked by the Stations of the Cross is the 1720 Petit Sanctuaire; the fieldstone chapel is "the oldest church in Canada to retain its primitive state" (ignoring the jarring modern addition, presumably). It's overshadowed by the massive octagonal basilica, a mid-twentieth-century concrete structure with a vertigo-inducing 38m-high vault best experienced when the 75-stop Casavant organ reverberates throughout the space.

Finally, the ruins of **Les Forges du Saint-Maurice**, 10,000 boul des Forges (mid-May to early Sept daily 9.30am–5.30pm, early Sept to early Oct until 4.30pm; $4; ⓣ819/378-5116 or 1-888/773-8888, ⓦwww.pc.gc.ca/forges), which put the town on the map as a supplier to the farmers and arsenals of Québec and Europe, is now a national historic site. Its pretty riverside grounds are 12km north of Vieux Trois-Rivières, linked to downtown by bus #4 – get on at the bus terminal on rue Badeaux – and Hwy 55 (exit 191).

Eating, drinking and nightlife

Most of the city's **restaurants** are located in the downtown core, their terraces lining rue des Forges between the waterfront and rue Royale. *Angeline*, 313 rue des Forges, has imaginative pasta and pizza choices. *Le Zenob*, 171 rue Bonaventure, is a relaxed **bar** with two leafy terraces that also sells sandwiches; for coffee and a snack, try *Café Morgane*, at 100 rue des Forges, a sleek coffee shop with three other outlets around town. For **nightlife**, the multistorey *Le Temple*, 300 rue des Forge, caters to all types.

Parc National de la Mauricie

Some 60km north of Trois-Rivières lies the mountainous area of the Saint-Maurice valley – known as the **Mauricie** – where the best of the landscape is demarcated by the **Parc National du Canada de la Mauricie** (year round; $7.80; ⓣ819/533-7272, ⓦwww.pc.gc.ca/mauricie). Situated on the southernmost part of the Canadian Shield, the park comprises soft-contoured hills, lakes and rivers, waterfalls and sheer rock faces. The one drawback is the lack of public transport;

to get there, take Hwy 55 north of Trois-Rivières to exit 226 and follow the signs to the St-Jean-des-Piles entrance.

The park offers numerous hiking trails of various lengths and abilities, ranging from the Cache Trail, a 1km walk leading to the Lac du Fou where a raised platform has a telescope for marine and wildlife watching, to the Laurentian Trail, a 75km trek which takes five to eight days to complete (reservation required; camping permit $39.20 for four nights). Information centres at the park's entrances have excellent maps and booklets about the park's well-maintained trails, canoe routes and bike paths, and also provide canoe rentals (for $18/day).

The park has hundreds of **camping** places (from $25.50 a pitch; May–Oct) allocated on a first-come, first-served basis, and they're rarely filled to capacity. If you'd rather sleep under a roof, there are also two **lodges** located 3.5km from the nearest parking lot: the *Wabenaki*'s two dormitories sleep up to 28 people and *Andrew*'s four rooms each sleep four (Ⓣ819/537-4555 for both lodges; weekdays starting at $26/person, weekends $50–60/person). Both open again in winter (mid-Dec to March) to accommodate cross-country skiers who use the park (trail permit $9.80).

Travel details

Trains

Montréal to: Bonaventure (3 weekly; 13hr 10min); Carleton (3 weekly; 12hr); Cornwall (4–5 daily; 1hr 5min); Gaspé (3 weekly; 17hr 30min); Jonquière (3 weekly; 8hr 55min); Kingston (4–5 daily; 2hr 30min); Matapédia (6 weekly; 10hr 10min); New York (1 daily; 11hr 30min); Ottawa (4–6 daily; 2hr 10min); Percé (3 weekly; 16hr 5min); Québec City (4–5 daily; 3hr); Rimouski (6 weekly; 7hr 40min); Rivière-du-Loup (6 weekly; 5hr 55min); Toronto (4–5 daily; 4hr 30min–5hr 30min; express daily except Sat; 4hr; sleeper daily except Sat; 8hr 50min); Washington, DC (1 daily; 16hr 10min including bus to St Alban's, Vermont).

Buses

Montréal to: Bromont (2 daily; 2hr); Chicoutimi (4 weekly; 4hr 55min); Chicoutimi via Québec City (5–6 daily; 6hr 30min); Granby (4–8 daily; 1hr 30min); Jonquière (4 weekly; 5hr 25min); Jonquière via Québec City (3–5 daily; 6hr 15min); Kingston (7 daily; 3hr); Magog (7–11 daily; 1hr 30min); Mont-Tremblant (3 daily; 2hr 40min); New York (6 daily; 8hr 30min); North Bay (2 daily; 7hr 40min); Orford (3 daily; 3hr); Ottawa (hourly; 2hr 20min); Québec City (hourly; 3hr); Rimouski (3 daily; 7hr); Rivière-du-Loup (4 daily; 5hr 30min); Ste-Adèle (6 daily; 1hr 25min); Ste-Agathe (6 daily; 1hr 45min); St-Jovite (5 daily; 2hr 15min); St-Sauveur (6 daily; 1hr); Sherbrooke (7–11 daily; 2hr 5min); Tadoussac (2 daily; 7hr 30min); Toronto (8 daily; 6hr 45min); Trois-Rivières (6–8 daily; 2hr); Val-David (6 daily; 1hr 30min), Montebello (6 daily; 1hr 30 min).

Sherbrooke to: Trois-Rivières (4 weekly; 2hr 10min); Québec City (2 daily; 3hr 30min).

Trois-Rivières to: Grand-Mère (3 daily; 1hr).

Flights

Montréal to: Baie-Comeau (3–4 daily; 1hr 30min); Bathurst (2–3 daily; 1hr 45min); Calgary (3–4 daily; 4hr 30min); Chicoutimi (5 daily; 1hr 5min); Fredericton (3–4 daily; 1hr 30min); Gaspé (2–3 daily; 2hr 40min); Halifax (10–12 daily; 1hr 25min); Îles-de-la-Madeleine (1–3 daily; 3hr 50min); Moncton (3–4 daily; 1hr 20min); Mont Joli (3–4 daily; 1hr 25min); Ottawa (9–11 daily; 40min); Québec City (13–20 daily; 50min); Saint John, NB (3–5 daily; 1hr 35min); St John's, NL (1–2 daily; 2hr 35min); Sept-Îles (3–6 daily; 2hr 45min); Toronto (19–40 daily; 1hr 15min); Vancouver (4–6 daily; 5hr 20min); Wabush (2 daily; 4hr 5min); Winnipeg (2–3 daily; 2hr 55min).

4

Québec City and Northern Québec

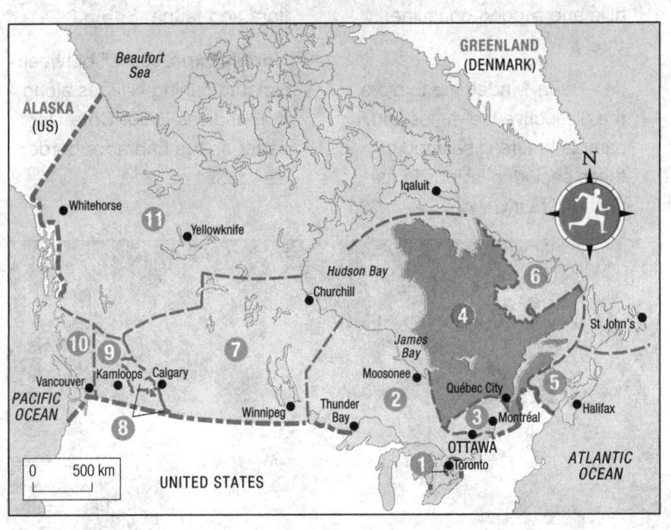

CHAPTER 4

Highlights

* **Vieux-Québec** The only walled city in North America is full of romantic nooks and crannies. See p.227
* **Mont-Sainte-Anne** A boggling number of ski runs in the winter as well as world class mountain biking and hiking during the summer just north of Quebec City. See p.296
* **Driving the Gaspé Peninsula** Hwy 132 encircles the peninsula, passing forested hills and rugged coastline. See p.308
* **Iles-de-la-Madeleine** Explore the distinctive red dunes and sample the fresh seafood of these secluded islands in the Gulf of St Lawrence. See p.323
* **Traversée de Charlevoix** This long-distance multi-use route bisects 100km of Charlevoix's most spectacularly wild terrain. See p.330
* **Tadoussac** Base yourself at this lively village and explore the Saguenay fjord or join a whale-watching trip. See p.333
* **Mingan Archipelago** Kayak around the eerie "flowerpot" islands inhabited by unique flora and fauna. See p.349
* **Nordik Express** Sail between isolated fishing villages along the roadless lower Côte-Nord as far as the Labrador border. See p.351

▲ Minke whale,Tadoussac

Québec City and Northern Québec

Forming the greater part of Canada's largest province, **Northern Québec** stretches from the temperate farmland in the south to the Arctic tundra in the north, covering over one million square kilometres. Much of this area is a monotonous blanket of dense boreal forest grafted onto a thin layer of soil spread over the Canadian shield – a horseshoe of ancient rock scoured clean during the last Ice Age. Nature rules supreme in northern Québec and the influence of the Arctic is strong – winters are long and among the coldest in eastern Canada, and the blazing summers are clipped short by northern frosts. Moose, caribou, wolverine and bears fill the forest while humans have barely made inroads. Civilisation is largely concentrated on the north shore of the **St Lawrence River**, around the main coastal hwy radiating eastward from Québec City. Mining communities, groups of aboriginal peoples and the hardy characters that work the immense hydroelectric installations on many of northern Québec's rivers are among the few with the will to penetrate deeper into this imposing wilderness.

Yet the coast has its own allure, not least the **whales** that come to feed and breed in the Gulf of St Lawrence from mid-May to mid-October, making it one of the best places in the world to learn about these incredible creatures. Away from the rural farmlands of **Charlevoix**, the further north you travel along the **Côte-Nord** from Québec City, the greater the distances between communities and the more self-contained they become. The isolation brings a noticeable change in attitude and you will find the northern Québécois genuinely interested in your travels and keen to demonstrate the tradition of 'northern hospitality'. In order to reach the more remote parks and settlements on secondary roads a **car** is pretty much essential, but the effort is worth it for a glimpse of the natural richness that initially drew settlers here in the first place.

Historic **Québec City** is the undisputed highlight of the region, sitting at the narrowing of the St Lawrence River like a symbolic gateway to the north (the word québec actually means 'narrowing' in the Algonquin language). It is also the most easterly point that connects the north and south shores of the river. Beyond the city, the waterway broadens dramatically and the only connection between

For a brief history of Québec, see p.213.

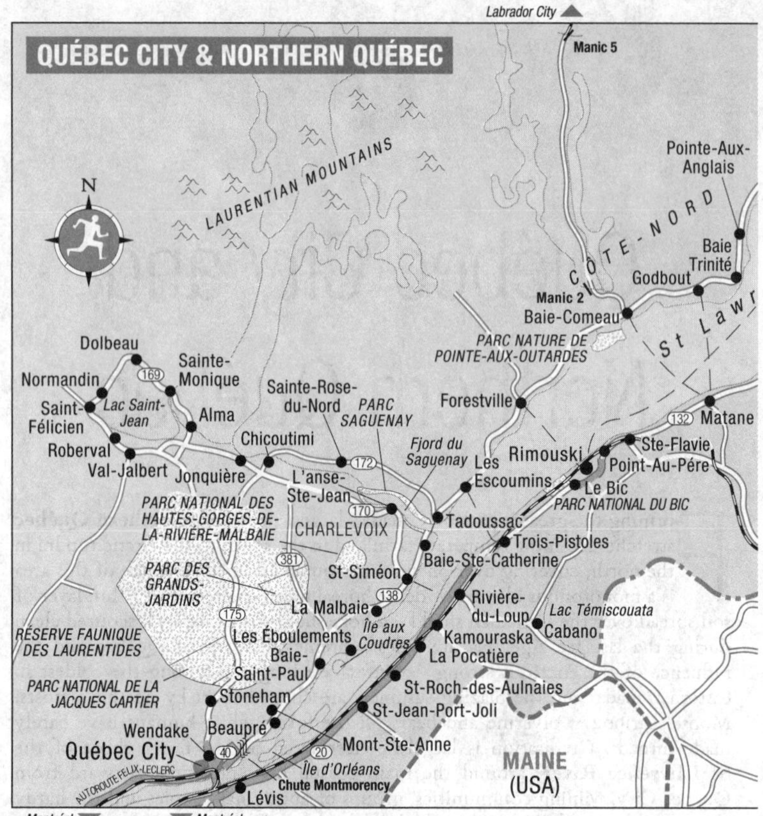

shores is by ferry. The mountainous **Gaspé Peninsula** forms the south shore of the river and presents a clear contrast to the flat wilds of the north. The **Chic Choc Mountains** create a rocky backbone along the centre of the peninsula and mark the end of the famous Appalachian Chain. More populated than the north shore, the Gaspé Peninsula can be easily negotiated by public transport or car and makes for a pleasing circuit out of Québec City.

Québec City

Spread over Cap Diamant and the banks of the St Lawrence River, **QUÉBEC CITY** (sometimes referred to just as "Québec") is one of Canada's most beautifully located and certainly its most historic city. Vieux-Québec, surrounded by solid fortifications, is the only walled city in North America, and a UNESCO World Heritage Site. In both parts of the Old City – Haute and Basse-Ville (Upper and

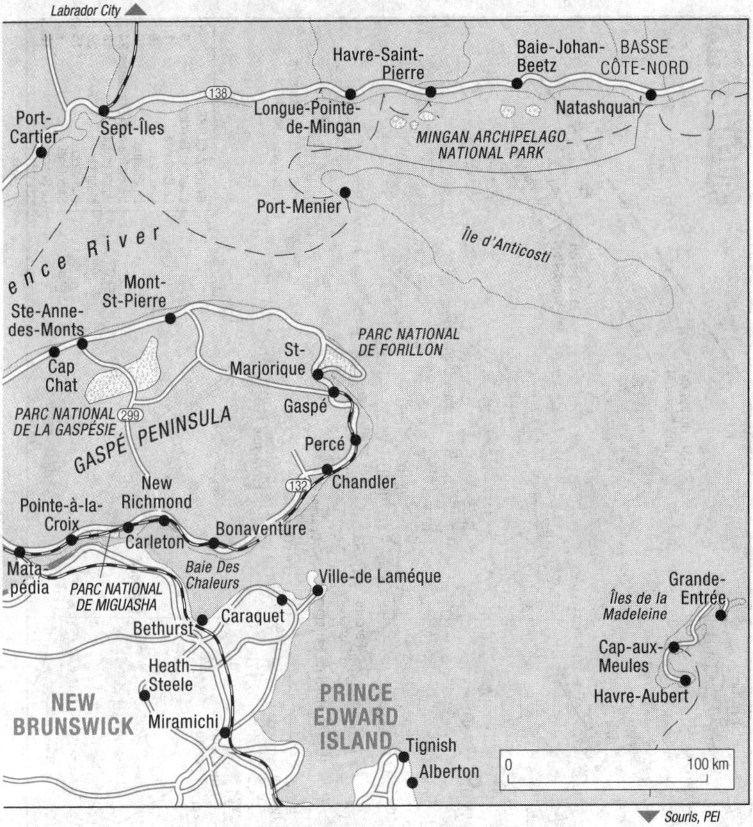

Lower Town) – the winding cobbled streets are flanked by seventeenth- and eighteenth-century stone houses and churches, graceful parks and squares, and countless monuments. Although some districts have been painstakingly restored to give tourists as seductive an introduction to Québec as possible, this is nevertheless an authentically and profoundly French-Canadian city. Over ninety percent of its 700,000 population are francophone, and it is often difficult to remember which continent you are in as you tuck in to a croissant and a steaming bowl of *café au lait* in a Parisian-style café. Moreover, despite the fact the city's symbol is a hotel, the **Château Frontenac**, the government remains the main employer.

Québec City is more than a shade provincial, often seeming too bound up with its religious and military past – a residue of the days when the city was the bastion of the Catholic Church in Canada. On the other hand, the Church can claim much of the credit for the creation and preservation of the finest buildings, from the quaint **Église Notre-Dame-des-Victoires** to the **Basilique-Cathédrale Notre-Dame de Québec** and the vast **Séminaire**. In contrast, the austere defensive structures, dominated by the massive **Citadelle**, reveal the military pedigree of a city dubbed by Churchill as the "Gibraltar of North America", while the battlefield of the **Plains of Abraham** is now a national historic park. Of the city's rash of museums, two are essential visits: the modern **Musée de la Civilisation**, expertly presenting all aspects of French-Canadian society, and the **Musée**

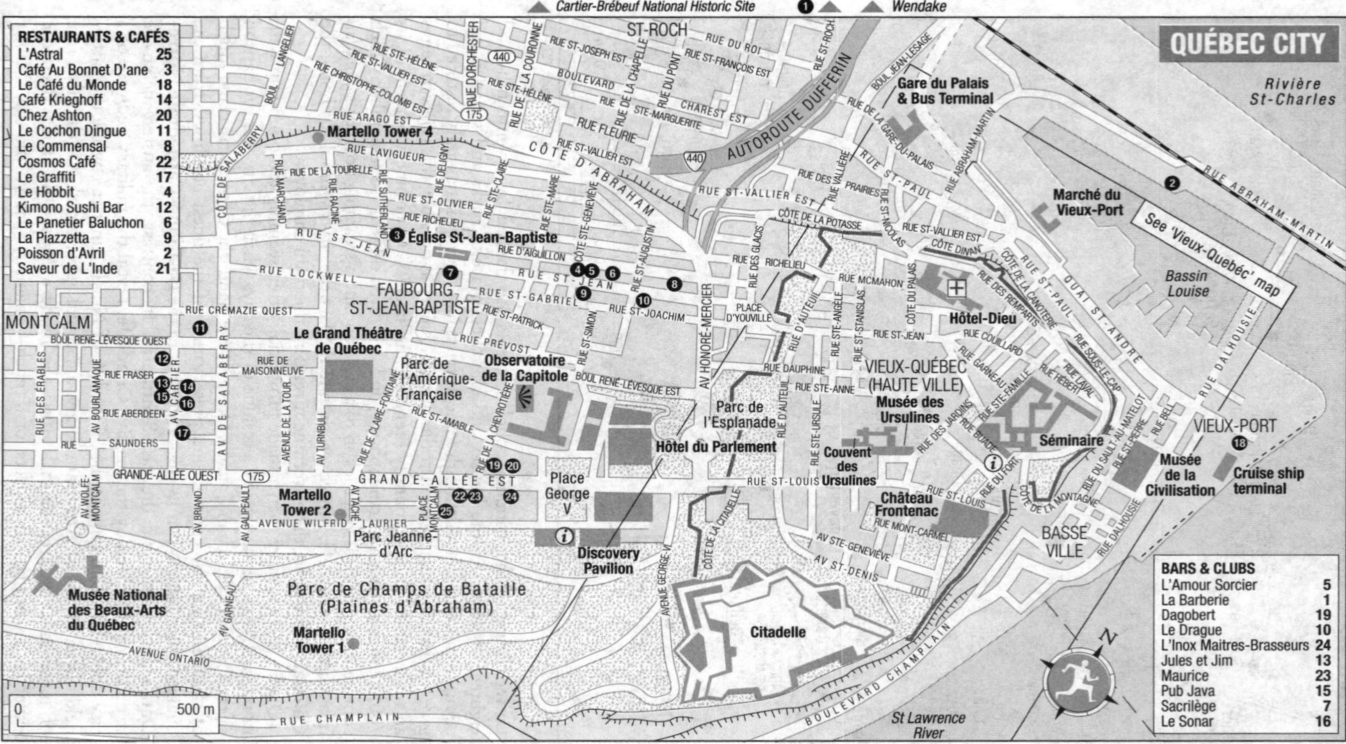
QUÉBEC CITY
Cartier-Brébeuf National Historic Site
Wendake
Lévis
RESTAURANTS & CAFÉS
L'Astral 25
Café Au Bonnet D'ane 3
Le Café du Monde 18
Café Krieghoff 14
Chez Ashton 20
Le Cochon Dingue 11
Le Commensal 8
Cosmos Café 22
Le Graffiti 17
Le Hobbit 4
Kimono Sushi Bar 12
Le Panetier Baluchon 6
La Piazzetta 9
Poisson d'Avril 2
Saveur de L'Inde 21
BARS & CLUBS
L'Amour Sorcier 5
La Barberie 1
Dagobert 19
Le Drague 10
L'Inox Maitres-Brasseurs 24
Jules et Jim 13
Maurice 23
Pub Java 15
Sacrilège 7
Le Sonar 16
See 'Vieux-Québec' map
Rivière St-Charles
St Lawrence River
Bassin Louise
Gare du Palais & Bus Terminal
Marché du Vieux-Port
Hôtel-Dieu
VIEUX-QUÉBEC (HAUTE VILLE)
Musée des Ursulines
Couvent des Ursulines
Séminaire
Musée de la Civilisation
Cruise ship terminal
VIEUX-PORT
BASSE VILLE
Château Frontenac
Citadelle
Parc de l'Esplanade
Hôtel du Parlement
Place George V
Discovery Pavilion
Observatoire de la Capitole
Parc de l'Amérique-Française
Le Grand Théâtre de Québec
Église St-Jean-Baptiste
FAUBOURG ST-JEAN-BAPTISTE
ST-ROCH
MONTCALM
Martello Tower 1
Martello Tower 2
Martello Tower 4
Parc Jeanne-d'Arc
Parc de Champs de Bataille (Plaines d'Abraham)
Musée National des Beaux-Arts du Québec
AUTOROUTE DUFFERIN
CÔTE D'ABRAHAM
GRANDE-ALLÉE EST
GRANDE-ALLÉE OUEST
RUE ST-JEAN
RUE ST-LOUIS
BOULEVARD CHAMPLAIN
RUE CHAMPLAIN
AV HONORÉ-MERCIER
BOUL RENÉ-LÉVESQUE EST
BOUL RENÉ-LÉVESQUE OUEST
RUE ST-PAUL
QUAI ST-ANDRÉ
RUE DALHOUSIE
RUE ABRAHAM-MARTIN
AV DE SALABERRY
AV CARTIER
RUE CRÉMAZIE OUEST
0 500 m

National des Beaux-Arts du Québec, west of the walls, which has the finest art collection in the province.

Outside the city limits, the town of **Lévis** and the Huron reservation, **Wendake**, make worthwhile excursions, while the churches and farmland of the **Côte-de-Beaupré** and the **Île d'Orléans** hark back to the days of the *seigneurs* and *habitants*. The gigantic **Basilique de Ste-Anne-de-Beaupré**, attracting millions of pilgrims annually, is one of the most impressive sights in Québec, and for equally absorbing natural sights there are the spectacular waterfalls at **Montmorency** and in the **Canyon Ste-Anne**, and the wildlife reserve in the **Laurentian mountains** north of the city.

A brief history of Québec City

For centuries the clifftop site of what is now Québec City was occupied by the **Iroquois** village of Stadacona, and although Jacques Cartier visited in the sixteenth century, permanent **European settlement** did not begin until 1608, when Samuel de Champlain established a fur-trading post here. To protect what was rapidly developing into a major inland trade gateway, the settlement shifted to the clifftop in 1620 when Fort St-Louis was built on the present-day site of the Château Frontenac. Québec's steady expansion was noted in London, and in 1629 Champlain was starved out of the fort by the **British**, an occupation that lasted just three years.

Missionaries began arriving in 1615, and by the time Bishop Laval arrived in 1659 Québec City and the surrounding province were in the grip of **Catholicism**. Yet in the city's earliest days the merchants of the fur trade wielded the most power and frequently came into conflict with the priests, who wanted a share in the profits in order to spread their message among the aboriginal peoples. **Louis XIV** resolved the wrangles, after being advised to take more interest in his kingdom's mercantile projects. By 1663 the entire French colony, which stretched from Newfoundland to the Gulf of Mexico, was known as New France and had become a royal province, administered by a council appointed directly by the crown and answerable to the king's council in France. Before the century ended, the long-brewing European struggles between England and France spilled over into the colony. It was at this time that the **Comte de Frontenac**, known as the "fighting governor", replaced Champlain's Fort St-Louis with the sturdier Château St-Louis, and began work on the now-famous fortifications that ring Vieux-Québec.

In 1759, during the Seven Years' War (also known as the French and Indian War), the most significant battle in Canada's history took place here, between the British under General **James Wolfe** and the French commander Louis Joseph, **Marquis de Montcalm**. The city had already been under siege from the opposite shore for three months when Wolfe and his four thousand troops scaled the cliff of Cap Diamant and engaged the hastily organized and ill-prepared French. The twenty-minute battle on the Plains of Abraham left both leaders mortally wounded and the city of Québec in the hands of the English, a state of affairs ultimately confirmed by the Treaty of Paris in 1763.

In 1775 – the year after the Québec Act, which allowed French-Canadians to retain their Catholic religion, language and culture – the town was attacked again, this time by the Americans, who had already captured Montréal. The British won the battle, and for the next century the city quietly earned its livelihood as the centre of a **timber-trade** and **shipbuilding** industry. Yet by the time it was declared the provincial capital of Lower Canada in 1840 the accessible supplies of timber had run out. The final blow came with the appearance of steamships that could travel as far as Montréal (earlier sailing ships had found it difficult to proceed beyond Québec City). Ceasing to be a busy seaport, the city declined into a centre of small industry and local government, its way of life still largely determined by the Catholic Church.

With the Quiet Revolution in the 1960s and the rise of Québec **nationalism**, Québec City became a symbol of the glory of the French heritage: the motto *Je me souviens* ("I remember"), for instance, placed above the doors of its parliament buildings, was transferred to the licence plates of Québec cars, to sweep the message across Canada. Though the city played little active part in the changes, it has grown with the upsurge in the francophone economy, developing a suburbia of shopping malls and convention centres as slick as any in the country.

Arrival and information

Québec City's **Aéroport Jean-Lesage** (Ⓦwww.aeroportdequebec.com), 20km west of the city, caters almost exclusively for domestic flights; most international flights arrive at Montréal. The twenty-minute trip to Vieux-Québec by taxi is fixed at $32.50. VIA Rail **trains** from Montréal arrive at the central Gare du Palais in Basse-Ville, while services from the Atlantic provinces stop at Charny, across the St Lawrence, occasionally at inconvenient times; a shuttle is available from Charny to Gare du Palais but reservations must be made in advance. The long-distance **bus terminal** (Ⓣ418/525-3000) is at 320 rue Abraham-Martin, adjoining the Gare du Palais. **Parking** downtown can be a pain: it's best to leave your vehicle outside the walls, near the tourist office off Grande-Allée or in the Vieux-Port area.

The main **tourist office** (late June to early Sept daily 8.30am–7.30pm; early Sept to mid-Oct daily 8.30am–6.30pm; mid-Oct to late June Mon–Sat 9am–5pm, Fri until 6pm, Sun 10am–4pm; Ⓣ418/641-6290 or 1-877/783-1608, Ⓦwww.quebecregion.com) is beside the Voltigeurs de Québec armoury, off Place Georges V at 835 av Wilfrid-Laurier, in the same building as the Discovery Pavilion of the Plains of Abraham. Information on the whole province (as well as Québec City) is available at the **Centre Infotouriste** (daily: late June to early Sept 9am–7pm; rest of year 9am–5pm; Ⓣ1-877/266-5687,

Québec City festivals

Québec City is renowned for its large annual **festivals**. The **Carnaval de Québec** (Ⓣ418/626-3716, Ⓦwww.carnaval.qc.ca) is in freezing early February, when large quantities of the warming Caribou – a lethal mix of red wine, spirits and spices – are consumed amid parades and ice-sculpture competitions, all presided over by the mascot snowman called Bonhomme Carnaval.

In July, the eleven-day **Festival d'Été** (Ⓣ1-888/992-5200, Ⓦwww.infofestival.com) is an equally cheery affair, especially as the provincial law prohibiting alcohol on the streets is temporarily revoked. The largest festival of francophone culture in North America, it attracts hundreds of artists, and everyone is roped in to the celebration, with restaurants offering discounts and all of Québec's major performers pitching up to dance, make music and lead the party from massive open-air stages all over town.

A month later, the **Fêtes de la Nouvelle France** (Ⓣ418/694-3311 or 1-866/391-3383, Ⓦwww.nouvellefrance.qc.ca) returns Basse-Ville to the seventeenth and eighteenth centuries. It's great fun if you're in the mood: thousands of Québécois from around the province dress up in period costume, often ones they've sewn themselves. It's also worth being in the city on **St-Jean Baptiste Day** (June 24), the provincial holiday, when an outpouring of Québécois pride spills onto the streets in a massive celebration, with the entire city decked with thousands of fleur-de-lis flags.

Ⓦwww.bonjourquebec.com) on the other side of Place d'Armes from the Château Frontenac, at 12 rue Ste-Anne.

City transport

Québec City's sights and hotels are packed into a small area, so **walking** is the best way to get around. Motorcycles are banned from Vieux-Québec. For sights further out, like the Musée National des Beaux-Arts du Québec, RTC **local buses** (Ⓣ418/627-2511, Ⓦwww.rtcquebec.ca) run from around 6am–1am (certain routes until 3am Fri & Sat). Fares are a standard $2.60 per journey by prepaid ticket, available at newsstands, grocery stores and supermarkets across town, as are one-day passes ($6.45; valid for two people Sat & Sun); the cash fare per journey is $3, exact fare only. If you need more than one bus to complete your journey, pick up a **transfer** (*une correspondance*) from the driver, which enables you to take the second bus for no extra charge. The main bus stop in Vieux-Québec is on its west side at Place d'Youville, near Porte St-Jean. The main transfer points for RTC buses are here and at Place Jacques-Cartier; many buses stop at both locations.

Accommodation

Accommodation in the historic heart of Québec City is easy to find and surprisingly affordable. In Vieux-Québec two **hostels**, and many budget **hotels** are as well located as those at the top end. As the city is one of Canada's most frequented tourist destinations, try to reserve in advance, particularly during the summer months and the Carnaval in February. Even at those times you're not likely to find the city completely full, as there are plenty of standard chain hotels outside the walls and the suburbs have masses of **motels** and **B&Bs**, all of them just a local bus ride away. Québec City's **campsites** are around 20km from the old town, convenient only for those with their own transport; we've listed the closest.

Hotels and B&Bs

Basse-Ville

Auberge St-Antoine 8 rue St-Antoine Ⓣ418/692-2211 or 1-888/692-2211, Ⓦwww.saint-antoine.com. Contemporary hotel divided into two buildings next to the Musée de la Civilisation. All rooms are tastefully decorated (some with a historic theme) and several have views of the river. Massage therapy, a private cinema, babysitters, indoor valet parking and free internet access available. 8

Hôtel Belley 249 rue St-Paul Ⓣ418/692-1694 or 1-888/692-1694, Ⓦwww.oricom.ca/belley. Eight-bedroom hotel near the Gare du Palais with spacious rooms full of period features. Breakfast is served next to a roaring fire in winter and on a sunny terrace in summer. 4

Hôtel Dominion 1912 126 rue St-Pierre Ⓣ418/692-2224 or 1-888/833-5253, Ⓦwww.hoteldominion.com. Fabulous boutique hotel with all the touches – feather pillows and duvets, subdued lighting, stylish modern decor and cool frosted-glass sinks lit from below. Some rooms have river views. 7

Hôtel Le Priori 15 rue du Sault-au-Matelot Ⓣ418/692-3992 or 1-800/351-3992, Ⓦwww.hotelpriori.com. Tastefully modernized old house on the "oldest street in North America" with a large courtyard for a breakfast spot. Many rooms have open fires or roll top baths and the suites are so comfortable, you may just want to move in permanently. 6

Jardin des Gouverneurs area

B&B des Grisons 1 rue des Grisons Ⓣ418/694-1461, Ⓦwww.bbcanada.com/2608.html. A late-nineteenth century home with high ceilings, wood-strip floors and antiques from various epochs. The larger of the five rooms have sofa-beds and all have shared bath. 4

Hôtel Cap-Diamant 39 av Ste-Geneviève Ⓣ418/694-0313 or 1-888/694-0313, Ⓦwww.hotelcapdiamant.com. Nine-bedroom guesthouse with Victorian furnishings and a courtyard to have breakfast in. All rooms are en suite, with a/c, minifridges and TVs. 6

Le Château Frontenac 1 rue des Carrières Ⓣ418/692-3861 or 1-866/540-4460, Ⓦwww.fairmont.com/frontenac. This opulent Victorian "castle", built for William Van Horne, president of CP Railways, opened in 1893, and has accommodated such dignitaries as Churchill, Roosevelt, Madame Chiang Kai-shek and Queen Elizabeth II. Thanks to its location and history it's the most expensive place in town, with splendid rooms and views, antique furnishings, internet access and first class service. Parking is extra. (See p.274) 8

Hôtel Le Château de Pierre 17 av Ste-Geneviève ☎418/694-0429 or 1-888/694-0429, ⓦwww.chateaudepierre.com. An 1853 mansion with fifteen plush rooms; all are en suite and those without a/c have balconies. 5

Hôtel Au Jardin du Gouverneur 16 rue Mont-Carmel ☎418/692-1704 or 1-877/692-1704, ⓦwww.quebecweb.com/hjg. On the corner of the Jardin des Gouverneurs, the seventeen decent-sized rooms here come with modern furnishings and adjoining bathrooms. 3

Hotel Maison du Fort 21 av Ste-Geneviève ☎418/692-4375 or 1-888 203-4375, ⓦwww.hotelmaisondufort.com. Charming hotel with eleven impeccably-designed, spacious rooms, some with exposed brick walls (6); there's also a two-room apartment with kitchenette (7).

Hôtel Manoir sur le Cap 9 av Ste-Geneviève ☎418/694-1987 or 1-866/694-1987, ⓦwww.manoir-sur-le-cap.com. Fourteen bright rooms, all with a private bath and TVs, with exposed beams or stone walls; a few have kitchenettes. 4

Hôtel Terrasse-Dufferin 6 place Terrasse-Dufferin ☎418/694-9472 or 1-800/694-9472, ⓦwww.terrasse-dufferin.com. The better rooms (6) in this 1830 private mansion have the best views in town, overlooking the St Lawrence, which makes up for the slightly plain decor; book months ahead. 4

Rue Ste-Ursule area

Hôtel Le Clos St-Louis 69 rue St-Louis ☎418/694-1311 or 1-800/461-1311, ⓦwww.clossaintlouis.com. Elegant hotel in two interconnected 1840s houses with Victorian decor: four-poster beds in some of the rooms, gilt mirrors and lots of antiques. A hot breakfast is included. 7

Hôtel Acadia 43 rue Ste-Ursule ☎418/694-0280 or 1-800/463-0280, ⓦwww.hotelacadia.com. Over forty ancestral dwellings with bare brick walls, original fireplaces, period furniture and the odd stained glass window. A few have shared bathrooms. 5

Hôtel La Maison Demers 68 rue Ste-Ursule ☎418/692-2487 or 1-800/692-2487. Parking and breakfast are included in the price of this family-run old house. The rooms aren't terribly fancy and can be rather small, but they are tidy and a few have balconies. 3

Maison Historique James Thompson 47 rue Ste-Ursule ☎418/694-9042, ⓦwww.bedandbreakfastquebec.com. A B&B in a historic 1793 house with sleigh beds, antiques throughout, a lovely sitting room and filling breakfasts. 4

Hôtel Le Manoir d'Auteuil 49 rue d'Auteuil ☎418/694-1173 or 1-866/662-6647, ⓦwww.manoirdauteuil.com. Lavish 1835 townhouse by the city walls, with Art Deco rooms. Free breakfast and a cheery owner. 4

Hôtel Manoir La Salle 18 rue Ste-Ursule ☎418/692-9953. A small century-old red-brick hotel, where only two of the eleven rooms are en-suite; one of these has a kitchenette. 2

Au Petit Hôtel 3 ruelle des Ursulines ☎418/694-0965, ⓦwww.aupetithotel.com. Situated in a peaceful cul-de-sac just off rue Ste-Ursule, the beds and rooms are a bit small but all are en suite. 3

Rue Ste-Anne

Auberge de la Place d'Armes 24 rue Ste-Anne ☎418/694-9485, ⓦwww.aubergeplacedarmes.com. Perfectly situated opposite the Anglican Cathedral, on the pedestrianized part of rue Ste-Anne. Rooms on the upper floor are a bit stuffy in summer; others have a/c. All rooms have shower but some share toilets. 6

Hôtel Clarendon 57 rue Ste-Anne ☎418/692-2480 or 1-888/554-6001, ⓦwww.dufour.ca. Québec City's oldest hotel, dating from 1870. Renovated in the 1930s, it has a classic Art Deco reception area and many of its modern rooms have good views of Vieux-Québec. 7

Hôtel Jardin Ste-Anne 109 rue Ste-Anne ☎418/694-1720 or 1-866/694-1720, ⓦwww.jardinsteanne.com. This century-old house has eighteen small but charming rooms (all with a/c) some of which have stone walls. There's also free wi-fi and a courtyard. 6

Elsewhere in Vieux-Québec

Hôtel Manoir des Remparts 3 1/2 rue des Remparts ☎418/692-2056, ⓦwww.manoirdesremparts.com. At the north end of Vieux-Québec on the ramparts, with views of the St Lawrence from the third-floor terrace. Simple hotel with bland, mostly en-suite rooms; others have dorm-type showers. 3

Hôtel Manoir Victoria 44 Côte du Palais ☎418/692-1030 or 1-800/463-6283, ⓦwww.manoir-victoria.com. A very grand, rambling manor that will not fail to impress, with a pool to die for, sauna, gym and luxuriously furnished rooms. 6

Motels, hostels, and campsites

Motels

Auberge Michel Doyon 1215 chemin Ste-Foy ⓣ418/527-4408 or 1-800/928-4408, ⓦwww.aubergemicheldoyon.com. One of the cheapest motels around, in the suburb of Ste-Foy. Basic but clean, with free parking. Ten-minute bus ride (#7) from Vieux-Québec. ❷

Hostels and the YWCA

Auberge de la Paix 31 rue Couillard ⓣ418/694-0735, ⓦwww.aubergedelapaix.com. Situated just off rue St-Jean this is by far the better of the city's two hostels, with four rooms that sleep between 2–8 people on each of its three floors. There's a large courtyard to hang out in, wi-fi and kitchen. The rate includes breakfast; $25.

Auberge International de Québec 19 rue Ste-Ursule ⓣ418/694-0755, ⓦwww.aubergeinternationaledequebec.com. The 300-bed HI hostel, in a former hospice run by nuns, is often full and can be impersonal, though it offers laundry facilities, free wi-fi, luggage lockers, kitchens and a bar. Dorms $28, private rooms $74.

YWCA 855 av Holland ⓣ418/683-2155, ⓦwww.ywcaquebec.qc.ca. Men are accepted as well as women here, though there are no double beds. Just off chemin Ste-Foy, about a 15min bus ride from Vieux-Québec; $15.

Campsites

Camping Aéroport 2050 rte de l'Aéroport ⓣ418/871-1574 or 1-800/294-1574, ⓦwww.campingaeroport.com. Take exit 305 nord off Hwy 440 onto rte de l'Aéroport – the campsite is around 5km north of the airport itself. It's not the most scenic of settings, but not a bad option. The decent range of services include wi-fi. Sites from $36.

Camping Municipal de Beauport 95 rue Sérénité, Beauport, off boul Rochette ⓣ418/641-6112 or 1-877/641-6113, ⓦwww.campingbeauport.qc.ca. Take exit 322 off Hwy 40; Bus #800 to Beauport, then #50 or #55. Large campground set back from the Montmorency River with boat rentals, swimming pool and wi-fi access. Early June to early Sept. $24/site.

The City

Québec City spreads from its historic heart into a bland suburbia but the highlights lie beside the St Lawrence River, with main attractions being evenly distributed between the upper and lower portions of what is known as **Vieux-Québec** (Old Québec). On the Cap Diamant, **Haute-Ville** (Upper Town) continues along the river from the old city walls and the furthest you need to wander from here is to the Musée National des Beaux-Arts du Québec, set in the extensive parkland of the Plains of Abraham that unfurls west of the magnificent Citadelle. The Terrasse Dufferin is also worth a stroll to watch street entertainers, unproductive students or the views over the river, but it gets crowded in the evening. It overlooks the second part of the old city, **Basse-Ville** (Lower Town), connected to Haute-Ville by funicular and several winding streets and stairs; if you're only in Québec City for a short while, head here straight from the Place d'Armes and then return to the upper town for the remainder of the sights. One of the main pleasures of the area, besides the wonderful old houses and small museums, is the Musée de la Civilisation.

Basse-Ville and Vieux-Port

The birthplace of Québec City, **Basse-Ville** (Lower Town), can be reached from Terrasse Dufferin either by the steep **escalier casse-cou** (Breakneck Stairs) or by the **funicular** alongside (daily 7.30am–11pm, until midnight in summer; ⓣ418/692-1132, ⓦwww.funiculaire-quebec.com; $1.75). The Basse-Ville station of the funicular is the 1683 **Maison Louis-Jolliet**, 16 rue du Petit-Champlain, built for the retired discoverer of the Mississippi, Louis Jolliet; it now houses a second-rate souvenir shop.

Dating back to 1685, the narrow, cobbled **rue du Petit-Champlain** is the city's oldest street, and the surrounding area – known as **Quartier du Petit-Champlain**

▲ Buskers entertaining on Place Royale, Basse-Ville

– is the oldest shopping area in North America. The boutiques and art shops in the quaint seventeenth- and eighteenth-century houses are not too overpriced and offer an array of excellent crafts, from Inuit carvings to the products of the glass-blowing workshop and gallery, **Verrerie La Mailloche** (July–Oct daily 9am–10pm, Nov–June Sat–Wed 9.30am–5pm, Thurs & Fri till 9pm; ⓣ418/694-0445, ⓦwww.lamailloche.com), at the base of the escalier casse-cou at 58 rue Sous-le-Fort. Older artefacts can be seen closer to the river, on the corner of rue du Marché Champlain and rue Notre-Dame, in the 1752 **Maison Chevalier** (May to late June & early Sept to mid-Oct Tues–Sun 10am–5pm; late June to early Sept daily 9.30am–5.30pm; Nov–April Sat & Sun 10am–5pm; ⓣ418/646-3167, ⓦwww.mcq.org; free), a grand town house and one-time London Coffee House, where merchants would meet throughout the nineteenth century. Its rooms excellently depict interior scenes comprising period furniture, costumes and domestic objects. Take a peek, too, into the vaulted cellars, where local artisans sell traditional works.

Place Royale and around

From here it's a short walk along rue Notre-Dame to **Place Royale**, where Champlain built New France's first permanent settlement in 1608, to begin trading fur with the aboriginal peoples. The square – known as Place du Marché until the bust of Louis XIV was erected here in 1686 – remained the focal point of Canadian commerce until 1759, and after the fall of Québec the British continued using the area as a lumber market, vital for shipbuilding during the Napoleonic Wars. After 1860 Place Royale was left to fall into disrepair, a situation reversed in the 1970s, when the scruffy area was renovated. Its pristine stone houses, most of which date from around 1685, are undeniably photogenic, with their steep metal roofs, numerous chimneys and pastel-coloured shutters, but it's a Legoland townscape, devoid of the scars of history. Fortunately, the atmosphere is enlivened in summer by entertainment from classical orchestras to juggling clowns, and by the Fêtes de la Nouvelle-France (see p.274), when everyone dresses in period costume and it once again becomes a chaotic marketplace.

In Maison Hazeur, a merchant's house dating in part to 1684, the **interpretation centre** (late June–early Sept daily 9.30am–5pm; early Sept–late June Tues–Sun 10am–5pm; ⓣ418/646-3167, ⓦwww.mcq.org; $6) at 27 rue Notre-Dame outlines the stormy past of Place Royale, the mercantile aspects and the changes in the look of the square from the days when it was inhabited by the Iroquois to its renovation – seek out the tucked away exhibit on level one rather than sitting through the hokey multimedia show. Domestic objects and arrowheads are on the upper floors, from where you can see Gilles Girard's *À rebrousse-temps*, an enigmatic three-storey sculpture that plays with the idea of determining an artefact's original purpose. The vaulted cellars have modern-looking displays of 1800s domestic scenes and kids can try on period costumes and act out a role.

The **Église Notre-Dame-des-Victoires** (May to mid-Oct daily 9.30am–5pm, rest of the year 10am–4pm; ⓣ418/692-1650; free), on the west side of the square, nearly always has a wedding in progress during the summer. It was built by Laval in 1688 but has been completely restored twice – after being destroyed by shellfire in 1759 and a fire in 1969. Inside, the fortress-shaped altar alludes to the two French victories over the British navy (in 1690 and 1711) that gave the church its name. Paintings depicting these events hang above the altar, while the aisles are lined with copies of religious paintings by Van Dyck, Van Loo and Rubens, gifts from early settlers to give thanks for a safe passage. The large model ship suspended in the nave has a similar origin.

Place Royale exits to the east past rue St-Pierre – the heart of the old financial district – onto **Place de Paris**, where a white cubic sculpture called *Dialogue with History* marks the disembarkation place of the first settlers from France. Visible to the south (but accessible only from rue St-Pierre), the crenellated **Batterie Royal** rampart was used to defend the city during the siege of 1759. The **ferry to Lévis** (6.20am–2.20am; ⓣ1-877/787-7483, ⓦwww.traversiers.gouv.qc.ca; $2.75 one-way; see p.298) leaves from the waterfront just to the southeast.

Musée de la Civilisation

A walk north along rue Dalhousie from Place de Paris brings you to one of Québec City's most impressive museums, the **Musée de la Civilisation** (late June to early Sept daily 9.30am–6.30pm; otherwise Tues–Sun 10am–5pm; $11; Nov–May free on Tues; ⓣ418/643-2158, ⓦwww.mcq.org), at no. 85. Designed by prominent Canadian architect Moshe Safdie, the museum references the steep-pitched roofs of the early settlers in a structure that incorporates a rooftop terrace with great views and three historic buildings – be sure to check out the vaulted cellars in the 1751 **Maison Estèbe**, which survived the British bombardment to eventually become the museum's gift shop (ask for the leaflet detailing the house's history). In the main foyer, a 1730s barque discovered on the site is displayed between a stone wall (the edge of the quay built a couple of decades later) and Astri Reusch's *La Débâcle*, a sculpture that symbolizes the break-up of the ice in the spring thaw.

Concentrating primarily on Canadian subjects but also diversifying into a worldwide perspective, the museum presents engaging temporary exhibitions that have ranged from whimsical pop culture interests to serious looks at earlier historical periods. The first of the two permanent exhibitions upstairs, **Memories**, expertly displays life in Québec from the early days of the settlers to the present (pick up an English-language text at the entrance). Cross the atrium for the **Encounter with the First Nations** exhibition, set up in consultation with all eleven of the First Nations of Québec. It presents the history and culture of these earlier residents using artefacts and videotaped oral histories; the larger items – including a *rabaska*, an enormous birch-bark canoe – were crafted in recent years.

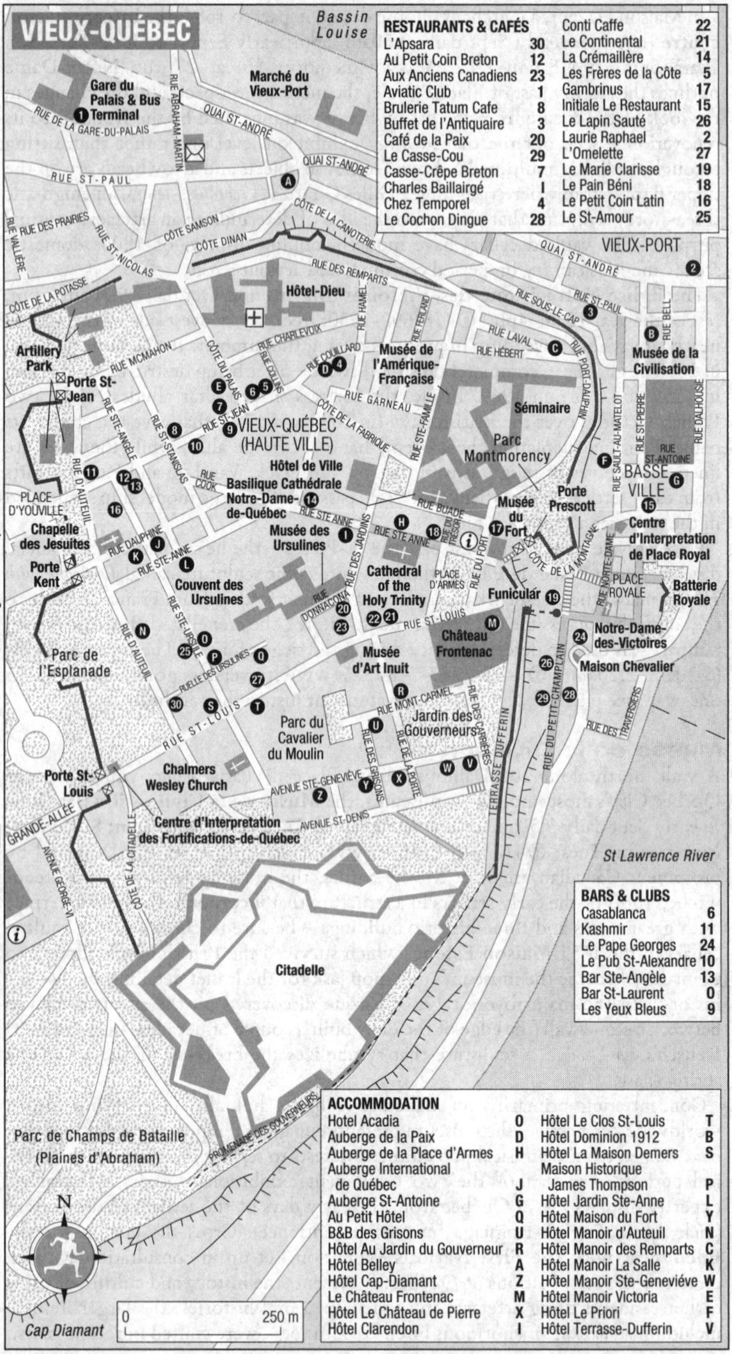

VIEUX-QUÉBEC
RESTAURANTS & CAFÉS
L'Apsara 30
Au Petit Coin Breton 12
Aux Anciens Canadiens 23
Aviatic Club 1
Brulerie Tatum Cafe 8
Buffet de l'Antiquaire 3
Café de la Paix 20
Le Casse-Cou 29
Casse-Crêpe Breton 7
Charles Baillairgé I
Chez Temporel 4
Le Cochon Dingue 28
Conti Caffe 22
Le Continental 21
La Crémaillère 14
Les Frères de la Côte 5
Gambrinus 17
Initiale Le Restaurant 15
Le Lapin Sauté 26
Laurie Raphael 2
L'Omelette 27
Le Marie Clarisse 19
Le Pain Béni 18
Le Petit Coin Latin 16
Le St-Amour 25
BARS & CLUBS
Casablanca 6
Kashmir 11
Le Pape Georges 24
Le Pub St-Alexandre 10
Bar Ste-Angèle 13
Bar St-Laurent O
Les Yeux Bleus 9
ACCOMMODATION
Hotel Acadia O
Auberge de la Paix D
Auberge de la Place d'Armes H
Auberge International de Québec J
Auberge St-Antoine G
Au Petit Hôtel Q
B&B des Grisons U
Hôtel Au Jardin du Gouverneur R
Hôtel Belley A
Hôtel Cap-Diamant Z
Le Château Frontenac M
Hôtel Le Château de Pierre X
Hôtel Clarendon I
Hôtel Le Clos St-Louis T
Hôtel Dominion 1912 B
Hôtel La Maison Demers S
Maison Historique James Thompson P
Hôtel Jardin Ste-Anne L
Hôtel Maison du Fort Y
Hôtel Manoir d'Auteuil N
Hôtel Manoir des Remparts C
Hôtel Manoir La Salle K
Hôtel Manoir Ste-Geneviéve W
Hôtel Manoir Victoria E
Hôtel Le Priori F
Hôtel Terrasse-Dufferin V
Bassin Louise
Gare du Palais & Bus Terminal
Marché du Vieux-Port
Rue de la Gare-du-Palais
Rue Abraham-Martin
Quai St-André
Rue St-Paul
Côte de la Canoterie
Côte Samson
Côte Dinan
Rue des Prairies
Rue Vallière
Rue St-Nicolas
Rue des Remparts
Vieux-Port
Côte de la Potasse
Hôtel-Dieu
Artillery Park
Porte St-Jean
Rue McMahon
Rue Charlevoix
Côte du Palais
Rue Collins
Rue Couillard
Rue Hamel
Rue Ferland
Musée de l'Amérique-Française
Rue Laval
Rue Hébert
Rue Sous-le-Cap
Rue Port-Dauphin
Musée de la Civilisation
Rue Bell
Rue Garneau
Séminaire
Rue St-Jean
Vieux-Québec (Haute Ville)
Côte de la Fabrique
Rue Ste-Famille
Parc Montmorency
Rue Sault-au-Matelot
Rue St-Pierre
Rue Dalhousie
Rue St-Antoine
Basse Ville
Rue Ste-Angèle
Rue St-Stanislas
Rue d'Auteuil
Rue Cook
Hôtel de Ville
Basilique Cathédrale Notre-Dame-de-Québec
Rue Buade
Musée du Fort
Porte Prescott
Place d'Youville
Chapelle des Jesuites
Rue Ste Anne
Musée des Ursulines
Rue du Trésor
Rue du Fort
Côte de la Montagne
Centre d'Interpretation de Place Royal
Rue Dauphine
Porte Kent
Couvent des Ursulines
Rue Donnacona
Cathedral of the Holy Trinity
Place d'Armes
Funicular
Rue Notre-Dame
Place Royale
Batterie Royale
Rue Ste-Ursule
Rue des Jardins
Rue St-Louis
Château Frontenac
Notre-Dame-des-Victoires
Maison Chevalier
Parc de l'Esplanade
Ruelle des Ursulines
Musée d'Art Inuit
Rue Mont-Carmel
Rue des Carrières
Rue du Petit-Champlain
Rue des Traversiers
Parc du Cavalier du Moulin
Jardin des Gouverneurs
Terrasse Dufferin
Rue des Grisons
Rue de la Porte
Chalmers Wesley Church
Porte St-Louis
Avenue Ste-Geneviève
Grande-Allée
Centre d'Interpretation des Fortifications-de-Québec
Avenue St-Denis
Côte de la Citadelle
Avenue George-VI
St Lawrence River
Lévis
Faubourg St-Jean-Baptiste
Musée National des Beaux-Arts du Québec
Citadelle
Promenade des Gouverneurs
Parc de Champs de Bataille (Plaines d'Abraham)
N
0 250 m
Cap Diamant

Vieux-Port and around

To the east and north, near the confluence of the St Charles and the St Lawrence rivers, lies the **Vieux-Port de Québec**, the busiest harbour in the province until its gradual eclipse by Montréal at the end of the 19th century. Much of the harbour has been renovated as a recreational area, with theatres, flats, sheltered walkways, restaurants and a marina packed with pleasure boats and yachts. The **Marché du Vieux-Port** (mid-March to Nov daily 9am–5pm; Jan to early March Tues–Sun 9.30am–5pm Ⓦwww.marchevieuxport.com) is a throwback to how the port used to be – its busy market stalls selling cheap, fresh produce from the local area.

Also on the south side of the Bassin Louise, the next street down from Quai St-André is rue St-Paul, heart of Québec's **antiques district**. Numerous cluttered antique shops, art galleries, cafés and restaurants now occupy warehouses and offices abandoned after the demise of the port. From rue St-Paul the steep Côte du Colonel Dambourgès leads to rue des Remparts on the northern borders of Haute-Ville (see below).

Haute Ville

The ten square kilometres of Vieux-Québec's **Haute Ville**, encircled by the city walls, form the Québec City of the tourist brochures. Dominated by the **Château Frontenac**, it holds a glut of historic architecture and several compelling museums. The whole area is undeniably enchanting, and simply strolling along its maze of streets is one of the city's great pleasures.

Place d'Armes and around

Haute Ville's centre of gravity is the main square, the **Place d'Armes**, with benches around the central fountain serving in the summer as a resting place for weary sightseers. It was here that Champlain established his first fort in 1620, on the site now occupied by the gigantic **Château Frontenac**, probably Canada's most photographed building. New York architect Bruce Price drew upon the French-Canadian style of the surroundings to produce a pseudo-medieval red-brick pile crowned with a copper roof. Although the hotel was inaugurated by the Canadian Pacific Railway in 1893, its distinctive main tower was only added in the early 1920s – during which time the hotel never closed – resulting in an over-the-top design that makes the most of the stupendous location atop Cap Diamant. Numerous notables, including Queen Elizabeth II, have stayed here, and the hotel has hosted one pair or more of newlyweds every night since it opened. The hotel has fifty-minute guided tours departing on the hour from the lower level (May to mid-Oct daily 10am–6pm; mid-Oct to April Sat & Sun noon–5pm, call for weekday times; reservations preferable Ⓣ418/691-2166, Ⓦwww.tourschateau.ca; $8.50).

Beside the Château Frontenac, where rue St-Louis enters the square, is the **Maison Maillou**, which houses the Québec chamber of commerce. Dating from 1736, this grey-limestone house, with metal shutters for insulation and a steeply slanting roof, displays the chief elements of the climate-adapted architecture brought over by the Norman settlers. On the west side of the square, on the spot where the Récollet missionaries built their first church and convent, stands the former **Palais de Justice**, a Renaissance-style courthouse designed in 1877 by Eugène-Étienne Taché, architect of the province's Parliament Buildings.

On the northeast corner of Place d'Armes, where rue Ste-Anne intersects with rue du Fort, is the **Musée du Fort** (April–Oct daily 10am–5pm, Feb, March & Nov Thurs–Sun 11am–4pm; Ⓣ418/692-2175, Ⓦwww.museedufort.com; $8), whose sole exhibit is a 37-square-metre model of Québec City circa 1750. You can only see it as part of the quaint thirty-minute sound and light show, when the

▲ The Château Frontenac, Québec City's best-known landmark

city's six major battles, including the battle of the Plains of Abraham and the American invasion of 1775, are re-enacted.

Parallel to rue du Fort is the narrow alley of **rue du Trésor** where French settlers paid their taxes to the Royal Treasury; nowadays it is a touristy artists' market. You're better to visit the row of stalls manned by local artisans in the churchyard running alongside the portraitists on the pedestrianized stretch of rue Ste-Anne. Nearby, the Centre Infotouriste (see p.274) occupies the former Union Hotel at 12 rue Ste-Anne.

Terrasse Dufferin and the ramparts

Fronting the Château Frontenac the wide clifftop boardwalk of the **Terrasse Dufferin** overlooks the narrowing of the river that was known to the aboriginal peoples as the *kebec* – the source of the province's name. Underlying part of the boardwalk are the foundations of Frontenac's Château St-Louis, which served as the governor's residence for two centuries until a fire destroyed it in 1834. The leafy park running alongside the boardwalk was the château's garden – hence its name, the **Jardin des Gouverneurs** (see p.285). To the south, a long flight of stairs leads up to the Promenade des Gouverneurs, a narrow boardwalk perched precariously on the cliff face below the Citadelle that leads to the Plaines d'Abraham (see p.288).

At the north end of the terrace – which offers charming views of the river – stands a romantic statue of **Champlain** and, beside it, a modern sculpture symbolizing Québec City's status as a UNESCO World Heritage Site. From here a **funicular** descends to Vieux-Québec's Basse-Ville (see p.277); save that for the weary walk back up and instead take the stairs down at the north end of the terrace to the **Porte Prescott**, one of the city's four rebuilt gates.

To stay in Haute Ville, continue across the top of the gate to **Parc Montmorency**; tucked between the upper and lower parts of the old city, its monuments recall the historic figures of the area. This land was granted by Champlain to Canada's first agricultural settler and seigneur, Louis Hébert, and was later the meeting place of Québec's first legislature in 1694. The park gives wonderful views of Québec's port and its massive grain elevators, as does the flanking rue Port Dauphin, which becomes **rue des Remparts**, where the cannons that once protected the city still point across to Lévis.

The ten-minute walk along rue des Remparts circles around the north side of the Séminaire past nineteenth-century homes to the **Hôtel-Dieu du Précieux Sang**, the oldest hospital north of Mexico. At the end of rue Remparts, turn left onto Côte du Palais; from here, you can turn right on rue McMahon to reach Artillery Park, or left on rue St-Jean and continue up the hill to the basilica.

Basilique-Cathédrale Notre-Dame de Québec

From Place d'Armes, you can follow rue du Trésor directly north towards the impressive bulk of the **Basilique-Cathédrale Notre-Dame de Québec** (daily 8am–4pm; free; ⓣ418/694-0665, ⓦwww.patrimoine-religieux.com). The oldest parish north of Mexico, the church was burnt to the ground in 1922 – one of many fires it has suffered – and was rebuilt to the original plans of its seventeenth-century forebear. Absolute silence within the cathedral heightens the impressiveness of the Rococo-inspired interior, culminating in a ceiling of blue sky and billowy clouds. The altar, a gilded replica of St Peter's, is surmounted by an elaborate baldachin uncharacteristically supported by angelic caryatids rather than columns due to the narrow space, and is topped by a statue of Jesus standing on a gilded sphere. The pewter sanctuary lamp, to the right of the main altar, was a gift from Louis XIV and is one of the few treasures to survive the fire. In the crypt more than nine hundred bodies, including three governors and most of Québec's bishops, are interred. Champlain is also rumoured to be buried here, though archeologists are still trying to work out which body is his. Unfortunately, the only part of the crypt you can see on the informative **guided tours** (daily every 30min 8.30am–3.30pm; reservations required; $2) is a mundane modern corridor.

Séminaire de Québec

Next door to the cathedral and sprawling to the north is the old **Séminaire de Québec**, founded by the aggressive and autocratic Monseigneur François de Laval-Montmorency in 1663 (see p.284). At its construction, the seminary was the finest collection of buildings the city had seen, leaving Governor Frontenac muttering that the bishop was now housed better than him. Primarily a college for priests, the seminary was also open to young men who wanted to follow other professions, and in 1852 it became Laval University, the country's first francophone Catholic university. Today, only the school of architecture remains; the other departments were moved to the western suburb of Ste-Foy.

Public access is limited mainly to the ever-expanding **Musée de l'Amérique Française** (late June to early Sept daily 9.30am–5pm; Sept–June Tues–Sun 10am–5pm, ⓣ418/692-2843, ⓦwww.mcq.org; $7; Nov–May free on Tues), whose four sections occupy a small part of the old Séminaire. The entrance – and departure point for one-hour guided tours of the seminary – is in the Welcome Pavilion in the Maison du Coin, next to the basilica. Upstairs, it has a small exhibition on the early colonists, and adjoins the Roman-style **chapel**, whose Second Empire interior houses Canada's largest collection of religious relics – bones, ashes and locks of hair of various saints, a few of which are on display. Laval's memorial chapel contains his ornate marble tomb, but not his remains, which were moved to the basilica when the chapel was deconsecrated in 1993. The whole interior is a bit of a sham, though: fed up with rebuilding after the chapel burnt down yet again in 1888, the church authorities decided to construct the pillars and coffered ceilings out of tin and paint over them; the stained glass windows have been painted on single panes of glass and even the tapestries are the result of some deft brushwork.

Monseigneur Laval

François-Xavier de Montmorency-Laval was born into a wealthy aristocratic family in northeast France. Educated by Jesuits, he briefly studied in Paris before giving up his hefty patrimony to join the church, and was ordained a priest in 1647 at the age of 24. Ten years later the Pope needed someone to oversee the spiritual development of New France and the Jesuits proposed Laval. He was swiftly made a bishop and sent to Québec. In the three decades of his incumbency, from 1659 to 1688, Laval secured more power than the governor and intendant put together, and any officer dispatched from France found himself on the next boat home if Laval did not care for him. Laval retired early due to ill health (brought on by a religious fervour that denied him blankets and proper food) but, unhappy with his successor, Bishop de St Valier, he continued to exert a stubborn influence on the running of the colony well into his dotage. Death finally came in 1708 after his feet froze on the stone floor of the chapel during his morning prayer session.

The wrought-iron gates between the Welcome Pavilion and the basilica lead into a vast courtyard flanked by austere white buildings; pass through the gates to visit the rest of the museum. Alternatively, take the underground corridor directly from the chapel; along the way a photo exhibit fills in the history of the Séminaire's buildings. Either way, you end up at the museum's **Pavillon Jérôme-Demers**, which displays a tiny sample of the eclectic items gathered by Québec's bishops and the academics at Laval – scientific instruments, an Egyptian mummy (with a remarkably well-preserved penis) – as well as ecclesiastical silverware and some of Laval's personal belongings. The museum's name derives from the exhibition on the second floor, **The Settling of French America**, which illustrates the history of the emigration and settlement of the more than nineteen million North Americans of French stock.

Hôtel de Ville and around

The edifices of the colony's once-powerful Church face the home of democratic power in the city today – the **Hôtel de Ville** (City Hall), which dates from 1883 and is surrounded by the park space of the Jardins de l'Hôtel de Ville, scene of numerous live shows in the summer. To the north, the shops on Côte de la Fabrique extend down the hill to the lively restaurants and bars of rue St-Jean; while to the south, the Hôtel de Ville is overlooked by the far more impressive Art Deco buildings of the **Hôtel Clarendon** and the **Édifice Price** (the city's first skyscraper), at nos. 57 and 65 rue Ste-Anne, respectively.

By the corner of rue Ste-Anne and rue des Jardins stands the first Anglican cathedral built outside the British Isles, the **Cathedral of the Holy Trinity** (daily late May to Oct 10am–5pm; free guided tours; Ⓣ418/692-2193, Ⓦwww.cathedral.ca). The king of France gave the site to the Récollet Fathers but their church burnt down in the late eighteenth century. Its replacement, constructed in 1800–04 on orders from George III, followed the lines of London's church of St Martin-in-the-Fields. The simple interior houses the 1845 bishops' throne, reputedly made from the wood of the elm tree under whose branches Samuel de Champlain conferred with the Iroquois. Many of the church's features came from London, including the silverware from George III and Victorian stained glass, shipped in vats of molasses for protection. The brass bars on the balcony denote the seats for the exclusive use of British sovereigns (or their representatives); humbler parishioners had wooden doors on the box pews to keep the winter cold out. In the courtyard are Les Artisans de la Cathédrale, Québec-based artisans whose small crafts and clothes stalls avoid tourist tack.

Couvent des Ursulines and around

Heading south along rue des Jardins from the Hôtel de Ville brings you to the narrow rue Donnacona, where a sculptured hand holding a quill – a monument to the women who, since 1639, have dedicated their lives to teaching young Québécois – rests on a pedestal. It seems to point the way to the **Couvent des Ursulines**, built by a tiny group of Ursuline nuns who arrived in Québec in 1639 calling themselves "the Amazons of God in Canada". Their task was to bring religion to the natives and later to the daughters of the settlers, a mission carried out in the classrooms of North America's first girls' school – the buildings still house a private school. They also cared for the *filles du roi*, marriageable orphans and peasant girls imported from France to swell the population. These girls were kept in separate rooms in the convent for surveillance by the local bachelors, who were urged to select a wife within fifteen days of the ship's arrival – a fine of three hundred *livres* was levied on any man who failed to take his pick within the period. Fat girls were the most desirable, as it was believed they were more inclined to stay at home and be better able to resist the winter cold.

A likeness of the Ursulines' first mother superior, Marie Guyart de l'Incarnation, can be seen in a posthumous portrait attributed to Pommier in the interesting little **Musée des Ursulines** (May–Sept Tues–Sat 10am–noon & 1–5pm, Sun 1–5pm; Oct–April Tues–Sun 1–4.30pm; Ⓣ418/694-0694, Ⓦwww.ursulines-uc.com; $6), housed in the former home of one of the first nuns. A painting by Frère Luc, though executed in France, pictures a Canadian version of the Holy Family: Joseph is shown presenting a Huron girl to Mary, while through the window one can glimpse Cap Diamant and the St Lawrence River flowing past. Other paintings, documents and household items testify to the harshness of life in the early days of the colony, but lace-work and embroidery are the highlights, particularly the splendid liturgical ornaments and vestments produced by the early Ursulines and shot through with gold and silver thread.

Marie de l'Incarnation's remains are entombed in the oratory adjoining the **chapel** (May–Oct Tues–Sat 10–11.30am & 1.30–4.30pm, Sun 1.30–4.30pm; free), rebuilt in 1902 but retaining sumptuous early eighteenth-century altar and sculptures. A plaque indicates General Montcalm's former resting place below the chapel (only his skull was found there during renovations, and this has subsequently been re-interred in a suburban military cemetery). The collection of seventeenth- and eighteenth-century paintings were acquired from post-Revolution France in the 1820s. Next to the museum, the **Centre Marie-de-l'Incarnation** (Tues–Sat 10am–11.30am & 1.30–4.30pm, Sun 1.30–4.30pm; closed Dec; Ⓣ418/694-0413; free) sells religious and historical books, and displays a few of Marie's personal effects.

On the corner of rue des Jardins and rue St-Louis – a touristy restaurant strip – stands **Maison Jacquet**, occupied by the restaurant *Aux Anciens Canadiens*. The name comes from Québec's first novel, whose author, Philippe Aubert de Gaspé, lived here for a while in the middle of the nineteenth century. Dating from 1677, the house is another good example of seventeenth-century New France architecture, as is the blue and white **Maison Kent** at no. 25 on the other side of rue St-Louis, which was built in 1649. Maison Kent was once home to Queen Victoria's father, the Duke of Kent, but it's best known as the place where the capitulation of Québec was signed in 1759 and now ironically houses the French consulate.

Jardin des Gouverneurs and around

Rue Haldimand, around the corner from the Musée d'Art Inuit, leads to the **Jardin des Gouverneurs**, whose wonderful prospect of the St Lawrence was once the exclusive privilege of the colonial governors who inhabited the Château

St-Louis, upon whose foundations the Terrasse Dufferin was built. The garden's Wolfe–Montcalm obelisk monument, erected in 1828, is rare in paying tribute to the victor and the vanquished. Converted merchants' houses border this grandiose area, and the nearby streets are some of the most impressive in Vieux-Québec – check out rue de la Porte and the parallel rue des Grisons on the park's west side, which boasts some fine eighteenth-century homes.

To escape the tourist hordes for a bit, follow rue Mont-Carmel, on the northern side of the square, to the almost unnoticed **Parc du Cavalier du Moulin**, a quiet little park perfect for a picnic. The remnant of a defensive bastion built atop Mont Carmel hill, this was part of the seventeenth-century French fortifications that protected the city's western side. You can't really see the walls from this angle, but you can see the rear facades of the houses on rue St-Louis.

From the Jardin des Gouverneurs, avenue Ste-Geneviève runs west past handsome nineteenth-century houses towards Porte St-Louis. En route, turn right onto rue Ste-Ursule for the **Chalmers-Wesley United Church** (late June to late Aug daily 10am–5pm; ⓣ418/692-2640; free) at no. 78, built in 1852 and one of the most beautiful in the city. Its slender, Gothic Revivalist spires are a conspicuous element of the skyline and, inside, the stained glass windows are worth a look. During summer there are weekly organ concerts on Sunday evenings at 6pm. Opposite at no. 71, the 1910 **Sanctuaire de Notre-Dame-du-Sacré-Coeur** (daily 7am–8pm; ⓣ418/692-3787; free) also has impressive stained glass windows.

The fortifications and Artillery Park

A left turn onto rue St-Louis from rue Ste-Ursule leads to the Porte St-Louis, one of the four gates in the city wall. It's surrounded by **Parc de l'Esplanade**, the main site for the Carnaval de Québec (see p.274), and departure point for the city's smart horse-drawn calèches. The park's **Centre d'interprétation des Fortifications-de-Québec** (May–Oct daily 10am–5pm; ⓣ418/648-7016, ⓦwww.pc.gc.ca/fortifications; $3.90), at 100 rue St-Louis, includes a powder house constructed in 1815 and a dull exhibition on the fortifications. Most visitors start their 4.5-kilometre stroll around the city wall from here. You can also take a ninety-minute tour focusing on the fortifications' military history with a costumed guide for $9.90.

The entrance to the Citadelle lies south of here along the Côte de la Citadelle. Alternatively, head north on rue d'Auteuil as it descends alongside the fortifications to Porte Kent, next to the **Chapelle des Jésuites** (Mon–Fri 11am–1pm; guided visits late June to Sept Thurs–Mon; free), at 20 rue Dauphine. Framed by the rose and powder-blue vault, the church's delicately carved altar and ecclesiastical sculptures are by **Pierre-Noël Levasseur**, one of the most illustrious artists to work on the early Québec parish churches.

Further north up rue d'Auteuil and immediately north of the **Porte St-Jean** lie the defensive structures of **Artillery Park**, raised in the early 1700s by the French in expectation of a British attack from the St Charles River, and subsequently a barracks for the Royal Artillery Regiment for more than a century. In 1882 it became a munitions factory, providing the Canadian army with ammunition in both world wars. The foundry, added in 1902, now houses an interpretation centre (April–Oct daily 10am–5pm; ⓣ418/648-4205, ⓦwww.pc.gc.ca/artillerie; $3.90), which has displays on the military pedigree of the city, including a vivid model of Québec City in 1808. It's also the starting point for one-hour guided tours ($3 extra) and visits of the site's four buildings, including the Officers' Quarters furnished as it was in 1830 and the massive Dauphine Redoubt. The latter typifies the changes of fortune here: used by the French as the barracks for their garrison, it became the officers' mess under the British and then the residence of the superintendent of the Canadian Arsenal.

The Citadelle

Dominating the southern section of Vieux-Québec, the massive star-shaped **Citadelle** (guided tours every 30min: July & Aug 9am–6pm; every hour: April 10am–4pm, May & June, Sept 9am–4pm, Oct 10am–3pm; once daily: Nov–March 1.30pm; ⓣ418/694-2815, ⓦwww.lacitadelle.qc.ca; $10) can only be visited on one of the worthwhile **guided tours**. The *tour de force* of Québec City's fortifications, the Citadelle occupies the highest point of Cap Diamant, 100m above the St Lawrence. This strategic site was first built on by the French, but the British constructed most of the buildings under orders from the Duke of Wellington, who was anxious about American attack after the War of 1812.

The complex of 25 buildings covers forty acres and is the largest North American fort still occupied by troops – it's home to the Royal 22nd Regiment, Canada's only French-speaking regiment. Around the parade ground are ranged various monuments to the campaigns of the celebrated "Van-Doos" (*vingt-deux*), as well as the summer residence of Canada's governor general and two buildings dating back to the French period: the Cap Diamant Redoubt, built in 1693 and thus one of the oldest parts of the Citadelle, and the 1750 powder magazine, now a mundane museum of weaponry and military artefacts.

In addition to the guided tours, the admission price includes the colourful Changing of the Guard (late June to early Sept daily 10am), which you can catch at the end of a 9am tour (otherwise arrive by 9.45am), and the Beating of the Retreat tattoo (early July to early Sept Fri–Sun 7pm, at the end of the 6pm tour).

Beyond Vieux-Québec

While there's plenty in Vieux-Québec to compel you to remain there for the duration of your stay, a handful of sights beyond the old city walls merit a day's outing. Paramount of these is the excellent **Musée National des Beaux-Arts du Québec**, which showcases Québécois and Inuit art. The museum lies at the western fringes of the expansive **Parc des Champs-de-Bataille**, site of a decisive battle in the city's history and a pleasant place for a picnic. A few blocks north of the park is stately **Grande-Allée** – many of the city's best restaurants and bars not within Vieux-Québec can be found on or just off it.

Faubourg St-Jean-Baptiste

To take a break from the tourist sights, head through the Porte St-Jean and across Place D'Youville to where rue St-Jean picks up again in the former *faubourg* – the name given to the settlements that once stood undefended outside the city walls – of **St-Jean-Baptiste**. The quarter's studenty atmosphere is more relaxed than the rest of Québec, with cheaper restaurants and great nightlife spots. A five-minute walk will bring you to the **Protestant Burying Ground** (May to mid-Nov daily 7am–11pm), Québec City's first Protestant cemetery and now the oldest one remaining in the province. Many historical figures were buried here between 1772 and 1860, including Lt Col James Turnbull, Queen Victoria's presumed half-brother. Further along on the same side of the street, **Maison Jean-Alfred Moisan** has been in the grocery trade since 1871, making it the oldest grocery store in North America. The tin ceilings and wooden furnishings provide a backdrop for fine foods and baked goods. The district's namesake, the **Église St-Jean-Baptiste** (late June to mid-Sept Mon–Fri & Sun 11am–4pm, Sat 9am–4pm), at 410 rue St-Jean, dominates the *faubourg*, its spire rising to 73m; the church's facade is a close reproduction of the Église de la Trinité in Paris.

Grande-Allée and the Parliament Buildings

Sweeping out from Porte St-Louis and flanked by grand Victorian mansions, the tree-lined boulevard of **Grande-Allée** is proclaimed the city's equivalent of the Champs-Élysées, with its bustling restaurants, hotels and bars. Adjacent to the *Loews Le Concorde* hotel, Place Montcalm has a monument to Montcalm and a more recent statue of Charles de Gaulle, the French president who declared from Montréal "Vive le Québec libre" in the 1960s, much to the separatists' delight. This area is now known as Parliament Hill, a new name that caused a lot of controversy, as Canada's Parliament area in Ottawa has the same title and anglophones thought it presumptuous of Québec City to label itself like a capital city.

There is indeed a hill here, and upon it, at the eastern end of Grande-Allée, stand the stately buildings of the **Hôtel du Parlement** (late June to early Sept Mon–Fri 9am–4.30pm, Sat & Sun 10am–4.30pm; early Sept to late June Mon–Fri 9am–4.30pm; guided tours every thirty minutes; ⓣ418/643-7239 or 1-866/337-8837, ⓦwww.assnat.qc.ca; free), designed by Eugène-Étienne Taché in 1877, using the Louvre for inspiration. The ornate facade includes niches for twelve bronze statues by Québécois sculptor Louis-Philippe Hébert of Canada's and Québec's major statesmen, while finely chiselled and gilded walnut panels in the entrance hall depict important moments in Québec's history, coats of arms and other heraldic features. From here the corridor of the President's Gallery, lined with portraits of all the Legislative Assembly's speakers and presidents, leads to the Chamber of the National Assembly, where the 125 provincial representatives meet for debate. You can't see much unless you take one of the free half-hour guided tours.

Among the government buildings clustered to the west of here, the Édifice Marie-Guyart, 1037 rue de la Chevrotière, is the tallest structure in the city. On its 31st floor, the **Observatoire de la Capitole** (early Feb to mid-Oct daily 10am–5pm; mid-Oct to mid-Feb Tues–Sun 10am–5pm; ⓣ418/644-9841, ⓦwww.observatoirecapitale.org; $5) offers a fairly stunning 360-degree panoramic view over Vieux-Québec, the Citadelle and beyond, with panels usefully providing background info on what you can see.

Parc des Champs-de-Bataille

West of the Citadelle are the rolling grasslands of the **Parc des Champs-de-Bataille** (Battlefields Park), a sizeable chunk of land stretching along the cliffs above the St Lawrence River. The park encompasses the historic **Plaines d'Abraham**, named after Abraham Martin, the first pilot of the St Lawrence River in 1620. The Plains were to become the site on which Canada's history was rewritten. In June 1759 a large British force led by **General Wolfe** sailed up the St Lawrence to besiege **General Montcalm** in Québec City. From the end of July until early September the British forces shuttled up and down the south side of the river, raking the city with cannon fire. Montcalm and the governor, Vaudreuil, became convinced Wolfe was planning a direct assault on the citadel from Anse de Foulon (Wolf's Cove), the only handy break in the cliff face; this was confirmed when lookouts observed a British detachment surveying Cap Diamant from across the river in Lévis. Montcalm thus strengthened the defences above Anse de Foulon, but made the mistake of withdrawing the regiment stationed on the Plains themselves. The following night the British performed the extraordinary feat, which even Wolfe had considered "a desperate plan", of scaling the cliff below the Plains via Anse de Foulon, and on the morning of September 16 Montcalm awoke to find the British drawn up a couple of kilometres from the city's gate. The hastily assembled French battalions, flanked by aboriginal warriors, were badly organized and rushed headlong at the British, whose volleys of gunfire mortally wounded Montcalm. On his deathbed

Montcalm wrote a chivalrous note of congratulations to Wolfe, not knowing he was dead. Québec City surrendered four days later.

The park's **Discovery Pavilion** (late June to early Sept daily 8.30am–5.30pm, early Sept to late June Mon–Fri 8.30am–5pm, Sat 9am–5pm, Sun 10am–5pm; ⓣ418/649-6157, ⓦwww.ccbn-nbc.gc.ca; $8 or $10 for a day-pass including other attractions), below the tourist office at 835 av Wilfrid-Laurier est, has maps, information panels and a multimedia show, which does a reasonable job of covering the after-effects of the battle.

The dead of 1759 are commemorated by a statue of Joan of Arc in a beautifully maintained sunken **garden** just off av Wilfrid-Laurier at Place Montcalm by the Ministry of Justice. More conspicuous, standing out amid the wooded parklands, scenic drives, jogging paths and landscaped gardens, are two Martello towers, built between 1805 and 1812 for protection against the Americans. Martello Tower 2, on the corner of Wilfrid-Laurier and Taché, hosts period dinner events (ⓣ418/649-6157 for information and tickets), while **Martello Tower 1** (late June to early Sept 10am–5pm; $4), further south in the park, has superb views of the river from its rooftop lookout. The views are almost as good from the base of the tower, and you don't have to pay for an unmemorable exhibition in order to reach the top; children get to dress up in costumes for the optional tour, though. Further west, outside the Musée National des Beaux-Arts du Québec, there's a monument to General Wolfe, whose body was shipped back to England for burial, pickled in a barrel of rum.

Musée National des Beaux-Arts du Québec

Canadian art had its quiet beginnings in Québec City and the full panoply of this output can be found on the western edge of the Parc des Champs-de-Bataille in the **Musée National des Beaux-Arts du Québec** (June to early Sept daily 10am–6pm, rest of the year Tues–Sun 10am–6pm, Wed until 9pm year-round; $15; ⓣ418/643-2150 or 1-866/220-2150, ⓦwww.mnba.qc.ca; bus #11). The Grand Hall, with its cruciform skylight, connects the museum's two buildings (its original home, the Pavillon Gérard-Morisset, and a renovated Victorian prison renamed the Pavillon Charles-Baillairgé) and also serves as the main entrance. For a chronological tour, start at the Pavillon Gérard-Morisset and then move on to the Pavillon Charles-Baillairgé.

Pavillon Gérard-Morisset

Gallery 7 on the second floor of the **Pavillon Gérard-Morisset** provides a good survey of Québécois art from the early seventeenth to late nineteenth centuries. As Québec churches were the primary art commissioners at the time, most of the earliest works are **religious** in nature, including the output of **Frère Luc**, represented here by *The Guardian Angel*. The most notable contributions to the collection are by two dynasties: the works of brothers **Pierre-Noël** and **François-Noël Levasseur** from the mid-1700s and the three generations of **Baillairgés** who succeeded them, their copious output including the architecture of churches as well as their interior decoration. Under the British, the subject matter broadened to include portraiture, seen here in **Antoine Plamondon**'s poised *Madame Tourangeau*, and Canadian landscapes by Québec-born **Joseph Légaré** and, more famously, Amsterdam-born **Cornelius Krieghoff**, noted for his romanticized landscapes of landmarks in the region.

Gallery 8, opposite, covers the period from 1860 to 1945, from the late-nineteenth-century **salons** to the development of **modernist art**. One that grabs your attention as you enter is **Horatio Walker**'s *Ploughing, the First Gleam at Dawn*, a romantic vision of the lives of the French-Canadian *habitants* who so engrossed him that he repudiated his Ontario roots. The tug-of-war of styles in Europe is played out in many of the subsequent works, including **Maurice Cullen**'s Impressionist-influenced view onto Basse-Ville, *Wolfe's Cove*, and the evocative scene of a horse-drawn carriage in a snowstorm, *Craig Street, Montréal*. Urban life is also admirably recorded by **Adrien Hébert**'s *Rue St-Denis*, which wonderfully captures the spirit of Montréal in the 1920s.

Downstairs, in gallery 2, the impact of **Alfred Pellan**, who returned from Paris in 1940 to teach at Montréal's École des Beaux-Arts, plays out in the development of post-war **figurative** and **abstract art**. His comparative radicalism, evident in his Cubist-influenced still life, *Flowers and Dominoes*, was the catalyst for a generation of Québécois artists to pick up on the avant-garde movements of the time. The move to non-figurative representation can be seen in **Jean Dallaire**'s softly muted abstract figures in his 1957 *Julie*, which contrasts with his surreally colourful and strident *Coq Licorne* (Unicorn Rooster) painted five years earlier. The process reaches its apogee with the Neo-Plasticism represented by **Fernand Leduc**'s boldly coloured geometric abstract *The Mountain Climber*.

At the same time, two of Québec's best-known artists were developing their signature styles. **Paul-Émile Borduas** applied the automatic writing technique of the surrealists to painting – his *Cabalistic Signs* is almost a doodle in oils. His progression to the increasingly spare canvases that have rooms devoted to them in Montréal's museums (Principal art) can also be noted here. Gallery 3, across the hall, is devoted solely to the work of **Jean-Paul Riopelle**. The gallery's highlight is his *L'Hommage à Rosa Luxemburg*, a 40-metre-long triptych in thirty segments, with ghostly spray-painted outlines of birds and man-made objects.

Pavillon Charles-Baillairgé

Armand Vaillancourt's *Tree on rue Durocher* sweeps up into the atrium of the former jail, leading visitors into the galleries and a few of the old prison cells. These lie en route to gallery 10, where "Je me souviens" portrays the personages and events in Québec's history through paintings and sculptures by some of the province's leading artists, and includes the studies for public works by sculptors Louis-Philippe Hébert and Alfred Laliberté. In the prison's tower, Montréal sculptor David Moore has created a unique two-storey sculpture of bodies scaling walls – just what you might expect in an old prison.

The third floor's Gallery 12 is devoted to Québec-born painter Jean-Paul Lemieux. His style varies wildly, from landscapes inspired by the Group of Seven, such as the Charlevoix-set *Afternoon Sunlight*, through a phase of folk-art-style painting (including a fun look at the Corpus Christi parade winding down côte de la Montagne), and ending with a series of uncluttered Expressionist portraits.

One of the most celebrated additions to the museum is the remarkable **Brousseau collection of Inuit Art**. Consisting of over 2600 pieces amassed from across the Arctic, the collection traces the development of Inuit art from the naive works of the mid-twentieth century to the highly narrative and intricately carved sculptures by contemporary artists. The few ancient items include simple ivory works from the nomadic Dorset and Thulé cultures.

Cartier-Brébeuf National Historic Site

Northwest of Vieux-Québec, on the banks of the St-Charles River (bus #4), the **Cartier-Brébeuf National Historic Site** (daily early May to early Sept 10am–5pm; rest of the year call for schedule; ⓣ418/648-4038, ⓦwww.pc.gc.ca/brebeuf; $3.90, including guided tour), at 175 de l'Espinay, has a double claim to fame. It marks the spot where Jacques Cartier spent the winter of 1535–36 in friendly contact with the people of the surrounding Iroquoian villages – a cordial start to a relationship that Cartier later soured by taking a local chief and nine of his men hostage. It is also where Jean de Brébeuf, with his Jesuit friends, built his first Canadian residence in 1625: Brébeuf is best known for his martyrdom near today's Midland in Ontario (see p.152). The **interpretation centre** features an excellent account of Cartier's voyages and of the hardship he and his crew endured during the winter and a backgrounder on the Jesuits' role in New France. The guided tour of the site leads to a mock-up of an Iroquoian longhouse and sweat lodge set within a palisade, where costumed guides demonstrate daily tasks, mostly for the benefit of the kids. Keep an eye out for the resident muskrat.

Eating

It is when you start **eating** in Québec City that the French ancestry of the Québécois hits all the senses: the city's restaurants present an array of culinary delights adopted from the mother country, from beautifully presented gourmet dishes to humble baguettes. The lively **cafés** are probably where you will want to spend your time, washing down bowls of soup and *croûtons* (toasted baguettes dripping with cheese) with plenty of coffee.

Vieux-Québec (upper and lower) is home to most of the gourmet **restaurants** and cafés; in Haute-Ville you'll generally find better value along rue St-Jean than rue St-Louis. Other areas have their fair share of eating spots as well – notably along rue St-Jean (quirky and cheaper) and, just outside the walls, Grande-Allée (generally touristy and expensive). Your best bet for good-value mid-price restaurants is to head for the numerous terrace-fronted establishments on avenue Cartier, near the Musée National des Beaux-Arts du Québec. Although prices in the city tend to be rather high, even the poshest restaurants have cheaper lunchtime and table d'hôte menus. Typical French-Canadian cooking – game with sweet sauces followed by simple desserts with lashings of maple syrup – is available at very few places in town, although the many *cabanes à sucre* on Île d'Orléans (see p.299) offer typical meals to tourists.

Cafés and diners

Brûlerie Tatum Café 1084 rue St-Jean. ⓦwww.tatum.qc.ca. All-day omelettes, light snacks and an impressive selection of coffee roasts are served at this stylish coffeehouse with exposed brick walls. 8am–11pm.

Buffet de l'Antiquaire 95 rue St-Paul ⓣ418/692-2661. An old-school diner popular with locals for breakfast (from 6am) and home-cooked comfort food like *poutine* and *pâté chinois* (shepherd's pie).

Café Au Bonnet D'ane 298 rue St-Jean ⓣ418/647-3031. While away a few hours at this hip café-bar, where you can munch on omelettes, pizzas and burgers at the quieter end of rue St-Jean.

Le Casse-Cou 90 rue du Petit-Champlain ⓣ418/694-1121. Cute little spot at the end of pedestrianized rue du Petit-Champlain for $5 breakfast fry-ups and decent light meals until 9pm.

Chez Temporel 25 rue Couillard ⓣ418/694-1813. Bowls of steaming *café au lait*, croissants and *chocolatines* make this café, near the *Auberge de la Paix* hostel, a perfect place for breakfast. Soups and sandwiches are available until 1.30am during the week, 2.30am on Fri & Sat and midnight on Sun.

L'Omelette 66 rue St-Louis ⓣ418/694-9626. Adequate tourist joint with omelette specialities; all-day breakfast from 7am. Evening meals include pizza and fish and start at $10.

Le Panetier Baluchon 764 rue St-Jean ⓣ418-522-3022, ⓦwww.panetier-baluchon.com. Small, but well-stocked café with freshly baked bread and decadent pies, as well as a nice selection of sandwiches.

Restaurants

Haute-Ville (within the walls)

L'Apsara 71 rue d'Auteuil ⓣ418/694-0232. Cambodian, Vietnamese and Thai food in a muted dining room across from the Parc de l'Esplanade. Three-course lunch is around $20, dinners around $30.

Aux Anciens Canadiens 34 rue St-Louis ⓣ418/692-1627, ⓦwww.auxancienscanadiens.qc.ca. This overly expensive and touristy restaurant (table d'hôte around $40) is in one of the oldest homes in Québec City. It serves refined Québécois specialities like *tourtière* (meat pie) and *pattes de cochon* (pigs' trotters) and house inventions such as duck glazed with maple syrup and caribou in blueberry-wine sauce.

Café de la Paix 44 rue des Jardins ⓣ418/692-1430, ⓦwww.cafedelapaix.ca. The desserts in the front window taste as good as they look, and the rest of the menu – pricey French classics (veal medallions with mushrooms) and game for around $30 – is equally delicious. Closed Sun.

Casse-Crêpe Breton 1136 rue St-Jean ⓣ418/692-0438. Diner-style restaurant where filling crêpes are made in front of you, from $5.25 for two ingredients. There's often a queue, but it's fast. 7am–11pm.

Charles Baillairgé At *Hôtel Clarendon* (see p.276), 57 rue Ste-Anne ⓣ418/692-2480. Opened in 1870, this is supposedly Canada's oldest restaurant and serves classic French cuisine. Expect to pay upwards of $40 for dinner; dress is formal.

Conti Caffe 32 rue St-Louis ⓣ418/692-4191. Sharing the kitchen of *Le Continental* next door, this casual Italian restaurant is the best choice on a street swamped with mediocre, touristy restaurants. Veal is a speciality – the medallions in porcini mushroom sauce are rich and succulent. The evening table d'hôte is great value at around $25.

Le Continental 26 rue St-Louis ⓣ418/694-9995, ⓦwww.restaurantlecontinental.com. Old-fashioned, if slightly stuffy, place down the street from the *Château Frontenac*. Excellent seafood, veal and flambéed dishes are among the options on the three-course table d'hôte starting at $35.

La Crémaillère 73 rue Ste-Anne ⓣ418/692-2216, ⓦwww.cremaillere.qc.ca. Superior French and Italian cuisine in a romantic, stone-walled nineteenth century residence. Most mains, such as a prawn and scallop casserole in a white butter sauce and roasted rack of lamb, are $30–40. If you have room for dessert, hone in on the delectable *pyramide au chocolat*.

Les Frères de la Côte 1190 rue St-Jean ⓣ418/692-5445. A friendly and crowded bistro that draws locals as well as tourists for steaks, smoked salmon and great mussels moderately priced between $10 and $20. Make sure to check the posted daily specials.

Gambrinus 15 rue du Fort ⓣ418/692-5144. Good Italian and French food on the corner of Place d'Armes, with seafood specialities and a table d'hôte regularly around $25. Musicians nightly.

Le Pain Béni 24 rue Ste-Anne ⓣ418/694-9485. You're spoiled for choice across the board at this cosy French and Italian bistro around the corner from the *Château Frontenac*. The superb menu includes exquisitely prepared items such as lamb ravioli and wild boar over parmesan risotto. Not a place to skip dessert, particularly the crème brulée.

Au Petit Coin Breton 1029 rue St-Jean ⓣ418/694-0758, ⓦwww.aupetitcoinbreton.com. A pretty good and reasonably priced creperie, particularly for brunch, where servers wear traditional Breton costume. Dishes start at $10.

Le Petit Coin Latin 8.5 rue Ste-Ursule ⓣ418/692-2022. Cosy café-bistro with a secluded courtyard. *Raclette* (heated cheese slivers with dried meats) is a speciality, but they also serve steaks and a caribou *tourtière* (meat pie) for heartier appetites. Breakfast (7.30–11.30am, until 4pm weekends) ranges from straightforward fry-ups to eggs Benedict.

Le Saint-Amour 48 rue Ste-Ursule ⓣ418/694-0667, ⓦwww.saint-amour.com. Romantic French restaurant with a glass-roofed winter garden. Excellent food at around $85 for two; try the foie gras.

Haute-Ville (outside the walls)

L'Astral 1225 cours du General-De Montcalm ⓣ418/647-2222, ⓦwww.lastral.ca. Rotating restaurant on the top floor of the *Hôtel Loews Le Concorde*. The international menu is generally expensive, starting at around $30, but the views can't be beaten.

Café Krieghoff 1089 av Cartier ⓣ418/522-3711. A typical French bistro *à la Québécois* that serves up some of the city's best coffee, big breakfasts and light meals, including traditional *croûtons* (a baguette topped with garlic butter and melted cheese), for around $16. Good spot to sit and read or write in the day, especially on the terrace.

Chez Ashton 640 Grande Allee est. Don't expect much in the way of atmosphere, but if you're looking to sample the best *poutine* in the city, consider *Chez Ashton* an essential stop. Served in a veritable tub, the several *poutine* varieties (each around $10) are all surefire artery cloggers but worth it just the same. Also at 54 Cote du Palais.

Le Cochon Dingue 46 boul René-Lévesque ouest ⓣ418/523-2013, ⓦwww.cochondingue.com. Near av Cartier, this branch draws locals, not tourists, as in Basse-Ville. Homestyle French cooking from $15.

Le Commensal 860 rue St-Jean ⓣ418/647-3733. Great buffet spot (the food is sold by weight) for vegetarians five minutes from Vieux-Québec's gates.

Cosmos Café 575 Grande-Allée est ☎418/640-0606, www.lecosmos.com. By far the best spot on the Grande-Allée – cool decor, great breakfasts and imaginative menu from $10. Crowded and lively at lunch and for the *cinq à sept* cocktail hour.

Le Graffiti 1191 av Cartier ☎418/529-4949. Chic French-Italian restaurant with decent lunch specials that also does a good Sun brunch (10am–3pm). The dinner menu includes mains like a succulent deer medallion with blueberry sauce and there's an impressive wine list.

Le Hobbit 700 rue St-Jean ☎418/647-2677. A popular local spot where a mixed studenty crowd come for the great vegetarian options, as well as burgers, pasta and bistro dishes like steak and trout filet.

Kimono Sushi Bar 1034 av Cartier ☎418/648-8821. Easily one of the best sushi bars in the city, with prices less than what you might expect. The stellar menu includes delicious choices like the Bonsai (soft shell crab *massago*) and TMT (smoked salmon tempura flakes).

La Piazzetta 707 rue St-Jean ☎418/692-2962. Trendy pizzeria with funky furnishings – the pizzas come close to perfection and are quite cheap – a good meal for two plus drinks will come to less than $40. There's another in Basse-Ville at 63 rue St-Paul (☎418/529-7489).

Saveur De L'Inde 1980 rue de Bergerville ☎418/683-0006. It takes some effort to get to this neighbourhood spot on a side street south of Boul Laurier, but if you're craving Indian food, this is *the* place to go. Most of the tasty staples, such as Tandoori chicken and lamb curry, cost under $20 and there's terrace seating.

Basse-Ville

Aviatic Club 450 rue Gare du Palais ☎418/522-3555, www.aviatic.ca. Surprisingly good international cuisine from $20 including sushi, Thai and Tex-Mex in a historic train station with a large patio alongside.

Le Café du Monde 84 rue Dalhousie ☎418/692-4455, www.lecafedumonde.com. This large and sleek Parisian-style bistro may be in the cruise ship terminal, but it's a hit with locals for its brash atmosphere and fantastic terrace overlooking the river. And the food – mussels, veal sweetbreads, *confit de canard*, steak tartare and the like – is also quite good.

Le Délice du Roy 33 rue St-Pierre ☎418/694-9161. Around the corner from Place Royale, this place dishes up hearty if plain traditional Québécois food for between $10 and $20.

Initiale Le Restaurant 54 rue St-Pierre ☎418/694-1818, www.restaurantinitiale.com. One of Québec City's best restaurants (and priced accordingly – $49 for table d'hôte), this is a chic place that does a lighter take on fine French classics.

Le Lapin Sauté 52 rue du Petit-Champlain ☎418/692-5325, www.lapinsaute.com. Very popular, informal bistro specializing in rabbit – even the breakfast menu ($10) includes a rabbit dish. Dinner for $20–30.

Laurie Raphael 117 rue Dalhousie ☎418/692-4555, www.laurieraphael.com. Warm but formal atmosphere in a restaurant focusing on *cuisine du marché* (market cuisine). Specialities include fish, sweetbreads, Québec venison and lobster from the Îles-de-la-Madeleine. The three course Chef Menu starts at $23 for lunch and $60 for dinner.

Le Marie Clarisse 12 rue du Petit-Champlain ☎418/692-0857, www.marieclarisse.qc.ca. Fine fish and market-fresh seafood in a tiny stone-walled restaurant at the foot of the *escalier casse-cou*. A four-course meal goes for $40–45; advance booking advised. A good spot for people-watching.

Poisson d'Avril 115 quai St-André ☎418/692-1010, www.poissondavril.net. Seafood and grilled steaks at this friendly nautical-themed restaurant near the Vieux-Port.

Bars and nightlife

Nightlife in Québec City is far more relaxed than in Montréal: an evening spent in an intimate bar or a jazz or blues soiree is more popular than a big gig or disco, except among the younger set. Few major bands tour here, except during the Festival d'Été in July, when everyone lets their hair down. Québec City's main bar and nightclub strip is around rue St-Jean; the stretch outside the city walls in the Faubourg St-Jean-Baptiste has studenty bars and gay nightspots. Places on Grande-Allée tend to cater to tourists, but there are a few decent clubs at either end of the strip. For up-to-date **information** check the local media.

Bars and music venues

L'Amour Sorcier 789 Côte Ste-Geneviève ⓣ418/523-3395. Popular, intimate lesbian bar with cheap beers, soft music (which gets louder and more danceable later on) and a great roof terrace.

La Barberie 310 rue Saint-Roch ⓣ418/522-4373, ⓦwww.labarberie.com Inviting microbrewery in Saint-Roch with a small selection of standout ales. Great spot to relax with a few pints or, better still, the carousel – eight 11oz glasses or eight 5oz flutes that do well to convey why this brewery is revered across the province.

Le Drague 815 rue St-Augustin ⓣ418/649-7212, ⓦwww.ledrague.com. A gay bar, café and nightclub, with cheap imported beers. Sun night drag shows are great fun.

L'Inox Maîtres-Brasseurs 655 rue Grande Alle ⓣ418/692-2877, ⓦwww.inox.qc.ca. The city's original brewpub serves artisanal cheeses and European sausages, a nice match with the fine ales and terrace seating.

Jules et Jim 1060 av Cartier. A long-time local hangout, this is a small, quiet place amid all the restaurants on av Cartier.

Le Pape-Georges 8 rue Cul-de-Sac ⓣ418/692-1320, ⓦwww.papegeorges.com. Tiny cellar of a bar near Place Royale with acoustic acts and pavement terrace serving wines by the glass, cheeses and smoked meats. Popular with the locals.

Pub Java 1112 av Cartier ⓣ418/522-5282. Good selection of imported and draught beers and you can even come back for breakfast. The Irish pub *Salon Galway* upstairs has large armchairs by the fireplace.

Le Pub St-Alexandre 1087 rue St-Jean ⓣ418/694-0015, ⓦwww.pubstalexandre.com. More than two hundred beers and forty single malts in this yuppie English-style pub.

Sacrilège 447 rue St-Jean ⓣ418/649-1985 ⓦwww.lesacrilege.net. Friendly and cheap watering hole with a popular terrace in back. In the Faubourg St-Jean-Baptiste.

Bar Ste-Angèle 26 rue Ste-Angèle ⓣ418/692-2171. A dark and smoky neighbourhood bar with a beamed ceiling and cosy nook that hasn't noticed it's in the middle of tourist central. Open from 8pm.

Bar St-Laurent 1 rue des Carrières. The *Château Frontenac* address may be a bit stuffy and alcohol pricey at the polished octagonal bar, but you needn't dress up and the view from the terrace is stupendous.

Les Yeux Bleus 1117 rue St-Jean ⓣ418/694-9118. Despite the name, there's no blues at this *boîte à chansons* tucked down an alleyway. You can catch acoustic acts in the dark and smoky interior or hang out on the crowded and lively terrace.

Clubs

Casablanca 1169 rue St-Jean ⓣ418/692-4301. Weekend dance club playing reggae, African and Arabic beats hidden away down a passageway off rue St-Jean. Only gets going around 11pm (Fri & Sat only). No cover.

Dagobert 600 Grande-Allée est ⓣ418/522-0393, ⓦwww.dagobert.ca. This sprawling old house has been one of the city's most raucous nightspots for decades. Young dressed-up-for-it clubbers head upstairs for the large Eighties-ish dance floor. Downstairs a slightly older crowd sit at tiered tables to catch cover bands from 10.30pm. There's rarely a cover charge.

Kashmir 1018 rue St-Jean ⓣ418/694-1648. Loud and packed full some nights, dead others, depending on the DJ or the band playing. Very young crowd, usually.

Maurice 575 Grande-Allée est ⓣ418/647-2000, ⓦwww.mauricenightclub.com. Happening club with a rotating crew of DJs that attracts a stylish 20s to mid-30s crowd for R&B and house nights (Wed–Sun only in winter). Dress up to get by the selective door policy. The small cover includes the more laidback *Charlotte* upstairs, though on the funk and latino nights it can be just as hopping.

Le Sonar 1147 av Cartier ⓣ418/640-733. Swish basement club-lounge that grooves to R&B on Thurs and house on the weekend after the tapas plates have been cleared away. Mid-20s to mid-30s crowd.

Performing arts and cinema

Québec City is not renowned for its high culture, but from May to September there are dance, theatre and music events at various outdoor venues, and throughout the year performances can be caught at the city's theatres. The liveliest periods are in February and July, when the entire city is animated by its two principal **festivals**: the excellent Carnaval and the equally frenzied Festival d'Été (see p.274). **Tickets** for most events can be purchased through the Admission agency (ⓣ1-800/361-4595, ⓦwww.admission.com) and Réseau Billetech (ⓦwww.billetech.com). For **information** on the city's goings-on, check out the listings section in the French daily newspapers *Le Soleil* and *Journal de Québec* and the free weekly newspaper *Voir* (Ⓦwww.voir.ca). The quarterly bilingual magazine for tourists *Voilà Québec* also carries information, as does the English *Québec Chronicle Telegraph* (Ⓦwww.qctonline.com), published every Wednesday.

Québec City has a smattering of **theatres**, all producing plays in French only. The city's main theatre for the performing arts is the Grand Théâtre de Québec (Ⓣ418/643-8131, Ⓦwww.grandtheatre.qc.ca), 269 boul René-Lévesque est, which has a programme of drama, opera, dance shows and classical music. For small-scale dramatic productions, check out the Théâtre de la Bordée (Ⓣ418/694-9721, Ⓦwww.bordee.qc.ca), 315 rue St-Joseph est, while Théâtre Le Capitole (Ⓣ418/694-4444 or 1-800/261-9903, Ⓦwww.lecapitole.com), 972 rue St-Jean, hosts dinner theatre, cabaret and flashy musicals. Canada's oldest symphony **orchestra**, L'Orchestre Symphonique de Québec (Ⓦwww.osq.org), performs at the Grand Théâtre, as does the Opéra de Québec (Ⓦwww.operadequebec.qc.ca) and the chamber ensemble Les Violons du Roy (Ⓦwww.violonsduroy.com). Other **classical concerts** can be caught at the Bibliothèque Gabrielle-Roy, 350 rue St-Joseph est. Seventeenth- and eighteenth-century music is performed at the chapel in the Séminaire in summer. In summer, **open-air venues** are particularly popular in Québec. The largest is the Agora (Ⓦwww.agoraportdequebec.ca), in the Vieux-Port at 120 rue Dalhousie, a huge amphitheatre used for a range of productions. A summer-long programme of activities is also enacted on open stages in the Jardins de l'Hôtel de Ville; at the Parc de la Francophonie beside Grande-Allée, just beyond the Parliament Buildings; and in the Place D'Youville. In Place Royale and at the Kiosque Edwin-Bélanger bandstand on the Plains of Abraham, there are various free classical music concerts in the summer.

The city's repertory cinema, Cinéma le Clap (Ⓦwww.clap.qc.ca; bus; #7), is in Ste-Foy at no. 2360 chemin Ste-Foy, and has the odd English film – pick up their monthly programme at cafés and bookstores.

Listings

Banks and currency exchange American Express, Place Laurier, 2700 boul Laurier, Ste-Foy (Ⓣ418/658-8820); Banque Royale, 700 Place d'Youville and 140 Grande-Allée est. Caisse Populaire DesJardins du Vieux-Québec, 19 rue des Jardins (summer daily 9am–6pm; winter Mon–Fri 10am–3pm, Thurs until 6pm) has exchange facilities and a 24hr ATM in Vieux-Québec, as does Banque Nationale, 1199 rue St-Jean (summer: Mon–Fri 9am–8pm, Sat & Sun 9.30am–8pm (May, June, Sept & Oct daily until 6pm only); winter: Mon–Thurs 9am–5pm, Fri 9am–4.30pm).

Bike rental Cyclo Services (Ⓣ418/692-4052; Ⓦwww.cycloservices.net), Marché du Vieux-Port, 160 quai St-André, is next to the bike trail. The tourist offices (see p.274) provide an excellent map of the cycling routes in and around the city.

Bookshops The two main English bookshops are in the suburb of Ste-Foy: Librairie Smith, Place Laurier, 2700 boul Laurier; and La Maison Anglaise, Place de la Cité, 2600 boul Laurier. In Vieux-Québec there's a small, but decent selection at Pantoute, 1100 rue St-Jean, and a counter selling travel books inside the tourist office on Place d'Armes.

Car rental Avis, *Hôtel Hilton*, 900 boul René-Lévesque est Ⓣ418/523-1075 (airport 418/872-2861); Budget, 380 boul Wilfred-Hamel ouest Ⓣ418/687-4220 and 29 Côte du Palais 418/692-3660 (airport 418/872-9885); Discount, 12 rue Ste-Anne Ⓣ418/692-1244; Hertz, 44 Côte du Palais Ⓣ418/694-1224 and 580 Grande-Allée est Ⓣ418/647-4949 (airport 418/871-1571); Thrifty, near the airport at 6375 boul Wilfred-Hamel Ⓣ418/877-2870.

Consulate US, 2 Place Terrasse-Dufferin Ⓣ418/692-2095.

Gay and lesbian Gai Écoute and Gay Line (Ⓣ1-888/505-1010; in English 7–11pm only).

Laundry Lavoir la Lavandière, 625 rue St-Jean (Mon–Sat 8am–9pm, Sun 9am–6pm); Lavoir Ste-Ursule, 17B av Ste-Ursule (daily 8am–9pm).

Medical emergencies 24hr medical advice and referral service Ⓣ418/648-2626. Hôtel-Dieu Hospital, 11 Côte du Palais (Ⓣ418/691-5042), is in Vieux-Québec; Jeffrey Hale Hospital, 1250 chemin

Ste-Foy (ⓣ418/683-4471), is better for English-speakers.

Post office 59 rue Dalhousie and 5 rue du Fort. All are open Mon–Fri 8am–5.30pm and have a free internet station (max 15min).

Taxis Taxi Coop ⓣ418/525-5191; Taxi Québec ⓣ418/525-8123.

Weather and road conditions Environment Canada (ⓣ418/648-7766, ⓦwww.weatheroffice.ec.gc.ca) for recorded weather forecast; Transports Québec (ⓣ1-888/355-0511, ⓦwww.mtq.gouv.qc.ca) for road construction and winter road conditions. Skiers can check snow conditions at ⓦwww.quebecskisurf.com.

Around Québec City

Options for day-trips on the fringes of the city include **Wendake**, to see Canada's only surviving Huron community, and **Lévis**, on the opposite shore of the St Lawrence River, less inundated by visitors than Québec City and with great views of its more illustrious neighbour. Also in easy striking distance of the city is tranquil, charming **Île d'Orléans** where the agricultural landscape is dotted with gîtes and auberges. Slightly further afield the tiny island of **Grosse Ile** has served as a secretive quarantine station for more than a century and is now a National Historic Site. Both the islands are just offshore of the **Côte-de-Beaupré** further to the northeast, which, though something of a city annexe, boasts the spectacular waterfalls of **Chute Montmorency** and the **Canyon Ste-Anne**. For those in

Winter sports around Québec City

You'll find good opportunities for everything from **cross-country skiing** to **ice-climbing** around Québec City, but most popular are the **skiing** and **snowboarding** at three resorts – Stoneham, Mont-Sainte-Anne and Le Massif. Some experts in search of big bowls and deep powder might find the terrain limited, but for most, the fine mogul fields, tricky glades, well thought-out terrain parks and extensive night-skiing more than compensate.

The ski resorts

Only 6km beyond the city limits off Rte 73 is **Stoneham** (late Nov to early April Mon–Fri 9am–10pm, Sat 8.30am–10pm, Sun 8.30am–9pm; ⓣ418/848-2411 or 1-800/463-6888, ⓦwww.ski-stoneham.com; day pass $51), which has limited expert terrain, but is set in a wind-protected horseshoe valley. Despite a minimal vertical drop of 421m and a modest 322 acres of terrain, it has been sculpted into an impressive ski area, thanks partly to its night-skiing operation, which keeps around two-thirds of the resort open after dark; the après ski can get wild.

The largest of Québec City's major ski areas is **Mont-Sainte-Anne** (mid-Nov to early May Mon 9am–4pm, Tues–Fri 9am–10pm, Sat 8.30am–10pm, Sun 8.30am–4pm; ⓣ418/827-4561 or 1-888/827-4579, ⓦwww.mont-sainte-anne.com; day pass $62), 40km away via Rte 440, which becomes Rte 138, northeast of town. It offers a well-balanced mix of terrain and comprehensive facilities. Centred on a single peak and covering 428 acres, it's easily navigable yet still provides a remarkably varied high-density trail system. The presence of novice runs extending from summit to base on both sides of the mountain is handy, while first-timers benefit from free access to bunny slopes adjoining the base area. The resort's greatest strength is its wealth of intermediate-level runs that make up almost half the ski zone. Most start from the resort's rapid gondola and follow a smooth and steep grade back to the minimal lift queues. Those hunting for steeper slopes, moguls, trees and high-speed carving should make for a cluster of black diamonds on the south side.

search of a longer jaunt into the great outdoors, the **Réserve Faunique des Laurentides** is within easy reach and there are a number of **ski hills** in the area.

Quebec City **buses** and bicycle paths run to Chute Montmorency and Wendake, a quick **ferry** trip lands you in Lévis and Intercar buses go daily to **Ste-Anne-de-Beaupré**.

Wendake

Just to the northwest of Québec City lies **WENDAKE**, the only **Huron reserve** in Canada. Its name derives from the Hurons' own name for their people – *Wendat*, meaning "people of the island". In 1650, French Jesuit missionaries led three hundred Huron from Ontario's Georgian Bay to the shores of the St Lawrence around today's Vieux-Québec, thereby saving the smallpox-weakened population from extermination at the hands of the Iroquois. As more French settlers arrived, the Hurons were successively relocated, ending up here beside the St-Charles River in 1697. Today, the central village core of the reserve retains typical Québécois wooden houses with sloping and gabled roofs, but is rather dilapidated – the main activities for visitors are at Onhoüa Chetek8e (see p.298), though there is also a pretty waterfall.

Arrival and information

In nice weather, the best way to get here is by bike – a 25km round-trip along the bike path (La Route Vert 6) from the Vieux-Port; all the climbing is on the way

The third main mountain in the area is **Le Massif** (early Dec to early April opening hours vary throughout the season but are at least 9am–3pm, longer at weekends; ⓣ418/632-5876 or 1-877/536-2774, ⓦwww.lemassif.com; day pass $61), 73km along Hwy 138 from Québec City. It has some of the most spectacular views of any resort in the world, and despite the presence of a couple of narrow, tricky and busy beginner runs, it's best at providing wonderful intermediate-level carving slopes. The mountain's grooming regime puts several black diamond runs within the capacity of intermediates – but watch out for the terrifying triple-diamond La Charlevoix.

Other sports

Tubing, ice-skating and an indoor climbing wall are available at Stoneham, while Mont-Sainte-Anne offers ice-skating, snowshoeing, dog-sledding, paragliding, sleigh riding and snowmobiling. The **Mont-Sainte-Anne Nordic Center** (mid-Dec to mid-April), 7km east of the main ski area, is a splendid local resource and the largest of its kind in Canada, boasting over 223km of trails. Day tickets cost $21, rentals another $21. For more of a wilderness experience cross-country skiers should also explore the rolling hills around Camp Mercier (see p.304). On the fringes of Québec City at Montmorency Falls (see p.301), is the world's largest **ice-climbing** school, L'Ascensation Ecole d'escalade (ⓣ1-800/762-4967, ⓦwww.rocgyms.com; rates vary).

Practicalities

Mont-Sainte-Anne and Stoneham have on-site **accommodation**, but more convenient are Québec City's hotels (see p.275), which are linked to all the resorts via a **ski shuttle**, the Hiver Express (ⓣ418/525-5191, ⓦwww.taxicoop-quebec.com; round-trips $25). Services run from sixteen downtown hotels and the tourist information office to both Stoneham and Mont-Sainte-Anne. Le Massif runs a complimentary shuttle that links with the Hiver Express, which departs from Mont-Sainte-Anne's shuttle parking area. All three resorts **rent** equipment (skis $25/day, snowboards $35/day). There's a better selection of higher end gear and lower prices in the stores along the hwy in Beaupré.

there, making the journey back to town an easy cycle. The STCUQ #801 bus runs from Place D'Youville to its terminus at Charlesbourg, from where the #72 goes to Wendake; get a transfer (*une correspondance*) and the 45-minute or so journey will set you back $2.75.

The Reserve and around

The bus arrives at the 1730 church of **Notre Dame-de-Lorette** on boul Bastien. This is Canada's only Huron church, and you'll find snowshoes on the altar and a small museum displaying old manuscripts and religious objects. To get into the church, you must first visit the **Maison Aroüanne** (late June to late Aug daily 10am–5pm; free) opposite, an early wooden house displaying a collection of Huron cultural objects, including ceremonial attire beaded with pearls and porcupine quills, drums of moose hide and feathered headdresses used for festive occasions. The waters of the **Chute Kabir Kouba** tumble into a 42m-deep canyon visible from the bridge just west of the church. For a closer look, take the path, which starts at the end of the car park directly opposite the church and leads to the slippery rocks below.

From Maison Aroüanne head along boul Valcartier and past the bike path Vert 6 (there's parking here) to follow signs to **Onhoüa Chetek8e** (May–Oct daily 8.30am–5pm, rest of the year call to arrange; $10; ⓣ418/842-4308, ⓦwww.huron-wendat.qc.ca), 575 rue Stanislas Kosca, a thirty-minute walk north. This replica of a seventeenth-century Huron village consists of wooden long houses, with Hurons in traditional garb and delicious native foods such as bison, caribou, trout and sunflower soup at the *Nek8arre* restaurant (May–Oct noon–3pm). You're greeted by a traditional welcome dance; participatory activities such as shooting arrows cost extra. The few souvenirs – mini totem poles, suede bags, moccasins and the like – in the shop not made by Huron artisans come from other First Nations reserves.

Lévis

LÉVIS is an attractive Victorian town, but the views of Québec make a visit here the real treat. The regular ferry leaves day and night (until 2am) from near Québec City's Place Royale, and costs $2.75 (ⓣ418/643-2019, ⓦwww.traversiers.gouv.qc.ca) for the fifteen-minute crossing – double that if you go back (whether or not you disembark). Most tourists stay on the ferry for the return trip, but those willing to scale the staircase (five-minutes' walk, to the right as you exit the ferry terminal) to the **Terrasse** on the heights of Lévis are rewarded with an even greater panorama; the vantage point is also accessible via the half-hour bus tour ($1) available at the tourist office in the Lévis terminal.

The Terrasse and its landscaped park lie at the northwestern end of the old quarter, **Vieux-Lévis**, whose main drag, avenue Bégin, has a small-town feel with low-rise modernized buildings. For a quick pastry, sandwich or salad, stop at the café and fine-foods grocery, *Aux P'tits Oignons*, 45 av Bégin, or at *Les Chocolate Favorits* at no. 32, which sells great home-made chocolates and ice cream. The streets between here and the river are wider than those in Québec City, lined with large single-family homes. The **Maison Alphonse-Desjardins** (Mon–Fri 10am–noon & 1–4.30pm, Sat & Sun noon–5pm; ⓣ418/835-2090, ⓦwww.desjardins.com/maisonalphonsedesjardins; free), 6 rue du Mont-Marie, is a particular delight with its cake-frosting-like facade facing onto a leafy park whose centrepiece is a statue of Father Joseph David Déziel, founder of Lévis. Inside, a permanent exhibition explains the evolution of the *caisse populaire* (cooperative credit union) in Québec, and the early twentieth-century interior furnishings convey the family lifestyle of the period. From here you can walk east a couple of blocks to rue St-Jean, where a second staircase leads back to the ferry terminal.

Île d'Orléans

From just northeast of Québec City to a short distance beyond Ste-Anne-de-Beaupré, the St Lawrence River is bottlenecked by the **ÎLE D'ORLÉANS**, a fertile islet whose bucolic atmosphere and handy location have made it a popular spot for holiday-making Québécois. More than most places on the mainland, Île d'Orléans, with its old stone churches, little cottages and seigneurial manors, has kept a flavour of eighteenth-century French Canada. This is largely because it was cut off from the mainland until 1935, when a suspension bridge was constructed from Hwy 440, about 10km out of the city, connecting it to the west end of the island.

Tourism and agriculture are the mainstays for the population of seven thousand: roadside stalls heave under the weight of fresh fruit and vegetables, jams, dairy products, home-made bread and maple syrup, and the island's restaurants and B&Bs are some of the best in the province.

Arrival and information

The island's **information office** (mid-June to early Sept Sun–Thurs 8.30am–7.30pm, Fri & Sat to 8pm; April to mid-June & early Sept–Oct daily 9am–5pm; rest of the year Mon–Fri 9am–5pm Sat & Sun 11am–3pm; ⓣ418/828-9411, ⓦwww.quebecweb.com/tourismeiledorleans), at 490 côte du Pont, is on the right at the top of the hill after the bridge from the mainland. It provides comprehensive details on the island's B&Bs and has self-guided driving tours (English available) for $10.

Accommodation

Budget travellers wanting to stay on the island should head straight for St-Jean's *Auberge Le P'tit Bonheur* (ⓣ418/829-2588, ⓦwww.leptitbonheur.qc.ca), at 183–186 Côte Lafleur, a **hostel** in an old stone manor with dorm beds ($23), private rooms (③), teepees ($35) and bike and cross-country ski rental.

▲ Ste-Pétronille, Île d'Orléans

Elsewhere, the selection of good **B&Bs** is bewildering; one of the standouts is *Le Vieux Presbytère* (ⓣ418/828-9723 or 1-888/828-9723, ⓦwww.presbytere.com; ④), at 1247 av Monseigneur D'esgly in St-Pierre, a charming inn with low ceilings, beams and antiques in an old presbytery just behind the village church. It has terrific river views and rents bicycles ($6/hr, $25/day). To **camp** head to the lovely and convenient *Camping Orléans* (ⓣ418/829-2953, ⓦwww.campingorleans.com; $39 unserviced, $47 hookup; mid-May to early Oct), at 357 chemin Royal in St-François near the village jetty, which has a small on-site pool.

Around the island

Encircling the island, Hwy 368 – called the chemin Royal for most of its length – dips and climbs over gentle slopes and terraces past acres of neat farmland and orchards, passing through the six villages with their churches evenly spaced around the island's periphery. A counter-clockwise tour of the island (turn right on chemin Royal from the hwy) and its villages are described below.

The first village you come to is **STE-PÉTRONILLE**, the island's oldest and most beautifully situated settlement and a district still characterized by the grand homes of the merchants who made their fortunes trading farm produce with Québec City. Wolfe observed the city from this spot before his bombardment. The white **Maison Gourdeau-de-Beaulieu** at no. 137 chemin Royal was the island's first permanent dwelling, built in 1648 and still the private residence of the Beaulieu family. Some of the best views can be had from rue Horatio Walker, named after the landscape painter who had his home and studio here. Known unofficially as the grand seigneur of Ste-Pétronille, **Horatio Walker** lived here from 1904 until his death in 1938. He despised his English heritage, continually emphasizing a French branch in his ancestry and refusing to speak English. His subject matter was almost entirely based on the Île d'Orléans and many of his paintings now grace Canada's larger galleries.

Until the 1950s the south shore of the island was the domain of sailors and navigators, with the village of **ST-LAURENT** being the island's supplier of *chaloupes*, the long rowing boats that were the islanders' only means of getting to the mainland before the bridge was built. At the **Parc maritime de St-Laurent interpretation centre** (mid-June to early Sept daily 10am–5pm; ⓣ418/828-9672; ⓦwww.parcmaritime.ca; $3), 120 chemin de la Chalouperie, you can get details of attractions like **La Forge à Pique-Assaut** (June to mid-Oct daily 9am–5pm; rest of year Mon–Fri 9am–noon & 1.30–5pm; ⓣ418/828-9300, ⓦwww.forge-pique-assaut.com; free), 2200 chemin Royale, which features a blacksmith's shop and an eighteenth-century bellows and sells forged metal crafts.

Further east is **ST-JEAN**, the island's prettiest village, which was similarly nautical; the cemetery of its red-roofed local church contains gravestones of numerous mariners. St-Jean's museum of antique furniture and domestic objects, is housed in the stately 1734 **Manoir Mauvide-Genest** (ⓣ418/829-2630, ⓦwww.manoirmauvidegenest.com; $8), at 1451 chemin Royal. At this one-time home of Louis XV's surgeon, the metre-thick walls withstood the impact from Wolfe's bombardment – you can still see dents in the wall.

From St-Jean, the road continues to the island's easterly tip and the village of **ST-FRANÇOIS**, where a precarious observation tower offers a view of both shores of the river. The village church was rebuilt in the early 1990s after a suicidal driver wrecked the 1734 church; the wall in front was added to avoid a repeat.

Among the French-Regime stone buildings in **STE-FAMILLE**, the **Maison Canac-Marquis**, 4466 chemin Royal, is a particularly fine example, but only the 1675 **Maison Drouin** (mid-June to mid-Aug daily 10am–6pm; mid-Aug to late Sept 1–5pm daily; ⓣ418/829-0330, ⓦwww.fondationfrancoislamy.org; $2), at no. 4700, with its exhibits on the architecture of these early houses, is open to the public. The richly decorated **church**, built in 1743, includes a painting of the Holy Family by Québec's foremost early painter, Frère Luc.

ST-PIERRE, to the west of Ste-Famille, is notable for its **church**, the oldest in rural Québec; constructed in 1718, it has pews with special hot-brick holders for keeping bottoms warm on seats. The town is the largest on the island, but is best known as the long-time home and final resting place of Félix Leclerc, the poet and singer–songwriter who penned "P'tit Bonheur" and the first musician to bring Québécois music international acclaim. The **Espace Félix-Leclerc** (mid-Feb to mid-Dec Tues–Sun 9am–6pm; ⓣ418/828-1682, ⓦwww.felixleclerc.com; $3), at 682 chemin Royal, covers a site that pays homage to Leclerc's life and work, and has several hiking trails and picnic tables.

Eating and drinking

Particularly good bets for **food** in Ste-Pétronille include *La Goéliche* (ⓣ418/828-2248, ⓦwww.goeliche.ca), at 22 chemin du Quai, which serves dishes such as filet mignon and rack of lamb, and *Le Bistro de bout de Lîlle*, at 148 du Bout de l'Île opposite rue Horatio Walker, which serves salads, pizza and *croque monsieur*. In St-Laurent, *Canard Huppé* (ⓣ418/828-2292, ⓦwww.canard-huppe.com), at 2198 chemin Royal, is a gourmand's treat, serving local duck and trout, while *Chez Bacchus* (ⓣ418/828-1388), at 1236 chemin Royal, is a more informal spot for pizza, grilled meat and drinks. *Le Vieux Presbytère* (see p.300) in St-Pierre also has a good restaurant serving game dishes. In Ste-Famille the local *boulangerie*, G.H. Blouin, at 3967 chemin Royal, is one of the island's oldest and best, with irresistible bread and pastries. Down the road at no. 3887, the convivial *Pub Le Mitan* (ⓦwww.microorleans.com) microbrewery has a terrace overlooking the river from which you can enjoy a variety of home-made ales.

Côte-de-Beaupré

The **Côte-de-Beaupré** stretches along the St Lawrence River past the **Basilique de Ste-Anne-de-Beaupré**, 40km northeast of Québec City, as far as the migratory bird sanctuary on Cap Tourmente, where you can see the greater snow goose in spring and autumn. There are two roads along the coast: the speedy Autoroute Dufferin-Montmorency (Hwy 440, then Hwy 138) and the slower Avenue Royale (Hwy 360), which local buses serve. The latter hwy gives a far better introduction to the province's rural life, passing through little villages with ancient farmhouses and churches lining the way. Beyond Ste-Anne-de-Beaupré, Hwy 360 leads to one of the best ski resorts in the province – **Mont-Sainte-Anne** (see p.313), which has everything from golf to world-championship mountain biking in summer.

Chute Montmorency

Some 9km northeast of Québec City the waters of the Montmorency River cascade 83m down from the Laurentians into the St Lawrence River, which makes the **Chute Montmorency** one and a half times the height of Niagara, though the volume of water is considerably less; tourists, however, flock here in numbers. The falls, named by Champlain in honour of the governor of New France, were the site of Wolfe's first attempted attack on the colony, but Montcalm's superior forces repelled Wolfe and his men. In those days – before a hydroelectric dam cut off much of the flow – the falls were far more impressive, but the cascade remains an awesome spectacle, especially in winter, when the water and spray become a gigantic cone of ice, known locally as the "sugar loaf". From the main car park (mid-April to late Oct $11.50, otherwise free) a **cable car** (late Jan to early April Sat & Sun 9am–4pm; mid-April to early June & late Aug to mid-Oct daily 8.30am–6.45pm; mid-June to late Aug until 7.30pm; closed Nov–Jan; $9.50 return) runs to the **interpretation centre** (daily 9am–8pm; June–Aug until 10pm; ⓣ418/663-3330, ⓦwww.sepaq.com/chutemontmorency; free), in the Manoir Montmorency, which also has a bar and restaurant with a terrace. You can also walk up to the centre, but this involves 487 steps. From the centre, a cliffside walkway leads to the bridge over the falls (wooded trails follow the river upstream) and onto the zigzag path down the other side. Local STCUQ bus #53 stops at the bottom of the falls, #50 at the top; both buses leave from Place Jacques-Cartier in Québec and take around fifty minutes, each costing $3.25. You can also cycle here – it's a 25km round-trip from the Vieux-Port and the path passes the **Domaine Maizerets** park, good for a pleasant break.

Ste-Anne-de-Beaupré

Pretty much the only reason to stop in **STE-ANNE-DE-BEAUPRÉ** is to see Québec's equivalent of Lourdes – the **Basilique de Ste-Anne-de-Beaupré**. About 39km northeast of Québec City (25min by Intercar coach from Gare Centrale; 3 daily; $6), it dominates the immediate area, its twin spires soaring above the St Lawrence shore. The church began in 1658 as a small wooden chapel devoted to St Anne (the Virgin Mary's mother). During its construction a crippled peasant was allegedly cured but the legend of St Anne's intercession didn't really get going until some Breton sailors were caught in a storm on the St Lawrence River in 1661 and vowed to build a chapel to St Anne if she saved them. The ship capsized at nearby Cap Tourmente but the sailors survived. Word of this miracle spread, and from then on everyone caught in the river's frequent storms prayed to St Anne. In 1876, the same year St Anne was declared patron saint of Québec, the church was distinguished as a basilica, to which the devout came on their knees from the beach or walked shoeless from Québec City; today, one and a half million pilgrims flock to the site every year in comfortable coaches.

The basilica and around

The neo-Romanesque granite cathedral with lofty symmetrical spires is the fifth church to stand here, fires and floods having destroyed the first four. The statue of St Anne between the steeples miraculously survived the 1922 destruction of the fourth church, even though the roof and both steeples fell in the blaze. The basilica seats 1500, though on St Anne's feast day (July 26) up to five thousand crowd in. Most of its decoration – countless stained-glass windows and massive murals – depict the miraculous powers of St Anne, though the wooden pews bear delightful animal carvings. Behind the ornate golden statue of St Anne, depicted holding her daughter Mary, is a chapel said to contain a portion of Anne's forearm, donated by the pope in 1960. Those who have been cured by her intervention have left a vast collection of crutches and wooden limbs hanging on the basilica's pillars near the entrance. The **information centre** in front of the basilica (daily 8.30am–4.30pm; ⓦwww.ssadb.qc.ca) runs free guided tours daily at 1pm from the basilica entrance. The hours of the basilica itself vary, but it is open 8am–4.30pm at a minimum, and 6am–10pm at the height of the midsummer pilgrimage.

Several little chapels are hidden in the basilica's shadow. The simple **Chapelle Souvenir** (early May to mid-Sept daily 8am–7pm), across the street behind the basilica, contains some of the stones from the second chapel and was built in the nineteenth century on the foundations of the transept of the third church (1676–1877), hence its north–south orientation. Nearby, the small white chapel of the **Scala Santa** (same hours) contains stairs that replicate those climbed by Christ on his meeting with Pontius Pilate. Glass boxes, embedded in each stair, contain lumps of earth from various holy places, and the devout accomplish the ascent on their knees. Another obligatory part of the penitential route is the nearby **Way of the Cross**, which curves steeply up the hillside. There are two daytime processions, and on some summer evenings torchlit processions wend their way through each station. Less athletic visitors can pay their respects to the basilica's collection of *ex votos* and treasures in the **Musée de Ste-Anne** (June to early Sept daily 9am–5pm; $2), which contains displays on the early churches and some of the surviving furnishings.

Practicalities

There's a glut of inexpensive **motels** sprawling along Rte 138 in Ste-Anne-de-Beaupré, with prices and standards fairly uniform between them. There are several pleasant **B&Bs** as well, including *Auberge Baker,* 8790 av Royale (Ⓣ418/824-4478 or 1-866/824-4478, Ⓦwww.auberge-baker.qc.ca; ❹), a wonderfully atmospheric B&B occupying a 150-year-old farmhouse set well back from the busy Rte 138. Rooms have rough-hewn beams and gloriously mismatched antique furnishings; guests have use of a communal kitchen.

The **restaurant** at the *Auberge La Camarine,* 10947 boul Ste-Anne, is the best in the area, serving an eclectic variety of French, Italian and Asian dishes, often fused and off a frequently changing menu. The food is of the highest standard but it doesn't come cheaply – mains start at around $40.

Mont-Sainte-Anne and around

Just up the hwy from Ste-Anne-de-Beaupre is the town of Beaupré, which gives access to **MONT-SAINTE-ANNE** (see p.313). The ski resort has successfully marketed itself as an off-season destination and is now the longest-standing venue on the **mountain bike** world-cup circuit. In summer you can explore the extensive cross-country mountain bike trails ($10.63), either staying around the base area to test your trials skills on the North-Shore-style wooden obstacles, or using the gondola ($16.75 round-trip) to explore one of the hardest downhill mountain bike courses in the world (there are easier routes down the mountain). Bikes can be rented at the base area with front-suspension models going for $35 for four hours; full-suspension for $75.

Hikers wanting to enjoy the remarkable views over the St Lawrence River and Québec City, as well as try out the several marked trails, can also take the gondola up the mountain. Yet one of the best hiking trails leaves out of the car park at the base area – head down the hill and over the bridge – to the **Chutes Jean-Larouse**, a twenty-minute walk. The trail leads to a series of dramatic waterfalls, though the latticework stairway that's been constructed alongside is just as dizzying and almost more impressive. The resort has a pleasantly wooded **campsite** (Ⓣ418/827-5281 or 1-800/463-1568, Ⓦwww.mont-sainte-anne.com; sites from $25).

For even grander waterfalls head some 6km further east along Hwy 138 to **Canyon Ste-Anne** (May to late June & early Sept to Oct daily 9am–4.30pm; late June to early Sept daily 9am–5.30pm; $11; Ⓦwww.canyonste-anne.qc.ca) about a thirty-minute drive from Québec City. Here, the river has carved a gorge where the water tumbles 74m, flanked by a chasm fringed with woodlands and short nature trails. A bridge crosses just before the precipice, giving views down the canyon, while in front of the falls a suspension bridge allows for splendid and terrifying views. With your own transport you can head 2km from the canyon towards the coast via Saint-Joachim to the **Cap-Tourmente National Wildlife Area** (mid-April to early Nov daily 8.30am–5pm, Jan–March weekends only 8.30am–4pm; Ⓦwww.sentiersquebec.com; $6). It's a favourite with snow geese, who stop to gather strength on its sandbars during their spring and autumn migrations. Another 250 species of bird also inhabit the park and naturalists are on hand to answer questions.

Réserve Faunique des Laurentides

The zone of the Laurentians 40km to the north of Québec City – via hwys 73 and 175 – is considerably wilder than the mountains near Montréal, thanks to the creation of the **Réserve Faunique des Laurentides**. The vast wooded terrain, with summits of more than 1000m towards the east, was once a hunting ground of the Montagnais, until the Hurons, armed by the French, drove the small population further north. The wildlife reserve became a protected area in 1895 to conserve the caribou herds, an intervention that was not a great success – very few exist today. Although it allows controlled moose-hunting, the reserve's main function is still to preserve native animals such as the beaver, moose, lynx, black bear and deer, all of which you may see in remote areas. Intercar (Ⓣ418/525-3000 or 1-888/861-4592) runs a **bus** service through the reserve from Québec City's bus station to Alma (3 daily; 2hr 45min) and Chicoutimi (4–5 daily; 2hr 30min).

The reserve's main entry point is at its southern end, along Hwy 175. At km 94, 9km north of the entrance, the Camp Mercier registration centre (daily 8.30am–4pm; Ⓣ418/848-2422 or 1-800/665-6527, Ⓦwww.sepaq.com) gives out **information**, including trail maps. The heavy snowfall makes the park an excellent place for cross-country skiing on a 120km network ($10.85/day). Hwy 175 traverses the reserve; halfway through is **L'Étape**, the only spot to fill your tank (or yourself) until just before Chicoutimi or Alma. Nearby there's **camping** beside Lac Jacques-Cartier at the rustic *La Loutre* campsite (late May to early Sept; Ⓣ418/846-2201; $26), and chalets available.

Parc national de la Jacques-Cartier

The southernmost sector of the reserve is set off as the **Parc national de la Jacques-Cartier** (Ⓦwww.sepaq.com; $3.50). A visitor centre (mid-May to late Oct), 10km west of Hwy 175, serves as the gateway to the Jacques-Cartier river valley, enclosed by 550m-high forested slopes. The park is ideal for canoeing, although the river runs beside a road for part of the way, detracting from the wilderness experience. You can rent canoes, kayaks, inflatable rafts and bicycles at the visitor centre, where you can also reserve a **campsite**. Pitches are available from $23.75, both near the visitor centre and in more peaceful spots further into the park.

Northern Québec

Northern Québec stretches out as two separate entities on either side of the St Lawrence River. The southern shore is the less remote, with the agricultural **Bas-Saint-Laurent** (Lower St Lawrence) the gateway to the rugged and lightly populated **Gaspé Peninsula**. East of here, stuck out in the middle of the Gulf of St Lawrence, are the majestic, treeless landscapes of the **Îles-de-la-Madeleine**, most easily reached by ferry from Prince Edward Island. The islands' fine shores

Tourist information in northern Québec

The areas to the north of Québec City and the offshore islands are divided into the following regional tourist associations, each providing an excellent free guide (including basic maps) of the region. All the main offices in each region will usually have guides for other regions. For general information contact Tourisme Québec (☎514/873-2015 or 1-877/266-5687, Ⓦwww.bonjourquebec.com).

Bas-Saint-Laurent ☎418/867-3015 or 1-800/563-5268, Ⓦwww.tourismebas-st-laurent.com.

Charlevoix ☎418/665-4454 or 1-800/667-2276, Ⓦwww.charlevoixtourism.com.

Côte-Nord ☎ 418/962-0808 or 1-888/463-0808, Ⓦwww.tourismeduplessis.com.

Manicouagan ☎418/294-2876 or 1-888/463-5319, Ⓦwww.tourismemanicouagan.com.

Gaspésie ☎418/775-2223 or 1-800/463-0323, Ⓦwww.tourisme-gaspesie.com.

Îles-de-la-Madeleine ☎418/986-2245 or 1-877/624-4437, Ⓦwww.tourismeilesdelamadeleine.com.

Saguenay–Lac-Saint-Jean ☎418/543-3536 or 1-877/253-8387, Ⓦwww.saguenaylacsaintjean.ca.

and strikingly eroded sandstone cliffs will appeal particularly to cyclists, walkers and solitude-seeking beach-goers.

The north shore of the St Lawrence covers an area that changes from trim farmland to a vast forest bordering the barren seashore. Further north, communities take on an isolated feel and the dominant role of nature in day-to-day life becomes more conspicuous. Immediately northeast of Québec City is the beautiful **Charlevoix** region, all peaceful villages and towns that bear the marks of Québec's rural beginnings. Often the winding hwys and back roads pass through a virtually continuous village, where the only interruptions in the chain of low-slung houses are the tin-roofed churches. The beguiling hills and valleys give way to dramatic ravaged rock just beyond the Charlevoix borders, where the **Saguenay River** crashes into the immense fjord that opens into the St Lawrence at the resort of **Tadoussac**, a popular spot for whale-watching and hiking. Inland, **Lac Saint-Jean** – source of the Saguenay River – is an oasis of fertile land in a predominantly rocky region, and its peripheral villages offer glimpses of native as well as Québécois life. Adventurous types following the St Lawrence can head beyond Tadoussac along the **Côte-Nord** through a sparsely populated region of spectacular empty beaches and dramatic rockscapes where the original livelihoods of fishing and lumber have largely given way to ambitious mining and hydroelectric projects. In the far northeast the supply ship *Nordik Express* serves the **Île d'Anticosti** and the roadless lower north shore as far as the Labrador border – the ultimate journey within Québec. The remoteness of the Île d'Anticosti and the sculptured terrain of the **Mingan archipelago** – a national park well served by boats from Havre-St-Pierre – is matched by the isolation of the fishing communities along the **Basse Côte-Nord**, where no roads penetrate and visits are possible only by supply ship, plane or snowmobile.

Bas-Saint-Laurent (Lower St Lawrence)

Heading east from Québec City along the southern shore of the **St Lawrence**, the most scenic route is Hwy 132, which sticks close to the shoreline showcasing the highlights of a region of fertile lands with farming and forestry covering gently rolling hills. The landscape is agricultural and dominated by long, narrow

The seigneurial system

In the seventeenth century the agricultural settlement of New France was conceived as an extension of European-style feudalism with the granting of **seigneuries** to religious orders, noblemen, merchants and, in a break from tradition, others of humble birth. The average seigneury covered around fifty square kilometres, part of it owned by the seigneurs, the rest rented by **habitants**, who were secure in their tenancy (they could sell the land or pass it on to their children) provided they met certain obligations. They had to pay a yearly tithe for the upkeep of the parish church, pay rent in kind (usually grain, as the seigneurs had a monopoly on milling), work on the roads and make themselves available for the militia.

In the early days the waterways provided the easiest form of transportation and so each *habitant's* farm had a river frontage of around a couple of hundred metres in length, with the rest of his land extending back in a narrow strip. One result of this was that *habitants* lived near their neighbours and, content with this decentralized way of life, long resisted the development of nuclear settlements. You can still see these ribbon farms and villages along the St Lawrence today. Legislation that passed land-ownership rights to the *habitants* ended the seigneurial system in 1854.

fields that are remnants of the old seigneurial system (see above. The stops worth making on the 180-kilometre trip to Rivière-Du-Loup are the woodcarving centre of **St-Jean-Port-Joli**, the seigneurial **St-Roch-des-Aulnaies** and the architecturally quaint **Kamouraska**.

St-Jean-Port-Joli

The first settlement of any note along Hwy 132, some 80km east of Lévis, is **ST-JEAN-PORT-JOLI**, where the long main street accommodates the galleries of the region's most popular **woodcarvers.** A traditional Québécois folk art, woodcarving flourished in the eighteenth and nineteenth centuries, but had almost expired by the 1930s, when the three Bourgault brothers (Médard, Jean-Julien and André) established their workshop here. Initially, religious statuary was their main source of income, but their folksy style and Francophile themes were adopted and popularized by the nationalists in the 1960s.

Along the main road, on the west side of the village, the **Musée des Anciens Canadiens** (daily May–June 9am–5.30pm, July–Aug 8.30am–9pm, Sept–Oct 8.30am–6pm; ⓣ418/598-3392, ⓦwww.museedesancienscanadiens.com; $5), at 332 av de Gaspé ouest, has an interesting collection of woodcarvings cut in white pine and walnut, many of which are the work of the Bourgaults. The most impressive piece is the giant *Les Patriotes*, a tribute to the Québécois rebels of 1837 who, under the leadership of Louis-Joseph Papineau, tried to drive out the British (see p.253). A few doors down, at no. 322, the **Maison Médard-Bourgault** (mid-June to early Sept daily 10am–6pm; ⓣ418/598-3880; $4) concentrates on the life and work of Médard Bourgault. He was the most talented of the brothers – he even carved the walls and furniture. The delicate and ornate interior of the village church, **Église St-Jean Baptiste** at no. 2, celebrates the work of an earlier generation of Québécois woodcarvers from the 1770s, the Baillairgé brothers. Any of the dozen or so galleries along the main road sell woodcarvings; the shop adjoining the museum is one of the best.

Practicalities

There are some pleasant **B&Bs**, of which *La Maison de L'Ermitage* (ⓣ418/598-7553, ⓦwww.maisonermitage.com; ❸), at 56 rue de l'Ermitage, has a lovely, turreted, red-and-white roof – if you're feeling particularly flush you can stay in one of the turrets (④). Numerous **motels** line Hwy 132, but one of the cheapest options is the De La Demi-Lieue **campsite** (ⓣ418/598-6108 or 1-800/463-9558, ⓦwww.campingunion; $24.89–33.89; May to late Sept), on the grounds of a former seigneury farther down the road at no. 589 Hwy 132 est.

The town has a few decent places to **eat**, including the inexpensive *La Boustifaille* (ⓣ418/598-3061, ⓦwww.rocheaveillon.com), at 547 av de Gaspé ouest, for gigantic portions of Québécois food for around $15, or the pricier *Café la Coureuse des Greves* (ⓣ418/598-9111), at no. 300 Hwy 204, where good breakfasts are served on the outdoor terrace. For high-end regional dining with views of the river, try the *Auberge du Faubourg* (ⓣ418/598-6455, ⓦwww.aubergedufaubourg.com; late April to Oct; ④), at 280 Hwy 132 ouest.

St-Roch-des-Aulnaies

About 14km east of St-Jean-Port-Joli is the village of **ST-ROCH-DES-AULNAIES**, where a gorgeous water mill and manor house have survived on a nineteenth-century seigneurial estate, formerly the home of a rich merchant. **La Seigneurie des Aulnaies** (late June to early Sept daily 9am–6pm; early June & Sept weekends only 10am–4pm; ⓣ418/354-2800, ⓦwww.laseigneuriedesaulnaies.qc.ca; $10.75), is named after the alder trees that grow along the banks of the Ferrée River and offers a fascinating glimpse into that era. The river powered Québec's largest bucket wheel in the estate's three-storey communal grist mill. Now refurbished and fully operational, the mill has frequent flour-grinding displays and mouthwatering muffins and pancakes in the café. Just upstream, the veranda-wrapped manor house has period rooms, guides in costume and diverting interactive displays on the seigneurial system.

Kamouraska

Some 40km further east along Hwy 132 from St-Roch-des-Aulnaies is **KAMOURASKA**, a pretty village where well-heeled citizens of Québec City once congregated to take the air. While they no longer visit to the same degree, it's not for lack of good air, which still has its way with the town's current residents, many of whom live to more than 100. The village boasts many examples of the Bas-St-Laurent region's most distinctive architectural feature, the Kamouraska roof. Extended to keep the rainwater off the walls, the arched and rounded eaves project from the houses in a design borrowed from the shipyards. One of the best examples is the **Villa St-Louis**, at 125 av Morel, a private residence once the home to Adolphe Basile-Routhier, the man who scripted the words to Canada's national anthem.

You may also spot several nets attached to wooden stakes emerging out of the river – these ensnare eels, traditionally the village's economic mainstay. The best collection of artefacts – crockery, farming tools and the like – is at the **Musée régional de Kamouraska** (June to mid-Oct daily 9am–5pm, mid-Oct to mid-Dec Tues–Fri 9am–5pm, Sat & Sun 1–4.30pm; ⓣ418/492-9783; $5), at 69 av Morel, a former convent. On the pier, you can board a small zodiac with Kamouraska Zodiac Aventure (ⓣ418/863-3132, ⓦwww.zodiacaventure.com; $35) for a ninety minute trip along the coast to spot local bird and marine life.

Practicalities

Kamouraska has no shortage of charming **B&Bs**. *Gîte Chez Jean et Nicole* (ⓣ418/492-2921, ⓦwww.gitechezjeanetnicole.ca; ④), at 81 av Morel, is one of the best, with cheerful rooms and a bountiful breakfast of regional and organic food. For views of the river, try the simple *Motel Cap Blanc* ⓣ418/492-2919,

ⓦwww.motelcapblanc.com; ③; May–Nov), at 300 av Morel. To try the local delicacy head for *Café du Clocher* (ⓣ418/492-7365), at no. 88 av Morel, which serves smoked eel as well as a range of vegetarian dishes under $20. For similar prices *Au Relais de Kamouraska* (ⓣ418/492-6246) at no. 253 is more family-orientated and also makes eel a speciality.

The Gaspé Peninsula

Bounded by the Gulf of St Lawrence to the north and west, and by the Baie des Chaleurs to the south and east, the **Gaspé Peninsula** is roughly 550km long, with a chain of mountains and rolling highlands dominating the interior and the northern shore. It has always been sparsely inhabited and poor, its remote communities eking out an existence from the turbulent seas and the rocky soil. But the landscape provides some wonderful scenery. Forested hills cut with deep ravines and vistas of craggy mountains tumble to a jagged coastline fronted by the St Lawrence River, where the winding coastal drive along Hwy 132 is a delight.

The Gaspé is well served by **bus**, with regular services travelling both the north and south coasts of the peninsula from Rimouski, Rivière-du-Loup and Québec City. Yet the interior and the peninsula's parks are difficult to explore without a car. VIA Rail links Montréal by **train** with Rivière du Loup and Rimouski, then follows the southern coast of the peninsula to Carleton and Percé, terminating in Gaspé town after more than seventeen hours – there's no service between Gaspé and Rimouski on the northern coast and some stations (like Percé) are miles from the towns they serve. As a major summer holiday spot the Gaspé gets especially busy during the last two weeks of July for Québec's **construction holiday**; if you travel during this period, book your accommodation and activities well in advance.

The north shore

Running parallel to Hwy 132, the Trans-Canada Hwy (Hwy 20) is a much faster route to the attractive town of **Rivière-du-Loup**, effectively the start of the Gaspé Peninsula. The subsequent principal towns strung along the north shore – **Rimouski**, **Matane** and **Gaspé** – are less appealing than its many smaller villages or the peninsula's two outstanding parks: the extravagantly mountainous **Parc national de la Gaspésie**, inland from **Ste-Anne-des-Monts**, and the **Parc national de Forillon**, at the tip of the peninsula, with its mountain and coastal hikes and wonderfully rich wildlife. Just to the south of the latter, the village of **Percé** is famous for the offshore **Rocher Percé**, an extraordinary limestone monolith that has been a magnet for travellers for more than a hundred years.

Rivière-du-Loup

A prosperous-looking place, whose hilly centre is complete with broad streets and handsome Victorian villas, **RIVIÈRE-DU-LOUP** owes its development to the timber industry and the coming of the railway in 1859. This established Rivière-du-Loup as a crossroads for traffic between the Maritimes, the Gaspé Peninsula and the rest of Québec. Its significance as an administrative and commercial centre has grown accordingly and today it is one of the more thriving towns on the peninsula.

Arrival and information

Highway 132 runs through the centre of Rivière-du-Loup. The town's **bus station** is on boulevard Cartier, beside the junction of hwys 132 and 20, about ten minutes' walk northeast of the centre. The **train** station (ⓣ1-888/842-7245) is on rue Lafontaine and rue Fraserville and only open when VIA Rail trains arrive here from destinations including Montréal, Gaspé and Halifax. A **car ferry** (mid-April to Jan; 2–5 trips daily; 65min; ⓣ418/862-5094, ⓦwww.travrdlstsim.com; $14, cars $38.80) provides a service to and from the marina to St-Siméon on the north shore (see p.331).

The **tourist office** (mid-June to Sept daily 8.30am–9pm; ⓣ418/862-1981 or 1-888/825-1981, ⓦwww.tourismeriviereduloup.ca) is at 189 boul de l'Hôtel-de-Ville.

Accommodation

For **accommodation**, try the *Auberge Internationale de Rivière du-Loup* (ⓣ418/862-7566 or 1-866/461-8585, ⓦwww.aubergerdl.ca), at 46 Rue de l'Hôtel-de-Ville, a hostel in an attractive wooden building; dorm beds are $25, breakfast included. The *Auberge de la Pointe* (ⓣ418/862-3514 or 1-800/463-1222, ⓦwww.aubergedelapointe.com; ⑤), at 10 boul Cartier, has comfortable rooms, a restaurant and its own health spa. Alternatively, aim for two magnificent **B&Bs** virtually across from each other on a gorgeous stretch of Hwy 132 west of town: *Auberge La Sabline* (ⓣ418/867-4890, ⓦwww.bbcanada.com/lasabline; ③), at 343 rue Fraser, and the summer residence of Canada's first prime minister, Sir John A. MacDonald, *Les Rochers* (ⓣ418/868-1435, ⓦwww.giteetaubergedupassant.com/rochers; ④), at no. 336. For **camping**, head to *Camping Municipal De La Pointe De Rivière-Du-Loup* (ⓣ418/862-4281, ⓦwww.campingquebec.com/riviereduloup; $20–32; mid-May to late Sept), taking exit 507 from Hwy 20 – it's off Hwy 132, near the harbour.

The Town

The river that gives the place its name crashes down a thirty-metre drop close to the centre, at the top of rue Frontenac, near **Parc de la Croix Lumineuse**, which offers a panoramic view of the mountains on the north shore. The town's **waterfall** is disappointing, however: although it generates a lot of noise and spray, even the specially built platform that crosses it fails to make the view enthralling. Similarly modest are the town's three museums. The central **Musée du Bas-Saint-Laurent** (June to mid-Oct daily noon–5pm; mid-Oct to May Wed–Sun 1–5pm; ⓣ418/862-7547; $5), at 300 rue St-Pierre, combines ethnological displays of the region with historical exhibits and works of modern art by local artists. The **Musée de bateaux miniatures et légendes du Bas-St-Laurent** (May to late June & late Aug–late Sept daily 10am–6pm, late June to late Aug 9am–9.30pm; ⓣ418/868-0800; $5), at 80 boul Cartier, houses an interesting collection of model boats built by local craftspeople. The most intriguing historical site in town is **Le Manoir Fraser** (daily mid-June to mid-Oct 10am–5pm; ⓣ418/867-3906; $5), at 32 rue Fraser, the home of Seigneur Fraser; instead of costumed guides, a computer-animated seigneur introduces you to his life and times. The red-brick manor house also has a fancy tearoom and garden.

Eating and drinking

There are plenty of good restaurants in the town centre, though most tend to be pricey. *Le Saint-Patrice* (ⓣ418/862-9895, ⓦwww.restaurantlestpatrice.ca), at 169 rue Fraser, is among the best, devoted to serving regional dishes, such as smoked fish, lamb and shellfish. On rue Lafontaine, near the river, less expensive alternatives include the cosy Southeast Asian bistro *Les Jardins de Lotus* (ⓣ418/868-1333, ⓦwww.jardinsdelotus.com) at no. 334 and *La Brulerie de l'Est* (ⓣ418/862-1616) at no. 419, a great spot for coffee and sandwiches. Closer to the centre, *L'Estaminet* (ⓣ418/867-4517, ⓦwww.restopubestaminet.com), at 299 rue Lafontaine, is a

Boat trips from Rivière-du-Loup

Rivière-du-Loup is a good place for **boat trips** on the St Lawrence River. Beginning at around $60 per person, these excursions are not cheap, but they are well organized and you may see beluga, minke and finback whales throughout the summer. All the companies are located by the marina at 200 rue Hayward; Croisières AML (Ⓣ418/867-3361 or 1-800/563-4643, Ⓦwww.croisieresaml.com; mid-June to mid-Oct) specializes in three-hour **whale-watching** trips on large boats. La Société Duvetnor (Ⓣ418/867-1660, Ⓦwww.duvetnor.com; mid-June to mid-Sept) has daily cruises to various midstream seabird and mammal sanctuaries, with overnight stops offered ($25–225/person; reservations required).

lively bar with 150 types of beer and fine pub food, including mussels with fries (from $7).

Trois-Pistoles

Heading northeast from Rivière-du-Loup along Hwy 132, with the far bank of the St Lawrence clearly visible, the coastal hwy passes through a succession of farming and fishing villages on its way to **TROIS-PISTOLES**, said to be named after a silver goblet worth three *pistoles* (gold coins) that a French sailor dropped into the river while trying to fill it with water in 1621.

The **information centre** is on Hwy 132 with a miniature windmill and lighthouse outside (late June to early Sept daily 9am–7pm; Ⓣ418/851-3698, Ⓦwww.ville-trois-pistoles.ca). A **car ferry** crosses to Les Escoumins (mid-May to Oct; 2–3 daily; 1hr 30min; Ⓣ418/851-4676 or 1-877/851-4677, Ⓦwww.traversiercnb.ca; $17.50, cars $39) on the Côte-Nord (see p.336).

The Town

The enormous church of **Notre-Dame-des-Neiges-de-Trois-Pistoles** (late June to early Sept daily 9am–4.30pm; Ⓣ418/851-1391; $3), built between 1882 and 1887, dominates the town. From a distance the church looks like something out of Disneyland, with a silver roof surmounted by four pinnacles. Inside, the vaulted ceiling is supported by massive marble columns, while the walls are dotted with nineteenth-century devotional paintings.

The most interesting museum in town is the **Parc de l'Aventure Basque en Amérique** (late June to early Sept daily 10am–8pm; mid-May to late June & early Sept to mid-Oct noon–4pm; Ⓣ418/851-1556; $6), at 66 rue du Parc. Built on the site of the first **Basque** village in Québec, the displays examine their early history in the region; an accompanying English-language booklet is available. The first weekend of July sees the centre host a Basque festival, during which the traditional stick-and-ball game of *pelota* is played. The town's other main museum is the **Musée St-Laurent** (late June to early Sept daily 9am–5pm; Ⓣ418/851-2345; $4), 552 rue Notre Dame ouest, which has a great ensemble of cars from the 1930s to the 1970s and an eclectic collection ranging from old packs of cigarettes to harpoons.

You can **sea-kayak** with Kayak de Mer des Îles (July–Aug; guided trips at 10am & 5pm; Ⓣ418/851-4637 or 1-877/851-4637, Ⓦwww.kayaksdesiles.com; $40), located at 60 av du Parc.

Practicalities

This isn't a bad spot to break your journey. If you do, try *Motel Trois-Pistoles* (Ⓣ418/851-4258 or 1-866/616-4258, Ⓦwww.moteltroispistoles.com; ❹),

64 Hwy 132 ouest, which has 32 slightly dated, but comfortable rooms, some with views of the river, and wi-fi. Just east of the town on Hwy 132 est at no. 124 is an excellent **B&B**, *Auberge Le Bocage des deux gamins* (ⓣ418/857-2828, ⓦwww.aubergelebocagedes2gamins.com; ❹), a former seigneurial manor with five charming rooms.

For a picnic lunch or hefty snack head to *La Fromagerie des Basques* (ⓣ418/851-2189, ⓦwww.fromageriedesbasques.ca), 69 Hwy 132 ouest, for exceptional artisan cheeses, bread, pastries and traditional beer, all made on site. Back in town, *La Belle Excuse*, 138 rue Notre-Dame Ouest (ⓣ418/857-3000), has table d'hote from $23.

Parc national du Bic and Le Bic

Heading east from Trois-Pistoles, Hwy 132 crosses a tedious landscape of fertile agricultural land, until it reaches the rocky wooded hummocks of the shoreline's **Parc national du Bic** (ⓣ418/8736-5035, ⓦwww.sepaq.com; year-round; visitor centre mid-May to mid-Oct daily 10am–5pm; park entry $3.50). At this naturalists' paradise, whose headlands push up tight against the river, it's possible to see herds of grey seals, especially at dusk. The park has three short hiking trails, a beach and shuttle buses (late June to late Aug every 30min 12.30–3pm; $5.70 return) that leave from the visitor centre up to Pic Champlain, and around the park (3 departures daily; 2hr; $15.50). You can also view the park from a **bicycle** (rental $30/day) and go on a guided **sea kayak** tour of the park's shoreline and nearby islands with Kayak Zodiac Archipel du Bic (ⓣ418/736-5232, ⓦwww.kayakzodiacarchipeldubic.com; ($48.25/4hr). The **campsite** (ⓣ418/736-4711 or 1-800/665-6527, ⓦwww.sepaq.com; $24.25–32; early June to early Sept) is pleasant, but highway noise is a problem.

Just beyond the park along Hwy 132, the elongated village of **LE BIC**, perched on a low ridge above its snout-shaped harbour, is a handsome medley of old and modern architectures and a good spot to stop for a bite to eat. The *Auberge du Mange Grenouille* (ⓣ418/736-5656, ⓦwww.aubergedumangegrenouille.qc.ca; ❸–❼; May to mid-Oct), at 148 rue Ste-Cécile, has a superb **restaurant** (reservations advised) with table d'hôte from $32–46 and attractively furnished double **rooms**. *Gîte de la Baie Hâtée* (ⓣ418/736-5668, ⓦwww.maisondelabaiehatee.com; ❸), at 2271 Hwy 132, is a stately **B&B** with views of the river, a restaurant and massage services. The **bakery**, *Folles Farines*, at 113 rue St-Jean Baptiste, has a wicked selection of tasty breads, croissants and thin-crust pizzas. Up the hill and facing the handsome church, *Chez Saint-Pierre* (ⓣ418/736-5051, ⓦwww.chezstpierre.ca), 129 du Mon St-Louis, is a sunny bistro with an imaginative menu and a terrace overlooking the town's rooftops.

Rimouski and around

Some 20km northeast of Le Bic, **RIMOUSKI** – "Riki" to its residents – appears quite unattractive from Hwy 132 thanks to a major fire that destroyed one-third of the buildings from the river to midtown in 1950, forcing the city to rebuild in 1960s strip-mall style. But forge past the highway and into the town, the administrative capital of eastern Québec, and you'll find a youthful city (thanks to the number of educational institutions), but not much in terms of sights, bar the interesting **Musée régional de Rimouski** (June–Sept Wed–Fri 9.30am–8pm, Sat–Tues until 6pm; rest of year Wed–Sun noon–5pm, Thurs until 9pm; ⓣ418/724-2272, ⓦwww.museerimouski.qc.ca; $4), at 35 rue St-Germain. It's housed in the oldest church in eastern Québec whose exterior has stayed intact; the three floors inside have been renovated and now focus on rotating exhibits on local history and contemporary art.

Arrival and information

The Orléans Express **bus** station (Ⓣ418/723-4923) is at 90 av Léonidas, while the **train** station (Ⓣ418/722-4737 or 1-800/361-5390) is at 57 de l'Évêché est. There's a **car ferry** to Forestville on the Côte-Nord (late April to Oct 2–4 trips daily; Ⓣ418/725-2725 or 1-800/973-2725, Ⓦwww.traversier.com; 55min; $25, cars $39), which only holds thirty vehicles so reservations are essential. The *Nordik Express* (see p.351) departs Rimouski every Tuesday.

Rimouski's **tourist office** (mid-June to early Sept daily 8.30am–7.30pm; early Sept to early Oct daily 8.30am–noon & 1–4.30pm; rest of the year closed weekends; Ⓣ418/723-2322 or 1-800/746-6875, Ⓦwww.tourisme-rimouski.org) is in the centre of town at 50 rue St-Germain ouest, on the waterfront, and has accommodation listings.

Practicalities

College **rooms** are available during the summer at *CÉGEP Residences* (Ⓣ418/723-4636 or 1-800/463-0617, Ⓦwww.cegep-rimouski.qc.ca/residenc; $30–35), 320 rue St-Louis. For **B&B** accommodation, *Chez Charles et Marguerite* (Ⓣ418/723-3938; ❸), 686 boul St-Germain ouest, has cheery rooms looking out onto fields leading down to the St Lawrence River. If you're considering **camping**, take the crossing to l'Île Saint-Barnabé, a tranquil island and popular bird migration site 3km offshore where there are fourteen sites (from $19.50). The ferry departs from the marina on Hwy 132 (Ⓣ418/723-2280; daily every 30min 9am–2.30pm late June to early Sept; $15.50).

Rimouski has a number of affordable places to **eat**, including the *Central Café* (Ⓣ418/722-4011, Ⓦwww.centralcaferimouski.com), 31 rue de l'Évêché ouest, a bistro with tasty salads and pizzas in a home decorated with birdcages. For something a bit more kitsch, plump for *Retro 50* (Ⓣ418/723-4858) across the street at 38 boul St-Germain est, a 1950s-themed diner. Just off Hwy 132, the hip brewpub *Le Bien, le Malt* (Ⓣ418/723-1339) at 141 av Belzile is a great spot for beer and live music.

Pointe-au-Père

A few kilometres east from Rimouski along Hwy 132, the small town of **POINTE-AU-PÈRE** holds not much more than the **Maison Lamontagne** (late June to early Sept daily 9am–6pm; Ⓣ418/722-4038, Ⓦwww.maisonlamontagne.com; $4), 707 boul du Rivage, the oldest house in eastern Québec; though there's not much inside worth the time or money, the gardens are free and quite educational. Further down the road, the **Musée de la Mer** (daily mid-June to Aug 9am–6pm; Sept–Oct until 5pm; Ⓣ418/724-6214, Ⓦwww.museedelamer.qc.ca; $9) is housed in a modern building resembling a tilting ship. The exhibit includes a 3D film on the *Empress of Ireland*, a luxury liner that sank offshore here in 1914, a disaster second only to the *Titanic*, with more than a thousand lives lost.

Sainte-Flavie

The small coastal town of **SAINTE-FLAVIE**, 30km east of Rimouski, is home to Gaspésie's **regional tourist office** (mid-June to mid-Sept daily 8am–8pm; rest of year 8.30am–4.30pm; Ⓣ418/775-2223 or 1-800/463-0323, Ⓦwww.tourisme-gaspesie.com) at 357 rue de la Mer. Nearby at no. 564, the **Centre d'art Marcel Gagnon** (daily: early May to mid-Oct 7.30am–10pm; mid-Oct to April 8am–9pm; Ⓣ418/775-2829 or 1-866/775-2829, Ⓦwww.centredart.net; free) offers a unique and memorable sight. The artist's outdoor work, *Le Grand Rassemblement* (The Great Gathering), groups more than eighty life-size statues and seven rafts, starting on a strip of land and then leading into the water. The works are especially remarkable at high tide, as the statues emerge out of the river, and the rafts seem to float.

Another visual feast lies 9km further east down Hwy 132. The **Jardins de Métis** (June & Sept 8.30am–6pm, July & Aug 8.30am–8pm; ⓣ418/775-2222, ⓦwww.jardinsmetis.com; $16) is a gigantic aristocratic mansion and garden complex with over 100,000 introduced species of plants neatly presented among forty acres of features such as miniature bridges and tumbling brooks – an impressive horticultural feat.

Matane

MATANE, 64km from Sainte-Flavie, appears to be dominated by oil refineries and cement works, but in fact fishing and forestry have long been the mainstays of the local economy. The Matane River, which bisects the town, is spanned by a pair of bridges – one beside the harbour (part of Hwy 132), the other a shorter affair a few hundred metres north, next to the fish ladder, which was built to help salmon spawn. At the **Barrage Mathieu-d'Amours** (mid-June to Sept 7.30am–9.30pm; ⓣ418/562-7006; $3), 260 av St-Jérôme, the dam's observation area allows visitors to watch salmon battling to get upstream.

The real reason to interrupt your journey in Matane is to catch one of the **car ferries** (ⓣ418/562-2500 or 1-877/562-6560, ⓦwww.traversiers.gouv.qc.ca) to the Côte-Nord (see p.344–353). There are two routes: to Godbout (April–Dec 1–2 daily; Jan–March 1 daily except Thurs & Sun; 2hr 10min; $14.05, cars $32.90); and to Baie-Comeau (April–Dec 1–2 daily; Jan–March daily except Thurs & Sun; 2hr 20min; same fares).

The town's **tourist office** (late June to mid-Sept daily 8.30am–8.30pm; rest of year Mon–Fri 8.30am–5pm; ⓣ418/562-1065 or 1-877/762-8263, ⓦwww.tourismematane.com) is beside Hwy 132, just west of the centre, in the lighthouse at 968 av du Phare ouest.

Practicalities

For **accommodation**, a good B&B is the *Gite des Îles* (ⓣ418/562-6688, ⓦwww.bbcanada.com/legitedesiles; ❸), at 29 av Desjardins, a riverside inn with comfortable rooms. Most of Matane's **hotels** and **motels** are pricey, but one of the best is *Auberge la Seigneurie* (ⓣ418/562-0021 or 1-877/783-4466, ⓦwww.aubergelaseigneurie.com; ❹), at 621 av St-Jérôme, a pretty brick house with comfortable rooms and free internet access. *Motel Le Beach* (ⓣ418/562-1350 or 1-888/570-1350, ⓦwww.lebeachmatane.com; ❷), 1441 rue Matane-sur-Mer, is one of the least expensive; it has sea views but is nothing special. There's a huge **campsite** (ⓣ418/562-3414, ⓦwww.campingmatane.com; $20–28; mid-June to Aug) at 150 rte Louis-Félix-Dionne southwest of the town centre – follow the river past the industrial park – where sites are pleasant amid trees.

Restaurant *Le Rafiot* (ⓣ418/562-8080, ⓦwww.lerafiot.com), at 1415 av du Phare ouest alongside Hwy 132, is a casual place and the best bet for shrimp, while *Italia Pizzeria* (ⓣ418/562-3646), 101 rue St-Pierre, serves great, moderately priced pizza.

Sainte-Anne-des-Monts

East of Matane the hwy hugs the shoreline, passing through increasingly rugged scenery where the forested hills of the interior push up against the rocky coast. A string of skimpy fishing villages breaks up this empty landscape – places like Capucins, with its fine headland setting, and **Cap Chat**, whose 76 towering wind turbines are visible for miles around. Of these, the 110m-tall **Éole de Cap-Chat** (mid-June to Oct daily 9am–5pm; ⓣ418/786-5719, ⓦwww.eolecapchat.com; $6) is the tallest and most powerful vertical-axis wind tower in the world.

Just 16km beyond Cap-Chat, unenticing **SAINTE-ANNE-DES-MONTS** sprawls along the coastline, its untidy appearance only offset by its relaxed atmosphere and its convenience – it's an easy place to break your journey before heading on to the cape, or inland to the Parc de la Gaspésie. The lone sight is the **Exploramer** (mid-June to mid-Oct daily 9am–6pm; ⓣ418/763-2500, ⓦwww.exploramer.org; $12.75) at 1 rue du Quai, a marine and birdlife discovery centre. Head to the aquarium downstairs, where you can handle starfish, sea cucumbers and scallops. The centre also offers zodiac excursions on the St Lawrence River to observe marine life (90min; $42).

The *Auberge Festive Sea Shack* **hostel** (ⓣ418/763-2999, ⓦwww.aubergefestive.com; dorm beds $24, cottages ❻), at 292 boul Perron est, has views over the river and offers kayak rental and a shuttle to Parc national de la Gaspésie, while the *Motel Manoir sur Mer* (ⓣ418/763-7844; ❷), at 475 1ère av ouest, has rooms backing onto the beach. For **B&B** accommodation, try *La Villa des Roses* (ⓣ418/763-3529; ❷) at 500 1ère av ouest.

Parc national de la Gaspésie

As you travel south from Sainte-Anne-des-Monts on Hwy 299, the snowcapped **Chic-Choc Mountains** – which make up most of the **Parc national de la Gaspésie** – can be spotted in the distance, a stark and forbidding backdrop to the coastal plain. The Chic-Chocs are the most northerly protrusions of the Appalachian Ridge, which extends deep into the US, and the serpentine road reveals the full splendour of their alpine interior. The sequence of valleys framed by thickly wooded slopes culminates in the staggering ravine that lies at the foot of the towering **Mont Albert**.

Arrival and information

The park's extremely helpful **interpretation centre** (mid-June to mid-Sept daily 8am–10pm, otherwise until 8pm; ⓣ418/763-5435 or 1-866/727-2427, ⓦwww.sepaq.com; $3.50) is located in the ravine, about 40km from Sainte-Anne-des-Monts. It rents hiking equipment and has details and maps of half a dozen well-signposted **hiking trails**; most are about a day's duration, though a couple around the centre are shorter. A **shuttle bus** (late June to late Sept daily 7.45am; $5.76 round-trip) links the park to Sainte-Anne-des-Monts; buses travel between the town's tourist office and the interpretation centre.

Park accommodation

The park has four **campsites**, two of which, *Camping La Riviere* and *Camping Mont Albert* (ⓣ418/763-1333; from $23.75/site), are conveniently near the interpretation centre. Close by is the smart, modern *Gîte du Mont-Albert* (ⓣ418/763-2288 or 1-866/727-2427, ⓦwww.sepaq.com; ❺–❼) which offers the only fixed **lodgings** in the park; room prices rocket during the summer and skiing seasons, but the location is very handy. It also has an excellent (pricey) **restaurant** specializing in regional produce such as pan-seared rabbit, caribou medallions and home-smoked salmon. The *Gîte* also controls a number of **huts** ($20.50) around the park, offering simple but reliable facilities.

The Park

Prospective hikers should come equipped with warm clothes, food and water, and log their intended route at the centre. The trails ascend to the summits of the area's highest mountains – including Mont Jacques-Cartier (1270m), Mont Richardson (1180m) and Mont Albert (1088m) – and are remarkable in that they climb through three distinctive habitats. Herds of Virginia deer thrive in the rich vegetation of the lowest zone, while moose live in the boreal forest, and caribou in the tundra near the peaks. This is the only place in Québec where the three species exist in close proximity.

Mont-Saint-Pierre

Heading east from Sainte-Anne-des-Monts towards the tip of the Gaspé Peninsula, the road often squeezes between the ocean and the sheer rock faces of the mountains, its twists and turns passing tumbling scree and picturesque coves. The view as you approach **MONT-SAINT-PIERRE** is particularly majestic, the curving seashore and the swelling mountains together framing this little community set at the mouth of a wide river valley. It's an unassuming resort dedicated to bathing and fishing, except during the colourful ten-day **hang-gliding festival** (Ⓣ418/797-2222, Ⓦwww.mont-saint-pierre.ca) at the end of July. During the rest of the summer you can fly in tandem with Carrefour Aventure (Ⓣ418/797-5033 or 1-800/463-2210) at 106 rue Prudent-Cloutier, who also rent sea kayaks and mountain bikes.

Practicalities

Several inexpensive **motels** line rue Prudent-Cloutier: try the basic *Chalets Auberge Bernatchez* (Ⓣ418/797-2733, Ⓦwww.users.mmic.net/chaletbernatchez; ❶) at no. 12, or *Le Délice* (Ⓣ1-888/797-2955, Ⓦwww.audelice.com; ❸) at no. 100, which offers guided trips up the mountain. *Auberge les Vagues* (Ⓣ418/797-1000; ❷), at no. 84, is a motel/hostel (dorm beds $20). There's also a large **campsite** (Ⓣ418/797-2250, Ⓦwww.mont-saint-pierre.ca; $20–33; mid-June to early Sept) at 103 rue Pierre-Godfroie-Coulombe.

For a bite to **eat**, the restaurant in *Le Délice* dishes up typical Gaspésian classics (think fish and seafood) at reasonable prices, while *Les Joyeux Naufragés* (Ⓣ418/797-2017), at 7 rte Pierre-Mercier, offers the same at similar prices.

Parc National de Forillon

At the very tip of the peninsula, the federally-run **PARC NATIONAL DE FORILLON** is the scenic culmination of the Gaspé, encompassing thick forest and mountains, crossed by hiking trails and fringed by stark cliffs along a deeply indented coastline. The splendour of the landscape is complemented by the **wildlife**: black bears, moose, beavers, porcupines and foxes are all common to the area. More than two hundred species of birds have also been seen, ranging from sea birds like gannets, cormorants and guillemots, to songbirds such as the skylark and chaffinch. From the coastal paths around Cap Gaspé itself, **whales**, such as humpbacks, fin whales and minke whales, and **harbour porpoises** can also be spotted (May–Oct).

Arrival and information

The park's **interpretation centre** (late May to mid-Oct 9am–5pm; Ⓣ418/892-5572, Ⓦwww.pc.gc.ca; $7.80.) is close to the lighthouse, near the village of Cap-des-Rosiers on the park's north side. It offers an overview of the natural and human history of the area and can advise on the park's hiking trails and other activities. There are also two **visitors' centres** off Hwy 132: one at Anse-au-Griffon (late May to early Sept daily 8.30am–9.30pm; Sept to mid-Oct 9am–4pm; Ⓣ418/368-5505 or 1-800/463-6769); the other on the south coast at Penouille (same hours; Ⓣ418/892-5661). **Whale-watching** excursions depart from Grande-Grave (June to early Oct 1–4 daily; Ⓣ418/892-5500 or 1-888/617-5500, Ⓦwww.baleines-forillon.com; $55).

The Park

Roughly triangular in shape, the park is sandwiched between the Gulf of St Lawrence and the Baie de Gaspé and encircled by hwys 197 and 132, the former crossing the interior to delineate the park's western limits, the latter mostly keeping to the seashore and threading through L'Anse-au-Griffon and Cap-des-Rosiers – tiny coastal villages with views onto the river and Forillon's wooded parkland. Make the time to take this route as the views are spectacular. You can also stop for a cup of tea at the **Manoir Le Boutillier** (mid-June to early Oct daily 9am–5pm; Ⓣ418/892-5150; $7; guided tours only), a restored 1850s house at 578 boul Griffon, in L'Anse-au-Griffon. Closer to the park, the much-photographed **lighthouse** at Cap-des-Rosiers is the tallest in Canada.

The park has nine hiking trails, the best of which, Les Graves, takes you to the tip of **Cap Gaspé**, otherwise known as "land's end" (4hr 30min; 15km). The trail extends from the end of the paved road beyond Grande-Grave, a restored fishing village originally founded by immigrants from Jersey. Their historical presence is enshrined in two sites situated along the trail following the southern coast of the cape. The first, **Hyman & Son's General Store and Warehouse** (early June to mid-Oct 10am–5pm; free with park entry) is a marvellous restoration of a 1920s general store; nearby **Anse-Blanchette** (mid-June to early Sept 10am–5pm; free with park entry), a fisherman's house dating from the same era, has also been painstakingly restored; the on-site barn frequently does duty as a stage for storytelling and musical acts. The path rises and falls until it makes the final steep ascent to the lighthouse, which is set on a 150m cliff with the ocean on three sides.

Park practicalities

The park's half-dozen **campsites** (all Ⓣ418/368-6050, Ⓦwww.pccamping.ca; from $25.50) are pleasantly situated and well maintained; Cap-Bon-Ami (early June to early Sept) has a particularly delightful setting just south of the interpretation centre. The villages edging the park offer plain accommodation, including L'Anse-au-Griffon's *Motel le Noroît* (Ⓣ418/892-5531; ❷), at 589 boul Griffon, and

▲ Parc National de Forillon coastline, near Anse-Blanchette

Cap-aux-Os's **hostel** (ⓣ418/892-5153, ⓦwww.gaspesie.net/aj-gaspe; dorm beds $20–24, private rooms $42–50), at 2095 boul Grande-Grève, with a café, laundry facilities and **mountain-bike rental**.

In L'Anse-au-Griffon's cultural centre, 557 boul Griffon, *Café de L'Anse* is a nice spot to eat, offering mostly seafood dishes, including a traditional *brandade de morue* (codfish brandade); it also has internet access.

Gaspé

The town of **GASPÉ** – its name derived from *Gespeg*, "the end of the land" in the Mi'kmaq language – straddles the hilly estuary of the York River and is a disappointment after the scenic drama of the national park. It's a humdrum settlement of about seventeen thousand people whose hard-pressed economy is reliant on its deep-water port.

Buses to Gaspé stop on the main street, rue Jacques-Cartier, at the *Motel Adams*. The **tourist office** (daily 8am–8pm; ⓣ418/368-6335, ⓦwww.tourismegaspe.org) is on the far side of the river from the town centre along Hwy 198; it has accommodation listings and town maps.

The town and around

Just to the east of the town centre, at 80 boul Gaspé, the **Jacques Cartier monument** looks out over the bay from the grounds of the town museum. It consists of six striking bronze dolmens carved in relief that record Cartier's visit (see p.318) and treatment of the natives in ambivalent terms, along with anodyne homilies on the nature and unity of humankind. The **museum** (late June to early Oct daily 9am–5pm; otherwise Mon–Fri 9am–noon & 1–5pm, Sat & Sun 1–5pm; ⓣ418/368-1534; $7), at 80 boul Gaspé, illuminates the social issues that have confronted the inhabitants of the peninsula: isolation from the centres of power, depopulation and, more recently, unemployment. Temporary displays concentrate mostly on local subjects, like the peninsula's artists and musicians. A good ten-minutes' walk west, near the top of rue Jacques-Cartier, stands the **Gaspé Cathedral**. Built in 1970, it's the only wooden cathedral in North America and its barn-like exterior has an extraordinarily dour and industrial appearance. The interior is completely different: the nave – all straight lines and symmetrical simplicity – is bathed in warm, softly coloured light that pours in through an enormous stained a glass window.

Just outside town, the white **Sanctuaire Notre Dame-des-Douleurs** (early June to mid-Sept daily 9am–5pm, rest of the year Mon–Fri 9am–4.30pm, Sunday 1–4pm; ⓣ418/368-2133; $3) is a popular pilgrimage site due to its alleged healing powers, supported by the collection of crutches, braces and canes found in the chapel entombing Father Watier, the sanctuary's founder. Up a slight incline behind the church, the replica of the Lourdes Grotto (replete with outdoor altar) and the Garden of Mary's Sorrows are both attractive, with remarkable religious sculptures. Next door, the **Site Historique Micmac de Gespeg** (June–Sept daily 9am–5pm; guided tours only; ⓣ418/368-7568; $8), at 783 boul Pointe-Navarre, is a replica of the aboriginal village that stood here in 1675, when trading with Europeans was in full swing. The site offers interesting insights into how to build tepees and animal traps and carve utensils, but the visit is overlong at 2hr 30min.

Practicalities

Most of Gaspé's **B&B** accommodation is superb, but *L'Emerillon* (ⓣ418/368-3063, ⓦwww.bbcanada.com/11809.htm; ④), at 192 rue de la Reine, is the best, located in a historic house with views of the bay and serving excellent breakfasts.

Jacques Cartier in Gaspé

Gaspé is the spot where the French navigator and explorer **Jacques Cartier** landed in July 1534, on the first of his three trips up the St Lawrence River. He stayed here for just eleven days, time enough to erect a wooden cross engraved with the escutcheon of Francis I, staking out the king's – and Christianity's – claim to this new territory. Cartier's first aim was to find a sea route to the Orient, but he also had more extensive ambitions – to acquire land for himself and his men, exploit the Indians as fur gatherers and discover precious metals to rival the loot the Spaniards had taken from the Aztecs. Naturally, Cartier had to disguise his real intentions on the first trip and his initial contacts with the Iroquois were cordial. Then, in the spring of 1536, he betrayed their trust by taking two of the local chief's sons back with him to Francis I. They were never returned, and when Cartier made his third trip in 1541 the Iroquois were so suspicious that he was unable to establish the colony he had been instructed to found. Desperate to salvage his reputation, Cartier sailed back to France with what he thought was a cargo of gold and diamonds; it turned out to be iron pyrite and quartz crystals.

One of the better-value **motels** in town is the modern *Motel Plante* (ⓣ418/368-2254 or 1-888/368-2254, ⓦwww.motelplante.com; ❶–❺) at 137 rue Jacques-Cartier, with basic doubles or two-floor suites with a kitchen.

Le Bourlingueur (ⓣ418/368-4323), across the river at 39 Montée de Sandy Beach, serves cheap, filling **breakfasts**, though the Chinese and Canadian dishes on the evening menu are rather pricey, with main courses costing $13. *Brise-Bise* (ⓣ418/368-1456, ⓦwww.brisebise.ca), at 135 rue de la Reine, is a great bistro and a swinging bar at night. If you're looking to splurge, go to *Café des Artistes* (ⓣ418/368-2255, ⓦwww.brulerieducafedesartistes.net) at 101 rue de la Reine Gaspé – it's one of the best restaurants on the peninsula for French cuisine. The upstairs cigar room nestled under the eaves is worth a visit whether you eat or not.

Percé

Once a humble fishing community, **PERCÉ** is a prime holiday spot, thanks to the tourist potential of the gargantuan limestone rock that rears up from the sea here facing the reddish cliffs of the shore. One of Canada's most celebrated natural phenomena, the **Rocher Percé** – so named for the hole at the western end – is nearly 500m long and 90m high, and is a surreal sight at dawn, when it appears bathed in an eerie golden iridescence. The town is now replete with tacky gift shops and mediocre restaurants and bars; off-season, when much of the resort closes down, Percé maintains a delightfully relaxed and sleepy feel.

Arrival and information

Hwy 132 bisects Percé and passes just to the north of the main wharf, close to the **tourist office** (late May to late-Oct daily 9am–7pm; ⓣ418/782-5448, ⓦwww.perce.info), which operates a free room-reservation service and keeps boat timetables. Arriving from Carleton or Gaspé, **buses** drop passengers in the centre of Percé at the Petro-Canada service station. The **train** station is 10km south of town on Hwy 132.

Accommodation

Most of Percé's **accommodation** is open during the summer months only, when advance booking is advised; in the off-season, you'll likely have to stay in Gaspé. There are numerous, charming motels along Hwy 132.

Le Macareux 262 Hwy 132 ⓣ418/782-2414 or 1-866/602-2414, ⓦwww.membres.multimania.fr/motelmacareux. The rooms (some with shared bath) are simple and clean, but the real pull is the proximity to the beach and the Rocher Percé, both just a short stroll away. ❶–❸

Le Mirage 288 Hwy 132 ⓣ418/782-5151 or 1-800/463-9011, ⓦwww.hotellemirage.com. One of the larger hotels in town, this rather pretty establishment has 67 rooms (some suites), all of which have great views of the Rocher Percé. There's also an on-site restaurant. ❸–❻

Hôtel La Normandie 221 Hwy 132 ouest ⓣ418/782-2112 or 1-800/463-0820, ⓦwww.normandieperce.com. There's been a hotel on this site since 1937 – no wonder, given its cliff-top location that offers superb views of the bay and *that* rock. Thirty-seven of the 45 bright and modern rooms have balconies. The on-site restaurant (early June to early Oct) offers table d'hôte for $23–48. ❺–❼

La Maison Rouge 125 Hwy 132 ⓣ418/782-2227, ⓦwww.lamaisonrouge.ca. A dynamic hostel which rents kayaks and runs excursions to l'Île-Bonaventure. Dorm beds ($20) are in a renovated barn, while private rooms (❸) are in the main building.

Camping Gargantua 222 rte des Failles ⓣ418/782-2852. Of the five nearby campgrounds (ask about the others at the tourist office), this one has the best views of you-know-what. Sites $22–30.

The town and around

At low tide it's possible (if you hurry) to walk around most of the Rocher Percé, starting from the lookout beyond the red-roofed houses at the end of rue Mont-Joli. Access to the rock now costs $1 – allegedly for upkeep of the belvedere and stairway leading to the stone beach; tide times are posted at the top. One of the most spectacular longer-range views of the monolith is from the top of **Mont Sainte-Anne**, which rises directly behind Percé town; the path is signposted from behind the church on rue de l'Église. The steep 3km walk takes about an hour each way. A separate trail leads from the path to **La Grotte**, a lovely spot with waterfalls and statues of the Virgin Mary nestled into the mountain's crevasses. Slightly more challenging is the hike up the western slope of Mont Blanc to the **Grande Crevasse**, a volcanically formed split in a rocky outcrop that's just a few millimetres wide but several hundred metres deep. The clearly marked path takes about an hour to walk in each direction and begins behind the *Auberge de Gargantua* restaurant (see p.320).

Apart from the rock, there's precious little to see in Percé, though the **Centre d'Interprétation du Parc de l'Île-Bonaventure-et-du-Rocher-Percé** (late May to mid-Oct daily 9am–5pm; free), some 2km to the south of the centre (exit Hwy 132 at route des Failles and turn left along route d'Irlande), has some

Boat trips from Percé

From the wharf in Percé **boat trips** operated by Les Traversiers de l'Île (1hr 30min–3hr; ⓣ418/782-2750, ⓦwww.croisieresgaspesie.com; $25–35) go around the nearby **Île Bonaventure** bird reserve (daily: late May to June & Sept to mid-Oct 8.15am–4pm; July & Aug 8.15am–5pm; $3.75), whose precipitous cliffs are favoured by gannets, kittiwakes, razorbills, guillemots, cormorants and puffins. You can arrange to disembark at the island's jetty, where all of the lengthy walking trails lead to the clifftops above the gannet colonies; one path includes a visit to **Le Boutillier**, a restored nineteenth-century fisherman's home. The wharf is also the departure point for **whale-watching** excursions (May–Oct); blue and humpback whales are often in the area, and you may also see porpoises, seals and the rarer white-sided dolphins. Zodiacs speed out with Bateliers de Percé (ⓣ418/782-2974 or 1-877/782-2974; $60), which also offer excursions in larger boats ($50) and trips to Île Bonaventure ($25). Les Croisières Julien Cloutier (ⓣ418/782-2161 or 1-877/782-2161; $50) offers two- to three-hour trips, which should be reserved in advance at the various ticket kiosks lining the main drag.

enjoyable displays on the area's flora and fauna. In the middle of town, in the old Charles Robin Company building formerly used for processing and storing fish, the **Musée la Chafaud** (daily late June to late Sept 10am–8pm; $5), at 142 Hwy 132, displays traditional and contemporary art and occasionally gets high-calibre exhibitions. A few kilometres west of Percé, **La Vieille Usine de l'Anse-à-Beaufils** (June to mid-Sept daily 10am–10pm; ⓣ418/782-2777, ⓦwww.lavieilleusine.qc.ca) showcases a wide range of local art in a renovated fish-packing plant that fronts a decent beach.

Eating and drinking

La Maison du Pêcheur (ⓣ418/782-5331, ⓦwww.maisondupecheur.restoquebec.com), 155 Place du Quai, has fine **seafood** dishes, while **snacks** and vegetarian dishes for under $20 can be had in the faintly bohemian atmosphere of *Les Fous de Bassan* (ⓣ418/782-2266), at 162 Hwy 132. For excellent food and great panoramas over town, try *Auberge Gargantua* (ⓣ418/782-2852), at 222 rte des Failles, where gourmet French cuisine will cost around $30, or *La Normandie* (ⓣ418/782-2112 or 1-800/463-0820; see p.319), at no. 221, for delicacies such as lobster baked in champagne.

The south shore

The **south shore** of the peninsula runs along the **Baie des Chaleurs**, a long wedge of sheltered ocean with relatively warm waters that separates the Gaspé from New Brunswick. For the most part, it's flatter and duller than the north here, though some of the seaside resorts-cum-fishing villages and farming communities dotting the coast are agreeable places to break your journey. **Carleton**, where the mountains return to tower over the coast, is tempting, especially as it's near the extraordinary fish and plant fossils of the **Parc de Miguasha**, a UNESCO World Heritage Site. This, along with **Bonaventure** further up the coast, is also one of the few long-established English-speaking settlements on the peninsula which is otherwise predominantly and proudly Québécois. Both Carleton and Bonaventure are centres of Acadian culture, established in 1755 in the wake of the British deportation of some ten thousand Acadians (see p.387).

Bonaventure

Southwest of Percé on Hwy 132, you'll pass through **Chandler**, an ugly lumber port, on the way to the most easterly resort on the bay, **BONAVENTURE**, whose tiny centre is beside Hwy 132. Bonaventure is best known for being a stronghold of **Acadian** culture. Their traditions and heritage are celebrated at the **Musée Acadien du Québec** (daily: late June to early Sept 9am–6pm; early Sept to mid-Oct 9am–5pm; mid-Oct to early May Mon–Fri 9am–noon & 1–4.30pm, Sun 1–4.30pm; early May to late June Mon–Fri 9am–noon & 1–4.30pm, Sat & Sun 1–4.30pm; ⓣ418/534-4000, ⓦwww.museeacadien.com; $8), 95 av Port-Royal, set in an imposing blue and white wooden building in the town centre. Highlights of the collection include some delightful handmade furniture dating from the eighteenth century and a range of intriguing photographs that encapsulate something of the hardships of Acadian rural life. On the opposite side of the main street **Cur de la mer** is, uniquely, a centre for the production of fish-leather products such as purses and wallets. The small shop sells a variety of examples and is worth a browse.

The wildlife observation centre, **Bioparc de la Gaspésie** (daily June to early Oct 9am–5pm; July–Aug until 6pm,; ⓣ1-866/534-1997, ⓦwww.bioparc.ca; $12.95), at 123 rue des Vieux-Ponts, showcases the region's animals – caribou, lynx, otters and mountain lions – in their respective ecosystems; it also offers recently built chalets (❼).

Bonaventure's **tourist office** (mid-June to Aug daily 9am–6pm; ⓣ418/534-4014, ⓦwww.ville.bonaventure.qc.ca), at 91 av Port-Royal, has background information on the town and accommodation lists.

Practicalities

Accommodation options include the well-appointed *Motel Grand-Pré* (ⓣ418/534-2053 or 1-800/463-2053, ⓦwww.motelgrandpre.com; ❺–❼), at 118 av Grand-Pré, and more reasonable **B&Bs** like the bohemian *Au Foin Fou* (ⓣ418/534-4413, ⓦwww.foinfou.qc.ca; ❷), 204 rte de la Rivière, and *Auberge du Café Acadien* (ⓣ418/534-4276; ❷), at 168 rue de Beaubassin. The latter is above the excellent *Café Acadien*, which serves imaginative French-Canadian **food**. *Cime Aventure* (ⓣ418/534-2333 or 1-800/790-2463, ⓦwww.cimeaventure.com), at 200 chemin Arsenault, has campsites ($23) and teepees (❷) alongside the Bonaventure River and comfortable cottages nestled in the woods (❻). They rent kayaks and canoes and run guided trips on the river (3hr to 6 days; prices vary).

Carleton and the Miguasha Peninsula

Just west of New Richmond, Hwy 299 runs north along the banks of the Cascapédia towards the Parc national de la Gaspésie (see p.314), while the coastal Hwy 132 continues to the popular bayside resort of **CARLETON**, where the mountains of the interior return to dominate the landscape. Founded in 1756 by Acadian refugees, Carleton is an unassuming little place that stands back from the sea behind a broad lagoon, linked to the narrow coastal strip by a couple of long causeways. The town has a bird sanctuary – a favourite haunt of wading species like the sandpiper and plover – and several accessible bathing beaches where you can rent kayaks. But what makes the place special is the contrast between the coastal flatlands and the backdrop of wooded hills that rise up behind the town. At 582m, **Mont Saint-Joseph** is the highest of these and is presided over by the **Oratoire Notre Dame-du-Mont-Saint-Joseph** (daily mid-June to early Sept 8am–7pm, early Sept to Oct 9am–5pm; ⓣ 418/364-2256; $4), a disappointing church that incorporates the walls of a stone chapel built on the site in 1935. A 3km maze of steep footpaths slip past streams and waterfalls before they reach the summit. You can also take the less adventurous option and drive up to see the splendid panoramic views over the bay and across to New Brunswick.

The hilly **Miguasha Peninsula**, some 20km to the west off Hwy 132, makes a pleasant excursion. Famous for its fossils, this tiny peninsula is home to the **Parc national de Miguasha** (ⓦwww.sepaq.com), where some of the area's better findings are displayed at the combined **research centre and museum** (daily: June–Aug 9am–6pm; Sept to mid-Oct 9am–5pm; otherwise Mon–Fri 8.30am–noon & 1–4.30pm; $12.25). Frequent and free guided tours take in the museum, the research area and a walk along the beach and cliffs.

Practicalities

Carleton is a good place to stay overnight and many **motels** line the main street, boulevard Perron. *Manoir Belle Plage* (ⓣ418/364-3388 or 1-800/463-0780, ⓦwww.manoirbelleplage.com; ❸–❻), at no. 474, has a touch of class, while a pleasant **B&B** with friendly owners, *Gite Les Leblanc* (ⓣ418/364-7601, ⓦwww.giteetaubergedupassant.com/Leblanc; ❷), is at no. 346. The town also has a well-situated **campsite** (mid-June to Aug; ⓣ418/364-3992, ⓦwww.carletonsurmer.com; $21), on the Banc de Larocque causeway. On the Miguasha Peninsula there's *Camping L'Erablière* (ⓣ418/794-2913, ⓦwww.campinglerabliere.qc.ca; $20), which enjoys a remote coastal setting at the tip and has simple chalets (❹).

For food, try *Le Bleu Marine* (☎418/364-6621), at 203 rte du Quai, which offers affordable lunchtime menus overlooking the beach. More substantial seafood **meals** are available at *Restaurant le Héron* (☎418/364-3881), at no. 561 – which is also where the **bus** stops – and the superb *Le Courlieu* (☎418/364-3388), at 474 boul Perron, which serves grilled seafood dishes for around $20 . If you're off to the Parc national de Miguasha, pack up a picnic at *La Mie Véritable*, a bakery at 578 boul Perron.

Pointe-à-la-Croix and around

Some 50km west of Carleton, **Pointe-à-la-Croix** is the site of the interprovincial bridge over to Campbellton, New Brunswick. During the summer, a **tourist booth** (Ⓦwww.pointe-a-la-croix.com) in the tiny wooden house by the turn-off for the bridge on Hwy 132 (daily 8am–8pm) offers a full range of information on the Gaspé Peninsula.

Just before the bridge, a right turn leads to the little waterside community of **LISTUGUJ** (Restigouche), the heart of a Mi'kmaq Indian reservation that functions on New Brunswick time because the children go to school in Campbellton. The village is home to the Mi'kmaq, an Algonquian-speaking people who spread across the Atlantic seaboard from Nova Scotia through to the Gaspé and east Newfoundland. Their history is a familiarly sad one: trading furs for European knives, hatchets and pots, the Mi'kmaq quarrelled with other aboriginal groups over hunting grounds until there was a state of perpetual warfare. In later years, the Mi'kmaq proved loyal allies to the French military cause, but, as with all other aboriginal groups, their numbers were decimated by European diseases and they remain a neglected minority. Yet this reserve is self-governing and one of the five richest in Canada (of eight hundred-odd reserves). The **Listuguj Arts and Cultural Centre** (May–Sept daily 9am–5pm; $5) offers a small display of traditional crafts and buildings from before European contact. The clothing, canoes and porcupine quill boxes are all made locally to rekindle interest in Mi'kmaq culture and traditional skills.

A couple of kilometres west of the bridge, back along Hwy 132, the national historic site of **La Bataille-de-la-Restigouche** commemorates a crucial naval engagement of 1760, which effectively extinguished French hopes of relieving their stronghold in Montréal, the year after the fall of Québec City. The French fleet, which had already taken casualties in evading the blockade of Bordeaux, was forced to take refuge in the mouth of the Rivière Restigouche and then, despite assistance from local Mi'kmaqs and Acadians, was overpowered by superior British forces. The site's excellent **interpretation centre** (June to early Oct daily 9am–5pm; Ⓦwww.pc.gc.ca/ristigouche; $3.90) contains relics of the French fleet, especially the frigate *Le Machault*, which has been partly reconstructed.

There's no need to stay in Pointe-à-la-Croix but if you're stuck, try an unusually regal **hostel**, *Auberge du Château Bahia* (☎418/788-2048, Ⓦwww.chateaubahia.com; dorms $24, private room $32.50–37.50), in **Pointe- à-la-Garde**, 6km east of Listuguj and signposted off Hwy 132 at 152 boul Perron. It's in an eccentric Renaissance-style wooden castle and the food is excellent. Rates include breakfast and banquet-style dinners are served ($12).

Matapédia

At the western tip of the Baie des Chaleurs, at the confluence of the Restigouche and Matapédia rivers, the tiny village of **MATAPÉDIA**, a Mi'kmaq term

New Brunswick is on **Atlantic time**, one hour ahead of Québec.

meaning "there where the two rivers meet", is surrounded by steep green hills and lies at the centre of an excellent salmon-fishing region. Not a lot else happens here aside from canoe and kayak trips down the area's several rivers, which can be organized by Nature Aventure (mid-May to late Sept; ⓣ418/865-3554, ⓦwww.matapediaaventure.com) in Parc Adams on rue d'Église. A two-hour canoe trip departing from Matapédia costs $35 per person while a multi-day canoe-camping trip starts at $199 per person.

There isn't a great choice of **restaurants** in town; *La Vieille Gare* (ⓣ418/865-2007), at 50 boul Perron ouest, has somewhat pricey seafood and, close by, the *Motel Restigouche* (ⓣ418/865-2155 or 1-877/865-2848, ⓦwww.matapedia.com; ❸), at no. 5, is the place to **stay** if you're into fishing and hunting; there's also an on-site restaurant.

From Matapédia, Hwy 132 cuts north across the interior of the peninsula, heading back up to Ste-Flavie (see p.312).

Îles-de-la-Madeleine

The archipelago of the **Îles-de-la-Madeleine** (Magdalen Islands), in the middle of the Gulf of St Lawrence some 200km southeast (and one hour ahead) of the Gaspé Peninsula and 100km northeast of Prince Edward Island (see pp.428–444), consists of twelve main islands, seven of which are inhabited. Six of these are connected by narrow sand spits and crossed by paved and gravel roads, while the last is only accessible by boat. Together these dozen islands form a crescent-shaped series of dunes, lagoons and low rocky outcrops that measures about 80km from end to end, with the main village and ferry port roughly in the middle at **Cap-aux-Meules**. The islands lie in the Gulf Stream, which makes the winters warmer than those of mainland Québec, but they are subject to almost constant winds, which have eroded the red-sandstone cliffs along parts of the shoreline into an extraordinary array of arches, caves and tunnels. These rock formations, the archipelago's most distinctive attraction, are at their best on the central **Île du Cap-aux-Meules** and the adjacent **Île du Havre-aux-Maisons**.

The islands' 15,000 inhabitants (most descended from Acadian settlers) are largely dependent on **fishing**, the lobster catch in particular. Despite international pressure, the annual seal hunt in late winter also still supports many islanders (seals can be easily spotted on the ice floes in March). Other sectors of the fishery are now suffering because of fish-stock depletion, and the islands' future livelihood revolves around **tourism**. Many residents worry about preserving their way of life and the fragile ecology of their beautiful islands. Tourists come to the archipelago for its wide-open **landscapes** and sense of **isolation** – it's easy to find a dune-laden **beach** where you can be alone with the sea. Throughout the islands, **powerful currents** and changeable weather conditions can make swimming dangerous, and the waters are occasionally home to stinging jellyfish.

Île du Cap-aux-Meules

The ferry from Souris, Prince Edward Island (see p.440), docks in the middle of the archipelago, at **Île du Cap-aux-Meules**, which boasts the islands' largest community – **CAP-AUX-MEULES**, on the eastern shore. A useful base for exploring the neighbouring islands, the town is the islands' administrative and business centre and their least attractive enclave. Yet just a couple of kilometres west of the village, there are fine views of the entire island chain from the **Butte du Vent**, the area's highest hill. Further west, on the other end of the island near

Îles-de-la-Madeleine practicalities

Getting there

Every month except February and March a CTMA **ferry** goes to Cap-aux-Meules **from Souris** on Prince Edward Island (Souris ⓣ902/687-2181; Cap-aux-Meules ⓣ418/986-3278; Montréal ⓣ514/937-7656, ⓦwww.ctma.ca/traversier-madeleine) – the number of weekly departures varies from five to ten depending on the season (a one-way ticket is $44.75 in high season; plus $83.75 for a car, $29 for a bicycle; 5hr). Reservations are mandatory in July and August and need to be made several months in advance. The CTMA-operated *Vacancier* cruise ship departs **from Montréal** for the islands every Friday (from $578 one-way; plus $302 for a car; 48hr).

Daily scheduled **flights** on Air Canada Jazz leave Gaspé town, Québec City, Montréal and Halifax; book two weeks in advance, and include a Saturday overnight stay for discount flights. Alternatives are Pascan Aviation (ⓣ450/443-0500 or 1-888/313-8777, ⓦwww.pascan.com) which flies from Montréal, Québec City and Bonaventure and ExactAir (ⓣ1-877/589-8923; ⓦwww.exactair.ca) which flies from Mont-Joli.

Arrival, information and transport

The islands' **airport** is at the north end of Île du Havre-aux-Maisons, some 20km from Cap-aux-Meules. Some flights have connecting buses to Cap-aux-Meules, but otherwise you'll have to take a **taxi** (about $25), or **rent a car** from Hertz (ⓣ418/969-4229) at the airport; book in advance in the summer. The **ferry terminal** at Cap-aux-Meules is near the **tourist office**, at 128 chemin Principal (late June to late Aug daily 7am–9pm; late Aug to late Sept daily 9am–8pm; Oct–May Mon–Fri 9am–5pm; first three weeks of June daily 9am–8pm; ⓣ418/986-2245 or 1-877/624-4437, ⓦwww.tourismeilesdelamadeleine.com), which operate a free room-reservation service with an emphasis on B&Bs; with few **inns**, **motels** and **hotels** on the islands, it's advisable to book a bed before you arrive. The tourist office also has details of cottage and apartment rentals, starting at roughly $250 per week. The cheapest way to stay is either at the **hostel** (where you can also camp) or one of the other half-dozen commercial **campsites** on the islands.

The best way to tour the principal islands is by **bike**; you can rent these at Le Pédalier (ⓣ418/986-2965; ⓦwww.lepedalier.com; $24/day, $90/week), at 545 chemin Principal in Cap-aux-Meules. They (and the tourist office) have an excellent map of the island's many well-marked routes. **Mopeds** can be rented from Cap-aux-Meules Honda (ⓣ418/986-4085), on Hwy 199 at La Vernière, southwest of Cap-aux-Meules.

Boat trips and watersports

Boat and **fishing trips** depart from near the ferry terminal during summer. Excursions en mer (ⓣ418/986-4745, ⓦwww.excursionsenmer.com) and Le Pluvier Aventurier (ⓣ418/986-5681, ⓦwww3.telebecinternet.com/lepluvier) offer similar services.

The islands' big attraction for many adventurous travellers is the strong winds that blow here. Between late August and late October conditions for **windsurfing** and **kitesurfing** are exemplary and the Canadian Professional and Amateur Windsurf Championship heads here every year. Contact Canada's first kitesurfing school, Aerosport Carrefour d'Aventures (ⓣ418/986-6677, ⓦwww.aerosport.ca), at 1390 chemin de La Verniére in Etang-du-Nord, for advice and rentals. Winds have also played their part in causing so many ships to founder around the coast, leaving behind some superb **wreck-diving**. For information and trips contact Le Repère du Plongeur (ⓣ418/986-3962, ⓦwww.repereduplongeur.com), 18 Allée Léo Leblanc. The Centre nautique de l'Istorlet (ⓣ418/937-5266, ⓦwww,istorlet.com), at 100 chemin de l'Istorlet in Havre-Aubert, offers guided **snorkelling** ($95) trips to see the seals that live around the islands' coastline as well as sea kayak outings ($50).

the fishing port of L'ÉTANG-DU-NORD, you'll find some extravagant coastal rock formations and a port where kayaking tours take off. In the opposite direction, the main road skirts the southern tip of the islands' longest lagoon before heading on across the Île du Havre-aux-Maisons.

Accommodation

Accommodation options include the basic *Motel Bellevue* (Ⓣ418/986-4477, Ⓦwww.ilesdelamadeleine.com/bellevue; ❹), 40 chemin Principal, and the large *Château Madelinot* (Ⓣ418/986-3695 or 1-800/661-4537, Ⓦwww.quebecweb.com/chateaumadelinot; ❺; June–Sept;), at 323 Hwy 199 in Fatima, with fine sea views, great food and comfortable rooms. There are several **campsites**: the peaceful *Le Barachois* (Ⓣ418/986-6065, Ⓦwww.campingbarachois.ca; from $19; May–Oct) is also in Fatima, at 87 chemin du Rivage; the dramatically-sited and wind-swept *Hostel and Camping Gros Cap* (Ⓣ418/986-4505 or 1-800/986-4505, Ⓦwww.parcdegroscap.ca; dorms $23, breakfast included; camping $20; May–Sept), at 74 chemin du Camping, in L'Étang-du-Nord offers expertly guided kayak tours from $39 and internet access.

Eating and drinking

For outstanding but pricey **seafood**, try *La Table des Roy* (Ⓣ418/986-3004, Ⓦwww.latabledesroy.com; closed Mon), 1188 chemin de La Verniére in La Vernière just west of Cap-aux-Meules; dinner will cost over $50. Cheaper options include: *Café la Côte* (Ⓣ418/986-6412) in L'Etang-du-Nord at 499 chemin Boisville ouest, with good sandwiches and pizzas and a view of the water; and *La Factrie* (Ⓣ418/986-2710), at 521 chemin Gros Cap, a fun and relatively inexpensive cafeteria-style lobster restaurant attached to a lobster-processing plant. Just short of the Dune de l'Ouest, the fantastic microbrewery *Á l'abri de la Tempete* (Ⓣ418/986-5005, Ⓦwww.alabridelatempete.com), 286 chemin Coulombe, is worth a detour. Housed in an old fish factory, it's an inviting place with several award-winning beers made from ingredients grown on the islands.

Île du Havre-aux-Maisons

Île du Havre-aux-Maisons' smooth green landscapes contrast with the red cliffs of its southern shore. Crisscrossed by narrow country roads and littered with tiny straggling villages, this island is best known for a unique oral tradition. The Acadians that settled here post-deportation were so irate with their treatment they decided never to utter the word "king" (*roi* in French) again, and eventually wound up dropping the letter "r" from their language altogether.

The striking arches and shapes of the coastal rocks around **Dune-du-Sud** are an understandably popular draw, as is the **Fumoir d'Antan** (daily 9am–5pm; Ⓣ418/969-4907, Ⓦwww.fumoirdantan.com; free tour), at 27 chemin du Quai, the last remaining traditional herring smokehouse on the islands. Down at the wharf, **Les Excursions de la Lagune** (Ⓣ418/969-4550, Ⓦwww.ilesdelamadeleine.com/excursions; June–Sept; $29) departs three times daily for a two-hour highly entertaining and educational tour of the lagoon on a glass-bottom boat. Deserted twin beaches edge the hamlet islet of **Pointe-aux-Loups** north of here, across the sand spit and along Hwy 199.

Practicalities

For a place to **stay**, the *Auberge la P'tite Baie* (Ⓣ418/969-4073, Ⓦwww3.sympatico.ca/auberge.petitebaie; ❸), at 187 Hwy 199, is your best bet, with lovely rooms and sea vistas. You can **camp** by the beach on the east side of the island at Camping Des Sillons

(May to mid-Oct; ⓣ418/969-2134, ⓦwww.chaletscampingdessillons.com; $19–30/site) which also has chalets (❸–❺). If you want some great **seafood**, try the restored convent *Au Vieux Couvent* (ⓣ418/969-2233, ⓦwww.domaineduvieuxcouvent.com), at 292 Hwy 199, which also has an energetic basement **bar** with regular live music – even without, the place gets packed nightly until 11pm.

Grosse-Île and Île de la Grande-Entrée

At the far northern end of the archipelago, the twin islets of anglophone **Grosse-Île** and francophone **Île de la Grande-Entrée** border the wildlife reserve of the **Pointe-de-l'Est**, whose entrance is beside the main road. On its south side, the reserve is edged by the enormous sandy expanse of La Grande Échouerie **beach**, whose southern end is framed by yet more splendid rock formations at Old Harry's Point. This is where Europeans first came to the islands in order to slaughter walruses, depleting the stock by 1800. Today, the 10km walk down the beach offers a good chance to spot seals, and there have been some – albeit very rare – walrus sightings. A kilometre past the rustic wharf at **Old-Harry**, a pretty white church with beautifully sculptured doors uses the islands as backdrop for biblical tales. A little further, the old red schoolhouse is home to the Council for Anglophone Magdalen Islanders and a **museum** (July & Aug daily 8am–4pm; Sept–June Mon–Fri 8am–4pm; ⓣ418/985-2116; free) tells the history of the anglophone population, most of whom are of Scottish descent. To learn more about seals head to the **Centre d'interprétation du Phoque** (June–Sept daily 10am–6pm; rest of year by appointment; ⓣ418/985-2833 or 1-888/537-4537, ⓦwww.loup-marin.com; $7.50) at 377 Hwy 199.

Practicalities

The lobster port of **Île de la Grande-Entrée**, the last island to be inhabited, has a couple of **accommodation** options: *Domaine de la Grenouille sur Mer* (ⓣ418/985-2365 or 514/645-9855; ❸), at 83 chemin des Pealey, and *La Salicorne* (ⓣ418/985-2833 or 1-888/537-4537, ⓦwww.salicorne.ca; ❸), at 377 Hwy 199, which has camping space as well as rooms and a great **restaurant**, *Madelinot*. The food is expensive but you can save money by opting to pay for full board; it's also open to non-guests. The inn also offers various activities, including trips to the caves on offshore Île Boudreau as well as hikes there to the southeast. A cheaper option for a meal is *Café de l'Est*, 503 chemin Principal, Old-Harry (ⓣ418/985-2155), which serves fish and mussels with chips.

Île du Havre-Aubert

To the south of Île du Cap-aux-Meules, **Île du Havre-Aubert** has one significant community, **HAVRE-AUBERT**, edged by round, sloping hills. It's the most attractive of the islands' communities, and its picturesque location and charm attract a lot of visitors. It is situated around **La Grave**, a pebbly beach flanked by a boardwalk and wooden buildings once used by sailors and fishermen and now transformed into bars, cafés, restaurants, souvenir shops and art galleries; the best spot to buy souvenirs is Les Artisans du Sable (ⓣ418/937-2917, ⓦwww.artisansdusable.com), at 907 Hwy 199. On the beach the **Aquarium des Îles** (early June to Aug daily 10am–6pm; Sept 10am–5pm; ⓣ418/937-2277; $7.50) displays fish and crustaceans found in the waters around the island, and there's a small seal tidal pool out back. Overlooking La Grave, the **Musée de la Mer** (mid-June to mid-Sept Mon–Fri 9am–6pm, weekends from 10am; call for hours off season; ⓣ418/937-5711; $5) has a series of displays on local fishing techniques and the history of the islands. Especially interesting is the exhibit focused on the more than four hundred shipwrecks that have occurred just offshore.

Set apart from Havre-Aubert, in the community of Bassin, the **Site d'Autrefois** (daily: June–Aug 9am–5pm; Sept 10am–4pm; Ⓦwww.ilesdelamadeleine.com/autrefois; $10) is a fanciful spot that tells the story of Madelinot life through life-sized mannequins of fishermen, boats and model houses. La Chevauché des Iles (Ⓣ418/937-2368; $25–40) also in Bassin, offers **riding** tours of the island.

Practicalities

You can **stay** on La Grave at *Chez Charles Painchaud* (Ⓣ418/937-2227, Ⓦwww.aubergechezcharles.ca; ③), at 930 Hwy 199, or *Le Berceau des Îles* (Ⓣ418/937-5614, Ⓦwww.berceaudesiles.com; ③), at 701 chemin principal in Havre-Aubert; the latter has more luxurious rooms. Both can arrange for pick-ups from the airport or ferry, organize winter and summer activities and even rent cars. *Auberge Chez Denis à François* (Ⓣ418/937-2371, Ⓦwww.aubergechezdenis.ca; ③), at 404 chemin d'en Haut, offers fine views of the strip.

Restaurants are of good quality in Havre-Aubert: even if you don't stay at *Auberge Chez Denis à François*, you should definitely try the seafood. *La Saline* (Ⓣ418/937-2230), at 1009 Hwy 199 in La Grave, is open for delicious evening meals and has live music in the adjoining bar. The much more expensive *La Marée Haute* (Ⓣ418/937-2492), 25 chemin des Fumoirs, is also only open at night and serves up some of Canada's finest seafood, including sea urchins and smoked seal. For chunky sandwiches, clam chowder served in a bread bowl, local beers and wi-fi, head for the convivial *Café de la Grave* (Ⓣ418/937-5244) in the old general store. *Le P'tit Mondrain* on chemin de La Grave is popular with locals, and its seafood is among the islands' cheapest.

Île d'Entrée

To the southeast, tiny anglophone **Île d'Entrée** is the only inhabited island not linked by land to the rest of the archipelago. Home to less than 150 people, this grassy hillock is encircled by footpaths and makes a pleasant day out, providing the sea is calm on the **ferry** trip from Cap-aux-Meules (May–Dec Mon–Sat 8am & 3pm; Ⓣ418/986-3278, Ⓦwww.traversiers.gouv.qc.ca; $30 return). Horses and cows roam freely on the slopes of the Îles-de-la-Madeleine's highest point, **Big Hill** (174m), accessible from the port by taking chemin Main and then chemin Post Office, and following the path across the fields to the top for a view of the whole archipelago. On your way towards the path, a tiny **museum** (June–Sept hours vary Ⓣ418/986-6622; free) displays island artefacts and historical household items. The only official lodging is the basic **B&B** *Chez McLean* (Ⓣ418/986-4541; ②). Otherwise, you'll probably end up in someone's home – ask around. There's a bar-restaurant and a grocery store near the port.

Charlevoix

Stretching along the **north shore** of the St Lawrence River east of Québec City, from the Beaupré coast to the Saguenay Fjord, the region of **Charlevoix**, named after the Jesuit historian Francois Xavier de Charlevoix, is a UNESCO World Biosphere Reserve. Species like the **arctic caribou** and **great wolf**, not usually associated with such southerly latitudes, can be seen in the more remote areas, and because the Ice Age that shaped the rest of eastern Canada missed this breathtaking portion of the Canadian Shield, numerous pre-glacial plants still thrive here. It consists of gently sloping hills, sheer cliffs and vast valleys veined with rivers, brooks and waterfalls, a landscape that Québec's better known artists – Clarence

Gagnon, Marc-Aurèle Fortin and Jean-Paul Lemieux – chose for inspiration. Though Charlevoix has been a tourist destination for years and especially popular with people from Québec City on weekend breaks, the land has been carefully preserved, and quaint villages and tin-roofed churches still nestle in an unspoiled countryside. The tourist office produces a brochure, *La Route des Saveurs de Charlevoix*, which is useful on a gastronomic trip: it lists agricultural producers and the restaurants that use local products.

Highway 138, the main route through Charlevoix, travels 225km from Québec City to Baie-Ste-Catherine on the Saguenay. The main towns along this hwy are served by Intercar **buses** from Québec City, but many of the quintessential Charlevoix villages – in particular those along the coastal Hwy 362 which starts from Baie-Saint-Paul – are not served by public transport. Be prepared to rent a car or bike; the expense is worth it.

Baie-Saint-Paul and around

One of Charlevoix's earliest settlements and longtime gathering place for Québec's landscape painters, the picture-perfect **BAIE-SAINT-PAUL** is tucked into the Gouffré Valley at the foot of the highest range of the Laurentian mountains. Dominated by the twin spires of the church, the streets wind from the centre of town flanked by houses that are more than two hundred years old – reason enough to make wandering around Baie-Saint-Paul the main attraction.

Arrival and information

The **tourist office** for Baie-Saint-Paul and the whole Charlevoix area is at the Belvédère Baie-Saint-Paul (daily: mid-June to early Sept 9am–7pm; rest of year 9am–4.30pm; ⓣ418/435-4160 or 1-800/667-2276, ⓦwww.baiesaintpaul.com) off Hwy 138 before you descend into town from the west, where there's a free museum detailing the geography of the area. There's also a tourist office in the heart of town at 6 rue St-Jean-Baptiste (same hours). The Intercar **bus** stops at *Restaurant La Grignote*, 2 chemin de l'Equerre (ⓣ418/435-6569), in the shopping centre by Hwy 138, twenty minutes' walk from downtown.

Accommodation

You shouldn't have any trouble finding rooms in Baie-Saint-Paul, as there's an excellent variety of **accommodation**, especially B&Bs.

Le Balcon Vert Turn left up Côte du Balcon Vert, about 3km east of town on Hwy 362 ⓣ418/435-5587, ⓦwww.balconvert.com. Probably the town's best bargain, this hostel/campsite has four-berth cabins (❷), private cabins with bathroom (❸), dorm beds ($22) and tent sites ($22). The views are tremendous and the on-site bar and restaurant (there are no guest kitchens) ensure a sociable vibe.

Domaine Belle-Plage 192 rue Ste-Anne ⓣ418/435-3321, ⓦwww.belleplage.ca. Comfortable double rooms with somewhat fussy decor are the name of the game at this waterfront establishment. Its sister venture, *Auberge le Cormoran* (ⓣ418/435-6030, ⓦwww.lecormoran.ca) next door at no. 196 has similar rooms and prices. ❷–❸

A La Lune Bleue 44 chemin de la Martine ⓣ418/614-5260, ⓦwww.alalunebleue.com. Just a few minutes' out of town and set in peaceful wooded grounds, the four designer rooms here each have their own bathroom and TV. ❸

Auberge La Maison Otis 23 rue St-Jean-Baptiste ⓣ418/435-2255 or 1-800/267-2254, ⓦwww.maisonotis.com. One of the best hotels in town, this has a pleasant, country-house feel to it. The thirty rooms (some with exposed beams) are a mixture of doubles, suites or apartments; some have jacuzzis and fireplaces. There's also an on-site restaurant and bar. ❺–❼

Auberge La Muse 39 rue St-Jean-Baptiste ⓣ418/435-6839 or 1-800/841-6839, ⓦwww.lamuse.com. Right in the centre of town, this beautiful Victorian-era inn has twelve large, prettily decorated rooms – including an "energizing suite". Facilities include a restaurant, health centre and gift shop selling food made on-site ❻

Auberge La Pignoronde 750 boul Mgr De Laval ⓣ418/435-5505 or 1-888/554-6004, ⓦwww.aubergelapignoronde.com. *La Pignoronde* has 28 spacious modern rooms (all with private bath), an indoor pool and attractive gardens. This is also a bit of a gourmand's paradise, with three separate dining rooms, all featuring local ingredients, as well as a vast wine list. ❸

The Town

From beside the church, the rue St-Jean-Baptiste slips through the commercial heart of the town edged by numerous quaint cottages characteristic of Québec's earliest houses, with curving roofs and wide verandas, many converted into commercial galleries. At 58 rue St-Jean-Baptiste, the **Maison de René-Richard** (ⓣ418/435-5571; daily 10am–6pm; free, guided tour $5) offers an insight into the works of René Richard, an associate of the Group of Seven. The 1852 house has been left exactly the same since Richard died in 1982; bilingual guided tours take you around his studio and living quarters, a rare glimpse at the Charlevoix of the 1940s when some of Québec's finest painters hung out here.

For an overview of the works of art produced in Charlevoix, visit the plush **Centre d'Exposition** (late June to early Sept Tues–Sun 11am–5pm; mid-Sept to mid-June Tues–Sun noon–5pm; ⓣ418/435-3681, ⓦwww.centredexpo-bsp.qc.ca; $6) at 23 rue Ambroise-Fafard, which has established an international reputation for the excellence of its temporary exhibitions of Québécois and international art. Every summer at a contemporary art symposium, the public can watch young Canadian and European artists at work in the nearby arena (ⓣ418/435.3681), 11 rue Forget.

Eating and drinking

There are plenty of good **places to eat** within a block or two of the church: *Vice Café*, 1 rue Ste-Anne (ⓣ418/435-0006), serves tasty crêpes and salads, and *Café d'Artistes*, 25 rue St-Jean-Baptiste (ⓣ418/435-5585), has desserts, coffees and thin-crust pizzas. Down the street at no. 43, the perpetually packed *Joe Smoked Meat* (ⓣ418/240-4949) lures meat lovers with juicy briskettes, while *Les Deux Soeurs* is an excellent patisserie-café across the street at no. 48 (ⓣ418/435-6591). *Le Mouton Noir*, 43 rue Ste-Anne (ⓣ418/240-3030), serves hearty country cooking, like smoked sausages with maple syrup, and dishes range from $18 to $35. The restaurant of the *Belle-Plage* (ⓣ418/435-3321) also serves traditional Québécois cuisine, with a buffet for around $16. For a **drink**, head to *Le Saint-Pub*, 2 rue Racine (corner of St-Jean-Baptiste), a terrific brewpub.

Parc national des Grands-Jardins

Baie-Saint-Paul makes a good base to explore the **Parc national des Grands-Jardins** (daily: June–Aug 8am–8pm; Sept–May 9am–5pm; ⓦwww.sepaq.com/pq/grj/en; $3.50), 42km away on Hwy 381 but with no public transport. Within the forests and lakes of the park, the 900m Mont-du-Lac-des-Cygnes gives the best of all Charlevoix panoramas. It's a three-hour (5km) climb from the Mont-du-Lac-des-Cygnes visitors' kiosk on Hwy 381 to the top and back along a clear but rocky path; you will need proper footgear. You can rent canoes ($38.10/day) and kayaks ($39.42/day) at the **Thomas-Fortin reception centre** and **chalets** (❺), huts (❺) and campsites ($23.75) are also available but must be reserved in advance (ⓣ1-800/665-6527).

Les Éboulements and around

From Baie-Saint-Paul the main route onwards is Hwy 138, but if you have your own transport you should opt for the coast-hugging detour of Hwy 362, which twists and turns through a succession of cliff-top villages along the river's shore.

Traversée de Charlevoix and other outdoor activities

Attracting hikers, mountain bikers and cross-country skiers, the long-distance **Traversée de Charlevoix** (Ⓣ418/639-2284, Ⓦwww.traverseedecharlevoix.qc.ca) begins near the Parc des Grands-Jardins on Hwy 381, crossing 105km of mountainous terrain including the Parc national des Hautes-Gorges-de-la-Rivière-Malbaie (see p.332) before ending at Mont Grand-Fonds near La Malbaie. Accommodation in cabins or cottages starts at $156.50 for the six nights needed to complete the hike.

Some of the province's most dramatic **skiing** is at **Le Massif** (Ⓦwww.lemassif.com; day pass $59) perched over the St Lawrence River to the west of town.

At 41 rue St-Jean-Baptiste, Randonnées Nature-Charlevoix (Ⓣ418/435-6275, Ⓦwww.randonneesnature.com) runs excellent hiking tours in the Parc des Grands-Jardins (see p.329) and tours around the **Charlevoix Crater** – one of the planet's largest – by bus (late June to early Sept; 1 daily; 2hr; $25). At the marina, L'Air du Large (Ⓣ418/435-2066, Ⓦwww.airdularge.com), 210 rue Ste Anne, rents bicycles, kayaks, canoes and paragliders and offers courses in kayaking and paragliding; they also run boat trips to explore nearby islands.

The first settlement on this route is **LES ÉBOULEMENTS**, which means "landslides" – named after the massive earthquake of 1663. Just west of the village at no. 157 rang St-Joseph is the eighteenth-century **Moulin Banal** (late June to early Sept daily 10am–5pm; $4), a working flour mill atop a pretty waterfall on the well-kept grounds of the **Manoir de Sales-Laterrière**. The manor and mill are among the few intact structures left from the seigneurial regime of New France. The manor (a school) is not open to the public but a path leads up from the mill, with interpretation panels on the grounds. At the entrance to the grounds is a charming chapel (1840) built of wood and relocated here from St-Nicholas, a village on the St Lawrence River.

From Les Éboulements, a steep secondary road leads to the pretty coastal village of **SAINT-JOSEPH-DE-LA-RIVE**, once a shipyard. The **Musée maritime de Charlevoix** (late June to early Sept daily 9am–7pm, rest of the year Mon-Fri until 4pm, weekends 11am–4pm; Ⓣ418/635-1131, Ⓦwww.musee-maritime-charlevoix.com; $5), at 305 rue de l' Eglise, has a few nautical displays, a workshop and boat-building yards. Pop into the local **church** on chemin de l'Église, where anchors prop up the altar and the font is a huge seashell from Florida.

l'Isle aux Coudres

The 16km-long island of **l'Isle aux Coudres**, where Jacques Cartier celebrated Canada's first Mass in 1535, is named after its numerous hazelnut trees. Missionaries were the first permanent settlers, arriving in 1748, and the growing population came to depend on shipbuilding and beluga-whale hunting for their livelihoods. Ship- and canoe-building still takes place here, but the main industry of its 1600 inhabitants is harvesting peat moss from the bogs in the centre of the island.

Access is on a free **car ferry** (8–26 trips daily 7am–11.30pm; 15min; Ⓣ418/438-2743, Ⓦwww.traversiers.gouv.qc.ca) from Saint-Joseph-de-la-Rive. The island's stone manors and cottages attract huge numbers of visitors, who drive and **cycle** around the 24km peripheral road that connects – in a clockwise direction – the three villages of **ST-BERNARD**, **LA BALEINE** and **ST-LOUIS**. The only real diversions along the way are the restored and working wind and adjacent water mills, **Les Moulins de l'Isle-aux-Coudres** (mid-May to mid-Oct daily

9.30am–5.30pm; Ⓣ418/438-2184, Ⓦwww.lesmoulinsiac.com; $8), in the southwest corner of the island, both dating from the early nineteenth century.

There is an **information centre** (mid-June to Aug daily 10am–7pm; Ⓦwww.tourismeisleauxcoudres.com) near the ferry dock in St-Bernard, with maps of the island. **Bikes** can be rented from Gérard Desgagnés (Ⓣ418/438-2332), 36 chemin de la Traverse, the lone road bisecting the island, or Vélo-Coudres (Ⓣ418/438-2118, Ⓦwww.charlevoix.qc.ca/velocoudres), 2926 chemin des Coudriers, which has a wider selection but is 5km from the dock at the eastern tip of the island, linked by free hourly shuttle.

Practicalities

Places **to stay** are unexciting, but many have reasonable restaurants. One of the best deals is *Motel Écumé* (Ⓣ418/438-2733, Ⓦwww.maisoncroche.com; ❷), at 808 chemin des Coudriers in La Baleine, a bizarre place with deliberately tilted windows and mismatched furniture in very basic rooms. The posh hotel *Cap-aux-Pierres* (Ⓣ418/438-2711 or 1-888/554-6003, Ⓦwww.dufour.ca; ❺), at 246 rue Principale in La Baleine, provides half-board accommodation and has a good restaurant. The *Motel l'Islet* (Ⓣ418/438-2423, Ⓦwww.quebecweb.com/lislet; ❸; May to mid-Oct), at 10 chemin de l'Islet, is a good bargain in an isolated spot near St-Louis on the west tip of the island. To **camp**, try the well-run *Camping Leclerc* (Ⓣ418/438-2217, Ⓦwww.famille-leclerc.charlevoix.net/; $22–30), at 333 chemin de la Baleine, in La Baleine.

For good, cheap **meals** head to *La Mer Veille* (Ⓣ418/438-2149) at 1833 chemin des Coudriers in St-Louis. Before heading off the island, be sure to pay a visit to *Boulangerie Bouchard*, 1648 chemin des Coudriers, which has all manner of freshly baked breads and pies.

La Malbaie

Hwys 362 and 138 converge about 50km from Baie-Saint-Paul at **LA MALBAIE** ("Bad Bay"), so called because Champlain ran aground here in 1608. Situated at the mouth of the Malbaie River, the town – an amalgamation of five villages – sprawls along the riverfront with little to detain you, though it's a good base for a day-trip to the **Hautes-Gorges** (see p.332); and the ritzy resort area **POINTE-AU-PIC** – back along Hwy 362 – is worth a quick look for its late nineteeth-century tourist-château. It makes for a delightful overnight stay – and you can wager the rest of your travel budget at the *Casino de Charlevoix* next door.

Arrival and information

The **tourist office** (mid-June to Sept daily 9am–7pm; rest of year Mon–Fri 9am–4pm, Sat & Sun 9am–5pm; Ⓣ418/665-4454), along the St Lawrence River at 495 boul de Comporté, has a full range of info on Charlevoix. **Buses** (Ⓣ418/665-2264) arrive nearby at Dépanneur Otis, 46 rue Ste-Catherine. The nearest **car ferry** across the river leaves from the hillside village of **Saint-Siméon** 25km northeast on Hwy 138, towards Rivière du Loup (see p.308).

Accommodation

Much of the classiest **accommodation** is in Pointe-Au-Pic, home to the luxurious *Le Manoir Richelieu* (Ⓣ418/665-3703 or 1-866/540-4464, Ⓦwww.fairmont.com; ❽), at 181 rue Richelieu, and many manor houses that have been converted into charming country inns. The *Auberge des 3 Canards* (Ⓣ418/665-3761 or 1-800/461-3761, Ⓦwww.auberge3canards.com; ❻), at 115 Côte Bellevue, has 49 comfortable rooms, most with their own private balcony overlooking the river and one of the area's finest restaurants. Cap-à-l'Aigle, an agricultural village to the east, has an excellent **B&B**, *Claire Villeneuve* (Ⓣ418/665-2288, Ⓦwww.quebecinformation.com/clairevilleneuve; ❷), at 215 rue St-Raphaël, a great example of Québécois rural architecture. If you have transport, head for Charlevoix's oldest and most beautifully situated **campsite**, *Camping Chutes Fraser* (Ⓣ418/665-2151, Ⓦwww.campingchutesfraser.com; $20–35, chalets $125; mid-June to early Sept), at 500 chemin de la Vallée, by the falls of the same name about 3km north of La Malbaie.

Outdoor activities

Descente Malbaie (Ⓣ418/439-2265, Ⓦwww.descentemalbaie.com), based just north of St Aimé des Lacs halfway to the Hautes-Gorges, run whitewater **rafting** in summer (around $50 for 2hr); overnight trips are also available. In winter the Rac du Mont Grand-Fonds (Ⓣ418/664-0095 or 1-877/667-0095, Ⓦwww.montgrandfonds.com; day pass $35) has **downhill skiing** and **snowboarding** on fourteen trails or **cross-country skiing** at the Centre de Plein Aire Les Sources Joyeuses (Ⓣ418/665-4858; $9) where 82km of trails – and 5km of ice-skating trails – are maintained. Instruction and equipment rental is available at both ski centres.

Eating and drinking

For **food** try *Le Manoir Richelieu*'s *Winston* bar and restaurant for inexpensive breakfasts. At the La Malbaie marina *Café de la Gare* (Ⓣ418/665-4272), 100 chemin du Havre, has a limited menu of items like paninis, mussels and nachos. For pub food head to *Club des Monts* (Ⓣ418/439-3711), 110 Ruisseau des Frênes, a busy bar with frequent live music.

Parc national des Hautes-Gorges-de-la-Rivière-Malbaie

One sight not be missed in the Charlevoix region is the **Parc national des Hautes-Gorges-de-la-Rivière-Malbaie**, a network of valleys slicing through a maze of lofty peaks 45km west of La Malbaie. To get there take Hwy 138 to **SAINT-AIMÉ-DES-LACS**, a small town 13km northwest of La Malbaie from where the way to the park is well marked. Admission is $3.50 and the park's excellent **information centre**, Félix-Antoine-Savard (daily mid-May to early Oct 7am–9pm; Ⓣ418/439-1227 or 1-800/665-6527, Ⓦwww.sepaq.com), is located beside the Malbaie River, just off rue Principale. You must leave your car here and rent a bike ($31.67/day) or take the frequent, free shuttle bus into the park as far as the Centre de services Le Draveur.

As you enter the park, cliff faces on all sides rise up to more than 700m, making it Canada's deepest canyon east of the Rockies. Its uniqueness lies not just in this astounding geology but also in the fact that all of Québec's forest species grow in this one comparatively small area. The best way to take in a sampling of the park's natural bounty is hiking the **L'Acropole-des-Draveurs** trail, a tiring but rewarding 10.5km trek leading to the canyon's highest point. It passes through a Laurentian maple grove on the way to the arctic–alpine tundra of the 800m summit and affords stunningly expansive views of the gorge; reckon five to six hours, round-trip. Shorter trails from the Centre de services Le Draveur offer less strenuous alternatives. From here you can take a leisurely ninety-minute river cruise ($29.68) or rent **canoes or kayaks** ($13.50/hr; $27/day) for the six-kilometre paddle along the calm "Eaux Mortes" of the river. These can be reserved at the Centre de services Le Draveur, while at the Félix-Antoine-Savard centre you can reserve sites at the park's three **campsites** ($18.50–23.75; June–Aug), and get permits for wild camping – some of which is only accessible by canoe.

The Saguenay and Lac Saint-Jean

The **Saguenay** is Québec's most schizophrenic region, encompassing some of the province's most spectacular scenery, tremendous marine life and also the dreariest of industrial towns. Fortunately, the two extremes are kept nicely separate along the Saguenay River, so that you can explore the rich landscapes along its fjord and source – **Lac Saint-Jean** – in peace. Best known for its **whale-watching** opportunities, the region is also exceptional for canoeing, backcountry hiking and cycle touring.

The main tourist centre of the region, **Tadoussac**, is best known as a whale-watching centre but also makes a great base to explore a number of other outdoor attractions in the vicinity. Many of these are centered on the national parks along the **Fjord du Saguenay**, another prime whale-watching spot, where both the land and sea are protected as a provincial park.

If you have time, continue west to the Upper Saguenay past the industrial centres of Chicoutimi and Jonquière and make a circuit of the flat farming country of **Lac Saint-Jean**. It's an ideal location to cycle, and the recently completed **Véloroute des Bleuets** allows you to travel the 256km around the lake without trucks forcing you off the road.

Tadoussac and around

One of Canada's oldest villages, **TADOUSSAC** is beautifully situated at the neck of the Saguenay Fjord and its confluence with the St Lawrence River, beneath rounded hills that gave the place its name; the Algonquian word *tatoushak* means "breasts". Basque whalers were the first Europeans to live here and by the time Samuel de Champlain arrived in 1603 it was a thriving trading post. The mid-nineteenth century saw Tadoussac evolve into a popular summer resort for the anglophone bourgeoisie, but today it's the best place in Québec, along with Bergeronnes and Les Escoumins just north along the coast, for **whale-watching** (see p.335). Mid- to late June is a good time to be here, when traditional Québécois folk singers, jazz pianists and rock guitarists all play a part in the popular **Festival de la Chanson** (Ⓦ www.chansontadoussac.com).

Arrival and information

Tadoussac is 78km north of La Malbaie and 227km from Québec City via Hwy 138. Traffic crosses the neck of the fjord by a free **car ferry** from Baie-Ste-Catherine to Tadoussac, but you may have to wait as long as an hour or two to board in midsummer. The nearest ferries across the St Lawrence River depart and arrive from Les Escoumins in the north (see p.336) and Saint-Siméon in the south (see p.331). Tadoussac's **bus station** (Ⓣ 418/235-4653) is at 443 rue du Bâteau-Passeur on Hwy 138 by the campsite. The **information centre** for the entire Côte-Nord is in a red-brick manor at 197 rue des Pionniers (daily: late June to early Sept 8am–9pm; early Sept to late June 9am–noon & 1–5pm; Ⓣ 418/235-4744 or 1-866/235-4744, Ⓦ www.tadoussac.com) and provides an accommodation service.

Accommodation

There's a wealth of **accommodation** in Tadoussac, with a number of fine B&B's. Many places are bilingual and can help arrange whale-watching tours.

Camping Tadoussac 428 rue du Bâteau-Passeur Ⓣ 418/235-4501, Ⓦ www.essipit.com. About 2km from the ferry terminal on Hwy 138, this is the best spot in the area for family-style camping ($25–40) – just make sure you arrive early during summer to get a spot. They also have five charming cottages (❻) and several larger, fully equipped houses (❻); late May to mid-Sept.

Maison Hovington 285 rue des Pionniers Ⓣ 418/235-4466, Ⓦ www.maisonhovington.com.

A century-old B&B with five beautifully decorated rooms. The bilingual owners will pick you up from the bus station. ④; mid-May to Oct.

Maison Majorique 158 rue du Bâteau-Passeur ⓣ418/235-4372, ⓦwww.ajtadou.com. This beatnik-type hostel is one of the best in Québec and – thanks to its own bar – determinedly lively and sociable. Canoes, cross-country skis, snowmobiles and snowshoes are all available for rent; various activities – guided hikes, snowshoe excursions and dog-sleigh trips – are organized in their relative seasons. All-you-can-eat breakfasts ($4) are optional. Dorm beds ($22); private and family rooms also available – call for prices.

Le Roupillon 141 rue du Parc ⓣ418/235-4353, ⓦwww.leroupillon.ca. A friendly, bilingual place with five themed rooms (including "Safari" and "Astral"), antique furnishings throughout and a relaxing lounge area with wood-burning stove. The owners can help arrange whale-watching tours. ④

Auberge la Sainte Paix 102 rue du Saguenay ⓣ418/235-4803, ⓦwww.aubergelasaintepaix.com. The best of the town's many B&Bs, this smartly-designed house is set on a hill overlooking the bay and has seven comfortable rooms. The exceedingly helpful owners can reserve whale-watching cruises with all of the town's operators. ④–⑥

Hôtel Tadoussac 165 rue du Bord-de-l'Eau ⓣ418/235-4421 or 1-800/561-0718, ⓦwww.hoteltadoussac.com. This red-roofed hotel is the pick (and the priciest) of the town's accommodation options, with surcharged riverview rooms, swimming pool, miniature golf and tennis courts. ⑦

The Town

The waterfront rue de Bord-de-l'Eau is dominated by the red roof and green lawns of the *Hôtel Tadoussac*, a landmark since 1864 and the focus of the historic quarter. Across the road is the oldest wooden church in Canada, the tiny **Chapelle de Tadoussac** (mid-June to mid-October daily 9am–9pm,; ⓣ418/235-4324; $2), built in 1747; visits are possible out of season by reservation. Tucked on the other side of the hotel, the steep-roofed wooden **Poste de Traite Chauvin** (mid-June to mid-Sept daily 9.30am–6.30pm, otherwise hours vary; $3) replicates – right down to the handmade nails – the first trading post on the north shore of the St Lawrence River, as described in Champlain's 1603 diary. It houses a small museum of beaver pelts and items pertaining to the fur trade, but a peek in from the doorway will suffice. Following the waterfront towards the harbour brings you to the modern **Centre d'Interprétation des Mammifères Marins** (daily: mid-May to mid-June & late Sept to late Oct noon–6pm; mid-June to late Sept 9am–8pm; ⓣ418/235-4701, ⓦwww.baleinesendirect.net; $8), at 108 rue de la Cale-Sèche, run by the nonprofit Group for Research and Education on Marine Mammals. This is a must if you intend to go whale-watching, as its excellent documentary films and displays explain the life cycles of the whales and the efforts being made to save their ever-diminishing numbers.

Outdoor activities

The Tadoussac sector of the Parc du Saguenay offers some easy **hikes** around the village and a 42km trek to Baie-Ste-Marguerite further along the fjord; an **information office** (mid-June to Sept daily 9am–5pm) in the car park just after the ferry terminal supplies maps of the trails. From near the Chapelle there is a two-hour walk along the beach; check tide times, as you'll have to clamber over rocks at high tide. The walk ends northeast of Tadoussac at the long terraced **sand dunes** on the Baie du Moulin-Baude, known locally as *le désert*. To reach the 112m-high dunes, you can also follow chemin du Moulin-Baude for 5km to the interpretation centre, the Maison des Dunes (early June to mid-Oct daily 9am–5pm; ⓣ418/272-1556 or 1-877/272-5229; $3.50). A little over a kilometre further on, the Sentier du Belvédiere is an ideal spot for a picnic with its expansive views of the river below and the dunes to the north.

Eating and drinking

Perhaps the most refined **meal** can be had at the *Hôtel Tadoussac* (see above), which has a vast dining room and a reasonably priced set menu ($20–30). *Chez Georges*

Whale-watching from the Tadoussac area

Whale-watching trips from Tadoussac and the surrounding communities are best done from mid-May to mid-October. Generally, prices for two- to three-hour trips from Tadoussac are around $45 in a large, sturdy and comfortable boat, and $50–60 in a zodiac, which provides a more exciting ride. The price drops the more northerly the starting-point: similar excursions from Bergeronnes and Les Escoumins cost around $35 in a zodiac. Officially, boats are not allowed to stray within 400m of the protected belugas, but the whales don't know that and often come thrillingly close to the craft.

If you can't afford a boat trip, or would rather leave the whales in peace, take the short **hike** around the Pointe de l'Islet from the marina in Tadoussac, which has lookout points for beluga-spotting. Improve your chances for a sighting by heading to even better lookout points along the shore: **Baie-Ste-Marguerite** (see p.339), west of Tadoussac, and **Cap-de-Bon-Désir** (see p.336), just past Bergeronnes, are the best. An array of interpretation centres supplement the whale-watching adventures, but don't miss the excellent **Centre d'Interprétation des Mammifères Marins** in Tadoussac (see p.334).

From Tadoussac and Baie-Ste-Catherine

If you're worried about missing a reservation in **Tadoussac** because of the ferry queue, ask to board at the quay in **Baie-Ste-Catherine** instead – many of the companies fill up their boats on both shores of the mouth of the Saguenay before heading off to see the whales. Some firms also run cruises up the Saguenay Fjord, as well as combined whale/fjord packages. Load up with brochures at the tourist office and compare what's on offer.

For trips in twelve person zodiacs, contact Otis Excursions (ⓣ418/235-4197, ⓦwww.otisexcursions.com), at 431 rue Bâteau-Passeur. Croisières AML (ⓣ418/237-4274 or 1-800/563-4643, ⓦwww.croisieresaml.com) gives you the option of a large boat or 24-person zodiac, while Croisières Groupe Dufour (ⓣ418/235-4421 or 1-800/561-0718, ⓦwww.dufour.ca) at the *Hôtel Tadoussac* (see p.334), offers whale safaris aboard a catamaran, a 48-person zodiac or a more sedate schooner.

From south of Tadoussac

Croisières Groupe Dufour (ⓣ418/692-0222 or 1-800/463-5250) offers a ten-hour trip from **Québec City** to Baie-Ste-Catherine for $115, with a pick-up and drop-off in **Ste-Anne-de-Beaupré**.

From north of Tadoussac

You'll spend less time on the water with the following companies, but their points of departure on the Côte-Nord are closer to where the whales are most likely to be, so you get about the same amount of contact time for less money. Heading north on Hwy 138, there's a turn-off on the right just after the overpass at **Bergeronnes**, where Les Croisières Neptune (ⓣ418/232-6716, ⓦwww.croisieresneptune.net) has a ticket office at 507 rue du Boisé for trips in zodiacs only. Croisière Essipit (ⓣ418/233-2266 or 1-888/868-6666, ⓦwww.essipit.com), 498 rue de la Mer, also uses the quay in Bergeronnes and has a wider variety of craft. Les Écumeurs (ⓣ418/233-2141, ⓦwww.lesecumeurs.com), at 4 Hwy 138, is the least expensive and launches its zodiacs from Les Escoumins, just south of the marine park (see p.336)

(ⓣ418/235-4393, ⓦwww.hotelgeorges.com), 135 rue du Bateau-Passeur, is in Tadoussac's oldest house and has seafood and steaks on the table d'hôte for $21. An inviting central option is *Café Bohéme*, 239 rue des Pionniers (ⓣ418/235-1180), which serves fresh salads and inventive dishes using local ingredients; they also have free wi-fi.

Cheaper food and great evenings of **drinking** can be had at *Le Gibard*, 135 rue Bord de l'Eau, which stays open until 3am, and at *Café du Fjord* (ⓣ418/235-4626), 154 rue du Bâteau-Passeur near the hostel, a young hangout with good music; they also have food, including a $16 dinner buffet. The best nightspot is *Le Père Coquart Café* (ⓣ418/235-1170; early June to Oct), at 115 rue Coupe de L'Islet, around the corner from *Le Gibard*. They serve food until 9pm when the place morphs into an intimate place to hear Québécois and other music.

North of Tadoussac

The landscape **north of Tadoussac** takes in lakes surrounded by granite outcroppings and boreal forest, interspersed with stretches of sandy beaches and salt marshes. The craggy terrain is the chief attraction here with lookout points and short trails in many of the villages, as well as interpretation centres for just about everything. The area is particularly known for cheaper and more convenient **whale-watching**, spectacular **diving** and first-rate **birdwatching**, particularly during the migratory seasons.

Bergeronnes

As accommodation fills up in Tadoussac in high season, you may wind up having to stay in **BERGERONNES**, 22km along Hwy 138. Otherwise if you're here it's generally for the good lookout post by a popular whale-feeding ground beside the Cap de Bon Désir lighthouse which now serves as the **Centre d'Interprétation et d'Observation de Cap-de-Bon-Désir** (mid-June to mid-Oct daily 9am–6pm; ⓦwww.quebecmaritime.qc.ca; $7), at 13 chemin du Cap-Bon-Désir, which has displays on whales. Also in town is the Archéo Topo (mid-May to mid-Oct daily 9am–8pm; ⓦwww.archeotopo.qc.ca; $5.50), at 498 rue de la Mer, a research and exhibition centre devoted to archeology along the Côte-Nord, where finds date back eight thousand years.

Accommodation is available at *Le Bergeronnette* (May–Oct ⓣ418/232-6642 or 1-877/232-6605, ⓦwww.bergeronnette.com; ❸), 65 rue Principale, which has simple rooms and a reasonable restaurant. *Camping Bon Désir* (ⓣ418/232-6297, ⓦwww.campingbondesir.com; $22–29; June–Oct), off the highway east of town, overlooks the river, and charges more for a pitch with a view.

Les Escoumins

Though whale-watching is popular at **LES ESCOUMINS**, the big deal here is the **diving**, especially at night when the phosphorescence creates an eerie underwater landscape. **Le Centre des Loisirs Marins** (interpretation centre: 9.30–11am & 1.30–3.30pm; $5), at 41 rue des Pilotes, is only worthwhile if you intend to dive (diving card required). The dive shop downstairs, Centre de plongée Atlan (ⓣ418/233-4242), rents out a complete set of gear for $55 per day. The only other reason to visit is for the excellent **birdwatching**; the Promenade du Moulin brings you to a rugged shoreline with hundreds of birds.

The town's **hostel**, *Auberge de la plongée* (ⓣ418/233-3289 or 1-800/375-3465; dorms $18), 118 rue St-Marcelin, is a bit shabby. If you want to **eat**, try the excellent burgers at *Auberge Manoir Bellevue* (ⓣ418/233-3325 or 1-888/233-3325, ⓦwww.manoirbellevue.com; ❸), 27 rue de l'Église, which also does a pricey table d'hôte for dinner and has comfortable rooms.

From Les Escoumins there's a **ferry** to Trois-Pistoles (see p.310), while the seasonal **ferry** (see p.312) to Rimouski leaves 59km along the coast from Forestville. While waiting in Forestville you can picnic next to the river or hang out on a pleasant beach, where camping is permitted.

Fjord du Saguenay

The **Fjord du Saguenay** is one of the world's longest, cutting through the Canadian Shield before merging with the St Lawrence River. A stupendous expanse of rocky outcrops, sheer cliffs and thick vegetation, the land flanking the fjord on both sides is protected as the **Parc du Saguenay and Parc Marin du Saguenay–St-Laurent** (Ⓣ418/235-4703 or 1-800/463-6769, Ⓦwww.sepaq.com), whose main entry is at Rivière-Éternité (see p.338). The marine park contains six different ecosystems and supports hundreds of marine species, but has had its work cut out for it. Since the park's creation, government initiatives have eliminated ninety percent of the pollutants from industrial plants in the immediate vicinity. Still, pollutants remain in the sediment and the number of St Lawrence River **beluga whales** is currently at one thousand, down from five thousand a century ago, placing them on Canada's list of endangered species. The area continues to attract whales because the mingling of the cold Labrador Sea waters with the highly oxygenated freshwater of the Saguenay River produces a uniquely rich crop of krill and plankton. The white St Lawrence River beluga lives in the area year-round, and from May to October it is joined by six species of migratory whales, including the minke, finback and **blue whale**.

The walls of the fjord itself extend to a depth of 270m in places, almost as much as the height of the cliffs above the waterline. Wedged between the two halves of the Parc du Saguenay are some of the most attractive parts of the Parc Marin du Saguenay–St-Laurent. But since **no bridges** cross the Saguenay for the 126km between Tadoussac and Chicoutimi, you may need to backtrack to explore both shores. For a taste of both the terrestrial and marine parks, drive along Hwy 170 as far as **Rivière-Éternité** on the south shore, and then double back. From Tadoussac, Hwy 172 runs parallel to the north side of the fjord past the turn-offs to Baie Ste-Marguerite and the pretty waterside village of **Ste-Rose-du-Nord** before reaching the bridge to **Chicoutimi**.

▲ Ice fishing on the Saguenay Fjord

The southern shore

Coming from Charlevoix, the best approach to the Parc du Saguenay is to drive along the wriggling Hwy 170 from Saint-Siméon, a road that strikes the **southern shore** of the Saguenay Fjord after about 50km, close to L'Anse-St-Jean. Both this town and Rivière-Éternité, 33km further west, are easy entry points to the park and arguably the most attractive places on the fjord to take a boat trip.

L'Anse-St-Jean

L'ANSE-ST-JEAN is famous for its Pont du Faubourg, the covered bridge on the back of the now-retired $1000 note. The village has a terrific view of the Saguenay Fjord and surrounding hills from the marina, and makes a good base to explore the park. L'Anse-St-Jean also boasts a particularly fine view of the Saguenay from the **L'Anse-de-Tabatière lookout**; the 500m trail begins at the lookout's car park. From the quay in L'Anse-St-Jean you can take a two- or four-hour **cruise** (June–Sept 1–3 daily; from $41) or join Fjord en kayak (May–Oct; ⓣ418/272-3024, ⓦwww.fjord-en-kayak.ca), 359 rue St-Jean-Baptiste, for three-hour trips ($48), or one- to five-day excursions (from $105). Alternatively, ride along the fjord on **horseback**: the Centre équestre des Plateaux (ⓣ418/272-3231, ⓦwww.cedp.ca), 34 chemin des Plateaux, offers three-hour rides ($60), as well as multiday excursions. Inland from L'Anse-St-Jean, you can ski at **Mont-Edouard** (ⓣ418/272-2927, ⓦwww.montedouard.com; $37 for full-day pass), with a 450m vertical and 28 trails.

L'Anse-St-Jean's best budget **accommodation** is *L'Auberge du boutdumonde* (ⓣ418/272-9979), 40 chemin des Plateaux, a beautifully-sited and charming hostel (dorms $25) that also has three private rooms ($50) and three campsites ($15). Other options are the clifftop cottages and condos at *Les Gîtes du Fjord* (ⓣ418/272-3430 or 1-800/561-8060, ⓦwww.lesgitesdufjord.com; ❺–❽), 354 rue St-Jean-Baptiste, as well as Camping de l'Anse (ⓣ418/272-2554, ⓦwww.campingdelanse.ca; $18–25), in a good position close to the fjord, with excellent facilities. For moderately priced **seafood** try *Le Maringoinfre* (ⓣ418/272-2385; $20–30 for dinner), 212 rue St-Jean-Baptiste.

Rivière-Éternité

Continuing along the fjord, scrappy **RIVIÈRE-ÉTERNITÉ**, 83km from Saint-Siméon on Hwy 138 and 61km east of Chicoutimi, is the main gateway to the Parc du Saguenay ($3.50). The park's **information centre** (mid-May to late-Sept daily 9am–9pm; late Sept to mid-Oct weekends only; ⓣ418/272-1556 or 1-800/665-6527, ⓦwww.sepaq.com), 3km from the village at 91 rue Notre-Dame, has trail maps and kayak routes and expert naturalists on hand. A smaller information post lies 1.5km from the village, on the park's border. Halfway between the two is the park's main **campsite** (sites $21–28); reservations are available from the information centre. Blackflies love this area, though the worst is over by late July; dress appropriately and bring repellent.

From the main information centre, a couple of short **hikes** and a long one are laid out through this sector of the park. The best short trip is the Statue Hike, an easy four-hour (7km) round-trip up the massive bluff of Cap Trinité, which flanks the deep-blue water of the Baie Éternité. The summit is topped by a huge statue known as *Our Lady of the Saguenay*, erected in 1881 by Charles-Napoléon Robitaille after he was saved from drowning in the river. The long-distance Les Caps hike (25km) follows the bay of the Éternité River back to L'Anse-St-Jean via massive plateaus, ravines, waterfalls and stunning views. It is an intermediate walk along clear paths and takes about three days. There are wilderness campsites and a couple of refuges along the way; registration with the information centre is required. A number of companies offer **water-taxi** services for backpackers, enabling you to hike as far as Tadoussac (one week) – you can even have your vehicle sent on to your destination by boat.

The northern shore

Running parallel to the Saguenay Fjord, Hwy 172 is a dramatic route along the less-frequented **northern shore** of the Saguenay that gives occasional panoramas over the water and provides access to a couple of pretty towns en route, where cruises are available or kayaks can be rented. The daily (except Sat) Intercar **bus** from Tadoussac follows the highway, terminating at Chicoutimi.

Baie-Ste-Marguerite

A 42-kilometre hiking trail from Tadoussac (follow the signs for 'Sentier Le Fjord') ends at **BAIE-STE-MARGUERITE**, where the main interpretation centre (early June to mid-Oct daily 9am–5pm; ⓣ418/272-1556 or 1-800/665-6527, ⓦwww.sepaq.com) for the northern part of the Parc du Saguenay ($3.50) is located. To get here by car, you need to travel 3km down a dusty gravel road that exits the hwy just after tiny Rivière-Ste-Marguerite, itself worth a quick stop for its covered bridge. The main draw here is **belugas**, and the interpretation centre has displays that cover all facets of them as well as the fjord in general; ask at the desk for an English-language guidebook. An easy three-kilometre trail leads through the woods to an observation platform, from where the belugas can frequently be spotted. Despite its appearances, the centre's cafeteria serves up good, hearty grub for hungry hikers from 7am in summer.

Ste-Rose-du Nord

About 80km from Tadoussac is the turn-off for **STE-ROSE-DU-NORD**, a tiny village of white houses crammed beneath the precipitous walls of the fjord, 3km from the main road. The seasonal **tourist office** (late June to mid-Sept 9.30am–7.30pm; ⓦwww.ste-rosedunord.qc.ca), 213 rue du Quai, has free maps of **hiking trails**, including the Plate-Forme trail leading to a fabulous panoramic viewpoint above the town. The **Musée de la Nature** (May to mid-Oct daily 8.45am–8.30pm, otherwise until 7pm; ⓦwww.musee-de-la-nature.com; $5.50), 199 rue de la Montagne, is a small but surprisingly informative museum housing an eclectic range of exhibits, including stuffed animals. The church of **Ste-Rose-de-Lima** (daily 8am–8pm), with its interior of wood, birch bark, branches and roots, is also worth a peek. Croisières du Fjord (late June to early Oct 1–2 departures daily; $45; ⓣ418/543-7630 or 1-800/363-7248, ⓦwww.croiseresdufjord.com) runs ninety-minutes **cruises** of the fjord's most stunning stretch. Sometimes there's a boat connection with Tadoussac as well; ask at the information centre for details.

If you're **staying** over, try *Auberge le Presbytère* (ⓣ418/675-1362 or 1-866/303-1326, ⓦwww.aupresbytere.com; ❸), 136 rue du Quai, a converted presbyterian sanctuary; it has an outstanding **restaurant**. Rooms are also available above the Musée de la Nature (ⓣ418/675-2348; ❷), while *Camping la Descente des Femmes* (ⓣ418/675-2581; June to mid-Oct) has sites for $17–22 and incredible views.

The Upper Saguenay and Lac Saint-Jean

The Saguenay Fjord's source – the vast **Lac Saint-Jean** – sits 210km inland, linked by the Rivière Saguenay. Along this stretch, a glut of aluminium and paper plants using the river as a power source has resulted in the growth of characterless industrial towns, the largest of which is **Chicoutimi**. Further west, beyond **Jonquière**, the lake's farmland periphery is still relatively untouched and offers the opportunity to stay on the Montagnais reserve at **Mashteuiatsh** near Roberval, a unique zoo at **Saint-Félicien** and the strange sight of **Val-Jalbert**, Québec's most accessible ghost town. A bike route connects the lake's towns and is an increasingly popular option for travellers from Montréal or Québec who pop their bike on the train or bus for a three- to five-day tour of the lake. In 1996, the Saguenay–Lac-Saint-Jean region was devastated by one of Canada's biggest catastrophes – a flood that wiped out homes and businesses in several towns. As the flood was an "act of God" no one received insurance, but those who lost their homes were assisted by donations from across the country.

From Lac Saint-Jean's southern shore it's about five hours to Montréal on Hwy 155 (via Trois-Rivières); from the southeast, you can take the moose-infested Hwy 169 until it joins up with Hwy 175 on its way to Québec City.

Chicoutimi

Since its founding by a Scottish immigrant in 1842, the regional capital of **CHICOUTIMI** has grown from a small sawmill centre into one of the province's largest towns. It's not a particularly enticing place, though the pedestrianized port area is pleasant enough. The town hosts one of Québec's best **festivals** – the mid-February ten-day **Carnaval Souvenir** when what seems like the entire population dresses in costumes from circa 1900; lumber camps, can-can clubs, operetta shows and period-authentic heavy drinking augment the pioneer atmosphere.

Arrival and information

Chicoutimi's **bus station** (ⓣ418/543-1403), 55 rue Racine est, is on the corner of rues Tessier and Racine, in the centre of town. Buses from Montréal, Québec City, Lac Saint-Jean and Tadoussac all connect here. The CITS local bus (ⓣ418/545-2487) links with Jonquière's **train station** (arrival point for trains from Montréal), running at least hourly from 7.15am–9.45pm. There's a municipal **tourist office** (Mon–Fri 8am–noon & 1.30–4.30pm; ⓣ418/698-3167 or 1-800/463-6565) at 295 rue Racine est.

If you're using Chicoutimi as a gateway to the Saguenay Fjord, you could opt for a **cruise**. Croisières du Fjord (ⓣ418/543-7630 or 1-800/363-7248, ⓦwww.croisieresdufjorde.com; $48; late June to Aug) goes as far as Cap Trinité, stopping both ways at Ste-Rose-du-Nord (see p.339), where they provide a coach back to Chicoutimi on the morning run (in the afternoon, the first Chicoutimi–Ste-Rose-du-Nord leg is by coach).

The Town

Outside Carnaval Souvenir time, the main local attraction is **La Pulperie de Chicoutimi** (June & Sept to mid-Oct Wed–Sun 9am–5pm; late June to Sept daily 9am–6pm; mid-Oct to early June Wed–Sun 10am–4pm; ⓦwww.pulperie.com; $10), 300 rue Dubuc. The Chicoutimi Pulp Company built the five austere brick buildings along the rapids in 1896. Left to rot in 1930, these gigantic ghosts of Chicoutimi's industrial past were restored to prime condition, damaged heavily in the flood of 1996 and renovated extensively again until the Pulperie was reopened in 2002. Exhibits explain the mill's history and include the strange **Maison du Peintre Arthur Villeneuve**. The former home of naive painter Arthur Villeneuve, the house is in effect one big painting, with murals covering inside and out. The subject matter is unadventurous, but the artist's work is bright and cheery, while scenes of 1950s Chicoutimi – when Villeneuve started his project after retiring as a barber – are intriguing.

Practicalities

Accommodation is readily available as the town hosts business conferences year-round. *Auberge Centre-Ville* (ⓣ418/543-0253, ⓦwww.aubergecentreville.com; ③),

104 rue Jacques-Cartier est, is a small, central **hotel** with free wi-fi, while *Le Montagnais* (ⓣ418/543-1521 or 1-800/463-9160, ⓦwww.lemontagnais.qc.ca; ⑥), 1080 boul Talbot, is a modern hotel with a full range of amenities further out.

There are numerous small **restaurants** on rue Racine, east of the tourist office. Try *La Cuisine Café-Resto* at no. 387, which has French food in the $10–20 range. For a more upmarket meal try the elegant *La Bourgresse* (ⓣ418/543-3178), 260 rue Riverin, where French cuisine is $20–40.

Jonquière

Some 15km west of Chicoutimi, **JONQUIÈRE** thrives due to its Alcan aluminium smelter, one of the largest in the world, and its two paper mills. A modern town with wide avenues and the world's only large-scale aluminium bridge (across the Saguenay), it can make a good stop for budget travellers because of an Allo-Stop office and train connections with Montréal.

The **tourist office** (Mon–Fri 8am–noon & 1.30–4.30pm; ⓣ418/548-4004 or 1-800/561-9196) is at 2665 boul du Royaume in the Centre des Congrès. **Buses** (ⓣ418/547-2167) terminate at 2249 rue St-Hubert and the **train** (ⓣ1-800/361-5390) station is at 2439 rue St-Dominique.

Practicalities

The *Auberge des Deux Tours* (ⓣ418/695-2022 or 1-888/454-2022, ⓦwww.aubergedeuxtours.qc.ca; ③), 2522 rue Saint-Dominique, is reasonable choice, or there's the *Holiday Inn Saguenay* (ⓣ418/548-3124 or 1-800/363-3124, ⓦwww.saguenay.holiday-inn.com; ⑥), 2675 boul du Royaume.

You can **eat** at the stately 1911 *Auberge Villa Pachon* (ⓣ418/542-3568 or 1-888/922-3568), 1904 rue Perron, whose pricey restaurant is excellent; meals start at over $50. Another expensive option is *L'Amandier* (ⓣ418/542-5395), 5219 chemin St-Andre, out of town but worth the trip for the bizarre dining room of carved plaster and wood. For an everyday meal head to Rue St-Dominique: *Le Puzzle*, no. 2497, is a fun place with cool decor.

Lac Saint-Jean

To the west of Chicoutimi, around **Lac Saint-Jean**, stretches a relatively untouched area whose tranquil lakeshore villages are linked by the circular route of Hwy 169. The huge glacial lake is fed by most of the rivers of northeastern Québec and – unusually for an area of the rocky Canadian Shield – is bordered by sandy beaches and a lush, green terrain that has been farmed for over a century. The local cuisine, especially the delicious coarse meat pie called a *tourtière* and the thick blueberry pie, is renowned throughout the province.

Easily the best way to take in the lake is on the relatively flat **Véloroute des Bleuets** (ⓦwww.veloroute-bleuets.qc.ca), a 256km **bike route** that encircles the whole lake. Much of it is in the form of a wide paved shoulder, but 60km of the route is completely car-free. The path passes close to most of the major attractions and through many of the villages around Lac Saint-Jean and there are beaches all along the lakeshore where you can cool off. The **train** from Montréal to Jonquière stops at Chambord on the south shore near Val-Jalbert and there's a **bus** from Québec City to Alma. A number of **B&Bs** and other services cater to two-wheeled visitors, and even the locals lay out a warm welcome – some set up garden chairs to rest on near the bike path. Gilles Girard minivan service (ⓣ418/342-6651 or 1-888/342-6651) can take some strain off by transporting your luggage around the lake for $40 per piece for a three- to four-day trip. The itinerary outlined below begins at Alma and heads west around the lake.

Alma and Saint-Gédéon

The dull aluminium-producing city of **ALMA**, 50km west of Jonquière, is useful for its **buses** – to Chicoutimi and Québec City and various points around Lac St-Jean – and is a practical starting point for the Véloroute des Bleuets. Liberté à Vélo (Ⓣ418/668-8430 1-877/668-8430, Ⓦwww.liberteavelo.ca) provides guided **tours** along the cycle route – a service which includes luggage transport. To **rent** a bike, try Equinox (Ⓣ418/480-7226, Ⓦwww.equinoxaventure.ca), 1385 chemin de la Marina, or Vélo Jeunesse (Ⓣ418/662-9785, Ⓦwww.velo-jeunesse.ca), 1691 av du Pont Alma, which has tandem bikes. The **information centre** (Mon–Fri 8am–noon & 1.30–4.30pm; Ⓣ418/668-3611 or 1-877/668-3611) is at 1682 av du Pont Nord.

In a clockwise direction beyond Alma, the path follows a shoreline inaccessible by hwy, joining up with highway 170 beyond **SAINT-GÉDÉON**, a popular beach town. For a treat, head for the lakefront *Auberge des Îles* (Ⓣ418/345-2589 or 1-800/680-2589, Ⓦwww.aubergedesiles.com; ❻), 250 rang des Îles, a lovely inn just north of St-Gédéon with a four-course menu of game and local flavours for around $35.

Val-Jalbert

One of the main attractions of the region, the historical village of **VAL-JALBERT** (daily: May to mid-June & late Aug to early Oct 10am–5pm; mid-June to late Aug 9.30am–5.30pm; Ⓣ418/275-3132 or 1-888/675-3132, Ⓦwww.valjalbert.com; $19.50) is 52km beyond Alma along the cycle route and 92km west of Chicoutimi along hwys 170 and 169.

The 72m-high Ouiatchouan waterfall, which dominates the town, led to the establishment of a pulp mill here more than a century ago, and by 1926 the village had around 950 inhabitants. In the following year, the introduction of chemical-based pulping made the mill redundant, and the village was closed down. Val-Jalbert was left to rot until 1985, when the government decided to renovate it as a tourist attraction. From the site entrance a bus (with on-board French commentary) runs around the main sights of the village, ending at the mill at the base of the falls. You can then wander around whatever catches your eye along the way – the abandoned wooden houses, a former convent (now a museum) or the general store (now a souvenir shop). From the mill, itself converted into an excellent crafts market and cafeteria, a **cable car** leads to the top of the falls, from where there are stunning views of the village and Lac Saint-Jean beyond. It is possible to stay in Val-Jalbert's renovated **hotel** above the general store (❸), in apartments in the converted houses on St George Street ($70–132 for one to six people), or in the **campsite** ($26) just outside the village. The site is officially closed from late October through April, but you can still gain access for free – it is a beautifully tranquil place to spend some time.

Mashteuiatsh

Some 10km west of Val-Jalbert, at **Roberval**, a turn-off leads to the Montagnais reserve of **MASHTEUIATSH**, also known as **Pointe-Bleue**. The reserve was created in 1856, and today around two thousand of eastern Québec's fifteen thousand Montagnais live here. Like many Canadian reserves, Mashteuiatsh is dry, in an attempt to reduce alcoholism and its attendant problems, yet the Montagnais suffer a great deal of prejudice from the surrounding white communities – so much so that there's no bus service, because Québécois bus drivers refuse to go there.

The village is situated on the lake and has an **information centre** (mid-June to Sept daily 8am–8pm) at 1427 rue Ouiatchouan. At the end of July a **powwow** is held on the waterfront by the four concrete teepee sculptures that represent the seasons. Up the hill, at 1787 rue Amishk, is the recently renovated **Musée Amérindien** (mid-May to mid-Oct daily 9am–6pm; rest of year Mon–Thurs 9am–noon & 1–4pm, Thurs 8am–noon & 1–4pm; Ⓦwww.museeilnu.ca; $9), where you start with a twenty-minute film showing traditional Montagnais life, much of it revolving around hunting and fishing. The permanent exhibition Pekuakami Ilnuatsh, which translates as "the Lac St-Jean Montagnais", continues the theme with artefacts and interpretation panels describing domestic life and the impact of European contact; temporary exhibitions highlight the works of aboriginal artists.

From August to September, the community organized Ashuapmushuaniussi (Ⓣ418/275-7200; call for current rates), at 1562 rue Ouiatchouan, leads **adventure trips** into the bush where you are immersed in traditional ways of life, relying on the woodland and river resources to build shelters, make fires and prepare food.

Saint-Prime and Saint-Félicien

Saint-Prime village, 13km west of Roberval, has a surprising little museum, the **Musée du fromage cheddar** (daily: early June & Sept 10am–5pm; late June–Aug 9am–6pm; Ⓦwww.museecheddar.org; $7.75), at 148 av Albert-Perron, where four generations of cheese-makers have worked since 1895. The one-hour guided tour covers the whole process of cheddar production (some of which is still exported to England). The unexpected part of the tour is upstairs, where the Perron family residence appears as it would have in 1922; a very convincing "Marie Perron" describes her life, how the best piece of furniture was reserved for the priest who visited once a year and why kitchen counters used to be so low – so children could make themselves useful. You also get to try a bit of the cheese produced by the modern cheese factory.

At the western extremity of the lake on the Ashuapmushuan River, **SAINT-FÉLICIEN** is the site of Québec's best zoo, the **Zoo Sauvage de Saint-Félicien** (June–Aug daily 9am–6pm; early May, Sept & Oct 9am–5pm; Ⓣ418/679-0543 or 1-800/667-5687, Ⓦwww.zoosauvage.com; $30), located on Chamouchouane Island. Don't let the giant car park put you off: the first part of the zoo is in a beautiful riverside setting. The rest mimics a number of ecosystems where over eighty, mainly Canadian, species roam free. It is the humans who are the ones in cages, hauled around on the back of a mini-train (provisions are made for disabled travellers). Highlights include the Arctic environment for the polar bears which allows you to see the magnificent animals swim underwater and the Asian section, which is home to Siberian tigers. The zoo also has an historical angle, with mock-ups of an aboriginal village, trading post, loggers' camp and settlers' farm, staffed by costumed guides. An English guidebook is available at the entrance.

Saint-Félicien's **information office** (late June to early Sept Mon–Fri 8.30am–8pm, Sat & Sun 9am–8pm; rest of year Mon–Fri 8.30am–noon & 1–4.30pm; Ⓣ418/679-9888) is at 1209 boul Sacré-Coeur. For **accommodation**, try the quaint *Auberge des Berges* (Ⓣ418/679-3346 or 1-877/679-3346; ④), 610 boul Sacré-Coeur, which has views of the lake.

Dolbeau-Mistassini and Saint-Monique

From Saint-Félicien the hwy and bike path separate, rejoining 15km inland at **Normadin**. Skip the visit to **Les Grands Jardins de Normandin** (it's overpriced and over-hyped) and continue clockwise around the lake to **DOLBEAU-MISTASSINI**, 28km further on. Dolbeau, the western half of town, is at its best during mid-July's ten-day **Western Festival**, with rodeos and people wandering around in stetsons and spurs. Mistassini, the region's blueberry capital, outdoes its neighbour in early August, with the **Festival du Bleuet**

(Ⓦwww.festivaldubleuet.qc.ca), one big blowout on everything blueberry – including a potent blueberry wine. Over the Mistassini River 7km up the road to St Eugéne d'Argentenay, the **Monastère des Pères Trappistes** sells its own organic produce; a large quantity of the berries are on offer in season, along with home-made chocolates (the chocolate-covered blueberry bar is regionally famous). Another worthwhile trip out of town is south in the direction of Ste-Marguerite-Marie, following route de Vauvert to its end where you'll find a 1km **beach** at the Centre Touistique Vauvert (Ⓣ418/374-2746). There's a restaurant and a few free places to pitch a tent; discreet no-trace camping on the beach is also tolerated.

For **accommodation** in Dolbeau-Mistassini, try the plesant *Auberge La Diligence* (Ⓣ418/276-6544 or 1-800/361-6162, Ⓦwww.hotelier.qc.ca; ❹), 414 av de la Friche. *Gîte Bonjour, Bienvenue* (Ⓣ418/276-1291; ❷), at 1824 boul Wallberg, is a good, inexpensive **B&B** choice.

Another 20km round the shore, a short walk just west of the village of **SAINTE-MONIQUE**, is a **hostel** and **campsite** on its own little island: the *Auberge de l'Île du Repos de Péribonka* (Ⓣ418/347-5649, Ⓦwww.iledurepos.com; ❸; dorms $24, camping from $17). Its location is useful for an excursion to **Parc de la Pointe-Taillon** (Ⓣ418/347-5371, Ⓦwww.sepaq.com; $3.50, parking $7), which also has rustic camping available 2–4km from the car park ($19 per site, no services); they'll give you a lift if needed. Occupying a finger of land that juts into Lac Saint-Jean, the park is bordered by long and often deserted beaches, and there are 45km of cycle trails, a portion of which coincides with the Véloroute des Bleuets. From Sainte-Monique, it's 29km round to Alma.

The Côte-Nord

The St Lawrence River was the lifeline of the wilderness beyond Tadoussac until the 1960s, when **Highway 138** was constructed along the **Côte-Nord** to Havre-St-Pierre, 625km away, and later Natashquan, another 145km distant. The road sweeps from high vistas down to the rugged shoreline through the vast regions of Manicouagan and Duplessis. Traditional sightseeing diversions are thin on the ground in the villages and towns en route, but there is plenty to reward a journey to this remote region, not least the strong native heritage and the panorama of spruce-covered mountains, the vast sky and the mighty St Lawrence. It is the river that holds much of what is most alluring in the Côte-Nord, from the striking beauty of the **Mingan Archipelago** to gazing at the northern lights aboard the **Nordik Express**.

The Intercar **bus** from Québec City to Tadoussac serves the Côte-Nord as far as Baie-Comeau, from where another travels to Sept-Îles, where you have no choice but to spend the night before continuing on to Havre-St-Pierre. At the time of writing there is no public transport to Natashquan; check with Intercar for the latest developments. At Natashquan the hwy gives out altogether and the only onward transport is by snowmobile, plane or the supply **ship** from Rimouski, which serves the wildlife haven of **Île d'Anticosti** and undertakes a breathtaking journey along the inlets of the windswept coastline of the **Basse Côte-Nord** (Lower North Shore).

Manicouagan

The Manicouagan refers largely to a string of settlements along the side of the St Lawrence in this region. The stretch between the two major industrial conurbations, **Baie-Comeau** and **Sept-Îles**, is rugged and desolate, the road twisting over passes and down to the occasional pretty fishing village like **Godbout**, but attractions are thin on the ground and most travellers here are just passing through on their way to the Mingan Coast (see p.348) or Labrador City (see p.499) via the Hwy 389 from Baie-Comeau or the railway from Sept-Îles. If you are on your way through, pause at Sept-Îles to explore some first-rate **Innu** museums and events – they will help to make more sense of the indigenous culture, which becomes more evident as you travel north.

Baie-Comeau and around

The road into western **BAIE-COMEAU** may be a fairly drab landscape of strip malls, but it's nothing compared to the city's east side, where a monstrous, belching newsprint mill plant sits. There's no reason to hang around Baie-Comeau, but while waiting for a northward bus or a ferry to Gaspé's Matane you might stroll through the quartier Sainte-Amélie in the eastern Marquette sector, where the streets are lined by grand houses dating from the 1930s. The **Église Sainte-Amélie** (daily June to mid-Sept 9am–6pm; rest of year 10am–5pm; free), at 38 av Marquette, is worth a peek for its frescoes and stained glass windows, designed by the Italian artist Guido Nincheri.

There's a seasonal **tourist information** office on the western edge of town at 3503 boul Laflèche (June–Aug daily 8am–8pm; ⓣ418/589-3610, ⓦwww.ville.baie-comeau.qc.ca). **Buses** terminate at 212 boul Lasalle (ⓣ418/296-6921); the departure point for the **car ferry** to Matane (see p.313) is beyond the eastern end of boul evard Lasalle on rue Cartier.

If you need to **stay** over, make the most of it and head for 8 av Cabot, where you'll find the rambling stone hotel *Le Manoir* (ⓣ418/296-3391 or 1-800/463-8567, ⓦwww.manoirbc.com; ④), which overlooks the St Lawrence River. *Le Manoir* is pricey for **eating** but has excellent dishes, including local seafood. For filling pizzas, head to *Pizza Royale* (ⓣ418/589-5427), 2674 boul Laflèche.

Parc Nature de Pointe-aux-Outardes

About 20km short of Baie-Comeau is the tip of a broad peninsula where the **Parc Nature de Pointe-aux-Outardes** (June to mid-Oct daily 8am–5pm; ⓣ418/567-4226, ⓦwww.parcnature.com; $5), is worth the admission price when migratory birds flock here around May and mid-September. Easy trails take in a variety of ecosystems including salt marshes and sand dunes, and ninety-minute guided tours of the plant and birdlife are included in midsummer. If you want to visit the beach (where the water is warm enough for swimming after a few hot sunny days), there's access at the Quai municipale on rue Labrie in Pointe-aux-Outardes.

Godbout and beyond to Sept-Îles

The attractive village of **GODBOUT**, situated on a crescent-shaped bay 54km from Baie-Comeau, is not just the most pleasant place hereabouts and a prime spot for salmon fishing, it also has the excellent **Musée Amérindien et Inuit** (mid-June to Oct daily 9am–10pm; ⓣ418/568-7306; $5), at 134 chemin Pascal-Comeau. The museum was founded by Claude Grenier, who spent ten years in the north in the 1970s on a government scheme to boost the Inuit economy by promoting aboriginal culture. Consequent commercialism has diluted the output since then, but the private collection of Grenier features nothing but genuine pieces, from the characteristic soapstone carvings to domestic artefacts.

Just down the road at no. 115, the old general store houses a seasonal **tourist office** (mid-June to early Sept Mon–Fri 8am–6pm, Sat & Sun 9am–6pm; ⓣ418/568-7462) with a few relics from its former life on display. The village is linked to Matane on the south shore by **car ferry** (see p.313).

For **accommodation**, you can get a simple room at *Hébergement Cormier* (Ⓣ418/568-7535; ❶) above the convenience store Dépanneur Proprio, 156 rue Pascal Comeau, where fishing licences are sold. Or, try one of the **B&Bs** facing the water, like the pretty, century-old *La Maison du Vieux Quai* (Ⓣ418/568-7453, Ⓦwww.gitemaisonduvieuxquai.com; ❸), at 142 rue Pascal-Comeau.

Pointe-des-Monts and Baie Trinité

Situated where the St Lawrence River merges into the Gulf of St Lawrence, scenic **POINTE-DES-MONTS**, 28km from Godbout (and a further 11km off the hwy), has changed little since the nineteenth century. There's not a lot to change – all that stands on this rocky outcrop is Canada's oldest **lighthouse** dating from 1830 and a small missionary **chapel** built in 1898. The lighthouse has a small **museum** (mid-June to mid-Sept daily 9am–5pm; Ⓦwww.pharepointe-des-monts.com; $5), whose nautical displays and history of the lighthouse-keeper provide distraction as you make your way to the top. The adjacent house contains a fairly expensive seafood **restaurant** and a **B&B**, while nearby chalets handle the overflow of this popular spot (Ⓣ418/939-2242; ❷; June–Oct). **Camping** is available at *Domaine de l'Astérie* (Ⓣ418/939-2327, Ⓦwww.campingquebec.com/domaindelasterie; mid-May to mid-Sept; $17–20), 2km before the lighthouse.

Back on the hwy the tiny hamlet of **BAIE TRINITÉ** would be easily missable if not for the **Centre national des naufrages du Saint-Laurent** (June to mid-Sept, daily 9am–8pm; Ⓣ418/939-2679, Ⓦwww.centrenaufrages.ca; $8). This fascinating museum tells the story of every shipwreck along the St Lawrence River through films and multimedia displays. A self-guided trail along the nearby shoreline allows you to visit the site of several of the shipwrecks and has designated **wilderness campsites**.

Réserve Faunique de Port-Cartier-Sept-Îles

From Baie Trinité it's 103km to the lumber and iron-ore centre of **PORT-CARTIER**. The town is the entrance to the **Réserve Faunique de Port-Cartier-Sept-Îles** (Ⓣ418/766-2524, Ⓦwww.sepaq.com; $3.50), a wildlife reserve with more than a thousand lakes, popular for its hunting and salmon and trout fishing. Information, permits and reservations are available from the administration offices at 24 boul des Îles in Port-Cartier. It's a bumpy 27km drive to the **registration centre** (late May to early Sept 7am–7pm; Ⓣ418/766-4743) at the southern tip of Lac Walker, where **campsites** ($16–23) and **cabins** (❺) are available, as well as canoe rentals and maps of the hiking trails.

Sept-Îles

The largest ore-exporting port in eastern Canada, **SEPT-ÎLES** is a good base for trips further north, owing to its **rail** links with Labrador. The town itself has as much character as a pile of iron ore, but it's pleasantly situated on the river's shore and you could spend an enjoyable day here thanks to two museums that explore native culture and, in August, the presence of one of Québec's foremost native-music festivals nearby. A trip to Île Grande Basque is also a worthwhile, easy adventure.

Arrival and information

Sept-Îles has a seasonal **tourist office** (mid-June to Aug daily 9am–6pm; Ⓣ418/968-1818) at 516 rue Arnaud, down by the waterfront in the Parc du Vieux-Quai, and another regularly open branch (daily late May to mid-Sept 7.30am–9.30pm; rest of year 8.30am–5pm; Ⓣ418/968-0022 or 1-888/880-1238, Ⓦwww.ville.sept-iles.qc.ca/tourisme) on the outskirts of town at 1401 boul

Innu Nikamu festival

One of the more offbeat Canadian music chart successes of recent years was the local aboriginal group Kashtin, the only nationally-known band to perform in a native tongue. Although Claude McKenzie and Florent Vollant have gone on to solo careers, they still appear occasionally at the excellent **Innu Nikamu Festival** of song and music (information ⓣ418/927-2181, ⓦwww.innunikamu.net), held in early August, 14km east of Sept-Îles in the Montagnais reserve of **Maliotenam**. Inspired by Kashtin's success, numerous other groups travel to the four-day festival to produce some of the best of Canada's contemporary and traditional native music. As well as the music, the festival includes native food and craft stalls; despite the reserve's alcohol ban, there is always a good buzz. There is no public transport to the reserve: by car, take Hwy 138 towards Havre-St-Pierre and turn right at the Moisie intersection for the Maliotenam entrance. Tickets, available at the gate, cost around $10.

Laure. The **bus station** (ⓣ418/962-2126) is at 126 rue Monseigneur-Blanche and has buses east to Havre-St-Pierre; the QNS&L **train station**, with two to three trains a week to Labrador City, is on rue Retty at the east end of town. The *Nordik Express* supply **ship** from Rimouski leaves Sept-Îles every Tuesday morning (for details see p.351)

Accommodation

The *Le Tangon* **hostel** (ⓣ418/962-8180 or 1-800/461-8585, ⓦwww.aubergeletangon.net; June to mid-Oct; dorms $16–20, private rooms $24–28), at 555 rue Cartier, is a cheap, cramped, family-run place with breakfast for $3.50; you can camp in the grounds for $10. Alternatively, try the luxurious *Hôtel Gouverneur Sept-Îles* (ⓣ418/962-7071 or 1-888/910-1111, ⓦwww.gouveneur.com; ❺), at 666 boul Laure. Two **campsites** lie 27km to the east, off Hwy 138 next to the salmon-filled Rivière Moisie: *Camping Laurent-Val* (ⓣ418/927-2899; $16–27; mid-May to late Sept) and *Camping de la rivière Moisie* (ⓣ418/927-2021; $16–28; late May to early Sept).

The town and around

The town is best appreciated along the waterfront. A 27km bike path leads from **Parc Rivière des Rapides**, with a three-kilometre walking trail and ice fishing in winter, to the beaches east of town; rent **bikes** from Rioux Vélo Plein Air, 555 boul Laure (ⓣ418/968-3470). The road down to the third beach, **Plage Routhier**, offers the best view of the seven islands that gave Sept-Îles its name. Along the way, the path passes through the Jardins de l'Anse – a good spot for birdwatching – and along the riverfront promenade in the **Parc du Vieux Quai**, where evening concerts of Québécois music are held under the yellow tent (late June to Aug Thurs–Sun; free). An interesting overview of local history is offered by **Le Vieux-Poste** (late June to mid-Aug daily 9am–5pm; ⓣ418/968-2070, ⓦwww.mrcn.qc.ca; $3), on boulevard des Montagnais, west of the centre. The reconstructed site, with its small chapel, store and postmaster's house, presents an absorbing portrayal of the Montagnais culture and is staffed by local Montagnais who produce crafts and food, which are sold at a decently priced handicrafts store.

The excellent **Musée Shaputuan** (Mon–Fri 8am–4.30pm; also late June to early Sept Sat & Sun 10am–4pm; ⓣ418/962-4000; $4), at 290 boul des Montagnais, presents the traditional life of the Innu (Montagnais) people as it is shaped by the seasons. Unlike most descriptive museums, the exhibits speak to the viewer – often literally via audio and video recordings. The museum is primarily a space for Innu who want to learn more about their own culture.

Just offshore, the largest island in the archipelago, **Île Grande Basque**, has 12km of easy walking trails and picnic spots; you can buy camping permits for $10 at the kiosk in Parc du Vieux Quai. From June to September, the quay is the departure point for regular **passenger ferries** (10 daily 10min; $15) and **cruises** offered by Les Excursions La Petite Sirène (Ⓣ418/968-2173, Ⓦwww.freewebs.com/la_petite_sirene; 1–3 daily; 2–4hr) and Croisière Petit Pingouin (Ⓣ418/968-9558; June–Sept 1–3 daily; 10min–3hr). Whales and a sea-bird sanctuary are the main attractions, but fishing trips are also available; you can also catch herring right from the quay in early summer. **Kayak tours** are another possibility: Vêtements des Îles (Ⓣ418/962-7223 or 1-800/470-7223, Ⓦwww.vetementsdesiles.com), 637 av Brochu, offers half-day guided tours around Île Grande Basque for $60 per person.

Eating and drinking

Sept-Îles has great seafood **restaurants**, including the rather expensive *Chez Omer* (Ⓣ418/962-7777) at 372 av Brochu, where dishes cost $20–30. Get cheaper seafood, pizza and pasta, as well as a few rounds of **drinks**, at nearby *Café du Port* (Ⓣ418/962-9311) on the same street at no. 495. Further down the road *Pub St-Marc* (Ⓣ418/962-7770) at no. 588 is a surprisingly stylish bar serving micro-brews, with a more expensive restaurant upstairs where there's great pasta and a vast selection of salads, all under $20.

The Mingan coast

There is little of specific interest along the stretch of shore east of Sept-Îles, known as the **Mingan coast** – blackfly-ridden in May and much of June – until you reach **Longue-Pointe-de-Mingan**, but the scenery changes dramatically with sand dunes followed by granite outcroppings of the Canadian Shield, then eerie landscapes of rounded grey boulders surrounded by scrubby vegetation. Most visitors make the journey for the stunning islands of the **Mingan Archipelago**, a unique environment of sculptured rock formations and profuse wildlife lying off the coast between Longue-Pointe-de-Mingan and **Havre-St-Pierre**, the region's largest town and a good base for visiting the archipelago. As the tourist season is short here accommodation can be at a premium, so book ahead.

If you want to break up the journey, park your car at the small **tourist office** (Ⓣ418/538-2512) 86km east of Sept-Îles (just after the Km61 marker – distances are measured from the Rivière Moisie) and visit the **Chutes Manitou** (June–Sept daily 9am–7.30pm; $2). Cross the river via the hwy bridge and walk five minutes on the marked trail along the river to a viewing point beside the rocky cascades. A more substantial waterfall is ten minutes further down the trail, with secluded pebble beaches along the way. It's dangerous to swim here; a couple of drownings have occurred.

Longue-Pointe-de-Mingan

Although Havre-St-Pierre is the more popular departure point for cruises of the Mingan Archipelago, it's worth stopping in **LONGUE-POINTE-DE-MINGAN** for the Centre de Recherche et d'Interprétation de la Minganie (mid-June to late Sept daily 9am–6pm; $7.50), 625 rue du Centre, a joint venture between Parks Canada and the Mingan Island Cetacean Study. In addition to a film and displays on whales and other marine life, the centre provides information on excursions to the islands, issues camping permits and, for the more adventurous, offers a day with one of the **whale researchers** (Ⓣ418/949-2845; June–Oct; $110). The latter are not cruises – you are with a marine biologist in a small boat from dawn until whenever their work is finished – but they are a unique experience. Less taxing cruises are offered by Excursions du Phare (Ⓣ418/949-2302, Ⓦwww.minganie.info; $55), 126 rue de la Mer, who lead trips to the westernmost islands – an important consideration if you want to see **puffins**, as most of the cruises from Havre-St-Pierre only visit the islands in the centre sector.

Practicalities

Longue-Pointe-de-Mingan has little accommodation and isn't much of a gourmet hot spot, but adequate **accommodation** and **seafood** is available at the restaurant of the basic *Hôtel-Motel de la Minganie* (Ⓣ418/949-2992; ❷), 905 chemin du Roi. Across the road are a few beachside campsites that are free if you book an excursion, otherwise $10. You can also camp a few metres down the road at 109 rue de la Mer, where the sites and facilities are larger at *Camping de la Minganie* (Ⓣ418/949-2320 or 1-866/949-2307, Ⓦwww.tourisme-loiselle.com; $17–22)

Havre-St-Pierre

The community of **HAVRE-ST-PIERRE** would have remained a tiny fishing village founded in 1857 by fleeing Acadaians but for the discovery in the 1940s of a huge deposit of **ilmenite**, the chief source of titanium. The quarries are 45km north of town, where fishing and tourism provide employment for the non-miners, the latter industry having received a major boost when the forty islands of the **Mingan Archipelago** (see p.350) were made into a national park in 1983. Before setting off to the park, check out the **interpretation centre** (June–Sept hours vary; Ⓣ418/538-3285), which shares a building with the **tourist office** on the wharf at 1010 Promenade des Anciens. The centre has temporary photographic displays and information on the flora, fauna and geology of the islands. It opens around 8.30am if the weather is too poor for the tour boats to depart. You can book cruises to the archipelago here or at one of the smaller kiosks further along the wharf, which is also the departure point for the *Nordik Express* (see p.351).

Away from the wharf, Havre-St-Pierre's old general store, the **Maison de la culture Roland-Jomphe** (daily mid-June to early Sept 9am–9pm; Ⓣ418/538-2512; $2), at 957 rue de la Berge, houses an interpretation centre that depicts the local history.

Practicalities

The **bus station** is at 843 rue de l'Escale (Ⓣ418/538-2033). For **accommodation**, a decent, basic option is the *Hôtel-Motel du Havre* (Ⓣ418/538-2800 or 1-888/797-2800, Ⓦwww.hotelduhavre.ca; ❹) at 970 rue de l'Escale. **B&Bs** include *Gîte Chez Francoise* (Ⓣ418/538-1329, Ⓦwww.gitechezfrancoise.com; ❸), 1122 rue Boréale, which has a room (with private bath) and kitchenette for $75 per night including breakfast, as well as three other impeccable rooms that share a bathroom. The *Auberge de la Minganie* **hostel** (Ⓣ418/538-1538; ❹; dorms $25, camping $10; May–Nov) is inconveniently situated 17km west of town on Hwy 138, but the bus from the west will let you off nearby, leaving you to walk the remaining 700m. An old fishing camp on a pretty bay with minimum renovations and lots of bugs, the hostel doesn't serve breakfast, but does have kitchen facilities and canoes for rent. You can **camp** at *Camping Municipal* (Ⓣ418/538-2415, Ⓦwww.havresaintpierre.com; $17–24) at the east end of rue Boréale.

For good seafood and smoked-salmon pizza, try the **restaurant** *Chez Julie* (Ⓣ418/538-3070) at 1023 Dulcinée. *Resto-Bar Les Moutons Blancs*, 1121 rue Boréale, has occasional live music and also serves seafood.

The Mingan Archipelago

Immediately offshore from Havre-St-Pierre, the **Mingan Archipelago National Park Reserve** (Ⓦwww.pc.gc.ca/mingan; $5.80) offers some of the most beautiful landscapes in Québec. Standing on the islands' white-sand shorelines are innumerable eight-metre-high **rocks** that have the appearance of ancient totem poles, with bright orange lichen colouring their mottled surfaces and bonsai-sized trees clinging to their crevices. These formations originated as underwater sediment near the equator. The sediment was thrust above sea level more than 250 million years ago and then covered in an icecap several kilometres thick. As the drifting ice melted, the islands emerged again, seven thousand years ago, at their present location. The sea and wind gave the final touch by chipping away at the soft limestone to create the majestic monoliths of today. But bizarre geology isn't the archipelago's only remarkable feature. The **flora** constitutes a unique insular garden of 452 arctic and rare alpine species, which survive here at their southerly limit due to the limestone soil, long harsh winters and cold Gulf of Labrador current. Other than the Gulf's whale populations, the permanent **wildlife** inhabitants of the park include puffins, who build nests in the scant soil of three of the islands from early May to late August, and 199 other species of birds.

Information is available from two visitor centres: 625 rue du Centre in Longue-Pointe-de-Mingan and 1010 Promenade des Anciens in Havre-St-Pierre. Biologists on some islands meet passengers from the cruise boats (mid-June to Aug) to explain aspects of the geology and flora.

Camping is allowed on Île Quarry and five other islands ($16) but the only transport besides a sea kayak is on a Havre-St-Pierre-based Plongée Boréale sea bus or sea taxi (Ⓣ418/538-3202, Ⓦwww.plongeeboreale.com; around $40, depending on destination). Obtain camping permits from the interpretation centre in Longue-Pointe or the wharfside kiosk in Havre-St-Pierre.

▲ Eroded rocks, Mingan Archipelago National Park Reserve

The Nordik Express

When the road ends at Natashquan, access further up the Basse Côte-Nord is by snowmobile in winter, floatplane or boat. The **Nordik Express supply ship** (Ⓣ418/723-8787 or 1-800/463-0680, Ⓦwww.relaisnordik.com; April–Jan) makes a weekly journey here on a trip that affords stunning views of a rocky, subarctic landscape so cold that icebergs occasionally float past the ship even in the height of summer. The boat is evenly split between its role as a freighter and passenger ship; the majority of its passengers are locals skipping between settlements or heading for a longer jaunt to Québec's bigger towns. Its voyage begins in **Rimouski** on Tuesdays, stopping in **Sept-Îles**, **Port-Menier** on Île d'Anticosti, **Havre-St-Pierre** and **Natashquan**, before calling in at the roadless communities along the Basse Côte-Nord, reaching **Blanc-Sablon** (see p.488), Québec's most easterly village on the Labrador border, on Fridays. The same route is then followed in reverse (the boat does not stop in Sept-Îles on the way back) to arrive back in Rimouski on Monday.

The journey up this stretch of the St Lawrence is far more impressive than the destinations. During the day, whales, dolphins, seals and a wealth of sea birds are a common sight; at night the **northern lights** often present an unforgettable display. At some stops the village inhabitants surround the boat, as its twice-weekly arrival is about all that happens hereabouts. With careful planning you can arrange to spend a couple of days in one community and catch the boat on the return voyage; each village receives at least one daytime visit, but either the upstream or downstream stop may be in the middle of the night. Most travellers just hop off at each port of call for the couple of hours needed to load and unload freight. A rented bicycle is particularly handy if you want to see much.

Stops include **Kegaska** village, with its large sandy beach, and **La Romaine**, a scrappy Innu town further on. Beyond here the land becomes increasingly rocky and picturesque, the coastline cut with many intriguing inlets. **Harrington Harbour**, a pretty village and easily one of the sightseeing highlights of the trip, is set on an island whose topography of large rounded rocks made it necessary to make the pavements out of wood. The village is best seen on the upstream journey, when the boat arrives in the daytime rather than at midnight. **Accommodation** is available at *La Maison de Amy* (Ⓣ418/795-3376; ⑤), which includes three meals a day. **Tête-à-la-Beleine** and, later on, **St Augustine** have similarly picturesque settings. At Tête-à-la-Beleine local boatmen are usually on hand to transport tourists from the ship out to the incongruous Chapelle de l'île Providence perched on a nearby hill. There is also a **hostel** here, *L'Auberge de l'Île Providence* (Ⓣ418/242-2015, Ⓔmecama@globetrotter.net; $35; June–Oct). The Coasters Association is the local residents' group and their website (Ⓦwww.coastersassociation.com) is a useful resource.

Fares on the ship are reasonable and it's possible either to travel all-inclusive (with three surprisingly good daily meals and a cabin berth) or to bed down on the aircraft-style seats and picnic on the deck or in the cafeteria. You can start and finish your journey from any of the stops along the coast, but the basic fare to travel the entire length of the route on a return trip to Rimouski is $479. The same trip with a spot in the most basic four-berth cabin is $853 and $1162 for a two-berth cabin with porthole and shower. Food is extra: breakfast $6, lunch $14, dinner $19; check the website for price changes. Non round-trippers can bring their car, although it's inaccessible during the voyage; fares are based on distance and the weight of the car. A one-way journey from Natashquan to Blanc-Sablon – useful if you are continuing to or returning from Newfoundland and Labrador – costs at least $221 for the car; for bikes, add $20 to the fare.

The Islands

One of the best ways to see the islands is by **sea kayak** or **two-man sail boats**. Expédition Agaguk (Ⓣ418/538-1588 or 1-866/538-1588, Ⓦwww.expedition-agaguk.com), 1062 av Boréale in Havre-St-Pierre, organize one- to six-day excursions (May–Sept) for $99 a day or $199 a day if you want them to supply camping equipment and local cuisine. Even if you have your own gear, this is an excellent place for tips on currents and other conditions. On prior request, they will also organize backcountry trips to the lakes and rivers to the north.

Boat tours (June–Sept) around portions of the archipelago are available from the wharf at Havre-St-Pierre, but they must be booked in advance: Croisiéres La Relève Jomphe (Ⓣ418/538-2865, Ⓦwww.hotelduhavre.ca) operates from kiosk no. 3; La Tournée des Îles (Ⓣ418/538-2547, Ⓦwww.tourismeduplessis.com/sites/tourneedesiles) runs the *Perroquet de Mer* from kiosk no. 2; and *Le Calculot*, a small boat whose captain's unrelenting commentary may spoil your trip; all have three daily trips for around $35. Cruises to see puffins in the park's west depart from Longue-Pointe-de-Mingan (see p.348).

Île d'Anticosti

In the Gulf of St Lawrence between the Jacques Cartier and Honguedo straits, the remote 220km-long **Île d'Anticosti** was once known as the "Graveyard of the Gulf", as more than four hundred ships have been **wrecked** on its shores. The island's vast expanse is made up of windswept sea cliffs and forests of twisted pine, crisscrossed by turbulent rivers and sheer ravines. Known as *Notiskuan* – "the land where we hunt bears" – by the natives, and a walrus- and whale-fishing ground by the Basques, Île d'Anticosti became the private domain of Henri Menier, a French chocolate millionaire, in 1873. He imported white-tailed Virginia deer, red fox, silver fox, beaver and moose in order to gun them down at his leisure. Today, a less exclusive horde of **hunters** and **anglers** come here to blast away at deer from the back of four-wheel-drives and to hoist the salmon from the rivers. For other travellers it presents an opportunity to explore an untamed area that's still practically deserted, with a population of about 280.

Getting there

The *Nordik Express* **supply ship** from Havre-St-Pierre to Port-Menier costs $41 one-way, from Sept-Îles $54. There is no boat from Port-Menier to Sept-Îles – it goes straight on to Rimouski instead. Sépaq Anticosti (Ⓣ418/890-0863 or 1-800/463-0863) offers flights to the island as part of a package from Montréal, Québec City, Mont-Joli and Havre-St-Pierre, while Exact Air (Ⓦwww.exactair.ca) has charter flights from Sept-Îles, Havre-St-Pierre and Île du Havre-aux-Maisons in the Îles-de-la-Madeleine.

Port-Menier and Parc national d'Anticosti

Menier established the tiny village of Baie Ste-Claire on the western tip in 1873; fewer than thirty years later the settlers moved to **PORT-MENIER** on the south side of this tip, and Baie-Ste-Claire's homes were left to the ravages of the salt air. The human population is still concentrated in the blue-roofed houses of Port-Menier, where the *Nordik Express* arrives once a week each from Havre-St-Pierre and from Sept-Îles (see p.351).

The town edges the westerly portion of the **Parc national d'Anticosti** (Ⓣ418/535-0156, Ⓦwww.sepaq.com; $3.50) whose protected landscapes are continued further east in the reserve's two other sectors – one deep in the interior, the other covering the island's eastern tip. The twisting gravel road crossing the island – jokingly called the "Trans-Anticostian" – provides access to the central and eastern portions of the reserve. Driving is the only way to get there: a four-wheel-drive is necessary, and it's not uncommon to get a few dents or a flat tyre. You can rent a car in Port-Menier at Location Pelletier (Ⓣ418/535-0204). En route, a rough track leads from the "main" road to Québec's largest cave. Discovered in 1982, the glacial **Caverne de la Rivière à la Patate**, 120km east of Port-Menier, has a modest opening leading into a cathedral-like chamber and a warren of 500m-long passages. Some 10km further on you can glimpse the canyon of the **Rivière Observation**, whose bleak walls rise to over 50m. The reserve's scenery is equally impressive and a good basis for its attempt to encourage **adventure tourism** during the summer months. SÉPAQ Anticosti, the government body responsible for the park, runs a variety of ecologically sound packages which, although pricey (starting at around $650/week/person, based on two people flying from Sept-Îles; Ⓣ418/535-0156, Ⓦwww.sepaq.com), include transport to the island, accommodation and four-wheel-drive vehicles.

Accommodation is available in Port-Menier at *Auberge de Port-Menier* (Ⓣ418/535-0122, Ⓦwww.sepaq.com; ⑤) or at the **hostels**: *Auberge Au Vieux Menier*, 26 chemin de la Faune (Ⓣ418/535-0111; ①; mid-June to mid-Oct), which also has camping for $10, will pick you up from the airport or wharf and organize excursions; or *Auberge Pointe-Ouest*, 20km west of Port-Menier (Ⓣ418/535-0155; ①), which also has camping ($10/day).

Basse Côte-Nord

Highway 138 used to end at Havre-St-Pierre, leaving the dozen or so villages along the rugged **Basse Côte-Nord** (Lower North Shore) cut off from the rest of Québec, as they had been for centuries – so much so that many inhabitants only speak English (most were and are descendants of fishermen from the Channel Islands and Newfoundland). Now a section of Hwy 138 links Havre-St-Pierre with **Natashquan** and three other villages on the 145-kilometre stretch. If you make the lonely journey by car – as yet there is no bus – you will receive a welcome unique to a people not long connected by road to the rest of Canada.

Baie-Johan-Beetz and beyond

The first settlement, 65km east of Havre-St-Pierre, is the village of **BAIE-JOHAN-BEETZ**, named after the painter and sculptor whose extraordinary and enormous **house** (late June to Sept daily 10am–noon & 1.30–4pm; guided tour every 30min Ⓣ418/648-0557 or 1-888/393-0557, Ⓦwww.baiejohanbeetz.com; $5) is open to the public; you can sleep in one of its seven historic bedrooms (③).

Beyond, you pass through tiny **Aguanish** and **Île-à-Michon**. At the end of the 780km road from Tadoussac, a small church, wooden houses and the old fishing huts are about all there is to see in **NATASHQUAN**, one-time home of revered Québécois poet Gilles Vigneault. The century-old general store has been reborn as an **interpretation centre** (mid-June to Sept daily 10am–5pm; Ⓣ418/726-3233; $5), focusing on local history; it's less impressive than the town's long sandy beach.

Accommodation is available in the ten-room *Auberge la Cache* (Ⓣ418/726-3347 or 1-888/726-3347, Ⓦwww.aubergelacache.com; ④) 183 chemin d'en Haut, whose restaurant is open June to August. B&Bs inlcude *Maison Chevarie* (Ⓣ418/726-3541; ③), 77 rue du Pré. You can **camp** along Hwy 138 at *Camping Municipal Chemin Faisant* (mid-June to early Sept; Ⓣ418/726-3697, Ⓦwww.guidecamping.ca/municipalcheminfaisant; $19–26).

Travel details

Trains

Sept-Îles to: Labrador City (2–3 weekly; 8hr 30min–10hr 30min); Schefferville (1 weekly; 11hr 15min).

Buses

Baie-Comeau to: Baie-St-Paul (2 daily; 5hr 30min); Godbout (1 daily; 50min); Port-Cartier (1 daily; 2hr 15min); Sept-Îles (1 daily; 3hr 30min).
Chicoutimi to: Alma (2 daily; 1hr); Dolbeau (2–3 daily; 3hr 30min); Jonquière (9 daily; 25min); St-Félicien (2 daily; 2hr 55min); Val-Jalbert (2 daily; 2hr 15min).
Dolbeau to: Alma (1 weekly; 1hr 15min); Péribonka (1 weekly; 30min).
Québec City to: Alma (3 daily; 2hr 45min); Baie-Comeau (2 daily; 6hr 5min); Baie-Ste-Catherine (2 daily; 3hr 20min); Baie-St-Paul (3 daily; 1hr 15min); Chicoutimi (5-6 daily; 2hr 30min); Dolbeau (2 daily; 5hr 25min); Forestville (2 daily; 4hr 45min); Jonquière (3–5 daily; 3hr); La Malbaie (3 daily; 1hr 50min); Les Escoumins (2 daily; 4hr 10min); Rimouski (5 daily; 3hr 55min); Rivière-du-Loup (4 daily; 2hr 20min); St-Félicien (2 daily; 4hr 25min); St-Siméon (2 daily; 2hr 20min); Sherbrooke (2 daily; 3hr 30min); Tadoussac (2 daily; 4hr); Val-Jalbert (2 daily; 3hr 45min).
Rimouski to: Bonaventure (2 daily; 6hr); Cap-aux-Os (summer 1 daily; 6hr 50min); Carleton (2 daily; 4hr 15min); Gaspé via Carleton (2 daily; 9hr 10min); Gaspé via Matane (2 daily; 6hr 50min); Matane (2–3 daily; 1hr 30min); Matapédia (2 daily; 2hr 50min); Mont St-Pierre (2 daily; 4hr 20min); New Richmond (2 daily; 5hr 30min); Percé (2 daily; 8hr 20min); Ste-Anne-des-Monts (2–3 daily; 2hr 50min); Ste-Flavie (2–3 daily; 30min).
Rivière-du-Loup to: Edmundston, NB (3 daily; 3hr).
Sept-Îles to: Baie-Comeau (1 daily; 3hr 30min); Havre-St-Pierre (1 daily; 2hr 30min).
Sherbrooke to: Trois-Rivières (4 weekly; 2hr 10min).
Tadoussac to: Chicoutimi (1 daily; 1hr 40min); Rivière Ste-Marguerite (6 weekly; 30min); Ste-Rose-du-Nord (6 weekly; 55min).
Trois-Rivières to: Grand-Mère (3 daily; 1hr).

Ferries

Baie-Ste-Catherine to: Tadoussac (1–3 hourly; 10min).
Blanc-Sablon to: St Barbe, NL (May–Dec 1–3 daily; 1hr 30min).
Matane to: Baie-Comeau (4 weekly–2 daily; 2hr 20min); Godbout (1–3 daily; 2hr 10min).
Québec City to: Lévis (1–3 hourly; 15min).
Rimouski to: Forestville (April–Oct 2–4 daily; 55min).
Rivière-du-Loup to: St-Siméon (April–Dec 2–5 daily; 1hr 15min).
St-Joseph-de-la-Rive to: Île-aux-Coudres (8 daily–2 hourly; 15min).
Trois-Pistoles to: Les Escoumins (May–Oct 2–3 daily; 1hr 15min).

Nordik Express

Continuous voyage (see p.351). Broken down into segments here for clarity.
Havre-St-Pierre to: Natashquan (1 weekly; 6hr 15min); Kegaska (1 weekly; 11hr 30min); La Romaine (1 weekly; 16hr); Harrington Harbour (1 weekly; 24hr 45min); Tête-à-la-Baleine (1 weekly; 29hr 15min); La Tabatière (1 weekly; 32hr 45min); St-Augustin (1 weekly; 37hr 15min); Blanc-Sablon (1 weekly; 43hr 45min).
Rimouski to: Blanc-Sablon (1 weekly; 78hr 30min); Sept-Îles (downstream only; 1 weekly; 11hr 30min).
Sept-Îles to: Havre-St-Pierre (1 weekly; 15hr 15min); Port-Menier (1 weekly; 7hr 45min).

Flights

Québec City to: Baie-Comeau (1–3 daily; 1hr 35min); Gaspé (1–2 daily; 2hr 10min); Halifax (1 daily; 1hr 40min); Îles-de-la-Madeleine (1–2 daily; 3hr 20min); Ottawa (2–7 daily; 1hr 10min); Sept-Îles (2–3 daily; 1hr 30min); Toronto (6 daily; 1hr 30min); Wabush (1–2 daily; 2hr 50min).

5

The Maritime Provinces

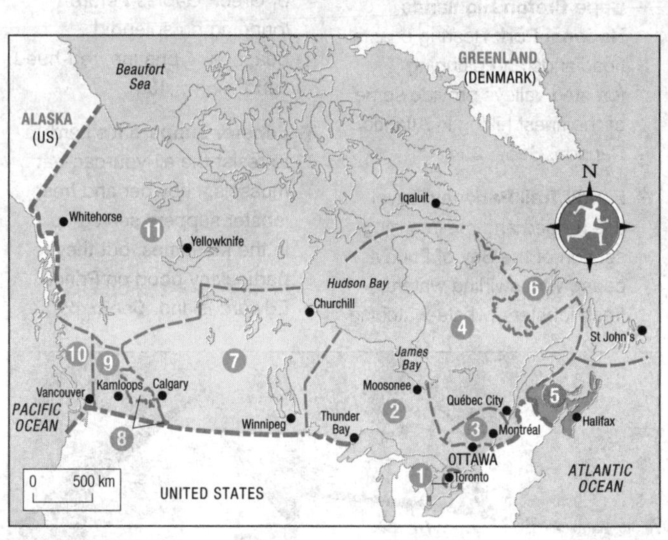

CHAPTER 5

Highlights

* **Halifax** The largest city in the Maritimes, jam-packed with pubs, restaurants and museums, and topped by the stirring militarism of the enormous Citadel. See p.360

* **Lunenburg** This handsome fishing port is small-town Nova Scotia at its prettiest, its hilly streets dotted with charming Victorian mansions. See p.374

* **Cape Breton Highlands National Park** Rearing coastal headlands and plunging forested valleys provide some of the finest hiking in Atlantic Canada. See p.394

* **Fundy Trail Parkway** Travel this rugged and mesmerizing section of the Bay of Fundy coast, with swirling waters, fresh lobsters, whale-watching and record setting tides. See p.419

* **Acadian culture** Soak up one of Canada's most resilient cultures - distinct French heritage, tasty cuisine, vibrant music and turbulent history - especially in New Brunswick. See p.427

* **Prince Edward Island National Park** Explore the extensive legacy of Anne of Green Gables before lounging on splendid beaches of pristine, red-hued sand. See p.436

* **Lobster suppers** It's hard to resist the all-you-can-eat mussels, chowder and fresh lobster suppers served up in the Maritimes, but they're particularly good on Prince Edward Island. See p.428

▲ Lobster boat, Nova Scotia

5

The Maritime Provinces

Canada's Maritime Provinces – **Nova Scotia, New Brunswick** and **Prince Edward Island** – are the country's three smallest provinces, and their combined population of around two million has been largely confined to the coasts and river valleys by the thin soils of the forested interior. Even today, the bulk of the Maritimes remains intractable – 84 percent of New Brunswick, for example, is covered by forest – and this rough and ready **wilderness** combines with a ruggedly beautiful **coastline** to form one of Canada's most scenic regions. The chunks of fertile **farmland** that punctuate the forests are also appealing, principally in the undulating fields of Prince Edward Island (PEI) and the lowlands around New Brunswick's Grand Falls, both of which produce massive crops of potatoes, and in Nova Scotia's Annapolis Valley, a major fruit-producing area. Yet all this was also at the heart of the epic struggle between England and France for North America in the eighteenth century, and it boasts a rich legacy of historic sights, many associated with the **Acadians**, who were usually caught in the middle.

Most travellers focus on **Nova Scotia**, where the busy provincial capital of **Halifax** makes an appealing base from which to explore the picturesque coastline, then head north to **Cape Breton Island**, featuring the mountainous splendour of **Cape Breton Highlands National Park**. Driving from the US or the rest of Canada, you'll pass through the often overlooked province of **New Brunswick**, with plenty of world-class diversions of its own: the gritty, revitalized port of **Saint John** (never "St John", and not to be mixed up with St John's, Newfoundland) and the **Bay of Fundy**, whose taper creates tidal variations of up to 12m. This phenomenon has a spectacular setting at both **Fundy National Park** and along the **Fundy Trail Parkway**. **Whale-watching trips** leave from a string of Fundy ports in both Nova Scotia and New Brunswick.

Last but certainly not least, **Prince Edward Island (PEI)** was linked to the mainland by the whopping Confederation Bridge in 1997 and possesses one of the region's most enticing culinary scenes. Leafy, laidback **Charlottetown** is well worth at least a couple of days, especially as it's just a short hop from the magnificent sandy beaches of the **Prince Edward Island National Park**.

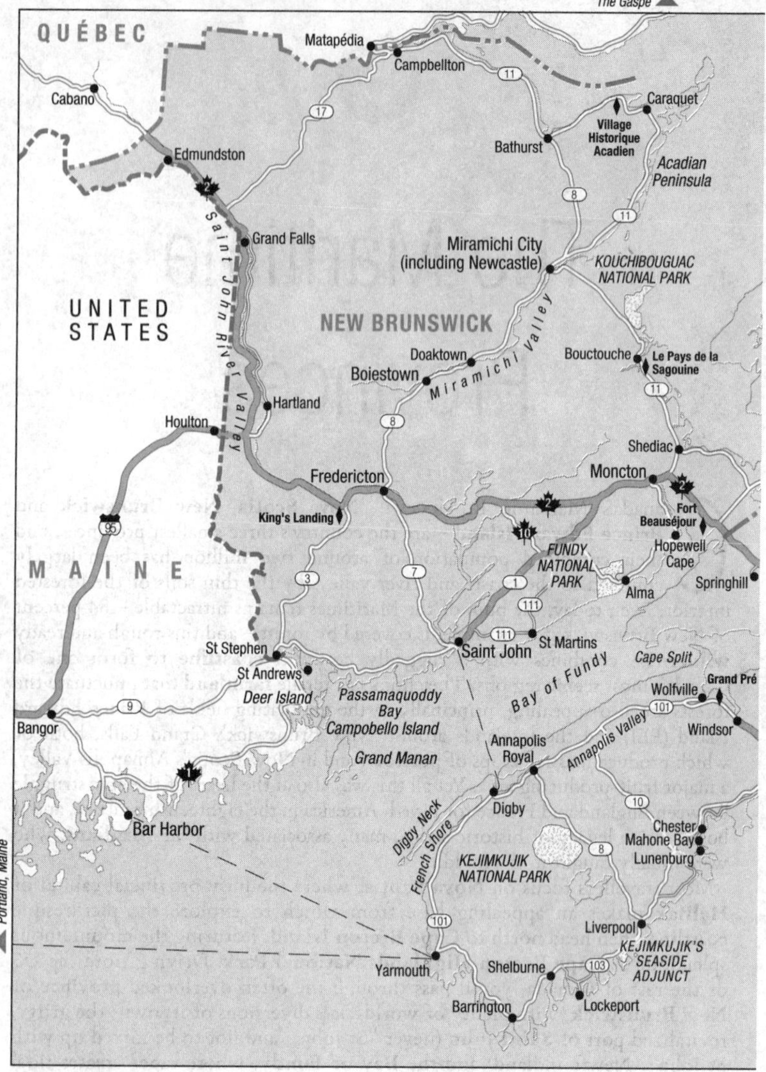

Nova Scotia

Visits to **Nova Scotia** usually begin at the lively capital, **Halifax**, which sits beside a splendid harbour on the south coast. With its exceptional restaurants, raucous nightlife and historic attractions, the city can easily fill a couple of days. From here, the most beguiling parts of the province fall into three regions: the **South Shore**, with **Lunenburg** and solitary **Lockeport** the most alluring targets; the forts,

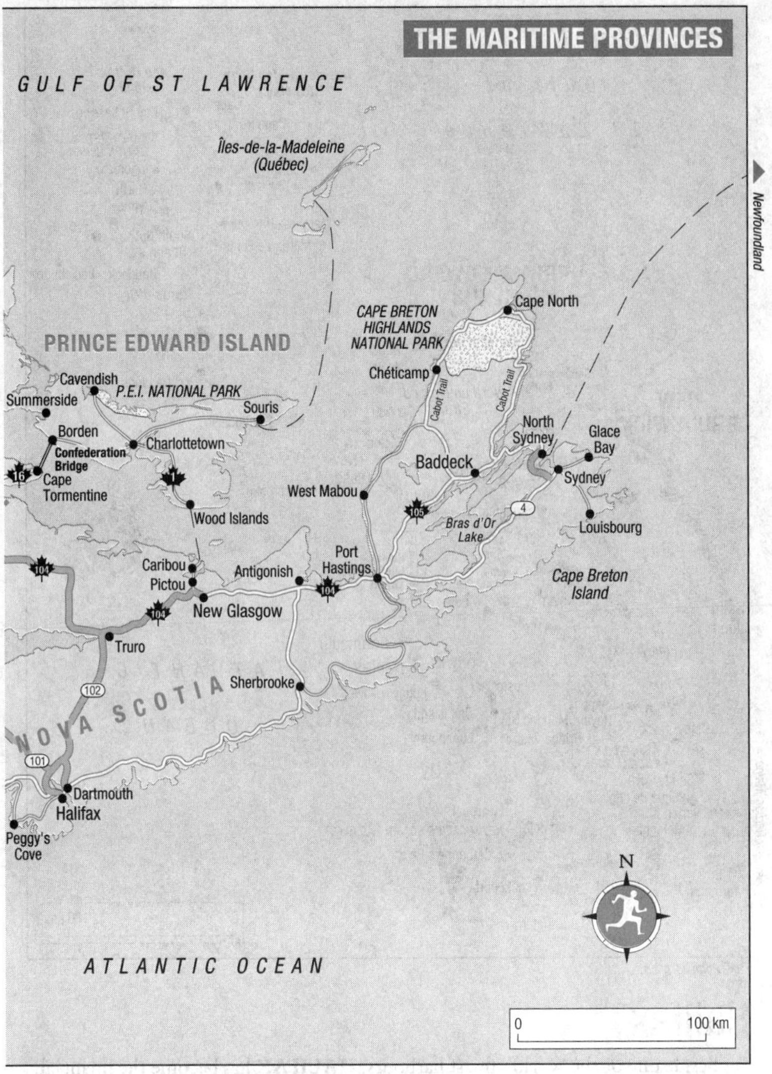

farms and villages of the **Annapolis Valley**; and **Cape Breton Island**, best appreciated by driving the circular **Cabot Trail**.

Southwest Nova Scotia, Truro and Sydney (on Cape Breton) are reasonably well served by **bus**, with daily connections from Halifax, bolstered by the Salty Bear services (see p.36). VIA Rail **trains** run between Halifax and Truro, then continue to New Brunswick's Miramichi and Québec. Elsewhere, you'll need a **car**, particularly if you're keen to see the wilder sections of the Cabot Trail.

Car ferries link North Sydney with Newfoundland; Caribou with PEI; and Digby with Saint John, New Brunswick.

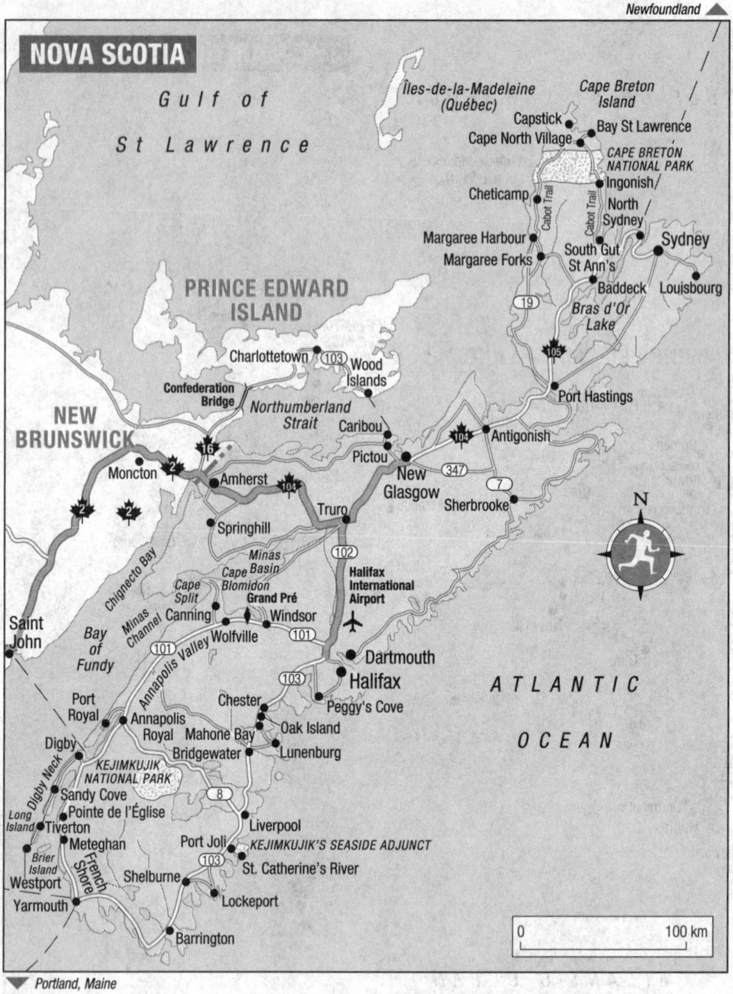

Halifax

Set beside one of the world's finest harbours, **HALIFAX** has become the financial, educational and transportation centre of the Maritimes, with its population of around 400,000 making it almost four times the size of its nearest rival, New Brunswick's Saint John. This pre-eminence has been achieved since World War II, but long before then Halifax was a naval town *par excellence*.

The British were the first to develop Halifax, founding a navy base here in 1749. The needs of the garrison called the tune throughout the nineteenth century and most **Haligonians**, as the locals are known, were at least partly employed in a service capacity.

In the twentieth century Halifax acted as a key supply and convoy harbour in both world wars, but since then its military importance has declined, even though Canadian navy ships still dock here. Workaday office blocks reflect the city's new commercial success, tumbling down to the harbour from the **Citadel**, the old British fortress that remains the city's most significant sight. Halifax retains a compact, thriving centre, with artists, street performers and students from prestigious Dalhousie University adding a grungy, alternative balance to the bankers and fashionistas.

Arrival

Most hotels have designated **parking** – otherwise aim for central MetroPark at 1557 Granville St and 1554 Hollis St ($2.50/hr, maximum $15/day) or Park Lane Parkade at Dresden Row and Sackville Street (Mon–Fri 6am–6pm; $2.50/hr; Mon–Fri 6pm–6am, Sat & Sun 24hr; $1/hr). On-street metered parking is also available ($1.50/hr, $3/hr on the waterfront; free 6pm–8am, weekends and holidays).

Halifax International Airport is located 35km northeast of the city centre and has its own extremely efficient **tourist information office** (daily 9am–9pm; ⓣ902/873-1223), where you can pick up free maps and the *Nova Scotia Doers' and Dreamers' Guide*. All the major car rental agencies have desks at the airport (see p.370). Airporter (ⓣ902/873-2091, ⓦwww.airporter.biz) runs a **bus shuttle** from the airport to the larger downtown hotels (24hr, every 30min/1hr; takes 40min–1hr depending on traffic; $21 one-way). For downtown in general get off at the *Delta Barrington* hotel, which is at Barrington and Duke streets, right in the centre. **Taxis** from the airport to the centre charge a flat fee of $53. Shuttle bus services run direct from the airport to numerous destinations, including Cape Breton, the Annapolis Valley and PEI (see ⓦwww.hiaa.ca for details).

Acadian Lines **buses** (ⓣ1-800/567-5151, ⓦwww.acadianbus.com) to Halifax (from Digby, Truro, Sydney and New Brunswick) pull into the **bus station** (ⓣ902/454-9321), 1161 Hollis St at Cornwallis Park. Sharing the same premises is the **VIA Rail station** (ⓣ1-888/842-7245, ⓦwww.viarail.ca), which handles just six **trains** a week, connecting Halifax with Truro, Moncton, the Gaspé and Montréal. From the train and bus station, it's a fifteen-minute walk into the centre, or catch bus #9 along Barrington Street (Mon–Fri every 20–30min, Sat & Sun hourly).

Information

Halifax has three downtown **tourist offices**: 1598 Argyle St at Sackville Street (late May to mid-Oct daily 9am–6pm; ⓣ902/490-5946 or 902/490-4000, ⓦwww.halifax.ca/visitors); the **Waterfront visitor information centre** (daily: May–Oct 8.30am–6pm; Nov–April 9am–4.30pm; ⓣ902/424-4248 or 1-800/565-0000), at the back of the Maritime Museum at the foot of Sackville Street; and a third inside the Scotia Square Mall, 5251 Duke St (Mon–Fri 8.30am–4.30pm, ⓣ902/490-5963). All will provide you with armfuls of maps and brochures, including the comprehensive *Halifax Visitor Guide*, and fix you up with accommodation. For entertainment listings and local news, grab a copy of free weekly *The Coast* (ⓦwww.thecoast.ca) widely available around town, or Halifax's main daily newspaper, the *Chronicle-Herald* (ⓦwww.thechronicleherald.ca); its Thursday listings are particularly good.

Nova Scotia information

Nova Scotia Department of Tourism within North America ⓣ1-800/565-0000, from elsewhere 902/425-5781, ⓦwww.novascotia.com. They run a free hotel reservation service via the phone lines or website.

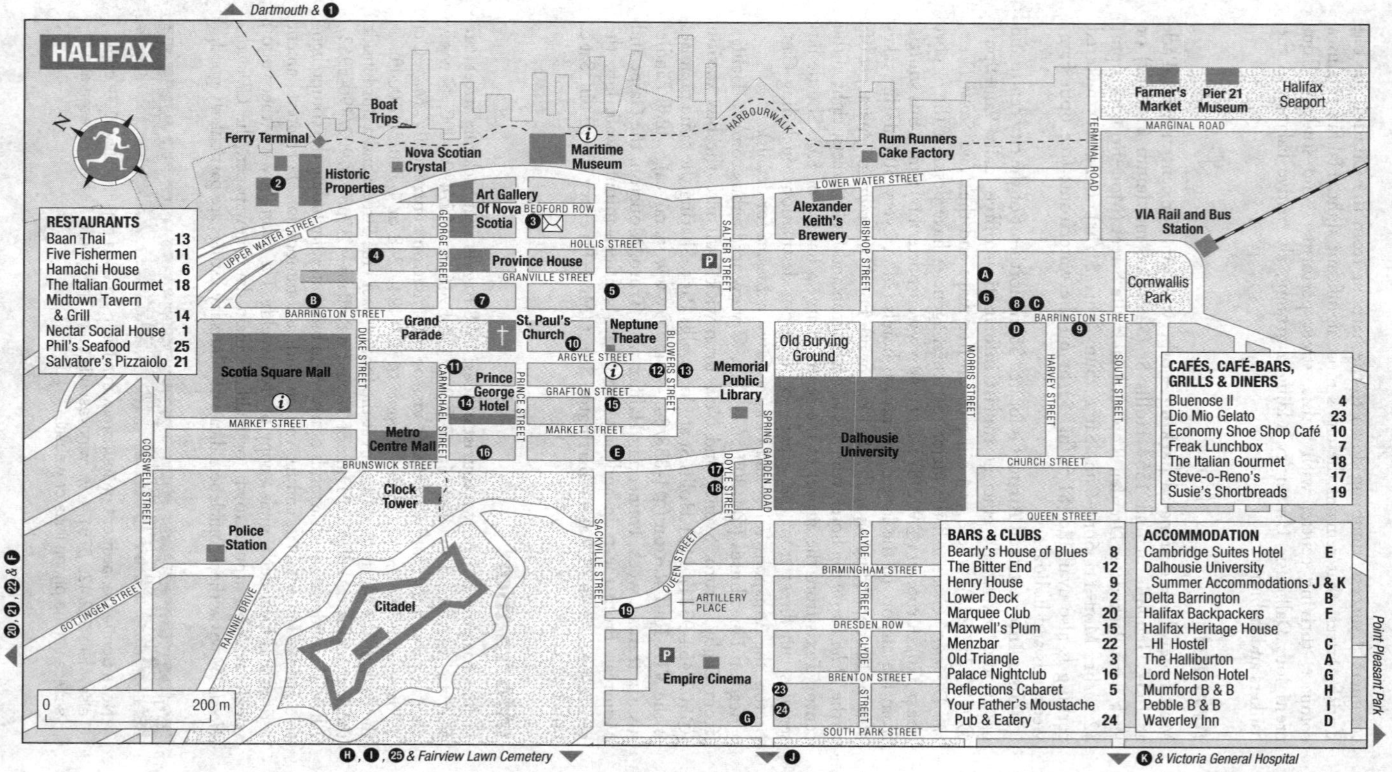

HALIFAX
Dartmouth & 1
RESTAURANTS
Baan Thai 13
Five Fishermen 11
Hamachi House 6
The Italian Gourmet 18
Midtown Tavern & Grill 14
Nectar Social House 1
Phil's Seafood 25
Salvatore's Pizzaiolo 21
CAFÉS, CAFÉ-BARS, GRILLS & DINERS
Bluenose II 4
Dio Mio Gelato 23
Economy Shoe Shop Café 10
Freak Lunchbox 7
The Italian Gourmet 18
Steve-o-Reno's 17
Susie's Shortbreads 19
BARS & CLUBS
Bearly's House of Blues 8
The Bitter End 12
Henry House 9
Lower Deck 2
Marquee Club 20
Maxwell's Plum 15
Menzbar 22
Old Triangle 3
Palace Nightclub 16
Reflections Cabaret 5
Your Father's Moustache Pub & Eatery 24
ACCOMMODATION
Cambridge Suites Hotel E
Dalhousie University Summer Accommodations J & K
Delta Barrington B
Halifax Backpackers F
Halifax Heritage House
HI Hostel C
The Halliburton A
Lord Nelson Hotel G
Mumford B & B H
Pebble B & B I
Waverley Inn D
Ferry Terminal
Boat Trips
Historic Properties
Nova Scotian Crystal
Maritime Museum
Harbourwalk
Rum Runners Cake Factory
Farmer's Market
Pier 21 Museum
Halifax Seaport
Marginal Road
Terminal Road
VIA Rail and Bus Station
Cornwallis Park
Lower Water Street
Upper Water Street
Art Gallery Of Nova Scotia
Bedford Row
Hollis Street
Province House
Granville Street
Barrington Street
Alexander Keith's Brewery
George Street
Salter Street
Bishop Street
Morris Street
Harvey Street
South Street
Grand Parade
St. Paul's Church
Neptune Theatre
Old Burying Ground
Argyle Street
Blowers Street
Memorial Public Library
Scotia Square Mall
Duke Street
Carmichael Street
Prince Street
Prince George Hotel
Grafton Street
Market Street
Metro Centre Mall
Brunswick Street
Spring Garden Road
Dalhousie University
Church Street
Queen Street
Doyle Street
Clock Tower
Cogswell Street
Police Station
Sackville Street
Citadel
Gottingen Street
Rainnie Drive
Artillery Place
Clyde Street
Birmingham Street
Dresden Row
Brenton Street
South Park Street
Empire Cinema
0 200 m
20, 21, 22 & F
H, I, 25 & Fairview Lawn Cemetery
J
K & Victoria General Hospital
Point Pleasant Park

City transport

The best way to see downtown Halifax is **on foot**, but for outlying attractions and accommodation **buses** operated by Metro Transit (ⓣ902/490-4000, ⓦwww.halifax.ca/metrotransit) are reliable and efficient. The flat fare is $2.25 in the Halifax area (exact change only). If you need to change buses on the same journey, ask for a free transfer ticket at the outset. The **ferries** that cross Halifax harbour from the downtown terminal to Dartmouth (see p.368) apply the same tariff. Free Metro Transit route maps and schedules are available from the tourist office. Between July and October you can also use the free **Fred** bus service (daily 10.30am–5pm), which runs on a forty-minute loop from Pier 21 through downtown and past the Citadel (look for the specially marked stops or call ⓣ902/423-6658). **Taxi** meters start at $3 and fares rarely top $7 for trips around downtown (see "Listings" p.371).

Accommodation

Finding **accommodation** in Halifax is rarely a problem. To get the flavour of the city your best bet is to stay in – or at least close to – downtown. Here you'll find a number of modern **hotels**, ranging from the comfortable to the luxurious, while there are plenty of more distinctive B&Bs a short walk or bus ride away. Halifax's **motels** are stuck out on the peripheries of town, inconveniently concentrated about 10km northwest of the centre along Bedford Hwy (Rte 2). The main budget alternatives are the **student rooms** city universities offer between mid-May and mid-August, and the two **hostels**. There is no city-centre campground.

Downtown

Cambridge Suites Hotel 1583 Brunswick St ⓣ902/420-0555 or 1/800-565-1263, ⓦwww.cambridgesuiteshalifax.com. Large, luxurious downtown hotel that offers spacious but affordable suites and studios, all decked out in a swish, contemporary style with flat-screen TVs; most rooms have superb views of the waterfront. ❻

Dalhousie University Summer Accommodations ⓣ902/494-8840 or 1-888/271-9222, ⓦwww.dal.ca/confserv. Dalhousie University offers rooms to tourists from around May 7 to Aug 23 in two principal locations; Howe Hall, 230 Coburg Rd, and newer Risley Hall, 1233 LeMarchant St (where you'll find the admin office), both on the main university campus, south of the centre along University Ave. Guests have access to the university's sports facilities. Single and double rooms available, usually with shared bathrooms – students and seniors receive substantial discounts. Singles ❷, doubles ❸

Delta Barrington 1875 Barrington St ⓣ902/429-7410 or 1-888/890-3222, ⓦwww.deltahotels.com. Modern luxury, in the middle of downtown, with weekend discounts of up to thirty percent. Internet (in-room and business centre) is $9.95/day. Attached to one of the city's larger shopping malls. ❻

Halifax Heritage House Hostel 1253 Barrington St ⓣ902/422-3863, ⓦwww.hihostels.ca. Only 300m from the train station and more central than *Backpackers*, this clean and agreeable HI hostel with private rooms and four- to six-bed dorms (members $26; nonmembers $31) has free phones, wi-fi and internet, a coin laundry, kitchen, patio and parking. Private rooms ❷

The Halliburton 5184 Morris St ⓣ902/420-0658 or 1-888/512-3344, ⓦwww.thehalliburton.com. Near the railway station off Barrington St, this long-established thirty-room inn occupies three adjacent buildings. The oldest, the original inn dating from 1809, has a Victorian period look to its public rooms, but the bedrooms beyond are firmly modern. The nicer – and larger – rooms, many of which have balconies, are in the other two buildings. Free breakfast and limited parking. ❼

Lord Nelson Hotel 1515 South Park St ⓣ902/423-6331 or 1-800/565-2020, ⓦwww.lordnelsonhotel.com. With its high coffered ceiling, the lobby of this popular brown-brick hotel is spacious and elegant, with Art Deco details dating from its 1920s construction. The two hundred-odd rooms do not quite live up to the lobby, but they are spacious, comfortable and furnished in smart modern style. ❻

Waverley Inn 1266 Barrington St ⓣ902/423-9346 or 1-800/565-9346, ⓦwww.waverleyinn.com. Elegant Victorian mansion, with thirty en-suite a/c rooms, sympathetically refurbished with splendid period furnishings. Oscar Wilde stayed here on his 1882 North American lecture tour, apparently turning up in green velvet pantaloons. The inn is situated about a five-minute walk from the train station. Rates include breakfast. ❼

North, West & South ends

Halifax Backpackers 2193 Gottingen St, North End ⓣ 902/431-3170 or 1-888/431-3170, ⓦwww.halifaxbackpackers.com. These clean, spacious six-bed dorms at just $20/night are the best deal in the city. *Alteregos Café* downstairs offers light meals, the shared kitchen is big and the owners invite all guests to a bbq every Fri. Laundry is just $1, and the wi-fi and internet is free. It's only ten minutes' walk to the Citadel, and there are plenty of student-friendly bars nearby. The North End has a reputation for crime but things have improved markedly since 2007 and it's rare to encounter trouble (though car theft is still a problem). Private rooms ❷

Mumford B&B 7015 Mumford Rd, West End (just off Rte 102) ⓣ902/446-0766, ⓦwww.mumfordbedandbreakfast.com. Family-friendly, very relaxed and welcoming B&B hosted by affable English expats. Both rooms are incredibly cosy with cable TV and shared bath. It's a fifteen-minute bus ride downtown. ❹

Pebble Bed & Breakfast 1839 Armview Terrace, South End ⓣ902/423-6687 or 1-888/303-5056, ⓦwww.thepebble.ca. You get fine Irish hospitality in this quiet, leafy residential neighbourhood just south of the centre, with gorgeous views across the North West Arm and fabulous breakfasts (they also have three dogs and a cat). The two luxurious suites are beautifully furnished, and the free phone calls, wi-fi, and glass of port in the evening are nice touches. ❼

The City

The commercial and social heart of modern Halifax clambers up the steep hillside from the harbourfront, its gridiron streets dotted with scores of heaving bars and restaurants. The city's main attractions – most notably the **Art Gallery**, the **Maritime Museum** and the Georgian **Province House** – all huddle close together in the lower part of town beneath Halifax's star turn, the **Citadel**.

The Citadel

Perched on a hill overlooking downtown, the present fortifications of **Halifax Citadel National Historic Site** (daily: early May to June & Sept to Oct 9am–5pm; July & Aug 9am–6pm; $11.70, $7.80 in shoulder season; Nov to early May 9am–5pm, free but all exhibits closed; parking $3.25; ⓦwww.pc.gc.ca) are Victorian, the fourth in a series dating from Edward Cornwallis's stockade of 1749. Although it never saw action, the fort was garrisoned by the British until 1906, and by Canadian forces during the two World Wars. Today it's an absorbing blend of museum, castle and historical re-enactments, with bagpipes blaring, marching "soldiers" of the Royal Artillery and 78th Highlanders in period uniform (c. 1869), and an elaborate ceremony to fire one of the old cannons every day at noon, which makes a terrific bang. If all this militarism leaves you cold, the Citadel is still worth a visit for the grand view over the city and harbour.

Start at the **information centre**, where a fifteen-minute video provides historical perspective. Here also is an **Army Museum**, which adopts an earthy soldier's outlook in the labelling of its wide collection of small arms. The **walls** themselves contain a string of **storehouses** stuffed with military bric-a-brac. Here you'll find a couple of reconstructed powder magazines, the former garrison school room and several exhibits exploring the Citadel's history, including a small theatre where a film (50min) details the development of Halifax. Free and entertaining **guided tours** (early May–Oct; 45min) of the Citadel depart from the information centre every hour or so.

▲ Preparing to fire the Halifax Citadel's cannon

Grand Parade and the Province House

From the Citadel, head down past the Clock Tower and follow Carmichael Street to reach the tree-lined, elongated square known as **Grand Parade**, the social centre of nineteenth-century Halifax. The southern edge of the Grand Parade borders the handsome **St Paul's Church** (Mon–Fri 9am–4.30pm; free), whose chunky cupola and timber frame date from 1750, making it both the oldest building in town and the first Protestant church in Canada. Look out for the piece of wood embedded in the plaster above the inner entrance doors, a remnant of the 1917 Halifax Explosion (see p.367).

Charles Dickens, visiting in 1842, described the graceful sandstone **Province House** (July & Aug Mon–Fri 9am–5pm, Sat & Sun 10am–4pm; rest of year Mon–Fri 9am–4pm; free; tours ⓣ902/424-4661), a couple of minutes' walk from Grand Parade down George Street on Hollis Street, as "a gem of Georgian architecture". Highlights of the free **guided tour** (self-guided in winter) include a peek into the old upper chamber, now the Red Chamber, with its ornate plasterwork and assorted portraits, including a dandified King George III and Queen Charlotte. The Nova Scotian legislature has been meeting in the Assembly Chamber since the house opened in 1819, a cosy space that partly resembles a Georgian dining room rather than a provincial seat of government.

Art Gallery of Nova Scotia

Across the road from Province House, the **Art Gallery of Nova Scotia** (daily 10am–5pm, Thurs till 9pm; $10; ⓣ902/424-7542, ⓦwww.artgalleryofnovascotia.ca), at 1741 Hollis St, occupies two adjacent buildings – one a stern Art Deco structure, the other an embellished Victorian edifice that has previously served as a courthouse, police headquarters and post office. The gallery is attractively laid out and although there is some rotation of the exhibits most of the pieces described here should be on view. Pick up a free **gallery plan** at the entrance in the more southerly of the two buildings, Gallery South. Guided tours begin here daily at 2.30pm, and 7pm on Thursday.

Floor 1 of **Gallery South** contains a delightful section devoted to the Nova Scotian artist **Maud Lewis** (1903–70). Lewis overcame several disabilities, including rheumatoid arthritis, to become a painter of some renown, creating naive, brightly coloured works of local scenes. Lewis's tiny cabin – awash with her bright paintwork – was taken from the outskirts of Digby (see p.382) for safe-keeping in 1984, and was finally placed here in 1997.

An underground passageway connects the Lower Floor of Gallery South with the Lower Floor of **Gallery North**. Gallery North's Level 1 has further temporary displays plus an enjoyable selection of **Canadian historical paintings** with the Maritimes to the fore. Close by, Room 4 holds several canvases by Cornelius Krieghoff (see p.87) and a small sample of the work of the **Group of Seven** (see p.88); look out for Lawren Harris's haunting *Algoma* landscape and J.E.H. MacDonald's diminutive *Lake O'Hara*. Room 6 features an eclectic selection of modern Canadian paintings drawn from the permanent collection: *Island in the Ice* by the Nova Scotian artist Tom Forrestall is perhaps the most striking work here, its sharp, deep-hued colours and threatening ice- and seascape enhanced by a tight control of space. Look out also for the work of Forrestall's mentor, **Alex Colville**, whose disconcerting paintings demonstrate a sort of Magic Realism of passive, precisely juxtaposed figures caught, cinema-like, in mid-shot.

The waterfront

From the art gallery, it's a short stroll north along Bedford Row to Water Street and the **waterfront** beyond, once at the heart of Halifax commercial life and now lined by a series of shops and tourist attractions linked by the traffic-free **Harbourwalk**. The much-vaunted **Historic Properties** (Ⓦwww.historicproperties.ca) comprises an area of refurbished nineteenth-century wharves, warehouses and merchants' quarters situated below Upper Water Street. The narrow lanes and alleys have a certain charm – all bars, boutiques and bistros – but there's not much to see unless you take one of several **boat tours** based on the wharf; Passage Privateers (Ⓣ902/406-8687, Ⓦwww.passageprivateers.com) offers enjoyable ninety-minute narrated tours (July & Aug 6 times daily; $19.95) around the harbour in a 65ft schooner, with a crew dressed in pirate-like garb.

Maritime Museum of the Atlantic

Heading southeast along the waterfront you'll come to the thoroughly absorbing **Maritime Museum of the Atlantic** (May & Oct Mon–Sat 9.30am–5.30pm, Tues until 8pm, Sun 1–5.30pm; June–Sept daily 9.30am–5.30pm, Tues until 8pm; Nov–April Tues 9.30am–8pm, Wed–Sat 9.30am–5pm, Sun 1–5pm; May–Oct $8.75, Nov–April $4.75; Ⓣ902/424-7490, Ⓦwww.museum.gov.ns.ca) at 1675 Lower Water St. The **ground floor** holds a series of small displays, including one on the Allied convoys that used Halifax as a port during both World Wars; a second on the Halifax Explosion (see p.367), illustrated by a first-rate video; and a third on the perilously sited Sable Island lighthouse, stuck out in the Atlantic southeast of Nova Scotia. **Upstairs**, a collection of small boats and cutaway scale models details the changing technology of shipbuilding in the 'Days of Sail', but it is the neighbouring **Shipwreck Treasures** section that attracts most attention, mainly because of its well-presented display on the **Titanic**, which sank east of Halifax in 1912.

Docked **outside** the museum are an early twentieth-century steamship, the CSS *Acadia*, and a World War II corvette, HMCS *Sackville* (daily 10am–5pm; $4 or $2 with museum ticket; Ⓦwww.hmcssackville-cnmt.ns.ca). The first is part of the museum, the second is an attraction in its own right; both can only be boarded in the summer (June–Sept).

The Halifax Explosion

Nothing in the history of the Maritimes stands out like the 1917 **Halifax Explosion**, the greatest man-made cataclysm of the pre-atomic age. It occurred during World War I when Halifax was the departure point for convoys transporting troops and armaments to Europe. Shortly after dawn on December 6, a Norwegian ship called the *Imo*, a vessel carrying relief supplies to Belgium, and a French munitions carrier called the *Mont Blanc* were manoeuvring in Halifax harbour. The Norwegian ship was steaming for the open sea, while the *Mont Blanc*, a small, decrepit vessel, was heading for the harbour stuffed with explosives and ammunition, including half a million pounds of TNT. As the ships approached each other, the *Imo* was forced to steer into the wrong channel by a poorly positioned tugboat. With neither ship clear about the other's intentions and each attempting to take evasive action, they collided, and the resulting sparks caused the ignition of the drums of flammable liquid stored on the *Mont Blanc*'s deck. A fire took hold, and the crew abandoned their vessel, which drifted under the force of the impact towards the Halifax shore.

A large crowd had gathered on the waterfront to witness the spectacle when the TNT **exploded**. The blast killed two thousand people instantly and flattened over three hundred acres of north Halifax, with fire engulfing much of the rest. Nothing remained of the *Mont Blanc*; part of its anchor weighing over half a ton was later found more than 4km away. To make matters worse, a **blizzard** deposited 40cm of snow on Halifax during the day, hampering rescue attempts. The bodies of many victims were not recovered until the spring.

Pier 21 and Alexander Keith's Brewery

From the museum it's a twenty-minute stroll to the **Halifax Seaport development** (Ⓦwww.halifaxseaport.com) of shops, bars and condos at the southern edge of downtown. The main attraction here is **Pier 21** (May–Oct daily 9.30am–5.30pm; Nov daily 9.30am–5pm; Dec–March Tues–Sat 10am–5pm; April Mon–Sat 10am–5pm; $8.50; Ⓣ902/425-7770, Ⓦwww.pier21.ca), expected to be designated Canada's National Museum of Immigration in 2010. Around 1.5 million immigrants and Canadian military personnel passed through Pier 21 between 1928 and 1971, and the museum features recordings and video testimonies of many of these people, enhanced with an assortment of interactive exhibits. Start with the thirty-minute multimedia presentation (shown frequently), which features compelling dramatisations of immigrant arrivals from the 1920s to the 1960s.

On the way back into town, stop in at **Alexander Keith's Brewery** (Ⓣ902/455-1474; Ⓦwww.keiths.ca) at 1496 Lower Water St, founded in 1820 and one of the oldest beer-makers in North America. Costumed guides conduct tours (May Sun–Thurs noon–5pm, Fri–Sat noon–8pm; June–Oct Mon–Sat noon–8pm, Sun noon–5pm; Nov–April Fri 5–8pm, Sat noon–8pm, Sun noon–5pm; $15.95), which are fun, especially if rounded off by a beer or meal at the on-site *Red Stag Tavern*.

Fairview Lawn Cemetery

If you have a car, it's worth considering the short ride out to **Fairview Lawn Cemetery**, in the North End of Halifax at the end of Windsor Street. The cemetery is the largest resting place of **Titanic** victims (121) marked with a simple white "Titanic" sign and small granite headstones. Most have their names engraved on the stones (some families have paid for larger memorials), but many occupants are still unidentified and wandering around the site can be a moving experience. Fans of the movie came here in droves in 1997 to lay flowers at the headstone of one "J. Dawson", though director James Cameron later confirmed there was no connection with the film's main character.

Dartmouth

Humdrum **DARTMOUTH**, across the harbour from Halifax, is often ignored by visitors, and although it's primarily an industrial centre the ferry ride over does provide the **best views** of the harbour and downtown Halifax. Turn left outside the ferry terminal and then take the first right for the five-minute stroll to the **Quaker House** (early June to Aug Tues–Sun 10am–1pm & 2–5pm; $2), at 57 Ochterloney St, a small, grey-clapboard residence sitting three blocks up the hill from the dock at King Street. After the American War of Independence, several Quaker whaling families emigrated from Nantucket to Dartmouth, but this is the only one of their houses to survive. The interior has been painstakingly restored to its 1785 appearance, its spartan fittings reflecting Quaker values. Among the exhibits are a two-hundred-year-old pair of shoes found under the floorboards during renovations in 1991, and the eye of a Greenland whale preserved in formalin.

Practicalities

The Dartmouth **ferry** leaves the Halifax waterfront from the Historic Properties at the foot of George Street and the journey takes about ten minutes (Mon–Sat 6.45am–11.30pm every 15–30min; Sun, except Jan & Feb, 10.30am–6pm every 30min–1hr; $2.25). Two road **bridges** (toll $0.75) also connect the twin cities. Bus #1 from Barrington Street at Duke Street uses the MacDonald, running just to the north of both city centres.

Eating

Halifax boasts a wide selection of downtown cafés, bars and restaurants within easy walking distance of Grand Parade; the more touristy spots are clustered down on the waterfront. **Seafood** is the leading local speciality, with **lobster** being a particular favourite – expect to pay about $30 for a medium-sized specimen. For something different, check out *Freak Lunchbox* (April–Aug Mon–Sat 9am–10pm & Sun 11am–7pm; Sept–March Mon–Sat 10am–9pm & Sun noon–6pm; ⓣ902/420-9151, ⓦwww.freaklunchbox.com), at 1723 Barrington St. A hip candy store with a cult following, it has a phenomenal range of sweets.

Downtown

Baan Thai 5234 Blowers St ⓣ902/446-4301, ⓦwww.baanthai.ca. There's often a line here to sample the city's best Thai food, but it's worth the wait. Inexpensive, with mains at around $12.95. Mon–Sat noon–2.30pm & 5–10pm, Sun 5–10pm.

Bluenose II 1824 Hollis St, at Duke ⓣ902/425-5092. Something of an institution, this long-established diner serves filling and fairly tasty meals. Seafood, in various guises, is the speciality, along with Greek dishes (lamb chops, souvlaki), excellent burgers and the signature rice pudding – service can suffer at busy times. Mains $10–20. Mon–Fri 7am–9pm, Sat & Sun 8am–10pm.

Dio Mio Gelato 5670 Spring Garden Rd, at Brenton ⓣ902/492-3467. Justly acclaimed ice cream, gelato and sorbetto with a mind-blowing choice of flavours – if it's all too much, you can't go wrong with amaretto and chocolate. Mon–Fri 8am–9pm, Sat & Sun noon–6pm.

Economy Shoe Shop Café 1663 Argyle St ⓣ902/423-7463, ⓦwww.economyshoeshop.ca. Everything here is imaginative – from the name and the off-beat decor through to the menu, offering tapas to Italian, but best known for its addictive nachos ($10–14), topped with marble cheddar and tomatoes. Daily 11am–2am.

Five Fishermen 1740 Argyle St, at Carmichael ⓣ902/422-4421, ⓦwww.fivefishermen.com. One of Halifax's best restaurants, where the house speciality is seafood. It's expensive perhaps (mains from $36), but the food is delicious and the all-you-can-eat mussel bar is included in the price of any main dish. The restaurant is on the first floor of a gorgeous 1816 building and its cosy interior, with its booths and stained glass, is decked out in antique nautical style. Reservations required. Daily from 5pm.

Hamachi House 5190 Morris St, at Barrington ⓣ902/425-7711, ⓦwww.hamachihouse.com. The best Japanese restaurant in town (with several off-shoots), serving fabulous sushi (sets from $13–25) as well as excellent *terriyaki*, rice and noodle dishes and *tempura*. Mains from $15. Daily 11am–midnight.

The Italian Gourmet 5431 Doyle St ⓣ902/423-7880, ⓦwww.italiangourmet.ca. A wide selection of good quality Italian meals (pizza slices $3.79), sandwiches ($10), salads ($7) and cheaper cakes are available at this large and relaxed deli-café. Mon–Sat 9am–8pm, Sun 9am–6pm.

Midtown Grill & Tavern 1744 Grafton St ⓣ902/422-5213. This venerable diner and pub has been in business since 1949, but moved into smart new digs in 2009. Daily specials include roast beef dinner (Thurs; $11) and ribs (Sat; $12), and DJs add a party atmosphere Fri & Sat nights. Mon–Sat 11am–2am, Sun 9pm–2am.

Steve-o-Reno's 1532 Brunswick St, just off Spring Garden. New Age-ish café-bar with bohemian decor and laidback vibes. The breakfasts are tip-top, with a bewildering range of coffees. Daily 9am–6pm.

Susie's Shortbreads 1589 Dresden Row ⓣ902/221-7075, ⓦwww.susiesshortbreads.com. Piles of the most addictive shortbreads you've ever tasted, from chocolate dipped and peanut butter, to snickerdoodle (cinnamon sugar) and coconut vanilla. Six cookies for $7. Closed Mon.

North End and West End

Phil's Seafood 6285 Quinpool Rd ⓣ902/431-3474. Fried fish fans should make the modest pilgrimage out to this local diner, home to the best fresh fish and home-cut chips in Halifax – it's a twenty-minute walk from the Citadel, just beyond the Quinpool Centre. Try the gingerbread for dessert.

Salvatore's Pizzaiolo 5541 Young St, North End ⓣ902/455-1133, ⓦwww.salvatorespizza.ca. This homely place knocks out the best thin-crust pizzas in the province, and at reasonable prices considering the quality (large starts at $13.75); try the clam pie marinato. Sun–Mon 4–10pm, Tues–Sat 11.30am–11pm.

Dartmouth

Nectar Social House 62 Ochterloney St ⓣ902/406-3363, ⓦwww.nectardining.com. Smartest option in central Dartmouth, with a creative menu of contemporary dishes such as strawberry avocado salad ($9), panko-crusted fish cakes ($9) and roasted vegetable risotto ($13). Sit outside on the tranquil patio in summer. Tues & Wed 11.30am–2.30pm & 5–9pm, Thurs & Fri 11.30am–2.30pm & 5–10pm, Sat 10.30am–2.30pm & 5–10pm, Sun 10.30am–2.30pm & 5–9pm.

Nightlife and entertainment

Halifax has more **bars** per head than anywhere else in Canada except St John's, Newfoundland, but it also has a vibrant **live music scene** with around forty of its café-bars and bars offering everything from blues and jazz through to indie and techno. Many of these places have live music on just a couple of nights a week, and detailed **entertainment listings**, along with local news features, are given in *The Coast* (see p.361). The *Chronicle-Herald* (ⓦthechronicleherald.ca) carries reviews and listings on Thursdays, and *Where* (ⓦwww.where.ca), a free monthly magazine supplied by the tourist office, has a section describing the city's most popular bars. The main **musical event** is the eight-day Atlantic Jazz Festival (ⓣ1-800/567-5277, ⓦwww.jazzeast.com), held in mid-July and featuring many of the biggest international names. Halifax also has a small but vibrant **gay scene**, centered on places like *MenzBar* in the North End at 2182 Gottingen St; check ⓦwww.gay.hfxns.org for the latest information.

Bars

The Bitter End 1572 Argyle St ⓣ902/425-3039, ⓦwww.bitterend.ca. Well-known for its martinis, this polished cocktail bar provides a quietly cool beginning to – or end of – a night on the tiles. Mon–Thurs 4.30pm–2am, Fri–Sun 11.30am–2am.

Henry House 1222 Barrington St, at South ⓣ902/423-5660, ⓦwww.henryhouse.ca. British-style pub with a charmingly intimate bar occupying a nineteenth-century stone building not far from the train station. Most of the ale is brewed on the premises – try the Peculiar, a fair approximation of the sultry grandeur of the legendary British ale.

Maxwell's Plum 1600 Grafton St, at Sackville ⓣ902/423-5090, ⓦwww.themaxwellsplum.com. Beer drinkers' heaven, with an outstanding sixty ales on tap, and around 150 different types of beer on offer altogether. Pitchers (from $14.95) and selected drafts (from $4.50) daily till 7pm.

Old Triangle 5136 Prince St, at Bedford ⓣ902/492-4900, ⓦwww.oldtriangle.com. An Irish-style pub with a whole network of cosy snugs and a warm and welcoming atmosphere. Live music every night, with Gaelic music at weekends.

Your Father's Moustache Pub & Eatery 5686 Spring Garden Rd at South Park ⓣ902/423-6766 ⓦwww.yourfathersmoustache.ca. There's a good range of ales here and they have frequent live acts – blues is a speciality. The seasonal rooftop patio is an excellent spot to have a pint.

Live music and clubs

Bearly's House of Blues 1269 Barrington St ⓣ902/423-2526, ⓦwww.bearlys.ca. Near the train station, this low-key bar has regular acts with the emphasis – you guessed it – on blues and bluegrass. Jam sessions on Sun nights, karaoke on Wed. Open Tues–Sun.

Lower Deck In the Privateer's Warehouse, one of the Historic Properties down on the waterfront ⓣ902/425-1501, ⓦwww.lowerdeck.ca. Traditional Maritime folk music is the speciality here with daily live acts and pub food, while the *Beer Market* (on the upper floor) reverts to a conventional DJ club Fri & Sat nights; cover $6–10.

Marquee Club 2037 Gottingen St, North End ⓣ902/429-2442, ⓦwww.themarqueeclub.ca. Upstairs, rock bands play to an energetic and enthusiastic audience. Downstairs, it's laidback acoustic jazz and blues. Tickets are usually $12–20, and $10 in advance. A ten-minute walk from the centre off Cogswell Street.

Palace Nightclub 1721 Brunswick St ⓣ902/420-0015, ⓦwww.thenewpalace.com. Massive, brash and noisy nightclub where Halifax's young more than get acquainted. Open Wed–Sun until 3.30am.

Reflections Cabaret 5184 Sackville St ⓣ902/422-2957, ⓦwww.reflectionscabaret.com. Halifax's biggest dance club with themed nights, both by music and disposition, though house tends to predominate. Cover $7–9. Mon–Sat 1pm–4am, Sun 4pm–4am.

Classical music, film and theatre

Empire 8 Park Lane 5657 Spring Garden Rd ⓣ902/422-2022, ⓦwww.empiretheatres.com. Mainstream cinema in the Park Lane Mall, just west of Dresden. Tickets around $9.

Neptune Theatre 1593 Argyle St ⓣ902/429-7070, ⓦwww.neptunetheatre.com. The doyen of Halifax's live theatres, offering a wide range of mainstream dramatic productions; closes for three months in summer. Tickets usually $15–45.

Symphony Nova Scotia Box office at the Dalhousie Arts Centre, 6101 University Ave ⓣ902/494-3820, ⓦwww.symphonynovascotia.ca. Professional orchestra that usually performs at the university's Rebecca Cohn Auditorium (University Ave and Le Marchant St). Concert season from Sept to May. Everything from Beethoven to Piaf, with standard tickets ranging $29–49.

Listings

Bike rental Idealbikes, 1678 Barrington St, at Prince (daily 10am–7pm; $25 for first day, $15/day thereafter; ⓣ902/444-7433, ⓦwww.idealbikes.ca).

Bookshops Halifax has several good bookshops on and around Barrington St, both new and second-hand. For used books, try John Doull Bookshop,, 1684 Barrington at Prince (Mon & Tues 9.30am–6pm, Wed–Fri 9.30am–9pm & Sat 10am–9pm; ⓣ902/429-1652, ⓦwww.doullbooks.com), and the café-cum bookshop Trident Booksellers, 1256 Hollis St near Pier 21 (Mon–Fri 8am–5.30pm, Sat 8.30am–5pm, Sun 11am–5pm ⓣ902/423-7100, ⓦwww.tridenthalifax.com).

Car rental Alamo (airport ⓣ902/873-3149); Avis (airport ⓣ902/429-0963); Budget (airport ⓣ902/492-7500) and at MetroPark, 1588 Hollis St (ⓣ902/492-7500); Discount (airport ⓣ902/468-7171); Dollar/Thrifty (airport ⓣ902/873-3527); Enterprise (airport ⓣ902/873-4700); Hertz (airport ⓣ902/873-2273), and at the Marriott Hotel, 1919 Upper Water St (ⓣ902/421-1763); National (airport ⓣ902/873-3505) and at the Westin Hotel, 1181 Hollis St (ⓣ902/423-0231).

Consulate US, Suite 904, Purdy's Wharf Tower II, 1969 Upper Water St ⓣ902/429-2480; British Honorary Consul in Dartmouth ⓣ902/461-1381 (emergencies only). German Honorary Consul, 1100 Purdy's Wharf Tower One, 1959 Upper Water St ⓣ902/420-1599 (emergencies only).

Internet access Free internet access at the Halifax North Memorial Public Library, 2285 Gottingen St (Tues–Thurs 10am–9pm, Fri & Sat

10am–5pm; ⓣ902/490-5723) and Spring Garden Road Memorial Public Library, 5381 Spring Garden Rd, at Grafton (Tues–Thurs 10am–9pm, Fri & Sat 10am–5pm, plus Sun in winter 2–5pm; ⓣ902/490-5700).

Post office 1680 Bedford Row and Prince (Mon–Fri 7.30am–5.15pm; ⓣ1-866/607-6301).

Taxis Casino Taxi ⓣ902/425-6666; Yellow Cab ⓣ902/420-0000.

Southwest Nova Scotia

The jagged coastline running southwest of Halifax to **Yarmouth**, a distance of 340km, boasts dozens of tiny fishing villages pressed tight against the shore by the vast forest that pours over the interior. Highlights include **Peggy's Cove**, an incredibly picturesque smattering of higgledy-piggledy clapboard houses dotted along a wild shore, and **Lunenburg**, with its stunning Victorian architecture. At workaday **Liverpool**, there's a choice of routes: you can cut across the peninsula to charming Annapolis Royal (see p.383) on Rte 8, past the wilderness splendours of **Kejimkujik National Park**, or – with more time – you can press on along the coast to **Lockeport**, with its old-fashioned air and fine sandy beaches, and ultimately **Yarmouth**. Beyond Yarmouth, the French-speaking **Acadian Shore** stretches to **Digby**, where the finger of land known as the **Digby Neck** offers whale-watching tours of national repute.

The southwest coast is popular with tourists, but not oppressively so, and once you get beyond Halifax day-trip range (effectively Lunenburg), the traffic should thin out considerably. **Public transport** is limited. **Acadian Lines** (see p.361) operates a once daily bus service from Halifax to Digby ($45) via the Annapolis Valley ($38), though currently this leaves at 6.40pm, reaching Digby at 11pm, which is far from ideal. Trius Tours (ⓣ1-877/566-1567) runs buses along the south shore to Yarmouth ($60), but again it's only once daily and departs at 5.30pm, arriving in Lunenburg at 7.05pm and Yarmouth at 10.30pm (coming back, the bus departs Yarmouth at 7.30am). There are also several shuttles (often cars or minivans) to the area: Kiwi Kaboodle (ⓣ866/549-4522, ⓦwww.novascotiatoursandtravel.com) offers a daily service between Lunenburg and Halifax ($35).

Peggy's Cove

From Halifax, Rte 333 cuts across dense forest before reaching a shoreline of ribbon fishing villages, glacial boulders, indented rocky bays and eventually tiny **PEGGY'S COVE**, 45km from the capital. Founded in 1811, the hamlet, with a resident population of just sixty souls, surrounds a rocky slit of a harbour, with a spiky timber church, a smattering of clapboard houses and wooden jetties on stilts. Stop at the plush visitor **information centre** (May–Oct daily 9am–5pm; ⓣ902/823-2253) to get local maps and information (especially if you're heading further south), before driving to the end of the road where a solitary **lighthouse** stands against the sea-smoothed granite of the shore – bizarrely, this acts as the local post office in the summer. Along the way you'll pass the **deGarthe Art Gallery** (May–Oct 10am–5pm; $2; ⓣ902/823-2256) where a collection of work by local artist William deGarthe is displayed, though it's his gripping **Fishermen's Monument** carved into the 30m granite rock-face in the garden outside that demands attention, an epic tribute to local fishermen still unfinished at his death.

Otherwise the main activity here is just wandering around the tiny harbour or giant granite boulders along the coast, soaking in the undeniable beauty of the place, despite the swarms of tourists in midsummer; try to visit at sunrise or sunset, when the coach parties leave the village to the locals.

Oak Island: Treasure or trick?

In 1795, three boys discovered the top of an underground shaft on tiny **Oak Island**, a low-lying, offshore islet a few kilometres west of Chester (it's signposted on Rte 3, but the causeway is closed to the public). The shaft, or "Money Pit", soon attracted the attentions of treasure hunters, who were convinced this was where a vast horde of booty had been interred. At first the betting was on Drake, Kidd or Morgan, but present favourites include the Templars and even the Rosicrucians. No treasure has ever been found, but the diggings became so dangerous the island's owners (treasure-hunter Dan Blankenship and the US-based Michigan Group), have closed it to the public (though they restarted the search themselves in 2009). The Oak Island Tourist Society (Ⓦwww.oakislandsociety.ca) organizes annual tours of the island, usually in June ($5), when they also display artefacts associated with the site at the posh *Oak Island Resort* (not be confused with the island itself), a few kilometres north on Rte 3. Check out Ⓦwww.oakislandtreasure.co.uk for the latest news.

The **Swissair Flight 111 Memorial** just beyond the village (open access) is a poignant reminder of the 229 people who lost their lives in the 1998 crash, which happened a few kilometres offshore. Take a few minutes to enjoy the awe-inspiring ocean views back towards the village.

Practicalities

Behind the lighthouse, *The Sou'wester* (Ⓣ902/823-2564) dispenses mundane meals, while the *Peggy's Cove B&B*, overlooking the harbour from the end of Church Road (Ⓣ902/823-2265 or 1-877/725-8732, Ⓦwww.peggyscovebb.com; ⑤), provides five simple but adequate rooms, each with its own sun deck; advance reservations are advised.

Chester

It's a thirty-minute drive north from Peggy's Cove to Hwy 103 and a further 40km west to **CHESTER**, a handsome and prosperous-looking village tumbling over a chubby little peninsula. Officially founded in 1759 and initially settled by colonists from Massachusetts, the village, with its fine old trees and elegant frame houses, has long been the favoured resort of yachting enthusiasts, whose principal shindig is the **Chester Race Week** regatta held in mid-August. Chester is also home to the first-rate **Chester Playhouse** (Ⓣ902/275-3933 or 1-800/363-7529, Ⓦwww.chesterplayhouse.ca; $25), right in the centre on Pleasant Street, which offers a lively programme of concerts and plays from mid-March to December and hosts the Summer Festival of contemporary music and Canadian-oriented drama (July & Aug).

A **passenger ferry** (Mon–Fri 4 daily from 7.10am, Fri also 8.30pm & 11pm; Sat 1pm & 7pm, last Sat of month also 8am; Sun 10am & 6pm; 50min; $5 return) sallies out from Chester bound for the offshore islet of **Big Tancook** (as distinct from neighbouring Little Tancook, which the ferry also visits), whose quiet country roads and benign scenery are popular with walkers, popping across for a day's ramble. There's somewhere to eat here too – *Carolyn's Café & Crafts* (Ⓣ902/228-2749, Ⓦwww.tancookislandrestaurantandcrafts.ca; June–Oct), just opposite the jetty; the café sells island maps and its website carries both a map and the ferry schedule. There's limited parking (free) near the ferry pier on Water Street in Chester, so get here early.

Chester's **tourist office** (May daily 11am–4pm; July & Aug daily 9am–7pm; June, Sept & Oct Mon–Sat 10am–5pm, Sun noon–5pm; Ⓣ902/275-4616, www.chesterns.com) is located in the old train station on the northern edge of town, beside Rte 3. They issue free town maps, which are very useful as Chester's layout is a tad confusing, plus Tancook island ferry timetables.

Practicalities

There's only a handful of **B&Bs** in town, including the affordable and rather modest *Mecklenburgh Inn*, whose four guest rooms (all en-suite with wi-fi) are in a good-looking 1902 clapboard house in the centre at 78 Queen St (902/275-4638, www.mecklenburghinn.ca; 4). For delicious **seafood** head for the *Rope Loft* (902/275-3430; May–Sept) down by the jetty on Water Street.

Mahone Bay

Just 25km southwest of Chester, **MAHONE BAY** spreads along the seashore, its elongated waterfront dominated by three adjacent **church towers**, which combine to create one of the region's most famous vistas. There's not much else to the place, though you might drop by the **Settlers' Museum**, 578 Main St (June–Sept Tues–Sat 10am–5pm, Sun 1–5pm; free), to examine its hotchpotch of period furniture and early nineteenth-century ceramics.

The **visitor information centre** (May Sat & Sun 10am–5pm; June & Sept daily 9.30am–6pm; July & Aug daily 9.30am–7.30pm, Oct daily 10am–5pm; 902/624-6151; www.mahonebay.com) is on the northern side of town on Rte 3.

Practicalities

Mahone Bay possesses some of the best **delis-cum-cafés** hereabouts; try *Jo-Ann's Deli & Bakeshop* (daily 9am–7pm; www.joannsdelimarket.ca) beside the main crossroads, which sells a superb selection of cakes, filled rolls, baguettes and sumptuous fruit pies ($12.95), or the *Biscuit Eater Books Café* (Wed–Sat 8.30am–4pm, Sun 10am–4pm; www.biscuiteater.ca) behind it at 16 Orchard St, a funky little place with new and used books, wi-fi and sublime oat cakes. For a beer on the waterfront, aim for the *Mug & Anchor* further south at 643 Main St (902/624-6378). You'll find plenty of free parking along the waterfront near the churches.

▲ Mahone Bay's famous church towers

If you decide to **stay**, the well-tended *Heart's Desire B&B* (☎902/624-8470, ⓦwww.heartsdesirebb.com; ❹), at 686 Main St, occupies an attractive 1920s building with pleasant views out across the bay, while the cosy *Kip & Kaboodle Backpackers Hostel* (☎902/531-5494, ⓦwww.kiwikaboodle.com) in Mader's Cove, 9466 Rte 3, 3.5km south of the village, is an excellent budget option, charging $25 for the first night and $20 thereafter for dorm beds (shared bath) with a free breakfast, wi-fi and shuttle into Lunenburg and Mahone Bay.

Lunenburg

Comely **LUNENBURG**, 10km south of Mahone Bay, perches on a narrow, bumpy peninsula, its central gridiron of streets clambering up from the main harbourfront flanked by brightly painted wooden houses. Dating from the late nineteenth century, the most flamboyant of these mansions display an arresting variety of architectural features from Gothic towers and classical pillars to elegant verandas and the so-called "Lunenburg Bump", where triple-bell cast roofs surmount overhanging window dormers, giving the town a vaguely European appearance – which is appropriate considering it was founded in 1753 by German and Swiss Protestants. They created a prosperous community with its own fleet of trawlers and scallop-draggers, though today the only fishing done here is for lobster, and since being declared a UNESCO Heritage Site in 1995 the town earns far more from the tourist industry.

Arrival and information

Parking on the waterfront costs a flat $3 per visit; you can also find spaces (2hr free) on Linden Avenue, just before the Fisheries Museum, but most of the street spaces in town are metered ($0.25/30min, $1/2hr). Trius **buses** from Halifax and Yarmouth pull in at the *Kwik-Way* grocery store (☎902/634-3307), at the edge of town on Rte 3. The town's **visitor centre** (daily: May–Sept 9am–8pm, Oct 9am–6pm; ☎902/634-8100, ⓦwww.explorelunenburg.ca) occupies an imitation blockhouse high up on Blockhouse Hill Road, a stiff 700m walk up from

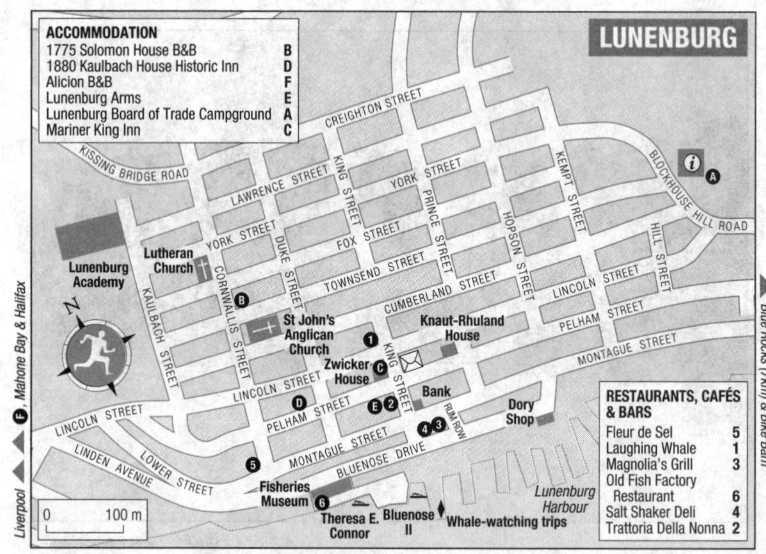

the harbourfront. They operate a free room-reservation service – especially useful in high season – and give out a leaflet detailing the town's architectural high points. You can **rent bikes** from the Bike Barn ($18/half day, $25/full day; tandems $45/day; ⓣ902/634-3426; ⓦwww.bikelunenburg.com) at 579 Blue Rocks Rd, 1.5km from the centre of town.

Accommodation

Visitors are spoilt for **accommodation**, with many of Lunenburg's historic houses turned into first-class **inns** and **B&Bs**. Given the town's tourist numbers, it's best to book well in advance for most of the places listed below.

1775 Solomon House B&B 69 Townsend St ⓣ902/634-3477, ⓦwww.bbcanada.com/5511.html. Clad in cedar shingles, this Georgian house has many of its original features, from its double entrance stairway outside to the plank floors within. There are three guest rooms, bedecked with period furniture, antiques, and bathrooms with claw-foot tubs. The freshly-baked scones at breakfasts are fabulous. 5

1880 Kaulbach House Historic Inn 75 Pelham St ⓣ902/634-8818 or 1-800/568-8818, ⓦwww.kaulbachhouse.com. One of the best preserved of Lunenburg's Victorian mansions, this comfortable inn, with its brightly painted exterior, has seven well-appointed guest rooms, most with sea views and all decorated in an attractive version of period style. The creative European breakfasts are delicious. 5–6

Alicion B&B 66 McDonald St, at Green ⓣ902/634-9358 or 1-877/634-9358, ⓦwww.alicionbb.com. Located a few minutes' drive from the central gridiron, this splendidly well-preserved 1911 mansion has three gorgeous guest rooms kitted out in a pleasing Edwardian style. 6

Lunenburg Arms 94 Pelham St ⓣ902/640-4040 or 1-800/679-4950, ⓦwww.eden.travel/lunenburg. Centrally located boutique hotel with a maritime theme and 24 rooms (most overlooking the harbour) equipped with wi-fi, cable, hardwood floors and fluffy bathrobes. There's a fancy spa and restaurant, *Tin Fish*, on site. 6

Lunenburg Board of Trade Campground 11 Blockhouse Hill Rd ⓣ 902/634-8100 or 1-888/615-8305, ⓔlunenburgvic@ns.aliantzinc.ca. Plain campground with fifty-five pitches (from $18) next door to the visitor centre. Water and free hot showers, plus internet. Great views – and big winds. May–Oct.

Mariner King Inn 15 King St ⓣ902/634-8509 or 1-800/565-8509, ⓦwww.marinerking.com. Bang in the centre of town, the luxurious *Mariner King* was sympathetically restored in 2009 with oodles of stripped wood and crisply modern furnishings and fittings. Five pleasant guest rooms, all with wall-mounted TVs, fancy coffee-makers and claw-foot baths. The gourmet breakfast is included. 5

The Town

Lunenburg has few specific sights and its charm is best appreciated by strolling the hilly streets away from the touristy waterfront, where you'll find rows of bright purple, pink, yellow and even lime-green clapboard houses. Take King Street from the harbourfront a couple of blocks to one of the finest of Lunenburg's mansions, the **Zwicker House** – now the *Mariner King Inn* (see above) – at no. 15. The house was built in the 1820s, but its exterior, including a fine illustration of the Lunenburg bump, was added later, probably in the 1870s. From here, it's a couple of minutes' walk to the **Kaulbach Inn** (see above), at 75 Pelham St, which has changed little since its construction for one of the town's premier families in the 1880s. The house is a simple clapboard frame, but perky dormer windows have been tacked on, as has the triple-bell cast roof of the "bump". To look inside an old Lunenburg home, visit the **Knaut-Rhuland House Museum** (mid-June to mid-Oct Mon–Sat 11am–5pm, Sun noon–4pm; ⓣ902/634-3498, ⓦwww.lunenburgheritagesociety.ca; $2), at 125 Pelham St, built in the 1790s and now staffed by guides dressed in period clothing.

From the museum, it's another short stroll to Lunenburg's fanciest building, **St John's Anglican Church** (May & Sept Sat & Sun noon–4pm; June Sat & Sun

11am–5pm; July & Aug Wed–Sat 11am–7pm; Ⓦwww.stjohnslunenburg.org), whose original oak frame was imported from Boston in 1754. This first church was plain and simple and by the early nineteenth century this just didn't match the expectations of the town's increasingly prosperous burghers, so they had it remodelled, once in the 1840s and again fifty years later. The end result is a superb illustration of decorative Gothic, its frilly wooden scrollwork punctuated by slender pinnacles that poke up from every one of its façades. All this Anglican brouhaha stimulated the Lutherans, who, in 1891, erected a **Lutheran Church** (July & Aug Mon–Fri 10am–4pm) in grand Victorian Gothic style, from its pointed windows through to its soaring spire, nearby at Cornwallis and Fox streets.

The Fisheries Museum and the waterfront

Everyone in Lunenburg eventually ends up at the pride and joy of the town, its **Fisheries Museum of the Atlantic** (May–June & Sept–Oct daily 9.30am–5.50pm; July & Aug Tues–Sat 9.30am–7pm, Sun–Mon 9.30am–5.50pm; $10 from late May to mid-Oct, otherwise $4; Ⓦwww.museum.gov.ns.ca/fma), housed in an old fish-processing plant by the quayside. The museum has an excellent aquarium, a room devoted to whales and whaling and displays on fishing and boat-building techniques. Another section explains the history of the locally built 1920s schooner *Bluenose* and its replica *Bluenose II* (see below), while the "August Gales" display has wondrous tales of mountainous seas and helmsmen tied to the mast to stop being swept overboard. Moored by the jetty, there's a trawler and a scalloper, but the real highlight is the *Theresa E. Connor*, a saltbank fishing **schooner** launched in 1938. Superbly restored, the schooner was one of the last boats of its type to be built, a two-masted vessel constructed to a design that had changed little since the early eighteenth century.

Unless it's out for a tour, the **Bluenose II** will be moored at the adjacent wharf. The original *Bluenose*, whose picture is on the 10¢ coin, was famed throughout Canada as the fastest vessel of its kind in the 1920s, although she ended her days ingloriously as a freighter, foundering off Haiti in 1946. The 1960s replica has spent years as a floating standard-bearer for Nova Scotia, based in Lunenberg, and embarks on a very popular cruise programme every summer (June–Sept) all over the province (and often further afield). The standard two-hour cruise is worth the $40; call Ⓣ902/634-4794 or 1-866/579-4909 ext 221 to make reservations, or check the schedule at Ⓦwww.museum.gov.ns.ca/bluenose. You can also take two- to three-hour **whale-watching** trips from here, operated four times daily from May to October by Lunenburg Whale Watching Tours (Ⓣ902/527-7175, Ⓦwww.whalewatchingnovascotia.com; $48).

Eating and drinking

Lunenburg has a good supply of restaurants and cafés, though standards do vary, partly because of the number of summer day-trippers; the main choices tend to be concentrated along the waterfront. Look out for two local culinary delights: the **Lunenburg sausage**, traditionally served at breakfast, and made of lean pork and beef, flavoured with coriander and allspice; and the **Solomon Gundy**, marinated herring with sour cream or occasionally mustard.

Fleur de Sel 53 Montague St Ⓣ902/640-2121, Ⓦwww.fleurdesel.net. High-end French restaurant offering an exquisite seasonal menu featuring dishes such as Lunenburg scallops ($29) and Quebec duck breast ($28). Late May to Oct Tues–Sun from 5pm (also Sun brunch 10am–2pm).

Laughing Whale 263 Lincoln St, at King Ⓣ902/527-3154, Ⓦwww.laughingwhalecoffee.com. Easily the best café in town, this coffee-roasting specialist uses only organically-grown, Fairtrade coffees and offers a tempting selection of snacks and blends; try the Ooh La La, a smoky sweet Peruvian coffee.

Magnolia's Grill 128 Montague St ⓣ902/634-3287. To save money, try this moderately priced place with its cosy diner-like booths and wide and inventive menu, featuring everything from burgers through to lobster, mussels and fish cakes. You'll pay under $30 for two, with drinks. Closed Sun.

Old Fish Factory Restaurant 68 Bluenose Drive ⓣ902/634-3333, ⓦwww.oldfishfactory.com. This seafood place has long been considered the prime spot on the waterfront, but although it still serves a splendid range of fish and shellfish, it's become a tad canteen-like. Dinners are pricey ($17 for a lobster roll), though lunches are better value (fish cakes for $10). May–Oct.

Salt Shaker Deli 124 Montague St ⓣ902/640-3434, ⓦwww.saltshakerdeli.com. A great standby with excellent views across the harbour, decent draught beers and justly popular pizza: the seafood version is $13, or you can try Stinky Charlie's (garlic) for $9. Tues–Sat 11am–9pm, Sun 11am–3pm.

Trattoria Della Nonna 9 King St ⓣ902/640-3112, ⓦwww.trattoriadellanonna.ca. The finest Italian restaurant in town, with pizzas from $14, pastas from $12 and classics such as *osso bucco alla Milanese* (braised veal shank) for around $30. Dinner daily from 5pm, lunch Thurs–Sun only.

Liverpool

Like its British namesake, **LIVERPOOL**, 70km from Lunenburg along Hwy 103, skirts the mouth of a Mersey River and has a strong seafaring tradition, but there the similarities end. Nova Scotia's Liverpool was founded in 1759 by Cape Cod emigrants, who established a fearsome reputation for privateering during both the American Revolution and the War of 1812. Today, Liverpool's largest employer is the Bowater Paper Mill and tourism has become increasingly important, boosted by the fine old houses grouped around the eastern end of **Main Street**. One of these, the **Perkins House** at no. 105 (June to mid-Oct Mon–Sat 9.30am–5.30pm, Sun 1–5.30pm; $2; ⓣ902/354-4058), has been restored to its late eighteenth-century condition, when it was the home of Simeon Perkins, who moved here from Connecticut in 1762. Perkins was a shipowner, a merchant, a colonel in the militia and a justice of the court, but he still had time to keep a detailed and revealing diary from 1766 until his death in 1812. Copies of this four-volume work are on display at the house, while the adjacent **Queens County Museum** (June to mid-Oct Mon–Sat 9.30am–5.30pm, Sun 1–5.30pm; mid-Oct to May Mon–Sat 9am–noon & 1–5pm; $2 June to mid-Oct, otherwise free) sometimes sells excerpts for a couple of bucks – and also possesses a diverting collection of early local photographs.

Liverpool's **visitor centre** is on the waterfront at 28 Henry Hensey Drive (May–Oct daily 9.30am–5.30pm, open till 7pm July & Aug; ⓣ902/354-5421), where you can also **park** for free.

Practicalities

Liverpool has one good place to **stay**, *Lane's Privateer Inn*, just across the bridge from the centre of town at 27 Bristol Ave (ⓣ902/354-3456 or 1-800/794-3332, ⓦwww.lanesprivateerinn.com; ❺). The inn occupies a spick and span, two-storey, motel-like structure built in the general style of an old timber house and the 27 guest rooms are in the annexe. The inn is also the best place to **eat**, either in the restaurant, where well-prepared steak and seafood dishes average $17, or in the adjoining café, which serves good coffees, teas and gourmet treats, including handmade Belgian chocolates.

Kejimkujik National Park

There's no better way to experience the solitude and scenery of the southwest Nova Scotian hinterland than to head northwest 70km from Liverpool along Rte 8 to the entrance to the **Kejimkujik National Park**. This magnificent tract of rolling wilderness has a rich variety of forest habitats interrupted by rivers and brooks linking about a dozen lakes. In the spring and autumn the park is alive with wild flowers, whose brilliant colours provide cover for an abundance of porcupines, black bears, white-tailed deer and beavers, as well as three types of turtle. The best time to visit is in the early spring and autumn, when the insects aren't too troublesome: blackflies peak between mid-May and late June. A park **entrance fee** of $5.80 per adult per day is levied from mid-May to mid-October.

Exploring the park

Hiking trails crisscross Kejimkujik, but the easiest way to explore the park and its flat-water rivers and lakes is by **canoe**. These can be rented from **Jakes Landing** (mid-May to mid-Oct; $7.75/hr, $29/day; Ⓣ902/682-5253; reservations recommended), roughly 10km by road from the entrance to the park. A couple of clearly defined, day-long canoe trips begin here, namely the delightful paddle among the islets of Kejimkujik Lake and an excursion up the Mersey River beneath a canopy of red maples. For overnight trips, the park has around fifty primitive **campsites** ($24.50) dotted along its canoe routes and hiking trails – these are a better bet than the large year-round campground at **Jeremys Bay** (reservations Ⓣ1-877/737-3783, Ⓦwww.pccamping.ca; $25.50), also 10km by road from the main entrance; for backcountry camping, register at the information centre.

Practicalities

The park's **information centre** (mid-June to Aug daily 8.30am–8pm; Sept to mid-June Mon–Fri 8.30am–4.30pm; Ⓣ902/682-2772, Ⓦwww.pc.gc.ca) is near the park entrance; they have detailed maps and dispense trail advice. If camping isn't your thing, the nearest **beds** are at the *Whitman Inn* (Ⓣ902/682-2226 or 1-800/830-3855, Ⓦwww.whitmaninn.com; ❸), 2km south of the park entrance on Rte 8, with eight rooms. The nearest town to Kejimkujik is Annapolis Royal (see p.383), 50km to the north.

Kejimkujik's Seaside Adjunct

Southwest from Liverpool on Hwy 103, it's about 25km to tiny **Port Joli**, from where a bumpy, 6.5km-long gravel road leads to **St Catherine's River** and the more accessible, western side of **Kejimkujik National Park Seaside Adjunct** (information kiosk mid-June to mid-Oct 9.30am–5.30pm; $3.90), a 22-square kilometre parcel of pristine coastline that provides an ideal half-day or day's hike. The Adjunct straddles the end of a beautiful but inhospitable peninsula where the mixed forests and squelchy bogs of the interior back onto the tidal flats, lagoons, headlands and beaches of the coast. You may catch sight of the rare piping plover, which nests here between May and early August. From the parking lot, the **Harbour Rocks Trail** follows the route of an old cart track straight down to the seashore, a fairly straightforward if sometimes wet and squelchy 5.2km (return) hike. There are no facilities, so carry food and water.

Lockeport

Well off the beaten track, 65km southwest of Liverpool via Hwy 103 and then Rte 3, the sleepy fishing village of **LOCKEPORT** sits on a tiny island connected to the mainland by a 1.5km-long causeway, fringed by the white sands of **Crescent Beach**. The beach is never crowded, the sea is deep and clear, and the village features a row of five contrasting houses built by the prosperous Locke family over a forty-year period in the nineteenth century. It's a languid, relaxing spot, where nothing much seems to happen except for the comings and goings of the odd fishing smack. It also boasts one first-rate **B&B**, *Seventeen South B&B*, 17 South St (Ⓣ902/656-2512 Ⓔshorebb@ns.sympatico.ca; ④), a tastefully modernized Cape Cod-style house with two spacious rooms perched on a wooded knoll in sight of the seashore and not far from the harbour; it's open year-round and the owners even throw in a canoe if you fancy a paddle. If the B&B is full, the tourist office (June–Aug daily 10am–6pm; Ⓣ902/656-3123, Ⓦwww.beachcentre.ca), in the **Crescent Beach Centre** (same hours) at the end of the causeway, has details of several beachside cottages. The centre houses displays on local ecology and traditional fishing and can hook you up with **boat tours**. Lockeport has a good **restaurant**, in the seasonal *Parrot's Pins Candlepin Café*, 10 Beech St (Tues–Sat 11am–2pm & 4–8pm; Ⓣ902/656-2695).

Shelburne

Founded by Loyalists in the 1780s – including two hundred freed black slaves – and once a major **shipbuilding** centre, historic **SHELBURNE** lies 35km northwest of Lockeport and 70km southwest of Liverpool on Hwy 103.

The Town

The town's fine clapboard houses and shingle wharf buildings have been preserved in the pristine **Historic District** that strings down from **Water Street**, the main drag, to Dock Street and the waterfront. Entry to all of Shelburne's historic attractions is $3 per site, or $8 for a combined ticket (see Ⓦwww.historicshelburne.com).

The **Shelburne County Museum** (June to mid-Oct daily 9.30am–5.30pm; mid-Oct to May Mon–Fri 10am–noon & 2–5pm; free mid-Oct to May; Ⓣ902/875-3219), on Maiden Lane, provides a broad overview of the town's history and its maritime heritage (pride of place goes to Canada's oldest fire pumper, made in London in 1740). The adjacent **Ross-Thomson House** (June to mid-Oct daily 9.30am–5.30pm; Ⓣ902/875-3141) is a Loyalist merchant's store and home, pleasingly restored to its appearance circa 1780s. The nearby **Dory Shop** (June–Sept daily 9.30am–5.30pm; Ⓣ902/875-3219) comprises a waterfront boat factory/museum. The flat-bottomed **dory**, rarely more than 5m long and built to ride the heaviest of swells, was an integral part of the fishing fleet during the days of sail. The Dory Shop produces three a year, but only for private use – the few dories used today in the offshore fishery are steel-hulled. Allow about an hour to visit the three sites, a little more if you throw in the **Muir-Cox Shipyard Interpretive Centre** (daily June–Sept 9.30am–5.30pm; Ⓣ902/875-2483), at the south end of Dock Street. You can also take a peek at the handful of heavyweight shingle buildings left over from the filming of the *Scarlet Letter* here in 1994 – you'll find them just off Dock Street.

Practicalities

There's no special reason to stay in Shelburne, but the **tourist office** (May, June & Sept Mon–Tues & Thurs–Sat 10am–5pm, Sun noon–5pm; July & Aug daily 9am–7pm; Ⓣ902/875-4547), at the north end of Dock Street, operates a free room-reservation service. The most agreeable **hotel** in town is the *Cooper's Inn*, which occupies a lavishly refurbished old shingle house at 36 Dock St (Ⓣ902/875-4656 or 1-800/688-2011, Ⓦwww.thecoopersinn.com; ⑥; May–Oct). Wooded, lakeside **camping** is available 5km west round the bay at the *Islands Provincial Park* (Ⓣ902/875-4304 or 1-888/544-3434; mid-May to Aug; $18–31).

For **food**, the *Charlotte Lane Café* (mid-May to late Dec Tues–Sat 11.30am–8pm; Ⓣ902/875-3314, Ⓦwww.charlottelane.ca), down an alley – Charlotte Lane – off Water Street, serves wholesome meals and smashing salads; and there's first-rate cuisine at the *Cooper's Inn* restaurant – try the steaks. For coffee and cake, there's the *Beandock Coffee* (Mon–Sat 9am–4pm, also Sun July & Aug; ⓣ902/875-1302), 10 John St at Dock Street. The best place for a drink is the outdoor deck of the *Sea Dog Saloon* (daily 11am–8pm; open till 2am Fri & Sat, closed Sun Sept–May; ⓣ902/875-2862, ⓦwww.theseadog.com), at 1 Dock St, which also sells live lobsters, has free wi-fi and rents kayaks (ⓣ902/875-1131).

Yarmouth

The cancellation of the Maine ferry service in 2009 was a major economic blow to **YARMOUTH**, hampering efforts to spruce up the town. Gallant efforts have been made to freshen up the harbourfront around the **Yarmouth Waterfront Gallery** (May–Oct daily 10am–5pm; ⓣ902/742-7089, ⓦwww.yarmouthwaterfrontgallery.com) at 90 Water St, where fifteen resident artists display their work. Efforts to brighten the appeal of Main Street, just up the hill, centre on the **Art Gallery of Nova Scotia, Western Branch** (mid-May to mid-Oct daily 10am–5pm; mid-Oct to mid-May Fri–Sun noon–5pm; $5; ⓣ902/749-2248) at no. 341, which displays pieces from the main collection in Halifax (p.365) over two floors of small but well-presented galleries. Back along Water Street at no. 112, the **W. Laurence Sweeney Museum** (May–Oct Mon–Sat 10am–6pm; $3; ⓣ902/742-3457) has preserved some of the actual wharf buildings and shacks that once dominated this part of town, crammed with all sorts of fishing and sailing paraphernalia going back to the 1920s.

There's **parking** along Main Street, or in the car parks just off it (2hr free). You can also park at the **Nova Scotia visitor centre** (daily: July & Aug 8am–7pm; June & Sept to late Oct 9am–5pm; ⓣ902/742-5033), on Main Street just uphill from the ferry terminal, which issues free leaflets and brochures.

Practicalities

The comfortable *Murray Manor* **B&B** (ⓣ902/742-9625 or 1-877/742-9629, ⓦwww.murraymanor.com; ❹), is at 225 Main St, opposite the visitors' centre, in an attractive Regency-style house with four pleasant rooms. Alternatively, the well-equipped *Comfort Inn* (ⓣ902/742-1119, ⓦwww.choicehotels.ca; ❺), at 96 Starrs Rd, Rte 3 on the outskirts of town, is the most popular option for drivers. The best place to **eat and drink** is *Rudder's* (ⓣ902/742-7311, ⓦwww.ruddersbrewpub.com) at 96 Water St on the harbourfront, which has a patio, brews its own beer and serves decent lobster suppers.

Côtes acadiennes: Baie Sainte-Marie

North from Yarmouth, Hwy 101 and the much slower Rte 1 slip across the flat coastline of the fifty-kilometre **Baie Sainte-Marie** district, part of the **Côtes**

Ferries between Yarmouth and Maine

In December 2009, **Bay Ferries** announced that it was cancelling the high-speed, car-carrying **catamaran** service from Yarmouth to Bar Harbor and Portland, Maine. Running for 22 years, the route had been making a loss for some time, and when the Nova Scotia government suspended financial support, the company could not continue. The economic fall-out is likely to be severe for the area; the Yarmouth mayor and many locals pledged to continue lobbying for a new service into 2010, but the prospects looked bleak at the time of writing. See p.402 for US border formalities.

acadiennes (Acadian Shores) whose straggling villages house the largest concentration of Acadians (see p.387) in the province. At **POINTE DE L'EGLISE**, 65km from Yarmouth and right next to the sea, is the massive **Église Sainte-Marie** (June–Oct daily 9am–5pm; $2;) whose soaring tower and steeple, finished in 1905, reach a giddy 56m making it the tallest wooden church in North America. Unfortunately, the museum inside holds some of the worst religious paintings imaginable, nineteenth-century dross with none of the medievalism suggested by the reliquaries beside the altar, among which are wooden shards purportedly from the Holy Cross. The best time to visit the region is early August, when the **Festival Acadien de Clare** (Ⓦwww.festivalacadiendeclare.ca) sees concerts, parades and special events celebrating Acadian culture.

You can **eat** cheaply at *Chez l'Ami* across the road from the church, a shack selling burgers, *poutine*, and old-fashioned ice cream. Other local culinary gems include *La Râpure Acadienne* (Ⓣ902/769-2172) just south of the village on Rte 1, where you can buy *râpure* to go, a stodgy chicken and potato concoction considered classic Acadian food, straight out of the oven. For more refined Acadian and French-inspired cuisine, head a few kilometres north to **GROSSES-COQUES** and *Chez Christophe* (Ⓣ902/837-5817, Ⓦwww.chezchristophe.ca), housed in an enchanting 1830s clapboard house and featuring live Acadian music Thursdays and Fridays. You can also stay at the guest house here (❸–❹).

Digby and around

It's around 35km from Pointe de L'Église to the fishing port of **DIGBY**, whose workaday centre spreads over a hilly headland that pokes out into the Annapolis Basin. The latter is connected to the Bay of Fundy by a narrow channel known as the **Digby Gut**, thereby subjecting Digby **harbour** to the swirling effects of the Fundy tides – and it's the pocket-sized harbour, with its rickety wooden piers, which is the most appealing part of town. Otherwise, Digby is notable for two things: its **smoked herring** or "Digby chicks", usually on sale at the north end of the harbour at **O'Neil's Royal Fundy Seafood Market** (Mon–Sat 10am–6pm, Sun noon–6pm), which also has a cheap seafood café; and its delicious **scallops**, which you can sample at the popular *Fundy Restaurant*, 34 Water St (Ⓣ902/245-4950; lunch from $14.95), the pick of several places lining the harbourfront Water Street and its continuation, Montague Row.

Arrival and information

You can **park** along Water Street (2hr; free), though spaces go fast in July and August. Acadian Lines **buses** to Digby stop at 77 Montague Row, from where it's a couple of minutes' walk north along the waterfront to the **tourist office** (mid-May to mid-Oct daily 9am–5pm; Ⓣ902/245-5714 or 1-888/463-4429 , Ⓦwww.digby.ca), which operates a room-reservation service and gives information on Digby Neck whale-watching trips.

Digby's **ferry port** is located 5km north of town; from here Bay Ferries (Ⓣ1-888/249-7245, Ⓦwww.bayferries.com) runs regular **car ferries** (1–2 daily; 3hr; passengers $30–40 one-way, cars $75–80 plus $20 fuel surcharge, bicycles $10) across the Bay of Fundy to Saint John, New Brunswick (see p.414), saving a long drive.

Accommodation

Digby has several appealing places to **stay**, beginning with the first-rate *Harbourview Inn* (Ⓣ902/245-5686 or 1-877/449-0705, Ⓦwww.theharbourviewinn.com; from ❺; May–Oct), 25 Harbourview Rd, just east of town on Hwy 1, a gorgeous 1899 B&B surrounded by gardens. There's also the bargain *Bayside Inn* (Ⓣ902/245-2247 or 1-888/754-0555, Ⓦwww.baysideinn.ca; ❷), 115 Montague Row, which

Digby Neck whale-watching

The nutrient-rich waters of the **Bay of Fundy** attract dozens of whales, and several local companies organize daily **whale-watching excursions** from late May to mid-October. Trips usually last between two and three hours, though those from Westport tend to last longer – between three and five hours. No one can guarantee you'll spy a whale, but there's every chance, beginning with finback and minkes in late spring, and humpbacks from mid- to late June. By the middle of July all three species are sighted and usually hang around the Bay of Fundy till late summer and autumn, which is when the rare North Atlantic right whale is seen.

Among several Digby Neck whale-watching companies, one of the most proficient is **Ocean Explorations Whale Cruises** ($59/half-day; ⓣ902/839-2417 or 1-877/654-2341, ⓦwww.oceanexplorations.ca), which uses zodiac boats and is based in tiny Tiverton on Long Island. Further along the Neck, based in the forlorn little fishing village of Westport, on Brier Island, are **Brier Island Whale & Seabird Cruises** ($49; ⓣ902/839-2995 or 1-800/656-3660, ⓦwww.brierislandwhalewatch.com) and **Mariner Cruises** ($49; ⓣ902/839-2346 or 1-800/239-2189, ⓦwww.novascotiawhalewatching.ca).

occupies a nineteenth-century clapboard house, has eleven rooms (seven en suite) and is equipped with an airy patio. The *Digby Backpackers Inn* (ⓣ902/245-5274, ⓦwww.digbyhostel.com) at 168 Queen St, one block from the waterfront, has budget dorms (❶) and private rooms (❸), with breakfast included.

Maud Lewis Memorial

If you've seen the "The Painted House" of **Maud Lewis** at the Art Gallery of Nova Scotia in Halifax (p.366), you might want to check out the poignant **Maud Lewis Memorial** on Hwy 101 in Marshalltown, just five minutes south of the Digby exit (on the right side of the road). The steel structure marks the spot where Maud lived and painted for 32 years; designed by Brian MacKay-Lyons, it mimics the actual size of the house.

Digby Neck

The 70km-long **Digby Neck** comprises a narrow finger of land that gingerly nudges out into the Bay of Fundy, sheltering the Acadian Shore from the full effects of the ocean. The Neck's further reaches are broken into two little islands – **Long Island** and, at the tip, **Brier Island** – and a pair of **car ferries** shuttle across the narrow channels between them, running every hour, 24 hours a day and charging $5 each for the return trip. Ferry times are coordinated, so it takes about two hours to reach Brier Island from Digby; ferry timetables are available at the Digby tourist office. The road along the Neck travels inland and is fairly monotonous, but then most people only venture down here to join a **whale-watching trip** (see box below). From either Digby or (even better) Annapolis Royal (see p.383), it's easy enough to complete both the drive along the Neck and the whale-watching cruise in a day.

The Annapolis Valley

The **Annapolis Valley**, stretching 110km northeast from Annapolis Royal to Wolfville, is sheltered from the winds and fog that afflict much of the province by a narrow band of coastal hills. This factor, combined with the fertility of the soil, makes the valley ideal for **fruit growing** and even **wine-making**, with the number of vineyards expected to reach twenty in the next few years. In the summer you'll see a tempting range of organic produce being sold on roadsides all over the valley.

Much of this is a legacy of French (later Acadian) settlers, who arrived in the 1600s and introduced the distinctive dykeland agriculture that still exists today. The string of little towns that dot the valley were settled by Loyalists from New England after the expulsion of the Acadians, but although several of them are pretty places, only two stand out: **Annapolis Royal**, with its handsome Victorian mansions and proximity to the historic site of **Port Royal**, and **Wolfville**, an amiable university town. Wolfville is also within easy striking distance of **Grand Pré National Historic Site** and the harsh scenery of **capes Blomidon** and **Split**.

Both towns are reachable on the once daily Acadian Lines **bus** service between Halifax and Digby (see p.381), while Kings Transit (Ⓦwww.kingstransit.ns.ca) operates local services between Wolfville and Digby (standard fare $3.50).

Annapolis Royal

With a population of just six hundred, **ANNAPOLIS ROYAL**, 40km northeast of Digby, spreads across a podgy promontory that lies tucked in between the Annapolis River and its tributary, the Allain River. The town maintains a relaxed and retiring air that's hard to resist, one that belies its turbulent past. Scots led by Sir William Alexander settled the district in 1629, but were forced to leave just three years later as part of an Anglo-French treaty. The town was occupied by French forces in 1636 (when it became the new Port Royal), and though subsequently it changed hands many times, this Acadian outpost prospered, even serving as the British capital of Nova Scotia after its capture in 1710 (Halifax assumed the role in 1749). The British – who had renamed the town again in honour of Queen Anne – finally expelled the Acadians in 1755, and the collection of elegant wooden mansions you see today were built by Loyalist settlers in later years.

▲ Nova Scotia's Annapolis Valley is rapidly becoming renowned for its vineyards and wine-making

Arrival and information

The main drag, **St George Street** (Rte 8), sweeps through the leafy southern outskirts to reach the end of the promontory, where it turns right to run parallel to the waterfront. The Acadian Lines **bus** between Halifax and Digby stops at the Annapolis Royal Inn on Rte 1, an inconvenient 1.3km west of St George Street and the town centre. The **tourist office** (daily: July & Aug 8am–8pm; mid-May to June & Sept to mid-Oct 10am–5pm; ⓣ902/532-5454) is on the other side of town, inside the tidal generating station on the Rte 1 bridge, about 1.4km north of the centre.

Accommodation

The town's best options are its B&Bs. The *Hillsdale House Inn* (ⓣ902/532-2345 or 1-877/839-2821, ⓦwww.hillsdalehouse.ns.ca; ⑤), at 519 St George St, occupies an elegant villa of 1849, while the *Queen Anne Inn*, opposite at no. 494 (ⓣ902/532-7850 or 1-877/536-0403, ⓦwww.queenanneinn.ns.ca; ⑤; May–Nov), is housed in a grand turreted and towered extravagance of the 1860s; rooms in both places are en-suite and kitted out in enchanting period style. The same goes for the well-tended *Bread and Roses Inn*, (ⓣ902/532-5727 or 1-888/899-0551, ⓦwww.breadandroses.ns.ca; ⑤; April–Nov), a spiky late Victorian mansion at 82 Victoria St. The well-equipped Dunromin **campsite** (ⓣ902/532-2808, ⓦwww.dunromincampsite.com; May to mid-Oct; $27–39; cabins $65–110), 1km beyond the tourist office on the far side of the Annapolis River, occupies a wooded, riverside location.

The Town

Edging St George Street just before it swings right along the waterfront are the substantial remains of **Fort Anne National Historic Site** (open access), whose grass-covered ramparts date from 1702. A few military buildings are inside, but the most significant survivor is the old **officers' quarters** in the middle. The British built these in 1797 and, surmounted by three outsize chimney stacks, they now house a small **museum** (mid-May to mid-Oct daily 9am–6pm; $3.90). Inside there's a copy of the original charter by which James I incorporated "Nova Scotia" in 1621, and a cheerful community tapestry tracing the town's history. If you want more of the flavour of early Annapolis Royal, ask at the museum (or your B&B) for details of the candlelight tours of the **old graveyard** (June to mid-Oct Tues, Wed, Thurs, Sun 9.30pm; 1hr) next to the fort – they're good fun and a snip at $7.

Five-minutes' walk from the fort – back along St George Street – lie the ten-acre **Annapolis Royal Historic Gardens** (daily: mid-May to June & Sept to mid-Oct 9am–5pm; July & Aug 8am–dusk; ⓦwww.historicgardens.com; $7.50). These feature a string of enjoyable "theme gardens", from the formality of a Victorian garden to an extensive rose collection in which the different varieties are arranged broadly in chronological order. The whole site slopes gently down towards the Allain River, with a dyke-walk offering views of mud flats and salt marshes and also twisting through elephant grass, a reed imported by the Acadians to thatch their cottages.

Eating and drinking

There are several **cafés** along the town's waterfront, including *Leo's Café* (June–Sept Mon–Sat 9am–8pm & Sun noon–5pm, otherwise Mon–Sat 9am–4.30pm; ⓣ902/532-7424), at 222 St George St, which serves up first-rate snacks and lighter meals, while the inexpensive *Fort Anne Café*, (closed Sun; ⓣ902/532-5254) opposite the entrance to the fort at 298 St George St, sells tasty and substantial meals from a traditional Canadian menu (don't be put off by the downbeat decor). *Ye Olde Towne Pub* at 9 Church St – just down the street from *Leo's* and across from the boatyard – serves good draught **beer**. The *Garrison House Inn* at 350 St George St is the best place for dinner (mains $15–30), set in an old wooden house dating from 1854 and featuring local haddock and lobster as well as more exotic dishes such as coconut curry.

Port Royal

In 1605, after their dreadful winter on the island of Saint-Croix in Passamaquoddy Bay, Samuel de Champlain and Pierre Sieur de Monts set up camp close to the current **Port Royal National Historic Site** (mid-May to mid-Oct daily 9am–5.30pm; www.pc.gc.ca; $3.90), on the north side of the Annapolis River 12km west of Annapolis Royal – Nova Scotia's first European settlement. This was a commercial venture not a colony or military installation; the hastily constructed *habitation*, designed by Champlain and similar to the fortified farms of France, was a square of rough-hewn, black-painted timber buildings where the French would trade with the Mi'kmaq for furs, particularly beaver pelts. Champlain left in 1607 (going on to found Québec), and the outpost was looted and destroyed by a party of desperate English colonists from Virginia in 1613.

The stronghold dominated the estuary from a low bluff, as does today's evocative **replica**, a painstaking reconstruction completed in 1940, relying solely on the building techniques of the early seventeenth century. Rooms inside have been furnished as they might have appeared at the time, with the Trading Room containing a selection of real beaver, timber wolf, bear, fox, and raccoon hides. There are **no buses** from Annapolis Royal to the site.

Wolfville and around

The orderly and well-heeled university town of **WOLFVILLE**, 110km northeast from Annapolis Royal, was originally called Mud Creek after the mud flats surrounding its tiny harbour. They are the creation of the Fundy tides, which rush up the Cornwallis River to dump the silt that is home to hundreds of herons and waders, with thousands of sandpipers arriving in early August on their annual migration from Arctic breeding grounds. Wolfville's other curiosity is the **Robie Tufts Nature Centre** on Front Street (take Elm Ave from Main St), once part of a dairy and now just a wooden shelter built around an old chimney with information boards on local flora and fauna, especially the **chimney swifts** that have been nesting here since the 1970s. It's best visited an hour before sunset on a summer's evening – usually from the second or third week in May till late August – when an enormous flock of them fly in circles above the centre, before suddenly swooping en masse into the chimney to roost for the night.

Arrival and information

Wolfville is on the Acadian Lines **bus** route connecting Halifax and Digby, but buses pull in on Highland Avenue, on the west side of town on the edge of the Acadia University campus, a good ten-minute walk from the tiny town centre – which consists of a few blocks of Main Street and several subsidiary side streets. The **tourist office** (July & Aug daily 9am–7pm; May–June & Sept–Oct Wed–Sat 10am–6pm, Sun noon-8pm; 902/542-7000, www.wolfville.info) is located on the east side of the town centre, just off Main Street on Willow Avenue. They have local accommodation lists and – a necessary preparation – details of the hike along Cape Split (see p.387).

Accommodation

The town has several splendid **inns** and **B&Bs**. Tempting choices start with the *Blomidon Inn* (☎902/542-2291 or 1-800/565-2291, www.blomidon.ns.ca), a five-minute walk east of downtown at 195 Main St, which occupies an ornate sea captain's mansion of 1882. The rooms in the main house (6) have lots of period detail, the rooms in the modern annexe (5) behind are less endearing and the suites (8) in the two-storey chalet at the back of the property are the epitome of modern luxury, albeit in retro style. *Victoria's Historic Inn & Carriage House* (☎902/542-5744 or 1-800/556-5744, www.victoriashistoricinn.com; 6) is an immaculately maintained grand mansion with fancy gingerbread scrollwork just 800m or so west of the centre at 600 Main St. It has sixteen guest rooms, both in the inn and the adjacent carriage house, each decorated in a plush Victorian style. A third and less expensive option is the three-roomed *Garden House B&B* (☎902/542-1703, www.gardenhouse.ca; 3), at 220 Main St just east of downtown, in an attractive old property of 1830.

Eating and drinking

For **food**, there are good paninis, lip-smacking muffins and great coffee at *Just Us! Café* (Mon–Fri 7am–9pm, Sat 8am–6pm & Sun 10am–7pm; www.justuscoffee.com), in the front of the old Art Deco Acadia Cinema at 450 Main St; and delicious salads, meats and seafood at the somewhat pricey and formal *Acton's Grill & Café* (daily from 5pm; ☎902/542-7525, www.actons.ca), at 406 Main St. The best restaurant in town is the *Tempest* (☎902/542-0588, www.tempest.ca; closed Mon), a gorgeous blue clapboard place at 117 Front St just off Main Street; expect an eclectic menu of lobster risotto, pad thai, fish cakes and even late night tapas. The *Library Pub* (☎902/542-4315) at 472 Main St is the pick of several bars in the centre, featuring an interesting roster of local wines.

East of Wolfville: Grand Pré

The expulsion of the Acadians from Nova Scotia in the 1750s is generally considered one of the darkest moments in Canadian history, which partly explains the reverence accorded the **Grand Pré National Historic Site** (mid May to mid-Oct daily 9am–6pm; weekends other times; $7.80; www.pc.gc.ca), 5km east of Wolfville along Rte 1. Established in the 1680s, this Acadian village was totally destroyed in 1755, and its inhabitants deported; almost forgotten, the tragedy was dramatized by Henry Wadsworth Longfellow in 1847, when he chose Grand Pré as the setting for his epic poem *Evangeline – A Tale of Acadie*. The poem follows the star-crossed love of the fictional Evangeline for her Gabriel, and though horribly sentimental it became extremely popular, turning the destruction of this particular community into a symbol of Acadian suffering and British callousness.

Displays in the visitor centre recount the history of the expulsions, but it's the multimedia presentation (every 30min) that really gets across just how devastating they were. Outside the site itself is a bit of an anti-climax – well-manicured gardens containing statues of Longfellow and Evangeline, and a memorial chapel built in 1922 that displays some vivid paintings of the expulsions. The most absorbing sights here are the on-going archeological digs, which finally began in 2001; so far they have located the remains of a house next to the chapel, but as yet not the original church.

The best place **to eat** around here is 2km west of the village on Rte-1, at the **Domaine de Grand Pré** winery (www.grandprewines.com), where *Restaurant Le Caveau* (May–Oct, lunch and dinner; ☎902/542-7177) utilises seasonal produce and the on-site wines; you can also take guided tours of the winery (May–Oct) daily at 11am, 3pm & 5pm ($7).

North of Wolfville: Cape Blomidon and Cape Split

The rugged, hook-shaped peninsula stretching north of Wolfville encompasses the dramatic scenery of **Cape Blomidon**, and of wilder and bleaker **Cape Split** beyond. To reach the peninsula from Wolfville, take Rte 1 west for a couple of kilometres and then turn north along Rte 358 for the 10km drive to the township of **CANNING**. Just after Canning, there's a choice of routes: stay on Rte 358 for Cape Split (see below) or take the signed 13km-long turning that leads down to **Blomidon Provincial Park** (mid-May to Aug), a narrow slice of seashore where steep sea cliffs back onto a lush, coastal forest. It's an entrancing spot with around 14km of footpaths and the park has a popular, shaded **campground** (Ⓣ902/582-7319, Ⓦwww.parks.gov.ns.ca; mid-May to Aug; $18–31).

Beyond the Blomidon turning, Rte 358 clambers the 3km up to the peninsula's highest point, the **Look-off Provincial Park**, from where the views over the Annapolis Valley and the Minas Basin are spectacular. You can savour the scenery at length if you bed down at the *Look-off Camping Park* (Ⓣ902/582-3022, Ⓦwww.lookoffcamping.com; mid-May to Sept; $27–31, cabins $60), one of the best-sited in the province. From the Look-off, it's a further 10km to **SCOTS BAY**, a scattered farming village that straggles along the edge of a wide and muddy bay. The road ends abruptly just beyond the village at the start of one of the region's most popular and moderate hiking trails that leads the 7km to the tip of **Cape Split Provincial Park Reserve**. Reckon on two hours each way and be sure to

The Acadians

Acadia – *Acadie* in French – has at different times included all or part of Maine, New Brunswick and Nova Scotia. The bulk of today's Acadians are the descendants of just forty French peasant families who arrived in the 1630s; slowly spreading along the **Annapolis Valley**, they lived a semi-autonomous existence in which trading with their English-speaking neighbours was more important than grand notions of loyalty to the French Empire. Consequently, when the British secured control of Port Royal (see p.385) under the Treaty of Utrecht in 1713, the Acadians made no protest.

In the 1750s, the tense standoff between the colonial powers highlighted the issue of Acadian loyalty. In **1755**, at the start of the Seven Years War, British government officials attempted to make the Acadians swear an **oath of allegiance** to the Crown. They refused, so Governor Charles Lawrence decided – without consulting London – to **deport** them en masse to other colonies. The process of uprooting and removing a community of around thirteen thousand was achieved with remarkable ruthlessness.

By the end of the year over half the Acadians had arrived on the American east coast, where they faced a cold reception – the Virginians even rerouted their allocation to England. Most of the rest spread out along the North Atlantic seaboard, establishing communities along New Brunswick's Miramichi Valley, on Prince Edward Island and in St-Pierre et Miquelon. Many subsequently returned to the Bay of Fundy in the 1770s and 1780s, but their farms had been given to British and New England colonists and they were forced to settle the less hospitable lands of the **Acadian Shore**, further west. For other deportees, the expulsion was the start of wider wanderings. Some went to Louisiana – these were the ancestors of the **Cajuns**, whose name is a corruption of "Acadian".

Today, the Acadian communities of the Maritime Provinces have largely resisted the pressures of assimilation and have recently begun to assert their cultural independence, most notably in New Brunswick, where the University of Moncton has become their academic and cultural centre.

pick up trail information at the Wolfville tourist office (see p.385) before you leave. The trail begins by threading up through thick forest beneath towering cliffs and passes heavily eroded rock formations before emerging onto a small open area, from where there are wondrous views across the Bay of Fundy.

Central Nova Scotia

Most visitors hurry through **central Nova Scotia**, the chunk of forested land north and east of Halifax, on their way to Cape Breton Island, PEI or New Brunswick. By and large they're right to do so, but there is the odd diversion hereabouts (like riding the Fundy **tidal bore**), and a couple of places make for a convenient overnight stay. An alternative route between Halifax and Cape Breton is along the **southeast shore**, an isolated region of skinny bays and the tiniest of fishing villages connected by the tortuous 320-kilometre Hwy 7. The coastal scenery is often quite delightful, but the only place worthy of attention is **Sherbrooke**, where around thirty old buildings have been preserved to create an enjoyable village museum.

Acadian Lines **buses** (p.361) run seven times daily from Halifax to Truro ($20), with three buses daily continuing northeast to Cape Breton Island ($48–67) and three buses pressing on northwest to New Brunswick's Moncton ($48). VIA Rail's Halifax–Montréal **trains** (p.361) also pass through Truro en route to Moncton. There's no public transport to either Pictou or Sherbrooke.

Truro

One place difficult to avoid in central Nova Scotia is **TRURO**, the region's largest town and a major crossroads, situated at the east end of the Minas Basin and so subject to the mighty Bay of Fundy tides. It's worth viewing the remarkable Fundy **tidal bore** here; aim for the *Palliser Motel* (Ⓣ902/893-8951, Ⓦwww.palliserrestaurantmotelandgifts.ca) on the edge of town (Hwy 102, exit 14), which overlooks the Salmon River. You can grab a table at the restaurant (reservations usually required for a river view) or just watch from the riverbank. The bore varies in height from just a ripple to over a metre (a truly magical sight);

Riding the tidal bore rapids

The Bay of Fundy is noted for its high tides, but while it can be intriguing to watch harbours around the bay fill up in a matter of minutes, don't confuse this with the hypnotic spectacle of the **Fundy tidal bore**. This only occurs higher up rivers towards the end of the bay: an advancing wave, ranging anything from two metres (very rare) to a few centimetres (the size depends on various factors, including the lunar cycle) powers upstream, smothering the riverbank. To get a closer look, you can take an exhilarating boat ride across the bore and crash through the one to six-metre rapids that temporarily form as the tide rushes over rocks and boulders. Three main operators run zodiac boats on the Shubenacadie River, south of Truro, all offering a similar experience: Tidal Bore Rafting Park (Ⓣ1-800/565-RAFT; Ⓦwww.raftingcanada.ca), 9km off Hwy 102 exit 10, on Rte 215 at Shubenacadie (4hrs for $70–80, 2hrs $55–65); Shubenacadie River Runners (Ⓣ1-800/856-5061, Ⓦwww.tidalborerafting.com) at 8681 Rte 215 in Maitland ($80 full day, $60 half-day); and Shubenacadie River Adventure Tours (Ⓣ1-888/878-8687, Ⓦwww.shubie.com) at 10061 Rte 215 in South Maitland (3hr tours from $70). Reservations are always crucial, and you should arrive 1hr in advance.

Ferries from Caribou, Nova Scotia, to PEI

Some 8km north of Pictou is **Caribou**, from where Northumberland Ferries operates frequent **car ferries** over to Wood Islands on Prince Edward Island (May to late June & mid-Oct to mid-Nov 5 daily, late June & Sept to mid-Oct 7 daily, July & Aug 8 daily, mid-Nov to late Dec 3–4 daily; 1hr 15min; $16 return, $63 for car and passengers; ⓣ902/566-3838 or 1-888/249-7245, ⓦwww.nfl-bay.com). The full return fare is only collected on the way off the island – either on the ferry or the Confederation Bridge (see p.430). Ferries operate on a first-come, first-served basis and queues are common in high season, when you should arrive about an hour and a half before departure. There are no ferries from late December to April.

check ⓦwww.centralnovascotia.com/tides.php or visit the **Truro Welcome Centre** (daily: May, June, Sept & Oct 9am–5pm, July & Aug 8.30am–7.30pm, ⓣ902/893-2922), in the centre of town on Victoria Square at Commercial Street, which has tide tables and will provide directions.

Pictou

Signs proclaim **PICTOU**, 170km from Halifax, as the "Birthplace of New Scotland" on the basis of the arrival in 1773 of the ship *Hector*, loaded with around two hundred settlers from the Highlands, the advance guard of the subsequent Scots migrations. Much of its historic appeal today relates to this landmark event, and the town even has a **Hector Festival** (ⓦwww.decostecentre.ca), a five-day affair in August featuring Scottish traditional dancing and plenty of bagpipes.

Arrival and information

You'll see the **visitor information centre** (May–Dec daily 9am–4pm; ⓣ902/485-6213, ⓦwww.townofpictou.ca) at the rotary on the outskirts of Pictou, while plenty of free **parking** can be found along the waterfront (Caladh Ave), near the Hector Heritage Quay.

Accommodation

Pictou is a convenient place to spend the night and there are several quality **inns** and **hotels** here. One of the best is the ornately decorated *Consulate Inn* (ⓣ902/485-4554 or 1-800/424-8283, ⓦwww.consulateinn.com; ④), at 115 Water St, housed in an elegant nineteenth-century mansion that once served as a US consulate, with ten comfortable suites and guest rooms. There's also the *Customs House Inn* (ⓣ902/485-4546, ⓦwww.customshouseinn.ca; ⑤), at 38 Depot St, which has eight spacious rooms with exposed brick walls and hardwood floors, in a stately 1870 red-brick and sandstone mansion on the waterfront. A third central choice is the attractive *Willow House Inn* (ⓣ902/485-5740, ⓦwww.willowhouseinn.com; ④), at 11 Willow St, whose four rooms and two suites, in a well-kept clapboard house built in 1840, are kitted out in a fetching version of late Victorian style.

The Town

Pictou's pride and glory is a replica of the *Hector*, an expensive ten-year project because the townsfolk insisted on using the original shipbuilding techniques. The boat was finally launched in 2000 and now either bobs around the harbour or can be viewed at the **Hector Heritage Quay** (mid-May to mid-Oct Mon–Sat 9am–5pm, Sun 10am–5pm; Tues, Weds & Thurs during July and August

9am–7pm; $7) on the waterfront, which gives the lowdown on the original harrowing twelve-week voyage of those first Scottish settlers. Conditions on the boat must have been unbelievably grim – just take a look below deck. It's all excellently done and spruces up Pictou's unassuming centre, where the narrow streets slope up from the harbour dotted with stone buildings.

The **Northumberland Fisheries Museum** (June to mid-Oct Mon–Sat 10am–5pm; ⓣ902/485-4972, ⓦwww.northumberlandfisheriesmuseum.com; $7), just along the waterfront from the *Hector* in the old train station at 71 Front St, includes a replica 1805 lighthouse, fisherman's bunkhouse and operating lobster hatchery. The town also has a **performing arts** centre (box office Mon–Fri 11.30am–5pm; ⓣ902/485-8848 or 1-800/353-5338, ⓦwww.decostecentre.ca), at 85 Water St, where much of the summer season is taken up by ceilidhs, pipe bands and Highland dancing.

Eating and drinking

You'll find plenty of excellent places to **eat** and **drink** in Pictou, especially along the waterfront, though most of these tend to open in the summer only.

Mrs. MacGregor's Tea Room 59 Water St ⓣ902/382-1878, ⓦwww.mrsmacgregors.com. Get to grips with the town's Scottish roots at this genteel tea room, serving soups, shortbread, scones and oatcakes, as well as premium pots of potent tea. The bread is home-made and the sticky toffee pudding highly addictive. Closed Mon.

Murphy's Fish & Chips 89 Water St ⓣ902/485-2009. There's not much to say about Murphy's – other than it's justly lauded as serving some of the best fish and chips in Canada. Daily till 7pm (closed holidays).

Sharon's Place Family Restaurant 12 Front St ⓣ902/485-4669. The most popular diner in town and a real local hangout; cheap, home-cooked food featuring fresh fish (haddock) and delicious burgers for under $10. Great coffee and milkshakes also.

Tak's Thai Kitchen 85 Caladh Ave ⓣ902/382-3088. This small kiosk on the waterfront knocks out some of the best food in town (you'll smell those Thai spices before you see it). Authentic pad thai ($12.95) and curries (from $9.95). Open for lunch and dinner May–Oct (cash only).

Sherbrooke

Developed as a timber town in the early nineteenth century, **SHERBROOKE** boomed when gold was found nearby in 1861, the start of a short-lived gold rush that fizzled out within twenty years. Most of the population checked out after the gold rush and Sherbrooke returned to the lumber trade, but without much success: the decline of the industry gradually whittled the population down to the four hundred of today. One result has been the creation of the open-air museum of **Sherbrooke Village** (June to mid-Oct daily 9.30am–5pm; $10; ⓣ902/522-2400, ⓦwww.museum.gov.ns.ca/sv), which encompasses those late nineteenth- and early twentieth-century buildings that are, for the most part, now surplus to requirements. It's a large site, several streets situated just beyond the modern part of the village beside St Mary's River, and costumed "interpreters" preside. Among the eighty-odd buildings highlights include the surprisingly grand Neoclassical Court House of the 1850s and the Victorian luxury of the high-gabled Greenwood Cottage nearby. Also of special note are the assorted baubles and throne-like chairs of the **Masonic Lodge**, which still meets on the second floor of the Masonic Hall.

The most agreeable of the three **places to stay** is *Daysago B&B* (ⓣ902/522-2811 or 1-866/522-2811, ⓦwww.bbcanada.com/1639.html; ❸), at 15 Cameron Rd, a 1920s house with river views and four rooms. *St Mary's Riverside Campground* (ⓣ902/522-2913, ⓦwww.riversidecampground.ca; mid-May to mid-Oct; $25.08) is near the sawmill. There's not much choice for **food**, but the *Main Street Café* (ⓣ902/522-2848) at 17 Main St, sells competent snacks and pizzas.

Cape Breton Island

From the lakes, hills and valleys of the southwest to the ripe, forested mountains of the north, **CAPE BRETON ISLAND** offers the most exquisite of landscapes, reaching its melodramatic conclusion along the fretted, rocky coast of the **Cape Breton Highlands National Park**. Encircling the park and some of the adjacent shore is the **Cabot Trail**, a 300-kilometre loop reckoned to be one of the most awe-inspiring drives on the continent. Allow time also for a **whale-watching cruise**: these are big business hereabouts and they are available at almost every significant settlement from May to October when fin, pilot, humpback and minke whales congregate off the island.

Cape Breton Island attracted thousands of **Scottish highlanders** at the end of the eighteenth century, mostly tenant farmers who had been evicted by Scotland's landowners when they found sheep-raising more profitable than renting farmland. Many of the region's settlements celebrate their Scots ancestry and Gaelic traditions in one way or another – museums, Highland Games and bagpipe-playing competitions.

These scenic and cultural delights attract thousands of summer tourists and, consequently, although there's a liberal sprinkling of **accommodation** across the island it's still a good idea to make reservations in advance. Two of the more

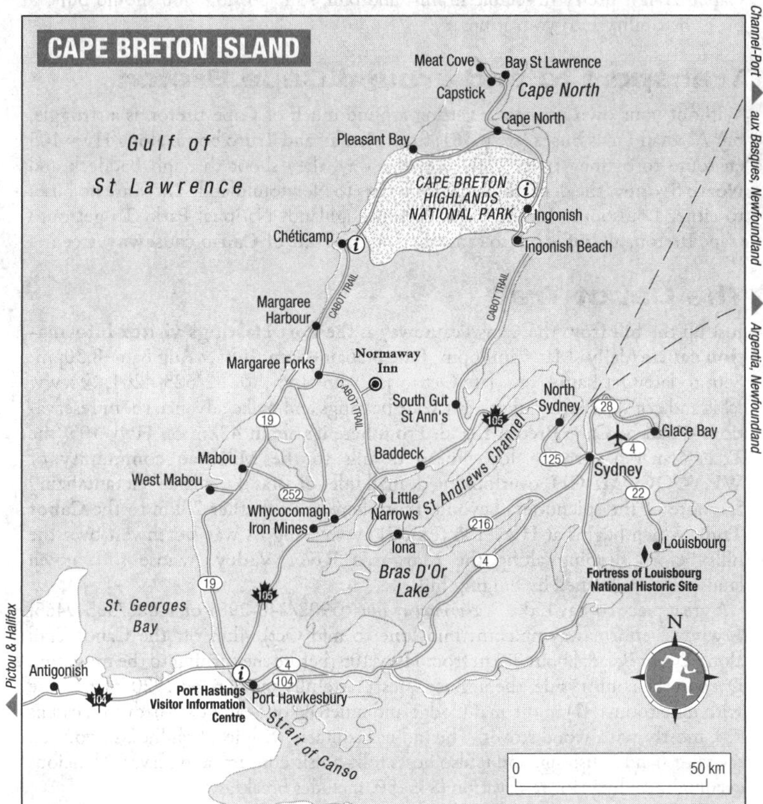

Gaelic music on Cape Breton Island

Cape Breton is not just about scenery and sights: the Scottish Highlanders who settled much of the island in the late eighteenth and early nineteenth centuries brought with them strong cultural traditions and today these are best recalled by the island's **musicians**, especially the fiddle players. Names to watch out for include Buddy MacMaster, Ashley MacIsaac, Natalie MacMaster and the Rankin family, not to mention Glenn Graham, Rodney MacDonald and Jackie Dunn – though it's impossible to pick out the "best" as each fiddler has their own particular style. Local tourist offices will gladly advise you on **gigs**, whether it be a ceilidh, concert or square dance, and listings are given in the weekly *Inverness Oran* (Ⓦwww.oran.ca), a local newspaper available at tourist offices and convenience stores. During the summer there's something happening almost every day – the Saturday night **Family Square Dance** at West Mabou Hall is especially well regarded (10pm–1am; $5). The largest festival is **Celtic Colours** (Ⓣ902/562-6700 or 1-877/285-2321, Ⓦwww.celtic-colours.com), with performances all across Cape Breton held over ten days in early to mid-October.

enjoyable targets are the busy resort of **Baddeck** and the quieter coastal community of **Chéticamp**.

Cape Breton's **weather** is notoriously unpredictable, even in summer. The Cabot Trail is pretty miserable in mist and rain, so if possible you should build a bit of flexibility into your itinerary.

Transport to and around Cape Breton

Without your own transport, getting around much of Cape Breton is a struggle, but Acadian Lines **buses** (see p.361) from Halifax and Truro bomb along Hwy 105 en route to Sydney twice daily. On the way, they shoot through Baddeck and **North Sydney**, the departure port for ferries to Newfoundland. There are no buses to either Louisbourg or the Cape Breton Highlands National Park. To get onto Cape Breton, all traffic has to cross the 1.4km **Strait of Canso causeway** (free).

The Cabot Trail

Just up the hill from the Canso causeway is the **Port Hastings visitor information centre** (daily: May 9am–6pm; June 8.30am–8pm; July & Aug 8am–8.30pm; Sept to late Oct 9am–7pm; late Oct to Jan 9am–4pm; Ⓣ902/625-4201, Ⓦwww.cbisland.com), where you can get your bearings and make advance room reservations on all of Cape Breton Island. From here it's about 48km on Hwy 105 (the Trans-Canada) through low, forested hills to the Mi'kmaq community of **WHYCOCOMAGH**, overlooking a small inlet of Bras d'Or Lake – a tantalizing foretaste of the splendours beyond. From here, it's a further 29km to the **Cabot Trail**, which begins at Hwy 105 (Exit 7) by weaving its way northwest over the hills before slipping along the **Margaree River Valley**, whose soft, green landscapes are framed by bulging hills.

A great place to stay is the *Normaway Inn* (Ⓣ902/248-2987 or 1-800/565-9463, Ⓦwww.thenormawayinn.com; mid-June to mid-Oct), 4km off the Cabot Trail along Egypt Road, about 28km from Hwy 105 (before the turning to the museum). Deep in the countryside, the inn occupies a tastefully maintained 1920s farmhouse with nine rooms (❹) in the main lodge and nineteen one- and two-bedroom cabins (❻), mostly with wood stoves. The inn has contacts with local ghillies, so you can try your hand at fishing, and it also hosts folk-music concerts and serves a delicious evening meal by prior reservation ($45–50, includes breakfast).

La Région Acadienne and Chéticamp

North from the Margaree Valley, the Cabot Trail offers captivating views of land and sea as it slices across the wide grassy littoral with a band of forested hills looming inland. The scattered dwellings hereabouts form **La Région Acadienne**, an **Acadian** enclave established in 1785 by French settlers deported from elsewhere in the Maritimes (see p.387). Despite being surrounded by English-speaking areas, the region was connected to the rest of Nova Scotia by road only in 1947, partly explaining the survival of Acadian culture. After 30km or so, the road slips into the district's main village, **CHÉTICAMP**.

Arrival and information

Chéticamp straggles along the main road for about 5km. Between the church – at the south end of the village – and Les Trois Pignons, at the north, is Le Quai Mathieu where a **tourist kiosk** (July–Sept; Ⓣ902/224-3349, Ⓦwww.cheticamp.ca), has the latest details on a variety of boat trips, several of which leave from the adjacent jetty. Go **whale-watching** with the highly reputable Whale Cruises (mid-May to mid-Oct 2–3 daily; 3hr; $28; Ⓣ902/224-3376 or 1-800/813-3376, Ⓦwww.whalecruisers.com) or Captain Zodiac (May 15 to late Oct; Ⓣ1-877/232-2522, Ⓦwww.novascotiawhales.com), just beyond the kiosk on the next wharf, who guarantees sightings or your money back (2hr tours at 9am, 11am & 1pm; $39).

The Village

The **Co-op Artisanale** (mid-June to Sept daily 8am–9pm; early May to mid-June & Oct Mon–Sat 9am–5pm, Sun 9am–6pm; free; Ⓣ902/224-2170, Ⓦwww.co-opartisanale.com), houses the tiny **Musée Acadien** in the basement, featuring old furniture, rare objects from the region's first chapel (1800), and a selection of simple hooked rugs, a characteristic craft of the area. The display is hardly spellbinding, but the co-operative's simple café-style *Restaurant Acadien* (daily: May to mid-June 11am–7pm; mid-June to late Oct 7am–9pm; Ⓣ902/224-3207) is top-notch and great value. The *poulet fricot* (chicken stew) is mouthwatering, as are the fruit pies and pea soup.

▲ The view on the Cabot Trail

Further up the road lies the soaring 55m-high silver steeple of **l'Église Saint-Pierre** (daily 8am–9pm), completed in 1893 with stones lugged across the ice from Chéticamp Island, just offshore. Inside, the lines of the cavernous nave are interrupted by two long galleries and oceans of elaborate wood and baroque plasterwork; the striking frescoes were added in 1957.

There's a much better exhibition of Acadian crafts at the north end of the village in **Les Trois Pignons** (daily: mid-May to June & Sept to mid-Oct 9am–5pm; July & Aug 8am–7pm; Ⓦwww.lestroispignons.com; $5), a cultural centre that proudly displays Acadian artefacts (with detailed explanations) collected by local eccentric Marguerite Gallant, as well as the hooked mats of Elizabeth LeFort, an artist of some local renown. Hooked rugs are still made in the village today, and you'll usually be able to watch one of the amiable volunteers demonstrating the ancient technique.

Practicalities

There are around twenty **motels** and **B&Bs** in and around Chéticamp with one of the best being *Ocean View Chalets & Motel* (Ⓣ902/224-2313 or 1-877/743-4404, Ⓦwww.oceanviewchalets.com; ❺; May to mid-Oct), whose well-maintained, shingle-clad chalets sit right by the seashore opposite Les Trois Pignons. Another popular option is *Merry's Motel* (Ⓣ902/224-2456, Ⓔmerrysmotel@capebretonisland.com; ❷; May–Oct) further along the main road, which has cheap but spotlessly clean rooms with free wi-fi and continental breakfast. More distinctive is *Chéticamp Outfitters Inn B&B* (Ⓣ902/224-2776, Ⓦwww.cheticampns.com/cheticampoutfitters; ❸; April–Nov), perched on a hilltop just off the main road about 4km south of the village and with riveting views over the surrounding shoreline.

For **food** there are plenty of options, though most only open June to August, and the best place is still *Restaurant Acadien* (see p.393).

Cape Breton Highlands National Park

The extensive **Cape Breton Highlands National Park** (Ⓦwww.pc.gc.ca), beginning 9km north of Chéticamp, offers some of the most mesmerizing scenery anywhere in the Maritimes – a mix of deep wooded valleys, rocky coastal headlands, soft green hills and boggy upland. Although visitors get a sniff of the park travelling by car – 120km of highway trimming all but its southern edge – the essence of the place is only revealed on foot.

Arrival and information

The park has two **information kiosks** – one at the west-coast entrance just beyond Chéticamp (daily: late June to late Aug 8am–8pm; mid-May to late June & late Aug to mid-Oct 9am–5pm; Ⓣ902/224-2306), the other at the east-coast entrance near Ingonish Beach (same details). There's also a **visitor centre** (same details) at the west-coast entrance with displays on local flora and fauna and a well-stocked bookshop. Both the visitor centre and the east-coast kiosk sell 1:50,000 maps, have details of the park's hiking trails (which are in peak condition from July to September), and issue backcountry camping permits ($9.80). There is a daily park entrance fee of $7.80 when the kiosks are staffed.

Accommodation: camping in the park

The park has six **campsites** ($17.60–38.20), all within easy reach of the road, and one **wilderness campsite** – Fishing Cove – along one of the more arduous 8km trails. Campground services vary and are only available from mid-May to mid-October, but you can camp in the park at any time of the year. Reservations (Ⓣ1-877/737-3783, Ⓦwww.pccamping.ca) are accepted at Chéticamp and Broad

Cove campgrounds (the only two with serviced sites and hook-ups), but the others assign sites on first-come, first-served basis.

Hiking in the park

Though much of the park is actually off-limits to the public, land bordering the Cabot Trail can be explored by twenty-five **hiking trails** signposted from the road, some of them the easiest of woodland strolls, others offering steeper climbs to small lakes, waterfalls and rugged coastal viewpoints. One of the most popular is the 9.2km-long **Skyline Loop Trail** (2–3hr), which clambers up the coastal mountains north of Corney Brook, a few kilometres up the coast from Chéticamp. Another good trail is the 7.4km **Franey Loop Trail** (3–4hr), a steep walk up through the mountains and lakes north of Ingonish Beach. Most of the wildlife inhabits the inner reaches of the park: garter snakes, red-backed salamanders, snowshoe hares and moose are common, while bald eagles, black bear and lynx are rarer. The only artificial sight is the **Lone Sheiling**, a somewhat battered 1930s replica of the stone shelters once built by Highlanders beside their mountain pastures. The hut is on the northern perimeter of the park in a valley that was settled by Scots in the early 1800s; it is accessible along a short and easy footpath from the road, providing a rare taster of the hardwood forests that make up the park's central (and strictly protected) zone.

Cape North

Another 30km or so beyond the northern perimeter of the park is **Cape North**, a forested hunk of hill and valley that juts out into the sea where the Gulf of St Lawrence meets the Atlantic Ocean. The Cabot Trail threads its way across the base of the cape, passing through the tiny village of **CAPE NORTH**, no more than a few lonely buildings straggling along the road. One of them houses the **North Highlands Community Museum** (July–Oct daily 9am–5pm; free; ⓣ902/383-2579, ⓦwww.northhighlandsmuseum.ca) an enthusiastic attempt to document the history of the area, with displays on local industries, lighthouses, early settlers and even a few bits and pieces recovered from the *Titanic*.

There are several **places to stay**, beginning with the handy *Macdonald's Motel & Cabins* (ⓣ902/383-2054; ❸; mid-May to mid-Oct), a modern affair at the village crossroads. Much more enticing is *Oakwood Manor B&B* (ⓣ902/383-2317, ⓦwww.capebretonisland.com/oakwood; ❹; May–Oct), whose en-suite guest rooms are in a charming 1930s clapboard farmhouse. To get there, take the Bay St Lawrence road north from Cape North village and, after about 1.3km, turn left at the sign, and drive down the 1.2km-long gravel road leading to the farm. For a bit more luxury, follow the signs to Dingwall and the *Markland Resort* (ⓣ902/383-2246 or 902/383-2246, ⓦwww.marklandresort.com; cabins ❺), which has its own beach and the on-site **Octagon Arts Centre**, with a decent programme of classical and Gaelic concerts in the summer.

To get off the beaten path, head up the North Cape to **MEAT COVE** (the cape itself is inaccessible), an incredibly picturesque spot at the end of a bumpy 8km-long gravel road from the hamlet of **CAPSTICK**, 22km north of the Cabot Trail. The idyllic **campsite** here (ⓣ902/383-2379; ⓦwww.meatcovecampground.com; June–Oct; sites $25) is full of the roar of the ocean, has kayaks and even its own **chowder hut** (June–Oct 8am–8pm). On the way, visit the windswept **Cabot Landing Provincial Park**, the spot where John Cabot may have "discovered" North America in 1497.

Ingonish

From Cape North village, heading east, the Cabot Trail skirts the edge of the national park for 30km, cutting across the interior before veering south along the coast to reach the pretty harbour at **INGONISH**. There's little in the village itself, though **Ingonish Beach**, around 10km south (before the village of the same name), is one of the most enticing in the national park, a thin strip of silky sand facing South Bay. Nearby, the easy 3.8km hike along **Middle Head** (drive through the grounds of *Keltic Inn* to get there) offers sublime views across both South and North bays.

Among several **places to stay** in the area, the *Glenghorm Beach Resort* (Ⓣ902/285-2049 or 1-800/565-5660, Ⓦwww.capebretonresorts.com; mid-May to late Oct) is on the main road halfway between Ingonish and the beach, its neat and trim motel rooms (⑤) and more luxurious suites (⑧) spreading out along a pleasant slice of seashore. The motels of Ingonish pale in comparison with *Keltic Lodge* (Ⓣ902/285-2880 or 1-800/565-0444, Ⓦwww.kelticlodge.ca; mid-May to mid-Oct), one of the province's finest hotel complexes, perched high above the cliffs amid immaculate gardens on Middle Head; features and facilities include beaches, restaurants, tennis courts and kayaks. You can stay in the main lodge (⑧), a handsome Edwardian mansion, or the modern *Inn at Keltic* (⑧), but the cottages (⑧) are perhaps more enjoyable, the best of them prettily located among the woods that cover much of the promontory.

The Gaelic Coast

Leaving the national park, the Cabot Trail threads its way down the 80km-long **Gaelic Coast** passing through **SOUTH GUT ST ANN'S**, the location of the Gaelic College of Celtic Arts and Crafts. The main focus of a visit here is the **Great Hall of the Clans** (June & Sept Wed–Sun 9am–5pm, July & Aug daily 9am–5pm; $7; Ⓣ902/295-3411, Ⓦwww.gaeliccollege.edu), which provides potted clan descriptions alongside wax models dressed in the appropriate tartan, exhibits tracing Scotland's military history, and pioneer artefacts from the nineteenth-century. Also inside is the **New Gaelic Heritage Learning Centre**, with interactive displays highlighting Gaelic language, dancing, piping, music, song, storytelling and textiles.

Baddeck

The amenable resort and yachting town of **BADDECK**, some 90km east of the Canso causeway along Hwy 105, enjoys a tranquil lakeside setting on St Patrick's Channel, an inlet of the tentacular Bras d'Or Lake. It is also home to the thoroughly absorbing **Alexander Graham Bell Museum and National Historic Site** (daily: May & late Oct 9am–5pm; June 9am–6pm; July to mid-Oct 8.30am–6pm; $7.80, Ⓦwww.pc.gc.ca), which overlooks the water on Chebucto Street at the northern end of the village. The museum is a mine of biographical information about the Scottish-born Bell – who started spending his summers here in 1885 – and gives detailed explanations of all his inventions. Most famous for the invention of the **telephone in 1876**, Bell also made extraordinary advances in techniques for teaching hearing-impaired children, a lifelong interest inspired by the deafness of his mother. He also worked on aircraft and boats, culminating in the first Canadian air flight here in 1909 – a replica of the *Silver Dart* is expected to be displayed in a new wing of the museum in the next few years. Bell's exploits culminated in 1919 with the launch of the world's first hydrofoil, the **HD-4** (of which there's a full-scale replica in the museum), which reached a speed of 70mph on the lake in front of town.

Arrival and information

Baddeck is on the Acadian Lines **bus** route between Halifax ($60; 6hr) and Sydney ($19; 1hr 30min), with two buses daily in each direction stopping at the Ultramar gas station 3.5km west of town on Hwy 105 (Exit 8). The **tourist office** (June–Oct daily 9am–7pm; ⓣ902/295-1911, ⓦwww.visitbaddeck.com) has lots of useful local information and sits at the resort's main intersection – Shore Road and the top of the short main drag, Chebucto Street.

Accommodation

Baddeck is a popular holiday spot, so there's a wide range of **accommodation**, but it fills up fast in high season, so book ahead. The nearest **campsite** is the *Bras d'Or Lakes* (ⓣ902/295-2329, ⓦwww.brasdorlakescampground.com; mid-June to Sept; $25–34), about 6km west on Hwy 105.

Auberge Gisele's Inn 387 Shore Rd ⓣ902/295-2849 or 1-800/304-0466, ⓦwww.giseles.com. Large, motel-like place overlooking the lake, with commodious bedrooms decked out in brisk, modern style and an excellent dining room. The deluxe rooms have fireplaces. May to late Oct. ❻

Heidi's B&B 64 Old Margaree Rd ⓣ902/295-1301. This handy option is in a large Victorian clapboard house with a new wing and wide terrace about 400m from the tourist office. It has six cosy rooms, three en-suite, and huge breakfasts. June to late Oct. ❸

Inverary Resort 368 Shore Rd ⓣ902/295-3500 or 1-800/565-5660, ⓦwww.capebretonresorts.com. This extensive and immaculately maintained complex is the best place in town. It dates back to 1850 and spreads down from Shore Rd to the bay. There are rooms in the main lodge ($179), the motel-like "Barn" behind it (❻) or you can choose from one of several different types of cottage (from ❼). May–Nov.

Silver Dart Lodge 257 Shore Rd ⓣ902/295-2340 or 1-888/662-7484, ⓦwww.maritimeinns.com. Popular hotel with spacious chalets spread over a hillside with decks and stunning views of the lake. Has a pool, hiking trails and free mountain bikes. Mid-May to mid-Oct. ❻

Tree Seat Bed & Breakfast 555 Chebucto St ⓣ902/295-1996, ⓦwww.baddeck.com/treeseat. Among several downtown B&Bs, this is one of the best, set in an attractive modern clapboard house next door to the Bell Museum; there are four guest rooms (two en suite; ❹) and the home-cooked breakfasts are first rate. May–Oct. ❸

Eating and drinking

Most visitors **eat** where they sleep, though there are plenty of other options in Baddeck, at least in the summer. The best café in town is the *High Wheeler*, on Chebucto Street (daily: May–June & Oct 7am–6pm, July–Aug 6am–10pm; ⓣ902/295-3006), which serves up a reasonable range of snacks and cakes, while the *Bell Buoy* (ⓣ902/295-2581, ⓦwww.bellbuoyrestaurant.com) at 536 Chebucto St, is a solid option for steaks and seafood (daily May–Oct). You should also check out *Baddeck Lobster Suppers* (early June–early Oct lunch and dinner, ⓣ902/295-3307), at 17 Ross St off Shore Road, which cooks up fresh lobsters (daily 4–9pm; $29.95) with unlimited chowder, mussels, rolls, biscuits, salads and desserts.

Sydney

Poor old **SYDNEY**, sprawling along the east bank of the Sydney River, 80km from Baddeck, was once the industrial dynamo of eastern Canada. From the late nineteenth century to the 1950s, its steel mills processed Newfoundland iron ore with Nova Scotian coke, but as gas and oil came on stream this arrangement became uneconomic and the subsequent decline has been severe and long-lasting: the city has regularly recorded an unemployment rate twice the national average. Still, it's worth a short tour to get a flavour for what passes as urban on Cape Breton.

Arrival and information

Acadian Lines buses pull into the **bus station** at 99 Terminal Rd (ⓣ902/564-5533), off Prince Street. From here, it's a good fifteen-minute walk west to the Esplanade.

There's free parking at the **Joan Harriss Cruise Pavilion**, which houses the Cape Breton Island **information centre** (late May to mid-Oct daily 9am–6pm; ⓣ902/539-9876, ⓦwww.downtownsydney.ca) and exhibits highlighting Cape Breton culture, as well as a café and free internet.

The Town

Given Sydney's economic troubles, it's hardly surprising the town lacks charm, though brave efforts have been made to reinvigorate the **North End** waterfront, along and around the **Esplanade** on Rte 4. Greeting cruise ships outside the information centre is the giant 17m painted-steel **Céilidh Fiddle**, symbol of the island's musical roots. Up the hill are Sydney's oldest buildings, including **St Patrick's Church** at 87 Esplanade, a solid stone structure built in 1828 that now holds a local history museum (June–Aug daily 9am–5pm; donation). One block behind the church, the shingled **Cossit House** at 75 Charlotte St (June–Aug Mon–Sat 9am–5pm, Sun 1–5pm; $2; ⓣ902/539-1572), was built for the town's first Anglican minister in 1787 and is staffed by costumed guides, while the wood-frame **Jost House** (June–Aug Mon–Sat 9am–5pm; $2; ⓣ902/539-0366) at 54 Charlotte St was built in 1786 and has been wonderfully preserved, its rooms crammed with historical bric-a-brac and a small maritime exhibit.

Practicalities

There are several **hotels** along the Esplanade, including the business-oriented *Delta Sydney* (ⓣ902/562-7500 or 1-800/268-1133, ⓦwww.deltahotels.com; ⑦), a large and well-equipped chain hotel at no. 300, and *Cambridge Suites* (ⓣ902/564-2017 or 1-800/565-9466 ⓦwww.cambridgesuitessydney.com; ⑥) next door at no. 380, which offers similar standards but tends to be a better deal for its larger, newer rooms.

For **food**, try *Joe's Warehouse Restaurant* (ⓣ902/539-6686, ⓦwww.joeswarehouse.ca), at 424 Charlotte St, for pastas, lobster and steaks, and *Katie Belle's Dining Room* (Mon–Sat 5–10pm; ⓣ902/567-3311) at the *Martin Arms*, 100 Kings Rd, for home-cooked meals and delectable pies and desserts. The *Governor's Pub*, at 233 Esplanade (ⓣ902/562-7646), is a cosy watering hole that served as the residence of Sydney's first mayor in the nineteenth century.

Ferries and flights from North Sydney and Sydney

Marine Atlantic (ⓣ1-800/341-7981, ⓦwww.marine-atlantic.ca) operates two **car ferry** routes to Newfoundland from **North Sydney**, 21km northwest of Sydney. The first, **to Channel-Port aux Basques** (2–4 daily), takes between five and six hours (6–8hr at night). One-way passenger tickets cost $28.75, $81.50 for cars. A four-berth cabin (reserve in advance), costs an additional $44.95 for day use, $111.75 at night; there are also dormitory bunks for $16.75. The second car ferry connects North Sydney **to Argentia**, 130km southwest of St John's (late June to early Sept, 3 weekly; mid-June & late Sept, 1 weekly; 14–15hr). One-way passenger tickets cost $80.50, $167.25 for cars. Vehicles must be booked in advance, as must four-berth cabins, which cost $152.75; dormitory bunks are $28.75.

Sydney airport, 10km northeast of Sydney, offers the shortest and least expensive flights (12.30pm Thurs & Sun; $190 one-way, $346 return; 1hr) from the mainland to St-Pierre et Miquelon (see p.465) with **Air St-Pierre** (ⓣ011/508/410000 or 1-877/277-7765, ⓦwww.airsaintpierre.com). There are also regular flights to Halifax with Air Canada Jazz and to Toronto with WestJet (May–Oct).

Glace Bay

Coal mining in **GLACE BAY**, just 24km northeast of Sydney on Rte 4, dates back to the 1860s, but the last mine closed in 1984 and today the only reminder of this mighty industrial past is the enlightening **Cape Breton Miner's Museum** (June–Oct daily 10am–6pm, Nov–May Mon–Fri 9am–4pm; ⓣ902/849-4522, ⓦwww.minersmuseum.com; $6) at 17 Museum St just south of the town centre. The museum features exhibits on the history of local coalfields, but the highlight is the underground tour of Ocean Deeps Colliery, led by retired but still energetic miners (additional $6). You can also visit the **Marconi National Historic Site** (June to mid-Sept daily 10am–6pm; free ⓣ902/295-2069) overlooking the cliffs at Table Head on Timmerman Street (north of the centre), which honours the first official wireless message, sent from this site across the Atlantic to England in 1902 by Guglielmo Marconi. The station closed in 1946, and today there is a small exhibition and trail to the original transmitter site.

Louisbourg

Stringing along the seashore 34km southeast of Sydney, the modern village of **LOUISBOURG** comes alive in the summer months when tourism supplements modest incomes from lobster and crab fishing. The crowds come for the **Fortress of Louisburg**, one of Canada's most enchanting historic monuments.

The visitor **information centre** (mid-May to mid-Oct daily 9am–5pm ⓣ902/733-2321) on Main Street is well-stocked with maps and leaflets from all over the province, and can help with accommodation. Louisburg is a little out-of-the-way and it makes sense to **stay the night** here. There's a spartan campground, the *Louisbourg Motorhome Park* (ⓣ902/733-3631 or 1-866/733-3631, ⓦwww.louisburg.com/motorhomepark; mid-May to mid-Oct; $13–26), down by the harbour in the centre of the village. For more comfort, any of the places listed below are a good choice.

Accommodation

Cranberry Cove Inn 12 Wolfe St ⓣ902/733-2171 or 1-800/929-0222, ⓦwww.cranberrycoveinn.com. Lavishly refurbished old house in fierce pink on the edge of the village (on the way to the fort), with seven gorgeous rooms, wi-fi, computer use and fine dining. May–Oct. ❺

Point of View Suites 15 Commercial Ext ⓣ902/733-2080 or 1-888-374- 8439, ⓦwww.louisbourgpointofview.com. Most convenient option for the fortress, with large, well-equipped and modern suites, some overlooking the water, and all with cable TV and kitchens. ❻

Louisburg Harbour Inn 9 Lower Warren St ⓣ1-888/888-8466, ⓦwww.louisbourgharbourinn.com. Fabulous bed and breakfast in an old sea captain's house just off Main St, with eight bright and modern en-suite rooms (six with harbour views). ❺

They also manage the equally appealing *Louisberg Heritage House* around the corner.

Stacey House B&B 7438 Main St ⓣ902/733-2317 or 1-866/924-2242, ⓦwww.bbcanada.com/thestaceyhouse. An attractive, high-gabled Victorian home, with four guest rooms dressed with period furnishings, hardwood floors and drapes. June to mid-Oct. ❷

Eating, drinking and entertainment

Lobster is a real treat in Louisbourg; the season runs mid-May to mid-July and you can buy them cheap and fresh from *H Hopkins* (ⓣ902/733-2424) on the waterfront. Among several **places to eat**, *L'il Café*, at 7543 Main St, is most likely to be open year-round, offering good coffee, tasty breakfast plates and lobster rolls – try the home-made cinnamon buns. Lobster is also served at the clapboard *Grubstake*, 7499 Main St (ⓣ902/733-2308, ⓦwww.grubstake.ca; mid-June to early Oct noon-8pm), as well as fish platters and home-baked pastries, while the

Lobster Kettle (Ⓦwww.lobsterkettle.com) at 41 Strathcona St, on the harbour, is also a solid bet for the local speciality. If you stay the night, check what's on at the **Louisbourg Playhouse** (Ⓣ902/733.2996 or 1-888/733-2787, Ⓦwww.louisbourgplayhouse.com) a modern shingle building at 11 Aberdeen St near the water, hosting music, comedy, theatre and dance.

Fortress of Louisbourg National Historic Site

A visit to the remarkably restored **Fortress of Louisbourg National Historic Site** (daily: May–June & Sept to mid-Oct 9.30am–5pm; July & Aug 9am–5.30pm; Ⓦwww.pc.gc.ca; June–Sept $17.60, May & Oct $7.30) begins just 2km beyond the village of Louisbourg at the visitor centre, where there's a good account of the fort's history. The French began construction in 1719, a staggeringly ostentatious stronghold that covered a hundred acres, encircled by ten-metre-high stone walls, to guard the Atlantic approaches to New France. Louisbourg was only attacked twice, but it was captured on both occasions, the second time by the celebrated British commander, James Wolfe, on his way to Québec in 1758, and it was levelled in 1760. Rebuilt in the 1960s, today it offers an extraordinary window into eighteenth-century colonial life, its streets and buildings populated by a small army of costumed role-players – English visitors (that admit their nationality), can expect some good-natured ribbing about being imprisoned for spying.

From the visitor centre, a free shuttle bus runs to the fort and settlement, whose stone walls rise from the sea to enclose more than four dozen restored buildings as they were in the 1740s; there are powder magazines, forges, guardhouses, warehouses, barracks and the chilly abodes of the soldiers, all enhanced by the dazzling coastal setting. Particular care has been taken with the **governor's apartments**, which have been splendidly furnished according to the inventory taken after the death of Governor Duquesnel here in 1744. Allow at least three hours to look round the fortress and sample the authentic refreshments available at the taverns and bakeries. The equally impressive story of Louisbourg's reconstruction is told in the small on-site museum.

New Brunswick

The province of **NEW BRUNSWICK** attracts less tourists than its Maritime neighbours, despite sharing a border with the US and offering some truly spellbinding scenery. In **Fredericton**, the capital, the province has one of the region's most appealing towns, a laidback place which offers the bonus of the Beaverbrook Art Gallery and a handsome historic district. It's just a short journey south to the funnel-shaped **Bay of Fundy**, with its dramatic tides and witheringly beautiful coastline, beginning with the likeable resort of **St Andrews** and **Grand Manan Island**. The province's big city is **Saint John**, and though hard times have left the

New Brunswick information

Tourism New Brunswick Ⓣ1-800/561-0123, Ⓦwww.tourismnewbrunswick.ca.

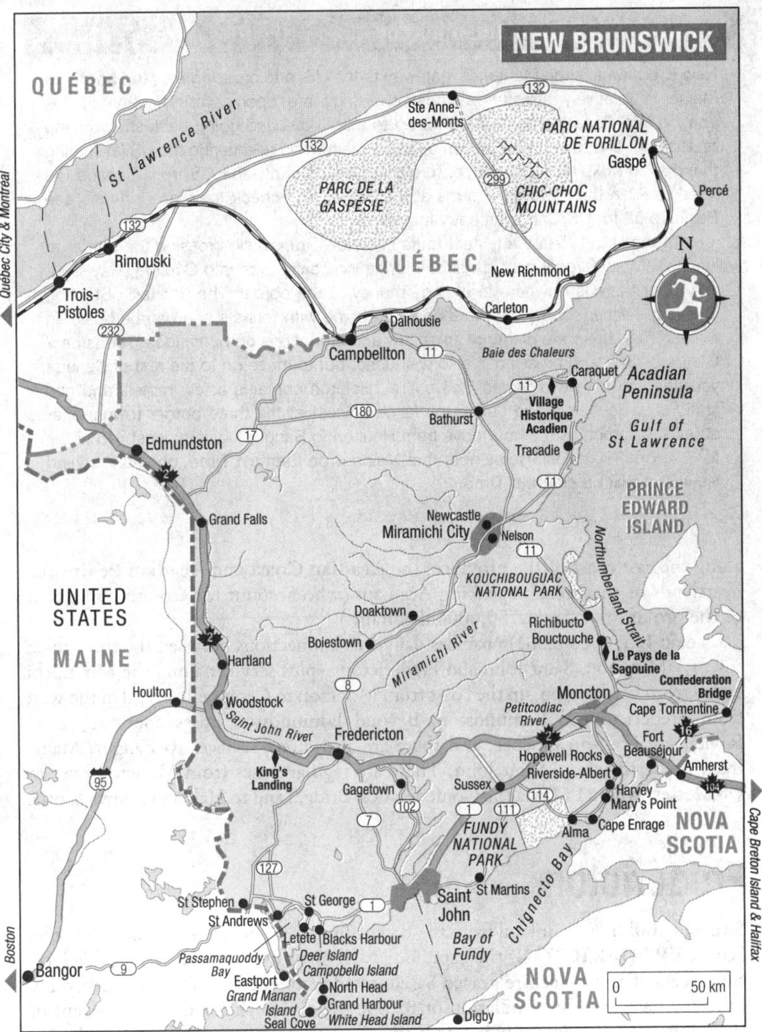

place frayed at the edges, it does boast a splendid sample of Victorian architecture. Not far away are the more pristine land- and seascapes of both the coastal **Fundy Trail Parkway** and **Fundy National Park**.

Moncton, in southeast New Brunswick, is the effective capital of modern **Acadia**, though the most absorbing Acadian districts are best visited on the way to **Québec**. The first route – which is both more scenically diverting and more direct – slices up the western edge of the province along the **Saint John River Valley** to French-speaking **Edmundston**, on the way to Rivière-du-Loup (see p.308). The second cuts northeast for the long haul up the **Miramichi River Valley** to the cluster of small towns that are known collectively as **Miramichi City**. Near here are the untamed coastal marshes of the **Kouchibouguac National Park** and,

Crossing the US-Canadian border

New Brunswick is the Maritimes' gateway to the US, and crossing the land border to Maine is relatively stress-free (most crossings are open 24hr). Non-Americans coming into Canada from the US for up to thirty days and going back should hang on to their I-94s, because they can be used again when re-entering the US (assuming they haven't expired). Otherwise, foreigners heading into the US from Canada will need to fill in the necessary forms at the border and check their visa status – see Basics p.52 for US/Canadian entry requirements.

From the US, I-95 is the fastest route into New Brunswick, crossing the border at Houlton, Maine. You'll pass a visitor information centre 2km into Canada (May–Sept only), but there is nowhere to change money at the border. The Calais/St Stephen crossing, further south, is a more popular choice with tourists and can be busier in the summer: there are plenty of amenities and attractions on both sides. The Lubec/Campobello Island crossing is also well-used, but to move on to the rest of Canada you need to take two ferries (see p.411). Houlton contains a few motels and gas stations while Calais and Lubec (by far the nicest of the three border towns) offer about the same. It's a 2 hour drive from Houlton to Bangor – give at least 4–5 hours for Boston (350 miles). Remember that Maine is on **Eastern Time**, one hour behind New Brunswick's **Atlantic Time.**

along the east coast of the province, the **Acadian Coast** and **Acadian Peninsula**, heartlands of the French-speaking Acadians (who account for around 35 percent of the province's current 750,000 inhabitants).

Acadian Lines (see p.361) provides daily **bus** connections between the three main towns – Moncton, Saint John and Fredericton – plus services along the Miramichi valley from Fredericton, up the coast from Moncton to Campbellton and in the west from Fredericton to Edmundston. Beyond Edmundston buses continue on to Rivière-du-Loup in Québec, and there are also direct services to Bangor, Maine from Fredericton and Saint John. There are regular buses from Moncton over to Charlottetown on PEI, via the Confederation Bridge, and to Halifax in Nova Scotia.

Fredericton

Situated 100km or so inland from the Bay of Fundy on the banks of the Saint John River, **FREDERICTON**, the capital of New Brunswick, has a well-padded air, the streets of its tiny centre graced by elms and genteel villas. There's scarcely any industry here and the population of 85,000 mostly work for the government or the university. Fredericton has few specific sights, but the **Beaverbrook Art Gallery** is outstanding, and there are several intriguing reminders of the British army in the **Historic Garrison District**.

Arrival and information

Driving into the city is usually hassle-free and you should find plenty of **parking** ($1/hr) – aim for the lot behind City Hall off Queen Street, or ask for a free Visitor Parking Pass at the visitor information centre (see p.403). The Acadian Lines **bus station** is at 101 Regent St at King Street, about five-minutes' walk south of the river and one block south of the main drag, Queen Street, with most destinations in the Maritimes served just once or twice a day. The direct bus to Bangor, Maine, leaves at 11.30am. Air Canada provides domestic flights from Toronto, Montréal, Ottawa and Halifax into Fredericton **airport** (Ⓣ506/460-0920, Ⓦwww.yfcmobile.ca), 16km southeast of town on Hwy 102; the taxi fare into the centre costs around $24 (Trius Taxi ⓣ506/454-4444). Avis, Budget, Hertz and National have counters at the airport. Downtown is easily covered on foot, but you can pick up **local buses** ($2) at King and York streets.

Fredericton's main **visitor information centre** is downtown in City Hall on the corner of Queen and York streets (daily: mid-May to late June & Sept to mid-Oct 8am–5pm; late June to Aug 8am–8pm; ⓣ506/460-2129, ⓦwww.tourismfredericton.ca); they will call ahead to reserve accommodation for free. In winter, information is available at the **Fredericton Tourism Office**, inside the old Militia Arms Store at 11 Carleton St (Mon–Fri 8.15am–4.30pm; ⓣ506/460-2041 or 1-888/888-4768). Check the **internet** for free across the road at Fredericton Public Library (Mon, Tues, Thurs 10am–5pm, Wed & Fri 10am–9pm, also Sat 10am–5pm mid-June to Sept).

Accommodation

You should try to avoid the humdrum motels on the city's outskirts (which still charge around $100) in favour of the downtown area, where there are a couple of tip-top **hotels** as well as an increasing number of **B&Bs**. For those strapped for cash, there's a downtown HI **hostel**. There are several **campgrounds** out of town, including *Heritage County Camping* (ⓣ506/363-3338, ⓦwww.heritagecamping.com; $22–29) in Lower Queensbury, west of the city on Hwy 105, and gay-friendly *Rivers Edge Camping Resort* (ⓣ506/459-8675 or 1-800/370-1644, ⓦwww.riversedgecamp.ca; $22–28), 19 Cottage Lane, Durham Bridge, off Rte 8, twenty minutes north of the city.

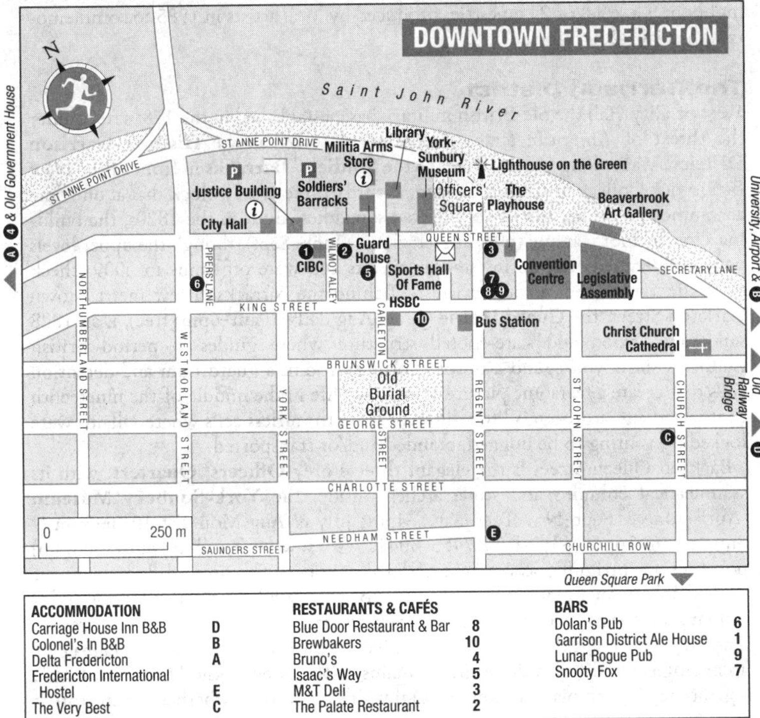

Carriage House Inn B&B 230 University Ave, at George ⓣ506/452-9924 or 1-800/267-6068, ⓦwww.carriagehouse-inn.net. This ten-room inn, on the east side of the city centre, occupies a grand Queen Anne-style house built in 1875, in one of the older residential areas. It comes complete with antique furnishings, ballroom, and capacious veranda. The rate includes a delicious breakfast. 6

Colonel's Inn B&B 843 Union St ⓣ506/452-2802 or 1-877/455-3003, ⓦwww.bbcanada.com/1749.html. On the north side of the Saint John River, this enjoyable B&B has three en-suite guest rooms decorated in appealing pastel shades. The breakfasts are great and the house itself, dating from 1894, offers splendid views back across to Fredericton's downtown, a 15-minute walk away via the old railway bridge. 4

Delta Fredericton 225 Woodstock Rd ⓣ506/457-7000 or 1-888/462-8800, ⓦwww.deltahotels.com. Modern high-rise hotel in an attractive retro style with dormer windows and stone finishings. Luxurious suites and posh doubles with views of the river; located a few blocks west of the centre. 7

Fredericton International Hostel 621 Churchill Row ⓣ506/450-4417, ⓦwww.hihostels.ca. Friendly HI hostel in a sparse, but well-kept older building about 500m south of downtown at the corner of Regent St. Kitchen facilities, laundry and internet access. Dorm beds $20, nonmembers $23; doubles $25, nonmembers $30.

The Very Best 806 George St at Church St ⓣ506/451-1499, ⓦwww.bbcanada.com/2330.html. This posh B&B, in a rambling 1840 mansion within easy walking distance of the centre, offers five tastefully renovated, en-suite guest rooms as well as an outside pool. 5

The City

Fredericton's centre, bounded by Brunswick Street to the south and York Street to the west, was laid out in the 1780s close to a curve in the **Saint John River**. Start your tour at **City Hall** (tours only: mid-May to mid-Oct daily 9.30am & 3.30pm; free; ⓣ506-460/2129), with its distinctive 35m clock tower. Inside the main highlight is a series of 27 tapestries produced by local artists in 1985 to commemorate the city's 200th birthday.

The Garrison District

West of City Hall the old British military base, established in the 1780s to counter the threat of American attack, is preserved today as the **Historic Garrison District**. Walk along Queen Street to the **Soldiers' Barracks** in front of the New Brunswick College of Craft & Design, a sturdy three-storey block that at one time accommodated more than two hundred squaddies. Built in the 1820s, the building's lower floor is home to eight craft shops (June–Sept), though the upper levels were condemned after an infestation of ants and were off limits in 2009 (check with the visitor centre for the latest). Behind the barracks, a few metres down Carleton Street, the **Guard House** (June–Aug daily 10am–6pm; free), is an 1828 sandstone, wood and slate-roofed structure where guides in period British uniforms show you round a restored orderly room, a guardroom and detention cells that create a fearsome picture of military life in the middle of the nineteenth century: the guardroom is little different from the airless cells where villains were locked up waiting to be flogged, branded and/or transported.

Back on Queen Street is the elegant three-storey **Officers' Quarters**, with its symmetrical columns and stone arches. Inside, the **York-Sunbury Museum** (April–June & Sept–Nov Tues–Sat 1–4pm; July & Aug Mon–Sat 10am–5pm & Sun noon–5pm; $3; ⓣ506/455-6041, ⓦwww.yorksunburymuseum.com) possesses an intriguing assortment of local bygones. The ground floor kicks off with displays on Fredericton under the British, while the second floor holds military uniforms, armaments and a reconstruction of a World War I trench. The third floor holds a couple of Native Canadian rooms, with a ragbag of archeological finds, plus the stuffed remains of the twenty-kilo "Coleman Frog", a giant-sized amphibian of dubious origins. It's not known whether the creature is real, but the local innkeeper, who produced it in the 1880s, claimed to have fed it on beer and buttermilk.

The museum overlooks **Officers' Square**, at the foot of Regent Street. Mostly grassed over today, the square still has space for the **Changing of the Guard** (July & Aug Mon–Thurs 11am & 7pm, Fri–Sun at 11am & 4pm, ⓣ506/460-2041), a re-enactment of British drill. On the river-side of the square, the **Lighthouse on the Green** (daily: June–Sept 10.30am–9.30pm; ⓣ506/460-2939), houses a café, an upper floor viewing deck and exhibits on the Saint John River (same hrs; $2), and **River Trails Bike Rentals** (daily: June 10.30am–6.30pm, July & Aug 10am–9pm, Sept 10.30am–5.30pm; $7/hr, $25/day; ⓣ506/476-7368), where you can pick up a bike to explore the city's 80km of bike trails.

Beaverbrook Art Gallery

Lord Beaverbrook, the newspaper tycoon, was raised in New Brunswick's Newcastle (see p.426) and moved to England in 1910 – becoming a close friend of Churchill and a key member of his war cabinet. In Fredericton his largesse was extended to the university, the Playhouse Theatre and the **Beaverbrook Art Gallery** (Mon–Sat 9am–5.30pm, Thurs till 9pm, Sun noon–5.30pm; Jan–May closed Mon; $8, Thurs after 5.30pm voluntary donation; ⓦwww.beaverbrookartgallery.org), by the river at the foot of St John Street. It's a first-rate gallery, where an eclectic and regularly rotated collection of mostly British and Canadian art is squeezed into a dozen or so rooms, sharing space with an imaginative programme of temporary exhibitions.

Salvador Dali's monumental *Santiago El Grande*, depicting St James being borne up towards a vaulted firmament on a white charger, usually takes pride of place at the **entrance**. Past this, Hogarth, Reynolds, Gainsborough, Constable, Turner, Landseer, Augustus John, Francis Bacon and Lowry represent the British and there's also a small sample of medieval paintings plus a haunting *Lady Macbeth Sleep-Walking* by Eugene Delacroix.

The extensive **Canadian collection** features well-known artists including Paul Kane (see p.87), the Group of Seven (see p.88) and Emily Carr, as well as lesser

▲ A sculpture in front of Fredericton's Beaverbrook Art Gallery

figures like the early nineteenth-century artist George Chambers, whose *"The Terror" Iced-in off Cape Comfort* is a wonderfully melodramatic canvas, the creaking ship crushed by the ice underneath a dark and forbidding sky. There's also a good selection of the works of the prolific **Cornelius Krieghoff** (see p.87), including two of his finest, *Merrymaking* and *Coming Storm at the Portage*.

Legislative Assembly Building and Christ Church Cathedral

The **Legislative Assembly Building** (guided tours: early June to mid-Aug daily 9am–7pm; mid-Aug to early June Mon–Fri 9am–4pm; free), the home of New Brunswick's parliament, stands opposite the art gallery, its robust and imposing sandstone and granite exterior topped by a ponderous tower and cupola. Completed in 1882, the interior holds a sumptuously decorated Assembly Chamber, adorned with portraits of George III and Queen Charlotte by Joshua Reynolds, as well as a splendid oak and cherry spiral staircase leading to the chamber's visitors' gallery.

The nearby **Christ Church Cathedral** (mid-June to Aug Mon–Fri 9am–6pm, Sat 10am–5pm, Sun 1–5pm; Sept to mid-June Mon–Fri 9am–4pm; free guided tours from mid-June to Aug), at King and Church streets, is rather modest in comparison, despite its status. Built between 1845 and 1853 in Gothic Revival style, its most distinguishing features are its elegant tapering 60m spire and the intricate grace of its red-pine hammerbeam ceiling.

Old Government House

With more time, drive or stroll east along the river to **Old Government House** (guided tours only: June to mid-Aug Mon–Sat 10am–4pm, Sun noon–4pm; free; ⓣ506/453-2505), the official residence of the Lieutenant-Governor of New Brunswick. Completed in 1828, the mansion was abandoned in the 1890s, and it wasn't until 1999 that the governors returned. Illuminating tours (45min) visit all the lavish main rooms on the first two floors (the third floor is reserved for the governor), and recount the history of the building and some of the notable events that took place here. There's free parking on-site.

Eating and drinking

Downtown Fredericton offers a reasonable range of **cafés** and **restaurants** and there are enough **bars** to entertain for a night or two. In the summer, there's also free outdoor theatre and live music down on Officers' Square. The Playhouse (ⓣ506/458-8344 or 1-866/884-5800, ⓦwww.theplayhouse.nb.ca), beside the Legislative Assembly Building, puts on a good variety of shows and is home to the province's only professional English-speaking **theatre** company, Theatre New Brunswick (Sept–April season). The tourist office has the details of all up-and-coming events.

Restaurants and cafés

Blue Door Restaurant & Bar 100 Regent St ⓣ506/455-2583, ⓦwww.thebluedoor.ca. Smart contemporary cuisine fusing Thai, Indian and European influences with local seafood and produce, with dinner entrees $17–27. Also a good bet for zippy martinis and a huge list of fine wines.

Brewbakers 546 King St, between Regent and Carleton ⓣ506/459-0067, ⓦwww.brewbakers.ca. First-rate wood-fired pizzas at affordable prices ($12–13), plus steaks and seafood ($12–16). Jam-packed at the weekend. Open Mon–Thurs 11.30am–10pm, Fri 11.30am–11pm, Sat 5–11pm & Sun 10am–3pm & 5–9pm.

Bruno's At the *Delta Hotel*, 225 Woodstock Rd ⓣ506/451-7935. This café-restaurant is noted for its lavish buffets where the emphasis is on pasta (daily lunch pasta bar $12.95) and seafood (Sat brunch buffet $12.95; Sun $20.95). Eat either inside or outside on the large riverside patio and watch the sunset. Daily 6am–8pm.

Isaac's Way 73 Carleton St ⓣ506/472-7937, ⓦwww.isaacsway.ca. One of the town's most popular restaurants, offering a consistently high-quality menu of salads, seafood, vegetarian dishes and pasta – look out for the $9 plate specials. Also has a full bar and large outdoor patio in summer.

M&T Deli 602 Queen at Regent St ⓣ506/458-9068. Fredericton's best deli, specializing in New York-style bagels, Montréal smoked meat and massive sandwiches ($5-6). Mon–Fri 7.30am–4.30pm.

The Palate Restaurant 462 Queen St ⓣ506/450-7911, ⓦwww.thepalate.com. Bright and breezy café-cum-restaurant with a lively, inventive menu featuring everything from Digby scallops to *porcini* and escargot brie. In the evening, main courses range from $15–24, and there's pita pizzas, paninis (both $9) and special brunch deals on Sat ($8). Mon 11am–3pm, Tues–Fri 11am–3pm & 5–9pm, Sat 10am–3pm & 5–9pm.

Bars

Dolan's Pub Pipers Lane, 349 King St ⓣ506/454-7474, ⓦwww.dolanspub.ca. Bustling bar with imported and domestic beers on draught and regular live folk music. Also does decent steak sandwiches ($7.95) and long happy hours (Mon–Thurs 4pm till close, Fri & Sat 4–8pm). Closed Sun.

Garrison District Ale House 426 Queen St ⓣ506/455-0300, ⓦwww.thegarrison.ca. Claims the largest selection of speciality beer in the province, including rare treats such as Dogfish Head 60 Minute IPA and Rogue Dead Guy Ale. Also does vast pub food menu and DJ nights on Sat. Closed Sun

Lunar Rogue Pub 625 King St ⓣ506/450-2065, ⓦwww.lunarrogue.com. Busy bar serving British and Maritime ales as well as an extensive range of malt whiskeys. Live music on most weekends. Summer patio. Open daily.

Southeast of Fredericton: Gagetown

Heading **southeast** to Saint John (see p.414) along leisurely Hwy 102, be sure to spend an hour or two in **GAGETOWN** (ⓦwww.villageofgagetown.ca), a pretty village whose graceful clapboard houses are sprinkled along the Saint John River about 60km from Fredericton (and 100km from Saint John). There are several engrossing craft and pottery shops here, a prim and proper Anglican church, and a grand old courthouse of 1836. The *Old Boot Pub* (Sept–May closed Mon & Tues: ⓣ506/488-3441), next door to Grimross at 48 Front St, offers decent beer, meals and live music at the weekends. There are also a couple of **places to stay**. The best is the well-kept *Step-Aside B&B* (ⓣ506/488-1808, ⓦwww.bbcanada.com/6860.html; May–Dec; ③–④), whose four guest rooms are in an 1880s white clapboard house down by the river at 58 Front St.

The Saint John River Valley

The **Saint John River Valley**, running northwest from Fredericton to **Edmundston**, a distance of 270km, is not consistently beautiful but does have its moments, especially when it slips through maple and pine forests or, to the north, where its low-lying hills and farmland are replaced by a more mountainous, heavily forested terrain. The valley towns which dot the Trans-Canada aren't particularly memorable, but the restored pioneer village of **King's Landing** is first-rate, as is the waterfall at **Grand Falls**.

King's Landing

Some 35km west of Fredericton on Rte 102 lies **King's Landing Historical Settlement** (June to mid-Oct daily 10am–5pm; $15.50; ⓦwww.kingslanding.nb.ca), a collection of historic buildings carefully relocated here in the 1960s to form the nucleus of an open-air museum of nineteenth-century rural life. Since then, further judicious purchases have added to the housing stock and, supplemented by a handful of replicas, there are now no fewer than seventy buildings spread out amid tranquil waterside woods and fields. King's Landing aims to provide a total experience to its visitors, with its "inhabitants" engaged in bread-making, horseshoeing, logging, milling, weaving and cattle-driving. Themed villages are not to everyone's taste, but this one works very well and several of the buildings are fascinating in their own right – particularly the **Jones House**, a stone dwelling built into the hillside in a manner typical of this area, the **Ingraham House**, once the property of a well-to-do farmer, and the fully operational sawmill.

Hartland and Grand Falls

Surrounded by forest, **HARTLAND**, some 90km beyond King's Landing, advertises itself exclusively on the size of its **wooden bridge**, which at 391m is by far the longest covered bridge in the world. It was completed in 1921 (replacing the 1901 original), the idea being to protect the timbers of the bridge from the elements by means of a long shed-like affair built in the manner of a barn. You can park on the Hartland side of the river, next to the local **information centre** (June–Sept daily 9am–6pm; Ⓣ506/375-4075).

North of Hartland, the scenery changes as the maples give way to a great undulating belt of potato fields. There's a surprise in store here at **GRAND FALLS**, 105km from Hartland, where, right in the centre of what is otherwise a nondescript town, a spectacular weight of water squeezes through hydroelectric barriers to crash down a 23-metre pitch. Even if the diversion of water through nearby turbines has deprived the falls of their original vigour, they're still impressive, as is the 2km-long gorge they've carved downstream, a steep-sided ravine encircling half the town. A 253-step **stairway** (daily: mid-May to June & Sept to mid-Oct 9am–6pm; July & Aug 9am–9pm; $5) leads down into the gorge, where pontoon boats make a 45-minute trip to the base of the falls ($25); the stairway begins just across the bridge from the **Malabeam Information Centre** (daily: May, June & Sept 10am–6pm, July & Aug 9am–9pm; Ⓣ506/475-7769, Ⓦwww.grandfalls.com), which perches on the bridge above the falls. There's nothing much else to see in Grand Falls, but straightforward **accommodation** is available right by the waterfall at the *Hill Top Motel*, 131 Madawaska Rd (Ⓣ506/473-2684 or 1-800/496-1244, Ⓦwww.sn2000.nb.ca/hilltop; ③–⑤).

Edmundston

Lying at the confluence of the Saint John and Madawaska rivers, wood-pulping **EDMUNDSTON** is the largest town in the north of New Brunswick, with a population of nearly eighteen thousand. It's a brash, modern place, where a profusion of flashing neon signs proclaim the proximity of the US, which lies just over the biggest of the town's three bridges. Edmundston is mainly French-speaking and, curiously, regards itself as the capital of an enclave known as the **Republic of Madawaska**, the snout-shaped tract of Canadian territory jutting out into the state of Maine. While the idea of an independent state here is preposterous, the town packages the Republic frivolously, with touches such as a coat of arms, a flag, honorary knights and a president (otherwise the mayor).

Practicalities

Acadian Lines **buses** pull in at 169 Victoria St, just off Boulevard Hébert before the Fournier Bridge over the Madawaska River into the town centre. There's a seasonal **tourist office** (daily late June to early Sept 9am–8pm) just off the Trans-Canada (Exit 18) near the top of Boulevard Hébert, which runs downtown.

Wild Canada

Although it has compelling urban spaces, you won't truly get a handle on the essence of Canada until you spend some time journeying through and soaking up its huge breadth of natural landscapes. This is a country that can at times still seem like an alluringly unexplored wilderness, with untamed rivers, quiet lakes, isolated coastline and lofty mountains. With abundant flora and fauna – much of it found in the extensive network of national and provincial parks – as well as countless opportunities for outdoor activities, it's nature that is likely to provide the most abiding memories of any Canadian visit.

Cliffs along the Bay of Fundy, New Brunswick ▲

l'Île-Bonaventure provincial park, Québec ▼

Landscapes

Canada encompasses virtually every possible terrain, from the desert-like Saskatchewan **badlands** and temperate **rainforests** of British Columbia, to New Brunswick's rugged **shores** and the wildlife-rich **forests** and parkland of the country's central interior.

Foremost in the public imagination are the jagged **mountains**, pristine lakes and massive glaciers of the Rockies, particularly in the Banff, Jasper, Yoho and Kootenay regions. Less well-known but equally awe-inspiring are Riding Mountain National Park in Manitoba, a vast piece of **escarpment** rising out of the **prairies**, and Ontario's Bruce Peninsula, home to fine, lakeside hiking and a magnet for divers. This medley of geography continues as you move into Québec's **Gaspé** region, particularly at Forillon and L'Île-Bonaventure parks, which combine rolling hills and wildflower-strewn meadows with glimpses of stunning waterscapes.

With all of this it's easy to forget the western and easternmost **coasts**. Yet Pacific Rim National Park's Long Beach in the west is one of the continent's greatest stretches of wild shoreline, and in the east, Prince Edward Island, Nova Scotia's Cape Breton **Highlands** and Newfoundland embrace a collection of sheer cliffs, quiet **beaches**, remote coves and atmospheric fishing villages.

Outdoor activities

Having so much variety and space makes Canada an outdoor enthusiast's dream destination. Wherever you are, you can be sure you're never that far away from an opportunity to **hike**, ride, **camp** or mountain-bike. You may have to plan a bit more carefully or travel a little farther if you want to downhill or cross-country **ski**, snowboard, ice-climb or give something like snowmobiling, dog-sledding or snow-shoeing a shot – but even then the 42 national and countless hundreds of provincial parks make indulging in the great outdoors easy. Urban tastes won't be disappointed either - **run** along Ottawa's Rideau Canal, **cycle** Vancouver's Stanley Park Seawall or inline **skate** Calgary's riverside pathways.

Fishing, **canoeing**, kayaking and other watery activities – including **whale-watching** – are widely available; Ontario alone has an estimated 250,000 lakes and 35,000km of waterways, 25,000km of which have been mapped out as superb canoe routes. Complementing the varied terrain and spectacular scenery is an invariably excellent infrastructure. In most places you'll be able to turn up, ask some questions, rent some gear and get going.

The best parks to...

▸▸ **Canoe** It's pure paddling pleasure in Ontario, with Point Pelee National Park's winding freshwater marshes and Algonquin National Park's network of lakes.

▸▸ **Drive** Jasper's Icefields Parkway is a superlative mountain drive, but the Cabot Trail in Nova Scotia's Cape Breton Highlands is a fine maritime alternative.

▸▸ **Hike** Banff's credentials can't be denied, but to escape the crowds, head to Gros Morne National Park, Newfoundland.

▸▸ **Raft** Nahanni National Park in the Northwest Territories just edges Jasper for wild white-water thrills.

▸▸ **Soak** In Radium or Banff Upper hot springs in the Rockies: both offer steaming waters to soothe the tired traveller.

▸▸ **Island hop** BC's lush Gulf Islands or the islets of Québec's Mingan Archipelago, both national park reserves.

▲ Humpback whale, St Lawrence River, Québec

▼ Banff Upper Hot Springs, Alberta

▼ Gros Morne National Park, Newfoundland

Wood bison, Wood Buffalo National Park, Alberta ▲

Bluenose caribou, Northwest Territories ▼

Flora and fauna

The best place for wildlife sightings are the **national parks** designated to help preserve specific plants or animals. These include Wood Buffalo, in the Northwest Territories and Alberta, designed to conserve the Wood **bison**, and Tuktut Nogait, in the Northwest Territories, which protects the calving grounds of the Bluenose **caribou**.

Still, a sighting of some sort – a swathe of spring wildflowers, a **moose** lumbering into the roadside trees, a **black bear** sniffing at the water's edge - is almost guaranteed in any park, and there are other top natural attractions that are also easily seen.

Among them are the **ancient cedars** – some over one thousand years old – in the rainforest of British Columbia's Mount Revelstoke National Park. Elsewhere, there's no need to go trekking to see the distinctive spiralled horns of **Dall sheep**; they'll probably be grazing happily near the highway in the Yukon. **Elk**, too, are common, and still amble around Banff's streets, despite rangers' best efforts to discourage them. Far more intimidating are **polar bears**, which can be seen near Churchill, Manitoba at Wapusk National Park, one of the world's largest denning areas for this magnificent animal. Aquatic encounters also abound, with **sea otters and sea lions** bobbing about off Vancouver Island's west coast. Plenty of **whales** seasonally patrol the same waters, as well as those off the coastal parks of Québec and the Maritimes.

Spring brings a carpet of **flowers** to most parks, especially high **alpine meadows**, but Nunavut's Auyuittuq or Sirmilik national parks are renowned for the remarkable June or July blooming of the otherwise barren tundra.

For central **accommodation**, head for the standard-issue comforts of the *Quality Inn*, 919 Canada Rd (Ⓣ506/735-5525 or 1-800/563-2489, Ⓦwww.choicehotels.ca; ⑤). A second, less expensive option is the homely, motel-style *Praga Hotel*, near the marina at 127 Victoria St (Ⓣ506/735-5567; ②), which is also a Chinese restaurant.

The Fundy Coast

In the southwest corner of New Brunswick, abutting the US state of Maine, the deeply indented **Bay of Fundy** boasts a sparsely populated shoreline of forest, rock and swamp. Easily the prettiest of the region's coastal villages is **St Andrews**, a Loyalist settlement turned seaside resort, 135km south of Fredericton and equipped with a battery of tantalizing inns and B&Bs. The other main attraction is the **Fundy Islands** archipelago at the mouth of Passamaquoddy Bay; **Campobello Island**, the site of Franklin Roosevelt's country retreat, and the far larger **Grand Manan Island**, a wild and remote spot noted for its imposing sea cliffs and rich birdlife.

St Andrews

Once a busy port and trading centre, **ST ANDREWS** is now an affluent resort town, with manicured gardens and neat rows of clapboard houses more reminiscent of New England than the fishing villages further north. It makes an obvious base for exploring the coast, with plenty of engaging attractions and activities in and around town.

Arrival and information

St Andrews is accessible by Acadian Lines **bus** from Saint John, Fredericton and Bangor, Maine; passengers are dropped on Water Street, a couple of blocks east of the pier. The **tourist office** (daily: early May to June 9am–5pm; July & Aug 8am–8pm; Sept to early Oct 9.30am–5.30pm; Ⓣ506/529-3556, Ⓦwww.townofstandrews.ca) is on Rte 127 as you enter town. They issue free tide tables and town maps, supply information on local bike rental, have the schedule for visits to Minister's Island, and will help you with accommodation.

Accommodation

St Andrews has a good choice of pricey **hotels** and B&Bs; advance bookings are essential during high season. *Kiwanis Oceanfront Camping* (Ⓣ506/529-3439, Ⓦwww.kiwanisoceanfrontcamping.com; May to mid-Oct; $25–34) has a great seaside location just over 1km east of the town centre along Water Street.

Fairmont Algonquin 184 Adolphus St Ⓣ506/529-8823 or 1-866/540-4403, Ⓦwww.fairmont.com/algonquin. The largest hotel in town is the a sprawling and well-equipped resort complex whose mock Tudor turrets and gables, dating from 1915, dominate the northwest of town, about 1.5km from the waterfront on Prince of Wales St. ⑦

Harris Hatch Inn 142 Queen St Ⓣ506/529-4995, Ⓦwww.harrishatchinn.ca. This B&B occupies an elegant, broadly Georgian mansion built in 1840, with shutters, fanlight and Neoclassical columns, a short walk from the pier. The four rooms and one apartment are all fairly spacious and very cosy, all with cable TV and wi-fi, and some with fireplaces. ④

Kingsbrae Arms 219 King St Ⓣ506/529-1897, Ⓦwww.kingsbrae.com. The most illustrious hotel in town, this sumptuous, immaculately maintained mansion overlooks the botanical gardens. There are just eight guest rooms here, six of them suites with balconies offering wide views of the gardens and the bay, and each is decorated in lavish modern style. ⑧

Montague Rose 258 Montague St ⓣ506/529-8963 or 1-888/529-8963, ⓦwww.themontaguerose.com. This inviting B&B is housed in a striking Second Empire-style home built in 1859, with three spacious rooms all with whirlpool or claw-foot tubs, satellite TV and DVD players. ⑤

Picket Fence Motel 102 Reed Ave ⓣ506/529-8985, ⓦwww.picketfencenb.com. Great budget option (at least by St Andrews standards), with seventeen basic units equipped with cable TV (internet in the office), just beyond Rte 127 (Mowat Drive), and a short drive from Water St. ③

The Town

The main drag, **Water Street**, tracks along a waterfront lined with cafés and craft shops – park along the street or in the nearby car park for free. The **pier** is packed with boat-tour companies: Quoddy Link Marine (ⓣ506/529-2600 or 1-877/688-2600, ⓦwww.quoddylinkmarine.com) operates first-class **whale-watching** cruises (late June to mid-Oct 1–3 daily; 3hr; $49), each of which has a naturalist on board; and Eastern Outdoors (ⓣ506/529-4662, ⓦwww.easternoutdoors.com) run **kayak tours** of Passamaquoddy Bay from $49 for a half-day.

The town is at its most enchanting among the antique clapboard houses of King Street, which leads up the hill from the pier. You can look inside a couple of them: the 1820 **Sheriff Andrews House** (late June to early Sept Mon–Sat 9.30–4.30pm, Sun 1–4.30pm; donation suggested), at no. 63, is staffed with costumed guides and filled with period furniture; the **Ross Memorial Museum** (June to mid-Oct Mon–Sat 10am–4.30pm; donation suggested), at 188 Montague St and King Street, is housed in a stately 1824 red-brick home and crammed with fine art assembled by a couple of nineteenth-century American collectors.

The only other sights are the 27-acre **Kingsbrae Garden** (mid-May to early Oct daily 9am–6pm; $9.75; ⓣ506/529-3335, ⓦwww.kingsbraegarden.com) on the crest of King Street, with its flowers, shrubs and trees, and at the west end of Water Street the squat, shingled **St Andrews Blockhouse** (June–Aug daily 10am–6pm; $0.95), the original wooden tower built in 1813 to protect the area from the Americans.

Minister's Island

You can also visit nearby **Minister's Island** (mid-June to mid-Oct 1–2 tours daily; 2hr; ⓣ506/529-5081, ⓦwww.ministersisland.ca; $14), whose undulating farmland is reached by car along a tidal causeway at low tide, or by boat (included in entry price; park on the mainland side). The island was once the property of Sir William Van Horne, the man who built the Canadian Pacific Railroad, and who constructed a grand stone mansion named **Covenhaven** here in the 1890s alongside a clutter of farm buildings. Highlights of the two-hour tour include a romp round the dilapidated mansion and inspection of the windmill, with its kerosene-powered reserve engines.

Eating and drinking

St Andrews has an excellent range of **cafés** and a few good **restaurants**. The inexpensive *Gables Restaurant Bar & Patio*, 143 Water St (ⓣ506/529-3440), is a funky little place serving lobster, PEI Mussels ($10.50), chowders ($5.99) and burgers ($8.50) from its bayshore location. The *Sweet Harvest Market*, just along the street at no. 182 (ⓣ506/529-6249; Tues & Wed 9am–3pm, Thurs–Sat 9am–5pm, Sun 11am–3pm), is a cosy café offering up hearty breakfasts, Java Moose coffee and especially tasty crab rolls and cinnamon buns. The *Red Herring Pub* at 211 Water St (daily noon–2am; ⓣ506/529-8455) serves good beer, tasty haddock and chips and is the best place in town for live music.

Campobello Island

US president Franklin D. Roosevelt loved **Campobello Island** for its quiet wooded coves, rocky headlands and excellent fishing – though he rarely returned after contracting polio here in 1921. The island, which is just 16km long by 5km wide, is now sprinkled with second homes and busy with day-trippers, though the southern half is protected as the **Roosevelt Campobello International Park**. Here, mixed forests, marshes, tidal flats, beaches and gullies are crossed by 24km of gravel road, which give access to a variety of gentle **hiking trails**. Several of these – including the refreshing 1.5km-long walk over to Friar's Head – begin beside the island's star turn, the red and green **Roosevelt Cottage** (late May to mid-Oct daily 10am–6pm; free) built in 1897, set among the woods by the seashore about 3km south of the ferry dock. One look at the place and you'll see that "cottage" is an understatement – it's a 35-room mansion built in a Dutch colonial style and packed with memorabilia, from the great man's childhood potty and the Christmas list he made when he was knee-high, through to the megaphone with which the children were summoned to dinner.

Arrival and information

Most visitors still come to Campobello Island **over the bridge** from Lubec in Maine. There's talk of a year-round ferry service from St Andrews, but until then the only way to reach the island directly from mainland Canada is the seasonal ferry via **Deer Island**. **Ferries** to Deer Island (Mon–Sat every 30min 7am–7pm, then hourly till 10pm; Sun same hours, hourly; 20min; free; first-come first-served; ⓣ506/453-3939 or 1-888/747-7006) leave from **Letete** on the southeast shore of Passamaquoddy Bay, 14km south of Rte 1 (and the village of St George). They dock at the island's northern shore, from where it's a 16km drive south to the **Deer Island–Campobello ferry** (late June to mid-Sept hourly 8.30am–6.30pm; 35min; car & driver $18, foot passenger $3; ⓣ506/747-2159, ⓦwww.eastcoastferries.nb.ca; first-come first-served) – look for the signs to Deer Island Point. Ferries also sail from this jetty to **Eastport in Maine** (late June to mid-Sept hourly 9am–6pm; 20min; car & driver $15, foot passenger $3; same contact details). Both ferries are quite small, so get there early.

Practicalities

There are several places to **stay** on the island, including *Lupine Lodge* (ⓣ506/752-2555 or 1-888/912-8880, ⓦwww.lupinelodge.com; ❻; late May to mid-Oct), whose delightful log cabins, with their Art Deco lines, occupy a clearing in the woods, in sight of the sea about 500m north of Roosevelt Cottage. The lodge itself dates from 1915 and holds a first-class and reasonably priced **restaurant** featuring local ingredients, including Fundy haddock and Maine shrimp. *Owen House* (ⓣ506/752-2977, ⓦwww.owenhouse.ca; ❺–❼; late May to mid-Oct) just south of the ferry at 11 Welshpool St, dates from 1835 and occupies a leafy spit overlooking the bay, with nine attractive en-suite rooms, two tranquil lounges and superb breakfasts (no wi-fi and no TV in rooms). Of the handful of small **diners** on the island, the pick is *Family Fisheries* (ⓣ506/752-2470) at Wilson's Beach, where lobster, lobster stews and lobster rolls top a tasty menu of shellfish, fish and chips and grills. Leave room for the home-made blueberry pie.

Grand Manan Island

At the mouth of the Bay of Fundy lies **Grand Manan Island**, a rugged nature hot-spot some 30km long that has remained remarkably undeveloped, at least compared to islands off the US coast further south. While day-trips can give you a decent taster, staying a couple of nights will allow a greater appreciation of the island's languid charm. **Hiking** trails cover the island: a geological fault essentially splits it in two, with the west side dominated by dark, imposing craggy cliffs of

Ferries to Grand Manan

To get to Grand Manan Island, catch the **car ferry** from **Blacks Harbour**, located 10km south of Rte 1 between St Andrews and Saint John (late June to mid-Sept 6–7 daily; mid-Sept to late June 3–4 daily; 1hr 30min–2hr; cars $32.55 return, passengers $10.90 return; ⓣ506/662-3724, ⓦwww.coastaltransport.ca). Spaces are allocated on a first-come, first-served basis so arrive at least an hour before the departure time, and be prepared to queue, especially in July and August; no fares are collected on the outward journey – you pay the whole deal on the way back.

volcanic origin, and the east by reddish sedimentary rock, whose crumblings have created some beautiful sandy – and occasionally magnetic – beaches. Grand Manan is also an ideal place to go **bird-** and **whale-watching**. The naturalist and painter James John Audubon first documented the island's assembly of puffins, gannets, guillemots, stormy petrels and kittiwakes during his visit in 1831; the best birdwatching times are in the spring migratory period (early April–early June), the summer nesting season and the autumn migration (late Aug through Sept).

Accommodation

There's a healthy supply of **accommodation** on Grand Manan, though it's all pleasantly low-key and distinctly folksy. Most places can be found in or around **North End**, where the ferry docks, but there are a few options elsewhere on the island.

Hole-in-the-Wall Park Campground 42 Old Airport Rd, North Head ⓣ506/662-3152 or 1-866/662-4489, ⓦwww.grandmanancamping.com. Offers some breathtaking cliff-top pitches, but they are popular, so arrive early or book ahead. Cliff-edge sites $25, $35 for cabins, hook-ups $5, laundry $2. May–Oct.

The Inn at Whale Cove Cottages 26 Whale Cove Cottage Rd, North Head ⓣ506/662-3181, ⓦwww.holidayjunction.com/whalecove. Tranquil property comprising three cosy, shaker-furnished en-suite rooms in the main shingle house dating from 1816 (5), a spacious one-bedroom bungalow (5) and two other larger properties with four bedrooms ($950/week) and two bedrooms ($800/week). The Willa Cather Cottage, built by the renowned author in the 1920s, is $950/week. All cottages come with kitchens and radios but no TVs or phones. To get there, turn off the main road in North Head and head 700m up Whistle Rd.

McLaughlin's Wharf Inn 1863 Rte 776, Seal Cove ⓣ506/662-8760, ⓦwww.mclaughlinswharfinn.com. To stay at the opposite end of the island try this B&B that began life as a hardware store in 1885,and now occupies a prime position on the harbour. It features six plain but comfy rooms, two shared bathrooms and one TV lounge. Breakfast and meals are served on the large deck right over the swirling Fundy tides. June–Sept. 4

Swallowtail Inn 50 Lighthouse Rd ⓣ506/662-1100 or 1-866/563-1100, ⓦwww.swallowtailinn.com. Just outside North Head, this especially unique B&B has six guest rooms (with satellite TV and scintillating views), in the former homes of two lighthouse keeper families – the lighthouse is still operational, as you will no doubt come to realize when the fog comes down and the fog horn goes off. June–Oct. 3

The Island: North Head

The ferry arrives at the north end of the island at Grand Manan's largest settlement, **NORTH HEAD**, just opposite the tiny **Whale and Seabird Research Station** (daily: June, Sept & Oct 10am–4pm; July & Aug 9am–5pm; donation suggested; ⓣ506/662-3804, ⓦwww.gmwsrs.org). The centre provides a thoughtful introduction to the several species of whale hereabouts, but to get a look at the real thing, take a trip with Whales-n-Sails Adventures (late June to late Sept; $65; ⓣ506/662-1999 or 1-888/994-4044, ⓦwww.whales-n-sails.com) on the wharf opposite.

Turning right at the ferry takes you towards the dramatically sited 1860 Swallows Tail Lightstation, perched on a small outcrop connected to the main island by a wooden bridge. The rocky coast to the north provides some of the island's best **hiking,** with trails leading to Fish Head and the **Hole in the Wall** rock formation, just over a kilometre away. Paths are narrow and quite rugged (marked with red disks), and if you don't fancy the hike, you can drive 2km up to **Hole in the Wall Park** ($4 late June to mid-Sept; free other times), where you can park within a few metres of the coast. Alternatively, you can take a **sea kayak** tour or rent a **bike** from Adventure High, back on the main road (Rte 776) at no.83 (Ⓣ506/662-3563, Ⓦwww.adventurehigh.com). Half-day guided kayak tours (May–Oct) are $55; seal-watching tours are $65.

Grand Harbour and White Head Island

Heading south from North Head, the main road hugs the coast to **GRAND HARBOUR**, the commercial and educational centre of the island, where the **Grand Manan Museum** (mid-June to mid-Sept Mon–Fri 9am–5pm; $5; Ⓣ506/662-3524), at 1141 Rte 776, houses all sorts of locally procured curios, as well as a small display recounting the history of the island and its inextricable link with the fisheries: special attention is paid to wrecks, the island's unusual geology and **Willa Cather**, the American writer that spent her summers here from the 1920s to 1940s. At the lower level (outside) you'll find a small **tourist office** (July & Aug daily 9am–5pm; Ⓣ506/662-3442 or 1-888/525-1655, Ⓦwww.grandmanannb.com), but you can also buy **walking guides** ($6) and good **road maps** ($3) from the museum shop. Pushing on south from Grand Harbour, it's 3.5km to **Ingalls Head**, from where a toll-free **ferry** (4–10 daily; 25min) scuttles over to **White Head Island,** a tiny islet whose blissfully untrammelled beach makes for a pleasant day-trip.

Seal Cove and Southwest Head

Back on Grand Manan, it's a brief drive southwest from Grand Harbour to **SEAL COVE**, a fishing village that still bears the signs of the once-thriving smoked herring industry. Restored smokehouses and rickety wharves crowd the small harbour, where the prize catch now is lobster. The village is also home to the dependable Sea Watch Tours (Ⓣ506/662-8552 or 1-877/662-8552, Ⓦwww.seawatchtours.com), who run **whale-watching** trips ($63) from mid-July to Sept (turn down SC Breakwater Rd); they also offer **birdwatching** tours ($85; 5hr 30min) from late June to mid-August to **Machias Seal Island** (18km south), the best place to see **puffins**. From Seal Cove the road winds on to windswept **Southwest Head**, where a small 1880 lighthouse guards some oddly-shaped cliffs, rock formations and more trails with stupendous views across the sea.

Eating and drinking

Local seafood – particularly lobster (May–July) and shellfish – take centre stage at the island's crop of cafés and restaurants. If you have access to a kitchen, look out for wholesalers like *Sunrise Seafood* (Ⓣ506/662-3237) in Woodwards Cove, which sells fresh fish straight off the boat. Don't forget to sample another Grand Manan treat – **dulse** (edible seaweed). It grows on the western shore, in the shade of the cliffs, and is sold all over the island.

Back Porch Café 43 Rte 776, North Head Ⓣ506/662-8994. Conveniently located near the ferry dock, with a porch that looks out over the harbour and a menu that features rich "chowdahs" ($3.50), salads ($4–5) and big sandwiches ($5–8). Mon–Sat 11am–7pm, Sun noon–7pm; closes 4pm out of season.

Fundy House 1303 Rte 776 (south of North Head) Ⓣ506/662-8341. No frills diner that knocks out the best lobster rolls ($9.95) on the island, made fresh from the tank. Will also sell and cook you a whole lobster to take home. Clam rolls ($5) and the home-made apple crisp and pies are just as good.

Inn at Whale Cove 26 Whale Cove Cottage Rd ⓣ506/662-3181. The seasonal dining room here is the best place for dinner on the island – reservations required. Menus change daily, but offer two or three choices for each course and feature an abundance of local and seasonal produce such as juicy scallops and lobster. Daily 6–8pm only.

North Head Bakery 199 Rte 776, North Head ⓣ506/662-8862. Bakes French artisan bread and pastries, making it a great place to stock up for a picnic; it's marked with just a "Bakery" sign. Must eats include the flaky croissants, small doughnuts and crumbly date slices. Tues–Sat 6.30am–5.30pm.

Saint John

The largest city in New Brunswick (pop. 126,000), **SAINT JOHN** is better known for its industrial prowess than its tourist attractions, home to iconic products such **Moosehead beer**, the mighty **Irving group** of companies and a booming oil and gas sector. Yet the surprisingly compact downtown area is crammed with diverting sights, from resplendent Victorian architecture to the absorbing **New Brunswick Museum** and the **Reversing Falls Rapids** on the Saint John River, a dramatic place to see the effects of the Fundy tides.

The French established a trading post here in 1631, but the city-proper was founded by Loyalist immigrants in the 1780s. In the nineteenth century Saint John thrived on the lumber and shipbuilding industries, and despite a devastating fire in 1877, it was sufficiently wealthy to withstand the costs of immediate reconstruction. Consequently, almost all the city's older buildings – at their finest in the **Trinity Royal Historic Preservation Area** – are late Victorian.

Arrival and information

Driving into uptown Saint John can be a baffling experience; the best strategy is to keep on Rte 1 and follow the signs from Exit 122. **Parking** by meter or in municipal lots (Mon–Fri 7am–6pm; $1.50/hr), is usually easy to find. From the Acadian Lines **bus depot**, at 19 Chesley Drive, it's a fifteen-minute walk east to Market Slip. Saint John's **ferry terminal**, 5km west of the centre across the mouth of the Saint John River, is served by Bay Ferries (ⓣ1-888/249-7245, ⓦwww.bayferries.com), which has services across the Bay of Fundy to Digby, Nova Scotia (see p.381 for details). There are no buses direct to the centre from the terminal – take a cab ($8) or call Diamond Taxi (ⓣ506/648-8888). **Saint John Airport** (ⓦwww.saintjohnairport.com), 15km east of the city centre on Loch Lomond Road, is a small affair with flights on WestJet from Toronto (mid-May to mid-Oct) and Air Canada from Halifax, Montréal and Toronto. City bus #32 runs into town (Mon–Fri hourly 6.05am–6.05pm; $2.50), and Diamond Taxi (see above) runs a shuttle service that meets all flights for $15, but only goes back and forth from the *Delta Brunswick Hotel* (call ahead). Private **taxis** cost around $30 to the centre. All the major car rental companies have counters at the airport.

The main **tourist office** (Mon–Sat 9am–5.30pm; ⓣ506/658-2855 or 1-866/463-8639, ⓦwww.tourismsaintjohn.com) is in the centre of town inside the Shoppes of City Hall mall off King Street. This is the best place to get the latest on local **boat trips**. There's also a small information desk at Barbour's Store (mid-June to mid-Sept daily 9am–7pm; ⓣ506/658-2939). Free **internet** and wi-fi is available at the library (closed Sun) inside Market Square mall.

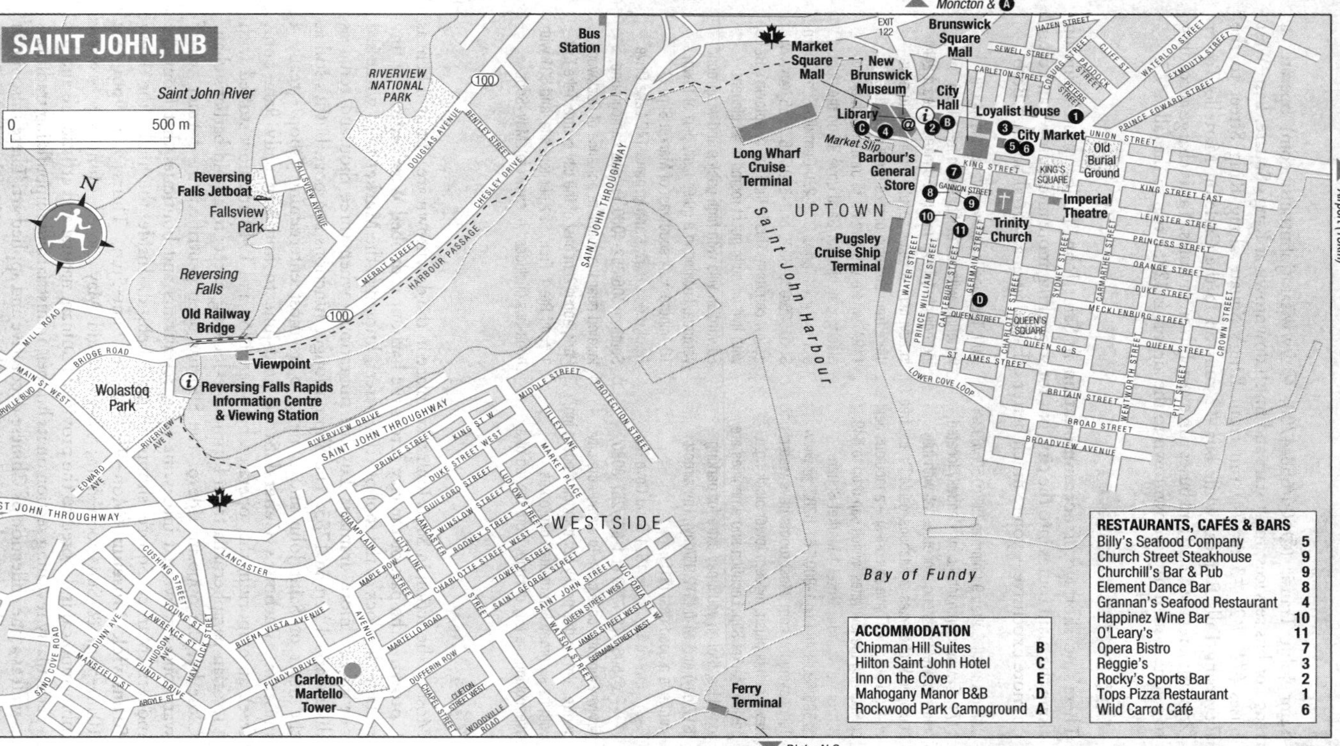
SAINT JOHN, NB
Moncton & A
Airport (15km)
Digby N.S.
E, Saint Andrews & Fredericton
0 500 m
N
Saint John River
RIVERVIEW NATIONAL PARK
Bus Station
Reversing Falls Jetboat
Fallsview Park
Reversing Falls
Old Railway Bridge
Viewpoint
Wolastoq Park
Reversing Falls Rapids Information Centre & Viewing Station
Market Square Mall
New Brunswick Museum
Brunswick Square Mall
City Hall
Loyalist House
Library
Market Slip
City Market
Old Burial Ground
Long Wharf Cruise Terminal
Barbour's General Store
KING'S SQUARE
Imperial Theatre
Trinity Church
UPTOWN
Pugsley Cruise Ship Terminal
QUEEN'S SQUARE
Saint John Harbour
Bay of Fundy
WESTSIDE
Carleton Martello Tower
Ferry Terminal
EXIT 122
ACCOMMODATION
Chipman Hill Suites B
Hilton Saint John Hotel C
Inn on the Cove E
Mahogany Manor B&B D
Rockwood Park Campground A
RESTAURANTS, CAFÉS & BARS
Billy's Seafood Company 5
Church Street Steakhouse 9
Churchill's Bar & Pub 9
Element Dance Bar 8
Grannan's Seafood Restaurant 4
Happinez Wine Bar 10
O'Leary's 11
Opera Bistro 7
Reggie's 3
Rocky's Sports Bar 2
Tops Pizza Restaurant 1
Wild Carrot Café 6

City transport

Saint John Transit (Ⓣ506/658-4700, Ⓦwww.saintjohntransit.com) operates a range of bus services; most start and finish downtown at King's Square. East–West buses (#1, #2, #3 or #4) run from King's Square along King Street to the Reversing Falls Rapids, while bus #2 runs on to the Carleton Martello Tower (25min); fares are $2.50 and buses run every fifteen minutes. **Taxis** charge according to a zone system: from downtown to the airport is $28; a trip to the falls is $7.

Accommodation

There's no shortage of **accommodation** in Saint John. Budget motels line up along the main routes into the city, but for something more interesting – and often no more expensive – you're much better off staying in a central hotel or B&B.

Chipman Hill Suites 9 Chipman Hill Ⓣ506/693-1171, Ⓦwww.chipmanhill.com. Centrally located suites in twelve historic properties, all with fully-equipped kitchenettes or kitchens, cable TV and free wi-fi (all buildings have laundries) – a fabulous deal considering the low rates, which can drop to $49. 3

Hilton Saint John Hotel 1 Market Square Ⓣ506/693-8484 or 1-800/561-8282, Ⓦwww.hiltonsaintjohn.com. Most rooms have waterfront views at this plush, modern tower block right beside Market Slip. Location and amenities are top-class, though you'll pay extra for parking ($17/day) and wi-fi ($12.95/day). The airport shuttle is a good deal ($15). 6

Inn on the Cove 1371 Sand Cove Rd Ⓣ506/672-7799 or 1-877/257-8080, Ⓦwww.innonthecove.com. To escape the city centre, aim for this pricey but tranquil modern inn, with its six ornately furnished bedrooms overlooking the Bay of Fundy from the top of a bluff. The food is as inventive as it is mouth-watering, with the emphasis on fresh local ingredients (dinner must be booked at least 24hr in advance). It takes about 10 minutes to drive there from downtown: take Rte 1 west to exit 119A, where you turn off to travel south along Bleury, watching for Sand Cove Rd on the right. 6

Mahogany Manor B&B 220 Germain St at Queen St Ⓣ506/636-8000 or 1-800/796-7755, Ⓦwww.sjnow.com/mm. This is the pick of uptown's B&Bs, with five en-suite guest rooms in an elegant Edwardian villa with high gables and wrapround veranda. Located in a quiet, leafy part of town, a 10-minute walk southeast of Market Slip. 5

Rockwood Park Campground 142 Lake Drive South Ⓣ506/652-4050. Popular campground located near the southern entrance of Rockwood Park, about 2km east of the city centre. Take Exit 125 off Rte 1. From $21 per tent site, and $31 with hook-ups (includes hot showers). May–Sept.

The City

Most of the action in Saint John takes place in the downtown area, known here as **Uptown** – the part of the city across the harbour is dubbed **West Side**. The tiny rectangular dock at the foot of King Street, known as the **Market Slip**, witnessed one of the more dramatic Loyalist migrations, when three thousand refugees disembarked here in 1783. The Slip no longer functions as a port, but it's still at the heart of Saint John and is next to its most entertaining "shop" (really a museum), **Barbour's General Store** (mid-June to mid-Sept daily 9am–6pm; free), an emporium that operated between 1860 and 1940 and now stuffed with Victorian paraphernalia from formidable-looking sweets to an old barber's chair. Close by, the opposite side of the Slip has been gentrified, the former wharf warehouses converted into wine bars, restaurants and boutiques that front the modern Market Square shopping mall behind. Inside the mall, the **New Brunswick Museum** (Mon–Wed & Fri 9am–5pm, Thurs 9am–9pm, Sat 10am–5pm & Sun noon–5pm; Nov to mid May closed Mon; $6; Ⓦwww.nbm-mnb.ca) is devoted to the province's human, natural and artistic life and has a particularly revealing section on its lumber, industrial and shipbuilding traditions as well as a fine collection of Chinese decorative and applied art. There's also much on the region's marine life, including the skeleton of a rare North Atlantic Right whale, and a thirteen-metre-high tidal tube constructed to illustrate the rise and fall of the Bay of Fundy tides.

Loyalist House and City Market

From Market Slip, it's a five-minute walk east on King Street and left along Germain Street to the white wooden **Loyalist House**, at 120 Union St (mid-May to June Mon–Sat 9am–4pm, Sun noon–4pm; July to mid-Sept daily 10am–5pm; $5; ⓣ506/652-3590). Completed in 1817 for merchant David Merritt – who fled colonial New York after the Revolution – the house boasts an attractive Georgian interior and is one of the oldest homes in the city. Thanks to Merritt's ancestors, who lived here until 1958 and never threw anything away, it's kitted out with a remarkable ensemble of original furnishings. Enthusiastic guides bring these pieces to life and provide a good introduction to the Loyalist story (see below); favourites include the disguised water-closet, a clock made in London around 1780 and a bed once slept in by the future Edward VII of England. If you visit in summer you may meet Saint John's mayor here: tradition dictates that the mayor serves tea and biscuits to visitors in the parlour every Wednesday (July & Aug Wed noon–3pm; free).

Just down the hill, back along Germain Street, is the entrance to the lively **City Market** (Mon–Thurs 7.30am–6pm, Fri 7.30am–7pm & Sat 7.30am–5pm), heaped with the characteristic foods of New Brunswick – **fiddleheads**, a succulent fern tip that tastes rather like asparagus, and **dulse**, dried seaweed.

Prince William Street

After the fire of 1877, the city's merchant class funded an ambitious rebuilding programme, epitomized by the brimmingly self-confident structures that grace the **Trinity Royal Historic Preservation Area**, especially along **Prince William Street** south of the Market Slip. Among the predominate red-brick are the grandiose Neoclassical and Second Empire facades of the Old Post Office at no. **115**, the Old City Hall at no. **116**, and the Nova Scotia Bank's Palatine Building at no. **124**.

Reversing Falls Rapids

Like just about everywhere else on the shores of the Bay of Fundy, Saint John is proud of its tides. What you have here are the impressive **Reversing Falls Rapids**,

The Loyalists

The forty thousand **United Empire Loyalists** who streamed north to British Canada in the aftermath of the American War of Independence accounted for a sizeable chunk of the New England population. Many had been subjected to reprisals by their revolutionary neighbours and most arrived virtually penniless. All but eight thousand settled in the Maritime Provinces, where they and their descendants formed the kernel of powerful commercial and political cliques. As a result, the Loyalists have frequently – and not altogether unfairly – been pilloried as arch-conservatives, but in fact they were far from docile royalists: shortly after their arrival in Canada they were pressing the British for their own elective assemblies. Crucially, they were also to instill in their new country an abiding dislike for the American version of republican democracy – and this has remained a key sentiment threading through Canadian history.

Before their enforced exile, the Loyalists conducted a fierce debate with their more radical compatriots, but whereas almost everyone today knows the names of the revolutionary leaders, the Loyalists are forgotten. The Loyalist argument had several strands: loyalty to Britain, fear of war, the righteousness or otherwise of civil obedience and, rather more subliminally, the traditional English Tory belief that men live most freely in a hierarchical society where roles are clearly understood.

created by a sharp bend in the Saint John River about 3km west of the centre. At low tide, the rapids flow quite normally, but the incoming tide forces them into reverse, causing a brief period of equilibrium when the surface of the water is totally calm, before a churning, often tumultuous, surge upstream; the visitor centres post **tide times**. Several vantage points are posted along the river, with **Fallsview Park** the closest to the fiercest cascades (best reached by taxi or car). Another way to reach the falls is by walking the 2km **Harbour Passage** from Market Slip, a pedestrian trail that hugs the river. This ends at a viewing station high above the rapids at the bridge on Rte 100. On the other side of the bridge you'll find more viewing points and two mediocre restaurants, both offering fine views of the gorge below. The first one (*Falls Restaurant*) also houses a **visitor information centre** (mid-May to mid-Oct daily 9am–7pm; ⓣ506/658-2937) that shows a film telescoping a day's tidal flow into fifteen minutes.

Reversing Falls Jet Boat operates "thrill" rides through the Reversing Falls during the summer from their jetty at Fallsview Park (June to Sept 10am till dusk; 20min; ⓣ506/634-8987 or 1-888/634-8987, ⓦwww.jetboatrides.com; $35.95). They also run (dry) **harbour tours** from the same place (or outside the *Hilton* when cruise ships are in town), which take in the falls for $35.35 (1hr).

Carleton Martello Tower

When you've finished with the river, it's another short drive or bus ride west via Rte 100 to the **Carleton Martello Tower** (June to early Oct daily 10am–5.30pm; $3.90) on Fundy Drive: beyond the falls viewing station, take the first left along Lancaster Avenue and follow the signs. The tower was raised in 1815, too late to be of much use in the War of 1812, and later served as a local museum, a detention centre for deserters in World War I and the focal point of the coastal defence system during World War II – hence the ungainly concrete structure plonked on top. The **visitor centre** tells the story of the tower and lays out the historical context, while inside the tower there's a reconstruction of a nineteenth-century barrack room and displays on World War II – plus stellar views over town and bay.

Eating, drinking and nightlife

Saint John is a boisterous, lively place to **eat and drink**, with some of the most enticing food options tucked away in the City Market (p.417), though these are usually closed by 6pm; visit on Saturdays for the most variety. Most of the bars listed below also serve food. Local **Moosehead** beer is served everywhere, though tours of the brewery are no longer given (visit the store instead at 49 Main St West). For **performance arts**, the city's leading venue is the Imperial Theatre, a refurbished Edwardian theatre at 24 King Square South (ⓣ506/674-4100 or 1-800/323-7469, ⓦwww.imperialtheatre.nb.ca).

Restaurants and cafés

Billy's Seafood Company 49–51 Charlotte St, City Market, ⓣ506/672-3474, ⓦwww.billysseafood.com. Facing Charlotte St and also open in the evenings, this market restaurant serves up fine fresh seafood such as lobster club wraps and *mahi-mahi* ($9.95), and there's an excellent oyster bar ($6.95 for six). Mon–Sat 11am–10pm & Sun 4–10pm (closed Sun Jan–March).

Church Street Steakhouse 10 Grannan St, alley off Prince William ⓣ506/648-2373, ⓦwww.grannanhospitalitygroup.com. Best steaks in the city, using prime Angus beef and starting at $21.69 for the 8oz Baseball Sirloin. The New York strip starts at $26.89, while the 16oz T-bone is $41.79 – a serious piece of meat. Mon–Sat 11.30am–11pm, Sun 11.30am–10pm.

Grannan's Seafood Restaurant Level 1, Market Square (on Market Slip) ⓣ506/634-1555. Among the string of pricey bars and cafés on Market Slip this is the best, where the catch of the day is a treat and you get everything from haddock and chips ($8.95) and cajun fish chowder ($8.95), to

Digby scallops ($24) and maple curry chicken pasta ($10.95). Daily 11am–midnight.

Reggie's 26 Germain St ☎506/657-6270. Well-lived-in diner near the city market, opened by Reggie Belliveau (now retired) in 1969, which still serves up superb chowders, all sorts of sandwiches, the signature bagel burger and whopping breakfasts from just $5. Daily 6am–5pm.

Tops Pizza Restaurant 215 Union St, at Sydney ☎506/634-0505. This old school pizza place and local favourite knocks out decent slices but also great lasagna, coleslaw and home-made soups – you can have a filling lunch for under $10. Booths and bar stools. Cash only.

Wild Carrot Café 47 Charlotte St, in City Market ☎506/632-1900, Ⓦwww.wildcarrotcafe.com. Small café stall inside the market knocking out wholesome and vegetarian snacks and light meals; huge variety of soup pots (from $3.32), wraps (from $5) and quiches (from $3.10). Open market hours only (closed Sun).

Bars

Churchill's Bar & Pub 8 Grannan St ☎506/648-2372. Congenial place that offers 24 drafts on tap, tangy martinis and delicious burgers. Daily from 11.30am

Happinez Wine Bar 42 Princess St ☎506/634-7340 Ⓦwww.happinezwinebar.com. To take a break from Saint John's beer-heavy pub scene, try this intimate wine bar, with exposed brick walls and exceptional wine list. Enjoy the compact 'hapito' patio outside in summer. Wed–Thurs 4pm–midnight, Fri 4pm–1am, Sat 5pm–1am.

O'Leary's 46 Princess St ☎506/634-7135, Ⓦwww.olearyspub.com. This local stalwart, an Irish pub with plenty of imported and domestic draught beers, has live music Wed–Sat, mostly folk, Irish or Maritime. Closed Sun.

Rocky's Sports Bar 2/F, Shoppes of City Hall (walk from Market Square) ☎506/652-5452, Ⓦwww.rockyssportsbar.com. This friendly place attracts locals as well as tourists, earning the title 'best sports bar in Canada' in 2009. Over 35 TVs cover all manner of sporting events, and there's plenty of snack food to accompany the beers. Daily 7.30am–1am.

The Fundy Coast east of Saint John

Some of the most alluring portions of New Brunswick's coastline can be found east of Saint John, a wild and mostly untouched region of rugged headlands, crumbling cliffs and dense, fog-bound forests trailing into the sea. The main sights are easily accessed via routes 114 and 195, collectively dubbed the **Fundy Coastal Drive** and ending up at the tidal bore city of **Moncton**.

The Fundy coast is a popular holiday spot in the summer, so it's a good idea to book **accommodation** in advance – most things are closed between November and June. Be prepared for patches of pea-soup fog: the Bay of Fundy is notoriously prone to them. You'll need a car to make the most of the area, as there is **no public transport** to either St Martins or the Fundy National Park.

St Martins and the Fundy Trail Parkway

The fishing village of **ST MARTINS** drizzles along the Bay of Fundy shoreline about 40km to the east of Saint John. To get there from downtown Saint John, take Rte 100 and exit at Loch Lomond Road (Rte 111). St Martins is a pretty ensemble of neat gardens and clapboard houses culminating (after 3km) at the **harbour**, a compact affair of lobster pots and skiffs set within a ring of hills. From here it's 8km east to the **Fundy Trail Parkway** (mid-May to mid-Oct daily 6am-8pm; Ⓦwww.fundytrailparkway.com; $4 per adult), one of the province's most magical destinations. The 13km-drive threads past craggy headlands, dense forest and stupendous viewpoints at almost every turn; you might see moose, porcupines and deer along the way. The road is also shadowed by a multi-use **trail** offering fine and comparatively easy hiking and biking, as well as access to several gorgeous beaches and falls. The parkway ends at the **Big Salmon River Interpretive Centre** (mid-May to mid-Oct daily 8am–8pm; ⓣ506/833-2019), whose exhibits give the historical low-down on the former lumber town of Big Salmon River, whose inhabitants packed up shop in the 1940s. From the centre, you can stroll down the hillside and cross the suspension bridge to the river below or negotiate the steep ninety-minute hike (2.7km) up into the hills to the hunting and fishing **lodge** built here in 1968 by the Hearst family – of newspaper fame and owners of the lumber mill. You can drive a little further from the centre, across the new bridge and up to a final viewpoint, the Cranberry Brook Lookout; the road should extend another 5km by 2010, and by the end of 2013 it will hopefully connect with Fundy National Park (see below), but until then you must return to St Martins to move on.

Practicalities

Accommodation in St Martins includes the first-rate *St Martins Country Inn* (ⓣ506/833-4534 or 1-800/565-5257, ⓦwww.stmartinscountryinn.com; ❹; April–Dec), whose high Victorian gables and fancy gingerbread scrollwork are at 303 Main St, which doubles as Rte 111; the inn has seventeen en-suite rooms decorated in broadly period style. An elegant second bet is the *Quaco Inn* (ⓣ506/833-4772 ⓦwww.quacoinn.com; ❹), a nineteenth-century clapboard property down by the water at 16 Beach St.

For **food**, try *Caves Restaurant* (daily till 7.30pm; ⓣ506/833-4698) at the harbour, justly praised for its seafood-crammed **chowder**, fresh lobster and waterside deck, while the *Coastal Tides Restaurant* (ⓣ506/833-1997) in the village at 7 Beach St, is good for a sit-down meal. On the edge of the village, *St Martin's Ice Cream Parlour* doles out scrumptious home-made ice cream in summer.

Fundy National Park

Bisected by Rte 114, **Fundy National Park** (ⓦwww.pc.gc.ca) encompasses a short stretch of the Bay of Fundy shoreline, all jagged cliffs and tidal mud flats, and the forested hills, lakes and river valleys of the central plateau behind. This varied scenery is crossed by more than 100km of **hiking trails**, mostly short and easy walks taking no more than three hours to complete – though the 45km Fundy Circuit links several of the interior trails and takes between three and five days. The pick of the hiking trails are along the Fundy shore and it's here you'll find the shady **Point Wolfe Beach Trail**, a moderately steep, 600-metre hike down from the spruce woodlands above the bay to the grey-sand beach below (15min). Of equal appeal is the 4.4km loop of the **Coppermine Trail** (1hr 30min–2hr), which meanders through the forests with awe-inspiring views out along the seashore. Serious hikers can walk 41km between the park and the Fundy Trail Parkway (see p.419) via the coastal **Fundy Footpath** (ⓦwww.fundyfootpath.info), accessible from the end of Goose River Path (7.9km; 2hr 30min) from Point Wolfe – most people take four days and camp along the way. Birdlife is more common in the park than larger **wildlife**, though you may see the odd moose, and several precocious raccoons in summer, which have become a real pest – feeding them is illegal.

Arrival and information

All the park's trails are described in a free booklet issued on arrival at either of the two Rte 114 **entrance kiosks** (mid-May to mid-Oct daily 8am–6pm; $7.80; free at other times). One is at the west entrance near Lake Wolfe, about 20km south of Rte 1; the other is about 20km to the east, on the coast next door to Alma. There is a **visitor centre** (daily: mid-May to mid-June & Sept to early Oct 8.15am–4.30pm; mid-June to Aug 8am–10pm; ⓣ506/887-6000) on Rte 114 near the east entrance, which features displays on local flora and fauna, organizes guided walks (June–Aug), issues backcountry permits ($9.80) and sells hiking maps and trail descriptions.

Park accommodation

The park has three **campgrounds**: all offer unserviced campsites ($15.70–25.50), while Chignecto North (mid-May to early Oct) and Headquarters (late June to Aug) offer serviced ($23.50–35.30) sites. Both serviced campgrounds are located near the east entrance (close to Alma) along with most of the park's tourist facilities. Campgrounds operate on a first-come, first-served basis, though reservations are taken (Ⓣ1-877/737-3783, Ⓦwww.pccamping.ca). There are also thirteen backcountry campgrounds ($9.80), which require registration with the visitor centre: you can register on arrival or ring ahead, which is certainly the better option in July and August. For a greater degree of isolation, take the 10km-long byroad southwest from the visitor centre to **Point Wolfe**, where the medium-sized, unserviced campground (late June to Aug) is tucked in among the wooded hills above the coast – and near the starting point of the Point Wolfe Beach and Coppermine trails (see p.420).

If you're after a roof over your head, there are a couple of modern **chalet complexes** just inside the park near the visitor centre. These are *Fundy Park Chalets* (Ⓣ506/887-2808 or 1-877/887-2808, Ⓦwww.fundyparkchalets.com; ④; May–Oct); and the marginally more comfortable, air-conditioned *Fundy Highlands Inn & Chalets* (Ⓣ 506/887-2930 or 1-888/883-8639, Ⓦwww.fundyhighlandchalets.com; ④; May–Oct). In both, the rooms come with kitchenettes. There's more accommodation close by in Alma (see below).

Alma

Just across the Salmon River from the east entrance to the national park, **ALMA** is a sleepy little village whose three hundred inhabitants make a tidy living from fishing, farming and tourism. All of Alma's facilities are clustered on a short stretch of its Main Street, including several **motels** and **hotels**. The pick is the trim *Captain's Inn B&B* (Ⓣ506/887-2017, Ⓦwww.captainsinn.ca; ⑤) with nine cosy rooms in a modern building of traditional design. There is also the clean, bayshore *Alpine Motor Inn* (Ⓣ506/887-2052 or 1-866/887-2052, Ⓦwww.alpinemotorinn.ca; ④; May–Oct); and the two-storey, motel-like *Parkland Village Inn* (Ⓣ506/887-2313 or 1-866/668-4337, Ⓦwww.parklandvillageinn.com; ⑤; April–Nov).

Food in Alma means **lobster**; the village contains three lobster pounds that sell the local Fundy Bay variety – prized for their firm, tasty meat – from large saltwater tanks. Try *Alma Lobster Shop* (mid-May to Sept daily 10am–6pm, Oct–Dec Sat & Sun noon–5pm; Ⓣ506/887-1987) overlooking the seashore, which sells both live and cooked lobsters; buy one to eat on the beach (you can get them to crack the shell open and get bread from the general store on Main St). In 2009 the price dropped to $6.90 per pound (whole lobsters for around $10). Most shops also sell scallops, smoked salmon, oysters and fresh fish. For something sweet, visit *Kelly's Bake Shop* (daily 10am–5pm; Ⓣ506/887-2460), on Main Street, for its enormous, delicious sticky buns and array of tempting cakes. *Fundy Take-Out Restaurant* (May–Oct; Ⓣ506/887-2261) near the river, is a no-frills shack that knocks out burgers, fried breaded clams and lobster rolls you can eat on picnic tables with *poutine*, while the best place for a sit-down meal is the *Tides Restaurant* (May–Oct) inside the *Parkland Village Inn* – their lobster chowder is a worthy house special and the views of the bay are fabulous.

Cape Enrage

From Alma, Rte 915 branches off Rte 114 to stick close to the coast, threading over the hills and along the valley past isolated farmsteads sheltering behind rugged sea-cliffs. The most dramatic scenery is at **Cape Enrage** (mid-May to early

▲ Lighthouse sign at Cape Enrage

Sept daily 8.30am–8pm; donation $4/person or $10/car; lighthouse tours $5), 6.5km down a side road off Rte 915, where the original 1848 lighthouse is glued to a great shank of rock soaring high above the sea. When the lighthouse was automated in 1988, the keepers moved away, and a Moncton schoolteacher initiated an ambitious plan to protect and develop the site with the enthusiastic help of his students. There's now a wooden walkway up to the foot of the lighthouse, a path down to the beach and the old keepers' house has been converted into a pleasant café (try the fish chowder). Students staff the cape from May to September and help run a programme of **adventure sports**, principally rappelling and climbing (2hr; $54). **Mountain bike** rentals are $8 per hour or $30 per day. In all cases, book ahead (ⓣ506/887-2273 or 1-888/280-7273, ⓦwww.capenrage.com). Though the facilities are locked up from October to April, you can usually still wander around the site.

Hopewell Rocks

The captivating shoreline of Hopewell Cape, where the Petitcodiac River flows into the bay some 35km northeast of Cape Engrage, is contained within the privately-managed **Hopewell Rocks park** (daily: mid-May to late June & early Sept to early Oct 9am–5pm; late June to late Aug 8am–8pm; late Aug to early Sept 8am–6pm; $8.50; ⓦwww.thehopewellrocks.ca), named for the gnarled red-sandstone pinnacles rising up to 15m above the beach. The interpretive centre at the park's upper section explains the cape's geology and the marine complexities of the Bay of Fundy, but you'll soon be wandering down the 828m footpath to the lower section – past several vantage points – and the primary formation, known as the flowerpot rocks (the shuttle bus is $1.50). The rocks were pushed away from the cliff face by glacial pressure during the Ice Age, and the Bay of Fundy tides have defined their present, eccentric shape. At high tide they resemble stark little islands covered in fir trees, but at low tide they look like enormous termite hills. Steps lead down to the beach and you can safely walk round the rocks two to three hours either side of low tide, or you can paddle round them at high tide by **renting a kayak** (June–Aug; $55; ⓣ1-877/601-2660, ⓦwww.baymountadventures.com). Your ticket is valid for two days to ensure you see both tides. You can still wander around the site when the park is officially closed, but at your own risk. From the Hopewell Rocks, it's 50km along the west bank of the Petitcodiac River to Moncton.

Moncton

The Petitcodiac River provides **MONCTON** with its most singular attraction, **the tidal bore**, which sweeps up from the Bay of Fundy, 35km downstream. Otherwise, Moncton is a booming but unremarkable commercial centre and transport junction surrounded by marshy flatlands – Greater Moncton is almost the same size as Saint John. This may sound unpromising, but the downtown area contains enough enticing restaurants, bars and hotels to make an overnight stay enjoyable, and the town is a convenient stop on the journey between Fundy National Park and PEI. Moncton's rejuvenation partly reflects the increasing confidence of local Acadians: the town hosts the province's only French-speaking university and is proud of its **bilingualism** – the result of Acadian ex-deportees settling here in the 1790s.

Arrival and information

Parking ($1–1.50/hr) is easy to find in downtown Moncton, with lots signposted along Main Street. **Greater Moncton International Airport** (ⓦwww.gmia.ca) is located 10km east of downtown near Dieppe, and hosts a surprising number of flights from Montréal and Toronto (via Air Canada and WestJet), and even Newark, USA (via Continental). Avis, Budget, Hertz and National have **car rental** desks at the airport; the only other way to get into town is to take a **taxi** (around $20; ⓣ506/857-2000).

Moncton **bus station** is on the west side of the town centre – about 1km west of Bore View Park – at 961 Main St. **Acadian Lines buses** (see p.361) arrive here from most major settlements in New Brunswick and twice or three times daily from PEI's Charlottetown; there are also buses to and from Halifax in Nova Scotia. Moncton's **train station** is nearby – behind the shopping mall, a couple of blocks further west along Main Street – with services running to Halifax and Montréal. Moncton's **tourist office** is inside the historic **Treitz Haus** in Bore View Park (daily: mid-May to early June & Sept 8.30am–4.30pm, early June to Aug 9am–7pm, Sept & Oct Sat & Sun 9am–5pm; ⓣ506/853-3590, ⓦwww.tourism.moncton.ca).

Accommodation

Moncton has a healthy supply of convenient downtown **accommodation**, while the cheaper motels line Mountain Road on the way to Magnetic Hill. Alternatively, several pleasant **B&Bs** are dotted among the leafy residential avenues to the north of Main Street.

Bonaccord House B&B 250 Bonaccord St at John St ⓣ506/388-1535, ⓦwww.bbcanada.com/4135.html. The pick of the B&Bs in town is this four-room late Victorian villa, north of the bus station, with trim picket fence and afternoon tea served on the veranda. ❷

C'mon Inn Hostel 47 Fleet St ⓣ506/854-8155, ⓦwww.monctonhostel.ca. Great budget option in a grand old house two blocks from the bus station with dorm beds from $24, as well as simple doubles and single rooms (shared bathrooms). Shared kitchen. ❶

Delta Beauséjour 750 Main St ⓣ506/854-4344 or 1-800/268-1133, ⓦwww.deltahotels.com. The most lavish hotel in town is this vast modern high-rise close to the centre, offering luxury rooms and all the extras. Parking $12.50, free internet. ⑥

L'Hotel St James 14 Church St ⓣ1-888/782-1414, ⓦwww.hotelstjames.ca. Boutique hotel with hardwood floors, flat-screen TVs, iPod docks, DVDs and full-length glass between bathroom and bed, right in the centre of town. It's definitely the coolest place to stay in Moncton, but the pub below can get noisy and the breakfast (included) is rather basic. ⑥

The Town

Moncton's premier attraction is the **tidal bore** (see Nova Scotia p.388), though at low tide you'll be in no doubt as to why the locals called the Petitcodiac the "chocolate river". The mud flats disappear after the bore arrives and the river level rises by up to 8m, a phenomenon best observed from tiny **Bore View Park**, just east of downtown at Main and King streets; you cannot **park** here – all the spaces are reserved for the adjacent police station.

The town's other oddity is **Magnetic Hill** (mid-May to mid-Sept daily 8am–8pm; $5; ⓦwww.magnetichill.com), an extraordinarily popular motorized attraction where your car appears to travel uphill when it is in neutral along an otherwise ordinary bit of road. You drive to what appears to be the bottom of the hill, put your vehicle in neutral and then coast backwards, apparently uphill – which is really rather weird. Magnetic Hill is located just off the Trans-Canada Hwy (Exit 450) about 9km northwest of downtown, and surrounded by a touristy "Wharf Village", zoo, water park and other kitschy attractions aimed at families.

Eating, drinking and entertainment

Moncton has plenty of choices when it comes to **food,** and **bars** throng the centre. The **Marché Moncton Market Complex** at 120 Westmoreland St, just off Main Street, also contains several tempting snack stalls (Sat 7am–2pm; *Shangrilla* and *Happy Wok* stalls also open Wed–Fri 11am–3pm; ⓦwww.marchemonctonmarket.ca). Both Theatre New Brunswick (ⓦwww.tnb.nb.ca) and the Symphony New Brunswick (ⓦwww.symphonynb.com) orchestra perform at the **Capitol Theatre**, 811 Main St (ⓣ506/856-4379 or 1-800/567-1922, ⓦwww.capitol.nb.ca).

Bars and restaurants

Le Château à Pape 2 Steadman St ⓣ506/855-7273, ⓦwww.lechateauapape.ca. Best place for a splurge, serving the finest Acadian cuisine from its premises in a gorgeous old house on the edge of Bore View Park; mains start at $18. Daily from 4pm.

Graffiti 897 Main St ⓣ506/382-4299. Specializes in moderately priced Mediterranean food, from Greek classics to pizza in a romantic, dimly it setting.

Jean's Restaurant 369 St George St ⓣ506/855-1053. No frills diner located about three blocks north of Main St at Weldon St (west of downtown), worth the trip for its clams alone ($10.99), not to mention its 1950s booths. Free parking on site.

Old Triangle Irish Alehouse 751 Main St ⓣ506/384-7474, ⓦwww.oldtriangle.com. Irish-themed pub food ($10–12) and plenty of live music (folk and Irish) accompany those fine pints of Guinness ($6.64) in this sister pub of the Halifax stalwart.

Pump House Brewery 7 Orange Lane, just off Main St (a few metres east of Bank of Montréal), ⓣ506/855-2337 ⓦwww.pumphousebrewery.ca. Popular brewpub that crafts some excellent seasonal beers; if the lauded blueberry ale is too fruity, try the hoppy harvest beers ($5.25). Pitchers are $13.75. The pub food is pretty good too.

Around Moncton: Fort Beauséjour

Providing panoramic views over the broad sweep of Chignecto Bay, **Fort Beauséjour National Historic Site** (June to mid-Oct daily 9am–5pm; $3.90) is stuck on a grassy, treeless hill about 50km south of Moncton and just 2km from the junction of Trans-Canada routes 2 and 16. The fort stands on the isthmus connecting New Brunswick and Nova Scotia and its strategic value was first recognized by the

French, who fortified the site in 1751. Four years later, the British captured the fort and promptly deported the local Acadians, who they thought might rebel. The British garrison stayed on until 1835 as a defence against the Americans.

Flush with the brow of the hill, the **remains** of the star-shaped fort include much of the original earthwork, the concentric ditches and mounds typical of the period, as well as a sally port and a couple of deeply recessed casements, used for general storage. The site also has a **museum** with intriguing displays on the history of the fort and of the Acadian farmers who settled the region in the 1670s. Some of the most interesting exhibits, like ancient clogs and farm tools, were recovered when the fort was repaired and restored in the 1960s. From Fort Beauséjour, it's just a few kilometres south to central Nova Scotia (see p.388) and about 50km east to the Confederation Bridge over to PEI (see p.430).

The Acadian Coast

From Moncton, Rte 11 cuts across to the Northumberland Strait at **Shediac**, the province's lobster capital, before heading north along what's been dubbed the **Acadian Coast** all the way to Miramichi (p.426). Settled in the years after the deportations of the 1750s, the string of pretty villages here are all French-speaking and proud of their Acadian roots. Highlights include **Le Pays de la Sagouine** (late June to late Aug daily 9.30am–5.30pm; $15.50; Ⓣ1-800/561-9188, Ⓦwww.sagouine.com), a sort of Acadian fantasy village set on the l'Île-aux-Puces in **BOUCTOUCHE**, 35km north of Shediac. Conceived by acclaimed Acadian writer Antonine Maillet (the name comes from her 1971 novel *La Sagouine*) and opened in 1992, costumed actors show off traditional Acadian crafts, cuisine and trades such as fishing, all enhanced with humorous tales and period costume. Actors also take part in musical performances throughout the day: the excellent dinner theatre is an additional $51. You have to speak at least some French to make the most of this, but there are daily tours in English at 10am and 2.30pm.

It's also worth checking out the **Irving Eco-Centre, La Dune de Bouctouche** (May–Oct Mon–Fri noon–5pm, Sat & Sun 10am–5pm; interpretation centre open daily 10am–7pm July & Aug; free, Ⓣ1-888/640-3300, Ⓦwww.irvingecocenter.com), along a 12km stretch of sparkling white sands off Rte 475, just north of the village, where you can view giant dunes from a 2km boardwalk and learn more about the ecology of the area. If you need somewhere to **stay**, try the modern and motel-like *Auberge Bouctouche* (Ⓣ506/743-5003, Ⓦwww.aubergebouctoucheinn.ca; ⑤) at 50 Industrielle St in the centre of the village.

Kouchibouguac National Park

Around 46km north of Bouctouche, Rte 11 skirts the coastal forests, salt marshes, lagoons and sandy beaches of the **Kouchibouguac** ("Koo-she-boo-gwack") **National Park**. Near the park's main **entrance** (mid-June to early Sept $7.80, April to mid-June & early Sept to Nov $3.90; free at other times) is the **visitor centre** (mid-May to early June & Sept to mid-Oct daily 9am–5pm; early June to Aug 8am–8pm; Ⓣ506/876-2443), where displays explore the area's complex ecology. From here, it's a few kilometres' drive to the sandy expanse of **Kellys Beach** – the park's main attraction, and there are several enjoyable **hiking trails** nearby, ranging from 1km to the 13km-long **Kouchibouguac River Trail**, which wriggles west along the riverbank (allow at least six hours).

The park has one fully serviced **campground**, *South Kouchibouguac* (mid-May to mid-Oct; $21.50–32.30), and one unserviced campground, *Cote-à-Fabien* (early June to early Sept; $15.70). Reservations (ⓣ1-877/737-3783, ⓦwww.pccamping.ca) are advised for South Kouchibouguac, but Cote-à-Fabien is first-come, first-served. If you're not camping, the park is easily visited on a day-trip from Miramichi (see p.426), or you can stay in one of the settlements nearby.

The Miramichi Valley

Running northeast from Fredericton, Rte 8 traverses the **Miramichi River Valley**, passing endless stands of timber en route to the **City of Miramichi**, an amalgamation of six tiny logging ports that flank the mouth of the river, and now home to a modest collection of engaging historic sites.

Doaktown

The 180-kilometre trip to Miramichi takes three to four hours from Fredericton, longer if you pause at **DOAKTOWN**, a favourite spot for **salmon fishing**. The season runs roughly between April and July, depending on the waters to be fished, and every angler has to buy a licence ($29–105). A raft of regulations controls the sport (there are seventeen different types of licence) but any local tourist office will have the details. The **Atlantic Salmon Museum** (mid-April to May Mon–Fri 9am–5pm; June to mid-Oct daily 9am–5pm; $5; ⓣ506/365-7787, ⓦwww.atlanticsalmonmuseum.com), beside Rte 8, illustrates the salmon's arduous life cycle, has a small aquarium and looks at different fishing techniques – but you're better off having a go at fishing yourself; ask at the museum for information on the town's numerous outfitters and guides.

Miramichi City: Newcastle and Nelson

Now incorporated within sprawling **MIRAMICHI CITY**, the old shipbuilding centre of **NEWCASTLE** (Miramichi West) sits on the north bank of the Miramichi River as it nears the sea. The principal attractions lie on **Beaubears Island** (mid-May to June & Sept to mid-Oct Mon–Sat 10am–4pm, Sun noon–4pm; July & Aug daily 10am–8pm; guided tours only) in the middle of the river, where the poignant **Boishébert National Historic Site** tells the story of the Acadians that fled here in 1755, and the **Beaubears Island Shipbuilding National Historic Site** preserves the fascinating remains of a nineteenth-century wooden shipbuilding yard. Start at the interpretive centre (same hours; $5) across the river from Newcastle, at 35 St Patrick's Drive in **NELSON-MIRAMICHI**, where you can pick up boat tours of the island ($15–25, includes centre admission).

It's also worth driving out to the beautifully designed **Metepenagiag Heritage Park** (May–Oct daily 9am–5pm; $8; ⓣ506/836-6118, ⓦwww.metepenagiagpark.com) in Red Bank, 28km upriver via routes 425 and 420, where the local Mi'kmaq tribe enthusiastically showcases their culture and history through thought-provoking multimedia presentations, interpretive trails, song, dance, art and displays of rare archeological finds from two nearby historic sites.

Newcastle makes a good base for the **Miramichi Folksong Festival** (ⓣ506/622-1780, ⓦwww.miramichifolksongfestival.com), held over five days in early August and generally reckoned to be one of the best of its kind, with fiddle music its forte. For gig details go to the **visitor centre** in **CHATHAM** (Miramichi East), 199 King St (late June to Aug daily 9am–9pm; ⓣ506/778-8444, ⓦwww.miramichi.org).

Practicalities

Places to stay in Newcastle include the modern, motel-like *Park Inn* (Ⓣ506/622-0302 or 1-800/285-9260, Ⓦwww.parkinn.com/miramichinb; ❹), near the bridge at 1 Jane St, and the *Canada's Best Value Inn & Suites* (Ⓣ506/622-1215 or 1-888/315-2378, Ⓦwww.canadasbestvalueinn.com; ❺), at 201 Edward St. Alternatively, the *Governor's Mansion B&B* (Ⓣ506/622-3036 or 1-877/647-2642, Ⓦwww.governorsmansion.ca; ❸), at 62 St Patrick's Drive in Nelson, occupies a handsome Victorian villa that was once the Lieutenant-Governor's residence. The mansion is graced by antique furnishings and holds eight guest rooms on the two upper floors; there are four additional rooms in a second old house, *Beaubear Manor*.

The Acadian Peninsula

The **Acadian Peninsula**, which protrudes some 130km into the Gulf of St Lawrence in the northeast corner of New Brunswick, is another part of the province where Acadians escaped the deportations (see p.387), and more than anywhere else in the Maritimes this is where they have maintained their traditional way of life. Many locals are still reliant on fishing and marshland farming, though frankly there's precious little to see and the best place to get a sense of the region's roots is **Caraquet**, on the north shore, home to the replica **Village Historique Acadien**. There are no **buses** along the peninsula.

Caraquet

Heading east from the mining town of **BATHURST**, Rte 11 bobs along the Acadian Peninsula's northern shore, trimming the edge of rolling countryside before reaching, after about 50km, the district's pride and joy, the **Village Historique Acadien** (June to early Sept daily 10am–6pm; $15.50; Ⓦwww.villagehistoriqueacadien.com). This holds around forty old Acadian buildings relocated from other parts of New Brunswick – only the church was built specifically for the village. Costumed actors emphasize the struggles of the early settlers and demonstrate traditional agricultural techniques as well as old methods of spinning, cooking and so on – all in an attractive rustic setting.

From the historic village, it's a further 16km east on Rte 11 to **CARAQUET**, a fishing port founded by Acadian fugitives in 1758. It now straggles along the seafront for some 13km and may not be much to look at, but it does have the **Le Musée Acadien de Caraquet** (May, June & early Sept Mon–Fri 10am–6pm; July & Aug Mon–Sat 10am–8pm & Sun 1–6pm; $3; Ⓣ506/726-2682, Ⓦwww.museecaraquet.ca), at 15 Blvd St-Pierre East (also Rte 145), which chronicles the life and times of the early settlers and has a small gallery devoted to the work of local artists (French labels only). At the west end of town, there's also the shrine of **Ste-Anne-de-Bocage** built to commemorate the founding families' trials and tribulations. Caraquet is the setting for the region's most important **Acadian Festival** (Ⓣ506/727-2787, Ⓦwww.festivalacadien.ca), a two-week programme of music and theatre held in early August, which begins with the blessing of the fishing fleet by a local bishop.

Among a bevy of Caraquet **accommodation** options, the pick is the *Hotel Paulin* (Ⓣ506/727-9981 or 1-866/727-9981, Ⓦwww.hotelpaulin.com; ❼), at 143 Blvd St-Pierre West, a smart and comfortable, family-operated inn with eight guest rooms in an attractive Victorian building. The **restaurant** here is first-rate, featuring traditional Acadian cuisine. Cheaper rooms are on offer at *Le Pignon Rouge*, a B&B in a nineteenth-century timber house at 338 Blvd St-Pierre East (Ⓣ506/727-5983, Ⓦwww.lepignonrouge.com; ❹; June–Sept).

Prince Edward Island

The freckly face and pert pigtails of Anne of Green Gables are emblazoned on much of **PRINCE EDWARD ISLAND**'s publicity material, and her creator, local-born novelist Lucy Maud Montgomery, was the island's most gushing propagandist, depicting the place floating "on the waves of the blue gulf, a green seclusion and haunt of ancient peace". Even today, Canada's smallest province remains thoroughly agricultural, with Islanders remarkably successful in controlling the pace of change. Fish and lobsters are still sold off fishing boats, doors remain unlocked and everyone seems to know everyone else; laws ban large billboards and there are no freeways. The French settled the what they called **Île-St-Jean** in the 1720s, but the British turned them out in the 1760s and renamed the island in 1799.

Charlottetown, the graceful capital, sits on the south coast, its tree-lined streets, wide range of accommodation and fine restaurants making it the best **base** for exploring the island. On the north coast, **Prince Edward Island National Park** is the island's busiest tourist attraction, with kilometres of magnificent sandy beach and a bewildering number of sights associated with **Anne of Green Gables**. PEI also has a growing reputation for **cuisine**; the island is home to organic farms, fine oysters, mussels and artisan producers of all kinds, from potato vodka and gouda cheese, to ice cream and home-made pickles. It remains best-known for the excellence of its **lobsters**, which are trapped during May and June and again in late August and September; the catch is kept fresh in salt-water tanks to supply the peak tourist season (this careful management is one of the reasons the lobster population is flourishing). Look out for posters advertising **lobster suppers**, inexpensive set meals served in several church and community halls during the lobster season.

▲ Lobster fisherman, Prince Edward Island

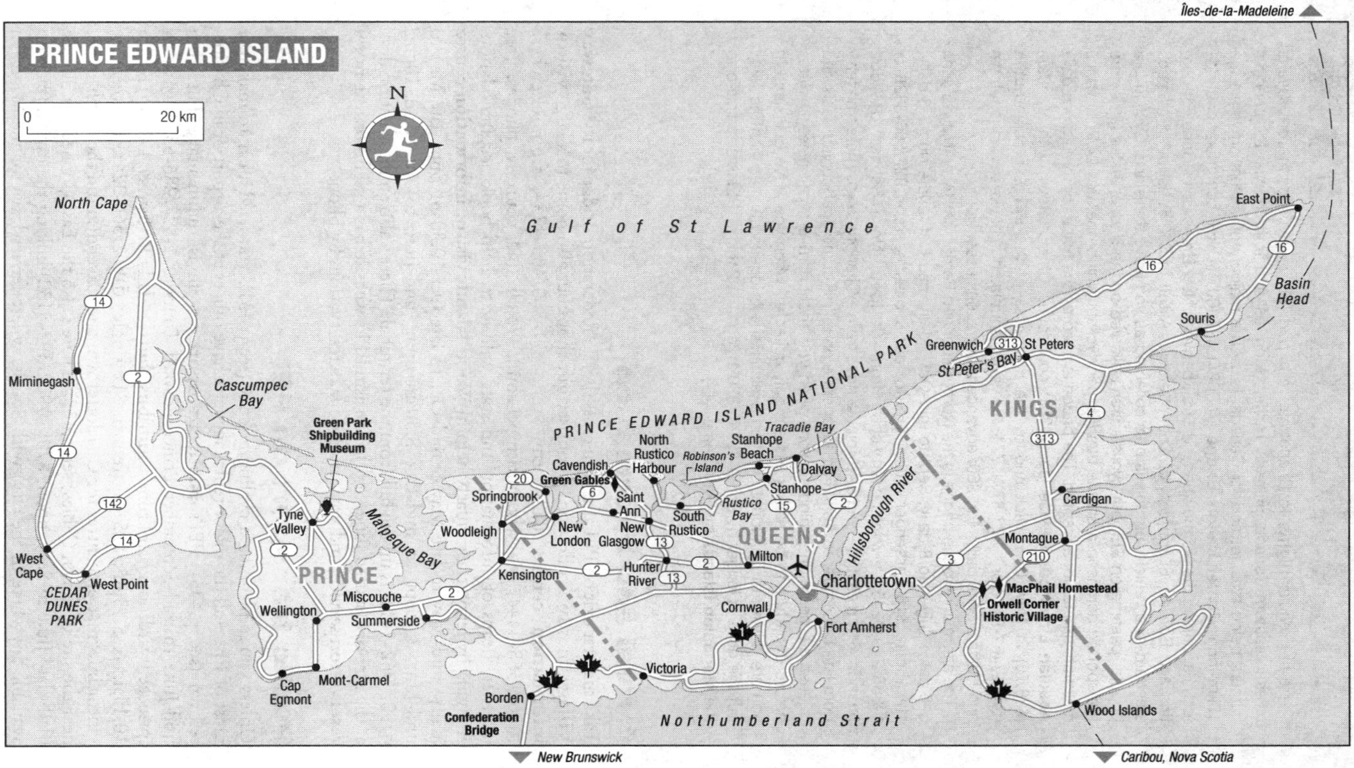

PRINCE EDWARD ISLAND
0
20 km
N
Îles-de-la-Madeleine
Gulf of St Lawrence
North Cape
Miminegash
West Cape
CEDAR DUNES PARK
West Point
Cascumpec Bay
Green Park Shipbuilding Museum
Tyne Valley
Malpeque Bay
PRINCE
Wellington
Miscouche
Summerside
Cap Egmont
Mont-Carmel
Woodleigh
Springbrook
Kensington
Borden
Confederation Bridge
PRINCE EDWARD ISLAND NATIONAL PARK
Cavendish
Green Gables
North Rustico Harbour
Robinson's Island
Saint Ann
New London
New Glasgow
Hunter River
South Rustico
Rustico Bay
Stanhope Beach
Stanhope
Tracadie Bay
Dalvay
QUEENS
Milton
Charlottetown
Hillsborough River
Cornwall
Fort Amherst
Victoria
Northumberland Strait
Greenwich
St Peters
St Peter's Bay
KINGS
Cardigan
Montague
MacPhail Homestead
Orwell Corner Historic Village
Wood Islands
Souris
East Point
Basin Head
New Brunswick
Caribou, Nova Scotia
1
2
3
4
6
13
14
15
16
20
142
210
313

Getting to PEI

There are regular **flights** to Charlottetown airport (Ⓦwww.flypei.com) from several cities in eastern Canada, primarily Halifax, Montréal and Toronto, with the principal carriers being WestJet and Air Canada Jazz. The majority of visitors arrive via the 13km-long **Confederation Bridge** (Ⓣ902/437-7300, Ⓦwww.confederationbridge.com) spanning the Northumberland Strait between New Brunswick's Cape Tormentine and Borden, 60km west of Charlottetown. A **toll** of $42.50 is levied on each standard-size vehicle, but this is only collected as you leave the island. Cycling is a popular pastime on PEI, but cyclists aren't allowed on the bridge; instead, they are transported across in a shuttle bus ($8 per cyclist), which operates 24/7; advance reservations are not accepted. The bridge is used by the twice- or three times daily **Acadian Lines bus** service (see p.361) connecting Charlottetown with Moncton ($36.75) in New Brunswick and by the minibuses of the **PEI Express Shuttle** (Ⓣ902/462-8177 or 1-877/877-1771, Ⓦwww.peishuttle.com) between Charlottetown and Halifax (once daily; 4hr; $60; advance reservations essential).

The alternative to the bridge is the Northumberland Ferries **car ferry** (May to June 5–6 daily; July–Aug 8 daily; Sept to mid-Oct 6 daily; mid-Oct to late Dec 3–5 daily; 1hr 15min; $16 passenger return, $63 for car & passengers; Ⓣ902/566-3838 or 1-888/249-7245, Ⓦwww.peiferry.com) from **Caribou**, Nova Scotia, to **Wood Islands**, 61km east of – and a 45-minute drive from – Charlottetown. There's no ferry from late December to April. Ferries operate on a first-come, first-served basis and queues are common in high season, when you should arrive about ninety minutes before departure to be safe; fares are only collected when you leave the island. If you are driving to Charlottetown from Halifax, the bridge is quicker than the ferry, but the drive is longer by about 80km (320km against 240km). PEI is also linked to the **Magdalen Islands** by ferry (see p.441).

Arrival and Information

Take the first exit on PEI after you cross the Confederation Bridge for the **Gateway Village**, mostly a collection of touristy gift shops but also home to a large **visitor information centre** (daily 9am–9pm; Ⓣ1-800/463-4734, from elsewhere Ⓣ902/368-4444, Ⓦwww.tourismpei.com). You'll find courtesy phones, free internet, heaps of information and staff willing to help book accommodation. Arriving by ferry, the similarly helpful **Wood Islands visitor information centre** (daily: mid-May to late May & mid-Oct to late Oct 10.30am–6pm, late May to mid-June & Sept to mid-Oct 8.30am–6pm, mid-June to Aug 8am–10pm; Ⓣ902/962-7411) is up the hill from the terminal. There's also an information desk at the **airport** (staffed June–Sept). Tourism PEI's website has a useful **online hotel reservation** service, and you can also make reservations by phone.

Public transport on PEI

Unless you're planning a cycling holiday (see p.431), you need a **car** to make the most of PEI – all the major rental agencies have offices at the airport or in Charlottetown (see p.435). PEI's **public transport** system is rudimentary, but from mid-June to mid-September Prince Edward Tours (Ⓣ1-877/286-6532, Ⓦwww.princeedwardtours.com) runs a **minibus shuttle** (daily 9.15am & 4.15pm, return 10.15am & 5.15pm; $25 day return, $15 single; Ⓣ902/566-3243) between the visitor information centres for Charlottetown and Cavendish (on the north shore, near the site of Green Gables; see p.438). There's also the East Connection Shuttle (daily late June to Sept, noon; $70; Ⓣ902/393-5132) linking the capital (pick up available anywhere in the city) with Souris, where ferries leave for the Magdalen

Cycling and hiking the Confederation Trail

Prince Edward Island's quiet roads and gentle terrain make it a great place for **cycling**, but although there are several **cycle-tour operators**, it's much less expensive (and entirely straightforward) to plan your own route: in Charlottetown, both Smooth Cycle (Ⓣ902/566-5530 or 1-800/310-6550, Ⓦwww.smoothcycle.com; $24.99/day; closed Sun), 330 University Ave, and MacQueen's (Ⓣ902/368-2453 or 1-800/969-2822, Ⓦwww.macqueens.com; $25/day), 430 Queen St, rent out all the necessary gear and will advise on trails. The most popular of these is the 279km **Confederation Trail** (Ⓦwww.tourismpei.com/pei-confederation-trail), a combined **hiking** and **cycling trail** that weaves its way across the bucolic heart of the island from east to west, partly following the route of PEI's old railway, which was closed in the 1980s. You won't see much of the coast from the trail, but you won't see any cars either, and it's a wonderful way to take in the idyllic countryside.

Islands. Trius Transit (Ⓣ902/566-9962, Ⓦwww.triustransit.ca) runs buses between Charlottetown and Summerside (Mon–Fri 6.43am, 7.50am, 2.40pm & 4.25pm; $7) from the Confederation Centre. Several Charlottetown companies operate **sightseeing tours**; try Abegweit (Ⓣ902/894-9966, Ⓦwww.abegweittours.ca), 157 Nassau St, which offers tours of the northern shore (daily 10.30am; $80; full day), Anne of Green Gables sights (daily 10.30am; $65; 7hr) and Charlottetown (7 daily; $11; 1hr).

Charlottetown

Pocket-sized **CHARLOTTETOWN**, the administrative and business heart of PEI since the 1760s, is the most urbane spot on the island, the comfortable streets of its centre hemmed in by leafy avenues of clapboard villas and Victorian red-brick buildings. In small-island terms, it also offers a reasonable **nightlife**, with a handful of excellent restaurants and a clutch of lively bars, though the best time to be here is in the summer, when the otherwise sleepy town centre is transformed by festivals, live music and street cafés.

Arrival and information

Tiny Charlottetown **airport** is 8km north of town; the **taxi** fare into the centre is fixed at $12 (with an additional $3 per additional person). Other locations are charged at $1.60 per km, with a $6 surcharge. Acadian Lines **buses** (p.361) from Moncton via the Confederation Bridge arrive and depart from an inconvenient depot 3km north of downtown out along Longworth Avenue/Mount Edward Road, at 156 Belvedere Ave. **Parking** in town is usually easy in one of several parkades or lots ($1/hr, max $6), or by meter (Mon–Fri 8am–6pm; $0.25/30min). **City buses** zip around town ($2; Ⓣ902/566-9962, Ⓦwww.triustransit.ca), though you probably won't need to use them, while **taxis** follow a zone system (no meters), with most journeys in downtown $6.

PEI's main **visitor information centre** (mid-May to mid-June & mid-Sept to early Oct daily 9am–6pm; mid-June to mid-Sept daily 9am–7pm; early Oct to Nov & Feb to mid-May Mon–Fri 10am–4pm; Ⓣ902/368-4444), on the harbourfront in the same building as Founders' Hall (see p.434), is a couple of minutes' walk from the town centre at the foot of Prince Street. The local daily **newspaper**, *The Guardian* (Ⓦwww.theguardian.pe.ca), makes for an enjoyable

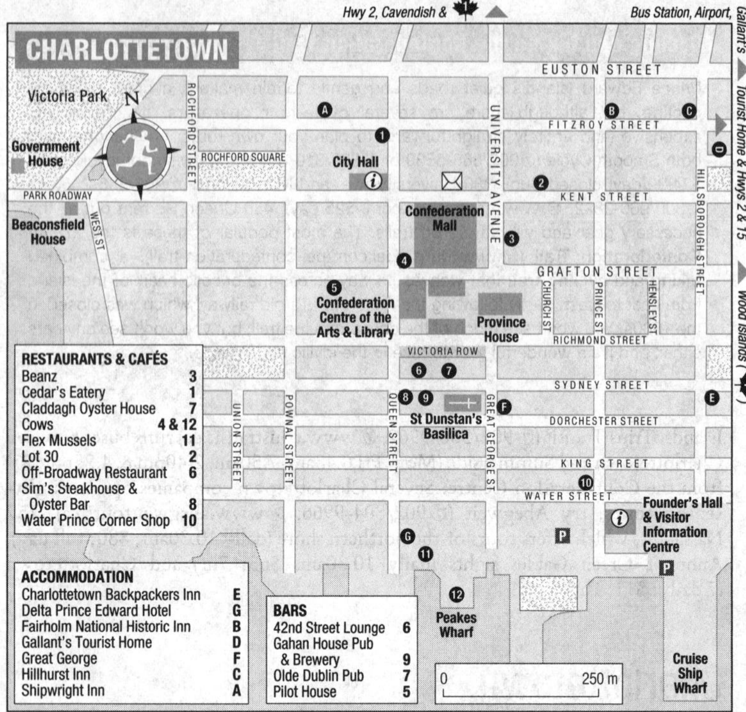

read, and there's a good quality, free monthly entertainment **listings magazine**, *The Buzz* (Ⓦ www.buzzon.com).

Accommodation

Charlottetown has a wide range of **accommodation** and things only get tight in the height of the summer season. There are plenty of chain **motels** on the outskirts of town (Rte 1), but to get the flavour of the place, try staying in the oldest part of the city – between Fitzroy Street and the waterfront. Options here include several reasonably priced **inns** and **B&Bs**, as well as a smattering of **hotels**. At the other end of the market there is one backpackers **hostel**.

Charlottetown Backpackers Inn 60 Hillsborough St Ⓣ902/367-5749, Ⓦwww.charlottetownbackpackers.com. Excellent HI-affiliated hostel with dorms ($28, $32 nonmembers) and a few cheap private rooms (3) in a renovated, three-storey house. There's a pool table, free internet, free parking and breakfast included, right in the heart of downtown.

Delta Prince Edward Hotel 18 Queen St Ⓣ902/566-2222 or 1-877/814-7706, Ⓦwww.deltahotels.com. Charlottetown's plushest chain hotel, in a high-rise overlooking the harbour; luxurious rooms with superb facilities including pool and health centre. 7

Fairholm National Historic Inn 230 Prince St Ⓣ902/892-5022 or 1-888/573-5022, Ⓦwww.fairholminn.com. A fine example of mid-nineteenth century architecture, this inn, with its elegant red-brick exterior, doubles up as a designated National Historic Site. The interior is appropriately plush with seven capacious guest rooms kitted out in period style and all with open fireplaces. 7

Gallant's Tourist Home 196 Kensington Rd Ⓣ902/892-3030 Ⓦwww3.islandtelecom.com/st.clair.gallant. This cosy budget option is more like a homestay than hotel, with affable hosts and hostel-like prices for private rooms with TV and shared bath. Meals are provided if required, family-style around the same table. It's a bit of a hike (or bus ride) from downtown. 1

The Great George 58 Great George St ☎902/892-0606 or 1-800/361-1118, ⓦwww.thegreatgeorge.com. Bang in the centre of town, opposite St Dunstan's, a row of fifteen old timber houses has been carefully renovated to hold this immaculate and atmospheric hotel. All the rooms are comfortable and tastefully decorated – the most appealing overlook the church. A continental breakfast is included. 7

Hillhurst Inn 181 Fitzroy St, at Hillsborough ☎902/894-8004 or 1-877/994-8004, ⓦwww.hillhurst.com. Classily renovated Georgian Revival mansion with finely carved interior. Nine large, en-suite guest rooms, each with ornate antique furnishings and two with whirlpools. It is open year-round, but by advance reservation only from Dec–April. Breakfast included. 6

Shipwright Inn 51 Fitzroy St ☎902/368-1905 or 1-888/306-9966, ⓦwww.shipwrightinn.com. Crammed with antiques, this rambling 1865 timber mansion (with a more recent extension) has nine individually decorated guest rooms managed by a couple of affable British expats. Very appealing – especially with its thoughtful additions (like popcorn, afternoon tea and muffins, videos and CDs), and its superlative breakfasts. 6

The Town

The island's most significant historical attraction is the **Province House National Historic Site** (June to early Oct daily 8.30am–5pm; early Oct to May Mon–Fri 9am–5pm; free), which sits right at the heart of Charlottetown, at the foot of University Avenue. A squat, Neoclassical structure completed in 1847 to house all three branches of the provincial government, its primary tenant today is the unicameral legislature. Yet its real claim to fame is as the location for the first meeting of the **Fathers of Confederation** in 1864, when representatives of Nova Scotia, New Brunswick, then-Canada (Ontario and Québec) and PEI met to discuss a union of the British colonies in North America. It took two more conferences before confederation was finally achieved in 1867, though PEI didn't join for a further six years, and only then because it was bankrupt after an ill-advised splurge on railway construction. On the ground floor, a seventeen-minute film provides a melodramatic account of that original meeting, after which tour guides introduce some of its restored nineteenth-century halls, including the reverentially preserved Confederation Chamber on the second floor. You can usually peek inside the Legislative Chamber, or if it's in session, walk up to the viewing gallery on the third floor to witness the vigorous but invariably polite debates within.

Next door, the **Confederation Centre of the Arts** (daily 9am–5pm, June–Sept till 8pm; free; ⓦwww.confederationcentre.com) is housed in a glass and concrete monstrosity built in 1964 to commemorate the centenary of the epochal meeting, but is best known today as the home of the Charlottetown Festival and Anne of Green Gables Musical (see p.434). The centre contains the island's main library, a couple of theatres, and an eclectic **art gallery** (mid-May to mid-Oct daily 9am–5pm; mid-Oct to mid-May Wed–Sat 11am–5pm, Sun 1–5pm; donation suggested), whose changing exhibitions always have a Canadian emphasis and often include a variety of nineteenth-century artefacts.

George Street and around

From the Confederation Centre, it's a couple of hundred metres south to the pretty terraced houses of Great George Street, which face the twin spires and imposing facade of **St Dunstan's Catholic Basilica** (daily 8am–5pm; free). Finished in 1919, the church has all the neo-Gothic trimmings, from blind arcaded galleries and lancet windows through to heavy-duty columns and a mighty vaulted ceiling. Some of Charlottetown's most historic clapboard and brick buildings are concentrated on and around **King Street** to either side of Great George Street, while **Victoria Row**, also near the church, has the city's finest example of commercial architecture, a long and impressive facade that now holds a series of restaurants and bars; in the summer the whole street is pedestrianized and smothered with al fresco diners.

The harbourfront and Founders' Hall

Below Water Street, the sequence of jetties that make up the **harbourfront** has been neatly refurbished with ice-cream parlours and restaurants, a yacht club, the incongruous hulk of the *Delta Hotel* and the souvenir shops of **Peake's Wharf**. Big cruise liners are often moored here, disgorging hundreds of day-trippers, many of whom make a beeline for **Founders' Hall** (Feb–April Tues–Sat 10am–3pm; early May Tues–Sat 9am–3.30pm; late May to early June daily 9am–4pm; late June daily 9am–6pm; July to mid-Aug Mon–Sat 9am–8pm; mid-Aug to early Sept daily 8.30am–9pm; early Sept to early Oct daily 8.30am–5pm; early Oct to Dec 23 Tues–Fri 9am–3pm; closed Dec 24–Jan 31; $7; Ⓦwww.foundershall.ca), at the foot of Prince Street, whose various multimedia displays, complete with a battery of sound effects and mock news reports, give an entertaining account of the deliberations of the Fathers of Confederation in the 1860s and the subsequent creation of each Canadian province, ending with Nunavut in 1999.

Beaconsfield House and Government House

From Founders' Hall, it's a pleasant ten-minute stroll northwest to **Beaconsfield House** (June–Aug daily 10am–4.45pm, regular guided tours; Sept–May times vary, call ahead; $4.25 Ⓣ902/368-6603), a resplendent late Victorian mansion whose fancy wooden trimmings and peaked roof overlook the harbour from the corner of West and Kent streets. The house was built in 1877 for James Peake, one of Charlottetown's leading shipbuilders, but he went bust five years after its completion. It changed owners and roles several times thereafter, until a local conservation society returned it to its former splendour in the 1970s. Across the way, the assorted greenery of **Victoria Park** edges the grandiose **Government House** (Mon–Fri 10am–4pm; free; Ⓣ902/368-5480), a splendid Georgian pile completed in 1834 and also known as Fanningbank. It's still the Lieutenant-Governor's residence and only open for guided tours in July and August.

Eating, drinking and entertainment

Charlottetown has a decent spread of **restaurants, cafés** and **bars**. In several cases restaurants share their premises with bars: food below, booze up above. Most places are open year-round, but everything changes in July and August, when people and tables fill the streets and sidewalks. You should also think about visiting at the end of September, when the **Fall Flavours Food Festival** (Ⓦwww.fallflavours.ca) highlights PEI cuisine through 130 events, from chocolate-making and clam-bakes, to oyster-tonguing and a lobster feast.

For **performing arts**, the Confederation Centre of the Arts (Ⓣ902/566-1267 or 1-800/565-0278, Ⓦwww.confederationcentre.com) hosts an extensive variety of acts, from rock and jazz through to comedians, magicians, theatre, opera and ballet. The centre is also the home to the main show of the annual **Charlottetown Festival** (mid-June to Sept), which – surprise, surprise – is a musical adaptation of *Anne of Green Gables*, running since 1965.

Cafés and restaurants

Beanz 38 University Ave, at Grafton. Great coffee ($1.15) and a range of tasty sandwiches and salads from around $4.75 at this agreeable little café. Especially popular at lunch times with the town's office workers. Mon–Fri 6.30am–6pm, Sat 8am–5pm & Sun 9am–4pm.

Claddagh Oyster House 131 Sydney St at Queen St Ⓣ902/892-9661, Ⓦwww.claddaghoysterhouse.com. Attractive modern restaurant set in a red-brick Victorian, specializing in delicious PEI oysters ($2.05 each); a ten-piece tasting plate costs just $19. Otherwise, the menu offers a competent selection of seafood and meat dishes with mains averaging $24. Daily from 5pm; it's beneath the *Olde Dublin Pub* (see below).

Cedar's Eatery 81 University Ave ⓣ902/892-7377 ⓦwww.cedarseatery.com. Charlottetown has had a relatively large Lebanese population since the 1880s, and this is one of their favourite haunts; think hummus, fragrant *kafta* and stuffed vine leaves. Mon–Sat 11am–11pm, Sun 4–10pm.

Cows 150 Queen St at Grafton St ⓣ902/892-6969, ⓦwww.cows.ca (also on Peake's Wharf May–Oct). Island institution, serving totally addictive ice cream in creative flavours like Moo Crunch and Gooey Mooey ($3.45 per scoop). Mon–Sat 10am–5pm, Sun noon–5pm. You can also tour the factory (June–Oct daily 9am–5.40pm; tours every 20min; $6; ⓣ902/370-3155) on the outskirts of town at 397 Capital Drive, on the North River Causeway (Rte 1).

Flex Mussels 2 Lower Water St at Peake's Wharf ⓣ902/569-0200, ⓦwww.flexmussels.com. Seasonal restaurant where mussels and assorted shellfish (great oysters) are prepared fresh to order – you get a mind-boggling choice of type, size and flavour, cooked with every kind of sauce imaginable, from $13 per order, with crispy $5 fries.

Lot 30 151 Kent St ⓣ902/629-3030, ⓦwww.lot30restaurant.ca. When local chefs want a treat they come here: Gordon Bailey's latest venture opened in 2008 and offers an exceptional dining experience, where the menu changes daily according to what fresh produce the chef picks up; poached lobster, organic pork and mussel-butter baked oysters often feature. Tues–Sun from 5pm.

Off-Broadway Restaurant 125 Sydney St at Queen ⓣ902/566-4620, ⓦwww.offbroadwayrestaurant.ca. Set in another gorgeous red-brick building with a creative menu of traditional and modern dishes – including the illustrious lobster caps (chunks of lobster; $13). Other house specialities include exotic crêpes and home-made desserts ($12–16). The decor is good fun – customers sit in dinky little wooden booths. Main courses average around $16.

Sim's Steakhouse & Oyster Bar 86 Queen St ⓣ902/894-7467, ⓦwww.simscorner.ca. Rapidly becoming the top restaurant in town, with delectable local oysters, a huge wine list and prime Canadian aged steaks – try the secret pepper sauce (steak $24–42). Features outdoor terrace and bbqs in summer. Daily from 4pm.

Water Prince Corner Shop 141 Water St ⓣ902/368-3212, ⓦwww.waterprincelobster.ca. It may look like a corner shop, but many locals swear by the seafood here – even if they are usually outnumbered by the tourists. The lobster dinners and chowders are perhaps the best on the island, but then the scallop burger is superb too. You can also buy fresh lobsters to go. Booking is essential. Moderately priced with mains from as little as $10. May–June & Sept to early Oct daily 10am–8pm; July & Aug daily 10am–10pm.

Bars

42nd Street Lounge 125 Sydney St ⓣ902/566-4620. Laidback lounge bar above the *Off-Broadway Restaurant*. A good range of brews, as well as comprehensive martini, cocktail and wine menus. Go on Thurs for 'Martini Madness' ($5.50 martinis).

Gahan House Pub & Brewery 126 Sydney St ⓣ902-626-2337, ⓦwww.gahan.ca. PEI's only microbrewery produces seven crisp handcrafted ales on-site, from the potent Sydney Street Stout to the lighter Harvest Gold Pale Ale. The pub food is equally comforting – try the signature Brown Bag Fish & Chips, ale-battered haddock (yes, served in a brown bag; $10.99).

Olde Dublin Pub 131 Sydney ⓣ902/892-6992, ⓦwww.oldedublinpub.com. Intimate and justifiably popular spot with imported and domestic ales, Guinness and Kilkenny included. Live folk music – mostly Irish – nightly from May to Sept. Above the *Claddagh* (see opposite).

Pilot House 70 Grafton St. Traditional pub-cum-diner in a fine nineteenth-century building, with booths to sit in and fish and chips (from its bar menu) to devour. Mon–Sat 11.30am–11.30pm.

Listings

Car rental Avis (airport ⓣ902/892-3706); Hertz 417 University Ave ⓣ902/566-5566 (airport 902/894-5774); National, on the harbourfront at Founders' Hall ⓣ902/628-990 (airport 902/628-6990).

Internet access Free at the harbourfront visitor information centre and at the Confederation Public Library, Richmond St (Mon & Fri–Sat 10am–5pm, Tues–Thurs 10am–9pm, Sun 1–5pm).

Pharmacy Shoppers Drug Mart, 128 Kent St ⓣ902/566-1200 (Mon–Wed 9am–6pm, Thurs & Fri 9am–9pm, Sat 9am–5.30pm), and 403 University Ave ⓣ902/892-3433 (daily 8am–midnight).

Post office 135 Kent St (Mon–Fri 8am–5.15pm).

Taxis City Cab, 168 Prince St ⓣ902/892-6567; Co-op Taxi, 91 Euston St ⓣ902/892-1111.

Prince Edward Island National Park

Pulling in thousands of visitors every summer, the gorgeous sandy beaches of **Prince Edward Island National Park** extend along the north shore for some 40km. Rarely more than one or two hundred metres wide, the main body of the park incorporates both the beaches and the sliver of low red cliff and marram grass-covered sand dune that runs behind – a barrier which is occasionally interrupted by slender inlets connecting the ocean with a quartet of chubby little bays. A narrow road runs behind the shoreline for most of its length, but **Rustico Bay** effectively divides the main body of the park into two: the smaller, more **westerly portion** runs from Cavendish – home of **Green Gables** – to North Rustico Harbour; the **easterly section**, which is wilder and more untrammelled, goes from Robinson's Island to Tracadie Bay, with a third, smaller section lying further east still at **Greenwich**, at the mouth of St Peter's Bay.

Park practicalities

There's a seasonal **information kiosk** at every entrance to the park (mid-June to late June 11am–6pm, late June to Sept 11am–7pm), which levy an entrance fee of $7.80 per adult per day ($3.80 in June); at other times entry is free. The **Greenwich Interpretation Centre** (daily: mid-May to mid-June & late Aug to early Oct 9am–5pm, late June to late Aug 9am–6pm) acts as the main visitor centre for the park, though the **Cavendish Visitor Centre** (daily: mid-May to June & Sept to mid-Oct 9am–5pm; July & Aug 8am–10pm), at Rte 6 and Rte 13, is more convenient for the western side.

The park has fourteen short **hiking trails**, easy strolls that take in different aspects of the coast from its tidal marshes and farmland through to its woodlands and dunes. The most strenuous is the 4km-long Woodlands Trail, up through a red-pine plantation near Dalvay, though perhaps the most scenic is the partly-boardwalked 4.2km-long Greenwich Dunes Trail.

The park has two **campsites**. The larger is the well-equipped, fully serviced *Cavendish Campground* (mid-June to late Aug), where there's a supervised sandy beach that's great for swimming. The quieter *Stanhope Campground* (mid-June to Sept), a short walk from the beach near the hamlet of Stanhope, is similarly well equipped. A few sites are allocated on a first-come, first-served basis, but most can be reserved (Ⓣ1-877/737-3783, Ⓦwww.pccamping.ca) – reservations are strongly advised. Pitches cost $25.50–35.30.

Robinson's Island and Stanhope Beach

The fastest route from Charlottetown to the more easterly section of the national park is the half-hour, 23km thump along Rte 15, which branches off Rte 2 on the north side of town. This takes you past the delightful *Dunes Studio Gallery and Café*, located just 600m beyond the Rte 6 and Rte 15 junction. The *Dunes* is a combined **café** (mid-June to Sept daily 11.30am–4pm & 5.30–10pm; Ⓣ902/672-2586, Ⓦwww.dunesgallery.com), pottery shop and art gallery (May–Oct daily 10am–6pm), which serves mouthwatering and reasonably priced snacks and meals from an imaginative menu of seafood and vegetarian dishes. Another 1km or so north on Rte 15 is the pick of the resort and cottage complexes hereabouts, the charmingly rustic *Shaw's Hotel and Cottages* (Ⓣ902/672-2022, Ⓦwww.shawshotel.ca), whose rooms (June–Sept; full board ❼) and year-round chalets occupy extensive grounds about ten-minutes' walk from the beach; *Shaw's* also does **canoe**, **kayak** and **bike rental** for guests and non-guests.

Inside the park, at the end of Rte 15, turn left along the coast for the causeway over to wooded **Robinson's Island** and right for the 5km trip along the seashore to **Stanhope Beach**, the setting for a string of perfectly placed beachside cottage complexes. These include the little red and white *Del-Mar Cottages* (Ⓣ902/672-2582 or 1-800/699-2582, Ⓦwww.delmarcottages.com; ⑤, sleeps up to four; June–Sept) and *Surf Cottages* (Ⓣ902/651-3300, Ⓦwww.peisland.com/surfcottages; $525 per week, sleeps up to three; mid-June to Sept).

Dalvay to Greenwich

Heading east from Stanhope Beach, it's about 6km to the end of the beach road and the pocket-sized hamlet of **DALVAY**, whose most conspicuous asset is the *Dalvay-by-the-Sea Inn* (Ⓣ902/672-2048 or 1-888/366-2955, Ⓦwww.dalvaybythesea.com; full board ⑧; mid-June to late Sept). The inn is an especially grand affair, a Victorian mansion that comes complete with high gables, rough-hewn stonework, a magnificent wraparound veranda and a croquet lawn. The inn holds 26 tastefully decorated rooms and has an ideal location inside the park just a couple of hundred metres from the beach. It's also worth stopping for **high tea** (July–Aug 2–4pm; $22 full service, $12 tea and scones), an elaborate affair involving sticky toffee pudding, fine china and heaps of exotic teas.

Along the coast to the east of Dalvay are two more segments of the national park, the first being the slender sandspit that shelters much of **Tracadie Bay** from the ocean. There are no roads to this section – just hiking trails; this also applies to the second segment, the partly wooded headland at the mouth of **St Peter's Bay**. Make a pit-stop here for *Rick's Fish & Chips* (Ⓣ902/961-3438 Ⓦwww.ricksfishnchips.com), just back from the bay on Rte 2, for some of the best fried haddock and seafood on the island.

From St Peter's, Rte 313 travels west from Rte 2 along the north shore of the bay, slipping through **GREENWICH** before grinding to a halt at the car park and the park interpretation centre (see opposite). From here, hiking trails drift across the headland, exploring its wild and especially beautiful beaches, dunes and wetlands.

To PEI National Park via New Glasgow

The 40km-long journey from Charlottetown to Cavendish and the western portion of the National Park covers some of PEI's most alluring scenery. Take Rte 2 west from the capital. After about 23km, turn north along Rte 13 to **NEW GLASGOW**, whose matching pair of black-and-white clapboard churches sit on opposite sides of an arm of Rustico Bay. In the centre of the village (Rte 224), the **Prince Edward Island Preserve Company** (mid-May to late June & early Sept to Oct daily 8.30am–5pm; late June to early Sept daily 8am–9.30pm Nov to late Dec Mon–Fri 9am–5pm; Ⓣ902/964-4300, Ⓦwww.preservecompany.com) is a great place to buy local jams, mustards and maple syrups, and the attached **café** (late May to late Oct) serves first-rate breakfasts, lunches and – in the summer – evening meals: try the cedar-planked salmon. There are **lobster suppers** available in the village at *New Glasgow Lobster Suppers*, on Rte 258 (June to mid-Oct daily 4–8.30pm; reservations Ⓣ902/964-2870, Ⓦwww.peilobstersuppers.com), though those at the church of **SAINT ANN**, a neighbouring hamlet about 5km west of New Glasgow along Rte 224, are generally considered better (mid-June to late Sept Mon–Sat 4–8.30pm; reservations Ⓣ902/621-0635, Ⓦwww.lobstersuppers.com). At both, a set meal including mussels, chowder, a 500g (1lb) lobster in its shell, salads, bread rolls and 'mile-high' lemon pie will cost around $30 (replace the lobster with beef or ham and it's $23). From New Glasgow, it's 10km to Cavendish along Rte 13.

Anne Country: Cavendish and around

Straggling **CAVENDISH**, clumped around the junction of Rte 6 and Rte 13, lies behind another stretch of fabulous national park **beach**. The west and east sections are not connected by road (both are signposted from Rte 6), but you can walk between them: the west side is better for swimming, while the east is noted chiefly for its crumbling red sandstone headlands. Yet the reason that so many people come to Cavendish – indeed, this is the most congested part of the island in July and August, and definitely the most commercialized – is because it lays claim to the key sights associated with the ubiquitous *Anne of Green Gables* (see p.439). Real fans will want to spend at least a day soaking up the attractions, but even the uninitiated will appreciate the old houses (and the genuine enthusiasm of the local guides).

The best place to start is the site of **Lucy Maud Montgomery's Cavendish Home** (daily: mid-May to June & Sept to mid-Oct 9am–5pm, July & Aug 9am–6.30pm; $4; ⓣ902/963-2969), on Rte 6, just east of Rte 13, where the author of Green Gables lived, on and off, between 1876 to 1911, and where she wrote her most famous novels. The farmhouse belonged to her grandparents, the Macneills, who raised Lucy after her mother died. Though it's the most historically significant site in town, there's not much to see, as the main buildings were knocked down in the 1920s, but the site has been beautifully maintained by the descendants of the family, and enhanced with signs pointing out important features and quotes from the author.

Green Gables Heritage Place and around

From the back of the Macneill site you can walk along the old homestead lane, across Rte 13 (through the "Haunted Wood") and into the back of **Green Gables Heritage Place** (May–Oct daily 9am–5pm; late March to April & Nov Sun–Thurs noon–4pm; call ahead other times; $7.15, ⓣ902/963-7871), the primary Anne pilgrimage site. The main entrance is on Rte 6, just 500m west of Rte 13. The two-storey timber house was built in 1831 and was once owned by the Macneill cousins of Montgomery, serving as her inspiration for the fictional *Green Gables* farm in the novel. The house has been modified several times since then, and the rooms have been decked out in authentic period furnishings, though few pieces are original to the house – the main aim was to faithfully match descriptions in the book, and Matthew's bedroom, the parlour and Anne's room are littered with items fans will recognise from the story. You can also explore the replica outhouses, and the **visitor centre**, which contains Lucy's original typewriter and scrapbooks.

Between the two sites, on the corner of routes 6 and 13, the old cemetery contains the **grave** of Montgomery, her husband and her mother. Lucy died in Toronto, but according to her last wish, was buried back on the island – the ceremony held here in 1942 is said to have been the closest thing to a state funeral PEI has ever had.

Further west along Rte 6, families will want to check out **Avonlea Village of Anne of Green Gables** (June 10am–5pm, July & Aug 10am–6pm, Sept 10am–4pm; $22, kids $16, free under 6, family $75; ⓣ902/963-3050, ⓦwww.avonlea.ca), where six of most famous episodes from the book (think slate being smashed on Gilbert's head) are brought to life by actors in a mock nineteenth-century village. The village does contain three originals: the Belmont School, where Montgomery taught in 1896; the Long River Church; and the Clifton Manse from New London, now a tearoom.

West of Cavendish

Serious aficionados can check out two other Anne-related properties: the **Birthplace of Lucy Maud Montgomery** (mid-May to early Sept daily 9am–5pm; $3; ⓣ902/886-2099) in New London, 13km west of Cavendish on Rte 6, a lovely old clapboard house where the author was born in 1874; and the home of Montgomery's aunt Annie Campbell, now the **Anne of Green Gables Museum** (daily: June & Sept 10am–4.30pm, July & Aug 9am–5pm; $4; ⓣ1-800/665-2663, Sat & Sun call ⓣ902/886-2884) in Park Corner, 8km west of New London on Rte 20. Montgomery spent much of her childhood playing here, and went on to base at least four novels on the house (including *Story Girl*). She was even married in the tiny parlour in 1911, and marriages still take place in exactly the same spot. All the rooms are littered with Montgomery memorabilia, and you can also take a **horse and carriage ride** to the beach (max 5 people; $50/30min, $80/1hr).

Practicalities

For **accommodation** in Cavendish, try *Shining Waters Country Inn & Cottages* (ⓣ902/963-2251 or 1-877/963-2251, ⓦwww.shiningwatersresort.com; May–Sept), 200m north of the route 6 and 13 crossroads on the way to the beach. They have rooms in the old inn (❸), a pleasant, homely structure with a wide veranda, as well as in a motel-style annexe (❺) and a string of modern chalet/cottages (❻). The National Park's **Cavendish campground** (see p.436) is another possibility; it's located just off – and signed from – Rte 6, just to the west of Green Gables House. Another appealing option is the *Cavendish Maples Cottages* (ⓣ1-888/662-7537, ⓦwww.cavendishmaples.com; ❻), 73 Avonlea Blvd (Rte 6), which offers beautifully finished one- to three-bedroom wood cabins, with kitchens, wi-fi and cable TV. For a little more historic character (and year-round accommodation), head over to the *Barachois Inn* (ⓣ1-800/963-2194; ⓦwww.barachoisinn.com; ❻) in nearby **NORTH RUSTICO**, featuring two gorgeous nineteenth-century properties with luxurious, Victorian-themed rooms.

For **eating**, you're better off heading to New Glasgow (see p.437), but the pick of the otherwise lacklustre Cavendish restaurants is *Chez Yvonnes*

Anne, Lucy and PEI

PEI may be the home of Confederation, juicy oysters and tasty lobsters, but even the most jaded golfers spend a couple of hours paying homage to **Anne of Green Gables**. The tear-jerking tale of a red-haired, pigtailed orphan girl that Mark Twain dubbed the "most lovable childhood heroine since the immortal Alice" has become a phenomenal worldwide sensation since it was published in 1908, and the vivid descriptions of rural PEI, handsomely captured in the 1985 TV miniseries has undeniably inspired many a trip here. Around six thousand Japanese visit every year; the book has been on school curricula there since the 1950s and remains extremely popular. Many visitors find it hard separating the fictional life of Anne Shirley and the real life of her creator **Lucy Maud Montgomery**, one of Canada's bestselling authors. In 1876, when Montgomery was just two, her mother died and her father migrated to Saskatchewan, leaving her in the care of her grandparents in Cavendish. Here she developed a deep love for her native island and its people, and although she spent the last half of her life in Ontario, PEI remained the main inspiration for her work. Completed in 1905 and published three years later (after being rejected five times), *Anne of Green Gables* remains her most popular book. Today, many Islanders remain conflicted over her legacy, hating the commercialization of the novel but deeply proud of the author's success.

(Ⓣ902/963-2070, Ⓦwww.chezyvonnes.com) on Rte 6, a solid family-friendly place serving steaks and seafood. In the centre of North Rustico, the *Fisherman's Wharf Restaurant* (daily: May–June & Sept–Oct 11am–9pm, July & Aug 8am–9pm; Ⓣ902/963-2669, Ⓦwww.fishermanswharf.ca;) is another tempting place to sample the island's **lobster suppers** (daily: May–June 4–9pm, July–Oct noon–9pm).

Points East Coastal Drive

The attractions on the eastern half of PEI are linked by what the tourism authorities have dubbed the **Points East Coastal Drive** (Ⓦwww.pointseastcoastaldrive.com), which essentially follows the main roads that hug the coast between Charlottetown and rugged **East Point** – you'll need one or two days to do it justice, even if you take shortcuts to the highlights, listed below.

Orwell

Some 30km east of Charlottetown, just off the Trans-Canada Hwy in the village of **ORWELL**, lies rustic **Orwell Corner Historic Village** (late May to June Mon–Fri 9am–5pm; July–Aug daily 9.30am–5.30pm; Sept to early Oct Sun–Thurs 9am–5pm; $7.50; Ⓦwww.orwellcorner.ca), originally settled by Scottish and Irish pioneers in the early nineteenth century but abandoned in the 1950s. The historic graveyard and a handful of buildings remained and in recent years these have been restored and supplemented by replicas of some of the early buildings, like the blacksmith's shop, barns and shingle mill. Care has been taken to give the interiors the authentic flavour of Orwell's past, from the farmhouse's darkened, cluttered living rooms and the austerity of the Presbyterian church to the cheeky graffiti carved into the schoolhouse desks. The gardens are splendidly maintained in period style, farm animals root around purposefully, and the village hosts a wide variety of special events, including ploughing contests and ceilidhs.

Cardigan

If you're short of time it's worth leaving the coastal drive at Orwell and cutting across the island on routes 3 and 4 to the turn-off to **CARDIGAN**, a friendly village at the head of Cardigan Bay that was a notable shipbuilding centre up to the 1920s. In the centre of the village, the **Cardigan Heritage Centre** (June–Oct daily 10am–5pm; Ⓣ902/583-2311) has a small display room dedicated to these glory years, while nearby Canada's **smallest library** (same hours) is a tiny kiosk that nevertheless contains two thousand books. You can get a splendid home-cooked meal at *Cardigan Lobster Suppers* (June–Oct daily 5–9pm; Ⓣ 902/583-2020, Ⓦwww.cardiganlobstersuppers.com), which offers decks over the water, unlimited chowder, fresh 1.5-pound lobsters, a large bowl of mussels and luscious desserts for $33.95.

Souris

From Cardigan, head back to Rte 4 for the 36km or so drive northeast to **SOURIS**, a busy fishing port and harbour, which curves round the shore of Colville Bay and has a regular car ferry service to the Magdalens (see p.323). There's not much to see here, but it makes a logical overnight stop. The stretch of shoreline between the centre of the town and the docks sees Souris at its best, and

Ferry to the Magdalen Islands

Operated by CTMA, a **car ferry** (Ⓣ418/986-3278 or 1-888/986-3278, Ⓦwww.ctma.ca) does the five-hour hop between **Cap-aux-Meules** on the Magdalen Islands (Îles-de-la-Madeleine, see p.323) and **Souris**, 81km northeast of Charlottetown from April to January (April–June & Sept 6 weekly, July & Aug 7–11 weekly; Oct–Jan 3–4 weekly). A one-way adult fare is $44 ($28 in winter), plus $80 ($57) per car.

here you'll find the first-rate *Matthew House Inn B&B* (Ⓣ902/687-3461, Ⓦwww.matthewhouseinn.com; ⑤; late June to early Sept), at 15 Breakwater St, which has eight attractive guest rooms with a period feel. The nearby *Dockside B&B* (Ⓣ902/687-2829 or 1-877/687-2829, Ⓦwww.colvillebay.ca; ③; mid-June to mid-Oct), at 37 Breakwater St, is a more economical option, occupying a 1960s house of expansive, open design with views out across the ferry terminal and ocean; it has four guest rooms, two of them en suite.

For **food**, check out the **Colville Bay Oyster Co** (Ⓣ902/687-2222, Ⓦwww.colvillebayoysterco.ca) 400m off Rte 330, just south of Souris at 83 Lower Rollo Bay on the left-hand side: it's just a small shack, but you can buy fresh oysters direct from the fisherman (usually June–Jan). Also in Rollo Bay (on Rte 2), the **Myriad View Distillery** (Ⓣ902/687-1281, Ⓦwww.straitshine.com) produces its unique brands of "moonshine", gin and vodka, all of which can be bought on site (open May–Dec; call ahead other times). In Souris itself, try the seafood at *Blue Fin* (Ⓣ902/687-3271), at 10 Federal Ave, just off Main Street, or the Portuguese-owned *Xitaka* (Ⓣ902/687-2734), at 116 Main St, which serves a fusion of Portuguese and Canadian staples. For a real treat, head for the *Inn at Bay of Fortune* (Ⓣ902/687-3745 Ⓦwww.innatbayfortune.com), ten minutes' drive west of Souris in Fortune Bay, internationally lauded for its menus of organic local dishes that change daily: expect plenty of seafood (mains around $15–20).

On to East Point

You can drive round the island's northeast corner along Rte 16 from Souris, ending at the lighthouse at **East Point** (Ⓦwww.eastpointlighthouse.com). Tours of the lighthouse (daily 10am–6.30pm; $4; Ⓣ902/357-2106), built in 1867, run mid-June to early September, and there's a craft shop on site (late May to early Oct daily). Nearby **North Harbour** is a raw fishing port, where freshly-caught tuna are snapped up by Japanese buyers, and the rows of fishing shacks make for a more authentic PEI picture.

Beyond here it's a long, lonely drive back to Charlottetown on Rte 16, enlivened somewhat by the **Prince Edward Distillery** in Hermanville (Ⓣ902/687-2586, Ⓦwww.princeedwarddistillery.com), producers of Canada's first and only vodka distilled from potatoes (they also make wild blueberry vodka), which you can buy at the on-site store.

The South Coast

The most diverting settlement on the **South Coast** is the old seaport of **VICTORIA**, overlooking the Northumberland Strait about 35km west of Charlottetown along the Trans-Canada Hwy. Though short on traditional sights, its gridiron of nineteenth-century clapboard houses is exceptionally picturesque – in July and August it can get packed with day-trippers. Victoria also has an attractive old **hotel**, the *Orient* (Ⓣ902/658-2503 or 1-800/565-6743, Ⓦwww.theorienthotel.com; ❸; mid-May to mid-Oct), while classically-trained chef Stephen Hunter runs the *Victoria Village Inn* (Ⓣ902/658-2483, Ⓦwww.victoriavillageinn.com; ❹), at 22 Howard St. His charming Victorian guest-house is open year-round, and also does superb **dinners** from June to September (6pm and 8pm), using local organic produce and fresh seafood.

There are several other places to **eat**, though most just open in the summer: one exception is the *Landmark Café* (daily from 11.30am; Ⓣ902/658-2286) near the Playhouse in the centre of the village, which serves excellent and moderately priced home-made meals, while *Island Chocolates* (mid-June to mid-Sept daily 9am–9pm) sells Belgian-style handmade chocolates and a fine coffee.

The village is home to the **Victoria Playhouse** (Ⓣ902/658-2025 or 1-800/925-2025, Ⓦwww.victoriaplayhouse.com), where a good range of modern plays and musical evenings are performed from late June through to late September.

Summerside

Some 37km further west, **SUMMERSIDE** is PEI's second largest settlement, a sprawling bayside town of fifteen thousand people that was once the island's main port. The historic downtown is a leafy, beautifully restored area of clapboard houses centred on the graceful nineteenth-century Trinity United Church on Spring Street and the nearby **Wyatt Heritage Properties** (Ⓣ902/432-1296, Ⓦwww.wyattheritage.com). Of several gorgeous buildings here, the **Wyatt House Museum** (June–Sept; tours Mon–Sat 10am–4pm; $5.50) at 85 Spring St is one of the most absorbing, built in 1867 and crammed with ornate furnishings and Victorian antiques.

You should also pop into the red-brick **International Fox Museum and Hall of Fame** (June–Sept Mon–Sat 10am–5pm; donation), a couple of blocks from the harbourfront at 286 Fitzroy St and Summer Street, which traces the history of the island's fox-ranching industry from its beginnings in 1894 to its heyday in the 1920s.

Summerside is best visited on a day-trip, but there are plenty of enticing places to **eat**. *Lobster House* (daily from 4pm; Ⓣ902/436-8439, Ⓦwww.lobsterhouserestaurant.ca), along Baywalk at 370 Water St, has a deck overlooking Bedeque Bay and serves thick lobster rolls, huge lobster suppers and all sorts of tasty seafood. The *Starlite Diner* (Ⓣ902/436-9075) at 810 Water St (out of town at the junction of routes 1A and 2) offers filling and excellent breakfasts and fish and chips in a retro 1950s dining room, while *St Eleanor's Dairy Bar & Take Out* (Ⓣ902/436-8683) on Bayview Drive (Rte 11) is a fabulous snack stop, serving cheap lobster rolls, burgers and ice cream.

North Cape Coastal Drive

The northern and western sections of PEI are deceptively large, with the **North Cape Coastal Drive** (Ⓦwww.northcapedrive.com) making a 300km loop around the coast from Summerside – driving straight to North Cape from here it's still 100km. You'll need to spend the night en route to get the most out of the region, the least developed and most traditional part of PEI.

La Région Évangéline

The most traditionally French part of the island was settled by Acadians in the eighteenth-century and is known as **La Région Évangéline** (Ⓣ902/854-3300,

Ⓦwww.regionevangeline.com). It's a few minutes' drive along Rte 2 from Summerside to **MISCOUCHE**, where the bright and informative **Acadian Museum** (July & Aug daily 9.30am–7pm; rest of year Mon–Fri 9.30am–5pm, Sun 1–4pm; $3) is a solid introduction to the island's French-speaking community and the traumatic deportations of 1755.

Continuing west, the **Cap Egmont headland** is a major centre of Acadian settlement, with tiny **MONT-CARMEL** dominated by the incongruous red-brick mass of the **Église Notre-Dame**. Built in 1898, this is the most important Acadian religious site in PEI, its stern lines and neat cemetery enhanced by a stunning location overlooking the sea. Further west along Rte 11 **CAP-EGMONT** village is home to the island's quirkiest sight, the **Bottle Houses** (daily: mid-May to late May & early Oct to mid-Oct 10am–4pm, June & Sept 10am–6pm; July & Aug 9am–8pm; $6; Ⓣ902/854-2987, Ⓦwww.bottlehouses.com). Édouard Arsenault built the three curious-looking buildings (one is a chapel) in the early 1980s from around thirty thousand bottles; the houses were reconstructed in the 1990s.

The cape itself is not worth seeing, and it's best to drive on to the pretty settlement of **ABRAM-VILLAGE** to eat: the *Centre Expo Festival* runs a bakery (June–Sept daily 10am–7pm; rest of year Thurs 1–4pm & Fri 10–4pm; Ⓣ902/854-3300, Ⓦwww.centreexpofestival.com), selling breads, pies and fabulous cinnamon rolls; in the summer they also serve lobster suppers. The best place **to stay** is *Chez Yvette* on Rte 124 (Ⓣ902/854-2966, Ⓦwww.chezyvette.ca; ❸) in nearby Urbainville, a clapboard home dating from the 1930s, with three neat bedrooms and two shared bathrooms.

Up West

The far northwest of PEI, or just **UP WEST** to the locals, is a long winding drive from Summerside, starting with the slightly hillier scenery along the northwest shore of **Malpeque Bay**, home of the famed and eponymous **oyster** variety (which you'll see listed on many PEI menus), the bulk of which are shipped overseas. The bay's reedy waters were once fringed by tiny shipbuilding yards and the scant remains of one of them have been conserved as part of the **Green Park Shipbuilding Museum** (June–Sept daily 9.30am–5.30pm; $5; Ⓣ902/831-7947) in Port Hill, on Rte 12. The museum also incorporates an interpretive centre, focusing on PEI's shipbuilding industry, and the restored **James Yeo house**, built in the 1860s.

The minuscule village of **TYNE VALLEY**, just 4km away, is home to the pleasant *Doctor's Inn B&B* (Ⓣ902/831-3057, Ⓦwww.peisland.com/doctorsinn; ❷), which occupies a big old house and has three modest but pleasantly appointed guest rooms. The owners run the adjoining two-acre organic garden, and you can have dinner ($45–55) at the inn (advance booking necessary).

It's about 50km from Green Park to the western tip of the island, where the remote and windswept **West Point Lighthouse** (June to late Sept daily 9am–9pm; $2.50) holds a small collection of photographs and memorabilia portraying the lives of the lighthouse keepers. One room in the lighthouse and eight more in the adjoining building, all en suite and decorated in cheery modern style, comprise the *West Point Lighthouse Inn* (Ⓣ902/859-3605 or 1-800/764-6854, Ⓦwww.westpointlighthouse.com; ❹; late May to Sept), which makes the most of a great seaside location, overlooking a long sandy beach. The lighthouse is surrounded by the **Cedar Dunes Provincial Park**, which has a **campground** about 500m down the coast (Ⓣ902/859-8785; June to mid-Sept; $23–30).

Travel details

Trains

Schedules and ticket prices from **VIA Rail** ⓣ1-888/842-7245, ⓦwww.viarail.ca.
Halifax to: Moncton (1 daily except Tues; 4hr 25min); Montréal (1 daily except Tues; 20hr); Truro (1 daily except Tues; 1hr 30min).
Moncton to: Halifax (1 daily except Tues; 4hr 25min); Montréal (1 daily except Tues; 15hr).

Buses

Acadian Lines (ⓣ1-800/567-5151, ⓦwww.acadianbus.com) operates the following services. Note that not all of these services are direct; some involve a change.
Charlottetown to: Moncton (2–3 daily; 3hr 30min).
Edmundston to: Fredericton (2 daily; 3hr 5min–3hr 40min); Halifax (10hr 5min–11hr 25min); Moncton (2 daily; 6hr); Rivière-du-Loup, Québec (3 daily; 1hr 45min).
Fredericton to: Bangor, Maine (1 daily; 7hr 40min); Edmundston (2 daily; 3hr 5min–3hr 40min); Halifax (2 daily; 6hr 40min); Moncton (2 daily; 2hr 30min); Montréal (1 daily; 12hr); Miramichi City (1 daily; 2hr 30min); Saint John (2 daily; 1hr 30min).
Halifax to: Annapolis Royal (1 daily; 3hr 50min); Baddeck (2 daily; 6hr–6hr 25min); Digby (1 daily; 4hr 20min); Edmundston (2 daily; 10hr– 5min 11hr 25min; Fredericton (2 daily; 6hr 40min); Moncton (3 daily; 4hr 20min); Montréal (2 daily; 20hr); North Sydney (2 daily; 6hr 45min–7hr 30min); Sydney (3 daily; 6hr 45min–8hr); Truro (7 daily; 1hr 30min); Wolfville (2–3 daily; 1hr 35min).
Moncton to: Bathurst (1 daily; 3hr 35min); Charlottetown (2–3 daily; 3hr 30min); Edmundston (2 daily; 6hr); Fredericton (2 daily; 2hr 30min); Halifax (3 daily; 4hr 20min); Miramichi City (1 daily; 2hr 10min); St Andrews (1 daily; 3hr 40min); Saint John (3 daily; 1hr 50min–2hr 10min).
Saint John to: Bangor, Maine (1 daily; 4hr 50min); Fredericton (2 daily; 1hr 30min); Moncton (3 daily; 1hr 50min–2hr 10min).
Sydney to: Halifax (3 daily; 6hr 45min–8hr); North Sydney (2 daily; 40min); Truro (3 daily; 4hr 40min–6hr 30min).
Currently, **Trius Tours** (ⓣ1-877/566-1567) operates a once daily service from Halifax to Yarmouth along Nova Scotia's southwest shore.
Halifax to: Chester (1 daily; 1hr); Liverpool (1 daily; 2hr 50min); Lunenburg (1 daily; 1hr 35min); Mahone Bay (1 daily; 1hr 20min); Shelburne (1 daily; 3hr 45min); Yarmouth (1 daily; 5hr).
Yarmouth to: Chester (1 daily; 4hr); Halifax (1 daily; 5hr); Liverpool (1 daily; 2hr 10min); Lunenburg (1 daily; 3hr 25min); Mahone Bay (1 daily; 3hr 40min); Shelburne (1 daily; 1hr 15min).

Ferries

Caribou, Nova Scotia to: Wood Islands, PEI (May to late June & mid-Oct to mid-Nov 5 daily, late June & Sept to mid-Oct 7 daily, July & Aug 8 daily, mid-Nov to late Dec 3–4 daily; 1hr 15min) with **Northumberland Ferries** (ⓣ902/566-3838 or 1-888/249-7245, ⓦwww.nfl-bay.com).
Digby, Nova Scotia to: Saint John, New Brunswick (1–2 daily; 3hr) with **Bay Ferries** (ⓣ1-888/249-7245, ⓦwww.bayferries.com).
North Sydney, Nova Scotia to: Channel-Port aux Basques, Newfoundland (2–4 daily; 5–6hr or 6–8hr) and Argentia, Newfoundland (late June to early Sept 3 weekly, mid-June & late Sept 1 weekly; 14–15hr) with **Marine Atlantic** ⓣ1-800/341-7981, ⓦwww.marine-atlantic.ca.
Saint John, New Brunswick to: Digby, Nova Scotia (1–2 daily; 3hr) with **Bay Ferries** (ⓣ1-888/249-7245, ⓦwww.bayferries.com).
Souris, PEI to: Cap-aux-Meules, on the Magdalen Islands (Îles-de-la-Madeleine), in Québec (April–June & Sept 6 weekly, July & Aug 7–11 weekly; Oct–Jan 3–4 weekly; 5hr) with **CTMA** (ⓣ418/986-3278 or 1-888/986-3278, ⓦwww.ctma.ca).
Wood Islands, PEI to: Caribou, Nova Scotia (May to late June & mid-Oct to mid-Nov 5 daily, late June & Sept to mid-Oct 7 daily, July & Aug 8 daily, mid-Nov to late Dec 3–4 daily; 1hr 15min) with **Northumberland Ferries** (ⓣ902/566-3838 or 1-888/249-7245, ⓦwww.nfl-bay.com).
Yarmouth, Nova Scotia to: Bar Harbor, Maine (June to mid-Oct 1 daily Mon & Tues; 3hr) and Portland, Maine (June & Sept to mid-Oct 1 daily Thurs, Fri & Sun, July & Aug 1 daily Wed–Sun; 5hr 30min) with **Bay Ferries** (ⓣ1-888/249-7245, ⓦwww.catferry.com).

6

Newfoundland and Labrador

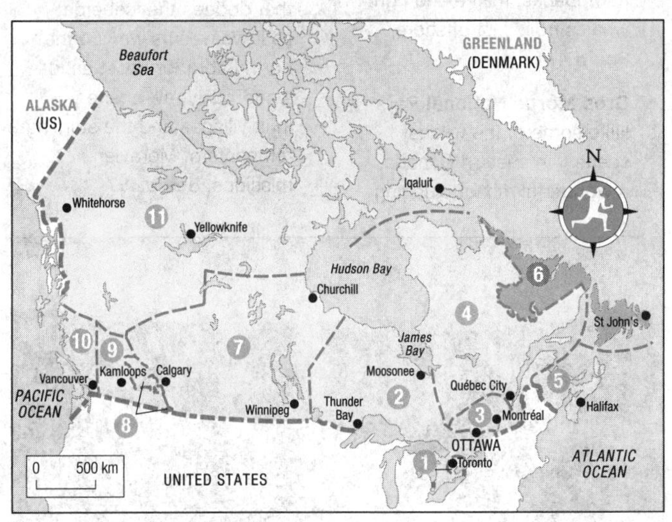

CHAPTER 6

Highlights

* **St John's** This lively port, with its fine coastal setting and raucous nightlife, provides the best introduction to Newfoundland culture, history and culinary traditions. See pp.450–459
* **Icebergs and whale-watching** Iceberg Alley, off the east coast of Newfoundland, can be studded with vast, shimmering lumps of ice in summer, and hundreds of humpbacks, minke and right whales frolic just offshore. See p.474
* **Gros Morne National Park** Hike some of the wildest scenery in eastern Canada, a wonderful mix of plunging fjords and rearing mountains, or take the boat tour across the dazzling waters of Western Brook Pond. See pp.476–480
* **Battle Harbour** Once the world's largest saltfish port, this wonderfully evocative and isolated village off the coast of southern Labrador is a magical place to spend the night. See p.491
* **The Northern Ranger** Summer-only steamship that dodges the icebergs as it weaves its way up the north Labrador coast amid wondrously raw scenery, Inuit villages and the startling remnants of Moravian missions. See p.497

▲ Gros Morne National Park, Newfoundland

6

Newfoundland and Labrador

The province of **Newfoundland and Labrador** joined Canada in 1949, a controversial move supported by just 52.3 percent of the population at the time. Even now, parts of Newfoundland seem like an entirely different country, and it's this unique sense of identity that makes it such a compelling destination. The island's harsh climate and relative isolation fostered a distinctive culture distinguished by a remarkable family of **dialects**, in essence an eclectic mix of old Irish and English. The dialects developed because the **outports** – ancient fishing settlements that were home to the first Europeans – could only be reached by boat, though today almost all are connected to the skein of side roads that plug into the **Trans-Canada Highway**. This sweeps 900km from the southwest corner of the island to the Avalon Peninsula, where **St John's**, the capital of the province, sits on the northeast shore. The rest of the island is largely untouched wilderness, a vast wonderland of snow-capped mountains, fish-filled rivers, mesmerizing fjords and clapboard fishing villages, clinging to a rocky shore.

Labrador, though part of mainland Canada, has been tied to the island of Newfoundland since the 1760s, yet here too you'll find a strong sense of identity – the central and northern regions of Labrador have a totally different history, one that blends recent arrivals with ancient Inuit and Innu traditions. Iron ore mines and hydroelectric schemes drive the economy, but these industrial blemishes are mere pinpricks in the barely explored **wilderness** that defines this part of the province. Unimaginably vast, Labrador boasts some of Canada's highest mountains, a jaw-dropping national park, a spectacular shoreline and a forested hinterland teeming with wildlife. A trip here is a true adventure.

Time zones and regional information

All of Newfoundland, as well as the Labrador coastal communities south of Cartwright (from L'Anse au Claire, on the Québec border, to Norman Bay), is on **Newfoundland Time.** Most of Labrador (Cartwright, Happy Valley-Goose Bay and Labrador West), as well as the Maritime Provinces, is on **Atlantic Time**, half-an-hour behind Newfoundland time. St Pierre et Miquelon also has its own time zone – half-an-hour ahead of Newfoundland Time. Most of your information needs can be met by **Newfoundland and Labrador Tourism** (ⓣ1-800/563-6353, ⓦwww.newfoundlandandlabradortourism.com).

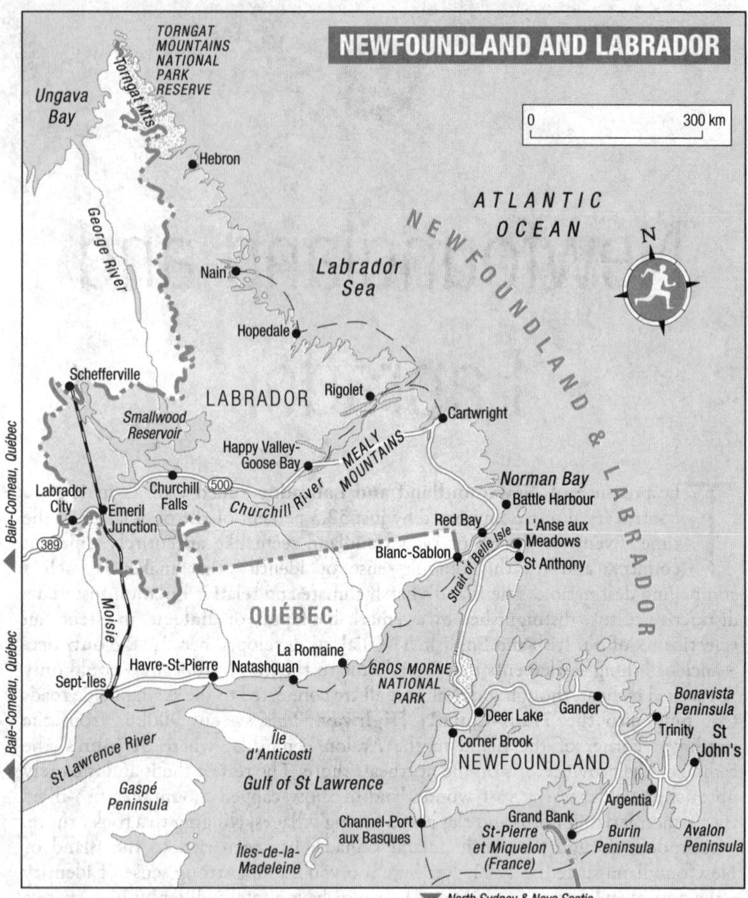

Newfoundland

Newfoundland's natural and historic charms are considerable, yet, astonishingly, the island rarely seems busy or crowded. You'll need a car to make the most of the place, though distances are vast, so it's worth weighing up itineraries carefully – even locals take over 12 hours to drive between St John's and St Anthony, a journey of over 1000km. Most visitors fly straight to **St John's**, which provides the best introduction to island life, not least for its museums, enticing restaurants, bars and flourishing folk music scene. The city is also within easy striking distance of the **Witless Bay sea-bird reserve**, the lighthouses of **Cape Spear** and the **East Coast Trail**, providing opportunities for everything from a short ramble to a full-scale expedition

Newfoundland's attractions don't end on the Avalon Peninsula though. Tiny **Trinity**, on the Bonavista Peninsula, is perhaps the most beguiling of all the old outports, though **Twillingate** comes a close second, while **Gros Morne National Park**, 700km west of St John's, features wondrous mountains and glacier-gouged lakes. Another 350km north of the park, at **L'Anse aux Meadows**, lie the scant but evocative remains of an eleventh-century Norse colony, as well as a remarkable hotel in the old lighthouse on **Quirpon** island.

Getting to and around Newfoundland

The only **scheduled international flights** to St John's are operated by Continental from Newark in the US – the closest direct flights from London now go to Halifax, Nova Scotia. **Air Canada** operates flights from St John's to Toronto, Montréal and Halifax; and to Deer Lake from Montréal and Toronto. In addition, Air Canada Jazz, WestJet and Porter Airlines also fly between Newfoundland and cities in Canada.

Regional carriers include **Air Labrador** (Ⓣ1-800/563-3042, Ⓦwww.airlabrador.com), which has flights between St John's and Deer Lake; St John's and Wabush in Labrador; and from Deer Lake to Goose Bay, St Anthony and Blanc Sablon. **Provincial Airlines** (inside Newfoundland Ⓣ1-800/563-2800, elsewhere Ⓣ709/576-1666, Ⓦwww.provincialairlines.ca) provides a regular service between St John's and Deer Lake and St Anthony, with other flights to Labrador's Goose Bay, Blanc Sablon and Churchill Falls. **Air St-Pierre** (Ⓣ508/41 00 00 or 1-877/277-7765, Ⓦwww.airsaintpierre.com) links St-Pierre et Miquelon with Montréal, Nova Scotia's Halifax and Sydney, New Brunswick's Moncton and St John's, Newfoundland.

For **ferries**, see p.398 for Nova Scotia, p.486 for Labrador and p.466 for St-Pierre et Miquelon. There are twelve other ferry routes connecting the remoter outports of Newfoundland; timetables and prices are at Ⓦwww.tw.gov.nl.ca/ferryservices.

The only long-distance **bus** on Newfoundland is operated by **DRL Coachlines** (Ⓣ709/263-2171 or 1-888/263-1854, Ⓦwww.drlgroup.com), a once-daily service running from Channel-Port aux Basques (at 8am) to St John's via the Trans-Canada Hwy, stopping at over twenty points on the way. The one-way fare costs $107 and the whole trip takes 13 hr 30min; confirm bus tickets and departure details before you set out. A patchy public transport network is provided by a string of **minibus/taxi** companies, most of which are based in St John's. **Marsh's** (Ⓣ709/747-2225) provides a once daily minibus service from St John's to Bonavista via Trinity with the journey to either costing $40; **Foote's Taxi** (Ⓣ709/832-0491 or 1-800/866-1181) operates a once-daily service to Grand Bank and Fortune from the capital for $45 per person; and **Newhook's Transportation** (Ⓣ709/682-4877) charges $30 for the trip from St John's to the Argentia ferry.

On the west coast, several operators run out of the Martin's Transportation office on Herald Avenue in Corner Brook (information at Ⓣ709/634-2659); the bus to St Anthony has been discontinued, but you can still get as far as Plum Point ($50; Ⓣ709/457-7719) on the north coast; Martin's (Ⓣ709/458-7845) runs between Corner Brook and Woody Point ($16) and Trout River ($18) in the Gros Morne National Park (Mon–Fri 4.30pm); Viking (Ⓣ709/458-8186) runs to Deer Lake ($5) and Rocky Harbour (Mon–Fri 4.30pm; $25); and Burgeo Bus Lines (aka D5 Trucking) runs to Burgeo (Mon–Fri 3pm; $38; Ⓣ709/886-6162). Buses usually depart from the Millbrook Mall (at Martin's Transportation), but always call ahead.

One final word about the **moose**: Newfoundland has thousands of them and they present a real danger to the motorist at dawn and dusk and to a lesser extent at night – so much so that many locals prefer not to drive at these times. The problem is that this large and powerful animal is drawn to vehicle headlights as if hypnotized and the results of a collision can be devastating for beast and human alike: on impact, cars typically knock the moose's legs away, leaving the animal's body to come barrelling through the windscreen.

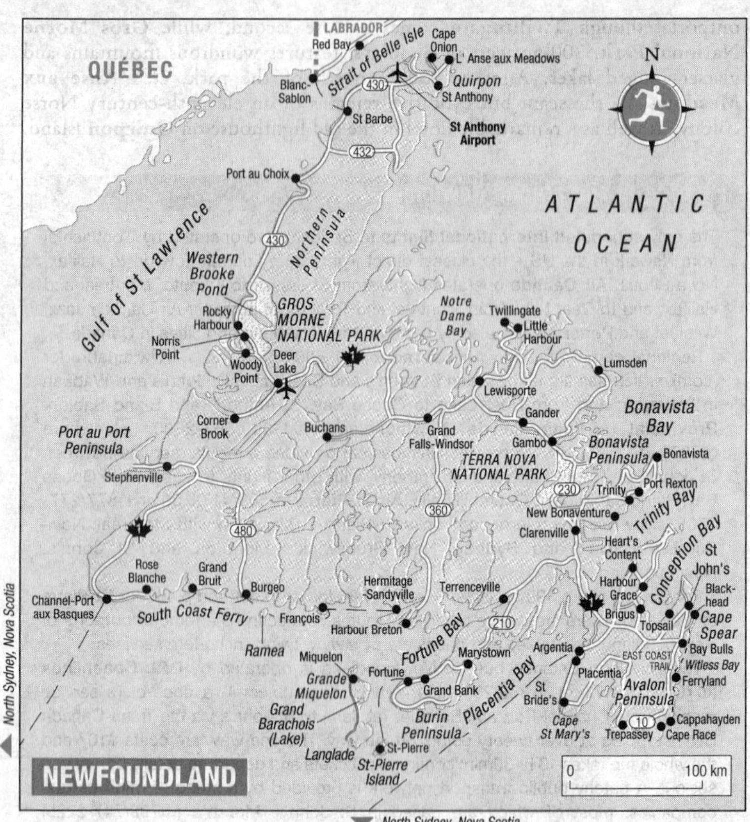

The southern coast of Newfoundland chips in with the wild and windswept Burin Peninsula, which is a quick ferry ride from French-speaking **St-Pierre et Miquelon**, a tiny archipelago that is – as an imperial oddity – a *département* of France.

St John's

For centuries life in **ST JOHN'S** has focused on its **harbour**, a dramatic jaw-shaped inlet approached through the 200-metre-wide channel of **The Narrows**. In its heyday, the port was crammed with ships from a score of nations; today, although traffic is not as brisk, it draws a mixed maritime bag of trawlers, container ships and oil construction barges. It still possesses a boisterous nightlife too, but the rough houses of the waterfront have been replaced by shops, slick office buildings and chic restaurants, and its inhabitants – of whom there are about 185,000 – are less likely to be seafarers than white-collar workers, artists and students from all over Canada. Yet the waterfront remains the social hub, sprinkled with lively **bars** that feature the pick of Newfoundland **folk music** – one good reason for visiting in itself.

Nonetheless, it's the overall appearance of the centre that pleases most, its higgledy-piggledy mix of the old and new clambering up the hillside to rows of brightly painted clapboard houses, with **Gower Street** being a prime example. **The Rooms** is the lavish home of the province's illuminating art and historical collections, but no visit to the city would be complete without a jaunt up **Signal Hill**, offering fabulous views over city and ocean. St John's is also a short drive from windswept **Cape Spear**, the continent's most easterly point.

Arrival, information and city transport

St John's international **airport** is about 6km north of the city centre. There's an ATM and a **tourist information desk** (daily 8am–12.30am; ⓣ709/758-8515) inside the terminal, well-stocked with maps and pamphlets, and it can also help book accommodation. You'll find all the major car rental firms at the airport (see p.459), but there's no public transport to the city centre; City Wide (ⓣ709/722-7777) has a monopoly on **taxis** with fares based on a zone system; most of downtown is $22.50, plus $2.50 for each additional passenger (coming back taxis use the meter; the fare is around $18).

DRL Coachlines (see p.449) **buses** from Channel-Port aux Basques terminate at the St John's campus of Memorial University, outside the Student Centre on Prince Philip Drive, about 3km northwest of the city centre. To get to the centre, take a taxi or Metrobus #10 to City Hall ($2.25). The **city tourist office** is one block up from the harbour at 348 Water St (Mon–Fri 9am–4.30pm, Sat & Sun 9am–5pm; ⓣ709/576-8106, ⓦwww.stjohns.ca).

The best way to explore St John's is on **foot**, but for more outlying attractions you might want to catch a bus. **Metrobus** (single fare $2.25; ten-ride pass $20; timetable information at ⓣ709/722-9400, ⓦwww.metrobus.com) has about a dozen routes serving most parts of the city.

▲ The St. John's waterfront

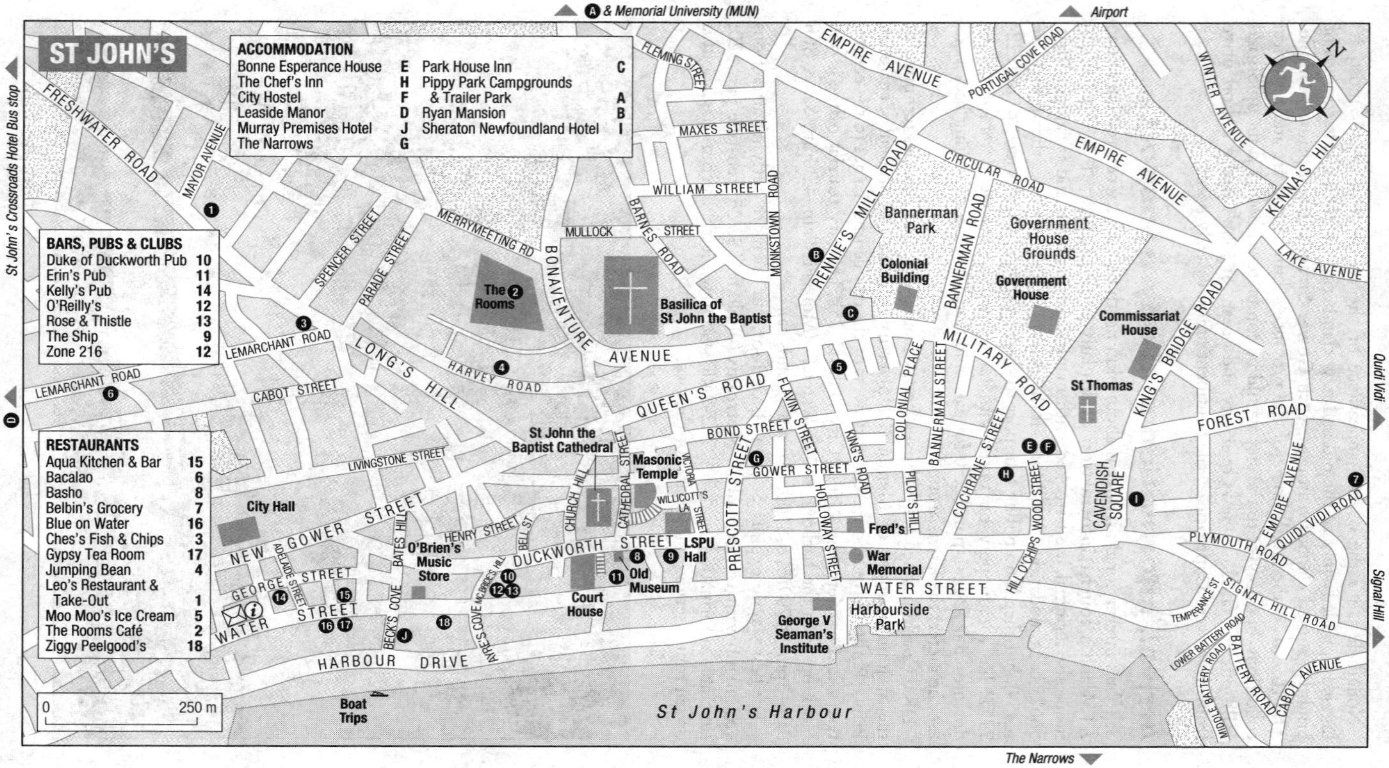

ST JOHN'S
ACCOMMODATION
Bonne Esperance House E
The Chef's Inn H
City Hostel F
Leaside Manor D
Murray Premises Hotel J
The Narrows G
Park House Inn C
Pippy Park Campgrounds & Trailer Park A
Ryan Mansion B
Sheraton Newfoundland Hotel I
BARS, PUBS & CLUBS
Duke of Duckworth Pub 10
Erin's Pub 11
Kelly's Pub 14
O'Reilly's 12
Rose & Thistle 13
The Ship 9
Zone 216 12
RESTAURANTS
Aqua Kitchen & Bar 15
Bacalao 6
Basho 8
Belbin's Grocery 7
Blue on Water 16
Ches's Fish & Chips 3
Gypsy Tea Room 17
Jumping Bean 4
Leo's Restaurant & Take-Out 1
Moo Moo's Ice Cream 5
The Rooms Café 2
Ziggy Peelgood's 18
0 250 m
A & Memorial University (MUN)
Airport
Quidi Vidi
Signal Hill
The Narrows
St John's Crossroads Hotel Bus stop
D
N
FRESHWATER ROAD
MAYOR AVENUE
SPENCER STREET
PARADE STREET
MERRYMEETING RD
LEMARCHANT ROAD
LONG'S HILL
HARVEY ROAD
CABOT STREET
The Rooms
BONAVENTURE AVENUE
MULLOCK STREET
BARNES ROAD
Basilica of St John the Baptist
FLEMING STREET
MAXES STREET
WILLIAM STREET
MONKSTOWN ROAD
RENNIE'S MILL ROAD
EMPIRE AVENUE
PORTUGAL COVE ROAD
WINTER AVENUE
CIRCULAR ROAD
KENNA'S HILL
LAKE AVENUE
Bannerman Park
Colonial Building
BANNERMAN ROAD
Government House Grounds
Government House
Commissariat House
KING'S BRIDGE ROAD
St Thomas
MILITARY ROAD
FOREST ROAD
QUEEN'S ROAD
BOND STREET
FLAVIN STREET
KING'S ROAD
COLONIAL PLACE
BANNERMAN STREET
COCHRANE STREET
GOWER STREET
PILOT'S HILL
WOOD STREET
HILL O'CHIPS
HOLLOWAY STREET
PRESCOTT STREET
VICTORIA STREET
WILLICOTT'S LA
Masonic Temple
St John the Baptist Cathedral
CATHEDRAL STREET
CHURCH HILL
LIVINGSTONE STREET
HENRY STREET
BELL ST
City Hall
NEW GOWER STREET
ADELAIDE STREET
GEORGE STREET
WATER STREET
BATES HILL
BECK'S COVE
O'Brien's Music Store
MC BRIDES HILL
AYRE'S COVE
DUCKWORTH STREET
LSPU Hall
Old Museum
Court House
Fred's
War Memorial
Harbourside Park
George V Seaman's Institute
HARBOUR DRIVE
Boat Trips
St John's Harbour
CAVENDISH SQUARE
EMPIRE AVENUE
QUIDI VIDI ROAD
PLYMOUTH ROAD
SIGNAL HILL ROAD
TEMPERANCE ST
LOWER BATTERY ROAD
MIDDLE BATTERY ROAD
BATTERY ROAD
CABOT AVENUE

Tours and boat trips

One of the most enjoyable **guided tours** of the city is the **St John's Haunted Hike** (June–Aug Sun–Thurs 9.30pm; $10; ⓣ709/685-3444, ⓦwww.hauntedhike.com; 1hr 15min), an intriguingly spooky walking tour delving into the city's dishevelled past that starts at the west entrance to the Anglican Cathedral. **Legend Tours** (ⓣ709/753-1497, ⓦwww.legendtours.ca) provides more conventional three-hour bus trips round the city centre, Signal Hill, Quidi Vidi and Cape Spear for $65; they operate year-round, weather permitting (daily 10am & 2pm).

The best place for **boat trips** is Bay Bulls (p.461), but in the summer Iceberg Quest (ⓣ709/722-1888, ⓦwww.icebergquest.com) runs four daily trips from Pier 7 in St John's out to Cape Spear, where you might spy whales (July & Aug), puffins and big chunks of ice (June). Thrill seekers should contact **Ocean Quest Adventure Resort** (ⓣ1-866/623-2664, ⓦwww.oceanquestadventures.com), at 17 Stanley's Lane in Conception Bay South (around 20km west of St John's), which runs boat trips and wreck dives around Bell Island in Conception Bay.

Accommodation

St John's has a healthy supply of downtown **hotels**, but – with one or two notable exceptions – its **B&Bs** are rather more distinctive. For those on a tighter budget, there are several chain **motels** along Kenmount Road (one of the main approach roads running east into the city from the Trans-Canada Hwy), a decent **hostel** and a **campground** within easy striking distance of the centre.

Bonne Esperance House 18-22 Gower St ⓣ709/726-3835 or 1-888/726-3835, ⓦwww.bonneesperancehouse.ca. Central B&B spread over three Victorian terrace houses that date to the 1890s. The interiors are decked out in broadly period style and each of the guest rooms, all en suite, feature antique furnishings; the breakfasts are particularly tasty. 6

The Chef's Inn 29 Gower St ⓣ709/753-3180, ⓦwww.thechefsinn.ca. Beautifully restored 1890s rowhouse on one of the prettiest streets in the city; four modern en-suite rooms enhanced with fluffy robes, wooden beds, cable TV and free w-fi; chef and owner Todd Perrin whips up gourmet breakfasts. 5

City Hostel 8 Gower St ⓣ709/754-4789. This solid backpacker option, right next to the *Bagel Café*, offers dorms ($27.50) and private rooms (some with private bath), all within stumbling distance of George St. You get free internet and laundry, a decent shared kitchen and very laidback staff. 3

Leaside Manor 39 Topsail Rd ⓣ709/722-0387, ⓦwww.leasidemanor.com. Wonderful, luxurious suites, ranging from the hip (open-plan with jacuzzis) to traditional (nineteenth-century decor with four-poster canopy beds). Opt for the Jellybean Row room if you like leopard pattern prints. Host Elaine Hann is great fun and a font of local information. 6

Murray Premises Hotel 5 Beck's Cove ⓣ709/738-7773 or 1-866/738-7773, ⓦwww.murraypremiseshotel.com. Perfect location for nightlife, one block from George St, featuring smart, boutique-like rooms carved out of an 1840s warehouse; the second-floor executive rooms are much nicer, with jacuzzi, flat-screen TVs and jet showers. The thin floors mean it can get a bit noisy. 7

The Narrows 146 Gower St ⓣ709/739-4850 or 1-866/739-4850, ⓦwww.thenarrowsbb.com. Infinitely cosy B&B in an old terrace house a short walk from the centre, with four en-suite guest rooms decorated in a neat and trim version of period style. 3–5

Park House Inn 112 Military Rd ⓣ709/576-2265 or 1-866/303-0565, ⓦwww.newfoundlandbedandbreakfast.nl.ca. This gorgeous old house, dating back to the 1870s, has been intelligently restored with all modern conveniences grafted onto all manner of period detail, from the wide wooden staircase to the expansive bay windows. Rooms come with wi-fi, cable TV and MP3/DVD player, while the handy location is just five minutes' walk from the town centre. 5

Pippy Park Campgrounds and Trailer Park Nagle's Place, Pippy Park ⓣ709/737-3669, ⓦwww.pippypark.com. Around 216 sites, both serviced ($35) and unserviced ($25), located about 4km west of the city centre, near the Confederation Building. To get there, proceed west along Allandale Rd; Nagle's Place is on the left, just beyond Prince Philip Drive. There are clean, accessible washrooms and a convenience store. May–Oct. Basic tent sites $20.

Ryan Mansion 21 Rennies Mill Rd ⓣ709/753-7926, ⓦwww.ryanmansion.com. Lavishly maintained 1911 Edwardian property, with utterly luxurious rooms; bathrooms come with steam rooms, heated marble floors, jacuzzis and Victorian tubs, while the beds are comfortable hardwood four-posters. 7

Sheraton Newfoundland Hotel 115 Cavendish Square ⓣ709/726-4980 or 1-886/716-8101, ⓦwww.starwoodhotels.com. The exterior of this chain hotel is all modern clunkiness, but the interior has a real sense of itself – as befits the city's most famous hotel, whose earliest incarnation dates back to 1926. All the rooms are kitted out in top-whack chain style and most have great views over the harbour. Indoor pool, fitness facilities and free internet access. 8

The City

Running the length of the centre, a stone's throw from the harbour, **Water Street** has long been the city's commercial hub, though the ship suppliers and fish merchants are gone, replaced by an engaging mix of shops, restaurants and bars. St John's finest buildings string along **Military Road**, culminating in the gargantuan **Catholic Basilica of St John the Baptist** and **The Rooms** museum and art gallery. Further afield, the prime objective is **Signal Hill**, not so much for the conspicuous Cabot Tower perched on top but for the panoramic views. With the exception of Signal Hill, all the main downtown attractions are within easy walking distance of each other. The appellation "cove", commonplace here, means a short side street, not a bay.

Harbourside Park

Tiny **Harbourside Park**, on Water Street, is the logical place to start a visit to the city: it was here – or at least hereabouts – that Sir Humphry Gilbert landed in 1583 to claim the island for England. A series of historical plaques in the park gives all the background, and behind are two bronze **dogs**, a **Newfoundland** and a **Labrador**. The early settlers were very reliant on their dogs and the Newfoundland breed, with its double-layered waterproof coat and webbed feet, was perfect for their requirements, though the Labrador – a cross between a Newfoundland and a Pointer – proved better for hunting.

From the Courthouse to Gower Street

From the park, it's a five-minute walk south along Water Street to the **Courthouse**, a monumental Romanesque Revival building of 1901 made of granite and equipped with rounded turrets, a tumble of different gables and a clock tower. Take the steps that run up beside the Courthouse and at the top, on Duckworth Street, turn right and it's a few metres to the **old Newfoundland Museum** (now a Career Work Centre), built in 1907. The main body of the building is sullen red brick, but the facade boasts a coat of arms and three finely cast panels – one each for the island's miners, loggers and fishermen. Opposite, Cathedral Street scuttles up to the **Masonic Temple**, completed in 1897 and now home to the **Spirit of Newfoundland** (ⓣ709/579-3023 or 1-877/661-3023, ⓦwww.spiritofnewfoundland.com) theatre company – performances usually feature a Newfoundland theme, and are often combined with dinner (tickets around $60).

The temple's cliff-face of a facade looks challengingly across to the bluestone **Anglican Cathedral of St John the Baptist** (mid-June to Sept Mon–Fri 10am–noon & 2–4pm, Sat 10am–noon; free) designed in Gothic Revival style by the English architect Sir George Gilbert Scott. Begun in 1847, much of the church burnt down in 1892 but Scott's son rebuilt it to the original plans, though the work was never fully completed. Inside, the stone walls are capped by a handsome vaulted timber ceiling and the stained glass is of exceptionally high quality. In summer you can enjoy tea and home-made cakes ($8) in the **Crypt Tea Room**

(July & Aug Mon–Fri 2.30–4.30pm), reached by the west door on the south side of the cathedral. The cathedral backs onto **Gower Street**, one of the city's most charming residential thoroughfares, its long line of brightly painted clapboard (or vinyl imitation) houses known locally as **Jellybean Row**.

Commissariat House

From the north end of Gower Street, it's a short stroll over to the robust Georgian clapboard of the **Commissariat House Provincial Historic Site** (May–Sept daily 10am–5.30pm; $3) on Kings Bridge Road. Completed in 1820, this was the home and offices of the assistant commissary general, who was responsible for keeping the British garrison in St John's paid, fed and clothed. Though all the rooms have been faithfully restored in austere 1830s style and you can wander around on your own, it's far better to be shown around by one of the knowledgeable guides (free), who will add the context; balancing the demands of spendthrift commanders with a penny-pinching Treasury back in London wasn't easy. Don't confuse the oil paintings of JA Turner upstairs with his more famous namesake – JA Turner was born 75 years later and spent most of his life in Australia. The stables outside house a small exhibition on the history of the site.

Government House and the Colonial Building

From Commissariat House, it's the briefest of walks along Military Road to the elegant red sandstone symmetries of **Government House** (Ⓣ709/729-4494, Ⓦwww.govhouse.nl.ca), completed at great expense in 1831. It has since served as the residence of the lieutenant-governor, the Queen's representative on the island. The only way to get inside is to call in advance to arrange a **free tour** (1hr 30min), normally on Tuesdays and Thursdays only, but you're free to stroll around the leafy grounds any time. Just along Military Road stands the limestone **Colonial Building**, a perfectly proportioned Neoclassical edifice fronted by a stirringly grand portico. It was here that the island's legislature met from 1850 until 1960, before moving to the Confederation Building on the waterfront. By 2012 the elegant interior should be **open to the public** as a provincial historic site.

Catholic Basilica of St John the Baptist

Continuing along Military Road, it's only a few minutes to the grandest of the city's churches, the **Catholic Basilica of St John the Baptist** (Mon–Fri 10.30am–4.30pm, Sat 9am–1.30pm, Sun 9am–noon; free; Ⓣ709/726-3660, Ⓦwww.thebasilica.ca), whose twin-towered limestone and granite mass overlooks the harbour from the crest of a hill. The church was completed in 1855, with the facade modelled on the great Romanesque churches of Italy. The interior is rather better, the 28 stained glass windows on the upper walls illuminating a delightfully ornate and embossed gold, maroon and deep-green ceiling. Look out for Irish sculptor John Hogan's *The Dead Christ*, at the Altar of Sacrifice, a moving statue created in 1854. You should also take a peek at the revered marble **Veiled Virgin**, carved in Rome by Giovanni Strazza in the 1850s, and now on display at the **Presentation Convent** (Mon–Fri 10.30am–noon & 2–4pm; free) next door. On the left side of the Basilica, in what used to be the old Bishop's Palace, the **Basilica Museum** (July–Aug Mon–Sat 10am–4pm, Sun noon–4pm; $2) displays an intriguing collection of religious artefacts, reliquaries and artwork.

The Rooms

Across from the Basilica, on Bonaventure Avenue, **The Rooms** (June to mid-Oct Mon–Sat 10am–5pm, Wed & Thurs till 9pm, Sun noon–5pm; mid-Oct to May Tues–Sat 10am–5pm, Sun noon–5pm; $7.50; Ⓦwww.therooms.ca) are lavish

The Beothuks

The Algonquian-speaking **Beothuks**, who reached Newfoundland in about 200 AD, were semi-nomadic, spending the summer on the coast and moving inland during the winter. They were the first North American natives to be contacted by English explorers, who came to describe them as "Red Indians" from their habit of covering themselves with red ochre, perhaps as some sort of fertility ritual or simply to keep the flies off. Neither side seemed to need or want anything from the other, and even after three hundred years of co-existence, hardly anything was known about the Beothuks. As settlers spread north from the Avalon Peninsula in the eighteenth century, they began to encroach on the Beothuks' ancient hunting grounds, pushing them inland. By the early 1800s, settlers' attitudes had hardened and the Beothuks that hadn't succumbed to European diseases were casually slaughtered. Some white settlers organized expeditions into the interior to catch one or two alive, but the last seen member of the tribe, a young woman named **Shanawdithit**, died of tuberculosis aged 29 in 1829. She spent the last years of her life in the protective custody of the attorney general in St John's, and it was here that she built a small model of a Beothuk canoe and made ten simple drawings of her people and their customs. No other Beothuks were ever found; she is considered the last of her people.

modern premises built to exhibit the island's best historical, ethnographic and fine art collections, though some of the art displays have more international themes. A rolling programme of temporary exhibitions occupies every nook and cranny with one exception – **Floor 3**, which has a permanent display that zips through the island's history. Beginning with the island's earliest inhabitants, the Maritime Archaic Peoples, and their successors, the Dorset Inuit and the Beothuks (see above), subsequent displays provide details on the island's early fishery, whaling, the arrival of the Vikings and early European settlement. Everything is illustrated with an assortment of archeological artefacts – there's even a miniature Norse boat-patching kit. Perhaps most interesting of all, and stored in the drawer of a small wooden cabinet, are the crude but particularly poignant drawings made by **Shanawdithit**, the last of the Beothuks, who, half-starved and desperate, surrendered herself to a European trapper in 1823.

Signal Hill

Rearing up above The Narrows, **Signal Hill National Historic Park** (open access) is a protuberant, grass-covered chunk of rock with views dramatic enough to warrant the strenuous half-hour (2km) walk up from the northern end of Duckworth Street (there's no city bus). Originally known as The Lookout, Signal Hill took its present name in 1704, when it became common practice for flags to be hoisted here to notify the city of impending arrivals. The hill was also an obvious line of defence, and the simple fortifications that were established after the last French occupation in 1762 were embellished every time there was a military emergency, right up until World War II.

The road to the summit is dotted with a string of attractions, beginning with the flashy **Johnson Geo Centre** (mid-May to mid-Oct Mon–Sat 9.30am–5pm, Sun noon–5pm; mid-Oct to mid-May Tues–Sat 9.30am–5pm, Sun noon–5pm; $11.50; Ⓦwww.geocentre.ca), which is devoted to earth sciences. An introductory film illustrates various natural phenomena, followed by a section each on the Earth, Newfoundland and Labrador's geology, the Earth's peoples and a "Stellarium", examining the stars. Special exhibits also focus on the *Titanic* and oil and gas.

Futher up lies Signal Hill **visitor centre** (mid-May to mid-Oct daily 10am–6pm; mid-Oct to mid-May Mon–Fri 8.30am–4.30pm; $3.90; ⓣ709/772-5367), whose well-chosen displays and dramatic twenty-minute multimedia presentation explore the military and civilian history of the hill, particularly the bitter struggle for the city between France and England in the eighteenth century. Just up the road is the **Queen's Battery**, whose antiquated guns peer over the entrance to the harbour. The plot of ground beside the battery, O'Flaherty Field, is used by the authentic nineteenth-century guns and drums of the **Signal Hill Tattoo** (July to mid-Aug Wed, Thurs, Sat & Sun at 11am & 3pm; $5; ⓣ709/772-5367).

Cabot Tower

Plonked on top of Signal Hill is **Cabot Tower** (daily: June–Aug 8.30am–9pm; rest of year 9am–5pm, closed mid-Jan to March; free), a short and stout stone structure completed in 1900 to commemorate John Cabot's voyage of 1497 and Queen Victoria's Diamond Jubilee. The tower holds a small display on electronic signalling, and outside in the car park there's a **plaque** honouring Guglielmo **Marconi**, who confirmed the reception of the first transatlantic radio signal here in December 1901. The views back over the city and out to sea are jaw-dropping, and half a dozen **hiking trails** fan out across the peak. The shortest is the comfortable 500m stroll back down Signal Hill to the Queen's Battery; another is the wild and windswept trek down the headland to The Narrows and onto Outer Battery Road, by means of which you can return to the city centre.

Quidi Vidi

Tiny **QUIDI VIDI** ("kiddy-viddy"), a couple of kilometres north of the city centre, is a well-known beauty spot, where a handful of old fishing shacks are backdropped by sharp-edged cliffs and set beside the deep-blue waters of a slender inlet. A spate of new construction has robbed the village of much of its charm, but it is home to both **Mallard Cottage Antiques** (May–Sept daily 10am–5pm; other times Wed–Sat 10am–4.30pm or call ⓣ709/576-2266), a creaky curio-filled house dating from the 1750s, and **Quidi Vidi Brewery**, which occupies the old fish plant. The brewery offers tours and tastings year-round (May–Oct hourly, call at other times; $10; ⓣ709/738-4040, ⓦwww.quidividibrewery.ca). From the centre of the village, it's a short walk east to **Quidi Vidi Battery Provincial Historic Site** (mid-May to early Oct daily 10am–5.30pm; $3; ⓣ709/729-2977), which overlooks the narrow channel connecting the village to the sea. The gun battery has been restored to its 1812 appearance, when it was readied against potential attack from the US.

To get to Quidi Vidi from the city centre, take Forest Road from beside the *Sheraton Newfoundland* hotel and keep going – or take Metrobus service #15 from Plymouth Road on the harbourside of the same hotel. En route, you'll travel the length of **Quidi Vidi Lake**, the site of the annual Royal St John's Regatta (ⓦwww.stjohnsregatta.org), held every August. This is one of the oldest sporting events in North America, featuring fixed-seat rowing races and a huge garden party.

Eating and drinking

St John's **restaurant** scene is very dynamic, with a string of fashionable places dotted around the city centre. Seafood remains the key ingredient on many menus, which often feature contemporary twists on Newfoundland classics, and there are plenty of fish and chip specialists. Traditional cuisine can be purchased at *Belbin's Grocery* (Mon–Fri 8.30am–8pm, Sat 8.30am–6pm, Sun 10am–6pm), 85 Quidi Vidi Rd, especially good for local fruit pies and seal flipper pie.

Newfoundland folk music

The English and Irish settlers who first colonized Newfoundland brought their music with them: step dances and square sets performed to the accompaniment of the **fiddle** and the **button accordion**, followed by the unaccompanied **singing** of locally composed and "old country" songs. The music was never written down, so as it passed from one generation to the next a distinctive Newfoundland style evolved, whose rhymes and rhythms varied from outport to outport – though its Irish and English roots always remained pronounced.

This traditional style of folk music has lingered on, as exemplified by the island's most famous fiddlers, **Rufus Guinchard** and **Émile Benoit**. The two died in the 1980s, but their approach was adopted by younger artists like singer-songwriters Jim Payne and Ron Hynes, musician-producer Kelly Russell and groups such as **Figgy Duff**. Currently, Celtic music is the big deal in the bars of St John's, but local musicians regularly perform in a more traditional idiom. In particular, look out for **Phyllis Morrissey** and **Anita Best**, not to mention two of the most popular bands, **Great Big Sea** and the **Irish Descendants. Hey Rosetta** is also an up and coming group.

St John's has two good specialist record shops – **O'Brien's Music Store**, 278 Water St (☎709/753-8135, Ⓦwww.obriens.nf.ca), and **Fred's**, 198 Duckworth St (☎709/753-9191, Ⓦwww.freds.nf.ca).

Aqua Kitchen & Bar 310 Water St ☎709/576-2782, Ⓦwww.aquarestaurant.ca. One of the new breed of restaurants to appear on the island with cool decor and an ambitious contemporary menu featuring caribou burger and seared scallops . Dinner entrees are $18–28. Mon–Fri noon–2pm & daily 5.30–10pm.

Bacalao 65 Lemarchant Rd ☎709/579-6565, Ⓦwww.bacalaocuisine.ca. Giving traditional home-cooked Newfoundland food a contemporary twist, chef Mike Barsley serves jiggs dinner as a cabbage roll appetizer, delicate cod tongues, local mussels ($12), caribou ($29), lobster in season and *bacalao* (cod) *du jour* ($26); expect to pay $50 a head for a good meal. Most of the ingredients are local, including the beers and fruit wines. Free parking on site.

Basho 283 Duckworth St ☎709/576-4600. Tak Ishiwata, a student of New York-based maestro Nobu Matsuhiro, opened his shrine to Japanese fusion cuisine in 2006 and rapidly became one of the hottest chefs in the city. Though the hype has died down somewhat, the food is still exceptional: think pan-seared caribou steak, sushi and iceberg martinis made with real chunks of Greenland bergs.

Blue on Water 319 Water St ☎709/574-2583, Ⓦwww.blueonwater.com. Chic restaurant decorated in sharp modern style and featuring local ingredients on its pricey but inventive menu – try the delicious rabbit and partridgeberry soup. Mains from $22. Mon–Fri 7.30am–10pm, Sat 9am–11pm, Sun 9am–9pm.

Ches's Fish & Chips 9 Freshwater Rd, 655 Topsail Rd & 8 Highland Drive ☎709/726-3434, Ⓦwww.chessfishandchips.ca. Legendary fish and chips since 1951, with several locations in the city; the main event is two pieces of crisp cod served with handmade chips, though the menu also offers cod bites, wings, chicken, burgers and shellfish.

Leo's Restaurant and Take-Out 27 Freshwater Rd ☎709/726-2658. Good spot to try local specialities like cods' tongues and, in season, seal-flipper pie, as well as first-rate fish and chips. Closed Sun.

Moo Moo's Ice Cream 88 Kings Rd ☎709/753-0999. Much loved ice cream counter inside *The Market* convenience store, serving sorbets and luscious ice cream with local flavours like partridgeberry (loganberry) and bakeapple (cloudberry).

The Rooms Café Bonaventure Ave ☎709/757-8097. Enjoy the best views of the city over a healthy salad, fish cakes ($12.95) or 'cod on the rocks' (cod and mussels; $16.95). Get here before noon to nab the best tables (no reservations). You don't need to pay the museum entrance fee to eat here, though the café opens the same hours (see p.455).

Ziggy Peelgood's Water St & Churchill Square. This chip van has cult status in St John's. The perfectly cooked fries are copied in many restaurants, and have provided 3am comfort food for generations of pub-goers.

Nightlife and entertainment

The city has dozens of **bars and pubs** – St John's is said to have more drinking places per square kilometre than any other city in the country. Most of the more popular joints are on Water and adjoining George streets and they can get mighty crowded (and boisterous) on weekends. At some point you're likely to be invited to be **screeched in**, a touristy but fun ritual for all newcomers – routines vary, but this usually involves kissing a stuffed cod, reading something written in Newfoundland slang, and downing the local brand of Screech Rum.

Most pubs also offer regular live **folk music**. Pick up a copy of the free weekly listings magazine *The Scope* (ⓦ www.thescope.ca) or ask at O'Brien's Music Store (see opposite). The best of the island's dozen folk festivals, the **Newfoundland and Labrador Folk Festival** (ⓣ 709/576-8508, ⓦ www.nlfolk.com), is held in Bannerman Park in St John's in early August. The **LSPU Hall** (ⓣ 709/753-4531, ⓦ www.rca.nf.ca), at 3 Victoria St, offers an inventive programme of **theatre** and **cinema**.

Duke of Duckworth Pub 325 Duckworth St ⓣ 709/739-6344. Popular bar just down the steps from Duckworth St towards Water St. Serves a wide range of Newfoundland ales (including Quidi Vidi and their own tasty brew, Duke's Own), but its speciality is English pints and fish and chips.

Erin's Pub 186 Water St ⓣ 709/722-1916, ⓦ www.erinspub.ca. Popular and well-established no-frills Irish pub, showcasing the best of folk acts Wed–Sun night. It also has the best Guinness in town.

Kelly's Pub 25 George St, at Adelaide ⓣ 709/753-5300. Lively spot with a youthful (drunken) clientele. Good range of beers and pub food (yet more lip-smacking fish and chips), with frequent live music.

Rose & Thistle 208 Water St ⓣ 709/579-6662, ⓦ www.roseandthistlepub.com. Small and long-established pub that pulls in the punters with creamy pints of Smithwicks and Guinness, and live folk bands (Thurs–Sun).

The Ship Solomon's Lane, at 265 Duckworth St ⓣ 709/753-3870. Down the steps from Duckworth St, this dark, earthy pub showcases an eclectic mix of live music that attracts everyone from grizzled old-timers who love their folk music to arty, black-clad students.

Zone 216 216 Water St ⓣ 709/754-2492. St John's only gay bar (above *Hava Java*,) is dark, cramped and sweaty. Fri & Sat only.

Listings

Bike rental Cychotic, 7 Lemarchant St, at Freshwater ⓣ 709/738-6222, ⓦ www.cychoticbikes.com. Mountain bikes $35/day or $45/2 days. Mon–Fri noon–6pm, Sat 10am–5pm.

Bookshops Afterwords (daily 9am–5.30pm; ⓣ 709/753-4690), 245 Duckworth St, has a large range of new and used Newfoundland titles. If the island dialect intrigues you, this is also the place to pick up the substantial *Dictionary of Newfoundland English* edited by Story, Kirwin and Widdowson.

Camping equipment The Outfitters, 220 Water St ⓣ 709/579-4453, ⓦ www.theoutfitters.nf.ca. Mon–Wed & Sat 10am–6pm, Thurs & Fri 10am–9pm, Sun noon–5pm.

Car rental Avis (airport ⓣ 709/722-6620); Budget (airport ⓣ 709/747-1234); Discount, 350 Kenmount Rd ⓣ 709/722-6699; Enterprise, 835 Topsail Rd, Unit 3, Mount Pearl ⓣ 709/738-3900; National (airport ⓣ 709/722-4307); Thrifty (airport ⓣ 709/722-6000).

Consulates UK ⓣ 709/579-2002.

Laundry Mighty White's, 152 Duckworth St (Mon–Thurs 8am–9.30pm, Fri & Sat 8am–7.30pm; ⓣ 709/753-7947) near the *Sheraton Newfoundland*.

Pharmacy Water Street Pharmacy, 335 Water St, at George (Mon–Sat 9am–6pm; ⓣ 709/579-5554).

Police ⓣ 709/729-8333.

Post office 354 Water St, at Queen (Mon–Fri 8am–5pm).

Shopping Good places to purchase handicrafts, knitwear and jewellery include The Cod Jigger, 245 Duckworth St; Devon House Craft Shop and Gallery, 59 Duckworth St; and Nonia, 286 Water St.

Taxis Bugden's ⓣ 709/726-4400; Casino ⓣ 709/579-5999. There's a rank outside the *Sheraton Newfoundland* and George St.

Weather Bulletins ⓣ 709/772-5534.

The East Coast Trail

Negotiating much of the length of the Avalon Peninsula, the **East Coast Trail** is a long-distance **hiking trail** that passes through fishing communities, provincial parks, national historic sites and a couple of ecological reserves. At present, the 220km stretch from Fort Amherst, on St John's harbour, to Cappahayden has been completed, but construction is under way to extend the trail another 320km; to Topsail, on Conception Bay in the north, Trepassey in the south and across to Placentia in the west (from Ferryland). It's an extraordinarily ambitious enterprise that should be complete by 2016, and one that is largely reliant on volunteer labour. The **East Coast Trail Association** (Ⓣ709/738-4453, Ⓦwww.eastcoasttrail.com) sells first-rate 1:25,000 waterproof topographical maps covering the whole trail ($26 per set of twenty), and guide books covering different sections of it. Only the first two – from St John's to Petty Harbour ($21.95), and from Petty Harbour to Bay Bulls ($28.95) – have been published, and are superb, with all sorts of information on everything from flora and fauna through to historical anecdotes and biographical snippets.

The East Coast Trail is linear, which means that if you're after a day's hiking you really need two cars and at least two people, but there are places to stay along the trail and it is possible to arrange to be picked up (and/or taken out) by taxi. The Association is glad to help and advise and also organizes a programme of group hikes for free. The 3.7km hike from the former fishing village of **Blackhead to Cape Spear** is one of the easier and more accessible portions of the trail and it covers a handsomely rugged stretch of coastline; allow one and a half to two hours. The

Around St John's: Cape Spear

In St John's, take the signposted turning off Water Street south of the centre and it's a 15km-drive via Rte 11 to **Cape Spear National Historic Site** (open access), a rocky, windblown headland that is nearer to Europe than any other part of mainland North America. The cape is crisscrossed by boardwalks, the most obvious of which leads up from the car park past the heritage shop and the modern lighthouse to the squat and rectangular Victorian **Lighthouse** (mid-May to mid-Oct daily 10am–6pm; $3.90), the oldest in the province. Built in the 1830s, the lighthouse's interior has been pleasantly decked out in nineteenth-century style, down to imitation barrels of sperm oil and the neatly made bed. The other specific attraction is the substantial remains of the World War II **gun emplacement** at the tip of the cape, but the views are really the main event, right along the coast and up to St John's. In spring and early summer, the waters off the cape are a great place to spy blue-tinged **icebergs**, and there's a reasonable chance of spotting **whales**.

The Avalon Peninsula

St John's sits on the northeast corner of the **Avalon Peninsula**, a jagged, roughly rectangular slab of land connected to the rest of Newfoundland by a narrow, tapering isthmus. Highlights include the varied attractions along the **Irish Loop**; **Heart's Content**, with its antique cable station; **Castle Hill**, from where there are panoramic views over Placentia Bay; and the sea-bird colonies of **Cape St Mary's**. With the exception of the cape, which is a tad too far away for comfort, all make good day-tripping destinations from St John's.

Southeast Avalon: The Irish Loop

The **Irish Loop** (a 312km combination of routes 10 and 90) covers the southeastern arm of the Avalon Peninsula, starting with **Bay Bulls** and the boat trips out to **Witless Bay Ecological Reserve**. From Bay Bulls, it's another short haul to **Ferryland**, where archeologists are exploring the site of the seventeenth-century English colony of **Avalon**, from which the whole peninsula received its name.

Bay Bulls and the Witless Bay Ecological Reserve

Straggling around the head of a deep and pointed inlet, 25km south of St John's, the village of **BAY BULLS** makes much of its living from **boat tours** to the four tiny offshore islets comprising the **Witless Bay Ecological Reserve**. The best time to visit is between mid-June and mid-July, when over 800,000 birds gather here – the reserve has the largest puffin colony in eastern Canada and there are also thousands of storm petrels, common murres, kittiwakes, razorbills, guillemots, cormorants and herring gulls. In addition, the area is home to the largest population of **humpback whales** in the world, and finback and minke whales are often spotted between June and August.

From May to September several companies offer daily **boat trips**, including O'Brien's Whale & Bird Tours (ⓣ709/753-4850 or 1-877/639-4253, ⓦwww.obriensboattours.com) and Mullowney's Puffin and Whale Tours (ⓣ709/334-3666 or 1-877/783-3467, ⓦwww.puffinswhales.com). Both run two-hour trips ($50–56) and reservations are advised. They'll provide transport to and from major hotels in St John's for roughly $25 return, though this has to be arranged in advance. From Bay Bulls, it's 45km south to Ferryland.

Ferryland

George Calvert, the first Lord Baltimore, was a favourite of King James I of England, who gave him a slab of land in Newfoundland to settle as a colony. Calvert obligingly sailed out to what is now **FERRYLAND** in 1620 and took a shine to the place, naming it the **Colony of Avalon** (mid-May to early Oct daily 10am–6pm; $9.50; ⓣ709/432-3200 or 1-877/326-5669), ⓦwww.colonyofavalon.ca) and dispatching a band of prospective colonists the following year. The settlers sent him such wonderful reports that he decided to move there himself a few years later, but he only lasted one winter. Archeologists have set about unearthing the remains of Calvert's colony at the base of a narrow and low-lying headland that hooks out into the ocean opposite today's Ferryland. They have discovered a surprising amount, including the foundations of several buildings, part of the original sea wall and even a small strip of cobblestone street. Start at the **Interpretation Centre**, which gives the historical background to Calvert's venture, before wandering 400m down to the archeological site itself (digs take place mid-June to Sept Mon–Fri 8am–4.30pm). Afterwards you can follow the gravel road leading to the stumpy Victorian **lighthouse** on Ferryland Head – allow 25 minutes each way for the walk. At the lighthouse is *Lighthouse Picnics* (June–Sept Tues–Sun 11.30am–5pm; ⓣ709/363-7456, ⓦwww.lighthousepicnics.ca), which offers tasty spreads featuring local ingredients and lip-smacking home-made lemonade; picnics (from around $21/person), have to be pre-booked.

Mistaken Point Ecological Reserve

It's another 58km south on Rte 10 to **PORTUGAL COVE SOUTH** and the gravel road turn-off for Cape Race and **Mistaken Point Ecological Reserve**, home to some incredibly well preserved Precambrian fossil remains *in situ*. Discovered in 1967, the site is considered one of the most important in the world (the fossils are around 575 million years old), but what makes it truly unique is that visitors are free to clamber all over the rocks to see them up close. Visitors must be accompanied **by an official tour guide**. Guided tour schedules (late May–early Oct daily 1pm; free) and information are available at the **interpretive centre** in Portugal Cove South (Ⓣ709/438-1100), which also arranges tours of the isolated Cape Race lighthouse, built in 1907, and the nearby 1904 Marconi wireless station (famous for receiving the Titanic distress call). Tours start at the centre and involve a 6km hike (1hr 30min); you can take a free minibus to save driving (book ahead).

Northwest Avalon: the Baccalieu Trail

The **Baccalieu Trail** (230km, primarily along routes 80 and 70) covers the northwestern section of the Avalon Peninsula (known as the Bay de Verde Peninsula), starting with Brigus and historic Cupids at the southern end of Conception Bay. From here, it's a short drive to the Victorian charms of Harbour Grace, and a little further to the landmark cable station at Heart's Content.

Brigus

Start at **BRIGUS**, about 80km from St John's, where the home of **Captain Robert Bartlett** has become the **Hawthorne Cottage National Historic Site** (daily mid-May to late June & Sept to mid-Oct 9am–5pm; late June to Aug 9am–7pm; $5; Ⓣ709/528-4004). Bartlett was a much sought-after ice navigator and Arctic explorer who helped get Peary to his base camp prior to his dash to the North Pole in 1909. The house is littered with his keepsakes, but just as interesting is the architecture. The family home, built in 1830, eschewed the clapboard of the traditional Newfoundland house for a decorative Regency style, complete with an elevated, wrought-iron, wraparound balcony. The cottage is in the old part of Brigus, a pint-sized pocket of good-looking Victorian houses that backs onto the bay.

Cupids

Tiny **CUPIDS**, a few kilometres north of Brigus, was the unlikely site of Canada's first English settlement, a venture established by Bristol merchant John Guy in 1610 that acted as a catalyst for the colonization of the rest of Newfoundland. The original settlement was all but abandoned by 1700, and it wasn't until the 1990s that it was rediscovered by archaelogists.

By the summer of 2010 the **Cupids Legacy Centre** on Seaforest Drive should be open, home to an exhibition hall, a family history resource centre, the Cupids Cove Plantation Archaeology Lab and a multipurpose community/arts centre. You can see some of the items recovered from the settlement site at **Cupids Museum** (mid-June to mid-Oct daily 10am–5pm; $2; Ⓣ709/528-3500) and visit the **dig site** (June–Sept Mon–Fri 9am–4.45pm, Sat & Sun 10am–4.45pm; $3; Ⓣ709/528-1344, Ⓦwww.baccalieudigs.ca) where 126,000 artefacts and the remains of four seventeenth-century buildings have been found since 1995.

Harbour Grace

HARBOUR GRACE, one of Conception Bay's prettiest settlements, sits on the bay's western shore, tucked in against Rte 70, 30km or so from Brigus and Cupids. The village stretches out along **Water Street**, which is most attractive near its northern end, where a handful of elegant clapboard houses flank a slender inlet and are overseen by three **churches**: the handsome Catholic Church of the Immaculate Conception; the modest Coughlan United Methodist effort next door; and the pretty neo-Gothic stonework of St. Paul's Anglican further up the road. The 1870 red-brick Customs House has been turned into the mildly entertaining **Conception Bay Museum** (mid-June to early Sept daily 10am–5pm; $2), featuring sepias of the village and its Victorian inhabitants, and an outdoor plaque commemorates

Peter Easton, the so-called "Pirate Admiral". Easton, who was based here between 1610 and 1614, ran a phenomenally successful fleet, manned by five thousand sailors who made their leader rich enough to retire to a life of luxury in the south of France. Next door, the tiny park has another plaque and wing-shaped monument honouring the early aviators who flew across the Atlantic from Harbour Grace between 1919 and 1937. The most famous was **Amelia Earhart**, the first woman to complete the journey solo in 1932. Earhart is also commemorated with a plaque on the grassy airstrip above the town – this was Canada's **first airfield** when it opened in 1927 (signs lead the way from town via a bone-shaking dirt track).

Heart's Content

In 1858, **HEART'S CONTENT**, 30km northwest of Harbour Grace on the shores of Trinity Bay, was the scene of the first attempt to connect North America with Britain by **telegraph cable**. After Queen Victoria and the American president James Buchanan had swapped inaugural jokes the cable broke. It was eight years before an improved version, running from Valentia in Ireland, could be installed and thereafter Heart's Content became an important relay station to New York, a role it performed until technological changes made it obsolete in the 1960s. Tight against the waterfront, in the centre of the village, the **Cable Station Provincial Historic Site** (mid-June to early Oct daily 10am–5.30pm; $3; ⓣ709/583-2160) contains an intriguing old cable operating room that has been preserved in pristine condition. It also houses displays on the history of telecommunications, including a replica of the original Victorian cable office and details of the problems encountered during the laying of the first telegraph lines. From Heart's Content, it's a pleasant 60km south along the eastern shore of Trinity Bay to the Trans-Canada Hwy just near the turning for Castle Hill National Historic Site.

Southwest Avalon: Castle Hill National Historic Site

The thumb-shaped promontory filling out the southwest corner of the Avalon Peninsula is a foggy wilderness of marsh and rock, whose westerly shoreline is negotiated by **Rte 100**, branching off the Trans-Canada some 80km from St John's. Just 5km short of the ferry terminal at **ARGENTIA** lies **Castle Hill National Historic Site** (open access; free), magnificently located above **Placentia Harbour**, one of Newfoundland's finest anchorages. The harbour's sheltered waters first attracted the French, who established their regional headquarters, "Plaisance", here in 1662, with Fort Royale (now Castle Hill) up above as the key defensive position completed in 1703. As the fortunes of war changed, the harbour and fort were successively occupied and re-fortified by the British in 1713, who maintained a garrison here until 1811. This history, as well as the process of cod fishing in the eighteenth century, is skillfully explored at the **visitor centre** (mid-May to mid-Oct daily 10am–6pm; $3.90). Little remains of the fort today – just a few stone walls and ditches – but make the trip for the views.

Practicalities

Argentia ferry terminal (see p.398 for ferry details) is a simple affair with little in the way of services. Drive 1km down the road for the **visitor information centre** (daily: April & May 9am–4pm, June–Oct 8.30am–6.30pm), which has a comprehensive collection of leaflets covering the whole province, and a small exhibit commemorating the massive naval base that stood here between World War II and 1994. **Eating** options are scant, but *Belle's Restaurant* (daily 11am–10pm; ⓣ709/227-1777), 2 Ocean Drive, in nearby **Placentia** has well-made Canadian staples.

St Bride's and Cape St Mary's

Immortalized in the much-loved ballad *Let Me Fish Off Cape St. Mary's*, these days the jagged headland, some 65km southwest of Placentia on Rte 100, is more famous for its seabirds, protected within **Cape St Mary's Ecological Reserve**. The reserve is best visited between early May and early August, when thousands of gannets, kittiwakes, razorbills and murres congregate on its rocky sea cliffs and stumpy sea stacks; you can get exceptionally close to this mind-boggling spectacle via paths overlooking the shore, the rocks so smothered with birds they look like snow-covered peaks. An **interpretive centre** (daily May & Oct 9am–5pm; June–Sept 8am–8pm; free; Ⓣ1-800/563-6353) close to the car park provides all the background information and from here a clearly marked footpath cuts across the cape. The main gannet colony and the most dazzling spectacle is generally considered to be 90m-high **Bird Rock**, just a few metres from the cliffs and a twenty-minute (1km) walk away. You can also join one of the reserve's **guided walks** ($7).

Cape St Mary's is just over 200km from St John's, which makes it rather too far away for a comfortable day-trip, but there are several places to **stay** in **ST BRIDE'S** (20km north of the reserve), beginning with the motel-style *Bird Island Resort*, whose assorted modern buildings spread out along the seashore (Ⓣ709/337-2450 or 1-888/337-2450, Ⓦwww.birdislandresort.com; ❸). There's also the spick and span *Capeway Motel* (Ⓣ709/337-2163 or 1-866/337-2163, Ⓦwww.thecapeway.ca; ❸–❹), which has seven unassuming en-suite rooms in what was once a convent.

The Burin Peninsula

Much of the **Burin Peninsula** is crossed by **Rte 210**, which forks off the Trans-Canada Hwy about 160km from St John's, a singularly lonely journey across boggy plateaux. About 140km from the main highway is the shipyard town of **Marystown**, the biggest settlement hereabouts. From here, it's a further 50km to the peninsula's most rewarding spot, the fishing village of **Grand Bank**, and a couple more to **Fortune**, the departure point for **passenger ferries** over to St-Pierre et Miquelon (see opposite).

Grand Bank and Fortune

Looking firmly out to sea, the older streets of **GRAND BANK** incorporate a charming assortment of late nineteenth-century clapboard houses, a few of which are equipped with the so-called "widow's walks", rooftop galleries from where the women watched for their menfolk returning from the Grand Banks cod fishing grounds. The boom years were 1890 to 1940 but today shellfish, particularly surf clams, provide the village with a modest income.

To see something of this tradition, visit the **Southern Newfoundland Seamen's Museum** (May–Aug daily 9am–4.45pm; free; Ⓣ709/832-1484), situated on Marine Drive in a modern building shaped like the sails of a schooner – look out for Atlantic Canada's largest mural on the exterior, a scene depicting the nineteenth-century wharf. The museum has all sorts of models, paintings and photographs of different fishing boats, plus a relief model of Newfoundland and the surrounding ocean showing exactly where the "Banks" are.

From Grand Bank, it's 5km or so to **FORTUNE**, a slightly smaller village and the departure point for the foot passenger ferries over to St-Pierre et Miquelon (see p.466); there's a **car park** near the ferry terminal ($6/day).

Practicalities

Grand Bank has one very recommendable **B&B**, the *Thorndyke* (ⓣ709/832-0820 or 1-866/882-0820, ⓦwww.thethorndyke.ca; ④; May–Sept), an especially well-maintained 1917 sea captain's house with five en-suite period rooms at 33 Water St. There's also the *Inn by the Sea* (ⓣ709/832-0202, ⓦwww.theinnbythesea.com; ④; May–Sept), whose four en-suite guest rooms occupy a 1940s clapboard house by the seashore on the north side of town on Blackburn Road, and a **motel**, *Granny's Motor Inn* (ⓣ709/832-2180 or 1-888/275-1098; ④), on Grandview Boulevard, which doubles as Rte 220.

St-Pierre et Miquelon

The tiny archipelago of **St-Pierre et Miquelon**, 20km off the coast of the Burin, has effectively been a full region of France since 1976 (officially a *collectivité d'outre-mer* in 2003), justifying the billing of the islands as "a little bit of France at your doorstep". The tag certainly pulls in several thousand visitors each year and also manages to put a gloss on the lack of actual attractions and the wetness of the climate, though the islands are still worth a day or two. The main appeal is the francophone atmosphere of the main settlement, **Ville de St-Pierre**, whose fine restaurants and simple guest-houses have a genuinely European flavour. All but seven hundred of the seven thousand islanders live here, with the remainder – mainly of Acadian and Basque descent – on **Grande Miquelon** to the north. The third and middle island, **Langlade**, or **Petite Miquelon**, has just a scattering of houses and is only inhabited in summer. The islands are thirty minutes ahead of Newfoundland time.

A brief history of St-Pierre et Miquelon

The Portuguese stumbled across the archipelago in 1520, but it was **Jacques Cartier** who claimed it for the French in 1536. Subsequently settled by fishermen from the Basque provinces, Normandy and Brittany, the islands were alternately occupied by Britain and France until the British gave them to the French in 1763.

After World War I, the French colonial authorities wanted to expand the local fishing industry, but their efforts became irrelevant with US **Prohibition** in 1920. Quite suddenly, St-Pierre was transformed from a maritime backwater into a giant transit centre for booze smuggling. It was an immensely lucrative business, but when Prohibition ended thirteen years later the St-Pierre economy collapsed. More misery followed during World War II, when the islands' governor remained controversially loyal to the collaborationist **Vichy regime**. Both the Canadians and the Americans considered invading, but it was a **Free French** naval squadron that got there first, crossing over from their base in Halifax and occupying the islands in late 1941 without a shot being fired.

St-Pierre currency and customs control

Since St-Pierre is part of France, local currency is the **euro** (€), made up of 100 cents. Canadian and US dollars are also widely accepted, but you'll usually get change in euros. For up-to-date exchange rates, check ⓦwww.oanda.com. There are several banks and ATMs in St-Pierre town.

To clear St-Pierre et Miquelon's **customs control**, Canadians, EU and US nationals need a **passport** (providing visa-free entry for up to thirty days); entry requirements are essentially the same as visiting France for other nationals, so check the latest requirements. For **medical emergencies**, dial ⓣ15, police ⓣ17.

There was further trouble in 1965 when a **stevedores' strike** forced the administration to resign. Charles De Gaulle promptly dispatched the navy, who occupied the islands for nine years. Perhaps surprisingly, the *St-Pierrais* remained largely loyal to France, and they certainly needed the support of Paris when the Canadians extended the limit of their territorial waters to two hundred nautical miles in 1977. The ensuing wrangle between Canada and France over the islands' claim to a similar exclusion zone was finally resolved in 1994, although the tightening of controls on foreign vessels has largely ended St-Pierre's role as a supply centre.

Arrival

Air St-Pierre (Ⓣ0508/41 00 00 or 1-877/277-7765, Ⓦwww.airsaintpierre.com) **flies** to St-Pierre et Miquelon from Montréal, Halifax and Sydney in Nova Scotia, Moncton in New Brunswick and St John's, Newfoundland. The least expensive flights are from St John's (3 weekly; 45min), where the company has a desk at the airport (Ⓣ709/726-9700); in summer a return flight costs in the region of €188/$277. The St-Pierre et Miquelon **airport** is 1.9km south of the town of St-Pierre; taxis run into the centre (around €5).

SPM Express (Newfoundland Ⓣ709/832-0429 or 1-800/563-2006; St-Pierre Ⓣ0508/41 53 93, Ⓦwww.spmexpress.net) operates **passenger ferries** (May & June, Sept & Oct Fri & Sat only; July & Aug 1 daily; check website for other times of year; 1hr 30min; $70.20 one-way, $103 return) from Fortune in Newfoundland to the town of St-Pierre. The ferry schedule means you almost always have to spend the night on St-Pierre; book your accommodation ahead. To sample St-Pierre on a **day-trip** from Fortune, contact St Pierre Tours (Ⓣ1-800/563-2006, Ⓦwww.spmtours.com), who organize nine-hour ferry and bus excursions (July & Aug Mon–Sat 1 daily) for $99.

Information and island transport

The main St-Pierre et Miquelon **tourist office** is in the centre of Ville de St-Pierre, just metres from the ferry dock on place du Général de Gaulle (June–Sept daily 8.30am–6pm; Oct–May Mon–Fri 8.30am–noon & 1.30–5pm; Ⓣ0508/41 02 00, Ⓦwww.tourismesaintpierremiquelon.fr). They supply all sorts of information about the archipelago, issue free maps and also have the timetable of the **local passenger ferry** linking Ville de St-Pierre with Miquelon village at the other end of the archipelago (Tues, Fri & Sun 1 daily; €14.50 or €22 return; 1hr). You can also **fly** between the two (2–4 daily; €17.50 one-way, €29 return). If you're after venturing beyond St-Pierre it is much easier to join a **guided tour**, and from mid-June to late September there are several **day-trips** to choose from. For example, the nine-hour excursion to Miquelon village via Langdale and the Grand Barachois lagoon costs about €60.

The islands' area **telephone code** is Ⓣ508; if calling from elsewhere, dial the international access code before this (011 from Canada or the US). To call Canada or the US from the island, dial 001 before the area code (dial 00 plus country code for other places). Electrical appliances run on 220 volts here, so US/Canadian appliances won't work unless they are compatible (most phone and laptop adapters can take both currents).

Ville de St-Pierre

The tidy streets of the **VILLE DE ST-PIERRE** nudge back from the harbour, altogether a pleasant ensemble of plain stone and brightly-painted clapboard buildings with a quintessentially French demeanour.

The central area makes for an enjoyable stroll, though there's nothing special to aim for, with the possible exception of the early twentieth-century **cathédrale**, on place Maurier, which does at least attempt to look imposing with its large stone bell tower. A short walk away, just to the north on rue Gloanec, is the **Zazpiak Bat**, a court on which the game of *pelote basque* is played – a reflection of the islands' strong Basque heritage. From here, it's about 700m southwest to **L'Arche Musée et Archives** (June–Aug Tues–Sun 10am–noon & 2–5.30pm; rest of year daily 2–5.30pm; free; Ⓣ0508/41 04 35, Ⓦwww.arche-musee-et-archives.net), on Rue du 11 Novembre, home to the islands' archives and featuring temporary displays on local history and culture. From the museum, it's a short walk back to the harbourfront and the main square, **place du Général de Gaulle**. Just off the square, the **Musée Héritage** (mid-June to mid-Sept Mon–Fri 2–6pm, Sat 10am–noon & 2–5pm; €4.50; Ⓣ0508/41 58 88, Ⓦwww.musee-heritage.fr) at 1 bis, rue Maître Georges Lefèvre, offers another cheerful look at the islands' history, with ten rooms crammed with antique bric-a-brac, including exhibits on the local Nuns of St Joseph, nineteenth-century schoolrooms and the fisheries.

Across the harbour from the town quayside lies the minuscule **Île aux Marins** (Sailor's Island), where the rocks were once strewn with thousands of drying cod fish. After centuries of use, the islet was abandoned in 1964, its assorted buildings pretty much left to their own weather-beaten devices. **Guided tours** (May–mid-Oct 2 daily; €20 including 10min boat trip; reservations Ⓣ0508/41 02 00) take in the church, the town hall, the old school (now the Musée Archipélitude), the lighthouse and a garish Stations of the Cross that leads to a small cemetery perched on a windy promontory. The church, **Notre Dame des Marins**, is the islet's most intriguing building, a large and good-looking structure whose original furnishings, dating from 1874, have survived, including a large black-wrapped catafalque, used for carrying coffins.

Practicalities

Ville de St-Pierre has a good supply of **accommodation**, though most of it is both modern and modest and reservations are strongly recommended from July to early September. Smarter **hotels** include the *Hôtel Île de France* (Ⓣ0508/41 03 50, Ⓦwww.hotelilede france.net; doubles €95), 6 rue Maître Georges-Lèfvre, and the workaday *Hôtel Robert* (Ⓣ0508/41 24 19; doubles €80), 10 rue du 11 Novembre, which was where Al Capone stayed during Prohibition; a small museum off the foyer has one of his straw hats and other memorabilia. For **pensions**, try the comfortable *Chez Hélène* (Ⓣ0508/41 31 08; doubles with shared bath €50), at 15 rue Beaussant.

St-Pierre's **restaurants** are splendid, combining the best of French cuisine with local delicacies such as *tiaude*, a highly seasoned cod stew. Prices are fairly high – reckon on about €25-30 for a main course – but it really is worth splashing out. One of the best is the restaurant at the *Auberge Quatre Temps* (Ⓣ0508/41 43 01), 14 rue Dutemple, which features the stylish *nouvelle cuisine* of chef Pascal Vigneau, blending local, French and even Réunion traditions. For a cheaper meal, head for *Le Maringouin'fre* (Ⓣ0508/41 36 79; closed Wed), 22 rue Général-Leclerc, where they serve delicious crêpes, and steaks and burgers at very affordable prices (€5–8).

Grande Miquelon and Langlade

At the north end of the archipelago, the stubby little island of **Grande Miquelon** comprises peat bog, marsh and a couple of hills which slope away from the only village, **MIQUELON**. The village has a couple of sights of some modest interest, beginning with **L'Eglise** (church) of 1865, whose sombre exterior hides a folksy interior filled with faux-marble columns and containing a good copy of a Murillo *Virgin* donated by Napoléon III – it's above the altar. Just down the street from the church at 5 rue Sourdeval is the cramped **Musée de Miquelon** (mid-June to mid-Sept daily 8.30am–noon & 1.30–5.30pm; €3; ⓣ0508/41 67 07), which displays all manner of items salvaged from local shipwrecks. Otherwise, the **tourist office** (call St-Pierre tourist office for hours) can provide you with details of local walks or you can rent a bicycle from them and cycle off towards Grand Barachois (see below). Of the handful of **places to stay** in Miquelon village, the simple, modern *Maxotel* (ⓣ0508/41 64 57; €70), 42 rue Sourdeval, has the advantage of a seashore location.

The archipelago's most unusual feature is the **Isthme de Langlade**, a sweeping ten-kilometre sandy isthmus linking Grande Miquelon with **LANGLADE**, otherwise **PETITE MIQUELON**. The isthmus began to surface above the ocean two hundred years ago as a result of sand collecting around a shipwreck and is now anything up to 2500m wide. There's a road along the length of the dune, but heavy seas can swamp parts of it, so be sure to stick to the guided tours. These stop at the **Grand Barachois**, a large saltwater pool at the northern end of the isthmus that's a favourite haunt of breeding seals. Langlade itself has a more varied landscape than the other islands – high hills, deciduous forests and rushing brooks – and is at its liveliest in summer, when the St-Pierrais arrive in droves to open up their summer homes.

The Bonavista Peninsula

Crossed by **Rte 230**, which leaves the Trans-Canada Hwy 200km west of St John's near Clarenville, the thickly wooded **Bonavista Peninsula** pokes out into the ocean for some 120km, its shredded shoreline confettied with bays, coves and islands. The English settled here in numbers during the seventeenth century, establishing dozens of tiny outports and one administrative centre, **Trinity**, with a gorgeous headland setting and medley of fine old buildings. Trinity is the ideal base for exploring the rest of the peninsula: it's close to several first-rate hiking trails and is within comfortable striking distance of the wild and windswept **Cape Bonavista**, right at the tip of the peninsula. Trinity also offers **whale-watching tours** and possesses a clutch of **B&Bs**, though the best accommodation is in neighbouring **Port Rexton** – another of the twelve settlements that are collectively known as **Trinity Bight**.

Trinity and around

Situated about 70km from the Trans-Canada Hwy, just off Rte 230, the narrow lanes of tiny **TRINITY** are edged by a delightful ensemble of white and pastel-painted clapboard houses, all set between a ring of hills and the deep and intricate Trinity Bight. The architectural high point is **St Paul's Anglican Church** of 1892, whose perfectly proportioned exterior is adorned by elaborate scrollwork. Inside, the graceful and dignified nave is divided into three, the side aisles entered through arches carved to resemble whale bones and the ceiling up above fashioned in the shape of an upturned boat. All of Trinity's other historic attractions (listed below) have a **combined admission ticket** of $10, and are open mid-May to mid-October (daily 10am–5.30pm, ⓣ709/464-3599, ⓦwww.trinityhistoricalsociety.com).

Opposite the church, there's the modest but entertaining **Trinity Museum**, in a classic saltbox home from the 1880s, which crowds together an eccentric collection of bygones arranged by theme: an old shoemaker's kit in the Washroom;

whaling gear in the Back Porch; an early cooperage in the Store Room; and a fire engine of 1811 in the shed next door, the oldest on the island. Other sites maintained by the local heritage society include the **Green Family Forge** on West Street, which displays artefacts associated with the town's blacksmiths between 1750 and 1955, including two fully-operational forges; and the nearby **Lester-Garland House**, a three-storey Georgian brick home with expertly reproduced period rooms. Entrance to just these three sites is a combined $7.50.

The three **Trinity Provincial Historic Sites** ($3 combined admission; donation suggested if visiting one site) include the yellow and green **Hiscock House** on Church Road, where guides in period costume explain the intricacies of early twentieth-century life. The **Lester-Garland Premises** back on West Street comprise an 1820s counting house and the early twentieth-century **Ryan General Store**, restored to its 1910 appearance. The third and final property is the **Trinity Interpretation Centre**, also on West Street, which contains general exhibits and information about Trinity and the surrounding area.

Practicalities

Trinity boasts several appealing **B&Bs**, foremost of which is the *Campbell House* (Ⓣ709/464-3377 or 1-877/464-7700, Ⓦwww.trinityvacations.com; ❺; mid-May to mid-Oct), in a handsome Victorian building at 49 High St. It has three double rooms, all en suite, and the breakfasts are first-class, featuring such local delicacies as partridgeberry crêpes. A second good choice, also in an older Victorian property, is the *Eriksen Premises B&B* (Ⓣ709/464-3698 or 1-877/464-3698, Ⓦwww.trinityexperience.com; ❹; May–Oct), West Street, which has seven en-suite rooms, mostly with sea views.

The best **restaurant** in town is the waterside *Twine Loft* (daily noon–3pm & 5–8pm; Ⓣ709/464-3377), just off High Street behind the *Artisan Inn*; seafood is the speciality, with meals (without wine) averaging $35 per person. Another good bet is the *Dock Marina Restaurant* (Ⓣ709/464-2133; June–Oct), on the water's edge near the Parish Hall, which serves well-prepared seafood and meat and does a good line in traditional Newfoundland cuisine.

South of Trinity: New Bonaventure

After about 15km, Rte 239 slips into **NEW BONAVENTURE**, a haphazard assortment of clapboard houses edging a rocky bay. On a rainy day it seems like the end of the world, but a side road pushes on even further – fork right over the hill as you descend into the village and continue for another 500m until you reach the church at the end of the road. The **church** seems surprisingly large considering New Bonaventure's size, and even larger when you realise the locals had to roam far and wide to collect the wood for its construction in the 1920s.

Beginning at the church, a six-hundred-metre-long gravel road leads down to the **Random Passage Site** (daily: June to mid-Sept 9.30am–6pm; mid-Sept to

Trinity whale-watching tours

Prince of Whales Adventures, 1 Ash's Lane in Trinity (Ⓣ709/464-2200, Ⓦwww.princeofwhalesadventures.com) runs an extensive programme of **whale-watching** excursions, designed to encourage close encounters between whales and humans. They can't guarantee contact, but there is an excellent chance of sighting minke, finbacks and humpbacks, particularly between mid-June and early August. Expertly run, these excursions take place daily during the whale season from June to October, and prices begin at $80 for a three-hour trip (9am, 1pm & 4pm).

mid-Oct 10am–5pm; $8; ⓦwww.randompassagesite.com), a replica early-1800s outport with fishing stages, roughly-hewn wooden shacks, a church and a school. The village was built in 2000 for the mini-series dramatizations of *Random Passage* and *Waiting for Time*, two romantic novels written by Newfoundland's Bernice Morgan, and telling the tale of the fictional Andrews family, who settled at a spot called Cape Random in the 1820s. Enthusiastic local guides are on hand to explain the basic plot if required – some of them are real characters themselves, and a few appeared in the series as extras. The whole project is run as a non-profit by the local community. The location is stunning, but the authentic mud and stone hovels emphasize the harsh nature of life here, and how everything revolved around the fishery.

Port Rexton

From Trinity, it's about 8km round Trinity Bight – via Rte 230 – to **PORT REXTON**, which actually consists of two pocket-sized outports (Robin Hood and Ship Cove) on either side of a headland. These twin communities once flourished on the back of the Labrador fishery, but things are very quiet today with a haphazard jigsaw of houses rambling across the foreshore. Overlooking Ship Cove from the side of a hill is the *Fishers' Loft Inn* (ⓣ709/464-3240 or 1-877/464-3240, ⓦwww.fishersloft.com; ❺; May–Oct), whose five separate houses – and 21 en-suite guest rooms and suites – are of recent construction, though they are built in various versions of traditional Newfoundland style. The interiors are superb, a well-conceived balance of the intimate and the smart from the wooden floors through to the handmade furniture. The views over Ship Cove and out across Trinity Bay are delightful and breakfasts, which feature local ingredients, are tasty and filling; their splendid, four-course **dinners** are by prior arrangement only.

Cape Bonavista

Some 50km north of Trinity, **Cape Bonavista** is witheringly beautiful, a desolate headland of dark-grey rock and pounding sea inhabited by hundreds of puffins. Explorer **John Cabot** is supposed to have first clapped eyes on the Americas here in 1497, exclaiming – or so it's claimed – "O buona vista!" ("O, happy sight") and, true or not, a statue has been erected in his honour. The cape has always been hazardous to shipping and it's overseen by a ten-metre red-and-white-striped **lighthouse** (mid-May to mid-Oct daily 10am–5.30pm; $3), which has been attractively restored to its appearance in 1870 when it was occupied by an 80-year-old lighthouse keeper, Jeremiah White, and his family; costumed guides give the background and the adjacent interpretive centre gives an overview of the island's crucial lighthouse system.

Bonavista village

The cape is 5km from the sprawling fishing village of **BONAVISTA**, which spreads out across the flattish headlands surrounding its double harbour. Settled by the English in the seventeenth century, Bonavista was long a successful trading centre and fishing station, a history explored at the **Ryan Premises National Historic Site** (mid-May to mid-Oct daily 10am–6pm; $3.90; ⓣ709/468-1600), sited in the nineteenth-century fish-processing complex. Inside you'll find the Bonavista Museum of local history, a multimedia exhibit on Labrador's seal fisheries, and the restored Ryan offices, circa 1900. There's more nautical stuff nearby at the **Ye Matthew Legacy** (mid-May to Sept daily 10am–6pm; $7.25; ⓣ709/468-1493, ⓦwww.matthewlegacy.com), which features a full-scale replica of **Cabot's ship**, the 28m-long *Matthew* with tours above and below deck; the attached interpretation centre has the historical low-down. Bonavista's other noteworthy sight is the plain white clapboard **Mockbeggar Plantation Provincial Historic Site** (mid-May to late Sept daily 10am–5.30pm; $3 or free with lighthouse ticket; Ⓣ709/468-7300), on Roper Street, once the home of F. Gordon Bradley, a lawyer-turned-politician who met here with Joe Smallwood throughout the 1940s to mastermind the island's bid for confederation. Though it was built around 1871 by a local merchant, the house has been returned to its appearance in 1939 when Bradley was on the brink of victory (he went on to serve in the Canadian cabinet in the 1950s), and comes complete with a full set of heavy-duty, Victorian and Edwardian furniture, much of it made by Bradley's father. Enthusiastic guides provide background and descriptions. The outhouses are also gradually being converted to display and activity spaces – the saltbox **Big Store** may date from 1733, which would make it the oldest building on the island.

Practicalities

The best **accommodation** in Bonavista is at *Elizabeth J. Cottages* (Ⓣ709/468-5035 or 1-866/468-5035, Ⓦwww.elizabethjcottages.com; ❼), two oceanside cottages on Harris Street. Each has two bedrooms and an outside deck, and is attractively furnished with hardwood floors, Persian rugs and all modern conveniences. Bonavista also has a handful of **B&Bs**, with one of the better options being *Butler's by the Sea* (Ⓣ709/468-2445 or 1-877/968-2445, Ⓦwww.bbcanada.com/1412.html; ❸), whose two well-appointed, en-suite rooms overlook the water at 15 Butler Crescent. In the centre of the village, on the waterfront, *Harbour Quarters* (Ⓣ1-866/468-7982, Ⓦwww.harbourquarters.com; ❻) is another plush option, open year-round in a converted 1920s general store. For **food**, try *Marsh's Snack Bar* (daily 10am–midnight; Ⓣ709/468-2639), near the lighthouse.

Central Newfoundland

The Trans-Canada Hwy cuts a long and lonely course across **central Newfoundland** on its way from Clarenville, at the base of the Bonavista Peninsula, to Deer Lake, a distance of 450km. Of the towns it encounters, **Gambo** commemorates the giant of Newfoundland politics, Joe Smallwood and **Grand Falls-Windsor** has a museum with a rare Beothuk focus. The highway also threads its way through **Terra Nova National Park**, with its arresting coastal scenery. The most obvious detour is the 100km dash north to the old fishing port and trading centre of **Twillingate**, set amid a craggy broken coastline that attracts icebergs by the score from April to June.

Terra Nova National Park

Heading north from Clarenville along the Trans-Canada Hwy, it's about 40km to the southern edge of **Terra Nova National Park** (admission fee of $5.80/adult mid-May to early Oct), whose coniferous forests, ponds and marshes border a deeply indented slice of rugged coastline. The road slices right through the park, giving clearly signed access to its various facilities, most of which are concentrated about 40km in at the head of **Newman Sound**. Here you'll find the **Salton's Brook Marine Interpretation Centre** (daily: mid-May to late June & Sept to early Oct 10am–5pm; late June–Aug 9am–7pm; Ⓣ709/533-2942), whose excellent displays explain and illustrate the park's flora and fauna. The centre also supplies oodles of information about guided walks, boat trips, safe swimming areas, diving, canoeing and sea kayaking.

Coastal Connections (Ⓣ709/533-2196, Ⓦwww.coastalconnections.ca) runs the **boat trips**, illuminating 2hr 30min cruises around the sound at 9.30am and 1pm daily (mid-June to mid-Sept) for $65 ($35 kids), taking in all the flora, fauna and marine life. **Ocean Quest Adventures** (Ⓣ1-866/623-2664 or 709/422-1111, Ⓦwww.oceanquestadventures.com) manages **kayak rentals** ($30/2hr, $50/half day, $80/day), **zodiac boat trips** ($65; 1hr 30min) and **dive trips** ($115). The Marine Centre also has the details of over a dozen **hiking trails**, from short strolls to full-scale expeditions, including the strenuous **Outport Loop Trail**, a 46km endurance test that takes sixteen hours to complete. En route are several primitive **campgrounds** ($15.70), permits for which must be arranged at the centre before you set out. Other highlights include the observation point at **Blue Hill** (199m), the park's highest point, the wooded **Southwest Brook Trail** (watch for beavers) and any of the **coastal trails** from the marine centre, which offer scintillating views across the sound. You might see **moose** anywhere in the park, usually ambling through the undergrowth.

Practicalities

In addition to the primitive campsites on the Outport Loop Trail (see above), the national park also has several serviced **campgrounds**, the largest being the all-year Newman Sound Campground (Ⓣ905/426-4648 or 1-877/737-3783, Ⓦwww.pccamping.ca; $25.50–29.40; resrevations advised), reached along a side road off the Trans-Canada Hwy just to the south of the Salton's Brook Marine turning. If camping seems too daunting, aim for the village of **CHARLOTTETOWN**, about 15km south of Newman Sound – and 50km from Clarenville – where there's a **motel**, the *Clode Sound* (Ⓣ709/664-3146, Ⓦwww.clodesound.com; May–Oct; ❸), with a reasonably priced **restaurant** (May–Sept daily 11am–2pm & 4.30–7.30pm) known for its fruit pies and apple crisps – and lots of fresh seafood.

Gambo and Gander

Around 32km beyond Terra Nova National Park, the Trans-Canada Hwy reaches the logging town of **GAMBO**, where the **Smallwood Interpretation Centre** (daily 11am–5pm; $3; Ⓣ709/674-4342,), off Rte 320, celebrates the life and times of its most famous son, Joe Smallwood. The larger-than-life Newfoundland premier dominated the political scene from 1949 to 1972, and remains a controversial figure. Most islanders would now agree that his main contribution was in squeezing through the vote for Confederation in the referendum of 1948, but his attempts to diversify the economy by attracting industry were often ill-considered and very costly. The on-site *Dianne's Café* overlooking the lake is a good place to grab lunch or a coffee, and as you leave town, stop at **Joe's Lookout** for stellar views across Gambo and the whole valley.

From Gambo it's 40km to **GANDER**, a workaday town built around an airport, once a major airforce base and re-fuelling stop for incoming flights from Europe. Today there's not much to see and it's really just a convenient pit-stop for food, accommodation and services. The local **information centre** on the main highway is open year-round (Mon–Fri 8.30am–5pm, Sat & Sun 10am–6pm Ⓣ709/256-7110, Ⓦwww.ganderchamber.nf.ca) and packed with leaflets on island-wide attractions. You'll also find plenty of **hotels**, the pick of which is the business-like *Hotel Gander* (Ⓣ709/256-3931, Ⓦwww.hotelgander.com) on the highway, which offers comfy modern rooms with wi-fi and all the amenities. For **eating**, fast-food chains dominate, though *Alcock & Brown's Eatery* inside the *Hotel Gander* does decent meals and *Che's* (Mon–Sat 11am–8pm, Sun noon–8pm) at Fraser Mall on

Airport Blvd (take the Magee exit from the highway, turn down Memorial, then right at Airport Blvd) does excellent fish and chips and a range of other seafood.

Twillingate

The isolated outport of **TWILLINGATE** makes a worthy detour, a blissfully untouched slice of rural Newfoundland noted for its stock of traditional fishing shacks, frolicking whales in summer and parades of towering icebergs – indeed, this is the self-proclaimed "iceberg capital of the world". The town is 100km north of Gander and the Trans Canada Hwy on Rte 340, at the end of a string of causeways and bridges negotiating the jigsaw of islets, headlands and inlets that distinguishes this part of the coast. Twillingate was settled by the English in the early eighteenth century after several decades of use by itinerant French fishermen, who gave the place its original name, "Toulinguet", from an island back home in Brittany. By the 1780s Twillingate had become the most important cod fishing station on the north coast on account of its fine, sheltered harbour. The boom times ended in the 1880s, when the switch from sail to steam curtailed Twillingate's role as a fishing station, but it remained a busy fishing port until the demise of the cod fishery in the 1990s. You can get a decent introduction to this history at the **Twillingate Museum** (mid-May to early Oct daily 9am–5pm; free; ⓣ709/884-2825, ⓦwww.tmacs.ca), just off Main Street. The best time to be in

▲ One of the many icebergs that drift into the waters around Twillingate

Twillingate iceberg-spotting

Between **April and June**, the myriad inlets near Twillingate can ensnare dozens of **icebergs** as they float down from the Arctic, though in these days of climate change it can be hard to predict their appearance: in 2009 the bays were chock full of ice, whereas bergs were extremely rare throughout the 2008 season. You won't forget the experience if you do encounter one: tinted in shades of aquamarine and white by reflections from the sea and sun, they seem like otherworldly cathedrals of ice, which stand out brilliantly from the blue-green ocean and, if you're particularly lucky, you might witness the moment when one of them rolls over and breaks apart, accompanied by a tremendous grating and wheezing and then an ear-ringing bang. Several local companies offer **iceberg-watching boat tours** with one of the best known being Twillingate Adventure Tours (mid-May to mid-Sept 3 daily; 2hr; $40; ⓣ709/884-5999 or 1-888/447-8687, ⓦwww.twillingateadventuretours.com). A second recommended operator is Twillingate Island Boat Tours (mid-May to Sept 3 daily; 2hr; $40; ⓣ 709/884-2242 or 1-800/611-2374, ⓦwww.icebergtours.ca), which also operates the **Iceberg Shop**, an arts and crafts shop and iceberg interpretive centre in an old barn in **DURRELL**, a couple of kilometres north of Twillingate. With both companies, boat tours should be booked ahead of time.

Landlubbers still stand a good chance of spotting an iceberg from the bright red and white **Long Point Lighthouse**, which occupies a commanding position on a high rocky cliff at the north end of Main Street; the approach is rocky and often slippery, so you'll need appropriate footwear. The **Long Point Centre**, across the street from the lighthouse (daily mid-May to mid-Oct 10am–9pm; free), has a tearoom, crafts shop and a small display on local culture and natural history. You should also check out ⓦwww.icebergfinder.com for a heads up on the latest berg activity.

Twillingate is during the four-day **Fish, Fun and Folk Festival** (ⓦwww.fishfunfolkfestival.com), held over the last full weekend of July and attracting folk musicians from all over the province.

Practicalities

One of the best places to **stay** in Twillingate is the *Hillside* (ⓣ709/884-1666, ⓦwww.bbcanada.com/nfhillside; ❸; June–Sept), an attractive, well-kept B&B in an 1870s clapboard house overlooking the harbour at 5 Young's Lane; it has three en-suite rooms, each decorated in brisk modern style. Alternatively, the *Toulinguet Inn* (ⓣ709/884-2080 or 1-877/684-2080, ⓦwww.bbcanada.com/9127.html; ❸; mid-May to Sept), down on the waterfront at 56 Main St, is in a 1920s building and has three smart, en-suite rooms. Finally, there's the *Beach Rock B&B* (ⓣ709/884-2292; ❸; May–Oct), which occupies a charmingly renovated, two-storey 1904 clapboard house. There are three rooms, all en suite, and breakfasts feature home-made bread and muffins; it is located on the seashore about 5km south of Twillingate, just off Rte 340 in the hamlet of **Little Harbour**.

For **food**, opt for the popular *R&J Restaurant* at 110 Main St North (ⓣ709/884-2212), with fabulous harbour views, addictive wedgefries, fish and chips and pizzas. A not-to-be-missed experience is the **All Around the Circle Dinner Theatre** (June to mid-Sept Mon–Sat 6pm; ⓣ709/884-5423) at the Crow Head Community Centre (near the lighthouse), which combines fine home-cooked fare with comedy, songs and dancing (from around $28). You should also visit the **Auk Island Winery**, 29 Durrell St (ⓣ1-877/639-4637, ⓦwww.aukislandwinery.com) for an introduction to the island's growing number of eminently drinkable **fruit wines**. If you visit the town in September, you'll be able to go **berry-picking**; thousands of bakeapples (cloudberries), partridgeberries and blueberries smother the slopes around the town.

Grand Falls-Windsor

GRAND FALLS- WINDSOR, 91km west of Gander along the Trans-Canada Hwy, sits among some of the island's best stands of timber, an expanse of **forest** that's been intensively exploited ever since Alfred Harmsworth, later Lord Northcliffe, opened a paper mill here in 1909. Harmsworth, the founder of Britain's *Daily Mirror* and *Daily Mail* newspapers, funded the project to secure a reliable supply of newsprint well away from Europe, which he believed was heading towards war. It was an immensely profitable venture, which also established the first Newfoundland community sited, as one contemporary put it, "out of sight and sound of the sea". Grand Falls today is an unprepossessing place built around the hulking mass of the AbitibiBowater paper mill that towers over the Exploits River – the mill closed in 2009 leaving hundreds out of work and an uncertain future for the town.

The **falls** themselves retain a certain rugged charm, hemmed in by jagged rocks and rapids, though they've been completely overshadowed by the now shuttered paper mill above them. You can take a look at them while visiting the **Salmonid Interpretation Centre** (mid-June to mid-Sept 8am–8pm; $6; Ⓣ709/489-7350, Ⓦwww.exploitsriver.ca), on the south bank of the river 2km from the centre. Exhibits highlight the history, biology and habitat of the **Atlantic Salmon**, while the observation level provides an underwater view of the migrating fish as they fight upstream to spawning grounds at Red Indian Lake. Also worth a look is the **Mary March Provincial Museum** (May to late Oct daily 9.30am–4.45pm; $2.50), at 16 St Catherine St, just to the south of the highway – take exit 18 (Cromer Ave). Its focus is the early history of Newfoundland, with a thought-provoking series of displays on its prehistoric cultures and the **Beothuks**. The Exploits Valley was the final Beothuk stronghold on the island, and was the home of the last known Beothuk, Shanawdithit (see p.456), and her aunt Demasduit.

Practicalities

The local **visitor centre** is just off the highway at exit 17 (June–Aug Mon–Fri 9am–8pm, Sat & Sun 10am–8pm; Ⓣ709/489-6332, Ⓦwww.grandfallswindsor.com). The best place to **stay** is the *Hill Road Manor B&B* at 1 Hill Rd (Ⓣ709/489-5451, Ⓦwww.hillroadmanor.com; ⑤), a large clapboard mansion with four spacious rooms enhanced with wi-fi and cable TV. Take exit 18A off the highway (see website for directions).

For **eating**, try *Clem's Restaurant* (Ⓣ709/489-2251) at the *Mt Peyton Hotel* right on the main highway, or *Gibson's*, (Ⓣ709/489-3664; closed Sun) at 12 Hardy Ave, where home-cooked dishes make a pleasant break from the fast-food strips surrounding the town.

Deer Lake

DEER LAKE, 210km west of Grand Falls, is another convenient pitstop, this time at the junction of the Trans-Canada Hwy and Rte 430, the road to the northern peninsular. The only real attraction here is the **Newfoundland Insectarium** (mid-May to mid-Oct Mon–Fri 9am–5pm, Sat 10am–5pm, Sun noon–5pm; July & Aug daily 9am–6pm; $10; Ⓣ709/635-4545, Ⓦwww.nfinsectarium.com), on Rte 430 towards Gros Morne, which features a tranquil pavilion of around one thousand dazzling butterflies, as well as a fascinating colony of leaf-cutter ants, an observation bee hive and tarantula section upstairs.

Arrival and information

If you fly into Deer Lake **airport**, metered taxis (☎709/635-2521) are around $7 into town, but realistically you'll need a car to get around: there are currently five **car-rental** offices at the terminal: Avis (☎709/635-5010), Budget (☎709/635-3211), Dollar/Thrifty (☎709/635-8211), Enterprise (☎709/635-4667) and National (☎709/635-3282). Star Taxi (☎709/634-4343) provides a shuttle service to Corner Brook for $22 per person (call in advance).

The information centre at the airport (☎709/635-1003) is open year-round. The DRL Coachline **bus station** is the Irving gas station on the highway just outside town, opposite the *Deer Lake Motel* (see below). The **visitor information centre** (daily June–Aug 9am–8pm; Sept & Oct 10am–7pm; ☎709/635-2202) is also beside the highway and supplies free town maps.

Practicalities

Deer Lake has half a dozen places to **stay**, one of the more convenient being the workaday *Deer Lake Motel* (☎709/635-2108 or 1-800/563-2144, ⓦwww.deerlakemotel.com; ④), on the highway, 2km from the airport. There are also several B&Bs in the centre among the grid of streets that stretch east from the highway as it sweeps round the edge of the lake. These include the *Lakeview B&B* (☎709/635-8104 or 1-888/635-8104; ⓦwww.lakeviewbb.ca; ③), in a modern, chalet-like building at 1 Young's Ave, with five, straightforward but pleasant en-suite rooms. Much fancier is the *Humberview B&B* (☎709/635-4818 or 1-888/635-4818, ⓦwww.thehumberview.com; ⑤), occupying a large and well-appointed, modern, two-storey brick house on the north side of the highway (exit 15) at 11 Humberview Drive.

Eating options are limited. Most travellers stick to the convenient restaurant at the *Deer Lake Motel*, or the *Big Stop* across the road at the Irving gas station, which serves hearty breakfasts and hefty lemon meringue pies. Look out for the daily specials here; *Big Stop* is a chain, but in Newfoundland the cooks are usually locals that tend to knock out superb home-made dishes in addition to the standard menu.

Gros Morne National Park

Some of Newfoundland's most mesmerizing scenery is contained within **Gros Morne National Park**, its bays, scrawny beaches, straggling villages and wizened sea stacks backclothed by bare-topped, fjord-cut mountains. The park's forested lower slopes are home to thousands of moose, woodland caribou and snowshoe hare, and **minke whales** regularly feed in Bonne Bay. Gros Morne has also attracted its fair share of artists and musicians, highlighted at the **Trails, Tales and Tunes festival** (ⓦwww.trailstalestunes.ca) held in Norris Point each May; Shirley Montague, singer Anita Best (see p.458), fiddler Daniel Payne and Bernard Felix, one of the world's top accordion players, all call the region home.

Most visitors come here during the short summer season (June–Sept), and other times you'll find many services shut – the exception is the peak **winter season** (Feb–April), when the park experiences another mini-boom in snowmobiling and cross-country skiing.

Arrival and information

You'll need a car to make the most of the park, as public transport is nonexistent and it's around 30km from Deer Lake to the entrance. It's possible – weather permitting – to drive into the park at any time, but from mid-May to mid-October there's an entry charge of $9.80 per person (pay at kiosks at the entrance, 10am–6pm).

The main **visitor information centre** (daily: late June to Aug 9am–9pm; mid-May to late June & Sept–Oct 9am–5pm; ⓣ709/458-2417, ⓦwww.pc.gc.ca), is situated beside Rte 430 as it approaches Rocky Harbour, 70km from Deer Lake. The centre has a series of edifying displays on the geology, botany, biology and human history of the park, as well as an introductory film. It has free maps, brochures on the park's key hiking trails and details of local boat excursions.

Accommodation

Rocky Harbour is the best **place to stay** in the park, not least because it's relatively compact and has a reasonable range of tourist facilities, but there are also some choice options in the **southern section**. The park runs five **campgrounds** (advance reservations ⓣ1-877/737-3783, ⓦwww.pccamping.ca), and you'll also find a number of backcountry **primitive campgrounds** dotted along the longer trails ($9.80). For these you have to register at the park visitor centre first. Privately-run campgrounds are also available (see below). **Reserving in advance** for all accommodation is a good idea anytime, but crucial in July and August and also in winter, when many places are closed.

Rocky Harbour and Cow Head (north side)

Berry Hill Campground Rte 430, Rocky Harbour ⓣ1-877/737-3783, ⓦwww.pccamping.ca. Of all the park-run campsites, this is the best, with 152 shaded, unserviced sites (with toilets and showers), 5km north of Rocky Harbour along Rte 430. Mid-June to mid-Sept; $18.60-25.50.

Gros Morne Cabins Main St, Rocky Harbour ⓣ709/458-2020, ⓦwww.grosmornecabins.com. Slightly nicer one- and two-bedroom timber cottages with fully-equipped kitchens, bbqs, cable TV and wi-fi, all overlooking the ocean. ❺

Gros Morne/Norris Point KOA Campground 5 Shearakin Lane (Norris Point access road from Rte 430) ⓣ709/458-2229 or 1-800/562-3441, ⓦwww.koa.com. Secluded campsite in wooded valley, overlooking the water; free wi-fi, laundry, games room, store and kayaks. Tent sites from $22.50 (no hook-ups) to $28 (water/electricity); cabins $55. Mid-May to mid-Oct.

Neddies Harbour Inn 7 Beach Rd, Neddies Harbour, Norris Point ⓣ709/458-3089 or 1-877/458-2929, ⓦwww.theinn.ca. The spectacular view from the sun deck and bar across Bonne Bay is the real highlight here, but the stylish rooms come a close second, decked out with local beechwood in a crisp, contemporary design reflecting the sensibilities of the Swiss owners; you also get fine dining on site and plenty of eco-friendly touches, like low-wattage lighting. ❼

Ocean View Motel 38-42 Main St, Rocky Harbour ⓣ709/458-2730 or 1-800/563-9887, ⓦwww.oceanviewmotel.com. Fabulous location in the heart of the village, overlooking the waterfront, with 52 modern rooms and a decent restaurant with sea views – upgrades to the building are in the works. ❺

Shallow Bay Motel & Cabins Cow Head, Rte 430 ⓣ709/243-2471, ⓦwww.shallowbaymotel.com. Solid choice at the northern edge of the park, where the real bonus is the waterside location – most rooms are right by the ocean, and some have decks. It's also convenient for the theatre (p.479) and is open all year. The gym, sauna and hot tub are pleasant extras. ❺

Woody Point (south side)

Red Mantle Lodge Shoal Brook, Rte 431 ⓣ1-888/453-7204 or 709/453-7204, ⓦwww.redmantlelodge.ca. Smart, modern hotel high above Rte 431 to Woody Point with views across the bay. Soak up the vistas over a continental breakfast prepared by the friendly hosts, and watch moose amble around the property at dusk. Signposted up a gravel road, off Rte 431. ❻

The Park

Gros Morne National Park is divided into two by the pristine arms of **Bonne Bay**; the northern section is accessible from Rte 430, while the southern area lies around Rte 431, which runs 36km from Rte 430 to the village of Woody Point. You could spend a week here **hiking** the fabulous trails, but if time is short make sure you at least visit the Discovery Centre and nearby Tablelands (ideally taking in a short hike), take the spell-binding boat tour of **Western Brook Pond**, and soak up local culture at the Gros Morne Theatre Festival.

Norris Point

From the visitor centre, it's 6km south to **NORRIS POINT** on the north shore of **Bonne Bay,** at the point where this deep and mountainous fjord divides into two inlets – East Arm and South Arm. The best way to see the bay is by guided **boat tour** with Bontours (July & Aug Mon, Wed & Fri 2pm; $27/2hr; ⓣ709/458-2874, ⓦwww.bontours.ca), departing from **Norris Point Waterfront**. The same company also operates a **water taxi** (foot passengers only; mid-June to Aug; 3 daily; 15min; $12 return) from Norris Point to **Woody Point** (see p.479). You can also tour the bay by **kayak** with nearby Gros Morne Adventures (rentals $30/1–2hr, $60/24hr; guided tours $50; ⓣ709/458-2722, ⓦwww.grosmorneadventures.com); on a clear day the bay serves up some rich sights, with whales, otters, seals and bald eagles sometimes spotted. They also arrange serious hikes around North Arm (6 nights; $1695) and rent mountain bikes for $35 per day.

Also at Norris Point Waterfront, the **Bonne Bay Marine Station** (late-May to Aug daily 9am–5pm; $6.25; ⓣ709/458-2874, ⓦwww.bonnebay.ca), a unit of Memorial University, offers guided tours (50min) of their research facilities and aquarium; tanks feature local lobsters, cod, skate and even a furry sea mouse.

Moving on to Rocky Harbour, stop at the Photographer's Lookout and Jenniex House (late June to early Sept daily 10am–8pm; ⓣ709/458-2896) just outside Norris Point, a 1920's clapboard home. It was moved to this spot in 1995, one of the most jaw-dropping locations in the park. Inside you'll find a craft shop and a traditional "mug up" – tea and muffins with molasses.

Rocky Harbour

It's 11km from Norris Point to **ROCKY HARBOUR**, the park's largest village, which curves around a long and sweeping bay with the mountains lurking in the background. Although there's nothing special to do or see here, nearby **Lobster Cove Head Lighthouse** (mid-May to mid-Oct daily 10am–5.30pm; free with park entry) offers stunning panoramas across the bay and a small exhibition on the history of the region. Completed in 1897, the upper section of the lighthouse is still in use and off-limits to the public. Rocky Harbour is also near several of Gros Morne's **hiking trails**, notably the lung-bursting, 16km Gros Morne Mountain Trail. The trail – for experienced hikers only – begins **at the signed trailhead** beside Rte 430, 7km east of the village, and climbs to the top of **Gros Morne Mountain** where, at 806m above sea level, the views are stupendous.

Western Brook Pond

The remote **Western Brook Pond**, reached by just one access point, 25km north of Rocky Harbour beside Rte 430, is one of eastern Canada's most enchanting landscapes, 16km of deep, dark-blue water framed by mighty mountains and huge waterfalls. From the access-point car park it's a forty minute (3km) walk on a well-maintained trail through forest and over bog to the edge of the lake. When you get to the end, don't skimp on the **boat trip** (reservations required; July & Aug daily 10am, 1pm & 4 pm; June & Sept daily 1pm; 2hr; $52 plus park ticket) operated by Bontours (see above). The boat inches its way between the cliffs right to the extreme eastern end of the lake, past several huge rockslides, dramatic hanging valleys and former sea caves now marooned high above the water.

Broom Point and Cow Head

Around six kilometres north of Western Brook Pond, **Broom Point** (mid-may to mid-Oct daily 10am–5.30pm; entry with park ticket) is a desolate, windswept promontory crowned with a picturesque smattering of fishing shacks, one of which has been turned into a small fishing museum – guides tell the story of the Mudge family fishing operation here (1941–75), and also the nearby paleo-eskimo site.

The village of **COW HEAD**, 11km north of Broom Point, is perched at the most northerly end of the park, and is noted chiefly for its **Gros Morne Theatre Festival** (late May to late Sept ⓣ1-877/243-2899, ⓦwww.theatrenewfoundland.com), based at the Warehouse Theatre in the centre of the village. Their programme of drama, music and cabaret, such as the much-loved *Neddy's Norris Nights*, always has a local slant and is thoroughly entertaining (tickets $22–25).

Woody Point and the southern section

The **southern section** of the park is just as rewarding as the northern side, with plenty to keep you occupied for several days. Rte 431 eventually rolls into minuscule **WOODY POINT**, a sleepy fishing village that was once the main port on Bonne Bay. Start with a visit to the **Discovery Centre** (daily: mid-May to late June and Sept to mid-Oct 9am–5pm; late June to Aug 9am–6pm, till 9pm Sun & Wed; free with park entry), 3km before you reach the village on Rte 431, which examines the area's geology, plant and animal life. The centre also runs guided tours of the nearby **Tablelands**, a forbidding landscape of bare and barren rock – at 450 million years old this is an incredibly significant geological site. If you can't make a tour, get a closer look on the **Tablelands Hiking Trail**, a 4km-long circular track that cuts across the main section. Another 8km along Rte 431 brings you to the 16km-long loop of the **Green Gardens Trail**, which twists its way to some secluded coves, caves and sea stacks and is equipped with three primitive campgrounds. Continuing down Rte 431, it's a further 4km to **Trout River Pond**, sandwiched by the yellowed bareness of the Tablelands and the massive cliffs bordering the Gregory Plateau. Here, in dramatic profile, you can see the extraordinary force of the uplift created by the collision of the North American and European continents 450 million years ago.

If you're staying the night in Woody Point (see p.477), check out the **Heritage Theatre** (ⓣ709/453-2304, ⓦwww.pondstage.com/woodypoint) in the centre of the village, which hosts an impressive roster of folk musicians and performers throughout the summer, including the **Writer's at Woody Point** festival (ⓣ709/458-3388, ⓦwww.writersatwoodypoint.com), which attracts the best Canadian literary talent every August.

Eating and drinking

Food options in Gros Morne are improving, though out of season you'll have very little choice. You can buy fresh **lobster** and fish steaks at *Harbour Seafoods* (daily 8am–8pm; ⓣ709/458-2821) in Rocky Harbour – they will cook and crack open lobsters at no extra charge.

Cat Stop Norris Point Waterfront ⓣ709/458-2821. Pub and café with a sun-drenched upper deck, perfect for early drinks and light snacks after a kayak or boat trip. Also hosts live folk music in the evenings.

Earle's Video & Convenience 111 Main St, Rocky Harbour ⓣ709/458-2577. This no-frills groceries/video store also serves a vast range of moose meat dishes, including the juicy moose burgers and moose pizza – the pizzas here are the best in the region and most dishes average around $10.

Java Jack's 88 Main St North, Rocky Harbour ⓣ709/458-3004, ⓦwww.javajacksgrosmorne.com. Fabulous café downstairs and an excellent restaurant up above, serving fresh fish (from $22.95), crab cakes ($8.95) and veggie dishes (lasagna $18.95), much of the produce coming from their organic garden. June–Sept.

Neddies Harbour Inn 7 Beach Rd, Neddies Harbour, Norris Point ⓣ709/458-3089 or 1-877/458-2929. This hotel restaurant serves superb gourmet dinners (5.30–9pm), featuring home-made pastas from $16, roast lamb and chicken ($26-28), and local desserts like steamed partridgeberry pudding ($8).

Ocean View Motel 38-42 Main St, Rocky Harbour ⓣ709/458-2730. Smart restaurant specializing in excellent seafood dishes for around $23 (seafood risotto, fresh fish), as well as local favourites like chowder and toutons and beans; the other main draw is the glorious view of the bay from the second floor dining room. June–Oct.

Old Loft Restaurant Water St, Woody Point ⓣ709/453-2294, ⓦwww.theoldloft.com. Fine dining in the southern section of the park, where tasty seafood and traditional island dishes ($15–24) are served up in a traditional 1930s clapboard fishing loft near the water.

The Northern Peninsula

Stretching out between Deer Lake and the township of St Anthony, a distance of about 450km, the **Northern Peninsula** is a rugged, sparsely populated finger of land separating the Gulf of St Lawrence from the Atlantic. Its interior is dominated by the spectacular **Long Range Mountains**, a chain of flat-topped peaks that are some of the oldest on earth, punctuated by the starkest of glacier-gouged gorges above the bluest of lakes – or "ponds" as the locals incongruously call them. **Rte 430** trails along the western edge of the peninsula, connecting the small fishing villages of the narrow coastal plain, but the region's most remarkable sight is the remains of the Norse colony at **L'Anse aux Meadows**, at the tip of the peninsula some 50km beyond St Anthony.

Port au Choix

Mysterious bone, stone and ivory artefacts were being discovered by locals in the small fishing village of **PORT AU CHOIX**, about 160km north of Rocky Harbour, as far back as 1904, but it wasn't until the 1960s that professional archeologists uncovered some astonishing finds: a mass of prehistoric bones, tools and weapons and several ancient cemeteries, ultimately yielding 117 skeletons from the Neolithic period. All these sites are now preserved within the **Port au Choix National Historic Site** (mid-June to early Sept daily 9am–6pm; early June & early Sept to early Oct daily 9am–5pm; $7.40), with its **visitor centre** set halfway along a bleak headland 2.5km from the village. Films, touch-screen presentations and artefacts dug up from the cemeteries introduce the various cultures that existed here, while **trails** lead out across the headland to the sites themselves – there's really not much left to see, but you'll probably spy plenty of caribou. The primary discovery, right in the middle of the village, is a cemetery belonging to the **Maritime Archaic Indians**, hunter-gatherers who lived here between 3500 BC and 1200 BC. You can also visit the **Philip's Garden site,** related to two later groups of settlers, the **Groswater** and **Dorset Paleoeskimo**, whose scant remains date from between two and three thousand years ago.

From Port au Choix, it's about 92km to the hamlet of **St Barbe**, where you can catch the ferry to Labrador (see p.486), and 212km to St Anthony.

Practicalities

Port au Choix has several unassuming **places to stay**, the pick being *Jeannie's Sunrise B&B* (ⓣ709/861-2254 or 1-877/639-2789, ⓦwww.jeanniessunrisebb.com; ❸), at 84 Fisher St, a trim modern place in the centre, with views out to sea.

Food choices are limited, but the *Anchor Café*, also on Fisher Street (Ⓣ709/861-3665), offers heaped plates of fresh cod, salmon and the local speciality, shrimp, for under $20.

St Anthony

Beyond St Barbe, Rte 430 slips through a handful of fishing villages and then cuts east across the peninsula, passing the byroad to L'Anse aux Meadows (see p.482) before thumping on to the fishing and supply centre of **ST ANTHONY**. This is the area's largest settlement, a humdrum port stretched around the wide sweep of its harbour. The best place to **view icebergs** (and eat) is **Fishing Point** and the lighthouse at the head of the harbour, where a small interpretation centre (June–Sept daily 9am–9pm; free; Ⓣ1-877/661-2500, Ⓦwww.fishingpoint.ca) introduces the ecology of the area. You can get closer to the bergs (and whales) with Northland Discovery Boat Tours (Ⓣ709/454-3092 or 1-877/632-3747, Ⓦwww.discovernorthland.com), which runs 2hr 30min cruises (mid-May to late Sept; 3 daily; $50) from the waterfront behind the Grenfell Interpretation Centre.

St Anthony airport is near Seal Bay, a rather distant 55km west of town on Rte 430 – and 72km from L'Anse aux Meadows. Onward transport is by taxi only (Ⓣ709/454-2630); it's around $30 to St Anthony. Bargain short-term **car-rental** deals are available at St Anthony airport; try National (Ⓣ709/454-8522).

Grenfell Historic Properties

St Anthony's primary land-based attraction is a group of memorials collectively dubbed the **Grenfell Historic Properties** (June–Sept daily 9am–6pm; Oct–May interpretation centre only Mon–Fri 9am–5pm; combined admission $10; Ⓣ709/454-4010, Ⓦwww.grenfell-properties.com), dedicated to the pioneering missionary doctor, Sir Wilfred Grenfell, an Englishman who first came here on behalf of the Royal National Mission to Deep Sea Fishermen in 1892. He never returned home and, during his forty-year stay, he established the region's first proper hospitals, nursing stations, schools and cooperative stores.

Start at the Grenfell Interpretation Centre, which introduces the subject with a film and two floors on Grenfell's life and times, before moving on to the Grenfell House Museum. Behind the museum, there's a pleasant woodland path leading – in twenty minutes – to the top of **Tea House Hill**, where Grenfell and his wife were buried. You should also see the remarkable ceramic murals depicting the culture and the history of Newfoundland inside the nearby hospital **Rotunda**, created by Montréal artist Jordi Bonet in 1967. The waterfront properties include the mildly engaging **Dockhouse Museum**, a 1920s boat repair shop and the **Ships Mast Display** of old ship masts and riggings.

Practicalities

For **accommodation**, try the sensitively renovated *Crow's Nest Inn B&B* (Ⓣ 709/454-4401 or 1-877/454-3402, Ⓦwww.bbcanada.com/8195.html; ❹), at 1 Spruce Lane, with eight spacious rooms equipped with cable TV and wi-fi, and offering fine views of the harbour. Alternatives are the memorable *Fishing Point B&B* (Ⓣ709/454-3117 or 1-866/454-2009, Ⓦwww.bbcanada.com/6529.html; ❸), a 1940s fishing shack with three en-suite rooms perched on the cliff on the road to Fishing Point, and the modern, motel-like *Haven Inn* (Ⓣ709/454-9100 or 1-877/428-3646, Ⓦwww.haveninn.ca; ❹), at 14 Goose Cove Rd.

For **food**, the *Lightkeeper's Seafood Restaurant* (Ⓣ1-877/454-4900), on Fishing Point, at the end of West Street, serves up tasty seafood such as *bacalao* (cod) fish cakes, pastas and thick soups. Next door, *Leifsburdir* (Ⓣ709/454-4900) is a replica sod hut where Viking feasts (featuring salmon, moose and cod; $45/person) are served at 7.30pm (call to check dates; July & Aug only) by costumed staff – very touristy but lots of fun, especially if you have a group.

L'Anse aux Meadows

L'Anse aux Meadows National Historic Site (June-Sept daily 9am–6pm; $11.70) is an extraordinary UNESCO World Heritage Site comprising the scant remains of the earliest verified European settlement in the Americas. It's also a tribute to the obsessive drive of **Helge Ingstad**, a Norwegian writer and explorer who from 1960 onwards hunted high and low to find Norse settlements on the North Atlantic seaboard. His efforts were inspired by two medieval Icelandic sagas, which detailed the establishment of the colony of **Vinland** somewhere along this coast in about 1000 AD – long regarded as myth by most scholars.

At L'Anse aux Meadows, a local named George Decker took Ingstad to a group of grassed-over bumps and ridges beside Epaves Bay; they turned out to contain the remnants of the only **Norse village** ever to have been discovered in North America. These comprised the foundations of eight turf and timber buildings and a ragbag of archeological finds, including a bronze cloak pin (which provided the crucial carbon dating for the site), a stone anvil, nails, pieces of bog iron, an oil lamp and a small spindle whorl. Ingstad concluded these were left behind by a group of about one hundred sailors, carpenters and blacksmiths who probably remained at the site for just one or maybe two years, using it as a base for further explorations.

The site was thoroughly excavated between 1961 and 1968, and again in the 1970s, and there followed an acrimonious academic debate about whether it was actually "Vinland"; on-site guides tend to assume it was, while the exhibition inside is more diplomatic, describing this site as a way station for trips further south in the Gulf of St Lawrence (where Vinland also may be located).

Whatever the truth, thousands of tourists come here every summer and begin at the **visitor centre**, where the Norse artefacts appear alongside exhibitions on the background to the site as well as Viking life and culture. From here it's a few minutes' walk to the cluster of gentle mounds that make up what's left of the original village, and another short stroll to a group of full-scale replicas centred around a **long house** – costumed role-playing interpreters enhance the experience with demonstrations of traditional activities such as cooking, weaving and boat-building.

Vinland and the Vikings

By 870 the **Vikings** had settled on the shores of Iceland, and by the start of the eleventh century there were about three thousand Norse colonists established in Greenland. The two **Vinland sagas** – the *Graenlendinga* and *Eirik's Saga* – give us the only extant account of further explorations west, recounting the exploits of Leif Eiriksson and Thorfinn Karlsefni, his merchant brother-in-law, who founded a colony they called **Vinland** in North America around 1000 AD. Crucially, the Norse settlers failed to establish reasonable relations with their native neighbours – whom they called *skraelings*, literally "wretches" – and the perennial skirmishing that ensued eventually drove them out of Vinland, though they did return to secure raw materials for the next few decades; it seems likely that **L'Anse aux Meadows** is the result of one of these foragings.

The Norse carried on collecting timber from Labrador up until the fourteenth century, when a dramatic deterioration in the climate made the trip from Greenland too dangerous. Attacks from the Inuit and the difficulties of maintaining trading links with Scandinavia then took their toll on the main Greenland colonies. All contact between Greenland and the outside world was lost around 1410 and the last of the half-starved, disease-ridden survivors died out towards the end of the fifteenth century – just as Christopher Columbus was eyeing up his "New World".

Norstead

Just 2km from the original Viking settlement, **Norstead** (June–Sept daily 9am–6pm; $10; ⓣ709/623-2828, ⓦwww.norstead.com) is an impressive replica of a Norse port replete with full-scale Viking ships, a touristy but extremely entertaining glimpse into Viking life one thousand years ago. Costumed interpreters lead hands-on activities, tell stories in the chieftain's hall and demonstrate ancient crafts like spinning and pot making.

Accommodation

Tourists visiting L'Anse aux Meadows have fuelled a mini-boom in local **B&Bs** and **inns**. One of the best of these is the *Tickle Inn* (ⓣ709/452-4321, off-season ⓣ709/739-5503, ⓦwww.tickleinn.net; ❸; June–Sept), whose four, cosy guest rooms share an attractive 1890s house in a superb location on the shores of a secluded cove at remote **Cape Onion**. Reservations are essential and evening meals – as well as boat trips along the rugged coast nearby – need to be booked in advance. The Cape is about 45km from L'Anse aux Meadows – backtrack along Rte 436, turn down Rte 437 and keep going. Even better is one of the most alluring hotels in Canada, the *Quirpon Lighthouse Inn* (ⓣ709/634-2285 or 1-877/254-6586, ⓦwww.linkumtours.com; ❽; May–Oct), out on isolated Quirpon Island ("kar-poon"), where eleven rooms in the two old lighthouse keeper's houses from 1922 have been intelligently upgraded. The inn boasts a spectacular location, standing next to the lighthouse with the cliffs jagging down below. A double room starts at $325 per night, but this does include the boat trip (15min) over and all meals; the dock in Quirpon village is 8km from L'Anse aux Meadows along a short gravel turning off Rte 436. Once here you can go whale- and iceberg-watching, rent kayaks and hike all over the island. A much cheaper and easier to access option is the all-year, four-room *Viking Nest B&B* (ⓣ709/623-2238 or 1-877/858-2238, ⓦwww.bbcanada.com/vikingnest; ❷), in a modern brick chalet in Hay Cove, 1km from L'Anse aux Meadows. The folks at the *Norsemen* (see p.398) also run an excellent B&B, *Valhalla Lodge* (❹), in nearby Gunner's Cove, which includes *Quoyle's House* (❼) the luxurious cottage once owned by **Annie Proulx**, author of *The Shipping News*.

Eating and drinking

The best place **to eat** is *The Norsemen* (mid-June to mid-Sept daily noon–9pm; ⓣ709/754-3105, ⓦwww.valhalla-lodge.com) near L'Anse aux Meadows, which serves fabulous locally-inspired dishes such as fish chowder, baked cod, bakeapple cheesecake and caribou tenderloin. You should also stop by the *Jam Stand* (ⓣ709/623-2434) at Gunner's Cove, for delectable local fruit jams, gifts and muffins, and *Dark Tickle* in St Lunaire-Griquet (June–Sept daily 9am–6pm, Oct–May Mon–Fri 9am–5pm; ⓣ709/623-2354, ⓦwww.darktickle.com), which sells all sorts of products made from local berries (tours daily 10am & 2pm; $5).

The Humber Valley and the southwest coast

From Deer Lake, it's a long-winded 270km along the Trans-Canada Hwy to **Channel-Port aux Basques**, from where ferries (see p.398) sail to North Sydney in Nova Scotia. En route, you should pause at the **Humber Valley** and the stunning falls and **zip-line** at Steady Brook. Channel-Port aux Basques is not particularly riveting, but it is a short drive from the handsome outport of **Rose Blanche**, which is itself the starting point for ferries to the remote outports of the **southwest coast**, most of which are still beyond the road network – if you're after a slice of traditional outport life, then this is the nearest you'll come.

The Humber Valley

South of Deer Lake, the Trans-Canada Hwy cuts through the magnificent **Humber Valley**, an increasingly steep and rugged gorge bristling with rocky outcrops and mountains rolling away on each side. The area has plenty of attractions in summer and winter, not least the majestic **Steady Brook Falls**, a sixty-metre cascade that ploughs over the edge of a narrow gorge into the valley. You can hike up to the viewpoint by taking exit 8 off the highway (at *George's Mountain Village*). Just behind *George's*, **Marble Zip Tours** (daily 9am–5pm; tours 9am, 1pm & 5pm; ⓣ709/632-5463, ⓦwww.marbleziptours.com) is one of Newfoundland's most adrenaline-pumping attractions, a series of six exhilarating zip-lines zigzagging across the falls and gorge, some 86 metres above the ground. Each tour (1–3hr depending on group size) is led by highly-qualified guides, who also run **caving tours** and a host of adventure activities – plans are also afoot to open a final 610-metre section of the zipline (making it North America's longest), to end at a new *Bay of Islands Microbrewery* in 2010. Nearby **Marble Mountain Ski Resort** (ⓣ1-888/462-7253, ⓦwww.skimarble.com; day passes $49), offers some of the best **skiing** east of the Rockies, and plenty of scenic hiking trails in summer, though the main activity for locals between June and September is **salmon fishing**: you'll need a licence (from $53) and a guide ($120/day); see ⓦwww.eurekaoutdoors.nf.ca for more details. In September you can pick wild **blueberries** at Pin's Brook (junction 12/13), and fill your bottles with fresh, clean **spring water** year-round – look for locals stopping on the highway at the small, signposted standpipe near *George's* (eastbound).

Practicalities

You'll find plenty of **accommodation** in the valley, including the deluxe chalets at the *Marble Inn Resort* (ⓣ709/634-2237; ⓦwww.marbleinn.com; ⑤), near *George's* and the ski area (exit 8), and the huge, luxurious villas at the *Humber Valley Resort* (ⓣ709/686-2500, ⓦwww.visithumbervalley.com; ⑧), which offer excellent value for groups and big families ($300 for three bedrooms). For **eating**, grab diner-type food at *George's*, or opt for the upscale, contemporary cuisine at *Madison's Grill* (ⓣ709/639-8846, ⓦwww.madisonsgrill.ca) inside the *Marble Inn Resort*. Corner Brook is just 10km from Steady Brook.

Corner Brook

CORNER BROOK, at the end of the Humber Valley some 50km from Deer Lake, is magnificently sited, surrounded by steep wooded hills dropping down to the blue waters of the Humber Arm. The city is Newfoundland's second biggest, a workaday pulp-and-paper town supplying newsprint to much of the world. The coast hereabouts was charted by Captain Cook, who now accounts for the city's most enjoyable attraction, the **Cook Historic Site**, to the west of the centre in a small park at the top of Crow Hill Road with fabulous views of the valley; get maps and directions at the **visitor centre** (June–Sept daily 9am–6pm; ⓣ709/639-9792), 15 Confederation Drive, just off the highway (exit 6).

Practicalities

Accommodation in Corner Brook tends to fill up fast, especially the popular *Comfort Inn* (ⓣ709/639-1980, ⓦwww.choicehotels.ca ⑥), at 41 Maple Valley Rd, just off the highway; book ahead. The *Glynmill Inn* (Ⓣ709/634-5181, Ⓦwww.glynmillinn.ca; ❺), at 1B Cobb Lane in town, has more character, a mock Tudor-style hotel with modern rooms.

For **food**, *Bay of Islands Bistro* (Ⓣ709/639-3500, Ⓦwww.bayofislandsbistro.com) at 13 West St, is top-notch, serving fancy dishes, including beautifully done salmon, beef, scallops and pork belly, while *Jennifer's* (Ⓣ709/632-7979), at 48 Broadway, offers tasty home-cooked seafood, steak and chicken. The best fish and chips on the west coast can be found 7km west of town at Mount Moriah (Rte 450), at tiny *C&E Takeout* (April–Oct) on Main Street. Corner Brook also has the best **nightlife** outside of St John's; try *Whelan's Gate Pub* (Ⓣ709/639-4283) at 14 Herald Ave.

Channel-Port aux Basques and beyond

Most people drive straight through **CHANNEL-PORT AUX BASQUES**, an important port and ferry terminal, but it does have a **tourist information office** (mid-May to mid-Oct daily 6am–8pm; Ⓣ709/695-2262), on the outskirts beside the Trans-Canada Hwy, and a substantial supply of affordable **accommodation**. In the newer part of the port, two options are the *Caribou Bed and Breakfast* (Ⓣ709/695-3408, Ⓦwww.bbcanada.com/2225.html; ❸; May–Sept), at 42 Grand Bay Rd, with five en-suite rooms; and the large, chalet-like *Hotel Port aux Basques* (Ⓣ709/695-2171 or 1-877/695-2171, Ⓦwww.hotelpab.com; ❹), at 2 Grand Bay Rd, 3km from the ferry.

Rose Blanche and the southwest coast

From Channel-Port aux Basques, it's a 45km drive east to end-of-the-road **ROSE BLANCHE**, a postcard-pretty village of steep lanes, brightly coloured houses and a fine old, granite lighthouse of 1871 (May–Oct daily 9am–9pm; $3; Ⓣ709/956-2052, Ⓦwww.roseblanchelighthouse.com). Nearby is a **B&B**, the *Hook, Line & Sinker* (Ⓣ709/956-2005; ❸; May–Oct).

From Rose Blanche it's still possible to travel by boat to **HERMITAGE**, about 180km to the east, passing majestic 150-metre cliffs and isolated fjords, but this is – in terms of time – a mammoth commitment involving several changes of ferry and several overnight stays of two or three days, as boats run to irregular timetables. Consequently, it's best to limit your ambitions and aim for **Ramea**, arguably the most dramatic of the coast's outports and just 83 nautical miles from Channel-Port aux Basques. To get there, take a **passenger ferry** (1 daily Mon, Wed, Fri, Sat & Sun; $4.75; 2hr 30min; Ⓣ709/292-4302, Ⓦwww.tw.gov.nl.ca/ferryservices) from Rose Blanche to picturesque **GRAND BRUIT**, where you can stay at the *Blue Mountain Cabins* (Ⓣ709/492-2753, Ⓦwww.bluemountaincabins.ca; ❸; June–Oct). At Grand Bruit, you change for the ferry (Tues 8.45am; $5.50; 3hr) to **BURGEO**, a much larger community from where Rte 480 makes the 150km journey north across the interior to the Trans-Canada. You can stay at *Gillett's Motel* (Ⓣ709/886-1284 or 1-888/333-1284, Ⓦwww.gillettsmotel.ca; ❹) at 1 Inspiration Rd, which also has a decent restaurant, the *Galley*.

There are frequent car ferries from Burgeo (1–2 daily; $3.75; 1hr 20min) to **RAMEA**, which perches on a tiny rugged island just offshore; there are a couple of pleasant B&Bs here, including the *Four Winds* (Ⓣ709/625-2002, Ⓦwww.fourwindsramea.ca; ❷) and the rooms and cottages of *Ramea Retreat* (Ⓣ709/625-2522, Ⓦwww.easternoutdoors.com/ramea; ❷).

Labrador

One of the last great unspoiled adventure destinations, **Labrador** is home to the planet's largest herd of caribou, wandering polar bears, awe-inspiring waterfalls and a string of pristine coastal communities that have preserved a raw, nineteenth-century quality despite the onset of wi-fi and SUVs. Travel here takes some planning and can be expensive, but the rewards are considerable; you can still hike or point your kayak anywhere into the interior (most of which is Crown land), and camp, fish or meditate for a couple of days, totally cut-off from civilization.

But Labrador also has a rich cultural heritage, with two of the most important historic sights in Canada, **Red Bay** and **Battle Harbour**, on the coast. Half the population of 29,000 lives here, while the remainder populate the towns of the **interior**; **Happy Valley-Goose Bay**, **Churchill Falls** and **Labrador West**, each offering quite different experiences. Labrador has a distinct identity to that of Newfoundland, despite a diverse ethnic mix of white settlers, Métis, Innu and Inuit; the **Labrador flag** is flown everywhere with pride. Summer is the most pleasant time to visit, though winter can be fun – especially if you travel by snowmobile – and has the added bonus of seeing the spectacular aurora borealis (northern lights; see also p.870).

Getting to Labrador

Flights from Newfoundland, Nova Scotia and Québec connect Labrador to the rest of the world, and are the simplest, quickest way there. Air Canada flies to Goose Bay from Halifax and to Wabush from Montréal, via Québec City and Sept-Îles. Air Labrador flies from St John's, Deer Lake and St Anthony in Newfoundland to their hub at Goose Bay, and Provincial Airlines flies from these and from Halifax to Goose Bay, Wabush and Lourdes de Blanc-Sablon; flights from the latter are always listed Blanc-Sablon local time, which is 30 minutes behind the neighbouring Labrador coastal communities in winter and 1hr 30min behind in summer. Flights from Montréal, Québec City and Halifax are around $800, and about half that for shorter hops from Newfoundland.

By ferry

For those driving, Labrador has **ferry** links from St Barbe on Newfoundland to Blanc-Sablon (mid-April to mid-Jan 1–3 daily; 1hr 45min; ⓣ1/866-535-2567, ⓦwww.labradormarine.com; $7.50 passengers, car and driver $22.75) on the Québec–Labrador border; reservations are recommended and all traffic must check in one hour before departure. Departures from Blanc-Sablon are listed in **Newfoundland time**, not local time (see above for flight information), so be careful if you plan to take the ferry and a flight on the same day.

The *Nordik Express* (see p.351) makes less frequent sailings and takes several days to find its way to Blanc-Sablon from Rimouski via numerous communities on the north shore of the St Lawrence River.

By train

The Québec North Shore and Labrador Railway runs an exhilarating 416km from Sept-Îles on Québec's North Shore to Schefferville, primarily serving the iron ore mines of Labrador West and First Nations communities. **Tshiuetin Rail Transportation Inc**, a First Nations venture, operates **trains** (reservations Mon–Fri 8am–noon & 1–4.30pm; ⓣ418/962-5530). The journey goes over high bridges,

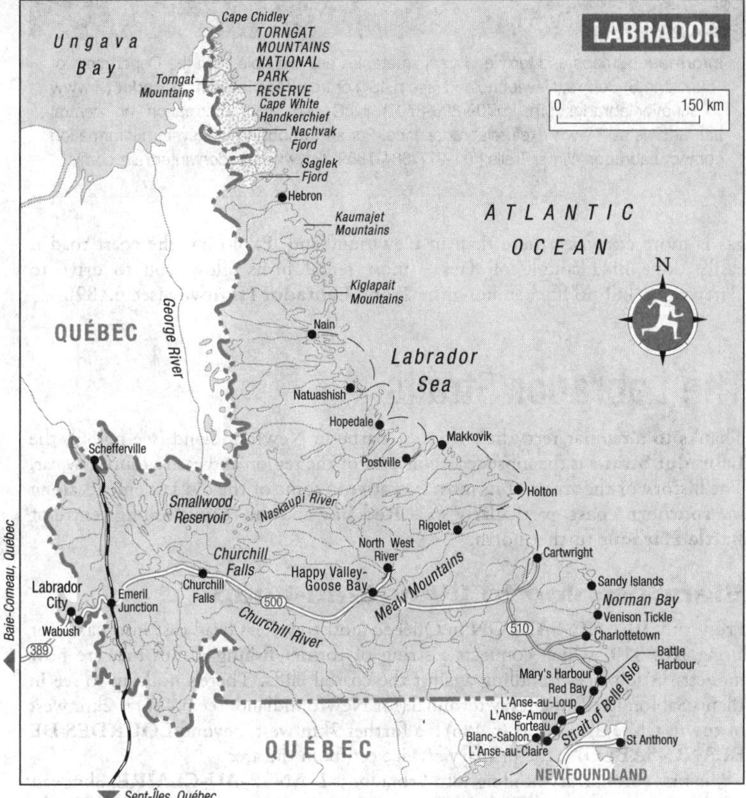

through dense forest and tundra and past waterfalls, deep gorges and rocky mountains, but travelling all the way to Schefferville is somewhat pointless; it's better to get off at Emeril Junction on the Trans-Labrador Hwy, 63km from Labrador City. Trains leave Sept-Îles for Emeril Junction Monday and Thursday at 8am (7hr) and arrive at 3pm; they depart on Tuesday and Friday at around noon and arrive at Sept-Îles at 7pm (around $60/one-way). A taxi is required to get back and forth from Labrador City (CJ Cabs ⓣ709/944-7757).

Transport on Labrador

Bar the **rail line** between Emeril Junction and Schefferville (see opposite), there is no land-based public transport in Labrador. The passenger-only *Northern Ranger* ferry sails weekly from Cartwright and Happy Valley-Goose Bay, and is the main lifeline for the northern coast (see p.497). If you want to reach the distant outposts quickly, the only choice is by **internal flights** with Air Labrador or Provincial Airlines. Between them they serve fourteen coastal communities, most with daily flights; it's around $400 return for Happy Valley-Goose Bay to Nain.

If you want to explore the south coast but don't have your own transport, you can **rent a car** from National in Lourdes de Blanc-Sablon (ⓣ418/481-2777 or 1-877/461-2777). Unless you have an SUV it's probably a good idea to rent one here – note, though, you only get 100km/day free (25 cents/km thereafter), and

Labrador information

Information, maps and ferry and train timetables are available from the Department of Tourism in St John's, Newfoundland (see p.451) or from **Destination Labrador** (@www.destinationlabrador.com; ⓣ709/896-6507) in Goose Bay. Information on central Labrador is at @www.explorelabrador.nf.ca. For snowmobiling trail system information contact Labrador Winter Trails (ⓣ1-877/884-7669, @www.labradorwintertrails.com).

gas is more expensive here than in Newfoundland. Exploring the coast road is easily done in a couple of days – most rental firms allow you to drive to Cartwright, but no further along the **Trans-Labrador Highway** (see p.489).

The Labrador Straits

Thanks to a regular ferry link from St Barbe in Newfoundland (see p.486), the **Labrador Straits** is the most accessible part of the region and easily toured by car. The history of the area is at its most evocative in some of the old settlements along the **southern coast**, particularly so at **Red Bay** and the rebuilt fishing centre of **Battle Harbour** further north.

Blanc-Sablon to L'Anse-au-Loup

From tiny **BLANC-SABLON** in Québec most travellers head east into Labrador along **Rte 510**, which connects a string of former fishing camps that are now modest, little places huddling against the coastal cliffs. There's nothing to see in Blanc-Sablon itself: the ferry terminal (for Newfoundland, see p.486) is 2km west of town, while the airport (p.486) is a further 7km west, beyond **LOURDES DE BLANC-SABLON,** the primary service centre in the area.

The first community heading into Labrador is **L'ANSE-AU-CLAIRE**, 8km east of the ferry terminal, which has the **area's main source of information**, the Gateway to Labrador visitor centre (mid-June to Sept daily 9.30am–5.30pm; ⓣ709/931-2360, @www.labradorstraits.net), housed in a 1909 church. From the beach just below the visitor centre, a 3.4km trail follows the original settlers path along the coast to the **Jersey Rooms**, the ruins of the abandoned nineteenth-century sealing settlement of L'Anse au Cotard. Families from Jersey occupied this tiny hamlet until the 1890s, and though there's not much to see, information boards along the route explain what was dug up here during the 2004 excavations.

Another 13km along Rte 510 is **FORTEAU**, at its liveliest during the annual three-day Bakeapple Festival in mid-August that celebrates the locally abundant cloudberry. A worthwhile hike out of Forteau is the Overfalls Brook Trail, which leads 1.3km from the village along the coast to a 30m-high waterfall. Another 6km east of town, the tiny **Labrador Straits Museum** (mid-June to mid-Sept Mon–Sat 9.30am–5.30pm; ⓣ709/927-7307, @www.labradorstraitsmuseum.ca; $5) is an endearing collection of local relics and curios, mainly from the 1920s and 1930s, though there are a few real gems: a wooden needle for mending codfish nets, a traditional *komatik* (sledge), bits from the 1922 wreck of HMS Raleigh and Labradorite from Nain. The story of the nearby 7500-year-old **burial mound** of a 12-year-old Archaic-Indian boy is also told in detail. You can see the mound itself – a well-defined heap of rocks – on the side road to **L'ANSE-AMOUR**, a few kilometres on and the oldest-known funeral monument in North America. Keep driving 2km through the village and you'll reach the 36m-high **Point**

Amour lighthouse (mid-June to mid-Oct daily 10am–5.30pm; ☎709/927-5826; $3), which provides fabulous 360 degree views from the top of its 128-step tower. Completed in 1857 and still in use, the history of lighthouse and the whole straits region is laid out in the adjacent lightkeeper's quarters, staffed by costumed guides.

Further up the coast, **L'ANSE-AU-LOUP** has all the basic services (including petrol) and the nearby **Pinware River Provincial Park** (late May to mid-Sept; ☎709/927-5516 or 1-800/563-6353; $5/vehicle; $23 camping). This is one of the most scenic stretches in the Labrador Straits, with a sandy beach, 1.2km hiking trail and the rushing, whitewater Pinware River as its centrepiece.

Accommodation

Most of the **places to stay** on this stretch of coast are either basic hotels or B&Bs; most offer dinner at an additional charge (non-guests are welcome).

Driving the Trans-Labrador Highway

Driving across Labrador is the most rewarding way to see the region, with new highways now making a monumental road-trip of around 1700km possible, from Newfoundland to Québec. Much of the route remains an unpaved, gravel road; it's possible to pass in a normal car, but it's best to opt for 4WD and to only attempt the trip in high summer. If you're renting, another problem might be your **rental policy**: most firms try to bar drivers from the section of the highway beyond Cartwright. They can't stop you ignoring this rule but if you have an accident insurance may not cover you. Check the latest situation; as the road is gradually paved (around 150km per year), the policy maybe be loosened. A greater barrier to renting is sheer distance; returning a car to Blanc-Sablon or anywhere in Newfoundland means driving a massive loop of almost 3000km through Québec and the Maritimes via at least two ferries, while one-way drop-off fees are exorbitant. If you have plenty of time, renting in Halifax makes more sense.

Trans-Labrador and Québec Highways: Blanc-Sablon to Baie-Comeau

Route 510:
Blanc-Sablon (the ferry port for Newfoundland) to Red Bay: 88km, paved (50min).
Red Bay to Mary's Harbour: 86km, gravel (50min).
Mary's Harbour to Cartwright Junction: 150km, gravel (2hr 30min; Cartwright an additional 87km on Rte 506).
Cartwright Junction to Happy Valley-Goose Bay: 296km, gravel (5hr).

Route 500:
Happy Valley-Goose Bay to Churchill Falls: 288km, gravel (4hr).
Churchill Falls to Labrador City: 238km, gravel (3hr).
Labrador City to Québec border (Fermont): 23km, paved (15min).

Route 389 (Québec):
Québec border (Fermont) to Gagnon: 177km, first 20km and last 90km paved (2hr 45min)
Gagnon to Manic-5: 180km, gravel (3hr).
Manic-5 to Baie-Comeau: 214km, paved (3hr).

The highway is one of the least frequented stretches of major road in eastern Canada, so make enquires about its current condition before driving. Fill up your tank every chance you get: there's nothing between Fermont and Manic-5, and as yet, between Port Hope Simpson and Goose Bay (detour into Cartwright). The speed limit on the highway is 70km/h, though locals and trucks often hit 100km/h where they can; the timings above assume a fairly conservative average.

Barney's B&B L'Anse-au-Loup ⓣ709/927-5634. In addition to the three rooms (two doubles and one double with a single bed) and ocean views, owner Mary Barney offers laundry and churns out delicious meals. Hiking trails aren't far off either, and there's some excellent trout and salmon fishing nearby. If you're staying here, drop by *Dot's Bakery* (Mon–Sat 7am–11pm), the best place to eat in the area, with great home-baked cakes, muffins and cookies, plus soups, sandwiches and light meals. ❷

Beachside Hospitality Home 9 Lodge Rd, L'Anse-au-Claire ⓣ709/931-2338, ⓦwww.bbcanada.com/10622.html. The five rooms here share two bathrooms, each with a jacuzzi tub, but the real treat is the free evening entertainment (on request) from host Norm Letto, a master of the accordion. ❷

Grenfell Louie A. Hall B&B 3 Willow Ave, Forteau ⓣ709/931-2916, ⓦwww.grenfellbandb.ca. Housed in a 1946 nursing station, this B&B has simple but pleasant rooms – each named after a nurse or staff member who worked at the station – and a common room. May–Oct. ❸

Northern Light Inn L'Anse-au-Claire ⓣ709/931-2332 or 1-800/563 3188, ⓦwww.northernlightinn.com. A modern, but rather basic motel with the most popular food options in town: the *Basque Restaurant* (daily 7am–9pm), which serves simple meals, and the *Greco* pizza take-out. ❹

Pinware River Provincial Park Rte 510, approximately 32 km southwest from Red Bay ⓣ709/729-2424 or 1-877/214-2267, ⓦwww.env.gov.nl.ca/parks. The facilities here are basic but the campground has flush and pit toilets, running water and hot showers. Tent sites $15.

Sea-View Restaurant and Cabins 33 Main St, Forteau ⓣ709/931-2840 or 1/866-931-2840. The motel-like rooms are basic, but the restaurant is known for its seafood; the scallops are under $15. Be sure also to try the Labrador Preserves (ⓦwww.preserves.nf.ca) jams sold here. ❹

Red Bay

It seems inconceivable today, but the sleepy village of **RED BAY** was once the world's largest whaling port, occupied by Basque fishermen years before the arrival of the Pilgrims in New England. Despite the abundance of broken red

Basque whalers at Red Bay

At its peak in the late sixteenth century, over two thousand men lived in Red Bay during the **whaling** season, producing half a million gallons of whale oil that was subsequently shipped back to Europe on a month-long voyage. Whale oil was used for light, lubrication and as an additive to drugs, soap and pitch; one 55-gallon barrel could fetch a price equal to $10,000 today – so for the **Basques** the discovery of Labrador's right-whale stocks was equivalent to striking gold. Yet as well as the treacherous journey from Spain to what they knew as Terranova, the Basques withstood terrible hardships to claim their booty. Once in Labrador, they rowed fragile wooden craft called *chalupas* into these rough seas and then attached drogues to the whales to slow them down. It was then a matter of following their prey for hours until the whale surfaced and could be lanced to death. Three factors brought the whale boom to an end: first, the Basques were so successful that within thirty years they had killed off more than fifteen thousand **right whales**; second, the industry became more hazardous with early freeze-ups in the 1570s; and, finally, the Basque ships and men were absorbed into the ill-fated Spanish Armada of 1588.

Serious study of Red Bay area began in 1977, when marine archeologists discovered the remains of three Basque **galleons** and four *chalupas*. Land excavations uncovered try-works (where the whale blubber was boiled down into oil), personal artefacts and, in 1982, a cemetery on Saddle Island where the remains of 140 young men were found. Many were lying in groups, indicating that they died as crew members when chasing the whales, but some had not been buried – suggesting at least part of the community died of starvation when an early freeze dashed their chances of getting home.

tiles on the beaches, their presence here was eventually forgotten, and only rediscovered in the 1970s after obscure documents in Spain led to the astounding discovery of the remains of a Basque ship buried in the harbour. Artefacts from the ship and subsequent land and marine archeological surveys can be viewed at the **Red Bay National Historic Site** (daily: June to early Oct 9am–6pm; $7.15; ⓣ709/920-2142, ⓦwww.pc.gc.ca/redbay).

Start at the **reception centre**, where the discoveries are introduced with a twenty-minute film and the most impressive relic is displayed: one of the small *chalupas* (see p.490) actually used by the whalers in the 1580s. In all, seven ships have been found – academics speculate that the largest vessel was the *San Juan*, which is known to have sunk here in 1565, but this has never been proven. Down the road, the **interpretation centre** contains two floors of artefacts recovered from the wrecks and nearby **Saddle Island**, including astonishingly well-preserved clothing worn by sixteenth-century sailors.

You can take a **boat trip** to Saddle Island (hourly departures from the interpretation centre daily 9am–4pm July-Sept; $2), where you can roam around the eerie whaler's cemetery and other labelled sites on a self-guided tour.

Practicalities

For **accommodation**, the *Whaling Station Cabins* (May–Oct; ⓣ709/920-2156; ❹), 61 East Harbour Drive, offers en-suite rooms with cable TV, some with kitchenettes. The *Whaler's Restaurant* (May–Oct daily 8am–8pm; ⓣ709/920-2156) opposite the interpretation centre is the most convenient place for a drink or meal.

Mary's Harbour and Port Hope Simpson

Beyond Red Bay, Rte 510 switches from asphalt to well-maintained gravel and heads inland to re-emerge 85km later at the coast by **MARY'S HARBOUR**, a settlement founded in 1930 by a handful of families after the hospital fire at Battle Harbour began an exodus to the mainland (see p.492). Today it's a surprisingly vibrant little town, living primarily on the seasonal crab fishery and tourism. It's also a sensible place to spend the night, though if you can afford it, the main attraction here is **Battle Harbour** 9km offshore – signs lead through the village to the ferry dock.

At Mary's Harbour you can stay and eat at the comfortable *Riverlodge Hotel* (ⓣ709/921-6948; ❺). Locals cook up hearty meals of roast beef, fried chicken, turkey and sometimes fresh fish and scallops in its restaurant. *Old Pete's Pub*, also on the premises, is a good place to share stories with fellow travellers and locals.

Heading north on Rte 510, it's 55km to **PORT HOPE SIMPSON**, another isolated fishing community and your last chance for gas and provisions before the long haul up to Cartwright. *Alexis Hotel* (ⓣ709/960-0228, ⓔburdencarol@yahoo.ca; ❹), just outside town, is a decent place to stay with cable TV, laundry and kayak rentals. *Campbell's Place* (ⓣ709/960-0606), at 98 Pioneer St, is a welcome pit-stop for its home-made sandwiches, soups, chilli and tempting cakes. It also offers four comfy en-suite B&B rooms (❸).

Battle Harbour

Spending a night or two on the island of **BATTLE HARBOUR** (mid-June to mid-Sept; $9 entry; ⓣ709/921-6325 or 709/921-6216, ⓦwww.battleharbour.com) is one of the most memorable experiences in Labrador. This beautifully restored fishing port is visited by towering icebergs in spring and humpback whales in summer; killer whales often cruise right off the dock. Established in the 1770s, Battle Harbour became one of the world's busiest saltfish, salmon and

▲ Battle Harbour

sealing ports in the nineteenth-century; Wilfred Grenfell opened a hospital here in 1893, it was home to a Marconi wireless station from 1904 and was the scene of Robert E. Peary's first news conference after he conquered the North Pole in 1909. A devastating fire in 1930 exacerbated long-term decline, and by the late 1960s most residents had been relocated to Mary's Harbour on the mainland – the last fish merchant was closed in the wake of the 1992 cod moratorium. Since then an epic restoration project by the Battle Harbour Historic Trust has resulted in a clutch of wonderfully evocative old wooden buildings opening to the public, a **visitor centre** and several walking trails; you can also **stay** in some of the old houses (see below). Many of the former residents of the town serve as guides and are as equally absorbing as the site itself – prepare for seriously traditional Labrador accents. Some houses are still privately owned (though these are summer homes – there are no permanent residents).

Ferries (daily 11am and 6pm, return at 4pm and 9am; 1hr 15min; $60 round-trip) from Mary's Harbour to Battle Harbour, depart from the Grenfell Mission wharf and visitor centre on Main Street.

Accommodation

Accommodation options include a restored merchant house – the *Battle Harbour Inn* (shared bath; ❻) – and a hostel-style fisherman's *Bunkhouse* ($35/person). Meals are provided at an extra cost of $8 for breakfast and $18 for dinner. Alternatively, you can stay in one of four cottages, including the self-catering *Grenfell House* (❻), and the rustic, three-bedroom *Issac Smith House* (❽), which has only oil lamps and wood fires, plus a modern kitchen and bath.

Cartwright

With the completion of the Trans-Labrador Hwy in 2009, tiny **CARTWRIGHT**, around 240km from Mary's Harbour, was left stranded 87km north of the main road via Rte 516. It remains a useful pit-stop on the drive to Happy Valley-Goose Bay nevertheless, with several attractions to justify the detour. The settlement is named after Captain George Cartwright, one of the first European traders to coexist with the natives when he established a post here in 1775. All that remains of his former shack, grandly titled **Caribou Castle**, is a large rock marking the boundary of his land, right at the end of Main Street facing the water. Nearby you'll find a small **memorial** to Cartwright in the old cemetery.

Today, Cartwright is best known for two things: some of the finest **salmon fishing** in the world (along the Eagle River; July only) and **Porcupine Strand**, a 56km-long sandy beach that can only be visited by boat or ATV (12km from Cartwright). The Vikings almost certainly visited the latter – their descriptions of the "Wunderstrand" are too precise to be anywhere else. Experience Labrador (Ⓦwww.experiencelabrador.com) can arrange fishing trips and excursions to the beach (mid-June to mid-Sept), where you can spend a day – or longer – hiking the beach, stumbling across historical remains, the odd moose and virtually no one else; it rates as one of Canada's great adventures.

Practicalities

The *Cartwright Hotel* (Ⓣ709/938-7414, Ⓦwww.cartwrighthotel.ca; ❹) is a friendly inn on the outskirts of town and the best place to seek **information** and local maps; it also serves good local cuisine in the *Sandwich Bay Dining Room* and has a pub, the *Eagle's Nest*. On the other side of the harbour (turn right when you hit Main St), near the water, the *Mug Up Restaurant* (Wed–Sat 4–9pm; longer in summer) also does great teas and meals. *Harbourview B&B* (Ⓣ709/938-7325; ❷), a few doors along, offers guided tours of the surrounding area as well as two comfortable rooms.

Happy Valley–Goose Bay and around

Sandwiched between the mighty Churchill River and the westernmost tip of sprawling Lake Melville, the town of **HAPPY VALLEY–GOOSE BAY** is the principal transport and administrative hub for the entire Labrador coast, as well as its largest settlement. If you're driving the Trans-Labrador Hwy, you'll almost certainly want to spend a couple of days here, and it's also the staging point for the epic boat journey north (see p.497). The city itself offers a few decent restaurants and bars, but much of the appeal lies in the surrounding spruce forest, sparkling lakes and rivers.

The town is a relatively recent creation, established when US forces built the **Goose Bay** airfield in 1941; this eventually became a sprawling NATO military base, housing up to twelve thousand military personnel. **Happy Valley**, where most of the shops and restaurants are located a few kilometres from the airfield, is a fairly quiet, laidback sort of place, originally developed to house the workers for the base. In 2006 NATO left, leaving the base managed by a handful of Canadian Air Force personnel, and the town struggling to adjust to potentially devastating social and economic changes. Against all the odds, it's done incredibly well since then: jobs related to the creation of **Nunatsiavut** (see p.496) and an independent Labrador Health Authority, as well as a resurgent mining sector, have led to a mini-housing boom, and the base is being converted into a major business park.

Arrival and information

From either Labrador West or Cartwright Junction you'll end up **driving** into the west side of Happy Valley-Goose Bay: a new bridge over the Churchill River means the Trans-Labrador Hwy bypasses the town, and rtes 510 and 500 meet a few kilometres on the outskirts; follow Rte 500 east till you hit Hamilton River Road: turn left for Goose Bay and the airport, and right for Happy Valley.

Happy Valley-Goose Bay **airport** is located on the former NATO base, in the old Goose Bay area of town. It has just one unreliable ATM, so make sure you bring cash. There's no public transport, so you'll have to rely on **taxis** (Cooney's;

☎709/896-3333). Meters start at $4, and fares should range between $10 for *Hotel North* and $15-20 for places in Happy Valley. Taxis around town use meters, but the fare to North West River is fixed at $50.

National (☎709/896-1072) and Budget (☎709/896-2976) have booths at the airport and charge about $60 per day, with the first 100km per day free. To get to town, head along Loring Drive and turn right at the traffic lights (the only ones in town) onto Hamilton River Road. Right on the corner is the **visitor centre**, 365 Hamilton River Rd (June–Aug daily 9am–8pm; rest of year closed weekends, call for times Mon–Fri ☎709/896-3489, Ⓦwww.tourismlabrador.com), which provides brochures and helps plan trips out of town.

The **ferry terminal** is 5km north of the visitor centre on the shores of Lake Melville: the *Northern Ranger* docks here (see p.497). You won't find much at the wharf: taxis into Goose Bay should be around $15–20, and $20–25 into Happy Valley.

Accommodation

Happy Valley-Goose Bay has a reasonable range of **accommodation**, though rooms can get booked up fast, so always reserve ahead. The least expensive options are the B&Bs.

Davis' B&B 14 Cabot Crescent ☎709/896-5077, Ⓦwww.bbcanada.com/davisbb. Centrally located B&B with four rooms with private bathrooms, wi-fi and cable TV; also has laundry and kitchen facilities. ❷–❸

Goose River Lodges Rte 520 ☎709/896-2600 or 1-877/496-2600, Ⓦwww.gooseriverlodges.ca. Around 10km north of town on the road to North West River, this tranquil resort has chalets ($95/night for four adults) as well as tent and serviced RV sites ($17–24) year-round. They also rent snowmobiles.

Hotel North 25/27 Loring Drive (☎709/896-9301 or 1-877/996-9301, Ⓦwww.atyp.com/hotelnorth. Relatively smart lodging, with standard, modern rooms, just five minutes from the airport; comes with wi-fi, satellite TV and fridges. ❻

Royal Inn 5 Royal Ave (☎709/896-2456 or 1-888/440-2456, Ⓦwww.royalinnandsuites.ca. This plush motel-like option is the best value in town; continental breakfast and internet access is free, rooms are new and comfy and it has self-service laundry ($1.50) and decent cable TV, all right in the centre of town. It's popular and can get very busy and noisy at times. ❹

The Town

The distinctions between the Goose Bay and Happy Valley sections of the town (around 4km apart) have largely disappeared since 2006, and new housing projects have effectively linked the two along the main drag, **Hamilton River Road**. There's no real centre, and you'll need a car to get around.

The town's two museums largely focus on its military heritage. The **Northern Lights Military Museum** (Mon–Sat 10am–5.30pm, Fri until 9pm; free), at 170 Hamilton River Rd, occupies a room in the basement of a general store and is stuffed with military memorabilia, primarily weapons and uniforms. The **Labrador Military Museum** (June–Sept Mon–Fri 9am–5pm; free; must call ☎709/896-6900 ext 2177 to arrange a visit), in a large hangar on Loring Drive near the airport, documents the history of the Canadian, British, American, Dutch and German military presence with displays of flags, insignia and radar apparatus. Particularly poignant are the references to the all-too-frequent fatal air crashes that have occurred here in past decades.

For a non-militaristic interlude visit **Slippers 'n Things** (Mon–Sat 9am–5pm; ☎709/896-5660, Ⓦwww.slippersnthings.com), at 55 Grenfell St, a delightful store selling traditional Labrador crafts, gifts and local books. On Saturdays they offer free toutons (fried bread dough) topped with home-made redberry jam or molasses, and coffee or tea.

Don't leave town without driving up to **Dome Mountain** (aka Pine Tree Lookout) around 16km from the visitor centre; there are no signs and the road becomes a potholed, jarring gravel track barely passable in a regular vehicle, but the views of the town, Churchill River, Lake Melville and the mountains are stupendous. To get there, drive towards the airport on Loring Drive, then take a left along Lahr Boulevard; take another left on River Road and follow this to the end – you'll need to turn left two more times before the dirt road rises up towards the old radar tower on the summit.

Eating and drinking

The best places to **eat** tend to be spread out all over town, and though there's not a huge choice, standards are improving. When it comes to nightlife, Happy Valley-Goose Bay is a lively **drinking** town and there are several decent pubs.

Mariner's Galley 25 Loring Drive ☎709/896-3388. Excellent option for breakfast, lunch and dinner, specializing in steaks and fine seafood; most popular joint for out-of-towners. The nautical theme is enhanced by the wooden ship centrepiece.

Maxwell's II/Bentley's Sports Bar 97 Hamilton River Rd ☎709/896-3583. The town's main spot for a night out, located right on the waterfront, features a sports bar showing all the big events and is very popular for dinner. Lunch specials are also good (from $8), as well as pastas ($11–16), salmon ($17.95), cod dishes ($11–13), steaks and grills (from $20). It morphs into a club late Fri and Sat nights. Daily happy hour 4–7pm.

Mulligan's Pub 368 Hamilton River Rd ☎709/896-3038. Tiny but congenial Irish pub that's always packed; has live music Wed and Sat, and a breezy patio in the summer.

Valley Restaurant and **Locals** nightclub, Grand St ☎709/896-7331. The place to come for all things caribou: steak ($12.99), burger ($5.49), soup ($2.99) included, but it also does decent pizzas. Local classics include the all-day breakfasts ($7–8), Jiggs dinner ($12.99) on Sun, cod tongues with gravy and fries and home-made pies from $3.29. Restaurant Mon–Fri 9am–6pm, Sat 9am–4pm, Sun 10am–4pm; the club takes over at the weekends.

Around Happy Valley-Goose Bay

Several tempting targets lie in the forests around Happy Valley-Goose Bay, but the most accessible and enjoyable are the mighty **Muskrat Falls** and the small settlement of **North West River,** central Labrador's most historic town.

Muskrat Falls

To experience the countryside around Happy Valley-Goose Bay at its most striking, make a trip to **Muskrat Falls**, a thunderous series of cascades on the Churchill River. To get there, drive out of Happy Valley on the Trans-Labrador Hwy (Rte 500) towards Churchill Falls. After about 40km, look for a small sign on the right pointing to a narrow dirt road on the left; drive along here for around 2km (you may have to walk this, depending on the condition of the road). From the end of the road it's a short hike to the falls lookout, while another rough, unmarked trail leads down to the bank of the river (around 800m), where you can view the falls from a spray-covered rocky outcrop. See the falls while you can; the area will be irrevocably transformed by the **Lower Churchill Project,** with construction of a dam, reservoir and power station expected to begin in 2012.

North West River

From the visitor centre in Happy Valley-Goose Bay paved Rte 520 heads north 38km to **NORTH WEST RIVER**, one of the oldest settlements in Labrador and picturesquely surrounded by three vast bodies of water: Grand Lake, Little Lake and the briney Lake Melville. In summer you'll see several make-shift camps along the road – these belong to local **Innu** from the community of **Sheshatshiu**. You'll pass their village just before crossing the bridge into North West River, but there's little point in stopping here.

North West River itself was a fur-trading post established by the French in 1743 and subsequently developed by Métis and English trappers. The **Hudson's Bay Company** arrived in 1836 and dominated the fur trade and life in the village until the construction of Goose Bay airbase started to draw the trappers away – today most of the 550 or so inhabitants work in Happy Valley-Goose Bay. The Hudson's Bay trading post closed in the 1970s, but just across the bridge the **Labrador Heritage Museum** (June–Sept Mon–Fri 9am–5pm; ⓣ709/497-8858; $2) on River Road incorporates the old Hudson's Bay store, restored to its 1930 appearance. Inside exhibits cover the history of the area, enhanced with a life-size reconstruction of a trapper's "tilt" (cabin) and a curious assortment of artefacts; look out for the disturbing tonsil snare, and a portable steel incubator – the guides know one of the babies transported in it (he's now in his 50s). The museum also has an intriguing account of the ill-fated 1903 **Wallace-Hubbard expedition** into the Labrador interior. American millionaire Leonidas Hubbard, his friend Dillon Wallace and guide George Elson hoped to cross from Lake Melville to Ungava Bay on the northern fringe of Québec, but they travelled up the wrong river valley and Hubbard eventually died of exhaustion in the wilderness. His Canadian-born wife Mina – who never forgave Wallace for abandoning him – completed the spectacular trek two years later. The museum is planning to run two-day expeditions 22km up the **Susan River** by canoe to the plaque marking Hubbard's death; call them for the latest.

From the jetty near the museum, **Jock Campbell** (ⓣ709/497-8544) runs boat trips across the lake on weekends and summer evenings: day-trips usually run to $100 per person, but he'll take you out for a quick spin for $20–30.

At the end of Portage Road, the houses stop abruptly to reveal a long sandy **beach** curling around the shore, a popular place to relax in the summer with fine views across to the mountains. The **North West River Beach Festival** (free) takes place here on the fourth weekend in July, featuring First Nations music and dance, as well as local snacks – look out for the Innu donuts.

At the other end of Portage Road, the **Labrador interpretation centre** (mid-June to mid-Sept Mon & Wed-Sat noon–4.30pm, Tues & Sun 10am-4.30pm; rest of the year Wed-Sun 1–4.30pm; free; ⓣ709/497-8566) has a temporary gallery (usually displaying local art) and an enlightening permanent display introducing the four main cultural groups of Labrador. The guides are extremely knowledgeable and are happy to explain the significance of the most intriguing artefacts on show; Innu tea dolls, the Innu shaking tent and a chunky sculpture made of serpentine by Inuit artist Gilbert Hay.

For a panoramic **view**, drive 2km beyond the museum up to **Sunday Hill** on a rather rough, potholed road; you'll be rewarded with sweeping vistas of both lakes, the lumpy outline of Mount Mokami and, in the distance, the Mealy Mountains.

Labrador North

The **north** is the most untouched and least visited part of Labrador. Up here, **Inuit** culture begins to assert itself; polar bears are common in winter; there are no cars in most of the settlements; arctic char are still hung in the street to dry; and activities change according to what is in season to hunt or trap. Things started to improve after most of the coast became part of **Nunatsiavut** (not be confused with Nunavut) in 2005, giving the Inuit special rights and ownership of 15,800 square kilometres. Based in Hopedale and Nain, the Nunatsiavut government (which remains nominally part of Labrador) has authority over local health, education and justice, with an elected president every four years. North of Nain, the hauntingly beautiful **Torngat Mountains National Park Reserve,** Canada's most isolated national park, beckons the adventurous.

The *Northern Ranger* (see below) from Happy Valley-Goose Bay takes three days to reach **Nain** – and a sudden storm can leave you stranded for days in one of the tinier midway settlements. Travelling only by plane and passenger ferry certainly creates lots of opportunity to spy whales, seals and all manner of northern wildlife plus **icebergs** – around three thousand drift over from Greenland every year.

North from Happy Valley-Goose Bay to Nain

Most of the coastal villages beyond Happy Valley-Goose Bay began as fur-trading posts in the nineteenth century, though some date back to the eighteenth-century missionary work of the **Moravian Brethren**, a small Czech evangelical sect active along the Labrador coast from the late 1700s to the 1950s.

One of the more interesting stops on the coast includes **RIGOLET** (Ⓦwww.thebigland.ca), another former Hudson's Bay trading post, which features a pleasant 2km boardwalk and the Net Loft Museum (filled with Hudson's Bay memorabilia). The prim, white 1782 Moravian mission still stands at **HOPEDALE,** 150km south of Nain (June–Sept by appointment; $5; Ⓣ709/933-3490), its hymn books printed in Inuktitut, the language of the Inuit. In town the *Amaguk Inn* (Ⓣ709/933-3750; ❻) provides comfortable motel-quality rooms and food, as well as small self-catering units.

Labrador's most northern settlement, **NAIN** has a population of just over one thousand, despite being the capital of Nunatsiavut. Fishing is still the primary activity here, though the town is also known for its adroit Inuit **carvers** and nearby **Labradorite** quarry at Ten Mile Bay (most of the stone is processed in Italy and used for floor tiles). The 1771 Moravian mission, converted into a museum called **Piulimatsivik** (Inuit for "place where we keep the old things"), burnt down

The Northern Ranger

Northern Labrador is the region at its most remote, yet the coast is fairly easy to explore, thanks to the weekly, summer-only **ferry service** of the **Northern Ranger**, which is becoming popular as a budget cruise. The foot-passenger only ship, run by Labrador Marine (Ⓣ1/866-535-2567, Ⓦwww.labradormarine.com), leaves once-weekly from Cartwright on a route that takes it to Nain via Happy Valley-Goose Bay, with stops at every larger community along the way. In most cases the hour or so the ferry spends at every stop is plenty to have a look around. Should you decide to stop for longer, you'll have to stay for several days until the ferry docks in again, and will have to ask around for somewhere to stay, though it's generally not too hard to find accommodation. The ferries run from mid-June to late November; soon after this, the Arctic ice pack closes in to seal up the area for the rest of year. The late-season schedule is notoriously unreliable since storms can delay sailings, sometimes for days.

Fares are very reasonable, based on the number of nautical miles travelled, with supplements for cabin space, which you should reserve well in advance, otherwise it's likely you'll have no option but to make yourself as comfortable as possible on the aircraft-style seats. A single trip from Happy Valley-Goose Bay to Nain costs around $67 for a basic berth and $444 for a standard cabin. Prices at the **onboard canteen** are reasonable but choice is limited and the meals are reminiscent of over-cooked school dinners so it's worth stocking up on provisions beforehand.

in 1999. Some artefacts were rescued, however – ask around to find where they are currently displayed. You can stay in town at the *Atsanik Lodge*, Sand Banks Road (ⓣ709/922-2910, ⓔatsanik52@aol.com; ⑤).

Torngat Mountains National Park Reserve

Nain is as far north as you can get using public transport in Labrador, and to travel onwards to the awe-inspiring wilderness of the **Torngat Mountains National Park Reserve** you need to rent a boat or charter a plane – both very expensive options (see below). If you can afford it, you'll have the utterly intoxicating experience of hiking in the highest range east of the Rockies, spot loads of polar bears and truly spectacular fjords. Base camp is usually the Saglek Bay station (July & Aug), just outside the park, from where boats and helicopters fan out to various spots inside the reserve (mostly for scientists), but the region is best visited with experienced guides like Torngat Mountain Labrador Tours in Nain (ⓣ709/896-0184 or 579-0995, ⓔwinstonw@nl.rogers.com), which offers canoeing, kayaking, walking and camping trips year-round – in igloos in the winter. At Nain you can also charter a boat to sail up the coast with Webb Services (ⓣ709/922-2865 or 922-2960), who will show you the deserted 1831 Moravian mission at **HEBRON** (the Inuit settlement was forcibly abandoned in 1959) and take you to the **Nachvak Fjord**, near Labrador's northernmost extremity, where the razorback mountains soar out of the sea at an angle of nearly eighty degrees to a height of 915m.

Labrador West

A vast expanse of forested mountains, lakes and tracts of tundra, **Labrador West** is punctuated by towns that live to serve the phenomenal mining and engineering projects that have sprouted up here since the 1960s. Tours of these mind-blowing facilities are the area's most obvious attractions, but **Labrador City** is also an important stop on the Trans-Labrador Hwy (p.489). This part of Labrador is also the best place to view the **Northern Lights** (Nov–March).

Churchill Falls

Few people would normally get excited about touring a power station, but the **Churchill Falls Hydro-Electricity Facility,** located 288km west from Happy Valley-Goose Bay, is not your average public utility. The sheer size of this mammoth project is overwhelming. The only way to appreciate its scale is to take a two-and-a-half-hour **tour** (daily 9am, 1.30pm & 7pm; free). Make reservations in advance by calling ⓣ709/925-3335 (Mon–Fri 8am–noon & 1–4.30pm).

The facility exploits the raw power of the **Churchill River** as it plunges 75m into McLean Canyon. Around 6700 square kilometres – an area three and a half

Labrador expedition cruises

Expedition cruises are a hassle-free and (usually) cheaper way to visit the Torngat Mountains and northern Labrador than going it alone. Cruise North Expeditions (ⓣ416/789-3752 or 1-866/263-3220, ⓦwww.cruisenorthexpeditions.com) is one of the best choices, offering trips from St John's to Kuujjuaq in Québec via the entire Labrador coast from around $2795. Wanderbird (ⓦwww.wanderbirdcruises.com) and Cruise Newfoundland and Labrador (ⓦwww.cruisenewfoundlandandlabrador.com) are also worth checking out.

times the size of Lake Ontario – was dammed for the development, a project conceived by the then premier, Joe Smallwood, to boost Newfoundland's economy. Wrangling with financial backers, and then with the Québec government, delayed its completion until 1971. Québec came out tops: it reserved the right to buy all the electricity for 65 years at a low fixed rate – Hydro Québec has since been selling this power on to the US at ten or twenty times what it pays Newfoundland and Labrador. The most infamous contract in Canadian history, it's been a source of deep bitterness for Labradorians ever since.

The company town of **CHURCHILL FALLS** – simply an outgrowth of the power plant – contains two **accommodation** options: the *Black Spruce Lodge* (Ⓣ709/925-3233; ❸), at 23 Cabot St, which has eight rooms, a common area and kitchen, and the smarter *Midway Travel Inn* (Ⓣ709/925-3211 or 1-800/229-3269; ❺), which also serves **food** (daily 7am–10pm).

Labrador City and Wabush

Some 238km west of Churchill Falls it's a shock to come across **LABRADOR CITY** and neighbouring **WABUSH**, two lively communities of wide streets, shopping malls and fast-food joints in the middle of nowhere. Both were established in the 1960s to serve the nearby **iron ore mines** which still dominate the local economy and, with a combined population of around ten thousand, they make up the largest concentration of people in Labrador. Don't expect grimy mining towns – both are modern and tidy places with plenty of families, lakeside parks, services and schools.

Wabush is the smaller of the two, located off the Trans-Labrador Hwy (Rte 500) on Rte 503, and you're better off focusing on Labrador City, just 4km away on the main highway (which is paved for this section).

Start at the **Gateway Labrador interpretation centre** (Mon–Fri 9am–5pm, Sat noon–5pm, Sun 1–4pm; $3; Ⓣ709/944-5399), on the main hwy on the edge of Labrador City, which doubles as the local visitor centre. Inside you'll find a gift shop and a well-presented **museum** outlining the history of Labrador West, from the early days of the fur trappers to the recent boom in mining and energy. Half of Canada's iron ore output is produced here from canyon-like open pit mines that are serviced by oversized 20m-long dump trucks. The only way to appreciate the super-human scale of what goes on here is to take a **mine tour**, which you can arrange at the Gateway Centre. The biggest and most mind-boggling facility belongs to **Iron Ore Company of Canada** in Labrador City; they normally offer regular tours from June to August (Wed & Sun 1.30pm) for $8, though the mine was shut over the summer of 2009 due to falling global demand for iron. You can also visit **Wabush Mines** (free), a slightly smaller operation. In both cases, call the Gateway in advance to check the current situation, or contact Destination Labrador (p.488).

Labrador West isn't just about industry though. Canada's longest and toughest snowmobile race, **Cain's Quest** (Ⓦwww.cainsquest.com) starts here every March, and there are plenty of forest parks and lakes around if you need to stretch your legs. The **Menihek Interpretive Trails** make an appealing place to hike in summer or cross-country ski in winter, with 34km of trails groomed for all ability levels by the Menihek Nordic Ski Club (Ⓣ709/944-5842, Ⓦwww.meniheknordicski.ca). The trails run around the adjacent **Smokey Mountain Ski Club** (Ⓣ709/944-2129), which offers nineteen downhill ski runs with a 300m vertical drop. You'll find both sites 3km off the Trans-Labrador Hwy (via a gravel road), just outside Labrador City (look for signs to Smokey Mountain Recreation Area). The most popular local winter activity is **snowmobiling**, which can conveniently be done from the *Northern Lights Lodge* (Ⓣ709/944-7475, Ⓦwww.labrador-frontier.com), which lies halfway to Churchill Falls beside a network of trails and offers rentals, guided tours and custom packages (they will pick you up from Wabush Airport).

Practicalities

Wabush Airport lies midway between the two towns on Rte 503. Budget (T 709/282-1234) and National (T 709/282-3059) have desks at the terminal and **taxis** (CJ Cabs T 709/944-7757) meet most flights: they normally use meters for trips around town, but charge fixed rates from the airport ($12 to Wabush or Labrador City).

For good-value **accommodation**, try the *PJ's Inn by the Lake B&B* (T 709/944-3438, W www.pjsinnbythelake.com; 3), at 606 Tamarack Drive, which has five comfy en-suite rooms, or head to the *Two Seasons Inn* (T 709/944-2661 or 1-800/670-7667, W www.twoseasonsinn.com; 4), on Avalon Drive, a smart, centrally-located hotel. To **camp**, head 10km west along Rte 500 to the Duley Lake Family Park (T 709/280-1128; $10), with an on-site store and a swimming beach.

Good choices for **eating** are *Jordan's Family Restaurant* (daily 7am–8pm; T 709/944-7772), at 215 Duke Ave, justly popular for its hearty breakfasts, and nearby *Heddy's* at 211 Drake Ave, given a smart makeover in 2009 and offering a variety of traditional Newfoundland and Labrador seafood dishes. All-you-can-eat **buffets** are also popular here, usually (and somewhat bizarrely) featuring Canadian and Chinese dishes: the restaurant inside the *Wabush Hotel* (T 709/282-3221; daily from 5.30pm), at 9 Grenfell Drive in Wabush, and *Charlie's* (T 709/282-3261) in Bruno Plaza at 118 Humphrey Rd, are the best examples.

A local joke goes that if it's hot for three days in a row the corner stores here run out of beer, and you'll certainly find plenty of **bars** in Labrador City. The *K Bar* (709/944-3876) also in Bruno Plaza, has a dancefloor and tends to attract a younger crowd, while the *Cabin Bar* (T 709/944-7575), at the *Sizzlers* restaurant in Carol Lake Shopping Centre on Avalon Drive, is a great place for live music and raucous karaoke nights.

Travel details

Trains

Emeril Junction to: Sept-Îles (2 weekly; 7hr).

Buses

St John's to: Argentia (1 daily; 2hr); Channel-Port aux Basques (1 daily; 13hr 30min); Clarenville (1 daily; 2hr 30min); Corner Brook (1 daily; 10hr 15min); Deer Lake (1 daily; 9hr); Fortune (1 daily; 5hr); Grand Falls (1 daily; 6hr 30min); Trinity (1 daily; 3hr).
Corner Brook to: Burgeo (1 daily; 2hr); Deer Lake (3 daily; 20min); Rocky Harbour (1 daily; 1hr 30min); Woody Point (1 daily; 1hr 30min).

Ferries

North Sydney, Nova Scotia to: Channel-Port aux Basques (2–4 daily; 5-6hr, 6-8hr at night).
North Sydney, Nova Scotia to: Argentia (late June to early Sept 3 weekly, mid-June & late Sept 1 weekly; 14–15hr).
Cartwright to: Nain (1 weekly; 84hr).
St Barbe to: Blanc-Sablon (mid-April to mid-Jan 1–3 daily; 1hr 30min).
Fortune to: St-Pierre (May & June, Sept & Oct Fri & Sat only; July & Aug 1 daily; 1hr 30min).

7

The Prairie Provinces

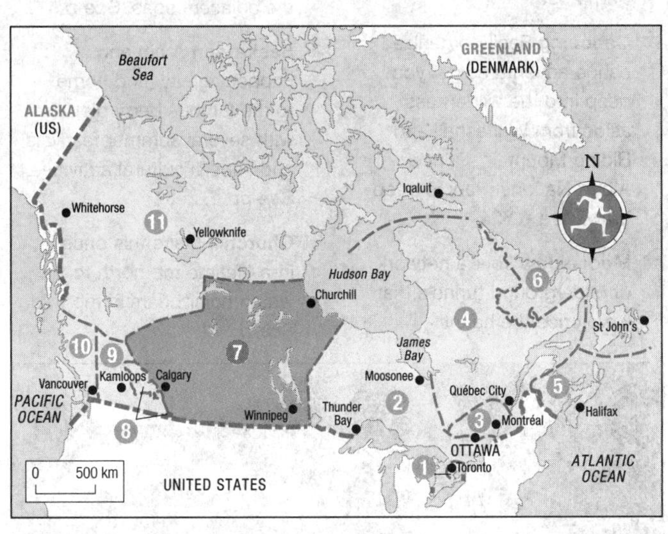

CHAPTER 7

Highlights

* **Winnipeg** A likeable and cultured city with a fine array of museums and restaurants. See pp.507–520

* **Rodeos** Central Canada is cowboy country, where devotion to beef takes on religious proportions and rodeos form the high points of social calendars; the Calgary Stampede is the best known. See p.555

* **Canoeing** Easily-organized canoe adventures get you deep into the wilderness; aside from Whiteshell and Riding Mountain, Prince Albert National Park is a top draw. See p.524

* **Moose Jaw** Tour a network of underground tunnels that were once the haunt of Chicago gangsters. See p.539

* **Grasslands National Park** Strike out off the beaten track to this beautiful – and under-visited – expanse of prairie landscape. See p.541

* **Little Manitou Lake** Experience near-weightlessness while floating in the salty lake waters, or at the adjacent spas. See p.571

* **Saskatoon** A hip and happening city (and home to the famous berry pie), with several summer festivals and superb cultural activities. See pp.572–577

* **Churchill** Make this once-in-a-lifetime trip north to watch polar bears in the wild. See p.597

▲ Canoeing in Prince Albert National Park, Saskatchewan

7

The Prairie Provinces

Spreading over the provinces of **Manitoba**, **Saskatchewan** and **Alberta** the vast lands between the Ontario border in the east and the Rocky Mountains in the west are usually lumped together in the common imagination as "**the prairies**". This is certainly not one of Canada's glamour regions, with the main cities caricatured as dull and the scenery as monotonous. In truth, this image is grossly unfair. Flat treeless plains – where isolated farms guard thousands of acres of swaying wheat or giant cattle herds – typify only the southernmost part of the region, and even then they're broken up by the occasional river valley and range of low-lying hills. The plains are divided into two broad geographical areas: semi-arid short **grasslands** on the US border, and a crescent-shaped **wheat-growing belt** to the north. This belt borders the low hills, mixed farms and sporadic forests of the **aspen parkland**, a transitional zone between the plains and the **boreal forest**, whose trees, rocky outcrops, rivers and myriad lakes cover well over half the entire region, stretching north to the Northwest Territories and the treeless **tundra** beside Hudson Bay.

The region's eastern gateway is **Winnipeg**, which demands a visit for its museums, restaurants and nightlife and can work as a base for exploring the varied lakes and plains of **Southeastern Manitoba**.

West of Winnipeg the **Trans-Canada Hwy** (Hwy 1) passes several **provincial parks** on its way over the Saskatchewan border to sprawling and easygoing **Regina**. A short hop beyond, the rejuvenating town of **Moose Jaw** lies north of the attractive coulees and buttes of **Grasslands National Park**. Then, at the Alberta border, **Cypress Hills Interprovincial Park** is another highlight as it includes the restored Mountie outpost of **Fort Walsh**. The first big town in Alberta is **Medicine Hat**, where **Hwy 3** begins, offering the most direct route to Vancouver. Continuing on Hwy 1, the ranching belt gives way to the intriguing and arid **Badlands** – once home to dinosaurs, which left abundant traces. The region is just about within the catchment area of **Calgary**, the oil town and self-styled cowboy city famous for the **Calgary Stampede**, as well as for being the main gateway for the Canadian Rocky Mountains.

The alternative route west from Winnipeg is the more interesting **Yellowhead Route** (Hwy 16), which passes through more attractive prairie towns before arriving at **Saskatoon**, Saskatchewan's largest city, with its attractive riverside setting, good restaurants and interesting sites devoted to Métis and Plains Indians. The Yellowhead route is also the natural gateway to two outstanding parks, **Riding Mountain National Park** in Manitoba and **Prince Albert National Park** in Saskatchewan; both parks are renowned for hiking and canoeing. In Alberta the Yellowhead beelines to **Edmonton**, Calgary's intense rival, and not just on the ice hockey rink. In many respects they're evenly matched, but **Edmonton** tends to be

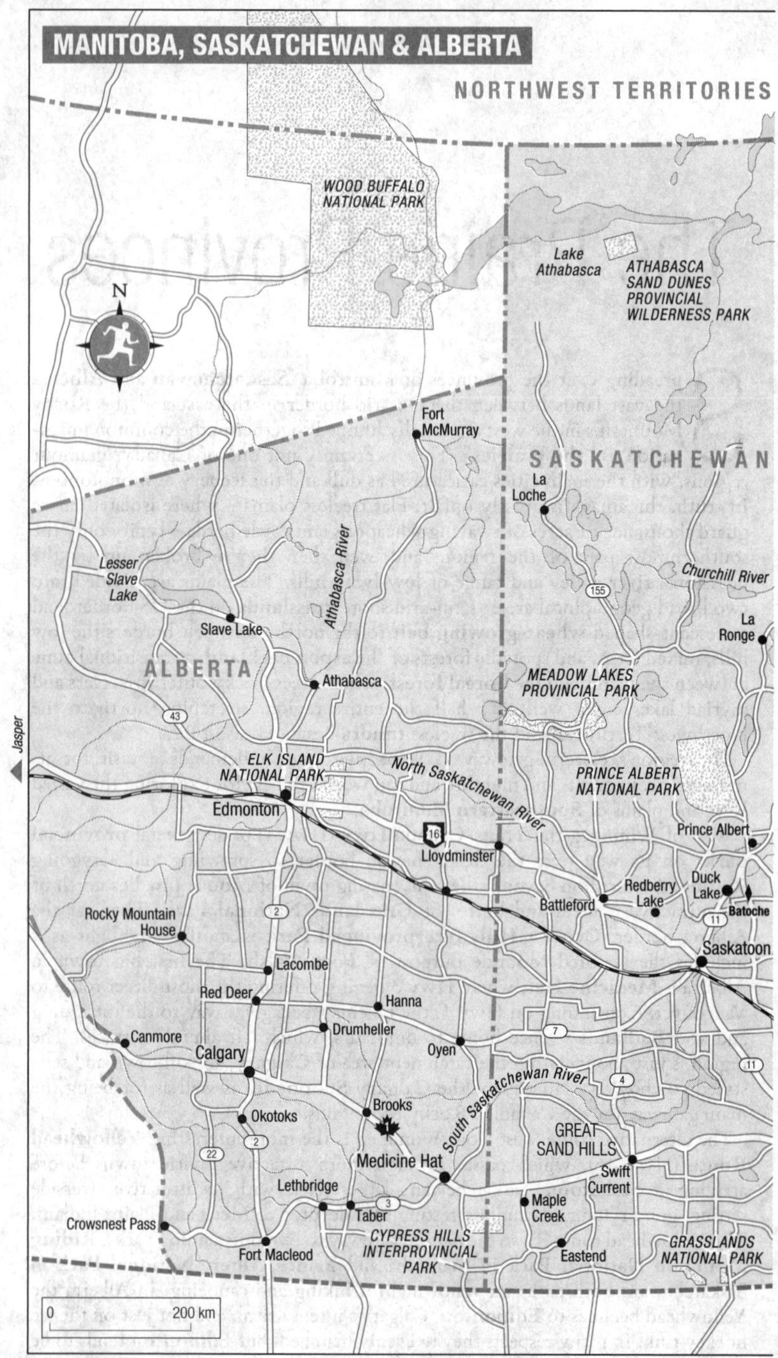
MANITOBA, SASKATCHEWAN & ALBERTA
NORTHWEST TERRITORIES
N
WOOD BUFFALO NATIONAL PARK
Lake Athabasca
ATHABASCA SAND DUNES PROVINCIAL WILDERNESS PARK
Fort McMurray
SASKATCHEWAN
La Loche
Churchill River
155
Lesser Slave Lake
Athabasca River
Slave Lake
La Ronge
ALBERTA
Athabasca
MEADOW LAKES PROVINCIAL PARK
43
Jasper
ELK ISLAND NATIONAL PARK
North Saskatchewan River
PRINCE ALBERT NATIONAL PARK
Edmonton
16
Prince Albert
Lloydminster
Duck Lake
Redberry Lake
Battleford
Batoche
11
Rocky Mountain House
2
Saskatoon
Lacombe
Red Deer
Hanna
Drumheller
7
Canmore
Oyen
Calgary
11
South Saskatchewan River
4
Brooks
Okotoks
1
GREAT SAND HILLS
2
22
Medicine Hat
Swift Current
Lethbridge
3
Maple Creek
Taber
Crowsnest Pass
CYPRESS HILLS INTERPROVINCIAL PARK
GRASSLANDS NATIONAL PARK
Fort Macleod
Eastend
0
200 km

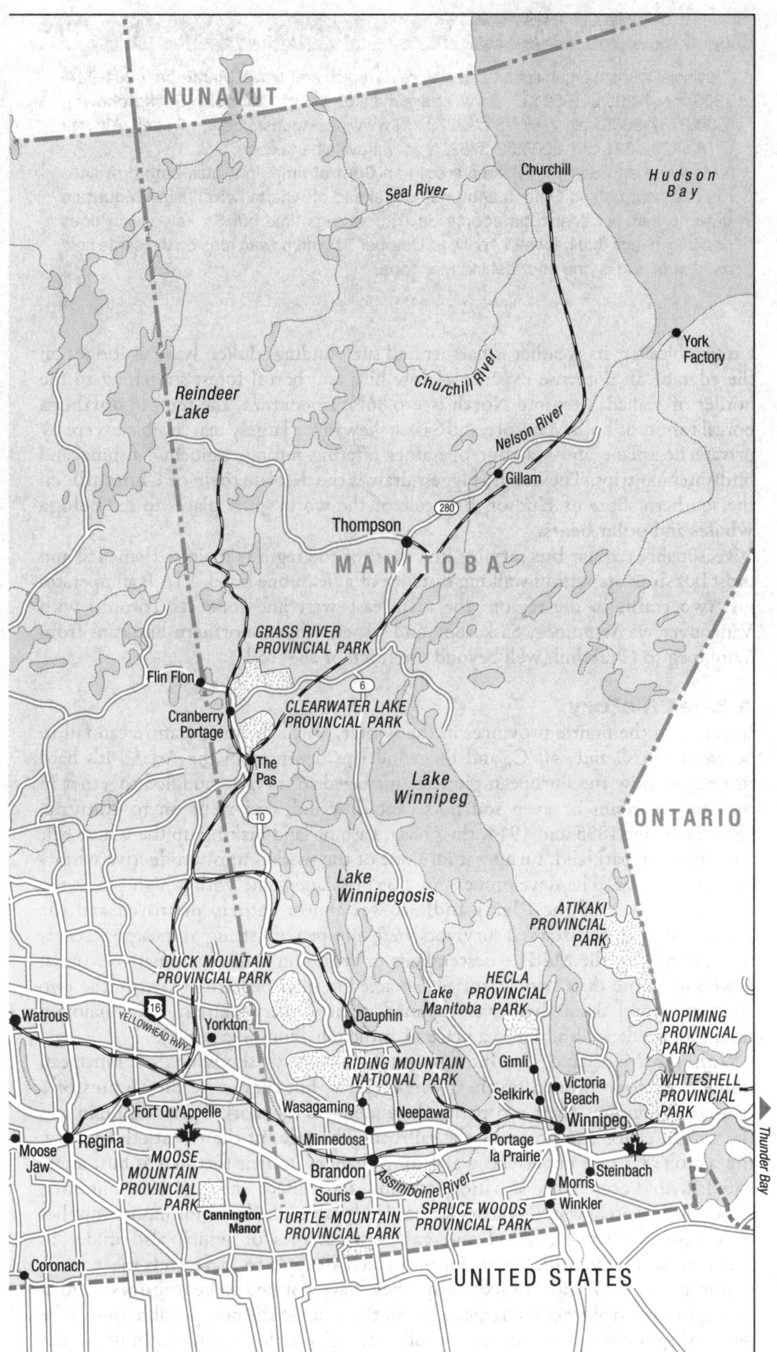
NUNAVUT
Hudson Bay
Churchill
Seal River
York Factory
Churchill River
Reindeer Lake
Nelson River
Gillam
280
Thompson
MANITOBA
GRASS RIVER PROVINCIAL PARK
Flin Flon
6
Cranberry Portage
CLEARWATER LAKE PROVINCIAL PARK
The Pas
Lake Winnipeg
10
ONTARIO
Lake Winnipegosis
ATIKAKI PROVINCIAL PARK
DUCK MOUNTAIN PROVINCIAL PARK
HECLA PROVINCIAL PARK
Lake Manitoba
Watrous
16
YELLOWHEAD HWY
Yorkton
Dauphin
NOPIMING PROVINCIAL PARK
RIDING MOUNTAIN NATIONAL PARK
Gimli
Victoria Beach
Selkirk
WHITESHELL PROVINCIAL PARK
Fort Qu'Appelle
Wasagaming
Neepawa
Winnipeg
Thunder Bay
1
Moose Jaw
Regina
Minnedosa
Portage la Prairie
MOOSE MOUNTAIN PROVINCIAL PARK
Brandon
Assiniboine River
Steinbach
Morris
Souris
Winkler
Cannington Manor
TURTLE MOUNTAIN PROVINCIAL PARK
SPRUCE WOODS PROVINCIAL PARK
Coronach
UNITED STATES

Information and time zones

Provincial tourism organisations for the prairie region are: **Travel Manitoba** ⓣ204-927-7800 or 1-800/665-0040, ⓦwww.travelmanitoba.com; **Tourism Saskatchewan** ⓣ306/787-9600 or 1-877/237-2273, ⓦwww.sasktourism.com; **Travel Alberta** ⓣ780/427-4321 or 1-800/252-3782, ⓦwww.travelalberta.com.

Manitoba and Saskatchewan are both on **Central time**. In winter, both provinces run one hour behind Ontario and one hour ahead of Alberta, which is on **Mountain time**. In summer, Manitoba adopts daylight savings time but Saskatchewan does not: this means that between April and October Saskatchewan runs on the same time as Alberta and is one hour behind Manitoba.

a touch bleaker; its weather is harsher and surroundings duller, lying as it does on the edge of an immense expanse of low hills and boreal forest stretching to the border of Canada's remote **North** (see p.864). In contrast, the remote **northern** boreal forests of both Manitoba and Saskatchewan are largely inaccessible except by private floatplane and via tour operators offering rafting, canoeing, fishing and birdwatching trips. The north's biggest draw is the desolate town of **Churchill**, on the southern shore of Hudson Bay, one of the world's best places to see **beluga whales** and **polar bears**.

Reasonably regular **bus** services link most of the region's main settlements, and most bus stops are within walking distance of at least one hotel. VIA Rail operates just two **trains** in the region: the main east–west line connects Toronto with Vancouver via Winnipeg, Saskatoon and Jasper, while a northern line runs from Winnipeg to Churchill, well beyond the reach of the road.

A brief history

If you're in the prairie provinces in the winter, when the temperature can fall to between -30°C and -40°C, and the wind rips down from the Arctic, it's hard to imagine how the European pioneers managed to survive, huddled together in remote log cabins or even sod huts. Yet they did, and went on to cultivate, between about 1895 and 1914, the great swath of land making up the wheat belt and the aspen parkland, turning it into one of the world's most productive wheat-producing areas. The development of this farmland came with a high price: the nomadic culture of the **Plains Indians** was almost entirely destroyed and the disease-ravaged, half-starved survivors were dumped in a string of meagre reservations. Similarly, the **Métis** – descendants of white fur traders and native women – who for more than two centuries had acted as intermediaries between the two cultures, found themselves overwhelmed, their desperate attempts to maintain their independence leading to a brace of futile rebellions (see p.578).

With the Métis and the Indians out of the way, thousands of European immigrants concentrated on their wheat yields, but they were the victims of a one-crop economy, their prosperity dependent on the market price of grain and the freight charges imposed by the railroad. Throughout the twentieth century, the region's farmers experienced alarming changes in their fortunes as bust alternated with boom; this situation continues to affect the prairie economies, although Saskatchewan in particular has lately diversified, exploiting its supplies of potash (fertilizer) and oil and gas, vast reserves of which also underpin Alberta's economy. Still, prairie farmers often struggle to make ends meet when wheat prices fall, and consequently they have formed **wheat pools**, which attempt to control freight charges and sell the grain at the best possible time. The political spin-off was the evolution of a strong socialist tradition, built on the

Provincial parks

Manitoba and, to a lesser extent, Saskatchewan are distinguished principally by their **parks**: thousands of acres of wilderness, lakes, rivers and forests boasting wonderful scenery, great hikes and hundreds of kilometres of canoe routes.

Entry to **Manitoba's** provincial parks (Ⓦwww.gov.mb.ca/conservation/parks) is free until 2011 when a small charge will be levied for cars; entry by foot or bike will remain free. Park campsites ($8.40–18.90) can be reserved from April to September by calling the Parks Reservation Service (Ⓣ204/948-3333 or 1-888/482-2267 Ⓦwww.prsltl.gov.mb.ca; $7.60/reservation).

Entry to **Saskatchewan's** provincial parks is $7 per day, $17 for three days, $25 weekly and $50 annually. Information is on Ⓣ306/953-3751 or 1-800/205-7070 or Ⓦwww.saskparks.net. Between mid-May and August you can reserve a campsite ($13–26) online in advance at most of the parks for a $10 fee; check the relevant section of the guide, but generally around half the campsites are on a first-come, first-served basis. A good walking guide is *Saskatchewan Trails*, by Robin and Arlene Karpan, which outlines over a hundred hikes in the province.

Entry to Alberta's provincial parks is free, but camping costs $5–22. At peak times the most popular campsites are largely reservation-only ($10/reservation); these can be made at Ⓦwww.albertaparks.ca for some campsites, while others need to be called direct – there's no centralized system but individual park numbers are available via Ⓣ780/427-9383 or 1-866/427-3582.

farmers' mistrust of the market. For many years Saskatchewan was a stronghold of the **Cooperative Commonwealth Federation (CCF)**, the forerunner of the New Democratic Party; in 1944 the CCF formed the country's first leftist provincial government, pushing through bills to set up provincially-run medical and social security schemes, which the rest of Canada eventually adopted.

Winnipeg

With 715,000 inhabitants, **WINNIPEG** accounts for half of Manitoba's population, and lies at Canada's centre, sandwiched between the US border to the south and the infertile Canadian Shield to the north and east. The city has been the gateway to the prairies since 1873, and became the transit point for much of the country's transcontinental traffic when the railroad arrived twelve years later. From the very beginning, Winnipeg was described as the city where "the West began", and its population, drawn from almost every European country, was attracted by the promise of the fertile soils to the west. But as early as the 1880s the city had developed a clear pattern of residential segregation, with leafy prosperous suburbs to the south along the **Assiniboine River**, and "Shanty Town" to the north. This division has proved hard to erase, and today the dispossessed still gather around the cheap flophouses just north of downtown; it's more a sad area than a dangerous one, but its reputation has hampered attempts to reinvigorate it: refurbished warehouses, new apartment blocks downtown and walkways along the Red and Assiniboine rivers haven't lured people out of the suburbs.

Still, Winnipeg makes for an enjoyable stopover, with all the main attractions within easy walking distance of each other: The **Manitoba Museum** has excellent displays on the history of the province and its various geographic areas; the happening **Exchange District** features good examples of Canada's early twentieth-century architecture; the Winnipeg **Art Gallery** has the world's largest Inuit art collection;

Winnipeg festivals

Winnipeg has an ambitious summer programme of open-air concerts, notably the nine-day **Jazz Winnipeg Festival** in late June (@www.jazzwinnipeg.com) and the **Winnipeg Folk Festival** (@www.winnipegfolkfestival.ca), a three-day extravaganza featuring over a hundred concerts, held in early July at Birds Hill Provincial Park, 25km northeast of the city. Apart from the music festivals, the biggest festival in Manitoba is **Folklorama** (@www.folklorama.ca), held during the first two weeks in August to celebrate Winnipeg's multiethnic population. The festival has over forty pavilions spread across town, each devoted to a particular country or region. The **Winnipeg Fringe Festival** (@www.winnipegfringe.com) is a ten-day event of theatrical productions, held in mid-July in the Exchange District. St Boniface's French-Canadian heritage is honoured annually in the **Festival du Voyageur** (@www.festivalvoyageur.mb.ca), ten days of February fun, whose events lead up to a torchlit procession and the Governor's Ball, where everyone dresses in period costume.

and, just across the Red River, the suburb of **St Boniface** has a delightful museum situated in the house and chapel of the Grey Nuns, who canoed here from Montréal in 1844. Winnipeg is also noted for the excellence and diversity of its restaurants and its flourishing performing-arts scene.

The city makes a useful base for exploring the region's immediate attractions (see pp.520–526), the most popular of which – chiefly **Lower Fort Garry** – are on the banks of the Red River as it twists its way to **Lake Winnipeg**, 60km north. On the lake itself, **Grand Beach Park** has the province's finest stretches of sandy beach, just two hours' drive from the city centre.

A brief history of Winnipeg

Named after the **Cree** word for murky water ("*win-nipuy*"), Winnipeg owes much of its history to the Red and Assiniboine rivers, which meet just south of the city centre at the confluence called **The Forks**. Fort Rouge was founded nearby in 1738 by the first European to reach the area, Pierre Gaultier; the settlement became part of a chain of fur-trading posts Gaultier built to extend French influence westwards and prospered from good connections north to Lake Winnipeg and Hudson Bay, and west across the plains along the Assiniboine.

After the defeat of New France in 1763, local trading activity was absorbed by the Montréal-based **North West Company** (NWC), which came to dominate the fur trade at the expense of its rival, the Hudson's Bay Company (HBC) – until Thomas Douglas, the **Earl of Selkirk**, bought a controlling interest in the HBC in 1809 and improved the business. Douglas resettled many of his own impoverished Scottish crofters around The Forks, buying from his own company a huge tract of farmland, which he named the Red River Colony, or Assiniboia. In 1821 the rival companies amalgamated under the "Hudson's Bay Company". For the next thirty years, the colony sustained an economic structure that suited both the farmers and the Métis hunters, and trade routes were established along the Red River to Minnesota, south of the border. But in the 1860s this collapsed with the decline of buffalo herds, and the Métis faced extreme hardship while the Hudson's Bay Company lost effective territorial control.

At this time, politicians in eastern Canada agreed the **federal union** of 1867, opening the way for the transfer of the Red River from British to Canadian control. The Métis majority – roughly six thousand compared to some one thousand – were fearful of the consequences and their resistance took shape round **Louis Riel** (see p.578), under whose dexterous leadership they captured the HBC's Upper Fort Garry and created a provisional government without challenging the crown's sovereignty. A delegation went to Ottawa to negotiate terms of admission into the Dominion, but their efforts were handicapped when the Métis **executed** an English settler from Ontario, Thomas Scott. The subsequent furore pushed prime minister John A. Macdonald into dispatching a military force to restore "law and order"; still, the Manitoba Act of 1870, which brought the Red River into the Dominion, acceded to many Métis demands and guaranteed the preservation of the French culture and language in the new province – although in practice little was done.

The eclipse of the Métis and the security of Winnipeg – as it became in 1870 – were both assured when the **Canadian Pacific Railway** routed its transcontinental line through The Forks in 1885. With the town handling the expanding grain trade and local industries supplying the vast rural hinterland, its population was swelled by thousands of **immigrants**, particularly from the Ukraine, Germany and Poland. By World War I, Winnipeg had become the third-largest city in Canada and the largest grain-producing centre in North America. More recently, the development of other prairie cities, such as Regina and Saskatoon, has undermined something of Winnipeg's pre-eminence, but it remains the transport hub of central Canada.

Arrival and information

Winnipeg **airport** (ⓦwww.waa.ca) is 7km west of the city centre. There's a tourist **information** desk (daily 8am–9.45pm) inside the airport concourse and a nearby complimentary hotel-booking phone. From outside the terminal building, Winnipeg Transit bus #15 (daily every 30min 5.51am–12.49am; $2.30) runs downtown, dropping passengers at or near most large hotels; taxis charge around $20. Greyhound and other long-distance **buses** operate from the airport, but drop passengers off at a heated shelter at 299 Fort St at the western entrance of Winnipeg Square, from which Greyhound shuttle buses also take passengers to the airport (daily: 8am, 11.15am & 5pm). The **train station** is on Main Street, just south of Portage Avenue.

Tours around Winnipeg

The sightseeing **boat trips** of Paddle Wheel Cruises (May–Oct daily 1pm; 2hr; ⓣ204/942-4500, ⓦwww.paddlewheelcruises.com; $17.75) leave from the dock at the end of Alexander Avenue on the banks of the Red River, as do their various evening dinner and dance cruises. Their **Historic Fort Cruise** (May–Aug Wed–Fri 9am–4.30pm; $26.75) takes you to Lower Fort Garry (see p.523) and back; one boat is a replica paddlewheel vessel. Leaving every fifteen minutes from a quay closer to the market the **water taxis** of Splash Dash (mid-May to mid-Oct daily 10am–sunset; 30min; ⓣ204/783-6633, ⓦwww.splashdash.ca; $10) provide shorter tours and are also handy for getting about ($3 one-way) to different spots along the river. The same company will rent you a canoe (daily 11am–9pm; $18/hr) to do the work yourself.

Walking tours are also popular. These include hour-long historical tours of the Forks (July to early Sept Thurs–Sun 2pm) and its archaeology (July to early Sept Thurs–Sun 1pm); tickets for both are sold at the Explore Manitoba Centre. Equally interesting are ninety minute tours of the Exchange District departing from the Old Market Square between June and early September. Tours at 10am explore the eastern half of the district, while the 2pm tour takes in the western half (each $6) and the daily tour at noon (Mon–Fri; $5) has a different route each day, including Banker's Row and the theatre district. Call ⓣ204/942-6716 or visit ⓦwww.exchangedistrict.org for the latest schedules.

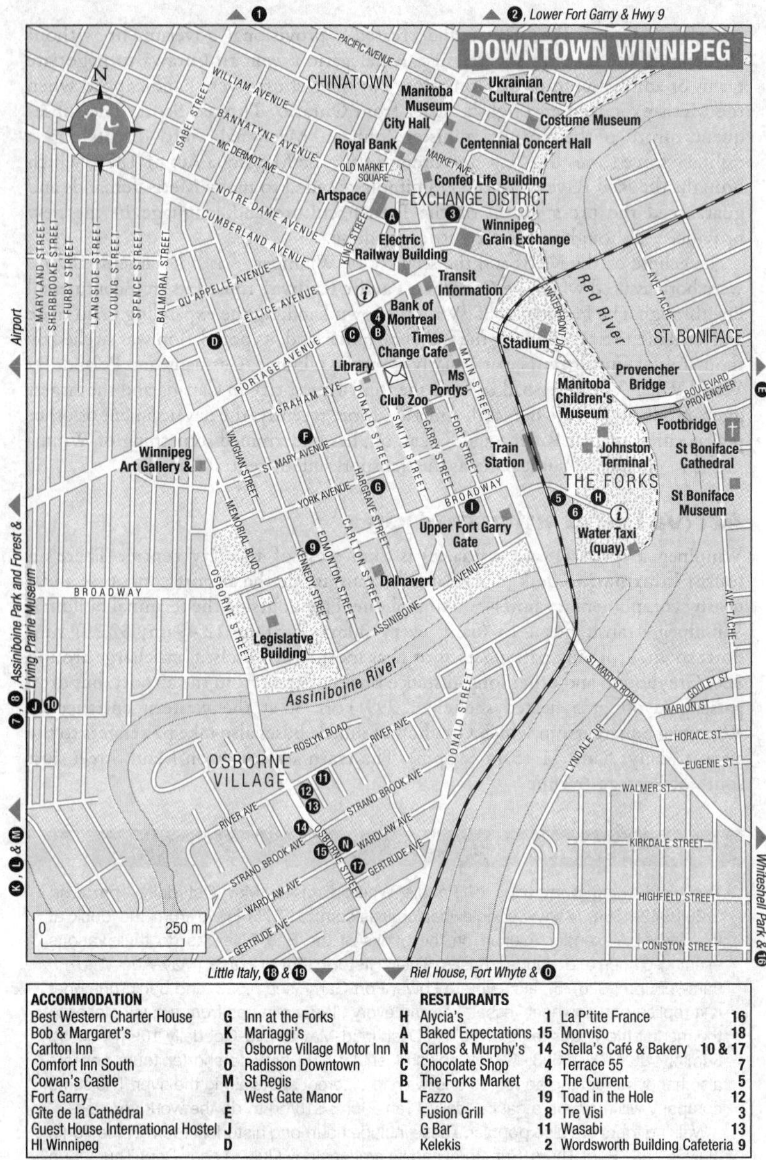

Winnipeg's tourist office, 259 Portage Ave (Mon–Fri 8.30am–4.30pm; ⓣ204/943-1970 or 1-800/665-0204, ⓦwww.destinationwinnipeg.ca), has a comprehensive range of leaflets and free maps for the city and province, as does the **Explore Manitoba Centre**, 25 Forks Market Rd (daily 10am–6pm; ⓣ204/945-3777 or 1-800/665-0040, ⓦwww.travelmanitoba.com), in The Forks, which is even stronger on provincial information.

City transport

You can stroll across the downtown core in twenty minutes or hop on the free **Downtown Spirit Bus** that circles between The Forks, Portage Avenue and Memorial Boulevard and is operated by **Winnipeg Transit** (Ⓣ204/986-5700, Ⓦwww.winnipegtransit.com), who also run buses to the suburbs. Tickets cost $2.30 per journey; ask the driver for a transfer for trips involving more than one bus, see p.520. For details of taxis and bike rental, see p.520. Tours (see p.509) are also a method of moving around the city.

Accommodation

Most of Winnipeg's **hotels** are within walking distance of the bus and train stations and are rarely full. Many modern hotels in standard-issue skyscrapers concentrate on business clientele and offer weekend discounts and sizeable reductions if you stay more than three nights. The major approach roads are dotted with **motels**, particularly the Pembina Hwy, running south from the city centre as Donald Street and Route 42, and along Portage Avenue, which runs west forming part of the Trans-Canada Hwy. Tourism Winnipeg has details of some thirty **B&Bs**, as does the Bed and Breakfast of Manitoba (Ⓦwww.bedandbreakfast.mb.ca).

Hotels and motels

Best Western Charter House 330 York Ave Ⓣ204/942-0101 or 1-800/782-0175, Ⓦwww.bwcharterhouse.com. A good location in the heart of downtown, one block from the Convention Centre; reasonable rates make up for the absence of character. ❸

Carlton Inn 220 Carlton St Ⓣ204/942-0881 or 1-877/717-2885, Ⓦwww.carltoninn.mb.ca. One of the more agreeable budget hotels, centrally located opposite the city's Convention Centre, with motel-style rooms, restaurant and small pool. ❸

Comfort Inn South 3109 Pembina Hwy Ⓣ204/269-7390, Ⓦwww.choicehotels.ca. One of several no-frills motels around the junction of the Trans-Canada and Pembina hwys, 11km south of downtown. It has an on-site restaurant and offers free local calls. ❺

Fort Garry 222 Broadway Ⓣ204/942-8251 or 1-800/665-8088, Ⓦwww.fortgarryhotel.com. Built in Neo-Gothic style between 1911 and 1914 and near the train station, this lavishly refurbished hotel has an elegant, balconied foyer leading to 250 rooms. Rates include a breakfast buffet. ❻

Inn at the Forks 75 Forks Market Rd Ⓣ204/942-6555 or 1-877/377-4100, Ⓦwww.innforks.com. Self-consciously hip boutique hotel in a tremendous central location at the confluence of the Assiniboine and Red rivers. Rooms have local art and internet access; there's also a slick spa and innovative restaurant. ❼

Mariaggi's Theme Suite Hotel 231 McDermot Ave Ⓣ204/947-9447 or 1-866/947-9190, Ⓦwww.mariaggis.com. You'll pay through the nose, but it's all to enjoy sumptuous Hawaiian, Mexican, Moroccan or African-themed suites or a tropical penthouse. ❼

Osborne Village Motor Inn 160 Osborne St Ⓣ204/452-9824, Ⓦwww.osbornevillage.com. Basic but decent choice in the heart of lively Osborne Village. Bands often play downstairs and the rooms (none are nonsmoking) are not sound-proofed. ❶

Radisson Hotel Winnipeg Downtown 288 Portage Ave Ⓣ204/956-0410 or 1-800/395-7046, Ⓦwww.radisson.com/winnipegca. One of the city's largest and smartest hotels, with fine views from the top floors, as well as a gym, saunas, whirlpool and swimming pool. Offers big discounts at weekends. ❺

St Regis 285 Smith St Ⓣ204/942-0171 or 1-800/663-7344, Ⓦwww.stregishotel.net. Early twentieth-century downtown hotel, with tastefully furnished rooms, free wi-fi, plus a dining room and coffee shop. The honeymoon suites have hot tubs. Under-18s stay free. ❸

B&Bs

Bob & Margaret's 950 Palmerston Ave Ⓣ204/774-0767, Ⓔbm950@mts.net. A fifteen-minute ride on bus #10 from downtown, this riverside B&B has one bedroom suite, with TV room, private bathroom and wi-fi. Bikes and canoes can be rented. ❹

Cowan's Castle 39 Eastgate Ⓣ204/786-4848, Ⓦwww.cowanscastle.tripod.com. A 1907 four-bed heritage home on the Assiniboine River, twenty minutes' walk to downtown. Serves delicious home-cooked breakfasts. ❷

Gîte de la Cathédrale 581 rue Langevin, St Boniface Ⓣ204/233-7792. Run by French

Manitobans, this B&B in the heart of St Boniface offers Québécois breakfasts of pancakes and maple syrup, omelettes and French toast. There are five flowery bedrooms with shared bathroom. ❷

West Gate Manor 71 West Gate ⓣ204/772-9788, ⓦwww.westgatemanor.ca. Six pleasant rooms with Victorian period furnishings in Armstrong Point, within walking distance of downtown. ❸

Hostels

Guest House International Hostel 168 Maryland St ⓣ204/772-1272 or 1-800/743-4423, ⓦwww.backpackerswinnipeg.com. Sociable hostel in a Victorian house with dorms ($25), private rooms (doubles $60) and living room walls decorated with aboriginal art. Facilities include a laundry, kitchen, game room, internet access and free wi-fi. To get there take bus #29 from Broadway to Sherbrook.

HI Winnipeg 330 Kennedy St ⓣ204/772-3022, ⓦwww.hihostels.ca. Old central motel on the free Downtown Spirit Bus route that's been converted into a hostel, but with many of the old facilities preserved, including a pub; there's also a kitchen and free wi-fi. Dorms $29 ($33 nonmembers), doubles $69 ($77 nonmembers).

Campsites

Conestoga Campground 1341 St Anne's Rd ⓣ204/257-7363. Located 13km southeast of town beside the Trans-Canada City ByPass (Hwy 100); most sites ($12–20) have electricity and water. June–Oct.

Traveller's RV Resort 870 Murdock Rd ⓣ204/256-2186 or 1-888/615-1995. Just off the Trans-Canada Hwy and some 14km southeast of the centre. A decent range of sites ($17.50–31) and facilities include mini-golf, a swimming pool and an amusement park next door. May–Sept.

Welcomestop 588 Trans-Canada Hwy, St François Xavier ⓣ204/864-2201 or 1-888/360-7999 ⓦwww.welcomestopcampground.com. In a small town on the Assiniboine River, 15km west of Winnipeg, this campground has a variety of sites ($16–31), most with water and electricity, as well as toilets, showers, a bbq area and free wi-fi. May–Sept.

The City

The traditional centre of Winnipeg is the intersection of **Portage Avenue** and **Main Street**. While you're here, have a look at the grand Neoclassical **Bank of Montréal** on the southeast side of the intersection, its fussily carved capitals contrast starkly with the clean lines of neighbouring skyscrapers. The intersection is also known as Canada's **windiest**.

North of here are the shops and markets of the **Exchange District** (where you'll also find the Manitoba Museum) and **Chinatown**. To the south of the intersection you'll find **The Forks**, a riverside development of shops, cafés and attractions that's usually packed with tourists and locals alike in the summer. Alternatively, you could head into **downtown** proper by walking west along Portage Avenue.

The Exchange District

The Exchange District is a rough rectangle of well-preserved old warehouses, commodity exchanges and commercial buildings. From the late 1970s on, many were converted into art galleries, boutiques, antique shops and restaurants creating a new, faintly bohemian area centred on **Old Market Square** with its weekend produce market, flea markets and buskers. This part of town was built during Winnipeg's boom, a period that peaked in 1882, but lasted only until World War I. The standard architectural design was simple and symmetrical, with plain brick walls topped off by decorative stone cornices. Yet one or two companies financed extravagant variations – notably the **Electric Railway Chambers Building** at 213 Notre Dame Ave, an imaginative blend of Italian Renaissance and early twentieth-century motifs, its terracotta facade lined with six thousand electric lights. Possibly the most gracious building in the district is the former **Winnipeg Grain Exchange** on Lombard Avenue. Built between 1906 and 1908, it was the largest of its type in Canada and grain offices still occupy some floors. Other imposing buildings are the ten-storey **Confederation Life Building**, at 457 Main St, which has a curved facade of white terracotta, and the massive **Royal Bank Building** at Main Street and William Avenue.

▲ The M.S. Paddlewheel Queen cruising down Winnipeg's Red River

Artspace, in a warehouse building at the corner of Arthur Street and Bannatyne Avenue, is a large artist-run centre with a cinema, several galleries and is a great place to see contemporary Canadian art, photography and wacky multimedia installations.

The Manitoba Museum

In the heart of the Exchange District, at 190 Rupert Ave, the **Manitoba Museum** (mid-May to early Sept daily 10am–5pm; rest of year Tues–Fri 10am–4pm, Sat & Sun 11am–5pm; planetarium and science gallery $18.50; Ⓦ www.manitobamuseum.ca; $8), provides an excellent introduction to the province's geography, history and peoples.

Highlights of the **natural history** section include an imposing polar bear diorama, a well-illustrated explanation of the Northern Lights and an evocative Boreal Forest gallery, complete with waterfall, moose family and a diorama of Cree food-gathering and rock-painting. There's also a disconcerting section devoted to Manitoba's more malicious insects – starring the "no-see-um", a deer fly that burrows into caribou nostrils. The **Grasslands Gallery** has a small display of Assiniboine Indian artefacts, along with a reconstructed teepee, a pioneer log cabin and a sod house of the sort that pioneers were forced to build in many parts of the treeless southern plains. Another replica is of the odd-looking Red River cart, whose massive wheels could tackle the prairie mud and mire.

The museum's most popular exhibit, moored in a massive display area that reproduces a seventeenth-century River Thames dockside, is an impressive full-scale replica of the **Nonsuch**, the ship whose fur-collecting voyage to Hudson Bay in 1668 led to the creation of the Hudson's Bay Company. The **Hudson's Bay Company Gallery** comprises more than ten thousand artefacts and documents which record its links with Manitoba and impact on Canada. A reconstructed trading post showcases goods that were exchanged for furs – everything from beads and guns to canned foods. There's also the last surviving York boat used for nineteenth-century river and lake travel, relics from the ill-fated Franklin Expedition's search for the Northwest Passage and beautiful native artworks and crafts, including carved ivory and immaculate beadwork. A reconstruction of the Company boardroom in London includes a huge ram's head used – unbelievably – as a snuff holder and passed around at dinner parties. The last section of the museum is the **Urban Gallery**, which recreates 1920s Winnipeg.

The museum also holds the **Planetarium** (May to early Sept daily; schedule varies; call ⓣ204/956-2830 for hours $7) and the **Science Gallery** (same hours; $6.50), with sixty interactive exhibits; a **Full Experience Pack** for the museum, planetarium and science centre costs $18.50, and allows three-day all-inclusive admission.

The history of the railway in Canada

Even before Confederation in 1867 Sir John A. Macdonald, Canada's first prime minister, had understood the necessity of physically linking what would become the new nation's disparate provinces. Lines of east–west communication were essential to counteract the natural tug of the US to the south, and both the Maritime Provinces and BC only joined Confederation on the condition that **rail** links would be built to transport their goods throughout the land. Railway construction of this scale was a huge undertaking for such a young country and outside finance was the only answer.

From 1855 to 1875, line construction in eastern Ontario and Québec culminated in the **Intercolonial Railway**, which linked central Canada with the Maritimes. Yet progress of the transcontinental line to the Pacific was impeded by the Riel rebellion in 1869–70 and in 1871 the Parliamentary Opposition labelled the entire scheme "an act of insane recklessness". Two years later Macdonald's Conservative government fell after implication in scandals involving the use of party funds in railway contracts. Alexander Mackenzie's subsequent Liberal government proceeded so slowly with railway plans that BC openly spoke of secession if construction was not speeded up. The eventual completion of the **Canadian Pacific Railway** (**CPR**) in 1885 finally made Canada "more than a geographical expression", and by the early twentieth century another coast-to-coast line had been completed.

Passage across the hitherto virtually impenetrable Canadian Shield was now feasible and the full agricultural potential of the prairies to the west could be realized. Between 1896 and 1913 more than one million people arrived by train to settle in the prairies, and wheat production rose to more than two hundred million bushels a year, up from twenty million. Ontario benefitted as well – some of the first major mineral finds there came to light during the railway construction. The years following World War I were a period of economic consolidation and the union of various smaller lines into a government-controlled nationwide system: the **Canadian National Railways** (**CNR**).

The impact of the Depression on Canadian railways was particularly severe, leading to stringent economies and pooling of competing lines. World War II saw a rise in profits, but over the subsequent decades the story has been one of gradual decline, with freight increasingly travelling by road and air, and passenger services pruned almost to extinction on some lines. By 1992, passengers could no longer cross Canada on the CPR, and one of the world's great train rides was gone forever. Grain and minerals are still moved by train, however, and the privately owned CPR is now exclusively a freight line. **VIA Rail**, the passenger branch of CNR, operates virtually all of Canada's passenger services, including the Hudson Bay line in roadless northern Manitoba.

Chinatown and around

Just northwest of the Exchange District lies **Chinatown**, originally settled in the 1920s by immigrants brought in to help build the railway. The area has many good restaurants and groceries, as well as shops selling silk fabrics and exotic herbs and spices – but no real sights. Just east of Chinatown, at 184 Alexander Ave East, is the **Ukrainian Cultural and Educational Centre** (Mon–Sat 10am–4pm; $2; ⓣ204/942-0218, ⓦwww.oseredok.org), which occupies a 1930s office building. One in seven Manitobans still describe themselves as Ukrainian, though most of their ancestors arrived around 1900. These were largely peasants united by language and custom, but divided by religion and politics – Orthodox against Catholic, nationalist against socialist. By 1940, the factions managed to form a coalition committed to the country's institutions and the promotion of Ukrainian interests. The collection of folk art in the fifth-floor museum of the complex is an excellent introduction to these traditions, with delightful examples of embroidery, weaving, woodcarving and the exquisite designs of *pysanky*, Easter egg painting.

A two-minute walk down Pacific Avenue – east behind the Ukranian Centre towards the Red River – reveals a woe-begone district of small warehouses. One of these once housed a T-shirt factory and has been converted into a **Costume Museum** (Mon–Sat 10am–5pm, Sun noon–4pm; $5; ⓣ204/989-0072, ⓦwww.costumemuseum.com). A group of local ladies who enjoyed dressing up began the collection which has since expanded into some 35,000 garments and accessories, mostly from the 1930s. Selections are now gathered together in themed bi-monthly exhibits. The display area is rather small but there's also a library, resource centre and an offbeat shop with interesting local designs.

Union Station and The Forks

South of Portage Avenue along Main Street rises the ponderous dome of the Beaux Arts-style **Union Station**, designed by the architects of New York's Grand Central Station; it has an indoor market and the **Winnipeg Railway Museum** (June–Aug Fri–Sun noon–5pm; May & Sept–Nov Sat & Sun noon–4pm; $5 ⓦwww.wpgrailwaymuseum.com). Across the street in a small park is the stone gate that's the sole remnant of Upper Fort Garry, a Hudson's Bay Company fort from 1837 to 1870 and thereafter the residence of Manitoba's lieutenant governors until 1883, when the fort was dismantled. The pointed dormers and turrets behind it belong to *Hotel Fort Garry*, a château-like structure built for the Grand Trunk Railroad.

Behind the station is a chunk of land known as **The Forks**, which borders the curve of the Red River. This area was once the start of the main Métis cart track (the Portage Trail) that led west across the prairies to Hudson's Bay Company posts, and the beginning of the principal trail north to Lake Winnipeg, linking the riverside farm lots and Lower and Upper Fort Garry. In later years, it was one of Canada's largest rail yards, as the CNR freight cars and cabooses dotting the grounds attest. Subsequent redevelopment has since turned The Forks into Winnipeg's premier attraction, thanks in part to the **Explore Manitoba Centre** (see p.510), half tourist information point, half museum, with six reasonably interesting themed displays on the province.

Nearby, the 1889 rail maintenance shed houses the **Manitoba Children's Museum** (May–early Sept daily 9.30am–6pm, early Sept–May Sun–Thurs 9.30am–4pm, Fri & Sat 9.30am–6pm; $6.75 ⓦwww.childrensmuseum.com), a hands-on, state-of-the-art enterprise that appeals equally to adults. Exhibits include a vintage steam-engine with Pullman carriages, a fully equipped mail office and close by, bear, lynx and raccoon costumes are on hand for kids to don while they explore a huge model of an oak tree and its ecosystem. For older kids, the highlight is probably the TV studio where they can experiment with lights and cameras.

A couple of minutes' walk away, two old railway buildings, **The Forks Market** (July to early Sept Mon–Sat 9.30am–9pm, Sun 9.30am–6.30pm; early Sept to June Sat–Thurs 9.30am–6.30pm, Fri 9.30am–9pm) and the Johnston Terminal both house shops, food stalls, bars and restaurants. Paths from the two lead down to the Assiniboine River via an outdoor amphitheatre. Nearby is **The Wall Through Time**, a curving brick barricade covered with plaques and inscriptions recording the historic events of the area. The riverside path continues north up to the Exchange District, beyond the bold, white **Provencher Pedestrian Bridge** with its striking cables and precariously overhanging restaurant, whose loos were locally dubbed "the million-dollar-toilets" for their extraordinarily expensive plumbing.

Downtown

Underground passageways and glass-enclosed overhead walkways link various malls and large stores along **Portage Avenue**, the city's main **downtown** shopping street, providing welcome relief from summer heat and winter cold. The largest complex is the ugly **Portage Place** mall, on the north side of the avenue, which has over 160 shops and an IMAX cinema (Ⓣ204/956-IMAX, tickets 204/780-SEAT, Ⓦwww.imaxwinnipeg.com). Other modern buildings on Portage are far more architecturally attractive: including the Paris Building at no. 259, with its splendid tiered facade and delicate cornice, and the Boyd Building at no. 388, with cream and bronze terracotta decoration.

At the western end of downtown Portage Avenue lies the uncompromisingly modern **Winnipeg Art Gallery** (Tues–Sun 11am–5pm, Thurs till 9pm; $8; Ⓣ204/786-6641, Ⓦwww.wag.mb.ca), 300 Memorial Blvd, the home of the world's largest public collection of Inuit art. There's also a decent selection of Gothic and Renaissance paintings and a reasonable assortment of modern European art, including works by Joan Miró, Marc Chagall and Henry Moore. Little is on display at any one time and much of the available space is usually given over to temporary (and often dire) exhibitions of modern Canadian art. Nevertheless, several temporary galleries devoted to the Inuit shine and are frequently arranged to explore a particular theme – from the symbolic significance of different animals to the role of women sculptors in isolated communities. The gallery also has a rooftop restaurant, *Storm*.

Legislative Building, Osborne Village and Dalnavert

Five minutes' walk south of the Art Gallery along Memorial Boulevard is the **Manitoba Legislative Building** (July & Aug hourly tours 9am–6pm; rest of year Mon–Fri by appointment; free; Ⓣ204/945-5813, Ⓦwww.gov.mb.ca/legtour), surrounded by trim lawns and flower borders. The building, made of local Tyndall stone embedded with fossils, has a central pediment decorated with splendidly pompous sculptures representing the ideals of Canadian nationhood. A half-kneeling figure, symbolizing progress, beckons his lazy neighbour to come to the land of promise, while a muscular male, with a team of powerful horses, idealizes the pioneer spirit. High above, a central square tower rises to a copper-green dome topped by the **Golden Boy**, a four-metre-high gold-plated bronze figure that's supposed to embody the spirit of enterprise and eternal youth. Inside, the marble columns and balconies of the foyer house two magnificent life-size bronze buffalo sculptures. The mural over the entrance to the legislative chamber depicting World War I scenes is by English artist Frank Brangwyn.

Behind the Legislative Building and across the Assiniboine River lies Osborne Street and **Osborne Village**, the studenty and bohemian part of town, with its inexpensive restaurants and bars. Southwest off Osborne Street is Corydon Avenue, whose several blocks and side streets comprise **Little Italy**.

A couple of blocks east of the Legislative Building at 61 Carlton St is **Dalnavert** (Wed–Fri 10am–5pm, Sat 11am–6pm, Sun noon–4pm; guided tours every 30min; $5; Ⓦwww.mhs.mb.ca), once home to Hugh John Macdonald, the son of Canada's first prime minister and, briefly, premier of Manitoba. Built in 1895 in Queen Anne Revival style, the house has been painstakingly restored, its simple red-brick exterior engulfed by a fanciful wooden veranda and the interior all heavy, dark-stained woods. Macdonald's conservatism, reflected in the decor, was mellowed by a philanthropic disposition – he even reserved part of his basement for some of the city's destitute.

St Boniface

The suburb of **St Boniface** lies to the east of downtown over the Red River (take bus #10, #50 or #56 from Portage Ave). A centre of early French-Canadian and Métis settlement, it was founded by two French-Canadian Catholic priests in 1818 and today retains something of its distinctive character – a quarter of its population still speaks French as a first language. St Boniface's main historic sights line the river along **avenue Taché**.

The cathedral and around

Walking south from the Provencher Bridge, the massive white-stone facade on the left is all that remains of **St Boniface Cathedral**, a huge neo-Romanesque structure built in 1908 and largely destroyed by fire in 1968. Its replacement, just behind, was designed with an interior in the style of a giant tepee. The large silver-domed building immediately to the east is the **Collège Universitaire de Saint-Boniface**, formerly a Jesuit college and now the French-speaking campus of the University of Manitoba. Here you'll see a controversial statue of Louis Riel that portrays him naked and deformed. Its original location was in the Legislative Building's grounds, but it caused such a storm of protest it was moved here in 1994. In front of the cathedral is the cemetery containing **Riel's grave**, whose modest tombstone gives little indication of the furore surrounding his execution in Regina on November 16, 1885. Only after three weeks did the authorities feel safe enough to move the body, which was then sent secretly by rail to St Boniface. The casket lay overnight in Riel's family home in the suburb of St Vital (see p.518) before its transfer to the cathedral, where most of the Métis population attended the funeral mass. That same evening, across the river, Riel's enemies burnt his effigy on a street corner, a symptom of a bitter divide that lasted well into the twentieth century.

The **Musée de Saint-Boniface** (May–Sept Mon–Fri 9am–noon, Sat & Sun 10am–5pm; Oct to mid-May Mon–Fri 9am–noon, Sun noon–4pm; $2; guided tours available with reservations Ⓣ204/237-4500, Ⓦwww.msbm.mb.ca) is housed in an attractive whitewashed building across from the cathedral. The oldest building in Winnipeg and largest squared-oak log building in North America, it was built between 1846 and 1851 as a convent for the Grey Nuns, a missionary order whose four-woman advance party had arrived by canoe from Montréal in 1844. The building was subsequently used as a hospital, school and orphanage. Inside, a series of cosy rooms are devoted to the Red River Colony, notably an intriguing collection of Métis memorabilia that includes colourful sashes – the most distinctive feature of Métis dress. You can also see the battered wooden casket used to transport Riel's body from Regina to St Boniface. There's a lovely little chapel, whose papier-mâché Virgin was made from an old newspaper that one of the original Grey Nuns found outside Upper Fort Garry when she walked across the frozen river to buy food.

The Riel House and Fort Whyte

The **Riel House** (mid-May to Aug daily 10am–6pm; $4; ⓣ204/257-1783, ⓦwww.parkscanada.gc.ca/rielhouse), at 330 River Rd in the suburb of **ST VITAL**, 10km south of downtown (bus #54 from Portage Ave), is just about worth the trip. The main feature of the site is a tiny clapboard house built by the Riels in 1880–81 and stayed in their possession until 1968. Louis Riel never actually lived here, but this was where his body was brought after his execution in 1885, and the house has been restored to its appearance at that time, complete with black-bordered photographs and a few artefacts left by his wife, Marguerite. Other period furnishings and fittings give a good idea of the life of a prosperous Métis family in the 1880s. Costumed guides provide an enjoyable twenty-minute tour of the house and garden, the sole remnant of the once sizeable Riel landholdings.

Across the Red River from St Vital the **Fort Whyte Centre** (July–Aug Mon–Fri 9am–5pm, Sat & Sun 10am–5pm, Sept–June Mon–Fri 9am–8pm, Sat & Sun 10am–5pm; $6; ⓦwww.fortwhyte.org), at 1961 McCreary Rd, is an environmental education complex dealing with the diversity of the prairie ecosystem's flora and fauna. It's largely an outdoor experience, with a wildlife observation tower, herd of bison, deer enclosure and a maze of self-guided trails through woodlands and marsh, plus an interpretive centre.

Assiniboine Park and the Living Prairie Museum

Some 8km west of the city centre and south of Portage Avenue, a great chunk of land has been set aside as **Assiniboine Park** (bus #66 from Broadway at Smith St), whose wooded lawns, gardens, cycling paths, playing fields and zoo attract hundreds of visitors every summer weekend. The park's English gardens of daisies, marigolds, roses and begonias bloom beneath columns of spruce trees and blend into the excellent **Leo Mol Sculpture Garden**, which contain the works of the Ukrainian artist. Dozens of Mol's graceful sculptures – deer, bears, nude bathers and other whimsical figures – are featured here, reflecting in ponds and in a glass-walled **gallery** (June to late Sept Tues–Sun 10am–8pm; free). Mol's studio is also on view just behind the gallery. The park's best-known feature is a large, half-timbered building in mock-Tudor style, home to the **Pavilion Gallery Museum** (Tues–Sun 10am–5pm; free) with a permanent collection of works by three local artists: Ivan Eyre, Walter J. Phillips and Clarence Tillenius. By the pavilion, the similarly Tudoresque bandshell of the **Lyric Theatre** (ⓦwww.partnersinthepark.org) has free performances by the Royal Winnipeg Ballet and the Winnipeg Symphony Orchestra, and hosts jazz, folk and drama festivals. The park's **zoo** (Jan to mid-May daily 10am–4pm; mid-May to late June Mon–Fri 9am–4pm, Sat & Sun 9am–6pm; late June to early Sept daily 9am–6pm; early Sept to Dec 10am–4pm; $4.78; ⓣ204/982-0660, ⓦwww.zoosociety.com) has over 1300 animals, a giant tropical conservatory and a steamy Palm House. A statue of Winnie the Pooh on the zoo grounds reminds you the fictitious bear was named after a real bear called Winnipeg. Adjoining the park to the south, the 700-acre nature reserve of Assiniboine Forest (sunrise–sunset; free), the largest in Canada, is home to deer, ruffled grouse and waterfowl.

A kilometre west and three blocks north of Assiniboine Park, the **Living Prairie Museum** (May–June Sun 10am–5pm; July & Aug daily 10am–5pm; free; ⓦwww.winnipeg.ca/publicworks), at 2795 Ness Ave, is worth a brief visit, its thirty acres of land forming Manitoba's largest area of unploughed tall-grass prairie. A visitor centre provides a wealth of information on the indigenous plants, whose deep-root systems enable them to withstand both the extreme climate and prairie fires. There's a daily programme of half-hour guided walks, or you can pick up a brochure and stroll alone. Come prepared with insect repellent: the bugs that thrive among the grass and wild flowers are particularly vicious. To get there take bus #24 from Portage Avenue.

Eating and drinking

Winnipeg boasts dozens of good, inexpensive places **to eat** and the wide variety of ethnic restaurants are particularly impressive, ranging from deluxe French, Italian and regional food establishments, to Ukrainian and French-Canadian restaurants. Many of the most interesting options cluster in the Exchange District, Osborne Village and Little Italy.

Restaurants

Alycia's 559 Cathedral Ave ⓣ204/582-8789. Long-established Ukrainian restaurant, 4km north of the centre, which also serves as an informal social centre. The food – borscht and *holubchi* (stuffed cabbage rolls) – is cheap and filling food. Mains $6–8. Closed Sun.

Baked Expectations 161 Osborne St ⓣ204/452-5176. Delicious burgers and salads, but especially known for its cheesecakes. Mains $4–9.

Carlos & Murphy's 129 Osborne St ⓣ204/284-3510. Huge portions of Mexican food for $5–10; eat out on the pleasant patio or inside, adjacent to the raucous and dingy bar.

The Chocolate Shop 268 Portage Ave ⓣ204/942-4855. Diner-style establishment that's Winnipeg's oldest restaurant (1918) and testing ground for a local culinary school. It has good bison burgers and great desserts. Mains $16–25.

The Current At the *Inn at the Forks* (see p.511) ⓣ204/944-2445 Known for its good regional food, created using local ingredients (dinner mains $18–38); sadly, the fantastic wild mushroom perogies ($11) only feature on the lunch menu.

Fazzo 905 Corydon Ave ⓣ204/478-1872, ⓦwww.fazzo.ca. Probably the pick of Corydon's Italians; a sleek contemporary place with minimalist decor, warm colours and lively chatter. Signature dishes ($13–24) include warm mushroom salad and *Ossobuco*, along with unusual choices like Cornish game hen. Live jazz on summer Sun.

The Forks Market The Forks. A converted railway shed incorporating an inexpensive food court where booths sell a variety of dishes from Caribbean to Greek to Chilean; *Yudyta's* does authentic Ukrainian food.

Fusion Grill 550 Academy Rd ⓣ204/489-6963, ⓦwww.fusiongrill.mb.ca. Though tucked in a shopping district midway between downtown and the airport this is a worthwhile trek for visiting foodies, thanks to the expert handiwork of a local celebrity chef who uses regional ingredients to craft fine gourmet dishes like pan-roasted pike or white truffle *perogies*. Mains $20–33. Closed Sun & Mon.

Kelekis 1100 Main St. Another true Winnipeg institution, located around 1km north of downtown and dishing out cheap but delicious portions of greasy fries, hotdogs and enormous hamburgers to people from all walks of life – including Pierre Trudeau – since 1931.

La P'tite France 241 St Mary's Rd ⓣ204/237-5868. Cheerful little place on a loveless artery south of St Boniface, serving inexpensive French dishes, often with a local twist. Classics include the boeuf bourguignon ($23), but consider the good-value six-course menu on Fri and Sat nights ($39) which gives the chef creative reign. Closed Sun & Mon.

Monviso 637 Corydon Ave ⓣ204/287-8807. In the heart of Little Italy, this restaurant, with outdoor patio, serves large portions pasta and other classic Italian dishes. Mains from $7.

Stella's Cafe & Bakery 166 Osborne St ⓣ204/453-8562. Breakfast specialist with items like baked eggs, along with all the trusty standbys, plus delicious home-made jam. Lunchtime soups and quiche are also great. There's a second location at 116 Sherbrook St.

Terrace 55 Food & Wine The Pavilion in Assiniboine Park ⓣ204/938-7275. Perfectly situated in a glass atrium on the back of the fake Tudor Pavilion, and an expensive favourite with Winnipeggers. Mains ($18–28) focus on local produce, fish and seafood.

Tre Visi 173 McDermot Ave ⓣ204/949-9032. Tiny, extremely popular Italian restaurant with good atmosphere and food. Mains $8–20. Reservations essential.

Wordsworth Building Cafeteria 405 Broadway Ave ⓣ204/944-8927. Overrun by lunching office workers thanks to well-priced specials and extensive salad bar. Breakfast and lunch only.

Wasabi 105–121 Osborne St ⓣ204/474-2332. Buzzing, trendy sushi bar in Osborne Village. Sushi from $1.50, $20 for a combo platter.

Nightlife and entertainment

Winnipeg supports a good range of theatre, ballet, opera and orchestral music and has some lively **nightlife**, in which live music also plays a big part. For listings, consult *Uptown* (Ⓦwww.uptownmag.com), widely available across the city, or check out the Thursday editions of the *Winnipeg Sun* or the *Winnipeg Free Press*.

Major performances by the Winnipeg Symphony Orchestra (Ⓦwww.wso.ca), the Manitoba Opera (Nov–May; Ⓦwww.manitobaopera.mb.ca) and the Royal Winnipeg Ballet (Ⓦwww.rwb.org) – Canada's finest dance company – are at the Centennial Concert Hall, 555 Main St (Ⓦwww.mbccc.ca), in the Exchange District. The city has several professional **theatre** groups: principally the Prairie Theatre Exchange (Ⓦwww.pte.mb.ca), in the Portage Place Mall, and the Manitoba Theatre Centre (Ⓦwww.mtc.mb.ca) at 174 Market Ave. Winnipeg's best downtown **cinema** is Cinémathèque, in Artspace at 100 Arthur St (Ⓣ204/925-3457, Ⓦwww.winnipegcinematheque.com), which concentrates on arthouse and Canadian releases.

Clubs and venues

Club 200 190 Garry St Ⓣ204/943-6045 Ⓦwww.club200.ca. A popular gay and lesbian club with karaoke nights and other weekly events.

G Martini Bar 454 River Ave Ⓣ204/284-3996, Ⓦwww.meijisushi.ca. Small, swank and lively martini bar that shares space with a sushi place.

Jazz on the Rooftop Winnipeg Art Gallery, 300 Memorial Blvd Ⓣ204/786-6641. Showcases frequent performances by some of Canada's best-known jazz musicians in the summer.

Ms Purdy's 226 Main St Ⓣ204/989-2344. Long-running women-only lesbian bar.

Palomino Club 1133 Portage Ave Ⓣ204/722-0454, Ⓦwww.palominoclub.ca. Best place for a good boot-scoot (that's line dancing, if you're wondering).

Times Change Café 234 Main St Ⓣ204/957-0982, Ⓦwww.highandlonesomeclub.ca. Rough-and-ready jazz and blues place. Live entertainment Thurs–Sun.

Toad in the Hole 112 Osborne St Ⓣ204/284-7201. Gregarious wood-panelled pub with British beer that packs out with sociable twenty and thirty-somethings; pool, darts and regular live music.

The Zoo 160 Osborne St Ⓣ204/452-9824. Rock and metal bar in *Osborne Village Inn* with live acts.

Listings

Bike rental HI Winnipeg $10/24hr.

Consulates UK, 229 Athlone Drive Ⓣ204/896-1380.

Internet Centennial Library, 251 Donald St Ⓣ204/986-6450. Osborne Cyber Café, 118 Osborne St (10am–midnight).

Laundry Zip-Kleen, 110 Sherbrook St Ⓣ204/772-5247.

Medical Health Sciences Centre, 820 Sherbrook St Ⓣ204/774-6511.

Post office 208 Provencher Boulevard Ⓣ204/987-5111.

Taxis Duffy's Ⓣ204/925-0101.

Weather information Ⓣ204/983-2050, Ⓦwww.winnipegweather.com.

Southeastern Manitoba

Tempting day-trips from Winnipeg abound in Southeastern Manitoba, with worthwhile cultural, historic and natural attractions all on offer. To the south, the workaday prairie town of **Steinbach** boasts the interesting Mennonite Heritage Village, while the unassuming neighbouring town of **Morris** is not to be missed in late July during its annual rodeo. East of here and on the Ontario border, **Whiteshell** and **Nopiming provincial parks** protect an inhospitable and sparsely inhabited region of lakes, rivers and forests on the granite landscapes of the Canadian Shield, providing a superb network of canoe routes between backcountry campsites.

The Manitoba Stampede

During the third week of July, be sure to pack up your spurs (or maybe just your camera) and head to the pleasant small town of **MORRIS**, 61km south of Winnipeg via Hwy 75, for the annual **Manitoba Stampede** and Exhibition. It's one of Canada's largest rodeos, yet still small enough to retain the feel of an authentic small-town hoedown.

North of Winnipeg, dreary suburbs fade into the seamless prairie landscape and the only major interruption is the **Red River** and the trading post of **Lower Fort Garry**. From here, birdwatchers should make a beeline to the marshlands of the **Oak Hammock Marsh Wildlife Area**, where thousands of migrating birds, particularly snow and Canada geese, drop in between April and September. Otherwise, the main hwys parallel the northbound Red River as it empties into **Lake Winnipeg**, a 400km-long finger of water that feeds the Nelson River on its way to Hudson Bay. It's a shallow lake and often has reasonable waves lapping at its shores, creating a real seaside atmosphere on its southeast shore in **Grand Beach Provincial Park**, where sand dunes stretch as far as the eye can see and Winnipeggers bathe in droves on summer weekends. The beaches of the lake's west shore are poorer, and the old fishing and farming villages of little interest, except for **Gimli**, which has its own windblown charm and a intriguing museum tracing its Icelandic history. Visiting the nearby **Narcisse Wildlife Management Area** is a must in April and May, when thousands of red-sided garter snakes gather to mate. Heading north along the lake's western coast you'll encounter scattered islands harbouring the unspoilt marshes and forests of **Hecla/Grindstone Provincial Park**.

Relying on **public transport** to explore this region is awkward but just about workable, with most key places having no more than one or two bus services per day. Lower Fort Garry is the only real exception, with its frequent bus and boat services from Winnipeg.

Steinbach

The sprawling minor town of **STEINBACH**, 63km southeast of Winnipeg, is worth visiting for its **Mennonite Heritage Village** (May & Sept 10am–5pm, Sun noon–5pm; June–Aug Mon–Sat 10am–6pm, Sun noon–6pm; Oct–April Mon–Fri 10am–4pm, outdoor buildings closed; Ⓣ204/326-9661 or 1-866 280-8741, Ⓦwww.mhv.ca; $10), a good reconstruction of a nineteenth-century pioneer settlement on the north edge of town off Hwy 12. It includes a church, a windmill and a couple of stores and farmhouses, but it's the general flavour of the place that appeals rather than any particular structure. Costumed guides provide an intriguing account of Mennonite history, augmented by displays in a tiny museum. For a Mennonite **meal**, try the inexpensive cafeteria-style *Livery Barn*, with borscht, stone-ground bread, smoked sausages and other delights.

Whiteshell Provincial Park

Dotted with holiday homes, lodges and campsites along a fairly extensive road system, **Whiteshell Provincial Park** is not a place where the wilderness is easily found but it does offer the great outdoors in return for minimum preparation and fuss. Summer weekends can get busy, but the busy spots are easily left behind and the canoeing is superb, with interesting overnight or multi-day trips easily organized.

Canada's Mennonites

There are about 100,000 **Mennonites** in Canada today, almost all descendants of those who joined a Protestant sect in the Netherlands in the early sixteenth century under the leadership of Menno Symons. The movement eventually divided into two broad factions: one group refused to have anything to do with the secular state and sustained a hostile attitude to private property; the more "liberal" clans were inclined to compromise on both issues. Many of the former – the Ammanites – moved to the US and then Ontario, settling in and around Kitchener-Waterloo, while the more liberal population migrated to Russia and then Manitoba in the 1870s. The Steinbach area today remains a Mennonite stronghold, and though few adherents wear the traditional black and white clothes or live on communal farms, most maintain the strong pacifist tradition.

The park takes its name from *megis*, a small, white shell sacred to the Ojibwa, who believe the creator blew through it to breathe life into the first human. These shells, left behind when the prehistoric lake that once covered the entire region disappeared, are concentrated along the park's two main rivers, the Whiteshell to the south and the Winnipeg to the north; the latter waterway was an important part of the canoe route the *voyageurs* of the North West Company followed on their way from Montréal to the Red River.

Falcon Lake and West Hawk Lake

Most park visitors head for **FALCON LAKE** and **WEST HAWK LAKE**, two well-developed but unexciting tourist townships either side of Hwy 1, near the Ontario border. Crowded throughout the summer, each has a range of facilities ranging from serviced campsites, resort hotels, fuel stations, grocery stores and miniature golf, through to boat and watersports equipment rental. Falcon Lake has the better supermarket, but West Hawk Lake is the more modest and sympathetic. The best places to **eat** in West Hawk Lake are the *Nite Hawk Café*, for home-made burgers, and *Pittman*, for juicy steaks ($23) and prime rib.

West Hawk Lake itself was formed by a meteorite and is the deepest lake in Manitoba, making it popular with scuba divers. On its south side the thirteen-kilometre **Hunt Lake Hiking Trail** passes through forests, across sticky, aromatic bogs and over rocky outcrops, to Little Indian Bay and back (8hr).

Caddy Lake

From West Hawk Lake, Hwy 44 cuts north towards **CADDY LAKE** (with campsites and two holiday lodges), the starting point for one of the area's most beautiful **canoe routes**, the 160-kilometre journey along the Whiteshell River to Lone Island Lake, in the centre of the park. The *Caddy Lake Resort* (Mon–Fri 8am–8pm-Sun 8am–9pm, ⓣ204/349-2596) rents canoes for $30 per day.

Experienced walkers could tackle the 60km **Mantario Hiking Trail** just to the east of Caddy Lake along Provincial Road 312. For beginners, there are the **Bear Lake** (8km) and **McGillivray trails** (4km), clearly signposted from Hwy 44 to the west of Caddy Lake; they reveal a good sample of the park – dry ridges dominated by jack pine, bogs crammed with black spruce and two shallow lakes brown from algae and humic acid. Opposite the start of the Bear Lake Trail, the **Frances Lake** canoe route makes for a pleasant overnight excursion, a twenty-kilometre trip south to the Frances Lake campsite, with three portages past the rapids and twelve hauls round beaver dams.

Wilderness trips

The **Manitoba Naturalists' Society** runs an excellent programme of Whiteshell wilderness adventures in July and August. The trips last for five days, cost $370 and are based at a cabin on secluded Lake Mantario. All equipment is provided, as are the services of fully experienced guides, who teach canoeing and survival skills. Reservations are essential. Check Ⓦwww.manitobanature.ca for details.

Rennie and Highway 307

Some 32km west of West Hawk, the village of **RENNIE** is home to the **park headquarters** (Mon–Fri 8.30am–noon & 12.45–4.30pm; Ⓣ204/369-5246), just east of town, with a comprehensive range of local trails and canoe route information. Between the headquarters and town, the **Alf Hole Goose Sanctuary** (late to May to mid-Oct daily 10.30am–6pm; free) is best visited in spring or autumn, when Canada geese pass through on their migration, but even in summer a couple of hundred are in residence. Rennie can be a base for excursions into the park, from the rather primitive *Rennie Hotel* (Ⓣ204/369-5308; ❸), but you're better off finding somewhere along the eighty-kilometre stretch of Hwy 307 that heads through the northwest section of the park, where there's a string of lonely campgrounds, lodges, trails and canoe routes. Be sure to pick up the free *Whiteshell Wanderer* magazine from the park headquarters; it lists a series of good hikes and interesting sites along the way, including petroforms, aboriginal designs made by placing stones on the ground. One great local lodging is the *Pinewood Lodge* (Ⓣ204/348-7549, Ⓦwww.mypinewood.com; ❺), alongside Dorothy Lake, 51km from Rennie. Run along ecological principles, it offers pretty luxurious rooms (and suites with jacuzzis and fireplaces) at very fair prices. The location is hard to beat and rates include canoe use plus access to an indoor pool, hot tub and fitness centre.

Nopiming Provincial Park

Some 100km north of Whiteshell Provincial Park, via Hwy 11 and Provincial roads 502, 313, 315 and 314, **Nopiming Provincial Park** is more remote (*nopiming* is Ojibwa for "entrance to the wilderness"), with a handful of lakeside campsites. This is a rocky area with granite shoreline cliffs above black-spruce bogs and tiny sandy beaches. The park's four campsites (all May–Sept; Ⓣ204/948-3333 or 1-888/482-2267; $9–11) lie close to the two gravel roads: Rte 314, which meanders across the 80km of its western edge, and the shorter Rte 315, a 30km track that cuts east south of Bird Lake to the Ontario border. Towards the south of the park, **BIRD LAKE** is a useful base, with a main settlement on the south shore that's equipped with a campsite ($9), grocery store and the cabins of the *Nopiming Lodge* (Ⓣ204/884-2281, Ⓦwww.nopiminglodge.com; ❻). There's also motorboat rental, canoe and guide rental for excursions to Snowshoe Lake, around falls and over rapids (55km). Nopiming Park is crossed by the Oiseau and Manigotagan waterways, whose creeks and rivers trickle or rush from lake to lake, forming no less than 1200km of possible canoe route.

Lower Fort Garry

Driving north out of Winnipeg on Main Steet, which becomes Hwy 9, it's about 32km to **Lower Fort Garry National Historic Site** (grounds open daily until

Backcountry canoeing in Manitoba

If you've already explored the superb canoeing in Whiteshell and Nopiming provincial parks or want some real wilderness, then you're spoilt for choice in Manitoba. Much of the best water is in the eastern half of the province in the remote Atikaki Provincial Wilderness Park, which has impressive stands of thick forest, several ancient pictograph sites and moose, timber wolves, coyotes and black bears. Its dramatic Bloodvein River to Lake Winnipeg is particularly outstanding, with rapids, falls and wild twistings balanced by peaceful drifts through quiet lakes and wild-rice marshes. In the far north the Hayes, Seal and Deer rivers all drain into Hudson Bay among Beluga whales and make for outstanding trips in sub-arctic waters.

All the above are very remote and only experienced, highly skilled and self-reliant backcountry canoeists should attempt trips here. You'll need to organise floatplane transportation and plan carefully using information from Paddle Manitoba (Ⓦwww.paddle.mb.ca) and Manitoba Conservation (Ⓦwww.gov.mb.ca/conservation), as well as purchase topographic, angling and illustrated maps, as well as aerial photographs; all are available from Canada Map Sales, Land Information Centre, 1007 Century St, Winnipeg (Ⓣ204/945-6666 or 1-877/627-7226, Ⓦwww.canadamapsales.com). Several outfitters offer trips that can spare you that level of preparation. Among them are Northern Soul (Ⓣ204-284-4072 or 1-866/284-4072, Ⓦwww.northernsoul.ca) and Wilderness Spirit (Ⓣ204-452-7049 or 1-866/287-1591, Ⓦwww.wildernessspirit.com), who both run trips to Hudson Bay and on several Atikaki rivers. These start at $600 for four days, but cost up to $4500 for a full-blown two-week adventure on the Seal River, the most remote of all.

sunset; visitor centre: mid-May to Aug daily 9am–5pm; $7.15). Built on the banks of the Red River, it was the headquarters of the Hudson's Bay Company between 1830 and 1847. It was the brainchild of George Simpson, governor of the company's northern department, an area bounded by the Arctic and Pacific oceans, Hudson Bay and the Missouri River Valley. Nicknamed the "Little Emperor" for his autocratic style, Simpson selected the site because it was downriver from the treacherous waters of the St Andrew's rapids but not prone to flooding, as Upper Fort Garry had been. The visitor centre presents a comprehensive history of the fort and the local fur trade, while beyond it several low, thick limestone walls protect reconstructions of company buildings, including the retail store, where a small museum is devoted to Inuit and Indian crafts, including some exquisite decorated skin pouches and an extraordinary necklace fringed by thin strips of sardine can. Next door, the combined sales shop and clerk's quarters has a fur loft packed with pelts, while the middle of the compound is dominated by the Big House, built for Governor Simpson in 1832. Guides in 1850s period costume stroll the grounds, ensuring a period atmosphere. The **restaurant** sells good *tourtière* – a Québécois meat pie – and bannock (freshly baked bread).

Lower Fort Garry can be reached via the frequent Beaver Bus (Mon–Fri 11 daily; Sat 7 daily; Sun 5 daily; $5.25 one-way; Ⓣ204/989-7007, Ⓦwww.beaverbus.com) service from Winnipeg, though it's more fun to catch the boat (see p.509).

Oak Hammock Marsh

The **Oak Hammock Marsh Wildlife Management Area** (daily: May–Aug 10am–8pm; Sept & Oct 8.30am–dusk; Nov–April 10am–4.30pm; $5) Ⓣ204/467-3300, Ⓦwww.ducks.ca/ohmic; is all that remains of the wetlands that once stretched from St Andrews, near the Red River, up to the village of Teulon, and to the west of Netley Creek. Most of this wetland was drained and farmed around the beginning of the twentieth century, but in the 1960s some of the area was restored to its original state and protected by a series of retaining dykes and a number of islands built to provide marshland birds a safe nesting place. To get here from Winnipeg take Hwy 7 north for 10km, turn east along Hwy 67 and follow the signs to the Main Mound Area, where an excellent interpretive centre has hands-on displays about the local environment and wildlife, a picnic site and a couple of observation decks, all connected by a system of dykes and boardwalk trails. The best time to visit is spring or autumn, when the grebes, coots and other residents are joined by thousands of migrating birds, including Canada geese. Another part of the area has been returned to tall-grass prairie, carpeted from mid-June to August with the blooms of wild flowers, including the purple blazing star and the speckled red prairie lily.

Grand Beach Provincial Park and around

The southeast shore of Lake Winnipeg has one major attraction, **Grand Beach Provincial Park**, whose long stretch of powdery white sand, high grass-crowned dunes and shallow waters have made it a favourite swimming spot with Winnipeggers since the 1920s; it can get very crowded at summer weekends. The beach divides into two distinct parts, separated by a narrow channel and spanned by a tiny footbridge: to the west are privately owned cottages, sports facilities, motor- and rowboat rental, grocery stores and a restaurant; to the east the beach is less developed, bar the large *Grand Beach Campground* (ⓣ1-888/482-2267; May–Sept; $12.60–15.75) nestling in the dunes. From the campsite office, the **Ancient Beach Trail** is an hour-long walk along the shore of a prehistoric lake that dominated southern Manitoba during the last Ice Age.

At **GRAND MARAIS**, just outside the park, you'll find an array of motels, beachside cottages and cabins (most May–Sept; ③–⑤), while 23km north the well-heeled twin townships of **HILLSIDE BEACH** and prettier **VICTORIA BEACH** have good sandy beaches but avoid catering to outsiders. The *Birchwood Motel* (ⓣ204/754-2596; ③), on the hwy 6km south of Victoria Beach is a good place to stay, thanks to a huge patio overlooking the bay.

Gimli

In 1875, some two hundred Icelanders moved to the southwestern shore of Lake Winnipeg, where they had secured exclusive rights to a block of land between today's Winnipeg Beach and Hecla Island, named after a volcano in their homeland. The next year the colonists were struck by a smallpox epidemic, yet managed to survive to founded the **Republic of New Iceland**, a large self-governing and self-sufficient settlement with its own Icelandic-language school, churches and newspaper. Their independence lasted just twenty years, for in 1897 they acquiesced to the federal government's decision to open their new homeland to other ethnic groups and by the 1920s, an identifiable Icelandic community ceased to exist. Nevertheless, Manitoba still has the largest number of people of Icelandic descent outside Iceland. The residents celebrate their heritage during the Islendingadagurinn (Icelanders' Day) festival, on the first weekend in August, when they dress up in Viking helmets and organize beauty pageants, concerts and firework displays. This rather commercial festival is held in the largest township, **GIMLI** (literally "paradise").

The **tourist office** is downtown on 7th Ave (May–Aug daily 10am–4pm; ⓣ204/642-7974), but there's really not much to attract visitors to this part of the lake, though Gimli's harbourside, with a fibreglass Viking statue and a massive wharf, is modestly attractive. The **New Iceland Heritage Museum** (May–Aug daily 10am–4pm; Sept–April Mon–Fri 10am–4pm, Sat & Sun 1–4pm; $5; ⓣ204/642-4001, ⓦwww.nihm.ca), at 62 2nd Ave, chronicles the history of New Iceland.

Practicalities

Gimli doesn't have a lot of **places to stay**, but the *Lakeview Resort*, 10 Centre St (ⓣ204/642-8565 or 1-877/355-3500; ❺), has comfortable suites and rooms, each with a balcony overlooking either Gimli or the lake. There's also a **campsite** near the beach, 8km south of town, *Idle-Wheels Trailer Park* (ⓣ204/642-5676; mid-May to Sept; $17). Most of Gimli's eating options cluster near the lakefront and are reasonable enough, but one place that's not obvious and worth seeking out is *Amma's Tearom*, 94 1st Ave (ⓣ204/642-7232), towards the southern end of 1st Avenue. This old-fashioned place is pure chintz pleasure, with a glut of floral and countrified decorations, and is ideal for high tea, a sandwich ($5.50) or slice of quiche. Try some Icelandic treats, like *rullupysla*, a sliced sausage.

The Interlake and Hecla/Grindstone Provincial Park

Known as the **Interlake**, the marginal farmland between Lake Winnipeg and lakes Manitoba and Winnipegosis to the west is pancake-flat and one of the most boring parts of the prairies. The only significant attraction is at the **Narcisse Wildlife Management Area**, 25km west of Gimli on Hwy 231 or 90km north of Winnipeg on Hwy 17, where thousands of red-sided garter snakes gather to mate in late April and early May, writhing around the bottom of a series of shallow pits in slithering heaps. It's not for the squeamish.

Some 70km north of Gimli, **Hecla/Grindstone Provincial Park** consists of several islands and a slender peninsula that jut out into Lake Winnipeg, almost touching the eastern shore. The park is approached along Hwy 8, which runs across a narrow causeway to the largest of the islands, **Hecla**, where the tourist township of **GULL HARBOUR** has a comprehensive range of facilities. Nearby, on the east side of the island, the original **Hecla Village** has a number of old houses, a church and a school dating from the early years of Icelandic settlement; a short heritage trail covers the highlights (guided tours available in summer), or you can strike out on one of the island's hiking trails through forest and marsh. Several are in and around the well-tended *Radisson Resort Hecla* (ⓣ204/279-2041 or 1-800/267-6700, ⓦwww.heclaoasis.com; ❼), which is beside a golf course and has extensive pool and spa facilities. Local **accommodation** also includes the *Solmundson Gesta Hus*, in Hecla Village (ⓣ204/279-2088, ⓦwww.heclatourism.mb.ca; ❸), a B&B with home-cooked dinners, and the **Gull Harbour Campground** (ⓣ204/948-3333 or 1-888/482-2267; $13–17; May–Sept) on the neck of land between Gull Harbour and the lake. The *Radisson Resort Hecla* has a casual **restaurant** with good pizzas and a fine-dining place with some of the best food in the region.

The Trans-Canada Highway

Slicing east–west across the prairies, the **Trans-Canada Highway** (Hwy 1), passes through Canada's most fertile farming region, with its swaying wheat and dazzling yellow rapeseed, for around 1500km before hitting the Rockies. Dotted with campsites and fast-food joints, it pushes past a series of charmless towns and soon the novelty of big skies and ever-changing cloud formations wears off, making the journey rather dull; many travellers with a little extra time on their hands prefer to push northwest towards **Saskatoon** via the **Yellowhead Highway**; if you're headed that way, turn to p.565. But this leg of the Trans-Canada Hwy needn't be dull if you're prepared to leave its main corridor. Several **provincial parks** offer the chance to stretch your legs and a few attractions, including **Cannington Manor**, Regina's **RCMP Heritage Centre** and the **Tunnels of Moose Jaw** are worthwhile. The only sights worth travelling far off the hwy for are the pristine and wonderfully empty **Grasslands National Park** in southern Saskatchewan and Alberta's **Badlands**, around Drumheller.

Winnipeg to Regina

West of Winnipeg, the Trans-Canada Hwy soon hits the workaday agricultural town of **Portage La Prairie**, located roughly halfway to **Brandon**, Manitoba's second largest city, which has a handful of Victorian mansions and a lively arts centre. Between them, **Spruce Woods Provincial Park** contains the exceptional dune landscape of Manitoba's only desert. South of Brandon, diversions include the pleasant little prairie town of **Souris** and **Turtle Mountain Provincial Park** on the US border. Over the provincial border in southeastern Saskatchewan, the lakes, hillocks and aspen, birch and poplar forests of **Moose Mountain Provincial Park** come complete with campsites, nature trails and a resort village, and are close to the delightful **Cannington Manor Provincial Historic Park**.

Portage La Prairie

The first major settlement 97km west of Winnipeg is food-processing centre **PORTAGE LA PRAIRIE**. East of the town is the mildly interesting **Fort la Reine Museum and Pioneer Village** (mid-May to mid-Sept Mon–Sat 9am–6pm, Sun noon–6pm; $8; Ⓦwww.fortlareinemuseum.ca), at the junction of Hwy 1A and 26. It's modelled on an original fort that served as the headquarters of Pierre Gaultier during his 1740s explorations and recreates nineteenth-century life through a trading post, log homestead and a trapper's cabin, among others.

Accommodation largely consists of chain motels along Saskatchewan Avenue (Hwy 1A): try the basic but clean *Westgate Inn Motel*, 1010 Saskatchewan Ave East (Ⓣ204/239-5200, Ⓦwww.westgateinn.com; ❸) where some units have kitchenettes, or the *Canad Inn*, 2401 Saskatchewan Ave West (Ⓣ204/857-9745 or 1-888/332-2623, Ⓦwww.canadinns.com; ❺), if you want a pool and hot tub. For **food**, try local rib joint *Bill's Sticky Fingers* at 210 Saskatchewan Ave East. Down the road at no. 818, *Essence Tea House* has great cheesecake.

The Manitoba Agricultural Museum

Some 47km west of Portage la Prairie in **AUSTIN**, the **Manitoba Agricultural Museum** (mid-May to Sept daily 9am–5pm; $5 Ⓦwww.ag-museum.mb.ca) has Canada's largest collection of early twentieth-century farm machinery, from gigantic steam tractors through to threshing machines and balers. The site also includes a homesteaders' village, which simulates late nineteenth-century life and has the province's largest collection of pioneer household articles. The immensely popular **Manitoba Threshermen's Reunion and Stampede** is held here every year in mid-July – four days of rodeo riding, threshing displays, ploughing competitions, square dancing, jigging and Central Canada's Fiddle Festival. You can camp in the museum grounds (mid-May to Oct; $12–15); otherwise, B&B **accommodation** is available next door at *The Oak Tree* (Ⓣ204/637-2029, Ⓦwww.bedandbreakfast.mb.ca; ❷).

Spruce Woods Provincial Park

About 40km west of Austin a southbound turn off Hwy 1 leads to the tiny unassuming community of **CARBERRY**, from where it's another 35km south along Hwy 5 to the unique and rewarding **Spruce Woods Provincial Park**. The park falls on either side of the Assiniboine River, whose loops meander slowly south and west. Several walking trails begin beside or near the road, including the **Epinette Creek Trails** to the north, which run through woodland and marsh; the longest of these is the 25km Newfoundland Trail. There are a number of unserviced campsites along the various paths.

Roughly 5km south of the Epinette Creek Trails, the **Spirit Sands Trails** cross an area of mixed-grass prairie before entering the shifting sand dunes and pots of quicksand that constitute Manitoba's only **desert**. These "Spirit Sands" were of great religious significance to the Ojibwa who, according to one of the earliest fur traders, Alexander Henry, told "of the strange noises heard in its bowels, and its nightly apparitions". If it's too hot to walk the 7km loop, try one of the horse-drawn **wagon tours** that leave from the start of the trail throughout the summer (May, June & Sept Sat & Sun noon & 2pm; July & Aug daily 10am, noon & 2pm; 1hr 30min; $11; times vary ⓣ204/827-2800). The whole park is filled with strange, bluish-green ponds formed by the action of underground streams, and has some rare animals, notably the hognose snake and the prairie skink (a lizard); there's also a lot of poison ivy about. About 1km south of the start of the Spirit Sands, there's a **visitor centre** (mid-May to early Sept ⓣ204/827-8850) and a range of tourist facilities at **KICHE MANITOU LAKE**, including a large campsite (ⓣ204/948-3333 or 1-888/482-2267; $16–19; mid-May to Sept), caravan park, grocery stores, restaurants, a beach and canoe rental. If you need to stay in Carberry, try the clean but dowdy *Carberry Motor Inn* (ⓣ204/834-2197; ❷), located in the town's business district.

Brandon

In 1881, the CPR routed the transcontinental railroad through Winnipeg and began to look for a refuelling depot in the western part of Manitoba. The ideal spot was on the east bank of the Assiniboine River, opposite today's **BRANDON**, 160km from Winnipeg, on the land of Dugald McVicar. With dollar signs in his eyes, McVicar attempted to sell his farm and sod hut to the CPR for around $60,000, prompting a railway negotiator to exclaim, "I'll be damned if a town of any kind is built here." It wasn't, and Brandon was founded 4km to the west. Today, the city is a major agricultural centre and host to Manitoba's largest livestock show – the Royal Manitoba Winter Fair – in late March and the Wheat City Stampede in late October.

Info on all these goings-on can be picked up at the smart **Riverbank Discovery Centre** (May–Sept Mon–Fri 8.30am–8pm, Sat & Sun 11am–8pm; Oct–April Mon–Fri 8.30am–5pm; ⓣ204/729-2141 or 1-888/799-1111, ⓦwww.brandon.com), a short drive south of Hwy 1 along 18th St North. This is also the starting point of several trails along the Assiniboine River, so pick up some self-guided tour leaflets , including the one covering downtown's historic buildings ($3). Some of these are on the Rosser Avenue, including the former Mutter Brothers Grocery Store, built in the Romanesque Revival style, but whose interior has been moved to the **Daly House Museum** (May–Sept Mon–Sat 10am–noon & 1–5pm, Sun 1–4pm; Oct–April Tues–Sat 10am–noon & 1–5pm; $5; ⓦwww.mts.net/~dalymus) at 122 18th St, the restored home of Brandon's first mayor. Back on Rosser Avenue the **Art Gallery of Southwestern Manitoba** (Mon–Sat 10am–6pm, Thurs till 9pm; free; ⓦwww.agsm.ca), at no. 710, has changing exhibitions, largely on the work of Manitoba artists and craftspeople.

Brandon's **bus station** (Ⓣ204/727-0643 or 1-800/661-8747) is at 141 6th St. It handles Greyhound buses running to Winnipeg, Regina and Saskatoon, as well as smaller places in southwest Manitoba, and also Grey Goose Lines, which runs buses south on Hwy 10. VIA Rail **trains** on the thrice-weekly Winnipeg to Vancouver run stop north of Brandon along Hwy 10; a taxi into town costs about $15.

Practicalities

Brandon isn't a bad place to break your journey, and has plenty of reasonable places to **stay**, many of which lie close to the Trans-Canada Hwy. One of these is the slightly eccentric *Barney's Motel*, 105 Middleton Ave (Ⓣ204/725-1540 or 1-866/825-8166; ❷), a place so scrupulously clean it'll cut your bill by ten cents for every dead fly you find; some rooms have kitchenettes. Also off the hwy is the *Super 8 Motel*, 1570 Highland Ave (Ⓣ204/729-8024 or 1-800/800-8000, Ⓦwww.super8.com; ❹), which is good value, with a free continental breakfast, plus pool and hot tub. Brandon's best address is the *Royal Oak Inn*, at 3130 Victoria Ave (Ⓣ204/728-5775 or 1-800/852-2709, Ⓦwww.royaloakinn.com; ❺). The *Meadowlark Campground* (Ⓣ204/728-7205 or 1-800/363-6434 Ⓦwww.meadowlarkcampground.ca; April–Oct; $27–31) is just off the Trans-Canada Hwy and west of *Barney's Motel*.

The best of the city's **restaurants** and **cafés** are on a couple of blocks along Rosser Avenue: The *Ginger Cat Café* at no. 934 is a comfortable coffee shop; the bland *Double Decker Tavern & Restaurant* at no. 943 has regular live music and does a good line in wings and bar food; and the excellent *Chilly Chutney* at no. 935 which, oddly, serves delicious east Indian curries and a full range of zesty Mexican items (mains $10–12).

Souris

Southwest of Brandon, an easy 43km drive through golden wheatfields dotted with **grain elevators** leads to pretty **SOURIS**, a quintessential prairie town on the steep banks of the Souris River. Squat false-gabled buildings line the wide tree-shaded main street with its parked half-ton trucks and sleeping dog or two, while tall Manitoba oaks or trembling aspen border the quiet side streets.

The main attraction is the vertigo-inducing cable **suspension bridge**, the longest of its kind in Canada. Beside the bridge at 26 Crescent Ave is the charming **Hillcrest Museum** (May, June & early Sept Sun 2–5pm; July & Aug daily 10am–6pm; $3). For something more active, try prospecting for fossils, agates, jaspers and other semi-precious stones in pits outside town. The Rock Shop, 8 1st St South (May–Sept Mon–Fri 10am–5pm, Sat & Sun noon–5pm; Oct–April Mon–Fri 10am–5pm, Sat 11am–5pm; Ⓦwww.sourisrockshop.com), sells some of the stones as well as the permit ($10/car), and can direct you to the pits; you can take away up to ten kilos of rock.

Turtle Mountain Provincial Park

Heading 97km south of Brandon along Hwy 10 will bring you to **Turtle Mountain Provincial Park**, a mixed area of marsh, rolling hills and deciduous forest, whose four hundred shallow lakes form an ideal habitat for the western painted turtle, after which the park takes its name; there's also a substantial moose population, most visible in late September. Turtle Mountain's main facilities are beside the main road at **ADAM LAKE**, where there's the large *Adam Lake Campsite* (Ⓣ 204/948-3333 or 1-888/482-2267; $15–19; mid-May to mid-Sept), a beach, a store, a **park office** (Mon–Thurs 10am–noon & 1–6pm, Fri & Sat 10am–10pm, Sun 1–4pm Ⓣ204/534-2028) and a number of walking and cross-country skiing trails. There's a smaller, prettier campsite at **MAX LAKE** (Ⓣ204/948-3333 or 1-888/482-2267; May–Sept; $12), south of Hwy 3 on Provincial Road 446. This campsite gives easy access to the **Oskar Lake Canoe Route**, a nineteen-kilometre paddle and portage excursion across ten of the park's lakes. Best in the spring or autumn, the route should be tackled in an anticlockwise direction to avoid climbing steep hills, and can be completed in one or two days. A number of backcountry campsites dot the lakeshores; there are no canoe-rental facilities.

On the southeastern edge of Turtle Mountain Park, straddling the US border, is the landscaped shrub and formal flower garden of the **International Peace Garden** ($10/vehicle, $5/person; ⓦwww.peacegarden.com). The dubious attractions on offer include a Peace Chapel, the starkly modern Peace Tower and a large, floral clock and ten steel girders from New York's collapsed World Trade Centers.

Moose Mountain Provincial Park and Cannington Manor

The first attraction of note after you enter **Saskatchewan** is **Moose Mountain Provincial Park** ($7), 60km south of the Trans-Canada Hwy on Hwy 9. It's a rough rectangle of wooded hills and lakes whose main resort, **KENOSEE LAKE**, is packed with holidaymakers during summer. The range of amenities here include a **parks office** (Mon–Fri 8am–5pm; ⓣ306/577-2600), restaurants, bars, sports facilities, waterslides and canoe and paddleboat rental, but it's still easy enough to escape the crowds in the surrounding poplar and birch groves.

For accommodation, the *Kenosee Inn* (ⓣ306/577-2099, ⓦwww.kenoseeinn.com; ④), offers standard rooms or rustic cabins and is near two golf courses, tennis courts and waterslides. Both the *Fish Creek* and *Lynwood* **campsites** (ⓣ306/577-2611; mid-May to early Sept; $17–26) lie on the western edge of the developed area, a good 2km from the busiest part of the park.

A short-lived experiment in transplanting English social customs to the prairies is the subject of the **Cannington Manor Provincial Historic Park** (mid-May to Aug Wed–Mon 10am–5pm; $4), a partly reconstructed Victorian village about 30km east of Kenosee Lake. Founded in 1882 by Edward Pierce, the would-be squire, the village attracted a number of British middle-class families determined to live as "gentlemen farmers", running small agricultural businesses, organizing tea and croquet evenings and even importing a pack of hounds to stage hunts. Their efforts failed when the branch rail line was routed well to the south, and by 1900 the settlement was abandoned.

The Qu'Appelle river valley

The slow-moving **Qu'Appelle River** flows 350km from Lake Diefenbaker (160km west of Regina) to the Manitoba border, its lush, deep and wide lake-filled valley acting as a welcome scenic break from the prairies, as well as an alternative east-west route to Hwy 1.

From the east, you leave the Trans-Canada Hwy at its junction with Hwy 9 to follow Hwy 247 west round the pleasantly quiet Round and Crooked lakes (both have several good campsites), the latter a 50km drive from Hwy 1. From Crooked Lake, leaving the valley and driving 68km along Hwy 22 brings you to the **Motherwell Homestead National Historic Site** (late May to Sept daily 9am–5pm; $7.80 ⓣ306/333-2116, ⓦwww.pc.gc.ca), 3km south of Abernethy. This large, square house, with its odd assortment of multicoloured fieldstones embedded in the exterior walls and wrought-iron "widow's walk" on the roof, was built in 1898 for local farmer and politician W.R. Motherwell, who moved himself – and this style of architecture – here from Southern Ontario.

From the homestead it's a 32km drive back to the Qu'appelle river valley and Fort Qu'appelle, which nestles at the foot of the grooved escarpments between a chain of eight little lakes known collectively as the **Fishing Lakes**. All are attractive and accessible by road but the nearest is **Echo Lake**, itself adjacent to the **Echo Valley Provincial Park** (Ⓣ306/332-3215; $7; camping $13–26), 8km west of Fort Qu'appelle.

Fort Qu'appelle

FORT QU'APPELLE itself centres on Broadway Street, whose most attractive building is the restored 1897 red-brick **Hudson's Bay Company store**, Canada's oldest surviving example. A five minute walk south down Bay Avenue, two blocks east of the store, leads to the town **museum** (June–Aug daily 1–5pm; $3), which has a small display on the area's European pioneers and the North West Mounted Police and is joined to the Hudson's Bay Company trading post of 1864. Three blocks to the south, the stone **obelisk** at Fifth Street and Company Avenue commemorates the 1874 signing of Treaty Number 4 between the Ojibwa, Cree and Assiniboine of the southern prairies and Lieutenant-Governor Alexander Morris. It was a fractious process. The Ojibwa insisted the HBC had stolen "the earth, trees, grass, stones, all that we see with our eyes", hectoring Morris to the point where he confined the more militant aboriginal leaders to their tents, thus undermining the unity of all the bands; the treaty was eventually signed in return for various land grants, pensions and equipment.

The **tourist office** is in the old CNR station at the junction of Boundary Avenue and Hwy 10 (June–Aug daily 10am–4.30pm; Ⓣ306/332-5266, Ⓦwww.fortquappelle.com). One of the town's three **motels**, the *Country Squire Inn* (Ⓣ306/332-5603; ❷), is beside Hwy 10 at the bottom end of Bay Street. There's also the attractive, lakefront *B-Say-Tah Point B&B* 4.5km west of town on Hwy 210 (Ⓣ306/332-5988; ❹), with free wi-fi and hot tub.

Restaurants on Broadway Street include the *Valley Bake and Coffee Shop* at no. 181, which is great for breakfast. Otherwise pickings are slim, though *Mings Garden* at no. 215 (closed Mon) is reasonable, as is the *Off Broadway Bistro*, 121 Boundary Ave (Ⓣ306/332-3939), where you can dine on turkey lasagne or *tourtière*.

Regina

REGINA, 575km west of Winnipeg, is Saskatchewan's capital, as well as its commercial and administrative services centre, which anchors a vast network of agricultural towns and villages. Yet despite its status, brash shopping malls and 200,000-plus population, Regina feels like a small and unremarkable prairie town. Still, it's a comfortable place to spend a couple of days (it gets more hours of sunshine than any other major Canadian city) and is an essential stop if you're keen on learning more about the Royal Canadian Mounted Police (RCMP), more commonly known as the **Mounties** (see p.536).

A brief history

Regina's origins stem from the 1881 decision of Edward Dewdney, lieutenant-governor of the Northwest Territories (which then spread west from Ontario as far

Seeing the city

The best way to see the centre is on **foot**, while for outlying attractions **Regina Transit** (Ⓦwww.reginatransit.com) runs good bus services; a standard one-way fare is $2.10 and most lines can be picked up downtown along either 11th Avenue or 12th Avenue, depending on the direction of travel as the Arctic and Pacific oceans) to move his capital south from Battleford to **Pile o'Bones** – an inconsequential place named for the heaps of bleached buffalo bones left along its creek by generations of native hunters – after the Canadian Pacific Railway was routed across the southern plains. The city was renamed Regina (Latin for "queen"), after Queen Victoria, but the site was far from being fit for royalty, let alone the average person: the sluggish creek provided a poor water supply, the clay soil was muddy in wet weather and dusty in the summer and there was no timber for building. Accordingly, the railway board refused to oblige and the end result was farcical: Government House and the Mounted Police barracks were built where Dewdney wanted them, but the train station was a three-kilometre trek south.

Regina became the capital of the newly created province of **Saskatchewan** in 1905 and settlers flocked here from the US and central Europe. The city soon overcame its natural disadvantages by extensive tree-planting, which provided shade and controlled the dust, and by damming the creek to provide a better water source. Yet Regina's success was based on the fragile prosperity of a one-crop (wheat) economy and throughout the twentieth century boom alternated with bust. Today, Regina's prosperity looks solid, thanks to sizeable oil reserves, uranium mines and the high price of agricultural commodities.

Arrival and information

Regina's **airport** (ⓣ306/761-7555, ⓦwww.yqr.ca) is about 5km west of the city centre. The taxi trip downtown costs roughly $10, or you can take the Hobo Express Shuttle bus (ⓣ306/949-2121) to Regina's downtown hotels or Moose Jaw ($27). A fifteen-minute walk east of the airport brings you to the junction of Regina Avenue and Pasqua Street, from where Regina Transit's **buses** #11 and #13 head for the city centre. The **bus station** is at 1717 Saskatchewan Drive, with services from Greyhound and provincial carrier, the Saskatchewan Transportation Company (ⓣ306/787-3340; ⓦwww.stcbus.com).

Tourism Regina operates a tourist bureau east of town on Hwy 1, really only accessible by car (May–Sept Mon–Fri 8.30am–6pm, Sat & Sun 10am–6pm;

▲ RCMP officers on the march in Regina

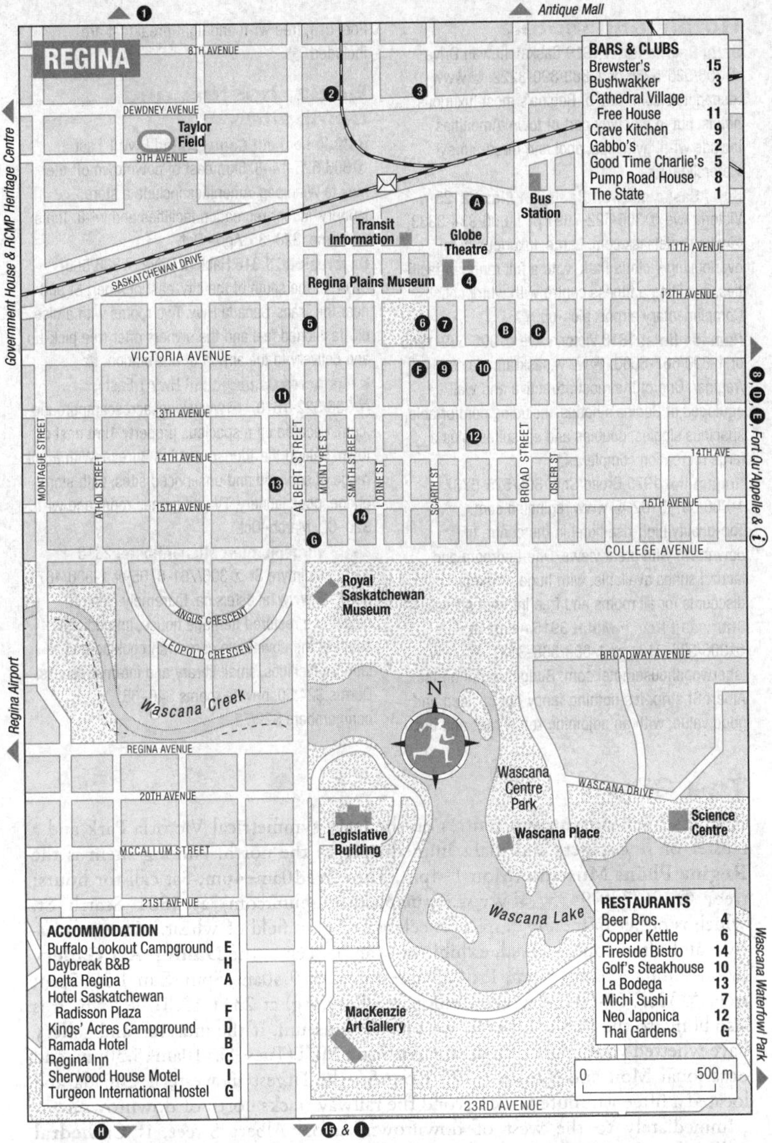

REGINA

BARS & CLUBS

Brewster's	15
Bushwakker	3
Cathedral Village Free House	11
Crave Kitchen	9
Gabbo's	2
Good Time Charlie's	5
Pump Road House	8
The State	1

ACCOMMODATION

Buffalo Lookout Campground	E
Daybreak B&B	H
Delta Regina	A
Hotel Saskatchewan Radisson Plaza	F
Kings' Acres Campground	D
Ramada Hotel	B
Regina Inn	C
Sherwood House Motel	I
Turgeon International Hostel	G

RESTAURANTS

Beer Bros.	4
Copper Kettle	6
Fireside Bistro	14
Golf's Steakhouse	10
La Bodega	13
Michi Sushi	7
Neo Japonica	12
Thai Gardens	G

Oct–April Mon–Fri 8.30am–4.30pm; ⓣ306/789-5099 or 1-800/661-5099, ⓦwww.tourismregina.com).

Accommodation

It's rarely difficult to find accommodation in Regina, which has plenty of central options, the cheapest of which are quite grim. Instead opt for the cluster of reasonably priced, standard **motels** east of the centre along Victoria Avenue East (also Hwy 1), or south of the centre, along Albert Street.

Hotels and motels

Delta Regina Hotel 1919 Saskatchewan Drive ⓣ306/525-5255 or 1-888/890-3222, ⓦwww.deltahotels.com. One of Regina's most luxurious hotels, but in a dowdy part of town. Amenities include wi-fi, gym, spa, pool and three-storey waterslide. ⑥

Hotel Saskatchewan Radisson Plaza 2125 Victoria Ave ⓣ306/522-7691 or 1-800/333-3333, ⓦwww.hotelsask.com. Large, luxurious hotel, overlooking Victoria Park, with a full range of facilities, including a fitness centre with whirlpool. Complimentary airport pick-up. ⑥

Ramada Hotel 1818 Victoria Ave ⓣ306/569-1666 or 1-800/667-6500, ⓦwww.saskramada.com/regina/. One of the most attractive and well equipped of Regina's hotels, including comfortable, spacious singles, doubles and en-suites, plus a large recreation complex. ④

Regina Inn 1975 Broad St ⓣ306/525-6767 or 1-800/667-8162, ⓦwww.reginainn.com. Top-quality high-rise hotel in the centre of downtown with great views. One-bedroom and jacuzzi suites available, with huge weekend discounts for all rooms and free internet access. ⑥

Sherwood House Motel 3915 Albert St ⓣ306/586-3131 or 1-888/586-3131, ⓦwww.sherwoodhousemotel.com. Budget motel on the Albert St strip; it's nothing fancy but is clean and good value, with an adjoining restaurant and bar. Pool use, free wi-fi and light breakfast are included. ③

B&Bs, hostels and campsites

Buffalo Lookout Campground Hwy 1 East ⓣ306/525-1448. 5km east of downtown off the hwy to Winnipeg. Amenities include a store, laundry, indoor recreation facilities and wi-fi. Tents welcome. $28–35. April–Oct.

Daybreak B&B 316 Habkirk Drive ⓣ306/586-0211. In the south of the city, east of Albert St and near the Trans-Canada Hwy. Two rooms with a nice old-fashioned feel and the owners offer free pick-up and delivery to the airport or bus station. ①

Kings Acres Campground Hwy 1 East ⓣ306/522-1610, ⓦwww.kingsacrescampground.com. Located on a spacious property 1km east of town, behind the Tourism Regina Bureau. With a full range of serviced and unserviced sites, with store, phone, pool, laundry, TV and games room and wi-fi. $20–32. March–Oct.

Turgeon International Hostel 2310 McIntyre St ⓣ306/791-8165 or 1-800/467-8357, ⓦwww.hihostels.ca. Extremely clean HI hostel in a restored heritage house, immediately south of the downtown core, with cooking and laundry facilities, small library and internet access. Dorms $24.50, private rooms $40–66; nonmembers $29/72.

The City

Regina's small **downtown** centres on the leafy symmetrical Victoria Park and a cluster of skyscrapers and malls immediately to the north. Among them is the **Regina Plains Museum** (Mon 1–4pm, Tues–Fri 10am–4pm, Sat call for hours; free; ⓣ306/780-9435, ⓦwww.reginaplainsmuseum.com) at 1801 Scarth St, which is rather mundane despite its celebrated glass field of wheat. More innovative, and often controversial, exhibitions can be seen at the **Dunlop Art Gallery** (Mon–Thurs 9.30am–9pm, Fri 9.30am–6pm, Sat 9.30am–5pm, Sun 1.30–5pm; free; ⓣ306/777-604, ⓦwww.dunlopartgallery.org) at 2311 12th Ave, which is also home to the Public Library, west of the museum. If the museum and gallery have whetted your appetite, visit the **Antique Mall** (Tues–Sat 10am–5.30pm, and occasional Mon and Sun) at 1175 Rose St, the largest in western Canada and located a fifteen-minute walk beyond the railway tracks north of downtown.

Immediately to the west of downtown, across Albert Street, is **Cathedral Village**, with 13th Avenue as its heart. It's an old, bohemian area with an eclectic mix of boutiques, coffee shops, craft shops, classy restaurants and the occasional hemp store.

Wascana Centre Park

Roughly eight times the size of its downtown, Regina's most distinctive feature is **Wascana Centre Park**, which begins three blocks south of 13th Avenue and extends southeast to the city limits, following the curves of **Wascana Lake**, which was created as part of a work project for the unemployed in the 1930s. The city's main recreation area, the park is equipped with a bandstand (performances May–Aug Sun 2–4pm), barbecue pits, snack bars, boating facilities and waterfowl ponds, but for the most part it's a cheerless combination of reed-filled water and bare lawn. Despite this, the attractions within it are another story and worth stopping by if you have time. The park is served by bus services #3 and #4 from downtown.

Royal Saskatchewan Museum and the Science Centre

In the northwest corner of the park, near College Avenue and Albert Street, the **Royal Saskatchewan Museum** (daily: May–early Sept 9am–5.30pm; early Sept–April 9am–4.30pm; donation $2; Ⓦwww.royalsaskmuseum.ca) is devoted to the province's geology and wildlife, with the star attraction a giant animated dinosaur called Megamunch. Informative dioramas portray aspects of aboriginal life in the First Nations Gallery. In the new Life Sciences Gallery the relationships between habitat, plants and animals are explored with a multitude of skilfully stuffed animals and plastic flora set against backdrops that evoke the diverse eco-regions of Saskatchewan. About fifteen minutes' walk southeast along the lakeshore is **Wascana Place** (Mon–Fri 8am–4pm Ⓣ306/522-3661), the park headquarters, which has information on all lake activities as well as some more general information on Regina. **Boat rentals** (canoes $10/hr) are available over the road below the *Willow on Wasana* restaurant, a short stroll south along the lakeshore.

Further east along the winding Wascana Drive is Regina's best tourist attraction, the **Saskatchewan Science Centre** (May to early Sept Mon–Fri 9am–6pm, Sat & Sun 11am–6pm; Ⓣ306/522-4629 or 1-800/667-6300, Ⓦwww.sasksciencecentre.com; $8). The open, airy building houses more than a hundred interactive scientific exhibits, many of them quite entertaining; try scoring goals against a virtual keeper. Of particular regional interest is a display on uranium mining and a gallery devoted to the soils and weather of Saskatchewan, where you can learn about what's involved in running a farm. There's also an IMAX cinema and planetarium (Mon–Wed 9am–6pm, Thurs & Fri 9am–8.30pm, Sat & Sun noon–6pm; $7.50; joint ticket with centre $12.75).

The Legislative Building and MacKenzie Art Gallery

On the other side of the lake, accessible from Albert Street, is the grand **Legislative Building** (daily mid-May to early Sept 8am–9pm; early Sept to mid-May 8am–5pm; free tours every 30min; 2hr), a self-confident cross-shaped structure of Manitoba limestone with an impressive domed tower at its centre. Tours take in the oak-and-marble-panelled Legislative Chamber and six small art galleries, the best of which houses Edmund Morris's portraits of local aboriginal leaders, presented to the province in 1911. A neighbouring corridor is occupied by paintings of the **Native Heritage Foundation**, with thirty-odd canvases featuring the work of contemporary Métis and native artists, notably Allen Sapp (see p.582).

A few minutes' walk south of the Legislative Building, just off Albert Street at 23rd Avenue, is the **MacKenzie Art Gallery** (Mon–Thurs 10am–5.30pm, Fri till 9pm, Sat & Sun noon–5.30pm; free; Ⓦwww.mackenzieartgallery.ca). Its spacious, modern galleries are devoted to temporary exhibitions by modern Canadian artists, plus there's a good permanent collection. It's also the stage for **The Trial of Louis Riel** (mid-July to Aug Wed–Fri; $12), a play based on transcripts of the September 1885 trial, which took place in Regina. The trial was *the* controversial event of the time in Canada: most Anglophones were determined Riel – who had returned from exile in the US and ended up leading his second rebellion in fifteen years – should hang as a rebel, whereas his French-Canadian defenders saw him as a patriot and champion of justice. Though Riel was subject to visions and

ons, the court rejected the defence of insanity on the grounds he knew what
as doing and found him guilty. For more on Riel, see p.578.

CMP Heritage Centre

All Mounties do their basic training at the **RCMP Heritage Centre** (daily 10am–5pm; $12; ⓣ306/522-7333 or 1-866/567-7267, ⓦwww.rcmpheritagecentre.com), 4km west of the city centre at 5907 Dewdney Ave West, accessible by bus #8 from 11th Avenue. But the centre also holds a wealth of information on the history of this most famous of police forces (see below), from its early contacts with the Plains Indians and Métis through to its present role as an intelligence-gathering and crime-fighting organization.

The Mounties

The heroes of a hundred adventure stories and eccentric, epic films (*Canadian Mounties versus the Atomic Invaders*), the **Mounties** have been the continent's most charismatic good guys since the mid-1870s. The **North West Mounted Police**, as they were originally called, were created in Ottawa in 1873 and tasked with restoring law and order in Saskatchewan and Alberta's "Whoop-up Country" in the aftermath of the Cypress Hills Massacre (see p.545). But there was no long-term strategy: the force's areas of responsibility were undecided and even their uniforms had been slung together from a surplus supply of British army tunics. Yet they did a brilliant job, controlling whiskey traders who had created pandemonium by selling liquor to the Plains Indians. What secured the force's future was the successful defusing of a very delicate situation in 1876. Fearing reprisals after his victory over General Custer at the Battle of the Little Bighorn, Chief Sitting Bull and five thousand Sioux moved north, establishing a camp at Wood Mountain, 350km east of Fort Walsh. Aware of the danger, Inspector James Walsh rode into the camp with just four other constables to insist the Sioux obey Canadian law. Walsh's bravery helped establish a rough rapport with Sitting Bull and greatly enhanced the force's reputation.

The Mounties became vital in administering the west, acting as law enforcement officers and justices of the peace. From the 1880s their patrols crisscrossed the territory, their influence reinforced by a knowledge of local conditions accumulated in the exercise of a great range of duties – including delivering the mail and providing crop reports. Despite this level of autonomy, the Mounties saw themselves as an integral, if remote, part of the **British Empire**, their actions and decisions sanctioned by the weight of its authority. They despised the individualism of the American sheriff and marshal; Mounties expected obedience because of the dignity of their office, not their speed with a firearm. Officers became respected for an even-handedness that extended, remarkably for the period, to dealings with the Plains Indians. Yet the force's conservative class prejudice was less positive in their approach to policing: socially disruptive violent crimes were their main priority, whereas prostitution and drunkenness were regarded as predictable and inevitable problems of the "lower orders".

After 1920, when the force become the **Royal Canadian Mounted Police**, this conservative undertow became more problematic. The RCMP consistently supported politicians – Prime Minister Richard Bennet among them – who used them to break strikes. They have also often been accused of bias in their dealings with the Québécois. In recent years their reputation has taken a further hit: accusations of widespread corruption, making errors that lead to the rendition of Canadian citizen Maher Arar to Syria and the Taser-related death of a man at Vanouver's airport in 2007. As evidenced by the coverage these incidents received, the Mounties remain a potent – and important – symbol of nationality.

Inside, a series of contemporary quotations illustrates the **Long March** that first brought the Mounties to the west from Ontario in 1874. Their destination was Fort Whoop-up, near present-day Lethbridge, Alberta, where they intended to expel American whiskey traders. Another small section deals with **Sitting Bull**, who crossed into Canada after his victory at the Battle of the Little Bighorn in 1876. Fearing reprisals from the furious American army, Sitting Bull spent four years in and around the Cypress Hills, where he developed a friendship with Police Inspector James Walsh; a picture of the chief and his braves also shows an audience of curious Mounties in pith helmets looking on. To reinforce the romantic Hollywood image of the Mounties, an on-site cinema has continuous free runnings of such glorified interpretations as the 1936 film *Rose Marie*.

On the **tour** of the grounds you're shown the various buildings, including mock-ups of houses where arrests and surveillance techniques are practised, the drill hall and the 1883 chapel – Regina's oldest building – a splendid structure furnished in dark, polished oak where you can escape the intense training activity outside.

If possible, try to time your arrival for either the closely choreographed **Sergeant Major's parade** (Mon–Fri 12.45pm) or the **Sunset Retreat Ceremony** (July to mid-Aug Tues 6.45pm).

Government House

A couple of kilometres west of the city centre, the stolid yellow-brick **Government House** (Tues–Sun 10am–4pm; tours every 30min; free; bus #1, #11 or #13; ⓣ306/787-5773, ⓦwww.governmenthouse.gov.sk.ca) at 4607 Dewdney Ave was the residence of the lieutenant-governors of the Northwest Territories and subsequently Saskatchewan from 1891 to 1945. Restored to its late-nineteenth-century appearance, the offices and reception areas downstairs are splendid, as is the balconied staircase leading up to the bedrooms. The men's billiards room is decorated with an enormous bison head and a lemon-water stand, where the governor and his cronies would dip their fingers to hide the smell of the cigars. There are also a couple of mementos of one of the more eccentric governors, Amédée Forget, whose specially designed "salesman's chair", beside the entrance, was meant to be uncomfortable, with protruding gargoyles sticking into the visitor's spine, legs shorter at the front than the back and a flesh-pinching crack cut across the middle of the seat. The rocking horse in the office was for Forget's pet monkey. **High tea** is usually served in the ballroom one weekend each month from 1–4pm.

Eating, drinking and entertainment

Regina has a clutch of lively, reasonably priced downtown **restaurants**, but many close early and some don't open at all on Sundays; in emergencies try the big hotels whose bars nearly always serve food daily until 9.30pm. The city's **nightlife** isn't inspiring, though university students help keep a strip of clubs and brewpubs ticking in the Old Warehouse District just north of downtown.

For local **theatre**, try the Regina Performing Arts Centre, 1077 Angus St (ⓣ306/779-2277) or the very popular central Globe Theatre at 1801 Scarth St (ⓣ306/525-6400 or 1-866/954-5623 ⓦwww.globetheatrelive.com). The Regina Symphony Orchestra (ⓦwww.reginasymphony.com) performs at the Saskatchewan Centre of the Arts, 200B Lakeshore Drive (ⓣ306/525-9999 or 1-800/667-8497), with most dates in the winter months. Check the *Leader-Post* newspaper for listings.

Regina's festivals

Regina's biggest bash is **Buffalo Days** (Ⓦwww.buffalodays.ca), a week-long festival in early August. It's a lot of raft and livestock exhibitions, plus rides and music shows and all ends in a massive fireworks display. A better live music event is the **Craven Country Jamboree** (Ⓦwww.cravencountryjamboree.com), a four-day mid-July rock festival held in Craven, a twenty-minute drive north of town. The early August **Regina Folk Festival** (Ⓦwww.reginafolkfestival.com) in Victoria Park is another big deal, but for something different, attend the First Nations Pow Wow (Ⓦwww.firstnationsuniveristy.ca), an aboriginal gathering in early April, featuring crafts, music and dancing.

Cafés and restaurants

Beer Brothers Bakery & Cuisine 1801 Scarth Street ⓣ306/586-2337, Ⓦwww.beerbros.ca. Sociable brick-and-beam place where everything on the menu uses beer as an ingredient: "beer is the new wine" they claim. Try the "'Brew'chetta", with garlic beer butter ($10), or the roasted Hoegaarden chicken ($23).

Cathedral Village Free House 2062 Albert St ⓣ306/359-1661, Ⓦwww.thefreehouse.com/cathedral. Busy bar and restaurant with locally brewed beers and good wood-fired pizzas, sandwiches and burritos. Try something a bit fancier like the excellent Freehouse bouillabaisse that combines halibut, salmon, scallops, shrimp, walleye and tiger prawns.

The Copper Kettle 1953 Scarth St ⓣ306/525-3545. Central Greek-Canadian place overlooking Victoria Park with a fabulous line in gourmet pizzas ($14–34).

Fireside Bistro 2305 Smith St ⓣ306/761-2305, Ⓦwww.firesidebistro.ca. Great bistro tucked in a leafy residential neighbourhood by Wascana Park with a sunny summer terrace. A reliable mix of burgers, sandwiches, salads and wraps (around $10) emerge for lunch; later on the range broadens, with some great seafood dishes – teriyaki salmon with wasabi cream ($18.50) and snapper and tiger prawns in chilli ($19.50) among the options.

Golf's Steak House 1945 Victoria Ave ⓣ306/525-5808. Special-occasion steakhouse with top-notch prime rib and charbroiled steaks.

La Bodega 2228 Albert St ⓣ306/546-3660, Ⓦwww.labodegaregina.ca. Hip restaurant with great patio where movies are screened on a neighbouring wall and which hosts a Tues drum night. The food is equally adventurous, with Thai mango and palm salads available and a confusing array of tapas and "tappetizers" that include odd bedfellows like sushi and bannock bruschetta; the execution is excellent and prices fairly steep.

Michi Sushi 1943 Scarth St ⓣ306/565-0141, Ⓦwww.michi.ca. Among the best Japanese restaurants in Canada, with excellent tempura ($10–16) and sushi ($2–10).

Thai Gardens 2317 Albert St ⓣ306/584-0347. Huge portions of tasty Thai and pan-Asian food; well-priced – with most items around $7 and located on the same block as the hostel on the south side of town. Takeout available.

Bars and clubs

Brewster's 1832 Victoria Ave East. One of a chain of three brewpubs known for their extensive range of beer. There's a second branch at 4180 Albert St.

The Bushwakker 2206 Dewdney Ave ⓣ306/359-7276, Ⓦwww.bushwakker.com. Successful chain brewpub (voted one of the best by Canada's *Globe and Mail* newspaper) with twelve types of beer and a large selection of single-malt scotches; excellent hearty bar food including pierogies and buffalo steaks. Live music frequently livens things up later on.

Crave Kitchen and Wine Bar 1925 Victoria Ave ⓣ306/525-8777. Slick wine bar with more than a hundred tapas to choose from. Closed Sun.

Gabbo's 2338 Dewdney Ave. One of several fairly basic nightclubs in a row of old warehouses; choose between them by following the crowds. Small cover Sat & Sun.

Good Time Charlie's In the *Plains Hotel*, 1965 Albert St. Relaxed and friendly downtown pub and also one of the best live music clubs in Regina, with something on almost every night: blues figures prominently and there's often a $3–5 cover charge.

The Pump Road House 641 Victoria Ave East. Ⓦwww.thepumproadhouse.com. Probably Saskatchewan's premier C&W venue, with a huge dancefloor. Wed–Sat.

Listings

Bike rental Western Cycle, 1550 8th Ave ⓣ306/522-5678.
Bookshops Book and Brier Patch, 4065 Albert St ⓣ306/586-5814.
Car rental Avis ⓣ306/757-1653 (airport 306/751-5460); Budget ⓣ306/791-6810; Thrifty ⓣ306/525-1000.
Internet Central Library, 2311 12th Ave ⓣ306/777-6000; downtown and the 13th Avenue district have a giant free wi-fi hotspot.
Laundry Cathedral Laundromat, 2911 13th Ave ⓣ306/525-2665.
Medical Regina General Hospital, 1440 14th Ave ⓣ306/766-4444; Cathedral Dental Clinic, 3032 13th Ave ⓣ306/352-9966.
Pharmacy 11th Ave Pharmacy, 11th Ave ⓣ306/569-9818.
Police ⓣ306/777-6500.
Post office 2200 Saskatchewan Drive.
Taxis Capital Cab ⓣ306/791-2222.

Southern Saskatchewan

From Regina the 400km drive west across **southern Saskatchewan** on Hwy 1 is monotonous, with **Moose Jaw**, the one-time Prohibition hangout of American gangsters, the only worthwhile stop. Well to the south of Hwy 1 things are far more interesting, with undulating farmland broken up by lakes and rivers, pockets of arid semi-desert and the odd range of wooded hills. Near the US border the weathered buttes and conical hills of the **Big Muddy Badlands** are best explored on tours, while west of here, **Grasslands National Park** protects an untrammelled prairie landscape – punctuated by the odd dramatic coulees or buttes – that hints at what the region must have looked like before the arrival of Europeans. Other beautiful landscapes lie closer to Hwy 1 and the quintessential cowboy town of Maple Creek, including the starkly beautiful **Great Sand Hills** and the forested hills and ridges of **Cypress Hills Interprovincial Park** with its restored Mountie outpost, **Fort Walsh**.

Apart from bus services along the Trans-Canada Hwy, the region's **public transport** system is dismal; to explore, you'll need a car.

Moose Jaw

MOOSE JAW, 70km west of Regina, was founded as a railway depot in 1882. Its name comes from a Cree word for "warm place by the river", although some believe it was named for the repairs made to a cartwheel by an early pioneer with the assistance of a moose's jawbone.

The city achieved some notoriety during US Prohibition in the 1920s, when liquor was smuggled south by car or train along the Soo Line to Chicago. For most locals this period of bootleggers, gangsters, gamblers and "boozoriums" (liquor warehouses) was not a happy one, and for years various schemes to attract tourists by developing the "Roaring Twenties" theme met with considerable opposition from the population that actually experienced them. Despite this, the Tunnels of Moose Jaw (see p.540) remain the most interesting attraction in town.

Today, the city is a quiet sort of place, with most using it as a quick pit stop before powering through to Alberta. But for the more leisurely visitor it's probably a better place to break your journey than further down the hwy at Swift Current.

Arrival and information

Moose Jaw's **bus station** (ⓣ306/692-2345) is at 63 High St East, a couple of minutes' walk from Main Street and two blocks north of Manitoba Street. The **tourist office** (July & Aug daily 9am–5pm; rest of year Mon–Fri 9am–5pm;

306/693-8097 or 1-866/693-8097, www.citymoosejaw.com/tourism) is on the east side of town alongside the Trans-Canada Hwy.

Accommodation

The town has several reasonably priced, central **hotels** and **motels**, including the *Capone's Hideaway Motel* (306/692-6422 or 1-877/443-3003, www.caponeshideawaymotel.com; ❷), at 1 Main St North, opposite the defunct train station, where rooms have been given a 1920s feel. Book well in advance for the four-star *Temple Gardens Mineral Spa*, 24 Fairford St East (306/694-5055 or 1-800/718-7727, www.templegardens.sk.ca; ❻), which has luxurious rooms (with jacuzzi), geothermal pools and facilities for massage, facials, reflexology and hydrotherapy treatments. The *Redland Cottage* **B&B** (306/694-5563, www.bbcanada.com/3418.html; ❺), in a tree-lined residential area at 1122 Redland Ave, has comfortable bedrooms and full breakfasts. The *River Park Campground*, 300 River Drive (306/692-5474; $20–30; mid-April to Sept) is 2km southeast of the centre.

The Town

Downtown, bisected north–south by Main Street and east–west by Manitoba Street, is fairly dispiriting, though a string of **murals** of early pioneer days concentrated along 1st Avenue NW do their best to cheer things up. That apart, some streets look as if they've changed little since the 1920s, the wide treeless avenues framed by solemn brick warehouses, hotels and porticoed banks. One block north of Manitoba Street, the best example is **River Street**, whose rough-and-ready *Royal* and *Brunswick* hotels were once favourite haunts of the gangsters.

Next door to "Tunnel Central" (see box below), Joyner's General Store, at 30 Main St North, is worth a quick look for the complicated **cash carrier system** used by department stores (before the invention of the till) that carried shoppers' cash by cable to the accountants upstairs. It's one of only two in the world still operating and was kept here despite Euro-Disney's attempts to purchase it. A replica of one of Moose Jaw's original electric trams, the **Moose Jaw Trolley**

The tunnels of Moose Jaw

A network of **tunnels** runs underneath River Street from the basements of some of the city's oldest buildings. No one knows who built these passageways – or why – but what is known is that Chinese railway workers extended and used them in the early 1900s, hoping to escape the $500 "head tax", a measure designed to force them to return to famine-stricken China after the completion of their railway work. Later, during Prohibition, Chicago gangsters used the tunnels to negotiate deals for Canada's liquor supplies and to hide out when things got too hot in Chicago.

The **Tunnels of Moose Jaw** (hours vary monthly but approximately: June–Sept Mon–Fri 10am–7pm, Sat & Sun 10am–8pm; Oct–May daily noon–5.30pm; tours every 20min; one tour $14, two tours $23 306/693-5261, www.tunnelsofmoosejaw.com) are two entertaining fifty-minute tours. The **Chicago Connection** tour is a light-hearted look at the capers of Al Capone's men in the tunnels, complete with a speakeasy, a police bust and an actor playing the particularly slimy Chief of Police. The more serious **Passage to Fortune** tour tells the horrific story of the Chinese immigrants, with recreations of a Chinese laundry, sweatshops, a herbalist and an opium den. Costumed guides ham it up along the way, helped by old movies and state-of-the-art animatronics. Tours begin at **Tunnel Central**, 16 Main St North, in a reception area with a beautiful copper ceiling and walls adorned with local photos from the early decades of the twentieth century.

(May–Oct 1.15pm, 3.15pm, 4.30pm & 7pm; 1hr 15min; $10), travels local sights with a guide who dwells on the town's shady past. It leaves from opposite the *Temple Gardens Mineral Spa* and from the *Heritage Inn* on Main Street. Moose Jaw's branch of the **Western Development Museum** (Jan–March Tues–Sun 9am–5pm; April–Dec daily 9am–5pm; $8.50; Ⓦwww.wdmuseum.sk.ca), lies about 2km from the centre, beside the Trans-Canada Hwy as it loops around the northern edge of town. Divided into sections covering air, land, water and rail transport, exhibits include a replica steamship, several CPR coaches, fragile old planes and a 1934 Buick converted to carry the chief superintendent along the rail line.

Eating and drinking

Worthwhile **places to eat** include the *Copper Café* in the 1910 Land Titles building at 76 Fairford St West, which has wonderful daily specials and is part of the Yvette Moore Gallery. Otherwise, the *Prairie Oasis Restaurant*, at Hwy 1 East and Thatcher Drive, specializes in freshly baked pies, while *Bobby's Place*, 639 High St East, is a bustling brewpub and the fairly formal *Hopkins Dining Parlour*, 65 Athabasca St West, in a pleasant Victorian house, has a wide-ranging menu and main courses from $20. For something more exotic, try the very good *Nit's Thai Food*, 124 Main St North (mains from $7).

The Big Muddy Badlands

At the end of the last Ice Age, torrents of meltwater produced a massive gash in the landscape near the US border south of Moose Jaw. Edged by rounded hills and flat-topped buttes rising up to 200m above the valley floor, the **Big Muddy Valley** is best explored with organized tours (May–Oct Sat–Mon & Thurs 9.30am; $45; Ⓣ306/267-3300) from dreary **CORONACH**, about 200km from Regina. Tours include: visits to Indian burial cairns; the dramatic **Castle Butte**, a sandstone formation rising above the plains that resembles the backdrop for a Western movie (without a guide you'll find it by turning west off Hwy 34 in the Big Muddy Valley along the only road); the small prairie town of **BIG BEAVER**, where Aust's general store is the social centre; and a couple of outlaw caves, the refuge of American rustlers and robbers like Butch Cassidy and Dutch Henry. Cassidy and his Wild Bunch gang established an outlaw trail that connected the Big Muddy with Mexico via a series of safe houses; their antics were curtailed by the arrival of a detachment of Mounties in 1904, led by a Corporal Bird, known ruefully as the "man who never sleeps".

The Coronach **tourist office** (mid-June to Aug 9am–7pm; Ⓣ306/267-3312) at the north end of Centre Street can provide information on the history and geography of the area. **Accommodation** in Coronach includes the *Country Boy Motel* (Ⓣ306/267-3267; ❸) at the junction of hwys 18 and 36, opposite the Pioneer Grain elevator. The only place to eat is the reasonable *Touch Of Class*, at 228 Centre, with its predictable pan-American choices.

Grasslands National Park

Directly west of the Big Muddy, accessible along Hwy 18, **Grasslands National Park** is predominantly mixed-grass prairie, a flat, bare badlands broken up by splendid coulees, buttes and river valleys – notably the wide ravine edging the Frenchman River in the western block. Far from the moderating influence of the oceans, the area has a savage climate, with an average low in January of -22°C and temperatures that soar to 40°C in summer. Even so, this terrain is inhabited by many species adapted to cope with the shortage of water: prairie grasses, rabbit brush and different types of cacti, as well as the graceful pronghorn antelope, rattlesnakes and Canada's only colonies of black-tailed prairie dog, all thrive here.

Arrival and information

Currently, the park consists of east and west sections separated by private ranches and farms, which the federal government eventually intends to buy, creating a single park stretching from Hwy 4 in the west to hwys 2 and 18 in the east. The **western** section is more scenic and accessible, its limited system of gravel tracks and roads cutting in from hwys 8 and 4, south and east of **VAL MARIE**, which itself houses the **Grasslands National Park Reception Centre** (mid-May to early Sept daily 8am–5pm; late Sept to Oct & April to late May Mon–Fri 8am–noon; ⓣ306/298-2257, ⓦwww.parkscanada.gc.ca/grasslands), at the junction of Hwy 4 and Centre Street. Park rangers provide advice on weather and road conditions, hand out maps, arrange for guided or self-guided eco-tours, issue camping permits and give tips on animal-spotting and hiking.

The few places to **stay** in town include the attractive *Convent Country Inn*, 4515 Hwy 4 (ⓣ306/289-4515, ⓦwww.convent.ca; ❷), a converted convent with lots of character that is also the best place to eat. Opposite is a well-worn **campsite** (May–Oct; $15–20).

The Park

There are no campsites within the park, but camping is allowed within 1km of its roads if you have purchased a $10 backcountry permit; take a good supply of water, a stout pair of walking shoes and a stick to sweep in front of you in tall grass or brush as a warning to **rattlesnakes**. Animal activity is at its height at dawn and dusk and during spring and autumn; whatever the season, you'll need a pair of binoculars.

One of the best **hikes** leads to 70 Mile Butte, a massive flat-topped promontory that is the highest point of land in the region, rising 100m above the valley floor with wonderful views of the waving prairie grasslands. To get there, drive south of Val Marie on Hwy 4, turn east at Butte Road and continue to the end of the road. While there is no marked trail, the way becomes obvious as you begin walking over the hills from the end of the road. Even just a couple of hours' walk will take you through exceptional country.

▲ Grasslands National Park, Saskatchewan

Swift Current and around

Driving west from Moose Jaw along the Trans-Canada Hwy, it's about 180km to **SWIFT CURRENT**, a small industrial city and farm-research centre.

It has limited attractions, the highlight of which is a **Mennonite Heritage Village** (late June to Aug Fri–Sun 2–7pm or by appointment; free; Ⓣ306/773-7685 Ⓦwww.mennoniteheritagevillage.ca) in Kinetic Park at 17th Avenue and South Railway Street East. This consists of a long, rectangular house and adjoining barn built between 1911 and 1915 and six buildings comprising **Doc's Town** (late June to Aug Sat & Sun noon–6pm and by appointment; $3; Ⓣ306/773-2944), an early twentieth-century replica prairie village with a fully functioning windmill, one-room schoolhouse and an old dancehall (now a tearoom), all transported here from rural Saskatchewan. The only other worthwhile stop is the **Art Gallery of Swift Current** (Mon–Thurs 2–5pm & 7–9pm, Fri–Sun 1–5pm; July & Aug closed Sun; free) at 411 Herbert St East, with its exhibitions of paintings, sculpture and ceramics by local and other Canadian artists.

Swift Current's **bus** station is at 143 4th Ave NW and its helpful **tourist office** (Mon–Fri 9am–5pm; Ⓣ306/778-9174, Ⓦwww.tourismswiftcurrent.ca), 44 Robert St West, lies at the junction of hwys 1 and 4.

Practicalities

Strung out along Hwy 1 north of the city, and along Hwy 4 south towards the US, are several comfortable **motels**, the best of which are the *Super 8 Motel*, 405 North Service Rd East (Ⓣ306/778-6088 or 1-800/800-8000; ❹) and the *Best Western Inn*, 105 George St (Ⓣ306/773-4660 or 1-800/773-8818, Ⓦwww.bestwestern.sk.ca; ❺). Both are just off the Trans-Canada Hwy, have pools and include a light self-service breakfast. Just north of the Trans-Canada Hwy is the small but convenient *Trail Campground* (Ⓣ306/773-8088; May to mid-Oct; $15–27). For **restaurants**, try *Carol's Diner*, 914 Central Ave North, which despite its dowdy appearance has good homecooked food.

Saskatchewan Landing Provincial Park

Reached by Hwy 4 and around 40km north of Swift Current is pretty little **Saskatchewan Landing Provincial Park**, covering both banks of the South Saskatchewan River, where it emerges from razorback hills to opens out into the large, artificial **Lake Diefenbaker**. The area was once an important and very difficult river crossing for aboriginal peoples and early settlers, and the staff at the park's **Goodwin House Visitors Centre** (June–Sept Mon–Fri 8am–4pm, Sat & Sun 10am–6pm; Oct–May Mon–Fri 8am–4pm), a beautiful century-old stone house, organize hikes through coulees and explain the significance of the crossing. There are also remains of several ancient teepee encampments in the area. You can **camp** in the north of the park at the *Bear Paw Campground* (Ⓣ306/375-5525; mid-May to Oct; $15–20) and rent kayaks ($7/hr) at the small marina.

Eastend

In 1994, one of only thirteen Tyrannosaurus Rex skeletons in the world was discovered near **EASTEND**, a tiny town 122km northwest of Grasslands National Park on Hwy 13. The T-Rex was named Scotty (after the bottle of scotch its discoverers consumed in celebration) and there is now a swish **T-Rex Discovery Centre** (daily: July & Aug 9am–9pm; Sept–June 9am–5pm; Ⓣ306/295-4009, Ⓦwww.trexcentre.ca; $8.45) about 1km north of town – worth hitting if you're travelling with children. After seeing a film on the difficulties involved in excavating Scotty, there's a small hands-on museum with replica bones of various dinosaurs.

The Hutterites

The **Hutterites**, the only prairie community to have maintained a utopian communal ideal, are members of an Anabaptist sect named after its first leader, Jacob Hutter. Originating in central Europe in the sixteenth century, they gradually moved east, ending up in Russia, which they abandoned for South Dakota in the 1870s. It was fifty years before they felt obliged to move again, their pacifism recoiling from the bellicosity that gripped their American neighbours during World War I. They moved north between 1918 and 1922, establishing a series of **colonies** where they were allowed to educate their children, speak their own language and avoid military service. In these largely self-sufficient communities tasks are still divided according to ability and skill, property is owned communally and social life is organized around a common dining room and dormitories. Economically prosperous, the Hutterite population continues to grow, with a new branch community being founded whenever the old one reaches a secure population of between one hundred and two hundred. Apart from the occasional skirmish with the outside world when they buy new land, the Hutterites have been left in peace and have resisted assimilation pressures more staunchly than the Mennonites (see p.543) and the Doukhobors (see pp.570, 708).

If you want to base yourself in Eastend for a more thorough exploration of the Grasslands park and the Frenchman River Valley, you could **stay** at the *Riverside Motel* (Ⓣ306/295-3630, Ⓦwww.dinocountry.com; ❷), just west of town on Hwy 13, which also has **camping** ($10–20), or at the basic but comfortable *Cypress Hotel*, 343 Red Coat Drive (Ⓣ306/295-3505; ❶), in the middle of town. For **food**, try *Jack's Café* on Red Coat Drive.

Maple Creek and the Great Sand Hills

From Swift Current it's another 130km along the Trans-Canada Hwy to **MAPLE CREEK**, situated 8km south of the hwy. Nicknamed "old cow town", it lies at the heart of ranching country, its streets full of pickup trucks, cowboy boots and stetsons; this all reaches wild heights in late September for the **Cowboy Poetry Gathering**, a literary celebration of the wrangler that draws cowboys from across North America.

Some of the late nineteenth-century brick storefronts have survived, and the trim and tidy **Old Timers' Museum** (May–Sept Tues–Sat 9am–5.30pm, Sun & Mon 1–5pm; $4), at 218 Jasper St, has good displays on pioneer life and the Mounties. The place is also the market town for a number of **Hutterite colonies** (see above), whose women stand out with their floral dresses and headscarves.

Perhaps Maple Creek's biggest selling point is its proximity to the Cypress Hills and the **Great Sand Hills**. The latter, north of the Trans-Canada Hwy on Hwy 21, incorporates a large area of giant sand dunes, home to hordes of kangaroo rats as well as mule deer and antelope. The best place to view the dunes is east off Hwy 21. From the village of **LIEBENTHAL** follow the road east in the direction of Fitters Ranch for 17.6km before turning off north for the final 2km to the dunes parking lot. You can also get here from **SCEPTRE**, 18.4km to the north of the dunes where the small **Great Sandhills Museum** (mid-May to early Sept Mon–Sat 10am–noon & 12.30–4.30pm, Sun 1–5pm; $3) on Hwy 32 has displays on the ecology of the hills and can provide printed directions.

The Cypress Hills

South of the Trans-Canada Hwy, the wooded ridges of the **Cypress Hills** rise above the plains in a 130-kilometre-long plateau that in places reaches a height of

1400m – the highest point in Canada between Labrador and the Rockies. This elevation left the area untouched by glaciers as they moved south during the Ice Age, scouring the land bare of vegetation. The Cypress Hills also have a wetter and milder climate than the treeless plains surrounding them, creating a rich variety of woodland, wetland and grassland. In turn, this comparatively lush vegetation supports a wealth of wildlife, including elk, lynx, bobcats, coyotes, plus about two hundred species of bird, over half of whom breed in the hills; keep an eye out for the colonies of long-necked wild turkeys, as well as the sage grouse, whose bizarre courting rituals involve the male swelling out his chest and discharging air with a sound like a gunshot. One surprise – considering the name – is the actual absence of cypress trees. The early French *voyageurs* seem to have confused the area's predominant lodgepole pines with the jack pines of Québec, a species they called *cyprès*. Literal-minded translation did the rest.

Two separate sections of the hills have been set aside as the **Cypress Hills Interprovincial Park**: Saskatchewan's **Centre Block** lies to the south of Maple Creek along Hwy 21; the larger **West Block** spans the Saskatchewan–Alberta border, accessible from Maple Creek along Hwy 271 in the east and via Alberta's Hwy 41

The Cypress Hills Massacre and the fate of the Plains Indians

From the mid-eighteenth century, the Cypress Hills lay in a sort of neutral zone between the **Blackfoot** and the **Cree**, whose intermittent skirmishing was small-scale until the 1860s, when the depletion of the Crees' traditional hunting grounds forced them west. Some three thousand Cree reached the Cypress Hills in 1865 and the violence began just four years later with the murder of the Cree peacemaker, Maskepetoon. Casualties in the ensuing war were high, with two smallpox epidemics making things worse.

In 1871 the Cree sued for peace, but both sides were exhausted, their morale, health and social structures further undermined by **whiskey traders** who'd moved into the region. These traders were mostly American and brought their liquor north in the autumn, returning south in late spring laden with furs and buffalo robes. Though it was illegal to supply the aboriginal people with booze, the traders spread out across the southern plains (aptly nicknamed **Whoop-up Country**), establishing dozens of posts whose occupants were protected from their disorderly customers by log stockades. In the spring of 1873, there were two such outposts beside **Battle Creek**, deep in the Cypress Hills. For reasons that remain obscure, though prevailing drunkenness no doubt played a part, this was the scene of a violent confrontation between a group of white wolf-hunters, whiskey traders and a band of Assiniboine. Equipped with the latest fast-action rifles, the hunters and traders riddled an Assiniboine camp with bullets, killing up to seventy before packing up and heading back across the US border. News of the incident, known as the **Cypress Hills Massacre**, filtered back to Ottawa and helped speed up the recruitment of the newly formed **North West Mounted Police**, who received their first posting west that autumn (see p.536).

The Mounties later attempted to have eight of the participants in the massacre extradited from the US, but failed. Three of these men were later arrested in Canada and a trial was held in Winnipeg in 1876, but due to confilcting testimony and a lack of evidence showing premeditation, all three were acquitted; no one was ever punished.

First Nations people appreciated the efforts the Mounties had made to ensure justice and were heartened somewhat by the thought that everyone was going to be seen as equal in the eyes of this new force tasked with maintaining law and order. The Mounties may have kept the peace, but the deeper truth was that they were a major part of a policy of containment and control of aboriginal peoples, spearheading a determined push that would force them on to reservations, thereby opening the area for European settlers.

in the west. The West Block is also attached to **Fort Walsh**, a partly refurbished Mountie station and replica trading post. The three north–south access hwys present no problems, but the east-west drive across the park – the **Gap Road** – is difficult since it includes two long stretches of gravel and clay track suitable only for high clearance four-wheel drive vehicles in dry weather. Call ⓣ306/662-5411 to check road conditions before travel.

The Centre Block

About 30km south of Maple Creek off Hwy 21, a paved side-road heads into the park's **Centre Block** (entry $7), a rough rectangle of hilly land dominated by a forest of lodgepole pines. At the centre, a pleasant tourist resort surrounds tiny **Loch Leven**, complete with canoe and bike rental facilities, shops and a petrol station. There's also a modest nature centre adjoining the **park office** (Mon–Thurs 8am–8pm, Fri–Sun 8am–10pm; ⓣ306/662-5411 or 1-800/205-7070, ⓦwww.cypresshills.com), which has useful maps and trail brochures. The resort is a popular holiday destination, but it's easy to escape the crowds along the half-dozen hiking trails. There's one **hotel**, the modern *Cypress Park Resort Inn* (ⓣ306/662-4477; ④), with rooms, cabins and apartments. Close by, there are several busy summer **campsites** ($13–24), which have to be booked at the campsite office (mid-May to Aug daily 8.30am–10pm) on Pine Avenue, west of the centre, or on ⓣ306/662-5484.

The West Block: Saskatchewan side

The eastern side of the park's **West Block** alternates between thick forest and open grassland and is broken up by steep hills and deep, sheltered ravines. Hwy 271 enters from the east and becomes increasingly bumpy as it twists towards **Fort Walsh National Historic Park** (mid-May to early Sept daily 9.30am–5.30pm; $9.80 ⓣ306/662-3590, off-season 662-2645), which has excellent displays on the Plains Indians, fort history and the development of the RCMP. A five-minute walk behind the information centre, Fort Walsh sits in a wide, low-lying valley, its trim stockade framed by pine forests. Built in 1875, the fort was abandoned in favour of Maple Creek just eight years later; in 1942 the RCMP acquired the land, and most of the present buildings date from that decade. Guides in period costumes enliven a tour of whitewashed log buildings, the whole site having returned to its original appearance. Close to the fort is a cemetery containing the tombstones of several North West Mounted Police officers. Every 45 minutes a minibus makes the trip from the information centre over the hills to Battle Creek, where Abel Farwell's whiskey trading post has been reconstructed to commemorate the 1873 Cypress Hills Massacre (see p.545). Guides will also take you to the actual site of the massacre.

The main **accommodation** in this part of the park is the *West Block Campground* (ⓣ306/662-5489 or 1-800/205-7070; May–Sept; $16), 5km north of Fort Walsh, in a dense stand of lodgepole pines with a brook running through it. It's in an isolated spot, so take your own food and drink. From the campsite you can make an expedition to the **Conglomerate Cliffs**, a few kilometres to the northeast near Adams Lake. These are strange-looking walls of rock, some 150m high, composed of multicoloured cobblestones.

The West Block: Alberta side

The lodgepole forests and deep coulees of the Alberta section of the West Block are centred on the resort of **ELKWATER**, 34km south of the Trans-Canada Hwy on Hwy 41. Curving round the southern shore of Elkwater Lake, the village has a comprehensive range of facilities, from boat and bike rental through to a sandy beach and saunas. There's also a **visitor centre** (mid-May to mid–Sept Mon–Fri 9am–7pm; ⓣ403/893-3833, ⓦwww.cypresshills.com), which runs guided walks throughout the summer.

For **accommodation**, try the *Elkwater Lodge* (ⓣ403/893-3811 or 1-888/893-3811, ⓦwww.elkwaterlodge.com; ⑥), which has suites and cabins, along with a saltwater pool and hot tub, while the *Elkwater Campground* has both simple and hook-up sites ($22–34). Southwest of Elkwater a paved road leads to Horseshoe Canyon and **Head of the Mountain**, where there are striking views over the hills towards Montana; other roads lead east to Reesor Lake and Spruce Coulee Reservoir. Beside the roads there are twelve other campsites (May–Aug), bookable on ⓣ403/893-3782.

Medicine Hat

Moving on from the Saskatchewan side of Cypress Hills will take you over the provincial border and into **Alberta**, where the first major town you'll encounter is **MEDICINE HAT**. Although only just over one hundred years old, the origin of its wonderful name has already been confused. The most likely story has to do with a Cree medicine man who lost his headdress fleeing a battle with the Blackfoot; his followers lost heart at the omen, surrendered, and were promptly massacred. These days you rarely see the town mentioned without the adage that it "has all hell for a basement", a quotation Rudyard Kipling coined in response to the huge reserves of natural gas below the town. The gas fields feed a flourishing petrochemical industry which blots the otherwise park-studded downtown area on the banks of the South Saskatchewan River.

The town's main landmark is the world's **tallest teepee** beside the Trans-Canada Hwy, a metal structure of twenty storeys, close to the town's **visitor centre**. The most rewarding attraction is **Medalta** (Mid-may to early Sept daily 9.30am–5pm; early Sept to mid-May Tues–Sat 10am–4pm; ⓣ403/529-1070, ⓦwww.medalta.org), at 713 Medalta Ave SE, one of a series of old pottery factories that clustered here in the early 1900s, drawn by cheap natural gas. To get there, drive from the visitor centre in the direction of downtown, following signs for the "Historic Clay District". The factory specialized in turning out sturdy tableware, or "war ware" as the simple cream-coloured pieces with their clean lines were dubbed, before mismanagement and a series of crippling strikes led to the factory's closure in 1954. It lay idle for half a century, until its reincarnation as an industrial heritage site. Partial refurbishment has helped provide spaces for exhibits, but it's the untouched parts, in their original battered state at the time of closure, that give the best feel for the place, as does the chance to watch replicas being handmade. Other museum highlights include samples of pottery personally commissioned by Haile Selassie for the Ethiopian court.

Practicalities

Inexpensive motels are easy to find around the fringes of town. Downtown, try the *Medicine Hat Inn*, 530 4th St SE (ⓣ403/526-1313 or 1-800/730-3887; ③) a basic but clean motel. Better is the smart and comfortable *Medicine Hat Lodge*, 1051 Ross Glen Drive (ⓣ403/529-2222 or 1-800/661-8095, ⓦwww.medhatlodge.com; ⑤), with a health centre, pool and gamut of 4-star facilities.

For coffee and snacks try *Café Mundo*, 579 3rd St SE, while for a novelty "Wild West" setting head to *Rustler's*, 901 8th St SW (ⓣ403/526-8004), one of the town's oldest restaurants. The best place for food is *DeVine*, 579 3rd St SE (ⓣ430/580-5510, ⓦwww.devinegrill.com), a stylish fusion-food place with a bustling outdoor patio and gourmet versions of burgers ($15), along with venison loin ($30) or grilled marlin ($27).

The Alberta Badlands

Formed by the meltwaters of the last Ice Age, the Red Deer River valley cuts a deep gash through the prairie – about 240km northwest of Medicine Hat and 140km east of Calgary – creating a surreal landscape of bare, sunbaked hills and eerie lunar flats dotted with sagebrush and scrubby, tufted grass. On their own, the **Alberta Badlands** would justify a visit, but what makes them an essential detour is the **Royal Tyrrell Museum of Paleontology**, one of North America's greatest natural history museums. It's 8km outside **Drumheller**, a dreary but obvious base to explore the surrounding area. You'll need your own transport to explore and get to the **Dinosaur Provincial Park**, home to the Tyrrell Museum Field Station and the source of many of its fossils.

To access the badlands region from Medicine Hat, continue along the Trans-Canada Hwy, braching north at either Brooks or, further on, Calgary. If you're coming from Calgary and are without your own transport, Greyhound **buses** from there to Drumheller (around $66 return) makes a day-trip easily possible; check ⓣ1-800/667-8747 or ⓦwww.greyhound.ca for the latest schedules.

Dinosaur Provincial Park

A 130km drive west of Medicine Hat on Hwy 1 and Hwy 876 leads to **Dinosaur Provincial Park** (ⓣ403/378-4342, ⓦwww.tpr.alberta.ca/parks). Nestled among some of the baddest of the badlands, the park's landscape is not only one of Canada's most otherworldly, but also one of the world's richest fossil beds. Over three hundred complete skeletons have been found and dispatched to museums across the world, representing 35 (or ten percent) of all known dinosaur species. The **Royal Tyrrell Museum Field Station** (daily: April to mid-May 9am–4pm; mid-May to Aug 8.30am–7pm; Sept to mid-Oct 9am–4pm; mid-Oct to March Mon–Fri 9am–4pm; $2.50; ⓣ403/378-4344), is the park's obvious hub and a starting point for five self-guided **trails**, the Badlands Trail and the Cottonwood Flats Trail being the most worthwhile. The centre also has a small museum, but the real meat of a visit is the excellent ninety-minute **bus tour** (April to mid-Oct several daily; $8), to an otherwise out-of-bounds dinosaur dig near the centre of the park. A few exposed skeletons have been left *in situ*, with panels giving background information. The station also organizes a variety of guided **hikes**, most notably the three-hour Centrosaurus Bone Bed Hike (Tues, Thurs, Sat & Sun 9.15am; $8), which visits a restricted area where hundreds of centrosaurus skeletons have been uncovered. All tours fill up quickly, so book ahead on ⓣ404/378-4344. The excellent Dinosaur Provincial Park **campsite** (ⓣ403/378-3700year-round but only serviced May–Sept; $20–26) is close to the Field Station and beside Little Sandhill Creek.

Drumheller

A downbeat town in an extraordinary setting, **DRUMHELLER** lies roughly ninety minutes' drive northeast of Calgary or a two-hour drive on a series of remote dirt roads from Dinosaur Provincial Park. Nestled at the bottom of a parched canyon and surrounded by the detritus and spoil heaps of its mining past, the otherworldliness of the landscape is heightened by its contrast to the vivid colours of the wheat and grasslands above. Its Red Deer River once exposed not only dinosaur fossils but also coal seams, which attracted the likes of Samuel Drumheller, after whom the town is named. The first mine opened in 1911, but within fifty years it was all over as oil and gas sounded mining's death knell. Today, Drumheller is sustained by agriculture, oil and tourism. There's not much to do in its tiny hardscrabble downtown, but the **Royal Tyrrell Museum** ensures visitors pass through in droves. The town has gone out of its way to try to tempt them in, with dino-mania at every turn; the **visitor centre** itself, at 60 1st Avenue West (daily 9am–9pm; ⓣ403/823-1331 or 1-866/823-8100) is beside a 26.2m T-Rex mock-up that you can climb (daily 9am–9pm; $3).

The Greyhound **bus station** (ⓣ403/823-7566) is at 308 Centre St in the middle of town. It's too long to walk from there to the Tyrell museum, particularly on a hot day, but Jack's Taxi (ⓣ403/823-2220) will take you for about $10.

Royal Tyrrell Museum

A sleek building packed with high-tech displays and blended skilfully into desolate surroundings, the **Royal Tyrrell Museum** (daily: mid-May to Aug 9am–9pm; Sept to mid-Oct 10am–5pm; mid-Oct to mid-May Tues–Sun 10am–5pm; $10; ⓦwww.tyrrellmuseum.com), 6km outside Drumheller, will appeal to anyone with even a hint of scientific or natural curiosity. Although it claims the world's largest collection of complete dinosaur skeletons (120,000 specimens), the museum is far more than a load of old bones. As well as skilfully and entertainingly tracing the earth's natural history, it's also a leading research centre and you can watch scientists painstakingly scratch, blow and vacuum dirt from fossils. Hands-on activities include fossil casting or the chance to dig in a realistic quarry; book ahead for both. There's also a gift shop and cafeteria, while outside you can spend the best part of an hour exploring a 1.4km hiking trail dotted with various infoboards.

Practicalities

Accommodation in Drumheller is limited and often hard to find, so try to book ahead. Even the **campsites** fill quickly on summer weekends. One good option is the *River Grove Campground and Cabins* (ⓣ403/823-6655) with its well-shaded campsites (May–Sept; $28–40) and basic cabins (④) a short walk northwest of downtown at 25 Poplar St. For primitive sites with plenty of shade try the friendly riverside *Pinters Campground* (May–Oct; ⓣ403/823-5810; $15–26) 6km southwest of town along Hwy 10 in Rosedale. Back in Drumheller, the well-kept *Badlands Motel*, 801 North Dinosaur Trail (ⓣ403/823-5155; ④) is a no-frills place on the fringes of the town en route to the Tyrell Museum. For a little more you can stay southeast of town at the *Super 8 Motel*, 680 2nd St SE (ⓣ403/823-8887 or 1-888/823-8882; ⑥), which has an indoor pool.

Drumheller's **restaurants** come and go with alarming regularity, but longstanding options include *Whif's Flapjack House* in the *Badlands Motel*, a good place to breakfast or grab a burger later on, and the reasonably priced *Sizzling House*, 160 Centre St (ⓣ403/823-8098), one of Alberta's best Chinese restaurants, which also has good Thai dishes.

Around Drumheller

Though the **Royal Tyrrell Museum** is clearly the major local draw, the rest of the semi-arid Red Deer Valley is dotted with viewpoints and minor sights. For a **scenic drive** take the 48km **Dinosaur Trail**; maps are available from Drumheller's visitor centre. Highlights include the Little Church (capacity six) and **Horsethief Canyon** and **Orkney Viewpoint**, both of which offer spectacular panoramas of the wildly eroded valley and are connected by a small car ferry at Bleriot (daily 10am–8.45pm; free).

For easy badland **hikes**, try **Horseshoe Canyon**, 19km southwest of Drumheller on Hwy 9, where a multitude of good trails snake around the canyon floor. Other sights are an easy drive southwest of town and include the near ghost town (population 27) of **Wayne**, with its atmospheric Wild-West-style *Last Chance Saloon* and *Rosedeer Hotel* (Ⓣ403/823-9189; ③), a place where miners used to drink and brawl and still a great place for a buffalo burger and beer; pleasant tree-encircled tent sites ($15) are also offered. Another 9km southeast on Hwy 10 a series of **Hoodoos** – slender columns of wind-sculpted sandstone topped with mushroom-like caps – make for a good photo, while another 6km further on is the **Atlas Coal Mine** (tours May–June daily 9.30am–5.30pm; July–Aug daily 9.30am–8.30pm; Sept & Oct daily 10am–4pm; $14 for full tours; Ⓣ403/822-2220, Ⓦwww.atlascoalmine.ab.ca). Tours here go underground but also examine the teetering wooden "tipple" dominating the site: once used to sort ore it's now a beautiful and rather wistful piece of industrial archeology. More wistful still are the ruins of the near-ghost town of **Dorothy**, 14km along Hwy 10 from Drumheller and worth a peek if you're traveling to or from Dinosaur Provincial Park.

Highway 3 through Southern Alberta

The most travelled route across southern Alberta is Hwy 1, through Calgary; but **Hwy 3**, branching off at **Medicine Hat**, takes a more southerly course across the plains before finally breaching the Rockies at Crowsnest Pass. Though a quieter and less spectacular route into the mountains, it's the quicker way to Vancouver and holds a couple of worthwhile diversions, including the **Carriage Centre** near Cardston and the **Head-Smashed-In Buffalo Jump** heritage site.

Lethbridge

LETHBRIDGE thrives on the back of oil, gas and some of Alberta's most productive agricultural land, none of which is of much consequence to people passing through, who the city attempts to sidetrack with the **Nikka Yuko Centennial Gardens** (daily: early May to June & Sept to mid-Oct 9am–5pm; July & Aug 9am–8pm; $7; Ⓣ403/328-3511, Ⓦwww.nikkayuko.com) in its southeastern corner in Henderson Lake Park. Built in 1967 as a symbol of Japanese and Canadian amity, the gardens were a somewhat belated apology for the treatment of Japanese-Canadians during World War II when 22,000 were interned, six thousand of them in Lethbridge. Four tranquil landscapes make up the gardens, along with a pavilion of cypress wood handcrafted in Japan and perpetually laid out for a tea ceremony.

Far removed from the gardens' decorum is **Fort Whoop-Up** (April–May & Oct Wed–Sun 1–4pm; June–Sept daily 10am–5pm; Nov–March Sat & Sun 1–4pm; $7; Ⓣ403/329-0444, Ⓦwww.fortwhoopup.com) on Scenic Drive at 3rd Avenue, a reconstruction of the wild whiskey-trading post set up in 1869 by American desperadoes from Montana. It became the largest and most lucrative of the many similar illegal forts which sprang up all over the Canadian prairies and led directly to the arrival of the North West Mounted Police in 1874. Aboriginal peoples came from miles around to trade anything – including the clothes off their backs – for lethal hooch, which was fortified by grain alcohol and supplemented by ingredients such as red peppers, dye and chewing tobacco. The fort was also the scene of the last armed battle in North America between aboriginal peoples (between the Cree and Blackfoot in 1870).

Lethbridge's **bus station** is at 411 5th St South (Ⓣ403/327-1551). The **tourist office** is at 2805 Scenic Drive (summer daily 9am–8pm; winter Mon–Sat 9am–5pm; Ⓣ403/320-1222 or 1-800/661-1222), at the corner of hwys 4 and 5.

Practicalities

Most city **motels** line Hwy 5, while downtown options include the good-value *Days Inn*, at 100 3rd Ave South (Ⓣ403/327-6000 or 1-800/661-8085; ❻), and the *Lethbridge Lodge Hotel*, at 320 Scenic Drive (Ⓣ403/328-1123 or 1-800/661-1232, Ⓦwww.lethbridgelodge.com; ❻), which boasts *Anton's*, an upmarket **restaurant** with modern North American food, and the cheaper *Botanica*. Downtown coffee and snacks can be had at *The Penny Coffee House*, 331 5th St South.

Fort Macleod and around

FORT MACLEOD, 50km west of Lethbridge, catches traffic travelling between the US and Calgary on Hwy 2, which eases around the town centre past the largely rebuilt wooden palisade of the **Fort Museum** (May Tues–Fri 9am–5pm; June daily 9am–5pm; July to early Sept 9am–6pm; early Sept to Oct Wed–Sun 10am–4pm; $7.50; Ⓦwww.nwmpmuseum.com), at 219 25th St. One for die-hard Mountie fans, this was the first fort established in Canada's Wild West by the North West Mounted Police, who got lost after being dispatched to raid Fort Whoop-Up in Lethbridge, allowing the whiskey traders to flee; finding Whoop-Up empty, they continued west under Colonel James Macleod to establish a permanent barracks here on Oldman Island on the river in 1874. The RCMP "musical ride", a display of precision riding, is performed four times daily in July and August by students in replica dress.

The town has several similarly priced **motels**, the most central being the *Fort Motel* on Main Street (Ⓣ403/553-3606; ❷), but the top choice is the *Sunset Motel* (Ⓣ403/553-4448, Ⓦwww.sunset-motel.ca; ❹), located on Hwy 3 at the western entrance to town. All fill quickly in summer.

Head-Smashed-In Buffalo Jump

The image of Indians trailing a lone buffalo with bow and arrow may be Hollywood's idea of how aboriginal peoples secured food, but the truth, while less romantic, was often far more effective and spectacular. Over a period of ten thousand years, Blackfoot hunters perfected a technique of luring buffalo herds into a shallow basin and stampeding them to their deaths over a broad cliff, where they were then butchered for meat (dried to make pemmican, a cake of pounded meat, berries and lard), bone (for tools) and hide (for clothes and shelter). Such "jumps" existed all over North America, but **Head-Smashed-In Buffalo Jump** (daily: July to early Sept 9am–5pm; rest of year 10am–5pm; $9; Ⓣ403/553-2731, Ⓦwww.head-smashed-in.com), 18km northwest of Fort Macleod on Hwy 785, is the best preserved. Its name is a literal description of how a nineteenth-century Blackfoot met his end after deciding the best spot to watch the jump was at the base of the cliff, apparently unaware he was about to be visited by five hundred plummeting buffalo. The modern **interpretive centre** delves deep into the history of the jump and native culture in general. Its highlight, a film entitled *In Search of the Buffalo*, recreates the thunderous death plunge using a herd of buffalo which were slaughtered, frozen and then somehow made to look like live animals hurtling to their deaths. Below the multilevel facility, a ten-metre-deep bed of ash and bones accumulated over millennia is protected by the threat of a $50,000 fine for anyone foolish enough to rummage for souvenirs. All manner of artefacts and objects have been discovered amid the debris, including knives, scrapers and sharpened stones used to skin bison. Metal arrowheads in the topmost layers, traded with white settlers, suggest the jump was used until the early nineteenth century.

Around the centre are a couple of kilometres of **trails**, the starting point for tours conducted by Blackfoot native guides. No public transport serves the site; taxis from Fort Macleod cost about $22.

Remington Carriage Centre

The **Remington Carriage Centre** (July to early Sept 9am–6pm; early Sept to May 10am–5pm; $9; ⓦ www.remingtoncarriagemuseum.com) is in **CARDSTON**, which is just off Hwy 2 and about 50km south of Fort Macleod. To get to the museum leave the town centre, cross the river and make for 623 Main St. Centring on horse-drawn vehicles and evoking the atmosphere of their nineteenth-century heyday, the museum is as brilliantly executed as its appeal is limited. The main hall boasts around sixty working carriages and around 140 in passive display, the exhibits cleverly integrated with "stories" that place them in their social and cultural context. You can ride the carriages (usually free), see working stables, admire magnificent horses from the centre's herd, and watch carriages being built and renovated. Guides are often in period dress and run regular guided tours.

Crowsnest Pass

Crowsnest Pass (1382m) is the most southerly of the three major routes into the Rockies and BC from Alberta, and less attractive than the Calgary and Edmonton approaches. As Hwy 3 pushes west out of Fort Macleod across glorious windblown prairie, it augurs well: the settlements are bleaker and more backwoods in appearance and the vast unbroken views to the mountain-filled horizon appear much as they must have to the first pioneers. But as the road climbs towards the pass the grime and dereliction of the area's mining heritage make themselves increasingly felt. Hopes a century ago that Crowsnest's vast coal deposits might make it the "Pittsburgh of Canada" were dashed by disasters, poor-quality coal, complicated seams, cheaper coal from BC and rapid obsolescence in the face of oil and gas. Today much of the area has been declared an historic district and turned into Alberta's only "eco-museum", a desperate attempt to bring life and tourist cash back to economically blighted communities. If mines and disaster sites don't appeal, the Crowsnest route west is of most use as a direct route if you're hurrying to Vancouver or aim to explore the Kootenays in southern BC. After breasting the pass, Hwy 3 drops into BC passing through Fernie (see p.703).

Bellevue and Hillcrest

Sleepy **BELLEVUE** is the first village west of Fort Macleod worthy of a stop. It's an oddball and close-knit spot with an old-world feel unusual in these parts, and is distinguished by a church the size of a dog kennel and a wooden teepee painted lemon yellow. It supports a small summer-only **tourist office** by the campsite and provides visitors with the opportunity to explore – complete with hard hat and miner's lamp – a wonderfully dark and dank 100m or so of the old **Bellevue Mine** (30min tours every half-hour mid-May to early Sept daily 10am–5.30pm; $10). The only local mine open to the public, it ceased production in 1962, but remains infamous for a 1910 explosion that destroyed the ventilator fan; thirty men died in the disaster, not from the blast, but by breathing so-called "afterdamp", a lethal mixture of carbon dioxide and carbon monoxide left after fire has burnt oxygen from the atmosphere.

As if this wasn't enough, Canada's worst mining disaster ever had occurred five years earlier at **HILLCREST**, a village immediately south of Bellevue (signed from Hwy 3), when 189 men were killed by an explosion and afterdamp. All were buried in mass graves in the Hillcrest Cemetery on 8th Avenue.

Bellevue has a quaint **campsite**, the *Bellecrest Community Association Campground* (May–Oct; by donation) beside the hwy just east of the village, with toilets, tap water and an on-site ten-seat church with recorded sermons. The site is also handy for the **Leitch Collieries Provincial Historic Site** (mid-May to early Sept daily 10am–5pm; winter site unstaffed; by donation), beside the main road east of the campsite. This was once the region's largest mining and coking concern; it was also the first to close (in 1915). Today, there are few old buildings, but boardwalk trails lead you past interpretive "listening posts" which fill you in on mining techniques.

The Frank Slide and Blairmore

The Crowsnest Pass trail of destruction, death and disaster continues beyond Bellevue. Dominating the skyline behind the village are the crags and vast rock fall of the **Frank Slide**, an enormous landslide that transformed Turtle Mountain, whose contours were once riddled with the galleries of local mines. On April 29, 1903 an estimated one hundred million tonnes of rock on a front stretching for over 1km and 700m high trundled down the mountain, burying 68 people and their houses in under two minutes. Amazingly, no miners were killed – they dug themselves out after fourteen hours of toil. The morbidly interesting **Frank Slide Interpretive Centre** (July to early Sept 9am–6pm; early Sept to May 10am–5pm; $9; ⓦwww.frankslide.com;), 1.5km off the Hwy and 1km east of the village of Frank, highlights European settlement in the area, the coming of the CPR and the technology, attitudes and lives of local miners. It's well worth wandering around the site and slide area. There's a 1.5-kilometre trail or you can walk up the ridge above the car park for good views and an idea of the vast scale of the earth movement; no one to this day quite understands the science of how boulders travelled so far from the main slide (several kilometres in many cases). "Air lubrication" – an occurrence by which the cascading rock compressed the air in front of it, creating a hovercraft-like cushion of trapped air on which it "rode" across the surface – is the best theory.

The scrappy settlement of **BLAIRMORE**, 2km beyond the slide, is redeemed only by the walks and dozen ski runs on Pass Powder Keg Ski Hill (day-pass $30; ⓣ403/562-8334, ⓦwww.passpowderkeg.ca) above it. Beyond Blairmore the road climbs towards **Crowsnest Pass** and, after a rash of sawmills, the natural scenery finally takes centre stage in a reassuring mix of lakes, mountains and trees protected by **Crowsnest Provincial Park**. A rustic provincial **campsite** ($10) overlooks the lake at Crowsnest Creek, 21km west of Blairmore.

Calgary

Though it's southern Alberta's likeable and booming focus, **CALGARY** is also an easy hour's drive east of where the prairies buckle into the **Rockies** to form some of the continent's most magnificent scenery. So it takes some self-restraint to give this city at the confluence of the Bow and Elbow rivers the day or two it deserves. Its compact, high-rise downtown core – which seemingly appeared overnight on the back of a 1970s oil bonanza – isn't too thrilling, but does contain the prestigious and extremely worthwhile **Glenbow Museum**. Immediately outside downtown are several lesser museums, historic sites and attractions that recall something of the city's origins as a frontier town. The city is probably best known as the home of the **Calgary Stampede**, a veritable cowboy carnival dubbed "the greatest outdoor show on earth", which takes place over ten days every July. It inspires most of the city (while irritating the remainder of it) and plenty of tourists to indulge in the boots-and-stetson image that's still a way of life in the surrounding. As such, Calgary's "Cowtown" nickname still has resonance – but not nearly as much relevance, given the wealth the oil and gas industry has brought to the city in the last forty years. These riches have seen the city's population grow to just over one million, many of whom live in an ever-growing cookie-cutter

▲ Calgary's skyline

suburban sprawl – albeit with the occasional superb view of the Rockies. Despite this Calgary is still an energetic place, harbouring a burgeoning **arts** and **culture** scene, excellent **restaurants** and cafés, splendid parks and some lively, trendy neighbourhoods good for just strolling around in.

The city is also a great hub for day-trips to the dinosaur remains in the strange **Badlands** around **Drumheller** to the east (see p.548) and to **Head-Smashed-In Buffalo Jump** (see p.551), an aboriginal site in the heart of Alberta's cowboy country to the south.

A brief history of Calgary

Modern Calgary is one of Canada's largest and youngest cities. It was once the domain of the **Blackfoot**, who ranged over the whole area for several thousand years. About three hundred years ago, they were joined by the **Sarcee**, forced south by war from their northern heartlands, and the **Stoney**, who migrated north with Sitting Bull into southern Saskatchewan and then Alberta.

Europeans first began to gather here in the late 1700s; explorer **David Thompson** wintered here during his travels, while the **Palliser expedition** spent time nearby en route for the Rockies. Settlers started arriving from around 1870, when hunters moved into the region from the United States, where they had hunted buffalo to the edge of extinction. In 1875, soon after the creation of the first North West Mounted Police stockade at Fort Macleod (see p.551), a second fort was built further north. A year later it was christened **Fort Calgary**, named after the Scottish birthplace of its assistant commissioner. The word *calgary* is Gaelic for "clear running water"; it was felt the ice-clear waters of the Bow and Elbow rivers were reminiscent of the "old country".

By 1883 a station had been built close to the fort, part of the new trans-Canadian **railway**. The township laid out nearby quickly attracted **ranchers** and British gentlemen farmers, cementing an enduring Anglo-Saxon cultural bias. By 1886, fires had wiped out most of the town's temporary wooden buildings and tents, leading to an edict declaring all new buildings should be constructed in sandstone and, for a while, Calgary was nicknamed "Sandstone City". It achieved

The Calgary Stampede

The annual **Calgary Stampede** brings around 1.25m spectators and participants to the city for ten days in early July. This is far more than a carefully engineered gift to Calgary's tourist industry, however, for the event is one of the world's biggest rodeos and comes close to living up to its "greatest outdoor show on earth" billing.

The competition end of things is taken very seriously. The rodeo is said to be North America's roughest and the combined prize money reaches $2 million. The first show in 1912 put up $100,000 and attracted sixty thousand people to the opening parade, with a line-up that included two thousand aboriginal people in full ceremonial garb and Pancho Villa's bandits in a show erroneously billed as a swan song for the cowboy of the American West ("The Last and Best Great West Frontier Days").

Stampede events

Things officially kick off on the first Friday of Stampede with the **parade**, timed to begin at 9am, though most spectators are in place along the route at 6am. The two-hour march involves around 170 entries, four thousand participants and 750 horses. For the duration of Stampede, downtown's **Olympic Plaza** (temporarily renamed Rope Square) offers free pancake breakfasts (8.15–11.30am) and entertainment every morning; events include live music, mock gunfights and aboriginal dancing, and square dancing also fills parts of Stephen Avenue Mall at 10am. If you want to really experience how the city celebrates Stampede move outside this central area, where you'll find entire neighbourhoods, shops, bars, churches and even local luminaries organizing their own festivities (usually a pancake breakfast; check ⓦwww.stampedebreakfasts.com for listings). **Nightlife** is a world unto itself, with Stampede locations giving way to music, dancing, mega-cabarets, plus lots of drinking, eating (it's barbecue heaven), fireworks and general partying into the small hours.

The Stampede's real action – the rodeo and allied events – takes place in **Stampede Park**, southeast of downtown and best reached by C-Train to Victoria Park–Stampede Station. This vast open area contains an amusement park, concert and show venues, bars, restaurants and a huge range of stalls and shows that take the best part of a day to see. Entrance is $14, which allows you to see all the **entertainment** except the rodeo and chuck-wagon races. Things to see include: the aboriginal village, where members of the Blackfoot, Blood, Sarcee, Stoney and Piegan first nations set up a teepee village (tours available); the John Deere Show Ring, scene of the World Blacksmith Competition; the Centennial Fair, which hosts events for children; the Agricultural Building, home to displays of cattle and other livestock; the outdoor Coca-Cola Stage, used for evening concerts; and Nashville North, an indoor country music venue.

To see the daily **rodeo** competition – bronco and bull riding, calf-roping, steer-wrestling, barrel racing and the rest – you'll need another ticket and unless you've bought these in advance it's hardly worth it: you'll likely be in poor seats and miles from the action. You'll also need a ticket (also best bought in advance) to watch the other big event, the ludicrously dangerous but hugely exciting **chuck-wagon** races. Both events are held in the Stampede Park grandstand.

Stampede practicalities

If you're coming to see the Stampede, plan ahead. **Accommodation** is stretched and prices can skyrocket for the duration. **Tickets** for the rodeo and chuck-wagon races range from $12–345; tickets for the finals of both events are a few dollars more; all tickets include park admission (waiving the need to pay $14). For ticket and all other general information, check ⓦwww.calgarystampede.com.

Shuttles to Banff and Lake Louise

Direct **buses** from the airport to **Banff** and **Lake Louise** mean you can be in Banff National Park a couple of hours after collecting your baggage. Services include: Banff Airporter (10 daily to Banff, $53; ⓣ403/762-3330 or 1-888/449-2901, ⓦwww.banffairporter.com); Brewster Transportation (2–3 daily to Banff, $55; 2–7 to Lake Louise, $71; 1 daily to Jasper, $133; ⓣ403/760-6934 or 1-800/760-6934, ⓦwww.brewster.ca). **Tickets** are available from separate desks in airport arrivals.

official city status in 1894, something it had taken rival Edmonton over a hundred years to achieve.

Cattle and the railway generated exceptional growth, though the city's rise was nothing compared with the prosperity that followed the discovery of **oil**. The first strike took place in 1914 in nearby Turner Valley. An oil refinery opened in 1923 and since then Calgary has rarely looked back. When prices soared during the oil crisis of the 1970s, the city exploded, becoming a world energy and financial centre – headquarters for some four hundred oil-related businesses.

Today, only Toronto acts as headquarters for more major Canadian corporations. Crucially though, Calgary has diversified into light manufacturing, high-tech, film, transportation and tourism, with 3.1 million visitors to the city every year.

Arrival and information

Approaching Calgary **by air** you're rewarded (in the right weather) with a magnificent view of the Rockies stretching across the western horizon; **Calgary International Airport** (ⓦwww.calgaryairport.com) is about 15km northeast of downtown. There's a small **information centre** (daily 10am–10pm) in arrivals, where you'll also find courtesy phones to hotels and car-rental agencies; most of the hotels are well away from the centre but at least usually served by courtesy shuttles. The cheapest way downtown is with Calgary Transit service #57 (every 20–30min 6am–midnight) which costs $2.50 but takes around an hour. A taxi downtown costs $30. Several airport hotels offer a shuttle service from the arrivals level bus bays #10 and #11. Otherwise, the Allied Downtown Shuttle Service (daily: 8am–midnight every 30min ⓣ403/299-9555, ⓦwww.airportshuttlecalgary.ca) provides transport between downtown pick-up points and the airport at bus bay #8; the Allied Shuttle counter is on the arrivals level near gate "C". Shuttles only stop at downtown locations if there is a booking, which can be made either over the phone or online.

Calgary's Greyhound **bus station** (ⓣ403/263-1234 or 1-800/661-8747) is somewhat inconveniently west of downtown at 8th Avenue SW and 850-16th St. From here, it's a twemty-minute walk along 9th Avenue SW, then north along 10th Street until you reach the end of the C-train line. Taxis to downtown are $6. The Calgary **tourist office** is in the base of the Calgary Tower at 101 9th Ave SW (daily 8am–5pm; ⓣ403/263-8510 or 1-800/661-1678, ⓦwww.tourismcalgary.com).

City transport

Almost everything in Calgary, barring Stampede locations and a few minor diversions, is a comfortable walk away from the centre – except in winter, when temperatures can make any excursion an ordeal. The city's much-vaunted **Plus 15** system (a reference to its height from the ground in feet) is a labyrinthine network of enclosed walkways designed to beat the freeze, enabling you to walk through downtown without setting foot outside.

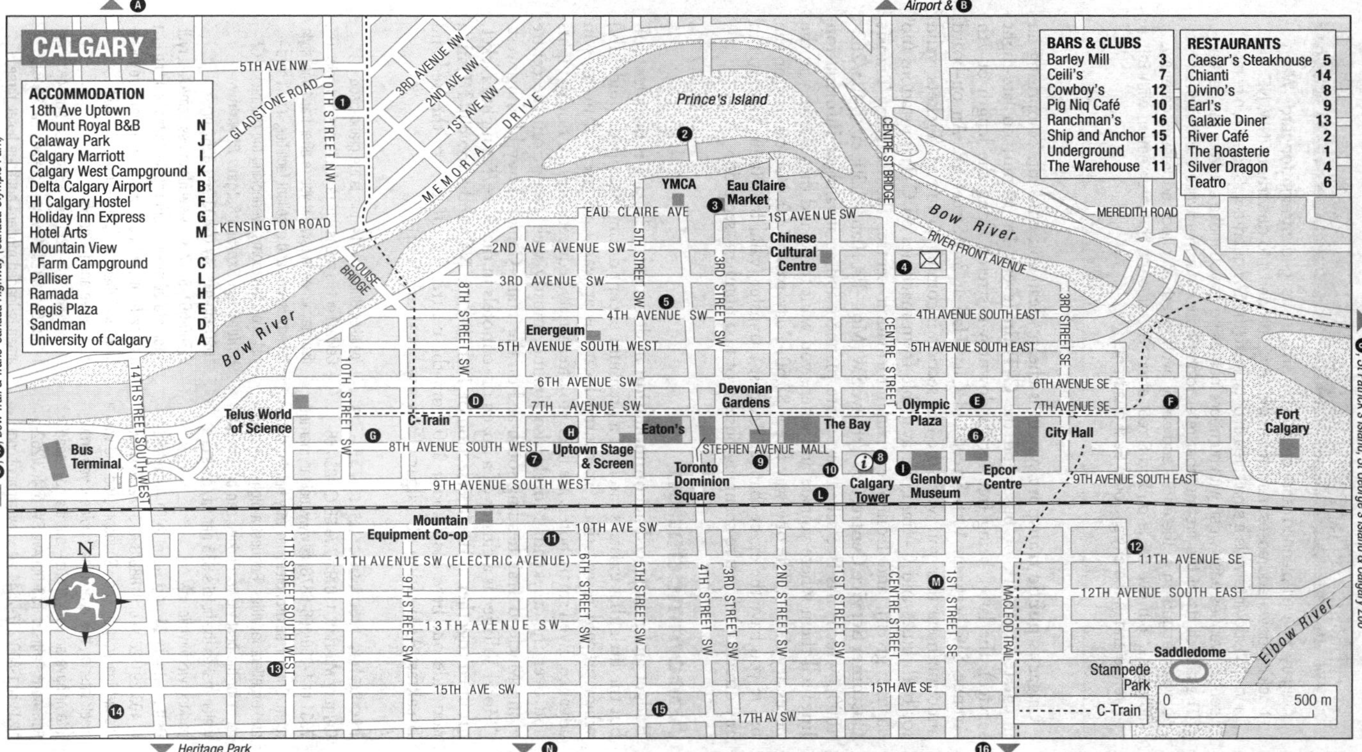
CALGARY
ACCOMMODATION
18th Ave Uptown
Mount Royal B&B N
Calaway Park J
Calgary Marriott I
Calgary West Campground K
Delta Calgary Airport B
HI Calgary Hostel F
Holiday Inn Express G
Hotel Arts M
Mountain View Farm Campground C
Palliser L
Ramada H
Regis Plaza E
Sandman D
University of Calgary A
BARS & CLUBS
Barley Mill 3
Ceili's 7
Cowboy's 12
Pig Niq Café 10
Ranchman's 16
Ship and Anchor 15
Underground 11
The Warehouse 11
RESTAURANTS
Caesar's Steakhouse 5
Chianti 14
Divino's 8
Earl's 9
Galaxie Diner 13
River Café 2
The Roasterie 1
Silver Dragon 4
Teatro 6
A
Airport & B
C, St Patrick's Island, St George's Island & Calgary Zoo
J, K, Bow Trail & Trans-Canada Highway (Canada Olympic Park)
Heritage Park
N
16
Prince's Island
Bow River
Elbow River
YMCA
Eau Claire Market
Chinese Cultural Centre
Energeum
Devonian Gardens
The Bay
Olympic Plaza
City Hall
Fort Calgary
Telus World of Science
C-Train
Eaton's
Uptown Stage & Screen
Toronto Dominion Square
Calgary Tower
Glenbow Museum
Epcor Centre
Bus Terminal
Mountain Equipment Co-op
Saddledome
Stampede Park
MEMORIAL DRIVE
LOUISE BRIDGE
CENTRE ST BRIDGE
RIVER FRONT AVENUE
MEREDITH ROAD
KENSINGTON ROAD
GLADSTONE ROAD
STEPHEN AVENUE MALL
MACLEOD TRAIL
11TH AVENUE SW (ELECTRIC AVENUE)
C-Train
0 500 m

Calgary addresses

Calgary is well-planned and orientation around its grid **straightforward**. When tracking down addresses, remember the city is divided into **quadrants** (NW, NE, SE and SW); downtown is a small area in or close to the SW quadrant. Streets run north–south, avenues east–west, with numbers increasing as you move out from the centre. The last digits of the first number refer to the house number while the quadrant is always tagged on at the end – and easily overlooked, so check addresses carefully. Thus 237-8th Ave SE is on 2nd Street at no. 37, close to the intersection with 8th Avenue and in the city's South East quadrant.

Calgary's **public transport** system is cheap, clean and efficient, comprising an integrated network of buses and the **C-Train** (every 15–30min; no late-night service), the latter being free for its downtown stretch along the length of 7th Avenue SW between 10th Street and City Hall at 3rd Street SE. An on-board announcement tells you when the free section is coming to an end. **Tickets**, valid for both buses and C-Train, are available from machines on C-Train stations (no change given), and from the main information centre, the **Calgary Transit Customer Service Centre**, 224-7th Ave SW (Mon–Fri 10am–5.30pm; ⓣ403/262-1000), which has free schedules, route planners and an invaluable **information line**: tell them where you are and where you want to go and they'll give you the necessary details. The one-way fare is $2.50, a day-pass $7.50. You can pay on the bus if you have the exact change. Request a transfer (valid for 90min for travel in any direction) if you're changing buses. For taxi numbers, see p.565.

Accommodation

Budget and mid-priced **accommodation** in downtown Calgary is not plentiful, but the little that exists is rarely at a premium except during Stampede (mid-July) when prepaid reservations, in central locations at least, are essential months in advance. Even smart hotels are likely to offer vastly reduced rates on Friday nights and over the weekend. **Motels** also abound, mostly well away from the centre along Macleod Trail heading south and on the Trans-Canada Hwy heading west. "Motel Village" is a cluster of a dozen or so motels in the $65–75 a night bracket, grouped together at the intersection of 16th Avenue NW and Crowchild Trail; a taxi ride out here costs about $10 from the centre. For B&Bs, try the Bed and Breakfast Association of Calgary (ⓦwww.bbcalgary.com).

Hotels, motels and B&Bs

Calgary Marriott 110-9th Ave SE ⓣ403/266-7331 or 1-800/896-6878, ⓦwww.calgarymarriott.com. Central, smart hotel with very helpful staff and excellent facilities. Request a higher, east side room for the best views. Parking can be a hassle, which makes the hotel's $35 per day on-site parking worthwhile. 8

Delta Calgary Airport Hotel 2001 Airport Rd ⓣ403/291-2600 or 1-888/890-3222, ⓦwww.deltacalgaryairport.com. Soundproofed and with a sleek interior, this is an ideal choice if you arrive late or have an early flight – but it's not cheap. 7

Fairmont Palliser 133-9th Ave SW ⓣ403/262-1234 or 1-800/257-7544, ⓦwww.fairmont.com/palliser. Built in 1914, this is the grand-daddy of Calgary hotels and is where dignitaries and celebrities stay when in town. If you're after traditional style, superb service and excellent facilities, it's all here – just avoid the rooms overlooking the rail tracks. 8

Holiday Inn Express Calgary Downtown 1020-8th Ave SW ⓣ403/269-8262 or 1-800/661-6017, ⓦwww.hiexpress.com/calgarydt. A ten-storey modern but slightly faded building just a block from the free C-Train. The rooms are more functional than flash, but some come with microwave and fridge. 7

Hotel Arts 119-12th Ave SW ⓣ403/266-4611 or 1-800/661-9378, ⓦwww.hotelarts.ca. Stylish amenity-loaded modern boutique hotel, three blocks from the centre of town. Room options – all quite plush – include pool, jacuzzi and luxury suites, and the on-site *Raw Bar* serves up some tasty fish and seafood. 7

Ramada Hotel Downtown 708-8th Ave SW ⓣ403/263-7600 or 1-800/661-8684, ⓦwww.ramadacalgary.com. A large, comfortable hotel at the heart of downtown, with predictably good rooms and a swimming pool. 5

Regis Plaza Hotel 124-7th Ave SE ⓣ403/262-4641. It's been here in one form or another since 1912, but is currently fairly unappealing, with 1970s decor. Still, it's cheap, clean and just two blocks from the Calgary Tower. Many of the rooms share bathrooms. 3

Sandman Hotel Downtown Calgary 888-7th Ave SW ⓣ403/237-8626 or 1-800/726-3626, ⓦwww.sandmanhotels.com. Excellent and first-choice mid-range hotel in a high-rise block, with three hundred clean, modern rooms, all with private bathrooms. Very handy for the free C-Train. 6

Travelodge/Thriftlodge 2750 Sunridge Blvd NE ⓣ403/291-1260; 2304-16th Ave ⓣ403/289-0211; and 7012 Macleod Trail ⓣ403/253-1111; book any on 1-888/578-578 or ⓦwww.travelodge.com. Inexpensive out-of-town chain motels; the first is convenient to the airport; the second north of town along the Trans-Canada Hwy; the third south along the arterial Macleod Trail. All have pools and free internet. 3

Uptown Mount Royal Bed and Breakfast 809-18 Ave SW ⓣ403/245-9371 or 1-800/556-1436, ⓦwww.mountroyalbb.com. A 1912 Edwardian house with two rooms, both with clawfoot tubs. The larger double room has a private entrance and deck, while the single room comes equipped with a fireplace. The gourmet breakfasts are superb, and you're within walking distance of downtown, Stampede Park and trendy 17th Ave. 6

Hostel and student rooms

HI-Calgary City Centre Hostel 520-7th Ave SE ⓣ403/269-8239, ⓦwww.hihostels.ca. Sociable hostel in a slightly seedy area close to downtown, two blocks east of City Hall and the free section of the C-Train. Rates fluctuate seasonally, but in high season are $30–39 for dorms ($34–43 nonmembers), $75 for private rooms ($83 nonmembers) and $82–92 for private en-suites ($90–100 nonmembers). Facilities include laundry, kitchen, bike storage, library and free wi-fi.

University of Calgary 3456-24th Ave NW 104 Cascade Hall ⓣ403/220-3202 or 1-877/498-3203, ⓦwww.ucalgary.ca/hotelandconference. Way out in the northwest suburbs, but cheap and with a huge number of private rooms (around $50–70) and apartments ($77–206) from early May–late Aug. All the student facilities – including great sports facilities – are on hand. Take the C-Train or bus #9. By car, head west from downtown along Hwy 1, then northwest on University Drive. The room-rental office is in the lobby of Cascade Hall on campus.

Campsites

Calaway RV Park 245033 Range Rd 33 ⓣ403/240-3822, ⓦwww.calawaypark.com. About 10km west of the city on the Trans-Canada Hwy towards Banff. It's also within walking distance of the Calaway Park amusement park – western Canada's largest. Full facilities, including showers and Stampede shuttle downtown. Mid-May to early Sept; $24–35.

Calgary West Campground 221-101 St SW ⓣ403/288-0411 or 1-888/562-0842, ⓦwww.calgarycampground.com. South of Hwy 1 on the western side of the city, close to Canada Olympic Park: 400 sites, laundry, store and outdoor pool. Mid-April to mid-Oct; $29–43.

Mountain View Farm Campground 244024 Range Rd 284 ⓣ403/293-6640, ⓦwww.calgarycamping.com. A 202-site full service campground on a farm 3km east of the city on the Trans-Canada (Hwy 1). Stampede shuttle and wi-fi for extra charge. April-Oct; $31–40.

The City

Downtown Calgary lies in a self-evident cluster of mirrored glass and polished granite. A monument to oil money, the area is about as sleek as an urban centre can be, but there isn't much of interest to see in the core itself. Though downtown is loosely centred on the largely pedestrianized **Stephen Avenue Mall** (8th Avenue between 1st Street SE and 3rd Street SW), any city tour should start with a trip to the **Glenbow Museum** or a jaunt up the **Calgary Tower**, across the street, to get your bearings. Thereafter, a good deal of the city lends itself to wandering on foot, whether around the mall-laden main streets or to **Prince's Island**, the nearest of many parks, gentrified **Kensington**, a busy shopping and café district north of the

Bow River and **17th Avenue SW**, which is packed with more shops, restaurants and cafés. The appeal of attractions further afield – **Fort Calgary**, **Heritage Park** and the **Calgary Zoo** – will depend on your inclinations. These sights, together with a crop of special interest **museums**, can be easily reached by bus or C-Train.

Glenbow Museum

The **Glenbow Museum** (Mon–Sat 9am–5pm, Sun noon–5pm; $14; ⓣ403/268-4100, ⓦwww.glenbow.org), 130-9th Ave SE, opposite the Calgary Tower, is – beside the Stampede– the only sight you'd make a special journey to Calgary for. The no-expenses-spared museum is a testament to sound civic priorities and the cultural benefits of booming oil revenues and its three floors of displays make a fine introduction to the heritage of the Canadian west.

The permanent collection starts with a section devoted to **sacred art** from around the world and an **art gallery** tracing the development of western Canadian **indigenous art**. Better still is the **European art** depicting aboriginal peoples. Two outlooks prevail – the Romantic nineteenth-century image of the "noble savage", and the more forward-looking analysis of contemporaries such as Paul Kane, a painter bent on accurately representing aboriginal cultures before their assimilation by white expansion.

The **second floor** runs the gamut of western Canadian history and heritage, including an outstanding exhibit on aboriginal peoples. In the treaties section, hidden in a corner almost as if in shame, the museum text skates over the injustices with a glossary of simple facts. On display are the original documents many chiefs were tricked into signing, believing they were peace treaties, when in fact the contracts gave away land rights to those who drafted them in deliberately incomprehensible legalese. **Native crafts** are also explored on this floor, with stunning displays of carving, costumes and jewellery; the emphasis is on the original inhabitants of Alberta – the Blackfoot – though the collection also examines the Inuit and the Métis. Following a historical chronology, the floor moves on to exhibits associated with the fur trade, Northwest Rebellion, the Canadian Pacific Railway, pioneer life, ranching, cowboys, oil and wheat. It all adds up to a glut of period paraphernalia, including a terrifying exhibit of frontier dentistry, an absurdly comprehensive display of washing machines and a solitary 1938 bra.

The top floor kicks off with a pointless display of Calgary Stampede merchandising, before moving on to a huge collection of military paraphernalia and a dazzling display of **gems and minerals**, said to be among the world's best.

Other downtown sights

The **Calgary Tower** (daily June–Aug 9am–10.30pm; Sept–May 9am–9.30pm; $14; ⓣ403/266-7171, ⓦwww.calgarytower.com), the city's favourite folly, is a good deal shorter and less imposing than the tourist material would have you believe. The 190m-tall sceptre (762 steps if you don't take the one-minute lift) stands somewhat overshadowed by downtown's more recent buildings. Yet its unusual shape has made it a long-term landmark and offers outstanding views, especially on clear days, when the snowcapped Rockies fill the western horizon, with the ski-jump towers of Canada Olympic Park in the middle distance. On the observation platform you'll also find a good-value snack bar with reasonable food, a cocktail bar and an expensive revolving restaurant.

Any number of shopping malls lurk behind the soaring high-rises, most notably Toronto Dominion Square (8th Ave SW between 2nd & 3rd Sts), the city's main shopping focus and the unlikely site of the **Devonian Gardens** (daily 9am–9pm; free). Like something out of an idyllic urban utopia, the three-acre indoor gardens support a lush sanctuary of streams, waterfalls and full-sized trees, no mean feat given it's located on the fourth floor of a glass and concrete glitter palace. Around twenty thousand plants round off the picture, comprising some 138 local and tropical species. Benches beside the garden's paths are perfect for picnicking on food bought in the mall below, while small concerts are often held on the small stages dotted around.

The **TELUS World of Science** (Mon–Thurs 9.45am–4pm, Fri 9.45am–5pm, Sat & Sun 10am–5pm; $14.25; Ⓣ403/268-8300, Ⓦwww.calgaryscience.ca), 701-11th St, lies one block west of the 10th Street SW C-Train line. Highlights include the interactive, regularly changing exhibits of the Discovery Hall and the **Discovery Dome**, a multimedia theatre complete with cinema picture images, computer graphics, slide-projected images and a vast speaker system. It's all best suited for families.

Eau Claire Market, Prince's Island, the Bow River and Kensington

North of downtown at the end of 3rd Street SW, **Eau Claire Market** (Ⓦwww.eauclairemarket.com) is a bright and deliberately brash warehouse mix of food and craft market, cinemas, buskers, restaurants, walkways and panoramic terraces. It brings some heart to the concrete and glass of downtown – the large communal eating area, in particular, is a good place to people-watch and pick up bargain takeaway Chinese, Japanese, wholefood and burger snacks.

A footbridge on the market's northern side connects **Prince's Island**, a popular but peaceful retreat offering plenty of trees, flowers, a kids' playground and enough space to escape the incessant stream of joggers pounding the walkways. Swimmers might be tempted by the adjacent broad, fast-flowing and icy-cold **Bow River**, but it's best to enjoy it from the shore (although you'll likely see people canoeing ot tubing down it in the height of summer). The river is the focus for Calgary's excellent 210km system of recreational **walking and bike paths** that run generally parallel the main waterways: maps are available from the visitor centre. Just east of the market lies the **Calgary Chinese Cultural Centre**, 197-1st St SW (daily 11am–5pm; $4; Ⓣ403-262-5071, Ⓦwww.culturalcentre.ca), its big central dome modelled on the Temple of Heaven in Beijing. It forms the focus for Calgary's modest Chinatown and large Chinese-Canadian population, most of whom are descendants of immigrants who came to work on the railways in the 1880s. It contains a small museum and gallery, gift shop and a restaurant.

A twenty-minute stroll west from Eau Claire along the river's south side will bring you to **Kensington**, a gentrified, somewhat studenty district on 10th Street NW and along Kensington Road. There's a couple of good used and new bookshops, a clutch of posh furniture and clothing stores and several restaurants, pubs and cafés, making it an ideal place to have a wander, meal or drink.

Fort Calgary

Fort Calgary (daily 9am–5pm; $11; Ⓣ403/290-1875, Ⓦwww.fortcalgary.ab.ca), the city's historical nexus, stands at 750-9th Ave SE, an easy five-block walk east of the City Hall C-Train stop. Built in under six weeks by the North West Mounted Police in 1875, the fort was the germ of the present city, and remained operative as a police post until 1914, when it was sold to the Canadian Pacific Railway. The whole area remained buried under railway tracks and derelict warehouses until 1974 when the city bought back the land and began to reclaim it.

Period photographs in the adjoining interpretive centre show how wild Calgary still was in 1876. Even more remarkable was the ground men in the fort were expected to cover: the log stockade was a base for operations between Fort Macleod, 160km to the south, and the similar post at Edmonton, almost 400km to the north. Only a few forlorn stumps of the original building remain and what survives is a pleasant forty-acre park at the confluence of the Bow and Elbow rivers, although a portion of a replica of the original log stockade has been built and is awaiting further funding. The interpretive centre traces Calgary's development and conducts "interpretive walks" along the river, and offers the opportunity to dress up as a Mountie.

Across the Elbow River to the east is **Hunt House**, built in 1876 for a Hudson's Bay official and believed to be Calgary's oldest building on its original site. Close by, at 750-9th Ave SE, on the same side of the river, is the renovated **Deane House Historic Site and Restaurant** (free tours Tues–Fri 11am–3pm, Sat & Sun 10am–3pm; ⓣ403/269-7747), built in 1906 by the Mountie Captain Superintendent Richard Deane. It subsequently served as the home of an artists' cooperative, a boarding house and a stationmaster's house.

St George's Island and Calgary Zoo

St George's Island is home to Calgary's most popular attraction: the **Calgary Zoo** (daily 9am–6pm; last admission 5pm; $18; ⓣ403/232-9300 or 1-800/588-9993, ⓦwww.calgaryzoo.org), 1300 Zoo Rd. It can be reached from downtown and Fort Calgary by riverside path, by C-Train northeast towards Whitehorn or by car (take Memorial Drive East to just west of Deerfoot Trail). Founded in 1920, this is now one of North America's best zoos, with some one thousand animals, 290 species and innovative and exciting displays in which the animals are caged in reasonably "natural" habitats. There are underwater viewing areas for polar bears and sea creatures, darkened rooms for nocturnal animals, a special Australian section, greenhouses for tropical birds and pens for the big draws like gorillas, tigers, giraffes and African warthogs. Check out the extended North American and Canadian Wilds, Aspen Woodlands and Rocky Mountains sections for a taste of a variety of fauna. Also worth a look are the Tropical, Arid and Butterfly gardens in the conservatory.

Gardens are dotted throughout the zoo, while a **Prehistoric Park** is accessible by suspension bridge across the Bow River. Its nineteen life-size dinosaur models are a poor substitute for the superb museum at Drumheller (see p.549). Picnic areas help make a day of the whole complex.

Inglewood Bird Sanctuary

Natural-history enthusiasts might also want to visit the **Inglewood Bird Sanctuary** (dawn–dusk; free), on the Bow River's forested flats, 3km downstream of the zoo and east of downtown. Some 230 species are present year-round and more during migratory cycles. Around 270 species have been recorded across the sanctuary, a portion of land once owned by Colonel James Walker, one of Calgary's original North West Mounted Police. You might see bald eagles, Swainson's hawks, ring-necked pheasants, warblers, grey partridges and great horned owls. Numerous duck, geese and other waterfowl are also present, and you may catch sight of muskrats, beavers, white-tailed and mule deer, foxes and long-tailed weasels. A visitor centre (May–Sept daily 10am–4pm; Oct–April Tues–Sun 10am–4pm) offers information, year-round walking trails and occasional natural history courses.

To get here, follow 9th Avenue SE to Sanctuary Road and follow signs to the parking area on the river's south bank. Bus #411 or #305 will both drop you off within an easy walk of the Sanctuary.

Heritage Park Historical Village

A sixty-acre theme park centred on a reconstructed frontier village 16km southwest of downtown, **Heritage Park** (mid-May to early Sept daily 9.30am–5pm; early Sept to early Oct Sat & Sun 9.30am–5pm; summer $19, museum only in winter $11; ⓣ403/268-8500 ⓦwww.heritagepark.ca) replicates life in the Canadian prairies before 1914 and panders relentlessly to the myth of the "Wild West". Full of family-oriented presentations and original costumes, this heritage offering is thorough enough for you never to feel obliged to see another like it. The working museum comprises more than 150 restored buildings, all transported from small-town locations. Each has been assigned to one of several communities – fur post, native village, homestead, farm – and most fulfil their original function. Thus you can see a working blacksmith, buy fresh bread, go to church and even get married. Transport is period appropriate, with steam trains, trams, a horse-drawn bus and stagecoaches. If you're here for the day you can pick up cakes and snacks from the traditional Alberta Bakery, or sit down to a full meal in the old-style *Wainwright Hotel*.

To get there by car, take either Elbow Drive or Macleod Trail south and turn right on Heritage Drive – the turn-off is marked by a huge, maroon steam engine). Alternatively, take the C-Train to Heritage Station and then a free shuttle bus (#502) that operates for most of the summer – call to confirm.

Eating

Alberta claims, with justification, to have some of the world's best **steaks**, so Calgary's cuisine can be heavily meat-oriented. There's also a healthy amount of places focusing on the fusion and Pacific Rim trends popular in western Canada. Most bars and even live-music venues double up as restaurants and invariably serve perfectly good, and often well-priced, food.

Cafés and restaurants

Caesar's Steak House 512-4th Ave SW ⓣ403/264-1222. Best place for a huge, perfect steak ($30–45) in the sort of wonderfully cheesy steakhouse – think dimly lit "Roman" decor – that's been around for decades. The rib-eye is considered by many to be the finest slab of meat in town. Closed Sun.

Chianti Café and Restaurant 1438-17th Ave SW ⓣ403/229-1600, ⓦwww.chianticafe.ca. A favourite local spot for years: dark, noisy, well priced and extremely popular (book ahead), with no-nonsense pasta basics and the odd fancy dish (mains $8–16). There's a patio for summer dining.

Divino's Wine and Cheese Bistro 113-8th SW ⓣ403/410-5555, ⓦwww.crmr.com/divino. Café and wine bar opposite the *Fairmont Palliser* hotel with faux mahogany-Tiffany chandelier interior, but good Italian food (mains $8–21) and particularly noteworthy desserts.

Earl's 315-8th Ave SW ⓣ403/265-3275. Ever-reliable mid-range chain, serving North American food at average prices. Right in the middle of Stephen Avenue Mall, so often quite busy, especially at lunch.

Galaxie Diner 1413-11th St SW ⓣ403/228-0001, ⓦwww.galaxiediner.com. Popular place with authentic diner decor and great breakfasts (try the burrito). Mon–Fri 7am–3pm, weekends till 4pm.

River Café Prince's Island Park ⓣ403/261-7670, ⓦwww.river-cafe.com. Along with *Teatro* (see below), this is the best of Calgary's restaurants: innovative Canadian cuisine – including game, smoked fish, roasted beet and crab apple borscht – an informal atmosphere and wonderful setting, across the bridge from the Eau Claire Market. Mains from $25. Book ahead.

The Roasterie 314-10th St NW. There are no meals, but with twenty kinds of coffee – you'll smell it roasting before you see it – snacks and newspapers, this artsy crowd coffee shop is more of a place to take a load off and people watch.

Silver Dragon 106-3rd Ave SE ⓣ403/264-5326. The first choice in town for a Chinese meal. It's been around for over thirty years and uses a team of fifteen Hong Kong-trained chefs to conjure up a menu of some two hundred dishes. Dim sum is served from 9.30am–2.45pm. Prices are moderate.

Teatro 200-8th Ave SE ⓣ403/290-1012, ⓦwww.teatro-rest.com. The place to come if you want to dress up a little and drop some money – perhaps appropriate, as it's located in the old Dominion Bank building. The fine Italian-influenced food (mains from $24) is on par with that of the *River Café*. Booking is essential.

Drinking and nightlife

Calgary is rarely a party town, except during Stampede and a brief period in summer when the weather allows barbecues and evening streetlife. Yet its **bars**, and **cafés** are all you'd expect of a city of this size. The vast majority of them are found in five distinct areas: **Kensington, Electric Avenue** (11th Ave SW between 5th and 6th streets), though much of the latter's action has moved to **17th Avenue SW**, where there's a more varied collection of pubs, bars and restaurants, and **4th Street SW**, a similarly more refined restaurant area.

The quality of **live music** is good – especially in jazz, blues and the genre closest to Calgary's heart, country. You'll find events listings in *ffwd* (ⓦwww.ffwdweekly.com) and Calgary's main dailies, the *Herald* and the *Sun*.

Bars and pubs

Barley Mill Eatery & Pub 201 Barclay Parade SW ⓣ403/290-1500, ⓦwww.barleymill.net. Busy pub in Eau Claire Market with an outside patio and a one hundred-year-old bar imported from Scotland inside; 25 draught beers, forty bottled brews and lots of whiskies.

Ceili's 803 8th Ave SW ⓣ403/265-1200, ⓦwww.ceilis.com. Large and lively Irish pub, with fish 'n' chips, pies and stews on the menu and standing room only after work.

Kensington Pub 207 10A St NW ⓣ403/270-4505, ⓦwww.kensingtonpub.com. A delightful gem of a neighbourhood pub without pretence, tucked away down a side street off Kensington Rd. The grub is good (try the chicken wings) and best accompanied by a pint or two of the local or UK/Irish brews on tap.

Ship and Anchor 534 17th Ave SW 403/245-3333, ⓦwww.shipandanchor.com. A long-established neighbourhood pub that's friendly and laidback – but gets very busy on weekends. Darts, fine music and excellent pub food make this a good place to start a big night out, or simply while away an evening.

Clubs and music venues

Beatniq Jazz and Social Club 811-1st St SW ⓣ403/263-1650, ⓦwww.beatniq.com. The main level of this place houses the *Bistro Piq Niq*, which isn't bad for food, but the real action is downstairs on Thurs–Sat nights, when excellent live jazz acts take to the stage. $10 cover.

Cowboy's 1088 Olympic Way SE ⓦwww.cowboysniteclub.com. Legendary – and often raunchy – bar that holds over 3500 people on two levels, with nightly live entertainment. It's usually heaving, thanks to promotions involving 25¢ beers and the club's policy to pay for the breast implants of female employees.

Ranchman's Steak House 9615 Macleod Trail South ⓣ403/253-1100, ⓦwww.ranchmans.com. A classic honky-tonk and restaurant, 8km south of downtown, known throughout Canada for live country and western music. Free dance lessons at 7pm Mon–Fri. Free admission before 8pm on Thurs. Closed Sun.

Underground 731-10th Ave SW. Hardcore, punk and metal bar with live bands every Fri and Sat and the cheapest beer in the city: jugs for $5.25.

The Warehouse 731-10th Ave SW ⓦwww.warehousenightclub.ca. Calgary's only truly late-night dance club, opens at 9pm and on weekend nights doesn't close until 7am. Drink specials help keep the party going. Located above *Underground*; the entrance is around the back.

Performing arts and cinema

Much of the city's highbrow cultural life occurs at the **Epcor Centre for the Performing Arts**, 205-8th Ave SE (ⓣ403/294-7455, ⓦwww.epcorcentre.org). Several of the city's professional theatre companies perform here, along with the Calgary Philharmonic Orchestra (ⓦwww.cpo-live.com) and the excellent Alberta Ballet Company (ⓦwww.albertaballet.com). The Calgary Opera's (ⓦwww.calgaryopera.com) home base is the Jubilee Auditorium at 1415-14th Ave NW. For repertory, arthouse, classic and foreign **films**, try the Uptown Stage & Screen, 612-8th Ave SW (ⓣ403/265-0120, ⓦwww.theuptown.com) or Plaza Theatre at 1113 Kensington Rd NW (ⓣ403/283-2222, ⓦwww.theplaza.ca).

Listings

Bookshops Pages on Kensington, 1135 Kensington Road NW ⓣ403/283-6655, ⓦwww.pages.ab.ca. For maps and travel books, check out Mountain Equipment Co-op (below).

Car rental Avis, 211-6th Ave SW ⓣ403/269-6166; Budget, 140-6th Ave SE ⓣ403/226-1550; Rent-A-Wreck ⓣ403/287-6800, ⓦwww.rentawreck.ca.
Medical Foothills Hospital, 1403-29th Ave ⓣ403/944-1110.
Library Central Library, 616 Macleod Trail SE (Mon–Thurs 10am–8pm, Fri–Sat 9am–5pm, Sun noon–5pm). Internet $2/2hr.
Outdoor gear Mountain Equipment Co-op, 830-10th Ave SW (ⓣ403/269-2420) large camping and outdoor store that also rents all manner of equipment.
Police 133-6th Ave SE ⓣ403/266-1234.
Post office 207-9th Ave SW ⓣ403/974-2078.
Taxis Advance Cab ⓣ403/777-1111; Checker ⓣ403/299-9999.
Weather Information ⓣ403/299-7878; road conditions ⓣ403/246-5853.

The Yellowhead Route (Highway 16)

Highway 16, one of central Canada's most appealing long-distance drives, is better known as **the Yellowhead Route** – taking its name from a light-haired Iroquois explorer and guide who was called *Tête Jaune* ("yellow head") by the *voyageurs*, French-speaking boatmen that plied the waterways transporting people, furs and supplies. It's a good alternative to the Trans-Canada Hwy, with more interesting sights along the way – including several towns, like **Dauphin**, where some of the culture of original groups has been preserved – and also more varied scenery. This not only includes vast tracts of prairie, but also some of the aspen parklands and boreal forest to the north. If you have the time you can easily make a foray into the enticingly wild **Prince Albert National Park**. The Yellowhead Route also runs through **Saskatoon** (781km from Winnipeg and 524km from **Edmonton**), a good place to break a journey and with several important historic sites in the vicinity.

Winnipeg to Saskatoon

The Yellowhead Route follows the Trans-Canada Hwy west out of Winnipeg as far as Portage la Prairie (see p.527), then leaves it to cut northwest for a more attractive journey across the prairies. It passes through the pretty little towns of **Neepawa** and **Minnedosa** before running south of **Riding Mountain National Park**, 250km northwest of Winnipeg, which protects attractive areas of deciduous and boreal forest, lake and grassland. Just north of the park lies the strongly Ukrainian town of **Dauphin**, which can form a base for exploring **Duck Mountain Provincial Park**, itself noted for fishing, birdwatching and canoeing. The park continues over the border in Saskatchewan and is close to the Doukhobor settlement of **Veregin** and the dreary prairie **Yorkton**. From here, the hwy embarks on one of its dullest stretches across the prairies towards Saskatoon, but don't miss **Little Manitou Lake** – Saskatchewan's Dead Sea.

Neepawa

Elms and cottonwoods line the streets of tiny pleasant **NEEPAWA**, some 90km west along Hwy 16 from Portage la Prairie. More varieties of lilies grow in the area around here than in any other part of the world – a fact celebrated during mid-July's **Lily Festival**.

In town, the oldest buildings dot the principal drag, Mountain Avenue. Notable among these are the neo-Romanesque Knox Presbyterian Church at Mill Street and 1st Avenue, with an unusual thick, turreted bell tower, and the tidy, late-Victorian County Court House, close to Mountain Avenue and Hamilton Street. In the old CNR station at the west end of Hamilton Street is the **Beautiful Plains Museum** (May–Aug Mon–Fri 9am–5pm, Sat & Sun 1–5pm; other times by appointment; $1; ⓣ204/476-3896 or 476-5292 off-season), with diverting displays on the life of the district's pioneers. Margaret Laurence (1926–87), one of Canada's best-known writers, lived in Neepawa in her early years and used the town (renamed Manawaka) as a setting for many of her novels, which portray strong women struggling against small town life, beginning with the highly acclaimed *The Stone Angel* and ending with *The Diviners*. You can visit her home, now the **Margaret Laurence Museum** (mid-May to Sept daily 10am–5pm; other times by appointment $3; ⓣ204/476-3612), at 312 1st Ave North.

The **bus station** is attached to the Petro Canada fuel station at 50 Main St.

Practicalites

For **accommodation**, try the *Garden Path B&B*, 536 2nd Ave (ⓣ204/476-3184; ❸), in a beautiful 1903 former lumber merchant's home, or one of the **motels**, west of town on Hwy 16; the spotless but simple *Vivian Motor Hotel* (ⓣ204/476-7400, ⓦwww.vivianmotorhotel.com; ❷) is a good choice.

The **restaurants** downtown are unappealing but *Prairie Seasons Bakery*, 370 Mountain Ave, is a pleasant spot for coffee and great cinnamon buns, as well as soups, made using traditional Hutterite recipes. On Hwy 16 (Main St), try the busy *Mr Ribs*, which has dinners from $8.

Minnedosa

The approach to **MINNEDOSA**, 28km west of Neepawa, is attractive thanks to its location in the flat of a long valley that slowly rises at each end. The town is famous for its four-day Rockin' the Fields festival (ⓦwww.rockinthefields.ca) in early August, but otherwise it's pretty quiet. There's not much here except for a **bison compound** near the Little Saskatchewan River (March–Oct; free), reached via a swinging bridge over the river or by turning off Main Street onto 2nd Avenue SE and driving five minutes along Beach Road to a viewing platform. You can also reach the compound and a pleasant **public beach** by following the two-kilometre **Heritage Village Walk** from a 1920s CPR caboose and diesel engine, located beside the boulder-strewn river at the bridge on Main Street.

Practicalities

Minnedosa's handful of **motels** includes the *Minnedosa Inn*, at 138 Main St (ⓣ204/867-2777; ❷). The attractive *Fairmount B&B*, (ⓣ204/874-2165, ⓦwww.bedandbreakfast.mb.ca; ❹), between town and Hwy 16 just off 9th Avenue SW, is a 1914 farmhouse decked out with early Canadiana and serving organic breakfasts.

For **food**, try the *Chipperfield Coffee Company*, at 50 Main St North in the town's first general store – it's worth a stop for coffee and ice cream. Otherwise there's the *Dari Isle Drive-In*, 11 6th Ave NE.

Riding Mountain National Park

About 56km north of Minnedosa on Hwy 10 is one of the region's best parks, **Riding Mountain National Park** ($7.80 entry), its name derived from fur trappers who changed from canoe to horseback to travel across its wooded highlands. It's still a vast expanse of wilderness, roughly 50km long and 100km wide, and provides some of Manitoba's finest hiking, biking and scenery. It's also known as the place where **Grey Owl** (see p.193) spent six months or so living with his wife and their pet beavers in 1931.

Arrival and information

The only significant settlement in the area is the tourist village of **WASAGAMING**, which sits beside Clear Lake on the park's southern edge. There's a scrawny beach here that gets overcrowded in July and August (try the beaches at the southwest and northern part of the lake where the water is shallower and warmer). The park's **visitor centre** (daily mid-May to late June & Sept to mid Oct 9.30am–5pm; July & Aug 9.30am–8pm; Ⓣ204/848-7275 or 1-866/787-6221, Ⓦwww.pc.gc.ca) is beside the main beach; you can get fishing licences, compulsory backcountry camping permits ($10) and other park information here. From mid-October to mid-May, when the centre is closed, the **administration office** opposite (Mon–Fri 8am–noon & 12.30pm–4pm) provides similar services. The **Pinewood Museum**, 154 Wasagaming Drive (July & Aug daily 1–4pm; free), relates the park's history.

Wasagaming's main **bus stop** is on the corner of Wasagaming Drive and Mooswa Drive.

Accommodation

Most park accommodation is open from May to September or October only. If you're not using one of the park's primitive campsites (see above), the other options are all in or around Wasagaming. *Clear Lake Lodge*, 143 Ta-Wa-Pit Drive (Ⓣ204/848-2345 or 1-877/848-8812, Ⓦwww.clearlakelodge.com; ❸), is a comfortable hotel choice, while the *Mooswa Resort*, Mooswa Drive (Ⓣ204/848-2533, Ⓦwww.mooswa.com; ❺), has modern A-frames and battered but clean motel rooms surrounding an outdoor pool. The village's only **campsite** is the park-run *Wasagaming Campground*, (Ⓣ204/848-7275 or 1-877/737-3783, Ⓦwww.pccamping.ca; May to mid Oct; $24–33; reservations advised) just beyond the main park gate. The only year-round possibility is the four-star *Elk Horn Resort* (Ⓣ204/848-2802, Ⓦwww.elkhornresort.mb.ca; ❻), with its slick spa and golf course, also in Onanole.

The Park

The park's eastern perimeter is formed by a 400-metre-high ridge studded with a dense evergreen forest of spruce, pine, balsam fir and tamarack. This soon gives way to a highland plateau whose mixed forests and lakes form the central, and most scenic, part of the park, bordered to the west by an area of aspen woodland, meadow and open grassland.

However you explore, it's the **wildlife** rather than the landscape that'll likely be the highlight. The optimal times for viewing are around dawn and dusk and some of the best spots readily accessible. There are elk and a carefully tended **buffalo** herd near Lake Audy, a 45-minute drive northwest of Wasagaming on a gravel road, where you can also spot elk on the lakeside trail. For **moose**, try the Moon Lake Trail, just off Hwy 10 or the nearby short Boreal Trail, which, though only 1km is usually a good bet for wildlife. **Bears** are commonly spotted alongside all the park hwys, so make plenty of noise if you want to avoid bumping into them while hiking or biking.

Most **hiking** trails in or near Wasagaming are short and easy, the longest being the **Clear Lake Trail** (24km) around the eponymous lake. The best trail from town is the 8km **Grey Owl Trail**, leading to the cabin where the man himself stayed. This trail connects with the nearest of the overnight routes, the **Cowan Lake Trail**, which branches off through a region of dense forest, small lakes and meadows; all the overnight trails have primitive campsites. If you have your own transport, the best trail for a half-day hike is the 6.4km **Gorge Creek Trail** near the East Park Gate. The rooty trail descends through thick stands of trees, continually re-crossing the tiny creek and delivering good views from the Riding Mountain escarpment along the way; the hike is frequently offered as an organized trip by the **visitor centre** as part of its summer events programme.

Also near the East Gate are some reasonably challenging **mountain bike** routes which have been developed to offer an alternative to the very gentle options around Wasagaming; the Tempo petrol station at the centre of town rents **bikes** (Ⓣ240/848-2535; $15/hr, $70/day). You can rent **canoes** and **powerboats** ($18/hr) from the jetty on Clear Lake.

Eating and drinking

The best of Wasagaming's **restaurants** is *TR McKoys*, 117 Wasagaming Drive, which has high-quality Italian food with pizza and pasta dishes from $12, as well as decent curries and steak. Alternatively, you could try the *Mountain Grill* at the *Elk Horn Resort* (see p.567). For breakfast try the *Whitehouse Bakery*, 104 Buffalo Drive, beside the Tempo station. The *Siesta Café*, 130 Wasagaming Drive, has locally roasted coffee, home-made cakes and internet access, but a nicer option for lengthy lingering is *Poor Michael's Bookshop* in Onanole, with its many secondhand books and craftsy items; and occasional musical events and readings.

Dauphin and around

Heading out of the park on Hwy 10, you'll soon hit **DAUPHIN**, founded as a French fur-trading post in 1739 just east of the Vermilion River. Today, it's a pleasant town that straggles across the flat prairie landscape and would be largely unremarkable, if it weren't for the preservation of its **Ukrainian** ancestry. You can see an excellent near-complete example of what life was like for Ukrainian immigrants at the nearby Wasyl Negrych Pioneer Farmstead (see p.568).

Dauphin's **bus station** is at Domo Gas, 201 Buchanan Avenue, a couple of minutes' walk from the town centre. The **tourist office** is at 100 Main St South (mid-May to Aug Mon–Thurs 10am–6pm, Fri–Sun 9am–7pm; Ⓣ204/622-3216 or 1-877/566-5669).

The Town

Those who cleared and settled this part of Manitoba between 1896 and 1925, assimilated rather more slowly into local culture, leaving onion domes of the Ukrainians' Orthodox churches in Dauphin and all along the fertile river valley to the west. The **National Ukrainian Festival** celebrates this ancestry and is held on the first weekend of August at a purpose-built complex on the edge of Riding Mountain Park, 12km south of Dauphin on Hwy 10. The complex has a splendid one-thousand seat hillside amphitheatre, ideal for the festival's music and dance performances and a tiny heritage village dedicated to early Ukrainian settlers (irregular hours free; Ⓣ204/638-9401).

Otherwise Dauphin's Main Street features good examples of early twentieth-century Canadian architecture, but the only real attraction is the **Fort Dauphin Museum** (May, June & Sept Mon–Fri 9am–5pm; July & Aug daily 9am–5pm; Oct–April by appointment; $3; Ⓣ204/638-6630), by the river at the end of 4th Avenue SW. This tidy wooden replica stockade of a North West Company trading outpost holds reconstructions of several sorts of pioneer building, including a trapper's cabin. With time to kill, nose around the huge CNR **railway station** at 101 1st Ave NW, which now houses the Dauphin Rail Museum (Mon–Fri noon–5pm; free) in a striking Romanesque Revival building. At the corner of 1st Street SW and 11th Avenue SW is the Ukrainian **Church of the Resurrection**, (call for hours Ⓣ204/638-5511) with its distinctive clustered domes.

The Wasyl Negrych Pioneer Farmstead

Canada's best-preserved and most complete Ukrainian homestead, the **Wasyl Negrych Pioneer Farmstead** (June–Aug daily 10am–5pm; $3; Ⓣ204/548-2326), lies near the village of Gilbert Plains, 30km west of Dauphin. Wasyl and Anna Negrych and their seven children arrived here from the Carpathian Mountains in 1897 to build their farmstead over the next few years. It ended up with ten buildings, including an 1899 home that replaced their first log house after it burnt down, three granaries, barns, a chicken coop, pigsty, garages and a bunkhouse with a fully-preserved working *peech* (the log and clay cookstove once the heart of every Ukrainian household). Amazingly, two of Wasyl and Anna's children ran the farmstead according to traditional practices until their deaths in the 1980s, never introducing electricity, sewers or phone lines.

Practicalities

For **accommodation** in Dauphin, the *Boulevard Motor Hotel*, 28 Memorial Blvd (Ⓣ204/638-4410 or 1-877/999-2228, Ⓦwww.boulevardhoteldauphin.com; ❷), is fairly downbeat but central. The *Canway Inn and Suites* (Ⓣ204/638-5102 or 1-888/325-3335, Ⓦwww.canwayinnandsuites.com; ❹), 4km south of town near the junction of hwys 5 and 10, has more appealing rooms – some with en-suite jacuzzis – plus a pool and sauna. The *Vermilion Trailer Park & Campground*, 21 2nd Ave NW (Ⓣ204/622-3125; May–Oct; $14–19), is ten minutes' walk north of Main Street. The **dining** scene in Dauphin is fairly desperate, but fast-food joints abound and at least the *Hong Kong Cafe*, at 123 Main St South, has reasonable Cantonese food.

Duck Mountain Provincial Park

Straddling the Manitoba–Saskatchewan border, **Duck Mountain Provincial Park** is a large slice of the Manitoba Escarpment run as two separate and strikingly different entities by the park authorities of each province.

In Manitoba

On the Manitoba side the park is huge and wild, comprising several thousand acres of thickly wooded rolling hills punctuated by meadows, bogs, streams and hundreds of tiny lakes. Most of the park is boreal forest, but many of its eastern slopes are covered by maple, burr oak and elm. Portions of this are regularly harvested for lumber, but care is taken not to disturb the black bears, moose, white-tailed deer and lynx that inhabit the park; it's not unusual to hear the cries of coyotes and wolves at night or the unmistakeable bugling of a bull elk among

Grain elevators

Though technically an American invention, there's hardly anything more distinctively Canadian Prairie than the **grain elevator**. These tall and traditionally wooden grain warehouses were utilitarian in design, built simply to store wheat prior to transport by rail. Yet with their clean, functional lines rising high above the plains, they've been likened to cathedrals, earned nicknames like "castles of the New World" and "prairie sentinels" and found their way into many a prairie heart.

The first Canadian grain elevators were built in the 1880s and by 1938 some 5800 dotted the region, each emblazoned with the names of the small towns they marked. But as transportation of grain switched from rail to road their numbers dwindled to the present seven hundred. In 2000, the Canadian Wheat Board decided to build massive central concrete terminals at main transit points, to which grain now travels by truck, making the old-style elevator increasingly redundant; indeed, some have already been dismantled, threatening to irrevocably change the prairie landscape. But there are holdouts, not least in **Inglis**, a tiny town on the west side of Riding Mountain National Park, where a row of 1920s wooden elevators beside an abandoned railway line lie preserved as a National Historic Site (Ⓦwww.ingliselevators.com).

the dense woodland. The park is noted for fishing, with pickerel, pike and trout in most of its lakes, and the delicious arctic char to the north.

Access is 100km northwest of Dauphin along two partly paved roads: the east–west Rte 367, which branches off Hwy 10 just north of Garland and cuts across the middle of the park to Hwy 83, a distance of 80km; and the south–north Rte 366, connecting the town of Grandview on Hwy 5 just 45km west of Dauphin with the village of Minitonas, 130km away.

Approached along the latter route, the park's best section is in the southeast corner, where **Baldy Mountain** (831m) is the highest point in Manitoba, complete with an observation tower providing views over the forest. A few kilometres north, the twin **West** and **East Blue Lakes** are among the park's finest – curving strips of clear water fed by underground springs. Between the lakes is the *Blue Lakes Campground* (ⓣ1-888/482-2267; May to mid-Sept; $10; unserviced sites only), close to both the **Blue Lakes Trail**, a six-kilometre cross-country hike, and the **Shining Stone Trail**, a short path along the peninsula that juts out into West Blue Lake. The campsite has a beach, grocery store and fuel station; the camp office advises on boat rental and fishing. For serviced sites, try *Childs Lake Campground* (ⓣ204/948-3333 or 1-888/482-2267; mid-May to mid-Sept; $13–17) on Rte 367 on the west edge of the park.

In Saskatchewan

The **Saskatchewan side** of Duck Mountain Park is highly regulated with much better, but far more crowded facilities than its Manitoba counterpart. It has toll booths at park entrances, a more extensive system of walking trails – including one wheelchair-accessible trail – and is open year-round. In winter, it has some of the best snowmobiling and cross-country skiing in the province.

Located some 100km northeast of Yorkton on hwys 9 and 5, this part of the park centres on the roughly circular **Madge Lake**, ringed with aspens, where you'll find a beach, several stores, canteens, recreational and picnic areas and places that rent canoes, paddleboats and ski equipment. The **parks office** (year-round; ⓣ306/542-3482) is near the lake and has full information on dates and times of the various activities.

The chalet-style *Duck Mountain Lodge*, overlooking the lake (ⓣ306/542-3466; ❸), is a relaxing place to stay; you can sleep in the large lodge, the two-bedroom town-house units with fireplaces or the woodland cabins nearby. There's also a campsite at Pickerel Point, 4km east of the main Saskatchewan entrance (ⓣ306/542-5500 or 1-800/205-7070; mid-May to early-Sept; $11–24).

Veregin

Coming from Duck Mountain on Hwy 5 the first town of any note is **VEREGIN**, a tiny place named after **Peter Veregin**, the leader of the pacifist Doukhobor sect (see p.708) whose seven thousand members migrated to Saskatchewan at the end of the nineteenth century. The town is home to the **National Doukhobor Heritage Village** (mid-May to mid-Sept daily 10am–6pm; rest of year by appointment; $4; ⓣ306/542-444). A modest museum traces the history of the sect and a large, square, refurbished two-storey prayer home contains Veregin's living quarters, complete with many original furnishings. The building, with its encircling veranda and wrought-iron adornment on both levels, dominates a large green lawn and faces the other village buildings, most of which were moved here from Doukhobor colonies in other parts of Saskatchewan. Lined up in a neat row are a farmhouse, blacksmith's shop, granary, bakery and bathhouse, the latter equipped with dried oak leaves used to cleanse the skin and make it fragrant. Another smaller prayer home features a Russian library and a display on Tolstoy, whose financial support helped the Doukhobors to migrate. On the grounds is an imposing bronze statue of the writer, donated by the Soviet Union.

Yorkton

Back on Hwy 16 and heading further west into Saskatchewan, **YORKTON** is the last sizeable place before you hit Saskatoon, 333km away. It was founded as an agricultural community in the 1880s by Ontarian farmers, although – as with so many other places hereabouts – it's the **Ukrainian** community that features most strongly in the town and surrounding area.

Yorkton's **bus station** is downtown at 35 1st Ave. Its **tourist office** (Mon–Fri 9am–noon & 1–5pm; ⓣ306/783-8707, ⓦwww.tourismyorkton.com) is at the junction of hwys 9 and 16.

The Town

The silver-painted dome and barrel roof of the nave of the white-brick **St Mary's Ukrainian Catholic Church** at 155 Catherine St, is the town's most distinctive feature. Inside, there's a large painting of the Coronation of the Virgin on the surface of the dome – about as close as you'll get in western Canada to the Baroque painted domes in Italian and German churches. The Ukrainian community also features strongly in Yorkton's branch of the **Western Development Museum** (Jan–March Tues–Fri 9am–5pm, Sat & Sun noon–5pm; Apr–Dec Mon–Fri 9am–5pm, Sat & Sun noon–5pm $8.50; ⓦwww.wdm.ca), which is devoted to the various ethnic groups who have settled in the region. You'll also find a replica of the interior of a 1902 Catholic church and a superb collection of early twentieth-century Fords and Buicks. The most startling sights are the bright-red, huge-wheeled early fire trucks, looking entirely too fragile to function. To see farmworkers and their fierce-looking machines in action, attend the **Threshermen's Show**, held in the museum grounds in early August.

Also in the city, at 49 Smith St and 3rd Avenue, is the **Godfrey Dean Art Gallery** (Mon–Fri 11am–5pm, Thurs 6–9pm, Sun 1–4pm; free), which has a small but striking permanent collection of Saskatchewan art, plus several galleries with temporary exhibitions. The town hosts the **Yorkton Short Film and Video Festival** (ⓦwww.yorktonshortfilm.org) in late May, the oldest of its kind in North America, started in 1947.

About 48km northwest of Yorkton off Hwy 16 is the attractive **Good Spirit Lake Provincial Park**, noted for its ecologically fragile sand dunes and the warm, shallow lake itself, which has exceptionally clear water. The south shore has fine beaches, a fuel station, mini golf, tennis courts, riding stables, dining and snacking facilities, plus a **campsite** (ⓣ306/792-4750; mid-May to Sept; $13–26).

Practicalities

Among several reasonably priced central **hotels** is the *Ramada Yorkton*, 100 Broadway St East (ⓣ306/783-9781 or 1-800/667-1585; ❺). A pleasant **B&B** is *Lazy Maples*, 111 Darlington St West (ⓣ306/783-7078; ❷); the owner is an excellent cook and offers Ukrainian pierogies for breakfast. You can **camp** in town at the well-shaded *Yorkton City Campground* (ⓣ306/786-1757; mid-May to Sept; $18–25), on Hwy 16A near the Western Development Museum.

Yorkton's **dining** scene is drab, though *Tapps Brewing Company*, 69 Broadway (ⓣ306/783-2522) is a lively brewpub with good bar food.

Little Manitou Lake

A mere 120km east of Saskatoon via Hwy 16 lies **Little Manitou Lake**. Set in a rather arid landscape it looks just like any other lake, until you submerge yourself in its murky waters – or try to, for its saline content is three times that of ocean water, and denser than Jordan and Israel's Dead Sea. You'll inevitably find yourself floating on the surface, feet up. The lake has also long been known for its healing properties; aboriginal peoples once camped on its shores and called it "lake of the healing waters".

Today, most people head to the tiny, rather ramshackle resort town of **Manitou Beach** on the lake's south shore to bathe in heated indoor mineral pools. You can experience near-weightlessness and sooth any rheumatic or arthritic pains in the heated comfort of Manitou Springs Mineral Spa (daily 9am–10pm; $14.95; Ⓣ306/946-2233 or 1-800/667-7672, Ⓦwww.manitousprings.ca), one of the largest and oldest mineral **spas** in Canada. You can also stay and eat in their hotel, whose rates (❺) include a dip in the spa.

Saskatoon and around

Set on the wide South Saskatchewan River at the heart of a vast wheat-growing area, **SASKATOON** is a commercial, manufacturing and distribution centre with a population of around 236,000 – making it Saskatchewan's largest city.

Ontario Methodists founded the town as a temperance colony in 1883 and named it after a local purple berry, but in spite of their enthusiasm the new settlement made an extremely slow start, partly because the semi-arid farming conditions were unfamiliar and partly because the 1885 Northwest Rebellion raised fears of Indian hostility. Although the railroad reached Saskatoon in 1890, there were still only 113 inhabitants at the beginning of the twentieth century. But the next decade saw a sudden influx of European and American settlers and, as the agricultural economy of the prairies expanded, a group of entrepreneurs nicknamed **boomers** came to both dominate and make Saskatoon the economic focus of the region. This success was underpinned by particularly sharp municipal loyalty: people who dared to criticize any aspect of the city, from the poor water quality to tyrannical labour practices, were dubbed **knockers**, and their opinions rubbished by the press. Yet the boomers established a city where solidarity overwhelmed differences in income and occupation.

These attitudes still tangibly prevail, making this a pleasant, well-groomed place, albeit one with just a trio of principal attractions – the **Mendel Art Gallery**, a branch of the **Western Development Museum** and, on the outskirts, **Wanuskewin**, a complex dedicated to the Plains Indians.

Further afield to the north, the highlights are the **Batoche National Historic Site** and **Prince Albert National Park**.

Saskatoon's festivals

Saskatoon's biggest and best shindig is the **Saskatchewan Jazz Festival** (Ⓦwww.saskjazz.com) in late June or early July; over five hundred musicians perform jazz, gospel and blues across the city, mostly for free. The **Shakespeare on the Saskatchewan Festival** (Ⓦwww.shakespeareonthesaskatchewan.com) sees plays performed in tents on the riverbank by the Mendel Art Gallery from early July to mid-August. The **Saskatoon International Fringe Festival** (Ⓦwww.saskatoonfringe.org), a week of alternative performances held at the beginning of August, features some comedy and theatre from all over the world. Also worthwhile is **Folkfest** (Ⓦwww.saskatoonfolkfest.ca), a large ethnic festival held in mid-August.

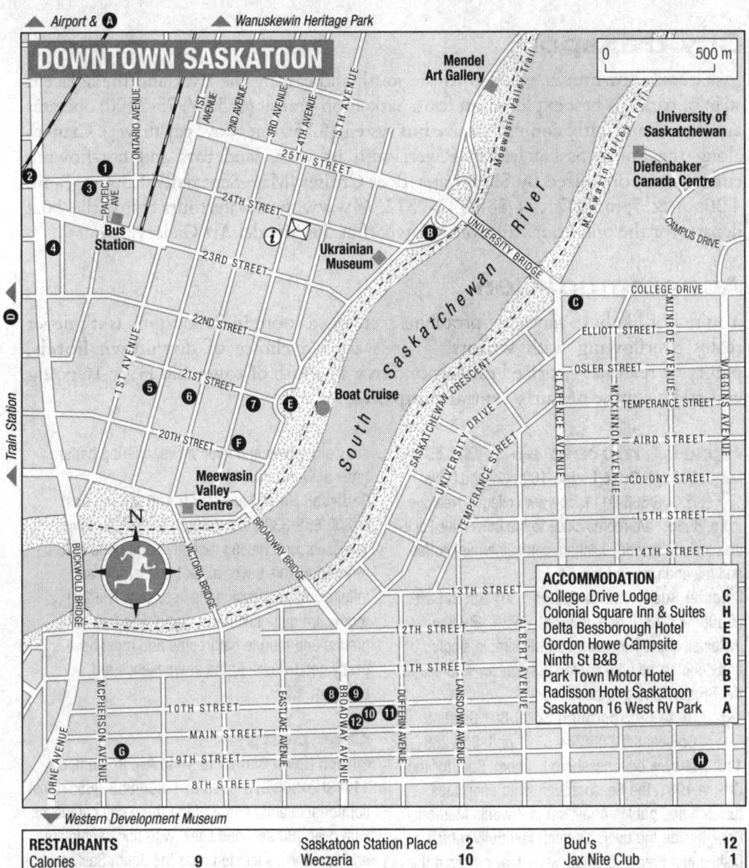

RESTAURANTS					
Calories	9	Saskatoon Station Place	2	Bud's	12
Freddie's Fifties Diner	4	Weczeria	10	Jax Nite Club	1
John's Steakhouse	7	**BARS & CLUBS**		The Odeon	5
Saigon Rose	3	Amigos Cantina	11	The Pat	C
Samurai	H	The Bassment	6	Stovin's Lounge	H
				Yard and Flagon Pub	8

Arrival and information

Saskatoon **airport** (Ⓦwww.yxe.ca) is 5km northwest of the city centre. There is no dedicated shuttle service to and from the airport but some hotels, including the *Park Town* (see p.574), operate their own; a taxi downtown will cost about $15. The **train station** is 7km west of the centre, on Chappell Drive, a five-minute walk from bus #3 on Dieppe Street; a taxi downtown costs about $17. More convenient is the city's **bus station** (Ⓣ306/933-8000), at 23rd Street East and Pacific Avenue in the centre.

The main **tourist office** (early May to early Sept Mon–Fri 8.15am–5.30pm; early Sept to early May Mon–Fri 8.15am–5pm; Ⓣ306/242-1206 or 1-800/567-2444, Ⓦwww.tourismsaskatoon.com) is at 101-222 4th Ave North. There's another tourist office at the corner of Avenue C North and 47th Street West (early May to early Sept daily 8.30am–5.30pm).

City transport

Saskatoon's downtown – edged to the south and east by the river and the adjacent strip of park – is best explored **on foot**. Saskatoon Transit (ⓣ306/975-3100) operates an efficient and fairly comprehensive **bus** system ($2.50 one-way; pay driver). **Cruises** along the South Saskatchewan River, with its weir, sand bars and fast-flowing currents, are organized by Shearwater Boat Cruises (May–Sept daily 1.30pm, 3pm, 4.30pm & 7pm; $17 ⓣ1-888/747-7572, ⓦwww.shearwatertours.com); the boat departs for the one-hour trip from the wharf at the Mendel Art Gallery.

Accommodation

You're not likely to have any problems securing a room in Saskatoon, as it's never really overflowing with visitors. There's a good choice of downtown **hotels**, plenty of reasonably priced **motels** on Hwy 11 south of town and Hwy 16 going east and a couple of fairly central **campsites**.

Hotels, motels and B&Bs

College Drive Lodge 1020 College Drive ⓣ306/665-9111, ⓦwww.collegedrivelodge.com. Budget a/c rooms close to the university. Facilities include laundry, kitchen, complimentary coffee and tea and free parking. ❷

Colonial Square Inn & Suites 1301 8th St East ⓣ306/343-1676 or 1-800/667-3939, ⓦwww.colonialsquaremotel.com. Eighty simple singles and doubles, all with cable TV & free wi-fi. Close to the Broadway Ave area. ❹

Delta Bessborough Hotel 601 Spadina Crescent ⓣ306/244-5521 or 1-800/268-1133, ⓦwww.deltabessborough.com. Built for the CNR in 1931, the Bessborough is an enormous turreted and gabled affair, set in Kiwanis Memorial Park, beside the river. It's been tastefully refurbished in a French château style that makes it the city's most striking building – but some claim it's haunted. ❼

Ninth St Bed & Breakfast 227 9th St East ⓣ306/244-3754, ⓦwww.bbcanada.com/949.html. Three attractive suites with shared bath, great gourmet breakfasts and bike rental. In the historic Nutana district and near the Broadway Ave area. ❸

Park Town Motor Hotel 924 Spadina Crescent East ⓣ306/244-5564 or 1-800/667-3999, ⓦwww.parktownhotel.com. Large hotel with standard rooms and river views, offering better rates at weekends. ❺

Radisson Hotel Saskatoon 405 20th St East ⓣ306/665-3322 or 1-800/333-3333, ⓦwww.radisson.com. Having recently undergone a $5m renovation, this tower-block hotel is now an infinitely more pleasing place to stay. The 291 rooms are quite luxurious, come with free wi-fi, granite and marble bathrooms and most have pretty good views. Rates at weekends are excellent. ❺

Campsites

Gordon Howe Campsite 1640 Ave P South, off 11th St ⓣ306/975-3328 or 1-866/855-6655. Most comfortable and central of the three city campsites, with over 130 serviced sites, with bbq, picnic area and laundry. It's located near the South Saskatchewan River, 4km southwest of the centre; take 22nd St out of town and follow Ave P south. Mid-April to mid-Oct. $17–30.

Saskatoon 16 West RV Park Hwy 16, 1.5km northwest of the city ⓣ306/931-8905 or 1-800/478-7833, ⓦwww.saskatoonrvpark.com. Twenty-five pull-through sites, plus fifty serviced sites with hook-ups and free wi-fi. The on-site shop sells local crafts. Mid-April to mid-Oct. $28.50–34.50.

The City

Most of Saskatoon's principal sights are on or near the **Meewasin Valley Trail**, a circular, nineteen-kilometre walking and cycle route that follows the narrow strip of park along both banks of the river between the Idylwyld Drive and Circle Drive bridges. At the start of the trail, the **Meewasin Valley Centre** (Mon–Fri 9am–5pm, Sat & Sun 10.30am–5pm; free; ⓦwww.meewasin.com), 402 3rd Ave South, provides tourist information and a useful introduction to the region's history. A few minutes' walk north from the centre, along the west bank, the

Ukrainian Museum of Canada (Tues–Sat 10am–5pm, Sun 1–5pm; $4; Ⓦwww.umc.sk.ca), 910 Spadina Crescent East at 24th Street East, is the more interesting of the city's two Ukrainian museums, representing the Orthodox as distinct from the Catholic tradition. Displays cover Ukrainian migrational history, traditional textile design, festivals and Easter-egg painting. The **Mendel Art Gallery** (daily 9am–9pm; free; Ⓣ306/975-7610, Ⓦwww.mendel.ca), overlooking the river from Spadina Crescent, just north of 25th Street East, features temporary shows of modern Canadian and international art and includes paintings by many of the country's renowned artists – Emily Carr, Lawren Harris and David Milne among them – and a good selection of Inuit sculpture.

Across the river from the gallery and over University Bridge is the campus of the **University of Saskatchewan** (Ⓦwww.usask.ca), which occupies a prime riverbank site just to the north of College Drive. Departmental collections include a **Museum of Antiquities** (mid-Jan to mid-Dec Mon–Fri 9am–4.30pm; free), in the Murray Building and the small **Kenderdine Gallery** (Mon–Fri 11.30am–4pm; free). Neither draw as many visitors as the **Diefenbaker Canada Centre** (Mon–Fri 9.30am–4.30pm, Thurs till 8pm, Sat & Sun noon–4.30pm; $7; Ⓣ306/966-8384), a museum, archive and research centre at the west end of the campus, beside the river. Prime Minister from 1957 to 1963, John Diefenbaker was a caricaturist's dream, with his large flat face, protruding teeth and wavy white hair; the museum's high point is its assortment of newspaper cartoons. He was buried just outside the centre in 1979. One of the finest **views** of the city is from the grounds of the centre.

On the south side of the river is the Saskatoon **Western Development Museum** (Jan–March Tues–Sun 9am–5pm; April–Dec daily 9am–5pm; $8.50; Ⓦwww.wdm.ca) at 2610 Lorne Ave South; take bus #1 from 2nd Avenue downtown. Its principal exhibit is "Boomtown", an ambitious reconstruction of a typical Saskatchewan small-town main street circa 1910, complete with boardwalk sidewalks and parked vehicles. More like a film set than a museum, its mixture of replica and original buildings include a school, general store, church, train station and a combined pool hall and barbershop.

Wanuskewin Heritage Park

Wanuskewin Heritage Park (daily 9am–4.30pm; $8.50; Ⓦwww.wanuskewin.com), twenty minutes' drive north of the city centre along Hwy 10 then Warman and Wanuskewin roads, is Saskatoon's principal tourist attraction and a lavish tribute to the culture of Northern Plains Indians. It's well worth the trip out here, as the commercial aspect is played down in favour of a sensitive interpretation of the Indians' spiritual relationship to the land and to living creatures.

Bordering the South Saskatchewan River in the attractive wooded Opamihaw Valley, the park embraces a string of marshy creeks and wooded ridges that have been used by aboriginal peoples for more than six thousand years. All along the trails are ecologically fragile plants and flowers that must not be picked. The nineteen sites are connected by trails and walkways to a visitor centre featuring reconstructions of teepees, a buffalo pound and a buffalo jump, as well as displays on traditional skills as diverse as tool-making and storytelling. The park can also arrange for overnight camping in teepees with breakfast, dinner cooked on the fire and interpretive programmes including storytelling and bannock-making (mid-May to Sept; reservation essential). The attached **restaurant** specializes in indigenous foodstuffs such as buffalo meat and bannock bread, and a gift shop has a full range of authentic arts and crafts by aboriginal people. Wanuskewin has been developed with the cooperation of local peoples, who provide most of the interpretive staff. There is no public transport; a **taxi** from downtown costs around $20.

Saskatoon berry pie

The thing to try while in town is **Saskatoon berry pie**, made with berries grown on the outskirts of the city. Perhaps the best place for a sampling is the *Berry Barn*, 830 Valley Rd (May–Sept daily 10am–9pm; April & Oct–Dec Mon–Thurs 10am–5pm, Fri–Sun 10am–9pm; ⓣ306/978-9797), located 11km southwest of town off Hwy 11. It's one of a number of places along this road that allows you to pick your own fruit, and also has a good restaurant serving hearty home-made food.

Eating

Saskatoon has an assortment of **restaurants** clustered in and around the downtown core and a couple of blocks of Broadway Avenue, south of the river. Broadway is the city's modest cultural centre, the home of the Broadway Theatre and a handful of more alternative shops and cafés.

Restaurants

Calories 721 Broadway Ave ⓣ306/655-7991, ⓦwww.caloriesrestaurants.com. Atmospheric French-style bistro (the chef grew up in Provence so, yes, this is the real deal), with great wine list. Mains from $22.

Freddie's Fifties Diner 140 Idylwyld Drive North ⓣ306/343-8437. Good spot for breakfasts, burgers and shakes, all eaten in crimson vinyl booths to the sounds of Elvis Radio – streaming from Graceland. Opens at 7am, closed Sun.

John's Steakhouse 401 21st St East ⓣ306/244-6384, ⓦwww.johnssaskatoon.com. Probably the best steaks in town, done any way you want in a fine-dining environment. Mains $29–62 Closed Sun.

Saigon Rose 69 24th St East ⓣ306/242-1351. Simple place with plastic tablecloths and fantastically cheap and filling Vietnamese and Chinese food; most dishes are $7–10.

Samurai At the *Delta Bessborough Hotel* (see p.574) ⓣ306/683-6926. Good but pricey Japanese sushi and *teppanyaki* restaurant. Mains $24-39.

Saskatoon Station Place 221 Idylwyld Drive North ⓣ306/244-7777, ⓦwww.saskatoonstationplace.com. Dine on steak and prime rib in Pullman cars in a converted train station. Lunch dishes average $11 for wraps, burgers and salads; dinners entrees are around $23. The Sun brunches are great.

Weczeria Food & Wine 616 10th St E ⓣ306/933-9600, ⓦwww.weczeriarestaurant.ca. Tiny, unpretentious French restaurant that delights gourmets with seasonal dishes made from locally grown ingredients. The menu changes daily and mains are in the $22–28 range.

Nightlife and entertainment

Nightlife is a little slow, but a few pubs and clubs can reward the determined, with a concentration in the old warehouse district on the corner of 24th Street and Pacific Avenue. While you're in town try a bottle of **Great Western Beer**, a local product whose future was threatened by the merger of Canada's two giant brewing companies, Molson and Carling O'Keefe. The workers bought the factory themselves and can now barely keep up with demand.

The Broadway Theatre, 715 Broadway Ave (ⓣ306/652-6556, ⓦwww.broadwaytheatre.ca), has the best of foreign and domestic **films**. For **theatre**, the Persephone, 100 Spanida Crescent (ⓣ306/384-7727, ⓦwww.persephonetheatre.org), is the best known of the city's professional companies; their season runs from October to May. Visiting ballet, theatre and opera appears at the TCU Place, 35 22nd St East (ⓣ306/975-7777 or 1-800/970-7328, ⓦwww.tcuplace.com). The *Star Phoenix* newspaper carries listings at the weekend.

Bars and clubs

Amigos Cantina 806 Dufferin Ave ⓣ306/652-4912, ⓦwww.amigoscantina.com. Excellent mostly Mexican restaurant that becomes a club at night with local bands often playing. Mains $12–15.

The Bassment B3 202 4th Ave North ⓣ306/683-2277, ⓦwww.saskatoonjazzsociety.com. Great jazz venue attracting international performers. Live jazz performances every Sat evening from Oct to April, usually starting at 8:30pm.
Buds 817 Broadway Ave ⓣ306/244-4155, ⓦwww.budsonbroadway.com. Rough-and-ready bar with nightly R&B acts, plus jam sessions Sat afternoon. $3–5 cover charge.
Jax Nite Club 302 Pacific Ave ⓣ306/934-4444 ⓦwww.jaxniteclub.com. One of several middling dance clubs in the warehouse area; follow the crowds.
Odeon 241 2nd Ave South ⓣ306/651-1000 ⓦwww.theodeon.ca. Saskatoon's hippest club, attracting the city's chic crowd. Occasional live music but mostly dance and techno.
The Pat 345 2nd Ave North. Vast middle-of-the road nightclub catering to just about everybody, though students dominate. Mostly Top 40, with occasional live music.
Stovin's Lounge At the *Delta Bessborough Hotel* (see p.574). A quiet and comfortable lounge, ideal for chatting and unwinding when all the other options sound like too much effort.
Yard and Flagon Pub 718 Broadway Ave ⓣ306/653-8883. Broadway bar with a lively rooftop that pulls in the university crowd.

Listings

Hospitals Saskatoon City Hospital, 701 Queen St ⓣ306/655-8000.
Laundries Off-Broadway Laundromat, 835b Broadway Ave ⓣ306/244-1344.
Police 130 4th Ave North ⓣ306/975-8300.
Post office 202 4th Ave North.
Taxi United Cabs ⓣ306/652-2222.
Weather ⓣ306/975-4266.

▲ A First Nation Cree man, Wanuskewin Heritage Park

Batoche National Historic Site

North of Saskatoon on Hwy 11, the briefest of detours will take you to the site of the Métis's last stand – and the last place where Canadians fought against Canadians. **Batoche National Historic Site** (May–Sept daily 9am–5pm; $7.80; ⓣ905/566-4321 or 1-888/773-8888, ⓦwww.pc.gc.ca) occupies a splendid site on the east bank of the South Saskatchewan River, just off Hwy 225. A **tourist office** has displays on Métis culture and provides a detailed account of the rebellion, supplemented by an exceptional 45-minute audiovisual presentation combining clips of re-enactments, spoken narration, music and tableaux of realistic mannequins. This provides an insight into the Métis way of life and a blow-by-blow account of the battle, but rather glosses over the cause of the conflict; the displays are perhaps too sympathetic to the Métis, instead of appreciating the government's concern to avoid Canada being split in half – the west was still very much an open territory at the time.

Behind the office, the main footpath leads to a refurbished Catholic church and adjacent rectory; all that are left of the original village. A few minutes' walk away, in the cemetery perched above the riverbank, memorials inscribed with the hoary commendation "a credit to his race" contrast with the rough chunk of rock that commemorates Riel's commander-in-chief, **Gabriel Dumont**. A stern and ferocious man, Dumont insisted he be buried standing up – so he could enjoy a good view of the river.

The Métis and the Northwest Rebellion

As the offspring of native women and white fur traders, the Métis were for centuries Canada's most marginalized group. Recognised neither as Canadians nor aboriginals, they were effectively denied rights and often forced to wander the country in poverty with nowhere to settle. The 1869–70 Red River rebellion in Manitoba, led by **Louis Riel**, won significant concessions from the Canadian government but failed to protect the Métis's way of life against the effects of increasing white settlement. Consequently, many Métis moved west to farm the banks of the **South Saskatchewan River**, where the men acted as intermediaries between aboriginals and the whites. Yet when government surveyors arrived in 1878 the Métis realized – as they had on the Red River twenty years before – their claim to the land they farmed was far from secure.

Beginning with the Métis, a general sense of instability spread across the region in the early 1880s, fuelled by the increasingly restless and hungry **Cree** peoples, as well as by the discontent of white settlers angry at the high freight charges levied on their produce. The leaders of the Métis decided to act and in June 1884 they sent a delegation to Montana, where Riel was in exile. Convinced the Métis were God's chosen instrument to purify the human race – and he their Messiah – Riel was easily persuaded to return and spent the winter unsuccessfully petitioning for confirmation of Métis rights.

In March 1885, Riel and his supporters declared a provisional government at **Batoche** and demanded the surrender of **Fort Carlton**, the nearest Mountie outpost, 35km to their west on the North Saskatchewan River. The police superintendent refused and the force he dispatched to re-establish order was badly mauled at **Duck Lake**. When news of the uprising reached the Cree, some 300km away, they attacked the local Hudson's Bay Company store, killing its nine occupants in the so-called **Frog Lake Massacre**. Within a couple of weeks, three columns of militia were converging on Big Bear's Cree and the meagre Métis forces at Batoche. The total number of casualties – about fifty altogether – does not indicate the full significance of the engagement, which for the Métis marked the end of their brief independence and influence. Riel's subsequent execution in Regina on November 16, 1885 was bitterly denounced in Québec and remains a potent symbol of the divide between English- and French-speaking Canada.

The church and cemetery are at the centre of the park's **walking trails**, which extend along the riverbank in both directions. Roughly 1km to the south, there's a military graveyard, a Métis farmhouse and the remains of some rifle pits; about the same distance to the north, there's the site of the old ferry crossing, more rifle pits and the foundations of several Métis buildings. With a knowledge of the history, the park becomes an extremely evocative spot.

Duck Lake and Fort Carlton

Back on Hwy 11, on the west side of the South Saskatchewan River, the tiny farming community of **DUCK LAKE** – where many buildings have outdoor murals depicting local history – is home to a regional **interpretive centre** (late May to early Sept daily 10am–5.30pm; $4.50; Ⓦwww.dlric.org), at 5 Anderson Ave, with displays on aboriginal, Métis and pioneer society from 1870 to 1905. Prize exhibits include some elaborate Cree costumes, an outfit that belonged to the Sioux chief Little Fox (an adviser to Sitting Bull) and Gabriel Dumont's gold watch, presented to him in New York where he was appearing in Buffalo Bill's Wild West Show. The building's huge tower gives views a long way over the prairies.

Continuing 25km west along Hwy 212, you'll reach **Fort Carlton Provincial Park** (mid-May to Aug daily 10am–6pm; $4), a reconstruction of a Hudson's Bay Company trading post circa 1860. Founded in 1810, the riverbank station was fortified in successive decades and became an important centre of the fur and pemmican trade, until the demise of the buffalo brought an end to its success. Reduced to a warehouse facility in the early 1880s, the fort was garrisoned by the Mounties during the Northwest Rebellion (see box opposite), but was finally burnt down and abandoned in 1885. The **visitor centre** provides an historical introduction to the fort, whose stockade shelters replicas of the clerk's quarters, a sail and harness shop, a fur and provisions store with piles of colourfully striped Hudson's Bay Company blankets and bottles of bright Indian trading beads and a trading shop, where the merchandise included gunpowder – which meant the clerks were forbidden to light a stove here, no matter what the temperature. There's an on-site **campsite** (mid-May to early Sept; $13). Take care when hiking or camping, as the wooded gullies of the North Saskatchewan River are home to a number of **black bears**.

Prince Albert National Park

Prince Albert National Park ($7.80), 230km north of Saskatoon, is a great tract of wilderness where the aspen parkland of the south meets the boreal forest of the north – it's a landscape of rivers and creeks, dozens of deep lakes, pockets of pasture and areas of spruce bog. The shift in vegetation is mirrored by the **wildlife**, with prairie species such as coyote and wild bison giving way to black bear, moose, wolf, caribou, osprey and eagle further north.

Arrival and information

The tourist village of **WASKESIU**, approached from the south by Hwy 263 and from the east by hwys 2 and 264, is the only settlement in the park. Spread out along the southern shore of Waskesiu Lake, it has all the usual facilities, plus a narrow sandy beach that gets ridiculously overcrowded in summer. The park's **nature centre**, on Lakeview Drive (July–Aug daily noon–4pm; Ⓣ306/663-4522), has a hands-on display on the southern boreal forest. In the centre of Waskesiu, at the junction of Lakeview Drive and Waskesiu Drive, the park's main **information centre** (mid-May to early Sept daily 8am–8pm; Ⓣ306/663-4522, Ⓦwww.pc.gc.ca) gives advice on wildlife and the condition of the hiking trails, along with weather forecasts. The information office also runs **guided walks** in July and August and issues backcountry camping permits ($9) for the primitive, seasonal **campsites** dotted along most of the more substantial trails.

Waskesiu's **bus stop** is in the centre close to Waskesiu Drive. Its stores sell a full range of outback **equipment**, but none rent out camping gear. **Canoe** and **kayak rentals** (Ⓣ306/663-5994) are available at three marinas within the park.

The Park

Several of the park's easier **hiking trails** begin in or near Waskesiu, most notably the thirteen-kilometre **Kingfisher Trail**, which loops through the forest just to the west of the resort. The best trails and **canoe routes** begin roughly 15km further north at the bottom end of **Kingsmere Lake**, accessible by boat or car from Waskesiu. They include a delightful week-long canoe trip along the western shore of Kingsmere Lake before heading through a series of remote lakes amid dense boreal forest. There's also a twenty-kilometre hike or canoe (a good overnight trip) to the idyllic spot of **Grey Owl's Cabin** (May–Sept), situated beside tiny Ajawaan Lake, near the northern shore of Kingsmere Lake. Grey Owl (see p.193) lived in this cabin from 1931 until 1937, the year before his death, and it was here that he wrote one of his better books, *Pilgrims of the Wild*, and where he, his wife and daughter are buried. For further information on these and other hiking and canoe routes, check at the park information office. Whatever you do in the park, remember to take **insect repellent**.

Park practicalities

Waskesiu's main street, Waskesiu Drive, runs roughly parallel to and just south of the lake, its western section curving round behind Lakeview Drive. Almost all the **hotels** and **motels** are on or near these two streets, including the *Lakeview Hotel*, 811 Lakeview Drive (Ⓣ306/663-5311 or 1-877/331-3302, Ⓦwww.lakeviewhotel.com; ④), and the more luxurious *All Season Waskesiu Lake Lodge*, Lakeview Drive (Ⓣ306/663-6161, Ⓦwww.waskesiulakelodge.com; May to mid-Oct; ⑤), with one- and two-bedroom apartments that include lakeside decks and barbecues. For **bungalow** and **cabin** accommodation try *Kapasiwin Bungalows* (Ⓣ306/663-5225 or 1-877/963-5225, Ⓦwww.kapasiwin.com; May to mid-Oct; ⑥), 2km round the lake to the east of the resort; its cabins form a quiet mini-resort with its own private beach. The wooded *Beaver Glen Campground* (Ⓣ1-877/737-3783; mid-May to Sept; $20–25) near Waskesiu Lake is popular with Rvers, or there are several other unserviced campsites ($9) along Hwy 263 and on kingsmere Lake, which all operate a self-registration system.

There are several low-priced **restaurants** and **snack bars** in Waskesiu. On the beachfront, *The Beach House* is good for cappuccinos, wraps and desserts. For more expensive dining, try the *Hawood Inn*, 851 Lakeview Drive, where main courses start at around $16 and include good cuts of local beef.

Saskatoon to Edmonton

From Saskatoon it's only another 275km to the Alberta border and the dull town of **Lloydminster** which straddles it. But **Redberry Lake** is a must for keen birdwatchers, and the **Battlefords** make another good short stop to see a refurbished Mountie stockade. In Alberta, and in the run up to Edmonton amid rippling hills, rivers, lakes, lonely farms and open prairie, lie the worthwhile **Elk Island National Park**, where bison roam, and the **Ukrainian Cultural Village**, a tribute to a major local immigrant group.

Redberry Lake

The **Redberry Lake World Biosphere Reserve** (Ⓦ www.redberrylake.ca; free), about 100km northwest of Saskatoon via hwys 16, 340 and then 40, is one of the province's best areas to view over two hundred species of birds. The north shore of Redberry Lake is home to several rare species, including piping plovers and white pelicans. There are trails around the lakeshore, as well as an interpretive centre (mid-May to mid Sept daily 9am–5pm, Ⓣ 306/549-4060) with videos and dioramas on the lake's fragile ecosystem. You can book guided walking tours ($5) and get information on a driving tour of the region at the centre. Within the reserve, the Redberry Lake Regional Park (May–Sept; $5) has **camping** ($12–25).

The Battlefords

Following the Yellowhead Hwy towards Edmonton, you'll come to the **Battlefords**, 140km from Saskatoon. Sedate little **BATTLEFORD**, with its trim riverside streets, lost its pre-eminence when the Canadian Pacific Railway routed its transcontinental line through Regina, which became the new capital in 1883. Twenty years later, its prospects were further damaged by the Canadian Northern Railway, which laid its tracks on the opposite bank of North Saskatchewan River. Consequently, Battleford stagnated and shrank, while its grimy rival **NORTH BATTLEFORD**, some 5km away, became a moderately successful industrial centre. Both towns have interesting museums and Battleford's **Saskatchewan Handcraft Festival**, held in mid-July, is one of the largest and best of its kind.

All long-distance and local buses use North Battleford **bus station**, at 2691-98th Street, 2km north of downtown.

Battleford

Battleford's **visitor information** is housed in the **Fred Light Museum** (mid-May to Aug daily 9am–8pm; free), 11 20th St East at the junction of hwys 4 and 40, which also has a substantial collection of early firearms, military uniforms and a replica of an old general store. It's thoroughly upstaged by **Fort Battleford National Historic Site** (mid-May to early Sept daily 9am–5pm; $7.80 Ⓦ www.parkscanada.gc.ca/battleford), which overlooks the river valley from the top of a steep bluff 1.5km south down Central Avenue. An information centre provides a general introduction while displays in the restored barracks next door explain its history, assisted by costumed guides. Within the replica stockade stand four original buildings, including the **Sick Horse Stable**, where the delicate constitutions of the Mounties' horses – most of which came from Ontario – were coaxed into accepting unfamiliar prairie grasses. The centrepiece of the park is the **Commanding Officer's Residence**, which has been returned to its 1880s appearance. The hewn-log house contains an enormous carved bed-head and a couple of magnificent black and chrome oven ranges, which must have been a nightmare to transport this far west. The house was not as comfortable as it seems today, principally because the high ceilings made it almost impossible to heat.

The town has the splendid *Eiling Kramer* **campsite** (Ⓣ 306/937-6212; May–Sept; $17–27), overlooking the river valley from beside Fort Battleford. For **food**, *Pennydale Junction*, in a converted 1908 CNR train station at 92 22nd St and Main Street, has great seafood, pizzas and steaks from $13.

North Battleford

On Hwy 16, just east of **North Battleford**, a branch of the **Western Development Museum** (Jan–March Tues–Sun 9am–5pm; April–Dec daily 9am–5pm; $8.50 Ⓦ www.wdm.ca) deals with local farming history. Inside, vintage vehicles and a "Jolly Life of the Farmer's Wife" exhibit of old ranges and laundry equipment recall older, harder, times. Outside, the Heritage Farm and Village contains 36 buildings saved from around the province, including tiny churches and homesteads, banks, a general store, creaky barns and a 1928 grain elevator. The museum is an excellent way to acquaint yourself with prairie history and is most fun on the second weekend in August when costumed locals bake bread and make crafts.

Downtown North Battleford forms a central gridiron north of the main road, Railway Avenue, which runs southeast to northwest. At its northwestern end, the old municipal library now houses the **Allen Sapp Gallery** (June–Sept daily 11am–5pm; Oct–May Wed–Sun noon–4pm; Ⓦwww.allensapp.com; free), 1 Railway Ave East, which showcases the work of local Cree Allen Sapp. One of the best-known Canadian contemporary native artists, Sapp trawls his childhood recollections of life on the Red Pheasant reserve in the 1930s for most of his material. His simply drawn figures are characteristically cast in wide prairie spaces, whose delicately blended colours hint at a nostalgic regard for a time when his people had a greater sense of community.

North Battleford's **tourist information centre** (June–Aug Mon–Fri 8am–8pm, Sat & Sun 9am–5pm; Ⓣ306/445-6226 or 1-800/243-0394, Ⓦwww.battlefordstourism.com) is on Hwy 16, 2km away from downtown, where most **hotels** tend to be the dispiriting haunts of the drunk and the dispossessed. Instead, stay beside Hwy 16 in the likes of the *Tropical Inn*, (Ⓣ306/446-4700 or 1-800/219-5244, Ⓦwww.tropicalinns.com; ❸), about 1km east of town. North Battleford is short on good **restaurants**, but has a few inexpensive places, including the Chinese place *Dragon Palace*, at 1292 101st St.

Lloydminster

Some 140km northwest of the Battlefords you hit the Saskatchewan–Alberta border and the drab city of **LLOYDMINSTER**, founded in 1903 by the Barr colonists, a group of two thousand British pioneers. It's a popular break in the journey along Hwy 16 and has a **tourist office** at 5001 50th Ave (Mon–Fri 8am–5pm; Ⓣ306/825-6180 or 1-800/825-6180). Both Tourism Saskatchewan and Alberta Tourism run seasonal **tourist offices** on either side of the border. The **bus station** is on the Alberta side at 5217-51st St.

Probably the most interesting thing about the city is its geographical location: the 4th Meridian runs right down 50th Avenue, the main street. A series of 30m-high metal border markers, shaped like the survey stakes used by the original surveyors when they laid out the border between the two provinces, line Hwy 16

Hotels and **motels** line 44th Street (the Yellowhead Hwy) and 50th Avenue (Hwy 17). The pick of these are the *Best Canadian Motor Inn*, 4320 44th St (Ⓣ306/825-4400 or 1-888/700-2264, Ⓦwww.bestcdn.com; ❺) with an indoor pool and cable TV, and the *Best Western Wayside Inn* (Ⓣ780/875-4404 or 1-800/658-4404; ❻), a sprawling complex just west of the city on Hwy 16 on the Alberta side. Check at the tourist office for **campsites**.

Elk Island National Park and the Ukrainian Cultural Village

The rolling aspen parklands of **Elk Island National Park** (Ⓦwww.parkscanada.gc.ca/elk; $7.80), 45km east of Edmonton along Hwy 16 draw visitors in numbers, thanks to the concentration of **wildlife**. Herds of plains and wood bison – a combined population of about eight hundred – are the particular highlight, but there are also good numbers of elk, moose, deer, beavers and coyotes. Viewing these animals is often easy, and the chances of watching free-roaming bison at close quarters from your vehicle along the main road is very good; if you don't see them here, you almost certainly will along some of the 16km of hiking paths criss-crossing the park. The park's interpretive centre (daily 8am–4pm July & Aug) by the gate has backgrounders on the animals, along with information on hiking, cycling, canoeing, skiing and snowshoeing. They can also advise on **camping** (Ⓣ905/566-4321 or 1-877/737-3783, Ⓦwww.pccamping.ca; $6–25.50; mid-May to early Oct).

A good side-trip from the park is a visit to the **Ukrainian Cultural Heritage Village** (mid-May to early Sept daily 10am–6pm, early Sept to early Oct Sat & Sun 10am–4pm; $8; Ⓣ780/662-3640, Ⓦwww.cd.gov.ab.ca/uchv), 5km east of Edmonton along Hwy 16. This reconstructed village celebrates the culture of the 250,000 Ukrainians who migrated here in the late nineteenth and early twentieth centuries, attracted by the familiar landscape and climate. The centrepiece is an impressive Ukrainian Greek Orthodox Church, surrounded with many seemingly authentic pioneer homes and businesses where costumed guides help bring the experience to life.

Edmonton

Alberta's provincial capital, **EDMONTON** is among Canada's most northerly cities and at times – particularly in the teeth of its bitter winters – can seem a little too far north for comfort.

Situated above the waters of the North Saskatchewan River, whose park-filled valley meanders below the high-rises of downtown, the proud and bustling city tries hard with its parks, restaurants, urban-renewal projects and festivals – which include August's world-class **Folk Music Festival**. Yet the **downtown** core has a somewhat unfinished feel to it (which perhaps helps contribute to people from fierce civic rival Calgary referring to the city as "Deadmonton"), despite having a handful of modest sites. It's fitting, then, that the premier attraction for many visitors is a shopping centre, the infamous **West Edmonton Mall**, which certainly has curiosity value but doesn't really merit a special journey. Far more worthwhile is **Old Strathcona**, a rejuvenated late-nineteenth-century district south of the North Saskatchewan River filled with heritage buildings, low-key museums and a booming restaurant, bar and **nightlife** scene, fuelled by a huge recent injection of oil money – and young workers – into the city. Another excellent attraction is the impressive **TELUS World of Science** museum.

Edmonton lands on many itineraries en route to somewhere else – particularly Jasper National Park or Northern Alberta and the Northwest Territories – so time will likely be limited, but if you have some to spare it's worth making the short trip east out of town to **Elk Island National Park** and the **Ukrainian Cultural Village** (see p.582)

Edmonton addresses

Addresses in Edmonton can look complicated. Avenues run east–west, with numbers increasing as you travel north, while streets run north–south, the numbers increasing as you move west. This is easy enough, but note that building numbers tend to be tacked onto the end of street numbers: for instance, 10021-104th Ave is building number 21 on 100th St, at the intersection with 104th Ave.

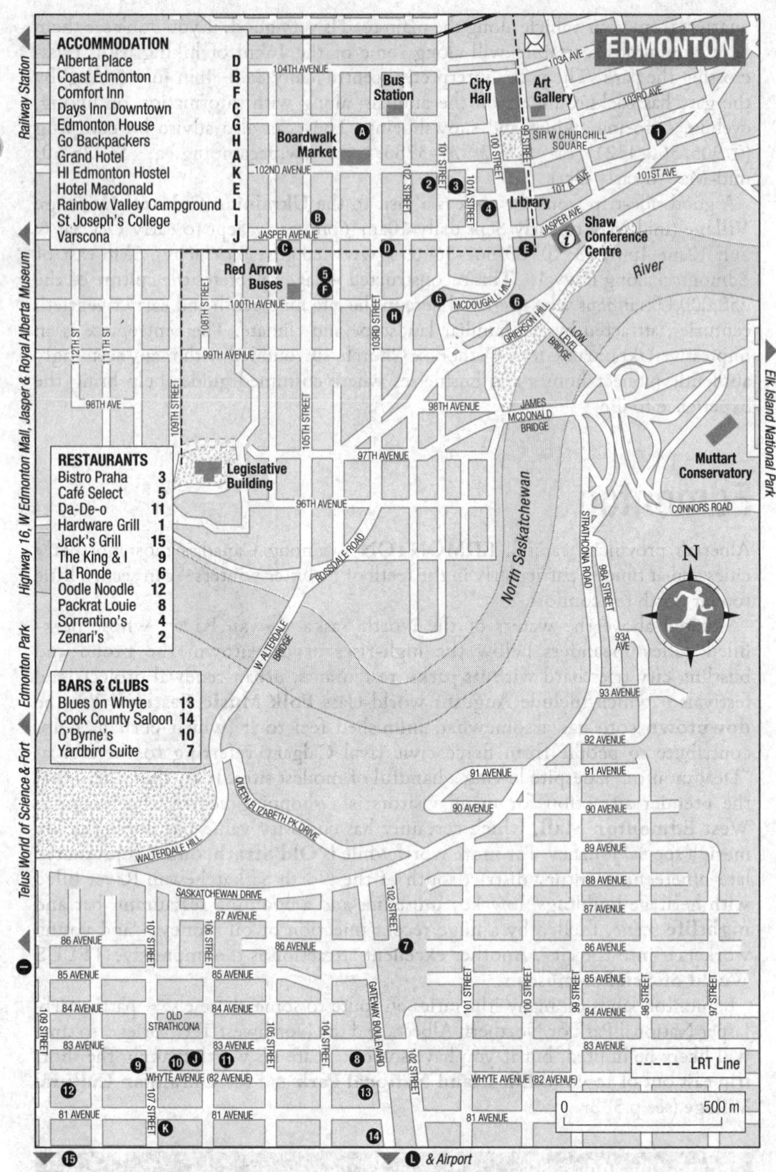

A brief history

Aboriginal peoples were attracted to Edmonton's location for thousands of years before the arrival of Europeans, thanks to the abundance of local **quartzite**, used to make stone weapons and tools. **Fur traders** arrived in the eighteenth century, attracted by river and forest habitats and some of Canada's richest fur-producing territory. The site lay at the meeting point of territory patrolled by the Blackfoot to the south and the Cree, Dene and Assiniboine to the north, providing a sort of no-man's-land where normally implacable enemies could coexist and trade with intermediaries like the North West Company, which built Fort Augustus on Edmonton's present location in 1795. The fort was joined later the same year by **Fort Edmonton**, the redoubtable log stockade of the Hudson's Bay Company.

The area soon became a major trading district but **settlers** arrived in force only after 1870, when the HBC sold its governing right to the Dominion of Canada. Worldwide demand for grain also attracted settlers to the region, now able to produce crops despite the poor climate thanks to advances in agricultural technology. The city only became firmly established with the Yukon gold rush of 1897, and only then through a scam of tragic duplicity. Prompted by the city's outfitters, newspapers lured prospectors with the promise of an "All Canadian Route" to the gold fields that avoided Alaska and the dreaded Chilkoot Trail (see p.896). In the event, this turned out to be a largely phantom trail across 3000km of intense wilderness. Hundreds of men perished as they pushed north; many of those who survived, or who never set off, ended up settling in Edmonton. World War II saw the city's role reinforced by its strategic position relative to Alaska, while its postwar growth was guaranteed by the 1947 Leduc oil strike; by 1956 some three thousand wells were in production within 100km of the city.

If Edmonton has achieved any fame since, it has been in the field of sports, as the home of **Wayne Gretzky**, the greatest player in ice-hockey history. Oil money continues to bankroll all sorts of civic improvements, though never quite manages to disguise the city's rather rough-and-ready pioneer roots.

Arrival and information

Edmonton is one of the easiest places to reach in western Canada. Its road and rail links are excellent and the international **airport** (Ⓦ www.flyeia.com), 29km south of downtown off Hwy 2 (Calgary Trail), is served by many airlines. There's a small tourist information desk (Mon–Fri 8am–midnight, Sat & Sun 9am–midnight; Ⓣ780/890-8382 or 1-800/268-7134) in the arrivals area. The Sky Shuttle **bus** (daily every 20–30min 6am–midnight; $15 one-way; Ⓣ780/465-8515) runs to downtown hotels, the university district and the western part of the city on three different routes, leaving from outside arrivals; buy tickets from the driver. A taxi dowtown costs around $50. The Jasper Connector service links Edmonton airport directly with Jasper (daily at 3.30pm; $100 one-way; Ⓣ780/852-4056 or 1-888/789-3641).

The **train station** is 3km northwest of downtown at 12360-121st St. The Greyhound **bus station**, 10324-103rd St (Ⓣ780/420-2400), is also within easy walking distance of downtown. **Red Arrow** buses serving Calgary (4–7 daily;

Edmonton festivals

There's almost always something good on in Edmonton (check Ⓦ www.festivalcity.ca for the latest). The finest event is easily the **Edmonton Folk Music Festival** (Ⓣ780/429-1899, Ⓦ www.edmontonfolkfest.org), held at Gallagher Park near the Muttart Conservatory in early August. Also well regarded are the **International Street Performers Festival** (Ⓣ780/425-5162, Ⓦ www.edmontonstreetfest.com), which attracts over one thousand street performers in early July, the **International Jazz City Festival** (Ⓣ780/432-7166) at the end of June and the increasingly popular August **Fringe Theatre Festival** (Ⓣ780/448-9000, Ⓦ www.fringetheatreadventures.ca), a ten-day theatrical jamboree that's turned into one of the largest festivals of its kind in North America. The more contrived and commercial **Capital Ex** (Ⓣ780/471-7210 or 1-888/800-7275; Ⓦ www.capitalex.ca) is a giant funfair, which for ten days in late July tries to steal some of Calgary's Stampede thunder.

Ⓣ403/531-0350 or 1-800/232-1958, Ⓦwww.redarrow.ca) use the *Holiday Inn Express Plaza* hotel at 10014-104th St as their station.

The central **tourist office** is at 9990 Jasper Ave (Mon–Fri 7am–7pm; Ⓣ780/496-8400 or 1-800/463-4667, Ⓦwww.edmonton.com).

City transport

The downtown area is easily negotiated **on foot**. Longer journeys can be made using Edmonton Transit (route and timetable **information** Ⓣ780/496-1611), an integrated **bus and light-rail** (LRT) system. Interchangeable tickets for bus and LRT cost $2.50; day-passes cost $7.50. You can buy tickets on buses or from machines in the ten LRT stations. Transfers are available from drivers upon boarding and can be used on other services for ninety minutes from the time of issue.

Accommodation

Due to its importance among business travellers Edmonton has no shortage of **hotels**, but there's quite a bit of reasonable budget accommodation too. **Motels** dot the arterial roads on the unlovely outskirts of the city, particularly along Stony Plain Road (northwest of downtown) and on the Calgary Trail (south). For **B&Bs** – which are virtually all well outside the centre and more expensive than many hotels – contact the visitor centre or browse the listings of the Alberta Central Bed & Breakfast Association (Ⓦwww.bbcanada.com).

Hotels and motels

Alberta Place Suite Hotel 10049-103rd St Ⓣ780/423-1565 or 1-800/661-3982, Ⓦwww.albertaplace.com. Large, well-equipped suites with kitchens and extra facilities; weekly rates available. 5

Coast Edmonton Plaza Hotel 10155-105th St Ⓣ780/423-4811 or 1-800/716-6199, Ⓦwww.coasthotels.com. Uninspired 299-room downtown hotel, handy for the LRT, with reasonable spa, pool and fitness facilities. Rooms are spotless, a bit dingy, but often substantially discounted online. 7

Comfort Inn & Suites 10425-100th Ave Ⓣ780/423-5611 or 1-800/613-7043, Ⓦwww.choicehotels.ca. Reliable downtown motel with parking. Local calls and a light breakfast included in the rates. 4

Days Inn Downtown 10041-106th St Ⓣ780/423-1925 or 1-800/329-7466, Ⓦwww.daysinn.com. Midsized and renovated central motel with parking just off Jasper Ave. 6

Edmonton House 10205-100th Ave Ⓣ780/420-4000 or 1-800/716-6199, Ⓦwww.edmontonhouse.com. Bigger (three hundred suites) and more expensive than the *Alberta Place*, but rooms have balconies, views, wi-fi and full kitchens in each unit. There's also an indoor pool and fitness centre. 7

Grand Hotel 10266-103rd St Ⓣ780/422-6365 or 1-888/422-6365, Ⓦwww.edmontongrandhotel.com. Handily near the bus station, this fine old hotel has been revamped to offer budget downtown accommodation with a bit of style. 4

Hotel Macdonald 10065-100th St Ⓣ780/424-5181 or 1-800/257-7544, Ⓦwww.fairmont.com/MacDonald. One of the big historic railway hotels once run by the CPR, and undoubtedly the first choice if you want to overnight in traditional style. Some rooms are a little small for the price, but there are lots of facilities, including pool and health club. 8

Varscona 8208-106th St Ⓣ780/434-6111 or 1-866/465-8150, Ⓦwww.varscona.com. Plush Old Strathcona boutique hotel, with every thinkable business amenity and many luxuries, including a fitness centre and nightly wine and cheese tastings, served by attentive staff. 6

Hostels, student rooms and campsites

Go Backpackers 10209-100th Avenue Ⓣ780/423-4146, 1-877/646-7835, Ⓦwww.gohostels.ca. Cheerful new downtown hostel with dorm beds ($26) and private rooms ($75), all with private washrooms. Also has a sociable communal area and decent kitchen facilities.

HI-Edmonton Hostel 10647-81st Ave Ⓣ780/988-6836 or 1-877/467-8336, Ⓦwww.hihostels.ca. This 104-bed hostel is in a former convent in the Old Strathcona district and has plenty of facilities, including laundry, library, bike rental, free wi-fi and roomy kitchen. Dorm beds

$29.50 ($33.50 nonmembers), plus some private rooms ($59/67).

Rainbow Valley Campground 13204-45th Ave NW ⓣ780/434-5531, ⓦwww.rainbow-valley.com. Within the city limits and off the Whitemud Freeway at 119th St and 45th Ave, in Whitemud Park. It's full by afternoon in summer, so arrive early or be sure to book in advance. Sites $26–30. Mid-April to early Oct.

St Joseph's College 11325-89th Ave ⓣ780/492-7681 ext 248, ⓦwww.stjosephscollege.ca. Small, cheap and popular student rooms ($24/night) that are out of the centre but well served by buses, and only a ten-minute walk from the Old Strathcona district; free wi-fi and communal bathrooms. May–Aug.

The City

Edmonton feels oddly dispersed, even in the six-block **downtown** area around Sir Winston Churchill Square and along the main east–west drag, **Jasper Avenue** (101st Ave). Bounded to the south by the North Saskatchewan River, this grid holds a few points of interest, though most of the younger and more cosmopolitan Edmonton resides south of the river in **Old Strathcona**. For the **West Edmonton Mall**, **TELUS World of Science**, and the **Provincial Museum**, you'll need to take transport west from downtown. To stretch your legs, wander up and down the big string of attractive **riverside parks**, or cross the Low Level Bridge to the **Muttart Conservatory**, another worthwhile sight consisting of four glass pyramids filled with flora and natural history displays.

Downtown

Downtown Edmonton only really comes alive on sunny days when office workers pour out for lunch; otherwise it's really not much of a place to linger. Yet with time to kill, the following low-key sites could keep you occupied. The **Art Gallery of Alberta** (Mon–Fri 10.30am–5pm, Thurs till 8pm, Sat & Sun 11am–5pm; $7; free Thurs after 4pm; ⓣ780/422-6223, ⓦwww.artgalleryalberta.com), 100-10230 Jasper Ave, is part of the Civic Centre on the north edge of Sir Winston Churchill Square and deals mainly in modern Canadian artists, though it also hosts many visiting exhibitions. More satisfyingly offbeat is the **Edmonton Police Museum and Archives** (Mon–Sat 9am–3pm; free; ⓣ780/421-2274), at 9620-103A Ave on the third floor of the central police station. It traces the long arm of Albertan law enforcement from the formation of what would become the RCMP in 1873 to present day.

Walk across the Low Level Bridge to the distinctive glass pyramids of the **Muttart Conservatory** (Mon–Fri 9.30am–5.30pm, Sat & Sun 11am–5.30pm; $9.75; ⓣ780/496-8735, ⓦwww.muttartconservatory.ca) at 9626-96A St, just south of downtown and the river. Its high-tech greenhouses reproduce tropical, temperate and arid climates, complete with trees, plants and occasional exotic birds. If you don't want to walk, take **bus** #85 (direction Capilano) travelling south on 100th Street.

Finally, you might stop by for a free guided tour of the domed sandstone **Alberta Legislature Building** (May to mid-Oct daily 9am–4pm; mid-Oct to April Mon–Fri 9am–4.30pm, Sat & Sun noon–5pm; free; ⓣ780/427-2826, ⓦwww.assembly.ab.ca; LRT station: Grandin) at 10800-97th Ave NW. Set in the manner of a medieval cathedral over an ancient shrine, it was built in 1912 on the original site of Fort Edmonton. Topped by a vaulted dome, it's a big city landmark, its interior reflecting the grandiose self-importance of the province's early rulers, who imported wood for their headquarters from as far afield as Belize; the marble came from Québec, Pennsylvania and Italy and the granite from British Columbia. Just north, amid adjacent parkland, stands the **Alberta Legislative Assembly Interpretive Centre**, where you can learn more than you probably want to about Alberta's political history and the building in which much of it took place (same hours).

Old Strathcona

The **Strathcona** district south of the North Saskatchewan River grew up at the end of the nineteenth century, thanks to a decision by the Calgary and Edmonton Railway Company (C&E) to avoid the expense of a bridge across the North Saskatchewan River by concluding a rail spur from Calgary south of the river. Today, the streets and many of the older buildings have been spruced up, new pavements laid and fake period street furniture added giving it a well-preserved feel. It's Edmonton's most wanderable and vibrant district, with cafés, nightlife and alternative arts also making it the best evening hangout. Plenty of buses run here from downtown, including #52 from 97th Street downtown, or you can walk across the river via the Walterdale or High Level bridges.

The area centres on **Whyte Avenue** (82nd Ave) between 109th and 103rd streets. Just to the north, on 83rd Avenue, is the **Old Strathcona Farmers' Market** (Sat 8am–3pm; free), a happy hunting ground for picnic supplies and craft goods. If you tire of wandering or sitting in cafés, you can give a little structure to your exploration by heading for one or both of the area's two small museums. Rail buffs should check out the **C&E Railway Station Museum** (June–Aug Tues–Sat 10am–4pm; winter by appointment; $2 donation; ⓣ780/433-9739), at 10447-86th Ave, a collection of railway memorabilia, costumes and photos housed in a replica of Strathcona's original 1891 station.

Royal Alberta Museum

Housed in a drab building in the western suburbs – a ten-minute drive from downtown – the **Royal Alberta Museum,** 12845-102nd Ave (daily 9am–5pm; $10; ⓣ780/453-9100, ⓦwww.royalalbertamuseum.ca), gives a good introduction to the history, culture, flora and fauna of western Canada. By far the best section concerns the virtual extinction of the region's **bisons**, while other displays include a rundown on the history and culture of Alberta's **aboriginal peoples**. Other engaging parts of the museum are the **Bug**, a showcase of live and often exotic insects, and "Earth's Changing Face", a geological display of gems, minerals, rocks and dinosaur exhibits. The museum also comes into its own when hosting temporary and travelling exhibitions of other collections and museums from around the world. To reach the museum by **bus**, take the #1 or #120 heading west to "Jasper Place" on Jasper Avenue.

Fort Edmonton Park

Located southwest of the city on a deep-cut bend of the North Saskatchewan River, the 158-acre **Fort Edmonton Park** (mid-May to late June Mon–Fri 10am–4pm, Sat & Sun 10am–6pm; late June to Aug daily 10am–6pm; Sept Sun 10am–6pm; $13.50; ⓣ780/442-5311, ⓦwww.edmonton.ca/fort) recreates the history of white settlement in Edmonton during the nineteenth century. Everything has been built from scratch and, while you can't fault the attention to detail, the pristine woodwork of the supposedly old buildings hardly evokes period authenticity (though the carpentry methods are those used around 1846). The heart of the complex is a facsimile of **Fort Edmonton**, a fur-trading post dominated by the Big House, former home of the fort's Chief Factor. Arranged around the house are the quarters of the 130 or so people who called the fort home and who are now represented by costumed guides pretending to be blacksmiths, shopkeepers and schoolteachers. Edmonton's later, pre-railway age is represented by a rendition of Jasper Avenue as it appeared in 1885, while two other streets simulate 1905 and 1920, complete with working steam engines and trams; rides are included in price of entry.

To get here take the LRT to University station and there pick up buses #4 or #106 to Fox Drive, about ten-minutes' walk from the site, which is off the Whitemud Freeway near the Quesnell Bridge.

TELUS World of Science

The splendid **TELUS World of Science** (daily 10am–7pm; $13.95 or $22.50 with IMAX; Ⓦwww.edmontonscience.com), at 11211-142nd St in Coronation Park, is one of Edmonton's better attractions. The complex includes both the **Margaret Zeidler Star Theatre**, Canada's largest planetarium, and an **IMAX** screen. The centre features a range of temporary exhibitions on scientific and technological themes and a **Challenger Centre**, with simulated "Astronaut Missions". There are also assorted displays on advanced communications technology and a selection of the various science demonstrations you can expect to see around the centre throughout the day – all of it best suited for the kids or entire families.

To get here by bus take #5 (to Westmount) travelling west on 102nd Avenue and ask the driver to tell you when you're close.

West Edmonton Mall

"The greatest indoor show on earth" is the claim of **West Edmonton Mall** (Ⓦwww.wem.ca) – a deliberate snipe at Calgary's "greatest outdoor show", the Stampede – and is worded as such to tempt you into becoming one of 28 million annual visitors to North America's largest shopping mall. Built at a total cost of $1.2 billion, the complex extends over the equivalent of 48 city blocks, boasts eight hundred-plus shops and has room for twenty thousand cars. There's also an on-site hotel and countless places to eat, none of them particulalrly remarkable. The mall's effect on Edmonton has been double-edged: it employs 23,000 people but crippled the downtown shopping area. Still, it certainly provides a lifeline for Edmontonians during their long, dark and bleak winters.

Size aside it's not the shops that make the mall unique, but the clutch of **extra attractions**. These include the world's largest indoor lake (122m long), part of a cluster of entertainments known as **Deep Sea Adventure**, that contains a full-sized replica of Columbus's *Santa Maria* and some two hundred different species of marine life. You can gape at sharks, sea turtles and penguins in the adjoining aquarium. Continuing with the water theme, the **World Waterpark** (Mon–Thurs noon–7pm, Fri & Sat 10am–7pm, Sun 11am–6pm; day-pass $36.95) is a superb collection of vast swimming pools, immense water slides and wave pools. Tack on to these attractions **Galaxyland**, a huge indoor amusement park, the **Ice Palace**, with its NHL-sized rink, or several other lesser amusements and you've filled a day – or been driven mad by the rampant consumerism of it all.

Bus services to the mall heading west out of downtown include #100. If you're coming here by car remember at which of its 58 entrances you've parked; maps are available throughout the main building. To save tired feet, you can rent a scooter for $10 an hour. Check the mall website for all details.

Eating, drinking and nightlife

Edmonton has some very good restaurants, plenty of them downtown. For a bit more nocturnal zip to go with your meal head out to **Old Strathcona** (see p.588). Ethnic options – notably restaurants serving Edmonton's populations of Ukrainian and Eastern European origin – complement the standard Italian-influenced cuisine or steak-and-salmon offerings.

There are any number of small-time clubs and other venues, especially in Old Strathcona, putting on **live music**. With larger places thin on the ground, big names tend to use the University of Alberta's **Jubilee Auditorium**, 87th Avenue and 114th Street (Ⓦwww.jubileeauditorium.com), which is also the venue for the Edmonton opera. Otherwise, the **Citadel Theatre**, 9828-101A Ave (Ⓣ780/425-1820 or 1-888/425-1820, Ⓦwww.citadeltheatre.com) or the **Francis Winspear Centre for Music**, 4 Sir Winston Churchill Square (Ⓣ780/428-1414 or 1-800/563-5081,

Ⓦ www.winspearcentre.com), home of the **Edmonton Symphony Orchestra** (Ⓣ 780/425-1414 or 1-800/563-5081, Ⓦ www.edmontonsymphony.com), also host events.

The best **listings** source is the free *Vue Weekly* (Ⓦ www.vueweekly.com), published on Thursdays and widely available across town, as well as the entertainment section of the *Edmonton Journal*. **Tickets** for most events – including Edmonton Oilers **ice hockey** games, played in Rexall Place, 7224 118th Ave NW – are available from Ticketmaster outlets around the city, including at 9930-102nd Ave, downtown on Churchill Square.

Restaurants

Bistro Praha 10168-100A St Ⓣ 780/424-4218. A good opportunity to sample Eastern European cuisine, Edmonton-style, in the city's oldest European-style restaurant. Slightly highbrow and expensive, though, with mains from $18.

Café Select 405-10018 106th Street NW Ⓣ 780/428-1629. Intimate and trendy without being intimidating. Serves fine, simple, moderately-priced bistro-type food, and is one of downtown's best choices for a late-night treat – open until midnight during the week and 2am at weekends; book ahead if possible.

Da-De-O 10548A-82nd Ave Ⓣ 780/443-0903, Ⓦ www.dadeo.ca. Upbeat Cajun diner with chrome-rimmed tables and great southern food. All the old favourites – oysters, gumbo, jambalaya and southern fried chicken – are very good and reasonably priced (mains from $15); start with the sweet potato fries.

Hardware Grill 9698 Jasper Ave Ⓣ 780/423-0969, Ⓦ www.hardwaregrill.com. The seasonally inspired Canadian cuisine in the best restaurant in Edmonton is served in a chic modern environment with dark hardwood floors, simple lines, elegant linen and prices to match (mains run $32–45). Book ahead.

Jack's Grill 5842-111th St Ⓣ 780/434-1113, Ⓦ www.jacksgrill.ca. Probably a tad too south of the city centre unless you have a car, but this is one of the top places in Edmonton for modern, innovative Pacific Rim cuisine. Many local ingredients are offered on the reassuringly short menu; mains cost around $30–40 and include items such as wild boar shoulder.

The King and I 8208-107th St Ⓣ 780/433-2222, Ⓦ www.thekingandi.ca. Superlative Thai restaurant where prices are nonetheless moderate. One good choice is the *galanga* cashew chicken ($17): chicken fillets in a sweet dark tamarind sauce with asparagus, ginger and cashews.

La Ronde 10111 Bellamy Hill Ⓣ 780/428-6611. Stunning views of Edmonton from the city's only revolving dining room (atop the *Crowne Plaza Château Lacombe*). The expensive (mains from $25) Albertan cooking – steaks, bison, berries – is good too. Dancing nightly and live entertainment Fri–Sun.

Oodle Noodle 10803-82nd Ave. Excellent, inexpensive Asian noodle house, where the food's speedily cooked to order and boxed for a quick chow down on the premises or a takeaway.

Packrat Louie 10335-83rd Ave Ⓣ 780/433-0123, Ⓦ www.packratlouie.com. Bright, young and welcoming bistro in Old Strathcona with generous portions of steaks, salads, chicken and other more sophisticated international dishes. Mains $14–20. Closed Sun.

Sorrentino's 10162-100th St Ⓣ 780/424-7500, Ⓦ www.sorrentinos.com. Downtown branch of an enormously successful local chain of family-run Italian restaurants with great atmosphere and serving good affordable food in a pleasant, stylish setting. Closed Sun.

Zenari's 10180-101st St NW Ⓣ 780/423-5409. Great Italian deli/houseware shop with a tremendous lunch counter for soups, salads, sandwiches and Italian staples, including gnocchi with tomato sauce ($9.95).

Bars and clubs

Blues on Whyte 10329-82nd Ave Ⓣ 780/439-3981, Ⓦ www.bluesonwhyte.ca. At the *Commercial Hotel*, this is one of the city's better live music clubs, with bands most nights and jam sessions on Sat.

Cook County Saloon 8010 Gateway Blvd Ⓣ 780/432-2665, Ⓦ www.cookcountysaloon.com. Deservedly popular Old Strathcona C&W venue, cited many times as Canada's best country nightclub, attracting twentysomethings in droves and packing out on weekend nights. Cover $5.

O'Byrne's 10616-82nd Ave Ⓣ 780/414-6766, Ⓦ www.obyrnes.com. Old Strathcona's popular version of an Irish pub has good food, live music, drink and reasonably authentic atmosphere. If this doesn't take your fancy, there are a dozen or so other bars an easy stagger away along Whyte Ave.

Yardbird Suite 11 Tommy Banks Way, corner of 102nd St and 86th Ave Ⓣ 780/432-0428, Ⓦ www.yardbirdsuite.com. Live music nightly (10pm–2am) in the city's top jazz venue; admission is lower for the Tues night jam session.

Listings

Car rental Avis ☎780/890-7596; Budget ☎780/448-2068; Driving Force ☎780/483-9559.
Laundry Jasper Place Coin Laundry, 11122-153rd St (7.30am–8pm).
Medical Royal Alexandra Hospital, 10240 Kingsway ☎780/477-4111.
Outdoor equipment Mountain Equipment Co-op, 12328-102nd Ave NW ☎780/488-6614.
Police ☎780/423-4567.
Post office 9808-103A Ave ☎780/944-3271.
Road conditions ☎780/471-6056, ⓦwww.ama.ab.ca.
Taxis Alberta Co-op ☎780/425-2525.
Weather Information ☎780/468-4940.

The Northern Prairies

Stretching from the edges of Lake Winnipeg and the Northern banks of the North Saskatchewan River all the way to the Northwest Territories and Nunavut, **northern Alberta, Manitoba and Saskatchewan** are inhospitable and sparsely inhabited expanses that account for roughly half the three provinces. The region divides into two slightly different zones, with the marginally richer flora and fauna of the **Interior Plains** lying south of the more spartan landscapes of the **Canadian Shield**, where shallow soils support a gigantic coniferous forest broken up by a complex pattern of lakes and rivers. The shield stretches north of a rough curve drawn between Flin Flon and Great Slave Lake (see p.928) in the Northwest territories. Both regions are hostile environments, with deep, cold winters alternating with brief, bright summers, when the first few centimetres of topsoil thaw out above the permafrost to create millions of stagnant pools of water; ideal conditions for mosquitoes and blackflies. There are compensations: out in the bush or along the shores of Hudson Bay you'll find a sense of desolate **wilderness** hard to experience elsewhere, all crossed by a staggering number of first-rate backcountry **canoe routes** and **wildlife** that includes caribou, **polar bear, bison** and all sorts of migratory birds.

Most of the region is inaccessible and the bulk of its limited hwy system was built to service the resource towns whose wealth is founded on mining or logging. These tend to provide the only convenient bases – don't expect much more – for the region's provincial and national parks.

Northern Alberta

The **Albertan north**, though equally vast is easily the most accessible of the three provinces, since many of its roads are new and provide a land link with its scattered northern communities around Wood Buffalo National Park and Yellowknife – both covered in Chapter 11. Unless you are on your way to either, nothing in the region is worth detouring for.

Edmonton is the gateway to the road network of the entire region: the **Yellowhead Hwy** heads 357km west to Jasper with the scenery only really picking up in the last hour. Numerous campsites and **motels** service the road at regular intervals, the main concentrations being at **EDSON**, halfway to Jasper, and **HINTON**, 79km from Jasper. The motels at both are pretty standard but fill up by 5pm almost every day, thanks to the local needs of transient oil industry employees.

Hwy 43 to Dawson Creek and the Alaska Hwy (see pp.889–894) are equally bleak in terms of diversions, while northbound travellers along **Hwy 2** to Peace River and the Mackenzie Hwy (see p.928) fare better with a few modest distractions offering stops, particularly for keen **birdwatchers.** Greyhound **buses** follow all these routes from Edmonton, supplemented by the VIA Rail **train** service from Edmonton to Jasper (and on to Vancouver or Prince Rupert).

Highway 43 to Dawson Creek and the Alaska Highway

Highway 43 out of Edmonton to BC rolls through terminally unexceptional towns, hills and prairie scenery on its 602km way west to Dawson Creek, the mile-zero of the **Alaska Hwy** (p.889). It's a mind-numbing day by car or bus, making the unfocused sprawl of **GRANDE PRAIRIE**, 463km from Edmonton, a relative highlight. If you end up stopping here, go first to the slick **tourist office** (June to early Sept daily 8.30am–8.30pm; ⓣ780/539-7688 or 1-866/202-2202, ⓦwww.northernvisitor.com) on Hwy 43, which bypasses the main part of town to the west. It's a good place to stock up on regional information and get free internet use. The centre also organizes a free bison barbeque (June–Aug Wed 4–6pm). Otherwise, the town's only real attraction is the reasonable **Grand Prairie Museum and Heritage Discovery Centre** (June–Aug Mon–Fri 8.30am–4.30pm, Sat 10am–4.30pm, Sun noon–4.30pm; $5; ⓣ780/523-5482) in Heritage Park on the western side of downtown. Local history exhbits and a few reconstructed pioneer buildings help shed light on recent times.

Grand Prairie's **bus station** is at 9918-121st St (ⓣ780/539-1111), while most of its many **motels** are on the strip known as Richmond Avenue (100th Ave), which links the southern part of the hwy-bypass to downtown.

Highway 2 to Peace River and the Mackenzie Highway

It's almost 500km from Edmonton to Peace River (see p.930) along Hwy 2; a long day watching a slow transition from prairie to boreal forests along a route which passes through little more than a handful of small towns. Luckily all are welcoming and deserve at least a quick stop to soak up a bit of small-town life and to stretch legs around a museum or nature reserve; all have a motel or two in case you need to break your journey.

Westlock

Not long after you've broken free of Edmonton's suburbs and satellite towns – 88km along Hwy 2 from downtown – is the prairie town of **WESTLOCK**. Its archetypal small-town feel is only accentuated by a visit to its cheerfully cluttered **tourist office** (late May to Aug daily 10am–5pm; free; ⓣ780/349-4444), where the collection of artefacts and knick-knacks that chart the course of the town's history include an antique threshing machine, aged aboriginal carvings and a lovingly restored 1920 automobile.

Slave Lake and Lesser Slave Lake Provincial Park

Another 165km northwest of Westlock on Hwy 2 brings you to the 100km-long **Lesser Slave Lake** and its gateway community **Slave Lake**. The sleek Lesser Slave Lake tourist office (Fri 9am–9pm, Sat–Mon 10am–6pm, ⓦwww.lesserslavelake.ca) on the southern side of town is helpful and well-stocked, though it doesn't take long to realise **Lesser Slave Lake Provincial Park**, stretching out along

Hwy 88 on the north side of Slave Lake, is really the only attraction. Here you can join locals on its long white-sand Devonshire Beach or explore inland parts of the park. Highlights there include the **Boreal Centre for Bird Conservation** (July–Aug Sun–Thurs 8.15am–4.30pm, Fri & Sat 8.15am–6pm, free; ⓣ780/849-8240), which provides an excellent introduction to the area's extraordinarily rich bird life. The **Marten Mountain Lookout**, some 30km north of Slave Lake along Hwy 88, has grand views spread over an otherwise relatively flat region. From the lookout you can also **hike** out to the pretty little **Lily Lake** – ideal for swimming and trout fishing – along a rough 6km trail (allow at least 2hr). Another good active option is **kayaking** on Lesser Slave Lake, with the bird refuge of **Dog Island**, 5km from the shore, the most tempting destination. Rentals and guided tours can be organised through Wildside (rentals from $40/day; ⓣ780/849-8375 or 1-877/305-2925, ⓦwww.wildside.ca).

The best of Slave Lake's slew of pricey **motels** along the hwy is the *Sawridge Hotel* (ⓣ780/849-4101 or 1-800/661-6657, ⓦwww.sawridge.com; ❻) which has a sauna and exercise room; fishing and kayaking packages are also available. **Campers** should head to the Marten River Campsite in the Provincial Park ($20/night). Head-and-shoulders above all the very average **restaurants** and fast food chains in town is the *Point Steakhouse* (ⓣ780/849-4133) off Albert Avenue on the north side of town, not least for its great lake views.

McLennan and the Kimiwan Lake Bird Sanctuary

If the bird observatory in the Lesser Slave Lake Provincial Park whetted your appetite, then make a point of stopping in **McLennan**, 166km from Slave Lake. It's not an over-statement to say that its **Kimiwan Lake Bird Sanctuary** (May–Aug 10am–5.30pm; ⓣ780/324-2004) is of international importance, with white pelicans among the hundreds of species – and 300,000 birds – that stop here on their migration routes. The sanctuary and and visitor centre are easily found beside the hwy on the eastern edge of downtown.

Northern Saskatchewan and Manitoba

In **Saskatchewan** the town of **Prince Albert** provides a gateway to the north, with all major hwy or bus journeys passing through or beginning here. Destinations include the uranium mining town **La Ronge**, beside the lakes and forests of the appealing **Lac La Ronge Provincial Park** and some of the north's longest and most varied canoe routes on the nearby **Churchill River**. But some of the most extraordinary backcountry adventures and landscapes lie in the far northwest of the province, where the **Athabasca Sand Dunes Provincial Wilderness Park** provides a unique getaway for well-heeled wilderness fans.

The layout of **Manitoba**'s far north is quite different, with Lake Winnipeg and Winnipegosis creating a vast natural barrier between it and the southern province. The largest towns up here – **Flin Flon** and **The Pas** – provide bases for the region's two main provincial parks, **Clearwater Lake** and **Grass River**. Even further north is **Thompson**, the penultimate stop on the remote railway line to the windswept town of **Churchill**, on the southern shore of Hudson Bay. Though far beyond the reach of the road network, this is the region's key tourist centre since, depending on the season, it's easy to see **beluga whales**, **polar bears** and the **northern lights**.

With distances so vast and the population so thin, public transport in Northern Saskatchewan and Manitoba is understandably poor, yet it's still possible to get to many places by bus or train. The **Saskatchewan Transportation Company** (T 306/933-8000 or 1-800/663-7181, W www.stcbus.com) provides two useful bus services: one connecting Saskatoon, Prince Albert, Waskesiu (mid-May to mid-Sept only) and La Ronge; the other heading up to The Pas and Flin Flon in Manitoba. All the main settlements in northern Manitoba are connected by daily Greyhound services, except Churchill, which forms the terminus of the only rail service in the region that runs from Winnipeg via The Pas and Thompson, with two departures in each direction every week.

La Ronge

Some 242km north of Prince Albert along Hwy 2, the scrawny, straggling resort of **LA RONGE** on the western edge of Lac La Ronge was home to an isolated Cree community until the road arrived in 1948. Since then, gold mines and forestry operations have started just to the north of town and the area's lakes and rivers have proved popular with visiting canoeists and anglers.

The town is fronted by La Ronge Avenue, which runs parallel to the waterfront, the location of the **bus station**. A few minutes' walk away, in Mistasinihk Place, is the office of the **Saskatchewan Parks Department** (Mon–Fri 8am–noon & 1–5pm; T 306/425-4234) and an interpretive centre (same hours) with exhibits on northern lifestyles, crafts and history. The **tourist office**, 207 La Ronge Ave (mid-May to mid-Sept Mon–Fri 8am–5pm; T 306/425-3056 or 1-866/527-6643, W www.laronge.ca) is 1.5km south of town beside Hwy 2.

La Ronge's several reasonably priced and central **hotels** and **motels**, include the *La Ronge Hotel*, 1120 La Ronge Ave (T 306/425-2190 or 1-800/332-6735, W www.larongehotelandsuites.com; 4) and a series of **campsites** strung along Hwy 102 north of town, the nearest of which is *Nut Point* ($13–20; mid-May to Aug), 1km away. One of the few places to **eat** that isn't run-of-the-mill is the vaguely Greek *Kostas*, 707 La Ronge Ave.

Lac La Ronge Provincial Park

La Ronge is on the western edge of **Lac La Ronge Provincial Park**, which incorporates Lac La Ronge and extends north to encompass a number of smaller lakes and a tiny section of the **Churchill River**, once the main route into the northwest for the *voyageurs*. The river swerves across the width of the province, from west to east, before heading on into Manitoba, its waterways providing some of the region's longest canoe routes. The parks department in La Ronge

Canoeing in northern Saskatchewan

Northern Saskatchewan has an abundance of **canoe routes** sprinkled across its thousands of lakes, but perhaps the two key places for an extended adventure is the turbulent white water of the **Clearwater River** in **Clearwater River Provincial Park** 700km north of Saskatoon and the fabulous **Churchill River** near La Ronge. For most the best bet is to take a guided trip with a company like the excellent Horizons Unlimited/Churchill River Canoe Outfitters (T 1-877/511-2726, W www.churchillrivercanoe.com), based in **MISSINIPE**, 80km north of La Ronge. Other outfitters are listed in the Tourism Saskatchewan (see p.56) guide to the north, that's available at most tourist offices. For independent and experienced wilderness travellers, The Ministry of Tourism, Parks, Culture and Sport (W **www.tpcs.gov.sk.ca/canoe**) is a good place to start with its detailed route descriptions. For topographic maps and canoe-route charts and booklets, plus secondary road maps, contact SaskGeomatics, 260-10 Research Drive, Regina (T 306/787-2799 or 1-866/420-6577).

(see opposite) provides a detailed description of the river and its history in the booklet *Saskatchewan's Voyageur Highway: A Canoe Trip*. The park is one of the few areas in the province where you can hike the Canadian Shield. The 15km **Nut Point Hiking Trail** leaves the campsites and runs along a narrow peninsula that juts into Lac La Ronge, crossing rock ridges through forests and over high, open ridges where you can view the enormous island-studded lake. Less strenuously, these waters are also good for fishing – the walleye, pike and lake trout are delicious. A number of La Ronge **tour operators** and **outfitters** run and equip fishing and canoeing trips into the park, most of them using lakeside holiday **lodges** and **cabins**; the parks department office has the details. There are also several **campsites** along Hwy 102 including the *Missinipe* (ⓣ306/635-4444 or 1-800/772-4064; $15–20; mid-May to early Sept) on Otter Lake, where the hwy crosses the Churchill River.

Lake Athabasca

The shallow soils of northern Saskatchewan are unable to support any form of agriculture, and its native peoples, the Woodland Cree, have traditionally survived by hunting, trapping and fishing. In recent times, this precarious and nomadic existence has been replaced by a more settled life on the reservations concentrated around **Lake Athabasca** in the extreme northwest corner of the province, close to the 60th parallel. The area has become a particular favourite of the hook-and-bullet brigade – and, in recent years, eco-tourists – but can only be reached by private floatplane. The most amazing landscapes in the area, not least because of their incongruity, are within the **Athabasca Sand Dunes Provincial Wilderness Park**, the world's most northerly sand dunes. Several companies organize excursions to the area that include flights, food, accommodation and boat rental; if you can afford around $3000 for a six-day trip, try Athabasca Camps (ⓣ1-800/922-0957, ⓦwww.athabascalake.com).

Flin Flon

The mining township of **FLIN FLON** – 138km from The Pas on Manitoba's Hwy 10, or 409km from Prince Albert on Saskatchewan's Hwy 106 – gouges copper, gold, lead and zinc from a massive seam discovered in 1914. Straddling the Manitoba–Saskatchewan border, it's a stark, rough-looking town, full of precipitously steep streets, where the houses are built on sheer rock in a barren landscape. Flin Flon takes its unusual name from the hero of an obscure dime-novel entitled *The Sunless City*, which one of the first prospectors was reading at the time of the discovery. In the book, Josiah Flintabbatey Flonatin builds a submarine and enters the bowels of the earth, where he discovers that everything is made of gold. There's not much to see in town, except in July, when the town hosts the **Trout Festival**, with a parade, a Queen Mermaid Pageant, the Great Northern Duck Race – and the tantalizing smell of frying fish.

Flin Flon's **bus station** is at 347 Main St, just over the Saskatchewan border in the adjoining settlement of **CREIGHTON**. About 4km east along Hwy 10A, the **tourist office**, 20 First Ave (May–Sept daily 8am–8pm; ⓣ204/687-7511, ⓦwww.cityofflinflon.com) runs the main **campsite** (May–Sept; $15–17) opposite a large statue of the intrepid Flintabbatey Flonatin. Otherwise, try the central **hotel** *Royal*, 93 Main St (ⓣ204/687-3437 or 1-800/308-2224; ❹), or, for budget accommodation, the *Flin Flon Friendship Centre Hostel*, 57 Church St (ⓣ204/687-3900; ❶). The place of choice to mooch around in is the *Orange Toad Café*, 115 Main St, with its selection of used books. Otherwise, try the basic **meals** at *Mugsy's*, 114 Main St, or the *Victoria Inn*'s restaurant, 160 Hwy 10.

Grass River Provincial Park

A 40km drive southeast from Flin Flon along Hwy 10 brings you to **Grass River Provincial Park**: several thousand square kilometres of evergreen forest, lake and river interspersed by the granite outcrops of the Canadian Shield. Its channels and lakes were first charted in the 1770s by Hudson's Bay Company employee Samuel Hearne and are still noted as excellent **canoe routes**. Hearne, who became the first European to reach the Arctic Ocean by land, witnessed both the development of the Grass River's fur trade and the cataclysmic effects of the smallpox epidemic that followed. He estimated that about ninety percent of the local Chipewyan population was wiped out in the space of a decade.

The most popular canoe route here runs 180km from the **Cranberry Lakes**, on the park's western perimeter, to its eastern boundary, where the southern tip of **Tramping Lake** lies near Hwy 39. It's an excursion of about ten days – all of the route's portages are short and fairly easy and there are lots of basic campsites on the way. The canoe route begins on the first of the three Cranberry Lakes close to **CRANBERRY PORTAGE**, a straggling township on Hwy 10, which runs along the western edge of the park; there's a small **information kiosk** in town.

If you're using Cranberry Portage as a base to explore the park, there are a few accommodation options: The small *Cranberry Portage Park* **campsite** (ⓣ204/472-3219; $10–12; mid-May to Sept), 1km west of Hwy 10 with its own beach; a couple of **hotels**, including the *Northern Inn*, 112 Portage Rd (ⓣ204/472-3231; ❷); and a handful of holiday **lodges** (mid-May to early Oct) along the lakeshore, such as the *Viking Lodge* (ⓣ204/472-3337; ❹) which also has campsites for $25. Most lodges have boat and canoe rentals, and can arrange guided trips and flights to the more remote lakes. There are other access points to Grass River Park along Hwy 39, which runs along its southern boundary. This road passes three small summer **campsites** (all $11) – *Gyles* (24km east of Hwy 10), *Iskwasum* (40km) and *Reed Lake* (56km) – where park entry points lead to circular canoe trips that can be accomplished within one day.

A worthwhile side-trip can be made from the park to **Wekusko Falls**, about 35km beyond the east boundary of the park along Hwy 39 and then south along a short stretch of gravel road (Hwy 596). Here the Mitishto River drops dramatically in a series of falls and rapids. You can view the spectacle from two suspension footbridges or along the walking trails below. A campsite here has showers (May–Sept; $15)

The Pas

Situated on the southern bank of the Saskatchewan River 400km north of Dauphin (see p.568) via Hwy 10, **THE PAS** is a former fur-trading and missionary centre founded in 1750. It's also a town with no specific sights, though it does host the annual **Northern Manitoba Trappers' Festival** over four days in late February; competitions include traditional pioneer skills like tree-felling, trap-setting, ice-fishing and muskrat-skinning, with the highlight being the World Championship Sled Dog Races and its 50km mushes. If you're in town in mid-August, you can join in the aboriginal celebrations honouring the Cree people during **Opasquiak Indian Days**.

The summer **tourist office**, 81 Edwards Ave (June–Aug daily 9am–5pm; ⓣ204/627-1100 ⓦwww.thepasarea.com), lies beside the tiny Devon Park and *Kinsmen Kampground* (ⓣ204/623-2233; mid-May to early Oct; $14–21) and close to the three-star *Kikiwak Inn* (ⓣ204/623-1800 or 1-888/545-4925; ❺). In the centre, near the train station, the comfortable *Wescana Inn*, 439 Fischer Ave (ⓣ204/623-5446 or 1-800/665-9468, ⓦwww.wescanainn.com; ❺), is also a good **place to eat**.

Clearwater Lake Provincial Park

Just 19km north of The Pas, the square-shaped lake and adjoining strip of coniferous forest that constitute **Clearwater Lake Park** are a favourite haunt of the region's anglers, who come here for northern pike, whitefish and highly prized trout. Park amenities are concentrated along Rte 287, a turning off Hwy 10, which follows the lake's southern shore past The Pas airport.

Beside the road there are two summer **campsites** (Ⓣ204/948-3333 or 1-888/482-2267; mid-May to mid-Sept; $18). For a **wilderness excursion**, Clearwater Canoe Outfitters (Ⓣ218/388-2254 or 1-800/527-0554; Ⓦwww.clearwateroutfitters.com) rents a full range of equipment and organizes canoe trips from $305 for three days, including the first night in their bunkhouse (otherwise $22/night); they also have B&B rooms (❹) and some beautiful cabins (❼).

Thompson

The sprawling nickel-mining town of **Thompson** at the end of Hwy 6 and 399km from The Pas is as far north as you can go on Manitoba's network of sealed hwys and a long haul from anywhere. Driving here you'll pass through hundreds of kilometres of boreal forest, with barely another vehicle in sight – part of the reason for this is that there's little reason to come here other than to catch the overnight train to Churchill, thereby cutting the cost and journey time of picking up the service in Winnipeg.

Thompson's **tourist office** (June–Sept 10am–5pm, Oct–May 1pm–5pm; Ⓣ204/677-2216, Ⓦwww.thompson.ca) is on the southeastern edge of town beside the hwy – walking distance from the Greyhound **bus station** – and can organize tours of local mines and suggest other ways in which to kill a few hours before your train leaves if you're not busy stocking up on groceries in the large downtown malls. The **railway station** is just southeast of the town centre – take Station Road, just south of Wal-Mart – but this desolate spot is prone to vandalism. Your better option is to either park at City Hall, 226 Mystery Lake Rd (just off the main drag), for free and take a taxi with Thompson Cab (Ⓣ204/677-6262), or park at the lakeside and pleasantly wooded *McReedy Campground* (Ⓣ204/778-8810; tent and RV sites $15) at the northern fringes of town for $7 per day and use their courtesy shuttle service to and from the station. If you need a **room**, try the dreary-looking but reasonable and very central *Interior Inn* (180 Thompson Drive Ⓣ204/778-5535; ❺) where the ample rooms are clean and have free wi-fi.

Churchill

Sitting on the east bank of the Churchill River where it empties into Hudson Bay, **CHURCHILL** has the neglected appearance of many remote northern settlements, its unkempt open spaces dotted with the houses of its mixed Inuit, Cree and white population. These grim buildings are heavily fortified against the biting cold of winter and the voracious insects of summer. That said, the town has long attracted a rough-edged assortment of people with a taste for the wilderness, and tourists flock here for the wildlife – particularly the **polar bears** – providing the town a lifeline now that Churchill's grain-handling facilities are underused.

A brief history of Churchill

In 1682, the Hudson's Bay Company established a fur-trading post at **York Factory** (see p.601), a marshy peninsula some 240km southeast of today's

▲ A polar bear warning sign in Churchill

Churchill. The impetus behind building a fort here was that the direct sea route from England was roughly 1500km shorter than the old route via the St Lawrence River, while the Hayes and Nelson rivers gave access to the region's greatest waterways. Within a few years, a regular cycle of trade had been established, with the company's Cree and Assiniboine go-betweens heading south in the autumn to **hunt and trade** for skins and returning in the spring laden with pelts they could exchange for the company's manufactured goods. The company was always keen to increase its trade, and it soon expanded its operations to Churchill, building the first of a series of forts here in 1717.

In the nineteenth century the development of faster trade routes through Minneapolis brought decline, and by the 1870s both York Factory and Churchill had become unimportant. The subsequent development of agriculture on the prairies brought a reprieve. Many of the politicians and grain farmers of this new west were determined to break the trading monopoly of Sault Ste Marie in northern Ontario and campaigned for the construction of a new port facility on Hudson Bay, connected **by rail** to the south through Winnipeg. In the 1920s the Canadian National Railway agreed to build the line, and it finally reached Churchill in 1929. Unfortunately, despite the efforts of the railway workers in the teeth of the ferocious climate, the port has never been very successful, largely because the bay is ice-free for only about three months a year.

Arrival and information

Churchill is well beyond the reach of Manitoba's hwys, but connected to Thompson (see p.597), The Pas (see p.596) and Winnipeg **by train**, with VIA Rail running three weekly services. The train station and adjoining Parks Canada Centre **tourist office** is in the centre of town (see p.599). There are also regular **flights** from Winnipeg with Calm Air (Ⓣ204/675-8858 or 1-800/839-2256, Ⓦwww.calmair.com) and Kivalliq Air (Ⓣ204/888-5619 or 1-877/855-1500, Ⓦwww.kivalliqair.com). Churchill's **airport** is 7km from the centre; a taxi to town costs around $15 (Churchill Taxi Ⓣ204/675-2345).

The Town

The obvious place to start any exploration of town is the railway station, which Parks Canada has refurbished into a swish **tourist office** (Mon–Sat 10am–8.30pm; Ⓣ204/675-8836, Ⓦwww.pc.gc.ca). Displays on the history of the fur trade and the Hudson's Bay Company are jazzed up by films dealing with arctic wildlife, **Prince of Wales' Fort** and the construction of the railway. These are supplemented by free evening lectures on archaeological history and climate change. This is also the place to pick up information on local tours (see box, p.600).

Exiting the railway station you quickly arrive in the middle of **Kelsey Boulevard**, the town's main street. For a quick orientation simply walk straight on from here to the large and rather forlorn **Town Centre Complex** overlooking Hudson Bay. The town's administrative offices are based here, as are its library (free internet) and various recreational facilities, including curling and hockey rinks, swimming pool, bowling alley and a cinema.

The Eskimo Museum

Just east down the road, the **Eskimo Museum** (June–Aug Mon 1–5pm, Tues–Sat 9am–noon & 1–5pm; Sept–May Mon & Sat 1–4.30pm; by donation), 242 La Vérendrye Ave, houses the Inuit collection of the Oblate Fathers of Mary Immaculate, whose missionary work began here around 1900. Animal-hide canoes and stuffed Arctic animals dominate the museum's one large room, which has Inuit art arranged in cases round the walls. It's a fine range of material, from caribou-antler pictographs and highly stylized soapstone figurines through to walrus-tooth scrimshaws and detailed ivory and stone carvings. The sculptures fall into two distinct periods. Up until the 1940s, the artistic work of the local Inuit was essentially limited to the carving of figurines in walrus ivory, modelled on traditional designs. However, in 1949 a Canadian painter, James Houston, travelled the east coast of Hudson Bay in Québec, encouraging the Inuit to vary their designs and experiment with different materials – which led, in particular, to the development of larger and more naturalistic sculptures carved in soapstone. One corner of the museum functions as a **gift shop** selling a wide range of prints and carvings, plus a good collection of books on the north.

The outskirts

A couple of minutes' walk north from the town centre, Churchill's grain elevators and silos stand at the base of a narrow peninsula that sticks out into the mouth of the Churchill River. At the tip, approached along a track, **Cape Merry National Historic Site** (check with Parks Canada for guided tour times – see above) has the remains of an eighteenth-century gun emplacement and a cairn commemorating the Danish explorer Jens Munck, who led an expedition forced to winter here in 1619; most of the crew died from cold and hunger. The cape is about a half-hours' walk from town and a brilliant spot at high tide to watch belugas in the bay, but take local advice first as to whether the area is currently safe; polar bears often potter among the rocks here.

On the other side of the estuary, **Prince of Wales' Fort National Historic Site** (July & Aug; for hours contact tourist office; $7.80) is a partly restored eighteenth-century stone fortress built to protect the trading interests of the Hudson's Bay Company from the French. Finished in 1771, this massive structure took forty years to complete, but even then it proved far from impregnable. When a squadron of the French fleet appeared in the bay in 1782 the fort's governor, Samuel Hearne, was forced to surrender without firing a shot because he didn't have enough men to form a garrison. The French spiked the cannon and undermined the walls, and after this fiasco the Company never bothered to repair

Churchill tour operators

Local wildlife **tour operators** have proliferated in Churchill, offering everything from snorkelling and kayaking with the whales to viewing polar bears from helicopters. They are all listed in the indispensable *Guide to Churchil* pamphlet which you can pick up at all major Manitoban tourist offices, and usually at the Churchill Parks Canada Visitor tourist office.

The best place to get a feel for what's on offer at any time of year is at **North Star Tours** (Ⓣ204/675-2356 or 1-800/665-0690), based in the Bayport Plaza on Munck Street. The outfit is run by jolly third-generation locals who organize an excellent minibus tour of local sites (3hr; $75) – which includes a good look for polar bears – but they won't hesitate to suggest, and even call, other companies for you if you have particular activities in mind. One of these is whale-watching specialist **Sea North Tours**, 39 Franklin St (mid-June to late Aug; Ⓣ204/675-2195 or 1-888/348-7591 Ⓦwww.seanorthtours.com), who offer trips by either zodiac or kayak (no experience necessary; $120/2hr 30min) and allow you to listen in on the belugas using stereo hydrophones. They also organize snorkelling trips ($170/2hr 30min), when visibility in the bay is good enough.

In the **polar bear season** (Oct & Nov), Great White Bear Tours (Ⓣ204/675-2781 or 1-866/765-8344, Ⓦwww.greatwhitebeartours.com) offer day-trips to find bears for $300, but a better option – if you've $6000 or so to spare and can book months in advance – are the week-long tours with **Frontiers North Adventures** (Ⓣ204/949-2051 or 1-800/663-9832, Ⓦwww.tundrabuggy.com), who have vehicles specially designed to avoid damaging the tundra; Churchill Wild (Ⓣ204/377-5090 or 1-866/846-9453, Ⓦwww.churchillwild.com) have similarly priced tours, while the *Lazy Bear Lodge* runs three-day tours for around half that price. Outside the main polar bear season consider splashing out on a flight with **Hudson Bay Helicopters** (Ⓣ204/675-2576 or 1-867/873-5146, Ⓦwww.hudsonbayheli.com), who can all but guarantee polar bear sightings, for $500 per hour.

the damage. The fort is only accessible as part of a guided tour of the Churchill River organized by Sea North Tours (see above).

East of town, a road runs behind the shoreline towards the airport, near to which lies the **polar bear "prison"**, a large hangar-like compound where dangerous bears are kept until they can be released safely. Bears are captured after wandering into town in search of food and, although most can be scared off quite easily, a handful return. These more persistent specimens are shot with tranquillizers and transported to the compound. It's a necessary precaution, as polar bears can run and swim faster than humans which they tend to regard as prey. Repeat bear offenders are given three chances, after which they are humanely destroyed.

Practicalities

With no campsites or hostels in Churchill, visitors are dependent on the town's uniformly drab **hotels** and handful of basic **B&Bs**. All are within easy walking distance of the train station, and all should be booked in advance; for a full list see Ⓦwww.churchill.ca. The **B&Bs** include the *Polar Bear Bed & Breakfast*, 26 Hearne St (Ⓣ204/675-2819; ❸), which lends out bikes to guests for free. The best of the hotels are the *Polar Inn*, 15 Kelsey Blvd (Ⓣ204/675-8878 or 1-877/765-2733, Ⓦwww.polarinn.com; ❺) and the *Northern Nights Lodge*, 101 Kelsey Blvd (Ⓣ204/675-2999; ❼), with an adjacent restaurant and mountain bikes for rent. The log cabin-style *Lazy Bear Lodge*, 313 Kelsey Blvd (Ⓣ204/633-9377 or 1-866/687-2327 Ⓦwww.lazybearlodge.com; ❽), has the most character as well as free wi-fi and a shuttle service from station or airport.

Churchill's handful of **restaurants** leave a lot to be desired, with the exception of the budget bistro and locals' hangout *Gypsy's Bakery*, 253 Kelsey Blvd, where you can get basic burger-and-fries food, or splash out a bit and sample delicious cuts of local caribou or the popular local fish, arctic char, for around $18. All the hotels also have their own restaurants, with the *Lazy Bear Lodge* probably the best – you can usually try muskox and other game here (mains around $25).

York Factory

The remote **York Factory National Historic Site** lies 240km southeast of Churchill, at the mouth of the Hayes and Nelson rivers. This was the central storehouse of the northwestern fur trade throughout the eighteenth century, its wooden palisades the temporary home of soldiers, explorers, travellers, traders and settlers bound for the Red River Colony at present-day Winnipeg. With the amalgamation of the North West and Hudson's Bay companies in 1821, it was here that the new governor **George Simpson** set about the delicate task of reconciling the feuds stirred by a generation of inter-company rivalry. In October he arranged his first formal joint banquet, 73 traders facing each other across two long and narrow tables. It was, according to a contemporary, "dollars to doughnuts [whether it would be] a feed or fight", but Simpson's diplomatic skills triumphed, leading to a successful reorganization of trading operations. In its heyday, there were some fifty buildings within the stockade, including a guesthouse, fur stores, trading rooms, living quarters and shops, but they were all destroyed in the 1930s,

Churchill's flora and fauna

Churchill occupies a transitional zone where the stunted trees of the taiga (subarctic coniferous forest) meet the mosses of the tundra. Blanketed with snow in the winter and covered by thousands of bogs and lakes in the summer, this terrain is completely flat until it reaches the sloping banks of the Churchill River and the ridge around Hudson Bay, whose grey-quartzite boulders have been rubbed smooth by the action of the ice, wind and water.

This environment harbours splendid **wildlife**, including **polar bears**, which start to come ashore when the ice melts on the bay in late June. They must then wait for the ice to form again to support their weight before they can start their seal hunt; a polar bear can detect a scent from 32km away and can pick up the presence of seals under a metre of snow and ice. The best months to spot bears are September, October and early November, just before the ice re-forms completely.

In mid-June, as the ice breaks on the Churchill River, the spreading patch of open water attracts schools of white **beluga whales**. As many as three thousand of these intelligent, inquisitive and vocal mammals spend July and August around the mouth of the river, joining the **seals**, who arrive in late March for five months. The area around the town is also on one of the major migration routes for **birds** heading north from April to June and returning south in August or early September. Nesting and hatching take place from early June until early July. A couple of hundred species are involved, including gulls, terns, loons, Lapland longspurs, ducks and geese. The star visitor is the rare Ross's Gull, a native of Siberia, which has nested in Churchill for some years. The *Birder's Guide to Churchill* by Bonnie Chartier lists them all and is available in the town at the Eskimo Museum.

Churchill is also a great place to see the **aurora borealis** (Northern Lights), whose swirling curtains of blue, green and white are common in the skies between late August and April; occasionally it's seen year-round but is at its best from January to March. Finally, in spring and autumn the tundra is a colourful sheet of moss, lichens, flowers and miniature shrubs and trees that include dwarf birch, spruce and cranberry.

with the exception of the **main warehouse** (1832), a sturdy wooden building that serves as a reminder of the fort's earlier significance. Wandering around the desolate site today, it's hard to imagine it was once the largest community in western Canada. Guided tours of the site are available (June to mid-Sept; contact the Parks Canada Visitor Reception Centre in Churchill $7.80).

This remote spot can only be reached by **charter flight** – weather permitting – from Thompson, Churchill or Gillam, a hydroelectric centre on the rail line between Winnipeg and Churchill.

Because of the disturbance to polar bears in the area, camping is not allowed at York Factory. The only **place to stay** is the *Nanuk Polar Bear Lodge* (Ⓣ306/296-4403, Ⓦwww.nanukpolarbearlodge.com; ❺) arranged in advance with the owners, who also run polar bear tours in August and September. There are no services and all supplies must be brought in.

Travel details

Trains

Calgary to: Vancouver with private Rocky Mountaineer Railtours (see p.37).
Edmonton to: Jasper (3 weekly; 5hr 30min) Vancouver (3 weekly; 27hr); Winnipeg (3 weekly; 20hr).
Jasper to: Prince Rupert via Prince George (3 weekly; 33hr).
Winnipeg to: Churchill (2 weekly; 48hr); Jasper (3 weekly; 26hr); Saskatoon (3 weekly; 11hr); The Pas (2 weekly; 14hr); Toronto (3 weekly; 31hr); Vancouver (3 weekly; 48hr).

Buses

With Greyhound unless otherwise indicated.
Calgary to: Banff (5 daily; 1hr 40min); Drumheller (1 daily; 1hr 50min); Edmonton (7 daily; 4hr); Lake Louise (4 daily; 2hr 40min); Regina (2 daily; 10hr); Saskatoon (4 daily; 11hr); Vancouver (4 daily; 15hr); Winnipeg (2 daily; 19hr).
Edmonton to: Grande Prairie (3 daily; 6hr); Hay River (1 daily; 16hr); Jasper (4 daily; 5hr); Peace River (2 daily; 7hr); Saskatoon (4 daily; 7hr); Vancouver (5 daily; 17hr); Whitehorse (mid-May to mid-Oct 1 daily; rest of year 3 weekly; 28hr); Winnipeg (4 daily; 20hr).
Regina to: Coronach (STC; 4 per week; 4hr); Medicine Hat (2 daily; 6hr 30min); Moose Jaw (STC & Greyhound; 6 daily; 1hr); Saskatoon (STC; 3 daily; 3hr); Swift Current (2 daily; 3hr 30min); Yorkton (STC; 2 daily; 2hr 35min).
Saskatoon to: Edmonton (4 daily; 7hr); Flin Flon (STC; daily; 12hr); La Ronge (STC via Prince Albert; 1 daily; 6hr); Lloydminster (3 daily; 3hr 15min); North Battleford (4 daily; 1hr 30min); The Pas (STC; 1 daily 9hr 30min); Waskesiu (via Prince Albert; mid-May to mid-Sept 1 daily; 3hr); Yorkton (3 daily; 4hr 30min).
Swift Current to: Eastend (STC; 2 weekly; 2hr).
Winnipeg to: Flin Flon (3 daily; 12hr); Gimli (1 daily; 1hr 30min); Grand Beach Provincial Park (1 daily; 1hr 15min); Kenora (2 daily; 2hr 40min); Neepawa (2 daily; 3hr); Portage La Prairie (6 daily; 1hr 15min); Regina (2 daily; 9hr); Riding Mountain (1 daily; 3hr); Saskatoon (4 daily; 12hr 30min); Sault Ste Marie (2 daily; 20hr); Steinbach (2 daily; 1hr); Sudbury (2 daily; 25hr); Thompson (2 daily; 9hr); Thunder Bay (2 daily; 9hr); Toronto (2 daily; 30hr); West Hawk Lake (2 daily; 2 hr).

Flights

Calgary to: Edmonton (25 daily; 50min); Montréal (29 daily; 5hr); Regina (9 daily; 1hr 25min); Saskatoon (9 daily; 1hr); Toronto (25 daily; 4hr); Vancouver (30 daily; 1hr 20min); to Winnipeg (11 daily; 2hr 10min).
Edmonton to: Montréal (4 daily; 5hr); Toronto (17 daily; 4hr 10min); Vancouver (19 daily; 1hr 25min).
Regina to: Toronto (4 daily; 3hr); Vancouver (2 daily; 3hr 30min).
Saskatoon to: Toronto (4 daily; 4hr); Vancouver (2 daily; 2hr 10min).
Winnipeg to: Churchill (3 daily; 3hr); Regina (3 daily; 1hr 10min); Saskatoon (3 daily; 1hr 20min); The Pas (4 daily; 1hr 15min); Toronto (13 daily; 2hr 20min); Vancouver (7 daily; 4hr).

8

The Canadian Rockies

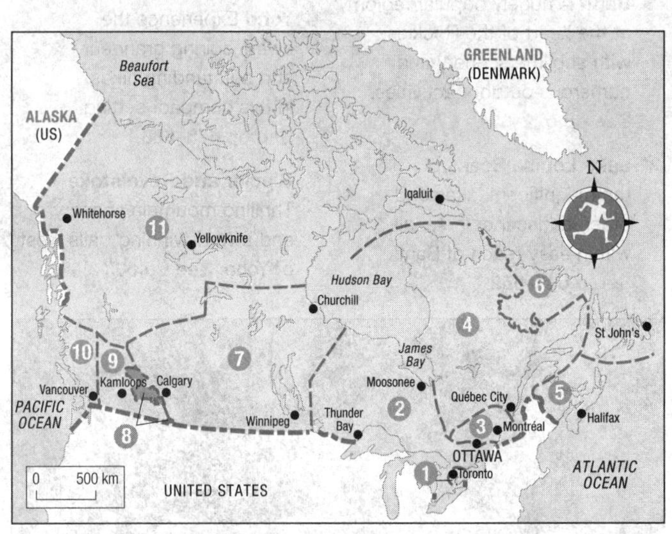

CHAPTER 8

Highlights

* **Waterton Lakes** There's superb hiking and stunning scenery at this small park on the US border. See pp.608–616
* **Kananaskis Country** As the crowds stream past to Banff, get out and draw breath in this collection of nine provincial parks, an ecological reserve and several recreation areas. See pp.616–620
* **Banff** A hugely popular region at the heart of the Rockies, with sublime scenery and numerous outdoor activities. See pp.622–639
* **Lake Louise** Soak up the magnificent lakes and other landscapes here, all within easy reach of Banff. See p.642–652
* **Rafting** Get up close and personal with the mountains, out on the water. See p.657
* **Jasper** Head north on the legendary Icefields Parkway for some memorable backcountry walks. See pp.658–670
* **Mount Robson** Explore west of Jasper for breathtaking vistas over the Rockies' highest peak. See pp.671–673
* **Yoho** Experience the awe-inspiring grandeur and outstanding hikes in this compact setting. See pp.673–683
* **Glacier and Revelstoke** Thrilling mountain scenery and award-winning trails west of Yoho. See pp.683–688

▲ An elk during winter, Banff National Park

8 The Canadian Rockies

Rising with overwhelming majesty from **Alberta's** rippling plains, the **Canadian Rockies** are one of the main reasons people come to Canada and few North American landscapes come as loaded with such high expectations. So it's a relief to find that the superlatives are scarcely able to do credit to the splendour or immensity of the region's forests, lakes, rivers and snow-capped mountains.

Joined with their smaller cousins in the US, the Canadian Rockies extend north of the US border almost 1500km to Canada's far north, where they merge with ranges in the Yukon and Alaska, forming the Continental Divide in the process – a vast watershed which separates rivers flowing to the Pacific and Arctic oceans from those flowing into the Atlantic. But the range is best known for its virtually unbroken north-south chain of national and provincial parks and the world-class ski resorts at its heart (see p.606).

At the southern end of the range, and coupled with Glacier National Park in the US, is small but impressive **Waterton Lakes National Park**. North of here lies a series of less-restrictively managed provincial parks, collectively known as **Kananaskis Country**. These exist partly to take the pressure off the adjacent **Banff National Park**, the region's best known and busiest park. Beyond its northern boundary the range is protected by the much less busy **Jasper National Park,** by far the largest park in the region. The western boundary of both Banff and Jasper parks is also the provincial border, so that adjacent areas are protected in a separate set of parks in BC: **Mount Robson Provincial Park**, just west of Jasper – which protects Mount Robson, the highest and most dramatic peak in the Canadian Rockies – and **Yoho** and **Kootenay national parks** west of Banff. Two smaller national parks, **Glacier** and **Mount Revelstoke**, lie separate and firmly in BC.

There's not a great deal to choose between the parks in terms of scenery – they're all sensational – and planning an itinerary that allows you to fit them all in neatly is just about impossible. It is also rather unnecessary, since to really experience the Rockies you're best off homing in on just one or two parks and then heading into the backcountry. But if you're here to see as much of the highlights as possible, it's best to start with Banff National Park, then head north along the otherworldly Icefields Parkway to Jasper and Mount Robson before doubling back – no hardship, given the scenery – to the Lake Louise and Banff area. Then, if you've time to spare, it's easy to head out to Yoho, Kootenay or

National Park passes

As with any national park, anyone entering any of the Rockies parks must buy a permit ($9.80 per day for most parks, or $67.70 for a National Parks annual pass; see p.46), available at the road entrances to parks and park information centres. Park centres are also the place to pick up the separate **backcountry Wilderness Pass** ($9.80 per person per night, or $68.70 for an annual pass; plus $11.70 reservation fee), required for overnight backcountry use. All backcountry areas in all parks have a quota, so it's vital to make bookings well in advance (up to three months) if you wish to walk – and camp – on some of the most popular trails requiring overnight stops. Reservations can be made by phone at ⓣ1-877/737-3783 or ⓦwww.pccamping.ca.

Kananaskis or pick up the Trans-Canada Hwy – a particularly enticing option if you're travelling to or from Vancouver – west to the smaller Glacier and Revelstoke national parks. Similarly, a visit to Waterton Lakes is most tempting if you are on your way to or from the US.

You can get to all the parks except Waterton by **bus**, but travelling by **car** is the obvious way to get the most out of the region. Once there, you'd be foolish not to tackle some of the 3000km of hiking and biking trails that crisscross the mountains, the vast majority of which are well worn and well signed. We've highlighted the best short walks and day-hikes in each area, and you can get more details from the excellent **park visitor centres**, which sell 1:50,000 topographical maps and usually offer small reference libraries of trail books; *The Canadian Rockies Trail Guide*, by Brian Patton and Bart Robinson, is invaluable for serious hiking or backpacking. Other activities – fishing, skiing, canoeing, whitewater rafting, cycling, riding, rock climbing and so on – are comprehensively dealt with in visitor centres, and you can easily **rent equipment** or sign up for organized tours in the bigger towns.

Don't **underestimate** the Rockies. Despite the impression created by the summer throngs in centres like Banff and Lake Louise, excellent roads and sleek park facilities, the vast proportion of parkland is wilderness and should be respected and treated as such.

Winter sports in the Rockies

With terrific terrain, reliable snow cover, uncrowded slopes and relatively low prices the Rockies are phenomenally tempting for a **ski or snowboard** vacation. The area is also ideal for a host of other **winter sports** like cross-country skiing, snowshoeing, dog-sledding and snowmobiling (though the latter is not allowed in national parks).

The season at most resorts runs from mid-December until the end of May, with the best conditions usually in March, when the days are getting warmer and longer, the snow is deepest and resort accommodation – hard to come by during Christmas week and at Easter – easier to find.

The best known, busiest and most expensive resorts are those in **Banff National Park**. All are within easy reach of the town of Banff, the best hub, and include the small, steep and taxing **Mount Norquay** (see p.634); the well-rounded intermediate-friendly **Sunshine Village** (see p.635); and the vast, varied and hugely challenging **Lake Louise** (see p.651). These three promote themselves with a common lift-ticket system. Locals make up a sizeable chunk of the business: weekends and holidays are peak times, leaving working weekdays particularly quiet. Smaller-scale alternatives within striking distance of Banff are in Kananaskis

Country. Here, **Nakiska** (see p.621) is one of the most user-friendly resorts on the continent, with state-of-the-art facilities and plenty of fine cross-country skiing. **Fortress Mountain** (see p.621), 15km south, is a much smaller area, where you're likely to share the slopes with school groups and families. A glorious three-hour drive north of Banff into **Jasper National Park** through craggy montane scenery along the Icefields Parkway lies **Marmot Basin** (see p.667). A far more modest affair than the ski areas surrounding Banff, it nevertheless has the advantage of being both quieter and less expensive. The town of Jasper, centre of the skiing area, is less commercial than Banff, and its surroundings remain more conspicuously wild, with almost limitless cross-country skiing possibilities.

Apart from these big names the region also contains many other equally worthy, though less accessible resorts, further west in the BC Rockies. Blessed with much the same light snow that's made the whole region famous – with the added advantage of milder temperatures – this area has the benefit of being located outside strictly regulated national park lands. The result has been not only the emergence of the world's highest concentration of heli-skiing operations, but also

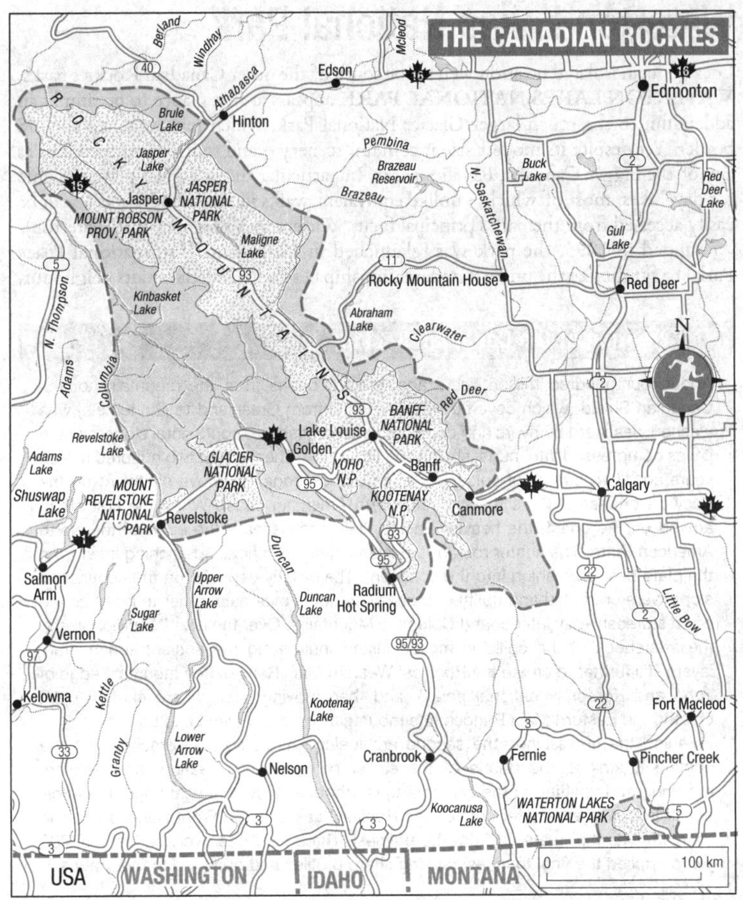

both heavy investment in the industry and an ongoing programme of rapid expansion at the resorts.

The closest to Banff is **Kicking Horse** (see p.683). Only a decade old, it's tipped by many to steal much of Banff's business, thanks to the fabulous quality of its expert terrain. South along the western fringe of the Rockies, **Panorama** (see p.701) is a fantastic mountain for cruising and carving, with a superlative setting for its quiet resort village. Another couple of hours' drive south is the cheerful family-orientated ski hill **Kimberley** (see p.702), where the quantity of spacious ideal beginner and intermediate terrain almost distracts from the presence of a few incredible mogul runs. Multi-day tickets here are interchangeable with those at **Fernie** (see p.703), with its bountiful mountain bowls and ridges, a resort – that with the recent Kicking Horse ski area (see p.683) – is likely to become Banff's greatest regional competitor for international ski trade. With all four resorts no more than a couple of hours' drive from their nearest neighbour, they make for an ideal multi-resort trip tackled as a loop (which can include Banff) from Calgary.

Waterton Lakes National Park

Located in an isolated position well to the south of the other Canadian Rockies parks, **WATERTON LAKES NATIONAL PARK** appears at first glance to be simply an addendum to the much larger Glacier National Park, which joins it across the US border. Yet despite its modest size it contains scenery – and trails – as stupendous as any of the bigger Canadian Rockies parks. In particular this is a great place to come for day-hikes, most of which – unlike equivalent walks in Banff and Jasper – can be easily accessed from the park's principal focus, **Waterton Village** (or just Waterton).

Founded in 1895, the park was relaunched in 1932 as an "International Peace Park" to symbolize the understated relationship between Canada and its neighbour.

The creation of the Canadian Rockies

About four hundred million years ago, eroded debris from the mountains of the Canadian Shield (which covered North America from Greenland to Guatemala) was washed westward by rivers and deposited on the offshore "continental slope", where it was compressed into muds, shales and limestone. Then, about two hundred million years ago, two strings of volcanic Pacific islands began to move eastward on the Pacific Continental Plate towards the North American coast. When the first string arrived off the coast, the heavier Pacific Plate slid beneath the edge of the North American Plate. The lighter rock of the islands stayed "afloat", detaching itself from the plate before crashing into the continent. The orderly deposits on the continental slope were crumpled and uplifted, their layers riding over each other to produce the coast's present-day interior and Columbia Mountains. Over the next 75 million years, the aftershock of the collision moved inland, bulldozing the ancient sedimentary layers still further to create the Rockies' Western Main Ranges (the mountain edge of Yoho and Kootenay national parks), and then moving east, where 4km of uplift created the Eastern Main Ranges (the mountains on a line with Lake Louise).

Behind the first islands the second archipelago had also now crashed into the continent, striking the debris of the earlier collision and creating more folding, rupturing and uplifting of the earlier ranges. About sixty million years ago, the aftershock from this encounter created the Rockies' easternmost Front Ranges (the line of mountains that rears up from the prairies). Three Ice Ages over the last 240,000 years applied the final touches, carving sharp profiles and dumping further debris.

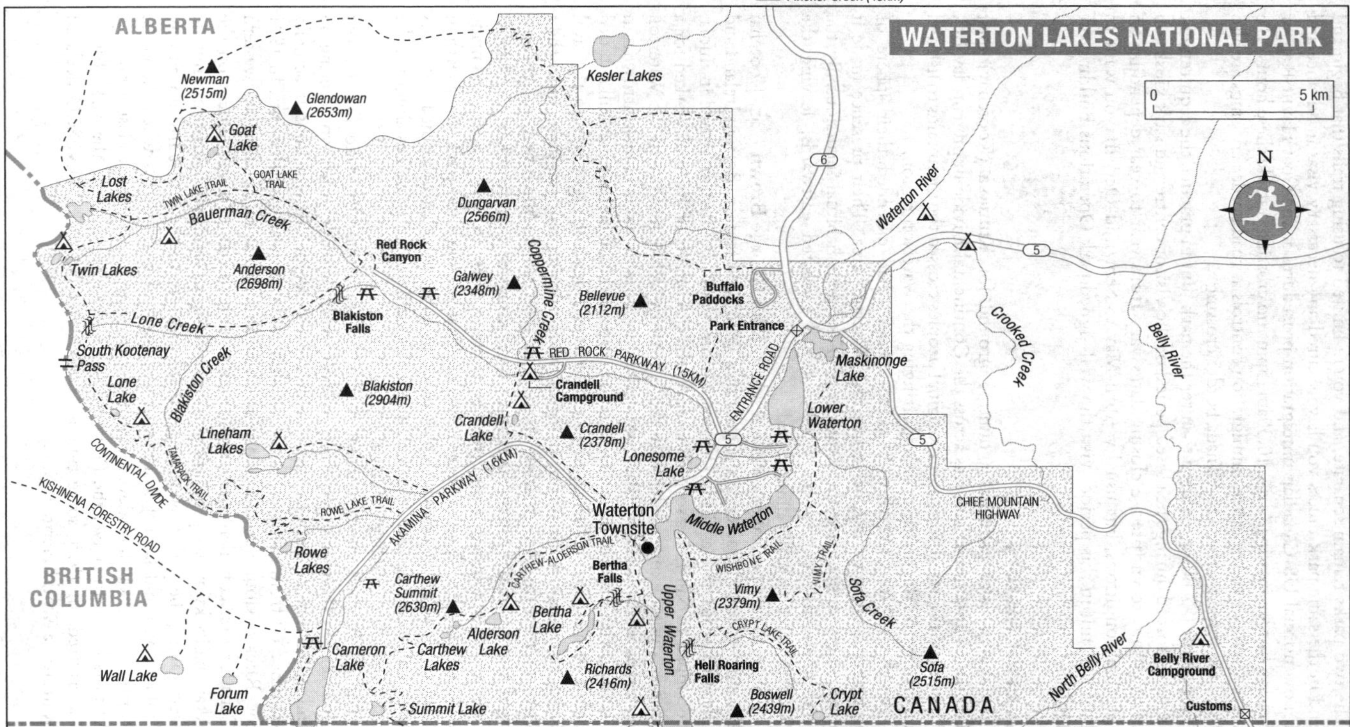
WATERTON LAKES NATIONAL PARK
0
5 km
N
Pincher Creek (48km)
Cardston (43km) & Lethbridge (130km)
Goat Haunt Ranger Station
Glacier National Park & Great Falls (MT)
ALBERTA
Newman (2515m)
Glendowan (2653m)
Kesler Lakes
Goat Lake
GOAT LAKE TRAIL
Lost Lakes
TWIN LAKE TRAIL
Bauerman Creek
Dungarvan (2566m)
Twin Lakes
Anderson (2698m)
Red Rock Canyon
Galwey (2348m)
Coppermine Creek
Bellevue (2112m)
Buffalo Paddocks
Park Entrance
Waterton River
Crooked Creek
Belly River
Lone Creek
Blakiston Falls
South Kootenay Pass
RED ROCK PARKWAY (15KM)
ENTRANCE ROAD
Maskinonge Lake
Lone Lake
Blakiston Creek
Blakiston (2904m)
Crandell Campground
Lower Waterton
Crandell Lake
Crandell (2378m)
Lineham Lakes
Lonesome Lake
CONTINENTAL DIVIDE
TAMARACK TRAIL
KISHINENA FORESTRY ROAD
AKAMINA PARKWAY (16KM)
ROWE LAKE TRAIL
Waterton Townsite
Middle Waterton
CHIEF MOUNTAIN HIGHWAY
Rowe Lakes
CARTHEW-ALDERSON TRAIL
Bertha Falls
WISHBONE TRAIL
VIMY TRAIL
BRITISH COLUMBIA
Carthew Summit (2630m)
Bertha Lake
Vimy (2379m)
Sofa Creek
Alderson Lake
Upper Waterton
CRYPT LAKE TRAIL
Wall Lake
Cameron Lake
Carthew Lakes
Hell Roaring Falls
Sofa (2515m)
North Belly River
Belly River Campground
Richards (2416m)
Forum Lake
Boswell (2439m)
Crypt Lake
Summit Lake
CANADA
Customs

The two parks remain separate, and you're limited to using trails that begin and end in the same park unless you have secured any necessary visas in advance and follow normal US-Canadian immigration procedures at the Goat Haunt Ranger Station border crossing (daily 10.30am–5pm; no crossing outside these hours). To drive from one to the other, immigration controls at road border crossings are also the same for any other US-Canada border crossing.

A **permit** ($7.80) is required to enter the park, but in practice the requirement is not enforced during the closed period of the visitor centre and park kiosks on Hwy 5 into town (precise closing dates vary from year to year depending on weather conditions, but usually April-May to Sept/mid-Oct). If you want to buy a permit in this period, visit the well-signed park Operations Building off Hwy 5.

A brief history

The region once provided a hunting ground for **Ktunaxa** (Kootenay) First Peoples, whose home base was across the Continental Divide in present-day BC. Up to nine thousand years ago aboriginal peoples crossed the mountains to fish and hunt bison on the prairie grasslands fringing the Waterton region.

By about 1700, the rival Blackfoot peoples had extended their sphere of influence from central Alberta into the Waterton area. Their presence made it increasingly difficult for the Ktunaxa to make their habitual incursions. By the mid-nineteenth century the Blackfoot had retreated eastwards, leaving the Waterton area virtually uninhabited.

The area's first permanent white resident, **John George Brown** – or "Kootenai Brown" – was a character straight out of a Wild West fantasy. Born in Ireland and allegedly educated at Eton, he spent time with the British Army in India, decamped to San Francisco, laboured in the gold fields of BC and worked for a time as a pony express rider with the US Army. While moving to the Waterton region he was attacked by Blackfoot natives, supposedly wrenching an arrow from his back with his own hands. He was then captured by Chief Sitting Bull and tied naked to a stake, but managed to escape at the dead of night to join the rival Ktunaxa people, with whom he spent years hunting and trapping, until their virtual retreat from the prairies. Marriage in 1869 calmed him down, and encouraged him to build a cabin (the region's first) alongside Waterton Lake. In 1895 a reserve was established, with Brown as its first warden. In 1910 the area was made a "Dominion Park"; a year later it was designated a **national park**, the fourth in Canada. Brown, then aged 71, was made its superintendent, but died five years later, still lobbying hard to extend the park's borders. His grave lies alongside the main road into Waterton Village.

For all Brown's environmental zeal it was he, ironically, who first noticed globules of **oil** on Cameron Creek, a local river, a discovery that would bring oil and other mineral entrepreneurs to ravage the region. Brown himself actually skimmed oil from the river, bottled it, and sold it in nearby settlements. In 1901 the Rocky Mountain Development Company struck oil, leading to western Canada's first commercial oil well, which soon dried up; a monument on the Akamina Parkway (see p.615) now marks its original location. Tourists meanwhile were giving the park a wide berth, thanks mainly to the fact it had no railway (unlike Banff and Jasper), a situation that changed in the 1920s when the Great Northern Railway introduced a bus link here from its Montana to Jasper railway. Visitors began to arrive, the *Prince of Wales* hotel was built, and the park's future was assured. In 1995, some time after the other big parks, UNESCO declared Waterton a World Heritage Site.

The natural environment of Waterton Lakes National Park

The unique **geological history** of Waterton becomes clear when you compare its scenery with the strikingly different landscapes of Banff and Jasper national parks. Rock and mountains in Waterton moved eastward during the formation of the Rockies (see p.608), but travelled as a single vast mass known as the Lewis Thrust. Some 6km thick, this monolith moved over 70km along a 300-kilometre front, the result being that rocks over 1.5 billion years old from the Rockies' "sedimentary basement" came to rest undisturbed on *top* of the prairies' far more recent sixty-million-year-old shales. Scarcely any zone of transition exists between the two, which is why the park is often known as the place where the "peaks meet the prairies", and its landscapes as "upside-down mountains". The effect was to produce not only slightly lower peaks than to the north, but also mountains whose summits are irregular in shape and very different from the distinctive sawtooth ridges of Banff National Park.

Flora and fauna

The huge variety of altitude, habitats and climate within the park mean plants and wildlife from prairie habitats co-mingle with the species of the purely montane, subalpine and alpine regions. The result is the greatest diversity of **flora and fauna** of any of the western national parks: 1200 plant species and 250 species of birds. Approaching the park on Hwy 5 from the north you pass through dry prairie **grassland**, home to native grasses such as grama and rough fescue; you should also see prickly wild rose (Alberta's floral emblem), sagebrush, buckbrush (yellow rose) and pincushion cactus. Entering the park you pass the **wetlands** of Maskinonge Lake on your left, while in the Blakison Valley and around *Belly River Campsite* is **aspen parkland**, a transitional zone between prairie and forest habitats.

Higher are the **montane forest** and subalpine zones, both rich in plant and animal life. On the eastern slopes above Cameron Lake are copses of four hundred-year-old subalpine trees, the park's oldest forest growth; you can also see vast spreads of "bear grass", a bright flower-topped grass which can grow up to a metre in height. Trees largely give out in the **alpine zone**, an area of which the park's Crypt Lake is a good example. See p.614 for more on these various habitats.

Birds are best seen on Maskinonge and Lower Waterton lakes, Linnet Lake, Cameron Lake and along the Wishbone Trail off Chief Mountain Hwy. The best time to look is during the migratory season between September and November; ospreys also nest close to Waterton Village. Maskinonge Lake is the place to sit in hope of seeing mink and muskrats; **beavers** can be seen on the Belly River. The park has about fifty black **bears**, but you'll be lucky to see them: your best bet is to scan the slopes of Blakison Valley in July and August as they forage for berries in readiness for hibernation. Grizzlies, moose and cougars are also prevalent, but rarely seen. White-tailed deer nibble up and down the Red Rock Canyon Parkway, while elk and mule deer often wander in and around Waterton village. Mountain goats are elusive, but you may glimpse one or two in the rocky high ground above Bertha, Crypt and Goat lakes. Bighorn sheep congregate above the visitor centre and the northern flanks of the Blakison Valley.

Waterton Village

WATERTON VILLAGE, the park's only base, accommodation source and services centre, is beautifully set on Upper Waterton Lake (at 150m, the Rockies' deepest lake). Most people are here to walk, windsurf, go riding or take boat trips on the lake. There are also a handful of town trails, and a trio of great hikes – Bertha Lake, Crypt Lake and the Upper Waterton Lakeshore – which start from the village (see p.614). Having long been a poor relation to the "big four" national parks in the Rockies, Waterton is now popular enough to warrant booking accommodation well in advance for much of July and August.

Arrival and information

Canadian **access** to Waterton by road is from Fort Macleod via either Hwy 3 west then Hwy 6 south (via Pincher Creek) or on Hwy 2 south to Cardston and then west on Hwy 5. Calgary is 264km and three hours' drive away; Lethbridge (which has the nearest airport), 130km (75min); and St Mary, Montana, 60km (45min). More than other Rockies' parks this is somewhere you really need your own transport to reach, with the nearest Greyhound depot at Pincher Creek 50km away; a cab from Crystal Taxi (Ⓣ403/627-4262) will cost around $65 for the run to town, otherwise there's no public transport to or within the park.

The national park **visitor centre** is on Entrance Road at the road junction just to the north (daily early May to mid-Oct 8am–7pm; Ⓣ403/859-5133); Waterton Village is easily navigable on foot, but if you need a **map**, the visitor centre can supply one. Further information is available from the Parks Canada office (Ⓣ403/859-2224, Ⓦwww.pc.gc.ca) and, outside the visitor centre's summer hours, at the park's administration office at 215 Mount View Rd (Mon–Fri 8am–4pm; Ⓣ403/859-2477). The Canadian Parks Service 1:50,000 **map** *Waterton Lakes National Park*, is useful if you're doing any serious walking. It's usually available from the visitor centre and outdoor stores in Waterton Village.

Accommodation

Waterton has a range of **hotel** accommodation, all of it in the village itself. In addition to the private campsites – and three Canadian Parks Service campsites, which are first-come, first-served, and fill quickly in summer – that are detailed below, the national park has provided nine designated **backcountry campsites**, where you'll find dry toilets and a surface-water supply; a few of them also have shelters and cooking facilities. To use any, you need a backcountry camping permit ($9.80 per person, plus $11.70 reservation fee) also issued on a first-come, first-served basis by the visitor centre or administration office.

Hotels and motels

Aspen Village Inn 111 Windflower Ave Ⓣ403/859-2255 or 1-888/859-8669, Ⓦwww.theaspenvillageinn.com. Quiet spot with mountain views opposite the municipal pool; 35 motel rooms and 16 "cottage" rooms, some with kitchenettes and one with a fireplace. May to mid-Oct. ⑤

Bayshore Inn 111 Waterton Ave Ⓣ403/859-2211 or 1-888/527-9555, Ⓦwww.bayshoreinn.com. This very comfortable hotel is just south of the marina, and 49 of its seventy units are on the lakefront. Choose from the "romantic", "deluxe" or "family" suites and lakefront or mountain view rooms. It also has an on-site spa, restaurant, bistro and "saloon". May to mid-Oct. ⑥

Crandell Mountain Lodge 102 Mountview Rd Ⓣ403/859-2288 or 1-866/859-2288, Ⓦwww.crandellmountainlodge.com. The seventeen nicely finished nonsmoking rooms in this pretty lodge are more intimate than some of the town's hotels; rooms with kitchenettes or gas fireplaces are available. ⑥

Northland Lodge 408 Evergreen Ave Ⓣ403/859-2353, Ⓦwww.northlandlodgecanada.com. Nine nonsmoking and cosy rooms (seven with private bathroom), south of the town site in the lee of the mountains and one block south of Cameron Falls. Mid-May to mid-Oct. ⑤

Prince of Wales Hotel Waterton Lake, off Hwy 5 Ⓣ403/859-2231, Ⓦwww.glacierparkinc.com. Famous and popular old hotel – the best in town if you want a place with a sense of history and unbeatable position – and one whose 1927 Gothic outline is in almost every picture of Waterton; worth it if you can afford the pricier lakeside rooms with views. Some rooms are rather small, however, so check what you're getting for between $179 and $799. Mid-May to mid-Sept. ⑦

Waterton Lakes Lodge 101 Clematis Ave Ⓣ403/859-2150 or 1-888/985-6343, Ⓦwww.watertonlakeslodge.com. A smart eighty-room resort hotel in the centre of the village, with health spa, recreational centre with 18m pool (summer only) and its own restaurant. Kitchenette rooms and suites available, while the "deluxe lodge" rooms come equipped with gas fireplaces, walk-in showers and two-person jacuzzi. Usually open mid-May to Oct, but at press time was open year-round. ❼

Campsites

Belly River Campground 26km southeast from the townsite, along the Chief Mountain Hwy (Hwy 6). The smallest (24 sites) and most primitive of the park-operated campsites works on a first-come, first-served basis, with self-registration. It has flush and dry toilets, kitchen shelters, fire rings and firewood, but no potable water, so be sure to bring your own for cooking and drinking. Mid-May to mid-Sept. $15.70.

Crandell Campground 8km northwest of Waterton on the Red Rock Parkway, off Hwy 5. With 129 unserviced sites this second of three park-operated sites (also first-come first-served) serves as a happy medium for those not keen on roughing it at *Belly River* or lounging in the relative comfort of the *Townsite Campground*. Flush toilets, piped water (no showers), kitchen shelters, some fire rings and firewood, food storage, recycling bins and a dump station are among the amenities. Mid-May to early Sept. $21.50.

Waterton Townsite Campground Off Vimy Ave ⓣ1-877/737-3783, ⓦwww.pccamping.ca. On the southern side of Waterton Village, this busy 238-site park-run campsite is the only one which can be booked in advance. Facilities include hot showers, flush toilets, kitchen shelters and food storage; no open fires. Mid-April to mid-Oct. $22.50 ($27.40 with showers) or $38.20 for full RV hook-up.

The village and around

There's a small assortment of shops, cafés and restaurants in the village proper, but none are really worth delaying getting out into the park for. With that in mind, two wonderfully scenic access roads from Waterton probe west into the park interior and provide picnic spots, viewpoints and the starting point for most other trails: the **Akamina Parkway** (open May–Oct) follows the Cameron Creek valley for 20km to Cameron Lake, a large subalpine lake where you can follow easy trails or rent canoes, rowing boats and paddleboats. The **Red Rock Parkway** (open May to Oct) weaves up Blakiston Creek for about 15km to the mouth of the water-gouged Red Rock Canyon. The road is one of the best places to see wildlife in the park without too much effort and, like the Akamina Parkway, has the usual pleasant panoply of picnic sites, trailheads and interpretive notice boards. If you're without transport for these roads see below for details of hiker shuttle services and car and bike rentals.

The third named road in the park, the **Chief Mountain Highway** (32km; open mid-May to Sept), runs east from the park entrance at Maskinonge Lake along the park's eastern border. After 7km it reaches a fine **viewpoint** over the mountain-backed Waterton Valley and then passes the park-run Belly River Campground (see above) before reaching the US–Canadian **border crossing** (open June to late Sept 7am–10pm). When this crossing is closed, depending on your direction of travel, you have to use the crossings on Alberta's Hwy 2 south of Cardston or Hwy 89 north of St Mary in Montana.

Cruises, water sports and other activities

Waterton Shoreline Cruises at the marina (ⓣ403/859-2362, ⓦwww.watertoncruise.com) runs scenic two-hour **cruises** (late June to Aug 4 daily, 2–3 daily in May, Sept & early Oct; $34 return) up and down the lake across the US–Canadian border to Goat Haunt in Montana, little more than a quayside and park ranger station, where there is a scheduled thirty-minute stop before the return to Waterton (after the ranger station closes in mid-Sept boats don't stop at Goat Haunt). You can take an early boat to Goat Haunt and then return on foot to Waterton on the **Waterton Lakeshore Trail**, an easy four-hour walk (13km one-way). The same company runs a ferry to various trailheads around the lake.

Windsurfing is also surprisingly popular, thanks to the powerful winds – anything up to 70km – that often roar across the lakes (Waterton is wetter, windier and snowier than much of Alberta). The beach at Cameron Bay on Upper Waterton Lake is a favourite spot for surfers to catch a breeze; the water is cold and deep, so use a wet suit. If you want to **swim**, head for the cheap outdoor heated pool on Cameron Falls Drive. **Bikes** can be hired from *Pat's*, 224 Mountain View Rd (ⓣ403/859-2660). **Fishing** is good on the lakes, but pick up the compulsory national park permit ($9.80) from the visitor centre or park office. Off the water, **riding** is available from the Alpine Stables (ⓣ403/859-2462, ⓦwww.alpinestables.com), located just east off the hwy, about 1km north of the visitor centre. Four kilometres north of town on the main hwy is the eighteen-hole **Waterton Lakes Golf Course** (ⓣ403/859-2114, ⓦwww.golfwaterton.com); green fees are $47 and club rental $7–20.

Hikes in Waterton National Park

Waterton Lakes' 255km of trails are among the best constructed in the Canadian Rockies, and also some of the most easily graded, well marked and scenically routed. Like Moraine Lake in Banff National Park – and unlike Banff and Jasper – you can also access superb walks easily without a car. Bar one or two outlying hikes, three key areas contain trails and trailheads: the **townsite** itself, which has two magnificent short walks; the **Akamina Parkway**; and the **Red Rock Parkway**. Most walks are day-hikes, climaxing at small alpine lakes cradled in spectacular hanging valleys. Options for backpacking are necessarily limited by the park's size, though the 36km **Tamarack Trail**, following the ridges of the Continental Divide between the Akamina Parkway (same trailhead as for Rowe Lakes – see opposite) and Red Rock Parkway, is rated as one of the Rockies' greatest highline treks (maximum elevation 2560m); the 20km Carthew–Alderson Trail from Cameron Lake to Waterton (maximum elevation 2311m), a popular day's outing, can be turned into a two-day trip by overnighting at the Alderson Lake campsite. To do it in a day, take advantage of the hiker shuttle service to the trailhead offered by Park Transport (ⓣ403/859-2378) based in the Tamarack Village Square on Mount View Road.

Waterton is a great park in which to base yourself for a few days' hiking: details of hikes are given below, but as a general guide to do the best of the hikes you'd first stroll the **Bear's Hump** for views of Waterton town and the lakes; then walk all or part of the **Bertha Lake Trail** (day or half-day) from the townsite. Next day take a boat to Goat Haunt and walk back on the **Waterton Lakeshore Trail**. Then try the **Crypt Lake Trail** from the townsite and/or the **Rowe Lake–Lineham Ridge Trail**, both ranked among the best day-walks in the Rockies. Finally, gird your loins for the longer **Carthew–Alderson Trail**, possible in a day.

Walks from Waterton Village

In and around the town there are various short loops: stroll to Cameron Falls, try the Prince of Wales from the Visitor Centre (2km; 45min) or climb the more demanding **Bear's Hump**, also from the centre (1.2km; 200m vertical; 40min one-way); the latter is one of the park's most popular short walks, switchbacking up the slopes to a rocky outcrop with great views of the Waterton Valley. More surprisingly good views can be had from the easily reached viewpoint near the Buffalo Paddock. Another obvious, and very simple, walk from the town is the Waterton Lakeshore Trail (13km one-way; 100m ascent; 4hr), which follows Upper Waterton Lake's west shore across the US border to Goat Haunt; regular lake ferries sail back to the townsite (see p.613).

The single most popular half-day or day's walk from the townsite is the classic **Bertha Lake Trail** from Waterton, 5.8km each way with an ascent of 460m (allow 4hr 30min for the round trip). It's a short, steep hike beginning on Evergreen Drive to a busy but remarkably unsullied mountain-ringed lake. There is an easy trail that runs right around the lakeshore (adding about another 5km to the trip). If you're not up to this, you can just do the first part of the trail and break off at Lower Bertha Falls (2.9km from the townsite; 150m ascent; 1hr); this deservedly popular section corresponds to the route of the *Bertha Falls Self-Guiding Nature Trail* pamphlet available from the Visitor Centre.

Another excellent, if challenging, walk out of Waterton is the unique **Crypt Lake Trail**, often touted as one of the best in Canada. The 8.6km hike (one-way; 675m ascent; 6–8hr) involves a boat trip ($15 round trip) across Upper Waterton Lake to the trailhead on the east side of the lake, a (perfectly safe) climb up a ladder, a crawl through a rock tunnel and a section along a rocky ledge with cable for support. The rewards are the crashing waterfalls and the great glacial amphitheatre containing Crypt Lake (1955m); rock walls tower 600m on three sides, casting a chill shadow that preserves small icebergs on the lake's surface throughout the summer. Allow time to catch a return boat.

Trails from the Akamina Parkway

Most of the trails accessed by the Akamina Parkway leave from the road's end near Cameron Lake. To stretch your legs after the drive up, or if you just want a stroll, try either the Akamina Lake (0.5km; 15min) or Cameron Lakeshore (1.6km; 30min) trails. The best of the longer walks is to Carthew Summit (7.9km one-way; 660m ascent), a superb trail that switchbacks through forest to Summit Lake (4km), a good target in itself, before opening out into subalpine meadow and a final climb to a craggy summit (2310m) and astounding viewpoint. The trail can be followed all the way back to Waterton Village (another 12km) – it's then the **Carthew–Alderson Trail** (see opposite), most of whose hard work you've done in getting up to Carthew Summit; from the summit it's largely steeply downhill via Carthew and Alderson lakes (1875m) to Cameron Falls and the townsite (1295m).

Another highly rated trail from the Akamina Parkway is equally appealing – the **Rowe Lakes Trail** (5.2km one-way; 555m ascent), which is accessed off the Parkway about 5km before Cameron Lake (it is also the first leg of the Tamarack Trail – see opposite). Most people make their way to the Rowe Basin (where there's a backcountry campsite) and then, rather than pushing on towards the Upper Rowe Lakes (1.2km beyond), either camp, turn around or – for stronger walkers – take the trail that branches right from the Upper Rowe path to walk to Lineham Ridge (another 3.4km and 540m ascent). This **Rowe Lake–Lineham Ridge** combination has been cited as one of the top five day-hikes in the Rockies. The stiffish walk is rewarded by Lineham Lake, sapphire blue in the valley far below, and a vast sea of mountains stretching to the horizon. Only come up here in good weather, as it's particularly hazardous when visibility's poor and the winds are up.

Trails from the Red Rock Parkway

Most trails on the Red Rock Parkway, such as the short Red Rock Canyon Trail (700m loop) and Blackiston Falls (1km; 30min), leave from Red Rock Canyon at the end of the road. The most exhilarating option from the head of the road is the **Goat Lake Trail** (6.7km; 550m ascent), which follows Bauerman Creek on an old fire road (flat and easy, but a little dull) before peeling off right at the 4.3-kilometre mark for the climb to tranquil Goat Lake and ever-improving views (there's a backcountry campsite at the lake). If you ignore the lake turn-off and follow the fire road for another 4km, you come to a junction: one trail leads north to Lost

Lake (2km), the other south to the spectacular Twin Lakes area (3.2km). This latter option will bring you to the long-distance Tamarack Trail (see p.614). Walk south on this from Twin Lakes (3.1km) and you can pick up the **Blackiston Creek Trail**, which will take you back to the head of the Red Rock Parkway.

Eating and drinking

Although there is a smattering of other restaurants and coffee shops (plus a chain or two) to provide some variety, most of the best food, drink and atmosphere is to be found in the hotel restaurants and bars of Waterton Village.

Bayshore Lakeside Chophouse *Bayshore Inn* 111 Waterton Ave ⓣ403/859-2211 or 1-888/527-9555, ⓦwww.bayshoreinn.com. One of the better and more elegant spots in town to treat yourself; the dining room overlooks the lake. Open all day for breakfast, lunch and dinner. Mains from $19–38.

Pat's 224 Mount View Rd ⓣ403/859-2266. Pat's, or Pat's Convenience Strore – though nobody uses its proper name – has been a Waterton fixture for over forty years, a useful general store (with an ATM, fuel for cooking stoves and other camping backup), garage, meeting place and friendly little café for coffee, snacks and sandwiches. You can also put together a picnic or trail lunch to take away.

Pizza of Waterton 103 Fountain Ave ⓣ403/859-2660. The dough for these good, cheap ($7–12) pizzas is made daily on the premises; they also have soups, salads and are licensed to serve alcohol. Open daily noon–10pm.

Windsor Lounge At the *Prince of Wales Hotel* ⓣ403/859-2231. One of several lounges, bars and dining rooms in this posh-looking hotel, open for non-patrons to enjoy afternoon tea, a good lunch or a refined hour with a drink and great lake views. Dress well, as the place is fairly smart.

Kananaskis Country

Most first-time visitors race straight from Calgary to Banff, ignoring **Kananaskis Country**, a dramatic foothill area that sprawls along the eastern boundary of Banff National Park. Created out of existing provincial parks to take pressure off Banff, Kananaskis remains almost the exclusive preserve of locals, who come to ski in the winter and to hike, bike and camp in the summer. The mountain scenery rivals that of the parks and the possibilities for outdoor pursuits even better, thanks to more liberal protection policies. **Canmore** is the region's natural focus, much as Banff is in the neighbouring national park – though in many other ways the towns are dissimilar. Plenty of excursions are possible on foot from Canmore, but to get deep into adjacent **provincial parks** you'll need your own transport.

Canmore

CANMORE competes with Banff, 28km away, for visitors, and, though less attractive, it's a decent alternative if you'd rather stay in a less busy place and can live without Banff's selection of restaurants and shops. Canmore began life in 1883 as a supply point for the CPR railroad, before booming as a mining centre after the company discovered coal in surrounding hills. It quickly became a boom town and lived off mining for almost a century until the last mine closed in 1979. Things looked bleak until it was decided Canmore would host the Nordic skiing events for the 1988 Calgary Olympics, which gave the town its impressive **Nordic Centre**. On the back of this and thanks to the town's location outside the restrictions of the national parks, the settlement grew. Occasional references to it as the "Aspen of Alberta" overstate the case, but certainly many adventurous types and artists are relocating here. It's a good place to visit as well as live, with good hiking, climbing, biking, skiing and

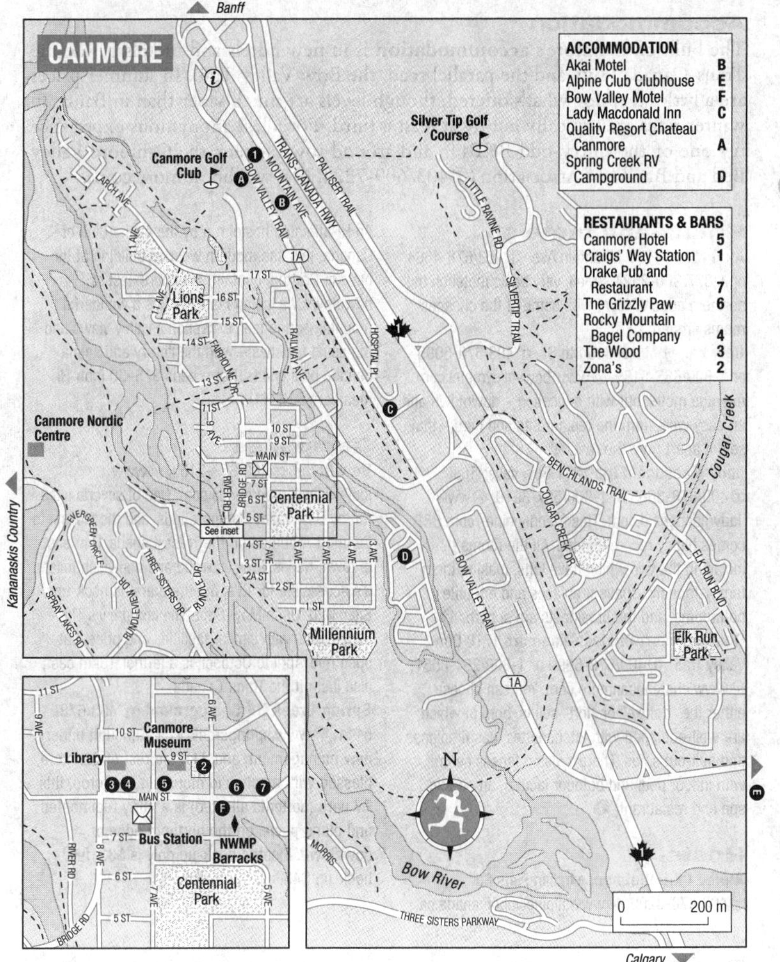

fishing on the fringes of town – and opportunities for many more activities, including caving and rafting, not much further away.

Arrival and information

Most shuttles between Calgary Airport and Banff (see p.623) make a stop at Canmore, with fares around $47 one-way. You can also take the Greyhound here from Calgary and Banff, with services arriving at the **bus station**, 801 8th St (Ⓣ403/678-4465). From here it's a long walk to the town's information centre, part of the **Travel Alberta visitor information centre**, 2801 Bow Valley Trail (June–Aug 8am–8pm; Sept–May 9am–6pm; Ⓣ403/678-5277 or 1-800/661-8888, Ⓦwww.discoveralberta.com), just off the Trans-Canada.

Downtown Canmore can easily be explored **on foot**, though a bike is useful on the extensive trail network in and around town. Gear Up, 1302 Bow Valley Trail (Ⓣ403/678-1636, Ⓦwww.gearupsport.com), is one of several places that **rents bikes**. For a taxi call Apex (Ⓣ403/609-0030).

Accommodation

The bulk of Canmore's **accommodation** is in new hotels and motels beside the Trans-Canada Hwy and the parallel road, the Bow Valley Trail. In summer prices are a little steep for what's offered, though levels are much saner than in Banff. In winter rates are typically cut by at least a third. For a less anonymous experience try one of the thirty-odd B&Bs in and around town; check the Canmore Valley Bed and Breakfast Association (Ⓣ403/609-7224, Ⓦwww.bbcanmore.com).

Hotels and motels

Akai Motel 1717 Mountain Ave Ⓣ403/678-4664 or 1-877/900-2524. Small, very basic motel on the northern edge of town with some of the cheapest rooms around. ❹

Bow Valley Motel 610 8th St Ⓣ403/678-5085 or 1-800/665-8189, Ⓦwww.bowvalleymotel.com. Average motel, but with a location – downtown and an easy walk from the restaurants and bars – that sets it apart from the rest. ❺

Lady Macdonald Inn 1201 Bow Valley Trail Ⓣ403/678-3665 or 1-800/567-3919, Ⓦwww.ladymacdonald.com. This friendly nine-room B&B comes highly recommended. All the rooms – including the two which have lofts, making them family-friendly – have fireplaces and en-suite bathrooms, and the breakfasts are superb. ❻

Quality Resort Château Canmore 1718 Bow Valley Trail Ⓣ403/678-6699 or 1-800/261-8551, Ⓦwww.chateaucanmore.com. You can choose either the "deluxe" or "loft" suites, both of which are well-equipped with kitchenettes, gas fireplaces and pull-out sofas. There's also a fitness centre with indoor pool and outdoor jacuzzi, an on-site spa and restaurant. ❼

Hostel

Alpine Club Clubhouse Indian Flats Rd Ⓣ403/678-3200, Ⓦwww.alpineclubofcanada.ca. An HI-affiliated hostel run by the Alpine Club of Canada, this fine modern wooden building at the base of Grotto Mountain, 5km northeast of downtown via Indian Flats Rd, has a wonderful mountaineering feel, exceptional valley views and the usual facilities – with the library and sauna definite plus points. Dorm beds $25–30 (non-HI members $36–41).

Campsites

Bow River Ⓣ403/673-2163, Ⓦwww.bowvalleycampgrounds.com. One of several sites run by Bow Valley Campgrounds, and the closest to Canmore, situated off the Trans-Canada 1km east of town; tables, fire-pit, wood and non-flush toilets. It's accessible for RVs, but there are no hook-ups. Sites $20. Open May–Sept. The company's Three Sisters site, with similar facilities and price, but open mid-April to October, is a farther 15km east, also just off the Trans-Canada.

Spring Creek RV Campground Ⓣ403/678-5111, Ⓦwww.springcreekrv.ca. Although under new management, and, like the rest of Canmore, blessed with a splendid mountain backdrop, this RV park (no tents allowed) is a fairly regimented and bland place, on the northern edge of downtown. Electric hook-up only is $33, full hook-up $45.

The Town

Canmore straddles the Trans-Canada Hwy, though its downtown area is entirely south of the road, and centred on relaxed Main Street (8th St). There are gallerys, shops, cafés, restaurants and a few sites to see on this strip and in other parts of town, but your best bet is to get out of the centre and explore. If you do get poor weather and are stuck in town, the **Canmore Museum and Geoscience Centre** (mid-May to early Sept Mon–Tues noon–5pm, Wed–Sun 10am–6pm; rest of the year Mon–Fri noon–5pm, Sat & Sun 11am–5pm; $3; Ⓦwww.cmags.org), 902 7th Ave, is a good option, and does a fine job of rooting around the town's past from its geological and First Nation origins to its Olympic glory days. If you don't want to wander too far afield, at the far end of Main Street is a spur of the extensive network of local **bike paths**, which leads down to and alongside the Bow River. Parts of it are reasonable for **fishing** for bull trout, brown trout and whitefish; the Green Drake Fly Shop, 102-512 Bow Valley Trail (Ⓣ403/678-9522), can provide tackle and advice.

Canmore Nordic Centre and Grassi Lakes

West of downtown and the Bow River the land begins to rise and the town starts to thin out, so that by the time Spray Lakes Road has climbed to the **Canmore Nordic Centre** (Ⓣ403/678-2400, Ⓦwww.canmorenordic.com), you're only left with views of the urban area. This state-of-the-art former Olympic facility is as popular in summer as in winter, since 70km of the total 300km cross-country network is maintained for mountain biking and suitable for every level of rider. Free trail maps are available, as are bike rentals. Beyond the Nordic Centre, Spray Lakes Road soon loses its asphalt cover and begins to climb in earnest, but just before it does there's a small turn-off to a parking lot beside a reservoir. This is the trailhead for an easy 2km hike up to **Grassi Lakes**, a series of small picture-book lakes high above town on a route that affords exceptional views over the valley. The trail up is rough and steep, though there's also the option of descending back down a rough access road, which is much easier going. On reaching the upper lake, be sure to take an easy scramble up the scree slope to four **pictographs** of human figures painted onto the first large boulder of the gorge.

Spray Valley Provincial Park

High above Grassi Lakes, Spray Lakes Road climbs out of view of Canmore to enter **Spray Valley Provincial Park**, the most accessible part of high-mountain Kananaskis Country. The main feature of the park is its 16km-long Spray Lakes Reservoir, which is used to generate electricity. Despite its industrial use the lake is a tranquil spot and surrounded by huge, impressively contorted mountains. The Spray Lakes West provincial campground (Ⓣ1-866/366-2267, Ⓦwww.kananaskiscountrycampgrounds.com; May–Sept, depending on weather; no reservations; $20) is strung out along the western shore and is an exceptionally attractive spot to pitch a tent, though facilities are basic and you need to bring all your own supplies except firewood ($6 per bundle). An added bonus is the great hiking trail that heads out from the campground to the small **Jakeroy Glacier**, perched high up in the goat range. The trail (4km; 4hr round-trip) begins opposite campsite no. 17 and is fairly well marked – at the only river crossing be sure to head straight on up the scree slope rather than right up to the waterfall – and climbs steeply through pine, willow, spruce and larch forests to a narrow hanging valley.

East of Canmore

The east side of Canmore is also good for shorter hikes. An easy informal trail with good views follows the course of **Cougar Creek** and it's possible to follow this all the way to the boundary of Banff National Park. An even better trail starts from Grotto Pond, 12km east of Canmore on Hwy 1A. It starts fairly unpromisingly, following a powerline road, but soon cuts into the woods to **Grotto Canyon**. There's no formal trail but the way up the steep-sided canyon is clear enough; look for pictographs around 300m into the canyon – on the left at about head-height at one of its narrowest points. Another 100m or so into the canyon is an impressive little waterfall. Beyond this the valley opens up, passing a cave and some strangely-shaped rock formations, known as hoodoos.

Eating, drinking and nightlife

Recently, several smarter **restaurants** serving imaginative regional food have opened up in Canmore, alongside a number of long-standing dependable downtown **pubs** for bar food.

Canmore Hotel 738 8th St Ⓣ403/678-5181, Ⓦwww.canmorehotel.com. Wild bar that looks like it's straight off the set of a Western and is barely more refined inside. Honky-tonk atmosphere and regular live music keeps the locals coming. Main courses cost between $7–19.

Craig's Way Station 1727 Mountain Ave ⓣ403/678-2656. Cheerful family-oriented place amid the motels on the north side of town. Good, full breakfasts served all day and inexpensive lunch and dinner options from $8.50–19.

Drake Pub & Restaurant 909 Railway Ave ⓣ403/678-5131. Locals' pub with two large, heated outdoor decks, two fireplaces and occasional live music. Fairly standard pub food is served; mains cost $10–19.

The Grizzly Paw Brewing Company 622 Main St ⓣ403/678-9983, ⓦwww.thegrizzlypaw.com. The Rockies' only microbrewery, with decent pub grub and reasonable beers; the Grumpy Bear Honey Wheat Ale is the most refreshing after a day in the outdoors. Live music on Tues nights.

Rocky Mountain Bagel Company 830 Main St. One of several decent cafés on Main St that's ideal for a simple breakfast, light lunch or just hanging out.

The Wood Restaurant & Lounge 838 Main St ⓣ403/678-3404, ⓦwww.thewood.ca. Log cabin that's a long-standing local favourite, with lots of Rocky Mountain charm. The huge patio-cum-beer-garden catches the sun until late and there's plenty of choice on the menu, with steaks, fish, pizzas, ribs and other North American staples at middling prices for lunch (burgers and curries at $10), but rather more in the evening, when mains cost from $18 to $40.

Zona's 710 9th St ⓣ403/609-2000, ⓦwww.zonaslatenightbistro.com. Chic bistro with earth-tone decor and highly inventive meals, including "Mo'rockin" molasses lamb curry. Main courses $12–18.

The Kananaskis Valley

The **Kananaskis Valley** is the mainstay of Kananaskis Country. Hwy 40, which intersects with the Trans-Canada Hwy 30km east of Canmore, travels south along its length, bisecting the high-mountain country, linking all the most significant provincial parks, and providing a ribbon to which most of the trails, campsites and scattered service centres cling. About 3km down the hwy is the **Barrier Lake Visitor Information Centre** (daily June to mid-Sept 9am–6pm; rest of year 9am–4pm; ⓣ403/673-3985), where you can get a full breakdown on outdoor activities.

Kananaskis Village

The only real settlement around is **KANANASKIS VILLAGE,** a rather soulless resort-village based around a golf course and ski area (see box, p.621) that can be used as a base. A number of hiking and biking trails radiate from here. Peregrine Sports (ⓣ403/591-7453) offers mountain bike, fishing rod and canoe rental and can advise on local conditions for these pursuits. Of the hiking trails, the 9km hike to **Ribbon Falls** is deservedly popular and arrives at the eponymous campsite ($10 per person); buy permits from the Barrier Lake Information Centre or on ⓣ403/678-3136. From here you can either head back, or with basic rock climbing skills head on and complete a loop by following the Galetea Creek trail below the hulking Mount Kidd. If you're fit and want to bag a peak, **Mount Allan** (2990m), just north of Kananaskis Village beckons: it's one of the few maintained trails in the Rockies that leads to a summit. Other than excellent **golf** (ⓣ403/591-7272 or 1-877/591-2525, ⓦwww.kananaskisgolf.com), the other organized pursuit in the area is **whitewater rafting**, run by Inside Out (ⓣ403/949-3305 or 1-877/999-7238, ⓦwww.insideoutexperience.com).

Practicalities

The best **accommodation** choice in Kananaskis Village is the comfortable *Delta Lodge* (ⓣ403/591-771 or 1-888/890-3222, ⓦwww.deltahotels.com; ❼) with its huge rooms, great mountain views and facilities (gym, spa, pool and outdoor hot tub). The hotel organizes a range of activities for kids, as well as offering an adult-only section for those who want to enjoy a bit of peace.

Nakiska and Fortress Mountain ski areas

Generally written off in favour of the local headline acts Sunshine Village and Lake Louise, **Nakiska** and **Fortress Mountain** are two ski areas in Kananaskis Country Provincial Park which, in good conditions (the snowphone for both is ⓣ403/244-6665), have skiing of a quality that justifies a trip even from Banff. Lift passes at the two are interchangeable.

Developed specifically for the 1988 Winter Olympics, **Nakiska** (ⓣ403/591-7777, ⓦwww.skinakiska.com) lies 25km south of the Trans-Canada Hwy, around an hour's drive from either Calgary or Banff, and beside Kananaskis Village. Designed from scratch, the ski area has a vertical drop of 735m (2412ft), is one of the most user-friendly on the continent and includes all the usual rental, instruction and childcare facilities. Intended for downhill racers, the runs here are mostly smooth and steep, making it a great intermediate mountain for cruising – seventy percent of the runs are blue – and a useful schoolroom for beginner boarders. The lack of snow at the ski area – only 250cm (98in) annually – is rarely a problem, since snowmaking covers 85 percent of the mountain, and though conditions can be a little crusty, the ski area's grooming helps. The area also maintains two competition-standard half-pipes and a terrain park.

Located 15km south of Nakiska on Hwy 40, **Fortress Mountain** (ⓣ403/591-7108, ⓦwww.skifortress.com) is very different. In place of smart regimented runs is largely untamed terrain, huddled beneath several vast, craggy rock outcrops. Particularly renowned for its tree-skiing, gullies and many natural obstacles as well as its well-maintained half pipe, Fortress offers a vertical drop of 280m (918ft) and spreads over 328 acres. The majority of its 47 trails are intermediate. The snowfall at Fortress is a reassuring 630cm (23ft), which, coupled with a sixty-percent snowmaking capacity, means decent conditions are virtually guaranteed.

Other options include the *Kananaskis Wilderness Hostel* (ⓣ403/591-7333 or 1-866/762-4122, ⓦwww.hihostels.ca; dorms $23 ($20 Oct–June), nonmembers $27/24, private room $58/61 (nonmembers $68/66), beside Ribbon Creek just off the Village access road. There are two good **campsites**: Sundance Lodges (ⓣ403/591-7122, ⓦwww.sundancelodges.com; mid-May to mid–Sept), which has regular sites ($28) hidden in the trees, cheerful hand-painted furnished tepees for $77 and thirty RV unserviced sites; and the impressive Mount Kidd RV Park (ⓣ403/591-7700, ⓦwww.mountkiddrv.com; tent sites $32.50, full RV hook-ups $48), which boasts hot tubs, saunas and tennis courts.

Peter Lougheed Provincial Park

Around 40km south of Kananaskis Village on Hwy 40, a short spur leads to Upper Kananaskis Lake, the head of the valley and the main focus of **Peter Lougheed Provincial Park**. This has the biggest concentration of accessible boating, fishing, camping and hiking possibilities in the region. Around 4km off Hwy 40 en route to the lake is the excellent park **information centre** (daily mid-May to Aug 9am–7pm; rest of year 9am–5pm; ⓣ403/591-6322, ⓦwww.tpr.alberta.ca/parks). Top trails include the rewarding half-day jaunt to Rawson Lake and the magnificent multi-day backpacking adventure over Burstall Pass to Banff, easily one of the best in the region. This hike is well detailed, along with many others in the Kananaskis area, in the definitive and widely available *Where Locals Hike in the Canadian Rockies* by Kathy and Craig Copeland.

Banff National Park

BANFF NATIONAL PARK is the most famous of the Canadian Rockies' parks and Canada's leading tourist attraction – so be prepared for the crowds that throng its key centres, **Banff** and **Lake Louise**, as well as the best part of its 1500km of trails, most of which suffer a continual pounding during the summer months. That said, it's worth putting up with every commercial indignity to enjoy the sublime scenery – and if you're camping or are prepared to walk, the worst of the park's excesses are fairly easily left behind. The best plan of attack if you're coming from Calgary or the US is to make straight for Banff, a busy and commercial town where you can pause for a couple of days to soak up the action and handful of sights, or stock up on supplies and make for somewhere quieter as quickly as possible. Then head 58km north along Hwy 1 to Lake Louise, a much smaller but almost equally busy centre with some unmissable landscapes, plus readily accessible short trails and day-hikes if you just want a quick taste of the scenery.

Two popular roads within the park offer magnificent vistas: the **Bow Valley Parkway** from Banff to Lake Louise is a far preferable route to the parallel Trans-Canada Hwy, and the much longer **Icefields Parkway** leads from Lake Louise to

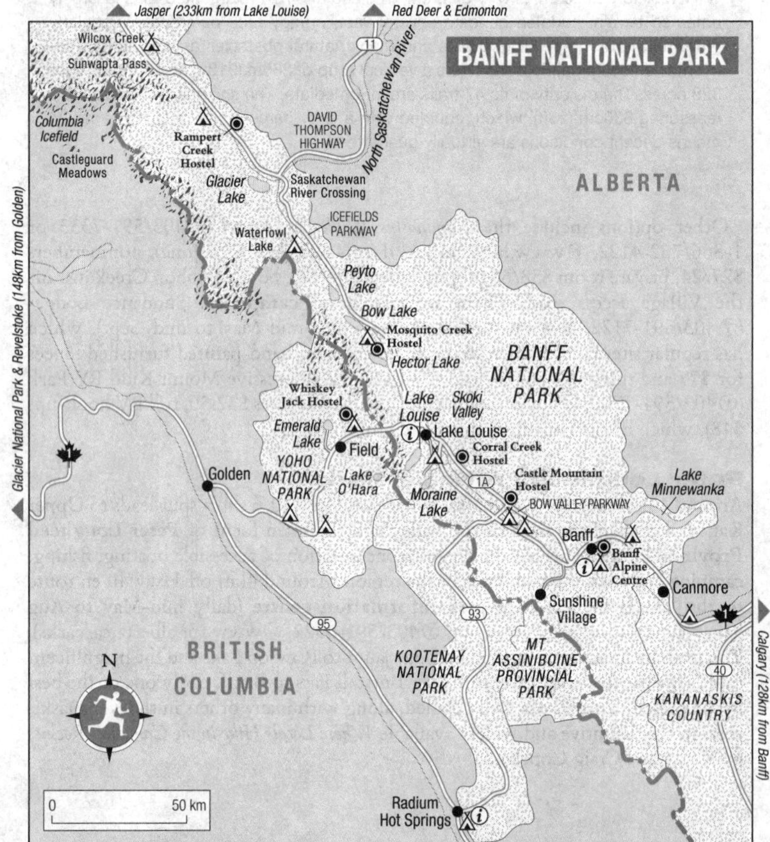

Jasper. Both are lined with trails long and short, waterfalls, lakes, canyons, viewpoints, pull-offs and a seemingly unending procession of majestic mountain, river, glacier and forest scenery.

A brief history

The modern road routes in the park provide transport links that have superseded the railway that first brought the park into being. The arrival of the **Canadian Pacific Railway** at the end of the nineteenth century brought to an end some ten thousand years of exclusive aboriginal presence in the region. This area had previously been disturbed only by trappers and the prodigious exploits of explorers like Mackenzie, Thompson and Fraser, who had sought to breach the Rockies with the help of native guides earlier in the century. Banff itself sprang to life in 1883 after three railway workers stumbled on the present town's Cave and Basin hot springs, its name coined in honour of Banffshire, the Scottish birthplace of two of the Canadian Pacific's early financiers and directors.

Within two years the government had set aside the Hot Springs Reserve as a protected area, and in 1887 enlarged it to form the **Rocky Mountains Park**, Canada's first national park. Yet the purpose was not entirely philanthropic; the new government-sponsored railway desperately needed passengers and profit, and spectacular scenery backed up by luxurious hotels was seen – rightly – as the best way to lure the punters. Cars were banned from the park until 1916.

Around four-and-a-half million visitors come to Banff every year and another four million pass through. Together they pump a staggering $800m or more annually into the local economy. Such numbers, despite the best efforts and intentions of the park authorities, inevitably have an effect on the environment. Scientists believe, for example, that the black and grizzly bear populations are dying out (combined numbers of both types of bear here are probably just 100 to 130), while numbers of wolves are declining at only a slightly lower rate than in areas where they have no protection at all (the park has just 35 or 40). Conversely, elk numbers exploded beyond internally sustainable limits to about 3200, almost entirely because they realized the town offered food (tasty suburban grass) and total safety from their natural predators (most have been relocated).

These are just a handful of symptoms of a greater ecological malaise. In response, a ceiling of ten thousand has been put on Banff's human population (it's currently around 7100), building is strictly controlled and areas are being closed to the public: the famous Bow Valley Parkway is closed to traffic for parts of the year and the airport is now all but closed, for it – like much of Banff town and the Bow River Valley – lies right in the path of major wildlife routes. Many of the big mammals require large areas to survive, larger even than the park. Experts suggest that Banff's ecosystem is on a knife edge: it may be saved and previous damage restored only if action is taken.

Banff

BANFF is the unquestioned capital of the Canadian Rockies, and with its intense summer buzz it can be a fun, busy and likeable base – but if you've come to commune with nature, you'll want to leave as soon as possible. Although the town is quite small, it handles an immense amount of tourist traffic, much of it of the RV and coach-tour variety. Anything up to fifty thousand visitors arrive daily in high season, making this the largest and busiest urban focus of any national park anywhere in the world.

Some contact with the town is inevitable, as it contains essential shops and services almost impossible to find elsewhere in the park. Many of the more rewarding **walks** locally are some way from the town – you'll need a car or have

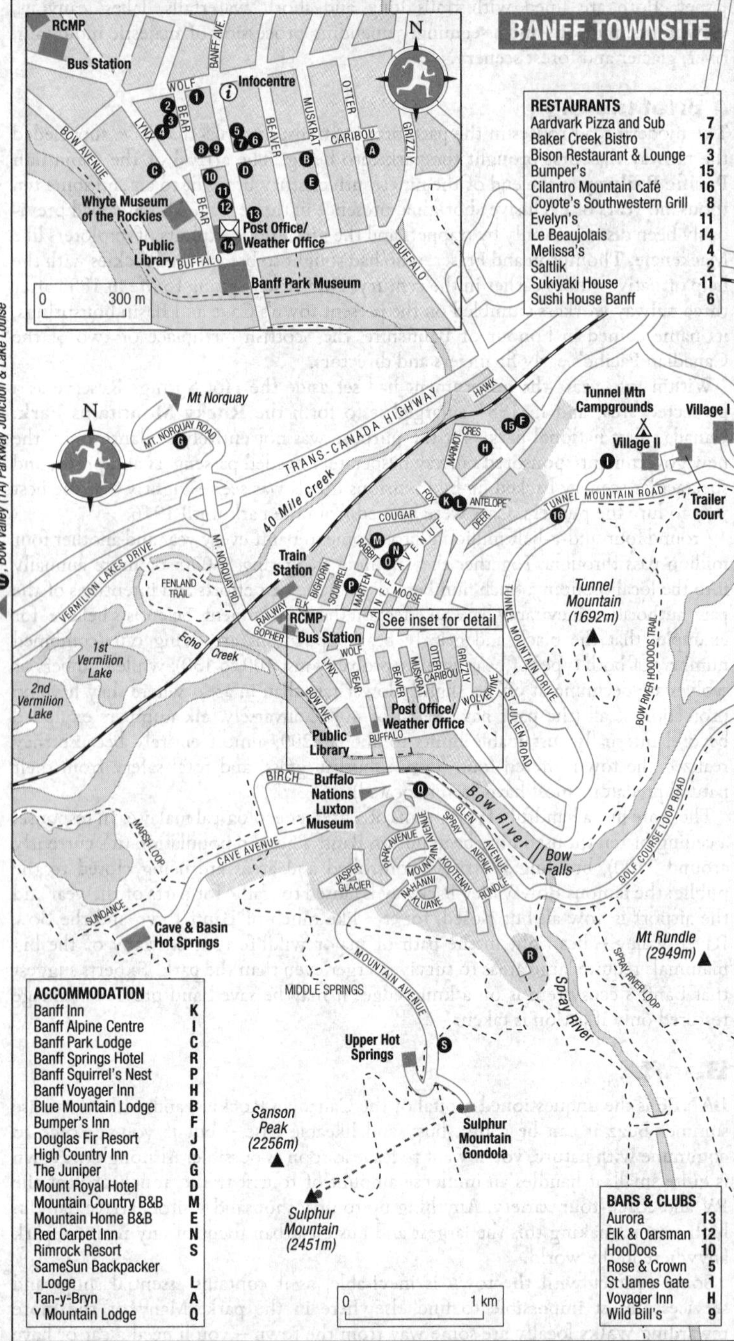
BANFF TOWNSITE
Cascade Ponds, Lake Minnewanka, Two Jack Lake & Bankhead
Park Entrance, Canmore & Calgary
17, Bow Valley (1A) Parkway Junction & Lake Louise
Mt Norquay
RESTAURANTS
Aardvark Pizza and Sub 7
Baker Creek Bistro 17
Bison Restaurant & Lounge 3
Bumper's 15
Cilantro Mountain Café 16
Coyote's Southwestern Grill 8
Evelyn's 11
Le Beaujolais 14
Melissa's 4
Saltlik 2
Sukiyaki House 11
Sushi House Banff 6
ACCOMMODATION
Banff Inn K
Banff Alpine Centre I
Banff Park Lodge C
Banff Springs Hotel R
Banff Squirrel's Nest P
Banff Voyager Inn H
Blue Mountain Lodge B
Bumper's Inn F
Douglas Fir Resort J
High Country Inn O
The Juniper G
Mount Royal Hotel D
Mountain Country B&B M
Mountain Home B&B E
Red Carpet Inn N
Rimrock Resort S
SameSun Backpacker Lodge L
Tan-y-Bryn A
Y Mountain Lodge Q
BARS & CLUBS
Aurora 13
Elk & Oarsman 12
HooDoos 10
Rose & Crown 5
St James Gate 1
Voyager Inn H
Wild Bill's 9
RCMP
Bus Station
Infocentre
Whyte Museum of the Rockies
Public Library
Post Office/ Weather Office
Banff Park Museum
0 300 m
See inset for detail
Train Station
Tunnel Mtn Campgrounds
Village I
Village II
Trailer Court
Tunnel Mountain (1692m)
40 Mile Creek
Echo Creek
1st Vermilion Lake
2nd Vermilion Lake
Fenland Trail
Buffalo Nations Luxton Museum
Bow River
Bow Falls
Cave & Basin Hot Springs
Middle Springs
Upper Hot Springs
Mt Rundle (2949m)
Spray River
Sanson Peak (2256m)
Sulphur Mountain Gondola
Sulphur Mountain (2451m)
Trans-Canada Highway
Vermilion Lakes Drive
Mt. Norquay Road
Tunnel Mountain Road
Tunnel Mountain Drive
Bow River Hoodoos Trail
Golf Course Loop Road
Cave Avenue
Marsh Loop
Sundance
Mountain Avenue
Spray River Loop
Banff Avenue
St Julien Road
0 1 km

Bears and other wild animals in Banff

Two types of **bears** roam the Rockies – black bears and grizzlies – and you don't want to meet either. They're not terribly common in these parts (sightings are all monitored and posted at park centres) and risks are pretty low on heavily tramped trails, but if you're camping or walking it's still essential to be vigilant, obey basic rules, know the difference between a black bear and a grizzly (the latter are bigger and have a humped neck), know how to avoid dangerous encounters, and understand what to do if confronted or attacked. Popular misconceptions about bears abound – that they can't climb trees, for example (they can, and very quickly) – so it's worth picking up the park service's **pamphlet** *You are in Bear Country* (also downloadable from the park site), which cuts through the confusion and lays out some occasionally eye-opening procedures. Be prepared, and if you don't want to be attacked, follow the cardinal rules: store food and garbage properly, make sure bears know you're there, don't approach or feed them, and, if you find yourself approached by one, don't scream and don't run.

Other wild animals can also be dangerous, and while you would be unlucky to encounter cougars, which are relatively rare, the chances of meeting elk are much higher. Generally, these are benign creatures, often seen grazing at roadsides, but can become aggressive if approached or if they are with young; don't clamber out of your car, or cross the hwy, to poke a camera in their faces.

to rent a bike to explore properly – but some surprisingly good strolls start just minutes from the main street.

Arrival and information

Banff is a ninety-minute **drive** from Calgary along the Trans-Canada Hwy. Several operators offer efficient shuttle services **from Calgary Airport** (see p.556). Daily Greyhound **buses** (ⓣ403/762-1092 or 1-800/661-8747, ⓦwww.greyhound.ca) also ply the route from the centre of Calgary (5 daily; 1hr 40min; $27 one-way), arriving in Banff's bus station at 100 Gopher St (7.30am–10.45pm; ⓣ403/762-6767 or 1-800/661-1152). Buses also arrive from Vancouver (4 daily; 13hr; $132).

Once in Banff it's easy to get around **on foot**, though a frequent town **bus** service, operated by Banff Transit ($2; ⓣ403/760-8294), provides transport to outlying areas, including the campgrounds on Tunnel Mountain Road and the *Banff Springs Hotel*.

The showpiece **visitor centre** is at 224 Banff Ave (daily: mid-May to mid-June and Sept 10–23 9am–7pm; mid-June to Sept 8am–8pm; Sept 24 to mid-May 9am–5pm; ⓣ403/762-8421, ⓦwww.banfflakelouise.com; park information ⓣ403/762-1550, ⓦwww.pc.gc.ca/banff). The centre is also the place to pick up a **park permit** if you haven't already done so (see box, p.606). Among the many free handouts, make a point of asking for the *Banff and Vicinity Drives and Walks* and *The Icefields Parkway* for **maps** of park facilities, the *Backcountry Visitors' Guide* for an invaluable overview of backpacking **trails** and campsites, and *Trail Bicycling in the National Parks* for conditions and a full list of mountain-bike trails. The centre has a selection of maps and guides you can consult for free; you can also buy excellent topographical maps from the "Friends of Banff National Park" shop (ⓣ403/762-8918) on the left, but many of the shorter and more popular trails are signed and well trodden, so you won't really need detailed maps unless you're venturing into the backcountry. You can also pick up details or book a place on the various **events** offered by the "Friends", which in past years have included free guided walks daily in the summer to Vermilion Lakes (10am; 2hr 30min),

Room and ski package operators

Banff Accommodation ⓣ403/762-0260 or 1-877/226-3348, ⓦwww.banffaccommodations.com.

Banff Central Reservations ⓣ403/705-4020 or 1-877/542-2633, ⓦwww.skibanff.com.

Ski Banff–Lake Louise (ski packages only) ⓣ403/762-4561 or 1-800/754-7080, ⓦwww.skibig3.com.

a Discovery Tour of the Cave and Basin Hot Springs (45min) and a Park Museum Wildlife Tour (45min). We've listed a number of other summer and winter **activities** on pp.634-635.

Accommodation

It's almost impossible to turn up after midday in Banff during July and August and find reasonably priced **accommodation**, so preplanning is essential; the visitor centre maintains a constantly updated vacancies board. There are also several private accommodation-finding services where you usually pay a small fee to the agency for sourcing a room (see box above).

The Bed & Breakfast and Private Home accommodation list at the information centre lists forty-plus places with **private rooms** and **B&Bs**, but don't expect too much – they're usually cheapish by Banff standards (typically around $100–140) and among the first places to go each day. Most of the town's **motels** are on the busy strip-cum-spur from the Trans-Canada into town, and charge high rates for basic lodgings – typically from $150 for doubles. Off-season (Oct–May), rates are usually considerably lower.

Campsites are not quite as bad (the town offers over a thousand pitches), but even these generally fill up by 2pm or 3pm in summer – especially the excellent government campsites. Beat the crowds by booking ahead on the Parks Canada reservation service (ⓣ1-877/737-3783, ⓦwww.pccamping.ca). In addition to the places listed here, there are lovely and less-developed park-run sites available along both the Bow and Icefields parkways to the north.

Hotels and motels

Banff Inn 501 Banff Ave ⓣ403/762-8844 or 1-800/667-1464, ⓦwww.banffinn.com. Fancy-looking 99-unit hotel, a five-minute walk from town, whose gables, loft windows, stucco and stone-clad walls make it stand out from neighbouring complexes. The smart and spacious rooms are much more run-of-the-mill, though some have fireplaces and jacuzzis. Other amenities include a steam room, hot tub, free wi-fi and underground parking. ❼

Banff Park Lodge 222 Lynx St ⓣ403/762-4433 or 1-800/661-9266, ⓦwww.banffparklodge.com. Quietly sophisticated, low-slung cedar and oak hotel, a block from the town centre and offering the best downtown deal. Scandinavian-style rooms are simple and airy; some have jacuzzis and fireplaces. Hotel facilities include two restaurants, a lounge, hot tub, steam room, indoor pool, laundry and dry cleaning service. ❽

Banff Voyager Inn 555 Banff Ave ⓣ403/762-3301 or 1-800/879-1991, ⓦwww.banffvoyagerinn.com. Predictably comfortable motel; one of the last of a number that line the road from the town centre. There's a chilly outdoor pool, a hot tub, sauna and the cheapest bar in town. ❺

Bumper's Inn 603 Banff Ave ⓣ403/762-3386 or 1-800/661-3518, ⓦwww.bumpersinn.com. Small, well-priced, 1970s motel on the northeastern fringe of town but only 50m from the nearest ski shuttle stop. Facilities are limited to the basics, but there is an eponymous on-site restaurant. ❻

Douglas Fir Resort Tunnel Mountain Rd ⓣ403/762-5591 or 1-800/661-9267, ⓦwww.douglasfir.com. Collection of low-rise wood-clad condo blocks in secluded wooded area on Tunnel Mountain, a fifteen-minute walk from the town centre. Ideally equipped for families or groups, units have a kitchen and lounge with fireplace as well as access to a host of leisure facilities, including squash courts and pool with waterslides. Laundromat and small convenience store on-site. 7

Fairmont Banff Springs 405 Spray Ave ⓣ403/762-2211 or 1-866/540-4406, ⓦwww.fairmont.com/banffsprings. One of the continent's most famous hotels – built in Scots Baronial style with turrets and cornices towering above its thick nine-storey granite walls – offering luxurious service that borders on pageantry. The glut of facilities, which include a world-class fitness and spa complex, several stores and restaurants, make the hotel almost entirely self-contained. Rates are extravagant but the winter season offers a chance to stay here for around half price. 8

High Country Inn 419 Banff Ave ⓣ403/762-2236 or 1-800/293-5142, ⓦwww.banffhighcountryinn.com. Mid-range motel with some luxury suites in a great central location. Facilities include a sauna, two hot tubs, an indoor pool and a Swiss-Italian restaurant, *Ticino*. 7

The Juniper 1 Juniper Way ⓣ403/762-2281 or 1-866/551-2281, ⓦwww.thejuniper.com. This recent "boutique" hotel breaks the predictable mould of most mid-range Banff hotels, offering a series of adjacent chalets with chic, pared-down contemporary interiors (the larger two- and three-bedroom chalets offer kitchenettes). The mountain views are some of the best from any Banff hotel, but *The Juniper*'s biggest drawback is the fact it lies 2km from the town centre at the foot of Mount Norquay. 7

Mount Royal Hotel 138 Banff Ave ⓣ403/762-3331 or 1-877/442-2623, ⓦwww.mountroyalhotel.com. The bland, three-storey exterior of this building amid downtown shops at the centre of town belies the perfectly acceptable – and near luxurious, in the case of the more expensive suites – decor. Most rooms have mountain views, and there's a large health club with whirlpool and exercise equipment. 7

Red Carpet Inn 425 Banff Ave ⓣ403/762-4184 or 1-800/563-4609, ⓦwww.banffredcarpet.com. Pastel shaded inside and out, this no-frills establishment is a clean, central and decent value option. There's free wi-fi and continental breakfast is included in the price. Guests can use the pool, sauna and hot tubs at the sister hotel, *High Country Inn*. 6

Rimrock Resort 300 Mountain Ave ⓣ403/762-3356 or 1-888/746-7625, ⓦwww.rimrockresort.com. Elegant and richly-furnished hotel in imposing, ten-storey angular building that nestles alone among thick stands of trees on the lower slopes of Sulphur Mountain, 3km south of town. The smart, modern rooms come with views of the Bow Valley, and you'd be hard pressed to beat the views from its superb French restaurant, *Eden*. There are also excellent and extensive fitness facilities and a free shuttle into town. 8

B&Bs

Banff Squirrel's Nest 332 Squirrel St ⓣ403/762-4432, ⓦwww.banffsquirrelsnest.com. Pleasant rooms on a quiet residential side street an easy walk from downtown. Rooms have queen beds and bathrooms en suite. Continental buffet breakfast included. 5

Blue Mountain Lodge 137 Muskrat St ⓣ403/762-5134, ⓦwww.bluemtnlodge.com. Friendly budget place in the centre of town with ten small rooms, all equipped with private bathrooms and spectacular mountain views. Common amenities include a guest kitchen, lounge and laundry facilities. 4

Mountain Country Bed & Breakfast 427 Marten St ⓣ403/762-3288, ⓦwww.banffmountaincountry.com. Large barn-shaped house close to downtown Banff and a block from the ski shuttle route. The large, dark-wood furnished rooms are equipped with private jacuzzi tubs, queen-size beds and duvets. Breakfast is of the light continental variety. 4

Mountain Home Bed & Breakfast 129 Muskrat St ⓣ403/762-3889, ⓦwww.mountainhomebb.com. Elegant 1940s tourist lodge converted into a B&B a couple of minutes' walk to downtown Banff. Spacious, antique-furnished en-suite guest rooms have down comforters on king-size beds, and the owners serve up delicious cooked breakfasts, with a daily, changing menu. 6

Tan-y-Bryn 118 Otter St ⓣ403/762-3696, ⓔtanybryn@telus.net. Eight simple and extremely reasonable B&B rooms (and one cheap "emergency" room) with private or shared bathrooms and in-room continental breakfast. Quiet residential district three blocks from downtown. No credit cards. 2

Hostels

Banff Alpine Centre 801 Hidden Ridge Way, off Tunnel Mountain Rd ⓣ403/762-4123 or 1-866/762-4122, ⓦwww.hihostels.ca. Friendly modern 216-bed hostel in great setting, but 3km from downtown and an $8 cab ride from the bus depot. Great facilities include large kitchen, laundry, lounge with fireplace, ski workshop and an adjoining inexpensive restaurant that can save trips downtown. Dorm beds are $35 (nonmembers $37.50); private doubles ($103/111) also available. No curfew.

SameSun Backpacker Lodge 449 Banff Ave ⓣ403/762-5521 or 1-877/972-6378 (for lodge and chalet), ⓦ www.banffhostel.com. Bohemian, sociable and chaotic one hundred-bed hostel on the strip just north of town, with a hot tub and sauna and all the more usual hostel facilities. Dorm beds cost $32. More beds, including private doubles (❹) are available in the new, co-owned *SameSun Banff Chalet* (ⓣ 403/762-4499) 50m away at 433 Banff Ave.

Y Mountain Lodge 102 Spray Ave ⓣ 403/762-3560 or 1-800/813-4138, ⓦ www.ymountainlodge.com. Clinically clean (but reasonably relaxed) hostel a short walk from downtown. Dorms cost $30–33, depending on the time of year, but if there are two of you a large spartan private room ($65–85 or $80–99 en suite) costs little more. In addition to a huge living room with gigantic stone fireplace, the hostel has a café with reasonable food, as well as a kitchen, laundry facilities and showers.

Campsites

Bow Valley Parkway There are three park campsites on or just off the Bow Valley Parkway road between Banff and Lake Louise, all within easy reach of Banff if you have transport (less than 30min drive): Johnston Canyon, Castle Mountain and Protection Mountain. See p.641 for full details.

Tunnel Mountain Village I ⓣ 450/505-8302 or 1-877/737-3783 (international), ⓦ www.pccamping.ca. A huge 618-pitch government-run campsite 4.3km from town, just off Tunnel Mountain Rd. It's also the nearest to downtown on the Banff Transit bus from Banff Ave. Reservations are accepted, but if these aren't available or if the site is full, arrive early for a first-come, first-served shot – it fills up quickly, thanks in no small part to the electricity and hot showers; $27.40. The nearby 320-site *Tunnel Mountain Trailer Court* ($32.30 electricity only, $38.20 full hook-up) is only for RVs. Both sites open mid-May to Sept.

Tunnel Mountain Village II ⓣ 450/505-8302 or 1-877/737-3783, ⓦ www.pccamping.ca. Also just off Tunnel Mountain Rd. and a bit closer to town (2.4km) than its sister location, this 188-pitch site is in summer available for group camping, RVs and walk-in tenting. The same rule for reservations at *Tunnel I* apply here. It has electricity, hot showers and is set amid trees, with lovely views, plenty of space and short trails close at hand. Bighorn sheep, elk and even the odd bear may drop in; $32.30; open year-round.

Two Jack Lakeside No reservations are taken at this 74-pitch government-run site, 12km northeast of town on the Lake Minnewanka Rd. It's a fully serviced site with showers and fire pits; $27.40. Open mid-May to mid-Sept.

Two Jack Main Another non-reservable government site, 13km northeast of town on Lake Minnewanka Rd. Its 380 sites have hot and cold running water and flush toilets, but no showers; $21.50. Open late May to early Sept.

The Town

With some of the world's most spectacular mountains on your doorstep, sightseeing in Banff might seem an absurd undertaking, yet it's good to have some rainy-day options. That said, it can seem quite odd that (given all the people who visit) there's next to nothing to do or see in Banff itself, save a couple of small museums, a cable-car ride and the chance to gape at the crowds on **Banff Avenue**, a thoroughfare lined with probably more souvenir stores and upmarket outdoor clothing and equipment shops than anywhere in North America.

Banff Park Museum

The downtown **Banff Park Museum** (daily mid-May to Sept 10am–6pm; Oct to mid-May 1–5pm; $3.90), at 93 Banff Ave, near the Bow River bridge, bulges with two floors of stuffed animals, many of which are indigenous to the park. In many ways the museum chronicles the changes of attitudes to wildlife in the park over the years; many Victorians wanted to see the park's animals without the tiresome business of having to venture into the backcountry – so they killed and stuffed the beasts for permanent display. The hunting of game animals in the park was banned in 1890, but not before populations of moose, elk, sheep, goats and grizzlies had been severely depleted. Game wardens only arrived to enforce the injunction in 1913, and even then they didn't protect the "bad" animals – wolves, coyotes, foxes, cougars, lynx, eagles, owls and hawks – which were hunted until the 1930s as part of the park's "predator-control program". Many of the stuffed victims in the museum date from this period. In summer the beautiful riverside **park** behind the museum is ideal for a snooze or picnic.

Whyte Museum of the Canadian Rockies

The excellent **Whyte Museum of the Canadian Rockies** (daily 10am–5pm; $7; Ⓦwww.whyte.org), next to the library at 111 Bear St, looks at the Rockies' emergence as a tourist destination through paintings and photographs, and at the early expeditions to explore and conquer the interior peaks. Pictures of bears foraging in Banff rubbish bins and of park rangers grinning over a magnificent lynx they've just shot give some idea of how times have changed. The museum, which opened in 1968, forms part of the Whyte Foundation, created in the 1958 by artists Peter and Catharine Whyte to collate and preserve as great a range of material as possible relating to the Rockies.

Buffalo Nations Luxton Museum

Across the river, dated displays of native history, birds and animals fill the **Buffalo Nations Luxton Museum** (daily: May to early Oct 11am–6pm, rest of the year 1–5pm; $8; Ⓦwww.buffalonationsmuseum.ca), an aboriginal peoples-run enterprise attractively housed in a huge wooden stockade at 1 Birch Ave. The museum takes its name from Norman Luxton, a local who ran a trading post here and forged a close relationship with Banff's Stoney native population over the course of sixty years. The exhibits aren't exciting, but the museum shop has some good crafts and other items if you're in spending mode.

The Fairmont Banff Springs Hotel

The **Fairmont Banff Springs Hotel** may be out of your league, but you can't spend much time in town without coming across at least one mention of the place, and it's hard to miss its landmark Gothic superstructure. Initiated in 1888, it got off to a bad start when the architect arrived to find the place being built 180 degrees out of kilter: while the kitchens enjoyed magnificent views over the river the guestrooms looked into thick forest. When it finally opened, with 250 rooms and a rotunda to improve the views, it was the world's largest hotel.

▲ The Fairmont Banff Springs hotel in winter, Banff National Park

The thinking behind the project was summed up by William Cornelius Van Horne, the larger-than-life vice-president of the Canadian Pacific Railway, who said of the Rockies, "if we can't export the scenery we'll import the tourists". One of the best ways to make the railway pay, he decided, was to sell people the idea of superb scenery and provide a series of jumbo hotels from which to enjoy it: the *Banff Springs* was the result, soon followed by similar railway-backed accommodation at Lake Louise and Yoho's Emerald Lake.

Don't bother with the hotel's guided tours: a voyeuristic hour or so can be spent looking around the hotel's first three floors on your own (pick up a map in reception) or taking a coffee, beer or afternoon tea in the second-floor café and Sunroom off the main reception. It's also worth walking out onto the terrace beyond the Sunroom for some spectacular views.

You can get out to the hotel either by walking along the south bank of the Bow River (taking in Bow Falls) or picking up the Banff Transit bus from downtown.

Sulphur Mountain Gondola

Banff is rightly proud of the **Sulphur Mountain Gondola** (daily: Feb to early April 10am–5pm; April–May 8.30am–6pm; June–Aug 8.30am–9pm; Sept to mid-Oct 8.30am–6.30pm; mid-Oct to Nov 8.30am–4.30pm; Dec & Jan 10am–4pm; $27.62; Ⓦwww.explorerockies.com), on Mountain Avenue, some 5km south of town. Buying tickets gets you crowds, great views and a commercialized summit (2255m), but also the chance to do some high-level hiking without the slog of an early morning climb – a glimpse of the remote high country if you're short of time or unable to walk the trails. The best times to take a ride are early morning or evening, when wildlife sightings are more likely, and when the play of light gives an added dimension to the views.

The gondola trundles 700m skywards at a stomach-churning 51 degrees to immense panoramas from two observation terraces. It takes just eight minutes for the glass-enclosed four-passenger cars to reach the high point, where there are two restaurants.

From the restaurants a one-kilometre path, the **Summit Ridge Trail**, has been blazed to take you a bit higher, while the short **Vista Trail** leads to the restored weather station and viewpoint on Sanson Peak. Norman Betheune "N.B." Sanson was the first curator of the Banff Park Museum, and between 1903 and 1931 made around a thousand ascents of the mountain – that's before the gondola was built – to take his weather readings. If, like him, you slog the 5.5km switchback trail up from the car park you can ride the gondola down for free.

If you're without transport, the only options for getting to the base station are to walk (dull and tiring) or take a taxi from downtown.

Cave & Basin Hot Springs

Banff boasts eight **hot springs**, and the next stop on the standard itinerary after the gondola ride was, for a long time, a plunge into their waters. In their early days these springs were vital to Banff's rise and popularity, their reputedly therapeutic effects being of great appeal to Canada's ailing Victorian gentry. Dr R.G. Brett, chief medical officer to the Canadian Pacific Railway, used his position to secure an immensely lucrative virtual monopoly on the best springs. In 1886 he constructed the Grandview Villa, a money-spinning sanatorium promising miracle cures and wonders such as "ice-cold temperance drinks". Its handrails were reinforced by crutches abandoned by "cured" patients, though Brett reputedly issued crutches to all arrivals whether they needed them or not.

There may be quieter places in western Canada to take the waters, but hot springs always make for a mildly diverting experience, and even if the crowds are a pain the prices are reasonable. The springs at the **Cave & Basin National Historic Site** southwest of downtown at the end of Cave Avenue, are the best places to indulge, though note that at the time of publication they were scheduled for closure until November 2011.

The original cave and spring, discovered on November 8, 1883 by three railway navvies prospecting for gold on their day off, are what gave birth to the national park. Having crossed the Bow River by raft, the workers discovered a warm-watered stream, which they followed to a small eddy of sulphurous and undergrowth-clogged water. Close by lay a small hole, the water's apparent source, which on further exploration turned out to be the entrance to an underground cave and warm mineral pool. The government quickly bought the three out, promoting travel to the springs as a means of contributing to the cost of the railway's construction. A small reserve was established in 1885, from which the present park eventually evolved. The first bathhouse was built in 1887, closed in 1975, restored and reopened in 1985 and closed again in 1993 – all because of corrosion and low visitor numbers.

At the time of publication, the pools were still shut to bathers, as was the site's **interpretive centre** (also closed to November 2011). You can walk here in a few minutes from town. From the foyer, where the faint whiff of sulphur is unmistakable, a short tunnel leads to the original cave, where the stench becomes all but overpowering. Smell aside, it's still a rather magical spot, with daylight shining in from a little hole in the roof and the limpid water inviting but tantalizingly out of bounds. Back down the tunnel and up the stairs brings you to a few rooms of displays, with a film show, some illuminating old photographs and several pertinent quotations, among which is the acidic comment of an early travel writer, Douglas Sladen: "Though it consists of but a single street," he grumbled about Banff in 1895, "it is horribly over civilized." Down the stairs from the displays at the rear brings you to the "basin", a small outdoor hot spring that's separate from the cave-spring system, but no less inviting. Alongside is a wooden hut theatre with a half-hour film show.

Upper Hot Springs

Unlike the Cave & Basin, there's no problem with swimming in the **Upper Hot Springs** (mid-May to mid-Oct daily 9am–11pm; rest of year Fri & Sat 10am–11pm, Sun–Thurs 10am–10pm; $7.30, towel ($1.90) and swimsuit ($1.90) rental available; ⓣ403/762-1515 or 1/800-767-1611), 4.5km from Banff town centre on Mountain Avenue. Originally developed in 1901, the springs have since undergone several renovations and now offer soaking at 38°C in a large outdoor pool, along with a day spa run by Pleiades (ⓦwww.hotsprings.ca or ⓦwww.pleiadesmassage.com) in conjunction with the park. Sadly, since 1998 the flow of natural spring water has dwindled so that from time to time the pool has to be topped up using tap water. Other attractions include a steam room and cold plunge, and the possibility of signing up for relaxing therapeutic massages ($55 for 30min) and other treatments. There's a good poolside restaurant with outside terrace, fresh juice bar and hot and cold snacks.

Lake Minnewanka

Lake Minnewanka lies a few kilometres north of Banff town centre and is easily accessed by bike or car from the Trans-Canada and the northern end of Banff Avenue on Lake Minnewanka Road. The largest area of water in the national park, its name means "Lake of the Water Spirit", and with the peaks of the Fairholme Range as backdrop it provides a suitably scenic antidote to the bustle of downtown. Various dams augmented the lake to provide Banff with hydroelectric power, though they've done little to spoil the views, most of which are best enjoyed from the various **boat trips** run by Lake Minnewanka Boat Tours (mid-May to early Sept sailings hourly on the hour from 10am to 6pm; $41.90; Ⓣ403/762-3473, Ⓦwww.explorerockies.com) that depart regularly from the quay in summer.

Walks and hikes in and around Banff

Banff Townsite is one of two obvious bases for walks in the park (the other is Lake Louise), and trails around the town cater to all levels of fitness. Short walks from town can provide an opportunity to see a remarkably wide range of **wildlife** and are particularly good for **birdwatching**. Longer day-hikes from the town are limited – you need transport and usually have to head a few kilometres along the Trans-Canada to reach trailheads that leave the flat valley floor for the heart of the mountains.

Short walks from downtown Banff

The best short stroll from downtown – at least for flora and fauna – is the **Fenland Trail**, a 1.5-kilometre loop west through the montane wetlands near the First Vermilion Lake (there are three, all can be accessed off Vermilion Lakes Drive). The lakes are the single most important area for birdwatching in the entire park. Marsh in this area is slowly turning to forest, creating habitats whose rushes and grasses provide a haven for wildlife, birds in particular. Ospreys and bald eagles nest around the lake, together with a wide range of other birds and waterfowl, including tundra swan, hooded merganser and northern shoveler You may also see beaver, muskrat, perhaps even coyote, elk and other deer. You can walk this and other easy local trails in the company of the "Friends of Banff" – see p.625 for more.

Immediately outside the Cave & Basin interpretive centre, the short Discovery Trail (15min) heads up the hill for a view over the historic site. Just below the centre, on Cave Avenue, is the start of the boardwalked **Marsh Loop Trail** (2km; 25min), another treat for birdwatching enthusiasts; in winter, Banff's own wolf pack has been known to hunt within sight of this trail. The area's low-elevation wetlands teem with waterfowl during the winter and spring migrations, with the chance to see – among others – Barrow's goldeneye and all three species of teal: cinnamon, blue-winged and green-winged. The warm microclimate produced here by the springs' warm waters supports mallards over the winter, as well as attracting seasonal rarities such as killdeer, common snipe and rusty blackbird. During the summer you might see belted kingfisher, common yellowthroat, willow flycatcher and red-winged blackbird.

Also accessed off Cave Avenue is the excellent **Sundance Canyon Trail** (3.7km), an easy and deservedly popular stroll along a paved path (watch out for cyclists and in-line skaters) to the picnic area at the canyon mouth; you can extend your walk along the 2.1km loop path up through the canyon, past waterfalls and back down a peaceful wooded trail.

For a shorter walk, and a burst of spectacular white water, stroll the level and very easy **Bow Falls Trail** (1km) from beneath the bridge on the south side of the river, which follows the river bank east to a powerful set of waterfalls and rapids just below the *Fairmont Banff Springs* hotel. The **Hoodoos Trail** on the other side of the river (starting at the eastern end of Buffalo St) offers similar views with fewer people, eventually linking up to Tunnel Mountain Road (3km) – making it a good way to walk into town if you're staying at the hostel and campsites – and beyond to viewpoints above the hoodoos (4.6km).

The most strenuous walk near town is to the summit of Tunnel Mountain. It's approached on a windy track (300m ascent) from the southwest from Tunnel Mountain Drive, culminating in great views over the townsite, Bow River and flanking mountains.

Day-hikes near Banff

Only a couple of longish day-hikes strike out directly from town: the **Spray River Circuit**, a flat, 13km round trip past the *Fairmont Banff Springs* hotel up the Spray River; and the Sulphur Mountain Trail, a 5.5-kilometre switchback that climbs 655m up to the Sulphur Mountain gondola terminal at 2255m (you're better off simply taking the gondola).

The **Cory Pass Trail** (5.8km; 915m ascent), combined with the Edith Pass Trail to make a return loop, is the best day-hike close to Banff. The trailhead is signed 6km west of the town off the Bow Valley Parkway, 500m after the junction with the Trans-Canada. The stiff climbing involved, and a couple of scree passages, means it's not for the inexperienced or faint-hearted. The rewards are fantastic, with varied walking, a high-mountain environment and spine-tingling views. From the pass itself at 2350m you can return on the Edith Pass Trail (whose start you'll have passed 1km into the Cory Pass walk), to make a total loop of a demanding 13km.

Another popular local day-hike, the trail to **Cascade Amphitheatre** (2195m), starts at Mount Norquay Ski Area, 6km north of the Trans-Canada Mount Norquay Road. This offers a medley of landscapes, ranging from alpine meadows to deep, ice-scoured valleys and a close view of the knife-edged mountains that loom so tantalizingly above town. Allow about three hours for the walk (7.7km; 610m ascent). For the same amount of effort you could tackle **Elk Lake** (2165m) from the ski area, though at 13.5km each way it's a long day's hike; some people turn it into an overnight hike by using the campsite 2.5km short of Elk Lake. Shorter, but harder on the lungs, is the **C Level Cirque** (1920m) walk, reached by a 4km trail from the Upper Bankhead Picnic Area on the Lake Minnewanka road east of Banff. Elsewhere, the Sunshine Meadows area (see p.639) has five high trails of between 8km and 20km, all possible as day-hikes and approached either from the Sunshine Gondola (if running) or its parking area, 18km southwest of Banff. There are also some good short trails off the Bow Valley Parkway, most notably the **Johnston Canyon** path (see p.641).

The best **backpacking** options lie in the Egypt Lake area west of Banff townsite, with longer trails radiating from the lake's campsite. Once you're in the backcountry around Banff, however, the combination of trails is virtually limitless. The keenest hikers tend to march the routes that lead from Banff to Lake Louise – the Sawback Trail and Bow Valley Highline, or the tracks in the Upper Spray and Bryant Creek Valley south of the townsite.

If you're planning long walks and overnight trips in backcountry you must have a **Wilderness Pass** ($9.80 a night from park centres). You should also book backcountry campsites (contact Parks Canada at Lake Louise or Banff visitor centres – see p.644 & p.625) and walks well in advance ($11.70 nonrefundable booking fee), as **quotas** operate for all backcountry areas – if the quotas fill, you won't be able to walk or camp or may have to make do with a second-choice hike. The most popular of the fifty-odd campsites are Marvel Lake, Egypt Lake, Luellen Lake, Aylmer Pass, Mystic Meadow, Fish Lakes, Paradise Valley, Hidden Lake, Baker Lake, Merlin Meadows, Red Deer Lakes and Mount Rundle. Be sure to pick up or send for the Parks Canada *Backcountry Visitors' Guide* pamphlet for further details of the system and of recommended routes.

Other Banff activities

Walking, hiking and backpacking are big draws for Banff visitors, but should you tire of lacing up your boots and shouldering a pack, then the information centre carries extensive lists and contact information for guides and outfitters for all manner of **outdoor activities**; for all kinds of **winter sports** see below.

Indoor climbing and swimming

There are free-**climbing** and bouldering walls at Mountain Magic, 224 Bear St (Ⓣ1-800/661-0399, Ⓦwww.mountainmagic.com), where gear rental is also offered (rock shoes, harness and helmet $20/day). The *Douglas Fir Resort* on Tunnel Mountain Drive (Mon–Fri 2–9.30pm, Sat & Sun 10am–9.30pm; $20) has two massive indoor **waterslides** and a pool. The only swimmable lake in the park is Johnson Lake northeast of town off Lake Minnewanka Road: the others are usually glacier-fed and thus too cold.

Biking and in-line skating

Mountain biking is popular, with plenty of rental places around town. One of the cheapest, Bactrax Bike Rentals, 225 Bear St, (from $10/hr or $35/day; Ⓣ403/762-8177, Ⓦwww.snowtips-bactrax.com) has easy bike tours from one to four hours (from $20) on paved routes around Sundance Canyon and Vermilion Lakes. More ambitious rides on the Icefields and Bow Valley parkways or around Moraine Lake can be arranged in Lake Louise at the *Château Lake Louise* hotel (see p.644). If you're exploring under your own steam, get the *Trail Bicycling Guide* from the information centre, which outlines some of the dedicated cycling trails: the best known are Sundance (3.7km one-way); Rundle Riverside (8km one-way); Cascade Trail (9km one-way); and the Spray River Loop (4.3km). The paved Sundance Canyon Trail near the Cave & Basin centre is a popular **in-line skate** run.

Boating and fishing

Boat trips can be taken on Lake Minnewanka, as can **fishing** trips with Lake Minnewanka Boat Tours (see p.632). Monod Sports, 129 Banff Ave (Ⓣ403/762-4571, Ⓦwww.monodsports.com), has all-day drift-boat fishing trips with Tightline Adventures (Ⓦwww.tightlineadventures.com) on the Bow River (catch and release only) at $500 for two people, and walk and wade trips ($225/person); trips include guide, instruction, tackle, waders, drinks and food.

Winter sports in and around Banff

Banff National Park comes close to paradise if you're a skier or snowboarder. The terrain here is some of the best and most varied in North America and three world-class resorts lie in the park: two close to Banff – **Mount Norquay** and **Sunshine Village** – and one in **Lake Louise** (see p.651). On top of great snow and pristine runs, you get crisp air, monumental mountains, sky-high forests, and prices and space that make a mockery of Europe's crowded and exorbitant winter playgrounds. The park also offers the full gamut of **winter activities**, embracing everything from skating, ice-fishing and toboggan trips to dog-sledding, snowshoeing and sleigh rides. What the brochures don't tell you is that here – as in Lake Louise – it can be bitterly **cold** for much of the skiing season.

Mount Norquay

Mount Norquay (Ⓣ403/762-4421, Ⓦwww.banffnorquay.com) is the closest resort to Banff, just 6km and ten minutes' drive from downtown. The mountain (the first in Canada to get a chairlift, in 1948) is as renowned for its uncrowded

Banff Fishing Unlimited (Ⓣ403/678-2486 or 1-866/678-2486, Ⓦwww.banff-fishing.com) has Bow River float trips and walk and wade trips (from $115/person) and half-day fishing cruises on Lake Minnewanka ($95/person in a group of six). Tackle can be rented from Performance Ski and Sports, 208 Bear St (Ⓣ403/762-8222). You need a national park licence ($9.80/day) to fish, available from tackle shops, most of the above companies or the information centre. To **rent canoes** for paddling on the Vermilion Lakes or quiet stretches of the Bow River, contact Blue Canoe ($34 for the first hr, then $20/hr; Ⓣ403/760-5007); the dock is on the river at Wolf Street.

Riding

Riding is easy to organize, with anything from one-hour treks to two-week backcountry expeditions available. The leading in-town outfitters are Holiday on Horseback, 132 Banff Ave (Ⓣ403/762-4551, Ⓦwww.horseback.com). One-, two- and three-hour rides start at $40, while a five-hour trip up the Spray River Valley costs $151. You can also take overnight trips either camping or with nights spent in a lodge.

Whitewater rafting

Best among adrenaline-rush activities is **whitewater rafting** on the Kicking Horse River, located a few kilometres up the road in Yoho but accessed by some eight companies in Banff and Lake Louise, most of them providing all necessary gear and transportation. Other gentler "float" trip options with the same companies are available on the Kananaskis, Kootenay and Bow rivers. Long-established Hydra River Guides, 211 Bear St (Ⓣ403/762-4554 or 1-800/644-8888, Ⓦwww.raftbanff.com), has a wide range of trips in paddle or oar rafts on the Kicking Horse. Wet 'n' Wild Adventures (Ⓣ403/344-6546 or 1-800/668-9119, Ⓦwww.wetnwild.bc.ca/rafting) has full ($115, including shuttle from Lake Louise) and half-day ($69) trips in the Kicking Horse Canyon, a half-day trip ($69) in the wilder lower part of the canyon for more advanced rafters, as well as easier, child-friendly trips, two-day trips, jet-boat rides and raft and riding packages. For family-friendly half-day trips ($69, $97 for a full day) on the Kootenay River, contact Kootenay River Runner (Ⓣ250/347-9210 or 1-800/599-4399, Ⓦwww.raftingtherockies.com), which also runs various parts of the Kicking Horse canyon. For gentle float trips, contact Canadian Rockies Rafting (Ⓣ403/678-6535 or 1-877/226-7625, Ⓦwww.rafting.ca), which charges $55 for two hours on the Bow River.

beginners' slopes as for its expert runs, the terrain breaking down as follows: Beginner (twenty percent), Intermediate (36 percent), Advanced (28 percent) and Expert (16 percent); there are 28 runs in total. The average snowfall is 300cm, and there's snow-making on 85 percent of the terrain. The season runs from December to mid-April. The highest elevation is 2133m, giving a vertical drop of 503m to the resort's base elevation at 1630m. Amenities include a visitor centre, ski school, rental shop, day-care and – on Fridays – the promise of night skiing (early Jan to March). Lift tickets are $55 a day.

Sunshine Village

Sunshine Village (Ⓣ403/277-7669, Ⓦwww.skibanff.com) is a stunning resort, situated way up in the mountains at 2160m, 18km southwest of Banff. If anything the scenery's better than Norquay's – you're higher – and you have the plus of the national park's only on-hill accommodation. With an incredible 10m of snow a year there's rarely a need for snow-making machines; it's all superb, soft, light powder that *Snow Country* magazine has repeatedly voted "The Best

Snow in Canada". A gondola carries skiers (and occasionally summer walkers) the 6km from the Healy Creek parking area to the self-contained Sunshine Village resort. There are 107 runs which can be accessed on the gondola, three high-speed detachable quads, a triple chair, four double chairs, two T-bars and two beginner rope tows. Terrain breaks downs as follows: Beginner (twenty percent), Intermediate (55 percent) and Expert (25 percent). The top elevation is 2730m at Lookout Mountain and there's 3358 acres of terrain to choose from. Lift tickets are $76 a day. Amenities include a day-lodge, day-care, ski school, rental shop and the 85-room *Sunshine Inn* (Ⓣ403/277-7669 or 1-877/542-2633; Ⓦwww.sunshinemountainlodge.com; ⑧).

Other winter activities

If you really want to see the park, head out on either **cross-country skis** or **snowshoes** on the myriad summer walking trails groomed for these purposes. Details of the full network are given in the *Nordic Trails in Banff National Park* pamphlet ($3) available from the town's visitor centre. Popular areas include Johnston Lake, Golf Course Road, Spray River and Sundance Canyon, along with several areas around Lake Louise (see p.651). An additional 300km of cross-country trails crisscross the Kananaskis region, many developed for Olympic competitions, radiating from Canmore Nordic Centre (see p.616). But if these networks aren't enough and you're interested in ski tours of Banff's backcountry, it's best to have the company of an experienced guide; see p.638 for information on guides and rentals.

One of the best **winter walks** in the area is the hike through the fairytale scenery of Johnston Canyon, on boardwalks suspended from its limestone walls to impressive pillars of glassy ice. Though icy, the boardwalks are navigable in winter with the right gear and knowledge. White Mountain Adventures (Ⓣ403/760-4403 or 1-800/408-0005, Ⓦwww.whitemountainadventures.com) and Discover Banff tours (Ⓣ403/760-5007 or 1-877/565-9372 or 0800/520-0904 toll-free in the UK, Ⓦwww.banfftours.com) offer trips down the canyon, as well as to the less spectacular Grotto Canyon. One of the highlights of either trip is to watch ice-climbers scaling the frozen columns. For more detailed **ice climbing** information visit the National Park desk in Banff's Information Centre (see p.625) where climbers should also register.

Of the large selection of local commercial tours, one of the best is **dog-sledding**. Discover Banff Tours (see above; starting at around $150 for four hours, one hour of sled time) or Snowy Owl Sled Dog Tours (Ⓣ403/678-4369, Ⓦwww.snowyowltours.com; starting at $150 for two hours). For **sleigh rides**, again contact Discover Banff Tours or Holiday on Horseback (from 45min for $27; Ⓣ403/762-4551, Ⓦwww.horseback.com). For **ice-fishing** contact Banff Fishing Unlimited (Ⓣ403/678-2486, Ⓦwww.banff-fishing.com).

For **ice-skating** or **tobogganing**, head to the *Fairmont Banff Springs* hotel where the outdoor rink is made particularly appealing by a fire beside it. Ice skates can be rented from The Ski Shop (Ⓣ403/762-5333) in the hotel; you can also rent sleds here for use on the unofficial run beside the rink.

Eating and drinking

Banff's hundred-plus **restaurants** run the gamut from Japanese and other ethnic cuisines to nouvelle-frontier grub. For cheap eats you're best sticking to hostel cafés, though Banff Avenue is lined with good little spots for coffee and snacks. For **groceries** try the big Safeway supermarket at 318 Marten St.

Cafés and restaurants

Aardvark Pizza and Sub 304a Caribou St. ⓣ403/762-5500, ⓦwww.aardvarkpizza.com. Tiny takeaway place with subs, wings, tacos, nachos, poutine (french fries with cheese curd, the favourite Québécois comfort food) and fantastic thick-crust pizzas. There's virtually nowhere to sit but with the best takeout food in town, and open until 4am, popularity's assured.

Baker Creek Bistro Baker Creek Chalets, Bow Valley Parkway ⓣ403/522-2182, ⓦwww.bakercreekbistro.ca. Romantic dining in a softly lit log cabin outfitted with deer-antler chandeliers, midway between Banff and Lake Louise on the Bow Valley Parkway. The menu has innovative steaks and pastas and good game dishes; apple cake is the house speciality. Mains from $24.

Fairmont Banff Springs 405 Spray Ave ⓣ403/762-6860, ⓦwww.fairmont.com/banffsprings. With around fifteen dining options under one roof, Banff's grandest hotel has plenty of variety, all open to non-guests. The *Bow Valley Grill* is the largest restaurant, its menu focused around reliably popular seafood and rotisserie-grilled meats. Other places to eat range from the 24-hour deli serving pizza, to the super-luxurious *Banffshire Club*, which stipulates formal attire and includes *Castello Ristorante* for top-class Italian foods and *Samurai*, which serves excellent sushi. For light snacks try *Grapes Wine Bar* which has good salads, a fine selection of pâtés and cheese and a highly esteemed fondue.

Bison Restaurant & Lounge Bison Courtyard, 211 Bear St ⓣ403/762-5550, ⓦwww.thebison.ca. Banff's best bistro recently got better, with the addition of a swinging downstairs lounge. Upstairs, the chic, contemporary interior, all light wood, large windows and splashy modern art, provides the perfect setting for excellent, creative Canadian cooking. The rooftop patio isn't bad either. Mains $24–45.

Bumper's At *Bumpers Inn*, 603 Banff Ave ⓣ403/762-2622, ⓦwww.bumpersinn.com. A busy, good-value steakhouse with adjoining laidback bar located a little outside downtown. Entrée prices start at around $20 and vegetarians can console themselves with a decent salad bar.

Cilantro At *Buffalo Mountain Lodge*, Tunnel Mountain Rd ⓣ403/760-3008. With a new menu in place, this spot has gone from average to pretty good, serving up with wood-fired pizzas, pasta (try the *buccatini* with elk meatballs) and a few meat and fish dishes. It's not too pricey (mains $15–28) and ideal if you're staying at the nearby hostel or campsites and want a modest treat.

Coyote's Southwestern Grill 206 Caribou St ⓣ403/762-3963, ⓦwww.coyotesbanff.com. Small, simple café just off the main drag, serving top-notch breakfasts. One of the best is the cream-cheese-filled French Toast with fruit ($9). But the hungry should try the huge Mountain Man Breakfast ($9.50), which includes two eggs, two pancakes, bacon or sausage and roasted potatoes. Evenings see fine renditions of pizza, pasta and Southwestern TexMex entrees ($15–25).

Elk and Oarsman 119 Banff Ave, above Ski Hub ⓣ403/762-4616, ⓦwww.elkandoarsman.com. Refined pub with a fine roof terrace, with excellent, if obvious, food – pizza, steaks, burgers and salads – albeit with a "gourmet" twist at good prices. There's also a good range of beers on tap, many of them local.

Evelyn's 201 Banff Ave ⓣ403/762-0352. A superb range of coffees wash down pastries and muffins here in a café that's popular enough to justify two other outlets, *Evelyn's Too*, at 229 Bear Ave, and *Evelyn's Again*, at 119 Banff AVe. All are open 7am–11pm, and put together deli sandwiches (around $5) that make ideal picnic food.

Le Beaujolais 212 Banff Ave, at Buffalo ⓣ403/762-2712. Longstanding gourmet restaurant whose reputation for fine French renditions of regional cuisine extends all over western Canada. Pick from a choice of three set-price menus, which help keep tabs on spending and range from two to six courses – though only the six-course meal includes drinks from the lavish wine list.

Melissa's 218 Lynx St ⓣ403/762-5511. Probably Banff's most popular daytime destination: big breakfasts, superb steaks, salads and burgers, plus a good upstairs bar, *Mel's*, for a leisurely drink, and a summer patio for food and beer in the sun. Recommended, particularly for lunch. Moderate prices with most main dishes in the $10–17 range.

Saltlik 221 Bear St ⓣ403/762-2467. A swanky second-floor nouvelle-steakhouse with wacky lamps and loud art in an otherwise understated but stylized interior. It does Alberta proud with its almost finicky preparation of the 10oz prime sirloin (around $20). But most entrées, including rotisserie chicken, smoked Alaskan black cod and sea bass, are under the $25 mark – but the price doesn't include the tasty sides (mushrooms, spinach, corn, shrimp) that you use to assemble your own meal. The wide selection of wines suffer little markup and the trendy first-floor bar is a good place for a drink before, after or with dinner, as it has the best bar menu in town; don't miss the crisp, seasoned shoestring fries.

Sukiyaki House 211 Banff Ave ⓣ403/762-2002. Sit low among Japanese visitors at the squat tables of this chic Japanese restaurant. With a broad menu, it's hard to choose, but almost impossible to go wrong; the easy option is to pick the Love Boat ($37), a well-priced and varied selection for two people.

Sushi House Banff 304 Caribou Street. Sushi delivered by train – a toy train that is – that circulates around the counter. Take what you fancy and get charged by the number of your dirty plates. Fresh, and good fun for a quick and inexpensive bite – if you don't mind being elbow-to-elbow with the other diners. All of Banff's other budget dining options line the same street.

Nightlife

With a huge number of summer travellers and a large, young seasonal workforce, plenty of people are looking for **nightlife** in Banff and the town has no shortage of **bars** – most within a short walk of one another – and several late-night clubs to stagger to afterwards. Among the less boozy entertainments are **billiards** upstairs at the ten-pin **bowling** at the *Fairmont Banff Springs* hotel and **films** at the Lux Cinema, 229 Bear St (ⓣ403/762-8595).

Aurora 110 Banff Ave ⓣ403/760-5300, ⓦwww.aurorabanff.com. Loud, pricey and popular bar, nightclub and pick-up joint usually gets going around midnight when twentysomethings gather to dance until 2am. Occasional live music on Fri and Sat evenings.

HooDoos Lounge 137 Banff Ave. Basement bar and nightclub that's the main competition for Banff's other major nightspot, the co-owned *Aurora*. If it's dead here it won't be in the *Aurora* and vice-versa. Live music or DJ nightly, with a small cover.

Rose & Crown 202 Banff Ave ⓣ403/762-2121, ⓦwww.roseandcrown.ca. Victorian-style pub with family-oriented restaurant serving decent bar food, which include fantastic hot wings. There's pool here and occasionally live music, particularly blues and funk, making it a cornerstone of town nightlife.

St James Gate 207 Wolf St ⓣ403/762-9355, ⓦwww.stjamesgatebanff.com. Genuinely dingy dark-wood pub, originally built in Ireland then reassembled here to become hugely popular with locals and visitors alike. The thirty beers on tap include good Guinness, as do many of the dishes on the satisfying bar menu; Guinness, crab and asparagus soup ($6), or Guinness, steak and mushroom pie ($11). Other menu items are equally earthy like the tasty Kilpatrick's cabbage and sausage soup ($6) and the juicy halibut fish and chips ($11) and decent meatloaf $12. Occasional live Celtic music.

Voyager Inn 555 Banff Ave ⓣ403/762-3301, ⓦwww.banffvoyagerinn.com. Workaday bar adjoining eponymous motel on the edge of town. Locals who appreciate the cheapest drinks in town – along with nightly specials – converge here.

Wild Bill's Legendary Saloon 203 Banff Ave ⓣ403/762-0333, ⓦwww.wbsaloon.com. Lively country-and-western bar with live bands and line-dancing lessons. There's also a pool hall and games room here, and before 8pm good TexMex and vegetarian food is served in a more family-oriented atmosphere.

Listings

Books Banff Book & Art Den, Clock Tower Mall, 94 Banff Ave (daily 9am–9pm; ⓣ403/762-3919, ⓦwww.banffbooks.com).

Car rental Avis ⓣ403/762-3222; Budget ⓣ403/226-1550; Hertz ⓣ403/762-2027.

Internet Public library, 101 Bear St (Mon–Fri 10am–8pm, Sat 11am–6pm, Sun 11am–5pm; ⓣ403/762-2661). $1/30min and same price to connect to wi-fi network.

Laundries Cascade Coin Laundry, Lower Level, Cascade Plaza, 317 Banff Ave ⓣ403/762-3444.

Medical Mineral Springs Hospital, 301 Lynx St ⓣ403/762-2222, ⓦwww.banffmineralspringshospital.ca. Dentist, 210 Bear St ⓣ403/762-2525. Gourlay's pharmacy, 229 Bear St ⓣ403/762-2516.

Outdoor equipment and guides Tents, outdoor gear and ski equipment to rent from Bactrax, 225 Bear St ⓣ403/762-8177, ⓦwww.snowtips-bactrax.com. Other rental stores and outlets line the same strip. Banff Alpine Guides (ⓣ403/678-6091) is a reliable local company for backcountry cross-country skiing tours. Good sources of rentals, repairs, accessories and advice are Trail Sports (ⓣ403/678-6764) in Canmore, at the Canmore Nordic Centre, and Mountain Magic (ⓣ403/762-2591), in Banff. Both stores rent snowshoes and can help with suggestions for local hikes.

Police ☎403/762-2228.
Post office 204 Buffalo St (Mon–Fri 9am–5.30pm, ☎403/762-2586).
Road conditions ☎403/762-1450.
Taxis Banff Taxi ☎403/762-0000.
Weather ☎403/762-1550 or 762-2088 (24hr recording).

Highway 1 and the Bow Valley Parkway

Two roads run parallel through the Bow Valley from Banff to Lake Louise (58km): the faster **Highway 1** (the Trans-Canada); and the quieter **Bow Valley Parkway**, on the north side of the river, opened in 1989 as a special scenic route. After Banff, there's only one link between the two roads, at Castle Junction, 30km from Lake Louise. Both routes are staggeringly beautiful as the mountains start to creep closer to the road. For the entire run, the mighty Bow River, broad and emerald green, crashes through rocks and forest. Despite the tarmac and heavy summer traffic, the surroundings are pristine and suggest the immensity of the wilderness to come. Sightings of elk and deer are common, particularly around dawn and sundown, and occasionally you'll spot moose.

Both roads offer some good **trails**: if you want to tackle one of the most highly rated day-walks in Banff National Park, make for the Bourgeau Lake Trail off Hwy 1 (see p.641); for a shorter walk, make for the Johnston Canyon on the Parkway.

Highway 1

Most people tend either to cruise **Hwy 1**'s rapid stretch of the Trans-Canada without stopping – knowing that the road north of Lake Louise is more spectacular still – or leap out at every trail and rest stop, overcome with the grandeur of it all. On Greyhound or Brewster **buses** you're whisked through to Lake Louise in about forty minutes; if you're driving, try, for the sake of wildlife, to stick to the 90kph speed limit. The vast fences that march for kilometre after kilometre along this section of the road are designed to protect animals, not only from traffic, but also from the brainless visitors who clamber out of their cars to get close to the bears occasionally glimpsed on the road. You won't have to be in the Rockies long during the summer before you're caught in a **bear jam**, when people – contrary to all park laws, never mind common sense – abandon their cars helter-skelter on the road to pursue hapless animals with cameras and camcorders.

Sunshine Meadows

A beautiful and unusually large tract of alpine grassland, **Sunshine Meadows** (Ⓦwww.sunshinemeadowsbanff.com), 18km southwest of Banff off Hwy 1, is cradled by Sunshine Village ski resort and straddles the continental divide. The area may be better known for its winter sports, but for the short summer season the valley is replete with hundreds of wild flowers and ideal for high-mountain hiking. Access to the valley is on foot on an arduous 6km access trail from the resort's car park, but an easier option is to take a shuttle bus. A service is run between early June and the end of September by White Mountain Adventures (☎403/760-4403 or 1-800/408-005, Ⓦwww.whitemountainadventures.com; $25 one-way from the car park, $55 from Banff), departing from both Banff (currently at 8.15am, returning at 2.30pm & 5.30pm) and the Sunshine Village parking lot (hourly from 9am, returning hourly).

Once you're in Sunshine Meadows two connecting gravel trails can be followed. The **Rock Isle Trail** loop starts at the Sunshine Meadows Nature Centre. After 1km, branch right to pass Rock Isle Lake on the left (take the left fork and you'd eventually come to Lake Assiniboine). Around 600m after the branch right you come to a fork: turn left and you loop around the Garden Path Trail (3.8km) past

Bow Valley parkway closures

In past years the 17km of the Bow Valley Parkway between Johnston Canyon and the east entrance off the Trans-Canada (the entrance closest to Banff) has been closed every day from March 1 to June 25 between 6pm and 9am. This lets animals forced down to look for food at lower altitudes by late snow to graze. Access at these times to the Johnston Canyon trails and campsite is from Hwy 1 only. Consult the visitor centre in Banff to confirm the latest arrangements.

Larix Lake, the Simpson Viewpoint and Grizzly Lake back to the fork. From here it's 500m to a 1.2-kilometre detour to the right to Standish Viewpoint (a dead end). Otherwise head straight on and after 2.8km you come to a junction and the Monarch Viewpoint, where a 1.6-kilometre walk takes you back to the Nature Centre (11.5km total with all loops and detours). Ask for a sketch map of this area from the information centre.

The Bow Valley Parkway

The **Bow Valley Parkway** boasts more scenic grandeur than Hwy 1 – which is saying something – and offers more distractions if you're taking your time: several trails, campsites, plus plenty of accommodation choices and one excellent eating option. The largest concentration of sightseers is likely to be found at the Merrent turn-off, enjoying fantastic views of the Bow Valley and the railway winding through the mountains.

If you have the time, the Parkway is the preferable route, and you should budget some time to walk one of the **trails** en route, in particular the easy but impressive Johnston Canyon Trail (see box opposite). En route, some of the various viewpoints and signed pull-offs deserve more attention than others. Around 8km down the hwy, look out for the **Backswamp Viewpoint**, where views one way extend to the mountains and the other across a river swamp area where you might see beaver, muskrat, ospreys and other birds, as well as the common butterwort, a purple-flowered carnivorous plant whose diet consists largely of marsh insects. In winter, Backswamp Viewpoint is also known locally as one of the most likely areas to spot wolves; at other times of the year you might also see bighorn sheep or mountain goats on the mountain slopes above.

About 3km further on you come to **Muleshoe Picnic Area**, also noted for its birds and wildfowl. Some of the area around shows signs of having been burnt in forest fires, though the park authorities deliberately torched these areas to encourage fresh undergrowth and the return of wildlife excluded from more mature forests. Some 11km on, a 400m trail takes you to a lovely little lake once known as Lizard Lake after the long-toed salamanders that thrived here. These were eaten when the lake was stocked with trout, and the name's now been changed to Pilot Lake. About 3km beyond is the trailhead for the **Johnston Canyon Trail,** deservedly the most popular in the area; 3km beyond that is **Moose Meadows**, where – name notwithstanding – you'll be mighty lucky to see any moose: habitat changes have forced them out.

Of interest to **birdwatchers**, Johnston Canyon is one of only two known breeding sites in Alberta of the black swift – you may see the birds flitting back to their nests at dusk – and is also a breeding place for American dippers, buxom grey birds that have the ability to walk along stream beds underwater and habitually nest below waterfalls. Elsewhere on the Parkway the various turn-offs give you the opportunity to spot species associated with montane forest and meadow zones, notably at the Muleshoe Picnic Area, 21km southeast of Castle Junction, where you might spot western tanagers, pileated woodpeckers and orange-crowned warblers.

Accommodation

The road's **accommodation** possibilities make a more rural alternative to Banff and Lake Louise, and are close enough to both to serve as a base if you have transport; as ever, you should book rooms well in advance. Four **lodges** are spaced more or less equally en route and, though expensive, they may have room when Lake Louise's hotels are stretched. The three national park **campsites** listed make for excellent camping retreats.

Lodges and hostels

Baker Creek Chalets 12km east of Lake Louise ⓣ403/522-3761, ⓦwww.bakercreek.com. Although it's somewhat over-manicured looking, this complex of log buildings offers some very comfortable accommodation. Choose from lodge suites or chalets, both of which have gas or wood fireplaces, full kitchens or kitchenettes and decks. There's also an excellent restaurant, the *Baker Street Bistro* (see p.637). 6

Castle Mountain Chalets 32km west of Banff, near Castle Junction ⓣ403/762-3868 or 1-877/762-2281, ⓦwww.castlemountain.com. The individual log cabins and chalets here can seem a bit too polished, but if creature comforts are what matters this makes an excellent choice. The log chalets for four with kitchenettes and fireplaces are more expensive, but the best options of all are the delightful deluxe cabins for four, five or six people, that come with full kitchens, dishwashers and jacuzzis. 7

Castle Mountain Wilderness Hostel 1.5km east of Castle Junction ⓣ403/762-2367 or 1-866/762-4122, ⓦwww.hihostels.ca. This is by far the least expensive possibility along the Parkway, but that doesn't make it any less charming. The common

Bow Valley Trails

Five major trails branch off the Bow Valley Parkway. The best short walk is the **Johnston Canyon Trail** (2.7km each way), 25km from Banff, an incredibly engineered path to a series of spray-veiled waterfalls. The Lower Falls are 1.1km, the Upper Falls 2.7km from the trailhead on the Parkway. From the upper falls you can continue on to the seven cold-water springs of the Ink Pots, which emerge in pretty open meadows, to make a total distance of 5.8km (215m ascent). Another short possibility is the **Castle Crags Trail** (3.7km each way; 520m ascent) from the signed turn-off 5km west of Castle Junction. Short but steep, and above the tree-line, this walk offers superb views across the Bow Valley and the mountains beyond. Allow ninety minutes one-way to take account of the stiff climb.

The best day-hike is to **Rockbound Lake** (8.4km each way), a steepish climb to 2210m with wild lakeland scenery at the end; allow at least two and a half hours one-way, due to the 760m ascent. Another fifteen-minutes' walk beyond Rockbound and Tower lakes at the end of the trail lies the beautiful Silverton waterfall. The other Parkway trails – **Baker Creek** (20.3km) and **Pulsatilla Pass** (17.1km) – serve to link backpackers with the dense network of paths in the Slate Range northeast of Lake Louise.

There are two outstanding trails along Hwy 1. The first is the trek to **Bourgeau Lake** (7.5km one-way), considered by many to be among the top five day-hikes in Banff; it starts from a parking area 10km west of Banff – allow two and a half to three hours for the 725m ascent. The second is the long day-hike to **Shadow Lake** (14.3km each way), where the lakeside campsite (at 1840m), in an impressive subalpine basin, gives access to assorted onward trails; the main trail starts from the **Redearth Creek** parking area 20km west of Banff – allow four hours for the 440m ascent.

room has a wood-burning stove and large bay windows, but the real sell is being so close to the cross-country and downhill skiing options and hiking and biking trails, all at a fraction of the cost of the more expensive places, year-round. Dorms for members $20 Oct–June, $23 July–Sept; nonmembers $24 & $27 over the same periods.

Johnston Canyon Resort 26km west of Banff, close to the trail that leads to Johnston Canyon ⓣ403/762-2971 or 1-888/378-1720, ⓦwww.johnstoncanyon.com. These rustic cabins – some with fireplaces, some with kitchenettes – set on the banks of the Johnston Canyon creek are all polished wood and provide a pleasing sense of tranquility. There's also an on-site restaurant, shop, garage, tennis court and BBQ. Mid-May to early Oct; ❻

Storm Mountain Lodge 5km south of Hwy 1 on Hwy 93 to Radium, 27km from Banff ⓣ403/762-4155, ⓦwww.stormmountainlodge.com. The fourteen log cabins here are the real deal when it comes to rustic accommodation. All were built in the 1920s, but the interiors are immaculate, well-decorated and boast wood-burning stone fireplaces, clawfoot tubs and hand-crafted log bed frames. There's a good restaurant and lounge, and hikers' lunches can be ordered if you're hitting the trails. ❼

Campsites

Castle Mountain 32 km from Banff (28km from Lake Louise), east off the Bow Valley Parkway. Set in a beautiful wooded area near Castle Junction, this 43-pitch, first-come, first-served site has no facilities beyond hot and cold running water, flush toilets and kitchen shelters – but it is close to a small store and restaurant. Open mid–June to early Sept; $21.50.

Johnston Canyon Campground 22km from Banff (30km from Lake Louise), south off the Bow Valley Parkway. This is the best equipped and closest site to Banff, which means its 132 pitches go quickly. It operates on a first-come, first-served basis, so arrive early and hope for the best if you want to take advantage of the easy access to hikes to Johnston Canyon (the trailhead of which is across from the site). Facilities include hot and cold running water, flush toilets and firepits. Open early June to mid–Sept; $27.40.

Protection Mountain 48km from Banff (17km from Lake Louise), just north of Castle Junction, off the Bow Valley Parkway. The most primitive of the three government-run campsites listed here has 89 pitches, none of which are reservable. Facilities include flush toilets, piped cold water, kitchen shelters and not much else. Open late June to early Sept; $21.50.

Lake Louise

Banff National Park's other main centre, **LAKE LOUISE**, is very different from Banff – less a town than two distinct artificial resorts. The first is a small mall of shops and hotels just off the Trans-Canada known as **Lake Louise Village**. The second is **the lake** itself, 4.5km from the village (and 200m higher) on the winding Lake Louise Drive, the self-proclaimed "gem of the Rockies" and – despite its crowds and monster hotel – a sight you must see. You can walk between the two (the uphill hike from the townsite to the lake is 2.7km on the Louise Creek Trail or 4.5km along the Tramline Trail), but you're better off saving the walking for around the lake and taking a taxi (ⓣ403/522-2020; around $10) from the village; save the two linking trails for coming down from the lake.

A third area, **Moraine Lake**, 13km south of the village, has almost equally staggering scenery and several magnificent and easily accessed trails. All three areas are packed in summer while in winter things slow down a little, though crowds still turn up for some of Canada's best powder **skiing** at the nearby resort (see box, p.651).

The mountains around offer almost unparalleled **hiking country** and the park's most popular day-use area. You'll have to weigh awesome scenery against the sheer numbers, for these are some of the most heavily used trails on the continent – fifty thousand-plus people in summer – though longer backpacking routes lead quickly away to the quieter spots.

If you do intend to hike – and the trails are all a little more accessible and manageable than at Banff – then in an ideal world you'd spend two or three days here: one to walk the loop around above Lake Louise (Lake Agnes–Big Beehive–Plain of the Six Glaciers–Lake Louise Shoreline) or the more

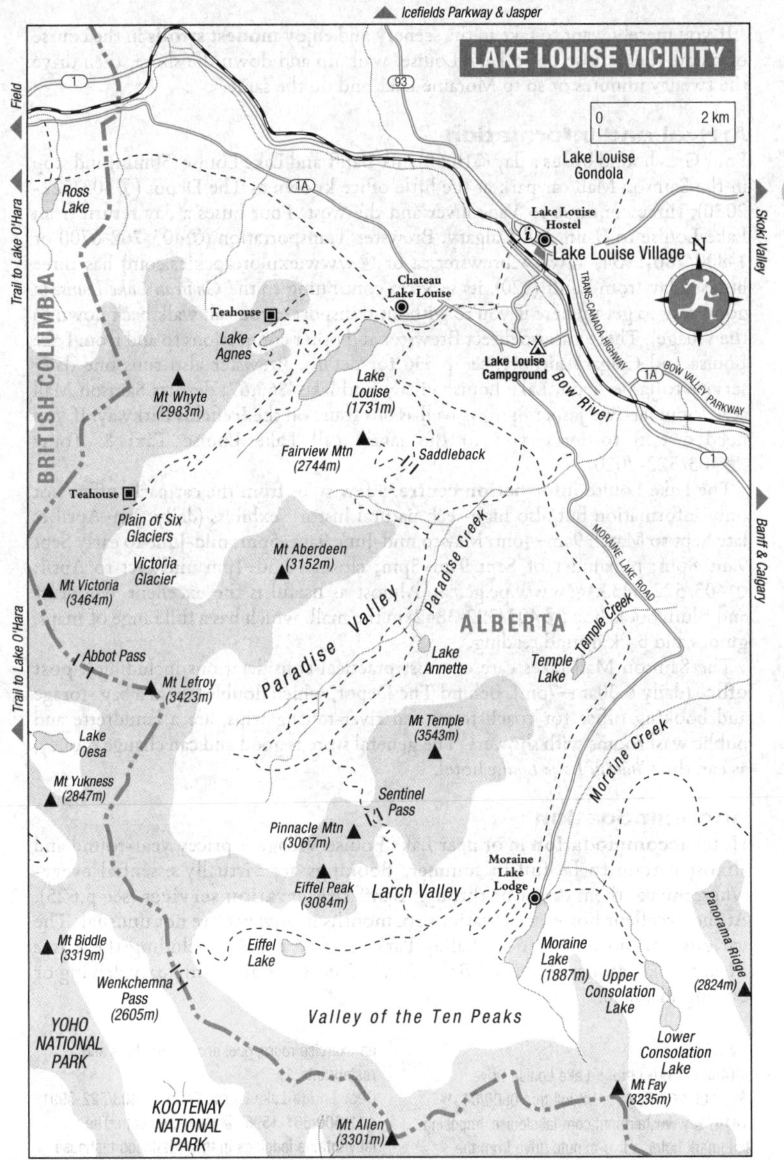

demanding Saddleback (at a push you could do both in a day if you were fit and keen). Then you'd bike, taxi, drive or take the shuttle bus to Moraine Lake (if you're not staying there), where in a day you could easily walk to Consolation Lake, return to Moraine Lake and then tackle the Moraine Lake–Larch Valley–Sentinel Pass or Moraine Lake–Larch Valley–Eiffel Lake trail. A third day could be spent in Paradise Valley between Lake Louise and Moraine Lake.

If you merely want to take in the scenery and enjoy **modest strolls** in the course of a day, then cruise up to Lake Louise, walk up and down the shore, then drive the twenty minutes or so to Moraine Lake and do the same.

Arrival and information

Four Greyhound **buses** a day ($16.60) link Banff and Lake Louise (50min) and stop in the Samson Mall car park at the little office known as The Depot (Ⓣ403/522-2080); three continue to Vancouver and the west. Four buses a day return from Lake Louise to Banff and Calgary. Brewster Transportation (Ⓣ403/762-6700 or 1-800/760-6934, Ⓦwww.brewster.ca or Ⓦwww.explorerockies.com) has three buses a day from Banff ($20), its services continuing to the *Château Lake Louise* (a good way to get up here if you're without transport – you can walk back down to the village). There are also direct Brewster and other connections to and from Lake Louise and Calgary airport; see p.556 for details. Brewster also runs one daily service to Jasper from Lake Louise village and lake ($66.67; departs Samson Mall at 4.15pm, arrives Jasper 8pm) as well as bus tours on the Icefields Parkway. If you need a taxi to ferry you to the lakes, call Lake Louise Taxi & Tours (Ⓣ403/522-2020).

The Lake Louise **information centre**, a few steps from the car park, offers not only information but also high-tech natural history exhibits (daily: Jan–April & late Sept to March 9am–4pm; May to mid-June 9am–5pm; mid-June to early Sept 9am–8pm; remainder of Sept 9am–5pm; closes 12.30–1pm mid-Oct to April; Ⓣ403/522-3833, Ⓦwww.pc.gc.ca). Almost as useful is the excellent Woodruff and Blum bookshop (Ⓣ403/522-3842) in the mall, which has a full range of maps, guides and background reading.

The Samson Mall takes care of most practical considerations including a **post office** (daily 6.30am–7pm). Behind The Depot, which doubles up as a bag storage and booking office for coach tours and river-rafting trips, are a laundrette and public washrooms with showers. The general store is good and can change money, as can the *Château Lake Louise* hotel.

Accommodation

Hotel **accommodation** in or near Lake Louise Village is pricey year-round and almost certain to be full in summer. Bookings are virtually essential everywhere; make them direct or through Banff's **reservation services** (see p.625). At the excellent hostel, reservations six months in advance are not unusual. The various options on the Bow Valley Parkway (see p.641), including the *Castle Mountain Wilderness Hostel* and *Baker Creek Chalets*, are all within easy driving or cycling distance.

Hotels

Château Lake Louise Lake Louise Drive Ⓣ1-800/257-7544 or UK toll free 0800/0441-1414, Ⓦwww.fairmont.com/lakelouise. Imposing landmark hotel, a five-minute drive from the townsite, with commanding views over Lake Louise from its 511 grand rooms and suites. The hotel is worth a look alone for the bizarre appeal of its fusion of alpine and neocolonial furnishings. Rooms and suites can cost over $500, but rates are savagely cut in the off-season (Oct–Dec), some rooms occasionally going for around $100, when good value ski packages are also offered. The hotel's battery of five-star facilities includes an exercise room, pool and several bars and restaurants. ⑧

Deer Lodge Lake Louise Drive Ⓣ403/522-3991 or 1-800/661-1595, Ⓦwww.crmr.com. The labyrinthine lodgings in this 1920s log teahouse contrast with the pomp of its neighbour, *Château Lake Louise*, a short walk away. This is far more relaxed and focused on escape; all rooms come with phones, but no TV. The rooftop hot tub has fantastic views and there's a sauna, restaurant and lounge. ⑦

Lake Louise Inn 210 Village Rd Ⓣ403/522-3791 or 1-800/661-9237, Ⓦwww.lakelouiseinn.com. The least expensive of the village hotels, with nine varieties of room, some with kitchens, balconies and gas or wood fireplaces. Facilities include a heated indoor pool and sauna. 6

Moraine Lake Lodge Moraine Lake ⓣ403/522-3733, or 1-877/522-2777, ⓦwww.morainelake.com. One of the most enticing and magnificently executed hotels in the entire Rockies: perfect if you're on honeymoon, or just want to splash out. Accommodation consists of a nicely landscaped collection of high-quality cabins and lodge rooms designed by eminent architect Arthur Erickson (also responsible for Vancouver's UBC Museum of Anthropology and the Canadian Embassy in Washington DC). Their open fires probably make the cabins best. The friendly staff and great privacy here gives it an edge over the more lacklustre hotels in the village and near Lake Louise. Open June–Sept. 8

Paradise Lodge and Bungalows Lake Louise Drive ⓣ403/522-3595, ⓦwww.paradiselodge.com. A short walk from Lake Louise, this is the pricier of the near-lake options, but with reasonable off-season rates for its 21 self-contained bungalows and 24 one- and two-bedroom suites (some with kitchens). Mid-May to mid-Oct. 7

Post Hotel Village Rd ⓣ403/522-3989 or 1-800/661-1586, ⓦwww.posthotel.com. Grand, log chalet-hotel that is the top spot in the village, with a noted restaurant and bar, but expect to pay $300-plus for a room here in summer. 8

Hostels

Lake Louise Alpine Centre 203 Village Rd ⓣ403/522-2201, ⓦwww.hihostels.ca. Standard-setting, mountain chalet-style 150-bed hostel just north of the village mall, offering dorm beds and private rooms. Clean, superior-quality facilities include communal kitchen, laundry, internet access, free wi-fi, a mountaineering library and a handy restaurant. Reservations are virtually essential (up to six months in advance) for summer and winter ski weekends. Dorm beds for members $31 Feb–May, $38 June–Sept, $26.50 Oct–Jan; nonmembers $35, $42 and $30.50, over the same periods. Private doubles in the same periods cost $87, $102 and $110 ($95/$110/$118).

Campsites

Lake Louise Campground ⓣ1-877/737-3783, ⓦwww.pccamping.ca. Lovely park-run site with 210 pitches 1km from the village, off Fairview Rd, that gets busy in the summer. Sites are close together, though the trees offer some privacy and, with the railway close by, it can be noisy. This is one of the national park campgrounds where reservations have been possible in past years from March of the year in question. There's hot and cold piped water, showers, flush toilets, kitchen shelters and provision for food storage. Open mid-May to late Sept, but in early spring and late fall tents are not permitted due to bears – check with park authorities before booking; $27.70.

Lake Louise Trailer Site Part of the above campsite (same number and website for reservations) but for RVs only. 189 drive through sites available in summer, thirty in winter. Facilities include hook-ups, hot and cold running water and showers. Open year-round; $32.30.

Lake Louise Village

Lake Louise Village doesn't amount to much, but it's an essential supply stop, with more or less everything you need in terms of food, shelter (at a price), information and equipment rental. Most of it centres round the Samson Mall and car park, with a smart hostel and a couple of hotels dotted along the service road to the north.

A short way from the village, the **Lake Louise Gondola** (daily: mid-May to mid-June & last three weeks of Sept 9am–4.30pm, mid-June to Sept 7 9am–5pm; $25.95) takes thirteen minutes to get to 2088m, partway up Mount Whitehorn (2669m). To reach it, pick up the free shuttle which operates from some village hotels or return to and cross over the Trans-Canada, and follow the road towards the ski area; the gondola is signed left after about 1km. You can choose between enclosed gondola cars, open chairs, or chairs with bubble domes. At the top are the usual sensational views – rated some of the best in the Rockies – a self-service restaurant, sun decks, picnic areas, souvenir shops and several trailheads through the woods and meadows. One takes you to the summit of Mount Whitehorn.

Lake Louise

Before you see **Lake Louise** you see the hotel: *Château Lake Louise*, a grandiose monstrosity that would surely never get planning permission today. Yet even so

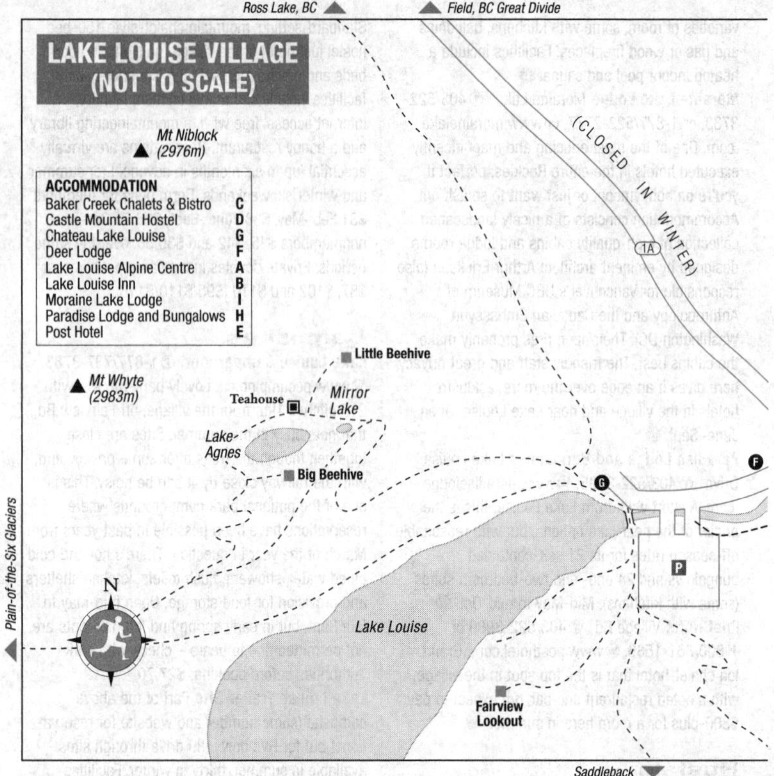

intrusive an eyesore fades into insignificance beside the immense beauty of its surroundings. The lake is brilliant turquoise, the mountains sheer, the glaciers vast; the whole ensemble is perfection. Outfitter Tom Wilson, the first white Canadian to see Lake Louise when he was led here by a local native in 1882, wrote: "I never, in all my explorations of these five chains of mountains throughout western Canada, saw such a matchless scene…I felt puny in body, but glorified in spirit and soul."

You can't help wishing you could have been Tom Wilson, and seen the spot unsullied by the hotel and before the arrival of the tourists and general clutter. Around ten thousand people come here daily in peak season to gawp, while noticeboards on the waterfront seem obsessed with the profoundly dull account of how the lake came by its name – it was named in honour of the fourth daughter of Queen Victoria. The native name translates as the "Lake of the Little Fishes". Wilson, showing precious little wit, originally called it Emerald Lake. More interesting is the account of Hollywood's discovery of the lake in the 1920s, when it was used to suggest exotic European locations. After Wilson's "discovery" all access was by rail or trail – the station, then known as Laggan, was 6km away; the first road was built in 1926.

The first hotel appeared in 1890, a simple two-bedroom affair which replaced a tumbledown cabin on the shore. Numerous fires, false starts and additions followed until the present structure made its appearance. Be sure to walk here, despite the paths' popularity.

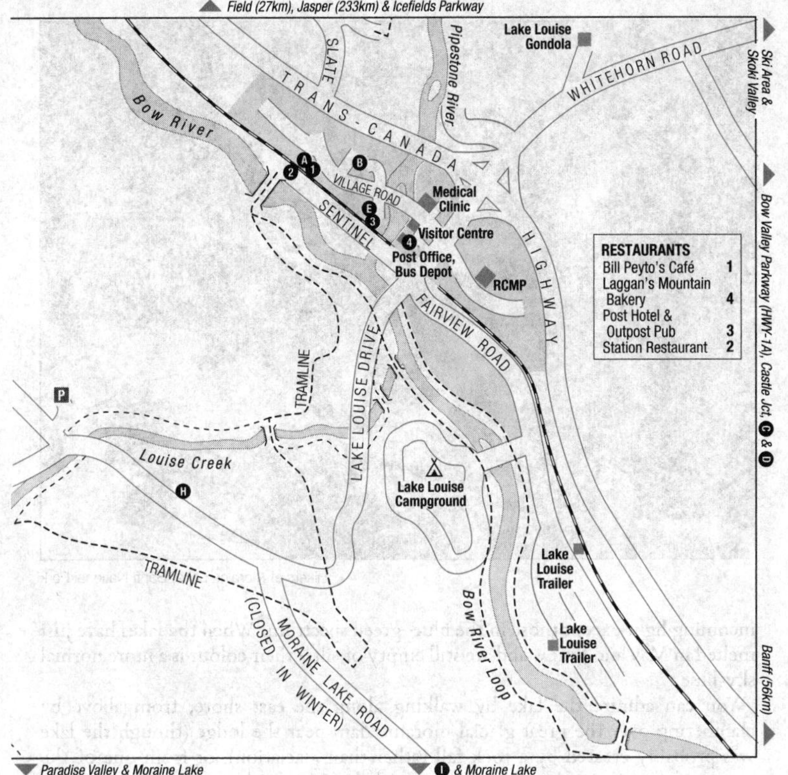

Moraine Lake

Not quite so many people visit Lake Louise as make the road journey 13km to **Moraine Lake**, which is smaller than its neighbour although in many ways its scenic superior. If you're without your own transport, you'll have to rely on a bike or taxi ($35) to get here or the park-run "Vista" bus shuttle (daily every 30min from outside the hostel and Lake Louise campsite; free on production of park pass). The last has been introduced because of the sheer number of visitors in cars and RVs trying to cram into the tiny car park and clogging the approach road.

No wonder they come, for this is one of the great landscapes of the region, has some cracking trails (see p.648) and the splendid yet discreet *Moraine Lake Lodge,* which is one of the best places to stay in the region (see p.645). Bar the *Lodge*, with its good little café and top-notch restaurant, nothing disturbs the lake and its matchless surroundings. The scene once graced the back of Canadian $20 notes, though the illustration did little justice to the shimmering water and the jagged, snow-covered peaks on the eastern shore that inspired the nickname "Valley of the Ten Peaks". The peaks are now officially christened the Wenkchemna, after the Stoney native word for "ten".

Moraine Lake is half the size of Lake Louise but is the most vivid turquoise imaginable. Like Lake Louise and other big Rockies lakes (notably Peyto on the Icefields Parkway), the peacock blue is caused by fine particles of glacial silt, or till, known as rock flour. Meltwater in June and July washes this powdered rock into the lake, the minute but uniform particles of flour absorbing all colours of

▲ Hikers at Moraine Lake, Banff National Park

incoming light except those in the blue–green spectrum. When the lakes have just melted in May and June – and are still empty of silt – their colour is a more normal sky-blue.

You can admire the lake by walking along the east shore, from above by clambering over the great glacial moraine dam near the lodge (though the lake was probably created by a rock fall rather than glaciation), or from one of the **canoes for rent** on the right just beyond the *Lodge* and car park. For the best overall perspective, tackle the Larch Valley–Sentinel Pass trail through the forest on the east shore (see p.649), but we strongly recommend checking with the visitor centre at Lake Louise for the latest on **bear activity**.

Hikes around Lake Louise

All the Lake Louise **hiking trails** are busy in summer, but they're good for a short taste of the scenery. They're also well worn and well marked, so you don't need to be a seasoned hiker or skilled map-reader. The two most popular finish up at teahouses – mountain chalets selling welcome, but rather pricey, snacks.

The signed **Lake Agnes Trail** (3.4km), said to be the most-walked path in the Rockies (but don't let that put you off), strikes off from the right (north) shore of the lake immediately past the hotel. It's a gradual 400m climb, relieved by ever more magnificent views and a teahouse beautifully situated beside mountain-cradled Lake Agnes (2135m); allow one to two hours. Beyond the teahouse, if you want more of a walk, things quieten down considerably. You can continue on the right side of the lake and curve left around its head to climb to an easily reached pass. Here a 200-metre stroll to the left brings you to **Big Beehive** (2255m), an incredible eyrie, 1km from the teahouse. Almost as rewarding is the trail, also 1km from the teahouse, to **Little Beehive**, a mite lower, but still privy to full-blown panoramas over the broad sweep of the Bow Valley.

Keener walkers can return to the pass from Big Beehive and turn left to follow the steep trail down to intersect another trail; turning right leads west through rugged and increasingly barren scenery to the second teahouse at the **Plain of the Six Glaciers** (2100m). Alternatively, the more monotonous Six Glaciers Trail (leaving out the whole Lake Agnes–Big Beehive section) leads from the hotel along the lakeshore to the same point (5.3km to the teahouse; 365m ascent). However, a better option is to follow the Lake Agnes and Big Beehive route to the Plain, then use the Six Glaciers Trail for the return to *Château Lake Louise*, which neatly ends the day's loop with a downhill stroll and an easy but glorious finale along the shore of Lake Louise (see our map to make sense of what is a pretty straightforward and very well-worn loop).

The main appeal of the less-used **Saddleback Trail** (3.7km one-way) is that it provides access to the superlative viewpoint of Fairview Mountain. Allow from one to two hours to Saddleback itself (2330m; 595m ascent); the trail to the summit of Fairview (2745m) strikes off right from here. Even if you don't make the last push, the Saddleback views – across to the 1200m wall of Mount Temple (3544m) – are staggering. Despite the people, this is one of the park's top short walks.

Skoki Valley hikes

The **Skoki Valley** region east of Lake Louise offers fewer day-hikes; to enjoy it you'll need a tent to overnight at any of the six campsites. The main access trail initially follows a gravel road forking off to the right of the Lake Louise Ski Area, off Hwy 1. Many people hike as far as Boulder Pass (2345m), an 8.6-kilometre trek and 640-metre ascent from the parking area, as a day-trip, and return the same way instead of pushing on to *Skoki Lodge*, 8km beyond. Various well-signposted long and short trails from the *Lodge* or the campsites are documented in the *Canadian Rockies Trail Guide*, found at the visitor centre.

Moraine Lake hikes

Each of the four basic routes in the **Moraine Lake** area are easily accomplished in a day or less, two with sting-in-the-tail additions if you want added exertion; all start from the lake, which lies 13km from Lake Louise Village at the end of Moraine Lake Road. Before hiking, check with the visitor centre in Lake Louise on the latest restrictions imposed to protect both the bears known to have made the area part of their territory as well as the tourists who hope to catch a glimpse of them. At the time of writing, walks in the Larch Valley and around were restricted. You must walk in groups of at least four people (there are often people waiting to join a group, so you should have no trouble making up the numbers).

The easiest walk is the 1km amble along the lakeshore followed by the 3km stroll to **Consolation Lake**, an hour's trip that may be busy but can provide some respite from the frenzy at Moraine Lake itself. This almost level walk ends with lovely views of a small mountain-circled lake, its name coined by an early explorer who thought it a reward and "consolation" for the desolation of the valley that led up to it. If you're tenting, fairly fit, or can arrange a pick-up, the highline **Panorama Ridge Trail** (2255m) branches off the trail (signed "Taylor Lake") to run 22km to the Banff–Radium hwy 7km west of Castle Junction.

The most popular walk (start as early as possible) is the Moraine Lake–**Larch Valley–Sentinel Pass Trail**, one of the Rockies' premier hikes, which sets off from the lake's north shore 100m beyond the lodge. A stiffish hairpin climb through forest on a broad track, with breathtaking views of the lake through the trees, brings you to a trail junction after 2.4km and some 300m of ascent. Most hikers branch right, where the track levels off to emerge into Larch Valley, broad alpine upland with stands of larch and majestic views of the encircling peaks. If you have the energy, push on to Sentinel Pass, in all some two hours' walk and

Other Lake Louise activities

Most operators – especially **rafting** companies – are based in Banff or elsewhere (see p.635 & p.670), though many offer pick-ups in Lake Louise, typically with a $10–15 add-on to their listed Banff prices; a handful operate trips directly out of Lake Louise itself. Companies actually based in or near the village include Wild Water Adventures (Ⓣ1-888/647-6444, Ⓦwww.wildwater.com), which runs half-day, full-day or two-day "gentle-water" or whitewater rafting trips on the Kicking Horse River in nearby Yoho National Park (half-day trips from $93 from Lake Louise).

Guided walks and cycling

If you don't want to hike alone, or wish to know more about what you're walking past, the national park and Friends of Banff (Ⓦwww.friendsofbanff.com) often run **guided walks** (from around $15) three or four times a week in July and August, usually along the Lake Louise lakeshore (2hr) and to the Plain of the Six Glaciers (6hr). Drop by the Banff visitor centre's Friends of Banff store to confirm latest timings and to reserve a place (the walks are popular) or call the Lake Louise visitor centre at Ⓣ403/522-3833.

Cyclists can rent bikes from Wilson Mountain Sports in the mall, or sign up for **cycling tours** (from $65 for half a day, $95 full day) and transfers that'll take you up to Bow Summit on the Icefields Parkway so you can pedal downhill or freewheel all the way back to Lake Louise.

Boating and fishing

Serious canoeists can rent craft from Wilson Mountain Sports for trips on the Bow River, while more sedate paddlers can **rent canoes** (June–Sept daily 10am–8pm; $50/hr) at *Château Lake Louise* to dabble on the lake itself (Ⓣ403/522-3511). Don't think about swimming: the water's deep and cold – the highest temperature in summer is 4°C.

Trout fishing is possible on the Bow River between Lake Louise and Banff, with support and advice available at the *Castle Mountain Chalets* on the Bow Valley Parkway (see p.640). Rental equipment is again on offer at Wilson Mountain Sports. Compulsory fishing permits ($9.80 daily) are available from the visitor centre.

Other activities

For **riding**, contact Brewster Lake Louise Stables at the *Château Lake Louise* hotel (Ⓣ403/522-3511 ext 1210, or 762-5454, Ⓦwww.brewsteradventures.com) and enquire about their two-hour trips along the shores of Lake Louise ($72), half-day tours ($113) to the Lake Agnes or Plain of the Six Glaciers (see p.649) or full-day treks to Paradise Valley and Horseshoe Glacier ($250, including lunch). Timberline Tours (Ⓣ403/522-3743, Ⓦwww.timberlinetours.ca) runs similar if slightly cheaper treks from the Lake Louise Corral behind the *Deer Lodge* hotel; ninety-minute rides locally ($65), three-hour rides to Lake Agnes ($95), four- to five-hour trips to the Plain of the Six Glaciers ($105/$115) and all-day trips to the Skoki Valley ($160) east of Lake Louise.

720m above Moraine Lake. At 2605m, this, along with the Wenkchemna Pass, is the highest point reached by a major trail in the Canadian Rockies. You can see what you're in for from the meadows – but not the airy views over Paradise Valley from the crest of the pass itself. You could even continue down into Paradise Valley, a tough, scree-filled descent, and complete an exceptional day's walk by picking up the Paradise Valley loop (see below) back to the Moraine Lake Road. Otherwise, return to the 2.4-kilometre junction and, if legs are still willing – you'll have done most of the hard climbing work already – think about tagging on the last part of the third Moraine Lake option.

This third option, the less-walked Moraine Lake–**Eiffel Lake–Wenkchemna Pass Trail**, follows the same climb from the lake as for the Larch Valley path before branching off left instead of right at the 2.4-kilometre junction. It's equally sound, virtually level and if anything has the better scenery (if only because less barren than Sentinel Pass) in the stark, glaciated grandeur to be found at the head of the Valley of the Ten Peaks. It's also much quieter once you're beyond the trail junction. At 2255m, Eiffel Lake is a 5.6-kilometre hike and 370-metre climb in total (allow 2–3hr) from Moraine Lake, and you don't need to go much further than the rock pile and clump of trees beyond the lake to get the best out of the walk. Ahead of you, a slightly rougher track continues through bleak terrain to Wenkchemna Pass (2605m), clearly visible 4km beyond. Having got this far, it's tempting to push on; the extra 350-metre climb is just about worth it, if lungs and weather are holding out, for the still broader views back down the Valley of the Ten Peaks. The views beyond the pass itself, over the Great Divide into Yoho and Kootenay parks, are relatively disappointing.

Paradise Valley

In 1894, the mountaineer Walter Wilcox deemed **Paradise Valley** an appropriate name for "a valley of surpassing beauty, wide and beautiful, with alternating open meadows and rich forests". North of Moraine Lake, it's accessed via Moraine Lake Road about 3km from its junction with Lake Louise Drive. The walk here is a fairly straightforward hike up one side of the valley and down the other, a loop of 18km with 385m of vertical gain. Most people take in the Lake Annette diversion for its unmatched view of Mount Temple's 1200-metre north face, and many overnight at the campsite at the head of the valley (9km from the parking area), though this is one of the busiest sites in the park. Others toughen the walk by throwing in the climb up to Sentinel Pass on the ridge south of the valley, which gives the option of continuing down the other side to connect with the Moraine Lake trails.

Winter sports in and around Lake Louise

Lake Louise is regarded by many as among the finest winter resorts in North America. In addition to **skiing** and **snowboarding** there are hundreds of kilometres of **cross-country** trails, numerous other winter activities, stunning landscapes and some of the best "powder" on the continent. The only drawback is the phenomenally low temperatures during January and February.

Ski areas

The core of the Lake Louise ski area is the **Front Side** (sometimes called the South Face). Climbing from the base area, this is particularly attractive to beginners and intermediates, who will find all the best groomed green and blue runs here. Tucked behind the Front Side, the **Back Bowls** are very different; flecked with above-tree-line black diamonds, offering wide-open runs particularly rewarding for those prepared to hike. From the Back Bowls a long, fairly flat run-out leads to the base of the **Ptarmigan** and **Larch** area, and some of the mountain's best glade runs. Slopes here face in several directions allowing you to follow the sun, and trees can give shelter from winds, a combination that makes this the best area to zero in on when conditions are harsh.

The 4200-acre terrain divides as follows: Beginner (25 percent), Intermediate (45 percent) and Advanced (thirty percent) and sees an average annual snowfall of 360cm. The top elevation is 2637m, giving a 1000m drop to the base elevation at 1645m. Lift tickets are around $75.95 a day ($61.50 half-day) and $74 ($60) in peak holiday periods and key weekends. The Ski Banff/Lake Louise **Tri-Area Pass** is good for between three and twelve days' skiing in Lake Louise, Mount Norquay and Sunshine Village (see p.635); a three-day pass is $239, six days $479. Call ⓣ403/762-4561 or 1-800/661-1431, or visit Ⓦwww.skibig3.com for further information.

Facilities in the ski area include three day-lodges, each of which has a restaurant and bar, a ski school, ski shop, rental shop, day-care, nursery and lockers. Free shuttles run from Lake Louise, while transfers from Banff cost around $15 return: these are included free if you buy the Tri-Area Pass. Free tours of the mountain are also available three times daily.

Cross-country skiing in Lake Louise is phenomenal, with plenty of options around the lake itself, on Moraine Lake Road and in the Skoki Valley area north of the village. For **heli-skiing**, contact RK Heli-Ski (ⓣ403/342-3889, ⓦwww.rkheliski.com), which has a desk in the *Château Lake Louise* (winter daily 4–9pm); one of their shuttle buses leaves from the hotel daily for the two-hour drive to the Purcell Mountains in BC.

For further information on skiing in and around Lake Louise, visit the official website (ⓦwww.skilouise.com) or call ⓣ1-877/956-8473.

Other winter activities

The *Château* is also the hub for **ice-skating** and **sleigh rides**, while several tour operations also offer pick-ups here for **dog sled** or **snowmobiling** tours. Brewster Lake Louise Sleighrides (ⓣ403/762-5454 or 522-1898 ext 1210, ⓦwww.brewsteradventures.com) offers 45-minute rides that cost $28 per person; reservations are necessary. You can hire skates (from Monod Sports ⓣ403/522-3837; from $12 per day) for **ice-skating** on the floodlit lake, probably one of the most inspirational spots imaginable.

Kingmik Dog-Sled Tours (ⓣ403/763-8887 or 1-877/919-7779, ⓦwww.kingmikdogsledtours.com) runs **tours** – from 35-minute romps ($145) to multi-day adventures ($275–300/day) – while Wet 'n' Wild adventures in Golden (ⓣ250/344-6546 or 1-800/668-9119, ⓦwww.wetnwild.bc.ca) offers all-inclusive **snowmobiling** trips out of Lake Louise for $200 per person for half a day, $265 for a full day.

Eating and drinking

Excellent **snacks** and **coffee** can be had in Lake Louise Village at *Laggan's Mountain Bakery & Deli* (daily 6am–7pm) on the corner of the mall opposite the general store. For something more substantial, try the relaxed and reasonably priced *Bill Peyto's Café* for full and varied meals from around $10 (daily 7am–9pm; ⓣ403/522-2200), within the hostel but open to all; in summer the outdoor eating area is a good place to meet people. The unique *Lake Louise Station Restaurant* (ⓣ403/522-2600, ⓦwww.lakelouisestation.com) is housed in the restored 1909 station building; choose between hearty Canadian food in the informal station building and the more formal and expensive restored railway-dining carriages. Some of the best (and pricier) meals can be found in the *Post Hotel* (see p.645). Reckon on $30–50 for a three-course dinner, less at lunch, when there is a restricted menu; reservations are essential in the evening. The best locals' hangout is the same hotel's *Outpost Pub*, a snug **bar** serving light meals from late afternoon. Other good drinking spots include the *Lake Louise Bar and Grill* (ⓣ403/522-3879) upstairs in the mall, and the lively *Explorers Lounge* in the *Lake Louise Inn* (see p.644).

The Icefields Parkway

The splendour of the **Icefields Parkway** (Hwy 93) can hardly be overstated: a road 230km from Lake Louise to Jasper through the heart of the Rockies, it ranks as one of the world's best drives. Its unending succession of huge peaks, immense glaciers, iridescent lakes, wildflower meadows, wildlife and forests – capped by the stark grandeur of the Columbia Icefield – is absolutely overwhelming. Fur traders and natives who used the route as far back as 1800 reputedly christened it the "Wonder Trail", though in practice they tended to prefer the Pipestone River Valley to the east, a route that avoided the swamps and other hazards of the Bow Valley. The present hwy was only completed in 1939 and opened in 1940 as part of a Depression-era public-works programme. Although about a million people a year make the journey to experience what the park blurb calls a "window on the wilderness", for the most part you can go your own way in relative serenity.

After 122km, at about its midway point, the Icefields Parkway crosses from Banff into Jasper National Park (about a 2hr drive); you might turn back here, but the divide is almost completely arbitrary, and most people treat the Parkway as a self-contained journey, as we do here. Distances in brackets are from Lake Louise, which is virtually the only way to locate places on the road, though everything mentioned is clearly marked off the hwy by distinctive brown-green national park signs. Pick up the Parks Canada *In the Shadow of the Great Divide* pamphlet from visitor centres for a detailed map and summary of all the sights and trailheads.

You could drive the whole hwy in about four hours, but to do so would be to miss out on the panoply of short (and long) trails, viewpoints and the chance just to soak up the incredible scenery.

Access and transport

Tourist literature often misleadingly gives the impression that the Parkway is highly developed. In fact, the wilderness is extreme, with snow often closing the road from October onwards, and there are only two points for **services**, at Saskatchewan Crossing (the one place campers can stock up with groceries, 77km from Lake Louise), where the David Thompson Highway (Hwy 11) branches off for Red Deer, and at the Columbia Icefield (127km).

Brewster Transportation (Ⓣ403/762-6767, Ⓦwww.brewster.ca) runs several tours and a single scheduled bus daily in both directions between Banff or Lake Louise and Jasper from late May to mid-October ($76.19 one-way from Banff, $66.67 from Lake Louise), though services at either end of the season are often weather-affected. A word with the driver will usually get you dropped off at hostels and trailheads en route.

Accommodation

Three **hostels** and twelve excellent park **campsites** (two year-round) are spaced along the Parkway at regular intervals; we've given details of each in the account below. It's essential to book the hostels as far in advance as you can, either direct if they have contact details, through the hostel at Banff or online at Ⓦwww.hihostels.ca. The frontcountry park campsites are available on a first-come, first-served basis. If you want more comfort, you'll have to overnight at Banff, Lake Louise or Jasper, as the only other accommodation – invariably booked solid – is hotels at Bow Lake, Saskatchewan Crossing and the Columbia Icefield.

North from Lake Louise

One of the biggest problems in the Rockies is to know what to see and where to walk among the dozens of possible trails and viewpoints. The Parkway is no exception. We've picked out the must-sees and must-dos along the 122-kilometre stretch of the Parkway from Lake Louise to the Columbia Icefield: the best view is at Peyto Lake; the best lake walk is at Bow Lake; the best waterfalls are the Panther–Bridal Falls; the best quick stroll is at Mistaya Canyon; the best short walk is at Parker Ridge; and the best walk if you do no other is Wilcox Pass.

The first **hostel** north of Lake Louise is *Mosquito Creek Wilderness Hostel* (26km; ⓣ778/328-2220 or 1-866/762-4122, ⓦwww.hihostels.ca; dorm beds $20 for members, $23 July–Sept; nonmembers $24/$27; private doubles $58 for members, $60 July–Sept; nonmembers $66/$68; open year-round, but closure dates may apply). It's a minimalist set-up of four log cabins that sleep 32, a kitchen, large common room and a wood-fired sauna; there's no telephone, electricity or showers. Slightly beyond is the first park **campsite**, *Mosquito Creek* (24km; $17.60 but free after mid–Sept for winter camping; year-round). Its 32 sites have hand-pumped well water, fire rings and wood and dry toilets, but no other facilities and one of the Parkway's two winter campsites. You're near the Bow River flats here, and the mosquitoes, as the campsite name suggests, can be a torment.

Two hikes start from close to the site: **Molar Pass** (9.8km; 535m ascent; 3hr), a manageable day-trip with good views, and **Upper Fish Lake** (14.8km; 760m ascent; 5hr), which follows the Molar Pass trail for 7km before branching off and crossing the superb alpine meadows of North Molar Pass (2590m). On the *Num-Ti-Jah Lodge* (see below) access road just beyond (37km), a great short trail sets off from beside the lodge to **Bow Lake** and **Bow Glacier Falls** (4.3km; 155m ascent; 1–2hr), taking in the flats around Bow Lake – one of the Rockies' most beautiful – and climbing to some immense cliffs and several huge waterfalls beyond (the trail proper ends at the edge of the moraine after 3.4km, but it's possible to pick your way through the boulders to reach the foot of the falls 900m beyond). If you don't want to walk, take a break instead at the picnic area on the waterfront at the southeast end of the lake.

The *Num-Ti-Jah Lodge* (ⓣ403/522-2167, ⓦwww.num-ti-jah.com; ❻; May–Oct) itself, just off the road, is one of the most famous old-fashioned lodges in the Rockies, built in 1920 by legendary guide and outfitter Jimmy Simpson (who lived here until 1972); book well in advance. It's the only privately owned freehold in the park – all other land and property is federally owned and leased. There's a **coffee shop** here if you need a break, or want to admire the *Lodge*'s strange octagonal structure, forced on Simpson because he wanted a large building but only had access locally to short timbers. Only guests are allowed in the lodge, but you can have dinner here or sign up for **riding**; rides include a one-hour trip to Bow Lake, a three-hour ride to Peyto Lake (see below) and a full-day excursion to Helen Lake.

Peyto Lake and beyond

Another 3km up the Parkway comes the pass at Bow Summit, source of the Bow River, the waterway that flows through Banff, Lake Louise and Calgary. (At 2069m this is the highest point crossed by any Canadian hwy.) Just beyond is the unmissable twenty-minute stroll to **Peyto Lake Lookout** (1.4km; elevation loss 100m), one of the finest vistas in the Rockies (signed from the road). The beautiful panorama only unfolds in the last few seconds, giving a breathtaking view of the vivid emerald lake far below; mountains and forest stretch away as far as you can see. Another 3km along the Parkway lies a viewpoint for the Peyto Glacier, part of the much larger Wapta Icefield.

After 57km you reach the Waterfowl Lakes **campsite** (116 sites with water, flush toilets, kitchen shelter and food storage but no showers; $21.50; mid-June to mid-Sept) and the **Chephren Lake Trail** (3.5km; 80m ascent; 1hr), which leads to quietly spectacular scenery with a minimum of effort. The next pause, 14km further on, is the **Mistaya Canyon Trail**, a short but interesting 300m breather of a stroll along a river-gouged "slot" canyon.

Saskatchewan Crossing and beyond

SASKATCHEWAN CROSSING (77km) is the lowest point on the road before the icefields; the 700m descent from Bow Summit brings you from the high subalpine ecoregion into a montane environment with its own vegetation and wildlife. Largely free of snow, the area is a favourite winter range for mountain goats, bighorn sheep and members of the deer family. The bleak settlement itself offers expensive food (restaurant and cafeteria), petrol, a spectacularly tacky gift shop and a 66-room **hotel-restaurant**, *Crossing*, that is surprisingly comfortable (ⓣ403/761-7000, ⓦwww.thecrossingresort.com; ❻; early March to Oct).

Some 12km north is the *Rampart Creek Wilderness Hostel* (ⓣ1-866/762-4122, wwww.hihostels.ca; dorm beds $20 for members, $23 July–Sept; nonmembers $24/$27; fall and spring closures may apply). There are 24 beds in two cabins and the "best sauna in the Rockies". Apparently this area is one of the best black bear habitats close to the road anywhere in the park.

Shortly before the spectacular **Panther Falls** (113.5km) the road makes a huge hairpin climb (the so-called "Big Hill"), to open up yet more panoramic angles on the vast mountain spine stretching back towards Lake Louise. The unmarked and often slippery one-kilometre trail to the falls starts from the lower end of the second of two car parks on the right.

Beyond it (117km) is the trailhead to **Parker Ridge** (2.4km one-way; elevation gain 210m; allow 1hr one-way, less for the return), which, at 2130m, commands fantastic views from the summit ridge of the Saskatchewan Glacier (at 9km, the Rockies' longest). If you're only going to do one walk after the Peyto Lake Lookout, make it this one: it gets cold and windy up here, so bring extra clothing.

Nearby **Sunwapta Pass** (2023m) marks the border between Banff and Jasper national parks and the watershed of the North Saskatchewan and Sunwapta rivers: the former flows into the Atlantic, the latter into the Arctic Ocean. From here it's another 108km to Jasper.

The Columbia Icefield

Just beyond Sunwapta Pass and covering an area of 325 square kilometres, the **Columbia Icefield** is the largest collection of ice and snow in the entire Rockies, and the largest glacial area in the northern hemisphere outside the Arctic Circle. It's also the most accessible of some seventeen glacial areas along the Parkway. Meltwater flows from it into the Arctic, Atlantic and Pacific oceans, forming a so-called "hydrological apex" – the only other one in the world is in Siberia. This is fed by six major glaciers, three of which – the Athabasca, Dome and Stutfield – are partially visible from the hwy.

Arrival and information

The busy **Icefield Centre** (ⓣ1-877/423-7433 or Parks Canada 780/852-6288, ⓦwww.explorerockies.com; daily May to mid-Oct 9am–5pm) provides an eerie viewpoint for the most prominent of these, the Athabasca Glacier, as well as offering the Parks Canada Exhibit Hall and information and slide shows on the glaciers and Canada's most extensive cave system – the Castleguard Caves, which honeycomb the ice but are inaccessible to the public. This is not a place to linger, thanks to the crowds and tour buses.

Accommodation

The 32-room *Glacier View Inn* (ⓣ780/852-6550; ❽) provides good but much-sought-after **accommodation** in the Icefield Centre between May and mid-October (rooms cost $250 from mid-June to Sept but half that the rest of the year). Brewster bus services between Jasper and Banff stop here: it's possible to take a Banff-bound Brewster bus out of Jasper at lunchtime (arrives at the Icefield at 3pm), see the Icefield, and pick up the evening Jasper-bound bus (leaves Icefield at 6.30pm) later the same day.

Two unserviced but very popular **campsites** lie 2km and 3km south of the Icefield Centre, respectively: the tent-only 33-site Columbia Icefield ($15.70; mid-May to mid-Oct, or until the first snow) site, and the 46-site Wilcox Creek site, which takes tents and RVs ($15.70; early June to mid-Oct).

Hikes and tours on and around the Icefield

You can walk up to the toe of the **Athabasca Glacier** from the parking area at Sunwapta Lake, noting en route the date-markers, which illustrate just how far the glacier has retreated (1.5km in the last one hundred years). You can also walk onto the glacier, but shouldn't, as it's riddled with dangerous crevasses; people are killed and injured every year on the glacier. Full-scale expeditions are the preserve of experts but you can join an **organized trip**.

Brewster's special "Snocoaches" run ninety-minute, five-kilometre rides over the glacier with a chance to get out and walk safely on the ice (daily every 15min or 30min: April & Oct 10am–4pm, May & Sept 9am–5pm, June–Aug 9am–6pm; April & Oct opening depend on weather; $49; book tickets at the Centre or call ⓣ1-800/760-6934). They're heavily subscribed, so aim to avoid the peak midday rush by taking a tour before 10.30am or after 3pm.

More dedicated types can sign up for the two Athabasca Glacier ice walks (3hr "Ice Cubed" walk mid-June to early Sept daily at 11am, except Thurs & Sun, $60; 5hr "Icewalk Deluxe" Thurs & Sun 11am, $70), led by licensed guides. Sign up on the spot at the front desk of the Icefield Centre – be sure to bring warm clothes, boots and provisions. Call ⓣ1-800/565-7547 or visit ⓦwww.icewalks.com for more information.

The Wilcox Creek campsite (see above) is also the trailhead for one of the very finest **hikes** in the national park, never mind the hwy: the **Wilcox Pass Trail** (4km one-way; 335m ascent; allow 2hr round trip), highly recommended by the park centres and just about every trail guide going. The path takes you steeply through thick spruce and alpine fir forest before emerging suddenly onto a ridge that offers vast views over the Parkway and the high peaks of the icefield (including Mount Athabasca). Beyond, the trail enters a beautiful spread of meadows, tarns and creeks, an area many people choose to halt at or wander all day without bothering to reach the pass itself. You could extend the walk to 11km by dropping from the pass to Tangle Creek further along the parkway.

Beyond the Columbia Icefield

If there's a change **beyond the Columbia** Icefield, it's a barely quantifiable lapse in the scenery's awe-inspiring intensity over the 108-kilometre stretch towards Jasper. As the road begins a gradual descent the peaks retreat slightly, taking on more alpine and less dramatic profiles in the process. Yet the scenery is still magnificent, though by this point you're likely to be in the advanced stages of landscape fatigue. It's worth holding on for two good, short trails at Sunwapta and Athabasca falls. About 17km beyond the icefield is the fourteen-berth, two-cabin *Beauty Creek Wilderness Hostel* (ⓣ778/328-2220 or 1-866/762-4122, ⓦwww.hihostels.ca; members $20 Oct–June, $23 July–Sept; nonmembers $24/$27; partial closure possible Oct–April). Some 9km further is the unserviced 25-site Jonas Creek **campsite** ($15.70; mid-May to early Sept).

A one-kilometre gravel spur leads off the hwy to **Sunwapta Falls** (175km from Banff, 55km from Jasper), fifteen minutes' walk through the woods from the road: they're not terribly dramatic unless in spate, but are interesting for the deep canyon they've cut through the surrounding valley. A short trail along the riverbank leads to more rapids and small falls downstream. The 35-pitch Honeymoon Lake

campsite ($15.70; late June to early Sept), with kitchen shelter, swimming and dry toilets is 4km further along the Parkway.

The last main stop before you're in striking distance of Jasper Townsite, **Athabasca Falls** (30km from Jasper), is impressive enough but the platforms and paths show the strain caused by thousands of tramping feet, making it hard to feel you're any longer in wilderness. One kilometre away is the excellent *Athabasca Falls* **hostel** (Ⓣ780/852-5959, Ⓦwww.hihostels.ca; members $20 Oct–June, $23 July–Sept; nonmembers $24/27; open daily May–Oct, closed Tues Dec–April; additional closures may occur in winter months), with forty beds in three cabins. About 3km back down the road is the 42-site Mount Kerkeslin **campsite** ($15.70; late June to early Sept), with swimming, kitchen shelter and dry toilets, spread over a tranquil riverside tract.

Rafting in the Rockies

Whitewater rafting has become very popular in the national parks. There are many operators, notably in Jasper, Golden (near Yoho National Park) and Banff. Depending on the river and trip you choose, some rafting tours are gentle journeys; others require you to be fit and a strong swimmer. Trips last anything from a couple of hours to a couple of days. Often you can choose between trips – gentle or severe – where you sit back and hang on while others do the work, or you join a trip where everyone paddles.

No previous experience is required for most tours but the most important thing to know is how rivers are **graded**. White water is ranked in six classes: Class 1 is gentle and Class 6 is basically a waterfall. The **season** generally runs from May to mid-September, with the "biggest" water in June and July, when glacial meltwater is coursing down rivers. Operators are licensed by the park authorities and should supply you with everything you need, from the basics of helmet and life jacket to wet suits, wool sweaters and spray jackets. They also provide shuttle services from main centres to the rivers, and many on longer trips include lunch, snack or barbecue in the price. On any trip it's a good idea to have a change of clothes, wear training shoes (or something you don't mind getting wet), bring a towel and have a bag for valuables.

At Banff the **Bow River** has no major rapids, so gentle one-hour float trips are offered through pretty scenery by several operators. Most companies in Banff or Lake Louise offer trips on one of two rivers to the west of the park. The **Kootenay River** in Kootenay National Park, two hours from Banff, is a Class 2–3 river. The **Kicking Horse River**, just an hour from Banff, is a much more serious affair. In and just outside Yoho National Park, it has Class 4 sections (including one called "Man Eater Hole") in its upper sections and stretches in the Lower Kicking Horse Canyon which give even seasoned rafters pause for thought.

At **Jasper**, the Class 2 **Athabasca River** (from Athabasca Falls, 35km south of the town) is scenic and provides gentle rafting for families or those who just want a quiet river trip from May to October. It also has one or two harmless whitewater sections. The **Sunwapta River**, 55km south of Jasper, is a Class 3 river with some thrilling stretches of water, magnificent scenery and good chances to spot wildlife. The **Maligne River**, 45km from town, is Class 2–3+ (including a lively 1.6-kilometre stretch of rapids) and the many operators who use it offer a wide variety of trips from July to September. The **Fraser River**, an hour west of Jasper in Mount Robson Provincial Park, is Class 4 in places but also has some gentle sections where the chance to watch salmon spawning at close quarters from mid-August to September provides an added attraction.

Operators in Jasper offer a wide range of trips for all ages and abilities; see p.668 for trip details and pricing.

Highway 93A, the route of the old Parkway, branches off the Icefields Parkway at Athabasca Falls and runs parallel to it for 30km. This alternative route has less dramatic views than the Parkway, as dense trees line the road, but the chances of spotting wildlife are higher.

Jasper National Park

Although traditionally viewed as the second-ranking of the Rockies' big-four parks after Banff, **JASPER NATIONAL PARK** covers an area greater than Banff, Yoho and Kootenay combined, and looks and feels far wilder and less commercialized than its southern counterparts. Its backcountry is more extensive and less travelled, and **Jasper Townsite** (or Jasper), the only settlement, is more relaxed and far less of a resort than Banff and has just half its population. Most pursuits centre on Jasper and the **Maligne Lake** area about 50km southeast of the townsite. Other key zones are **Maligne Canyon**, on the way to the lake; the Icefields Parkway (covered on pp.652–658); and the **Miette Hot Springs** region, an area well to the east of Jasper and visited for its springs and trails.

The park's **backcountry** is a vast hinterland scattered with countless rough campsites and a thousand-kilometre trail system considered among the best in the world for backpackers. Opportunities for day and half-day-hikes are more limited and scattered than in other parks. Most of the shorter strolls from the townsite are just low-level walks to forest-circled lakes; the best of the more exciting day-hikes start from more remote points off the Maligne Lake road, Icefields Parkway (Hwy 93) and Yellowhead Hwy (Hwy 16).

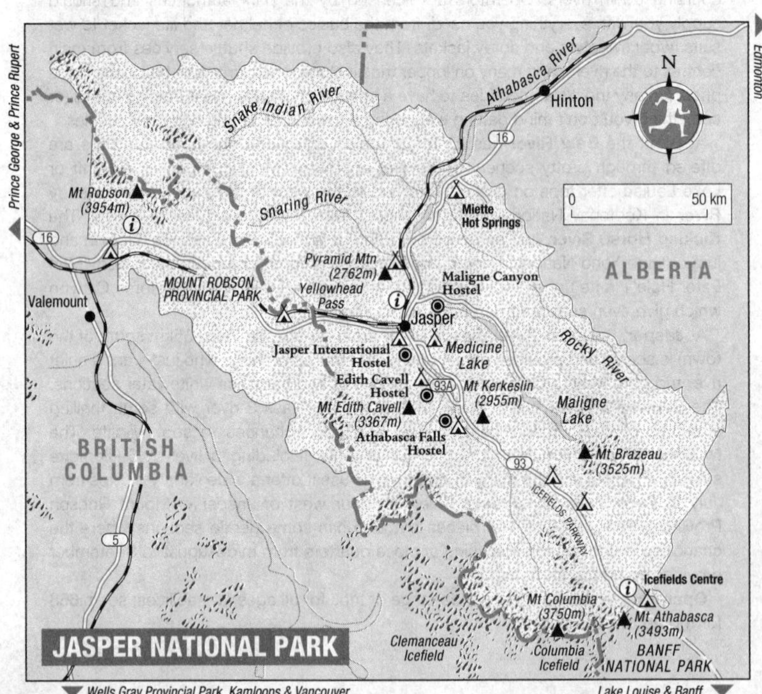

A history of the park

Permanent settlement first came to the Jasper area in the winter of 1810–11. The great explorer and trader David Thompson left **William Henry** at Old Fire Point (just outside the present townsite), while he and his companions pushed on up the valley to blaze a trail over the Athabasca Pass that would be used for more than fifty years by traders crossing the Rockies. In the meantime, Henry established **Henry House**, the first permanent European habitation in the Rockies (though its exact location has been lost). In 1813 the North West Company established Jasper House at the eastern edge of the park's present boundary. Named after Jasper Hawes, a long-time company clerk there, it moved closer to Jasper Lake in 1829. By 1884, and the collapse of the fur trade, the post had closed. By 1900, the entire region boasted just seven homesteads.

Jasper traces its real origins to the coming of the railway in the late nineteenth century. The Canadian Pacific had made Banff and Yoho boom in 1885 when it spurned a route through the Jasper region in favour of a more southerly route. The **Grand Trunk Pacific Railway** hoped for similar successes in attracting visitors when it started to push its own route west in 1902, and the Jasper Forest Park was duly created in 1908.

By 1911 a tent city known as **Fitzhugh**, named after the company's vice president, had grown up on Jasper's present site, and the name "Jasper" was adopted when the site was officially surveyed. Incredibly, a second railway, the **Canadian Northern Railway** (CNR), was completed almost parallel to the Grand Trunk line in 1913, the tracks at some points running no more than a few metres apart. Within just three years, the line's redundancy became obvious, consolidation took place west of Edmonton, and Jasper became a centre of operations for the lines in 1924, greatly boosting its importance and population.

The first road link from Edmonton was completed in 1928 and official national-park designation came in 1930.

Jasper townsite

JASPER's small-town feel comes as a relief after the razzmatazz of Banff: its streets still have the windswept, open look of a frontier town and, though the mountains don't ring with quite the same majesty as Banff, you'll probably feel the town better suits its wild surroundings. Situated at the confluence of the Miette and Athabasca rivers, its core centres around just two streets: **Connaught Drive**, which contains the bus and train terminal, restaurants, motels and park information centre, and – a block to the west – the parallel **Patricia Steet**, lined with more shops, restaurants and the odd hotel.

Arrival and information

Jasper's strength is its ease of access from Edmonton, with plenty of **transport** options and approaches, as well as a wide range of onward destinations. Driving time from Edmonton (362km) or Banff (287km) is around four hours; from Kamloops (443km) and Calgary (414km) it's five or six hours; from Vancouver (863km) nine or ten hours.

Greyhound (Ⓣ780/852-3926 or 1-800/661-8747, Ⓦwww.greyhound.ca) runs four **buses** daily from Edmonton (5hr; $60.65 one-way) along the Yellowhead Hwy (Hwy 16), plus onward services (2–4 daily) to Kamloops (5hr; $64) and Vancouver (11hr 30min; $126) via scenic Hwy 5 and Prince George (2–4 daily; $64). Brewster Transportation (Ⓣ780/852-3332 or 1-800/661-1152, Ⓦwww.brewster.ca) operates services to Banff (4hr 45min; $76.19) via Lake Louise (3hr 45min; $66.67) and continuing to Calgary and Calgary Airport (1 daily; 8hr 40min; $127), and also runs day-trip tours to Banff, taking in sights on the Icefields

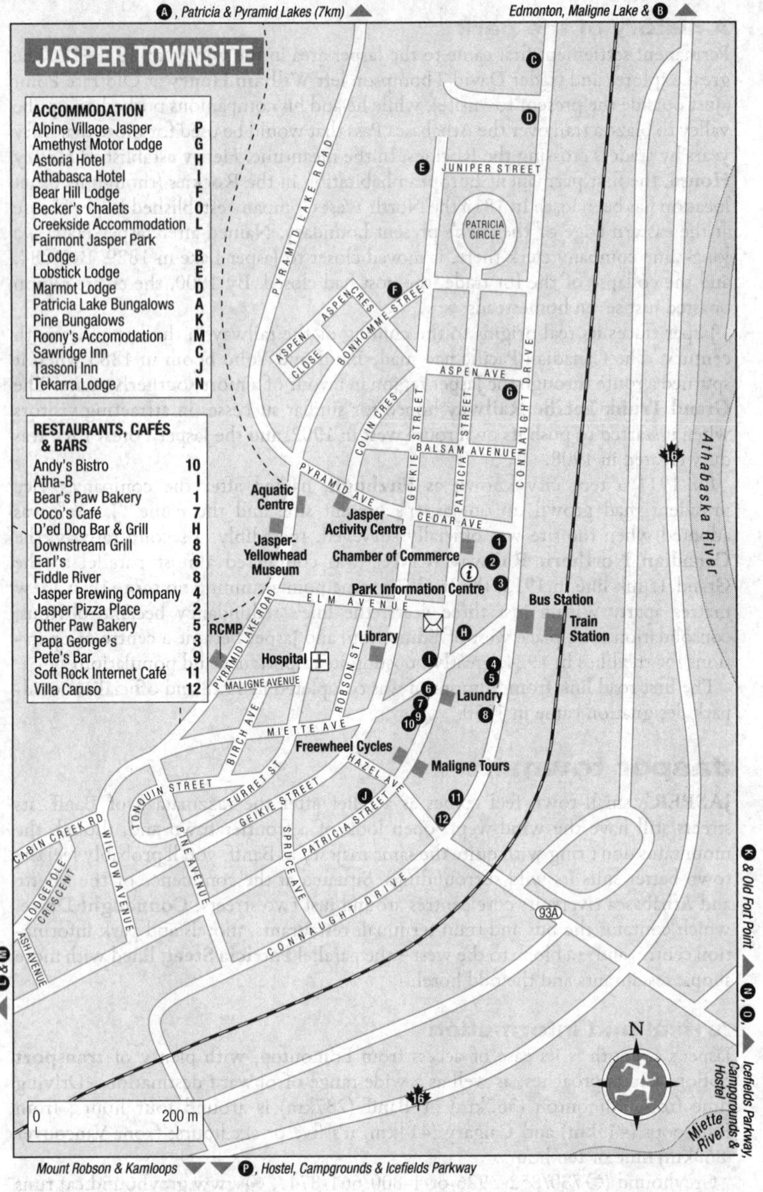

Parkway; weather can play havoc with Brewster's schedules in October and April. Both companies share the same **bus station**, located in the train station building at 607 Connaught Drive.

VIA Rail **trains** operate to Jasper from Winnipeg and Edmonton and continue to Vancouver (via Kamloops) or Prince Rupert (via Prince George). This is the only scheduled rail route through the Rockies, so summer places are hard to come by, but at other times there's little need to book a seat. Fares are considerably more – and journey times longer – than those of equivalent buses. The **ticket office** is open on train days only (Ⓣ780/852-4102 or 1-888/VIA-RAIL, Ⓦwww.viarail.ca).

Jasper's superb national park **visitor centre** (daily Nov to early April 9am–4pm early April to mid-June & Oct 9am–5pm, mid-June to Aug 8.30am–7pm, Sept 9am–6pm; Ⓣ780/852-6176) is at 500 Connaught Drive, 50m east of the bus station, back from the road on the left in the open grassy area. This is for park-related and campsite information only, and sells compulsory **national park permits** ($9.80 daily) and backcountry wilderness permits ($9.80), and lets you register for backpacking trails.

The centre also has a shop (good for **maps**) run by the Friends of Jasper (Ⓣ780/852-4767, Ⓦwww.friendsofjasper.com), who offer **guided walks** and other summer activities. For information on the town of Jasper, contact the Jasper Chamber of Commerce (June to early Sept daily 9am–7pm; rest of year Mon–Fri 9am–5pm; Ⓣ780/852-3858, Ⓦwww.jaspercanadianrockies.com) at 409 Patricia St, behind the park office.

Accommodation

Beds in Jasper are not as expensive or elusive as in Banff, but hotel rooms are still almost unobtainable in late July and August. Ask at the Chamber of Commerce for the *Private Home Accommodation List* or go to Ⓦwww.stayinjasper.com; Jasper has rooms in around 120 **private homes**, from $75–150 for a double.

Most **motels** are spaced out along Connaught Drive on the eastern edge of town; prices drop sharply off-season. An often cheaper and in many ways more pleasant option is to plump for motels made up of collections of **cabins**; most are within a few kilometres of town. The four park-run **campsites** close to the townsite and the three local hostels all fill up promptly in summer. You can make reservations for Whistlers, Pocahontas and Wapiti (Ⓣ1-877/737-3783, Ⓦwww.pccamping.ca) – but don't forget the hostels and campsites strung along the Icefields Parkway.

Hotels, motels and chalets

Alpine Village 2.5km south of town on Hwy 93A Ⓣ780/852-3285, Ⓦwww.alpinevillagejasper.com. An assortment of 41 serene one- and two-room cabins, including twelve deluxe cabins and lodge suites, most with great mountain views, and some with wood-burning fireplaces. There's also a big, outdoor hotpool. May to early Oct. ❼

Amethyst Motor Lodge 200 Connaught Drive Ⓣ780/852-3394 or 1-888/852-7737, Ⓦwww.mtn-park-lodges.com. Within easy walking distance of downtown this workaday 97-room motel is devoid of alpine pretensions. Most rooms have balconies or a patio and there are two outdoor jacuzzis. ❼

Astoria Hotel 404 Connaught Drive Ⓣ780/852-3351 or 1-800/661-7343, Ⓦwww.astoriahotel.com. Downtown Alpine-look hotel, family owned and run since 1920s, with mini fridges in all its fairly basic rooms, the bulk of which have mountain views. ❼

Athabasca Hotel 510 Patricia St Ⓣ780/852-3386 or 1-877/542-8422, Ⓦwww.athabascahotel.com. Despite the grand lobby dotted with the disembodied heads of wild animals, rooms (some without private bathroom) are very plain, functional and cramped – but the downtown location is fantastic. Try to get a room higher up in the building if the din of the hotel's lounge bar is likely to disturb. ❻

Bear Hill Lodge 100 Bonhomme St Ⓣ780/852-3209, Ⓦwww.bearhilllodge.com. Thirty-nine simple but comfortable bungalows, suites, chalet and lodge units on the northwest edge of the townsite in a pleasant wooded setting (wildlife sometimes wanders through). There's a lovely spa with jacuzzi and sauna, too. ❻

Becker's Chalets 5km south of Jasper on Hwy 93 Ⓣ780/852-3779, Ⓦwww.beckerschalets.com. Ninety-six of the best local one-, two-, three- and four-bedroom log cabins, most with wood-burning stoves or fireplaces and full kitchens or kitchenettes. May to mid-Oct. ❻

Fairmont Jasper Park Lodge Lac Beauvert Ⓣ780/852-3301 UK 1-800/441-1414, Ⓦwww.fairmont.com/jasper. Reminiscent of a summer camp, this collection of luxurious log cabins blends in well with its surroundings on the secluded shores of Lac Beauvert 6km northeast of Jasper. The vast main lodge is replete with large lounges, several restaurants, an outdoor heated pool, on-site spa and an underground mall. 8

Lobstick Lodge 94 Geikie St ⓣ780/852-4431 or 1-888/852-7737, ⓦwww.mtn-park-lodges.com. Arguably the pick of the east end motels, with large, simply furnished and clean rooms – try to avoid the dingy basement; some rooms have kitchenettes. There's also an indoor pool and three outdoor jacuzzis. 7

Marmot Lodge 86 Connaught Drive ⓣ780/852-4471 or 1-888/852-7737, ⓦwww.mtn-park-lodges.com. Cheapest motel in town and one of the biggest; spreading over three separate buildings. Rooms, all decorated with aboriginal peoples items, range dramatically in size, and some units have kitchens, fireplaces and fine mountain views. Communal amenities include a hot tub and sauna. 7

Patricia Lake Bungalows 5km northwest of downtown on Pyramid Lake Rd ⓣ780/852-3560 or 1-888/499-6848, ⓦwww.patricialakebungalows.com. This complex of cabins, cottages and bungalows makes for a pleasant out-of-town base. Some of the 38 units have fine views over Patricia Lake, and several come equipped with kitchens. There are more secluded (and expensive) options, all with full kitchens and fireplaces, alongside the main complex at *The Grove* (8). Fishing, boat, canoe and paddle boat rentals are available. May to mid-Oct. 6

Pine Bungalows 2km east of Jasper on the Athabasca River at 2 Cottonwood Creek ⓣ780/852-3491, ⓦwww.pinebungalows.com. The 72 wooden cabins here sleep two–six people and have no telephones or TVs, so make the most of the peaceful forested and riverside setting. Most of the cabins have kitchens and 41 of them come with fireplaces; there are also motel-style rooms available. Open May to mid-Oct. 7

Sawridge Inn 82 Connaught Drive ⓣ780/852-6590 or 1-888/729-7343, ⓦwww.sawridgejasper.com. Plush and expensive hotel on the eastern edge of town. Some rooms look onto an atrium, while others have balconies to take advantage of the exterior views. There's also an on-site day spa. 7

Tekarra Lodge 1km south of town on the Athabasca River off Hwy 93A. ⓣ780/852-3058 or 1-800/709-1827, ⓦwww.tekarralodge.com. Forty-two quiet, wooden cabins, all with hardwood floors, stone fireplaces and fully-equipped kitchens; B&B rooms also available. Open May–Oct. 6

B&Bs

Aspen Lodge 8 Aspen Crescent ⓣ780/852-5908, ⓔaspnlodg@telusplanet.net. A self-contained one-bedroom suite with two bathroms and a kitchen area, located on a quiet street about a 10-minute walk from downtown. Best suited to a couple or small family. 4

B&G Accommodation 204 Colin Crescent ⓣ780/852-4345, ⓦwww.explorejasper.com. Three well-priced rooms with shared bathroom and a private entrance three blocks from downtown. 2

Creekside Accommodation 1232 Patricia Crescent ⓣ780/852-3530, ⓦwww.creeksideaccommodation.com. Two bright, clean rooms with private or shared bath, on the southwest edge of town near Cabin Creek and very close to Pyramid Mountain hiking trails. 3

Roony's Accommodation 1114 Patricia Crescent ⓣ780/852-4101 or 5907, ⓦwww.roonys.com. Just out of the town centre comprising two nice rooms that can sleep a total of six, with and without private baths. 3

Tassoni Inn 706 Patricia St ⓣ780/852-3427, ⓦwww.visit-jasper.com/TassoniInn.html. Two bright and newly renovated rooms less than a block from the town centre, each with two double beds and a private bathroom. Guests can make use of the patio and have access to free wi-fi. 4

Hostels

Jasper International Hostel 1 Skytram Rd, 7km south of town via Hwy 93 ⓣ780/852-3205 or 1-866/762-4122, ⓦwww.hihostels.ca. Large, sterile and highly institutional hostel, the biggest of three in the vicinity of Jasper. The 4km uphill walk from Hwy 93 is a killer, but shuttles and taxis ($15) run from downtown. Dorms $20–26 for members, $24–30 for nonmembers. Private doubles $58–63 ($66–71). It has all the usual hostel facilities, plus free wi-fi and a library. The 84 beds fill up quickly in summer, so arrive early or book.

Maligne Canyon Hostel Maligne Lake Rd, 11km east of town ⓣ778/328-2220 or 1-866/762-4122, ⓦwww.hihostels.ca. Two cabins in lovely setting with beds for 24 in six-bed rooms; there's no running water, showers or flush toilets, but purified water is available for cooking. The Maligne Lake Shuttle from downtown or Alberta Hostel Shuttle drop off here daily in summer. Dorms $20–23 for members, $24–27 for nonmembers. Open all day, year-round but may have closures in winter.

Mount Edith Cavell Hostel Edith Cavell Rd, 13km off Hwy 93A, 23km south of town ⓣ778/328-2220 or 1-866/762-4122, ⓦwww.hihostels.ca. Cosier than the *Jasper International*, close to trails and with great views of the Angel Glacier. Sleeps 32 in two cabins and has an outdoor wood-burning sauna. Dorms $20–23 for members, $24–27 for nonmembers. Private doubles $58–60 for members, $66–80 for nonmembers. Open mid-June to mid-Oct; 12km ski-in only in winter.

Campsites

Pocahontas 45km east of Jasper, 1km off Hwy 16 on Miette Rd. One of two to the northeast of Jasper on this road. It has 130 pitches, hot and cold water and flush toilets but no showers. Open mid-May to mid-Oct; $21.50.

Snaring River 13km east of Jasper on Hwy 16. Simple 66-site park-run facility, with tap water, kitchen shelter, dry toilets only and no showers. Open mid-May to early Sept; $15.70.

Wabasso 16.5km south of Jasper on Hwy 93A. A 228-pitch riverside park-run site with flush toilets, hot water but no showers. Wheelchair-accessible. Open mid-June to early Sept; $21.50.

Wapiti 5.4km south of Jasper and 2km south of *Whistlers* (see below) on Hwy 93. Big 362-pitch park-run place with flush toilets and coin showers that accepts tents but also caters for up to forty RVs. Ninety sites remain open for winter camping from Oct. Wheelchair-accessible. Open year-round; summer $27.40; winter (with water and flush toilets) $17.60.

Whistlers 3.5km south of Jasper just west off Hwy 93. Jasper's main 704-site park-run campsite is the largest in the Rockies, with three sections, and prices depending on facilities included. Brewster buses usually stop here if you ask and taxis and shuttles run from Jasper. Wheelchair-accessible. Open early May to early Oct; tents $27.40, RVs $38.20.

The town and around

Apart from the **Yellowhead Museum & Archives** (mid-May to early Sept daily 10am–5pm; early Sept to Oct Thurs–Sun 10am–5pm; Ⓦwww.jaspermuseum.org; $5), at 400 Pyramid Rd, with its fur trade and railroad displays and a cable car, nothing here even pretends to be a tourist attraction; this is a place to sleep, eat and stock up. If you want to know a little more about the town or park from the locals, contact the Friends of Jasper National Park (Ⓣ780/852-4767, Ⓦwww.friendsofjasper.com), which offers guided walks between July and August, or pick up *Jasper: A Walk in the Past* , by Merna Foster, from local bookshops. A lot of people head 58km northeast of town for a dip in Miette Hot Springs (see p.667).

Jasper Tramway

With little on offer in town you need to use a bike, car or the shuttle services to get anything out of the area. The obvious trip is on Canada's longest and highest cable car, the **Jasper Tramway** (daily April to mid-May and late Aug to early Oct 10am–5pm; mid-May to late June 9.30am–6.30pm; late June to late Aug 9am–8pm; $29; Ⓣ780/852-3093, Ⓦwww.jaspertramway.com), 7km south of town on Whistlers Mountain Road, off the Icefields Parkway. In peak season you may have a long wait in line for the 2.5-kilometre ride, whose two thirty-person cars take seven minutes to make the 1000m ascent. It drops you at an interpretive centre, expensive restaurant and an excellent viewpoint (2285m) where you can take your bearings on much of the park. A steep trail ploughs upwards and onwards to the Whistlers summit (2470m), an hour's walk that requires warm clothes year-round and reveals even more stunning views. A tough but rather redundant 10km trail follows the route of the tramway from *Jasper International Hostel*.

Maligne Lake Road

Bumper to bumper with cars, campers and tour buses in the summer, the **Maligne Lake Road** runs east from Jasper for 48km, taking in a number of beautiful but rather busy and overdeveloped sights before reaching the sublime Maligne Lake (pronounced *ma-leen*). If you have time to spare, and the transport, you could set aside a day for the trip, whitewater raft the Maligne River or walk one of the trails above Maligne Lake itself.

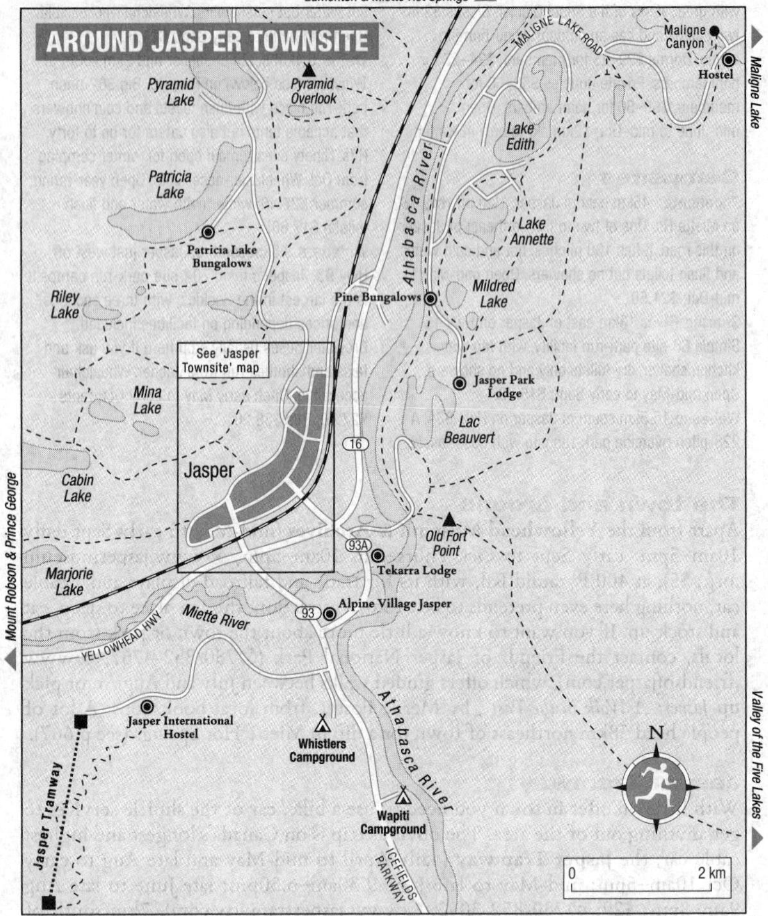

Maligne Tours (Ⓣ780/852-3370 or 1-866/625-4463, Ⓦwww.malignelake.com), at 627 Patricia St, runs a **bus**, the Maligne Lake Shuttle (Ⓦwww.malignelakeshuttle.com), to the lake eight times daily ($20 one-way, $40 return), with drop-offs (if booked) at *Maligne Canyon* hostel and the northern and southern ends of the Skyline Trail, one of the park's three top backpacking trails (see p.666). Joint tickets are offered for the shuttle and other activities organized by the company, notably the cruises (see p.668), raft trips and horse rides on and around Maligne Lake.

The often rather crowded **Maligne Canyon** is 11km out of Jasper, with an oversized car park and a tacky café/souvenir shop. This heavily sold excursion promises one of the Rockies' most spectacular gorges: in fact the canyon is deep (50m), but almost narrow enough to jump across – many people have tried and most have died in the attempt. In the end the geology is more interesting than the scenery; the violent erosive forces that created the canyon are explained on the main trail loop, an easy twenty-minute amble that can be extended to 45 minutes (few people do this, so the latter part of the trail is often quiet), or even turned into a hike back to Jasper. In winter, licensed guides lead tours (more like crawls) through the frozen canyon.

Next stop is picture-perfect **Medicine Lake**, 32km from Jasper, which experiences intriguing fluctuations in level. Its waters have no surface outlet; instead the lake fills and empties through lake-bed sink holes into the world's largest system of limestone caves. They re-emerge some 17km away towards Jasper (and may also feed some of the lakes around Jasper Townsite). When the springs freeze in winter, the lake drains and sometimes disappears altogether, only to be replenished in the spring. The lake's strange behaviour captivated local natives, who believed spirits were responsible, hence the name. Few people spend much time here, preferring to press on to Maligne Lake, so it makes a quietish spot to escape the headlong rush down the road.

Maligne Lake

At the end of Maligne Lake Road is the stunning **Maligne Lake**, 22km long and 92m deep, and surrounded by snow-covered mountains. The largest lake in the Rockies, its name comes from the French for "wicked", and was coined in 1846 by a Jesuit missionary, Father de Smet, in memory of the difficulty he had crossing the **Maligne River** downstream. The road peters out at a warden station, three car parks and a restaurant flanked by a picnic area and the start of the short, self-explanatory Lake Trail along the lake's east side to the Schäffer Viewpoint (3.2km loop; begin from Car Park 2).

A small waterfront area is equipped with berths for glass-enclosed boats that run ninety-minute narrated **cruises** on the lake to Spirit Island: the views are sensational. Maligne Tours (see opposite) at 627 Patricia St in Jasper, books ninety-minute boat tours on the lake (daily hourly on the hour: first ice-free period to early June 10am–3pm; early June to late June & Sept to early Oct 10am–4pm; July–Aug 10am–5pm; $55). The boats are small and reservations are vital during peak times, especially as tour companies often block-book entire sailings. The same company also rents canoeing, fishing, boating and any other equipment you may need; rental reservations are also essential in summer.

▲ Kayakers on Maligne Lake, Jasper National Park

There are no **accommodation** or camping facilities here, but two backcountry campsites on the lakeshore can be reached by canoe; get details from Jasper's information centre.

Hiking in Jasper National Park

The range of hiking trails on offer in and around Jasper is vast, far more than we can outline here, though we've sketched out some ideas below; at a glance, the best stroll is Maligne Canyon; the best short walk is Wilcox Pass; the best easy day-hike is Cavell Meadows; the best moderate day-hike is Opal Hills; the best strenuous day-hike is Sulphur Skyline; and the best backpacking trail is the Skyline Trail.

Hikes close to town

A winding road heads 5km north from Jasper to **Patricia** and **Pyramid lakes**, pretty moraine-dammed lakes full of rental facilities for riding, boating, canoeing, windsurfing and sailing. Short **trails**, generally accessible from the approach road, include the Patricia Lake Circle, a 4.8-kilometre loop by the Cottonwood slough and creek offering good opportunities for seeing birds and beavers during early morning and late evening. The island on Pyramid Lake, connected by a bridge to the shore, is an especially popular destination for a day out: continue on the lake road to the end of the lake and you'll find everything a little quieter.

Slightly closer to town on the east side of the Athabasca River, **Lake Edith** and **Lake Annette** are the remains of a larger lake that once extended across the valley floor. Both are similarly busy day-use areas. Their waters are the warmest in the park, thanks to the lakes' shallow depth. In summer you can lie out on sandy beaches or grassy areas. A clutch of picnic sites are the only development, and the wheelchair-accessible Lee Foundation Trail meanders around Lake Annette (2.4km).

Few other hikes from town are spectacular, but the best of the bunch, the **Old Fort Point Loop** (6.5km round trip), is recommended. Despite the trailhead being just thirty minutes' walk out of town, it's remarkably scenic, with panoramic views and lots of quiet corners. To reach the trailhead (1.6km from town) use the Old Fort Exit, following Hwy 93A across the railway and Hwy 16 until you come to the Old Fort Point–Lac Beauvert turn-off, then turn left and follow the road to the car park beyond the bridge. The Valley of the Five Lakes Trail (4.6km) is also good, but the path starts 10km south of town off the Icefields Parkway. For full details of all park walks, ask at the information centre for the free *Day-hiker's Guide to Jasper*.

Half and full-day hikes

If you haven't travelled to Jasper on the Icefields Parkway (see pp.652–658), remember several of the national park's top trails can be accessed from this road, including the **Wilcox Pass Trail**, one of the finest half-day-hikes anywhere in the Rockies.

If you're at Maligne Lake and want a longer walk, one of Jasper's best day-hikes, the **Opal Hills Circuit** (8.2km round trip; 460m vertical ascent), starts from the picnic area to the left of the uppermost Maligne Lake car park, 48km east of Jasper. After a heart-pumping haul up the first steep slopes, the trail negotiates alpine meadows and offers sweeping views of the lake before reaching an elevation of 2160m; the trip takes about four hours, but you could easily spend all day loafing around the meadows.

The **Bald Hills Trail** (5.2km one-way; 480m ascent) starts with a monotonous plod along a fire road from the same car park, but ends with excellent views; allow four hours for the round trip, which goes as high as 2170m.

To get to the trailhead for another outstanding day-hike, **Cavell Meadows** (3.8km one-way; 370m ascent) – named after a British nurse who was executed for helping the Allies during World War I – drive, cycle or taxi 7.5km south on the Icefields Parkway, then 5km along Hwy 93A and finally 14km up Mount Edith Cavell Road; there's a daily shuttle bus from Jasper and it takes bikes so you can ride back down. If you're driving, an alternating one-way system has been instigated to reduce traffic flow up Mount Edith Cavell Road every day from 10am to 9.30pm between mid-June and mid-October; contact the park information centre for latest timings. The walk's scenery is mixed and magnificent – but the hike is popular, so don't expect solitude. As well as Cavell's alpine meadows, there are views of Angel Glacier and the dizzying north wall of Mount Edith Cavell. Allow two hours for the round trip; the maximum elevation reached is a breathless 2135m.

Further afield – you'll need transport – another superlative short, sharp walk starts from Miette Hot Springs, 58km northeast of Jasper. The **Sulphur Skyline** (4km one-way; 700m ascent) offers exceptional views of knife-edged ridges, deep gorges, crags and remote valleys. Take water with you and allow two hours each way for the steep climb to 2070m. The trailhead is signed from the Miette Hot Springs complex, reached from Jasper by heading 41km east on Hwy 16 and then 17km south; in the past the shuttles have made the trip in summer – check with the visitor centre. The **springs** (mid-June to early Sept daily 8.30am–10.30pm, mid-May to mid-June and early Sept to mid-Oct daily 10.30am–9pm, \$6.05 or \$8.55 day-pass; ⓣ780/866-3939 or 1-800/767-1611, ⓦwww.hotsprings.ca) themselves are the hottest in the Rockies and have to be cooled for swimming; there's one pool for soaking, another for swimming, with massages by appointment and not included in the pass price. You can rent bathing suits, towels and lockers for an extra \$4–6. Other trails from the springs make for the **Fiddle River** (4.3km one-way; 275m ascent) and **Mystery Lake** (10.5km one-way; 475m ascent).

Backpacking trails

Jasper's system of **backpacking trails** and 111 backcountry campsites makes it one of the leading areas for backcountry hiking in North America. To stay overnight in the backcountry, pick up a wilderness permit (\$9.80) within 24 hours of your departure from the park information centre in Jasper Townsite or at the Columbia Icefield. All trails and campsites operate quota systems; contact the park information office for details and book yourself a backcountry campsite(s) – and thus trail place – as soon as you can. Reservations cost \$11.70. Trails remain busy even into September: the busiest are Skyline, Maligne Lake, Brazeau and Tonquin Valley.

The office staff offer invaluable advice, and issue excellent low-price strip maps of several trails. Overnight hikes are beyond the scope of this book – talk to staff or get hold of a copy of *The Canadian Rockies Trail Guide* – but by general consent the finest long-distance trails are the **Skyline** (44km; 820m ascent) and **Jonas Pass** (19km; 555m ascent), with the latter often combined with the **Nigel** and **Poboktan** passes (total 36km; 750m ascent) to make a truly outstanding walk. Not far behind come two hikes in the Tonquin Valley – **Astoria River** (19km; 445m ascent) and **Maccarib Pass** (21km; 730m ascent) – and the **Fryat Valley** (3–4 days). Others to consider are Maligne Pass and the long-distance North and South Boundary trails (the latter both over 160km).

Winter sports in and around Jasper

The park has plenty of winter activities and a first-rate ski area in **Marmot Basin** (early Dec to late April; ⓣ780/852-3816, ⓦwww.skimarmot.com), a

Other Jasper activities

There are a number of tour operators in Jasper that offer trips and tours for everything from fishing to guided hikes and walks.

Sundog Tours, 414 Connaught Drive (ⓣ780/852-4056 or 1-888/786-3641, ⓦwww.sundogtours.com), runs its own tours and acts as a one-stop booking agent for a huge range of others, including seeing the park and Icefields by **helicopter** (from $149), train (5hr from $95), guided nature hikes (3hr locally $49, 6hr on Mount Edith Cavell Meadows $69) or whitewater rafting ($55 and up). Maligne Tours, 616 Patricia St (ⓣ780/852-3370, ⓦwww.malignelake.com), offers **boat cruises** on Maligne Lake, guided hiking and fishing trips, canoe rentals and rafting excursions.

If you need to **rent outdoor equipment**, the best bet is On-Line Sport & Tackle, 600 Patricia St (ⓣ780/852-3630), or the Totem Ski Shop, 408 Connaught Drive (ⓣ780/852-3078 or 1-800/363-3078, ⓦwww.totemskishop.com).

Biking and camping

You can **rent bikes** in town from On-Line Sport & Tackle ($10/hr, $25/3hr, $40/day) or from Freewheel Cycles, 618 Patricia St (same rates; ⓣ780/852-3898, ⓦwww.freewheeljasper.com). At the latter, drop in and ask for their *Mountain Biking Trail Guide*. Out of town you can rent bikes at the *Jasper International Hostel*; at the *Fairmont Jasper Park Lodge* on the shore of Lac Beauvert; and at *Patricia Lake Bungalows*, 4.8km northwest of town on Pyramid Lake Rd. To rent **camping equipment** (plus bikes and fishing tackle) make for Source for Sports, 406 Patricia St (ⓣ780/852-3654, ⓦwww.jaspersports.com). A three-person tent costs $15/day.

Fishing and riding

For **fishing** tours, information and advice, try Maligne Tours or On-Line Sport & Tackle (see above), along with Currie's Guiding, 414 Connaught Drive (ⓣ780/852-5650, ⓦwww.curriesguidingjasper.com).

Riding enthusiasts should contact Pyramid Stables, 4km from Jasper on Pyramid Lake Road (ⓣ780/852-3562), who run day-treks and one-, two- and four-hour trips (from $39/65/120; full-day rides from $130) around Patricia and Pyramid lakes. Ridgeline Riders at Maligne Tours (see above) and Skyline Trail Rides (ⓣ780/852-4215 or 1-888/852-7787, ⓦwww.skylinetrail.com) at *Jasper Park Lodge* also organize rides.

twenty-minute drive from the townsite, and a resort that has the advantages of cheaper skiing and far less crowded runs than its Banff rivals. Scenically it's every bit as spectacular, and the quality of the snow is superb; it's best for intermediate skiers and riders. Eight lifts serve 1500 acres of terrain with a vertical drop of 700m and a choice of 75 trails. Lift passes cost $66.62 per day ($47.62 in January) and equipment rental is available at the resort. Daily shuttle buses head here from downtown hotels; for local taxis call Jasper Taxi ⓣ780/852-3600 or Heritage Cabs ⓣ780/852-5558.

Jasper's range and quality of **cross-country skiing** is excellent, for its summer backcountry trails lend themselves superbly to winter grooming. Pick up the *Cross-Country Skiing* leaflet from the park information centre. To buy or rent cross-country skis try Totem Ski Shop, 408 Connaught Drive (ⓣ780/852-3078, ⓦwww.totemskishop.com), and for a guiding service contact Beyond the Beaten Path (ⓣ780/852-5650). You can **ice-skate** on parts of Pyramid Lake and Lac Beauvert that are cleared for the purpose. Source for Sports, 406 Patricia St (ⓣ780/852-3654, ⓦwww.jaspersports.com), and most other rental shops and hotels offer skate rentals.

Eating and drinking

Jasper has enough **restaurants** to ensure variety and a reasonable choice for a week-long stay, though hearty North American food dominates local menus.

Wholly unpretentious, generally gritty and regularly raucous, **nightlife** in Jasper's limited number of **bars** tends to make up in enthusiasm what it lacks in style. Yet many of the hostels and campsites are too far out of town for people to get in, so the fun there is generally of the make-your-own variety. For alternative evening entertainment – local theatre, cinema, music or dance– consult the town's summer or winter guide available from the tourist office.

Cafés and restaurants

Andy's Bistro 606 Patricia St ⓣ780/852-4559 or 1-877/232-6397, ⓦwww.andysbistro.com. Staid but popular and unpretentiously upscale place serving good Swiss food and some interesting gamey options (main courses cost $24–48). It only seats 45, so reservations in high season are recommended. Open daily from 5pm.

Bear's Paw Bakery 4 Cedar Ave ⓣ780/852-3233, ⓦwww.bearspawbakery.com. Slightly tucked away, but always busy with locals. Freshly baked buns, cakes and pastries with coffee, plus big sandwiches, other snacks and great trail food such as date squares and carrot cake. Has just a couple of tables and most people here take away. Open daily 6am–6pm. There is a newer offshoot, *The Other Paw*, opposite the station at 610 Connaught Drive.

Coco's Café 608 Patricia St ⓣ780/852-4550. Tiny, earthy and fun café with a glut of fabulous home-made items including tasty egg (free range) breakfasts, wraps, sandwiches, cakes and smoothies. Most items are available to take away and great for picnic lunches. Open daily 7am–7pm or later.

Earl's 600 Patricia St ⓣ780/852-2393. Branch of Canada-wide chain with cheerful staff and a dependable, mid-priced and generally North American menu (main courses from $10), though the burgers, a huge rib platter and perfectly broiled salmon steaks are offset by the presence of some eclectic options like sushi and Thai stir-fry. There's also a cocktail bar. Open daily 11am–11pm.

Fiddle River 620 Connaught Drive ⓣ780/852-3032. Stylish restaurant with dried flower and oil lamp decor, mountain panoramas and excellent fresh seafood at prices that reflect its distance from the sea; expect to pay $35–40 per person for three courses. Main courses range from basic beer-battered cod fish and chips to more exotic seafood jambalaya and green curry grilled swordfish. Open from 5pm daily.

Jasper Park Lodge Lac Beauvert ⓣ780/852-3301, ⓦwww.fairmont.com/jasper. The area's most prestigious lodging has several restaurants. Choices include a large bar menu at the *Tent City Sports Lounge* and the 500-seat *Beauvert Dining Room*, particularly recommended for its buffet breakfast and Sun brunch (from $20). A notch above these, the *Moose's Nook Northern Grill* serves local "mountain" food, which generally includes excellent whiskey-soaked salmon, venison and bison; mains are $28–42. The lodge's best restaurant – and the only one really worth the trek out here if you are based in town – is the *Edith Cavell Dining Room*, where you can expect to part with around $80 for five courses from an expertly crafted menu that's basically French with some Canadian accents. Daily 6–10pm.

Jasper Pizza Place 402 Connaught Drive ⓣ780/852-3225. Despite the open kitchen and everyday bar furnishings that make for a chain-restaurant ambience, the wood-fired pizzas (from $10.50) include Dijon mustard, escargot, smoked oysters and palm hearts. The small salads like the spinach, mushroom and citrus and honey ($6) are less exciting but still good. Other options include a gargantuan lasagne ($12), burgers and pita-pizzas that are ideal for a quick snack. Pool tables in the basement invite you to hang out after your meal, plus there's a rooftop patio. Daily 11am–11pm. Closed Nov.

Papa George's In the *Astoria Hotel* (see p.661), 404 Connaught Drive ⓣ780/852-3351, ⓦwww.papageorgesrestaurant.com. Though it looks plain and dowdy this locals' favourite is one of the town's oldest restaurants (it opened in 1924) and has excellent, varied food and gargantuan portions. Dinner mains are $15–42, but a quick lunch comes in at around $6–10. Breakfasts are also good and inexpensive. Daily 7am–2.30pm & 5–9.30pm (later in summer).

Soft Rock Café 622 Connaught Drive ⓣ780/852-5850. Good breakfast choice with encyclopedic selection of coffee and mouth-watering waffles heaped with fresh fruit and cream and satisfying all-day breakfasts. The best place in town to both browse the web ($8/hr) and pick up fantastic, massive cinnamon buns. Daily 7.30am–10pm (7am–4pm on winter weekends).

Villa Caruso 640 Connaught Drive ⓣ780/852-3920, ⓦwww.villacaruso.com. Upmarket steakhouse with subdued lighting, wood accents and orange hues the backdrop for meat feasts, largely focused on flame-grilling Alberta's best cuts, though seafood, pasta and pizzas are also available. Execution of dishes is unexciting but the pleasant ambience compensates; mains are $18–37 or $10–13 at lunch. The adjoining fireside lounge is particularly tempting for a drink before or after your meal.

Bars

Atha-B In the *Athabasca Hotel* (see p.661), 510 Patricia St. Uninspired, but large and occasionally rowdy, this is Jasper's most reliably busy venue, with nightly dancing – mostly to mainstream chart hits – and regular live music. Small cover.

De'd Dog Bar and Grill In the *Astoria Hotel* (see p.661), 404 Connaught Drive. Regularly unruly sports bar that's almost inevitably full of extrovert, thirty something locals. Other diversions here include pool, darts, big-screen sports and a bar menu with great burgers ($6). The generous happy hour runs 5–7pm.

Downstream Grill 620 Connaught Drive ⓣ780/852-9449 ⓦwww.downstreambar.com. Funky, spacious, airy bar with several sofas to relax on, below the *Fiddle River* restaurant (see p.669). Good bar food at reasonable prices.

Jasper Brewing Company 624 Connaught Drive ⓣ780/852-4111, ⓦwww.jasperbrewingco.ca. Excellent recent addition to Jasper's eating and drinking scene, with smart, wood-beamed contemporary interior and seven of its own-brewed and many other beers. The food is imaginative and well-cooked but somewhat pricey; try the Jamaican jerk pork chop ($25) or pesto linguini ($15).

Pete's Bar 614 Patricia St ⓣ780/852-6262. Big, bustling young bar with big screens – frequently for snowboarding videos – pool, darts and, on weekend nights, live music, varying from blues to Irish; locals jam here on Tues.

Silverwater Lounge At *Château Jasper*, 96 Geikie St ⓣ1-888/852-7737, ⓦwww.mpljasper.com. Recently renovated, this is a relaxed, smoochy sort of place, with a sleek contemporary interior that features comfortable chairs and a cosy fire: there's also a summer terrace, but this is a lounge that is better suited to an indoor cocktail or cosy nightcap.

Villa Caruso 640 Connaught Drive. Elegantly laidback fireside martini and cocktail bar (adjoining a restaurant) with piped jazz and blues; as relaxing and stylish a place as you'll find to sip a drink in town.

Listings

Car rental Hertz ⓣ780/852-3888, ⓦwww.hertz.com and National ⓣ780/852-1117; both at the train station. Book in advance if you want to pick up cars here: they go quickly, especially on days when trains arrive from Vancouver and Edmonton. Avis, 414 Connaught Drive ⓣ780/852-3970, ⓦwww.avis.ca.

Bookshop Jasper Camera and Gift, 412 Connaught Drive ⓣ780/852-3165.

Hospital Seton General, 518 Robson St ⓣ780/852-3344.

Internet access Soft Rock Internet Café, 633 Connaught Drive.

Laundry Coin Clean, 607 Patricia St ⓣ780/852-3852.

Library 500 Robson St (Mon–Thurs 10am–8pm Fri & Sat 10am–5pm). Has a huge number of park books.

Pharmacy Cavell Drugs, 602 Patricia St ⓣ780/852-4441.

Police ⓣ780/852-4848.

Post office 502 Patricia St ⓣ780/852-3041.

Rafting tour operators Maligne Rafting Adventures, 627 Patricia St (ⓣ780/852-3370 or 1-866/625-4463, ⓦwww.mra.ab.ca) offers four-hour trips ($99) on parts of the Sunwapta River, two-hour raft trips ($64) on small but lively rapids and three-hour trips ($89) suitable for families and children, both on the Athabasca River; there are also overnight trips to the Kakwa (three days $599) and Athabasca rivers, Class-3 rides on the Sunwapta (4hr; $79) and Fraser rivers (5hr; $99), with two departures each daily. Jasper Raft Tours, at Jasper Adventure Centre, Chaba Movie Theatre, 604 Connaught Drive (ⓣ780/852-2665 or 1-888/553-5628, ⓦwww.jasperrafttours.com) offers good trips for first-timers: two- to three-hour jaunts twice daily in summer on the Athabasca River in comfortable oar rafts. Tickets cost $55 and include shuttle to and from the river, with possible pick-ups from your hotel by prior arrangement. White Water Rafting (ⓣ780/852-7238 or 1-800/557-7238, ⓦwww.whitewaterraftingjasper.com) offers similar trips on several rivers, ranging in price from $55–115. Trips last between two and six hours-plus; call ahead for details on all trips.

Mount Robson Provincial Park

The extensive **MOUNT ROBSON PROVINCIAL PARK** borders Jasper National Park to the west and protects Mount Robson (3954m), the highest peak in the Canadian Rockies.

The park's scenery equals anything anywhere else in the region, and Mount Robson itself is one of the most staggering peaks you'll ever encounter. The preceding ridges creep up in height hiding the massive peak itself from view until the last moment.

The overall impression is of immense size, thanks mainly to the colossal scale of Robson's south face – a sheer rise of 3100m – and to the view from the road, which frames the mountain as a single mass isolated from other peaks. A spectacular glacier system, concealed on the mountain's north side, is visible if you make the popular backpacking hike to the Berg Lake area (see p.672).

The source of the mountain's name has never been agreed on, but could be a corruption of Robertson, a Hudson's Bay employee who was trapped in the region in the 1820s. Local natives called the peak Yuh-hai-has-hun (the "Mountain of the Spiral Road"), an allusion to the clearly visible layers of rock, which resemble a road winding to the summit. It was first climbed in 1913, and is still considered a dangerous challenge.

Arrival and information

Trains don't stop anywhere in the park, but if you're travelling by bus you can ask to be let off at Yellowhead Pass or the **Mount Robson Visitor Centre** (daily: early May to early June & Sept 3–30 8am–5pm; early June to early Sept 8am–7pm; first week of Oct 9am–4pm; ⓣ1-800/435-5622), located at the Mount Robson viewpoint near the western entrance to the park, where **maps** and information on the various hikes in the park are available. **Facilities** in the park itself are minimal, so stock up on food and fuel before entering if you can. Otherwise, most amenities are found near the visitor centre, including a **café/garage**. Around 16km beyond the park's western boundary is Tête Jaune Cache, where you can continue north on Hwy 16 to Prince George (for routes to Prince Rupert, northern BC and the Yukon), or take Hwy 5 south, past Wells Gray Provincial Park to Kamloops and a whole range of onward destinations; the latter route is covered on p.739.

Accommodation

The few accommodation options in the park are made up of a couple of campsites and lodges, one of which organizes rafting, helicopter and riding tours. **Backcountry camping** in the park is only permitted at seven wilderness campsites dotted along the Berg Lake Trail (see p.672); to use these you have to register and pay an overnight fee at the visitor centre.

Mountain River Lodge 13990 Swift Current River Rd, at Hwy 16 ⓣ250/566-9899 or 1-888/566-9899, ⓦwww.mtrobson.com. This really is quite a spectacular setting, overlooking the Fraser River and onto Mt Robson itself. Take your pick from the main lodge B&B rooms (❻) or go for a more private, self-catering cabin (❼); the latter all have a bbq and fireplace, with free firewood. The friendly hosts dish up good breakfasts and speak German.

> Yellowhead Pass marks the boundary between the Jasper park, which is in Alberta (on **Mountain time**), and the Mount Robson park, which is in BC (on **Pacific time**, one hour behind).

Provincial campsites in BC

Tent and RV sites at many public **campsites** in BC's provincial parks can be reserved through Discover Camping (March to mid-Sept Mon–Fri 7am–7pm, Sat & Sun 9am–5pm Pacific time; ⓣ604/689-9025 or 1-800/689-9025, ⓦwww.discovercamping.ca. Reservations can be made up to three months in advance but no later than 48 hours before the first day of arrival. A nonrefundable booking fee of $6.30 per night, up to a maximum of three nights ($18.90), is charged. General information on the parks is on ⓣ250/387-4550 or 1-800/663-7867, ⓦwww.env.gov.bc.ca/bcparks.

Mount Robson Lodge 5km west of the park on Hwy 16 ⓣ250/566-4821 or 1-888/566-4821, ⓦwww.mountrobsonlodge.com. The eighteen log-sided riverfront cabins here sleep two–six people, have electricity, heat, private bathrooms and most come with kitchenettes, but there are no telephones or TVs – the idea is to soak up the views on hand and disconnect from the world. This is also the site for the **Robson Shadows Campground** which has 25 sites for tents and RVs ($15–18) along the Fraser River, including space for group camping in a large meadow. There's a tap for drinking water, a fire pit (firewood costs extra) and showers are included in the price. Both accommodation options serve as a good base for those keen on doing some hiking, canoeing, fishing and riding; daily rafting trips are also offered on-site through the Mount Robson Whitewater Rafting (see lodge website for details). Open mid–May to mid–Oct. Cabins ❸–❻

Mount Robson Provincial Park Campground On Hwy 16, 22km north of Valemount ⓣ250/566-4811 (April–Sept only), ⓦwww.env.gov.bc.ca/bcparks. Three different campsites make up this government-run ground. Two of them – Robson River and Robson Meadows – are a short walk west of the visitor centre on Hwy 16, while the third, Lucerne, is about 10km west of the Alberta-BC border. Robson River has 19 sites ($19) on a first-come, first-served basis, with hot showers and toilets; open mid–May to early Sept. Robson Meadows has 125 sites ($19), which you can reserve (see above) or get on a first-come, first-served basis if available. It has the same facilities as Robson River, but families may find it more appealing for the playground and an amphitheatre that hosts interpretive programmes; open mid–May to Sept. Lucerne has 36 sites ($15) on a first-come, first-served basis, with dry toilets, pumped well water and no showers; open mid-May to mid–Sept.

Hiking in the park's west: Berg Lake Trail

Starting 2km north of the park visitor centre, the **Berg Lake Trail** (22km one-way; 795m ascent) is perhaps the most popular short backpacking trip in the Rockies, and the only trail that gets anywhere near Mount Robson. If you plan to **camp** ($5) while doing the trail, you must make reservations by phone (see box above).

You can do the first third or so as a comfortable and highly rewarding day-walk, passing through forest to lovely glacier-fed Kinney Lake (6.7km; campsite at the lake's northeast corner). If you trek the whole length you'll traverse the stupendous Valley of a Thousand Waterfalls – the most notable being sixty-metre Emperor Falls (14.3km; campsites 500m north and 2km south) – and eventually enjoy the phenomenal area around Berg Lake itself (17.4km to its nearest, western shore). Mount Robson rises an almost sheer 2400m from the lakeshore, its huge cliffs cradling two creaking rivers of ice, Mist Glacier and Berg Glacier – the latter, one of the Rockies' few "living" or advancing glaciers, is 1800m long by 800m wide and the source of the great icebergs that give the lake its name.

Beyond the lake you can pursue the trail 2km further to Robson Pass (21.9km; 1652m ascent; campsite) and another 1km to Adolphus Lake in Jasper National Park. The most popular campsites are the Berg Lake (19.6km) and Rearguard (20.1km), both on Berg Lake itself; but if you've got a Jasper backcountry permit you could press on to Adolphus where there's a less-frequented site.

Once you're camped at Berg Lake, a popular day-trip is to Toboggan Falls, which starts from the southerly Berg Lake campsite and climbs the northeast (left) side of Toboggan Creek past a series of cascades and meadows to eventual views over the lake's entire hinterland. The trail peters out after 2km, but you can easily walk on and upward through open meadows for still better views.

The second trail in the immediate vicinity is Robson Glacier (2km), a level walk that peels off south from the main trail 1km west of Robson Pass near the park ranger's cabin. It runs across an outwash plain to culminate in a small lake at the foot of the glacier; a rougher track then follows the lateral moraine on the glacier's east side, branching east after 3km to follow a small stream to the summit of Snowbird Pass (9km total from the ranger's cabin).

Hiking in the park's east: Yellowhead Mountain and Mount Fitzwilliam Trail

Both road and rail links to the park from Jasper climb through **Yellowhead Pass** (1131m), 20km west of Jasper Townsite, long one of the most important native and fur-trading routes across the Rockies. The railway meanders alongside the road most of the way, occasionally occupied by epic freight trains hundreds of cars long.

Two more hikes start from Yellowhead Lake, at the eastern end of the park. To get to the trailhead for **Yellowhead Mountain** (4.5km one-way; 715m ascent), an excellent day-hike, follow Hwy 16 for 9km down from the pass and then take a gravel road 1km on an isthmus across the lake. After a steep two-hour climb through forest, the trail levels out in open country at 1830m, offering sweeping views of the Yellowhead Pass area.

The **Mount Fitzwilliam Trail** (13km one-way; 945m ascent), which leaves Hwy 16 about 1km east of the Yellowhead Mountain Trail but on the other side of the hwy, is a more demanding walk, especially over its last half. If you don't want to backpack to the endpoint – a spectacular basin of lakes and peaks – you could walk through the forest to the campsite at Rockingham Creek (6km).

Yoho National Park

Wholly in BC on the western side of the Continental Divide from Lake Louise, **YOHO NATIONAL PARK**'s name derives from a Cree word meaning "wonder" – a fitting testament to the awesome grandeur of the region's mountains, lakes and waterfalls. Yet it's a small park, whose intimate scale makes it the one favoured by Rockies' connoisseurs. As in other national parks, it was the railway that spawned tourism in the area: the first hotel in Field was built by the CPR in 1886 and within a few months sixteen square kilometres at the foot of Mount Stephen (the peak to Field's east) had been set aside as a special reserve. By 1911, Yoho had become Canada's second national park.

The Trans-Canada Hwy divides Yoho neatly in half, climbing from Lake Louise over the **Kicking Horse Pass** to share the broad, glaciated valley bottom of the Kicking Horse River with the old Canadian Pacific Railway. The only village, **Field**, has the park visitor centre, some services and limited accommodation (the nearest full-service towns are Lake Louise, 28km east, and **Golden**, 54km west). Other expensive accommodation is available at the central hubs, **Lake O'Hara**,

Although in BC, Yoho runs on **Mountain time**.

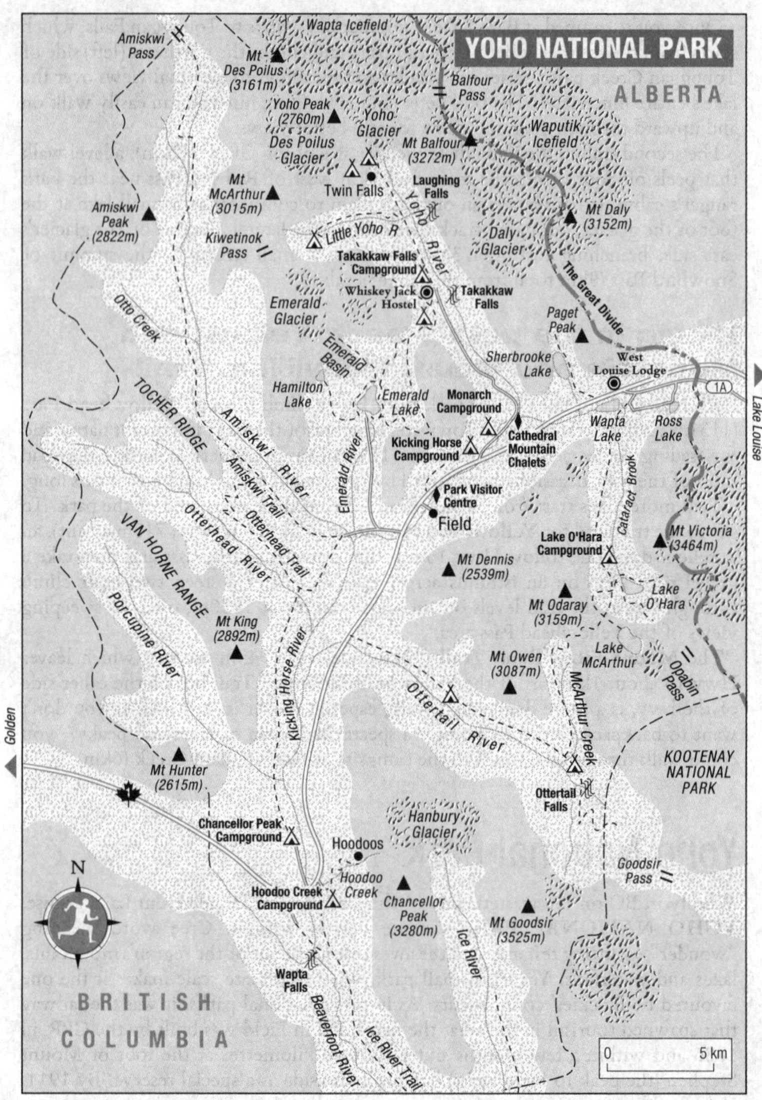

the **Yoho Valley** and **Emerald Lake**, from which radiate most of the park's stunning and well-maintained **hiking** trails (see p.678) and a couple of lodges just off the Trans-Canada. These areas – not Field – are the focal points of the park, and get very busy in summer.

Field

No more than a few wooden houses backed by an amphitheatre of sheer-dropped mountains, **FIELD** looks like an old-world pioneer settlement, little changed from its 1884 origins as a railroad-construction camp, named after Cyrus Field, sponsor of the first transatlantic communication cable, who visited Yoho that year. Field does have a few interesting attractions nearby – the Burgess Shale and the Spiral Tunnels – but it's mostly used as a base for those **hiking** in Yoho (see p.678).

Arrival and information

There are no passenger **trains** to Field, but the village is a flag stop for Greyhound buses (5 daily in each direction) – wave them down from the Petro-Canada just east of the turn-off from the hwy to the village, though most stop anyway to drop packages.

Yoho's park **visitor centre** (daily: May to mid-June 9am–5pm; mid-June to early Sept 9am–8pm; second and third week of Sept 9am–7pm and 9am–5pm respectively; late Sept to March & April 9am–4pm; ⓣ250/343-6783, ⓦwww.pc.gc.ca), marked by a distinctive blue roof about 1km east of Field, sells park permits ($9.80 daily), takes backcountry registrations (nightly permit $9.80, reservations $11.70), takes bookings for Lake O'Hara (see p.678), has displays, lectures and slide shows – notably on the famous Burgess Shales (see p.677) – and advises on trail and climbing conditions. It also gives out a useful *Backcountry Guide* with full details of all trails and sells 1:50,000 **maps** of the park. If you intend to camp at Lake O'Hara it's essential to make **reservations** at the information centre.

Field's railway history

Regular passenger services no longer come through Field, but the **railway** is still one of the park "sights", and among the first things you see whether you enter from east or west. That it came this way at all was the result of desperate political and economic horse trading. The Canadian Pacific's chief surveyor, Sandford Fleming, wrote of his journey over the proposed Kicking Horse Pass route in 1883: "I do not think I can forget that terrible walk; it was the greatest trial I ever experienced." Like many in the company he was convinced the railway should take the much lower and more amenable Yellowhead route to the north.

The railway was as much a political as a transportational tool, designed to unite the country and encourage settlement. A northerly route would have ignored great tracts of valuable prairie near the US border (around Calgary), and allowed much of the area and its resources to slip into the hands of the US. So, against all engineering advice, the railway was cajoled into taking the Kicking Horse route, and thus obliged to negotiate four-percent grades, the greatest of any commercial railway of the time.

The result was the famed **Spiral Tunnels**, two vast figure-of-eight galleries within the mountains; from a popular viewpoint about 7km east of Field on Hwy 1, you can watch the front of goods trains emerge from the tunnels before the rear wagons have even entered. More notorious was the **Big Hill**, where the line drops 330m in just 6km from Wapta Lake to the flats east of Field. The first train to attempt the descent plunged into the canyon, killing three railway workers. Runaways became so common that four blasts on a whistle became the standard warning for trains careering out of control (the wreck of an engine can still be seen near the main Kicking Horse Park campground). Lady Agnes MacDonald, wife of the Canadian prime minister, rode down the Big Hill on the cowcatcher (a metal frame in front of the locomotive to scoop animals off the track) in 1886, remarking that it presented a "delightful opportunity for a new sensation". She'd already travelled around 1000km on her unusual perch; her husband, with whom she was sharing the symbolic trans-Canada journey to commemorate the opening of the railway, managed just 40km on the cowcatcher. Trains climbing the hill required four locomotives to pull fifteen coaches; the ascent took over an hour, and exploding boilers (and resulting deaths) were frequent.

Enquire at the park centre for details of activities arranged by the "Friends of Yoho" (Ⓣ250/343-6393, Ⓦwww.friendsofyoho.ca) and the two free summer guided walks: "Emerald Lakeshore Stroll" and "Walk into the Past".

Accommodation

Yoho's popularity and accessibility mean there is huge pressure on its very limited **accommodation**: if you're really stuck, you can make for one of the motels in Golden (see p.682). Field has just one officially listed hotel, the *Kicking Horse Lodge*, a fine base if you have transport, with two other lodges on the hwy just to the north and a third at Lake O'Hara; otherwise there is a hostel in the Yoho Valley and a luxury hotel in the adjacent Emerald Valley.

You can also try one of the fully furnished suites in **private homes** (Ⓦwww.field.ca/accommodations) in Field – of which there were twenty or so at last count. Bar one or two exceptions, these are all similarly priced – from $75 in low season to about $175 for a double in high – and all within a few minutes' walk of each other in Field's small grid of streets.

The most central and popular **campsites** are listed below. **Wilderness camping** is allowed in the Amiskwi, Otterhead, Lower Ice River and Porcupine valleys, but check at the visitor centre first: you must be at least 3km from any road, 100m from water, 50m from a trail and purchase the $9.80 backcountry pass. The park's **backcountry** sites (all $9.80) are: McArthur Creek (ten sites); Float Creek (four sites); Yoho Lake (eight sites); Laughing Falls (eight sites); Twin Falls (eight sites); and Little Yoho (ten sites). The only facilities are dry toilets (except Float Creek) and bear poles. Between one and three sites at each can be reserved ($11.70 fee) up to three months in advance at the visitor centre.

Hotels

Cathedral Mountain Lodge 3km off Hwy 1 on Yoho Valley Rd Ⓣ250/343-6442 or 1-866/619-6442, Ⓦwww.cathedralmountain.com. Beautifully situated in the lee of Cathedral Mountain, 4km east of Field and fifteen minutes' drive from Lake Louise, this fabulous collection of luxury log cabins – there are no phones or televisions – is ideally placed for exploring the Yoho Valley immediately to the north. Open late May to early Oct. ❽

Emerald Lake Lodge 1km west of Field, off Hwy 1 Ⓣ250/343-6321 or 1-800/663-6336, Ⓦwww.crmr.com. One of the Rockies' historic "railway hotels" (like the *Banff Springs* and *Château Lake Louise*), with the style, grandeur and prices to match – it was voted the number two resort in the country by *Conde Nast Traveller* in 2009. Advance reservations are essential; expect to pay $300 or more in high season, less outside summer. ❽

Kicking Horse Lodge 100 Centre St Ⓣ250/343-6303 or 1-800/659-4944, Ⓦwww.trufflepigs.com. Attractive wooden building with fourteen plain but acceptable rooms; family rooms have kitchens. Not far from the lodge you can eat well at the co-owned *Truffle Pigs Bistro*, a relaxed and funky spot for great coffee, home-baked breads and cakes and larger meals. ❻

Lake O'Hara Lodge Lake O'Hara Ⓣ250/343-6418, or 250/678-4110 in winter Ⓦwww.lakeohara.com. You need to reserve weeks in advance and be prepared to part with a large amount of money to stay at this stunning 1920s mountain lodge. There are eight rooms in the main lodge, eleven two-person cabins along the lakeshore and four-person cabins overlooking the lake. Open mid-June ro late Sept & Feb to mid-April. In winter, access is by ski or snowshoe only. ❽

West Louise Lodge 11km west of Lake Louise, off Hwy 1 Ⓣ250/343-6001 or 1-888/682-2212, Ⓦwww.west-louise-lodge.com. A fifty room lodge just inside the park boundary that's bigger and less expensive than the rival *Cathedral Mountain Lodge*. The nicest rooms have balconies and overlook Wapta Lake; there are often rooms from as little as $59. Amenities include a café, restaurant and indoor pool. ❺

Private homes

Alpine Guesthouse 313 2nd Ave Ⓣ250/343-6878 or 1-866/634-5665, Ⓦwww.alpineguesthouse.ca. A spacious establishment at the edge of the village and at the base of Mt Stephen, with spectacular views. It sleeps up to seven in two rooms, plus sofa bed in the living room. There's a full kitchen, games room, internet access and the hosts speak Dutch, German, Spanish and Italian. ④

Bear's Den Guesthouse 414 1st St W ⓣ250/343-6439, ⓦwww.bearsdenguesthouse.ca. It's all a bit modern and fairly plain compared with the rustic feel of other local accommodation, but there's a large kitchen/dining area and accommodation for six in a double room, a second room with double bed and a pair of twin beds. The owners speak German. Minimum three-night stay in high season. ⑦

Burgess Lookout Guest Cabin 302 2nd Ave ⓣ1-877/343-6452, ⓦwww.burgesslookoutguest cabin.com. A cute, dolls' house of a cabin, with steeply pitched roof, wood-burning stove, sitting room, kitchen and lovely views. Sleeps two–three. Minimum two-night stay late June to end of Sept. ⑦

Canadian Rockies Inn 308 Stephen Ave, at Wall St ⓣ250/343-6046 or 1-877/343-6046, ⓦwww .bbcanada.com/british_columbia. The three rooms here – all with fine views – each have a private bathroom and entrance. The main floor suite has a full kitchen, while the other two suites have fridges. The two-bedroom suite can accommodate up to six people. ⑦

Coyote's Den Guesthouse 213 2nd Ave ⓣ250/343-6034, ⓔcoyotesden@redshift.bc.ca. Three bedrooms on the main floor of a standalone wooden house, with full access to living room and kitchen. Ideal for families or groups. Continental breakfast included. ⑤

Old Church Guesthouse 308 Kicking horse Ave (ⓣ250/343-6345, ⓦwww.oldchurchguesthouse .ca. A two-bedroom suite that sleeps four is available, but it's all in the rather low-ceilinged lower level of the former 1960s United Church building. There's a living room and fully-equipped kitchen, too. ⑥

Hostels

Fireweed Hostel Field; call for directions ⓣ250/343-6999 or 1-877/343-6999, ⓦwww .fireweedhostel.com. This smart, excellent little hostel has room for 25 in four- and six-bunk rooms; there's also a private two-bedroom suite. The bunk rooms beds are solid but comfy, with duvets and mattress toppers. The shared showers are excellent and there's a big, well-equipped kitchen, plus a lounge and dining room. Dorms $40 ($30 Oct–May), private rooms $160 ($90 Oct–May).

Whiskey Jack Hostel Just beyond the end of Yoho Valley Rd, 500m south of Takakkaw Falls ⓣ1-888/762-4122, ⓦwww.hihostels.ca. An appealing option, if only because of its proximity to Takakkaw Falls. There are 27 beds in three nine-bed dorms, all of which have hot showers and flush toilets. Dorms $23 for members, $27 for nonmembers; open late June to Sept and reservations are recommended.

Campsites

Hoodoo Creek/Chancellor Peak 22km west of Field, off Hwy 1. A thirty-pitch first-come, first-served site with a cold-water hand pump, dry toilets and no showers. About 1km west of Hoodoo Creek is the Chancellor Peak campsite, with 59 sites and the same facilities. Both open early June to early Sept; $21.50.

Kicking Horse 3km east of Field, off Hwy 1, near the junction with Yoho Valley Rd for Takakkaw Falls. The most central of the five park-run campsites, this 92-pitch site is first-come, first-served. It's pleasingly forested (the riverside pitches are best), though it echoes somewhat with the rumble of trains day and night. It has the same facilities as Hoodoo Creek, but with hot showers. In summer a separate overflow site is often opened (no showers), but even this fills up and you should aim to arrive extremely early. Open late May to early Oct; $27.40.

Monarch 3km east of Field, within walking distance of the Kicking Horse site. With 46 first-come, first-served pitches in a big meadow, this is the second of the park's major campsites. It has pumped well water, dry toilets and a kitchen shelter with a wood stove. Open May & early June to early Sept; $17.60.

Takakkaw Falls 17km east of Field, at the top of Takakkaw Falls Rd. Only 300m from the falls' day-use car park and with great views of the falls from most of the 35 sites, this is one of the best bases for local hikes (see p.678). It's first-come, first-served and for walk-in tent camping only. Amenities include pumped well water, dry toilets and a kitchen shelter with stove. Open mid-June to Sept; $17.60.

The Burgess Shale

Yoho today ranks as highly among geologists as it does among hikers and railway buffs, thanks to the world-renowned **Burgess Shale**, a unique geological formation situated close to Field. The shale – layers of sedimentary rock – lie on the upper slopes of Mount Field and consist of the fossils of some 120 types of soft-bodied marine creatures from the Middle Cambrian period (515–530 million years ago), one of only three places in the world where the remains of these unusual creatures are found. Soft-bodied creatures usually proved ill-suited to the fossilization process, but here the fossils are so well preserved and detailed that in some cases scientists can identify what the creatures were eating before they died.

Plans are in hand to open a major new museum in Field devoted to the shale, but in the meantime access is restricted to protect the fossils and fossil-hunting is strictly prohibited. The area can only be seen on two **guided hikes** to Walcott's Quarry (760m ascent; 20km round-trip; departs 8am Fri–Mon; $100) and the trilobite beds on Mount Stephen (780m ascent; 6km round-trip; departs 10am Sat & Sun; $75). Qualified guides lead the walks, which are limited to fifteen people and run between late June and October. For details and reservations, contact the Burgess Shale Geoscience Foundation (ⓣ250/343-3006, ⓦwww.burgess-shale.bc.ca).

Hikes in Yoho National Park

Hiking in Yoho is magnificent. If you have time for just a single day walk, make it the **Iceline–Whaleback–Twin Falls Trail**, rated among the top five day-hikes in the Rockies. If you're short of time and want a quick taste of the park before moving on, side roads from the Trans-Canada lead to Emerald Lake and the Yoho Valley. We recommend picking up the *Yoho National Park Backcountry Guide* and the Lake O'Hara pamphlet; both are available at the visitor centre.

Lake O'Hara

The **Lake O'Hara** area is one of the Rockies' finest all-round enclaves – with staggering scenery, numerous lakes and an immense diversity of alpine and subalpine terrain. It's a great base for concentrated hiking: you could easily spend a fortnight exploring the well-constructed trails that strike out from the central lodge and campsite. The setting is matchless, with Lake O'Hara itself framed by two of the peaks that also overlook Lake Louise across the ridge – mounts Lefroy (3429m) and Victoria (3464m). The one problem is **access**, which is severely restricted to safeguard the mountain flora and fauna.

Arrival and information

To get there, turn off the Trans-Canada Hwy onto Hwy 1A (3.2km west of the Continental Divide), cross the railway and turn right onto the gravel road leading to the parking area (1km). This fire road continues all the way up to the lake (13km), but it's not open to general traffic or bikes: **no bikes** are allowed on the road or anywhere else in the Lake O'Hara region. This makes getting here difficult, but it's worth it if you want to hike some of the continent's most stunning scenery.

Anybody can walk the 13km up the road, or the more picturesque **Cataract Brook Trail** (12.9km), which runs roughly parallel to the road, but a quota system applies for the bus up here: 42 people daily, plus campers in the 30-site campground at the end, for which reservations are compulsory.

Aim instead for the special **bus** from the car park up to the lake; priority is given to those with reservations or those with bookings at the *Lake O'Hara Lodge* (see p.676), the thirty-pitch **campsite** or Alpine Club huts. **Reservations** for bus and campsite can be made with Parks Canada three months in advance by phone only (April–May Mon–Fri 8am–noon & 1–4pm; daily June–Sept 8am–noon & 1–4pm; Oct 1–4pm; ⓣ250/343-6433, ⓦwww.pc.gc.ca). There are baggage **restrictions**: one large or two small bags per person; maximum weight 25 kg; maximum length, width and height 158cm.

If you're going **for the day**, the 8.30am and 10.30am buses are best (there are also 3.30pm and 5.30pm departures, with returns at 9.30am, 11.30am, 2.30pm, 4.30pm and 6.30pm from mid-June to Sept; and outbound at 10am and 3pm with returns at 11am and 4pm in early Oct); the maximum number in a party is six. To use the

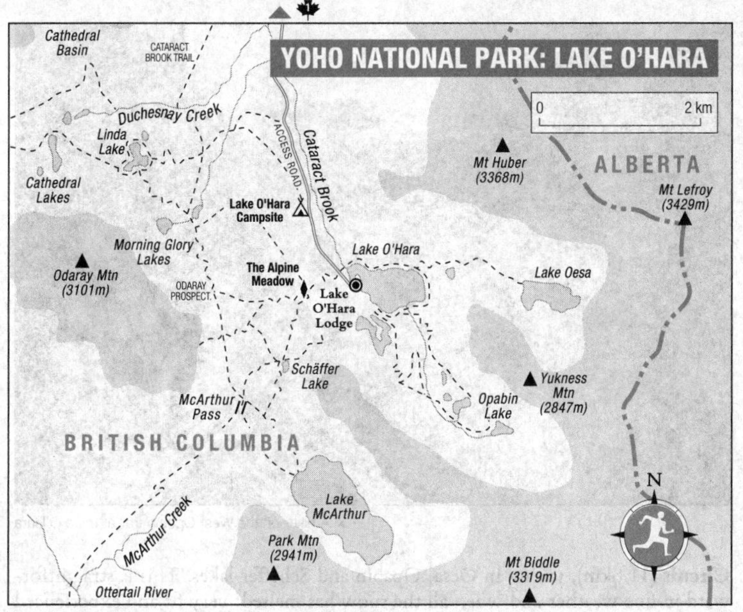

campsite you have to have dates ready (up to a maximum of three nights), state the number of people, the number of sites required (maximum of two per party, one tent per site) and your preferred bus time. The reservation fee for bus (day-use or camp) is $11.70 and the return bus fare is $14.70, payable by credit card over the phone.

Hikes from Lake O'Hara

The **Lake O'Hara region** divides into five basic zones, each of which deserves a full day of exploration: Lake Oesa, the Opabin Plateau (this area and others are often closed to protect their grizzlies), Lake McArthur, the Odaray Plateau and the Duchesnay Basin.

If you have time to do only one day-hike here, the classic (if not the most walked) trails are the **Wiwaxy Gap** (12km; 495m ascent), or the **Opabin Plateau Trail** (3.2km one-way; 250m ascent), from the *Lake O'Hara Lodge* to Opabin Lake. Despite the latter's brevity, you could spend hours wandering the plateau's tiny lakes and alpine meadows on the secondary trails that crisscross the area. Most people return to Lake O'Hara via the **East Circuit Trail**, but a still more exhilarating hike – and a good day's outing – is to walk the **Yukness Ledge**, a section of the Alpine Circuit (see below) that cuts up from the East Circuit just 400m after leaving Opabin Lake. This spectacular high-level route leads to the beautiful Lake Oesa, from where it's just 3.2km down to Lake O'Hara. Oesa is one of many beautiful lakes in the region, and the **Lake Oesa Trail** (3.2km one-way; 240m ascent) from Lake O'Hara is the single most walked path in the Lake O'Hara area. Close behind comes the **Lake McArthur Trail** (3.5km one-way; 310m ascent) that leads to the largest and most photographed of the lakes in the area. The **Odaray Plateau Trail** (2.6km one-way; 280m ascent) is another highly rated, but rather overpopular hike.

The longest and least-walked path is the **Linda Lake–Cathedral Basin** trip, past several lakes to a great viewpoint at Cathedral Platform Prospect (7.4km one-way; 305m ascent). The most challenging hike is the high-level **Alpine**

▲ A hiker on the West Opabin trail at Lake O'Hara

Circuit (11.8km), taking in Oesa, Opabin and Schaffer lakes. This is straightforward in fine weather and when all the snow has melted; very fit and experienced walkers should have little trouble, though there's considerable exposure and some scrambling. At other times it's best left to climbers, or left alone completely.

The Yoho Valley and Emerald Lake

Less compact an area than Lake O'Hara, the **Yoho Valley** and nearby **Emerald Lake** are far more accessible for casual visitors, and offer some great sights – the Takakkaw Falls in particular – and a variety of top-rated trails. The lake and valley combine to form one of the Rockies' most important backpacking zones. Though popular and easily reached – access roads head north from the Hwy to both the Emerald and Yoho valleys – the region is not quite as crowded as Lake O'Hara to the south. The scenery is equally mesmerizing, and if fewer of the trails are designed for day-hikes, many of them interlock so that you can tailor walks to suit your schedule or fitness.

If you plan to do a lot of walking, or simply want to stay overnight, but not in a tent, the *Whiskey Jack* HI **hostel** (see p.677) is just beyond the end of the Yoho Valley Road, 500m south of Takakkaw Falls. Close by is the *Takakkaw Falls* **campsite** (see p.677): trails to the north lead to four further backcountry campsites.

The Emerald Lake Road leaves the Hwy about 2km west of Field and ends, 8km on, at the *Emerald Lake Lodge* (see p.676). Like the Yoho Valley Road, this road offers access to easy strolls and a couple of good day- or half-day hikes.

Hikes in the Yoho Valley

Most trails in the **Yoho Valley area** start from the Takakkaw Falls campsite and car park at the end of the Yoho Valley Road; the road leaves the Trans-Canada about 5km east of Field (signed from the Kicking Horse campsite), a narrow and switchbacking route unsuitable for trailers and RVs and open in the summer only. It's 14km from the Hwy to the parking area. The cascades' total 254-metre drop makes them among the most spectacular road-accessible falls in the mountains. Many of the area's trails connect, and some run over the ridge to the Emerald Lake region, offering numerous permutations.

For a stroll from the main trailhead at the campsite after a drive or cycle, walk to **Point Lace Falls** (1.9km one-way; minimum ascent) or **Laughing Falls** (3.8km one-way; 60m gain). Another shortish, extremely popular walk from the same car park is the **Yoho Pass** (10.9km; 310m ascent, 510m height loss), which links to Emerald Lake and its eponymous lodge (though you'll need transport arranged at the lake). A southern branch from this hike will take you over the Burgess Pass and down into Field, another manageable day-trip with fine overviews of the entire area.

The most tramped path in the Yoho Valley is the **Twin Falls Trail** (8.5km one-way; 290m ascent) from the Takakkaw Falls car park. This easy six-hour return journey passes the Laughing Falls and has the reward of the Twin Falls cataract at the end, plus fine scenery and other lesser waterfalls en route. Stronger walkers could continue over the highly recommended **Whaleback Trail** (4.5km one-way; 1hr 30min) to give some quite incredible views of the glaciers at the valley head. A complete circuit returning to Takakkaw Falls with the Whaleback is 20.1km.

If you're allowing yourself just one big walk in Yoho it's a hard choice between the Takakkaw Falls–Twin Falls–Whaleback Trail just described or the **Iceline–Little Yoho Valley–(Whaleback)–Twin Falls** combination. The latter is often

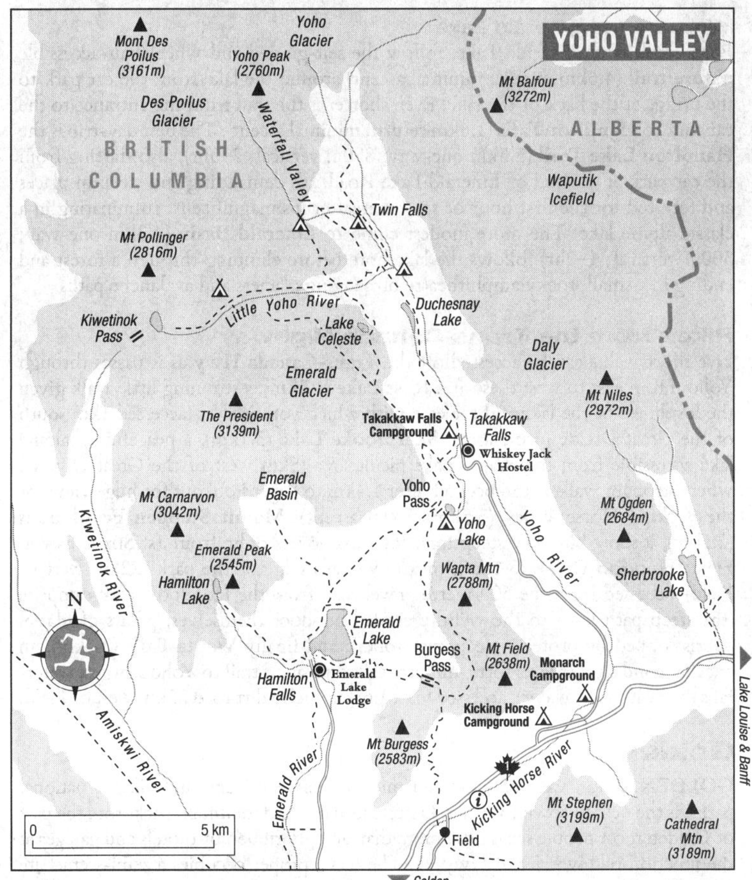

cited as one of the top five day-walks in the Rockies, and on balance might be the one to go for, though both options duplicate parts of one another's route. The Iceline (695m vertical gain) also starts close to the Takakkaw Falls car park, climbing west through a large avalanche path onto a level bench with jaw-dropping views of the Emerald Glacier above and the Daly Glacier across the valley. It contours above Lake Celeste (a trail drops to this lake, making a shorter 17km circuit in all back to the car park) and then drops to the Little Yoho Valley and back to Takakkaw Falls for a 19.8-kilometre circuit. If you're very fit (or can camp overnight to break the trip), tagging on the Whaleback before returning to Takakkaw Falls makes a sensational 27-kilometre walk with 1000m of ascent. Most people will want to do this as a backpacking option (there are four backcountry sites up here) – though the Iceline–Little Yoho walk coupled with the trek west to the **Kiwetinok Pass** (30km; 1070m) is also in many people's list of top-five day/backpacking Rocky Mountain walks. Juggling further with the permutations brings the Whaleback into this last combination to make one of the best backpacking routes in the Rockies: Iceline–Little Yoho Valley–Kiwetinok Pass–Whaleback (35.5km; 1375m ascent), a route up there with the Rockwall Trail in Kootenay, Skyline in Jasper and Berg Lake in Mount Robson Provincial Park.

Hikes around Emerald Lake

For a stroll from Emerald Lake, follow the self-guided and wheelchair-accessible **nature trail** (4.6km circuit; minimal ascent) around the lake from the car park to the bridge at the back of the lake. Even shorter is the trail from the entrance to the car park to **Hamilton Falls** (1.6km return; minimal ascent). The best day-trip is the **Hamilton Lake Trail** (5.5km one-way; 850m vertical; 2–3hr), also starting from the car park at the end of Emerald Lake Road. It's demanding and steep in places and forested for the first hour or so – thereafter it's magnificent, culminating in a classic alpine lake. The more modest climb to **Emerald Basin** (4.3km one-way; 300m vertical; 1–2hr) follows the lakeshore before climbing through a forest and ending in a small, rocky amphitheatre of hanging glaciers and avalanche paths.

Hikes from the Trans-Canada Highway

Five short walks can be accessed off the **Trans-Canada Hwy** as it passes through Yoho. From east to west these are: **Ross Lake** (1.3km), a stunning little walk given the loveliness of the lake and the ease with which you reach it (accessed 1km south of the Great Divide picnic area); **Sherbrooke Lake** (3.1km), a peaceful subalpine lake accessible from the Wapta Lake picnic area (5km west of the Great Divide), where stronger walkers can peel off after 1.4km to Paget Lookout for huge views of the Kicking Horse Valley (3.5km; 520m ascent); **Mount Stephen Fossil Beds** (2.7km), a short but very steep trail, for fossil lovers only, from 1st Street East in Field; **Hoodoo Creek** (3.1km), on the western edge of the park (22km west of Field), accessed from the 600-metre gravel road from the Hoodoo Creek campsite (the steep path leads to the weirdly eroded hoodoos themselves, pillars of glacial debris topped by protective capping stones); and finally **Wapta Falls** (2.4km), an excellent and almost level forty-minute walk on a good trail to Yoho's largest waterfalls (by volume of water), accessed via a 1.6-kilometre dirt road 25km west of Field.

Golden

GOLDEN, 54km west of Field and midway between Yoho and Glacier national parks, is the nearest town to either. Despite its name and mountain backdrop, the part of Golden most people see is little more than an ugly ribbon of motels and garages at the junction of Hwy 1 and Hwy 95. The town proper occupies a semi-scenic site down by the Columbia River, below the hwy strip; here you'll find the municipal campsite, more accommodation and many of the companies offering rafting and other **tours**.

The town is changing, thanks to the ongoing development of **Kicking Horse** (Ⓣ1-888/706-1117, Ⓦwww.kickinghorseresort.com), the most significant BC **ski resort** in the area, which is 13km from Golden, with an eight-person gondola and a 1245m vertical rise."

Arrival and information

The bus **station** (Ⓣ250/344-2917) is just north of the chamber of commerce, along the Trans-Canada. In Golden, all the "South" streets are on one side of the river, all the "North" streets on the other.

The chamber of commerce (year-round: Mon–Fri 9am–6pm & Sat 10am–5pm; Ⓣ250/344-7125 or 1-800/622-4653, Ⓦwww.goldenchamber.bc.ca), at 500 10th Ave North, provides **information**, as does the BC **visitor centre** (daily: Jan to mid-May & mid-Oct to Dec 9am–4pm; mid-May to late June & early Sept to early Oct 9am–5pm; late June to early Sept 9am–8pm), at 111 Golden Donald Upper Rd.

Practicalities

All the **motels** on the strip, like the *Park Inn-Golden* (Ⓣ250/344-6315 or 344-5153, Ⓦwww.selkirkinn.com; ④) on Hwy 1, look over the road or onto the backs of garages opposite. None of them have great views, but at least the *Sportsman* (Ⓣ250/344-2915 or 1-888/989-5566, Ⓦwww.sportsmanlodge.ca; ⑤), at 1200 12th St North, is off the road.

Around 16km northwest of Golden, the *Blaeberry Mountain Lodge* (Ⓣ250/344-5296, Ⓦwww.blaeberrymountainlodge.bc.ca; ④), at 1680 Moberly School Rd, is first-rate and beautifully situated; accommodation consists of simple but comfortable log cabins and a lodge. The owners will often pick you up in Golden if you're travelling without your own transport.

The town's **campsite**, the Golden Municipal Campground (Ⓣ250/344-5412 or 1-866/538-6625, Ⓦwww.goldenmunicipalcampground.com; $20; May to mid-Oct), is on the banks of the river at 1407 9th St South, three blocks east of the main street. It has flush toilets, hot showers, washhouses, firewood and is adjacent to a swimming pool and tennis courts.

In town, a good place to **eat** is the *Eleven 22 Grill* (Ⓣ250/344-2443; Ⓦwww.eleven22.ca; from 5pm daily) at 1122 10th Ave South. It has a wide range of dishes (from Greek and Asian to fondues); mains cost $11–24.

Glacier National Park

GLACIER NATIONAL PARK is part of the Selkirk and Columbia Mountains rather than the Rockies, but on the ground little sets it apart from the magnificence of the other national parks, and all the park agencies include it on an equal footing with its larger neighbours. Yet to a great extent it's the domain of ice, rain and snow; the weather is so atrocious that locals like to say it rains or snows four days out of every three, and in truth you can expect a soaking three days out of five. Despite this, the park is a big draw for **climbers** and, to a slightly lesser extent, **day-hikers** and **backpackers**. As the name suggests, **glaciers** – 422 of them – form its dominant

Glacier and Revelstoke parks run on **Pacific time**, an hour behind Yoho NP and Alberta.

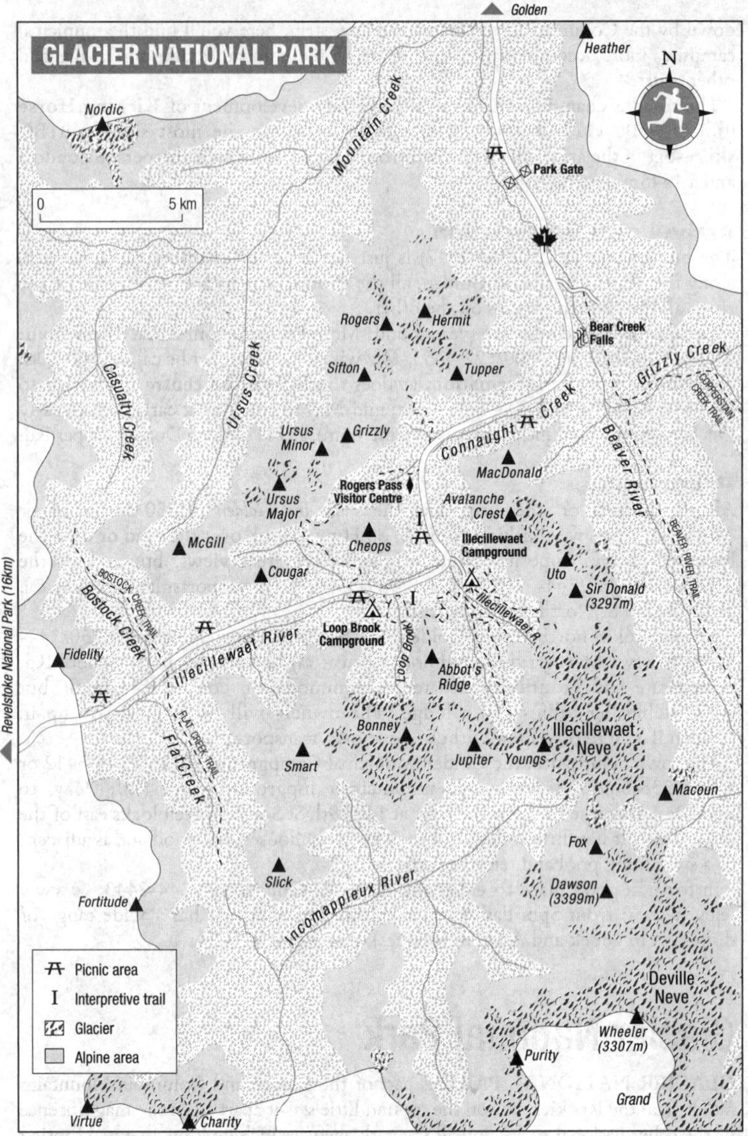

landscape, with fourteen percent of the park permanently blanketed with ice or snow. Scientists have identified 68 new glaciers forming on the sites of previously melted ice sheets in the park – a highly uncommon phenomenon. The main ice sheet, the still-growing **Illecillewaet Neve**, is easily seen from the Trans-Canada Hwy or from the park visitor centre.

The Columbia range's peaks are every bit as imposing as those of the Rockies – Glacier's highest point, **Mount Dawson**, is 3399m tall – and historically they've presented as much of a barrier as their neighbours. Aboriginal peoples and then railwaymen shunned the icefields and the rugged interior for centuries until the discovery of **Rogers Pass** (1321m) in 1881 by Major A.B. Rogers, the chief engineer of the Canadian Pacific Railway.

Despite the railway's best efforts the pounding of repeated avalanches eventually forced the company to bore a tunnel under the pass, and the flow of visitors fell to almost nothing. In the 1950s the pass was chosen as the route for the Trans-Canada Hwy, whose completion in 1962 once again made the area accessible. This time huge snowsheds were built, backed up by the world's largest **avalanche-control system**. Experts monitor the slopes year-round, and at dangerous times they call in the army, who blast howitzers into the mountains to dislodge potential slips.

Arrival and information

Glacier is easy to get to, but it doesn't tie in well with a circuit of the other parks; many people end up traversing it at some point simply because the main route west passes this way, but comparatively few stop, preferring to admire the scenery from the road. The visitor centre is a flag stop for Greyhound **buses**, which zip through up to four to seven times a day in each direction.

The **Rogers Pass visitor centre** (daily: May to mid-June & early Sept to early Oct 8.30am–4.30pm; mid-June to early Sept 7.30am–8pm; last 3 weeks of Oct & first week of Nov closed; Dec–April 7am–5pm; ⓣ250/814-5232 or 837-7500, ⓦwww.pc.gc.ca), 1km west of Rogers Pass, is a draw in itself, attracting some 160,000 visitors annually. It sells park permits ($7.80), has good walking **maps** and houses a variety of high-tech audiovisual aids. In summer (July & Aug), book here for **guided walks** (1–6hr), some of them fairly strenuous, featuring flowers, wildlife and glaciers. Walks start at the Illecillewaet Campground Welcome Station. Also ask about trips to the **Nakimu Caves**, some of the largest in Canada; you need to apply for a permit to enter them and be led by a guide. If you're heading for the backcountry, pick up *Footloose in the Columbias*, a hiker's guide to Glacier and Revelstoke national parks. Next to the visitor centre, a **garage** and a **shop** are the only services on the Trans-Canada between Golden and Revelstoke, an hour's drive east and west respectively.

Accommodation

Hotel **accommodation** is best sought in Golden (see p.682), although we've listed two in-park options below, both of which tend to be full in season. If you don't manage to get into either of the three first-come, first-served, park-run **campsites** (or want more facilities) there are three commercial campsites west of the park on the Trans-Canada Hwy towards Revelstoke. **Wilderness camping** is allowed anywhere if you register with the visitor centre, pay for a nightly backcountry camping permit ($9.80) and pitch more than 5km from the road.

Glacier Park Lodge Just east of the Rogers Pass visitor centre ⓣ250/837-2126 or 1-888/567-4477, ⓦwww.glacierparklodge.ca. This excellent establishment has fifty rooms, six of which are suites. There's a sauna, outdoor pool and jacuzzi,a lounge with a fireplace and free wi-fi. The "family" dining room offers a weekend buffet and the lodge cafeteria is open from 7am–5pm. ④

Heather Mountain Lodge 24km east of the Rogers Pass visitor centre ⓣ250/344-7490 or 1-866/344-7490, ⓦwww.heathermountainlodge.com. There are 22 rooms in this spacious, fir- and larch-beam lodge; all units have private bathrooms and good views of the mountains. The main lodge has two large fireplaces, a deck with a jacuzzi, a dining room and a slightly more relaxed second-floor lounge.

Hillside Lodge 13km west of Golden, 500m off Hwy 1 ⓣ250/344-7281, ⓦwww.hillsidechalets.com. With sixty acres of space, finding something more secluded here isn't difficult. Choose from one or two-bedroom chalets, the slightly smaller "chalet units", a summer-only suite with a private jacuzzi or B&B rooms in the main lodge. There's a guest lounge in the main lodge and plenty of trails leading off the property, good for short strolls down to the Blaeberry River. ⑥–⑧

Canyon Hot Springs Resort Campground 35km east of the Rogers Pass visitor centre ⓣ250/837-2420, ⓦwww.canyonhotsprings.com. Close to the park's borders, with about two hundred secluded sites for tents ($29) and RVs ($39), as well as cabins for two (❺) and chalets for four (❽). The on-site hot springs –piped from two miles awy to fill an outdoor pool and hot pool – make it all the more attractive to the weary traveller. Open May to late Sept.

Illecillewaet Campground 3km west of the Rogers Pass visitor centre. This is the closest of the three park-run campsites to the visitor centre. It has sixty pitches and is the trailhead for six walks. Facilities include flush toilets, water, kitchen shelters and firewood ($8.80). Open late June to early Sept; $21.50.

Loop Brook Campground 5km west of the Rogers Pass visitor centre. The twenty sites here have the same facilities as the Illecillewaet. It's self-serve check-in, but park staff will register visitors in the evening. Open July to early Sept; $21.50.

Mount Sir Donald Campground 1km west of the Loop Brook site. You can only stay at one of the fifteen primitive sites here in July and August, and fires are not permitted. It's also self-serve check-in and park staff will eventually show up to register you. $15.70.

Hiking in Glacier National Park

Some of the park's 21 trails (140km of walking in all) push close to glaciers for casual views of the ice – though only two spots are now safe at the toe of the Illecillewaet – and the backcountry is noticeably less busy than in the Big Four parks to the east.

The easiest short strolls off the Hwy are: the **Abandoned Rails Trail** (1.2km one-way; 30min), along old rail beds to abandoned snowsheds between the Rogers Pass visitor centre and the Summit Monument (suitable for wheelchairs); the **Loop Trail** (1.6km) from the viewpoint just east of the Loop Brook campsite, full of viewpoints and features relating to the building of the railway; the **Hemlock Grove Boardwalk** (400m), a stroll through old-growth stands of western hemlock trees, some more than 350 years old (wheelchair-accessible; trailhead midway between Loop Brook campsite and the park's western boundary); and the **Meeting of the Water Trail** (30min) from the Illecillewaet campsite, the hub of Glacier's trail network. Six manageable day-hikes from the campsite give superb views onto the glaciers, particularly the Great Glacier, Avalanche Crest and Abbott's Ridge trails. Other hikes, not centred on the campsite, include **Bostock Creek** (9km) and **Flat Creek** (9km), a pair of paths on the park's western edge heading north and south, respectively, from the same point on the hwy.

Among the backpacking routes, the longest is the **Beaver River Trail** (30km-plus), which peels off from the hwy at the Mount Shaughnessy picnic area on the eastern edge (also a favourite mountain-bike route). The single best long-haul trail is the **Copperstain Creek Trail** (16km), which leaves the Beaver River path after 3km, and climbs to meadows and bleak alpine tundra from where camping and onward walking options are almost endless.

Mount Revelstoke National Park

The smallest national park in the region, **MOUNT REVELSTOKE NATIONAL PARK** is a somewhat arbitrary creation, put together at the request of local people in 1914 to protect the Clachnacudainn Range of the Columbia Mountains. The lines on the map mean little, for the thrilling scenery in the 16km of no-man's-land between Glacier and Revelstoke is largely the same as that within the parks. The mountains here are especially steep, their slopes often scythed clear of trees by avalanches. The views from the Trans-Canada Hwy, as it peeks out of countless tunnels, are of forests and snowcapped peaks aplenty and, far below, the railway and the Illecillewaet River crashing through a twisting, steep-sided gorge.

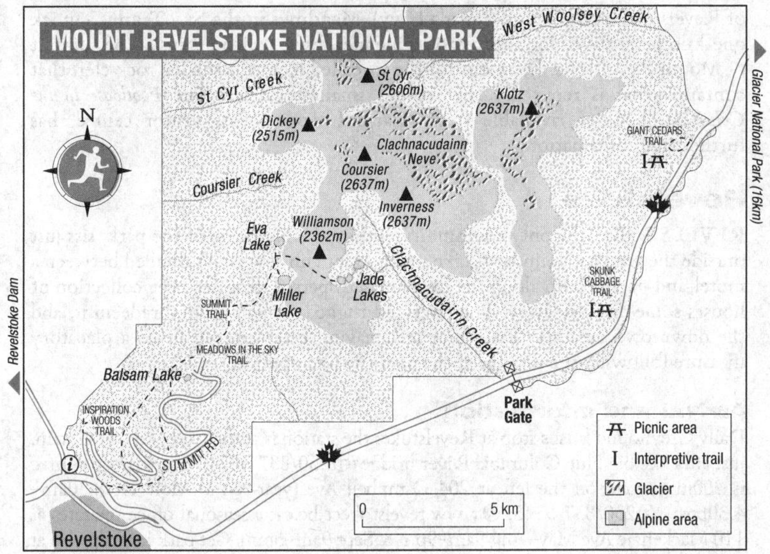

Arrival and information

The main access to the park interior is the very busy **Meadows-in-the-Sky-Parkway**, which is only open during the snow-free season (May to early June & Sept to early Oct 9am–5pm; mid-June to early Aug 7am–10pm; remainder of Aug 7am–8.30pm; the road is gated and locked outside these hours). It strikes north from the Trans-Canada Hwy at the town of Revelstoke and winds 26km to the top of the eponymous mountain (1938m) through forest and alpine meadows noted for glorious displays of wildflowers; there is a park **welcome station kiosk** (staffed mid-June to early Aug 7am–10pm) at the start of the road, but when it's closed you have to visit the park administration office in the Revelstoke post office (300 3rd St West for information; year-round Mon–Fri 8.30am–noon & 1–4.30pm; ⓣ250/837-7500).

You can walk partway up the mountain on the **Summit Trail** (10km one-way; 4hr), which begins from the car park at the base of the mountain on Summit Road, to Balsam Lake. From there, you can continue to the top or take a regular shuttle bus (daily: 10am–4.20pm during snow-free periods) to the summit from a car park at Balsam Lake. The daily **park fee** is $7.80.

Hikes in Mount Revelstoke Park

Many of the longer of the park's ten official **trails** start from the summit; serious backpackers prefer to head to **Eagle Lake**, off Summit Road, rather than take the more popular **Miller Lake Trail** (6km one-way). The award-winning **Giant Cedars Trail** is a wooded one-kilometre jaunt with ten interpretive exhibits off the road on the park's eastern edge, its boardwalks negotiating a tract of ancient forest crammed with eight hundred year-old western red cedars and rough-barked western hemlock (the trailhead begins at the Giant Cedars Picnic Area, 30km east of Revelstoke on the Trans-Canada Hwy). You could also try the **Skunk Cabbage Boardwalk** (1.2km), an easy trail through temperate forest and wetland inhabited by muskrat, beaver and numerous birds (trailhead is 28km east of Revelstoke on the Trans-Canada Hwy). **Meadows in the Sky Trail** is a quick one-kilometre paved loop through alpine meadows, which begins at the summit of Mount Revelstoke. Look out for the so-called Icebox, a shaded rock cleft that contains what is reputedly the world's smallest glacier. The *Footloose in the Columbias* booklet, available from Glacier's Rogers Pass visitor centre, has further trail information.

Revelstoke

REVELSTOKE, the only community within striking range of the park, sits just outside the western boundary. Like many mountain towns, it's divided between a motel-and-garage strip along the hwy and a dispersed, frontier-type collection of houses some distance away. The river and rugged scenery around redeem it, and the downtown area also has a nice feel, having been spruced up as a placatory measure following the disaster at the dam site (see opposite).

Arrival and information

Daily Greyhound **buses** stop at Revelstoke; the station is at the west end of the strip, just after the big blue Columbia River bridge (Ⓣ250/837-5874). The **visitor centre** is 200m beyond on the left at 204 Campbell Ave (year-round Mon–Fri 8.30am–4.30pm; Ⓣ250/837-5345, Ⓦwww.revelstokecc.bc.ca; a seasonal office operates at 110 Mackenzie Ave May–Aug 9am–9pm & Sept 9am–5pm). Get park information at either location, or visit the **Park administration office** on 3rd Street in the **post office** building (see p.687) or the Rogers Pass visitor centre. The park office also has a store for the Friends of Mount Revelstoke and Glacier National Parks (Ⓣ250/837-2010, Ⓦwww.friendsrevglacier.com) that is useful for **maps** and guides.

Accommodation

Revelstoke has plenty of **accommodation**, including half a dozen campsites. Backcountry camping in the park is $9.80, with tent-pads, outhouses and food-storage poles provided at Eva and Jade lakes, but no camping is allowed in the Miller Lake area or anywhere within 5km of the Trans-Canada and Summit Road. Registration at the Park Administration office is obligatory.

Hotels, motels and hostels

Peaks Lodge 4km west of Revelstoke on Hwy 1 Ⓣ250/837-2176 or 1-877/814-2123, Ⓦwww.peakslodge.com. It won't win any awards for decor, but the setting – at the base of Boulder Mountain – is rustic enough, with a choice of rooms in the main lodge, a three-storey motel or more private cabins. It's convenient for hikes, birdwatching and the like. ❹–❺

Regent Hotel 112 First St East Ⓣ250/837-2107, Ⓦwww.regentinn.com. It's safe to say this centrally-located hotel is probably the best in town. The rooms have "standard" and "premium" town or mountain views, massive beds and large bathtubs. If you're looking for more privacy or need group accommodation, you can plump for the one- and two-bedroom units in the "The Annex", just across the street. Hotel amenities include an on-site restaurant and pub, a sometimes boisterous club and a breakfast café.

Revelstoke Gateway Inn 1500 1st St Ⓣ250/837-2164 or 1-877/837-8337 Ⓦwww.revelstokegatewayinn.com. One of the cheapest motels in town; some rooms have kitchenettes and the more roomy two- and three-bedroom family suites have fully-equipped kitchens. There's free internet access and a continental breakfast is included in the price. ❹

SameSun Hostel 400 2nd St West Ⓣ250/837-4050, Ⓦwww.samesun.com/Revelstoke. Cheap private, semi-private and dorm beds ($24) and private rooms (from $53) convenient for local restaurants and supermarkets. Well run and offers free wi-fi in the common area, bike rentals and kitchen facilities. ❶

Campsites

Lamplighter Campground Ⓣ250/837-3385, Ⓦwww.revelstokecc.bc.ca/lamplighter. Off Hwy 1 before the Columbia River bridge; take Hwy 23 south towards Nakusp and turn into Nixon Rd (first left). A peaceful, fully serviced fifty site tent and RV ground within walking distance of downtown. Open May–Sept; tents $22, RVs $29.

Williamson Lake Campground 1818 Williamson Lake Rd ⓣ250/837-5512, ⓦwww.williamsonlakecampground.com. Pleasant, fifty site lakeside campsite 4km south of the town centre. There are free hot showers, flush toilets, laundry, a beach, canoe and rowboat rentals and a mini-golf course. Tents $21, RVs $25.

The town and around

Downtown, there's the small but polished **Revelstoke Railway Museum** (May, June, Sept daily 9am–5pm; July & Aug daily 9am–8pm; March–April & Oct–Nov Thurs–Tues 9am–5pm; Dec–Feb Fri–Tues 11am–4pm; $8), which has a steam engine, snowploughs and assorted memorabilia relating to the building of the stretch of the CPR between Field and Kamloops. If you want to relax close to town, try warm-watered **Williamson Lake**, a favourite swimming spot for locals.

A trip to Canada's largest dam may sound dull, but the **Revelstoke Dam** (daily late May to mid-Oct 10am–5pm; $6) makes an interesting outing. Located 5km north of town on Hwy 23, the 175-metre tall barrier holds back the waters of the Columbia River, around 500km from its source. Its sleek, space-age **visitor centre** offers a two-hour self-guided tour, which omits the fact that insufficient mapping during the construction caused a landslide that threatened to swamp Revelstoke: millions had to be spent or it would have been curtains for the town.

Eating and drinking

Eating possibilities include the *Frontier Restaurant* on the Trans-Canada Hwy, part of the eponymous motel near the visitor centre, which serves up superior steak-and-salad meals at reasonable prices, with friendly service and a genuine cowpoke atmosphere. In town, the *One-Twelve Restaurant & Lounge* in the *Regent Inn* at 112 Victoria Rd (ⓣ250/837-2107; ⓦwww.regentinn.com) is a favourite, with good food (mains cost $15–30), a lively pub and dancefloor.

Kootenay National Park

KOOTENAY NATIONAL PARK, lying across the Continental Divide from Banff in BC, is the least known of the four contiguous parks of the Rockies, and the easiest to miss out – many people prefer to follow the Trans-Canada Hwy through Yoho rather than commit themselves to the less enthralling westward journey on Hwy 3 imposed by Kootenay. Yet the park's scenery is as impressive as that of its neighbours and if you're not determined to head west you could drive a neat loop from Banff through Kootenay on Hwy 93 to **Radium Hot Springs** (the only town in this area), then head north on Hwy 95, and back on the Trans-Canada through Yoho to Lake Louise and Banff. You could drive this in a day and still have time for a few short walks and a dip in Radium's hot springs to boot.

Kootenay lends itself to admiration from a car, bus or bike, mainly because it's little more than a sixteen-kilometre-wide ribbon of land running either side of Hwy 93 for around 100km (the hwy here is known as the **Kootenay** or **Banff–Windermere Parkway**). All its numerous easy **short walks** start immediately off the hwy. Options for **day-hikes** are more limited, though the best of the longer walks are as good as anything in the Rockies and can be extended into outstanding two-day (or more) backpacking options. If you want no more than a stroll from a car or bike follow the **Marble Canyon** and **Paint Pots** trails; for something a bit longer go for the **Stanley Glacier** walk; if you're after the best day-hike the choice is the **Kindersley Pass Trail**, though it's a close-run thing with the Floe Lake Trail

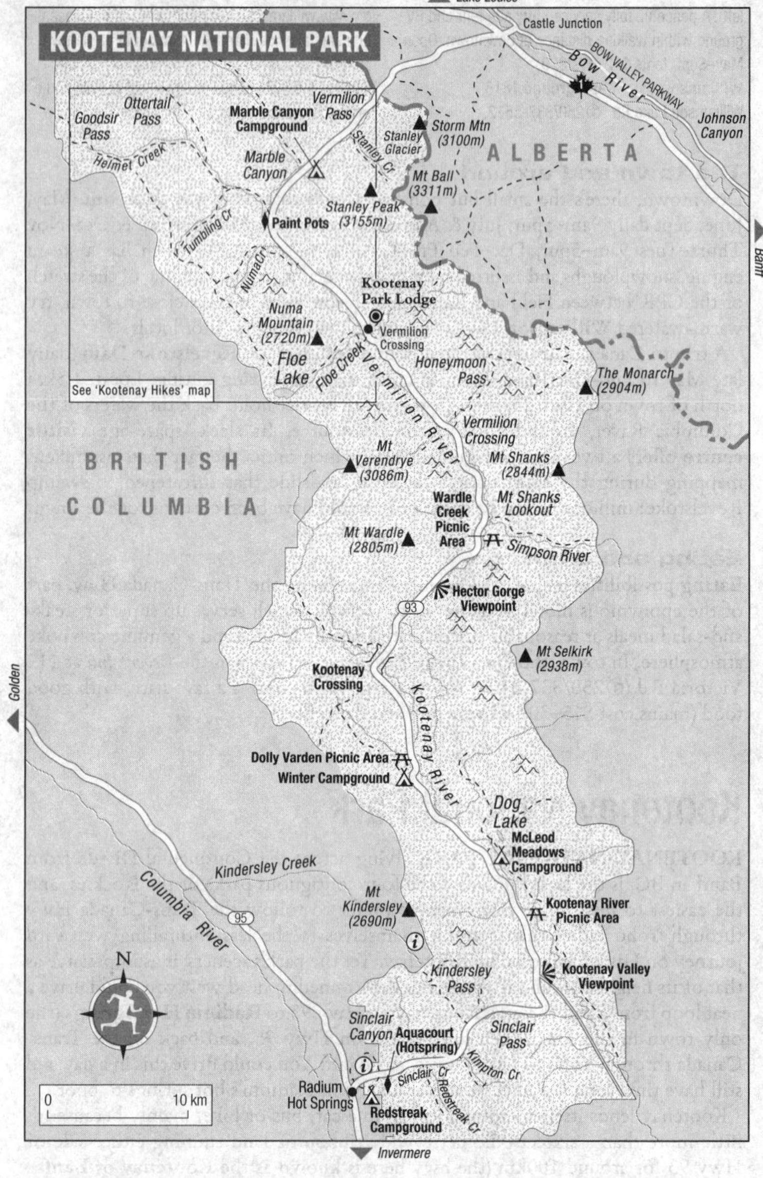

to Floe Lake and its possible continuation northwest over the Numa Pass and down Numa Creek back to the hwy. If you have time do both of latter two hikes – they're two of the top ten or so walks in the Rockies. If you have more time, the Rockwall Trail (Floe Lake–Numa Pass–Rockwell Pass–Helmet Falls) is widely considered among the Rockies' top three or four backpacking routes. See p.694 and our maps to make sense of these routes.

Arrival and information

The only practicable access to Kootenay is on Hwy 93, a good road that leaves the Trans-Canada Hwy at Castle Junction (in Banff National Park), traverses Kootenay from north to south, and joins Hwy 95 at Radium Hot Springs at the southern entrance. Radium offers the only practical accommodation options, bar a trio of park-run campsites and handful of rooms at Vermilion Crossing, a summer-only huddle of shop, cabins and petrol station midway through the park. The two daily Greyhound **buses** east and west on the southern BC route between Cranbrook, Banff and Calgary stop at Vermilion Crossing and Radium. **Park permits** ($9.80) are required for entry.

If you come from the east you can get **information** from the Kootenay Park Lodge visitor centre at Vermilion Crossing (daily: mid-May to mid-Oct; ⓣ403/762-9196). Coming from the south, the main park **visitor centre** (daily: mid-May to mid-June & second week of Sept 9am–5pm; mid-June to early Sept 9am–7pm; mid-Sept to early Oct 9am–4pm; ⓣ250/347-9505, ⓦwww.pc.gc.ca) is at 7556 Main St East, at Redstreak Road, in Radium Hot Springs. The centre provides a free *Backcountry Guide to Kootenay National Park*, all you need walk-wise if you're not planning anything too ambitious. The park entrance itself is on Hwy 93, farther east and close to the Radium Hot Springs Pools (see p.695).

Kootenay, has a "Friends" organization (ⓦwww.friendsofkootenay.ca), which helps run **guided walks** and other activities: walks should be booked at the visitor centre.

Accommodation

Camping options handily outweigh those of the indoor variety in the park A dozen or more **backcountry sites** with pit toilets and firewood are scattered within easy backpacking range of the hwy; you'll need a **permit** ($9.80) from the visitor centres. If you stay at the Redstreak campsite listed below, the Redstreak Campground Trail (2.2km) takes you from the northwest corner of the site to the **Radium Hot Springs Pools**, while the Valleyview Trail (1.4km) takes you from the site entrance into Radium village, avoiding Redstreak Road.

Dolly Varden Campground 36km north of Radium Hot Springs village, on Hwy 93. The seven drive-through sites at this primitive site are for winter camping only. Amenities include pit toilets and kitchen shelters. Open from early Oct; $15.70.

Kootenay Park Lodge Hwy 93 at Vermilion Crossing. It's the only indoor option in the heart of the park, so you'll need to book your spot in one the ten rustic cabins here well in advance. Most of them have fireplaces and several come with a hotplate or microwave; one cabin has a fully-equipped kitchen. There's also an on-site restaurant (mid-May to Sept), small library and a shop selling coffee, sandwiches, gifts and clothing. Open mid-May to Sept. ❻

Marble Canyon 7km south of the Banff-Kootenay boundary. A high-altitude campsite that's close to an interpretive trail along the Marble Canyon Gorge. There are 61 sites and amenities include flush toilets, piped cold water and kitchen shelters with stoves. Open late June to early Sept; $21.50.

McLeod Meadows 27km north of Radium Hot Springs village. Situated along the Kootenay River, the 98 sites here are spacious, and the scenic Dog Lake (see p.694) is a 2.5km stroll away. Amenities include flush toilets, piped cold water and kitchen shelters. Open early June to late Sept; $21.50.

Redstreak Campground 2.5km above Radium Hot Springs village, off Redstreak Rd ⓣ1-877/737-3783 for reservations or 250/347-9567, ⓦwww.pccamping.ca. This is the only park-run campsite that accepts reservations (for stays during the third week of May & mid-June to early Sept only). Its proximity to Radium village and the hotsprings themselves, as well as its amenities – flush toilets, hot showers, playgrounds, a theatre and partial or full RV hook-ups – make its 242 sites a justifiably popular place to stay. Open early May-late Sept; tents $27.40, RVs $32.30 or $38.20.

Hikes in Kootenay National Park

There's a nice spread of short and some much longer walks and hikes in the park, many of them providing the chance to see an excellent range of wildlife. The best of these are the **Kindersely Pass Trail** (day-hike), in the park's southern half, and the **Rockwall Trail** (day-hike or multi-day backpacking), in the park's northern half. The rest of the longish day-walks are in the park's northern half, accessed on the west side of the hwy from the Marble Canyon, Paint Pots, Numa Creek and Floe Lake parking areas.

If you're doing any of these hikes, we recommend checking in at the visitor centre for the latest trail conditions and advice. You can also pick up the *Kootenay National Park Backcountry Guide* from the visitor centre or download it from the Parks Canada website (www.pc.gc.ca).

Vermilion Pass and around

Vermilion Pass (1637m) marks the northern entrance to the park, the Continental Divide's watershed and the border between Alberta and BC. Little fanfare accompanies the transition – only the barren legacy of a huge forest fire (started by a single lightning bolt) that ravaged the area for four days in 1968, leaving a 24-square-kilometre blanket of stark, blackened trunks. Take the short **Fireweed Trail** (1km) through the desolation from the car park at the pass to see how nature deals with such disasters, indeed how it seems to invite lightning fires to promote phoenix-like regeneration. The ubiquitous lodgepole pine, for example, specifically requires the heat of a forest fire to crack open its resin-sealed cones and release its seeds.

At Vermilion Pass a broad carpet of lodgepole pines have taken root among the blasted remnants of the earlier forest, while young plants and shrubs are pushing up

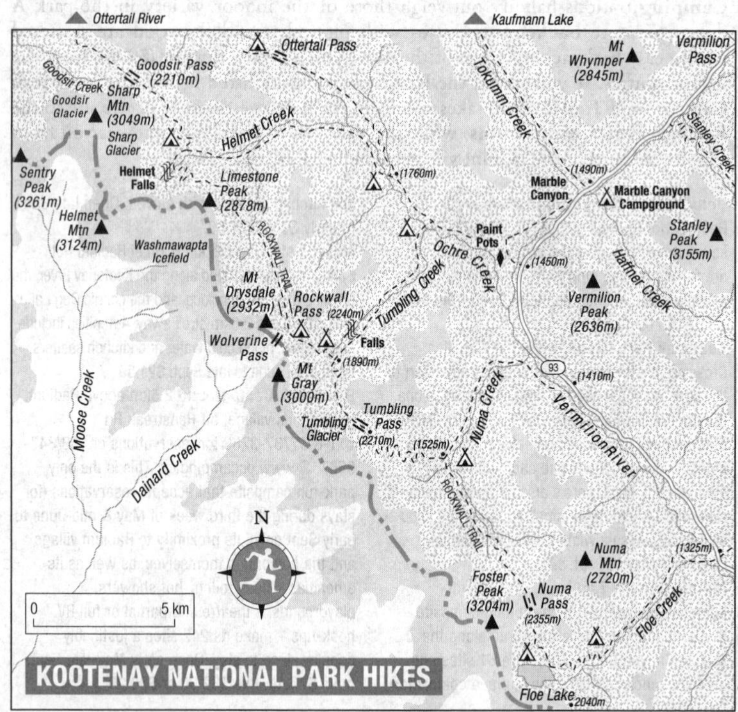

into the new clearings. Birds, small mammals and deer, elk and moose are being attracted to new food sources and, more significantly, **black and grizzly bears** are returning to the area. Burning takes place in the park, and some trails may be closed as a result: latest details are posted at the park centre or the Parks Canada website.

Stanley Glacier, Marble Canyon and Kaufmann Lake Trail

About 3km south of Vermilion Pass, the small, well-defined **Stanley Glacier Trail** (4.2km; 365m ascent; 1hr 30min) strikes off up Stanley Creek from a parking area on the eastern side of the hwy. In its first 2km the trail provides you with a hike through the Vermilion Pass Burn (see opposite), but more to the point pushes into the beautiful hanging valley below Stanley Peak (3155m). Here you can enjoy close-up views of the Stanley Glacier and its surrounding recently glaciated landscapes. The area is also known for its fossils, and for the chance to see marmots, pikas and white-tailed ptarmigan.

Marble Canyon, 8km south of Vermilion Pass, the site of a park-run **campsite**, has an easy trail (800m) that's probably the most heavily trafficked of Kootenay's shorter hikes. The track crosses a series of log bridges over Tokumm Creek, which has carved through a fault in the limestone over the last eight thousand years to produce a 600m-long and 37m-deep gorge. In cold weather this is a fantastic medley of ice and snow, but in summer the climax is the viewpoint from the top of the path onto a thundering waterfall as the creek pounds its way through the narrowest section of the gorge. The rock here was once mistakenly identified as marble – hence the canyon's name; the white marble-like rock is actually dolomite limestone.

One of the park's better long hikes, the **Kaufmann Lake Trail** (15km one-way; 570m ascent; allow 4–6hr one-way), also starts from the Marble Canyon car park. It climbs to one of the park's loveliest high-mountain lakes, where there's a campsite. The first few kilometres of the trail – easy valley and meadow walking – make for an appealing stroll of about an hour.

The Paint Pots and Helmet Creek Trail

You could extend the Marble Canyon walk by picking up the Paint Pots Trail south, which puts another 2.7km onto your walk, or drive 2km south and stroll 1km to reach the same destination. Either way you come first to the Ochre Beds (after 800m) and then (1.5km) to the **Paint Pots**, one of the Rockies' more magical spots: red, orange and mustard-coloured pools prefaced by damp, moss-clung forest and views across the white water of the Vermilion River to the snow-capped mountains beyond.

The pools' colours are created by iron-laden water bubbling up from three mineral springs through clay sediments deposited on the bed of an ancient glacial lake. Aboriginal peoples from all over North America collected the coloured clays from the ponds and ochre beds to make into small cakes, which they baked in embers. The fired clay was then ground into powder – **ochre** – and added to animal fat or fish oil to use in rock, tepee or ceremonial body painting. The Stoney and Ktunaxa peoples saw these oxide-stained pools and their surroundings as inhabited by animal and thunder spirits – which didn't stop European speculators in the 1920s from mining the ochre to manufacture paint in Calgary.

The car park is the trailhead for three longer (day-hike or backpack) routes, all of which branch off from the Ochre Creek Valley. The first is the rather dull Ottertail Pass Trail. The second is the **Tumbling Creek Trail** (10.3km; 440m ascent to the intersection with the Rockwall Trail) and the third is the **Helmet Creek Trail** (14.3km; 310m ascent, another intersection with the Rockwall Trail), a long day-hike to the amazing 365-metre **Helmet Waterfalls**.

The Rockwall Trail

The **Rockwall Trail**, an incredible thirty-kilometre (55km including approach trails; 1450m ascent), backpacking high-level trail, is the most popular backcountry, long-distance hike in the park. It follows the line of the mountains on the west side of Hwy 93, and can be joined using the Tumbling Creek, Helmet Creek, Floe Lake and Numa Lake trails. You could hike the trail in about two days, making one 55km loop, or do a series of three shorter loops using the adjoining trails listed above. The trail proper usually doesn't open until early to mid-July.

There are five backcountry campsites along the trail, but a quota system is in place to limit the enviromental impact, so **reservations** are recommended. You can do so up to three months in advance by contacting the visitor centre (see p.695) in Radium Hot Springs.

Floe Lake and Numa Creek trails

The best of the day-hikes after Kindersley Pass (see opposite) is the easier **Floe Lake Trail** (10.5km; 715m ascent), in the park's northern section, up to a spell-binding lake edged by a 1000m sheer escarpment and a small glacier. There are campsites on the route, and another tie-in to the Rockwall Trail. The **Numa Creek Trail** (6.4km; 115m ascent), further to the north, is less enthralling – though you could use it as a downhill leg to add to the Floe Lake Trail.

Vermilion Crossing and Mount Assiniboine Provincial Park

Vermilion Crossing, 20km south of the Paint Pots Trail, is gone in a flash, but it's the only place, in summer at least, to find petrol and food in the park. You can also stop to walk the **Verendyre Creek Trail** (2.1km), accessed west off the hwy, an easy stroll, but forest-enclosed, and with only limited views of Mount Verendrye as a reward. One of the Rockies' tougher walks heads east from the Crossing, up over Honeymoon Pass and Redearth Pass to Egypt Lake and the Trans-Canada Hwy in Banff National Park, while to the south equally demanding trails provide the only westside access into the wilderness of **Mount Assiniboine Provincial Park**.

Sandwiched between Kootenay and Banff, this wilderness park was created in honour of Mount Assiniboine (3618m), a sabre-tooth-shaped mountain with one of the most dramatic profiles imaginable, whose native Stoney name means "those who cook by placing hot rocks in water". The **Simpson Road Trail** (8.2km) leads to the park boundary, and then divides into two paths (20km and 32km) to Lake Magog in the heart of Assiniboine. Some 8.5km beyond the Crossing look out for the Animal Lick, a spot where animals come down to lick nutrients from a natural mineral source: with luck you may see elk, mule deer and even moose here. Over the next few kilometres, for similar reasons, you might also see **mountain goats** by banks at the side of the road.

Kootenay Crossing

Kootenay Crossing is no more than a ceremonial spot – it was where the ribbon was cut to open Hwy 93 in 1923 – though a clutch of short trails fan out from its park warden station, and the nearby Dolly Varden campsite (see p.691) is the park's only specific site for winter camping. **Wardle Creek** nearby is a good place to unpack a picnic if you're determined to stick to the road.

Around 11km south of the Kootenay Crossing is the **McLeod Meadows** campsite (see p.691), and immediately behind it to the east the easy **Dog Lake Trail** (2.5km), much tramped as an after-dinner leg-stretcher by campers (the trail can also be accessed from the hwy at the picnic area 500m south). The path offers glimpses of the Kootenay Valley through the trees, and ends in a marsh-edged lake whose temperate microclimate makes it ideal for nature study. You may see deer, elk and coyotes, and – if you're lucky – bears and moose. Several types of orchid also bloom here in early summer (June & July). About 11km further on, the **Kootenay Valley Viewpoint** offers one of the broadest views on the hwy, with great vistas of the Mitchell and Vermilion mountain ranges, and with them the inevitable hordes in search of a photo opportunity.

Sinclair Pass and the Kindersley Pass Trail

For its final run down out of the park, the hwy doglegs west through the **Sinclair Pass**, a red-cliffed gorge filled with the falling waters of Sinclair Creek and the start of the **Kindersley Pass Trail** – if you have time and energy for only one long walk in Kootenay, make it this one. It's a strenuous 9.8-kilometre trail that climbs to Kindersley Pass and then cuts northeast for the steep final push to Kindersley Summit (2210m). Here you can enjoy the sublime prospect of an endless succession of peaks fading to the horizon away to the northeast. Rather than double back down through the open tundra, many people push on another 2km (trail vague) and contour around the head of the Sinclair Creek valley before dropping off the ridge (the Kindersley–Sinclair Col) to follow the well-defined **Sinclair Creek Trail** (6.4km) down to meet the hwy 1km from the starting point (do the hike this way round – the Sinclair Creek Trail is a long, dull climb).

If this seems too much of a slog, Sinclair Pass offers three far easier short trails, all marked off the hwy to the west. The best is the **Juniper Trail** (3.2km), accessed just 300m inside the park's West Gate. The trail drops to Sinclair Creek and over the next couple of kilometres touches dry canyon, arid forest slopes of juniper and Douglas fir and thick woods of western red cedar before emerging at the hot springs, or Aquacourt, 1.4km up the road from the start. The **Redstreak Creek Trail** (2.7km), 4.5km east of the West Gate, starts off as a good forest walk, but tails off into dullness, as does the **Kimpton Creek Trail** (4.8km), also on the south side of the road and canyon, accessed 7.5km east of the West Gate.

Radium Hot Springs

RADIUM HOT SPRINGS is far less attractive than its evocative name suggests but, as the service centre for Kootenay, its tacky motels and garages are likely to claim your attention and money. The town spreads across the flats of the Columbia Valley, 3km from the southern/western entrance at the junction of Hwys 93 and 95. For **information** visit the park centre, which has a Chamber of Commerce desk (hours as for park centre – see p.691; ⓣ250/347-9331 or 1-888/347-9331, ⓦwww.radiumhotsprings.com).

The Hot Springs

The **hot springs** (hot pool: daily mid-May to mid-Oct 9am–11pm; mid-Oct to mid-May Sun–Thurs noon–9pm, Fri & Sat noon–10pm; cool pool: daily mid-May to late June & early Sept to mid-Oct 1pm–8pm; late June to early Sept 9am–11pm; mid-Oct to mid-May Fri 6–9pm & Sat noon–9pm; ⓣ250/347-9485 or 1-800/767-1611, ⓦwww.hotsprings.ca) are open year-round and, together with the park visitor centre, are nicely away from the settlement, 2km north of town off Hwy 93; park authorities administer the springs.

Aboriginal peoples used the springs for centuries, and commercial white development started as early as 1890 when Roland Stuart bought the area for $160. Traces of supposedly therapeutic radium found in the water turned Stuart's investment into a recreational gold mine. When the government appropriated the springs for inclusion in the national park, it paid him $40,000 – a small fortune, but considerably less than what they were worth, which at the time was estimated to be $500,000. The pools today are outdoors, but serviced by a large, modern centre. In summer, four thousand people per day take the plunge into the odourless 45°C waters, enough to discourage any idea of a quiet swim, though in late evening or off-season you can escape the bedlam and pretend more easily that the water is having some sort of soothing effect. The radium traces sound a bit worrying, but 300,000 visitors a year don't seem to mind.

Practicalities

If possible, aim to **stay** in Invermere (see p.700) or one of the newer **motels** creeping up the Sinclair Valley around the hot springs area away from downtown: they're more expensive, but more attractively sited than the town's mirror-image motels. Try the big 120-room *Radium Resort*, 1km south of the springs at 8100 Golf Course Rd (ⓣ250/347-9311 or 1-800/667-6444, ⓦwww.radiumresort.com; ⑥), for all the trimmings, including swimming pool and massage therapist. Almost alongside the park entrance are the fourteen-room *Alpen* (ⓣ250/347-9823 or 1-888/788-3891, ⓦwww.alpenmotel.com; ⑤) and nine-room *Crescent* (ⓣ250/347-9570 or 1-888/295-8822; ③) motels. The *Radium International Hostel*, at the Misty River Lodge at the edge of the park (ⓣ250/347-9912, ⓦwww.radiumhostel.bc.ca; ①), has a kitchen, common room, bicycle storage and rental and two dorms with five or six beds ($26) and private rooms from $67.

Travel details

Trains

Banff to: Calgary and Vancouver with private Rocky Mountaineer Railtours (see Basics, p.37).
Jasper to: Edmonton (3 weekly; 5hr 30min); Prince Rupert via Prince George (3 weekly; 20hr); Vancouver (3 weekly).

Buses

Banff to: Calgary (5–8 daily; 1hr 30min); Calgary Airport (5–8 daily; 2hr); Golden (4 daily; 1hr 55min); Jasper (1 daily; 4hr 45min); Lake Louise (4–7 daily; 55min); Radium Hot Springs (1-2 daily; 2hr); Revelstoke (4 daily; 4hr 25min); Vancouver via Fort Macleod, Cranbrook, Nelson, Osoyoos and Hope (1–2 daily; 22hr); Vancouver via Kamloops (4 daily; 13hr); Vancouver via Vernon, Kelowna and Penticton (3 daily; 14hr).
Canmore to: Banff (5 daily; 15–25min); Calgary (4 daily; 1hr 15min); Lake Louise (4 daily; 1hr 15min); Vancouver (4 daily; 15hr 15min).
Jasper to: Banff (1 daily; 4hr 45min); Edmonton (6 daily; 4hr 30min); Lake Louise (1 daily; 3hr 45min); Prince George (1 daily, 5hr 15min); Vancouver via Mount Robson, Tete Jaune Cache and Kamloops (2 daily; 11hr 15min).
Lake Louise to: Banff (4–7 daily; 55min); Calgary (4–7 daily; 2hr 30min); Calgary Airport (5–8 daily; 3hr); Jasper (1 daily; 3hr 45min); Radium Hot Springs via Kootenay National Park (1hr 10min); Vancouver via Cranbrook, Nelson, Osoyoos and Hope (1–2 daily; 21hr); Vancouver via Kamloops (4 daily; 12hr); Vancouver via Vernon, Kelowna and Penticton (3 daily; 13hr).
Radium Hot Springs to: Banff via Lake Louise (1 daily; 2hr 5min); Calgary via Lake Louise and Banff (1 daily; 4hr 10min); Vancouver (3 daily; 13hr 25min).

The BC Interior

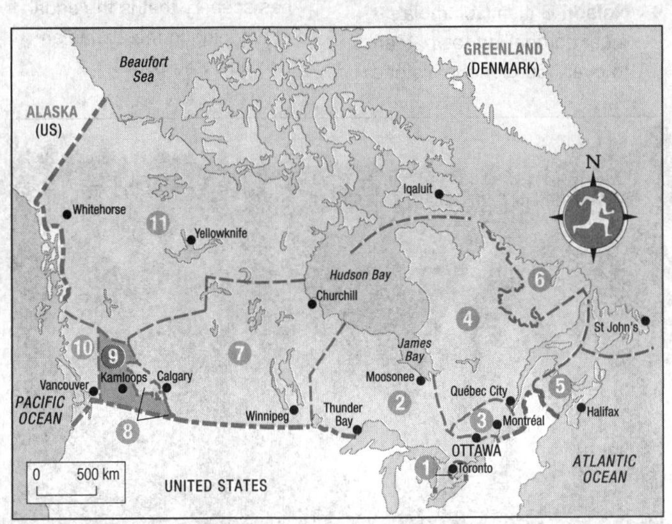

CHAPTER 9 Highlights

* **Fernie** Stay in this scenic, funky town and enjoy the longest ski season in the British Columbia Rockies. See p.703
* **The Kootenays** A pristine region of lakes, mountains, forests, hot springs and charming old-world villages. See p.709
* **Nelson** British Columbia's most compelling town, thanks to over 350 glorious historic buildings and a thriving cultural and alternative lifestyle scene. See p.712
* **Osoyoos** Beware the rattlesnakes slithering through the surreal, scrub-covered landscape of Canada's only desert. See p.727
* **Wells Gray Provincial Park** This vast tract of wilderness has scenery that is the equal of anything in the Canadian Rockies. See p.740

▲ Helmcken Falls, Wells Gray Provincial Park

9

The BC Interior

It says something about the magnificence of British Columbia's **interior** that you can enter it from the Rockies or Vancouver and find landscapes every bit as spectacular as those you've just left. Unfortunately, whatever your approach, both major routes through the region confine you to some of its least interesting areas. The most obvious and quickest east–west line, the **Trans-Canada Highway** (Hwy 1) isn't worth considering in its entirety unless you're in a hurry: little west of Revelstoke compares to what you can find further north or south. Nor does **Hwy 3**, which rumbles along the US border, offer convincing reasons for sticking to it religiously.

The most rewarding option for travellers heading west along the Trans-Canada Hwy is to detour south along the meandering **Columbia River Valley** (Hwy 93/95) and back north into the outstanding **Kootenay** region – an idyllic assortment of mountains and lakes and several towns, including **Nelson** and **Rossland**, that make fun bases. From the Kootenay's you can head west to the arid **Okanagan**: an almost Californian enclave of orchards, vineyards, warm lakes and resort towns, whose beaches and scorching summers draw hordes of holidaymakers from all over Canada and the western US. Running almost parallel west of the Okanagan the awesome **Fraser Canyon** makes for the most interesting corridor to the region for travellers heading to or from Vancouver, transporting them via **Kamloops** at its northern end. Though an unexceptional regional transport hub, Kamloops is the main gateway for the laidback **Shuswap** region – the lakes and rivers of which salmon swim to in dramatic numbers every autumn – and the magnificent **Wells Gray Provincial Park**.

The Columbia River Valley and Purcell Mountains

Heading south from Radium Hot Springs and Kootenay National Park (see p.689), or Golden, hwys 93 and 95 travel through scenery as spectacular as anything in the big Rockies parks to the north. The route follows the bottom of the broad **Columbia River** valley, bordered to the east by the soaring, craggy Rockies and to the west by the more rolling **Purcell Mountains**. At **Cranbrook** (see p.705) these hwys meets Hwy 3, which you can follow east via Fernie, Crowsnest Pass and Alberta, or west towards Vancouver along the US border – over which there are numerous crossings along the way. Greyhound **buses** ply all these routes.

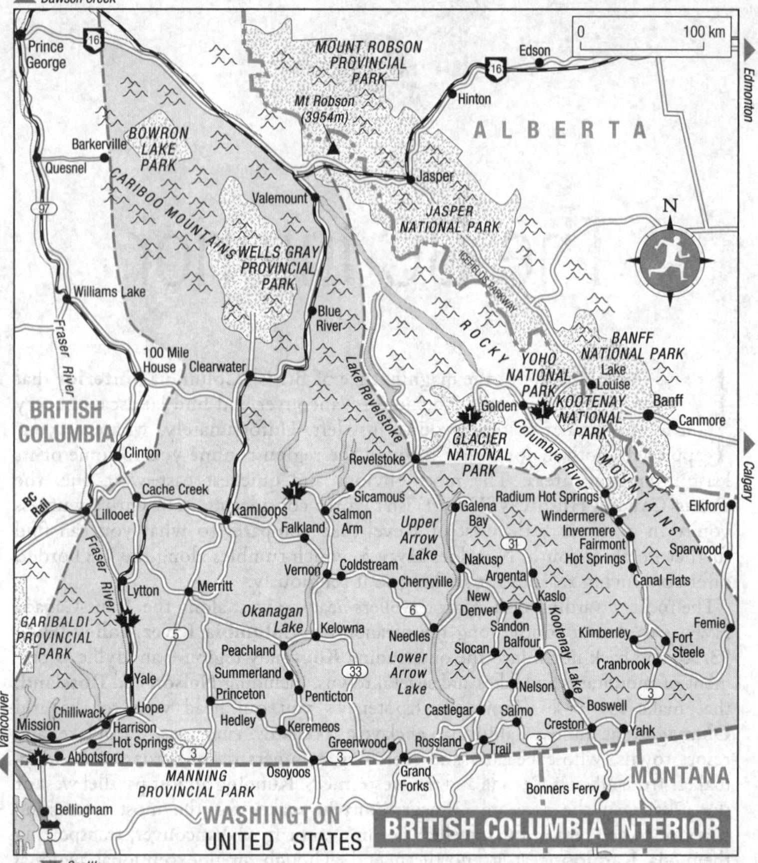

Invermere and around

About 16km south of Radium Hot Springs, on the western shore of Windermere Lake, **INVERMERE** is a feel-good summer resort with the usual range of aquatic temptations. However, droves of anglers, boaters and beach bums mean summer vacancies may be in short supply; call the main **visitor centre** (Mon–Fri 8.30am–4.30pm; Ⓣ250/342-2844, Ⓦwww.vchamber.ca) near the junction of Hwy 93 and Hwy 95 for B&B possibilities.

Of the town's handful of **motels** – the tidy *Mountain View Lodge* at 747 12th St (Ⓣ250/342-6618 or 1-877/442-6618, Ⓦwww.mtnviewlodge.ca; ⑤) has kitchenettes and wi-fi. Smarter is the downtown *Best Western Invermere Inn* at 1310 7th Ave, with its outdoor hot tub and fitness room (Ⓣ250/342-9246 or 1-800/661-8911, Ⓦwww.invermereinn.com; ⑥). The nearest provincial **campground**, with vehicle and tent sites, is 7km north at Dry Gulch Provincial Park ($19; May to mid-Sept).

For **food**, the popular *Blue Dog Café* at 1213 7th Ave is particularly good for vegetarians, serving lentil burgers and falafels ($8.50).

Panorama and the Purcell Wilderness

From Invermere the minor Toby Creek Road climbs 18km west to **Panorama Mountain Village** (central reservations ⓣ250/342-6941 or 1-800/663-2929, ⓦwww.panoramaresort.com; Nov to late-April; day-pass $72), a **ski resort**, with nine lifts and over 120 groomed runs, whose slick facilities and range of accommodation options provide summer lodgings for **golfers** visiting the Greywolf course and **mountain bikers** hurtling down lift-accessed routes (day-pass $39).

The chief appeal of the area in summer is **hiking**, particularly up the road toward the **Purcell Wilderness Conservancy Provincial Park** (the road stops 9km short of the park), one of the few easily accessible parts of the Purcell Mountains. If you have a tent and want a robust hiking experience, you could tackle the 61km **trail** through the area to Argenta (see p.715) on the northern end of Kootenay Lake, an excellent cross-country route that largely follows undemanding valleys except when crossing the Purcell watershed at Earl Grey Pass (2256m). Check ⓦwww.env.gov.bc.ca/bcparks for trail information.

Fairmont Hot Springs

Back in the Columbia River Valley, Hwy 93/95 heads south following the shores of Lake Windermere en-route to the ugly modern upmarket resort of **Fairmont Hot Springs** which spills over the Columbia's flat flood plain and feeds off the appeal of the hot springs themselves. The pools were commandeered from the Ktunaxa (Kootenay) peoples in 1922 for exploitation as a tourist resource; the calcium springs (daily 8am–10pm; $10 or $5 after 9pm) were particularly prized by Europeans because they lack the sulphurous stench of many BC hot dips. Locals have now opened some cheaper, makeshift pools above the resort, which are proving very popular. If you don't fancy splurging to stay in a room at the swish *Fairmont Hot Springs Resort*, (ⓣ250/345-6000 or 1-800/663-4979, ⓦwww.fairmonthotsprings.com; ❼) you could try its big RV-only **campsite** (sites $23–49), one minute from the pools – or the riverside *Spruce Grove Resort* (ⓣ250/345-6561 or 1-888/629-4004; ❹, sites $24–32), 2km south of Fairmont, with an outdoor pool.

Highway 93/95: Fairmont Hot Springs to Kimberley

Just 4km south of Fairmont Hot Springs, Hwy 93/95 curves around the **Dutch Creek Hoodoos**, fantastically eroded river bluffs created (according to Ktunaxa legend) when a vast wounded fish crawling up the valley expired at this point; as its flesh rotted, the bones fell apart creating the hoodoos.

Some 23km beyond is the turn-off for **Whiteswan Lake Provincial Park**, a handkerchief-sized piece of unbeatable scenery at the end of a twenty-kilometre gravel logging road; the park has five **campgrounds** ($15; May–Sept) but few trails, as its main emphasis is on boating and trout fishing. Three of the campgrounds are at Whiteswan Lake itself, the other two at Alces Lake; also keep an eye open for the undeveloped **Lussier Hot Springs** at the entrance of the park (17.5km from the main road), reached by a steep downhill trail. The same access road (called the Lussier River Rd after it passes the park) continues another 30km from Alces Lake to **Top of the World Provincial Park**, a far wilder and gorgeous alpine region with good hiking trails. You need to be completely self-sufficient – the five walk-in campsites ($5; June–Sept), reached by an easy six-kilometre trail (200m elevation gain) from the parking area at the end of the road offer water, firewood and spaces for twenty in the Fish Lake cabin ($15; June–Sept).

Continuing south on Hwy 93/95, a blanket of trees begins to encroach the Columbia Valley en route to Kimberley. One worthwhile stop along the way is **Wasa**, 30km north of Kimberley, located in Wasa Lake Provincial Park; the lake is warm enough for summer swimming and you can **camp** here ($19/night).

Kimberley

KIMBERLEY, 94km south of Fairmont Hot Springs and 30km north of Cranbrook, is Canada's second highest city (1117m), but perhaps its silliest, thanks to a tourist-tempting ruse in the 1970s to transform itself into a Bavarian village. The result is a masterpiece of kitsch that's almost irresistible: buildings have been given a plywood-thin veneer of authenticity, piped Bavarian music dribbles from shops with names like *The Yodelling Woodcarver*, and even the fire hydrants have been painted to look like miniature replicas of Happy Hans, Kimberley's lederhosened mascot. The ploy might seem absurd, but there's no doubting the economic rewards from the influx of tourists and European immigrants – Germans included – who've provided authentic cafés and restaurants and a variety of family-oriented summer and winter activities. Most of the Teutonic gloss is around the **Bavarian Platzl** on Spokane Street in the small downtown area. If nothing else, you can leave Kimberley safe in the knowledge that you've seen **Canada's Biggest Cuckoo Clock**, a fraudulent affair which amounts to little more than a large wooden box that twitters inane music.

If you're around between early December and April, you can escape Kimberley's kitsch for **skiing** and other winter activities at **Kimberley Alpine Resort** (Ⓣ250/427-4881 or 1-800/258-7669, Ⓦwww.skikimberley.com), 4km west of town. It has five lifts and eighty runs, the longest of which covers more than 6km. A day-pass is $64.

Kimberley's **visitor centre** is at 270 Kimberley Ave (daily 9am–8pm; Ⓣ250/427-3666 or 1-866/913-3666, Ⓦwww.kimberleychamber.com).

Practicalities

The nearest **campsite** is the *Kimberley Riverside Campground* (Ⓣ1-877/999-2929, Ⓦwww.kimberleycampground.com; $21–33; mid-April to Oct), 7km south of the town centre then 3km west on St Mary's River Road; it has full service sites and facilities include a pool. For **accommodation** in town, try *The Edge Pub and Hostel,* 275 Spokane St (Ⓣ250/427-7744, Ⓦwww.theedgepubandhostel.com; dorms summer/winter $15/20; ❷), a lively establishment on the Platzl, or the central, boutique-style *Château Kimberley*, 78 Howard St (Ⓣ250/427-1500 or 1-866/488-8886, Ⓦwww.chateau-kimberley.com; ❺).

Back in town and opposite the clock at 170 Spokane St you can get a room upstairs at *Chef Bernard* (Ⓣ250/427-4820; ❸), who offers a hot tub and free wi-fi, but whose main business is a twee but excellent café and **restaurant**, where the owner – heartily sick of Bavaria – often plays Irish fiddle music as a mark of defiance. Another good place is the *Snowdrift Cafe*, at 110 Spokane St, which is excellent for filling breakfasts and cheap lunches, including good vegetarian dishes for around $8. Farther afield is the *Old Bauernhaus,* 280 Norton Ave (Ⓣ250/427-5133; dinner only, closed Tues & Wed), about fifteen-minutes' walk from the town centre towards the ski area off Dewdney Road. The Bavarian food is good (schnitzel $18), but the draw here is the location, a 350-year-old post-and-beam building dismantled and brought from its original site in southern Bavaria. For pub food, **drinking** and occasional **live music**, try *The Edge Pub* (see above).

Highway 3: Crowsnest Pass to Rossland

Unless you're crossing the US–Canada border locally, BC's slightly tawdry necklace of border towns between the Alberta border and Hope (see p.731) along **Hwy 3** is as good a reason as any for taking a more northerly route across the province. Few of the towns amount to much; if you have to break the journey, do it in **Salmo** or **Castlegar**, towns on which some of the Kootenays' charm has rubbed off. Things are more interesting around **Osoyoos** and **Keremeos**, where the road enters a parched desert landscape then descends to Hope through the gripping mountain scenery of the Coastal Ranges, passing through **Manning Provincial Park**.

Sparwood and Elkford

In rounding **Crowsnest Pass** (see p.552) Hwy 3 leaves Alberta for BC but its surroundings remain largely despoiled by mining. The service town of **SPARWOOD** lies 19km from the provincial line and provides no real reason to stop other than to stock up on provisions and turn onto the scenic Hwy 43, to follow the Elk River 35km upstream to **ELKFORD**. Nestled against a wall of mountains to the east and gentler hills to the west, Elkford claims to be the "wilderness capital of British Columbia" – ambitious, but perhaps justified if you're prepared to carry on up either of two rough gravel roads to the north. The more westerly follows the Elk River a further 70km to **Elk Lakes Provincial Park** close to the Continental Divide, one of the wildest road-accessible spots in the province; the road ends at a trailhead and backcountry campsite ($5; June–Sept). A slightly better road to the east heads 55km into the heart of unbeatable scenery below **Mount Armstrong** (2792m). Both areas offer excellent chances of spotting wildlife, including cougars, deer, moose, elk or bighorn sheep.

Before striking out along either road, it's essential to pick up maps and information at the Elkford **visitor centre** at 4A Front St (Mon–Fri 8.30am–5pm; ⓣ250/865-4614 or 877/355-9453, ⓦwww.tourismelkford.ca), on your right as you enter town. It will also give directions to nearby **Josephine Falls**, a few minutes' walk from the parking area on Fording Mine Road.

For **accommodation** in town, try the *Elkford Motor Inn*, 808 Michel Rd (ⓣ250/865-2211, ⓦwww.elkfordmotorinn.com; ④), next to the shopping centre, which has its own pub and reasonable restaurant, or the *Hi Rock Inn* at 2 Chauncey St (ⓣ250/865-2226 or 1-866/865-2226, ⓦwww.hirockinn.com; ④), with spotless rooms and free wi-fi. You can **camp** at Elkford's municipal campsite (ⓣ250/865-2650; $15; May–Oct).

Fernie and around

If you choose to skip Elkford, Hwy 3 will usher you alongside the rapid, ice-clear Elk River into a bowl of knife-edged mountains, where **FERNIE** couldn't hope for a better introduction. Though logging and open pit coal mining form its economic backbone, Fernie's appeal as a **recreation centre** has brought in a more liberal demographic, reflected in the number of art galleries, health food shops and hemp stores. Meanwhile, its popularity as a **ski resort** has led to a spate of lacklustre condos.

Arrival and information

Fernie's main **visitor centre**, at 102 Commerce Rd (daily 9am–5pm; ⓣ250/423-6868 or 1-877/433-7643, ⓦwww.ferniechamber.com), stands alongside a reconstructed wooden oil derrick 2km north of town on Hwy 3. Greyhound **buses** pull into and depart from the Edge of the World shop at 902 6th Ave (Ⓣ250/423-9292).

The town and around

The town's first impressions – the bland, motel and mall-lined hwy – don't do it justice. But beyond this strip are pleasant tree-lined streets, boutique shops and small wooden houses. Fernie's **museum** (daily 9.30am–5pm; Ⓣ250/423-7016), on the corner of 2nd Avenue and 4th Street, runs a small **visitor centre** where you can pick up details of the heritage walking tour of downtown, whose best buildings cluster along the main street, 2nd Avenue, between 3rd and 7th streets, monuments to the rebuilding of town following a destructive fire in 1908.

For a challenging hike, try the full-day **Three Sisters Trail**, which starts from the main visitor centre on Hwy 3, or head some 2km west of town along Hwy 3 to **Mount Fernie Provincial Park**, which has plenty of **hiking** and **biking** trails, picnic areas and a pleasant forty-pitch campsite (reservations see p.672; $15; mid-May to mid-Sept). Canyon Raft Company (Ⓣ250-423-7226 or 1-888/423-7226, Ⓦwww.canyonraft.com) will take you on day or overnight whitewater **rafting** trips down the Elk or Bull rivers.

Fernie's population doubles in the winter, as skiers flock to the **Fernie Alpine Resort** (Nov–May; day-pass $75; Ⓣ250/423-4655 or 1-866/633-7643, Ⓦwww.skifernie.com), 5km west of town and 2km off the main hwy. It claims the longest ski season in the BC Rockies, has a whopping 107 trails and gets an average of nine metres of snowfall annually. In the summer, the resort opens its lifts (Fri–Sun) to both **hikers** and **mountain bikers** (day-pass $39), and maintains a sizeable network of trails for the latter.

Practicalities

Most accommodation options not at the resort lie alongside Hwy 3. The boutique *Park Place Lodge*, 742 Hwy 3 (Ⓣ250/423-6871 or 1-800/381-7275, Ⓦwww.parkplacelodge.com; ❺), has an indoor pool, fitness centre and room service, while the friendly, well-run *Powder Mountain Lodge* at no. 891 (Ⓣ250/423-4492 or 1-877/562-2783, Ⓦwww.powdermountain.com; ❸), has an outdoor pool, kitchen, social areas, wi-fi and a handful of dorm beds for $31. There are more hostel beds at the basic, HI-affiliated *Raging Elk Hostel*, 892 6th Ave (Ⓣ250/423-6811, Ⓦwww.ragingelk.com), which has dorm beds for $27 and a private single and double rooms for $55.

Eating in Fernie is concentrated along 2nd Avenue. Good coffee and a quick snack can be had at *Freshies*, 561 2nd Ave, while breakfasts are scrumptious (gourmet omelettes $7) at the hip *Blue Toque Diner*, 601 1st Ave, in the Arts Station next to the gallery and theatre. The *Curry Bowl*, 931 7th Ave, serves a range of outstanding Asian fusion dishes (mains $11–13) and has a wide selection of beers, including the locally brewed Fernie Griz. For **drinks**, try the gritty *Royal Hotel*, 501 1st Ave, which has a pool table and live music.

Kikomun Creek Provincial Park

From Fernie Hwy 3 heads southwest to the unsullied village of **Elko** and a junction with Hwy 93 to the US border, 91km away. Elko is gone in a flash, but you might want to stop and camp at the excellent **Kikomun Creek Provincial Park** (reservations see p.672; $24; May–Sept), on the eastern shore of the artificial Lake Koocanusa, a signed 3km drive west of town.

From Elko, Hwy 3 heads northwest to Cranbrook 60km away. About 17km short of Cranbrook on Hwy 93/95 is the impressive **Fort Steele Heritage Town** (daily May–June & Sept–Oct 9.30am–5pm, July–Aug 9.30am–6.30pm, Nov–April

10am–4pm; $5 or $25 including train and wagon rides and theatre; ⓣ250/417-6000, ⓦwww.fortsteele.bc.ca), a reconstructed c.1900 village of some 55 buildings in a superb mountain-ringed setting.

Cranbrook and around

The regional service, transport hub and ex-forestry town of **CRANBROOK**, 96km from Fernie, is one of the most dismal in the province. A strip of motels and marshalling yards dominates a soulless downtown area. The only worthwhile sight is the **Canadian Museum of Rail Travel** (mid-April to mid-Oct 10am–6pm; rest of year Tues–Sat 10am–5pm; tours $5.25–11.95; ⓣ250/489-3918, ⓦwww.trainsdeluxe.com), 57 Van Horne St, which centres around the restored luxurious passenger cars of trains which chugged between Montréal and Vancouver in the 1920s.

The Greyhound **bus station** (ⓣ250/426-3331) is at 1229 Cranbrook St, 1.5km up the same road from the **visitor centre** at no. 2279 (Mon–Fri 8.30am–5pm, Sat & Sun 9am–5pm; ⓣ250/426-5914 or 1-800/222-6174, ⓦwww.cranbrookchamber.com).

The *Lazy Bear Lodge*, 621 Cranbrook St North (ⓣ250/426-6086 or 1-888/808-6086, ⓦwww.lazybear-lodge.ca; ❸), is a good, inexpensive **accommodation** option on Hwy 3. Far better is the large, modern *Heritage Inn*, 803 Cranbrook St North (ⓣ250/489-4301 or 1-888/888-4374, ⓦwww.heritageinn.net; ❺), with its pool, hot tub and inclusive hot breakfasts. The most appealing local **campground** is the *Jimsmith Lake Provincial Park* (June–Sept; $15), 4km southwest of town, despite the lack of showers.

The strip offers plenty of cheap **eating** options, but make for *Allegra*, 1225 B Cranbrook St North (ⓣ250/426-8812; closed Mon & Tues), which serves Mediterranean cuisine (mains $14–27).

Moyie Lake and Yahk

Following Hwy 3 west from Cranbrook, you reach the tiny community of **MOYIE** on the edge of lovely **Moyie Lake**. There are local **campsites** here, including the excellent one at **Moyie Lake Provincial Park** (reservations, see p.672; $24; May–Sept), with short trails and sandy swimming beach; it's 1km along Munro Lake Road west from Hwy 3/95 and the northernmost point of Moyie Lake.

Southwest of Moyie Hwy 3 crosses a **time zone** (clocks go forward one hour) en route to the unspoilt village of **YAHK**, some 35km away. Yahk's no more than a few houses and antique shops nestled amid the trees and great for a quiet stopover at the *Cozy Quilt Motel*, 8849 Hwy 3 (ⓣ250/424-5558 or 1-877/717-5558, ⓦwww.cozyquilt.ca; ❸), or camping at **Yahk Provincial Park** ($20; May to mid-Sept) east of town.

Creston

Don't stop in prosperous little **CRESTON**, 83km east of Salmo, unless you're a birdwatcher. Creston overlooks a broad mountain-flanked valley that's home to the idly meandering Kootenay River. Over the years the river has repeatedly burst its banks, creating a rich alluvial plain beloved by farmers, and producing the lush medley of orchards and verdant fields. The flood plain and its wetlands – the so-called "Valley of the Swans" – is a haven for birds and waterfowl, particularly the 7000-hectare **Creston Valley Wildlife Management Area** (ⓣ250/402-6900, ⓦwww.crestonwildlife.ca), 10km northwest of town off Hwy 3. This has one of the world's largest nesting **osprey** populations, while some 250 other species have been recorded in the area (not to mention otters, moose and other animals). For full details visit the sanctuary's Wildlife Centre (mid-May to early-Oct daily 9am–4pm; $7).

If you do end up in downtown Creston, you might pause at the **Stone House Museum**, 219 Devon St (mid-May to Oct daily 10am–3.30pm, Nov to mid-May by appointment; $3; ⓣ250/428-9262), known for its replica Kootenay (Ktunaxa) canoe. Similar canoes, with their down-pointed ends, are only found in parts of eastern Russia, underlining the fact that millennia ago, migrations took place across the Bering Strait into North America. If you're not driving, another temptation is the **Columbia Brewery**, 1220 Erickson St (mid-May to mid-Oct tours Mon–Fri 9.30am, 11am, 1pm & 2.30pm ⓣ250/428-9344,), whose Kokanee beers you'll find in most of the region's bars and restaurants.

Practicalities

Use the **visitor centre**, 1607 Canyon St (daily July & Aug 8am–6pm, Mon–Fri Sept–June 9am–4pm; ⓣ250/428-4342, ⓦwww.crestonbc.com) if by mischance you need **accommodation**, but better still limit your stop to picking up coffee, snacks or picnic provisions at the *Creston Valley Bakery*, 113 10th Ave (closed Sun) or **eating** at the *Otherside Café*, 1021 Canyon St, which serves hearty vegetarian and Asian fusion dishes for around $8 (closed Sat & Sun).

Kootenay Pass and Salmo

A classic stretch of scenic road, Hwy 3 climbs west from the fruit-growing plains around Creston then over **Kootenay Pass** (1774m), making it one of the highest main roads in the country. It's frequently closed by bad weather and there are no services for 70km, so check your petrol before setting out. If you're cycling, brace yourself for a 46km uphill slog, but the reward is an unexpected and stunning lake at the pass, where there's a pull-off picnic area and views of high peaks in the distance.

Some 38km north of Kootenay Pass, tiny **SALMO** somehow manages to retain a pioneer feel with its tidy wooden buildings, despite the large volume

British Columbia's polygamy probelm

In recent years, Creston has found itself on the map no thanks to **Bountiful**, a community of 1200 fundamentalist Mormon polygamists who live southeast of town near the US border, in a sprawling collection of drab houses.

The community was founded in 1946 by six men whom the Mormon church – which banned polygamy in 1890 – had excommunicated. The descendants of these men make up almost the entire community, which has rapidly multiplied thanks to teachings which insist men must have three or more wives – and as many children as possible – to enter heaven, and that a woman's role is to serve men. Community leaders decide who marries whom in a process which sometimes pairs 15-year-old girls with men three times their age. Leaders are alleged to have organized the swapping of under-age girls with similar communes in the US to maintain better "breeding stock".

The community doesn't take well to tourists coming to gawk or to the publicity generated by claims of widespread sexual abuse. The latter has helped force the Canadian government to end its tolerance, which long rested on the notion that Canada's constitutional guarantee of religious freedom trumps the Criminal Code. Although charges against two community leaders – one of whom has 25 wives and 101 children – were thrown out, legal action may resume once the BC Supreme Court has decided whether criminal code provisions that make polygamy illegal don't clash with the Canadian Charter of Rights and Freedoms.

of traffic converging on it along Hwy 3 and Hwy 6. In early August, ten thousand ravers, hippies and world-class DJs also descend on their way to the Salmo River Ranch, 6km east of town, for the five-day **Shambhala Music Festival** (Ⓦwww.shambhalamusicfestival.com). In winter there's **skiing** 2km east of town at the Salmo ski area. The Chamber of Commerce (July & Aug daily 10am–4pm, Sept–June Mon–Fri 10am–4pm; Ⓣ250/357-2596, Ⓦwww.salmo.net) is at 4th Street and Railway Avenue.

Salmo practicalities

If you need to **overnight**, try the *Reno*, at 123 Railway Ave (Ⓣ250/357-9937 or 1-866/357-9937, Ⓦwww.renomotel.ca; ❹), one block east of the bus terminal. For **camping**, the *Selkirk Motel and RV Sites*, 307 2nd Relief Rd (Ⓣ250/357-2346 or 1-888/368-6336; sites May–Oct $17–23.50; ❷), is 4km west of town on Hwy 3.

For **food**, *Charlie's Pizza and Spaghetti House* (Ⓣ250/357-9335) is an old-style diner on 4th Street serving hunger-crushing breakfasts, as well as wraps and burgers (dinner mains $12–18). Just up the road, the *Silver Dollar Pub* is the town's favourite **bar**, with pool tables, a jukebox and lots of good ol' boys in an atmospheric wooden interior.

Castlegar

CASTLEGAR, 42km west of Salmo on Hwy 3, is a strange, diffuse place with no obvious centre, probably because roads and rivers – the Kootenay meets the Columbia here – make it more a transport hub than a community. In the early 1900s it was famous for its immigrant **Doukhobors** (see p.708)

Castlegar's **visitor centre**, 1995 6th Ave (July & Aug daily 8am–7pm; rest of year Mon–Fri 9am–5pm; Ⓣ250/365-6313 or 1-888/365-6313, Ⓦwww.castlegar.com) is off the main road as you come into town from Grand Forks. The town has the major regional **airport**; the landing strip is alongside Hwy 3A.

The town

Much of the community's heritage has been collected in the **Doukhobor Village Museum** (May–Sept daily 10am–5pm; $8; Ⓣ250/365-5327, Ⓦwww.doukhobor-museum.org), at 112 Heritage Way, just right off the main road after you cross the big suspension bridge over the Kootenay River. A Doukhobor descendant is on hand to take you through the museum, which houses displays of farm machinery, handmade tools, superb archive photographs and traditional Russian clothing. For a further taste of Doukhobor culture, visit the evocative **Zuckerberg Island Heritage Park** (May–Oct Wed–Sat 10am–5pm; by donation; Ⓣ250/365-6440) off 7th Avenue, named after a local teacher of Doukhobors who built a log Russian Orthodox Chapel House and other buildings and memorials here after coming to the town in 1931; it is reached by a ninety-metre pedestrian suspension bridge.

Practicalities

There are some half-dozen places to stay in and around town: the best **motel** – small, and with a nice view and an RV site ($20–30) – is the *Cozy Pines*, 2118 Crestview Crescent (Ⓣ250/365-5613, Ⓦwww.cozypines.com; ❷), on Hwy 3 on the western edge of town. Closer in is the modern and attractive *Fireside Motor Inn*, 1810 8th Ave at the junction of Hwys 3 and 22 (Ⓣ250/365-2128; ❺). About 3km west of town on Hwy 3 is the *Castlegar RV Park and Campground*, (Ⓣ250/365-2337, Ⓦwww.castlegarrvpark.com; $18–28; April–Oct), with wi-fi, hot showers, laundry and restaurant. There are also regional and provincial park **campsites** in the vicinity, including the *Pass Creek Regional Park*, which has a nice, sandy beach (Ⓣ250/365-6244; $15; April–Oct), 2km west off Hwy 3A at the Kootenay River

The Doukhobors

The **Doukhobors** were members of a southern Russian sect who fled that country in 1899 after being persecuted for their religious and political views. Fiercely pacifist, they rejected secular government and ignored the liturgy and procedures of the organized church, believing God resided in each individual rather than in a building or institution. Their proto-communist views made them unpopular with the tsars, with their leader **Peter Veregin**, a keen advocate of communal labour and the collective ownership of property.

The flight from Russia was aided by the Quakers and by the novelist Leo Tolstoy, both of whom identified and supported the Doukhobors' pacifist and other ideals. Around 7500 left in the first wave, bringing their lifestyle to western Canada, and to **Saskatchewan** in particular. Initially, authorities were sympathetic to their beliefs and granted religious, educational and housing concessions. In 1905 sect members refused to swear an oath of allegiance to the dominion government and then, in 1907, when the Canadian government insisted all Doukhobor homesteads be registered as private property, things fell apart and the colonists were divided. Over a third accepted the government's proposals, despite the bitter opposition of the collectivists, who showed their contempt for worldly possessions by destroying their belongings; some even burnt their clothes and organized Canada's first naked demonstrations. Irretrievably divided, some stayed behind to create a prosperous, pacifist and Russian-speaking community, which remained separate and distinct until the 1940s, while Veregin and his supporters left for southern BC.

By the 1920s BC had around ninety Doukhobor settlements, each with a population of around sixty. They had arrived in **Castlegar** in 1908, establishing at least 24 villages in the area, each with Russian names meaning things like "the beautiful", "the blessed" or "consolation". Accomplished farmers, they laboured under the motto "Toil and a Peaceful Life", creating highly successful orchards, farms, sawmills and packing plants. Although their way of life waned after Veregin's death in 1924 (he was killed by a bomb planted in his railway carriage), the Doukhobors' considerable industry and agricultural expertise transformed the Castlegar area. Today, the Doukhobors number around fifteen thousand across the region (though those with Doukhobor roots total about thirty thousand) and Russian is still spoken. There's also a breakaway radical sect, the Freedomites, or Sons of Freedom, infamous for their eye-catching demonstrations (including fires and naked parades) against materialism and other morally dubious values.

Bridge. For cheap **eating**, *Gabriel's Restaurant*, 1432 Columbia Ave (Ⓣ250/365-6028), serves light meals ($12–24).

Rossland

Picturesque **ROSSLAND**, which relies on the lead and zinc smelter in nearby **Trail** for employment, was founded on gold mining – some $125 million-worth ($5 billion at today's prices) of which was gouged from the surrounding hills in the early 1900s.

The town's major draw is the **Red Mountain Resort** (mid-Dec to early-April; day lift-pass $59; Ⓣ250/362-7384 or 1-800/663-0105, Ⓦwww.redresort.com); 3km west of Rossland on Hwy 3. It's 1,500 acres of skiable terrain is particularly remarkable for its expert-level tree skiing. In summer the area around the resort and Rossland is excellent for **mountain biking**; many of the area's fine trails are detailed in several free leaflets from the visitor centre. Rent **bikes** from *Revolution Cycles and Service*, 2044 Columbia Ave (Ⓣ250/362-5688).

If you are keen on learning about the town's gold-mining heritage, a tour of the Le Roi Gold Mine – once one of the world's largest, with 100km of tunnels – and the adjoining **Rossland Historical Museum** (mid-May to mid-Sept daily 9am–5pm; mine tours May, June & Sept every 1hr 30min, July & Aug every 30min; museum & mine $10, museum $5; Ⓣ1-888/448-7444, Ⓦwww.rosslandmuseum.ca) will entertain with fascinating technical and geological background.

The **visitor centre,** 2185 Columbia Ave (May–Sept daily 9am–5pm; Ⓣ250/362-5666 or 1-888/725-0599, Ⓦwww.rossland.com), in the museum at the junction of the town's two main roads (Hwy 3B & Hwy 22), is useful for details of the **Nancy Greene Provincial Park**, nestled in the Monashee Mountains, and which has a ten-pitch campground (no showers; May–Sept; $10) northwest of town.

Practicalities

For **accommodation**, there's the *Mountain Shadow Hostel*, 2125 Columbia Ave (Ⓣ250/362-7160, Ⓦwww.mshostel.com; dorms $20; private rooms $60), and several resort hotels, including the upmarket twelve-unit *Ram's Head Inn*, (Ⓣ250/362-9577 or 1-877/267-4323, Ⓦwww.ramshead.bc.ca; ❻).

The locals' choice for **food** is the *Sunshine Café* (breakfast & lunch only; closes 3pm) on Columbia Street. The *Gypsy at Red* at the base of the ski hill, 4430 Red Mountain Rd (lunch Thurs–Sun and dinner daily) has award-winning desserts and tasty Angus sirloin steak ($23).

Grand Forks and around

GRAND FORKS is not grand at all – it's a small and quite perfunctory transit settlement built on a river flat. The Greyhound **buses** that drop by daily are probably the main event. The **visitor centre** is at Central Avenue South (July–Aug daily 9am–6pm Sept–May Mon–Fri 8.30am–4.30pm; Ⓣ250/442-2833 or 1-866/442-2833, Ⓦwww.grandforkschamber.com). The history of Doukhobor settlers (see p.708) is charted at the small **Hardy Mountain Doukhobor Village Historic Site** (June–Aug daily 9am–6pm; $2) on Hardy Mountain Road. For a further taste of all things Russian, sample the home-made Eastern European (and Mexican) food at the *Borscht Bowl*, 258 Market Ave (Ⓣ250/442-5977) – its namesake dish comes in different sizes.

About 25km north of town, 19km long **Christina Lake** – which claims some of BC's warmest water – is a modestly unspoilt summer resort with lots of swimming, boating and camping opportunities. A dozen or so motels sprout along its shore, mostly at the southern end.

If you're travelling onward along Hwy 3 from Grand Forks, turn to p.727 for **Osoyoos**, which is 126km further west. If you have time to spare, be sure to explore the Kootenays, covered in the following section.

The Kootenays

The Kootenays are one of the most attractive and unvisited parts of BC, and centre on two major north–south valleys which harbour **Kootenay Lake**, the **Upper** and **Lower Arrow Lakes** and three adjacent mountain ranges – the Purcells, Selkirks and Monashees – whose once-rich mineral deposits formed the kernel of the province's early mining industry. **Nelson** is the key spot, slightly peripheral to the Kootenays' rugged core, but a lovely place, and one of the few provincial towns offering real attractions in its own right. Scattered lakeside hamlets, notably **Kaslo** and **Nakusp**, make excellent bases for excursions into mountain scenery which has a pristine quality rarely found elsewhere. Water-based activities – **canoeing** and

fishing in particular – are excellent, and you can also explore the ramshackle mining heritage of near-ghost towns like **Sandon** and **New Denver**. Many of these towns and villages also have more than their fair share of artists, painters, writers, healers and New Age enthusiasts, lending the region considerable cultural and alternative-lifestyle lustre.

Getting around the region is tricky without **private transport**, which is a shame because the roads here are among the most beautiful in the province. The most **scenic routes** – and these are some of the loveliest drives in BC – are Hwy 31A from Kaslo to New Denver, and dramatic Hwy 6, which leads south of New Denver along the Slocan Valley and west to Vernon. Your best Kootenay strategy would be to enter from Creston and exit via Vernon, setting you up nicely for the Okanagan (see pp.720–727).

Kootenay Lake and around

Starting just north of Creston, Hwy 3A picks a slow, twisting course up the eastern shore of **Kootenay Lake** to the free car ferry at Kootenay Bay. Apart from the ample scenic rewards of the lake and the mountains beyond, the hwy is almost completely empty for all of its 79km, and none of the villages marked on maps are more than scattered houses hidden in the woods.

Boswell and Gray Creek

The only noteworthy sight in the lake area is the **Glass House** (May, June, Sept & Oct daily 9am–5pm; July & Aug 8am–8pm; $6; ⓣ250/223-8372), 7km south of **BOSWELL**, which ranks high on the list of Canada's more bizarre offerings. Constructed entirely from embalming bottles, the house was built by David Brown in 1952, after 35 years in the funeral business – "to indulge", the wonderfully po-faced pamphlet tells you, "a whim of a peculiar nature". The retired mortician travelled widely, visiting friends in the funeral profession until he'd collected 600,000 bottles to build his lakeside retirement home. The family continued to live here until curious tourists took the upper hand.

Nearby **accommodation** is provided by the seven-unit *Kootenay Lake Lodge Resort*, 12622 Hwy 3A (ⓣ250/223-8181 or 1-877/610-6960, ⓦwww.kootenaylakelodge.com; ④), a rustic log lodge with private beach, wood-fired cedar baths and RV sites ($10).

At **GRAY CREEK**, a few kilometres onward, check out the superb **Gray Creek Store**, which boasts the once-in-a-lifetime address of 1979 Chainsaw Avenue and claims, with some justification, to be "The Most Interesting Store You've Ever Seen". The shop basically *is* Gray Creek – it's the sort of place you go to get your chainsaw fixed and where real lumberjacks come for their red-checked shirts.

The closest and easiest to reach **campsite** is 13km south of Gray Creek and 20km south of Kootenay Bay (see below), at small Lockhart Beach Provincial Park ($15; May–Sept), which has RV and tent sites. A bit more exotic, *Tipi Camp* (ⓣ250/227-9555 or 1-866/800-2267, ⓦwww.tipicamp.bc.ca; mid-June to mid-Sept; $95/night including transport and vegetarian meals) lies on Pilot Peninsula and is reached by a twice daily twenty-minute boat taxi from Gray Creek; bring your own bedding. From Gray Creek, the Gray Creek Forest service road (July–Oct) leads 85km east to Kimberley (see p.702), not a short cut by any means, but scenic and adventurous driving; stock up on supplies before setting off.

Crawford and Kootenay bays

CRAWFORD BAY and **KOOTENAY BAY** are the most fleeting of settlements, though the latter is also the **ferry terminal** for boats to Balfour on the western shore. Crawford Bay, 3.5km from the terminal, boasts the Kootenay

Forge (Ⓦwww.kootenayforge.com), where in summer you can often watch blacksmiths working, and a number of other artisan shops, from traditional broom-makers to weavers. The area has also long been famous for the **Yasodhara Ashram**, 527 Walkers Landing Rd (Ⓣ250/227-9224 or 1-800/661-8711, Ⓦwww.yasodhara.org), a spiritual centre offering a range of multi-day courses (from $75/day). As a place to **stay**, this side of the ferry crossing is a touch brighter. The *Wedgwood Manor Country Inn* (Ⓣ250/227-9233 or 1-800/862-0022, Ⓦwww.wedgwoodcountryinn.com; ❺), a 1910 heritage building set amid fifty acres of gardens and estate, is extremely pleasant; book well in advance. The local **campsite** is the nicely wooded *Kokanee Chalets, Motel, Campground & RV Park* on Hwy 3A (Ⓣ250/227-9292 or 1-800/448-9292, Ⓦwww.kokaneechalets.com; mid-April to Oct), with tent and RV sites ($23–36) and motel and chalet rooms (❹) a short walk from the beach.

The Kootenay Lake ferry (daily 6.30am–9.40pm; free; Ⓣ250/229-4215) leaves every fifty minutes from June to September, and every two hours the rest of the year. The nine-kilometre, forty-minute **crossing** is beautiful.

Balfour and Ainsworth Hot Springs

BALFOUR is a fairly ramshackle and dispersed collection of motels, garages and cafés – albeit in verdant surroundings – gathered to catch the traffic rolling on and off the ferry. The handiest **motel** for those passengers is the *Balfour Beach Inn and Motel*, 8406 Busk Rd (Ⓣ250/229-4235, Ⓦwww.balfourbeachinn.com; ❺), with a heated indoor pool but convenient also for the small, pebbly beach just north of the terminal. The *Dog & Duck* by Balfour's jetty serves perfectly decent pub food.

A better place to stay is **AINSWORTH HOT SPRINGS**, about 16km north of Balfour on Hwy 31. The tasteful *Ainsworth Hot Springs Resort* (Ⓣ250/229-4212 or 1-800/668-1171, Ⓦwww.hotnaturally.com; ❻) is ideal if you want to stay over while soaking in the waters of the **mineral springs.** There's only one pool, but a wonderful network of hot spring caves (daily 10am–9.30pm; day-pass $14, single visit $9) and you don't need to stay in the resort to sample the springs. The nicest local **motel** is the eight-room *Mermaid Lodge and Motel* (Ⓣ250/229-4969 or 1-888/229-4963, Ⓦwww.themermaidlodge-motel.com; ❷) alongside the springs and pools. Cave enthusiasts might want to take a one-hour guided tour of **Cody Caves** (late June to early Sept 10am–4pm; $15; Ⓣ250/353-7364 Ⓦwww.codycaves.ca), 12km up a rough gravel side road off Hwy 3, 3km north of town. From the end of the road it's a twenty-minute walk to the caves, which has extensive galleries.

Kokanee Glacier Provincial Park

RV **campgrounds** line Hwy 3A from Balfour to Nelson, but the most attractive camping option is at **Kokanee Creek Provincial Park** (reservations see p.672, $24; May–Sept), about 10km west of Balfour or 19km northeast of Nelson, with its sandy beach, mosquito problem and interpretive centre (May–Sept daily 9am–9pm; Ⓣ250/825-4723) with trail advice.

From here, Kokanee Glacier Road leads 16km up to **Kokanee Glacier Provincial Park**, which straddles the Slocan Range of the Selkirk Mountains, and a park entrance at Gibson Lake. There's a trailhead here for the 2.5km jaunt around the lake and another trail leading 4km uphill to the lovely Kokanee Lake, where it levels out and continues another 3km to Kaslo Lake. Two kilometres further you reach backcountry campsites and the *Kokanee Glacier Cabin* (reserve in advance at Ⓣ403/678 3200 Ⓦwww.alpineclubofcanada.ca; $36 per person; June–Oct). Other approaches to the park are from Hwy 31, 10km north of Ainsworth, driving 13km up Woodbury Creek into the park; from Hwy 6, some 14km north of Slocan, where you drive 13km up Enterprise Creek; and from Hwy 6, 8km south of Slocan, where you follow a road up Lemon Creek for 16km.

Nelson

NELSON – 34km west of Balfour on Hwy 3A – is one of BC's best towns, and one of the few interior settlements in which you could happily spend two or three days; longer, if you use it as a base for touring the Kootenays by car. The elegant town is home to more than its share of baby-boomers, the dreadlocked and refugees from the 1960s and later mainstream, a hangover that's nurtured a friendly, civilized and close-knit community, a healthy cultural scene and a liveliness – manifest in alternative cafés, nightlife and secondhand-clothes shops – you'll be hard pushed to find elsewhere in the province outside Vancouver. The town's Chinese medicine school, as well as the Kootenay School of the Arts, attract students from all over North America and there are, apparently, more artists and craftspeople here per head than any other town in Canada. It's a young place, permeated with immense civic pride, which was given a further boost by the filming here of *Roxanne*, Steve Martin's spoof version of *Cyrano de Bergerac*. Producers chose the town for its idyllic lakeside setting and 350-plus homes from the late nineteenth to the early twentieth-century, factors which for once live up to the Canadian talent for hyperbole – in this case a claim to be "Queen of the Kootenays" and "Heritage Capital of Western Canada".

Arrival and information

Nelson's **bus station** is on the lakeshore at 1128 Lakeside Drive. The **visitor centre**, 225 Hall St (June–Aug daily 8.30am–6pm; Sept–May Mon–Fri 8.30am–5pm; ⓣ250/352-3433 or 1-877/663-5706, ⓦwww.discovernelson.com) is on the northeast edge of downtown at the corner of Lake Street.

For **car rental**, try Rent-a-Wreck, 524 Nelson Ave (ⓣ250/352-5122), or Budget, 205 Lakeside Drive (ⓣ1-888/368-7368). Up the road in the *Prestige Lakeside Resort*, Captain Erik's Watertoys (ⓣ250/551-5502, ⓦwww.captaineriks.com), rents **boats** and offers wakeboarding lessons. *Gerick Cycle and Sports*, 702 Baker St (ⓣ250/354-4622), or *The Sacred Ride*, 213 Baker St (ⓣ250/354-3831), both rent **bikes** and have trail maps of the many **mountain-biking** routes.

Accommodation

Nelson has a reasonable spread of **accommodation**; central choices include hostels, charming boutique hotels and a wide range of B&B options. Most motels are on Hwy 31A at the north end of town or over the Nelson Bridge on the north side of the lake.

Dancing Bear Inn 171 Baker St ⓣ250/352-7573 or 1-877/352-7573, ⓦwww.dancingbearinn.com. A beautifully renovated hostel between Kootenay St and Hwy 3A. Dorm beds are $21 for HI members, $25 for nonmembers. There's a kitchen, resource library for local recreation, plus internet and wi-fi access. ❷

Hume Hotel 422 Vernon St ⓣ250/352-5331 or 1-877/568-0888, ⓦwww.humehotel.com. This charming, 1898 four-storey hotel is the best central, mid-range choice. It has cosy, old-world rooms (some with views) and complimentary breakfast in the downstairs restaurant. ❺

Kokanee Creek Provincial Park 20km northeast of town on Hwy 3A. With 168 pitches on a forested site, this campsite ($24) offers access to sandy beaches and nature trails; mosquitoes can be a problem though.

Mountain Hound Inn 621 Baker St ⓣ250/352-6490 or 1-866/452-6490, ⓦwww.mountainhound.com. A wonderfully restored boutique hotel located in the thick of the action. ❹

New Grand Hotel 616 Vernon St ⓣ250/352-7211 or 1-888/722-2258, ⓦwww.newgrandhotel.ca. Boutique hotel with retro rooms – including some well-priced singles. ❸

North Shore Inn 687 Hwy 3A ⓣ250/352-6606 or 1-800/593-6636, ⓦwww.nshoreinn.com. On the north side of town, this thirty-unit motel is simple, clean and offers good value. ❹

Prestige Lakeside Resort 701 Lakeshore Drive ⓣ250/352-7222 or 1-877/737-8443, ⓦwww.prestigeinn.com. The most luxurious hotel in town, this is part of Nelson's rather crass ongoing lakefront redevelopment; it has a spa, gym, marina, shops and all the other resort trimmings. ❼

Stanley House 420 Railway St ⓣ250/352-3777, ⓦwww.stanleyhousebb.com. There are three ornate rooms in this 1908 B&B, housed in a lovely Victorian-era home. ❹

The Town

Nelson forms a 24-odd block tree-shaded grid of streets laid over the hilly slopes that edge down to the westernmost shores of Kootenay Lake. Most homes are immaculately kept and vividly painted, and even the commercial **buildings** along the parallel main east-west streets – Baker and Vernon – owe more to the vintage architecture of Seattle and San Francisco than to the drab Victoriana and worse of much of eastern Canada. If you want to add purpose to your wanderings, pick up the *Heritage Walking Tour* or the *Heritage Motoring Tour* pamphlets from the visitor centre. Highlights of the routes are the courthouse on Ward Street and City Hall (at the corner of Ward and Vernon streets), both designed by F.M. Rattenbury, also responsible for Victoria's *Empress Hotel* and BC's legislature. Also check out the old railway station and the *Hume Hotel*.

If walking tours aren't your thing, the town's **shops** may be, particularly those of its artists and craftspeople. In summer they club together to present **Artwalk**, a crawl round about a hundred of the town's artists' studios and little galleries (the visitor centre has details). If you don't want to walk in town, take the restored **Streetcar 23** (Sat & Sun May to mid-June & early-Oct, daily mid-June to Sept; $3), a tram running the length of the lakeshore waterfront from a point about two hundred metres north of the visitor centre on Hall Street. Particularly good galleries include the Craft Connection, 441 Baker St, and the Mermaid Gallery, 410 Kootenay St, which sells paintings, jewellery and pottery. For secondhand books and CDs – and a great little café-restaurant – make for *Packrat Annie's* at 411 Kootenay St. Another shop worth a stop is Still Eagle, 557 Ward St, the province's first hemp store. On a similar theme, Holy Smoke, 512 Hendryx St, sells marijuana paraphernalia and adopts a liberal attitude to the drug that riles local law enforcement.

Other attractions include the **Mining Museum** (daily 9am–3pm; free), next to the visitor centre. The area owes its development to the discovery of copper and silver ore on nearby Toad Mountain at the end of the nineteenth century. Although the mines declined fairly quickly, Nelson's diversification into gold and lumber, and its roads, railway and waterways, saved it.

The **Touchstone's Nelson: Museum of Art and History** (May–Sept Mon–Sat 9am–5pm, Oct–April Tues, Wed & Fri–Sat 10am–5pm, Thurs 10am–8pm; $10, by donation Thurs 5–8pm; ⓣ250/352-9813, ⓦwww.nelsonmuseum.ca), 502 Vernon St, is housed in the former City Hall building and hosts art exhibitions and Nelson's historical archives. Back outside, walk to Lakeside Park near the Nelson Bridge, where there are surprisingly good sandy **beaches**, picnic areas and waterfront paths. For a workout with the sweetest of rewards, the one-hour climb to **Pulpit Rock**, starting on the north side of the lake, offers an eagle's eye view over Nelson.

If you're in town between May and mid-October on a Saturday, make a point of stopping by the Cottonwood Falls **farmers' market** (May to mid-Oct 9.30am–3pm), near the old railway station in Cottonwood Falls Park, with organic fruit, vegetables, delicious breads and local arts and crafts. The local ski hill, **Whitewater Winter Resort**, 12km south of Nelson off Hwy 6 (Dec–April; day-pass $56; ⓣ250/354-4944 or 1-800/666-9420, ⓦwww.skiwhitewater.com), may be small, but often compensates with great powder. Its three lifts serve 1180 acres of mostly good steep terrain and there's also 20km of cross-country trails.

Eating, drinking and nightlife

Nelson's choice of **restaurants** is broad, and the quality so high it's hard to go wrong just wandering around and choosing something tempting.

All Seasons Café 620 Herridge Lane ⓣ250/352-0101. In a restored heritage home, this top-flight restaurant is one of the Kootenays' best dining experiences. It serves superb West Coast (or what it calls "left-coast") food and boasts a wine list that has won a prestigious *Wine Spectator* Award of Excellence. Mains from $19. Open daily for dinner from 5pm.

El Taco 306 Victoria St. For Mexican chow you can down with a glass of sangria, tuck into one of the tasty burritos, quesadillas and taco mains ($5–10).

The Full Circle 101–402 Baker St. For superb breakfasts ($11) follow the locals to this café.

Fusion 301 301 Baker St. This swanky tapas bar has a buzzing outdoor patio and also dishes up creative mains ($12–18). Closed Mon.

Max & Irma's Kitchen 515 Kootenay St ⓣ250/352-2332. Simple, tasty thin-crust pizzas ($14) from a wood-fired oven. Closed Sun.

Mike's Place At the *Hume Hotel* (see p.712). This usually packed spot sells the full range of Nelson Brewing Company beers (founded in 1893); top tipple is the flagship Old Brewery Ale. There's usually dancing from 9pm (Fri–Sat) at the adjoining *Taffy Jack's* nightclub. The *Hume's* more elegant bar, *The Library*, as its name suggests, offers a quieter drinking experience.

Outer Clove 353 Stanley St ⓣ250/354-1667. For novelty value you could do worse than spoil your breath at this restaurant where virtually everything from decor to dessert features garlic (it's better than it sounds). Mains $9–17. Closed Sun.

Kaslo

KASLO, 70km north of Nelson and 25km north of Ainsworth Hot Springs (see p.711), must rate as one of British Columbia's most attractive and friendliest little villages. Huddled at the edge of Kootenay Lake and dwarfed by towering mountains, its half-dozen streets are lined with picture-perfect wooden homes and flower-filled gardens. It started life as a sawmill in 1889 and turned into a boom town – there were 27 bars, compared with two today – with the discovery of silver in 1893; diversification, and the steamers that plied the lakes, saved it from the cycle of boom and bust that ripped the heart out of so many similar towns. Today, Kaslo remains an urbane and civilized community whose thousand or so citizens work hard at keeping it that way, supporting a cultural centre, art galleries and a concert society.

Arrival and information

Getting to Kaslo without your own transport is difficult, with only weekly shuttle buses serving Nelson on Wednesdays in both directions and leaving from the senior's hall on 4th and Front Street in Kaslo (ⓣ1-877/843-2877, ⓦwww.busonline.ca). Finding your way around Kaslo is easier, as is getting information – everyone is disarmingly helpful. The **visitor centre**, 324 Front St (mid-May to mid-Oct daily 9am–5pm; ⓣ250/353-2525 or 1-800-663-4619, ⓦwww.kaslovisitorguide.com), is beside the sternwheeler.

More or less opposite, Kaslo Kayaking (ⓣ250/353-9649, ⓦwww.kaslokayaking.ca) rents **kayaks** and offers lessons and guided tours to view aboriginal petroglyphs on lakeside cliffs. Kootenay Mountain Holidays (ⓣ250/353-7122, ⓦwww.skihikebc.com) offers guided wilderness walking tours. For hiking or a jeep tour into the wilderness, try the highly knowledgeable Top Down Tours (ⓣ250/353-7347, ⓦwww.jeephikekootenays.com).

Accommodation

For such a small place, there are a number of good accommodation options in Kaslo and the surrounding area, especially for **camping**.

Beach Gables 243 Front St ⓣ250/353-2111. The best central accommodation in town, near the visitor centre, with uninterrupted lake views and two themed rooms. ❸

Kaslo Motel 330 D Ave ⓣ250/353-2431 or 1-877/353-2431, ⓦwww.kaslomotel.ca. Also downtown, this has standard motel rooms or three-bed cabins. The site used to be an ice rink and the cabins themselves were built by Japanese-Canadians interned in Kaslo during World War II. ❷

Kaslo Municipal Campground Foot of Ave A, by the lake ⓣ250/353-2662, ⓦwww.kaslo.ca. Picnic area and shelter, and a childrens' playground. A pleasant location, with serviced and unserviced sites ($15–20), hot showers and sani-dump facilities available locally. May–Sept.

Kootenay Lake Guest House 232 B Ave ⓣ250/353-2551, ⓦwww.kaslohostel.com. Kaslo's welcoming hostel has dorm beds for $25 or private rooms for $50. There are bike and kayak rentals, plus a large communal kitchen and lounge area. ❷

Lakewood Inn 6km north of Kaslo on Kohle Rd ⓣ250/353-2395, ⓦwww.lakewoodinn.com. Further north up the lakeshore, offering fully-equipped lakeside log cabins, trailers and tent and RV sites ($20–25) with private beach and boat rentals. ❹

Mirror Lake Campground 5777 Arcola Lake Rd ⓣ250/353-7102, ⓦwww.mirrorlake.kaslobc.com. Beautifully situated 5km south of town on the main road to Ainsworth, this campsite is packed with facilities, including firepits, washrooms, showers, a laundry and store, games room, playground and sandy beach. Tent and RV sites $21–24. April–Oct.

The Town

Kaslo's main attraction is the SS *Moyie*, 324 Front St (tours mid-May to mid-Oct daily 9am–5pm; $7; ⓣ250/353-2525, ⓦwww.klhs.bc.ca), the oldest surviving **sternwheeler** in North America, which ferried people, ore and supplies along the mining routes from 1898 until the advent of reliable roads. Similar steamers were the key to the Kootenays' early prosperity, their shallow draught and featherweight construction allowing them to nose into the lakes' shallowest waters. Inside is a collection of antiques, artefacts and photographs from the steamer's heyday. Drop in on Kaslo's thriving **arts centre**, the Langham Cultural Society, on A Avenue opposite the post office (ⓣ250/353-2661, ⓦwww.thelangham.ca), for theatrical performances and art exhibitions. The 1893 building began life as a hotel-cum-brothel for miners and was also used as an internment centre for Japanese-Canadians during World War II. The **Kaslo Jazz Festival** (ⓣ250/353-7548, ⓦwww.kaslojazzfest.com) in early August has some top-notch acts that perform on a floating stage on Kootenay Lake.

Kaslo makes an ideal base for tackling the **Purcell Wilderness Conservancy** (see p.701) and for pottering around some of the charming lakeshore communities. The visitor centre can advise on getting to tiny **Argenta**, 35km north, a former refugee settlement of Quakers who in 1952 came from California, alienated by growing militarism, to start a new life; Argenta is also the western trailhead for the difficult 61km **Earl Grey Pass Trail** over the Purcell Mountains to Invermere (see p.700). This area offers a good chance of seeing **ospreys**: the Kootenays' hundred or so breeding pairs represent the largest concentration of the species in North America.

Eating and drinking

For food and drink, try the rightly renowned *Treehouse Restaurant*, 419 Front St, the town's social hub (mains $6–15). An intimate place for coffee and snacks is the *Silver Spoon Bakery* at 301 Front St (closed Mon). The *Kaslo Hotel*, 430 Front St, has an appealing terrace and a good range of standard pub food, as well as some fancier dishes in its restaurant (mains around $20).

Kaslo to Slocan

From Kaslo, the scenic Hwy 31A ascends alongside the Kaslo River, a crashing torrent choked with branches and fallen trees and hemmed in by high mountains and cliffs of dark rock through the Selkirk Mountains to the **Slocan Valley**. Near its high point the road passes a series of stunningly picturesque lakes: **Fish Lake** is deep green and has a nice picnic spot at one end; **Bear Lake** is equally pretty; and **Beaver Pond** is an amazing testament to that animal's energy and ingenuity. Just 5km short of New Denver lies the turn-off to the intriguing near-ghost town of **Sandon**, before reaching **New Denver**, **Slocan** and the untamed wilds of **Valhalla Provincial Park**.

Sandon

SANDON, one of five ghost towns in the area, lies 13km east of New Denver via Hwy 31A and a gravel side road that climbs through scenery of utmost grandeur. The ragtag remains of Sandon form quite the contrast to its lovely surroundings, as a number of its current population (around a dozen) run a haulage company and are keen renovators of old machinery – giving much of the settlement the feel of a scrapyard.

Otherwise there are few relics of Sandon's silver-mining heyday, when the town had 24 hotels, 23 saloons, an opera house, a thriving red-light district and five thousand inhabitants – it even had electric light well before Victoria or Vancouver. Still, you can pop into old City Hall and pick up a walking tour pamphlet ($1) from the **visitor centre** (usually July–Sept daily 10am–5pm), which vividly documents the area's Wild West mining history, harking back to an era when Slocan produced the lion's share of Canada's silver. Then head for the **museum** (July–Sept daily 10am–5pm; $4) in the old general store, with photos and domestic and commercial artefacts.

Don't miss the hike up **Idaho Peak** (2280m) one of the most accessible and spectacular walks in the area. A 12km gravel access road from behind the museum leads into alpine pastures and a car park, from where it's a steep 3km to the summit of Mount Idaho and back, with views emerging all the way up to the spectacular panorama at the Forest Service lookout point. **Cycling** is also popular in this area, especially along the 17km **Galena Trail**; contact the Spoke 'n' Dog (see p.718) for rentals and information.

▲ Cycling the Galena Trail

There's no **accommodation** in Sandon, but RVers are welcome to an electric hook-up ($10) beside the visitor centre, which can also advise on the many places you can **camp** for free on crown land along the creek.

New Denver

After the Sandon turn-off, Hwy 31A drops into the **Slocan Valley**, a minor but still spectacular lake-bottomed tributary between the main Kootenay and Columbia watersheds. It meets Hwy 6 at **NEW DENVER**, formerly known as Eldorado after its mineral riches. Born of the same silver-mining boom as Kaslo, and with a similarly pretty lakeside setting and genuine pioneer feel, New Denver is quieter than its neighbour, the tree-lined streets mercifully free of neon, fast food joints and most evidence of tourist passage. If you're heading north from New Denver, see p.718.

Well signposted from Hwy 6, the moving **Nikkei Internment Memorial Centre** (May–Sept daily 9.30am–5pm; Oct–April by appointment; $6; ⓣ250/358-7288), 306 Josephine St, is Canada's only museum dedicated to the 22,000 Nikkei (Canadians of Japanese ancestry) who, in 1942, were forcibly relocated from the west coast to remote internment camps in the BC interior after Pearl Harbor. Beautiful Japanese gardens now surround the wooden shacks and outhouses the Nikkei were forced to build. Although the majority of Nikkei were Canadian citizens, they were all labelled "enemy aliens" and stripped of their possessions, homes and businesses. It wasn't until 1988 that the Canadian government formally apologized to Japanese–Canadians and awarded them token monetary compensation.

The **visitor centre** in New Denver is at 202 6th Ave (late June to early Sept daily 9am–5pm; ⓣ250/358-2719, ⓦwww.newdenver.ca or www.slocanlake.com).

Practicalities

As a stopover, New Denver is appealing but not quite as enticing as Kaslo. The most exotic **accommodation** possibility is the *Villa Dome Quixote,* 602 6th Ave (ⓣ250/358-7242, ⓦwww.domequixote.com; ❸), an ecologically-sound domed lodge with ten rooms. *Glacier View Cabins*, 8th Avenue and Hwy-6 (ⓣ250/358-7277, ⓦwww.glaciercabins.com; ❸), offers individual cabins just off Hwy 6 in town, while the *Valhalla Inn*, 509 Slocan Ave (ⓣ250/358-2228, ⓦwww.valhallainn.biz; ❷) is a beach-hut-type motel with pub and restaurant. The best choice for **camping** is four kilometres north of town on Hwy 6 at the *Rosebery Provincial Park* campground ($15; early May to mid-Sept). Set on the banks of Wilson Creek, it's a lightly forested site with lake and mountain views, flush toilets and cold pumped water; campfires are allowed.

For **food** in New Denver try 6th Avenue, where at no. 210 you'll find the relaxed *Apple Tree Sandwich Shop* and the bistro *Panini* at no. 306.

Slocan and Valhalla Provincial Park

Southbound out of New Denver, Hwy 6 follows the tight confines of the Slocan Valley for another 100km of ineffable mountain and lake landscapes. Be certain to stop at the **Slocan Lake Viewpoint**, 6km out of New Denver, where a short path up a small cliff provides stupendous views.

At the southern end of Slocan Lake, you'll hit **SLOCAN**, another former mining village and the best access point for trips into the 125,000-acre **Valhalla Provincial Park**, a wilderness area with very few developed facilities, on the western side of Slocan Lake.

Slocan's **visitor centre**, 1020 Griffin Rd (daily July & Aug 11.30am–7.30pm; ⓣ250/355-2266 or 1-800/355-2023, ⓦwww.slocancity.com), at the *Springer*

Creek Campground, has up-to-date timetables for the **minibus** service between Nelson and Slocan (4 daily; ⓣ1-877/843-2877, ⓦwww.busonline.ca).

If you're not interested in what the park holds but still want some of what the outdoors has to offer, try **floating** down the Slocan River, a lazy way to spend a summer's day. For **kayak** or **canoe** rentals, as well as guided **whitewater rafting** trips, contact Smiling Otter Wilderness Adventures (ⓣ250/355-2373, ⓦwww.smilingotter.com). The Slocan Rail Trail is a popular fifty-kilometre **cycling** route from Slocan south to Crescent Valley; for bike rental and shuttle service, contact the *Spoke 'n' Dog B&B and Cycling*, 6285 McKean Rd (ⓣ250/226-6752, ⓦwww.spokendog.com; ④), in Winlaw, halfway along the route.

Gravel roads from Slocan also lead east from Hwy 6 to **Kokanee Glacier Provincial Park** (p.711). Pick up detailed directions and further information about either park at the New Denver or Slocan visitor centres.

Exploring the park

A popular wildflower-lined trail leads 7.2km from Slocan past many good fishing and swimming spots along the western shore of the lake to Evans Beach, the most accessible part of the park. From the small campsite here the Evans Creek trail leads to equally attractive spots beside lakes en route to Beatrice Lake, where the fishing is excellent. Most other park trailheads need to be accessed by boat and Slocan Valla Ventures (ⓣ250/358-7775) operate a useful water taxi service from Slocan. These trails include the steep and difficult 8.8km Sharp Creek Trail to the New Denver Glacier – the park's real scenic highlight – and the easy 4km Nemo Creek Crail, which passes Nemo Falls, spectacular rock formations, an old cabin and a massive ageing cedar and hemlock forest. Much of the upper valleys in the park are prime grizzly bear habitat, so extreme care should be taken if backcountry camping, which is possible in many good spots around the park.

Practicalities

There are about half-a-dozen **accommodation** options, most in rustic settings with mountain or lake views. Try *Lemon Creek Lodge* (ⓣ250/355-2403, ⓦwww.lemoncreeklodge.com; ④, campsites $15–21), 7km south of Slocan on Kennedy Road – it has great **food** and rents bikes and kayaks. For camping, head to *Springer Creek RV Park and Campground* (ⓣ250/355-2266; $15–22; mid-May to Sept) in Slocan.

North from New Denver: Summit Lake and Nakusp

From New Denver Hwy 6 strikes north and after 30km passes **Summit Lake**, a perfect jewel of water, mountain and forest served by the Summit Lake Provincial Park **campsite** (see p.672). A road runs south from here into the mountains and to a small **ski** area (Dec–March, day lift-pass $21; ⓣ250/265-3312, ⓦwww.skisummitlake.com).

Some 17km beyond Summit Lake, **NAKUSP** has a wonderful, typically-Kootenays lakefront setting: beside the huge **Upper Arrow Lake** with the snowcapped Selkirk Mountains to the east providing the majestic backdrop. You can happily wander around the town for an hour along the main street, Broadway, stroll the lakefront path, go boating or swimming at the public **beach**. There's also plenty of fishing and hiking, details of which are available at the visitor centre, at 92 6th Ave (May–Sept Mon–Sat 9am–5pm Sun 10am–5pm; Oct–April Tues–Sat 10am–2pm; ⓣ250/265-4234 or 1-800/909-8819, ⓦwww.nakusparrowlakes.com), located beside the post office on Broadway.

The main attraction are the excellent **Nakusp Hot Springs**, a well-signposted complex 13km northeast of town (daily 9.30am–9.30pm; $9, day-pass $12.50; ⓣ250/265-4528 or 1-866/999-4528). It's generally sociable and it's not unusual for late-night informal parties to develop around the two outdoor pools. Partying is also a big part of Nakusp's other claim to fame: the **Nakusp Music Fest** (ⓦwww.nakuspmusicfest.ca) in which an array of rock and folk acts and fans swarm upon the town in mid-July.

BC Transit (ⓦwww.bctransit.com) provides **buses** to and from Nelson and many other local destinations, but only a couple of times a week. The full schedule is posted on the wall of the helpful visitor centre.

Practicalities

For **accommodation**, Hwy 6 west along the lake is dotted with cabins, resorts and campgrounds. Downtown, try the *Kuskanax Lodge*, 515 Broadway (ⓣ250/265-3618 or 1-800/663-0100, ⓦwww.kuskanax.kootenays.com; ❸), a more upmarket sort of place. The *Leland Hotel*, 96 4th Ave SW (ⓣ250/265-4221; ❹) is right on the lake and has been operating as a hotel since 1892. The lovely *Hotsprings Guesthouse* (ⓣ250/265-3069, ⓦwww.enjoynakusp.com; ❹), lies one kilometre north of town on Hwy-23N and on the lakeshore. **Campers** would do best to aim for the lovely *Nakusp Hot Springs* **campsite** (ⓣ250/265-4528; $15–22), near the hot springs; non-campers could try the adjoining seven-unit *Cedar Chalets* (ⓣ250/265-4505, ⓦwww.nakusphotspringschalets.com; ❷).

For food, breakfast and snacks head for the *Broadway Deli Bistro*, 408 Broadway, which also offers lunch options, including Mexican dishes for $5–9. The *Leland Hotel* has a cheerful pub, a lakefront terrace and reasonable bar food, while *Woodfired Pizza n' More*, 312 Broadway, is a higher-end dining option with good schnitzel ($14) and baked salmon ($18).

Nakusp to Revelstoke or Vernon

From Nakusp, branch off up **Hwy 23**, which heads 105km north to Revelstoke, (see p.688) or continue along **Hwy 6** in the direction of Vernon (194km; see p.721). Both are spectacular journeys involving a free ferry crossing at **Galena Bay** (hourly sailings 5am to midnight; half-hourly sailings at selected peak times in summer) and **Fauquier**, respectively (half-hourly 5am–10pm): both are 58km from Naksup where the latest crossing times are posted by the road where the hwys leave town.

There's almost nothing en route or at **GALENA BAY**, but the hamlet of **FAUQUIER** consists of a handful of buildings including a garage, a store and the *Arrow Lake Motel* (ⓣ250/269-7622; ❸), with a restaurant and on the lakeside near the ferry; call ahead to check that it's open, as it's the only option in the area. There's also a **campsite** off Hwy 6 at the northern entrance to the hamlet, the *Tukaluk* (ⓣ250/269-7355), with twenty sites for $15–25. The **free** five-minute **ferry** across Lower Arrow Lake arrives at **NEEDLES**, which is no more than a ferry ramp. There's an unofficial **campsite** at Whatshan Lake, 3km off the hwy just after Needles, but otherwise Hwy 6 is a gloriously empty ribbon as it burrows through the staggering Monashee Mountains. After cresting Monashee Pass (1198m), the hwy begins the long descent through the **Coldstream Valley** towards the Okanagan. Snow dusts the mountains here almost year-round, crags loom above the meadows that increasingly break the forest cover and beautiful flower-filled valleys wind down to the hwy. The first sign of life in over 100km is the *Gold Panner* **campsite** (ⓣ250/547-2025, ⓦwww.goldpannercampground.com; $22-28; April–Oct), 55km east of Vernon and a good spot to overnight or to explore the utter wilderness of **Monashee Provincial Park** to the north. The park is reached by rough road from **CHERRYVILLE**, a hamlet 10km further west. **LUMBY**, 22km beyond, is scarcely more substantial, although **rooms** at the *Twin Creeks Motel* (ⓣ250/547-9221, ⓦww.twincreeks-motel.com; ④) is worth considering if it's late, given the Okanagan lodgings ahead could well be packed. The village also boasts a simple riverside **campsite**, 2215 Shield Ave (ⓣ250/547-2005; $18-23; May–Sept) and there's a seasonal **visitor centre** on the hwy at 1882 Vernon St (July & Aug 9am–5pm; ⓣ250/547-2300, ⓦwww.monasheetourism.com). Beyond the village, the road glides through lovely pastoral country, with orchards, verdant meadows, low, tree-covered hills, and fine wooden barns that look like inverted longboats. Vernon (see p.721) is a 26km drive away.

The Okanagan

The vine- and orchard-covered hills and warm-water lakes of the **Okanagan**, located in south-central BC, are in marked contrast to the rugged beauty of the region's more mountainous interior, and have not only made the region one of Canada's finest fruit-growing areas but also one of its most popular holiday destinations. Yet unless you want (occasionally) rowdy beach life or enjoy mixing with families on their annual holiday, you'll probably want to ignore the area altogether in summer. Three main centres – **Vernon**, **Kelowna** and **Penticton**, ranging from north to south along the hundred-kilometre-long **Okanagan Lake** – together contain the lion's share of BC's interior population. All have fairly unpleasant downtown cores that embrace concrete, cars and unbridled construction, with an array of accommodation and tacky attractions. Things improve immeasurably if you can slip away from the towns and head for the hills or quieter stretches of lakeshore.

The almost year-round lushness that makes this "the land of beaches, peaches, sunshine and wine" means that, in the relative peace of **off season**, you can begin to experience the region's considerable charms: fruit trees in blossom, quiet lakeside villages and free wine tastings in local vineyards. You can also expect room rates to halve. Kelowna is the biggest and probably best base at any time of the year. Greyhound **buses** ply Hwy 97 on their way between Osoyoos and Kamloops or Salmon Arm.

Ogopogo

When travelling through the Okanagan Valley, you'll find it hard to avoid **Ogopogo**, the famed monster of Okanagan Lake, whose smiling dragon-like face appears on all manner of postcards, billboards and bumper stickers – someone even thought to market bags of green jellybeans as his "droppings". Its name comes from a 1920s music-hall song – "his mother was an earwig, his father a whale; a little bit of head and hardly any tail; and Ogopogo was his name" – but the myth is much older. The aboriginal Salish peoples believed in a creature called **N'ha-a-itk**, meaning "Lake Demon", who was apparently a demon-possessed man punished by the gods for murdering a tribal brother. To appease him, the Salish would sacrifice animals whenever crossing near **Rattlesnake Island**, around which the monster supposedly lurked. The Salish people warned early white settlers, who decided to set up armed patrols along the shores in case of an attack. Today, holidaymakers would be thrilled to spot BC's Loch Ness monster, and numerous sightings are claimed every year.

The O'Keefe Ranch

Some 12km north of Vernon on Hwy 97, stands the **Historic O'Keefe Ranch** (May, June & Sept to mid-Oct daily 9am–5pm; July & Aug daily 9am–6pm; $12; Ⓣ250/542-7868, Ⓦwww.okeeferanch.ca), a collection of early pioneer buildings and a tidy little museum that's well worth a half-hour's pause. In addition to a proficient summary of nineteenth-century frontier life, the museum contains an interesting section on the role of aboriginal peoples in the two world wars. Some 25 percent of eligible men immediately volunteered for service – a tour of duty that did little to resolve their national dilemma, which the museum sums up pithily with the observation that they belong to that "unhappy group who lost the old but are unable to obtain the new".

Vernon

The beach scene is less frenetic in **VERNON** than elsewhere in the region. Located near the northern edge of Okanagan Lake, the town attracts fewer of the bucket-and-spade brigade, though the emphasis on fruit and the great outdoors is as strong as ever, and the main hwy through town is bumper-to-bumper with motels, fast-food joints and garish neon signs. It's easier to find a place to stay here than in Kelowna – but there are fewer reasons for wanting to.

Vernon's **visitor centre**, 701 Hwy 97 (May–Aug daily 8.30am–6pm; Sept–May Mon–Fri 8.30am–4.30pm; Ⓣ250/542-1415 or 1-800/665-0795, Ⓦwww.vernontourism.com), is well south of the centre. The Greyhound **bus station** is on the corner of 30th Street and 31st Avenue.

The town and around

Downtown Vernon centres on Main Street (30th Ave) and despite numerous listed buildings, is a charmless, downtrodden thoroughfare dominated by impatient traffic. At the southern entrance to town, sprawling **Polson Park** is a green sanctuary, but for **beaches** head 8km south of Vernon to **Kalamalka Provincial Park**, which sits on the stunning blue-green eponymous lake. The most popular strip of sand here is the tree-fringed Kal Beach, with convenient parking just across the railway, and a large pub with a terrace at its eastern end.

Other outdoor recreation (but no camping) is on hand at **Silver Star Mountain Resort** (Nov–April day lift-pass $71; Ⓣ250–542-0224, Ⓦwww.skisilverstar.com), a steep 22-kilometre drive to the northeast on 48th Avenue off Hwy 97, where in summer a **ski lift** trundles to the top of Silver Star Mountain (1915m) for wide views and meadow-walking opportunities; the most-used trail wends from the summit back to the base area. This is also a very popular **mountain biking** centre and chairlift uplift and bike hire available. For guided summer interpretive hikes as well as winter snowshoeing trips, contact Outdoor Discoveries (Ⓣ250/545-7446, Ⓦwww.outdoordiscoveries.com). A shuttle bus services the mountain on demand ($45 one-way from Kelowna; Ⓣ250/938-0321, Ⓦwww.allcanadianescapes.com). On the other side of the valley, Paraglide Canada offer an eagle's-eye view of the area with tandem rides from the top of **Vernon Mountain** (Ⓣ250/503-1962, Ⓦwww.paraglidecanada.com; from $185).

Heading **south from Vernon**, be sure to take Mission Road to Commonage Road into Cars Landing on the western shore of Okanagan Lake – a quiet detour that offers something of the beauty for which the area is frequently praised, but which can be somewhat obscured by the commercialism of towns to the south. From the road, weaving through woods and small bays, the lake looks enchanting.

Practicalities

The most pleasant places to stay if money isn't too much of an issue are either the *Best Western Vernon Lodge*, 3914 32nd St (ⓣ250/545-3385 or 1-800/663-9400, ⓦwww.bestwesternvernonlodge.com; ❺), nine blocks from Main Street on Hwy 97, with 127 air-conditioned rooms, or *Tiki Village*, 2408 34th St (ⓣ250/503-5566 or 1-800/661-8454, ⓦwww.tikivillagevernon.com; ❺), fifteen minutes' walk southwest of downtown with thirty rooms, an outdoor pool and on-site Japanese restaurant. There's a **hostel** at Silver Star Mountain, the *SameSun Silver Star,* 9898 Pinnacles Rd (ⓣ250/545-8933, ⓦwww.samesun.com; ❸), with dorm beds $30 a night. **Campgrounds** near town all get busy during high season, and the nicer option is the more rural Ellison Provincial Park, 16km to the southwest on Okanagan Lake (reservations see p.672; $24; March–Nov), with a beach and hiking trails.

There are plenty of **eating** choices. Downtown, try *El Portillo*, 2706 30th Ave (ⓣ250/545-9599) for good coffee, sandwiches, pastries and regular live music. At 2915 30th St, *Eclectic Med* (ⓣ250/558-4646) has an extensive menu that is eclectic indeed, with Mediterranean, North African and Asian mains from $16–36. *Sir Winston's*, 2705 32nd St, is the downtown **pub** of choice.

Kelowna

If you want a summer suntan, big crowds and cheek-by-jowl nightlife – all rare in interior BC – then **KELOWNA** ("grizzly bear" in Salish) – is the place to come. But Kelowna is also famous for its fruit – growing virtually all of Canada's apricots, half its pears and plums and a third of its apples – eternally indebting it to one Father Pandosy, the French priest who founded a mission here in 1859 and planted apple trees two years later. Today, Kelowna ranks as a sprawling metropolis compared with other interior towns and its approaches come as a very unpleasant surprise to the unsuspecting visitor – particularly the conglomeration of motels, garages and fast-food outlets on Hwy 97 to the north. Still, the lakefront and beaches, though heavily developed, aren't bad, the **downtown** can make a good respite from mountains and forests and the town is a good base to **tour local vineyards**.

▲ Grape-stomping competition at one of the Okanagan's many vineyards

Arrival and information

Kelowna has a major regional **airport** 12km north of town on Hwy 97; there are regular shuttles and local buses to the centre. The Greyhound **bus station,** 2366 Leckie Rd in Orchard Park Mall, lies on Hwy 97 3km east of the centre; local buses #9 and #11 run to downtown. The **visitor centre,** 544 Harvey (May–Sept daily 8am–8pm; Sept–May Mon–Fri 8am–5pm, Sat & Sun 10am–5pm; ⓣ250/861-1515 or 1-800/663-4345, ⓦwww.tourismkelowna.com) is five blocks back from the lake.

To **rent a bike**, try Sports Rent at 3000 Pandosy St or hook up with Monashee Adventure Tours, 1591 Highland Drive North (ⓣ250/762-9253 or 1-888/762-9253, ⓦwww.monasheeadventuretours.com), for cycling tours to wineries and other parts of the Okanagan. There's also plenty of action on the lake; **jet skis** and **boats** can be rented from $85 for two hours from Kelowna Marina (ⓣ250/861-8001, ⓦwww.kelownamarina.ca) at the end of Queensway Avenue.

Accommodation

There are a staggering number of motels and campgrounds in and around town. Yet accommodation of any kind can be a major headache in the height of summer; some places may only accept reservations for three days or more. The **motels** on northbound Hwy 97 are the only dependable option for vacancies (and then only early in the morning), but it's a neon- and traffic-infested area well away from downtown and the lake; prices drop the further out you go).

Hotels and hostels

Grand Okanagan Lakeside Resort 1310 Water St ⓣ250/763-4500 or 1-800/465-4651, ⓦwww.grandokanagan.com. The top money-no-object choice in town, with a choice of spacious, modern rooms, villas and vacation homes. The complex includes a good spa, fitness centre and a casino. ❽

Kelowna International Hostel 2343 Pandosy St, near Guisachan Rd and the hospital ⓣ250/763-6024, ⓦwww.kelowna-hostel.bc.ca. Beds cost $18–20 at this charming, intimate hostel south of downtown. The owner will pick you up from the bus station. Laundry and kitchen facilities available and a pancake breakfast and wi-fi use are included in the cost. ❷

Prestige Hotel 1675 Abbott St ⓣ250/860-7900 or 1-877/737-8443, ⓦwww.prestigehotelsandresorts.com. Across from City Park and close to the beach, this is one of the best options in town. Rooms have modern, country-style furnishings, and theres's access to an indoor pool, hot tub and fitness centre . ❼

SameSun Hostel 245 Harvey Ave ⓣ250/763-9814 or 1-877/972-6378, ⓦwww.samesun.com. Enormous hostel just across from the beach has thirty private rooms and one hundred dorm beds at $28. From the bus station take bus #10 or #11 to Queensway. ❸

Travelodge Abbott Vila 1627 Abbott St ⓣ250/763-7771 or 1-800/578-7878, ⓦwww.travelodge.com. A few doors down from the *Prestige*, you could do worse than this busy, central option. ❺

Camping

Bear Creek Provincial Park 9km west of town on Westside Rd, off Hwy 97 on the west side of the lake A good option if you want to be further away from the crowds, this campsite has showers and most facilities. $24; March–Nov.

Fintry Provincial Park 34km north of town. On the attractive lakeside site of a former orchard, facilities here include showers and firepits but no electricity. Sites from $24; April–Oct.

Hiawatha RV Park 3795 Lakeshore Rd ⓣ250/861-4837 or 1-888/784-7275, ⓦwww.hiawatharvpark.com. Reasonably close to the action and backing onto Lakeshore Rd, with a separate tenting area, laundry, heated pool and free hot showers. Sites from $39–51; March–Oct.

The town and around

The main attractions in downtown Kelowna are the public beach off **City Park**, a green space fronting downtown, and the strips along Lakeshore Road south of Kelowna's famed pontoon bridge, which tend to attract a younger, trendier crowd: **Rotary Beach** here is a windsurfers' hangout, and **Gyro Park**, just north, is where

Touring Kelowna's vineyards

Kelowna's visitor centre can point you to dozens of good general fruit and food tours, but the best option is to take a **wine tour** around some of the twenty local **vineyards**. At one time these produced crisp, fruity white and dessert wines, but now successful red wines and drier whites are common. It's worth visiting a couple vineyards since the valley's microclimates and differing soil types allow neighbouring vintners to produce completely different wines. A number of local companies also run wine tours – a far better option than driving, given the generosity of samples. The visitor centre has a list that includes Wildflower Trails and Winery Tours (ⓣ250/979-1211 or 1-866/979-1211, ⓦwww.wildflowersandwine.com). Should you strike out on your own don't miss:

Summerhill Pyramid Winery 4870 Chute Lake Rd (tours daily noon, 2pm, 4pm & 6pm; $5; ⓣ250/764-8000 or 1-800/667-3538; ⓦwww.summerhill.bc.ca). Located in a beautiful spot with a top-notch restaurant and wines aged in a replica Egyptian pyramid – there's even organic champagne.

Cedar Creek Estate Winery 5445 Lakeshore Rd (daily May–Oct 11am, 1pm & 3pm, Nov–April by appointment; $5; ⓣ250/764-8866, ⓦwww.cedarcreek.bc.ca). Voted Canada's winery of the year in 2005 and 2006 and always a top contender.

Mission Hill Family Estate 1730 Mission Hill Rd (tours daily: July–Sept 11.30am, 12.30pm, 2.30pm & 3.30pm, Sept to mid-Oct 11am & 2pm, mid-Oct–end-Oct 2pm; $7; ⓣ250/768-6448, ⓦwww.missionhillwinery.com). Lying on the west side of the lake, its buildings wouldn't look out of place in Tuscany.

The wineries join together in early May, early August and early October to lay on annual spring, summer and autumn **wine festivals** (ⓦwww.owfs.com) when free wine tastings, gourmet dinners, grape stomps and vineyard picnics take place to lure the connoisseur and novice alike. More background can be found at Kelowna's **BC Wine Museum**, 1304 Ellis St (Mon–Fri 10am–6pm, Sat 10am–5pm, Sun 11am–5pm; by donation), basically a glorified shop with a few exhibits.

the town's teenagers preen. Across the bridge **Bear Creek** and **Fintry Provincial Parks** are 2km and 14km up the lake's west bank, respectively; both are lovely spots with great beaches and campgrounds, but they are also horrendously popular.

Kelowna has a growing arts scene, and is justifiably proud of its six-block **cultural district**, centred around Cawston Avenue and Water Street. Its main attractions are the Rotary Centre for the Arts, 421 Cawston Ave (Mon–Fri 8am–8pm, Sat noon–8pm; ⓣ250/717-5304, ⓦwww.rotarycentreforthearts.com), with its gallery, theatre, studios and café, and the small but impressive Kelowna Art Gallery, 1315 Water St (Tues, Wed, Fri & Sat 10am–5pm, Thurs 10am–9pm, Sun 1–4pm; $5; ⓣ250/762-2226; ⓦwww.kelownaartgallery.com).

Getting away from Kelowna's crowds isn't easy, but you can almost shake them off by climbing **Knox Mountain**, the high knoll overlooking the city to the north, just five minutes' drive (or a 30min walk) from downtown. It offers lovely views over the lake and town, particularly at sunset, and there's a wooden observation tower to make the most of the panorama.

Come winter, the focus moves 54km southeast of Kelowna off Hwy 33 to **Big White Ski Resort** (mid-Nov to mid-April; day-pass $71; ⓣ250/765-3101 or 1-800/663-2772, ⓦwww.bigwhite.com). The dry winters make this something of a powder paradise; with sixteen lifts, 7,355 skiable acres and 118 runs – over half of which cater to intermediate skiers. The full range of accommodation options here include the *Halfmoon Hostel* (ⓣ250/765-7920 or 1-877-562-2783; ❹) with dorms for $32 a night.

Eating, drinking and nightlife

Most **eating** places are crammed into the downtown core and cater to a range of tastes and budgets.

Bohemian Cafe and Catering Co 524 Bernard Ave ⓦwww.bohemiancater.com. Usually packed with gossiping girlfriends, this cavernous hangout does hearty breakfasts (with home-made bread and jam) and lunches for around $9–13.

Bouchons Bistro 105-1180 Sunset Drive ⓣ250/763-6595. This fine-dining restaurant serves French cuisine such as duck confit, rabbit and steak medallions. Mains $22–35.

Grateful Fed Psyche Deli 509 Bernard Ave. Open for breakfast; serving various burgers and wraps ($8–11) later on – with good veggie selections too; come nightfall, it often hosts live music, as the paraphernalia-festooned walls suggest.

Rose's Pub 1352 Water St. If you're in town to sink a beer and people-watch, make for this lakeside terrace heaving with sun-struck partiers.

Siam Orchard 279 Bernard Ave. Follow the crowds here for terrific value Thai food (the vegetarian pad Thai is a bargain at $7.50). Closed Mon.

Penticton

PENTICTON is a corruption of the Salish phrase *pen tak tin* – "a place to stay forever"; while this is not a name the town deserves, it is far more laidback and inviting than Kelowna, 68km to the north. Its summer daily average of ten hours of sunshine ranks it higher than Honolulu, making tourism its biggest industry after fruit (this is "Peach City"). That, along with Penticton's proximity to Vancouver and the US, keeps prices high and ensures the town and beaches are swarming with watersports jocks, cross-country travellers, RV skippers and lots of happy families. Off the beaches, there's some festival or other playing virtually every day of the year to keep the punters entertained, the key ones being the **Wine Festival** in May and late September; and the **Peach Festival** in August.

Arrival and information

Penticton **airport** is 8km south of downtown. The Greyhound **bus station**, 307 Ellis St (ⓣ250/493-4101), is just off Main Street. Downtown is small and easy to negotiate, particularly after a visit to the big **visitor centre**, 533 Railway St (June–Sept daily 8am–8pm, Oct–May Mon–Fri 9am–6pm, Sat & Sun 10am–5pm; ⓣ250/493-4055 or 1-800/663-5052, ⓦwww.tourismpenticton.ca), off Hwy 97 on the north side of town. The adjacent BC Wine Information Centre sells wines at vineyard prices.

Accommodation

Although Penticton brims with **accommodation**, finding a room in summer isn't easy. Most cheaper **motels** line the messy southern approach to the town along Hwy 97. Among the best and most central choices are the luxurious *Penticton Lakeside Resort*, 21 Lakeshore Drive West (ⓣ250/493-8221 or 1-800/663-9400, ⓦwww.rpbhotels.com; ❼), and *Days Inn Conference Centre*, 152 Riverside Drive (ⓣ250/493-6616, ⓦwww.daysinnpenticton.ca; ❼), with indoor and outdoor pools. The HI **hostel**, 464 Ellis St (ⓣ250/492-3992 or 1-866/782-9736, ⓦwww.hihostels.ca; ❸) is in an old bunkhouse downtown, one block south from the bus station, with dorms (members $20, nonmembers $24) and private rooms.

Recommended **campsites** include: *South Beach Gardens*, 3815 Skaha Lake Rd (ⓣ250/492-0628, ⓦwww.southbeachgardens.net; $33–41; June–Sept); *Camp-Along RV Resort*, 6km south of town off Hwy 97, in an apricot orchard overlooking Skaha Lake (ⓣ250/497-5584 or 1-800/968-5267, ⓦwww.campalong.com; $27–43; April–Sept); or the site at Okanagan Lake Provincial Park, 22km north of Penticton, with sites ($24; March–Oct) overlooking the lake.

The town and around

Most leisure pastimes in Penticton take place on or near Okanagan Lake, ten blocks from the town centre. **Okanagan Beach** is the closest sand to downtown and is usually covered in oiled bodies for most of its one-kilometre length; **Skaha Beach**, 4km south of town on Skaha Lake, is a touch quieter and trendier; both beaches close at midnight and sleeping on them is out of the question. Also overlooking Skaha Lake are the famed Skaha Bluffs, one of North America's premier **rock climbing** spots. Skaha Rock Adventures, 113–437 Martin St (Ⓣ250/493-1765, Ⓦwww.skaharockclimbing.com) run tours for beginners for $125 per day. More restful is the favourite method of cooling off in the summer: **floating** down the Okanagan River Channel to Skaha Lake for a couple of hours in an inflatable boat or tube; Coyote Cruises, 215 Riverside Drive (Ⓣ250/492-2115, Ⓦwww.coyotecruises.ca), rents tubes and offer a return shuttle for $10.

The **Penticton Museum** (Tues–Sat 10am–5pm; donation), at 785 Main St, has a panoply of predictable Canadiana and you can take tours around the *SS Sicamous* (May–Sept daily 9am–9pm; Oct–April daily 9am–5pm; $5), a beached **paddlesteamer** off Lakeshore Drive on the Kelowna side of town. Just off Main Street there's the **Penticton Art Gallery** (Tues–Fri 10am–5pm, Sat & Sun noon–5pm; $2, free Sat & Sun), 199 Front St, which often carries high-quality shows and backs onto lovely Japanese gardens. More tempting perhaps, and an ideal part of a day's stopover, is a trip to the **Red Rooster Winery** (daily: April–Oct 10am–6pm, Nov–March 11am–5pm; Ⓣ250/492-2424, Ⓦwww.redroosterwinery.com), at 891 Naramata Rd, with an on-site art gallery housing a replica of *The Baggage Handler*, a controversial sculpture known to locals as "Frank"; it was banished from its original home in a downtown Penticton traffic circle after its nudity offended locals – one incensed vandal even hacked off Frank's privates. For another unique experience, **Elephant Island Winery** (May to mid-Oct 10.30am–5.30pm, mid-Oct to May by appointment; Ⓣ250/496-5522, Ⓦwww.elephantislandwine.com), 2730 Aikens Loop, in Naramata, 15km north of town, makes highly regarded fruit wines. If you are vineyard hopping and want to avoid drink driving, Top Cat Tours (Ⓣ250/493-7385, Ⓦwww.topcattours.com) offer five-hour **guided tours**, lunch included, for $80.

Winters in Penticton centre 33km west of town at the **Apex Mountain Resort** (Nov–April; day-pass $60; Ⓣ250/292-8222 or 1-877/777-2739, Ⓦwww.apexresort.com), with four lifts and 67 runs – almost half of which are intermediate level, though the resort is famed for its black diamond mogul runs.

Eating and drinking

For something low-key try the funky *Fibonacci Rostery and Café*, 219 Main St, serving organic coffee and vegetarian wraps. Down towards the lake and around the corner at 67 Front St, *The Dream Cafe* (Ⓣ250/490-9012, Ⓦwww.thedreamcafe.ca) has oodles of bohemian atmosphere and delectable Indian, Middle Eastern and Asian-inspired cuisine (mains $11–24) and also hosts quality live music. Back on Main Street, vine-covered *Theo's* at no. 687 (Ⓣ250/492-4019) is a friendly and crowded Greek place with big portions (mains $13–26). For something more upmarket, search out the very popular but eccentric *Salty's Beach House*, 988 Lakeshore Drive (Ⓣ250/493-5001), with its South Seas setting of palm trees and fishing nets and a spicy menu of Caribbean, Thai, Indonesian and Malaysian food (mains around $20). For **drinks**, make for the perennially popular *Barking Parrot* in the *Penticton Lakeside Resort*, with unbeatable views and live music on the outdoor patio.

Osoyoos

From Penticton, travelling south on Hwy 97 will bring you to **OSOYOOS**, (the Syilx'tsn word for "gathered together"), surrounded by half-bare, scrub-covered, ochre hills, in one of Canada's strangest landscapes. With a mere 25cm of rain per year, this is a bona fide **desert**, with lizards, cacti and snakes: 23 types of invertebrate are endemic. Temperatures are regularly 10°C higher than in Nelson, less than a morning's drive away, enabling exotic fruit like bananas and pomegranates to be grown and prompting local buildings to favour the odd adobe building. The town is otherwise distinguished by its position beside **Lake Osoyoos**, Canada's warmest freshwater lake, with an average summer temperature of 24°C. Hwy 97, which passes through the town as an ugly strip, is the main route into the Okanagan region from the south. In summer the place comes alive with swimmers and boaters and with streams of American RVs slow-tailing their way northwards to the real action.

The relative lack of crowds and strange scenery might persuade you to do your beach-bumming in Osoyoos, though you may be pushed to find space in any of the town's twenty or so **hotels** and **motels** during high season; for help, contact the **visitor centre** (daily: June 9am–5pm; July & Aug 8am–6pm; Sept–May 9am–4pm; ⓣ250/495-5070, ⓦwww.destinationosoyoos.com), at the corner of hwys 3 and 97, outside the Greyhound **bus stop** (ⓣ250/495-7252).

The town and around

A visit to the **Desert Centre** (daily: late April to mid-May & Sept 10am–2pm; mid-May to mid-Sept 9.30am–4.30pm; $7; ⓣ250/495-2470 or 1-877/899-0897, ⓦwww.desert.org), on Hwy 97 just north of town, is a good way to learn a little more about the region's oddball environment. There are tours over a 1.5km boardwalk through a small area of desert, a fascinating ecosystem of some one hundred rare plants, including tiny cacti and sage, as well as three hundred animals from rattlesnakes to pocket gophers that are now all under serious threat. For a similar experience with a bonus cultural punch, visit the slick **Nk'Mip Desert Culture Centre** (early March–early Tues–Sat 9.30am–4pm early May–early Oct daily 9.30am–4.30pm; $12; ⓣ250/495-7901 or 1-888/495-8555, ⓦwww.nkmipdesert.com), at 1000 Rancher Creek Rd on Hwy 3 just east of town, run by the Osoyoos Indian Band. It features a reconstruction of a native village and 2km of trails through a desert landscape with an unnerving number of "rattlesnake alert" signs. You'll also find the **Nk'Mip Cellars** (tours May–Oct 4pm; $55; ⓣ250/495-2985, ⓦwww.nkmipcellars.com) here, Canada's first aboriginal-owned winery.

Practicalities

Good **accommodation** choices include the *Avalon Inn*, 9106 Main St (ⓣ250/495-6334 or 1-800/264-5999, ⓦwww.avaloninn.ca; ❻) or the more expensive *Best Western Sunrise Inn,* 5506 Main St (ⓣ250/495-4000 or 1-877/878-2200, ⓦwww.bestwesternosoyoos.com; ❼), with its indoor pool and restaurant. The swankiest spot is the *Spirit Ridge*, 1200 Rancher Creek Rd (ⓣ250/495-5545, ⓦwww.spiritridge.ca; ❽), a luxurious place with a top-notch spa and nine-hole golf course. For **campsites**, try the *Nk'Mip Campground and RV Park*, 8000 45th St (ⓣ250/495-7279; $38-48), 1km from Hwy 3 East, or the popular and picturesque Hayes Point Provincial Park (ⓣ1-800/689-9025; $24), 2km south of town on 32nd Avenue off Hwy 97.

Local **restaurants** are almost entirely fast food, but the *Wildfire Grill*, 8526 Main St (ⓣ250/495-2215; closed Sun & Mon), is a fine dining favourite (mains $18–25). For a caffeine fix or a quick bite try *Delights*, 8323 Main St, a bakery and café with inexpensive Asian dishes for $7–9.

Highway 3 west of Osoyoos

From Osoyoos, it's 248km to Hope (see p.731) along Hwy 3. The road begins by meandering out of the US border zone into the beautiful and fertile rural landscape around the fruit-growing centre of **Keremeos**, then follows the serene Simikameen valley to quietly attractive **Hedley**. Some 38km to the west of Hedley Hwy 3 hits **Princeton** – a dispersed collection of mostly drab houses amid lacklustre low hills – before doglegging sharply south and conveniently twisting through the attractive and worthwhile **Manning Provincial Park**.

Keremeos

Pretty little **KEREMEOS**, whose attractive siting rivals Nelson's (see p.712), spreads over a dried-up lake bed, with hills and mountains rising from the narrow plain on all sides. Thanks to a climate that blesses the region with Canada's longest growing season, lush, irrigated orchards surround town – offset in spring by huge swaths of flowers across the valley floor – and you can pick up fruit and vegetables – including cherries, apricots, peaches, pears, apples, plums and grapes – from stands dotted more or less everywhere. Try **wine tasting** at the organic **St Laszlo Vineyards** (9am-9pm, ⓣ250/499-2856), 1km east of town on Hwy 3.

Keremeos itself is a rustic, two-street affair almost unspoilt by neon or other urban clutter. There are a couple of local **motels**, including the cheaper *Similkameen Motel* (ⓣ250/499-5984; ❷), 1km west of the centre in open country surrounded by lawns and orchards, and the nicer *The Elks* (ⓣ250/499-2043 or 1-888/499-7773; ❹), also with landscaped gardens and wi-fi. The *Pasta Trading Post,* 629 7th Ave (ⓣ250/499-2933, ⓦwww.pastatradingpost.com; ❺), is a B&B in century-old antique-filled house that's also a wonderful place to **eat** locally grown organic produce, with mains ranging from $5–20 (closed Tues).

Hedley

West from Keremeos, Hwy 3 travels 29km along the extremely picturesque and ever-widenening Similkameen Valley to **HEDLEY**. This old gold-mining hamlet is today little more than a single street with great scenery and a couple of motels. The **visitor centre**, 712 Daly St (mid-May to Aug daily 9am–5pm; rest of year Thurs–Mon 9am–4pm; donation for museum; ⓣ250/292-8787, ⓦwww.hedleybc.ca), is part of a small but interesting **museum** with archive photos and mining memorabilia. Pick up details of the self-guided walking tour around the village's period buildings.

To **stay**, try the *Colonial Inn Bed & Breakfast* (ⓣ250/292-8131, ⓦwww.colonialinnbb.ca; ❺), an historic 1930s house built by the Kelowna Exploration Gold Mining Company to wine and dine potential investors; it has just five rooms and sixteen RV sites ($27). The *Gold House B&B*, 644 Colonial Rd (ⓣ250/292-8418 or 1-866/676-4653, ⓦwww.thegoldhouse.com; ❹), 200m off Hwy 3, is equally historic, having been the 1904 Gold Assay Office. About 1km east of Hedley, off the hwy, lies **Bromley Rock Provincial Park**, a lovely picnic stop looking down on the white water of the Similkameen River. It also has seventeen campsites ($15). West of the village is the small, pine-tree dotted Stemwinder Provincial Park **campsite** ($15; April–Oct). **Eat** and **drink** at *The Hitching Post*, 916 Scott Ave (ⓣ250/292-8413; closed Tues), in a downtown heritage building, serving generous portions of seafood, steak and ribs with dishes from $17–29.

Manning Provincial Park

Manning Provincial Park, hard on the US border 147km from Hedley and 64km east of Hope, is one of the few parks in the Coast and Cascade ranges. It

Skiing and snowboarding

You'd expect a country that's near snowbound for half the year to be ideal for winter sports, and Canadians have become masters at making the most out of winter – the country is studded with venues for every possible cold-weather activity. Ice hockey is the undisputed national obsession, but cross-country skiing, snowshoeing, tobogganing, snowmobiling and ice-skating are all national pastimes too. Yet it's downhill skiing and snowboarding that have spawned the greatest industry of all, with conditions – and scenery – stunning enough to lure visitors halfway around the world.

Mont Tremblant resort, Québec ▲

Skiing off the beaten track at Lake Louise, Alberta ▼

Canada's ski resorts

Almost three hundred ski resorts dot Canada, yet most visiting skiers head to just a handful in the **Rocky Mountains**, interior **British Columbia** and southern **Québec**. The season runs from mid-December until the end of May, with the **best conditions** usually in March, when the snow is at its deepest, the days get warmer and longer and resort accommodation – hard to secure during Christmas week, the mid-February school holidays and at Easter – is easy to find.

Canada's resorts have a great balance of terrain, from rolling beginner runs to more challenging expert slopes. Service and **efficiency** is also a strong point: fast lifts whisk you away from short queues to immaculately **groomed** slopes, where snow-making equipment is at the ready, just in case. Yet what really distinguishes these resorts – those in the Rockies, particularly – from their US counterparts is that the mountains are more scenically stunning.

The Rocky Mountains

Most of Canada's best skiing and snowboarding is in the **Rockies**, much of it around **Banff**; shuttles serve a trio of resorts – **Norquay**, **Sunshine** and **Lake Louise** – from town, and another half-dozen hills are within day-trip distance. Winter in Banff is far less busy than summer, which means cheaper prices, a more relaxed pace and more subdued nightlife. The big drawback is the temperature which, particularly in the early season, can be bitterly cold (think -25 to -30°C). Yet low temperatures help preserve powdery snow; and in any case, the wild beauty of the surrounding national park more than compensates for the chill.

British Columbia

Just west of the main spine of the Rockies and in British Columbia there are a series of slightly smaller resorts ideal for shorter breaks. These include: **Kicking Horse**, known for its epic backcountry-style terrain; **Panorama**, with its big vertical drop, impressive range of slopes and purpose-built village; and **Kimberley**, where a mix of uncrowded blue and black runs lie close to the eponymous Bavarian-themed town. The most remote of these resorts – but still only three hours' drive from Calgary or Banff – is the excellent **Fernie**, which deserves its reputation for varied terrain and great powder.

With much of the best snow and terrain in the Rockies, it's perhaps surprising to find Canada's biggest ski town, **Whistler**, host of the 2010 Winter Olympics, far to the west, close to Vancouver. It's got the continent's biggest vertical drop, highest piste mileage and a wide variety of exciting runs above and through the tree line, but is also the best resort to party, which can make it a bit hectic and pricey. A greater weakness is its propensity to bad weather rolling in from the ocean. This can provide good snow, but often as not also brings rain and days on end without the sun in sight.

The BC interior has brighter conditions. **Sun Peaks**, near Kamloops, has a Tirolean-style ski village and varied terrain with some fabulously steep pistes; the area is also home to some of Canada's best **heli-skiing**. Further south in the Okanagan Valley is **Silver Star**, a tiny 1890s-style village with many easy and intermediate slopes and a splendid bowl of expert trails. Even further south, near Kelowna, is BC's highest ski area, **Big White**, which peaks at 2318m, and has reputation for powder.

▲ Backcountry skiing at Kicking Horse, BC

▼ Snowboarding in powder at Whistler, BC

▼ Heli-skiers on a BC mountain top

Riding the rail at Mont Tremblant's terrain park, Québec ▲

ross-country skiing in Gaspésie Provincial Park, Québec ▼

Québec

Though the icy snow is not nearly as good as what you'll get out west, and conditions can be equally cold, eastern Canada also has **world-class** skiing. Its hills might appear less imposing but don't be fooled – they hold a fantastic range of trails, excellent **mogul** runs and impressive **terrain parks**. The most notable locations are in **Québec**, where French culture, language and cuisine forms an extra attraction, as do the shorter flight times for Europeans and east coast Americans.

Its 95 runs, European-style village and excellent après-ski nightlife make **Mont Tremblant**, 120km northwest of Montréal, Québec's most popular resort. No less superb though are its Québec City-area rivals: **Stoneham**, with excellent night skiing; **Mont-Ste-Anne**, with clusters of black diamond and wooded runs; and **Le Massif**, whose views over the St Lawrence River are spectacular. As elsewhere, prices tumble in the winter.

Other winter sports

Plenty of other outdoor pursuits can provide an entertaining day off from the Canadian pistes. Places for low-tech activities like **sledding**, snowshoeing and **ice-skating** are easily found, while operators providing guided horse-drawn **sleigh rides** or snowmobile trips abound. In some areas, particularly around Banff and Jasper, there's good ice climbing, **canyon crawling** and **ice-fishing**.

Cross-country skiing is especially popular and well-maintained trails provide a chance to really immerse yourself in the surrounding terrain. Among the best areas are Alberta's **Canmore Nordic Centre** and Quebec's **Gaspésie and Gatineau parks**, the latter just 15 minutes from Ottawa.

parcels up a typical assortment of mountain, lake and forest scenery, so even if you're just passing through it's time well spent walking at least one of the short **trails** off the road, including the 700-metre Sumallo Grove loop, 10km east of the park's western entrance. The most popular drive within the park is the fifteen-kilometre side road to **Cascade Lookout**, which overlooks an amphitheatre of mountains. A gravel road carries on another 6km from there to **Blackwall Peak**, the starting point for the **Heather Trail** (10km one-way), renowned for its swaths of summer wild flowers. Other manageable day-hikes leave the south side of the main hwy, the majority accessed from the Lightning Lake Road. In the winter, the park is good for downhill and cross-country **skiing** as well as snowshoeing.

For park information and trail leaflets, ask at the front desk of the *Manning Park Resort* (Ⓣ250/840-8822 or 1-800/330-3321, Ⓦwww.manningpark.com; ⑧), on Hwy 3 almost exactly midway between Princeton and Hope, which has cabins, chalets and hotel rooms. There are also four provincial **campsites** (reservations see p.672) on and off the hwy, those close to the road being Coldspring, Hampton and Mule (each $15). A fourth, Lightning Lake ($24), has free hot showers and flush toilets, but you'll need to reserve a site in advance.

The Fraser Valley

Some 65km northwest of Manning Provincial Park at the town of Hope, Hwy 3 meets the **Fraser River Valley**, which forms the corridor for the busy Trans-Canada Hwy between Vancouver and interior BC. All road and rail routes west roll along the 154km meandering course of the Fraser's lower reaches: the Trans-Canada Hwy (Hwy 1) being the quickest while the **Lougheed Highway** (Hwy 7) on the river's north shore is less busy. Diversions along the latter include **Harrison Hot Springs** and the archeological dig at **Xá:ytem**.

Meanwhile, travellers heading east from **Hope** can either take the brisker Coquihalla Hwy (see below) to Kamloops or follow the **Trans-Canada Hwy** along the **Fraser Canyon** to see one of BC's grandest waterways squeezed between the high ridges of the Cascade and Coast mountain ranges. Long regarded as impassable, the canyon has forced the highway to pass through seven tunnels and along a series of perilous rock ledges hundreds of metres above the swirling waters. The Canadian Pacific Railway and Canadian National Railway also pass this way.

Harrison Hot Springs

An easy 41km drive through pretty farmland on Hwy 7 from Hope, **HARRISON HOT SPRINGS** populates the southern edge of Harrison Lake, which aboriginal peoples have visited for centuries for its healing properties. The waters were not

The Coquihalla Highway

Anyone travelling east-west in any sort of hurry, travels the 182km between Hope and Kamloops on the **Coquihalla Hwy** (Hwy 5). Bring enough food and fuel as there are no services along the way; be prepared to pay a toll at the wind- and snow-whipped Coquihalla Pass (1244m). The scenery is unexceptional in the west, but things look up considerably east of the pass. Here, forests, mountains and crashing rivers add much drama – despite being somewhat compromised by old mines, road-building scars, forest fire-ravaged landscapes and the devastating effects of the Pine Beetle infestation, which has often necessitated large-scale clear-cuts.

popularized until their 1858 "discovery" by gold prospectors and shortly after, the town became BC's first resort. Today, tourism remains Harrison Hot Spring's main industry, as you'll see from the number of modern apartment buildings and motels lining the lake. Yet it's all mercifully free of too much neon and tat and remains a scenic spot, thanks to the beautiful mountain views.

The **visitor centre** is at 499 Hot Springs Rd (June–Sept Thurs–Mon 9.30am–5.30pm; early Oct to May Sat & Sun 10am–4pm; Ⓣ604/796-5581, Ⓦwww.tourismharrison.com) in an old logging-camp bunkhouse. There is no Greyhound service to Harrison Hot Springs, but local buses link the town with Chilliwack (4 daily; Ⓦwww.busonline.ca; $3).

The town and around

The lake itself is 60km long – making it one of BC's largest – and its waters very clean, but perishingly cold. The only swimming option is in the artificial lagoon on the lake's shore; to get onto the lake itself, you can rent boats, windsurfing equipment and jet-skis from the deck in front of the upmarket but rather ugly *Harrison Hot Springs Resort*. The **springs** are a short walk along the shore – past the *Harrison Hot Springs Resort* – but they're a scalding hot 73°C at source. To make the waters suitable for soaking, they're cooled and redirected to the **Harrison Hot Springs Public Pool** (Mon–Thurs 9am–8pm, Fri & Sat 9am–9pm; $8.50) at the intersection of Hot Springs Road and the Esplanade in town.

Alternatively, head for free hot springs in a series of tubs in a remote setting at **Clear Creek Hot Springs**, reached by driving 50km north up the east side of Harrison Lake and then a further 30km on a series of extremely rough logging roads. If your car isn't up to the challenge, you might have to journey the last 10km on foot. For detailed directions, ask at the **visitor centre**. You can also ask there for a map of the Agassiz-Harrison Mills **Circle Farm Tour** (Ⓦwww.district.kent.bc.ca), which takes you to fifteen local farms, including a hazelnut orchard, a cheese-maker's, a Coho salmon farm and a corn barn, all within a 25km radius.

Practicalities

One of the cheapest **motels** is the *Bungalow,* 511 Lillooet Ave (Ⓣ604/796-3536, Ⓦwww.bungalowmotel.com; ❺), with self-contained lakeside cabins and an ice-cream bar. *Harrison Heritage House and Cottages,* 312 Lillooet Ave (Ⓣ604/796-9552 or 1-800/331-8099, Ⓦwww.bbharrison.com; ❺) is a pricey but beautiful **B&B** in one of the village's few heritage buildings, and also has three riverside cottages (❻). The *Harrison Hot Springs Resort & Spa* (Ⓣ604/796-2244 or 1-866/638-5075, Ⓦwww.harrisonresort.com; ❻), a favourite of Clark Gable's in the 1950s, is a friendly place with indoor and outside pools piped from the springs. There are several private campsites around, but head instead for nearby Sasquatch Provincial Park (reservations see p.672; $15, day-use parking $5).

Eating options are mostly along the Esplanade by the lake. *Ravens*, at no. 160 (Ⓣ604/796-8717), has a large patio overlooking the lake, with seasonal menus (mains $14–27) and largely local ingredients: the salmon's excellent. For a treat, head to the *Harrison Hot Springs Resort*'s *Copper Room* for the rack of lamb ($39).

Mission and Xá:ytem

From Harrison Hot Springs another 41km drive west along Hwy 7 brings you to **Xá:ytem** (Mon–Sat 10am–4.30pm;; Ⓣ604/820-9725, Ⓦwww.xaytem.ca), BC's oldest aboriginal dwelling site, on the eastern outskirts of **MISSION**. People have lived continuously here for nine thousand years, and an ongoing archeological dig has uncovered numerous lithic artefacts, including arrowheads and stones used for cutting and chopping – some were made from obsidian from Oregon, an indication of early trade routes. A Stó:lo long house serves as the site's interpretation centre, and inside you can learn more about the excavations.

Hope

Reputedly christened by pioneers familiar with Dante, **HOPE** – as in "Abandon all hope..." – is a pleasant mountain-ringed town 158km east of Vancouver that achieved a certain fame as the place wasted in spectacular fashion by Sylvester Stallone at the end of *First Blood*, the first Rambo movie. Despite the number of roads converging here – the Trans-Canada Hwy, Hwy 3 and the Coquihalla Hwy – it remains a remarkably unspoilt stopover. In the past it was rivers, not roads that accounted for the town's growth: the Fraser River (Simon Fraser himself passed through in 1808) and two of its major tributaries, the Skagit and Coquihalla rivers, meet at the townsite. The aboriginal villages here were forced to move when a Hudson's Bay post was established in 1848, the status quo being further disturbed when the gold rush hit in 1858.

Arrival and information

The **visitor centre,** 919 Water St (daily July & Aug 8am–8pm; May, June & Sept 8am–6pm; rest of year Mon–Fri 10am–4pm; ⓣ604/869-2021 or 1-866/467-3842, ⓦwww.hopebc.ca) is the building next to the restored home gold mill. Most of what happens in Hope happens on Hwy 1, here known as Water Avenue. The Greyhound **bus station** lies at the junction of Fort Street and 3rd Avenue, with an office in the Midtown Laundromat at 800 3rd Ave.

The town and around

The town **museum** (May–Sept daily 10am–4pm; donation) is in the same building as the visitor centre, and offers the usual hand-me-downs of Hope's erstwhile old-timers. Time permitting, drop by **Memorial Park** downtown, where trees ravaged by rot have been given a new lease on life by local chainsaw sculptors. Nearby, the **Christ Church National Historic Site**, built in 1861, is one of BC's oldest churches still on its original site.

Hiking, fishing, canoeing and even gold panning are all popular around the hundreds of local lakes and rivers; get details from the visitor centre. Of the hikes, the **Rotary Trail** (3km) from the end of 7th Street to the confluence of the Fraser and Coquihalla rivers is popular, as is the more demanding **Mount Hope Loop and Lookout Trail** (4km), with a view worth the climb. Another popular walking expedition is the dark jaunt through the five colossal **Othello-Quintette Tunnels** (closed Nov–April) of the Hope-Midway Kettle Valley Railway, opened in 1916 but abandoned in 1959 after countless avalanches, mudslides and rock falls. The tunnels are reached by a short trail from the **Coquihalla Canyon Provincial Park** parking area, 6km northeast of town off the Coquihalla Hwy. This was one of the backcountry locations used during the filming of *First Blood*, and offers spectacular views over the cliffs and huge sand bars of the Coquihalla Gorge. **Kawkawa Lake**, 3km northeast of the Hope town centre, on Kawkawa Lake Road is another popular mountain retreat, with plenty of relaxing and swimming opportunities.

Practicalities

Cheap **motels** proliferate along Old Hope Princeton Way. In town, the *Best Continental Motel*, 860 Fraser Ave (ⓣ604/869-9726, ⓔbcmhope@hotmail.com; ④), is a block back from the main hwy and is handy for the bus station. On the banks of the

Simon Fraser

The Fraser River is named after **Simon Fraser**, one of North America's most remarkable early explorers who, as an employee of the North West Company established western Canada's first white settlements: Fort McCleod (1805), Fort St James (1806), Fort Fraser (1806) and Fort George (1807). Having traced the route taken by fellow explorer Alexander Mackenzie across the continent, he set out in 1808 to establish a route to the Pacific and secure it for Britain against rival US claims. Instead, he travelled the entire 1300-kilometre length of a river – the Fraser – under the mistaken impression he was following the Columbia. "We had to pass where no man should venture," he wrote, making most of the journey on foot guided by local natives, pushing forward using ladders, ropes and improvised platforms to bypass rapids too treacherous to breach by boat. Reaching the river's mouth, where he would have glimpsed the site of present-day Vancouver, he realized his error and deemed the venture a commercial failure, despite the fact he had successfully navigated one of the continent's greatest rivers for the first time. Few people felt the need to follow Fraser's example until the discovery of **gold** near Yale in 1858; prospectors promptly waded in and panned every tributary of the lower Fraser until new strikes tempted them north to the Cariboo.

Coquihalla River 8km east of town, *Kw'o:kw'e:hala*, 67400 Tunnels Rd (Ⓣ604/869-3799 or 1-877/326-7387, Ⓦwww.eco-retreat.com; ⑦), offers exclusive getaways in restored historic cabins; you could easily kill a few days here, melting in the wood-fired sauna or burning off the gourmet organic meals with a burst of hiking or river tubing. **Campsites** include the *Othello Tunnels Campground & RV Park,* 67851 Othello Rd, (Ⓣ604/869-9448 or 1-877/869-0543, Ⓦwww.othellotunnels.com; $22–27), 8km east of Hope, with a rainbow trout fishing pond that delights the kids.

Food facilities are limited. For snacks, try the buzzing *Blue Moose Coffee House*, at 322 Wallace St. For more substantial dishes, opt for the Korean and Japanese cuisine at *Kimchi*, 821A 6th Ave (Ⓣ604/869-0070; closed Sun), with *udon* and sushi from $9.

Yale

YALE, about 25km north of Hope, opens the Fraser Canyon with a ring of plunging cliffs. Sitting at the river's navigable limit, it was once a significant site for Canada's aboriginal peoples, providing an important point of departure for the canoes of the Stó:lo ("People of the River"). A Hudson's Bay Company post, The Falls, appeared here in the 1840s, later renamed in honour of James Murray Yale, commander of the HBC post at Fort Langley. Within a decade it became the largest city in North America west of Chicago and north of San Francisco.

Today, Yale is a small town of about two hundred, though a visit to the **Yale Heritage Site** (mid-April to early May Sat & Sun 10am–5pm; early May to mid-Oct daily 10am–5pm; $5; Ⓣ604/863-2324, Ⓦwww.historicyale.ca) on the corner of Hwy 1 and Douglas Street, offers an exhaustive account of the town's golden age. If large rocks impress you, then have a peek at **Lady Franklin Rock**, the vast river boulder which blocked the passage of steamers beyond Yale – all goods heading north to the goldfields had to transfer at this point to wagon trains bound for the Cariboo Wagon Road; ask locals for directions. For a longer jaunt, take Hwy 1 a kilometre south out of the village to reach the trailhead of the **Spirit Cave Trail**, a three-hour walk with fine views of the mountains.

The *Fort Yale Motel* (Ⓣ604/863-2216, Ⓦwww.fortyalemotel.net; ③) at the entrance to the canyon, is the only motel in town. The heritage-listed *Teague House B&B* (Ⓣ604/863-2336 or 1-800/363-7238, Ⓦwww.fraserraft.com; ④) has a communal kitchen and operates whitewater rafting trips down the Fraser River. If you're **camping**, you might want to backtrack 10km towards Hope on Hwy 1 to the *Emory Creek Campground*, a large, peaceful wooded site with river walks (May–Oct; $19).

Hell's Gate

Around 20km north of Yale on Hwy 1 is the famous **HELL'S GATE**, where – in a gorge almost 180m deep – the huge swell of the Fraser is squeezed into a 38-metre channel of foaming water that crashes through the rocks with awe-inspiring ferocity. For a good view of the canyon, travel 10km north of Yale on Hwy 1 to the **Alexandra Bridge Provincial Park**, where an old section of the hwy drops to the Alexandra Bridge for some startling panoramas. Eight kilometres further there's some resort-like commercialism to negotiate – and an "Air-Tram" cable car (daily: early April to mid-May & early Sept to mid-Oct 10am–4pm, mid-May to early Sept 10am–5pm; $17; ⓣ604/867-9277, ⓦwww.hellsgateairtram.com) to pay for – before getting down to the river. Close by there are also displays on the various provisions made to help migrating **salmon** complete their journeys, which have been interrupted over the years by the building of roads and railways. The Fraser River is one of the key runs for Pacific salmon, and every summer and autumn they fill it as they head for tributaries and upstream lakes to spawn (see p.737).

Lytton

LYTTON, 50km north of Hell's Gate, marks the start of BC's arid interior. Lying at the junction of the Fraser and Thompson rivers, it's a small lumber town and a main centre for **whitewater rafting**. The most notorious stretch is along the Thompson River from Spences Bridge to Lytton, home to rapids with intimidating names like *Jaws of Death* and *Witch's Cauldron*. Various companies run several trips a week from May to August and are listed at **visitor centre**, 400 Fraser St (June–early Sept daily 9am–5pm, rest of year call for times; ⓣ250/455-2523, ⓦwww.lytton.ca). These include *Kumsheen Rafting Resort*, 5km east of Lytton on Hwy 5 (ⓣ250/455-2296 or 1-800/663-6667, ⓦwww.kumsheen.com). The resort offers lovely antique-furnished tent-cabins (❹), camping (rentals available) and RV sites

▲ Whitewater rafting on the Thompson River

from $26, and has an outdoor pool and restaurant. For something central, try the *Totem Motel and Lodge*, 320 Fraser St (ⓣ250/455-2321, ⓦwww.totemmotellytton.com; ④). The Skihist Provincial Park, 6km east of town, has camping sites ($19) with views of the Thompson River canyon.

Cache Creek

CACHE CREEK, 337km from Vancouver and 84km west of Kamloops, has a reputation as a hitchhiker's black hole and indeed is the sort of sleepy place you could get stuck in for days. It's known as the "Arizona of Canada" for its extraordinary rocky landscapes and baking summer climate, which settles a heat-wasted somnolence on its dusty streets. The parched, windswept mountains here are anomalous volcanic intrusions in the regional geology, producing a legacy of hard rock and semi-precious stones – including jade – that attract climbers and rock hounds. You can watch semi-precious stones being worked at several places, or check out **Hat Creek Ranch** (May–Sept daily 9am–5pm, July–Aug till 6pm; $9; ⓣ1-800/782-0922, ⓦwww.hatcreekranch.com), a collection of original buildings including a log stopping house, the last of its type, and a reconstruction of a Shuswap village. It's located ten minutes north of Cache Creek by the junction of hwys 97 and 99 (the original Cariboo Wagon Rd) and offers camping ($10–15), teepees (②) and cabins (④). Otherwise, try one of several **motels**, including the *Bonaparte*, Hwy 97 North (ⓣ250/457-9693 or 1-888/922-1333; ④), with its large heated pool.

Kamloops

Almost any trip in southern BC brings you sooner or later to **KAMLOOPS**, a sprawling town 355km northeast of Vancouver and 110km west of Salmon Arm, which has been a transport centre from time immemorial. Its name derives from the Shuswap word for "meeting of the rivers" and today it marks the meeting point of the Trans-Canada and Yellowhead (South) hwys, the region's principal transcontinental roads, as well as the junction of the Canadian Pacific and Canadian National railways. One of the larger towns in interior southern BC, it's a bland and unobjectionable place that has yet to shake off its Wild West heritage. There's no particular need to stick around, but it makes a convenient provisions stop, especially for those heading north on Hwy 5 or south on the Coquihalla Hwy, neither of which has much in the way of facilities. Otherwise the most compelling times to visit are during the **Kamloops Pow Wow**, held the first weekend in August (ⓣ250/828-9782; $10/day) and the mid-March **Kamloops Cowboy Festival**, which celebrates cowboy poetry, music and even has a cowboy church (ⓦwww.bcchs.com; $10/day).

Arrival and information

The **visitor centre**, 1290 West Trans-Canada Hwy (mid-May to mid-Oct daily 8am–6pm, rest of year Mon–Fri 9am-6pm; ⓣ250/374-3377 or 1-800/662-1994, ⓦwww.tourismkamloops.com), is 6km west of downtown. In the summer, there's a visitor centre downtown at 103-340 Victoria St (mid-June to Aug Mon–Fri 11am–3pm).

The Greyhound **bus station** (ⓣ250/374-1212), on Notre Dame Avenue off The Trans-Canada Hwy, is a crucial interchange for buses to all parts of the province. Kamloops also has a key regional **airport**, 7km northwest of the centre. It's connected to downtown by a BC Transit bus or the airport shuttle (ⓣ250/314-4803; $14). The **train** station is 11km north of Kamloops, off Hwy 5 on CNR Yard Access Road.

Accommodation

Kamloops' huge volume of **accommodation** is aimed at the motorist and consists of thick clusters of motels, most of which blanket the town's eastern margins on Hwy 1 or out on Columbia Street West.

Executive Inn 540 Victoria St ⓣ250/372-2281 or 1-800/663-2837, ⓦwww.executiveinn.kamloops.com. Make for this central hotel if you want top-of-the-range comfort after a long journey, with an in-house casino and restaurant. ❻

Fountain Motel 506 Columbia St ⓣ250/374-4451 or 1-888/253-1569, ⓦwww.fountain.kamloops.com. This is a basic and budget option, closer to town but with pool access. ❹

Plaza Heritage Hotel 405 Victoria St ⓣ250/377-8075 or 1-877/977-5292, ⓦwww.plazaheritagehotel.com. Downtown hotel whose rooms have been restored to their original, rather floral, grandeur, to provide a real sense of history – without foregoing modern amenities such as wi-fi. ❻

Silver Sage Tent and Trailer Park 771 Athabasca St East ⓣ250/374-2488. The nearest campsite, but if you've got a car aim for the far more scenic facilities at Paul Lake Provincial Park ($15) (see below).

Thriftlodge 2459 Trans-Canada Hwy ⓣ250/374-2488 or 1-800/661-7769, ⓦwww.thriftlodge.kamloops.com. This is probably the cheapest of all, but it's about the last building on the eastbound hwy out of town; local phone calls and light continental breakfast included. ❹

The town and around

Rough-edged Kamloops is determinedly functional and not a place to spend a happy day wandering. Perhaps the most interesting thing about the city is its surroundings, dominated by the strange, bare-earthed brown hills locals like to say represent the northernmost point of the Mojave Desert. There's no doubting the almost surreal touches of near-desert, which are particularly marked in the bare rock and clay outcrops above the bilious waters of the Thompson River and in the bleached scrub and failing stands of pines that spot the barren hills. A good way to see the scenery is to take a seventy-minute ride on the **Kamloops Heritage Railway** (July & Aug Fri–Mon 7pm, Sat 11am; $17; ⓣ250/374-2141, ⓦwww.kamrail.com), a restored steam-powered heritage train that hisses and whistles its way through the countryside; it departs from 510 Lorne St, downtown.

The city itself does have the modern 2400-work **Kamloops Art Gallery** (Mon–Wed, Fri & Sat 10am–5pm, Thurs 10am–9pm, Sun noon–4pm; $5; ⓣ250/377-2400, ⓦwww.kag.bc.ca), 465 Victoria St, which showcases Canadian artists, particularly those from BC. The **Kamloops Museum** (Tues–Wed, Fri & Sat 9.30am–4.30pm, Thurs 9.30am–7.30pm; by donation), at 207 Seymour St, is one of the more interesting provincial offerings, with illuminating archive photographs, artefacts, period set-pieces and a particularly well-done section on the Shuswap. For a more complete picture of local First Nations history and traditions, call at the **Secwepemc Museum & Heritage Park** (Mon–Fri 8am–4pm; ⓣ250/828-9749, ⓦwww.secwepemc.org; $6), just over the bridge on Hwy 5. North American ginseng has become one of the region's prime crops and the opulent **Sunmore Ginseng Spa**, 925 McGill Place (ⓣ250/372-2814, ⓦwww.sunmore.com) offers pampering sessions to weary travellers. Treatments such as the ninety-minute ginseng body wrap are priced around $125. Next door to the spa is a ginseng factory with free tours and a showroom.

Most other diversions lie a short drive out of town; the visitor centre has details, with a special bias towards the dozen-plus golf courses and two hundred or so trout-stuffed lakes dotting the hinterland. The nearest and most popular lake is the 402-hectare **Paul Lake Provincial Park**, northeast of town (take Hwy 5 north for 5km and then Paul Lake Road east for 17km), with swimming and a campsite ($15). To get up close and personal with grizzly bears, wolves, moose and cougars – albeit with the animals languishing safely behind a fence – visit the

Sun Peaks

It may not receive half the attention lavished on Whistler, but BC's second-largest winter destination, **Sun Peaks Resort**, 53km northeast of Kamloops along Hwy 5 and Sun Peaks Road, has some pretty impressive statistics of its own: 3,678 acres of terrain, 122 runs, eleven lifts and 40km of cross-country trails (late Nov to mid-April; day lift-pass $71; ⓣ250/578-5399 or 1-800/807-3257, ⓦwww.sunpeaksresort.com). Come summer, Sun Peaks attracts mountain bikers to its lift-accessed bike park (day-pass $38) as well as hikers and golfers. The ever-increasing accommodation options – all bookable through the resort – range from the budget *Sun Peaks International Hostel* (ⓦwww.sunpeakshostel.com; dorms $26, private rooms ❸) to the luxurious *Delta Sun Peaks Hotel* (ⓦwww.deltahotels.com; ❼). The resort's rapid expansion has not been without controversy: some members of the Secwepemc First Nation protest over what they claim to be an "illegal land grab".

British Columbia Wildlife Park (May–June 9.30am–5pm, July–Aug 9.30am–8pm; $13; ⓣ250/573-3242, ⓦwww.bczoo.org), at 9077 Dallas Drive, a zoo and animal rehabilitation centre 15km east of Kamloops.

Eating and drinking

Kamloops has plenty of eating options, with competition fierce along Victoria Street. There are also lively **bars** here, but it's worth venturing a block beyond for Kamloops' famous cowboy drinking dens.

Brownstone 118 Victoria St ⓣ250/851-9939. Fine dining establishment in a 1904 heritage building that's entertained the likes of Harrison Ford and Jennifer Lopez. Mains $18–36. Closed Sun & Mon.

Cactus Jacks 417 Seymour St ⓣ250/374-7289, ⓦwww.cactusjackssaloon.com. Down your beer with the local cowboys and cowgirls at this bona fide western bar (a block south of Victoria St) and enjoy attractions like mechanical bull riding or line dancing. Closed Sun–Tues.

Peter's Pasta 149 Victoria St ⓣ250/372-8514. For fresh and reliable Italian meals (mains $10–18), slurp your linguine at this always-packed restaurant. Closed Sun & Mon.

Ric's Mediterranean Grill 227 Victoria St ⓣ250/372-7771. On Victoria St, Ric's plays second-fiddle to only the *Brownstone*, with fine steaks ($19–37) and good seafood options, including the delicious Caribbean lobster ($29).

Swiss Pastries & Café 359 Victoria St. Snack food is served in generous portions at this popular café, which really is run by Swiss people. It does good muesli, cappuccino, pastries and excellent sandwiches.

Highway 97

Passing through landscapes of Eden-like clarity and beauty, **Hwy 97** is the best northern entrance to (or exit from) the Okanagan. The grass-green meadows, grazing cattle and low wooded hills here are the sort of scenery pioneers must have dreamed of and most of the little hamlets en route make charming spots to stay; and if you have time and transport any number of minor roads lead off to small lakes. Hwy 97 peels off the Trans-Canada 26km east of Kamloops, its first good stop being **MONTE LAKE**, 21km on, which is served by the excellent *Heritage Campsite & RV Park* (ⓣ250/375-2434; April–Oct; $20–30). **WESTWOLD**, 5km beyond, is a dispersed ranching community of clean, old wooden houses and large pastures that present a picture of rural life. **FALKLAND**, 13km beyond, is an unassuming place with a rustic village atmosphere. Country lanes lead north and east from here to **Bolean Lake** (10km), **Pillar Lake** (13km) and to **Pinaus Lake** (10km).

The Shuswap

Some 56km east of Kamloops along Hwy 1, the sleepy lakeside town of **CHASE** marks the western extent of the Shuswap region, whose centrepiece is Shuswap Lake. Taking their names from the largest single native BC tribe, the region and lake offer 1000km of navigable waterways and 32 provincial parks, making them ideal for **fishing**, swimming, water-skiing or **houseboating**. But the big draw is the spectacle of the annual migrations of **spawning salmon** every October. Though stocks have been depleted over the last century or so, Shuswap Lake still provides an important sanctuary for hatched salmon fry before they make their long journey down the Thompson and Fraser rivers to the sea. Up to two million fish brave the run from the Pacific up to their birthplace in the Adams River. During spawning time, people also migrate here in droves, with around 250,000 visitors coming during the peak week alone. **Salmon Arm** is the largest of the somewhat bland resorts in the area.

Spawn to be wild

At times it seems impossible to escape the **salmon** in BC. Whether on restaurant menus, in rivers or in photographs of grinning fishermen clutching their catch, the fish is almost as much a symbol of the region as the mountains and forests are. Five different species inhabit the rivers and lakes of western Canada: **pink**, **coho**, **chum**, **chinook** and **sockeye**.

Though they start and finish their lives in fresh water, salmon spend about four years in the open sea. Mature fish make their epic migrations from the Pacific to **spawn** in the BC rivers of their birth between June and November, swimming about 30km a day; some chinook travel more than 1400km up the Fraser beyond Prince George, which means almost fifty days' continuous swimming upstream. Though the female lays as many as four thousand eggs, only about six percent of the offspring survive. On the Adams River near Salmon Arm, for example, it's estimated that of four billion sockeye eggs laid in a typical year, one billion survive to become fry (hatched fish about 2cm long), of which 75 percent are eaten by predators before becoming smolts (year-old fish). Only five percent of these then make it to the ocean. In effect, each pair of spawners produces about ten mature fish; of these, eight are caught by commercial fisheries and only two return to reproduce.

These returns clearly put the salmon's survival and BC's lucrative **fishing industry** on a knife edge. Salmon accounts for two-thirds of BC's $1 billion annual revenues from the fishing industry, its third-highest earner after forestry and energy products. Commercial fishing suffered its first setback in BC as long ago as 1913, when large rockslides at Hell's Gate in the Fraser Canyon disrupted many spawning runs. Although fish runs were constructed to bypass the slides, new pressures have since been heaped on the salmon, including fish farms, mining, logging, urban and agricultural development and the dumping of industrial and municipal wastes. Much of the concern surrounds farmed salmon: the incidence of disease among them is high, and the Atlantic salmon preferred by BC farms threaten to escape in numbers that will undermine wild populations through interbreeding and competition for resources.

An increasingly important line of defence, **hatcheries** have been built on rivers on the mainland and Vancouver Island to increase the percentage of eggs and fry that successfully mature. Meanwhile, overfishing remains a major concern, although various measures have been implemented by the government, including a moratorium on large-scale drift nets and the closure of the Fraser and Thompson rivers to all salmon fishing. Despite these measures, Greenpeace estimates hundreds of stocks of salmon in BC and Yukon are either extinct or at risk.

Squalix and Roderick Haig-Brown Provincial Park

The hamlet of **SQUALIX**, 11km east of Chase on Hwy 1, has a couple of interesting overnight options and is close to one of the best easily accessible provincial parks in the Shuswap, **Roderick Haig-Brown Provincial Park**. The park provides a great view of the salmon migrations from signposted viewing platforms. If you're thinking of dangling a line, pick up the *Fishing in Shuswap* leaflet from the visitor centre in Chase or Salmon Arm; don't forget to get a licence at the same time. **Birdwatching** is another local draw, as the bay in Shuswap Lake is one of the world's last nesting areas of the western grebe. The park is 5km north of Squalix on a signposted side road.

The HI-affiliated waterfront **hostel**, *Squalix General Store and Caboose Hostel* (ⓣ250/675-2977 or 1-888/675-2977; ❷), just off the Trans-Canada Hwy, offers dorm beds (members $17, nonmembers $21) in converted railway carriages, and you can put up a tent for $8; Greyhound bus drivers will usually stop here on request. Just 4km northwest of Squalix, the plush lakeside *Talking Rock Resort and Quaaout Lodge*, 1663 Little Shuswap Rd (ⓣ250/679-3090 or 1-800/663-4303, ⓦwww.talkingrock.ca; ❼) is owned and run by the Little Shuswap Indian Band; it has a sweat lodge and a restaurant serving native dishes such as 'bird in clay' ($37).

Salmon Arm

SALMON ARM, 108km east of Kamloops, was named for an era when it was possible to spear salmon straight from the lake, and fish were so plentiful that they were shovelled onto the land as fertilizer, but today the town's simply the largest and most practical hub for the Shuswap.

Greyhound **buses** arrive at 50-10th St SW (ⓣ250/832-3131), just off Hwy 1 and some 300 metres west of the **visitor centre** at 200 Trans-Canada Hwy Southwest (mid-May to Sept daily 8am–8pm; Sept to mid-May Mon–Fri 8.30am–4.30pm; ⓣ250/832-2230 or 1-877/725-6667).

Practicalities

Virtually all of Salmon Arm's **motels** are strung out along the hwy. The *Salmon River Motel and RV Park*, 910 40th St SW (ⓣ250/832-3065; motel ❸, March–Dec; RV $25, April–Oct), 1km west of downtown, is inexpensive and offers **camping** space. A far better hotel is the *Best Western Salmon Arm Inn*, 61 10th St SW (ⓣ250/832-9793 or 1-888/832-5595, ⓦwww.bestwestern.com; ❻), with its

Houseboating on Shuswap Lake

Houseboating on Shuswap Lake is a hugely popular way to idle away a week or two and the pleasant waterfront village **SICAMOUS**, 31km east of Salmon Arm along Hwy 1, has specialized in their rental. A few houseboats rent by the night, but most tend to be let weekly: the season runs May to September with prices from around $900 per week for eight people, but there are many larger (up to 22 people) and pricier options.

Agencies include: *Bluewater Houseboats* (ⓣ250/836-2255 or 1-800/663-4024, ⓦwww.bluewaterhouseboats.ca); *Sicamous Creek Marina & Admiral Houseboats* (ⓣ250/836-4611 or 1-866/704-4611, ⓦwww.admiralhouseboats.com); or the *Twin Anchors Houseboat Association* (ⓣ250/836-2450 or 1-800/663-4026, ⓦwww.twinanchors.com). The **visitor centre**, 110 Finlayson St (Mon–Fri 9am–5pm, July & Aug daily 9am–5pm; ⓣ250/836-3313, ⓦwww.sicamouschamber.bc.ca), by the government dock has full listings.

pool, hot tub and wi-fi. Campers will also find better facilities at the *Salmon Arm Camping Resort* (☎250/832-6489 or 1-800/562-9389, Ⓦwww.salmonarmkoa.com; $32–49; May–Oct), a big wooded campsite with a heated swimming pool 3km east of town.

For **food** and drink, try the *Hideaway Pub & Bistro*, on the Trans-Canada Hwy Southwest, which does cheap pub food and ribs, or if you're with kids try *PJ's Family Restaurant*, diagonally opposite the *Best Western*. *Table 24*, a block north of the Trans-Canada Hwy at 20 Hudson Ave Northeast, is the smartest and most expensive place in town (mains around $20) and often has good fish dishes.

Highway 5 and Wells Gray Provincial Park

Northbound **Highway 5** (or Yellowhead South Hwy) heads upstream along the North Thompson River, coursing through high hills and rolling pasture between Kamloops and **Clearwater** and beyond. It is one of the most scenically astounding routes in this part of the world, following the river as it carves through the Monashee Mountains from its source near **Valemount** to the final meeting with the main Yellowhead Hwy (Hwy 16) at Tête Jaune Cache, a total distance of 338km. The entire latter half of the journey is spent sidestepping the immense **Wells Gray Provincial Park**, one of the finest protected areas in BC.

Greyhound **buses** cover the route on their run between Kamloops and Prince George via Clearwater (daily in each direction), as do VIA Rail **trains**, which connect Kamloops with Jasper via Clearwater (3 weekly in each direction).

Clearwater

A dispersed logging and ranching community 125km north of Kamloops, **CLEARWATER** is invisible from Hwy 5. Unless you need a place to stay or arrive by rail there's no need to stop here, except if you're planning to spend time exploring Wells Gray Provincial Park.

Everything you need, apart from the odd shop, is on or just off the hwy, including the town's visitor centre, at 425 East Yellowhead Hwy (May daily 10am–4pm; June–early Oct daily 9am–6pm; ☎250/674-2646, Ⓦwww.clearwaterbcchamber.com).

Practicalities

For a place to **stay**, try the lovely *Half Moon Guesthouse*, 625 Greer Rd (☎250/674-4199, Ⓦwww.halfmoonhostel.com; ❸), about 4km north of town and just off Clearwater Valley Road, which organizes tours into the park. One block from the visitor centre, the big *Clearwater Valley Resort & KOA Campground*, 373 Clearwater Valley Rd (☎250/674-3909 or 1-888/837-1161, Ⓦwww.clearwatervalley.com), has a combination of rooms (❺), cabins (❹), camping and RV sites ($25–31; March to mid-Oct), with a heated pool and a restaurant. Much grander is the 64-room *Clearwater Lodge* (☎250/674-3080 or 1-888/383-2388, Ⓦwww.clearwaterlodge.bcresorts.com; ❺) also with a swimming pool, near the Hwy 5 turn-off for the park. A number of **campsites** are within walking distance of the visitor centre: the best is the *Dutch Lake Resort and RV Park* (☎250/674-3351 or 1-888/884-4424, Ⓦwww.dutchlake.com; cabins ❺, pitch $31–34; April–Oct), with a lakeside setting. There are also three simple campsites within the park (see p.672).

For **food**, the *Wells Gray Inn* at 228 East Yellowhead Hwy (☎250/674-2214, Ⓦwww.wellsgrayinn.ca; ❹) has a good on-site restaurant and grill (mains

$12–40). A local favourite is the *Flour Meadow Bakery and Café,* 444 Clearwater Valley Rd (closed Sun), just beyond the KOA campground, with good coffee, home-made bread and lunchtime soup and sandwich deals. If you plan to spend the day exploring the park, stock up on picnic supplies at the **supermarket** at 74 Young St, 1km west of the Dutch Lake Resort.

Wells Gray Provincial Park

WELLS GRAY PROVINCIAL PARK is the equal of any of the Rocky Mountain national parks to the east: if anything, its wilderness is probably more extreme – so untamed, in fact, that many of its peaks remain unclimbed and unnamed. **Wildlife** sightings are common – you may encounter black and grizzly bears, mountain goats, cougars, timber wolves, coyotes, weasels, martens, mink, wolverines and beavers. We recommend consulting the park visitor centre in Clearwater or ⓦwww.env.gov.bc.ca/bcparks for information on bear, cougar and wolf safety; attacks are not common but have been known to occur. The excellent Wells Gray Provincial Park **visitor centre** is at the intersection of Hwy 5 and Clearwater Valley Road in Clearwater.

Accessing the park

Seeing the park is straightforward if you have transport and only want a superficial – but still rewarding – glimpse of the interior. A 63-kilometre **access road** strikes into the park from Hwy 5 at Clearwater and ends at Clearwater Lake, allowing you to see all the obvious scenic landmarks in a day. To get into Wells Gray without your own transport, you'd have to hitch from Clearwater up the 63-kilometre main access road – feasible at the height of summer, but highly unlikely at any other time.

There are some less-travelled gravel roads into other sectors of the park from **Blue River**, 112km north of Clearwater on Hwy 5, and from the village of **100 Mile House**, on Hwy 97 west of the park.

Activities in Wells Gray Provincial Park

With some 250km of maintained trails and dozens of other lesser routes, the 1.3 million acre park is magnificent for **hiking**. We've outlined short walks and day-hikes from the park's access road (see p.741), but serious backpackers can easily spend a week or more on backcountry hikes, most of which are in the southern third of the park and link together for days of hiking and wilderness camping. Pick up a free *BC Parks* map-pamphlet at the Clearwater visitor centre; if you're thinking of doing any backcountry exploration you'll want to invest in their more detailed maps and guides. Steep switchbacks, muddy conditions, thick brush and large deadfall as well as tramping across sharp lava flow and loose rock make the going slow on many of the more remote trails. The longest one-way trail connects Clearwater Lake to Kostal Lake trail (26km) and begins on the main Wells Gray Park Road, just across from Clearwater Lake campground.

Another of the park's big attractions is **canoeing** on Clearwater and Azure lakes. The former is at the end of the access road and can be linked with a short portage to make a fifty-plus-kilometre dream trip for paddlers; rent canoes ($50/day, $200/week) from Clearwater Lake Tours (ⓣ250/674-2121, ⓦwww.clearwaterlaketours.com; mid-May to Oct) on the south end of Clearwater Lake. For excellent guided interpretive hikes in the park, contact Go-Outdoors (ⓣ250/674-0204, ⓦwww.go-outdoors.ca). Several local operators run **tours** featuring **whitewater rafting**, riding, fishing, boating and floatplane excursions around the park; the Clearwater visitor centre will have details.

Park accommodation

If you're not using Clearwater as a base, there are options in or much closer to the park. These include the log cabins at *Wells Gray Ranch* (ⓣ250/674-2792, ⓦwww.wellsgrayranch.com; ❻; early May–early Oct), just within the park entrance, 27km from Hwy 5 on Clearwater Valley Road, which offers organized riding and canoeing trips. The slightly larger but equally lonely *Helmcken Falls Lodge* (ⓣ250/674-3657, ⓦwww.helmckenfalls.com; ❼; late Dec–March & May to mid-Oct) is in the park itself, 35km from Hwy 5, and has similar facilities and activities at slightly higher prices.

The best **camping** in Wells Gray is at the park's three provincial campsites (all $15; May–Oct) along the park access road. Many other backcountry campgrounds ($5) dot the shores of the park's major lakes; Clearwater Lake Tours operates a water-taxi service which drops you off at any site on Clearwater Lake, picking you up at a prearranged time.

Sights and hikes along the access road

Even if you're not geared up for the backcountry, the **access road** to the park from Clearwater opens up a medley of waterfalls, walks and viewpoints that make a detour extremely worthwhile. The road is paved for the first 42km into the park boundary, but the remaining 36km to Clearwater Lake is gravel. Most sights are well signed.

About 10km north of Clearwater, a short walk from a well-signed car park brings you to the 61-metre **Spahats Falls**, the first of several mighty cascades along this route. You can watch the waters crashing down through layers of pinky-red volcanic rock from a pair of observation platforms, which also provide an impressive and unexpected view of the Clearwater Valley. A few hundred metres further up the road, a 15km gravel lane peels off into the **Wells Gray Recreation Area**; a single trail from the end of the road strikes off into alpine meadows. About 15km further up the main access road, a second 4WD track branches east to reach the trailhead for **Battle Mountain** (19km), with the option of several shorter hikes like the Mount Philip Trail (5km) en route.

Green Mountain Lookout, reached by a rough, winding road on the left just after the park entrance, offers one of the most enormous roadside panoramas in BC: as far as you can see, there's nothing but an almighty emptiness of primal forest and mountains.

The next essential stop is **Dawson Falls**, a broad, powerful cascade (91m wide and 18m high) just five-minutes' walk from the main access road, signed "Viewpoint". Beyond, the road crosses an ugly iron bridge and shortly after meets the start of the **Murtle River Trail** (14km one-way), a particularly good walk that takes in the more spectacular Majerus and Horseshoe waterfalls .

Back on the main access road, the next turn-off, almost immediately beyond Dawson Falls, leads to **Helmcken Falls**, the park's undisputed highlight. The site is heavily visited, and it's not unknown for wedding parties to come up here to get dramatic matrimonial photos backed by the luminous arc of water plunging into a black, carved bowl fringed with vivid carpets of lichen and splintered trees, the whole ensemble framed by huge plumes of spray wafting up on all sides. At 137m, these are two and a half times the height of Niagara Falls.

Continuing north, the park access road rejoins the jade-green Clearwater River, passing picnic spots and short trails that wend down to the bank for close-up views of one of the province's best whitewater-rafting stretches. Next up is **Ray Farm**, home to John Bunyon Ray, who in 1912 was the first homesteader in this area; it now consists of picturesquely ruined, wooden shacks scattered in a lush clearing. The last attraction before the end of the road is **Bailey's Creek** where, in August and September, the robust chinook salmon attempt to jump the rapids before giving up and spawning a kilometre downstream. The park road ends at **Clearwater Lake**, where there are some boat launches, a provincial campsite ($15; May–Oct) and a series of short trails.

Blue River and Valemount

Clearwater is the best base for forays into Wells Gray, but you may find the **accommodation** options at Blue River and Valemount useful, though the latter is a whopping 225km north of Clearwater on Hwy 5.

BLUE RIVER, 100km north of Clearwater, has far fewer possibilities. Its cheapest option is the *Blue River Motel*, 791 Spruce St (Ⓣ250/673-8387, Ⓦwww.wiegele.com; ❸), with one- and two-bedroom units two blocks off the hwy. For **camping**, try the *Blue River Campground and RV Park*, at Myrtle Lake Road and Cedar Street (Ⓣ250/673-8203, Ⓦwww.bluerivercampground.ca; $16–32; May–Oct), which also has teepees (❶) and cabins (❷), plus offers canoe rentals and a variety of fishing, canoeing and riding tours.

VALEMOUNT has around thirty motels and a dozen-plus campsites. One block off the hwy at 1475 5th Avenue is the *Yellowhead Motel* (Ⓣ250/566-4411, Ⓦwww.yellowheadmotel.com; ❹), while just down the road at no.1465 is the *Super 8 Valemount* (Ⓣ250/566-9171, Ⓦwww.canoemountainlodge.com; ❹). About 1km north of town is the modern and RV-oriented *Irvin's Park and Campground*, at 360 Loseth Rd (Ⓣ250/566-4781 Ⓦwww.irvins.ca; $21–35; April–Oct).

From the Yellowhead Hwy junction north of Valemount, it's 270km to Prince George (see p.869) and 77km east to the BC-Alberta border.

Travel details

Trains

Kamloops to: Vancouver (3 weekly; 10hr).

Buses

Cranbrook to: Kamloops (1 daily; 10hr); Kelowna (2 daily; 9hr 40min); Kimberley (1 daily; 30min); Nelson (1 daily; 4hr 5min); Vancouver (2 daily; 16hr).
Kamloops to: Kelowna (1 daily; 2hr 25min); Vancouver (3 daily; 5hr); Vernon (1 daily; 1hr 40min).
Kelowna to: Castlegar (1 daily; 5hr); Nelson (1 daily; 5hr 50min); Penticton (2 daily; 1hr 15min); Vancouver (5 daily; 6hr).
Nelson to: Fernie (1 daily; 5hr 30min); Kamloops (1 daily; 12hr); Vancouver (2 daily; 12hr).

Flights

Castlegar to: Vancouver (3 daily; 1hr 10min).
Cranbrook to: Vancouver (5 daily; 1hr 30min).
Kamloops to: Prince George (1 daily; 1hr 5min); Vancouver (8 daily; 1hr).
Kelowna to: Prince George (1 daily; 1hr 10min); Vancouver (10 daily; 1hr); Victoria (1 daily; 1hr 20min).
Penticton to: Vancouver (3 daily; 1 hr).

10

Vancouver and Vancouver Island

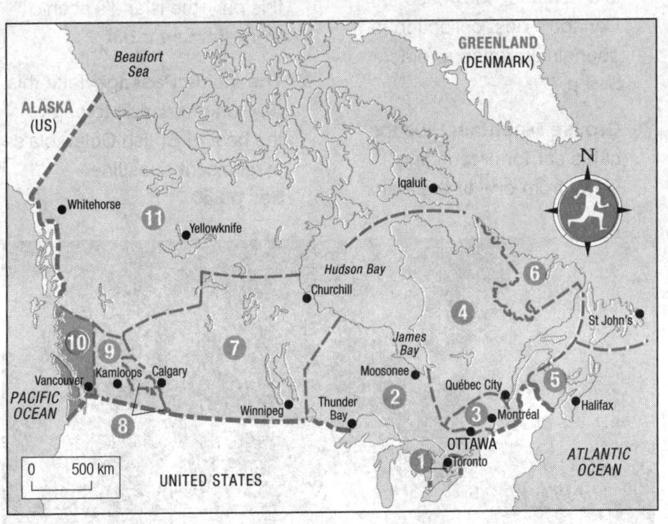

CHAPTER 10 Highlights

* **Stanley Park** North America's largest urban park is an oasis of ancient forest, beaches, gardens and peaceful trails. See p.765
* **Granville Island** A superb market and specialist stores are the main attractions of this hugely popular enclave. See p.767
* **Museum of Anthropology** Vancouver's finest museum is a beautiful showcase for Canada's best collection of aboriginal art and artefacts. See p.770
* **Grouse Mountain** Ride the cable car for astounding views from one of the major peaks on Vancouver's North Shore. See p.772
* **Whistler** Come here for superlative outdoor activities in the summer or winter. See pp.791–800
* **Victoria** British Columbia's Anglophile capital is one of Canada's most charming cities. See pp.806–819
* **Pacific Rim National Park** Beautiful Long Beach makes this park the island's scenic highlight. See p.835
* **The Inside Passage** Take this day-long ferry ride to enjoy the best of British Columbia's magnificent coastline. See p.860

▲ Biking the Stanley Park Seawall, Vancouver

10

Vancouver and Vancouver Island

Vancouver and Vancouver Island stand apart from the rest of British Columbia, the big-city outlook and bustling, cosmopolitan streets of Vancouver, Canada's third-largest metropolis, and Victoria, the provincial capital, dramatically at odds with the interior's small towns, remote villages and vast tracts of wilderness. And while Vancouver Island has scenery that occasionally matches that of the interior, its landscapes are generally more modest, the island's intimate and self-contained nature and relatively small extent creating a region that feels very different to the rest of mainland BC.

Vancouver is one of the world's great scenic cities, its watery and mountain-ringed setting equalling those of Sydney and Rio de Janeiro. Long after the many fine galleries and museums, and the even better restaurants, have faded, the memory of the Coast Mountains rearing above Burrard Inlet, or the beaches and semi-wilderness of Stanley Park, will probably linger. Vancouver is also a sophisticated and hedonistic city, having more in common with the West Coast ethos and outlook of San Francisco than, say, Toronto or Ottawa to the east.

With all its natural advantages, not to mention one of the world's finest ports, it is no wonder most of Vancouver is booming, the Downtown core growing rapidly in a wave of gleaming new condominiums; the city's eastern fringes, however, remain grittier and, in places, downright impoverished. The boom, and Vancouver's enhanced international profile, received an additional boost after the city was awarded the 2010 Winter Olympics, the honour in no small part due to the proximity of **Whistler**, 125km north of Vancouver, a modern centre for skiing, snowboarding and other winter sports, and for hiking, in-line skating, golf and, above all, mountain biking, in the summer (the resort now has as many summer as winter visitors). Beyond Whistler stretch the endless forests and ranch country of the Fraser Valley and **Cariboo** region, not without interest, but not one of BC's most compelling destinations.

The so-called Sea to Sky Highway (Hwy 99) to Whistler is the tempting of two obvious road excursions from Vancouver. The other is the 150-kilometre **Sunshine Coast** (Hwy 101), distinguished by occasional stretches of fine coastal scenery, but experienced by most travellers only as far as Horseshoe Bay, one of several points of embarkation for ferries to Vancouver Island.

Most visitors to the island start in Victoria, easily reached by ferry or seaplane from Vancouver or nearby ferry terminals. Few break their journey en route

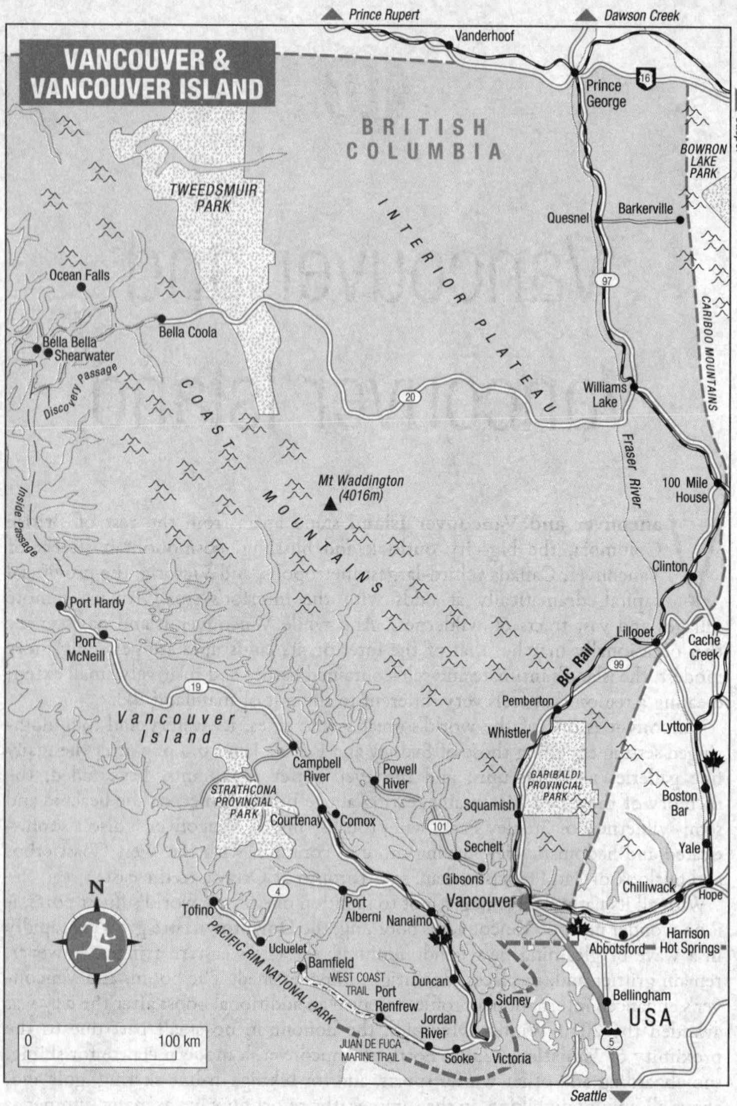

between the cities, missing out on the **Gulf Islands**, an archipelago scattered across the Strait of Georgia between the mainland and Vancouver Island. If you have time, the islands' laid-back vibe, numerous small galleries, glorious seascapes and often bohemian population make them great places in which to catch your breath for a few days.

You can also reach the islands from **Victoria**, a city that pre-dates Vancouver and which was the focus of the earliest white settlement in the region, only surrendering its primacy after the mainland gold rushes of the mid-19th century and the eventual arrival of the transcontinental railway in Vancouver in 1887. Today, the city is considerably smaller than Vancouver, a comfortable and easygoing place of

Reserving provincial campsites

Tent and RV sites at many public **campsites** in British Columbia's provincial parks can be reserved through Discover Camping (April to mid-Sept Mon–Fri 7am–7pm, Sat & Sun 9am–5pm Pacific time; ⓣ604/689-9025 or 1-800/689-9025). Reservations can be made up to three months in advance but no later than 48 hours before the first day of arrival. A nonrefundable booking fee of $6.30/night, up to a maximum of three nights ($18.90), is charged. Reservations can also be made at ⓦwww.discovercamping.ca. General information on the parks is on ⓣ250/387-4550 or 1-800/663-7867, ⓦwww.env.gov.bc.ca/bcparks.

solid, small-town values, a pretty waterfront, numerous gardens, excellent restaurants, one superb museum and a decidedly English ambience that it rather overplays to lure its (mostly US) visitors.

Away from Victoria, Vancouver Island moves quickly from the gentle, pastoral country of the south to the jagged peaks of **Strathcona Provincial Park** and the ravishing landscapes of the **Pacific Rim National Park**, one of the region's undoubted highlights. Of the visitors that venture farther north, most are either fishermen or whale-watchers bound for **Campbell River** or **Telegraph Cove**, respectively, or those intending to catch a ferry from Port Hardy along the **Inside Passage** or **Discovery Passage** to Prince Rupert or Bella Coola, two of western Canada's most stunning journeys.

Vancouver

Cradled between the ocean and snowcapped mountains, **VANCOUVER** has a dazzling Downtown district that fills a narrow peninsula bounded by Burrard Inlet to the north, English Bay to the west and False Creek to the south. Greater Vancouver sprawls south to the Fraser River. Edged around its idyllic waterfront are fine beaches, a dynamic port and a magnificent swath of parkland, not to mention the mirror-fronted ranks of skyscrapers that look across Burrard Inlet and its bustling harbour to the residential districts of North and West Vancouver. Beyond these comfortable suburbs, the Coast Mountains rise in steep, forested slopes to form a dramatic counterpoint to the Downtown skyline and the most stunning of the city's many outdoor playgrounds. Small wonder, given Vancouver's surroundings, that Greenpeace was founded here.

Vancouver's two million or so residents exploit their spectacular natural setting to the hilt, and when they tire of the immediate region can travel a short distance to the vast wilderness of the BC interior. Whether it's sailing, swimming, fishing, hiking, skiing, golf or tennis, locals barely have to move to indulge in a plethora of **recreational whims**. Summer and winter the city oozes hedonism and healthy living – it comes as no surprise to find that you can lounge on beaches Downtown – typically West Coast obsessions that spill over into its sophisticated **arts and culture**. Vancouver claims a world-class museum and symphony orchestra, as well as opera, theatre and dance companies at the cutting edge of contemporary arts. Festivals proliferate throughout its mild, if occasionally rain-soaked, summer

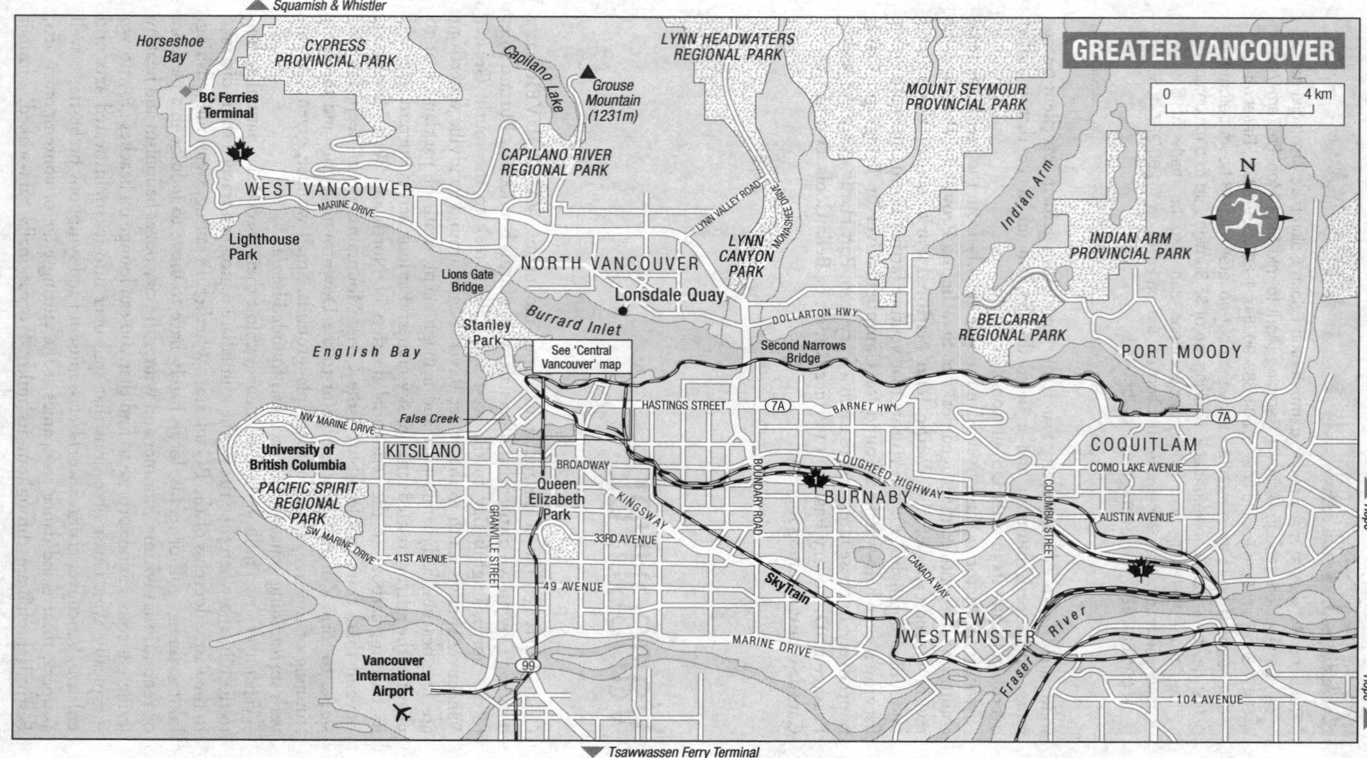
GREATER VANCOUVER
0
4 km
N
Squamish & Whistler
Horseshoe Bay
BC Ferries Terminal
CYPRESS PROVINCIAL PARK
Capilano Lake
Grouse Mountain (1231m)
LYNN HEADWATERS REGIONAL PARK
MOUNT SEYMOUR PROVINCIAL PARK
CAPILANO RIVER REGIONAL PARK
WEST VANCOUVER
MARINE DRIVE
Lighthouse Park
LYNN VALLEY ROAD
MONASHEE DRIVE
LYNN CANYON PARK
Indian Arm
INDIAN ARM PROVINCIAL PARK
NORTH VANCOUVER
Lions Gate Bridge
Lonsdale Quay
Burrard Inlet
DOLLARTON HWY
BELCARRA REGIONAL PARK
Stanley Park
English Bay
See 'Central Vancouver' map
Second Narrows Bridge
PORT MOODY
HASTINGS STREET
7A
BARNET HWY
NW MARINE DRIVE
False Creek
KITSILANO
COQUITLAM
University of British Columbia
BROADWAY
LOUGHEED HIGHWAY
COMO LAKE AVENUE
BOUNDARY ROAD
PACIFIC SPIRIT REGIONAL PARK
Queen Elizabeth Park
KINGSWAY
BURNABY
COLUMBIA STREET
Hope
AUSTIN AVENUE
SW MARINE DRIVE
33RD AVENUE
41ST AVENUE
GRANVILLE STREET
CANADA WAY
49 AVENUE
SkyTrain
NEW WESTMINSTER
Fraser River
MARINE DRIVE
99
Vancouver International Airport
104 AVENUE
Tsawwassen Ferry Terminal

while numerous music venues provide a hotbed for up-and-coming rock bands and a burgeoning jazz scene.

Much of the city's prosperity stems from a **port** so laden with the raw materials of the Canadian interior – lumber, wheat and minerals – that it ranks as one of North America's largest. It began by exporting timber in 1864 in the shape of fence pickets to Australia and today it handles around 82.7 million tonnes of cargo annually, turns over $40 billion in trade and processes some three thousand ships a year from almost a hundred countries. The port owes its prominence to Vancouver's much-trumpeted position as a gateway to East Asia, and its increasingly pivotal role in the **Pacific Rim** market.

Vancouver is a new, multicultural city, and much of the city's earlier immigration focused on its extraordinary **Chinatown**, just one of a number of ethnic enclaves – Italian, Greek, Indian and Japanese in particular – which lend the city a refreshingly gritty quality that belies its sleek, modern reputation. So too do some of the city's semi-derelict eastern districts, whose worldly lowlife characters, addicts and hustlers are shockingly at odds with the glitz of more lush residential neighbourhoods. Low rents and Vancouver's cosmopolitan young have also nurtured an unexpected **counterculture**, distinguished by varied restaurants, secondhand shops, avant-garde galleries, clubs and bars – spots where you'll probably have more fun than in many a Canadian city. And at the top of the scale there are **restaurants** as good – and as varied – as any in North America.

Vancouver's growth and energy is almost palpable as you walk its streets. The Downtown population, currently around 600,000, is the fastest growing on the continent and in response the Downtown area is spreading to the older and previously run-down districts southeast of the old city core. Development over the last decade is symbolized by a superb library and performing-arts complex that constitutes the most expensive capital project ever undertaken in the city. The city is also North America's largest **film and TV** production centre after Los Angeles and New York. Yet, in the peculiar way that seems second nature to Canadians, the changes are being handled in a manner that's enhancing rather than compromising the city's beguiling combination of pleasure, culture, business and natural beauty.

A brief history of Vancouver

Vancouver in the modern sense has existed for a little under 120 years. Over the course of the previous nine millennia the Fraser Valley was home to the Tsawwassen, Musqueam and another twenty or so aboriginal tribes, who made up the **Stó:lo Nation**, or "people of the river". The fish, particularly salmon, of this river were the Stó:lo lifeblood. Over the millennia these people ventured relatively little into the mountainous interior, something that remains true to this day. The Stó:lo inhabited about ten villages on the shores of Vancouver's Burrard Inlet before Europeans arrived. A highly developed culture, they were skilled carpenters, canoe-makers and artists, though little in the present city – outside its museums – pays anything but lip service to their existence. Vancouver Island is the nearest best bet if you're in search of latter-day tokens of aboriginal culture.

Europeans appeared in notable numbers during the **eighteenth century**, when Spanish explorers charted the waters along what is now southwestern British Columbia. In 1778 **Captain James Cook** reached nearby Nootka Sound while searching for the Northwest Passage, sparking off immediate British interest in the area. In 1791 José Maria Narvaez, a Spanish pilot and surveyor, glimpsed the mouth of what would eventually be christened the Fraser River from his ship, the *Santa Saturnia*. This led to wrangles between the British and Spanish, disputes quickly settled in Britain's favour when Spain became domestically embroiled in the aftermath of the French Revolution. **Captain George Vancouver** officially claimed the land for Britain in 1792, but studying the river from a small boat decided that it seemed too shallow to be of practical use. Instead he rounded a headland to the north, sailing into a deep natural port – the future site of Vancouver – which he named "Burrard" after one of his companions. He then traded briefly with several Squamish tribespeople at X'ay'xi, a village on the inlet's forested headland (the future Stanley Park). Afterwards the Squamish named the spot Whul-whul-Lay-ton, or "place of the white man". Vancouver sailed on, having spent just a day in the region – scant homage to an area that was to be named after him a century later.

Vancouver's error over the river was uncovered in 1808, when Scottish-born **Simon Fraser** made an epic 1368-kilometre journey down it from the Rockies to the sea. In 1827 the Hudson's Bay Company set up a fur-trading post at **Fort Langley**, 48km east of the present city, bartering with the Stó:lo for furs and salmon, the latter being salted and then packed off to company forts across Canada. Fort Langley was kept free of homesteaders, despite being the area's first major white settlement, their presence deemed detrimental to the fur trade. Major colonization of the area only came after the Fraser River and Cariboo gold rushes in 1858, when **New Westminster** bustled with the arrival of as many as 25,000 hopefuls, many of whom were refugees from the 1849 Californian rush. Many also drifted in from the US, underlining the fragility of the national border and the precarious nature of British claims to the region. These claims were consolidated when BC was declared a crown colony with New Westminster as its capital. Both were superseded by Fort Victoria in 1868, by which time the gold rush had dwindled almost to nothing.

In 1862 three British prospectors, unable to find gold in the interior, bought a strip of land on the southern shore of Burrard Inlet and – shortsightedly, given the amount of lumber around – started a brickworks. This soon gave way to the Hastings Sawmill and a shantytown of bars that by 1867 had taken the name of **Gastown**, after "Gassy" – as in loquacious – Jack Leighton, proprietor of the site's first saloon. Two years later Gastown became incorporated as the town of **Granville** and prospered on the back of its timber and small coal deposits. The birth of the present city dates to 1884, when the **Canadian Pacific Railway** decided to make it the terminus of its transcontinental railway. In 1886, on a whim of the CPR president, Granville was renamed Vancouver, only to be destroyed on June 13 that year when fire razed all but half a dozen buildings. The setback proved short-lived, and since the arrival of the first train from Montréal in 1887 the city has never looked back.

Arrival and information

Vancouver International Airport (Ⓣ604/207-7077, Ⓦwww.yvr.ca) is situated on Sea Island, 13km south of the city centre. International flights arrive at the majestic main terminal; domestic flights at the smaller and linked old Main Terminal. There's a **tourist information** desk (daily 7am–midnight; Ⓣ604/688-5515) as you exit customs and immigration. Close by are desks for direct bus services from the airport to Victoria (Pacific Coach Lines) and Whistler. There are also services for Bellingham Airport and Sea-Tac Airport (Seattle) in the US. Domestic passengers also have a tourist information desk (daily 7am–midnight) just before the terminal exit.

The best way to get into Vancouver from the airport is on **SkyTrain** (see p.756), the light rail system, on the Canada Line. Trains run from about 5.10am to

12.57am, taking 26 minutes to make the journey to Waterfront station close to Canada Place and the heart of Downtown. Fares are $5 ($2.50 after 6.30pm weekedays and all day Sat and Sun and public holidays).

You can also take the private **Airporter bus** (6.45am–1.10am; $14 single, $12 return; ⓣ604/946-8866 or 1-800/668-3141, ⓦwww.yvrairporter.com), which leaves every fifteen minutes from a bay to the left immediately outside the main door of the international arrivals; from domestic arrivals you can walk here if you need Airporter information or wait at the domestic arrivals pick-up outside the terminal; buy **tickets** from the driver or at the bus stop by international arrivals. Resourceful staff and a pamphlet with a useful map help you figure out which drop-offs on the shuttle's three routes are most useful. Returning to the airport, buses run round the same pick-up points, including the bus depot. **Taxis** to town cost about $25–30.

Pacific Coach Lines (ⓣ604/662-7575 or 1-800/661-1725, ⓦwww.pacificcoach.com) runs direct buses from the airport to **Victoria** (7 daily; $48) and **Whistler** (7 daily; $51.45). Other **bus services from the airport** are run by Perimeter (ⓣ604/717-6600 or 1-888/717-6600, ⓦwww.perimeterbus.com) for services to **Whistler**; Quick Shuttle (ⓣ604/940-4428 or 1-800/665-2122, ⓦwww.quickcoach.com) to **Bellingham** Airport, Downtown **Seattle** and Sea-Tac Airport; and Malaspina Coach Lines (ⓣ604/885-2217 or 1-877/227-8287, ⓦwww.malaspinacoach.com) to the **Sunshine Coast**, Powell River, Whistler, Pemberton and **Nanaimo** on Vancouver Island.

By bus

Vancouver's main **bus terminal** is used by Pacific Coach Lines to and from Victoria and Vancouver Island, Malaspina Coach Lines to and from the Sunshine Coast (see "Arrival" for contact details for both lines), and all Greyhound services (ⓣ604/482-8747 or 1-800/661-8747, ⓦwww.greyhound.ca; to and from BC, Alberta, Yukon and long-haul destinations including Seattle and the US). It is in a slightly dismal area alongside the VIA Rail Pacific Central train station at 1150 Station St; ticket offices for all companies are inside on the right as you enter.

It's too far to walk to Downtown from the bus terminal, so bear left from the station through a small park to the Science World–Main Street SkyTrain station, from where it's a couple of stops to Downtown (take the train marked "Waterfront"); tickets ($2.50) are available from platform machines. Alternatively, you could take a taxi Downtown from the station for about $7–9.

By train

Skeletal **VIA Rail** services operate out of Pacific Central Station (ⓣ1-888/842-7245, ⓦwww.viarail.ca); they run to and from Jasper (3 weekly; see p.659), where there are connections (also 3 weekly) for Prince George and Prince Rupert, and on to Edmonton and the east. There is one service run by **VIA–Amtrak** (ⓣ 1-800/872-7245, ⓦwww.amtrak.com) between Vancouver and Seattle.

Information

The Vancouver **visitor centre** is almost opposite Canada Place (see p.761) at the foot of Burrard Street in the Waterfront Centre, 200 Burrard St at the corner of

For information on moving on from Vancouver, see p.786.

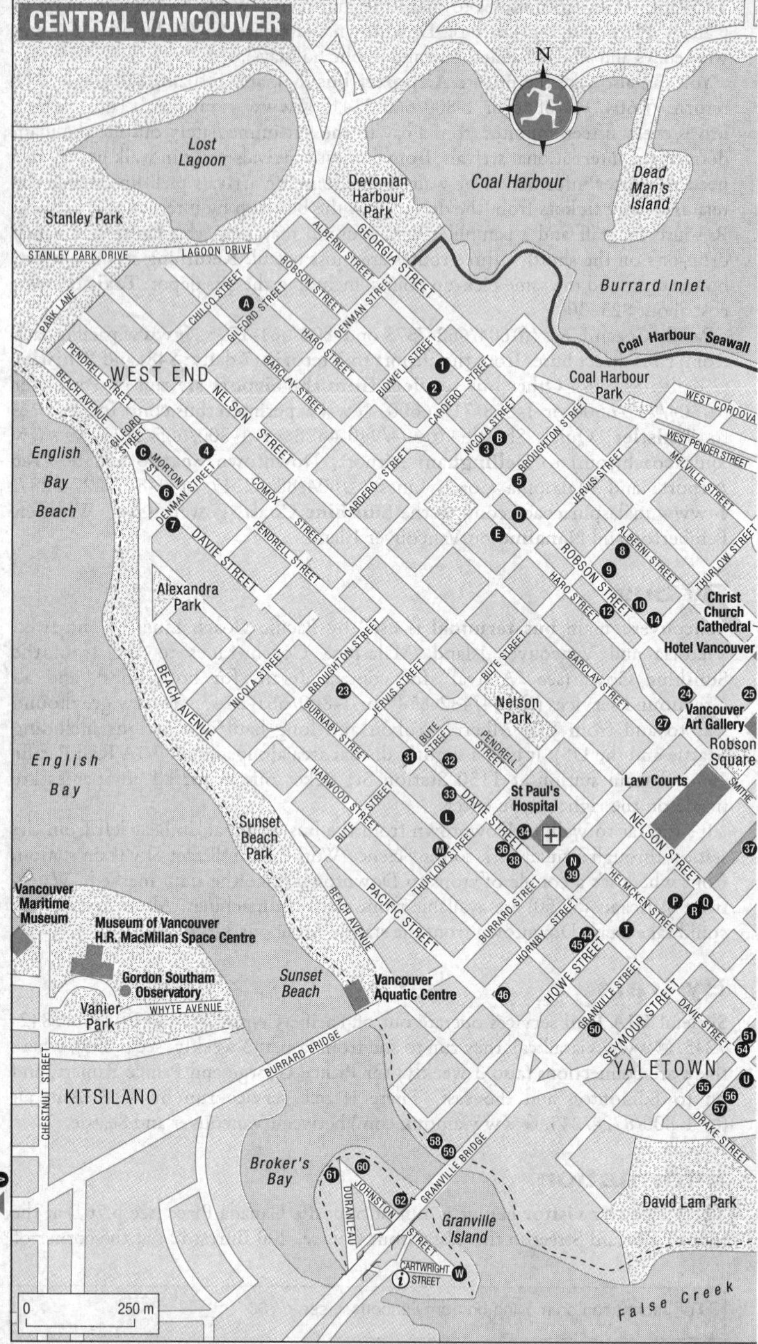
CENTRAL VANCOUVER
Lions Gate Bridge & North Vancouver
N
Lost Lagoon
Stanley Park
Devonian Harbour Park
Coal Harbour
Dead Man's Island
Burrard Inlet
Coal Harbour Seawall
Coal Harbour Park
WEST END
English Bay Beach
English Bay
Alexandra Park
Nelson Park
St Paul's Hospital
Law Courts
Robson Square
Vancouver Art Gallery
Christ Church Cathedral
Hotel Vancouver
Sunset Beach Park
Sunset Beach
Vancouver Aquatic Centre
Vancouver Maritime Museum
Museum of Vancouver
H.R. MacMilian Space Centre
Gordon Southam Observatory
Vanier Park
KITSILANO
YALETOWN
David Lam Park
Broker's Bay
Granville Island
False Creek
STANLEY PARK DRIVE
LAGOON DRIVE
PARK LANE
CHILCO STREET
GILFORD STREET
ALBERNI STREET
GEORGIA STREET
ROBSON STREET
DENMAN STREET
HARO STREET
BIDWELL STREET
BARCLAY STREET
NELSON STREET
CARDERO STREET
NICOLA STREET
BROUGHTON STREET
JERVIS STREET
WEST CORDOVA
WEST PENDER STREET
MELVILLE STREET
THURLOW STREET
PENDRELL STREET
BEACH AVENUE
MORTON ST
COMOX STREET
DAVIE STREET
BUTE STREET
BURNABY STREET
HARWOOD STREET
PACIFIC STREET
BURRARD STREET
HORNBY STREET
HOWE STREET
HELMCKEN STREET
GRANVILLE STREET
SEYMOUR STREET
DRAKE STREET
SMITHE
WHYTE AVENUE
CHESTNUT STREET
BURRARD BRIDGE
GRANVILLE BRIDGE
DURANLEAU
JOHNSTON STREET
CARTWRIGHT STREET
0
250 m

North Vancouver & Lonsdale Quay

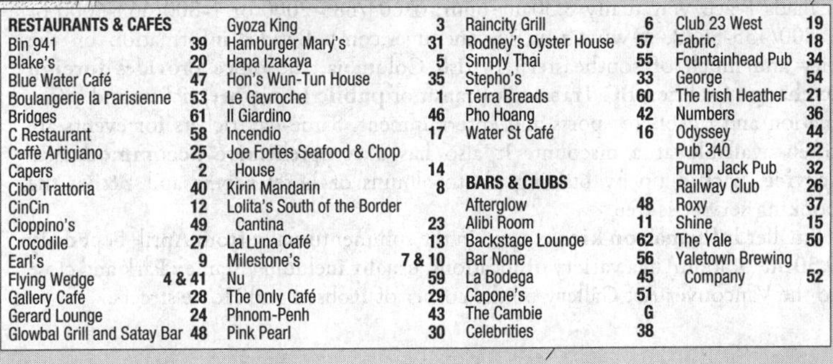

RESTAURANTS & CAFÉS

Bin 941	39
Blake's	20
Blue Water Café	47
Boulangerie la Parisienne	53
Bridges	61
C Restaurant	58
Caffè Artigiano	25
Capers	2
Cibo Trattoria	40
CinCin	12
Cioppino's	49
Crocodile	27
Earl's	9
Flying Wedge	4 & 41
Gallery Café	28
Gerard Lounge	24
Glowbal Grill and Satay Bar	48
Gyoza King	3
Hamburger Mary's	31
Hapa Izakaya	5
Hon's Wun-Tun House	35
Le Gavroche	1
Il Giardino	46
Incendio	17
Joe Fortes Seafood & Chop House	14
Kirin Mandarin	8
Lolita's South of the Border Cantina	23
La Luna Café	13
Milestone's	7 & 10
Nu	59
The Only Café	29
Phnom-Penh	43
Pink Pearl	30
Raincity Grill	6
Rodney's Oyster House	57
Simply Thai	55
Stepho's	33
Terra Breads	60
Pho Hoang	42
Water St Café	16

BARS & CLUBS

Afterglow	48
Alibi Room	11
Backstage Lounge	62
Bar None	56
La Bodega	45
Capone's	51
The Cambie	G
Celebrities	38
Club 23 West	19
Fabric	18
Fountainhead Pub	34
George	54
The Irish Heather	21
Numbers	36
Odyssey	44
Pub 340	22
Pump Jack Pub	32
Railway Club	26
Roxy	37
Shine	15
The Yale	50
Yaletown Brewing Company	52

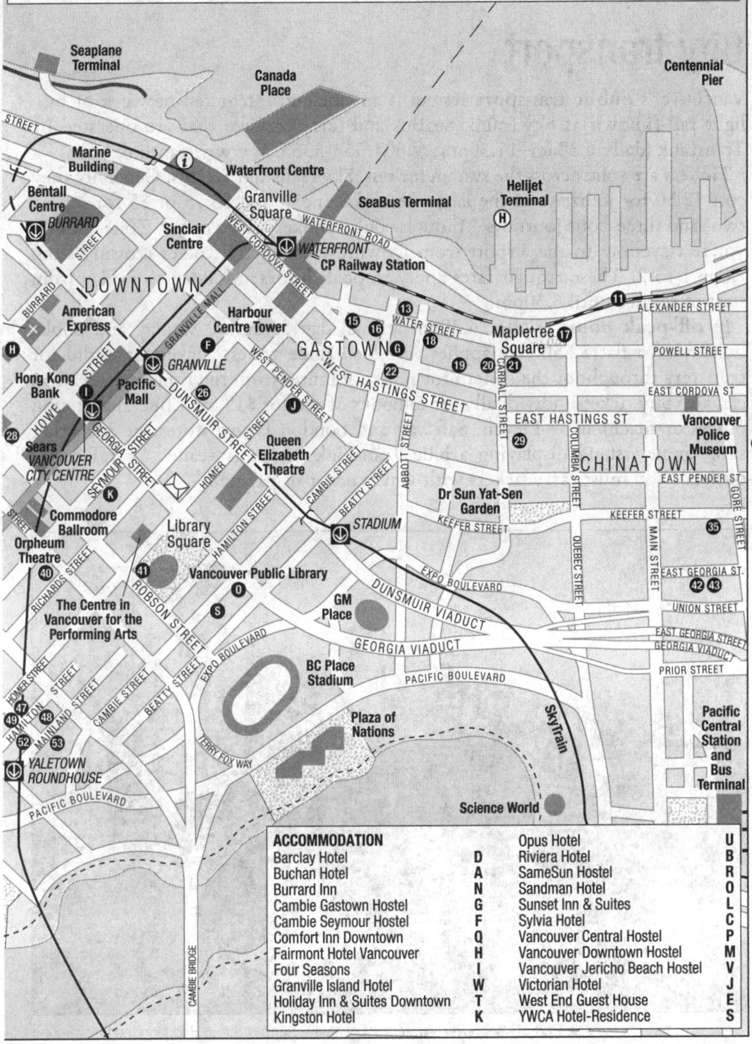

ACCOMMODATION

Barclay Hotel	D
Buchan Hotel	A
Burrard Inn	N
Cambie Gastown Hostel	G
Cambie Seymour Hostel	F
Comfort Inn Downtown	Q
Fairmont Hotel Vancouver	H
Four Seasons	I
Granville Island Hotel	W
Holiday Inn & Suites Downtown	T
Kingston Hotel	K
Opus Hotel	U
Riviera Hotel	B
SameSun Hostel	R
Sandman Hotel	O
Sunset Inn & Suites	L
Sylvia Hotel	C
Vancouver Central Hostel	P
Vancouver Downtown Hostel	M
Vancouver Jericho Beach Hostel	V
Victorian Hotel	J
West End Guest House	E
YWCA Hotel-Residence	S

Canada Place Way (daily 8.30am–6pm; ⓣ604/683-2000 or 1-800/663-6000 or 1-800/435-5622, ⓦwww.tourismvancouver.com). Besides information on the city and much of southeastern British Columbia, the office provides **foreign exchange** facilities, BC TransLink (transit or **public transport**) tickets and information and tickets to sports and entertainment. Same-day tickets for events are often available at a discount. It also has a comprehensive **accommodation service**, backed up by bulging photo albums of hotel rooms and B&Bs; the booking service is free.

Smaller **information kiosks** open in the summer (usually from April–Sept daily 9.30am–5.30pm) in a variety of locations, usually including Stanley Park and close to the Vancouver Art Gallery on the corner of Robson and Howe streets.

City transport

Vancouver's **public transport** system is an efficient, integrated network of bus, light rail (known as SkyTrain), SeaBus and ferry services that are operated by TransLink (daily 6.30am–11.30pm; ⓣ604/953-3333, ⓦwww.translink.bc.ca).

Tickets are valid across the system for bus, SkyTrain and SeaBus. Generally they cost $2.50 for journeys in the large, central Zone 1, and $3.75 or $5 for longer two- and three-zone journeys – though you're unlikely to go out of Zone 1 unless you're travelling to the airport from Downtown, which involves crossing from Zone 1 to 2. These regular fares apply in **peak hours**: Monday to Friday from start of service until 6.30pm.

In **off-peak hours** – after 6.30pm and all day Saturday, Sunday and public holidays – a flat $2.50 fare applies across all three zones. Tickets are valid for **transfers** throughout the system for ninety minutes from the time of issue. You can also buy tickets individually (or in books of ten for $19 for Zone 1) at station offices or machines, 7-Eleven, Safeway and London Drugs stores, or any other shop or newsstand displaying a blue TransLink sticker (so-called "FareDealer" outlets). You must carry tickets with you as proof of payment.

▲ Part of Vancouver's waterfront, with the Burrard Street Bridge in the background

The simplest and cheapest deal if you're going to be making three or more journeys in a day is to buy a **DayPass** ($9), valid all day across all three zones (weekly passes are not available). If you buy these over the counter at stores or elsewhere (not in machines) they're "Scratch & Ride" – you scratch out the day and month before travel.

See "Listings" on p.783 for details of **car and bicycle rental** and **taxis**.

Buses

You can buy tickets on the bus, but exact change is required; ask for a transfer ticket if the driver doesn't automatically give you one. If you have a pass or transfer, simply show the driver. Normal buses stop running around midnight, when a rather patchy "Night Owl" service comes into effect on major routes until about 4am. Blue **West Van buses** (Ⓣ604/985-7777) also operate in the city (usually to North and West Vancouver destinations, including the BC Ferries terminal at Horseshoe Bay) – TransLink tickets are valid on these buses as well.

SeaBuses

The **SeaBuses** ply between Downtown and Lonsdale Quay in North Vancouver, and they're a ride definitely worth taking for its own sake: the views of the mountains across Burrard Inlet, the port and the Downtown skyline are superb. The Downtown terminal is Waterfront Station in the old Canadian Pacific station buildings at the foot of Granville Street. There is only a ticket machine here, but you can get a **ticket** (same price as bus tickets) from the newsagent immediately on your left as you face the long gallery that takes you to the boats. Two four hundred-seat catamarans make the thirteen-minute crossing every fifteen to thirty minutes (6.30am–12.30am). Arrival in North Vancouver is at Lonsdale Quay, where immediately to the left is a bus terminal for connections to Grouse Mountain and other North Vancouver destinations. Bicycles can be carried on board.

Ferries

The city also has a variety of small **ferries**, run over similar routes at similar prices by two companies: Aquabus (Ⓣ604/689-5858, Ⓦwww.theaquabus.com) and False Creek Ferries (Ⓣ604/684-7781, Ⓦwww.granvilleislandferries.bc.ca). These provide a useful, frequent and fun service (daily 7am–10.30pm, winter until 8.30pm). Aquabus runs boats in a continuous circular shuttle from the foot of Hornby Street to the Fish Docks on the seawalk to Vanier Park and the museums ($3), to Granville Island ($3) and to the Yaletown dock by the road loop at the east foot of Davie Street ($4). False Creek Ferries also runs to Granville Island and to Vanier Park from Granville Island (and the Aquatic Centre) just below the Maritime Museum – this is a good way of getting to the park and its museums (see p.768). You buy **tickets** on board with both companies. They also run east up False Creek, with connections from Granville Island to Science World and the Plaza of Nations. You can catch the Aquabus boat from a number of

Information and hotel reservations

Tourism British Columbia Ⓣ1-800/HELLO-BC (435-5622) Toll-free in North America, or 604/435-5622 or 250/387-1642 outside North America, Ⓦwww.hellobc.com.
Tourism Vancouver Ⓣ604/683-2000, Ⓦwww.tourismvancouver.com.

points on False Creek, the most useful for Granville Island and Vanier Park visits being at the Arts Club Theatre on Granville Island, the foot of Hornby Street Downtown or – with False Creek Ferries – below the Aquatic Centre at the foot of Thurlow and northern end of Burrard Bridge, on Granville Island.

SkyTrain

Vancouver's light-rail line – **SkyTrain** – links the Downtown Waterfront Station (housed in the CPR building with the SeaBus terminal) and the southeastern suburb of New Westminster. Only the first three or four stations – Waterfront, Burrard, Granville and Stadium – are of any practical use to the casual visitor. A new sixteen-station extension, the 26-kilometre Canada Line, serving South Vancouver, including the airport, opened in 2009.

Accommodation

Vancouver has a surprisingly large number of inexpensive **hotels**, but some – mainly in the area east of Downtown – are horribly dingy. If you're on a low budget, you're better off in the **hostels** or the excellent **YWCA**. Mid-range hotels are still reasonable, but Vancouver is a tourist city and space can get tight in summer: you'll need to **book ahead**. Many of the nicer options are in the West End, a quiet residential area bordering Vancouver's wonderful Stanley Park, only five or ten minutes' walk from Downtown. Another option, if you're here to explore the parks on the city's fringe, is to take advantage of the far less convenient hotels on the North Shore. Vancouver is not a camper's city: the majority of the in-city **campsites** are for RVs only and will turn you away if you only have a tent.

Hotels

Gastown, Chinatown and the area between them hold central Vancouver's cheaper **hotels**. Parts of these areas are not safe at night, especially backstreet Chinatown. If you really need to stick to the rock-bottom price bracket, and don't fancy the hostels or YWCA, as a last resort go for one of the invariably dodgy hotels north of the Granville Street Bridge. Further up the scale, you should book in advance for the best and most popular places such as the *Sylvia* and *Kingston*.

The **North Shore** embraces North Vancouver – the area across the Burrard Inlet opposite the Downtown peninsula – and West Vancouver, a mix of residential and open country. The main reason you may want to stay here is to access the hikes and other outdoor activities in Grouse Mountain and the Capilano River, Mount Seymour and Lyon Canyon parks. However, there's no point staying here if you

Bed and Breakfasts

B&B accommodation can be booked through agencies, but most of them operate as a phone service only and require two days' notice – it's better to try the Visitor Centre's accommodation service first (see p.751). Though seldom central or cheap – reckon on $90-plus for a double – if you choose well you can have beaches, gardens, barbecues and as little or as much privacy as you want. **B&B agencies** have accommodation throughout the city, in Victoria (see p.806), the Gulf Islands and beyond: one of the best is Ⓦwww.bbcanada.com.

want to get to grips with Downtown. The city's reservation services (see p.751) can help out with North Shore lodging, but North Vancouver also has its own **visitor centre** at 102–124 West 1st St (Ⓣ604/987-4488, Ⓦwww.nvchamber.bc.ca) with information on the area's accommodation.

Out of season, hotels in all categories offer reductions, and you can reckon on thirty percent discounts on high-season prices. Even the smartest hotels will introduce an extra bed into a double room at very little extra cost if there are three of you.

Central Vancouver

Barclay Hotel 1348 Robson St, between Jervis and Broughton Ⓣ604/688-8850, Ⓦwww.barclayhotel.com. A good bargain, the *Barclay* is one of the nicer of several hotels at the north end of Robson St, with ninety rooms and a chintzy French rustic ambience. 6

Buchan Hotel 1906 Haro St, between Chilco and Gilford Ⓣ604/685-5354 or 1-800/668-6654, Ⓦwww.buchanhotel.com. Some smallish rooms, past their prime, but still a genuine bargain given the peaceful residential location, only a block from Stanley Park and English Bay Beach. 3–6

Burrard Inn 1100 Burrard St, between Davie and Helmcken Ⓣ604/681-2331 or 1-800/663-0366, Ⓦwww.burrardinn.com. A fairly central and pleasantly dated motel with standard fittings: some rooms look onto a charming garden courtyard, and some have kitchens. 5

Comfort Inn Downtown 654 Nelson St Ⓣ604/605-4333 or 1-888/605-5333, Ⓦwww.comfortinndowntown.com. There have been lodgings of sorts in this heritage building for years, but after a 1950s retro-inspired refit, complete with lots of black and white photographs and period neon, this 82-room boutique hotel now has a hip and stylish look. Rooms all come with high-speed internet access, voicemail and a/c. The location isn't the best but is convenient for the restaurant and clubs of both Yaletown and the lower end of Granville St. 6

Fairmont Hotel Vancouver 900 West Georgia St at Burrard Ⓣ604/684-3131 or 1-800/441-1414, Ⓦwww.fairmont.com/hotelvancouver. This traditional old hotel is the city's most famous and prestigious. It's the place to stay if money's no object and you want old-world style and Downtown location. Whether you stay here, the ground floor *900 West* restaurant and bar is good, as are the various other restaurants, including *Griffins* on the same floor. Doubles among the 550 rooms range from $269–589, but low-season rates around $190 are available. 8

Four Seasons Hotel Vancouver 791 Georgia St at Howe Ⓣ604/689-9333 or 1-800/332-3442, Ⓦwww.fourseasons.com/vancouver. A Four Seasons hotel rarely disappoints, and Vancouver's is no exception. The location is central, a block from Robson and the Vancouver Art Gallery, and the 385 rooms occupy a 28-storey high-rise building above the Pacific Centre mall. Rooms are enormous, the service immaculate, and the common parts stunning. If you're staying or not, you should definitely think about taking the buffet breakfast which is served on the Garden Terrace – it's one of the best in the city (from $13). Doubles start from about $400 for an executive suite. 8

Granville Island Hotel 1253 Johnson St Ⓣ604/683-7373 or 1-800/663-1840, Ⓦwww.granvilleislandhotel.com. You're away from central Downtown in this polished, modern hotel, which has a good bar and restaurants and a spectacular waterfront setting. But on the other hand you're in the heart of one of the city's trendiest and most enjoyable little enclaves. Free internet access in rooms, some of which have water views. 7

Holiday Inn Hotel & Suites Downtown 1110 Howe St, between Davie and Helmcken Ⓣ604/684-2151 or 1-800/663-9151 in Canada and the US (also 1-800/HOLIDAY), Ⓦwww.holidayinnvancouverdowntown.com. Reasonably central, large and – unlike the dingier hotels nearby – you'll know what to expect, though at this price there's plenty of alternative choice around town. Lots of facilities, including sauna, pool and kids' activity centre, plus rooms with kitchenettes for self-catering. 7

Kingston Hotel 757 Richards St at Robson Ⓣ604/684-9024 or 1-888/713-3304, Ⓦwww.kingstonhotelvancouver.com. This popular bargain is handily sited for Downtown and its clean and nicely decorated interior affects the spirit of a "European-style" hotel. Rooms are available with or without private bathroom and there's a modest but free breakfast to start the day. Along with the *Sylvia*, it's by far the best hotel at its price in the city, so book well ahead. Long-stay terms available. 3

Opus Hotel 322 Davie St Ⓣ604/642-6787 or 1-866/642-6787, Ⓦwww.opushotel.com. Outside, the *Opus* is just another former Yaletown warehouse, but inside it's a bold palette of decorative colours and materials (mosaic, marble and expensive fabrics). The 97 rooms are equally fetching – expensive linens, firm beds, CD players, big windows and great bathrooms. The cool *Opus Bar* and *Elixir* French brasserie mean you need never leave the hotel precincts for food, drink and evening relaxation – though with the temptations of Yaletown just seconds away, this would be a mistake. Rooms start from $339, but off-season rates are far more manageable. 8

Riviera Hotel 1431 Robson St, between Nicola and Broughton ⓣ604/685-1301 or 1-888/699-5222, ⓦwww.rivieraonrobson.com. Reasonably priced central motels such as this place, around midway between Stanley Park and the Vancouver Art Gallery, are rare; the one- and two-room suites are slightly dated, but they have kitchenettes if you want to cook for yourself. 6

Sandman Hotel Vancouver City Centre 180 West Georgia St at Beatty ⓣ604/681-2211 or 1-800/726-3626, ⓦwww.sandmanhotels.com. Flagship of a mid-price chain with hotels all over western Canada and well placed at the eastern edge of Downtown. Rooms are bland but fine and spacious as far as chain hotels go, which makes this first choice if you want something one up from the *Kingston*. 6

Sunset Inn & Suites 1111 Burnaby St, at Thurlow ⓣ604/688-2474 or 1-800/786-1997, ⓦwww.sunsetinn.com. One of the best West End "apartment" hotels and a good spot for a longer stay – spacious studio, double or triple rooms (all with kitchens and balconies) with on-site laundry and many nearby shops. Ten minutes' walk to Downtown. 5

Sylvia Hotel 1154 Gilford St ⓣ604/681-9321, ⓦwww.sylviahotel.com. A local landmark located in a "heritage" building, this is a popular place with an excellent reputation, making reservations essential. It's by the beach two blocks from Stanley Park, and its snug bar, quiet, old-world charm and sea views make it one of Vancouver's best. Rooms are available at different prices depending on size, view and facilities. 6–7

Victorian Hotel 514 Homer St at West Pender ⓣ604/681-6369 or 1-877/681-6369, ⓦwww.victorianhotel.ca. The family-run *Victorian* is situated about as far east as you'd want to be, but remains within easy walking distance of Gastown and the rest of Downtown. Built in 1898 as one of the city's first guesthouses, it has been carefully restored so that many of its 26 rooms have a period feel, with high ceilings, hardwood floors, elegant bathrooms and old features such as original fireplaces and mouldings. Prices vary by up to $60 between double rooms, depending on whether they have private bathrooms and/or kitchenettes. All rooms have phones and small TVs, and a continental breakfast is included. 5

West End Guest House 1362 Haro St at Jervis ⓣ604/681-2889, ⓦwww.westendguesthouse.com. A wonderful, small guesthouse with an old-time parlour and bright rooms, each with private bathroom; book well in advance. Full breakfast included. 7

YWCA Hotel-Residence 733 Beatty St between Georgia and Robson ⓣ604/895-5830 or 1-800/663-1424, ⓦwww.ywcahotel.com. Despite its name, Vancouver's main "Y" is open to all and is excellent, offering the city's best inexpensive accommodation. It was purpose-built in 1995 in a handy east Downtown location close to the stunning central library. Top-value rooms (especially for small groups) are spread over eleven floors with a choice of private, shared or hall bathrooms. There are no dorm beds. Most rooms have TVs, plus there are sports and cooking facilities, wi-fi access, lounges, a/c, laundry rooms, as well as a cheap cafeteria and rooms with mini-kitchens. Rates for the various configurations of rooms come in two bands: A (June–Oct), B (rest of the year). Singles cost $68/61 in the two bands; doubles $82/70 with shared bathroom or $125/84 with private bathroom. Four-person rooms (two double beds) are also available from $142/94, plus $10 for each additional adult.

The North Shore

Best Western Capilano Inn & Suites 1634 Capilano Rd ⓣ604/987-8185 or 1-800/644-4227, ⓦwww.bestwesterncapilano.com. Virtually on the junction of Marine Drive and Capilano Rd, this 74-room establishment is one of several chain motels just east of the Lions Gate Bridge. Standard rooms or rooms with kitchenettes for an additional $20, as well as laundry, restaurant and outdoor summer pool. 5

The Grouse Inn 1633 Capilano Drive ⓣ604/988-7101 or 1-800/779-7888, ⓦwww.grouseinn.com. Close to Downtown road links – one block east of the Lions Gate Bridge and one block south of Hwy 1 at Exit 14. Choose between 80 regular or larger superior rooms and one or two-bedroom kitchen suites (the kitchens cost an extra $29). 5

Lonsdale Quay Hotel 123 Carrie Cates Court ⓣ604/986-6111 or 1-800/836-6111, ⓦwww.lonsdalequayhotel.com. Tastefully appointed rooms and a location right on the Lonsdale Quay waterfront (with fabulous harbour views) and above the quay's superb market (see p.772): escalators from the market itself lead you to the hotel reception on the third floor. Posted room rates are as low as $80 off season, but you're far more likely to pay up to $225. 6

North Vancouver Hotel 1800 Capilano Rd ⓣ604/987-4461 or 1-800/663-4055 in Canada and the US, ⓦwww.northvancouverhotel.ca. One block north of the Capilano Rd and Marine Drive intersection. Rates include continental breakfast, and some rooms have kitchens and/or microwaves and fridges. ⑥

Hostels

Vancouver has three good Hostelling International **hostels**, plus a handful of other reasonable privately run hostels. There are some poorly run and occasionally dangerous "hotels", "hostels" and "rooming houses", particularly on Hastings Street a few blocks either side of Main Street; don't stay at any of them.

Cambie Gastown Hostel 300 Cambie St at Cordova ⓣ604/684-6466 or 1-888/395-5335, ⓦwww.cambiehostels.com. A private hostel located in Vancouver's oldest hotel and pub (built in 1897) just off Gastown's main streets, and so with a much nicer and more central position than many of the city's hostels. Beds are arranged in two-, four- or six-bed bunk rooms, and there are laundry, luggage-storage and bike-storage (but no cooking) facilities. There's a deservedly popular and inexpensive bar-grill with good patio (the *Cambie Saloon & Grill*) downstairs, so aim for beds away from this area if you want a relatively peaceful night's sleep. Also check out the linked and good-value *General Store & Bakery* nearby at 312 Cambie St. No curfew. $27/person in a dorm room (Oct–April $24); private double rooms from $54/person (off season $30). Weekly rates available.

Cambie Seymour Hostel 515 Seymour St at West Pender ⓣ604/684-7757 or 1-888/395-5335, ⓦwww.cambiehostels.com. This is the second, newer, calmer and more central of the *Cambie*'s hostels. Like the Gastown hostel, the management has made an effort to ensure rooms in this heritage building are pleasant, secure and well kept, and provide laundry, storage, internet and food and drink in the shape of a café and *Malone's Bar & Grill* next door. No curfew. Pricing is slightly different to the Gastown hostel. Doubles in a bunk room cost $27/person (Oct–April $24) and $58/person for a double bed ($52 off season).

SameSun Hostel 1018 Granville St at Nelson ⓣ604/682-8226 or 1-888/844-7875, ⓦwww.samesun.com. *Samesun* has followed up the success of a popular hostel in Toronto with a zippy, bright hostel in Vancouver, although their chosen location on Granville St – while central and away from the worst of this street's tawdriness – is not the city's quietest. The hostel has 250 beds in two- and four-bed rooms, and offers a free shuttle from the bus/train station, secure lockers, modern kitchen and common area (with free wi-fi), games room and computer access. No curfew. From $25/person.

Vancouver Central Hostel 1025 Granville St ⓣ604/685-5335 or 1-888/203-8333, ⓦwww.hihostels.ca. Vancouver's newest and smartest HI hostel on busy Granville St is a far cry from the humble days of hostelling. It offers 226 beds in private double rooms with TV and en-suite bathrooms, four-bed dorms and a/c in most rooms. Family rooms are also available. Facilities include a kitchen, pub, reading lounge, free wi-fi, computer access and shuttle runs to the other city HI hostels and the Pacific Central Station. Dorm beds: members $37.50 Oct–Jan, $45 in peak summer and Easter periods; nonmembers $41.50, $49 in peak periods. Private en suite doubles: members $77, $82 and $109 at peak; nonmembers $85, $90 and $117 at peak. Private doubles without en-suite are a few dollars cheaper.

Vancouver Downtown Hostel 1114 Burnaby St at Thurlow ⓣ604/684-4565 or 1-888/203-4302, ⓦwww.hihostels.ca. Located in a former nunnery and health-care centre in the city's West End. There are 223 beds split up between shared and private rooms (maximum four/room). Bike rental and storage as well as laundry, kitchen, free wi-fi, computer access and storage lockers are available. A free shuttle (look for the blue HI logo) operates between this hostel, the Jericho Beach hostel and the Pacific Central railway and bus terminal; if there's no bus, call the hostel to find when the next one is due. No curfew. Reservations essential. Dorm beds: members $27, $29 and $31.50 in peak periods; nonmembers $31, $33 and 35.50 at peak. Private doubles: members $75, $80 and 90 at peak; nonmembers $83, $88 and 98 at peak.

Vancouver Jericho Beach Hostel 1515 Discovery St, off NW Marine Drive ⓣ604/224-3208 or 1-888/203-4852, ⓦwww.hihostels.ca. Canada's biggest HI hostel has a superb and safe position surrounded by lawns by Jericho Beach south of the city. A former barracks, the 286-bed hostel fills up quickly, occasionally leading to a three-day limit in summer. There are dorm beds and ten private rooms (sleeping up to six) which go quickly and free bunks occasionally offered in return for a couple of hours' work; family rooms also available. Facilities include kitchen, licensed café (April–Oct), bike rental and storage, storage lockers, free wi-fi, computer access and an excellent cafeteria. Dorm beds: members $22, $26 in July & Aug; nonmembers $26, $30 in July & Aug; Doubles: members $63, $76 in July & Aug; nonmembers $71, $84 in July & Aug.

Campsites

In a city famed for its natural beauty and opportunities for outdoor activities it's something of a disappointment – and a municipal failing – that not only are there no public or private **campsites** in or near the city centre, but also none of the handful of sites that do exist could be described as memorable. To pitch a tent or hook up an RV you'll have to head to North Vancouver or the suburbs of Richmond and Burnaby, neither of which are places you'd choose to camp.

Burnaby Cariboo RV Park 8765 Cariboo Place, Burnaby ⓣ604/420-1722, ⓦwww.bcrvpark.com. A 237-pitch site about 16km east of the city centre with luxurious facilities (indoor pool, jacuzzi, laundry, free showers and convenience store) and a separate tenting area away from the RVs (for which there are full hook-ups). Take the Gaglardi Way exit (#37) from Hwy 1, turn right at the traffic light, then immediately left. The next right is Cariboo Place. Open year-round. $36.50/tent site, $51.50–55/RV site.

Capilano RV Park 295 Tomahawk Ave, North Vancouver ⓣ604/987-4722, ⓦwww.capilanorvpark.com. This is a pretty unattractive place but it is the city's most central site for trailers and tents, located beneath the north foot of the Lion's Gate Bridge and a short walk from the Park Royal Shopping Centre: exit Capilano Rd South or Hwy 99 exit off Lion's Gate Bridge. There are full RV facilities and hook-ups, plus swimming pool, free showers, washrooms and laundry, ice and water. Reservations (with deposit) are essential June–Aug. $30–45/site.

Park Canada Recreational Vehicles Inn 4799 Hwy 17, Delta ⓣ604/943-5811 or 1-877/943-0685, ⓦwww.parkcanada.com. Convenient for the Tsawwassen ferry terminal to the southwest, this 145-pitch site has partial and three-way hook-ups for RVs and some separate tent sites. There are free showers, washrooms, laundry, heated pool and grocery store. The site's also right next to a waterslide and golf course. Tent sites $27.50, RV sites $27.50–$33.50.

The City

Vancouver is not a city that offers or requires lots of relentless sightseeing. Its breathtaking physical beauty makes it a place where often it's enough just to wander and watch the world go by – "the sort of town", wrote Jan Morris, "nearly everyone would want to live in". In summer you'll probably end up doing what the locals do, if not actually sailing, hiking, skiing, fishing or whatever, then certainly going to the beach, lounging in one of the parks or spending time in waterfront cafés.

Still, there are a handful of sights that make worthwhile viewing by any standards. You'll inevitably spend a good deal of time in the **Downtown** area and its Victorian-era equivalent, **Gastown**, now a renovated and less than convincing pastiche of its past. **Chinatown** could easily absorb a morning and contains more than its share of interesting shops, restaurants and busy streets. The former warehouse district of **Yaletown**, on Downtown's southeast fringes, is also a great area to explore for its own sake: a compact grid of streets full of chic one-off stores, cafés, galleries and good, contemporary restaurants and bars. For a taste of the city's sensuous side, hit **Stanley Park**, a huge area of semi-wild parkland and beaches that crowns the northern tip of the Downtown peninsula. Take a walk or a bike ride here and follow it up with a stroll to the **beach**. Be certain to spend a morning on **Granville Island**, by far the city's most tempting spot for wandering and people-watching. If you prefer a cultural slant on things, hit the formidable

Museum of Anthropology or the museums of the Vanier Park complex, the latter easily accessible from Granville Island.

At a push, you could cram the city's essentials into a couple of days. If you're here for a longer stay, you'll want to venture farther from Downtown: trips across Burrard Inlet to **North Vancouver**, worth making for the views from the SeaBus ferry alone, lend a different panoramic perspective of the city, and lead into the mountains and forests that give Vancouver its tremendous setting. The most popular trips here are to the Capilano Suspension Bridge, something of a triumph of PR over substance, and to the more worthwhile cable-car trip up **Grouse Mountain** for some staggering views of the city.

Downtown

You soon get the hang of Vancouver's **Downtown** district, an arena of streets and shopping malls centred on **Robson Street**. On hot summer evenings it's like a latter-day vision of *La Dolce Vita* – a buzzy meeting place crammed with bars, restaurants, late-night stores, and bronzed youths preening in bars or cafés, or ostentatiously cruising in open-topped cars. At other times a more sedate class hangs out on the steps of the Vancouver Art Gallery or glides in and out of the two big department stores, Sears and The Bay. Downtown's other principal thoroughfares are **Burrard Street** – all smart shops, hotels and offices – and **Granville Street**, partly pedestrianized with plenty of shops and cinemas, but curiously seedy in places, especially at its southern end near the Granville Street Bridge. New development is taking Downtown's reach farther east, and at some point you should try to see the **public library**, opened in 1995, at 350 West Georgia St, a focus of this growth and a striking piece of modern architecture.

Canada Place and the Harbour Centre Building

For the best possible introduction to Vancouver, you should walk down to the waterfront and **Canada Place** (walkways open 24hr, information Ⓣ604/775-7200, Ⓦwww.canadaplace.ca; free), the Canadian pavilion for Expo '86, the huge world exhibition held in the city in 1986, and another architectural tour de force that houses a luxury hotel, cruise-ship terminal and two glitzy convention centres. For all its excess, it makes a superb viewpoint, with stunning vistas of the port, mountains, sea and buzzing boats, helicopters and floatplanes. The **port** activity, especially, is mesmerizing. Canada Place's design, and the manner in which it juts into the port, is meant to suggest a ship, and you can walk the building's perimeter as if "on deck", stopping to read the boards that describe the immediate cityscape and the appropriate pages of its history. Inside are expensive shops, an unexceptional restaurant and an IMAX cinema (from $12; Ⓣ604/682-IMAX, Ⓦwww.imax.com/vancouver).

An alternative to Canada Place's vantage point, the nearby **Harbour Centre Building** at 555 West Hastings, is one of the city's tallest structures. On a fine day it's definitely worth paying to ride the stomach-churning, all-glass SkyLift elevators that run up the side of the tower – 167m in a minute – to the fortieth-storey observation deck, with its staggering 360-degree views (daily: May to mid-Oct 8.30am–10.30pm; mid-Oct to April 9am–9pm; $13; Ⓣ604/689-0421, Ⓦwww.vancouverlookout.com). Admission is valid all day so you can return and look out over the bright lights of Vancouver at night.

The Vancouver Art Gallery

Centrally located in the imposing old city courthouse is the rather exorbitant **Vancouver Art Gallery**, at 750 Hornby St (daily 10am–5.30pm, Tues & Thurs until 9pm; May–Sept $20.50, $19.50 rest of the year; Ⓣ604/662-4700, Ⓦwww.vanartgallery.bc.ca). The permanent collection has over eight thousand works and is valued at over $100 million. Yet the only part of the collection you can be sure of seeing is the Emily Carr portion on the top floor. The other three floors are given over to (admittedly often excellent) touring shows and a rotating display of parts of the permanent collection.

The permanent collection features a rather sparse international assortment, with some of the lesser works of Warhol and Lichtenstein, and Italian, Flemish and British paintings spanning the sixteenth to twentieth centuries. In recent years the gallery has made a determined effort to concentrate on contemporary works – videos, sculptures, installations and, in particular, photo-based and photoconceptual art. In the last area the gallery boasts the largest such collection in North America, including wonderful pieces by Cindy Sherman (notably her "self" portraits), Jeff Wall, Rachel Whiteread, Jenny Holzer and the magnificent monumental photographs by Andreas Gursky.

You can't be sure you'll see these, although the fact that there are three or four temporary shows means there's often something of interest. The steep admission fee means casual visitors are taking a rather expensive chance unless you know you want to see a particular exhibition. What ultimately redeems the place are the powerful and almost surreal works of **Emily Carr**, who was born on Vancouver Island in 1871 and whose paintings – characterized by deep greens and blues – evoke something of the scale and intensity of the West Coast and its aboriginal peoples. The **gallery café**, with its sun-trap of a terrace, is also excellent.

Gastown

An easy walk east of Downtown – five minutes from Canada Place and concentrated largely on Water Street – **Gastown** is a determined piece of city rejuvenation aimed squarely at tourists, distinguished by new cobbles, fake gas lamps, *Ye Olde English Tea Room*-type cafés and a generally over-polished patina. The name derives from "Gassy" (as in loquacious) Jack Leighton, a retired sailor turned publican and self-proclaimed "mayor", who arrived on site by canoe with his native wife and a mangy yellow dog in 1867, quickly opening a bar to service the nearby lumber mills, whose bosses banned drinking on or near the yards. Leighton's statue stands in **Maple Tree Square**, Gastown's heart, focus of its main streets and reputed site of this first tavern. Trade was brisk, and a second bar opened, soon followed by a village of sorts – "Gassy's Town" – which, though destroyed by fire in 1886, formed in effect the birthplace of modern Vancouver. Over the years, the Downtown focus moved west and something of Gastown's boozy beginnings returned to haunt it, as its cheap hotels and warehouses turned into a skid row for junkies and alcoholics. By the 1970s the area was declared a historic site – the buildings are the city's oldest – and an enthusiastic beautification programme was set in motion.

The end product never quite became the dynamic, city-integrated spot the planners had hoped, and was slated for years by locals as something of a tourist trap, though recent signs suggest that interesting cafés, clubs and restaurants are slowly beginning to make themselves felt. It's certainly worth a stroll for its buskers, Sunday crowds and occasional points of interest.

Probably the most surprising aspect of Gastown, however, is the contrast between its manicured pavements and the down-at-heel streets immediately to the south and east. The area between Gastown and Chinatown is both a thoroughly unpleasant skid row and, nearer Gastown, a haven for secondhand clothes shops, bookshops, galleries, new designers and cheap five-and-dimes. In places, this area recalls Gastown's bad old days: unpleasantly seedy, pocked with the dingy bars and hotels, and inhabited by characters to match.

Vancouver Police Museum

One sight worth hunting out in the area between Gastown and Chinatown is Vancouver's **Police Museum** at 240 East Cordova St (Mon–Sat 9am–5pm; shorter hours possible in winter; $7; ⓣ604/665-3346, ⓦwww.vancouverpolicemuseum.ca), a bizarre and fascinating little museum, housed in the city's old Coroner's Court Building, that is easily seen and leaves you well placed for a short two-block walk south to the centre of Chinatown.

The building has its own place in Vancouver folklore, not least for the fact that it was here that the actor **Errol Flynn** was brought after he died in Vancouver in 1959. Flynn arrived in the city in October 1959 with his best acting days well behind him. With him was his "personal assistant", a 17-year-old blonde girl not known for her secretarial skills. Within two days Flynn had dropped dead in his rented West End apartment. The body was brought to the Coroner's Court, where the pathologist conducting the autopsy is said to have removed a piece of Flynn's penis and placed it in formaldehyde to keep as a souvenir. The horrified chief coroner, a rather more fastidious operator, is said to have pulled rank and reattached the missing piece of member to the corpse with sticky tape. The body was then dispatched to Los Angeles for burial. This was not the end of the story, for it emerged that somewhere between the West End and the morgue, a key to a Swiss safety-deposit box that Flynn wore round his neck had disappeared. When Flynn's lawyers opened the box three years later, the stock certificates and half a million dollars in cash they had expected to find were nowhere to be seen.

The **autopsy room** is still there, together with a suitably macabre selection of mangled and preserved body parts arranged around the walls; check out the **morgue**'s cooler, penultimate resting place of many over the years. Other rooms include a **forensics lab**, a simulated autopsy room, police cell and radio room, while a variety of themed displays include sections on notorious local criminals, weapons seized from criminals (some pretty unusual), crime-scene reconstructions, gambling, uniforms, counterfeit money and a sizeable collection of firearms. More light-hearted exhibits include a collection of model police cars from around the world. The museum's gift shop has an interesting line in police-related gifts and souvenirs.

Chinatown

Vancouver's vibrant **Chinatown** – clustered mainly on Pender Street between Carrall and Gore streets and on Keefer Street from Main to Gore – is a city apart. Vancouver's 100,000 or more Chinese make up one of North America's largest Chinatowns and are the city's oldest and largest ethnic group after the British-descended majority. Many crossed the Pacific in 1858 to join the Fraser Valley gold rush; others followed under contract to help build the Canadian Pacific Railway. Most stayed, only to find themselves being treated appallingly. Denied citizenship and legal rights until as late as 1947, the Chinese community sought safety and familiarity in a ghetto of their own, where clan associations and societies provided for new arrivals and the local poor – and helped build the distinctive houses of recessed balconies and ornamental roofs that have made the area a protected historic site.

Unlike Gastown's gimmickry, Chinatown is all genuine: shops, hotels, markets, tiny restaurants and dim alleys vie for attention amid an incessant hustle of jammed pavements and the buzz of Chinese conversation. Virtually every building replicates an Eastern model without a trace of self-consciousness, and written Chinese characters feature everywhere in preference to English. Striking and unexpected after Downtown's high-rise glitz, the district brings you face to face with Vancouver's oft-touted multiculturalism, and helps explain why Hong Kong immigrants continue to be attracted to the city. Yet it's a district with a distinct edge, and

▲ Vancouver's Chinatown night market

visitors should avoid the area's more dingy streets at night and parts of East Hastings near Main Street just about any time.

Apart from the obvious culinary temptations (see p.776), Chinatown's main points of reference are its **shops**. Some of the best boast fearsome butchery displays and such edibles as live eels, flattened ducks, hundred-year-old eggs and other stuff you'll be happy not to identify. Check out the open-air **night market** at Main and Keefer streets (May–Sept Fri–Sun 6pm–midnight), a wonderful medley of sights. Keefer Street is **bakery** row and it's worth dropping in to one of the local **herbalists** to browse amongst their panaceas: snakeskins, reindeer antlers, buffalo tongues, dried sea horses and bears' testicles are all available if you're feeling under the weather. Ming Wo, 23 East Pender St, is a fantastic cookware shop, with probably every utensil ever devised. Most people also flock dutifully to the 1913 **Sam Kee Building**, at the corner of Carrall and Pender streets; at just 1.8m across, it's officially the world's narrowest building.

Chinatown's chief cultural attraction is the small **Dr Sun Yat-Sen Garden**, (May to mid-June & Sept daily 10am–6pm; mid-June to Aug daily 9.30am–7pm; Oct daily 10am–4.30pm; Nov–April Tues–Sun 10am–4.30pm; $10; Ⓦ www.vancouverchinesegarden.com), at 578 Carrall St near Pender Street. This 2.5-acre park is billed as the first authentic, full-scale classical Chinese garden ever built outside China. Named after the founder of the first Chinese Republic, who was a frequent visitor to Vancouver, the park was created for Expo 86. The whole thing is based on classical gardens developed in the city of Suzhou during the Ming dynasty (1368–1644) to achieve a subtle balance of Yin and Yang: small and large, soft and hard, flowing and immovable, light and dark. Every stone, pine and flower was carefully placed and has symbolic meaning. Hourly free guided tours on the half-hour explain the Taoist philosophy behind the carefully placed elements.

Science World

Although much of the **Expo site** around Canada Place, and at other points to the south and east, has been levelled or is undergoing rigorous redevelopment, you can see one of the main surviving structures just south of Chinatown. The geodesic dome, at 1455 Quebec St, is a striking city landmark and now home to **Science World** (Mon–Fri 10am–5pm, Sat & Sun 10am–6pm; Science World $19.75, Omnimax $10 for a single feature; joint ticket for Science World entry and one Omnimax film $19.50; ⓣ604/443-7440 or 24-hour recorded line ⓣ604/443-7443, ⓦwww.scienceworld.bc.ca). Probably only children will be satisfied by the various high-tech, hands-on displays, which include the opportunity to make thunderous amounts of noise on electronic instruments and drum machines. Galleries deal with all manner of science-related themes, but probably the best things here for adults are the building itself and the vast screen of the Omnimax Cinema at the top of the dome.

Stanley Park

One of the world's great urban spaces, **Stanley Park** is Vancouver's green heart, helping lend the city its particular character. At nearly one thousand acres, it's the largest urban park in North America – a semi-wilderness of dense rainforest, marshland and beaches. Ocean surrounds it on three sides, with a road and parallel cycleway/pedestrian promenade following the Seawall all the way round the peninsula for a total of 10.5km. From here, views of the city and across the water to the mountains are particularly worthwhile. Away from the coastal trail network and main draw – the aquarium – the interior is nearly impenetrable scrub and forest, with few paths and few people. There are also plenty of open, wooded or flower-decorated spaces to picnic, snooze or watch the world go by around the park, particularly near its eastern entrances.

The peninsula was partially logged in the 1860s, but in 1886 the newly formed city council – showing typical Canadian foresight and an admirable sense of priorities – moved to make what had become a military reserve into a permanent park. Thus its remaining first-growth forest of cedar, hemlock and Douglas fir, and the swamp now known as Lost Lagoon, were saved for posterity in the name of Lord Stanley, Canada's governor general from 1888 to 1893.

Park practicalities

The park is a simple though rather dull **walk** from most of Downtown: Beach Avenue to the south and Georgia Street to the north are the obvious approaches if you're on foot, leading to either end of the Seawall. Alternatively, walk along the Coal Harbour waterfront path parallel to West Cordova Street or grab a Stanley Park **bus** #19 from the corner of Burrard and Pender streets Downtown, which drops you just inside the park by Lost Lagoon. Other buses that will take you close to the park are the #1 (Beach) to Davie Street and Beach Avenue and the #3 (Robson) to Denman Street.

The unstaffed Brockton interpretive centre (daily May–June & Sept 9am–6pm, July & Aug 9am–8pm, rest of the year 9am–4pm, but hours may vary) is about a 100m along the Seawall promenade as you walk or cycle in a clockwise direction round the park. A neat **itinerary** would be to stroll or cycle all or part of this Seawall and then walk back to Denman Street, where you can pause at one of several cafés before heading down Denman to English Bay Beach. The corner of Denman and Georgia streets has a cluster of **bike rental** outlets; from Denman it's just a minute's pedalling to the park.

In the park

Taking time in the park, especially on a busy Sunday, gives a good taste of what it means to live in Vancouver. The first thing you see is the **Lost Lagoon**, a fair-sized lake that started life as a tidal inlet, and got its name because its water all but disappeared at low tide. Dozens of waterfowl species inhabit its shoreline. Just east are the pretty Rose Garden and Vancouver Rowing Club, before which stands a statue of Scottish poet Robbie Burns. From here you can follow the Seawall path all the way, or make a more modest loop past the **totem poles** and round Brockton Point. The nine poles here, the last added in 2009, are copies, or loaned replacements, the deteriorating originals – mostly brought from Vancouver's Alert Bay region in the 1920s – having been moved to various museums between 1986 and 1992.

A brisk walk around the Seawall **path** takes about two hours. Moving around anticlockwise, odd little sights dot the promenade, all signed and explained, the most famous being the *Girl in a Wetsuit* statue, a rather lascivious update of Copenhagen's *Little Mermaid*. If you want a more focused walk, the **Cathedral Trail**, northwest of the Lost Lagoon, takes you past some big first-growth cedars. **Beaver Lake**, carpeted green with water lilies, is a peaceful spot for a sleep or a stroll. **Lumberman's Arch**, near the aquarium (see below) was raised in 1952 to honour those in the lumber industry, an odd memorial given that the industry in question would probably give its eye teeth to fell the trees in Stanley Park. Its meadow surroundings are a favourite for families and those looking for a good place for a nap. **Prospect Point**, on the park's northern tip, is a busy spot but worth braving for its beautiful view of the city and the mountains rising behind West Vancouver across the water. There's a café-restaurant here, popular for its outdoor deck and sweeping views. Southwest of here lies **Siwash Rock**, an outcrop which has defied the weather for centuries, attracting numerous native legends in the process, and which is distinguished by its solitary tree (not visible from the road, but quickly reached by path).

Though people do swim in the sea at beaches around the park's western fringes, most bathers prefer the **swimming pool** next to Second Beach, which is just west of Lost Lagoon. Facilities – cafés, playgrounds, golf, outdoor dancing – proliferate near the Downtown margins. Guided **nature walks** are also occasionally offered around the park; ask for details at the park's visitor centre.

Vancouver Aquarium Marine Science Centre

The **Vancouver Aquarium Marine Science Centre** is the park's most popular destination (daily: late June to early Sept 9.30am–7pm; rest of year 9.30am–5pm; $22; Ⓦwww.vanaqua.org). The aquarium is ranked among North America's best, and with over a million visitors a year claims to be the most-visited sight in Canada west of Toronto's CN Tower. It contains over eight thousand living exhibits representing some six hundred different species. The complex has been targeted by animal-rights campaigners for its treatment of performing beluga and killer whales, not to mention cooped-up seals and otters. Given the aquarium's reputation as a tourist attraction, however, as well as its role as a research centre, the campaigners have a long, uphill battle. The whales in particular are huge draws, but you can't help feeling they should really be in the sea, for all the hoopla surrounding their $14 million marine-mammal area.

There are several key areas to see. The **Arctic Canada** section concerns itself with the fragile world of the Canadian north, with a chance to see whales face to face through glass and hear the sounds of whales, walruses, seals and other creatures in this icy domain. The **Amazon Gallery** displays the vegetation, fishes, iguanas, sloths and other creatures of the rainforest in a climate-controlled environment, while the **Pacific Northwest Habitat** performs a similar role for otters, beavers and other creatures of the waters of BC.

Yaletown

Yaletown is a small, hip and genuinely captivating grid of interesting shops, cafés and restaurants centred on Homer, Hamilton and Mainland streets between Drake

Street to the south and Smithe Street to the north. It takes its name from the many Canadian Pacific railway workers who settled here in the 1880s, having followed the line west from the town of Yale 180km away in BC interior. At the time, it had more saloons per acre than anywhere in the world and was considered one of North America's most lawless enclaves.

For most of the twentieth century it was a warehouse and packing district, but over the last decade or so has been transformed, helped by the spread of a booming Downtown south and east, and the ranks of condominiums that have sprouted on the north shore of False Creek. At street level, the broad, raised walkways provide the perfect stage for café terraces, while the narrow, lofty or otherwise unusual old warehouse spaces have become often dramatically designed bars and restaurants.

You can get here on the new stretch of SkyTrain using Yaletown-Roundhouse station, but it's an easy walk from central Downtown. If you're walking, be sure to come via the striking **Vancouver Public Library** (Ⓦwww.vpl.vancouver.bc.ca) at Robson and Homer streets. It's become one of the city's iconic buildings, resembling a postmodern Roman Colosseum.

Moving on, Granville Island is the obvious next destination, easily reached by ferry (see p.755) from Yaletown Landing on the north shore of False Creek at the foot of Davie Street.

Granville Island

Granville Island (Ⓦwww.granvilleisland.com), huddled under the Granville Street Bridge south of Downtown, is the city's most enticing "people's place" – the title it likes for itself – and pretty much lives up to its claim to be the heart of Vancouver. Friendly, easy-going and popular, its shops, markets, galleries, marina and open spaces are juxtaposed with a light-industrial setting whose faint whiff of warehouse squalor saves the area from any sense of pretentiousness.

The island was reclaimed from swampland in 1917 as an ironworks and shipbuilding centre, but by the 1960s the yards were derelict and the place had become a rat-infested dumping ground for the city's rubbish. In 1972 the federal government agreed to bankroll a programme of residential, commercial and industrial redevelopment that retained the old false-fronted buildings, tin-shack homes, seawall and rail sidings. The best part of the job had been finished by 1979 – and was immediately successful – but work continues unobtrusively today, the various building projects only adding to the area's sense of change and dynamism. Most people come here during the day, but there are some good restaurants, bars and the Arts Club Theatre, which are all enough to keep the place buzzing at night.

Virtually the first building you see on the island if you enter by road (rather than ferry) augurs well: the **Granville Island Brewery**, 1441 Cartwright St (tours only: daily noon, 2pm & 4pm; $9.75; Ⓣ604/687-2739, Ⓦwww.gib.ca), a small but interesting concern offering guided tours that include tastings of its additive-free beers.

Dominant among the maze of shops, galleries and businesses, the **Granville Island Public Market** (daily 9am–7pm) is the undisputed highlight of the area. On summer weekends it's where people go to see and be seen and it throngs with arts-and-crafts types, and a phalanx of dreadful buskers. The quality and variety of **food** is staggering, with dozens of kiosks and cafés selling ready-made titbits and potential picnic ingredients. Parks, patios and walkways nearby provide lively areas to eat and take everything in. Other spots to look out for include Blackberry Books, the Kids Market (a shopping mall for children and parents; it also has a water park) and the bright-yellow *Bridges*, a pub/restaurant/wine bar, which has a nice patio and great views of False Creek and English Bay.

Island practicalities

The most direct approach to Granville Island is to take **bus** #50 from Gastown or Granville Street. The walk down Granville Street and across the bridge is deceptively long, not terribly salubrious, and so probably only worthwhile on a fine day when you need the exercise. Alternatively, and more fun, private **ferries** ($3, pay on board) ply the route almost continuously between the island and little quays at the foot of Hornby Street or the Aquatic Centre at the foot of Thurlow Street. They also connect from Granville Island to Science World (hourly) and, more significantly, to Vanier Park (half-hourly). A logical and satisfying day's **itinerary** from Downtown would take you to Granville Island, to the museums and back by ferry. You might also choose to **walk** from the island along the False Creek seawall (east) or west to Vanier Park and Kitsilano Beach.

There's a **visitor centre** on the second floor at 1661 Duranleau St for Island-related information only (daily 9am–6pm; ⓣ604/666-5784, ⓦwww.granvilleisland.bc.ca), with a small, non-permanent kiosk on the street at this address usually open the same hours, May to September only. Many of the island's shops and businesses close on Mondays, so if you want a **bus back** to Downtown do *not* take the #51 from the stop opposite the information centre (it will take you in the wrong direction): walk out of the island complex's only road entrance, and at the junction the #50 stop is immediately on your right.

Vanier Park museum complex

A little to the west of Granville Island, **Vanier Park** conveniently collects most of the city's main museums: the **Vancouver Museum**, the **Maritime Museum** and the **H.R. MacMillan Space Centre**. The complex sits on the waterfront at the west end of the Burrard Bridge, near Kitsilano Beach and the residential-entertainment centres of Kitsilano and West 4th Avenue; Vanier Park itself is a fine spot to while away a summer afternoon. You could easily incorporate a visit to the museums with a trip to Granville Island using the **ferry**, which docks just below the Maritime Museum. Coming from Downtown, take the #22 Macdonald **bus** south from anywhere on Burrard or West Pender streets – get off at the first stop after the bridge and walk down Chestnut Street to the park. The park is pleasant but open and has a few nice patches of sandy beach on its fringes.

The Museum of Vancouver

The Museum of **Vancouver**, 1100 Chestnut St (July & Aug Mon–Sun 10am–5pm, Thurs 10am–8pm; rest of the year Tues, Wed, Fri–Sun 10am–5pm, Thurs 10am–8pm; $11; ⓦwww.museumofvancouver.ca), traces the history of the city and the lower British Columbian mainland, and invokes the area's past in its very form: the flying-saucer shape is a nod to the conical cedar-bark hats of the Northwest Coast natives, former inhabitants of the area. The fountain outside, looking like a crab on a bidet, recalls the animal of native legend that guards the port entrance.

Though it's the main focus of interest at Vanier Park, the museum is not as captivating as you might expect and a visit needn't take more than an hour or so. A patchy collection of baskets, tools, clothes and miscellaneous artefacts of aboriginal peoples – including a huge whaling canoe, the only example in a museum – homes in on the eight thousand years before European arrival. After that, the main collection, weaving in and out of Vancouver's history up to World War I, is full of offbeat and occasionally memorable insights – notably the accounts of early explorers' often extraordinary exploits, the immigration section (which recreates what it felt like to travel steerage) and the forestry displays. The twentieth-century section is a disappointment, much of it looking more like an antique shop than a museum.

The H.R. MacMillan Space Centre

In the same building as the Museum of Vancouver is the **H.R. MacMillan Space Centre** (Tues–Sun 10am–5pm; evening laser shows at varying times: see website for latest details; Space Centre $15, additional Virtual Voyage rides $7, evening laser shows $10.75; ⓣ604/738-7827, ⓦwww.spacecentre.ca), which incorporates the MacMillan Planetarium and a range of space-related displays and shows. Its main draws are its forty-minute star shows – the standard planetarium fare, held several times daily – and very loud, very brash evening laser and music extravaganzas, which are very popular: arrive in good time or make reservations.

Many of the centre's exhibits are high-tech and hands-on, especially in the so-called Cosmic Courtyard, where interactive displays allow you to battle an alien, design a spaceship, guide a lunar robot or plan a voyage to Mars. Many displays also involve lots of impressive computer and other audiovisual effects, notably the Virtual Voyages Simulator, a flight simulator complete with the "motion" you might encounter during space travel and other journeys. The "rides" on the simulator last about five minutes and experiences range from collisions with a comet to trips on a roller coaster and simulated space flights to the planets.

Vancouver Maritime Museum

The **Vancouver Maritime Museum**, 1905 Ogden Ave (May–Sept daily 10am–5pm; Oct–April Tues–Sat 10am–5pm, Sun noon–5pm; $10; ⓦwww.vancouvermaritimemuseum.com), is a short walk from the Vancouver Museum and features lovely early photographs evoking turn-of-the-century Vancouver, though the rest of the presentation doesn't quite do justice to the status of the city as one of the world's leading ports. An exception is the renovated *St Roch*, a two-masted schooner once used by the RCMP in Canada's Arctic; it was the first vessel to navigate the famed Northwest Passage in a single season, and the first to make the trip from west to east; it now sits impressively in its own wing of the museum, where it can be viewed by guided tour only. Outside, just below the museum on **Heritage Harbour** (quay for ferries to and from Granville Island), you can admire (for free) more restored vessels, including a half-scale replica of a Norwegian Viking ship.

Kitsilano

The leafy district (west from Burrard to Alma sts, and from the waterfront to about 16th Avenue) beyond Vanier Park is **Kitsilano**, or Kits. This former hippie and alternative-lifestyle neighbourhood is now a desirable and much-gentrified enclave, but with shades of its past in the shape of laidback cafés, interesting shops, good restaurants and the easygoing charm of **Kitsilano Beach** and its wonderful **waterfront swimming pool** (late May to mid-June Mon–Fri noon–8.45pm, Sat & Sun 10am–8.45pm; mid-June to early Sept Mon–Fri 7am–8.45pm, Sat & Sun 10am–8.45pm; rest of Sept Mon–Fri 7am–7.15pm, Sat & Sun 10am–7.15pm; $5.15; ⓣ604/731-0011). Walk here from Vanier Park and the museums on the coast path (30min) or, from downtown, take **bus** #22 southbound on Burrard Street. Both beach and streets are nice places to idle away a summer afternoon and evening, while the **shoreline path** is a lovely place for a stroll. The Jericho Beach **hostel** (see p.759) is nearby, should you want to spend more time here.

The Museum of Anthropology and around

Located well out of Downtown on the University of British Columbia campus, the **Museum of Anthropology** (mid-May to mid-Oct daily 10am–5pm, Tues until 9pm; rest of year Tues 10am–9pm, Wed–Sun 10am–5pm; $11, $6 on Tues 5–9pm; Ⓦ www.moa.ubc.ca), 6393 NW Marine Drive, is by far Vancouver's most important museum. Emphasizing the art and culture of the natives of the region, and the Haida in particular, its collection of carvings, totem poles and artefacts is unequalled in North America.

Much is made of the museum's award-winning layout, a cool and spacious collection of halls designed by Arthur Erickson, the eminent architect also responsible for converting the Vancouver Art Gallery. Particularly outstanding is the huge **Great Hall**, inspired by native cedar houses, which makes as perfect an artificial setting for its thirty-odd **totem poles** as you could ask for. Huge windows look out to more poles and Haida houses, which you're free to wander around, backed by views of Burrard Inlet and the distant mountains. Most of the poles and monolithic carvings, indoors and out, are from the coastal tribes of the Haida, Salish, Tsimshian and Kwakiutl, all of which share cultural elements. One of the museum's great virtues is that few of its displays are hidden away in basements or back rooms, but are beautifully presented in the Great Hall and Multiversity Galleries close by: the latter opened in January 2010, part of a large renovation project that, among other things, also added a pleasant café.

Most of the permanent collection revolves around **Canadian Pacific** cultures, but the **Inuit** and **Far North** exhibits are also outstanding, as are the jewellery, masks and baskets of Northwest native tribes, all markedly delicate after the blunt-nosed carvings of the Great Hall. Look out especially for the argillite sculptures, made from a jet-black slate found only on BC's Haida Gwaii or Queen Charlotte Islands. The **African** and **Asian** collections are also pretty comprehensive, if smaller, but appear as something of an afterthought alongside the indigenous artefacts. Also on the site is a less arresting three-gallery wing designed to house the Koerner Collection, an assortment of six hundred European ceramics dating from the fifteenth century onwards.

▲ Totem poles in the Museum of Anthropology's Great Hall

The museum saves its best for last. Housed in a separate rotunda, **The Raven and the Beast**, a modern sculpture designed by Haida artist Bill Reid, is the museum's pride and joy and has achieved almost iconographic status in the city. Carved from a 4.5-tonne block of cedar and requiring the attention of five people over three years, it describes the Haida legend of human evolution with stunning virtuosity, depicting terrified figures squirming from a half-open clam shell, overseen by an enormous and stern-faced raven. As beautiful as the work is, its rotunda setting makes it seem oddly out of place – almost like a corporate piece of art.

To get to the museum, catch a bus south from Granville Street marked UBC and stay on until the end of the line. The campus is huge and disorienting: to find the museum, turn right from the bus stop, walk along the tree-lined East Mall to the very bottom (10min), then turn left on NW Marine Drive and walk till you see the museum on the right (another 5min). In the foyer pick up a free mini-guide or the cheap larger booklet – a worthwhile investment, given the exhibits' almost total lack of labelling, but still pretty thin.

Around the museum

Turn right out of the museum entrance and a five-minute walk leads to the **Nitobe Memorial Garden** (April–Oct daily 9am–5pm; call for winter hours; $6, joint ticket with Botanical Garden $12; Ⓦwww.nitobe.org), a small Japanese garden good for a few minutes of peace and quiet. It's considered to be one of the world's most authentic Japanese gardens outside of Japan (despite its use of many non-Japanese species), and is full of gently curving paths, trickling streams and waterfalls, as well as numerous rocks, trees and shrubs placed with Oriental precision. Cherry blossom season (April–May), or after a rare Vancouver snowfall, are particularly good times to visit.

Beyond the garden lies the greater seventy-acre area of the university's **Botanical Garden**, 16th Avenue and SW Marine Drive (Mon–Fri 9am–5pm, Sat & Sun 9.30am–5.30pm; $8; Ⓦwww.ubcbotanicalgarden.org), established in 1916, making it Canada's oldest such garden. Nongardeners will probably be interested only in the macabre poisonous plants of the Physick Garden, a recreated sixteenth-century monastic herb garden – though most plants here are actually medicinal rather than lethal – and the swaths of shrubs and huge trees in the Asian Garden. The BC Native Garden, the Alpine Garden and the Food Garden are all also worth a look.

North Vancouver

Perhaps the most compelling reason to visit **North Vancouver** (known as North Van) is the trip itself – preferably by SeaBus – which provides views of not only the Downtown skyline but also the teeming port area, a side of the city otherwise easily missed. Most of North Van itself is residential, as is neighbouring **West Vancouver**. You'll probably cross to the north shore less for these leafy suburbs than to sample the outstanding areas of natural beauty here: **Lynn Canyon**, **Grouse Mountain**, **Capilano Gorge** (the most popular excursion), **Mount Seymour** and **Lighthouse Park**. All are found in the mountains that rear up dramatically almost from the West Van waterfront, the proximity of Vancouver's residential areas to genuine wilderness being one of the city's most remarkable aspects. Your best bet if you wish to hike, and want the wildest scenery close to Downtown, is Mount Seymour.

Most of North Van is within a single bus ride of **Lonsdale Quay**, the north shore's SeaBus terminal. **Buses** to all points leave from two parallel bays immediately in front of you as you leave the boat; blue West Van buses are run by an independent company but accept TransLink tickets. If you've bought a ticket to come over on the SeaBus, remember you have ninety minutes of transfer time to ride buses from the time of purchase, which should be long enough to get you to most of the destinations below.

The **Lonsdale Quay Market**, 123 Carrie Cates Court (daily 9am–7pm; restaurants remain open later; Ⓦwww.lonsdalequay.com), to the right of the buses, is alone worth making the crossing for. While not as vibrant as Granville Island Market, it's still an appealing place, with great food stalls and takeaways, plus walkways looking out over the port, tugs and moored fishing boats.

Grouse Mountain

The trip to **Grouse Mountain** – named by hikers in 1894 who stumbled across a blue grouse – is a popular one. This is mainly due to the **cable cars** – North America's largest – which run from the 290-metre base station at 6400 Nancy Greene Way to the mountain's 1250-metre summit (daily 9am–10pm; $37.95; Ⓦwww.grousemountain.com). A favourite among people learning to **ski** or **snowboard** after work, the mountain's brightly illuminated slopes and dozen or so runs are a North Vancouver landmark on winter evenings. In summer, it's possible to walk up on the aptly named Grouse Grind Trail from the base station, but it's a tough and not terribly varied or scenically rewarding hike, so you'd do better to settle instead into the inevitable queue for the cable-car ticket office (get here early if you can).

After two stomach-churning lurches over the cables' twin towers you reach the summit, which, with its restaurants and tourist paraphernalia, is anything but wild. Yet the views are stunning, sometimes stretching as far as the San Juan Islands 160km away in Washington State. Have a quick look at the interpretive centre off to the right when you leave the cable car. A 3-D film is shown in the theatre downstairs (admission covered by your cable-car ticket). Of the two cafés, *Altitudes Bistro* has panoramic views, but fills up quickly. The smarter restaurant *The Observatory* (Ⓣ604/998-4403) serves dinner accompanied by a fine prospect of the sunset and city lights below; the cable-car ride is free with a restaurant booking. Ask at the interpretive centre, or small information desk just beyond the centre, about easy **guided walks**.

Walk up the paved paths away from the centre and you come to the scene of the "World Famous Lumberjack Show" (three daily; free), involving various crowd-pleasing sawing and wood-chopping displays. Other attractions nearby include a Wildlife Refuge and displays by birds of prey. Also here is the **Peak Chairlift** (also included in your ticket), which judders upwards for another eight minutes to the mountain's summit; views of the city and Fraser delta are even better. Check with the office at the lower cable-car base station for details of long **hikes** – many are down below rather than up at the summit proper. The best easy stroll is to **Blue Grouse Lake** (15min); the Goat Ridge Trail is for experienced hikers. More rugged paths lead into the mountains of the West Coast Range, but for these you'll need maps.

To get directly to the base station of the cable car from Lonsdale Quay, take the special #236 Grouse Mountain **bus** from Bay 8 to the left of the SeaBus terminal.

North Vancouver information

Vancouver's main visitor centre (see p.751) has plenty of **information** and accommodation listings for North Van, but you might also want to consult the area's own office, the North Vancouver Visitor Infocentre, 102–124 West 1st St, North Vancouver (Mon–Fri 9am–5pm; Ⓣ604/987-4488 or 980-5332, Ⓦwww.nvchamber.bc.ca).

You can also take a #246 Highland bus from Bay 7 and change to the #232 Grouse Mountain at Edgemount Village.

Lynn Canyon Park

Among the easiest targets for a quick taste of backwoods Vancouver is **Lynn Canyon Park** (year-round dawn to dusk; Ⓦwww.metrovancouver.org/services/parks), a quiet, forested area with a modest ravine and suspension bridge which, unlike the more popular Capilano Suspension Bridge (see below), you don't have to pay to cross. Several walks of up to ninety minutes take you through fine scenery – cliffs, rapids, waterfalls and over the eighty-metre-high bridge over Lynn Creek – all just twenty minutes from Lonsdale Quay. Take bus #228 from the quay to its penultimate stop at Peters Street, from where it's a ten-minute walk to the gorge; alternatively, take the less-frequent #229 Westlynn bus from Lonsdale Quay, which drops you about five minutes closer. Before entering the gorge, it's worth popping into the **Ecology Centre** (June–Sept daily 10am–5pm; rest of the year Mon–Fri 10am–5pm, Sat & Sun noon–4pm; suggested donation $2; Ⓦwww.dnv.org/ecology), 3663 Park Rd, off Peters Road, a friendly and informative place where you can pick up maps and pamphlets on park trails and wildlife.

Capilano River Regional Park

Lying just off the approach road to Grouse Mountain, **Capilano River Regional Park**'s most publicized and overrated attraction is – given the high admission – the inexplicably popular seventy-metre-high and 137-metre-long **suspension bridge** (the world's longest pedestrian suspension bridge) over the vertiginous Capilano Gorge (daily: Jan–Feb & Oct–Nov 9am–5pm, March–April & last three weeks of Sept 9am–6pm, May 9am–7pm, June to first week of Sept 8.30am–8pm, Dec 10am–9pm; admission May–Oct $28.95, reduced rates in winter except Dec; Ⓦwww.capbridge.com). The first bridge here was built in 1889, though the present structure dates from 1956. Although part of the park, the footbridge is privately run as a money-making venture.

Elsewhere in the park stick to the paths – and avoid the pedestrian toll, which buys you miscellaneous tours, forestry exhibits, trails and a visit to a native carving centre, which don't amount to much. More interesting is the **salmon hatchery** just upstream (daily: June–Aug 8am–8pm; May & Sept 8am–7pm; April & Oct 8am–4.45pm; Nov–March 8am–4pm; free; Ⓦwww-heb.pac.dfo-mpo.gc.ca), a federal operation designed to help salmon spawn and thus combat declining stocks. The building is well designed and the information plaques interesting, but it's a prime stop on city coach tours, so it can often be packed.

Capilano is probably best visited on the way back from Grouse Mountain: from the cable-car station it's an easy downhill **walk** (1km) to the north end of the park, below the Cleveland Reservoir, source of Vancouver's often disconcertingly brown drinking water. From there, marked trails – notably the **Capilano Pacific Trail** – follow the eastern side of the gorge to the hatchery (2km). The area below the hatchery is worth exploring, especially the Dog's Leg Pool (1km), which is along a swirling reach of the Capilano River, and if you really want to stretch your legs you could follow the river the full 7km to its mouth on the Burrard Inlet. Alternatively, you could ride the #236 Grouse Mountain bus to the Cleveland Dam or the main park entrance – the hatchery is quickly reached via a side road (or the Pipeline Trail) from the signed main entrance left off Nancy Greene Way. This comes not far after the busy roadside entrance to the Capilano Suspension Bridge (on the bus, ring the bell for the stop after the bridge).

Mount Seymour Provincial Park

At 8668 acres, **Mount Seymour Provincial Park** is the biggest of the North Vancouver parks, the most easterly and the one that comes closest to the flavour of high-mountain scenery. It's 16km north of Vancouver, with four major **trails** that are manageable in a day. The easiest hikes go out to Goldie Lake, a half-hour stroll, and to Dog Mountain, an hour from the parking area (one-way), with great views of the city below. Still better views, requiring more effort, can be had on the trails to First and Second Pump. The wildest and most demanding hike bypasses Mount Seymour's summit and runs by way of an intermittently marked trail to the forest- and mountain-circled Elsay Lake.

For **information** on the park, call ⓣ604/986-9371 or 986-2261 in winter for skiing and other seasonal information, visit ⓦwww.env.gov.bc.ca/bcparks, or ask at Vancouver's Downtown tourist information centre. To get here by **bus**, take the #239 from Lonsdale Quay to Phibbs Exchange and then the #215 to the Mount Seymour Parkway (1hr) – from there you'll then have to walk or cycle up the thirteen-kilometre road to the heart of the park. If you're driving, the road climbs to over 1000m and ends at a car park where boards spell out clearly the trails and mountaineering options available. Views are superb on good days, particularly from the popular **Vancouver Lookout** on the parkway approach road, where a map identifies the city landmarks below. There's also a café, toilets and a small information centre (summer only). In winter this is the most popular family and learners' **ski area** near Vancouver (ⓦwww.mountseymour.com).

Adjacent to the park to the northwest is the **Lower Seymour Conservation Reserve**, a 14,000-acre area of mostly temperate rainforest in the lower part of a glacier-carved valley. It's situated at the northern end of Lillooet Road and, if going by public transport, you need to take the #229 Lynn Valley bus to Dempsey Road and Lynn Valley Road. From here it's a ten-minute walk over Lynn Creek via the bridge on Rice Lake Road. You're far better off coming up here on a bike, for the 40km of trails in the area offer some of the best **mountain biking** close to Downtown. Or you can follow various sixty- and ninety-minute marked **hiking trails**.

Cypress Provincial Park

Cypress Provincial Park, most westerly of the big parks that part-cover the dramatic mountains and forest visible from Vancouver's Downtown, is among BC's most visited day-use park and probably the most popular of the north shore's protected areas. It takes its name from the huge old red and yellow cedars that proliferate here. Something of a hit with locals who prefer their wilderness just slightly tamed, its trails can be rugged and muddy, but they're always well marked, and even just a few minutes from the parking area you can feel in the depths of the great outdoors.

There are several good trails, including the three-kilometre **Yew Lake Trail** – wheelchair-accessible – and the main park trail, which climbs through forest and undergrowth, occasionally opening up to reveal views. The trail also shadows part of Cypress Creek, a torrent that has cut a deep and narrow canyon. For more **information**, ask at the Downtown tourist information centre or visit ⓦwww.env.gov.bc.ca/bcparks. To get here, take the #253 Caulfield/Park Royal **bus**. The park also has two closely linked **ski** and **snowboard** areas: the Alpine skiing area at Cypress Bowl (ⓦwww.cypressmountain.com) and the Nordic ski area at Hollyburn just to the southwest. Day passes cost $56.19.

Lighthouse Park

Lighthouse Park, (search for "Lighthouse" at ⓦwww.westvancouver.net) just southwest of Cypress Provincial Park, offers a seascape semi-wilderness at the extreme western tip of the north shore, 8km from the Lion's Gate Bridge. Smooth granite rocks and low cliffs line the shore, backed by huge Douglas firs up to 1500 years old, some of the best virgin forest in southern BC. The rocks make fine sun beds, though the water out here is colder than around the city beaches. A map at the car park shows the two trails to the 1912 Point Atkinson **lighthouse** itself – you can take one out and the other back, a return trip of about 5km which involves about two hours' walking. Although the park has its secluded corners (no camping allowed), it can be disconcertingly busy during summer weekends. The West Van #250 **bus** makes the journey all the way from Georgia Street in Downtown.

Eating and drinking

Vancouver's **restaurants** are some of Canada's finest. If you want to eat well, you'll be spoilt for choice – and won't have to spend a fortune. **Chinese** and **Japanese** cuisines have the highest profile (though the latter tend to be expensive), followed by **Italian**, **Greek** and other European imports. **Vietnamese** and **Thai** are more recent arrivals and can often provide the best starting points if you're on a tight budget. Specialist **seafood** restaurants are surprisingly thin on the ground, but those that exist are excellent and often remarkably cheap. **Vegetarians** are well served by a number of specialist places.

Countless **cafés** are found mainly around the beaches, in parks, along Downtown streets, and especially on Granville Island. The city also has a commendable assortment of **bars**, many a cut above the functional dives and sham pubs found elsewhere in BC.

The definitions of bar, café, restaurant and nightclub can be considerably blurred: food in some form – usually substantial – is available in most places, while daytime cafés and restaurants also operate happily as night-time bars.

Cafés, bakeries and diners

Little Italy, the area around Commercial Drive (between Venables Street and Broadway), is good for cheap, cheerful and trendy cafés, though as new waves of immigrants fill the area Little Italy is increasingly becoming "Little Vietnam" and "Little Nicaragua". The heavily residential **West End**, notably around Denman and Davie streets – Vancouver's "gay village" – is also booming, having gained a selection of interesting shops and restaurants.

Blake's 221 Carrall St, near Water. One of several cosy and relaxed places on this short Gastown stretch of Carrall St for a coffee, sandwich or snack; a good place to while away an hour writing a postcard or reading the newspaper.

Boulangerie la Parisienne 1076 Mainland St, at Helmcken. A Yaletown café and bakery with striking and very pretty all-blue interior that – true to its name – opens up French-style on to the pavement in summer.

Caffè Artigiano 763 Hornby St, at Robson ⓣ604/696-9222, ⓦwww.caffeartigiano.com. Across from the Vancouver Art Gallery, this café serves the best coffee in town. You can also choose from a full crop of croissants and other pastries, plus grilled sandwiches and light pasta dishes – though food quality is not on the level of the coffee. Other branches include those at 1101 West Pender St, at Thurlow, plus branches further afield at 740 West Hastings St and 2154 West 41st St.

Capers 1675 Robson St. Now merged with the Whole Foods empire, Capers is a three-branch chain of pristine supermarkets selling natural and organic foods, many of which can be bought as sandwiches and snacks in the on-site cafés. There are branches in West Vancouver (too far from Downtown to be useful to most casual visitors) and at 2285 West 4th Ave.

Flying Wedge 3499 Cambie St ⓣ604/874-8284, ⓦwww.flyingwedge.com. If you want pizza, this is the place; cheap, thin-crust pie by the slice (but no alcohol) at eight outlets, including Library Square, Cornwall Ave (for Kits beach) and just south of the Burrard St Bridge.

Gallery Café Vancouver Art Gallery, 750 Hornby St. Relaxed, stylish and pleasantly arty place at the heart of Downtown for coffee, good lunches and healthy, high-quality food (especially desserts); also has a popular summer patio.

Hamburger Mary's 1202 Davie St, between Bute and Jervis ⓣ604/687-1293, ⓦwww.hamburgermarys.ca. These may well be the best burgers in the city, though there are plenty of other things on the menu. Lots of people end the evening with a snack at this former West End diner. Outside tables are available when the weather is fine. Open very late (usually until 3am).

La Luna Café 117 Water St, between Cambie and Abbot. One of only a couple of places on Gastown's main street that has the character to raise it above the usual tourist-oriented cafés in this part of the city.

Sophie's Cosmic Café 2095 West 4th Ave at Arbutus ⓣ604/732-6810, ⓦwww.sophiescosmiccafe.com This excellent 1960s-style diner is a Kits institution and is packed out for weekend breakfasts and weekday lunch; it's renowned for its vast, spicy burgers, milkshakes, tasty desserts and whopping breakfasts.

Terra Breads Granville Island Public Market ⓣ604/685-3102, ⓦwww.terrabreads.com. Tremendous rustic, grainy and fresh-baked breads are the speciality here, with black olive, rosemary, focaccia, cheese, onion, rye, raisin, grape, pine nut and other variations also available. You can also pick up the odd accompaniment and sandwich to combine with a drink from elsewhere. Also has locations in Kitsilano and False Creek.

Restaurants

Restaurants are spread around the city but are thinner on the ground in North and West Vancouver. Places in Gastown are generally tourist-oriented, with some notable exceptions, in marked contrast to Chinatown's bewildering plethora of authentic and reasonably priced options. Downtown offers plenty of chains and huge choice, particularly with top-dollar places and fast food: the local *White Spot* chain has some thirty locations in Vancouver, offering good and glorified fast food – the branch at 1616 West Georgia St between Seymour and Granville streets is the most central Downtown outlet. Superior chains like *Earl's*, *Milestones* and the excellent *Cactus Club Café* and *Burgoo* are also highly commendable. The old warehouse district of **Yaletown**, part of Downtown's new southeasterly spread, is also a key – and still developing – eating and nightlife area. Similar places line 4th Avenue in Kitsilano and neighbouring West Broadway, though these require something of a special journey if you're based in or around Downtown: try them for lunch if you're at the beach or visiting the nearby Vanier Park museums.

Asian and Chinese

Gyoza King 1508 Robson St, near Nicola, Downtown ⓣ604/669-8278. Choose, tapas-style, from more than twenty types of Japanese *gyoza* – succulent fried dumplings with a variety of fillings (try the vegetable and spinach) with a soy dipping sauce. Or go for noodle and robust *o-den* soups and *katsu-don* (breaded pork chop with rice). All very pleasing when chased down with one of many choices of beer. Main courses from $9–20. Open Mon–Thurs 5.30pm–1am, Fri 5.30pm–1.30am, Sat 6pm–1.30am, Sun 6–11.30pm.

Hapa Izakaya 1479 Robson St, near Broughton ⓣ604/689-4272, ⓦwww.hapaizakaya.com. Small, individual dishes and low prices are the lure, along with a boistrous, busy and entertaining atmosphere. There are sushi-like raw fish options (try the fresh tuna with chopped spring onions and garlic bread), as well as tasty hotpots and other meat dishes. Mains cost from about $8–12, and the opening times mean you can eat and drink (sake, martinis, wine) long and late. Open Sun–Thurs 5.30pm–midnight, Fri & Sat 5.30pm–1am. Second location in Kitsilano.

Hon's Wun-Tun House 108-268 Keefer St, at Gore ⓣ604/688-0871. Started life as a cheap, basic and popular place known for the house specialities, "potstickers" – fried meat-filled dumplings – and ninety-odd soups (including fish ball and pig's feet). Success has spawned other branches and a slight smartening-up, but the good food and low prices (mains from around $6–11) are mercifully unchanged. No alcohol or credit cards. Daily 11am–11pm.

Kirin Mandarin 1166 Alberni St, near Bute ⓣ604/682-8833, ⓦwww.kirinrestaurant.com.

Among the first of the city's smart Chinese arrivals with an elegant decor that's a world away from old-fashioned Chinatown. The superior food is relatively costly, with mains from $15, but you're repaid with great views of the mountains. Daily 11am–2.30pm, 5–10.30pm. Other locatiions include West Van.

Phnom-Penh 244 East Georgia St, near Gore ⓣ604/682-5777. Excellent, cheap Vietnamese and Cambodian cuisine, especially seafood, in a friendly, family-oriented restaurant. Most dishes cost around $5–10. Daily 10am–10pm.

Pho Hoang 238 East Georgia St, near Gore ⓣ604/682-5666; also at 3610 Main at 20th ⓣ604/874-0810. One of the many Vietnamese *pho* (beef soup) restaurants now springing up all over the city. Choose from thirty soup varieties with herbs, chillis and lime at plate-side as added seasoning. Open for breakfast, lunch and dinner. Daily 11am–10pm.

Pink Pearl 1132 East Hastings St, near Glen ⓣ604/253-4316, ⓦwww.pinkpearl.com. Big, bustling and old-fashioned with a highly authentic feel but in a dingy part of town. The moderately priced food (mains from $12–25, dim sum from about $4–7) has a Cantonese slant, strong on seafood and great for dim sum. It frequently emerges as the city's top Chinese restaurant in dining polls. Mon–Thurs, Sun 9am–10pm, Fri–Sat 9am–11pm.

Simply Thai 1211 Hamilton St, at Davie ⓣ604/642-0123, ⓦwww.simplythairestaurant.com. This plain, modern but inviting Yaletown restaurant is packed at lunch (11.30am–3pm) and dinner, thanks to the keen prices (mains from $8) and good, authentic food – the chefs are all from Bangkok.

Sun Sui Wah 3888 Main St ⓣ604/872-8822, ⓦwww.sunsuiwah.com. This sophisticated restaurant has won deserved rave reviews from critics and locals alike, especially for its seafood, with numerous regular dishes and special catches of the day (pick from the tank or order from the menu if you are squeamish). Main dishes start at around $12, but prices for the more exotic offerings can be three or four times that. Dim sum is available (also with a seafood emphasis), as are meat and vegetarian options. Open daily for lunch 10am–3pm and dinner 5–10.30pm.

Fish and seafood

Blue Water Café 1095 Hamilton St, at Helmcken ⓣ604/688-8078, ⓦwww.bluewatercafe.net. This big restaurant has quickly become one of Yaletown's most popular fixtures, thanks to the sushi, fish and seafood, and to the attractive terrace and interior. There's an open kitchen for the fish and seafood staples, with mains around $25 (great halibut dishes, BC sablefish or salmon with pumpkin seed gnocchi), plus Eastern and Western bars (for sushi, ceviche or caviar), and an Ice Bar, where you can indulge in chilled vodkas and freshly squeezed fruit juices. Service is amiable and unstuffy and the quality is excellent. Daily 5am–midnight.

C Restaurant 2-1600 Howe St, near Pacific Blvd ⓣ604/681-1164, ⓦwww.crestaurant.com. The lengthy menu here, which contains Southeast Asian influences, might include a choice from the "raw bar" – say a trio of scallop, wasabi salmon and smoked chilli tuna – and unusual fish such as Alaskan arctic char. Views from the dining room are splendid. Bank on around $30 for main courses. Mon–Fri 11.30am–2.30pm & 5.30–11pm, Sat 5.30–11pm, Sun 11am–2pm & 5.30–11pm.

Joe Fortes Seafood and Chop House 777 Thurlow St, near Robson ⓣ604/669-1940, ⓦwww.joefortes.ca. This long-established oyster bar-cum-chophouse and seafood restaurant is a city institution, noted as a hip place for high-spirited singles, Robson Street shoppers, visitors and workers, partly seduced by the great bar (drinks and oysters) upstairs on the year-round heated roof garden and terrace. The restaurant plays it straight food-wise: fish and seafood presented simply and without contemporary frills – and in generous portions. Mains cost from $20. The atmosphere is lively and casual, the saloon-style decor heavy on the mahogany and stained glass. Open daily 11am–11pm.

Rodney's Oyster House 1228 Hamilton St ⓣ604/609-0080. Not one of the most up-front Yaletown locations – it's tucked away in a relatively quiet dead-end street – but if you're after oysters, this fishing-shack lookalike is the place. Expect anything up to eighteen varieties, from locally harvested bivalves to exotic Japanese *kumamotos*, all laid out on ice, and priced from about $1.50 to $3.50 each. More substantial main courses cost from $15–20. Open Mon–Sat 11am–11pm, Sun 3–10pm.

French

Cioppino's Mediterranean Grill 1133 and 1129 Hamilton St ⓣ604/688-7466, ⓦwww.cioppinosyaletown.com. It's hard to categorize this inviting Yaletown restaurant with warm, cherrywood interior – the name comes from San Francisco's *cioppino* fish stew, but some food is French-influenced, other Italian. It's an attractive and convenient place if you are in this part of town. If the food seems too expensive (main courses cost from about $23–45), head for the *Cioppino* wine bar next door for a drink. Mon-Fri noon–2.30pm & 5.30–11pm, Sat 5.30–11pm.

Le Crocodile 100-909 Burrard St, entrance on Smithe ⓣ604/669-4298, ⓦwww.lecrocodilerestaurant.com. Plush French-Alsace upmarket bistro that pushes *Bishop's* (see p.779) close for the title of the city's best restaurant and, unlike its rival, it's located Downtown. The menu has something for traditionalists and the more adventurous alike. A memorable meal is guaranteed, but at a price, with main courses ranging from $20 to $40. Mon–Sat 11.30am–2pm, 5.30–10pm.

Le Gavroche 1616 Alberni St, at Cardero ⓣ604/685-3924, ⓦwww.legavroche.ca. The similarly priced *Le Crocodile* may just take the culinary plaudits, but this other top French restaurant (with a West Coast twist) is not far behind. A formal but amiable place and rated as one of the most romantic spots in the city. Daily from 5.30pm.

Lumière 2551 West Broadway, near Trafalgar, Kitsilano ⓣ604/739-8185, ⓦwww.lumiere.ca. Local food critics regularly name this Vancouver's best restaurant. Cooking is "contemporary French", and a touch lighter than *Le Crocodile*, though prices are equally elevated. Visitors based in Downtown will need to take a cab here; you'll also need to book, for the simple, tasteful dining room accommodates just fifty people. Wed–Sun 5.30–11pm.

Greek

Ouzeri 3189 West Broadway, at Trutch, Kitsilano ⓣ604/739-9995, ⓦwww.ouzeri.ca. A friendly and fairly priced restaurant (mains from $10) that is the first port of call if you're at the hostel or beach in Kitsilano. Tues–Sat 11.30am–3.30pm, Mon & Sun 4.30–10pm.

Stepho's 1124 Davie St, between Thurlow and Bute ⓣ604/683-2555. This West End restaurant has simple interior, fine food, efficient service and is very popular, thanks in part to the fair prices, with mains from $5 to 10. Daily 11am–11.30pm.

Indian

Akbar's Own 1905 West Broadway at Fir St, ⓣ604/736-8180. Not as fancy as Vij's, (see below), but a good, no-nonsense restaurant on a quiet stretch of Broadway in Kitsilano. Traditional Mughlai and Kashmiri specialities include shrimp *pakora* ($8) delicately fried in chickpea flour, and chicken tikka butter marsala ($11). Mon–Fri 11.30am–2pm, Mon–Sat 5–10pm.

Vij's 1480 West 11th Ave, near Granville ⓣ604/736-6664, ⓦwww.vijs.ca. The Indian cooking here has won just about every award going in Vancouver for Best Ethnic Cuisine. The menus change regularly and always include some excellent vegetarian options. Main courses cost from $15 to 25. The only problem is that you can't book. Daily 5.30–10pm.

Italian

Cibo Trattoria *Moda Hotel* 900 Seymour St ⓣ604/602-9570, ⓦwww.cibotrattoria.com. By far one of the best new restaurants in the city, thanks to the cooking of British chef Neil Taylor (ex-River Café in London). The elegant setting belies the down-to-earth food, with mains from $18. Open Mon–Sat from 5pm.

CinCin 1154 Robson St, between Thurlow and Bute ⓣ604/688-7338, ⓦwww.cincin.net. An excellent Downtown option, with stylish, buzzy setting; try to book an outside table in summer. The food merits the prices (mains from $16) and includes top-grade home-made pastas and desserts. The wine list is one of the best in the city. Mon–Fri 11am–11pm, Sat 9am–10.30pm.

Il Giardino 1382 Hornby St, at Pacific ⓣ604/669-2422, ⓦwww.umberto.com. Sublime and expensive food (mains from $15 to 35) with a bias towards pasta and game served to a trendy and casually smart thirtysomething clientele. Weekend reservations are essential, especially for the nice vine-trailed terrace. Mon–Fri 11.30am–3pm, 6–11.30pm, Sat 6.30–11pm.

Incendio 103 Columbia St, near Alexander, Gastown ⓣ604/ 688-8694, ⓦwww.incendio.ca. This pizzeria is in a heritage building a block east of Maple Tree Square, making it hidden enough to escape the attention of the crowds rampaging through central Gastown. It features excellent wood-fired thin-crust pizzas (over twenty varieties), calzone, good salads and a range of well-made and inventive pastas such as fettucine with capers and a tomato and lime-butter sauce. Pizzas and main courses start at around $9. A second branch has opened in Kits at 2118 Burrard St (ⓣ604/736-2220). Open Mon–Thurs 11.30am–3pm & 5–10pm, Fri 11.30am–3pm & 5–11pm, Sat 5–11pm, Sun 4.30–10pm.

Mexican

Bin 941 941 Davie St ⓣ604/683-1246, ⓦwww.bin941.com. Bin 942 at 1521 West Broadway ⓣ604/734-9421. No one seems to have a bad word for *Bin 941*. Both outlets are tiny, on the slightly crazy side of funky, and packed long and late with people drawn by the up-tempo bars and some of the city's best – and best-value – bite-size food. The menu's "tapatizers" include great fries ($4 for a mountain of hand-cut Yukon Gold potato fries), jumbo scallops, tiger-prawn tournedos, crabcakes, charred bok choy and many more. Open for dinner daily until 2am.

Lolita's South of the Border Cantina 1326 Davie St, near Jervis ⓣ604/696-9996, ⓦwww.lolitasrestaurant.com. One glance from outside at the boldly-coloured dining room here gives you a pretty good idea of what to expect inside: a rather self-conscious but fun, funky and friendly neighbourhood café-restaurant that requires no dressing up, offers filling and unfancy Mexican (and other) food and prices (from $7) that aren't going to hurt your pocket. That said, it's stranded in a residential part of town, and you're unlikely to be passing by unless you're travelling the length of Davie St. If you are nearby, it's a good place for a snack, light meal or invigorating late-night beer or tequila cocktail. Open Mon–Thurs 4.30pm–2am, Fri–Sun 3pm–2am.

Vegetarian

The Naam 2724 West 4th Ave, near Stephens, Kitsilano ⓣ604/738-7151, ⓦwww.thenaam.com. The oldest and most popular health-food and vegetarian restaurant in the city. Comfortable and friendly ambience with live folk and other music and outside eating some evenings. Choose right, and you can fill up here from as little as $5. Open 24hr.

West Coast

Bishop's 2183 West 4th Ave, near Yew, Kitsilano ⓣ604/738-2025, ⓦwww.bishopsonline.com. Consistently ranked one of Vancouver's best restaurants, though it's some way from Downtown. Although there's a frequent film-star and VIP presence, the welcome is as warm for everyone. The light and refined "contemporary home cooking" – Italy meets the Pacific Rim – commands high prices (mains start at around $30) but is worth it. First choice for the big, one-off splurge, but booking is essential. Mon–Sat 5.30–11pm, Sun 5.30–10pm.

Bridges 1696 Duranleau St, Granville Island ⓣ604/687-4400, ⓦwww.bridgesrestaurant.com. Unmissable big, yellow restaurant upstairs, pub and informal bistro (the best option) downstairs, with a large outdoor deck and decent prices (mains from about $13). A reliable and very popular choice for a drink or meal on Granville Island. Bistro daily 11am-11pm, restaurant daily 5.30–10pm.

Earl's 1185 Robson St, near Bute ⓣ604/669-0020. Come here first if you don't want to mess around scouring Downtown for somewhere to eat. The mid-priced, and often innovative, high-quality food (main courses range from around $10–20) is served in a big, open and casual dining area, with outside terrace in the summer. Daily 11.30am–1am.

Glowbal Grill & Satay Bar 1079 Mainland St, near Helmcken ⓣ604/602-0835, ⓦwww.glowbalgrill.com. This is the perfect place to catch up on the hip, buzzy dining typical of Vancouver, and of Yaletown in particular – not to mention the classic fusion of Asian and West Coast cuisines that characterizes so much of the city's cooking. The simple, clean-lined Modernist-inspired dining room is divided between a long raised bar and semi-isolated tables with banquettes below. Mains from $18; or enjoy smaller, lighter meals in the *AFTERglow* lounge, with suitably funky music and inventive cocktails. Daily 11.30am–1am.

Milestone's 1145 Robson St between Bute and Thurlow ⓣ604/682-4477, ⓦwww.milestonesrestaurants.com; also at 1210 Denman St ⓣ604/662-3431, 1109 Hamilton St at Helmcken ⓣ604/684-9112, and 2966 West 4th Ave in Kits. Popular mid-market chain with cheap drinks and food (especially good breakfasts) in very generous portions and reasonable prices (a pasta main dish costs around $15). The Denman St location is more laidback, while the Yaletown site is popular, with an outdoor terrace. Mon–Fri 10.30am–10.30pm, Sat & Sun 9.30am–midnight.

Nu 1661 Granville St, near Granville Island ⓣ604/646-4668, ⓦwww.whatisnu.com. Not "new", as the name might suggest, but from the French for "naked". Easy-to-eat finger food and classic West Coast meat and fish staples from around $20 for a main course. The dining room has a vaguely nautical, cruise-ship theme, appropriately enough, given its location on the north shore of False Creek. Open Mon–Fri 11am–1am, Sat 10.30am–1am, Sun 10.30am–midnight.

Raincity Grill 1193 Denman St, at Morton ⓣ604/685-7337, ⓦwww.raincitygrill.com. The candles and a position in the West End overlooking English Bay make for a romantic dining experience, but it is the food and wine, both of which make the most of BC and Pacific Northwest ingredients (more than one hundred varieties of Northwest and Californian wines by the glass are available), which are the chief attraction here. Mains from about $20. Mon–Fri 5–10pm, Sat & Sun 10.30am–2pm & 5–10pm.

Water Street Café 300 Water St, at Cambie ⓣ604/689-2832. The café-restaurant of choice if you wind up in Gastown (located close to the famous steam clock). An airy and casual atmosphere that offers a short but well-chosen menu and decent prices – a pasta main course will cost around $13; consider booking an outside table if you're going to be here for lunch.

West 2881 Granville St, near West 13th ⓣ604/738-8938, ⓦwww.westrestaurant.com. Year after year, *West* challenges *Bishop's* and *Lumière* for the title of Vancouver's best restaurant. The restaurant's credo – "True to our region, true to the seasons" – is a shorthand way of saying what most of the city's West Coast and many other restaurants are saying: that the emphasis is on exceptional, locally sourced ingredients, and a menu that changes according to what is seasonally available. Main courses cost from $30, but high prices bring consistently high-quality food, with menus changing three or four times a week. Mon–Fri 11.30am–11pm, Sat & Sun 5.30–11pm.

Pubs and bars

AFTERglow 1082 Hamilton St, near Helmcken ⓣ604/642-0577. The very mellow bar attached to the *Glowbal Grill* (see p.779), with its candlelight, intimate seating and easy listening grooves, is a good place for a pre- or post-dinner drink – or for a night's drinking without pause for food.

Alibi Room 157 Alexander St, between Columbia and Main ⓣ604/623-3383, ⓦwww.alibi.ca. Unashamedly hip bar-restaurant and a crowd that is trendy, but not so trendy that it spoils what is a good place for drinks and – perhaps – dinner. Excellent and eclectic food is served upstairs, with a short, modern menu at surprisingly reasonable prices; downstairs you can drink and venture onto the small dancefloor.

Backstage Lounge Arts Club Theatre Company, 1585 Johnston St, Granville Island ⓣ604/687-1354, ⓦwww.thebackstagelounge.com. Part of the theatre complex, this place has a waterfront view, easygoing atmosphere, decent food and puts on blues, jazz and other live music Fri and Sat evenings.

Bar None 1222 Hamilton St ⓣ604/689-7000, ⓦwww.dhmbars.ca. Busy, reasonably smart and hip New York-style Yaletown bar and club where you can eat, drink, watch TV, smoke cigars (walk-in humidor), play backgammon or shoot pool and listen to live music.

Bin 941 941 Davie St, between Burrard and Hornby ⓣ604/683-1246, ⓦwwwbin941.com. This is a great place to eat (see p.778), but vast numbers of people come here (be prepared to wait in line – there are no reservations) primarily to drink, attracted by the place's high energy and cramped good vibes.

Bridges 1696 Duranleau St, Granville Island ⓣ604/687-4400. You can eat here (see p.779), but when the sun's shining it's a close-run thing between the busy patio here and the *Dockside Brewing Company* as to which is the nicest place to have a waterside drink on Granville Island: *Bridges* is more central and thus more convenient.

The Cambie 300 Cambie St ⓣ604/684-6466. An obvious place to drink if you're staying at the linked hostel (see p.758), but the roomy (but invariably crowded) outdoor area and cheap pitchers of beer bring in a fair number of locals and other passing trade. Inside, it's all pool tables and down-to-earth drinking.

Dockside Brewing Company *Granville Island Hotel*, 1253 Johnston St, Granville Island ⓣ604/685-7070, ⓦwww.docksidebrewing.com. Beer buffs may want to try this stylish lounge to sample some of the establishment's on-site micro-brewery's ales. The atmosphere is relaxed and the generally well-heeled crowd thirtysomething. Things tend to be livelier early in the evening, and in summer there's a fine outdoor patio.

George 1137 Hamilton St, at Helmcken ⓣ604/628-5555, ⓦwww.georgelounge.com. If you want a smart, urban bar, this is a good bet, a place that appeals to a young, beautiful set, with easy-on-the-palate cocktails, well-priced wines by the glass, just-right subdued lighting and a choice between sitting at the long bar or on the sofas of the lounge.

Gerard Lounge *Sutton Place Hotel*, 845 Burrard St, at Robson ⓣ604/682-5511. The smooth, wood-panelled lounge and piano bar with leather chairs and tapestries all make this a very elegant Downtown drinking spot. Also, it's the place to see the stars currently filming in town.

The Irish Heather 210 Carrall St, near Water ⓣ604/688-9779, ⓦwww.irishheather.com. A definite cut above the usual mock-Irish pub, with an intimate bar, live Irish music some nights, excellent food, good Guinness (apparently it sells the second largest number of pints of the stuff in Canada); and an unexpectedly pretty outdoor area in the back.

La Bodega 1277 Howe St, near Drake ⓣ604/684-8815, ⓦwww.labodegavancouver.com. One of the city's best and most popular places, with tapas and excellent main courses, but chiefly dedicated to lively drinking. It's packed later on, so try to arrive before 8pm. Closed Sun.

Sylvia Hotel 1154 Gilford St, at Beach ⓣ604/688-8865. This nondescript but easy-going hotel (see p.758) bar is popular for quiet drinks and superlative waterfront views, and is a pleasant place to stop in after a stroll on English Bay Beach.

Yaletown Brewing Company 1111 Mainland St ⓣ604/681-2739, ⓦwww.drinkfreshbeer.com. An extremely large and unmissable bar and restaurant with their own six-beer on-site brewery. Very popular, and leading the way in the funky Yaletown revival.

Nightlife and entertainment

Vancouver gives you plenty to do come sunset, laying on a varied and cosmopolitan blend of **live music**. **Clubs** are more adventurous than in many other Canadian cities, particularly those on and around Main Street and Commercial Drive, in the city's eastern half. Summer nightlife often takes to the streets, with outdoor bars and (to a certain extent) beaches becoming venues in their own right. The city also hosts a range of **festivals**, from jazz to theatre, and the **performing arts** are as widely available as you'd expect in a city as culturally dynamic as Vancouver.

Vancouver is also a welcoming city for **gays and lesbians**. Davie Village, which runs from Burrard Street along Davie Street to Denman Strett, is where the highest concentration of long-established gay clubs, pubs and stores are, while there's more of a lesbian scene on **Commercial Drive** ("The Drive"). For information on gay and lesbian **events**, check ⓦwww.xtra.ca. The main draw in Vancouver's gay calendar is **Pride** (ⓣ604/687-0955 or 737-7433, ⓦwww.vancouverpride.ca), which usually takes place over three days during the first long weekend in August.

Comprehensive **listings** appear in the *Georgia Straight* (ⓦwww.straight.com), a free weekly published on Thursday and available across the city.

Half-price and last-minute same-day **tickets** are available via "Tickets Tonight" (ⓦwww.ticketstonight.ca) at participating venues, or through the outlet at the main visitor centre at 200 Burrard St (see p.751).

Live music and clubs

Capone's 1141 Hamilton St ⓣ604/684-7900, ⓦwww.caponesrestaurant.net. This Yaletown restaurant has live jazz seven nights a week, mostly performed by local talent.

Cellar Restaurant & Jazz Club 3611 West Broadway, Kitsilano ⓣ604/738-1959, ⓦwww.cellarjazz.com. A seventy-seat red-walled basement with black booths and low tables offering some of the best live jazz in the city four or more nights a week (generally Wed–Sat). Join the enthusiastic crowd for top local outfits or big international names.

Commodore Ballroom 868 Granville St at Smithe St ⓣ604/681-7838, ⓦwww.livenation.com. The *Commodore* is the city's best midsized venue. There is an adventurous music policy and both local and national DJs frequently spin.

Fabric 66 Water St, at Abbott ⓣ604/683-6695, ⓦwww.fabricvancouver.com. Central Vancouver's best-known music venue, with live bands nightly. The mid-Gastown location attracts a varied clientele – it's also known as a pick-up spot. There's bar food and a piano lounge until 9pm, when the band strikes up.

Pub 340 340 Cambie St, at West Hastings ⓣ604/602-0644. A 110-person capacity venue that never pretends to be other than what it is: a no-nonsense pub, with cheap beer and food, and live music nightly from loud and enthusiastic rock, punk, electronic and hardcore metal bands.

Railway Club 579 Dunsmuir St, at Seymour ⓣ604/681-1625, ⓦwww.therailwayclub.com. Long-established favourite with excellent bookings, wide range of music (folk, blues, jazz) and a casual atmosphere. Has a separate "conversation" lounge, so it's ideal for a drink (and weekday lunches). Arrive before 10pm at weekends – the place is tiny.

Roxy 932 Granville St, at Nelson ⓣ604/684-7699, ⓦwww.roxyvan.com. Nightly live bands with emphasis on retro 1950s to 1970s music. Casual and fun place for college crowd and people in from the burbs.

Shine 364 Water St ⓣ604/408-4321, ⓦwww.shinenightclub.com. Conveniently located and happening Gastown club which attracts some of the city's top DJs. Understated decor, with comfortable retro 1960s couches and all-white colour scheme provide a sophisticated setting for house, reggae, soul, R&B, hip-hop and other sounds. Dress up a bit.

The Yale 1300 Granville St, at Drake ⓣ604/681-9253, ⓦwww.theyale.ca. The top place in the city to hear hardcore blues and R&B. Relaxed air, big dancefloor and occasional outstanding international names. Often jam sessions with up to fifty players, on Sat (3–8pm) and Sun (3pm–midnight). Closed Mon & Tues.

Gay and lesbian

Celebrities 1022 Davie St, near Burrard ⓣ604/681-6180, ⓦwww.celebritiesnightclub.com. High-profile and showcase club, with Davie St's largest dancefloor, the latest lighting and sound systems and a roster of the city's top DJs. Also numerous theme and one-off nights, plus excellent entertainers.

Club 23 West 23 West Cordova St ⓣ604/662-3277, ⓦwww.club23.ca. A cool, dark split-level club, perfect for the various theme nights held here, such as "Sin City" fetish nights.

Fountainhead Pub 1025 Davie ⓣ604/687-2222, ⓦwww.thefountainheadpub.com. A popular and pleasantly buzzing place at the heart of Davie Village for good food, drink and a large, heated patio from which to spy on all the street action. Tends to attract a slightly older, more mellow crowd.

Numbers 1042 Davie St, at Burrard ⓣ604/685-4077, ⓦwww.numbers.ca. This is a cruisy multilevel venue that has been in business for over twenty years, with a gay disco, kitsch mirrored dancefloor, movies and pool tables. Tends to attract a slightly more mature crowd.

Odyssey 1251 Howe St, near Davie ⓣ604/689-5256, ⓦwww.theodysseynightclub.com. A young gay and bisexual club with house and techno disco and theme shows on most nights. Expect to queue on Fri & Sat.

Pump Jack Pub 1167 Davie ⓣ604/685-3417, ⓦwww.pumpjackpub.com. A spacious spot and Vancouver's leather bar of choice. Arrive early to guarantee a cruisey window-side bar. There are pool tables and uniform nights. Expect queues at the weekends.

Performing arts

The main focus for the city's performing arts is the **Queen Elizabeth Theatre** (ⓣ604/299-9000, ⓦwww.city.vancouver.bc.ca/theatres), 600 Hamilton St at Dunsmuir Street, which plays host to visiting theatre, opera and dance troupes and even the occasional big rock band, along with the **Centre in Vancouver for the Performing Arts** (ⓣ604/602-0616, ⓦwww.centreinvancouver.com), opposite the central library at 777 Homer St. The refurbished **Orpheum Theatre** (ⓣ604/665-3050, ⓦwww.city.vancouver.bc.ca/theatres), 884 Granville St at Smithe Street, is Vancouver's oldest theatre and headquarters of the Vancouver Symphony Orchestra.

Classical music

Music-in-the-Morning PO Box 95024, Kingsgate ⓣ604/873-4612, ⓦwww.musicinthemorning.org. This began modestly in someone's front room 25 years ago; it has now grown past its morning moniker, organizing innovative and respected concerts of old and new music with local and visiting musicians at various times of the day.

Vancouver Chamber Choir ⓣ604/738-6822, ⓦwww.vancouverchamberchoir.com. One of two

Festivals

Among Vancouver's major festivals are the annual **International Jazz Festival** (late June to early July), organized by the Coastal Jazz and Blues Society (ⓣ604/872-5200, ⓦwww.coastaljazz.ca); **Vancouver International Folk Music Festival** (ⓣ604/602-9798 or 1-800/985-8363, ⓦwww.thefestival.bc.ca); and the July **Sea Festival** (ⓣ604/684-3378) – nautical fun, parades and excellent fireworks around English Bay.

The chief arts event is the **Fringe Festival** (ⓣ604/257-0350, ⓦwww.vancouverfringe.com), modelled on the Edinburgh equivalent. There's also an annual **Bard on the Beach Shakespeare Festival** (ⓣ604/739-0559, ⓦwww.bardonthebeach.org; June–Aug) in Vanier Park and an **International Comedy Festival** (ⓣ604/683-0883, ⓦwww.comedyfest.com) in early August on Granville Island. Many of the city's arthouse cinemas join forces to host the **Vancouver International Film Festival** (ⓣ604/685-0260, ⓦwww.viff.org), an annual showcase for more than 150 films running from late September to mid-October.

professional, internationally renowned choirs in the city. They perform at the Orpheum and on some Sunday afternoons at the *Hotel Vancouver*.

Vancouver Opera 500-845 Cambie St ⓣ604/638-0222, ⓦwww.vancouveropera.ca. Four operas are produced annually at the Queen Elizabeth Theatre and productions currently enjoy an excellent reputation.

Vancouver Recital Society 304-873 Beatty St ⓣ604/736-0363, ⓦwww.vanrecital.com. Hosts two of the best and most popular cycles in the city: the summer Chamber Music Festival (at St George's School) and the main Vancouver Playhouse recitals (Sept–April). Catches up-and-coming performers plus a few major international names each year.

Vancouver Symphony Orchestra 601 Smithe St ⓣ604/876-3434, ⓦwww.vancouversymphony.ca. Presents most concerts at the Orpheum or Chan Shun Hall on Crescent Rd off NW Marine Drive, but also sometimes gives free recitals in the summer at beaches and parks, culminating in a concert on the summit of Whistler Mountain.

Theatre and cinema

Arts Club Theatre Main box office at 1585 Johnston St, Granville Island ⓣ604/687-1644, ⓦwww.artsclub.com. A leading light in the city's drama scene, performing at three venues: the Stanley Industrial Alliance Stage, 2750 Granville St at 12th, is the company's main venue and runs larger musicals, 20th-century classics and acclaimed productions from around the world; the Granville Island stage offers mainstream drama, comedies and musicals; the next-door bar shows small-scale revues and cabarets.

Theatre Under the Stars (TUTS) Malkin Bowl, Stanley Park ⓣ604/687-0174 or 257-0366, ⓦwww.tuts.ca. Summer productions here are fun and lightweight, but can suffer from being staged in one of Canada's rainiest cities.

Vancouver Playhouse Theatre Company Hamilton St, at Dunsmuir ⓣ604/665-3050, ⓦwww.vancouverplayhouse.com. One of western Canada's biggest companies. It usually presents six top-quality shows with some of the region's premier performers and designers during its Oct–May season.

Cinemark Tinseltown 88 Pender St, at Abbott ⓣ604/806-0799, ⓦwww.cinemark.com. Just two blocks south of the heart of Gastown, this multi-screen in the International Village complex is the most modern of the city centre's first-run cinemas, with big screens, underground parking and good seating.

Empire Granville 7 855 Granville St, between Robson and Smithe ⓣ604/684-4000, ⓦwww.empiretheatres.com. Once there were a dozen or so cinemas on this strip: this is now the last one, a multiplex, and an obvious Downtown choice to catch a big-budget first-run movie.

Pacific Cinémathèque 1131 Howe St, near Helmcken ⓣ604/688-3456, ⓦwww.cinematheque.bc.ca. Shows a good range of arthouse, overseas and experimental films; the best non-mainstream cinema in the city. The programmes can be hit or miss, but any film buff will find something to tempt.

Dance

Anna Wyman School of Dance Arts 707-207 West Hastings St ⓣ604/685-5699, ⓦwww.annawyman.com. This school specializes in contemporary dance and puts on four major performances each school year, involving all students, at the Centennial Theatre in North Vancouver. The school also performs several shows each year around the lower mainland, as well as free outdoor performances at Granville Island and at Robson Square near the Art Gallery.

Ballet British Columbia Sixth Floor, 677 Davie St ⓣ604/732-5003, ⓦwww.balletbc.com. The province's top company performs – along with visiting companies – at the Queen Elizabeth Theatre.

Scotiabank Dance Centre 677 Davie St ⓣ604/606-6400, ⓦwww.thedancecentre.ca. Also known as the Vancouver Dance Centre, this is a major source of information on dance in Vancouver and beyond, and provides studio and rehearsal space for around thirty companies; it's open to the public for workshops, classes, exhibitions and other events. Contact it for details of the major Dancing on the Edge Festival (ⓦwww.dancingontheedge.org).

Listings

Bike rental Bayshore Bicycles & Rollerblade Rentals, 745 Denman St (ⓣ604/688-2453, ⓦwww.bayshorebikerentals.ca); Spokes, 1798 West Georgia St, at Denman (ⓣ604/688-5141, ⓦwww.vancouverbikerental.com).

Buses Airporter (ⓣ604/946-8866 or 1-800/668-3141, ⓦwww.yvrairporter.com) for shuttle from Vancouver Airport to bus depot and Downtown; BC Transit for city buses, SeaBus and SkyTrain (ⓣ604/953-3333, ⓦwww.translink.bc.ca);

Greyhound (ⓣ604/662-3222, 482-8747 or 1-800/661-8747, ⓦwww.greyhound.ca) for BC, Alberta, Yukon and long-haul destinations including Seattle and the US; Malaspina Coach Lines (ⓣ1-877/227-8287, ⓦwww.malaspinacoach.com) for the Sunshine Coast, Powell River, Whistler, Pemberton and Nanaimo; Pacific Coach Lines (ⓣ604/662-8074 or 1-800/661-1725, ⓦwww.pacificcoach.com) for Victoria; Perimeter (ⓣ604/266-5386 or 717-6600, ⓦwww.perimeterbus.com) for services between Whistler and Vancouver Airport; Quick Shuttle (ⓣ604/940-4428 or 1-800/665-2122, ⓦwww.quickcoach.com) for Bellingham Airport, Downtown Seattle and Sea-Tac Airport.

Car rental Alamo, 1185 West Georgia St (ⓣ604/684-1401, ⓦwww.alamo.ca); Avis, 757 Hornby St (ⓣ604/606-2869, ⓦwww.avis.ca); Budget, 416 West Georgia St (ⓣ604/668-7000 or 1-800/268-8900 in Canada, 1-800/527-0700 in US, ⓦwww.bc.budget.com); Hertz, 1270 Granville St (ⓣ604/606-4711 or 1-800/263-0600, ⓦwww.hertz.com); Lo-Cost, 1835 Marine Drive (ⓣ604/986-1266 or 1-800/986-1260, ⓦwww.locostrental.com).

Consulates Australia: Suite 2050, 1075 West Georgia St ⓣ604/684-1177; Germany: Suite 704, World Trade Centre, 999 Canada Place ⓣ604/684-8377; New Zealand: Suite 1200, 888 Dunsmuir St ⓣ604/684-7388; Republic of Ireland: Suite 210, 837 Beatty St ⓣ604/683-9233; United Kingdom: Suite 800, 1111 Melville St ⓣ604/683-4421; United States: 1075 West Pender St ⓣ604/685-4311.

Currency exchange International Securities Exchange, 1169 Robson St (ⓣ604/683-4686); Vancouver Bullion & Currency Exchange, 800 West Pender St (ⓣ604/685-1008, ⓦwww.vbce.ca).

Directory enquiries ⓣ411.

Emergency services ⓣ911.

Hospitals St Paul's Hospital, 1081 Burrard St (ⓣ682-2344); Vancouver General Hospital, 855 West 12th Ave (ⓣ604/874-4111) or BC Children's Hospital, 4480 Oak St. (ⓣ604/875-2345). In North Van, Lions Gate Hospital, 231 East 15th St. (ⓣ604/988-3131).

Internet Free wi-fi at the Vancouver Central Library, 350 West Georgia St (ⓣ604/331-3600, ⓦwww.vpl.ca); or from any of the many internet cafés dotted around town, for $3–4hr, including *Internet Coffee*, 1104 Davie St, at Thurlow (ⓣ604/682-6668).

Laundry Davie Laundromat, 1061 Davie St (ⓣ604/682-2717); Scotty's One Hour Cleaners, 834 Thurlow St (ⓣ604/685-7732).

Left luggage At Pacific Central Station ($2/24hr) and at CDS Baggage at the city airport national and international arrivals (from $2/item for 24hr).

Lost property BC Transit, Stadium SkyTrain station, 590 Beatty St (ⓣ604/682-7887); West Vancouver Transit (ⓣ604/985-7777).

Parking Main Downtown garages are at The Bay (Richards St, near Dunsmuir), Robson Square (Smithe St, at Howe) and the Pacific Centre (Howe St, at Dunsmuir).

Pharmacies Shopper's Drug Mart, 1125 Davie St (ⓣ604/669-2424), is open 24hr and has five other outlets open Mon–Sat 9am–midnight, Sun 9am–9pm. London Drugs, 1650 Davie St (ⓣ604/669-2884) is open daily until 11pm. Carson Midnite Drug Store, 6517 Main St, is open daily until midnight. The Safeway supermarket pharmacy at Robson and Denman sts is open until midnight.

Police Non-emergency 24hr (ⓣ604/717-3321); RCMP (ⓣ604/264-3111); Vancouver City Police, 2120 Cambie St (ⓣ604/665-3535 or 717-3535, ⓦwww.vancouver.ca/police).

Post office Main office at 349 West Georgia St (Mon–Fri 8am–5.30pm; ⓣ604/662-5722 or 1-800/267-1177, ⓦwww.canadapost.ca). Outlets are also in many 7-Eleven and Shopper's Drug Mart stores.

Shopping Most of Vancouver's smartest clothes and other shops – and several upmarket malls (notably the Pacific Centre) are found on or around Burrard St and the central stretch of Robson St. Gastown has a smattering of specialist stores, plenty of souvenir stores and some excellent galleries of aboriginal art. Yaletown boasts many design and homeware stores, along with plenty of interesting one-off shops. Edgier galleries, vintage and fashion stores are found on East Vancouver's Main St and Commercial Drive. Vancouver is also an excellent place to shop for outdoor gear, notably at the outstanding Mountain Equipment Co-op at 130 West Broadway and Columbia St (ⓦwww.mec.ca).

Taxis Black Top (ⓣ604/731-1111 or 681-2181); Vancouver Taxi (ⓣ604/871-1111); Yellow Cab (ⓣ604/681-3311 or 681-1111).

Trains VIA Rail (ⓣ604/669-3050 or toll-free in Canada only ⓣ1-888/842-7245, 1-800/561-3949 in the US, ⓦwww.viarail.ca); Amtrak (ⓣ1-800/872-7245, ⓦwww.amtrak.com); Rocky Mountain Railtours (ⓣ604/606-7200 or 1-800/665-7245, ⓦwww.rockymountaineer.com) for expensive rail tours through the Rockies.

The Sunshine Coast, Whistler and the Cariboo

Apart from Vancouver Island, Victoria and the Southern Gulf Islands, covered in the next section, two other major excursions from Vancouver are possible, each of which can easily be extended to embrace longer itineraries out of the city. Both are part of mainland southern British Columbia, but owing to the lie of the land and the paucity of roads in this region, both can only realistically be accessed from Vancouver.

The first, and less enticing, is the 150-kilometre **Sunshine Coast**, the only stretch of accessible coastline on mainland British Columbia, and a possible springboard to Vancouver Island: ferries depart from Powell River, the coast's largest town, to Comox on Vancouver Island. Most people on short trips make the run to Powell River and then turn tail for Vancouver – there is no alternative route back to the city and no onward road route after the village of Lund and the end of Hwy 101 beyond Powell River.

The second, and far more tempting trip is the inland route to **Garibaldi Provincial Park**, which contains the best scenery and hiking country within striking distance of Vancouver, and then on to the world-class summer and winter resort of **Whistler**. The latter is worth visiting at any time of year, with winter an obviously busy time and summer almost equally popular, thanks to the area's many outdoor activities. En route to Whistler you'll pass through **Squamish**, one of North America's premier destinations for windsurfing, climbing and – in season – eagle-watching.

Beyond Whistler the roads and countryside empty quickly, the roads picking up the Fraser River at **Lillooet**, a striking scenic interlude before the more workaday ranching country and immense forests of the **Cariboo** region. On the coast, and only accessible via a single mountain road or by sea, is **Bella Coola**, best seen as part of a longer itinerary that takes in Vancouver Island and the Discovery Coast ferry service (see p.860). Continuing north from the Cariboo provides access to Prince George and the north (see p.869), but it's a long and pretty dull haul.

The Sunshine Coast

A mild-weathered stretch of sandy beaches, rugged headlands and quiet lagoons running northwest of Vancouver, the **Sunshine Coast** sees heavy tourist traffic, though its reputation is considerably overstated and the scenic rewards are slim compared to the grandeur of the BC interior. Even as a taste of the province's mountain scenery it leaves much to be desired, and the best that can be said of the region is that in summer it offers some of western Canada's best diving, boating and fishing. If you are just coming out for the day, the best parts of the trip are the various **ferry crossings** en route: the first is from Horseshoe Bay at the western extreme of West Vancouver to Langdale. From there, it's a short drive to Gibsons Landing, (often known simply as Gibsons) where you pick up Hwy 101 for the 79-kilometre run along the coast to Earl's Cove, and the beautiful (and slightly longer) crossing to Saltery Bay, where the boat provides views of some fine maritime landscapes. The road continues 35km to Powell River before coming to an abrupt conclusion 23km later at the village of Lund.

Moving on from Vancouver

Vancouver is at the hub of transport links to many parts of western Canada. Deciding where to move **onward from the city** – and how to go – presents a wealth of possibilities. We've listed the basic alternatives, together with cross-references to more detailed accounts of the various options.

The Yukon and Alaska

You can **fly** to **Whitehorse** (see p.894) in the Yukon directly from Vancouver, but there are no nonstop flights to Alaska from the city: all go via Seattle in the US. Flying to Seattle or taking a bus to Sea-Tac Airport takes around three hours from Vancouver Airport or various downtown hotels and other locations (see p.783). You can **drive** to Alaska through southern British Columbia to **Dawson Creek**, where you can pick up the **Alaska Hwy** (see p.889), which runs through the Yukon to Fairbanks; allow at least three days. Alternatively, drive to Prince George, head west towards Prince Rupert and then strike north up the **Cassiar Hwy** (see p.886) to connect with the Alaska Hwy in the Yukon. Using **public transport** you could take a Greyhound bus to Prince George (one day), connecting with another Greyhound to Dawson Creek and Whitehorse (two days). Buses link Whitehorse with other Yukon and Alaskan destinations. To travel to Alaska **by boat** from Vancouver you need to go via Bellingham (in the US), Prince Rupert or Port Hardy on Vancouver Island (see p.858).

BC, Calgary and the Canadian Rockies

Two main **roads** strike east from Vancouver towards Alberta and the Canadian Rockies – the **Trans-Canada Highway** and **Hwy 3**, both served by regular Greyhound buses. Both give access to **the Okanagan** (see p.720), and the **Kootenays** (see p.709). VIA trains run three times weekly through the region via Kamloops to **Jasper** and **Edmonton**; there is no train service to Calgary. Buses serve the **Cariboo** region, in the central part of the province (see p.801). Several itineraries can be put together by combining car or public transport journeys in the **BC interior** with BC Ferries' connections from Port Hardy on Vancouver Island to either Bella Coola or Prince Rupert.

It takes between ten and twelve hours to drive to **Calgary** on the Trans-Canada Hwy, and about ninety minutes less to reach **Banff**; express-service Greyhound buses operate over the same route. Frequent one-hour flights connect Vancouver and Calgary, and charter operators and no-frills airlines offer highly competitive rates on this route (though cheap flights often leave very early or very late in the day).

Vancouver Island

Ferries sail between Vancouver and three points on **Vancouver Island** – Swartz Bay (for Victoria), Nanaimo and Comox. Most leave from Tsawwassen and Horseshoe Bay terminals, about thirty minutes' drive south and west of Downtown, respectively. Foot passengers can buy inclusive bus and ferry tickets from Vancouver to Victoria or Nanaimo. Drivers should make advance reservations for all summer crossings (see p.809). **Public transport** connects to the **Pacific Rim National Park** and to Port Hardy on the island's northern tip for ferry connections to Prince Rupert and Bella Coola.

Highway 101

Highway 101 runs almost the length of the coast from **Gibsons**, which is 5km from the ferry terminal at Langdale for boats coming from **Horseshoe Bay** at the end of Marine Drive and the western edge of West Vancouver. You can reach the ferry terminal here from the city by taking bus #250 or the #257 express westbound from points on West Georgia Street Downtown. Given that the coast is hardly worth full-scale exploration by car, and that the two ferry crossings provide two of the trip's highlights, you might consider saving the price of a rental and going by **bus**; it's feasible to get to **Powell River** in a day. Malaspina Coachlines (Ⓣ1-888/227-8287, Ⓦwww.malaspinacoach.com) runs two buses to Powell River at 8.30am (daily) and at 4.15pm daily, except Saturday (5hr 45min; $58 one-way). Returns leave at 6.45am daily and 2.45pm Friday to Sunday. Bus tickets include the price of the ferry crossings en route. Buses also run from the airport daily, except Saturday, at 4pm (6hr 45min; $73).

Gibsons to Powell River

Soon reached and well signposted from North and West Vancouver, **Horseshoe Bay** is the departure point for the first of the Hwy 101 **ferry** crossings, a thirty to forty-minute passage through the islands of fjord-like Howe Sound. There are regular sailings year-round, and tickets cost $11.85 for adults and $39 for cars: bikes cost $2; all tickets cost a little less outside the late June to early September peak period. Each ticket is valid for one Horseshoe Bay-Langdale (return), Earl's Cove-Saltery Bay (return) or single journeys on both the Horseshoe Bay-Langdale and Earl's Cove-Saltery Bay crossings. Ferries also go from here to Nanaimo on Vancouver Island, with hourly sailings in summer and every other hour off-season. Tickets cost $13.50 per adult and $45 for cars (less off-season and less for cars year-round outside weekends). For information on either of these services, contact BC Ferries in Vancouver (Ⓣ604/669-1211, 250/386-3431 or 1-888/223-3779, Ⓦwww.bcferries.com), or pick up a timetable from the visitor centre Downtown.

Gibsons, the terminal on the other side of Howe Sound, is spread widely over a wooded hillside – the nicest area is around the busy marina and public wharf, a better bet if you're pausing than Upper Gibsons a little further down the hwy, which is little more than a busy strip. If you have time to kill, check out the **Sunshine Coast Maritime Museum & Archives** on Molly's Lane (June–Aug Tues–Sat 10.30am–4.30pm; free; Ⓦwww.sunshinecoastmuseum.ca), which contains displays of maritime and frontier memorabilia. For more on the town and details of local trails, beaches and swimming areas, visit the **infocentre** at 417 Marine Drive (daily 9am–6pm; Ⓣ604/886-2374 or 1-866/222-3806, Ⓦwww.gibsonschamber.com).

Farther west on Hwy 101 is Pender Harbour, a string of small coastal communities of which **Madeira Park** is the most substantial; whales occasionally pass this section of coast – which, sadly, is the source of many of the whales in the world's aquariums – but the main draws are fishing and boating. **Earl's Cove** is nothing but the departure ramp of the second ferry hop – a longer crossing (45min) that again offers fantastic views, including an immense waterfall that drops off a "Lost World"-type plateau into the sea.

From Saltery Bay, the opposite landing stage, it's a couple of kilometres up the road to the best of all the provincial parks in this region, **Saltery Bay Provincial Park**. Everything here is discreetly hidden in the trees between the road and the coast, and the campsite ($15) – beautifully situated – is connected by short trails to a couple of swimming beaches. Farther along on the main road, the standout accommodation is the *Oceanside Resort Motel*, which also has eleven cabins, 7km short of Powell River, which sits on a superb piece of shoreline (Ⓣ604/485-2435 or 1-888/889-2435, Ⓦwww.oceansidepark.com ❸).

Powell River and beyond

Given its seafront location, **Powell River** has its scenic side, but like many BC towns its unfocused sprawl and nearby sawmill slightly dampen the appeal. If you're catching the **ferry** to Courtenay on Vancouver Island (4 daily; 75min), you might not see the town site, as the terminal is 2km to the east at Westview, and some of the **buses** from Vancouver are timed to coincide with the boats; if your bus doesn't connect, you can either walk from the town centre or bus terminal or call a taxi (Ⓣ604/483-3666). The local **infocentre** (summer daily 9am–5pm, winter Mon–Fri 9am–5pm; Ⓣ604/485-4701 or 1-877/817-8669, Ⓦwww.discoverpowellriver.com), at 111-4871 Joyce Ave, has maps showing the many trails leading inland from the coast hereabouts; they can also advise on boat trips on Powell Lake, immediately inland, and tours to Desolation Sound farther up the coast. The most central of several **campsites** is the 81-site *Willingdon Beach Municipal Campground* on the seafront off Marine Avenue at 6910 Duncan St (Ⓣ604/485-2242, Ⓦwww.willingdonbeach.ca; tent $17.50, RV $24).

The northern end-point of Hwy 101 – which, incidentally, starts in Mexico City, making it one of North America's longest continuous routes – is the hamlet of **Lund**, 28km up the coast from Powell River. **Desolation Sound Marine Provincial Park**, about 10km north of Lund, offers some of Canada's best boating and scuba diving, plus fishing, canoeing and kayaking. There's no road access to the park, but a number of outfitters in Powell River run tours to it and can hire all the equipment you could possibly need – try Westview Live Bait Ltd, 4527 Marine Ave, for **canoes**; Coulter's Diving, 4557 Willingdon Ave, for **scuba gear**; and Spokes, 4710 Marine Drive for **bicycles**. The more modest **Okeover Provincial Park**, immediately north of Lund, has an unserviced campsite ($15).

The Sea to Sky Highway

A fancy name for Hwy 99 between North Vancouver and Whistler, the **Sea to Sky Highway** has a slightly better reputation than it deserves. It undoubtedly scores in its early coastal stretch, where the road clings perilously to an almost sheer cliff and mountains come dramatically into view on both sides of Howe Sound. Views here are better than along the Sunshine Coast, though plenty of campsites, motels and minor roadside distractions fill the route until the mountains of the Coast Range rear up beyond **Squamish** for the rest of the way to Whistler.

If you've a **car** you're better off driving only as far as **Garibaldi Provincial Park**, as the section between Pemberton and Lillooet, the Duffy Lake Road, is very slow going and often impassable in winter, though the drive is a stunner, with wonderful views of lakes and glaciers. Regular buses (see "Perimeter bus" details on p.783) connect Vancouver and Whistler (some continue to Pemberton), which you can easily manage as a day-trip (it's 2hr 30min one-way to Whistler from Vancouver by bus).

Britannia Beach

Road and rail lines meet with some squalor at tiny **Britannia Beach**, 53km from Vancouver, whose **BC Museum of Mining** (daily Feb–Nov 9am–4.30pm; Dec–Jan Mon–Fri 9am–4.30pm; $18.50; Ⓣ1-800/8964044, Ⓦwww.bcmuseumofmining.org) is the first reason to take time out from admiring the views. Centring on what was once one of the largest producer of copper in the British Empire – 56 million tonnes of ore were extracted here before the mine closed in 1974 – the museum is housed in a huge, derelict-looking building on the hillside and is chock-full of hands-on displays, original working machinery, a 235-tonne monster mine truck and archive photographs. You can also take guided underground tours (every 30min) around about 350m of the mine's galleries on small electric trains. And if parts of the complex look familiar it's because the mine has been used as a location in *The X-Files* and numerous other films and TV programmes.

Continuing north you pass several small coastal reserves, the most striking of which is **Shannon Falls Provincial Park**, 7km from Britannia Beach, signed right off the road and worth a stop for its spectacular 335-metre **waterfall**. Six times the height of Niagara, you can see it from the road, but it's only five minutes' walk to the viewing area at the base.

Squamish

The sea views and coastal drama end 11km beyond Britannia Beach at **SQUAMISH**, known for its excellent climbing and windsurfing in particular, but, by the high scenic standards of BC, a largely scrappy, unattractive place whose houses spread out over a flat plain amid warehouses, logging waste and old machinery.

Arrival and information

Most of the relevant parts of the town are concentrated on or near Cleveland Avenue, off Hwy 99, including the new and aptly named **Squamish Adventure Centre** (May–Sept daily 9am–5pm; Oct–April Mon–Fri 9am–5pm, Sat & Sun 10am–2pm; ⓣ604/815-4994 or 1-866/333.2010, ⓦwww.tourismsquamish.com), at 102-38551 Loggers Lane, which houses the visitor centre, a café and shop. Most of the central accommodation is here, as well as a big supermarket.

If you want to **rent equipment**, Vertical Reality Sports Centre at 37835 2nd Ave (ⓣ604/892-8248, ⓦwww.verticalrealitysports.com) has climbing shoes and mountain bikes. For other **mountain bike hire**, contact Tantalus (ⓣ604/898-2588), by the Greyhound depot at 40446 Government Rd, or Corsa Cycles (ⓣ604/892-3331, ⓦwww.corsacycles.com) at 800-1200 Hunter Place: rates for both start at about $45 for a day's hire. If you are here to climb, there are several **guides**, available from bookstores in Vancouver as well as the climbing shops in Squamish: Kevin McLane's *The Climbers' Guide to Squamish* (Elaho, $34.95) is a good place to start.

Accommodation

August Jack Motor Inn 37947 Cleveland Ave ⓣ604/892-3504 or 1-888-892-3502, ⓦwww.augustjack.com. The most central of the choices in Squamish, right off Hwy 99 and on Cleveland St, won't win any awards for decor, but it's clean, comfortable and some rooms have kitchenettes for $15 extra. Wi-fi access in most rooms, as well as the lobby. ❹

Garibaldi Budget Inn 38012-3rd Ave ⓣ604/892-5204 or 1-888-313-9299, ⓦwww.garibaldibudgetinn.com. A slightly cheaper option than *August Jack*, but still perfectly suitable and excellent value for what's on offer. Rooms are spotless, have a fridge and microwave and, in some cases, great views of the surrounding mountains. Check the website for a $10 discount coupon. ❸

Howe Sound Inn & Brewing Company 37801 Cleveland Ave ⓣ604/892-2603 or 1-800/919-2537, ⓦwww.howesound.com. If you can afford to spend more, then definitley plump for this spot and one of its twenty simple but modern rooms, great food and plenty of tasty beer from its own on-site microbrewery, tours of which can be arranged. Other amenities include a sauna and wi-fi access. ❺

Squamish Inn On The Water On Mamquam Blind Channel, off Hwy 99 ⓣ604/892-9240 or 1-800/449-8614, ⓦwww.innonthewater.com. Arriving from Vancouver, take a sharp right turn off Hwy 99 on to River Rd, following the signs to this superlative hostel. It's clean and friendly, with a kitchen, common room and a choice of dorm-style rooms (from $28.50), one-family suite (from $140), a private-entrance suite with waterfront and mountain views (from $80) and private rooms (from $70). Faciilities include internet access, fireplace lounge, home theatre and bbq.

The Town

At a glance, all the town has by way of fame is the vast granite rock overshadowing it, "The Stawamus Chief", which looms into view to the east just beyond Shannon Falls and is claimed to be the world's "second-biggest free-standing rock" (after Gibraltar, apparently). The town rates as one of Canada's top – if not *the* top – spot for **rock climbing**. Around 200,000 climbers from around the world come here annually, swarming to more than four hundred routes covering the 625-metre monolith: the University Wall and its culmination, the Dance Platform, is rated Canada's toughest climb.

The rock is sacred to the local Squamish, whose ancient tribal name – which means "place where the wind blows" – gives a clue as to the town's second big activity: **windsurfing**. There are strong, consistent winds, but the water is cold, so a wet suit's a good idea (there are rental outlets around town). Most people head for the artificial **Squamish Spit**, a dyke separating the waters of the Howe Sound from the Squamish River. The area is run by the Squamish Windsports Society (Ⓦwww.squamishwindsports.com) and is 3km from town.

Rounding out Squamish's outdoor activities is the tremendous **mountain biking** terrain – there are 63 trails in the area ranging from gnarly single-track routes to readily accessible deactivated forestry roads. The best areas are the Valley Cliff Trails (stream-bed, single-track and woodland trails); Mamquam Forest Service roads (active logging roads with fine views of the Mamquam Glacier); the Cat Lake and Brohm Lake trails; and the Alice Lake trails, which include an abandoned railway for an easy ride.

The town has one more unexpected treat, for the Squamish River, and the tiny hamlet of Brackendale in particular (10km to the north on Hwy 99), which is the world's best place to see **bald-eagles**. In winter, around two thousand eagles congregate here, attracted by the migrating salmon. The best places to see them are the so-called Eagle Run just south of the centre of Brackendale, and on the river in the Brackendale Eagles Provincial Park.

If you want to base yourself locally while seeing the eagles, contact the Sunwolf Outdoor Centre (Ⓣ604/898-1537 or 1-877/806-8046, Ⓦwww.sunwolf.net), signposted off Hwy 1 – take a left onto Squamish Valley Road at the Alice Lake junction 2km past Brackendale, continue for 4km and the centre is on the right. It has ten three-person cabins on the shore of the Cheakamus River for $90; some have kitchens for an extra $10. To see the eagles from a raft costs $99 per person, including light lunch; a raft trip plus cabin accommodation costs $134 per person, if two share a cabin.

Garibaldi Provincial Park

After about 5km the road north of Squamish enters the classic river, mountain and forest country of the BC interior, and the journey up to Whistler is a joy, with only the march of electricity pylons to take the edge off an idyllic drive.

Unless you're skiing, **Garibaldi Provincial Park** is the main incentive for heading this way. It's a huge and unspoilt area that combines all the usual breathtaking ingredients of lakes, rivers, forests, glaciers and the peaks of the Coast Mountains (Wedge Mountain, at 2891m, is the park's highest point). Four rough roads access the park from points along Hwy 99 between Squamish and Whistler, but you'll need transport to reach the trailheads at the end of them. Other than camping, the only accommodation close to the park is at Whistler.

There are five main areas with trails, of which the **Black Tusk/Garibaldi Lake** region is the most popular and probably most beautiful, thanks to its high-mountain views. Further trails fan out from Garibaldi Lake, including one to the huge basalt outcrop of **Black Tusk** (2316m), a rare opportunity to reach an alpine summit without any rock climbing. The other hiking areas from south to north are **Diamond Head**, **Cheakamus Lake**, **Singing Pass** and **Wedgemount Lake**. Outside these small, defined areas, the park is untrammelled wilderness. For more **information**, including good advice on trails, visit Ⓦwww.garibaldipark.com or get the dedicated BC Parks pamphlet from visitor centres in Vancouver and elsewhere; its information can also be accessed at Ⓦwww.env.gov.bc.ca/bcparks.

Whistler

WHISTLER, 56km beyond Squamish and 125km from Vancouver, is Canada's finest four-season resort, and frequently ranks as one of the world's top-five winter ski destinations. Skiing and snowboarding are the main activities, but all sorts of other winter sports are possible and in summer the lifts keep running to provide supreme highline hiking and other outdoor activities (as well as North America's finest summer skiing). It is a busy place – over two million lift tickets are sold here every winter, more than at any other North American resort. Fortunately, it also has one of the continent's largest ski areas, so the crowds are spread thinly over the resort's two hundred-plus trails and twelve alpine bowls.

The resort consists of two adjacent but separate mountains – **Whistler** (2182m) and **Blackcomb** (2284m) – each with their own extensive lift and chair systems (but a joint ticket scheme). The mountains can be accessed from a total of five bases, including lift systems to both mountains from the resort's heart, the purpose-built and largely pedestrianized **Whistler Village**, the tight-clustered focus of many hotels, shops, restaurants and après-ski activity. The gondola for Whistler Mountain also leaves from the Village. Around this core are two other "village" complexes, **Upper Village** (for the gondola to Blackcomb Mountain), about a kilometre to the northeast, and Village North, about 700m to the north. Around 6km to the south of Whistler Village is **Whistler Creekside** (also with a gondola and lift base), which has typically been a cheaper alternative but has undergone a fifty-million dollar redevelopment that has seen its accommodation and local services duplicating those of its famous neighbour. Further development took place in the build-up to the 2010 Winter Olympics, largely based in and around Whistler.

Arrival

There are several ways of **getting to** Whistler. If you're driving from Vancouver, allow about two and a bit hours for the 125-kilometre drive.

Perimeter (Ⓣ1-888/717-6066, Ⓦwww.perimeterbus.com) runs a shuttle **bus** from Vancouver airport and various Vancouver hotels to Whistler Bus Loop and a selection of Whistler hotels. Reservations are required year-round for the service and a return ticket must be purchased if you want to take advantage of a pickup from selected Vancouver hotels (mid-April to mid-Dec, six daily; there are eight southbound departures; mid-Dec to April, 11 daily; 2hr 30min–3hr; $49 plus tax one-way); winter schedules can be affected by bad weather on the Sea to Sky Hwy.

Greyhound (Ⓣ604/482-8747 in Vancouver, Ⓣ604/932-5031 in Whistler, 1-800/661-8747 from anywhere in North America, 604/904-7060 from outside North America and 0800 731 5983 from the UK; Ⓦwww.greyhound.ca) runs seven–eight daily bus services from Vancouver's bus depot (see p.751) to the Village (2hr 20min; $27.90 one-way) via Britannia Beach, Whistler Creek and other stops.

Part of the old BC Rail freight line from North Vancouver to Prince George is open to passenger traffic. The Whistler Mountaineer (Ⓣ1-888/403-4727, Ⓦwww.whistlermountaineer.com) departs daily from May to early October from North Vancouver station at 8.30am, arriving in Whistler at 11.30am. The return trip leaves at 3pm. It's designed as an excursion trip rather than a passenger service and costs $119 one-way, $199 return. Bookings must be made in advance by phone only.

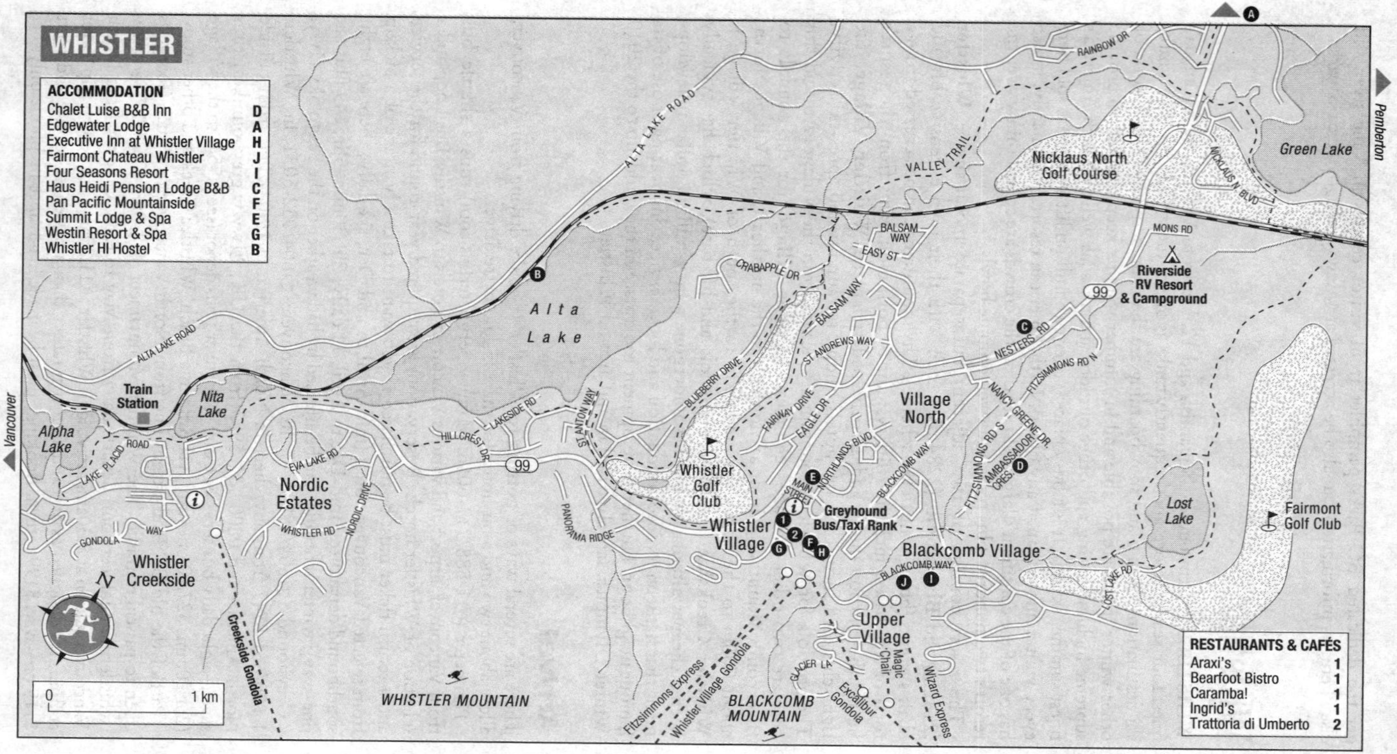

WHISTLER

ACCOMMODATION	
Chalet Luise B&B Inn	D
Edgewater Lodge	A
Executive Inn at Whistler Village	H
Fairmont Chateau Whistler	J
Four Seasons Resort	I
Haus Heidi Pension Lodge B&B	C
Pan Pacific Mountainside	F
Summit Lodge & Spa	E
Westin Resort & Spa	G
Whistler HI Hostel	B

RESTAURANTS & CAFÉS	
Araxi's	1
Bearfoot Bistro	1
Caramba!	1
Ingrid's	1
Trattoria di Umberto	2

Pemberton
Vancouver
Green Lake
Nicklaus North Golf Course
Riverside RV Resort & Campground
Alta Lake
Nita Lake
Alpha Lake
Train Station
Lost Lake
Fairmont Golf Club
Whistler Golf Club
Village North
Whistler Village
Blackcomb Village
Upper Village
Greyhound Bus/Taxi Rank
Nordic Estates
Whistler Creekside
WHISTLER MOUNTAIN
BLACKCOMB MOUNTAIN
Creekside Gondola
Fitzsimmons Express
Whistler Village Gondola
Excalibur Gondola
Magic Chair
Wizard Express
ALTA LAKE ROAD
VALLEY TRAIL
RAINBOW DR
NICKLAUS N. BLVD
MONS RD
NESTERS RD
FITZSIMMONS RD N
FITZSIMMONS RD S
NANCY GREENE DR.
AMBASSADOR CRES.
BLACKCOMB WAY
NORTHLANDS BLVD
MAIN STREET
EAGLE DR
FAIRWAY DRIVE
ST ANDREWS WAY
BALSAM WAY
EASY ST
CRABAPPLE DR
BLUEBERRY DRIVE
ST ANTON WAY
LAKESIDE RD
HILLCREST DR
PANORAMA RIDGE
EVA LAKE RD
NORDIC DRIVE
WHISTLER RD
LAKE PLACID ROAD
GONDOLA WAY
LOST LAKE RD
GLACIER LA
99
0 1 km
N

If you're staying in or near the Village, you probably won't need **local transport**, but WAVE (Ⓣ604/932-4020) runs a shuttle bus service around Whistler Village, Village North and Upper Village as well as buses to Whistler Creek and other destinations ($2 flat fare, day-pass $5, weekly pass $20). Buses have racks for skis and bikes. If you need a taxi call Ⓣ604/938-1515, Ⓦwww.resortcabs.com.

Information

For **information** on Whistler-Blackcomb call Ⓣ604/904-8134 (1-866/218-9690 toll free in North America or 0800/587-1743 toll free in the UK, Ⓦwww.whistlerblackcomb.com). Tourism Whistler (Ⓣ604/932-3928) is another source of information, including booking accommodation and activities, and runs the Whistler Activity and Information Centre, in the green-roofed Conference Centre near the Village Square (daily 9am–5pm; Ⓣ604/932-0606 or 1-800/WHISTLER toll free in North America and 0808/180-0606 toll free in the UK, Ⓦwww.whistler.com). The **Chamber of Commerce** is in Whistler Village at 4230 Gateway Drive, off Village Gate Boulevard (Mon–Thurs 8.30am–6.30pm, Fri–Sat 8.30am–7.30pm; Ⓣ604/932-5592, Ⓦwww.whistlerchamberofcommerce.com), and can assist with general information, tickets for events and last-minute accommodation. **Information kiosks** open daily 9am–5pm between May and early September at several points, including the main bus stop and the Village Gate Boulevard at the entrance to Whistler Village.

Accommodation

If you're here in summer and not on a package tour, all local **accommodation** can be booked through the excellent Whistler Central Reservations (Ⓣ 604/932-0606, 1-800/944-7853 toll-free in North America and 0800/731-5983 toll-free in the UK, Ⓦwww.whistler.com). In winter, reservations for those not on a package tour should be made well in advance (Sept at least), as many hotels have a thirty-day cancellation window and may insist on a minimum of three days' stay; prices are highest at this time. In winter there's no such thing as budget accommodation, unless you stay at the hostel; with ever greater numbers of visitors in the summer, prices – and availability – of beds are increasingly a problem outside the ski season. Still, you don't have to stay in a "conventional" hotel, as there is a wide range of chalets, condos, apartments and houses to rent. These, as well as many hotels, often have kitchen facilities. Virtually all types of accommodation, from B&B to condo, list nightly and weekly rates, and in season there's likely to be a minimum stay.

Hotels

Chalet Luise B&B Inn 7461 Ambassador Crescent Ⓣ604/932-4187 or 1-800/665-1998, Ⓦwww.chaletluise.com. Open May–Nov. Eight rooms in a peaceful garden setting that is convenient for the Village, lifts and various summer hiking trails. The European owners pride themselves on providing big, home-made breakfasts. 6

Edgewater Lodge 8020 Alpine Way, 3km north of the Village Ⓣ604/932-0688 or 1-888/870-9065, Ⓦwww.edgewater-lodge.com. Set on a lovely forested waterfront promontory that pushes into Green Lake, the twelve luxurious rooms here enjoy sublime views, and you can canoe and hike virtually from the front door. 6

Executive Inn at Whistler Village 4250 Village Stroll Ⓣ604/932-3200 or 1-800/663-6416, Ⓦwww.executivehotels.net. Located at the heart of the Village, this "European-style" hotel has 37 rooms, each with big picture windows, kitchenettes, fireplaces and two-person jacuzzis. 4

Fairmont Château Whistler 4599 Château Blvd, Upper Village Ⓣ604/938-8000 or –800/257-7544; Ⓦwww.fairmont.com/whistler. This was the resort's obvious first choice until the arrival of the *Four Seasons*, which has left the vast English-manor-house-meets-French-château affair looking a little dated and its huge lobby and overall stylistic effect a little bombastic. You won't be disappointed here, thanks to some great facilities (including indoor and outdoor pools, fine spa, tennis and golf course) and ski-in/ski-out access to Blackcomb Mountain, but if you have the money, the *Four Seasons* is the preferred choice. 9

Four Seasons Resort Whistler 4591 Blackcomb Way, Upper Village ⓣ604/935-3400 or 1-888/935-2460, ⓦwww.fourseasons.com. It's fair to say this is currently Whistler's luxury resort hotel of choice. Service reaches the *Four Seasons*' group's usual elevated standards, and the fabulous panoramic rooms, black-slate bathrooms, suites and town-house-style accommodation are the largest and most polished of their sort in town. Gas-burner fireplaces in the cosy wood-interior rooms are typical nice touches. All manner of facilities are available, along with every aid and guidance imaginable when it comes to skiing or indulging in other outdoor (or indoor) activities. 9

Haus Heidi Pension Lodge B&B 7115 Nesters Rd ⓣ604/932-3113 or 1-800/909-7115, ⓦwww.hausheidi.com. An eight-room inn that has been run by the same family for over 25 years, close to the Village, lifts and valley trails. A generous breakfast is included in the price. 6

Pan Pacific Mountainside 4320 Sundial Crescent ⓣ604/905-2999 or 1-888/905-9995, ⓦwww.panpacific.com. There's nowhere closer to the lifts than the older of Whistler's two Pan Pacifics – you can ski from the front door to the Whistler Mountain gondola station a few steps away. The contemporary lodge style is pleasant, and the 121 units include compact studios and one- and two-bedroom suites with kitchens. There's an outdoor pool, and the "Irish" pub and lounge are popular après-ski locations. 5

Summit Lodge & Spa 4359 Main St ⓣ604/932-2778 or 1-888/913-8811, ⓦwww.summitlodge.com. A peaceful boutique-style hotel, with 81 rooms, all with kitchenettes, balconies and fireplaces. Granite worktops and cherry-wood decor add more than a dash of style, along with details such as free hot chocolate nightly, a ski shuttle, heated outdoor pool and above-average spa. 5

Westin Resort & Spa 4090 Whistler Way ⓣ604/905-5000 or 1-888/634-5577, ⓦwww.westinwhistler.com. With almost one thousand beds and set in a prime location on the mountain-side below the main run into the Village this is not exactly an intimate place – but the rooms are spacious and well finished, with granite and cedar trim providing luxurious touches. Facilities include a spa and indoor and outdoor pools. 9

Hostels

Hostelling International Whistler 5678 Alta Lake Rd ⓣ604/932-5492, ⓦwww.hihostels.ca. A 25-bed hostel with four- and eight-bed dorms 7km from the Village right on the shores of Alta Lake. One of the nicest hostels in BC, it's a signposted fifty-minute walk from Whistler Creek or ten-minute drive to the Village centre; local buses leave the gondola base in the Village four times a day for the hostel (15min; $2). As it's popular year-round, reserve many weeks, if not months ahead. Beds for members $30, nonmembers $34, private doubles $75/83.

Campsites

Riverside RV Resort and Campground ⓣ604/905-5533 or 1-877/905-5533, ⓦwww.whistlerlogcamping.com. Whistler's only central campsite is 1.4km north of Whistler Village at 8018 Mons Rd, and also has fourteen five-person log cabins for $119–229 and 107 sites combined, for RVs and tents (rates vary month to month; check website for details).

Whistler Village

WHISTLER VILLAGE is the key to the resort, a rather characterless and pastel-shaded conglomeration of hotels, restaurants, mountain-gear shops and more loud people in fluorescent clothes than are healthy in one place at the same time. It's all a far cry from February 1966 when what was then known as London Mountain (local population 25) first started skiing operations. Apparently the International Olympics Committee had let drop in the early 1960s that the region satisfied all the criteria for a successful Winter Olympic bid, and development began soon after. Over the years, Whistler would make no fewer than three failed bids, losing out to Sapporo in 1972, Innsbruck in 1976 and Lake Placid in 1980. But the fourth time was lucky, and Whistler secured the lion's share of the 2010 winter games.

The brouhaha that accompanied the awarding of the games led to a fury of investment, building and upgrading, especially in Whistler Village, which took shape in the late 1970s (until then its site had been the community's rubbish tip). Whistler's name is said to derive either from the distinctive shriek of the marmot, or the sound

Skiing and snowboarding practicalities

The **skiing and snowboarding season** for Whistler and Blackcomb is one of the longest in North America, often running for almost two hundred days from November to early June, weather permitting. The yearly average snowfall is an impressive ten metres, while the average winter alpine temperature rarely falls below –5C (compare this with a chillier –12C in Banff). Whistler sits in an area of temperate rainforest, and rain can certainly be a problem at lower altitudes; what falls as rain in the Village is often falling as snow higher up.

Blackcomb closes at the end of April, while Whistler stays open until early June. Then the mountains switch places, as Whistler closes and Blackcomb reopens in early June for glacier skiing and snowboarding. Lifts open at 8.30am (9am from late Feb) and close at 3pm until late January, 3.30pm until late February, and at 4pm from late February. The Tube Park on Blackcomb is open Monday to Friday noon–8pm and 11am–8pm at weekends and holidays. **Summer hours** (June 5–July 30), for glacier skiing or high-level hiking are noon–3pm daily.

Lift tickets give you full use of both Whistler and Blackcomb mountains, and it will take days for even the most advanced skier or snowboarder to cover all the terrain. The best advice is to pick one mountain and stick to it for the day, or use the PEAK 2 PEAK, a $50-million, 4.4-kilometre gondola 415m above the valley floor that links the mountains; see the main text below for the relative merits of each. Lift tickets include access to PEAK 2 PEAK and are available from the lift base in Whistler Village, but the queues can be horrendous. Plan ahead and purchase your tickets and check all lift and other information online at ⓦwww.whistlerblackcomb.com or book by phone on ⓣ604/904-8134 or 1-866/218-9690 toll free in North America. Discounts are available for online booking, but you must book another element, such as rentals, lessons or accommodation. Your hotel can often set you up with tickets if you pre-book far enough in advance. **Prices** increase slightly in peak season – over Christmas and New Year and from mid-February to mid-March – and lift tickets are subject to a seven-percent tax.

You can rent equipment from outlets at the Whistler and Blackcomb lifts, but it is first-come, first-served, and you need to be there first thing (8am) to beat the queues. Alternatively, Summit Ski (ⓣ604/932-6255 or 1-888/608-6225, ⓦwww.summitsport.com) has several outlets around the Village, including the *Delta Whistler Resort* and Market Pavilion. Intermediate and expert skiers can join the **free tours** of the mountains: contact the infocentre for latest departure times.

Under-6s ski free. Daycare is available for children up to the age of 12, (from $35–139), but should be booked well in advance. Contact the information centre or search for "daycare" at ⓦwww.whistler.com or ⓦwww.whistlerblackcomb.com.

of the wind whistling through Singing Pass up in the mountains. Whatever its origins, almost forty years' worth of investments, plus the money associated with the Olympics, have paid off; the resort's services, lifts and general overall polish are almost faultless, and those of its nearby satellites are not far behind.

Whistler Mountain

Winter-sports enthusiasts can argue long and late over the relative merits of **WHISTLER MOUNTAIN** and its rival, Blackcomb Mountain (see p.796), both accessed from lifts at Whistler Village's lifts (the Blackcomb base is a little closer to the Upper Village). Both are great mountains, and both offer top-notch skiing and boarding, as evidenced by world-class events like the annual Snowboard FIS World Cup and the World Ski and Snowboard Festival in April – both held on Whistler. If this makes the slopes sound big-scale and intimidating, they're not, and if you

▲ The view from one of Whistler Mountain's many trails

become lost, confused or just want advice, there are eighty or so red-jacketed "Mountain Hosts" to answer questions.

Each mountain has its own distinctive character, and traditionally Whistler has been seen as the more homely of the two mountains, somewhere you can ski or board for days on end and never have to retrace your steps. One of Whistler's great advantages over Blackcomb is the sun, which the mountain catches much earlier: Seventh Heaven run aside, much of Blackcomb doesn't see the sun until after 11.30am.

The Whistler resort's combined ski area is 8171 acres, with a total of 38 lifts and over two hundred **trails**: Whistler Mountain's share of the ski area is 4757 acres and its breakdown of terrain is twenty percent beginner, fifty-five percent intermediate and twenty-five percent expert. Common consent has Whistler as the better mountain for beginners and intermediates – if you're attending ski school it's a mid-station.

Whistler's twenty **lifts** include two high-speed gondolas, six high-speed quads, two triple and one double chairlift and nine surface lifts. Helicopter drops make another one hundred runs and glacier runs available. If you want the fast track to the best skiing on a quality powder day, take the Harmony and Peak chairlifts. Snowboarders are blessed with a half-pipe and park, though most boarders prefer Blackcomb, if only because it has fewer dull traverses where you have to unbuckle your board. Total vertical drop is 1530m and the longest run is 11km.

Blackcomb Mountain

BLACKCOMB MOUNTAIN, the "Mile-High Mountain", is a ski area laden with superlatives: the most modern resort in Canada, North America's finest summer skiing (on Horstman Glacier), the continent's longest unbroken fall-line skiing and the longest *and* second longest lift-serviced vertical falls in North America (1609m and 1530m).

Blackcomb is slightly smaller than Whistler, at 3414 acres, and has a similar breakdown of **terrain** (fifteen percent beginner, fifty-five percent intermediate and thirty percent expert). Blackcomb is steeper and has more narrow runs than

Whistler, which can test beginners' stopping abilities to the limit. The exception for beginners is for **children**, where the under-6s should learn at the small hill at the base of Blackcomb, avoiding the bustle of the lift to mid-station on Whistler.

The seventeen **lifts** include one high-speed gondola, seven express quads, three triple chairlifts and seven surface lifts. There are over a hundred marked trails, two glaciers and five bowls along with two half-pipes and a park for snowboarders. Runs such as Ruby, Sapphire, Garnet and Diamond are some of the world's best steep and avalanche-controlled powder, but it takes two chairlifts to reach them. Even if you're not skiing, come up here (summer or winter) on the ski lifts to walk, enjoy the **view** from the top of the mountain, or to eat in the restaurants like *Rendezvous* or *Glacier Creek*. The *Crystal Hut*, a cosy log cabin, is one of the best and deservedly popular at lunch.

Mountain biking

The phenomenal rise in the popularity of **mountain biking** in and around the resort sees an estimated 100,000 visitors annually coming to Whistler specifically to take to two wheels. The oft-made observation is that what Hawaii is to the global surfing community, Whistler is to the mountain-biking fraternity. Some predict that by the time the Winter Olympics come and go in 2010, biking could be bigger in Whistler than skiing.

The resort's popularity is not all down to terrain and happy accident. It always did have hundreds of free trails, with a total of 100km of single-track and 80km of double-track trails, plus around 200km of lift-serviced trails, the last factor vital, for there's nothing better than having a ski lift do all the hard work of carrying your bike up the mountain and letting gravity do the work – and provide the pleasure – coming down. What has made a big difference, however, is the deservedly celebrated **Whistler Mountain Bike Park** (ⓣ604/938-7275, ⓦwww.whistlerbike.com; daily mid-May to early or mid-Oct, 10am–5pm, plus 5–8pm on some lifts mid-June to early Sept, depending on the light). This includes those 200km of lift-serviced trails, two jump park areas, three or four access lifts (Whistler Gondola, Fitzsimmons, Magic and Garbanzo), three skills centres for all abilities (green circle, blue square and black diamond), expert staff on site, banked cruisers and dirt trails through canopied forest, a BikerCross park (fun to watch even if you don't take part), and self-guided rides over 1200-metre vertical trails.

It'll **cost** you $51 for a day-pass in high season (from mid-June), $40–44 the rest of the time, and $45/39 for seniors and youth 13–18. Children 7–12 are charged $28/23; children under 12 must be accompanied by adults. Two- and three-day passes are also available. These prices cover riding, entry to the Magic Bike Park and access to the lifts from 10am–8pm. You can also rent a high-quality "Park" bike from $65 for half a day (or from $10/hr) from the park's eight various outlets (including the *Westin*, *Four Seasons* and *Pan Pacific* hotels, and *Glacier Lodge*, *Crystal Lodge*, *Whistler Mountainside* and Blackcomb Base), or $99.99 for the whole day. Lesser "Youth Park" models cost $50/65. You can also rent individual bits of protective gear, or a full armour package (arm, leg, glove, chest and helmet) for $44.99 ($39.99 with a bike rental).

You can buy lift-only passes, rent equipment and do your own thing by visiting other rental outfits such as Cross Country Connection (ⓣ604/905-0071, ⓦwww.crosscountryconnection.ca), which has bikes from $12 per hour, and also offers tours and lessons. If you want to research routes and further information, then ⓦwww.whistlermountainbike.com is an excellent resource.

If you're a beginner, stick with the **Valley Trail**, the 30km paved pedestrian and cycle route in the valley around Whistler Village. You can rent bikes from outlets around the resort, including so-called "cruiser" bikes designed for beginners or those who want a more sedate and comfortable ride.

Other outdoor activities at Whistler

In addition to skiing (see p.795), mountain biking (see p.797) and hiking (see below), Whistler offers a wealth of **outdoor activities** year-round. For further information on the activities below, contact the various visitor centres (see p.793) or visit Ⓦwww.whistler.com, which can book and advise on most activities. Numerous **rental outlets** around the resort provide bikes, in-line skates and other equipment.

Summer activities

From June through August, Whistler River Adventures (Ⓣ604/932-3532 or 1-888/932-3532, Ⓦwww.whistlerriver.com; from $109 for a three-hour trip, one hour on the water) has **jet boating** on the Green River to below the Nairn Falls, with a good chance of spotting wildlife such as moose and bears. It also has a range of **rafting** trips priced from $89 for four-hour trips (one hour on the river): beginners are taken to the Green River, while experts can plump for the Class-IV thrills of the Elaho or Squamish River rapids. The same company offers half- and full-day catch-and-release **fishing** trips in surrounding rivers from about $175 per person.

Whistler Core, at the Whistler Conference Centre (Ⓣ604/905-7625, Ⓦwww.whistlercore.com; daily 10am–10pm, except autumn noon-9pm), offers indoor facilities for **climbing** year-round and an outdoor summer climbing wall. A day's drop-in indoor climbing costs $17.50. A variety of guides and guided tours are available from $175 for a half-day climb.

You can **play tennis** at several public courts, or ask at the visitor centre for details of hotels such as the *Delta Whistler Resort*, *Fairmont Château Whistler* and *Château Whistler Resort* that allow players to use their courts and provide racket rental. Call Meadow Park Sports Centre (Ⓣ604/938-7529) for information on free public courts.

Hiking in and around Whistler

You can ride the ski lifts up both mountains for tremendous views and easy access to high-altitude **walking** trails (June to early Sept daily 10am–8pm; early Sept to late Sept daily 10am–5pm, late Sept to mid-Oct Sat & Sun only 10am–5pm; lift passes $41.95 or $39.95 bought online).

Pick up the sheet of hiking trails from the information centres (see p.793), or buy the 1:50,000 *Whistler and Garibaldi Region* **map**. The two most popular high-level day walks are the **Rainbow Falls** and **Singing Pass** trails (both five to six hours). Other good choices are the easy and mostly level 4km trail to Cheakamus Lake or any of the high-alpine hikes accessed from the Upper Gondola station (1837m) on Whistler Mountain or the Seventh Heaven lift on Blackcomb. Among the eight walks from Whistler Mountain gondola station, consider the **Glacier Trail** (2.5km round-trip; 85m ascent; 1hr) for views of the snow and ice in Glacier Bowl. The slightly more challenging **Little Whistler Trail** (3.8km round-trip; 265m ascent; 1hr 30min–2hr) takes you to the summit of Little Whistler Peak (2115m) and gives grand views of Black Tusk in Garibaldi Provincial Park; time your hike to return to the gondola station for the last ride down (times vary according to season).

If high-level hiking seems too daunting (it shouldn't be – most are less than 5km, save the Musical Bumps-Singing Pass trail at 21km) there are plenty of trails for bikers, walkers and in-line skaters around the Village. The **Valley Trail** system starts on the west side of Hwy 99 by the Whistler Park Golf Course and takes you through parks, golf courses and peaceful residential areas: the 30km of trails on and around **Lost Lake**, entered by the northern end of the Day Skier car park at Blackcomb Mountain, wend through cedar forest and past lakes and creeks; the eponymous lake is just over a kilometre from the main trailhead. There are also numerous operators offering guided walks to suit all abilities.

After any of these activities there are umpteen **spas** for massage, mud baths and treatments that soothe all aches and pains. For utter luxury, try the spa at the *Fairmont Château Whistler* (Ⓣ604/938-2086, Ⓦwww.fairmont.com).

Winter activities

For **snowshoe tours** for novices contact Outdoor Adventures@Whistler (Ⓣ604/932-0647, Ⓦwww.adventureswhistler.com; from $79 for ninety minutes' snowshoeing or $109 for an evening tour by Green Lake followed by dinner).

For **sleigh rides**, Blackcomb Horsedrawn Sleigh Rides (Ⓣ604/932-7631, Ⓦwww.blackcombsleighrides.com), offers a range of tours with or without lunch or dinner, with four tours (hourly from 5pm) every evening in winter ($55 for 40–50 min). Tours follow the ski trails to the woods for great views and a stop in a cabin for a mug of hot chocolate. For $105 you get a sleigh ride and dinner.

You can ride **snowmobiles** with Outdoor Adventures (see above), Blackcomb Snowmobile (Ⓣ604/932-8484, Ⓦwww.blackcombsnowmobile.com) or Canadian Snowmobile Adventures (Ⓣ604/938-1616, Ⓦwww.canadiansnowmobile.com), all of which offer similar tours and prices; check websites for pricing details. Blackcomb Snowmobile also offers a range of dog-sled rides: the "Mountain Mushing" tour (4 daily; 2hr 30min) costs $145.

For **cross-country skiing**, the best spots are the 32km of groomed and patrolled trails around Lost Lake and the *Fairmont Château Whistler* golf course, all easily accessible from Whistler Village. Check with the visitor centre and resort websites for more background information. Visit Ⓦwww.crosscountryconnection.ca for more details and rental information.

Eating

Whistler Village and its satellites are loaded with cafés and around a hundred restaurants. These can come and go at an alarming rate, and none – given the resort's purpose-built nature – have much in the way of original interiors or atmosphere. Most hotels have one or more restaurants, always open to non-residents. In smarter places such as the *Four Seasons*, where the *'Fifty Two 80 Bistro* (Ⓣ604/966-5280) – named after Whistler and Blackcomb Mountain's "vertical mile" – has been winning plaudits, these can be of very high quality, if rather expensive.

Araxi's Restaurant 4222 Village Square Ⓣ604/932-4540, Ⓦwww.araxi.com. A top-rated restaurant of long standing that serves up expensive Italian and West Coast-style food, with inventive pasta and very high-quality seafood bar and dishes. The wine list runs to 27 pages and 11,000 bottles, but there's a good choice of wines by the glass. A meal for two here will cost $80-plus, with mains from about $30 – expensive, but you're paying for probably the best food in town.

Bearfoot Bistro 4121 Village Green Ⓣ604/932-3433, Ⓦwww.bearfootbistro.com. A few years ago this was a simple French bistro: today it has a reputation of one of Canada's best restaurants, with superlative French food served in a variety of tasting menus (from $90–200-plus) that change from day to day. Reservations are essential.

Caramba! Restaurante 12-4314 Main St Ⓣ604/938-1879, Ⓦwww.caramba-restaurante.com. On the face of it, the Mediterranean food in this casual but buzzy Lower Village spot – pastas, pizzas, roast meats – might seem unremarkable, but the regular queues out of the door bear witness to the quality of the food and dining experience. Main courses start at about $12, but run as high as $32.

Ingrid's Village Café 102-4305 Skiers Approach Ⓣ604/932-7000, Ⓦwww.ingridswhistler.com *Ingrid's* is a favourite among locals and resort workers for breakfast (it opens 7.30am–6.30pm), coffee and snacks. Prices are fair – the daily soup special will cost around $5, a veggie burger a dollar or so more – and the quality good.

Trattoria di Umberto 4417 Sundial Place Ⓣ604/932-5858. You can pay less for Italian food in Whistler, but this well-established place (one of the sister restaurants of *Il Giardino* in Vancouver; see p.778) scores by virtue of its cosy setting and accomplished, straightforward cooking. Expect to part with up to about $50 for three courses for two, without wine.

Nightlife

Whistler enjoys year-round **nightlife** and après-ski activity, with visitors being bolstered by the large seasonal workforce. Clubs come and go, but certain establishments have carved out well-defined niches, including *Moe Joe's*, *Buffalo Bill's*, *Savage Beagle* and *Tommy Africa's* for dancing. For peace and quiet, hit any of the bars and lounges in the luxury hotels such as the *Four Seasons* and *Fairmont Château Whistler* hotel. Some clubs may charge a cover – anything from $10–30 – on busy nights, or for live music.

Buffalo Bill's Bar & Grill 4122 Village Green ⓣ604/932-6613, ⓦwww.buffalobills.ca. Across from the Whistler gondola, this thirtysomething bar/club has comedy nights, hypnosis shows, video screens, a moderate dance floor and live music.
Garfinkels Club 1-4308 Main St, Village North ⓣ604/932-2323, ⓦwww.garfswhistler.com. If you fancy yourself hip, between 20–25 and don't mind sports bars, then "Garf's" is for you. It's a good dance place week round, but Thurs is the big night, with indie, funk and classic dance tracks.
Moe Joe's 4115 Golfer's Approach ⓣ604/935-1152. Fri nights are popular at *Moe Joe's*, one of the best places in Whistler for dancing. It's smaller and more intimate than *Garf's* but attracts a similar clientele and expouses a similar musical policy.
Savage Beagle 4222 Village Square ⓣ604/938-3337, ⓦwww.savagebeagle.com. Like *Buffalo Bill's*, the long-established and split-level *Savage Beagle* appeals to a slightly older, thirtysomething crowd, with a lounge upstairs (with a great selection of drinks) and a dancefloor downstairs. Tues is the key night.
Tommy Africa's 4216 Gateway Drive ⓣ604/932-6090, ⓦwww.tommyafricas.com. This is the best-known dance club in the Village and usually the most musically adventurous. The big night here is Mon.

North to Lillooet

About 25km northeast of Whistler, Hwy 99 funnels down to two slow lanes at **PEMBERTON**, known primarily for its potatoes, of all things, where apartments are now mushrooming in the wake of Whistler's popularity. Beyond, you're treated to some wonderfully wild country. Patches of forest poke through rugged mountainsides and scree slopes, and a succession of glorious lakes culminate in Seton Lake, whose hydroelectric schemes feed power into the grid as far south as Arizona.

At the lumber town of **LILLOOET**, founded as Mile 0 of the 1858 Cariboo Wagon Road to the goldfields to the north (see p.801), the railway meets the Fraser River, which marks a turning point in the scenery as denuded crags and hillsides increasingly hint at the *High Noon*-type ranching country to come. In July and August, the rocky banks and bars of the sluggish, mud-coloured river immediately north of town are dotted with vivid orange and blue tarpaulins. These belong to aboriginal peoples who still come to catch and dry salmon as the fish make their way upriver to spawn. It's one of the few places where this tradition continues and it's worth a stop to watch. The town's name, changed from Cayoosh Flat in the 1860s, is a misrendering of Leel-wat, one of the aboriginal peoples who lived to the north.

The town boasts a handful of central **hotels and motels** if you need to stay: try the *Mile 0 Motel*, 616 Main St (ⓣ604/256-7511 or 1-888/766-4530, ⓦwww.mileomotel.com; ❸), which has kitchenettes in some units and overlooks the river and mountains. The nearest **campsite** is the riverside *Cayoosh Creek* on Hwy 99 within walking distance of downtown (ⓣ604/256-4180 or 1-877/748-2628, ⓦwww.cayooshcampground.ca; $21–26; mid-April to mid-Oct). The **visitor**

centre/museum is in the old church at 790 Main St (mid-May to Sept Mon–Sat 9am–5pm, longer hours July & Aug; ⓣ604/256-4308, ⓦwww.lillooetbc.com).

From Lillooet, Hwy 99 heads east for 50km to Hwy 97; you can then either turn south towards Cache Creek (see p.734), or snake your way north to the gold fields of the Cariboo.

The Cariboo

The Cariboo is the name given to the broad, rolling ranching country and immense forests of British Columbia's interior plateau, which extend north of Lillooet between the Coast Mountains to the west and Cariboo Mountains to the east. The region contains by far the dullest scenery in the province, and what little interest it offers – aside from fishing and boating on thousands of remote lakes – comes from its **gold-mining** heritage. Initially exploited by fur traders to a small degree, the region was fully opened up following the discovery of gold in 1858 in the lower Fraser Valley. The building of the **Cariboo Wagon Road**, a stagecoach route north out of Lillooet, spread gold fever right up the Fraser watershed as men leapfrogged from creek to creek, culminating in the big finds at Williams Creek in 1861 and Barkerville a year later.

Much of the old Wagon Road is today retraced by lonely **Highway 97** (the Cariboo Hwy), which runs through hour after hour of straggling pine forests and past the occasional ranch and small, marsh-edged lake – scenery that strikes you as pristine and pastoral for a while but which soon leaves you in a tree-weary stupor. If you're forced to stop over, there are innumerable lodges, ranches and motels on or just off the hwy; you can pick up material on the region at the Vancouver tourist office or information centres en route.

Clinton and Williams Lake

A compact little village surrounded by green pastures and tree-covered hills, **CLINTON** marks the beginning of the heart of Cariboo country. The town has a couple of **B&Bs**, a **campsite**, *Clinton Pines Campground,* 1204 Cariboo Ave (ⓣ250/459-0030; ⓔclintonpines@explornet.com; $18–24) and a **motel** – the *Nomad* (ⓣ250/459-2214 or 1-888/776-6623, ⓔnomad@bcwireless.com; ❷).

The three tiny settlements beyond Clinton at 70, 100 and 150 Mile House are echoes of the old roadhouses built by men who were paid by the mile to blaze the Cariboo Wagon Road – which is doubtless why 100 Mile House is well short of one hundred miles from the start of the road. Visit ⓦwww.southcaribootourism.com for details of the fishing, riding and other local outdoor pursuits.

WILLIAMS LAKE, 14km north of 150 Mile House and still 238km south of Prince George, is a busy and drab transport centre huddled in the lee of a vast crag on terraces above the eponymous lake. It has plenty of motels, B&Bs, boat launches and swimming spots south of the town – but it's hardly a place you'd want to spend any time, unless you're dead-beat after driving or around on the first weekend in July for its famous **rodeo**. The year-round **visitor centre** is at 1660 South Broadway (May–Sept daily 9am–5pm; Oct–April Mon–Fri 9am–4pm; ⓣ250/392-5025 or 1-877/967-5253, ⓦwww.williamslakechamber.com).

Bella Coola

Highway 20 branches west from Williams Lake, a part-paved, part-gravel road that runs 456km to **BELLA COOLA**, a wilderness-enveloped village in a superb setting. Most of the road ploughs through the interminable forest or ranching country of the Cariboo Plateau, but there are services, campsites and the odd hotel at regular intervals and the last very worthwhile 100km or so traverses the high and stunningly spectacular peaks of the Coast Mountains and **Tweedsmuir Provincial Park**, which at a million hectares is BC's largest.

Arrival and information

Once you **drive** through Tweedsmuir Park on Hwy 20 you'll encounter the notorious "Hill", a winding and precipitous stretch of road barely tamed by the various upgradings over the years. Until 1953 there was no road link here at all. Instead, there was a sixty-kilometre gap in the mountain stretch, a missing link the province refused to bridge. In response the locals of Bella Coola built the road on their own, completing the so-called Freedom Road in three years. No **buses** serve Bella Coola, and beyond the village there is no onward road route. You can **fly** in to and out of the airport at nearby Hagensborg (Pacific Coastal Airlines Ⓣ250/982-2225, Ⓦwww.pacific-coastal.com), but it's not really convenient. The most scenic way to reach Bella Coola is on a Discovery Coast Passage **boat** from Port Hardy; see p.860 for full details of this service.

Bella Coola's **visitor centre** is in the Co-op grocery store at 450 Mackenzie St (June 2 to Sept 6 Mon–Fri 9am–5.30pm; Mon & Wed July & Aug 7am–5.30pm for early ferry arrivals; Ⓣ250/799-5202 or 1-866/799-5202, Ⓦwww.bellacoola.ca).

Accommodation

Accommodation in town is provided by a handful of B&Bs and inns: try the *Bella Coola Valley Inn* (Ⓣ250/799-5316 or 1-888/799-5316, Ⓦwww.bellacoolavalleyinn.com; ❺), the closest hotel to the ferry terminal, and the *Bella Coola Motel* (Ⓣ250/799-5323, Ⓦwww.bellacoolavalley.com; ❸) at the corner of Burke and Clayton streets; both places are downtown.

Near **Hagensborg** there's also the *Bella Coola Mountain Lodge* on Hwy 20 16km east of Bella Coola (Ⓣ250/982-2298, Ⓦwww.coastmountainlodge.com; ❸) or camp in the heart of the village at *Gnome's Home Campground & RV Park* (Ⓣ250/982-2504, Ⓦwww.gnomeshome.ca; $15–18; April–Oct). Bella Coola itself currently has no dedicated campsite.

The town and around

Bella Coola itself was formerly the domain of the Bella Coola, or Nuxalk, an aboriginal people who prospered thanks to the surfeit of salmon in local rivers and were visited by Alexander Mackenzie as early as 1793; Mackenzie's arrival here on July 22 marked the conclusion of his successful attempt to become the first man to cross North America. In 1869 the Hudson's Bay Company opened a trading post, though permanent white settlement only began in 1894. One house belonging to a company clerk is now all that remains of the post.

Besides the small museum in the old schoolhouse and surveyor's cabin (June–Sept Sun–Fri 10am–5pm; $2.50 Ⓣ250/799-5767, Ⓦwww.bellacoolamuseum.ca) and glorious scenery, there's not much to see in Bella Coola.

Language, heritage and buildings here – notably the square-logged barns – all show a Scandinavian touch (Norwegian settlers were early pioneers; many of today's inhabitants can trace their ancestry to 120 Norwegians led here from Minnesota in 1894 by a pastor determined to found a Utopian society). **Hagensborg**, a village with accommodation (see above) 18km east of Bella Coola, preserves a particularly strong Nordic flavour. About 10km from the village, roughly midway to Bella Coola, are the **Thorsen Creek Petroglyphs**, a hundred or so rock drawings; the visitor centre should be able to provide a guide to explore the site.

Visiting Tweedsmuir Provincial Park

If you want to **explore** the park, (Ⓦwww.env.gov.bc.ca/bcparks) it's best to do so as a day or multi-day trip from Bella Coola; the main sights and trails are too far from Hwy 20 to see as you pass through on the way to town.

One of the park's chief sights are the **Hunlen Falls**, 260m of plunging water, though it's a struggle to see them – you need to leave the road near Atnarko River (midway through the park) and take the rough road the 13km to the trailhead for the falls and Turner Lake. From here it's another 16km of walking, with an elevation gain of 2000m. This is typical of a trail system that is still relatively undeveloped, and there are few day-hikes or easy trails from the hwy; an exception is the 8km round-trip to a series of pretty lakes from a trailhead 16km west of the Atnarko River campsites (see below).

There are limited **accommodation** options: the *Tweedsmuir Lodge* (Ⓣ250/982-2402, Ⓦwww.tweedsmuirparklodge.com; ⑥), 60km east of Bella Coola on the Atnarko River, but in the park itself, has ten lodge rooms and chalets, two with kitchenettes. There are also two simple BC provincial campgrounds on the north side of the river (June–Sept; $15).

Highway 97: north of Williams Lake

North of Williams Lake on Hwy 97, the **Fraser River** re-enters the scenic picture and, after a dramatic stretch of canyon, reinstates more compelling hills and snatches of river meadows. Yet this also marks the start of some of the most concerted **logging operations** in all of BC, evidenced by increasing numbers of crude pepper-pot kilns used to burn off waste wood. By **QUESNEL**, home of the "world's largest plywood plant", you're greeted with scenes from an environmentalist's nightmare: whole mountainsides cleared of trees, hill-sized piles of sawdust, and unbelievably large lumber mills surrounded by stacks of logs and finished timber that stretch literally as far as the eye can see. If you're stuck for accommodation (there are a dozen or so hotels) or tempted by any of the many mill tours, contact the **visitor centre** in Le Bourdais Park at 703 Carson Ave (mid-May to early Sept Mon, Wed, Fri & Sun 9am–6pm, Tues, Thurs & Sat 9am–9pm; early Sept to mid-May Tues–Sat 9am–4pm; Ⓣ250/992-8716 or 1-800/992-4922, Ⓦwww.northcariboo.com).

Barkerville

Most people who take the trouble to drive Hwy 97 detour from Quesnel to **Barkerville Historic Town** (June–Sept daily 8am–8pm; $8 entry only, $23.50 for entry, theatre and stagecoach ride; Ⓣ250/994-3332 Ⓦwww.barkerville.ca), 90km to the east in the heart of the Cariboo Mountains, the site of the Cariboo's biggest gold strike and an invigorating spot in its own right, providing a much-needed jolt to the senses after the sleepy scenery to the south. In 1862 a Cornishman named Billy Barker idly staked a claim here and after digging down a metre or so was about to pack up and head north. Yet urged on by his mates, he dug another couple of spadefuls and turned up a cluster of nuggets worth $600,000. Within months Barkerville, as it was later dubbed, had become the largest city in the region, and rode the boom for a decade until the gold finally ran out. Today, 125 buildings have been restored and are filled with costumed staff, and the main administrative building has displays on mining methods and the gold rush.

If you're continuing from Quesnel north to Prince George and beyond, turn to Chapter 11, "The North", beginning on p.869.

There are two **accommodation** options: the *St George Hotel* (Ⓣ250/994-0008 or 1-888/246-7690, Ⓦwww.stgeorgehotel.bc.ca; ❻), a restored 1890s heritage building; or the *Kelly and King House B&Bs* (Ⓣ250/994-3328, Ⓦwww.kellyhouse.ca; ❹), with two separate locations, also at the heart of Barkerville.

In **WELLS**, 8km west of Barkerville, are the *Hubs Motel*, 12438 Barkerville Hwy (Ⓣ250/994-3313, Ⓦwww.hubsmotel.ca; ❷); the *Wells Hotel*, 2341 Pooley St (Ⓣ250/994-3427 or 1-800/860-2299, Ⓦwww.wellshotel.com; ❸), a restored 1933 heritage country inn with licensed café and breakfast included; and the *White Cap Motor Inn*, 3885 Ski Hill Rd (Ⓣ250/994-3489 or 1-800/377-2028, Ⓦwww.whitecapinn.com; ❸), which has RV and camping spaces for $21–27.50. You can **camp** at the linked 168-pitch *Government Hill*, *Forest Rose* and *Lowhee* sites of Barkerville Campgrounds (Ⓣ250/994-3297, Ⓦwww.barkervillecampgrounds.ca), adjacent to the old town, for $16–20 per night. Wells has to **visitor centre** at 11900 Hwy 26 (daily mid-May to Aug 9am–6/7pm; Ⓣ250/994-2323 or 1-877/451-9355, Ⓦwww.wellsbc.com).

Vancouver Island

The proximity of **VANCOUVER ISLAND** to Vancouver makes it one of western Canada's premier tourist destinations, though its popularity is slightly out of proportion to what is, in most cases, a pale shadow of the scenery on offer on the region's mainland. The largest of North America's west-coast islands, it stretches almost 500km from north to south, but has a population of almost 750,000, mostly concentrated around **Victoria**, whose small-town feel belies its role as BC's second metropolis and provincial capital. While Victoria makes a convenient base for touring the island and merits a couple of days in its own right, there's little else in any of the island's other sizeable towns to justify an overnight stop (the countryside is another matter).

Vancouver Island's main attraction is the outdoors and, increasingly, **whale-watching**, an activity which can be pursued from Victoria, **Tofino**, **Ucluelet**, **Telegraph Cove** and several other places on the island. The scenery is a mosaic of landscapes, principally defined by a central spine of snowcapped mountains that divide it between the rugged and sparsely populated wilderness of the west coast and the more sheltered lowlands of the east. Rippling hills characterize the northern and southern tips, and few areas are free of the lush forest mantle that supports one of BC's most lucrative logging industries.

The beaches at **Parksville** and **Qualicum** lure locals and tourists alike, while the stunning seascapes of the unmissable **Pacific Rim National Park** and the mountainous vastness of **Strathcona Provincial Park** are the main destinations for most visitors. Both parks offer the usual panoply of outdoor activities, with hikers being particularly well served by the national park's **West Coast Trail**, a demanding and very popular long-distance path.

Lovely, short ferry rides will take you from the ferry terminal north of Victoria to various of the **Southern Gulf Islands**, each dulcet little retreats with plenty of places to stay, good restaurants, galleries, craftspeople and an easygoing way of life.

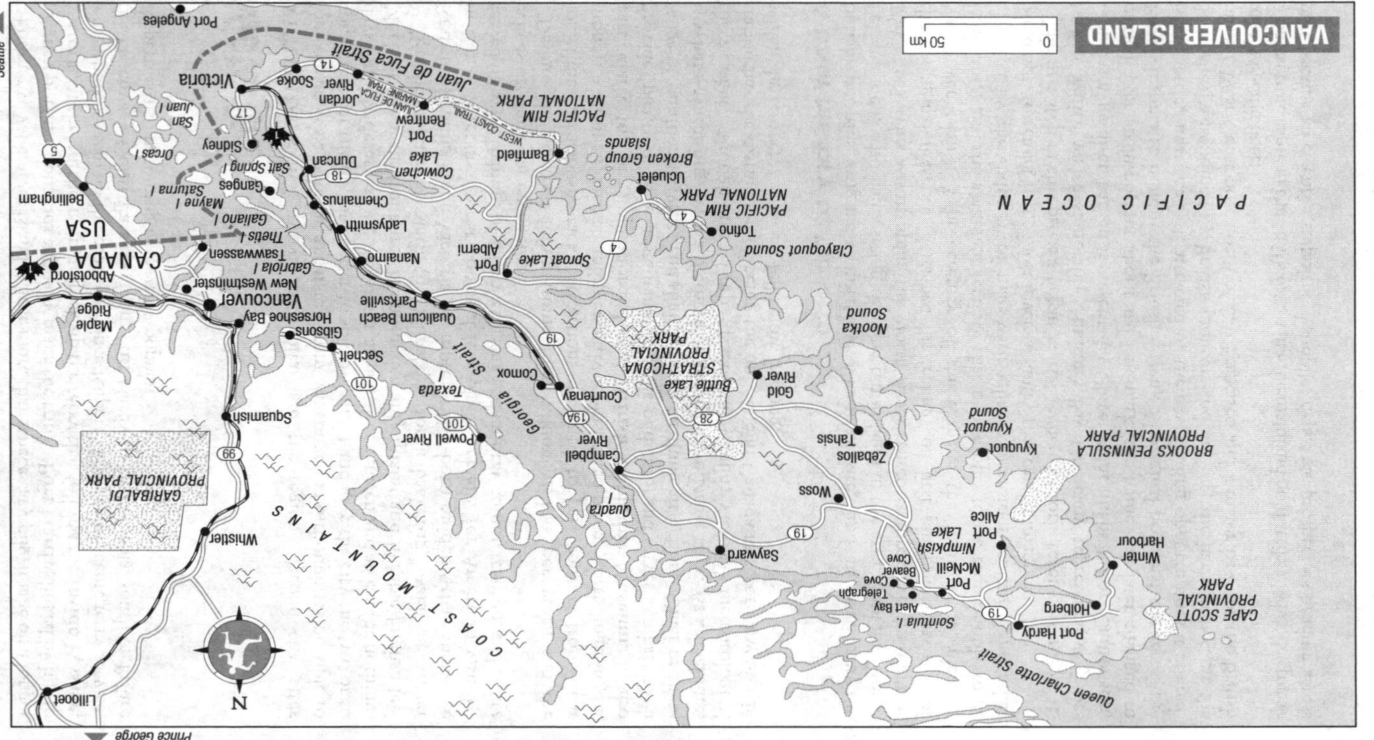
VANCOUVER ISLAND
0
50 km
Seattle
Prince George
N
Lillooet
GARIBALDI PROVINCIAL PARK
Whistler
99
Squamish
Maple Ridge
Abbotsford
CANADA
USA
Bellingham
5
Vancouver
New Westminster
Horseshoe Bay
Gibsons
Sechelt
101
Powell River
Texada I
Tsawwassen
Gabriola I
Thetis I
Galiano I
Mayne I
Saturna I
Orcas I
San Juan I
Salt Spring I
Ganges
Sidney
17
Victoria
Port Angeles
Sooke
14
Jordan River
Juan de Fuca Strait
JUAN DE FUCA MARINE TRAIL
Port Renfrew
WEST COAST TRAIL
PACIFIC RIM NATIONAL PARK
Duncan
18
Chemainus
Ladysmith
Nanaimo
Cowichen Lake
Parksville
Qualicum Beach
Port Alberni
Sproat Lake
Bamfield
Broken Group Islands
Ucluelet
4
Tofino
Clayoquot Sound
COAST MOUNTAINS
Georgia Strait
Comox
Courtenay
19A
19
Campbell River
Quadra I
STRATHCONA PROVINCIAL PARK
Buttle Lake
28
Gold River
Nootka Sound
Tahsis
Zeballos
Kyuquot
Kyuquot Sound
BROOKS PENINSULA PROVINCIAL PARK
Woss
Sayward
Port Alice
Nimpkish Lake
Port McNeill
Beaver Cove
Telegraph Cove
Alert Bay
Sointula I.
Port Hardy
Holberg
Winter Harbour
CAPE SCOTT PROVINCIAL PARK
Queen Charlotte Strait
PACIFIC OCEAN

For many, Vancouver Island is little more than a necessary pilgrimage on a longer journey north. Thousands annually make the trip to **Port Hardy**, linked by bus to Victoria, at the northern tip, to pick up the ferry that follows the **Inside Passage**, a breathtaking trip up the coast to Prince Rupert. The newer scenic ferry service, the **Discovery Coast Passage**, from Port Hardy to Bella Coola, south of Prince Rupert, is also becoming deservedly popular.

Victoria

VICTORIA is BC's provincial capital and the region's second city after Vancouver. It's a popular excursion from Vancouver, and though it's possible to come here for the day, it's better to stay overnight and give the city the two or so days it richly deserves. Victoria is not named after a queen and an era for nothing. Much of the waterfront area has an undeniably quaint and likeable English feel – "Brighton Pavilion with the Himalayas for a backdrop," said the writer Rudyard Kipling – and Victoria has more British-born residents than anywhere in Canada. Yet its tourist potential is exploited chiefly for American visitors, served up with lashings of fake Victoriana and chintzy commercialism, and ersatz echoes of empire at every turn.

Despite the seasonal influx (some four million visitors per year), and the sometimes atrociously tacky attractions designed to part tourists from their money, it's a small, relaxed and pleasantly sophisticated place, worth lingering in, particularly for the inspirational **Royal British Columbia Museum**. It also provides plenty of pubs, restaurants (and the odd club) and serves as a base for a range of outdoor activities and slightly more far-flung attractions. Chief of these is **whale-watching**, with a plethora of companies offering trips. As a final lure, the weather – though often damp – is extremely mild; Victoria's meteorological station has the distinction of being the only one in Canada to record a winter in which the temperature never fell below freezing.

A brief history of Victoria

Salish peoples originally inhabited Victoria's site, and in particular the Lekwammen, who had a string of some ten villages in the area. Captain George Vancouver, who was mapping the North American coast apparently ignorant of the aboriginal presence, described his feelings on first glimpsing this part of Vancouver Island: "The serenity of the climate, the innumerable pleasing landscapes, and the abundant fertility that nature puts forth, require only to be enriched by the industry of man with villages, mansions, cottages and other buildings, to render it the most lovely country that can be imagined."

The first step in this process began in 1842 when Victoria received some of its earliest **white visitors**, notably Hudson's Bay Company representative James Douglas, who disembarked at present-day Clover Point and built **Fort Camouson**, named after an important aboriginal landmark (the name was later changed to **Fort Victoria** to honour the British queen). Aboriginal peoples from across the island settled near the fort, attracted by the new trading opportunities it offered. Soon they were joined by British pioneers and in time, the harbour became the busiest West Coast port north of San Francisco and a major base for the British navy's Pacific fleet.

Boom time came in the 1850s following the mainland gold strikes, when Victoria's port became an essential stopoff and supplies depot for prospectors heading across

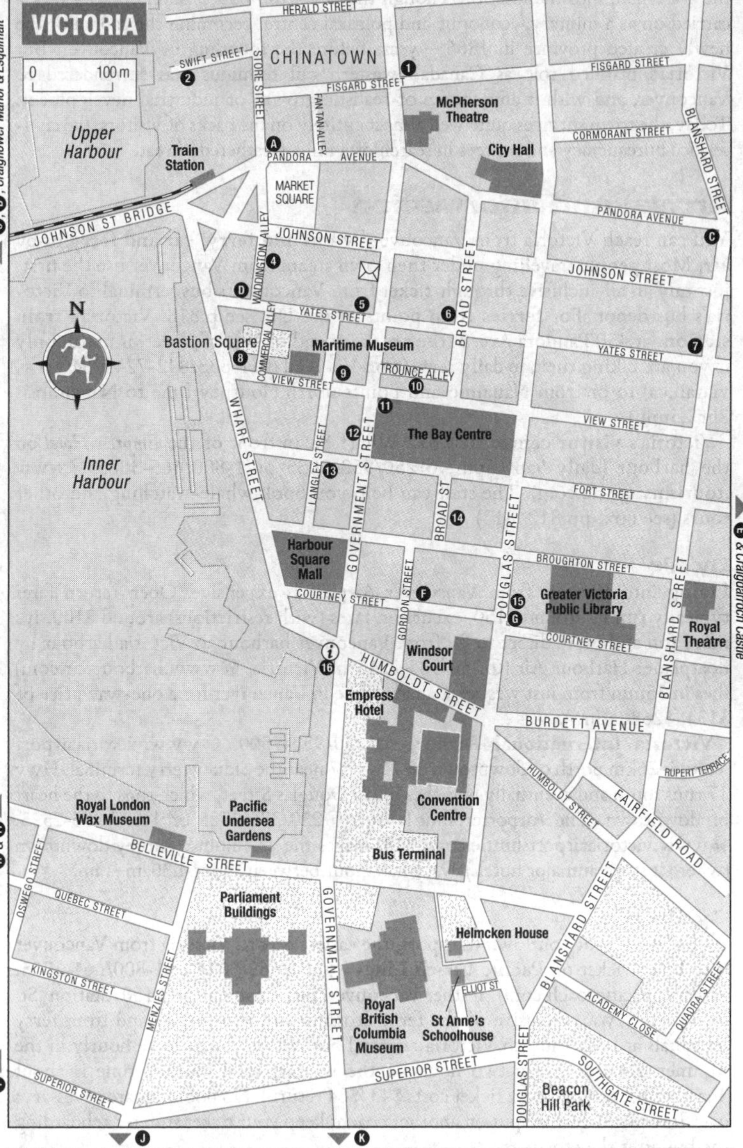

ACCOMMODATION

Heathergate House	J
James Bay Inn	K
Laurel Point Inn	H
Magnolia Hotel & Spa	F
Ocean Island Backpacker's Inn	C
Prior House	E
Ryan's	I
Selkirk Guest House	B
Strathcona Hotel	G
Swans Suite Hotel & Brewpub	A
Victoria Youth Hostel	D

RESTAURANTS, CAFÉS & BARS

Barb's Place	17
Big Bad John's	15
Brasserie L'Ecole	1
Canoe	2
Darcy's Pub	8
Demitasse Coffee Bar	6 & 7
Earl's	11
Il Terrazzo	4
Milestones	16
Murchie's	12
Pagliacci's	14
Rebar	9
The Reef	5
Swans Brewpub	A
Spinnakers Gastro Brewpub	3
The Tapa Bar	10
The Temple	13

the water and into the interior. Though the gold-rush bubble soon burst, Victoria carried on as a military, economic and political centre, becoming the capital of the newly created province in 1866 – years before the founding of Vancouver. But Victoria's planned role as Canada's western rail terminus was surrendered to Vancouver, and with it any chance of realistic growth or industrial development. Today, the town survives quite well almost entirely on the backs of visitors, the civil-service bureaucracy and retirees in search of a mild-weathered retreat.

Arrival and information

You can reach Victoria from Vancouver by **bus and ferry**, **car and ferry** or by **air**. Most people travelling under their own steam from Vancouver use the first; just buy an all-inclusive through-ticket from Vancouver's bus terminal to Victoria's bus depot. For **ferries** from points in the US, see p.818. Victoria's **train station**, at 450 Pandora Ave, at the northern end of Wharf Street, is useful only if you are taking the one daily service on Via Rail (Ⓣ1-888/842-7245, Ⓦwww.viarail.ca) to or from Nanaimo and points north (journey time to Nanaimo is 2hr 25min).

Victoria's **visitor centre** is at 812 Wharf St, in front of the *Empress Hotel* on the harbour (daily 9am–5pm; Ⓣ250/953-2033 or 1-800/663-3883 Ⓦwww.tourismvictoria.com). The staff can help you book whale-watching and other tours (see box, pp.812–813).

By Air

Flying into Victoria from Vancouver Airport is expensive. Open return fares typically run to around $150, excursion fares (with restrictions) around $100. It's more fun and more direct to fly from Vancouver harbour to Victoria harbour by floatplane: Harbour Air (Ⓣ250/384-2215 in Victoria, Ⓦwww.harbour-air.com) flies in 35min from just west of Canada Place in Vancouver for a one-way price of $134 ($268 return).

Victoria International Airport (Ⓣ250/953-7500, Ⓦwww.victoriaairport.com) is 26km north of downtown on Hwy 17 near the Sidney ferry terminal. Hwy 17 runs south and eventually branches off to Douglas Street, which runs to the heart of downtown. The Airporter shuttle bus (Ⓣ250/386-2525 or 1-877/386-2525, Ⓦwww.victoriaairportshuttle.com; $18) makes the 45-minute journey downtown (where it stops at major hotels) every half-hour between about 4.30am–1am.

By Bus

If you're without your own transport, the easiest way to Victoria from Vancouver is to buy a ticket on **Pacific Coach Lines** (Ⓣ604/662-8074 or 1-800/661-1725, Ⓦwww.pacificcoach.com) at the Vancouver bus terminal at 1150 Station St, which takes you, inclusive of the ferry crossing and journeys to and from ferry terminals at both ends, to Victoria's central bus station. Buses leave hourly in the summer, roughly every two hours in the winter; total journey time is about 3hr 30min and a one-way ticket costs $43 ($84 return). No bookings are necessary: overflow passengers are put on another coach; keep your ticket stub for reboarding the bus after the crossing.

A similar all-inclusive bus-ferry arrangement operated by Greyhound (6 daily; 2hr 55min; $17 plus BC Ferries fee) also operates from Vancouver **to Nanaimo** on Vancouver Island (113km north of Victoria) via the Horseshoe Bay Terminal, located about fifteen minutes north of West Vancouver on Hwy 1. You can reach the Horseshoe Bay Terminal by taking bus #250 or #257 from Georgia Street. The ferry charges ($13.50) are the same for foot passengers on the Horseshoe Bay-Nanaimo and Tsawwassen-Swartz Bay (Victoria) services.

You can also reach Victoria directly **from Vancouver Airport** by inclusive coach-ferry (7 daily; $48 single). The Pacific Coach Lines bus desk is in international arrivals; journey time is about 3hr 30min. If you intend to visit Victoria before Vancouver, and are flying, then it usually only costs a little more to fly direct to the city from farther afield: it's not usually worth flying to Vancouver and then taking the bus-ferry option to save money.

The **bus terminal** is downtown at 700 Douglas St, close to the Royal British Columbia Museum. Pacific Coach Lines' buses (Ⓣ250/385-4411, Ⓦwww.pacificcoach.com) from Vancouver or Vancouver airport drop you here, and it is the base for Greyhound (Ⓣ250/388-5248 or 1-800/661-8747, Ⓦwww.greyhound.ca) for onward connections.

By Car

BC Ferries operates four routes to Vancouver Island across the Georgia Strait from mainland BC (information on Ⓣ1-888/223-3779 anywhere in North America, otherwise Ⓣ250/386-3431, Ⓦwww.bcferries.com). Reservations are essential in summer to avoid long waits. The route used by most Vancouver–Victoria drivers is the **Tsawwassen–Swartz Bay** connection, also the route used by Pacific Coach Lines' buses. Ferries ply the route almost continuously from 7am–9pm (sixteen sailings daily in summer, minimum of eight daily in winter). Car tickets in high season (from late June to early Sept) cost $45. Bicycles cost $2 year-round. You need to add on per-person fares, which are $13.50.

The Mid-Island Express **Tsawwassen–Nanaimo** (Duke Point terminal), midway up the island, has eight or so departures daily on the two-hour crossing. More boats cover the 1hr 40min **Horseshoe Bay–Nanaimo** (Departure Bay terminal) route, from a terminal about fifteen minutes' drive from West Vancouver. Fares for both these routes are the same as for Tsawwassen to Swartz Bay. The fourth route is **Powell River–Comox**, Powell River being some 160km northwest of Vancouver on the Sunshine Coast.

City transport

The most enjoyable means of transport are the tiny Inner Harbour **ferries** (Ⓣ250/708-0201, Ⓦwww.victoriaharbourferry.com) that run around the harbour. Stops include Fisherman's Wharf, *Ocean Pointe Resort* and West Bay Marina, but they're worth taking just for the ride: try an evening mini-cruise ($20) around the harbour: buy tickets (from $2.25, depending on route) on ferries in the Inner Harbour or book at the visitor centre. You're unlikely to need to take a local **bus** if you stick to the downtown area, but if you do venture out, most services run from the corner of Douglas and Yates streets. The fare within the large central zone is $2.25 – tickets and the DayPASS ($7) are sold at the visitor centre, 7-Eleven stores and other marked outlets, or you can pay on board (exact fare only).

Accommodation

Victoria fills up quickly in the summer, and most of its limited budget **accommodation** is well known and heavily patronized. Top-price hotels cluster around the Inner Harbour area; **hostels** and more downmarket alternatives are scattered all over, though the largest concentration of cheap **hotels** and **motels** is around the Gorge Road and Douglas Street areas northwest of downtown.

Reservations are virtually obligatory in all categories, though the accommodation service (Ⓣ1-800/663-3883, Ⓦwww.tourismvictoria.com) will root out a room if you're stuck. This will likely be in one of the city's vast selection of **B&Bs**;

prices for many are surprisingly elevated, though owners of many of the more far-flung places will pick you up from downtown.

Victoria's commercial **campsites** are full to bursting in summer, with most space given over to RVs. Few of these are convenient for downtown – given that you'll have to travel, you might as well head for one of the more scenic provincial park sites. Most are on the Trans-Canada Hwy to the north, or on Hwy 14 east of Victoria.

Hotels, motels and B&Bs

James Bay Inn 270 Government St, at Toronto ⓣ250/384-7151 or 1-800/836-2649, ⓦwww.jamesbayinn.com. This Edwardian building, just two blocks south of the BC Parliament, was where famed Canadian artist Emily Carr died as a patient when it was a priory. Today, it is – relatively speaking – one of Victoria's more reasonably priced options, with 45 simply furnished rooms, and a restaurant and pub in the basement. 6

Laurel Point Inn 680 Montréal St ⓣ250/386-8721 or 1-800/663-7667, ⓦwww.laurelpoint.com. Don't be put off by the size of this two hundred-room resort-style hotel. All the rooms have a balcony and good harbour view, thanks to a position on a well-landscape promontory (with a Japanese garden) on the Inner Harbour. The contemporary aesthetic is simple and clean, and a far cry from the chintzy look of many of Victoria's hotels. There are two wings, north and south – you want to be in the southern one, designed by Arthur Erickson (see p.770) in 1989. Here, the rooms are all pale wood and dark marble, with Japanese-style sliding doors, Asian works of art and airy, stylish bathrooms. 7

The Magnolia Hotel & Spa 623 Courtney St ⓣ250/381-0999 or 1-877/624-6654, ⓦwww.magnoliahotel.com. This 63-room boutique hotel lays on the character thick, the small lobby setting the period Edwardian tone, though the effect, especially in the high-quality rooms (the best have harbour views and fireplaces) and superb bathrooms, is never stuffy. The on-site spa is one of the best in the city. 7

Strathcona Hotel 919 Douglas St ⓣ250/383-7137 or 1-800/663-7476, ⓦwww.strathconahotel.com. Large, modern hotel where rooms include baths and TVs. There's a British-style pub and restaurant, plus a club downstairs with booming live and DJ music which may not be to all tastes. 5

Swans Suite Hotel & Brewpub 506 Pandora Ave ⓣ250/361-3310 or 1-800/668-7926, ⓦwww.swanshotel.com. Brewpub aside, the appeal of the thirty rooms here is the setting, a converted 1880s grain store that means many of the suites and larger rooms are quirky, loft-style spaces, often on a split level and with exposed beams and bold, original artwork. The one- and two-bedroom suites take up to six people, making them perfect for families, and there are fully equipped kitchens and dining and living rooms. Doubles 7, suites 9

Bed and breakfasts

Heathergate House 122 Simcoe St ⓣ250/383-0068 or 1-888/683-0068, ⓦwww.heathergatebb.com. This small B&B offers three rooms plus a separate two-bed cottage within walking distance of the Inner Harbour and the sights. All rooms are en suite. There's a private floor for guests with a lounge and TV room. 5

Prior House 620 St Charles St ⓣ250/592-8847 or 1-877/924-3300, ⓦwww.priorhouse.com. A very smart six-room B&B; once the home of Victoria's lieutenant governor – ask for his suite, complete with bathroom with chandelier. About 2.5km east of downtown in the smart Rockland area, so it's better if you have transport. 8

Ryan's 224 Superior St ⓣ250/389-0012 or 1-877/389-0012, ⓦwww.ryansbb.com. A very pretty 1892 heritage building south of the Royal BC Museum and a five-minute walk to downtown; all seven rooms are nicely decorated and have private bathrooms. 7

Selkirk Guest House 934 Selkirk Ave ⓣ250/389-1213 or 1-800/974-6638, ⓦwww.selkirkguesthouse.com. Fine waterfront home dating from 1909, northwest of the Inner Harbour. It can be difficult to find, so call ahead or check their website map for directions. It's well placed for bike and walking trails (it's on the Galloping Goose Trail) and you can rent boats and canoes. 6

Hostels

Ocean Island Backpacker's Inn 791 Pandora Ave, at Blanshard ⓣ250/385-1788 or 1-888/888-4180, ⓦwww.oceanisland.com. A good, reasonably central location in the northeast corner of downtown. The restored 1893 heritage building has a wide variety of dorms and rooms (singles and doubles with and without bathroom) on a sliding scale depending on the time of year, the day of the week (more on Fri and Sat) and whether you have a HI card. Facilities include internet access, free wi-fi, a café and laundry. Dorm beds cost $19; private doubles cost from $28, family rooms from

$36. Weekly and monthly rates are available on dorms and rooms.

Victoria Youth Hostel (HI) 516 Yates St, at Wharf ⓣ250/385-4511 or 1-888/883-0099, ⓦwww.hihostels.ca. Large, modern, welcoming and extremely well-run place just a few blocks north of the Inner Harbour. The bunk rooms can be noisy but you can buy earplugs at reception. The notice boards are packed with useful information on the city, and facilities include free wi-fi, laundry and bike storage. Rates for dorms and private rooms fluctuate according to the time of year: Members from $20–26, nonmembers from $24–30; private rooms $58–68 for members, $66–76 for nonmembers.

Campsites

Fort Victoria RV and Park Campground 340 Island Hwy 1A ⓣ250/479-8112, ⓦwww.fortvictoria.ca. Closest site to downtown, located 6km north of Victoria off the Trans-Canada Hwy. Take bus #14 (for Craigflower) from the city centre; it stops right by the gate. Large three thousand-pitch site mainly for RVs but with a few tent sites; free hot showers, plus laundromat. RV sites $37 for two people.

Goldstream Provincial Park 2930 Trans-Canada Hwy ⓣ604/689-9025 or 1-800/689-9025, ⓦwww.discovercamping.ca. Bus #50 from Douglas St downtown. Although 16km northwest of the city off Hwy 1, this site is set in old-growth forests of cedar and Douglas fir and is Victoria's best camping option. Flush toilets and free hot showers, with plenty of hiking, swimming and fishing opportunities. $24/site.

Thetis Lake Trans-Canada Hwy at 1938 West Park Lane ⓣ250/478-3845, ⓔthetislake@shaw.ca. Runs a close second to Goldstream Provincial Park's campsites for the pleasantness of its setting, and is only 10km north of downtown. Family-oriented, with 150 sites, as well as laundry and coin-operated showers. $20 for two people.

The City

The Victoria that's worth bothering with is very small: almost everything worth seeing, as well as the best shops and restaurants, is within walking distance of the **Inner Harbour** area and the Old Town district behind it. On summer evenings this area is alive with strollers and buskers, and a pleasure to wander around as the sun drops over the water. Foremost among the daytime diversions are the **Royal British Columbia Museum** and the **Empress Hotel**. Most of the other trumpeted attractions are dreadful, and many charge entry fees out of proportion to what's on show. Otherwise you might drop by the modest **Maritime Museum** and think about a trip to the celebrated **Butchart Gardens**, some way out of town, but easily accessed by public transport or regular all-inclusive tours from the bus terminal. If you're around for a couple of days you should also find time to walk around **Beacon Hill Park**, a few minutes' walk from downtown to the south.

The Royal British Columbia Museum

The Royal British Columbia Museum (daily 10am–5pm, National Geographic IMAX Theatre daily 10am–8pm; museum $15, IMAX Theatre $11, combined ticket $24, IMAX double feature $16.75; ⓦwww.royalbcmuseum.bc.ca) is a short stroll along the waterfront from the visitor centre at 675 Belleville St. Founded in 1886, it is arguably the **best museum in Canada**, and regularly rated, by visitors and travel-magazine polls, as one of North America's top ten. All conceivable aspects of the province are examined, but the aboriginal peoples section is probably the definitive collection of a much-covered genre, while the natural-history sections – huge recreations of natural habitats, complete with sights, sounds and smells – are mind-boggling in scope and imagination. Allow at least two trips to take it all in.

The **second floor** contains full-scale reconstructions of some of the many natural habitats found in BC. The idea of recreating shorelines, coastal rainforests and Fraser Delta landscapes may sound far-fetched, yet all are incredibly realistic, down to dripping water and cool, dank atmospheres. Audiovisual displays and a

Whale-watching from Victoria

The waters around Victoria are not as **whale**-rich as those around Tofino on the west coast of Vancouver Island, but there's still a very good chance of spotting the creatures. Three pods of orcas (**killer whales**) live in the seas around southern Vancouver Island, around a hundred animals in all, so you may see these, though **minke** are the most common whale spotted, with occasional **greys** and **humpbacks** also present. Few outfits offer guaranteed sightings, and many cover themselves by telling you that if you don't see whales you stand a good chance of seeing Dall's **porpoises**, harbour or elephant **seals** and California and Steller **sea lions**.

While there are many outfits to choose from, they offer almost identical trips at the same prices, typically around \$80 to \$100 for a three-hour outing. There's usually a naturalist, or at least a knowledgeable crew member, to fill you in on what you're seeing (or not). The only real variables are the **boats** used, so you need to decide whether you want a rigid-hull cruiser (covered or uncovered), which is comfortable and sedate (and usually the most expensive at around \$100), a catamaran (\$75–90), or a high-speed aluminium-hull inflatable known as a "Zodiac" (\$80–1000), which is

tumult of information accompany the exhibits (the beaver film is worth hunting down), most of which focus on the province's 25,600km of coastline, a side of BC usually overlooked in favour of its interior forests and mountains.

On the **third floor** is the mother of all the tiny museums of bric-a-brac and pioneer memorabilia in BC. Arranged from the present day backwards, it explores in great detail every aspect of the province's social history over two centuries. Prominently featured are part of an early twentieth-century town, plus comprehensive displays on logging, mining, the gold rush and farming.

On the mezzanine off the **third floor** is a superb collection of **aboriginal peoples'** art, culture and history. It's presented in gloomy light which creates a solemn atmosphere, in keeping with the tragic nature of many of the displays. The collection divides into two epochs – before and after the coming of Europeans – tellingly linked by a single aboriginal carving of a white man, starkly and brilliantly capturing

▲ Whale-watching near Victoria

infinitely more exhilarating, but can offer a sometimes bumpy ride and lacks toilets on board.

The two companies below have been around longer than most; the visitor centre (see p.808) has details on others.

Seacoast Expeditions Located at the *Coast Victoria Harbourside*, 146 Kingston St (Ⓣ250/383-2254 or 1-800/386-1525, Ⓦwww.seacoastexpeditions.com) – a ten-minute walk across the Johnson Street bridge or a three-minute harbour ferry crossing (it also has a shuttle-bus pick-up from downtown hotels). Victoria's founding whale-watching company, Seacoast has been in the business for over two decades and offers between four and six three-hour trips daily between April and October ($89).

Five Star Charters 651 Humboldt St (Ⓣ250/388-7223 or 1-800/634-9617, Ⓦwww.5starwhales.com). Has been in business since 1985 and in the past claimed the highest percentage of whale sightings out of all the tour operators. It runs two daily three-hour trips from mid-April through September ($99). Trips are in twelve-passenger open cruiser or forty-person "Supercat" boats.

the initial wonder and weirdness of the new arrivals. The whole collection takes a thoughtful and oblique approach, taking you to the point where smallpox virtually wiped out in one year a culture that was eight millennia in the making.

Helmcken House and around

Helmcken House (irregular hours – check the RBCM website for the latest details; $5) stands adjacent to the museum. The oldest house in BC still on its original site, built in 1852, it is a predictable heritage offering showcasing the home, furnishings and embroidery talents of the Helmcken family. Dr John Helmcken was Fort Victoria's doctor and local political bigwig, and his house is a typical monument to stolid Victoria values. Upstairs it contains various attic treasures and some fearsome-looking medical tools. It's probably only of interest if you've so far managed to avoid any of Canada's many thousands of similar houses.

Just behind the house there's another old white-wood building, the **St Anne's Pioneer Schoolhouse**, originally purchased by a Bishop Demers for four sisters of the Order of St Ann, who in 1858 took it upon themselves to leave Québec to come and teach in Victoria. Built between 1843 and 1858, it's believed to be the oldest building in Victoria still in use.

The Parliament Buildings

The huge Victorian pile of the **Parliament Buildings** (early Sept to April Mon–Fri 8.30am–5pm for regular guided or self-guided tours (guaranteed guided tour at 4pm); late May to early Sept Mon–Fri 8.30am–5pm for regular guided or self-guided tours (guaranteed guided tour at 5pm), Sat–Sun 9am–5pm guided tours only; times may vary according to parliamentary business; all tours free; Ⓣ250/387-3046 or 1-800/663-7867 in BC) one block west of the museum at 501 Belleville St, is old and imposing in the manner of a large and particularly grand British town hall. Beautifully lit at night by some three hundred tiny bulbs, the domed building is framed by the sea and well-kept gardens – take time out on the front lawns, distinguished by a perky statue of Queen Victoria and a giant sequoia, a gift from the state of California.

Designed by the 25-year-old Francis Rattenbury, who was also responsible for the nearby *Empress Hotel*, the building was completed in 1897, at a cost of $923,000, in time for Queen Victoria's jubilee. Figures from Victoria's grey bureaucratic past are duly celebrated, the main door guarded by statues of Sir James Douglas, who chose the site of the city, and Sir Matthew Baillie Begbie (aka the "Hanging Judge"), responsible for law and order during the heady days of gold fever. Sir George Vancouver keeps an eye on proceedings from the top of the dome.

Beacon Hill Park

The best park within walking distance of the town centre is **Beacon Hill Park**, south of the Inner Harbour and a few minutes' walk up the road behind the museum. Victoria is sometimes known as the "City of Gardens", and at the right times of the year this park shows why. The city's biggest green space, it has lots of paths, ponds, big trees and quiet corners, and plenty of views over the **Juan de Fuca Strait** to the distant Olympic Mountains of Washington State (especially on the park's southern side); the park was a favoured retreat of celebrated artist Emily Carr, who painted several of its scenes.

The gardens in the park are by turns well tended and wonderfully wild and unkempt, a far cry from its earliest days, when it was known by the local Salish as "Meeacan", their word for a belly, as the hill was thought to resemble the stomach of large man lying on his back. They also claim the **world's tallest totem pole**, as well as the "Mile Zero" marker of the Trans-Canada Hwy and – that ultimate emblem of Englishness – a cricket pitch. Some of the trees are massive old-growth timbers you'd normally only see on the island's unlogged west coast. In spring, there are swaths of daffodils and blue camas flowers, the latter a floral monument to Victoria's earliest aboriginal inhabitants, who cultivated the flower for its edible bulb. Some thirty thousand other flowers are planted in the gardens annually.

The Empress Hotel

A town is usually desperate when one of its key attractions is a hotel, but in the case of Victoria the **Empress Hotel**, at 721 Government St, is so physically overbearing and plays such a part in the town's tourist appeal that it demands some

The Butchart Gardens

If you're into things horticultural, trek out to the celebrated and much-hyped **Butchart Gardens**, 22km north of Victoria at 800 Benvenuto Ave, Brentwood Bay on Hwy 17 towards the Swartz Bay ferry terminal (daily: mid-June to Aug 9am–10pm, first two weeks of Sept & Dec 9am–9pm; rest of the year 9am–sunset; rates $16.25 in early Jan, then on a sliding scale through the year to $29.50 between mid-June and Sept; ⓣ250/652-4422 or 652-5256 for recorded information, ⓦwww.butchartgardens.com). The gardens are renowned for the stunning **firework displays** that usually take place each Saturday evening from early July to early September, and are often followed by open-air concerts. If the music isn't to your taste, you can just stroll around the illuminated gardens during the late-evening summer opening hours.

The gardens were started in 1904 by Jennie Butchart, wife of a mine-owner and pioneer of Portland Cement in Canada and the US, her initial aim being to landscape one of her husband's quarries. The garden now covers fifty breathtaking acres, comprising rose, Japanese and Italian gardens and lots of decorative details. About half a million visitors a year tramp through the foliage, which includes over a million plants and seven hundred different species.

To get here by public transport take **bus** #75 for "Central Saanich" from downtown. Otherwise, there are regular Gray Line summer **shuttles** (daily May–Oct, roughly hourly ⓣ250/388-6539) from the main bus terminal, where tickets ($9 one-way) are obtainable not from the main ticket office but a separate Gray Lines desk.

sort of attention. If you want to **take tea**, which is why most casual visitors come, you can do so in either the Tea Lobby or the Library; there you can enjoy scones, biscuits, cakes and, of course, tea over six courses – but you have to abide by the dress code and be prepared for an enormous outlay.

The hotel's **Crystal Ballroom** and its lovely Tiffany-glass dome form the most opulent area on view, but the marginally less ornate entrance lounge is the top place for the charade of afternoon tea. There's also a reasonably priced bar and restaurant downstairs. For a bigger treat, take dinner amid the Edwardian splendour of *The Empress Room*.

The old town

The oldest part of Victoria focuses on **Bastion Square**, original site of Fort Victoria, from which it's a short walk to Market Square, a nice piece of old-town rejuvenation, and the main downtown shopping streets. Bastion Square's former saloons, brothels and warehouses have been spruced up and turned into offices, cafés and galleries.

The modest **Maritime Museum** at 28 Bastion Square (daily 9.30am–4.30pm; $10; Ⓦ www.mmbc.bc.ca) is of interest mainly for the former provincial courthouse in which it's housed, a lovely chocolate and vanilla coloured building. Displays include old charts, uniforms, ships' bells, old photographs, lots of models and a BC Ferries section on the second floor. On the top floor is the restored vice-admiralty courtroom, once the main seat of justice for the entire province.

Two blocks away to the north of the museum lies the attractive **Market Square** (Ⓣ 250/386-2441, Ⓦ www.marketsquare.ca), the old heart of Victoria but now a collection of some 35 speciality shops and cafés around a central courtyard (bounded by Store, Pandora and Johnson streets). This area boomed in 1858 following the gold rush, providing houses, saloons, opium dens, stores and various salacious entertainments for thousands of chancers and would-be immigrants. On the Pandora Avenue side of the area was a ravine, marked by the current sunken courtyard, beyond which lay **Chinatown** (now centred slightly further north on Fisgard St), the oldest on North America's west coast. Here, among other things, 23 factories processed ninety thousand pounds of opium a year for what was then a legitimate trade and – until the twentieth century – one of BC's biggest industries.

Other attractions

Outside the Inner Harbour, Victoria has a scattering of **minor attractions** that don't fit into any logical tour of the city – and at any rate are only quick-stop diversions – the most compelling of which is Craigdarroch Castle.

Craigdarroch Castle and the Art Gallery of Greater Victoria

Craigdarroch Castle (daily: mid-June to early Sept 9am–7pm; rest of year 10am–4.30pm; $12; Ⓦ www.craigdarrochcastle.com) is perched on a hilltop at 1050 Joan Crescent in Rockland, one of Victoria's more prestigious neighbourhoods. It was built by Robert Dunsmuir, a caricature of a Victorian politician, strike-breaker, robber baron and coal tycoon, who was forced to put up this gaunt Gothic pastiche to lure his wife away from Scotland. Only the best was good enough, from the marble, granite and sandstone of the superstructure to the intricately handworked panels of the ceilings over the main hall and staircase. Among the 39 rooms there's the usual clutter of Victoriana and period detail, in particular some impressive woodwork and stained and leaded glass.

The **Art Gallery of Greater Victoria** (May to early Sept Mon–Sat 10am–5pm, Thurs 10am–9pm, Sun noon–5pm; closed Mon the rest of the year; $12; Ⓦ www.aggv.bc.ca) is near Craigdarroch Castle at 1040 Moss St, just off Fort Street. It's of little interest unless you're partial to contemporary Canadian paintings and the country's best collection of Japanese art; the building, housed in the 1890 Spencer Mansion, boasts the only complete Shinto shrine outside Japan. It also has a small permanent collection of Emily Carr's work as well as a temporary exhibition that changes every six weeks.

The Emily Carr House, Point Ellice and Craigflower Manor

Ten rooms are open to the public at **Emily Carr House** (May–Oct Tues–Sat 11am–4pm; $6), about two blocks from the Inner Harbour at 207 Government St. This was the early home of BC's best-known artist, born here during a blizzard in 1871 in the old wooden bed still visible in what would become her bedroom. The building was constructed in 1864, and has been painstakingly restored to its former state. Fans of Carr may want to pay homage, but the works on the walls are copies.

Point Ellice House and Gardens

The 1861 Victorian-Italianate **Point Ellice House and Gardens** (guided tours May–Sept daily 11am–5pm; $6; ⓣ250/380-6506, ⓦwww.pointellicehouse.ca) at 2616 Pleasant St is magnificently recreated but less enticing than Craigdarroch Castle because of its slightly shabby surroundings. These can be overlooked if you make a point of arriving by sea, taking one of the little Harbour Ferry services to the house (10min) from the Inner Harbour. The restored Victorian-style gardens here are a delight on a summer afternoon. The interior – one of the best of its kind in western Canada – retains its largely Victorian appearance thanks partly to the reduced circumstances of the O'Reilly family, whose genteel slide into relative poverty over several generations (they lived here from 1861 to 1974) meant that many furnishings were simply not replaced. Tea is served on the lawns in the summer; it's a good idea to book ahead.

Craigflower Manor and Farmhouse

In its day, **Craigflower Manor and Farmhouse** (currently closed for restoration after a Jan 2009 fire; ⓣ250/387-4697; $6) at 110 Island Highway, about 9km and fifteen minutes' drive northwest from downtown, was among the earliest of Victoria's farming homesteads, marking the town's transition from trading post to permanent community. Built in 1856, its 39 rooms offer a clutter of Victoriana and period detail, in particular some fine woodwork and stained glass. Its owner, Kenneth McKenzie, was a Hudson's Bay Company bailiff, who recruited fellow Scottish settlers to form a farming community on Portage Inlet. The house soon became the foremost social centre in the fledgling village – mainly visited by officers because McKenzie's daughters were virtually the only white women on the island.

Eating, drinking and nightlife

Although clearly in Vancouver's culinary shadow, Victoria still has many **restaurants**, some extremely good, offering greater variety – and higher prices – than you'll find in most other BC towns. **Pubs** tend to be plastic imitations of British equivalents, with one or two worthy exceptions, as do the numerous **cafés** that pander to Victoria's self-conscious afternoon-tea ritual. Good snacks and pastry shops abound, while at the other extreme there are budget-busting establishments if you want a one-off treat or a change from the standard menus that await you on much of the rest of the island.

There's a smattering of **bars**, as well as **live music** venues and **clubs** to keep you happy for the limited time you're likely to spend in the city. **Listings** appear in the *Times-Colonist* (ⓦwww.timescolonist.com) newspaper and in a variety of free magazines distributed to shops, cafés and hotels, including the *Monday* magazine (Ⓦ www.mondaymag.com). **Tickets** for most offerings are available from the city's main performance space, the McPherson Playhouse, 3 Centennial Square, at Pandora and Government streets (Ⓣ 250/386-6121 or 1-888-717-6121, Ⓦ www.rmts.bc.ca).

Cafés, tea and snacks

Barb's Place 310 St Lawrence St, Fisherman's Wharf Ⓣ 250/384-6515, Ⓦ www.barbsplace.ca. A much-loved floating shack that offers classic home-cut chips, fish straight off the boat and oyster burgers and chowder to boot; the small bathtub-size ferries from the Inner Harbour drop you close by. Open March–Oct.

Demitasse Coffee Bar 1320 Blanshard St Ⓦ www.demitassevictoria.com. A popular, elegantly laidback hole-in-the-wall café with excellent coffee, salads, bagels, lunch-time snacks and an open fire in season. Second location at 1320 Broad St.

Empress Hotel 721 Government St Ⓣ 250/348-8111. Try tea in the lobby, with tourists and locals alike on their best behaviour amid the chintz and potted plants. A strict dress code allows no dirty jeans, anoraks or sportswear.

Murchie's 1110 Government St Ⓣ 250/383-3112, Ⓦ www.murchies.com. Grab a seat at this 110-seat "beverage bar", the best place for basic tea, coffee and cakes in the centre of Victoria's shopping streets. Also has an on-site shop.

Rebar 50 Bastion Square Ⓣ 250/361-9223, Ⓦ www.rebarmodernfood.com. A great place serving teas, coffees and health food (usually organically grown) at lunch and dinner, but most remarkable for its extraordinary range of freshly squeezed juices, smoothies, "power tonics" and frighteningly healthy wheatgrass drinks, including "Astro Turf": a blend of carrot, spinach, parsley and wheatgrass.

Restaurants

Brasserie l'Ecole 1715 Government St Ⓣ 250/475-6260, Ⓦ www.lecole.ca. This multi-award-winning restaurant serves the best French country cooking in town, with classic moules, frites, steaks, local fish and other staples, all made with immaculate and well-sourced local ingredients. Menus change daily. The dining room is pleasantly small and intimate, much like the wine list, which doesn't dazzle with big names, just decent, unpretentious selections to match the cooking. Main courses from about $18. Tues–Sat 5.30–11pm.

Canoe 450 Swift St Ⓣ 250/361-1940, Ⓦ www.canoebrewpub.com. One of Victoria's most popular places to eat and drink, with an impressive setting – this was once Victoria's power station, and the interior retains an old industrial feel, with sturdy walls and vast beams. The patio is superb, with views towards the harbour and the Johnson St bridge, and the atmosphere lively and convivial. Best of all, the food is excellent, whether you take the more refined restaurant offerings upstairs (mains from $12) or the simple bar snacks and pub food (oysters, pizzas, burgers) downstairs (from $5). And the beer, of course, is excellent. Sun–Wed 11.30am–11pm, Thurs 11.30am–midnight, Fri & Sat 11.30am–1am.

Earl's 1199 Government St Ⓣ 250/381-1866, Ⓦ www.earls.ca. You'll find an *Earl's* in many western Canadian towns, but the restaurants are none the worse for being part of a chain: good – not fast – food, with a lively, pleasant interior and friendly service. Always reliable, and fair prices, with mains from around $10. Mon–Thurs & Sun 11.30am–10pm, Fri & Sat 11.30am–11pm.

Il Terrazzo 555 Johnson St, in Waddington Alley Ⓣ 250/361-0028, Ⓦ www.ilterrazzo.com. Smooth, laidback ambience with lots of red brick and plants and a summer patio that provides the setting for good North American versions of Italian food. With *Pagliacci's* (see below), this is the best place in town for Italian food, but it's costly, with mains costing from $14–37. Lunch Mon–Fri 11.30am–3pm, dinner daily 5–10pm.

Milestone's 812 Wharf St Ⓣ 250/381-2244, Ⓦ www.milestonesrestaurants.com. Popular mid-priced place for burgers, pastas, steaks and the like, right on the Inner Harbour beneath the visitor centre, so expect lots of bustle, passing trade and good views. Prices are keen, with mains starting at $8 and running to around $25. Mon–Fri from 11am, Sat from 10am, Sun from 9am.

Pagliacci's 1011 Broad St, between Fort and Broughton Ⓣ 250/386-1662. The best restaurant in Victoria if you want a fast, furious atmosphere, live music, good Italian food and excellent desserts. Prices are good, with mains from $12. A rowdy throng begins to queue almost from the moment the doors are open. Mon–Thurs 11.30am–10pm, Fri & Sat 11.30am–11pm, Sun 10am–10pm.

The Tapa Bar 620 Trounce Alley Ⓣ 250/383-0013, Ⓦ www.tapabar.ca. This buzzy place has inexpensive tapas (plates from $7) – try the excellent *gambas al ajillo* (prawns in garlic sauce), wines by the glass and a long list of martinis. Mon–Thurs 11.30am–11pm, Fri–Sat 11.30am–midnight, Sun noon–10pm.

The Temple 525 Fort St ⓣ250/383-2313, ⓦwww.thetemple.ca. The chic, sleek main dining room here has a wraparound bar (in glowing glass), a double chaise lounge-bed for reclining couples and an imposing fireplace (the more intimate Velvet Room has a couple of cosier tables). There's a DJ later in the evening, but the emphasis remains on good Pacific Northwest cooking and a seasonal menu, with small dishes from around $9, more substantial ones up to $20 or more. Mon–Thurs 4pm to midnight, Fri & Sat 4pm–2am.

Bars and pubs

Big Bad John's 919 Douglas St. Next to the *Strathcona Hotel* this is by far Victoria's most atmospheric bar, with bare boards and authentic old banknotes and IOUs pasted to the walls. It also hosts occasional live bands and singers, usually of a country-music persuasion.

Darcy's Pub 1127 Wharf St ⓣ250/380-1322, ⓦwww.darcyspub.ca. This "Irish pub" has a prime site on the edge of Bastion Square, offers predictable food and beer and has live music seven nights a week.

Spinnakers Gastro Brewpub 308 Catherine St, near Esquimalt Rd, ⓦwww.spinnakers.com. Thirty-eight beers, including several home-brewed options, a restaurant, live music, occasional tours of the brewery and good harbour views draw a mixed clientele. Catch bus #6 to Esquimalt Rd from Douglas St.

Swans Brewpub 506 Pandora Ave ⓦwww.swanshotel.com This pretty and highly popular hotel-café-brewery (see p.810), a former winner of the National Brewpub of the year award, is located in a 1913 warehouse and is the place to watch Victoria's young professionals at play. Several foreign and nine home-brewed beers on tap, with the *Neptune Soundbar* nightclub in the basement.

Clubs and live music

The Cambie 856 Esquimalt Rd ⓣ250/382-7161, ⓦwww.thecambie.com. A long-established venue recently taken over by the Cambie Hostels group, which has retained the no-frills pub atmosphere, cheap drinks and bands most nights. Take bus #6 from Douglas St and ask to be dropped at the bingo hall.

Element 919 Douglas St. ⓣ250/383-7137, ⓦwww.elementnightclub.ca. The biggest, best and noisiest of the live-music venues, this club is part of *Strathcona Hotel*. Varied live bands, including the occasional big name, and dancing nightly.

Evolution 502 Discovery St ⓣ250/388-3000, ⓦwww.evotheclub.com. One of Victoria's more interesting clubs and discos, thanks to plenty of techno, rave and alternative sounds.

Hermann's Jazz Club 753 View St, between Douglas and Blanshard ⓣ250/388-9166, ⓦwww.hermannsjazz.com. Dimly lit club thick with 1950s atmosphere that specializes in Dixieland but has occasional excursions into fusion and blues.

Listings

Bike rental Cycle BC Rentals, at 950 Wharf St for motorbikes and scooters (ⓣ250/385-2453), and 707 Douglas St for bicycles (ⓣ250/380-2453; toll free for both locations 1-866/380-2453, ⓦwww.cyclebc.ca) rents bikes (from $7 an hour, $24 daily), scooters and motorbikes.

Bus information Airporter shuttle bus from Victoria Airport (ⓣ250/386-2525 or 1-877/386-2525). Pacific Coast Lines Vancouver service (ⓣ604/662-8074 in Vancouver or 250/385-4411 at the Victoria bus terminal, ⓦwww.pacificcoach.com); for services on the island, Greyhound (ⓣ1-800/661-8747, ⓦwww.greyound.ca). Both operate from the bus terminal at 700 Douglas St.

Car rental Avis, 62B-1001 Douglas St (ⓣ250/386-8468 or 1-800/879-2847) and Victoria Airport (ⓣ250/656-6033, ⓦwww.avis.com); Budget, 757 Douglas St and Victoria Airport (ⓣ250/953-5300 or 1-800/668-9833, ⓦwww.budgetvictoria.com); National, 767 Douglas St (ⓣ250/386-1213 or 1-877/222-9058) and Victoria Airport (ⓣ250/656-2541).

Doctor and dentist Cresta Dental Centre, Tillicum Centre, 3170 Tillicum Rd (ⓣ250/384-7711) and the Tillicum Medical Centre at the same address (ⓣ250/381-8112) both accept walk-in patients.

Equipment rental Sports Rent, 1950 Government St, at Discovery (ⓣ250/385-7368, ⓦwww.sportsrentbc.com), has a colossal range of equipment, including bikes, in-line skates, all camping, hiking, climbing and diving gear.

Ferries BC Ferries (ⓣ250/386-3431 or 1-888-223-3779, ⓦwww.bcferries.com). From the US: Port Angeles to Victoria with Black Ball Transport (ⓣ250/386-2202 or 360/457-4491, ⓦwww.cohoferry.com); Seattle to Victoria, with Victoria Clipper (ⓣ250/382-8100, 206/448-5000 or 1-800/888-2535, ⓦwww.clippervacations.com/ferry); Anacortes to Sidney, with Washington State Ferries (ⓣ1-888/808.7977, ⓦwww.wsdot.wa.gov/ferries); and Friday Harbour to Sidney, with Victoria Express (ⓣ250/361-9144 or in the US 360/452-8088, ⓦwww.victoriaexpress.com).

Hospital Victoria General Hospital, 35 Helmcken Rd (☎250/727-4212).
Post office 714 Yates St, at Douglas (☎250/953-1352). Mon–Fri 8.30am–5pm.
Taxis Blue Bird Cabs (☎250/382-4235); Empress Cabs (☎250/381-2222); Victoria Taxi (☎250/383-7111).
Train information VIA Rail, 450 Pandora Ave (☎250/383-4324 or 1-800/561-8630 in Canada and 1-800/561-3949 in the US, www.viarail.ca).

The Southern Gulf Islands

Scattered between Vancouver Island and the mainland lie several hundred tiny islands, most no more than lumps of rock, a few large enough to hold permanent populations and warrant a regular ferry service. Two main clusters are accessible from Victoria: the **Southern Gulf Islands** and the San Juan Islands, both part of the same archipelago, except that the San Juan group is in the United States.

You get a good look at the Southern Gulf Islands on the seaplanes from Vancouver (see p.808) or on the ferry from Tsawwassen – twisting and threading through their coves and channels, the ride sometimes seems even a little too close for comfort. The coastline makes for superb **sailing**, and an armada of small boats crisscrosses between the islands for most of the year. Hikers and campers are also well served, and **fishing** is good, with the surrounding waters holding some of the world's biggest salmon. The climate is mild, though hardly "Mediterranean" as tourist blurbs claim, and the vegetation is particularly lush. There's also an abundance of marine wildlife (sea lions, orcas, seals, bald eagles, herons, cormorants). All this has made the Gulf Islands the dream idyll of many people from Washington State and BC, whether they're artists, writers, pensioners or dropouts from the mainstream. For full details of what's happening on the islands, grab a copy of the *Gulf Islander*, distributed on the islands and the ferries.

Planning a visit

BC Ferries (☎250/386-3431 or 1-888/223-3779, www.bcferries.com) sails to five of the Southern Gulf Islands – **Salt Spring**, **Pender**, **Saturna**, **Mayne** and **Galiano** – from Swartz Bay, 33km north of Victoria on Hwy 17. (A few other North Gulf Islands, notably Gabriola, can be reached from Chemainus and Nanaimo; see p.827 & p.828.) Reckon on at least two crossings to each daily, but be prepared for all boats to be jammed solid during the summer. Visit the website or pick up the company's *Southern Gulf Islands* timetable, widely available on boats and in the mainland visitor centres; it's invaluable if you aim to exploit the many

Gulf Islands Water Taxi

The **Gulf Islands Water Taxi** (☎250/537-2510, www.members.unet.ca/~watertaxi) has been a feature of island life since 1978, complementing the BC Ferries service and carrying visitors, schoolchildren, fishermen and others on two scheduled routes from the Visitors' Dock below the *Oystercatcher Bar & Grill* in Ganges. The **first route** runs Salt Spring (Ganges Harbour) to Galiano (Sturdies Bay) and on to Mayne Island (Miners Bay); currently September to June, two daily departing at 6.45am and 4.30pm from Salt Spring; $25 round-trip between any two points, $15 one-way, no extra charge for bicycles. Prices are the same on the **second route**, which runs from Salt Spring (Ganges Harbour) to Saturna (Lyall Harbour) and on to Pender (Port Washington). An "Island Hopping" **third route** operates in summer (Sat 9am & 3pm from Ganges) calling at Galiano and Mayne. All services are timetabled so that you can realistically make short day or sightseeing trips to other islands from Salt Spring.

inter-island connections. Ferries take cars, bikes and motorbikes, though with a car you'll need to make a **reservation**. There's next to no public transport on the islands, so what few taxis there are can charge what they wish. It costs around $2 to take bikes on board, and **cycling** can be a great way to see the islands: most are small (if hilly), with few roads.

Have your **accommodation** worked out well in advance in summer. **Campers** should have few problems finding sites, most of which are located in the islands' provincial parks, though at peak times you'll want to arrive before noon to ensure a pitch – there are reservations in some parks (see p.747 for booking information). For help with B&Bs, use the *BC Approved Accommodation Guide* and the BC tourism website (see Ⓦwww.hellobc.com).

Salt Spring Island

SALT SPRING (pop. 10,000) is the biggest, most populated and most visited of the islands – its population triples in summer – though if you're without transport think twice about coming here on a day-trip as getting around is pretty tough. Most enjoyment on Salt Spring, as with the other Gulf Islands, is to be had from sinking back into its laidback approach to life: grabbing a coffee at a café overlooking the water, browsing galleries, cycling the backroads or hiking the odd easy trail.

Arrival and information

Salt Spring is served by Harbour Air seaplanes from Vancouver (see p.808) and has three ferry terminals: **Fulford Harbour** in the south, with sailings from Victoria's Swartz Bay (ten daily, more in summer; 35min; foot passengers $9.45, cars $28); **Vesuvius Bay** in the northwest, with sailings from Crofton, near Duncan, on Vancouver Island (13 daily; 20min; same fares); and **Long Harbour**, midway down the east coast, which connects to points on the BC mainland, notably Tsawwassen, usually via other islands. Long Harbour is also the main terminal for inter-island travel. The Salt Spring Island Transit System connects the ferry terminals with **GANGES**, the island's main village, on the east coast 5km from Long Harbour, but check with the Victoria or local visitor centre (see below) for the latest.

Ganges has a small **visitor centre** (daily: July & Aug 9am–5pm, April–June & Sept–Oct 10am–4pm, Nov–March 11am–3pm; Ⓣ250/537-5252, Ⓦwww.saltspringtourism.com) at 121 Lower Ganges Rd, and a rapidly proliferating assortment of galleries, tourist shops and holiday homes.

Accommodation

The visitor centre is the place to check out the island's relatively plentiful **accommodation**. You can choose from the hundred or more, often rather expensive, **B&B** options (whose owners can arrange to pick you up from the ferry), or one of the so-called "resorts" – usually a handful of houses with camping, a few rooms to rent and little else. Each of the ferry terminals also has a range of mid-price **motels**, notably *Harbour House*, 121 Upper Ganges Rd, Ganges (Ⓣ250/537-5571 or 1-888/799-5571, Ⓦwww.saltspringharbourhouse.com; ❺); and the 28-unit *Seabreeze Inn* in a park-like setting above Ganges Harbour at 101 Bittancourt Rd (Ⓣ250/537-4145 or 1-800/434-4112, Ⓦwww.seabreezeinne.com; ❺).

The island's best **campsite** is in Ruckle Provincial Park – a magnificent, waterfront, 78-pitch site ($15 in summer, $10 in winter) at Beaver Point, reached by following Beaver Point Road from the Fulford Harbour ferry terminal (10km).

The island

Besides loafing about Ganges, there are a number of **beaches** on the island worth visiting. The best strips are on the more sheltered east side – Beddis Beach in particular, off the Fulford to Ganges road – as well as at Vesuvius Bay in the northwest and at Drummond Park near Fulford in the south.

Beddis Beach can be seen en route to one of the best parks in the Gulf Islands, the **Ruckle Provincial Park**, a swath of lovely forest, field and maritime scenery tucked in the island's southeast corner 10km east of Fulford Harbour. It has 15km of trails, most leaving from trailheads at Beaver Point, the rocky headland that marks the end of the access road – the best path marches north from here along the coast of tiny coves and rocky headlands to Yeo Point. The park also has an outstanding campsite ($15) at the end of the access road (see opposite). **Mount Maxwell Provincial Park** lies midway up the west coast; the eponymous mountain provides a tremendous 588-metre viewpoint. The park is accessed on Cranberry Road, which strikes west midway down the island off the main Ganges to Fulford road. Visit Ⓦwww.env.gov.bc.ca/bcparks for more information on both parks.

Between April and October, head for the **Saturday Market** (Sat 8am–4pm; Ⓦwww.saltspringmarket.com), in Ganges' Centennial Park, for food and crafts. Community spirit reaches a climax during the annual **Artcraft** crafts fair (late June to mid-Sept), held in Ganges' Mahon Hall, that displays the talents of the island's many dab-handed creatives. The other main focus for cultural events is the **ArtSpring** centre, 100 Jackson Ave in Ganges (Ⓦwww.artspring.ca), which hosts a summer performing arts festival (July & Aug).

Eating and drinking

In Ganges, there are numerous **cafés** and coffee shops for high-quality sandwiches: for something more ambitious, try the appealing *Tree House Café-Restaurant*, 106 Purvis Lane (Ⓣ250/537-5379, Ⓦwww.treehousecafe.ca), which serves breakfast, lunch and dinner and has places to sit outside and low-key live (often acoustic) music most nights. For a treat, the place to go is *House Piccolo*, 108 Hereford Ave, Ganges (Ⓣ250/537-1844, Ⓦwww.housepiccolo.com, dinner only), which serves high-quality European and Scandinavian food and has won *Wine Spectator* magazine awards.

Galiano Island

Long and finger-shaped, **Galiano** (pop. 1071) is just 27km from north to south and barely five kilometres wide, but it remains one of the more promising islands to visit if you want variety and a realistic chance of finding somewhere to stay. There are two ferry terminals: **Sturdies Bay** in the southeast, which takes boats from the mainland (foot passengers $14.85, cars $47.60), and **Montague Harbour** on the west coast, which handles the Vancouver Island crossings from Swartz Bay (foot passengers $9.80, cars $31). You can also get here with the Gulf Islands Water Taxi and there are inter-island BC Ferries connections (1–4 daily) from Salt Spring via Pender and Mayne.

If you're **canoeing**, stick to the calmer waters, cliffs and coves off the west coast. **Hikers** can walk almost the entire length of the east coast, or climb Mount Sutil (323m) or Mount Galiano (342m) for views of the mainland mountains. To reach the trailhead for the latter, take Burrill Road south from the ferry at Sturdies Bay and along Bluff Road through the forest of Bluffs Park. A left fork, Active Pass Drive, takes you to the trailhead (total 5km from the ferry).

The locals' favourite **beach** is at Coon Bay at the island's northern tip, but there are excellent marine landscapes and beaches elsewhere, notably at **Montague Harbour Provincial Marine Park** (Ⓦwww.env.gov.bc.ca/bcparks), 10km from the Sturdies Bay ferry terminal on the west side of the island. It has stretches of shell and pebble foreshore, a café, shop, three-kilometre waterfront trail to Gray Peninsula (though you can easily do your own foreshore walks) and, more to the

▲ A view of Galiano Island from Salt Spring Island

point, a glorious provincial **campsite** ($19). Booking is essential in summer; see website for details.

Practicalities

For a decent place to **stay**, right on Studies Bay is the very pleasant ten-room *Galiano Oceanfront Inn & Spa*, 134 Madrona Drive (ⓣ250/539-3388, ⓦwww.galianoinn.com; ⑦); rates include gourmet breakfast. For **food and drink**, the island's main pub, the *Hummingbird Inn* (ⓣ250/539-5472), is about 2km from Sturdies Bay at 47 Sturdies Bay Rd. The food there is reasonable, as it is at *La Bérengerie* (ⓣ250/539-5392, ⓦwww.galianoisland.com/laberengerie; ③), a genteel restaurant about 2km from Montague Harbour on the corner of Montague and Clanton roads; it usually rents three B&B rooms upstairs.

North and South Pender islands

The somnolent bridge-linked islands of **North** and **South Pender** muster about a two thousand people between them, many of whom will try to entice you into their studios to buy local arts and crafts. Otherwise you can swim, snooze or walk on one of the many tiny **beaches** – there's public ocean access at some twenty points around the island. Two of the best are Hamilton Beach near Browning Beach on the east coast of North Pender and Mortimer Spit just south of the bridge that links the two islands. The latter is also the place to pick up trails to Mount Norman and Beaumont Provincial Marine Park.

Ferries come to North Pender from Swartz Bay (up to 7 daily; 40min direct or 2hr via Galiano and/or Mayne; foot passengers $9.80, cars $31) and Tsawwassen (foot-passengers $14.85 one-way; cars $47.60).

Practicalities

There's a handful of **B&Bs**, and a small wooded **campsite** at Prior Centennial Provincial Park, 6km south of the Otter Bay ferry terminal (March–Sept; $15). For the only **hotel**-type rooms, try the twelve-room *Inn on Pender Island*, prettily situated in 7.5 acres of wooded country near Prior Park at 4709 Canal Rd, North

Pender (Ⓣ250/629-3353 or 1-800/550-0172, Ⓦwww.innonpender.com; ❻), or the *Poets Cove Resort & Spa*, a plush resort at 9801 Spalding Rd, South Pender (Ⓣ250/629-2100 or 1-888/512-7638, Ⓦwww.poetscove.com; ❽), which has a pool, marina, bistro-pub, restaurant, store, tennis, harbour views, canoe, boat and bike rentals, and a choice of rooms or cabins. Alternatively, try the three fully equipped self-catering cottages 500m sharp left from the ferry at *Arcadia by the Sea*, 1329 MacKinnon Rd, North Pender (Ⓣ250/629-3221 or 1-877/470-8439, Ⓦwww.arcadiabythesea.com; ❺; May–Sept), with tennis court, outdoor pool and private decks.

Mayne Island

Mayne is the first island to your left (Galiano is on your right) if you're crossing from Tsawwassen to Swartz Bay – which is perhaps as close as you'll get, since it's the quietest and most difficult to reach of the islands served by ferries. One-way tickets from Tsawwassen (via Galiano/Montague Harbour) in high season cost $14.85 for foot passengers, $47.60 for cars. It also has few places to stay, which may be as good a reason as any for heading out here – particularly if you have a bike to explore the island's quiet country roads.

Best of several **beaches** is Bennett Bay, a sheltered strip with warm water and good sand. It's reached by heading east from the island's principal community at Miner's Bay (5min from the ferry terminal at Village Bay on the west coast) to the end of Fernhill Road and then turning left onto Wilks Road. If you want a **walk**, try the 45-minute climb up Mount Parke in the eponymous regional park; it starts near the Fernhill Centre on Montrose Road.

Practicalities

Village Bay – don't be fooled by the name: there's no village – has a summer-only **visitor centre** booth (daily 9am–6pm; no phone, Ⓦwww.mayneislandchamber.ca) that should be able to fill you in on the limited **hotel** and **B&B** possibilities. Try the *Blue Vista Cottage Resort*, eight fully equipped cabins overlooking Bennett Bay at 536 Arbutus Drive, 6km from the ferry (Ⓣ250/539-2463 or 1-877/535-2424, Ⓦwww.bluevistaresort.com; ❹), with ferry pick-up, sandy beach, park-like setting and bike, canoe and kayak rental. The *Tinkerer's B&B* on Miner's Bay at 417 Sunset Place off Georgina Point Rd (Ⓣ250/539-2280, Ⓦwww.jjtinkerers.com; ❺; May–Sept), 2.4km from the ferry, is nicely offbeat: it rents bikes, provides hammocks and offers "demonstrations of medicinal herb and flower gardens".

The best **food** around is at the waterfront *Oceanwood Country Inn*, 2km south of the ferry at 630 Dinner Bay Road (Ⓣ250/539-5074, Ⓦwww.oceanwood.com; ❼; March–Nov, but may open during winter – call ahead), which also has twelve smart rooms, sauna, oceanfront hot tub and a superb, quiet garden setting.

Saturna Island

Saturna, to the south, has daily **ferries** from Swartz Bay on Vancouver Island (2–3 daily; foot passengers $9.80 return, vehicles $31) and from Tsawwassen but only via Mayne. The island boasts some good **beaches**, the best being at Russell Reef and Winter Cove Marine Park (no campsite) on its northwest tip. There's walking, wildlife and good views to the mainland from Mount Warburton Pike (497m) and on Brown Bridge in the southwest of the island.

Practicalities

For general **information** on Saturna, visit Ⓦwww.saturnatourism.com. The island is another **B&B** hideaway: try the three-room waterfront *Lyall Harbour B&B*

(ⓣ250/539-5577 or 1-877/473-9343, ⓦwww.lyallharbour.com; ❺), 500m from the ferry at 121 East Point Rd in Saturna Point. A slightly larger place to stay is the *Eastpoint Ocean Cottages*, 753 Tumbo Channel Rd (ⓣ250/539-9809, ⓦwww.eastpointresort.com; ❺; March–Dec), situated in a park-like setting near a gradually sloping sandy beach; the five cabins are fully equipped and you can choose between one- and two-bedroom units; in July and August there's generally a minimum stay of a week. There are no campgrounds and only a handful of **places to eat**, notably the pub-restaurant at the modern, waterfront *Saturna Lodge*, 130 Payne Rd (ⓣ250/539-2254, ⓦwww.saturna.ca; ❻; mid-Feb to late Nov), which also has six rooms; rates include breakfast.

Highway 14: Victoria to Port Renfrew

Highway 14 runs west from **Victoria** to **Port Renfrew** and is lined with numerous beaches and provincial parks, most – especially those close to the city – heavily populated during the summer months. The 107km route is covered in summer by shuttles serving the West Coast Trail (see p.847) and Juan de Fuca Trail (see opposite) but also popular for the ride alone.

Victoria city buses go as far as **SOOKE** (38km), and you can also cycle here on the Galloping Goose cycle trail. Sooke is the last place of any size, so stock up on supplies if you're continuing west. It's best known for its excellent art galleries, a clutch of good restaurants and **All Sooke Day** in mid-July, when lumberjacks from all over the island compete in various tests of forestry expertise. Check out the small **Sooke Region Museum** (daily: 9am–5pm, July & Aug until 6pm; ⓣ250/642-6351, ⓦwww.sookeregionmuseum.com; donation), across the Sooke River Bridge at 2070 Phillips and Sooke streets, to bone up on the largely logging-dominated local history; the **visitor centre** (daily 9am–5pm) lies in the same building. Sooke has a surfeit of **accommodation**, with a bias towards comfortable B&Bs. Many make the trip here just for the **food** at *Sooke Harbour House*, 1528 Whiffen Spit Rd (ⓣ250/642-3421, ⓦwww.sookeharbourhouse.com; ❽), one of the finest restaurants on the West Coast; it's expensive, but has a surprisingly casual atmosphere. It also has 28 top-notch and rather costly **rooms**.

The mostly empty beaches beyond Sooke are largely grey pebble and driftwood, but none the worse for that. The first key stop, 20km beyond Sooke, is **French Beach Provincial Park** (ⓦwww.env.gov.bc.ca/bcparks). An infoboard here fills in the natural history background of the foreshore and rich Douglas fir and Sitka forest, and there are maps of trails and the highlights on the road farther west. There's good walking on the fairly wild and windswept beach, and a 69-pitch provincial park campsite (summer $15, winter $10) on the grass immediately away from the shore. About 3km beyond, the 25 log cabins of *Point No Point*, 10829 West Coast Rd (ⓣ250/646-2020, ⓦwww.pointnopointresort.com, ❻), make a tremendous place to overnight near the water.

Sandy, signposted trails lead off the road to beaches over the next 9km, including **Jordan River**, a logging community known for its good surf. Just beyond is the best of the beaches on this coast, part of **China Beach Provincial Park** (no camping), reached after a fifteen-minute walk from the road through rainforest. West Coast Trail Express buses make stops at all these parks and beaches on request.

Port Renfrew and the Juan de Fuca Marine Trail

The road is partly gravel from China Beach on – past Mystic and Sombrio beaches to **PORT RENFREW**, a logging community that's gained from being the western starting point of the **West Coast Trail** (see p.847). A second trail, the

West Coast Trail Express

The **West Coast Trail Express** (☎250/477-8700 or 1-888/999-2288, Ⓦwww.trailbus.com), provides an invaluable complement to the relatively limited scheduled bus services on Vancouver Island. **Reservations** are required for services between May 1 and June 15 and September 15–30. They are also highly recommended for all other services. Cancellations require 10 days' notice.

It offers a shuttle service (May–Sept only; currently leaves Victoria at 6.30am) from Victoria daily to and from **Gordon River** ($55), **Port Renfrew** ($55), **Pachena Bay** ($80) and **Bamfield** ($80), thus providing access to the trailheads of the West Coast Trail and to points in the Pacific Rim National Park, such as Bamfield, that would otherwise be difficult to reach without your own transport. It also provides non-daily **inter-town shuttles** between most combinations of these destinations – and others such as Nitinat ($55) and **Nanaimo** (connections to Pachena Bay and Bamfield; $90). **Departure points** are as follows: Victoria (700 Douglas St); Nanaimo (Departure Bay ferry terminal); Pachena Bay (trailhead car park); Bamfield (Trails Motel); Gordon River (trailhead office); Nitinat (Nitinat Junction, 7km from the Nitinat village); Port Renfrew (at the road intersection by the Port Renfrew Hotel by the Lighthouse Pub sign).

Another service serving the Juan de Fuca Trail runs from Victoria to Port Renfrew and back ($55) **along Hwy 14** with stops at Sooke (at the Payless Gas station), French Beach ($40), Jordan River ($50), China Beach ($50), Sombrio Beach ($50) and Parkinson Creek ($50). Pick-ups, unless specified, are the same as for the West Coast bus or at the junction of the individual trailheads with Hwy 14. Transport between trailheads is $25.

Juan de Fuca Marine Trail, also starts from near Port Renfrew, running east towards Victoria for about 50km. This does not have the complicated booking procedure of the West Coast Trail, but the scenery is also less striking and the going far easier for the less experienced walker. Car parks and hwy access points are also dotted along its length, allowing you to enjoy strolls or day-hikes. Beyond China Beach is the start of the **Juan de Fuca Provincial Park**, designed to protect the beaches and coastal rainforest strip explored by the trail (summer frontcountry camping $15, winter $10; backcountry camping $5).

Practicalities

Accommodation in town is limited: try the four cottages on the San Juan River at *Gallaugher's West Coast Fish Camp* off Beach Road at 5222 Heritage Drive (☎250/647-5409, Ⓦwww3.telus.net/gallaughers; ❺; May–Oct). South of the village on a logging road (6km) is the Juan de Fuca trailhead at **Botanical Beach**, a sandstone shelf and tidal-pool area that reveals a wealth of marine life at low tide. If you're driving and don't want to retrace your steps, think about taking the gravel logging roads from the village on the north side of the San Juan River to either Shawnigan Lake or the Cowichan Valley. They're marked on most maps, but it's worth picking up the **detailed map** of local roads put out by the Sooke Combined Fire Organization (ask at the Victoria visitor centre). Heed all warnings about logging trucks.

Highway 1: Victoria to Nanaimo

If you leave Victoria with high hopes of Vancouver Island's lauded scenery, **Highway 1** – the final, western leg of the Trans-Canada – will come as a disappointing introduction to what you can expect along most of the island's southeast coast. After a lengthy sprawl of suburbs, blighted by more billboards than you'd see in supposedly less scenic cities, the landscape becomes suddenly wooded and immensely lush; unfortunately the beauty is constantly interrupted by bursts of dismal motels and other hwy junk.

Buses make the trip between Victoria and Nanaimo (up to 6 daily). One **train** a day (more in summer) also covers this route – and beyond to Courtenay – but it's usually a single-carriage job, gets booked solid in summer and stops at every stump.

Goldstream Provincial Park

Thetis Lake Regional Park, 11km out of Victoria, is good for swimming, with forested trails and sandy beaches on two lakes backed by high cliffs; there's a busy beach near the car park, which is quieter round the shore, or beyond at the bottom of the hill at Prior Lake. Prettier still is **Goldstream Provincial Park** (Ⓦwww.env.gov.bc.ca/bcparks), 5km beyond Langford and 20km from Victoria city centre, where you'll find an ancient forest of Douglas fir and western red cedar and a large provincial park **campsite** with good facilities and a visitor centre (summer frontcountry camping $24, winter $10). There's also a network of marked **trails** to hilltops and waterfalls designed for anything between five minutes and an hour's walking. Try the paths towards Mount Finlayson (3hr hard walk to the summit) for views of the ocean – views you also get if you carry on up the hwy, which soon meets Saanich Inlet, a bay with a lovely panorama of wooded ridges across the water. Look out for the Malahat Summit (31km from Victoria) and Gulf Islands (33km) viewpoints.

Duncan

DUNCAN, 60km north of Victoria, begins inauspiciously, with a particularly scrappy section of hwy spoiling what would otherwise be an exquisitely pastoral patch of country.

Duncan's **visitor centre** is at 381 Trans-Canada Hwy opposite the supermarket on the main road (early April to June Mon–Sat 9am–5pm; July & Aug daily 9am–6pm; Sept to early April Tues–Sat 10am–4pm; Ⓣ250/746-4636 or 1-888/303-3337, Ⓦwww.duncancc.bc.ca), close to the **bus station**, which has up to six daily connections to and from Victoria (1hr 10min). It's not worth staying in Duncan – though there are plenty of motels and campsites– but for **meals** you could try the *Arbutus Café*, 195 Kenneth St, at Jubilee (Ⓣ250/746-5443), which has excellent Italian- and Pacific Rim-influenced food. The local vineyards are also worth visiting; one of the best is the **Vigneti Zanatta Winery**, 5039 Marshall Rd (tastings, sales, tours and restaurant Wed–Sun noon to 4.30pm; Ⓣ250/748-2338, Ⓦwww.zanatta.ca), which has been in business for over forty years; as well as their wine, you can buy meals at the lovely (but expensive) restaurant.

Quw'utsun Cultural Centre

Out of Victoria, the first real reason to pull over is Duncan's **Quw'utsun Cultural** Centre, 200 Cowichan Way (generally open to drop-in visitors April–Sept Tues–Sat 10.30am–3pm; Ⓦwww.quwutsun.ca), on your left off the hwy in the unmissable wooden buildings next to Malaspina College. Duncan has long been the self-proclaimed "City of Totems", reference to a rather paltry collection of poles – arranged mostly alongside the main road – that belong to the local Cowichan tribes, historically BC's largest aboriginal group. The tribes, about three thousand strong locally, still preserve certain traditions, and it's been their energy – along with cash from the civic authorities, attuned as ever to potentially lucrative tourist attractions – that has put up the poles and pulled the project together. Much of the emphasis is on aboriginal crafts, especially the ubiquitous lumpy jumpers for which the area is famous, but there is a good twenty-minute film and tour of the centre and (for a varying admission) you can usually expect to find historical displays and demonstrations of dancing, knitting, carving, weaving and native cooking.

British Columbia Forestry Discovery Centre

Vancouver Island is one of the most heavily logged areas in Canada, and the **BC Forest Discovery Centre** (June to early Sept daily 10am–5pm; early April to May Thurs–Mon 10am–4pm; early Sept to mid-Oct Thur–Mon 10am–4.30pm; check website for winter hours; $14; Ⓦwww.bcforestmuseum.com), 1km north of Duncan on Hwy 1, preserves industry-related artefacts; but with industry bigwigs as museum trustees, you can't help feeling it's also designed to be something of a palliative in the increasingly ferocious controversy between loggers and environmentalists.

Ranged over a hundred-acre site next to a scenic lake, the well-presented displays tell everything you want to know about trees and how to cut them down. The narrow-gauge **steam train** round the park is a bit gimmicky, but a good way of getting around; check out temporary exhibitions and artefacts and archive material in the Main Exhibit Gallery in particular. There's also the usual array of working blacksmiths, sawmill, a farmstead and an old logging camp.

The Cowichan Valley

Striking west into the hills from Hwy 1 north of Duncan, Hwy 18 enters the **Cowichan Valley** and fetches up at the 32-kilometre long Lake Cowichan, the largest freshwater lake on the island. Rather than drive, the nicest way up the valley is to walk the **Cowichan Valley Footpath**, following the river 18km from Glenora (a hamlet southwest of Duncan at the end of Robertson Road) to Lake Cowichan Village on the lake's eastern shore. You could do the trip in a day, camp en route, or turn around at Skutz Falls and climb up to the Riverbottom Road to return to Duncan, which would be a half-day walk.

A road, rough in parts, circles **Lake Cowichan** (it's 75km round the lake by road – allow 2hr) and offers access to a gamut of outdoor pursuits, most notably fishing; the area is touted, with typical smalltown hyperbole, as the "Fly-Fishing Capital of the World". The water gets warm enough for summer swimming (the aboriginal name for the area, *Kaatza*, means the "land warmed by the sun"), and there's also ample hiking in the wilder country above.

For details of the area's many tours, trails and outfitters contact the **visitor centre** at Lake Cowichan Village, 125 South Shore Rd (mid-May to early Sept daily 10am–5pm; early Sept to mid-May 10am–2pm; closed Dec & Jan; Ⓣ250/749-3244, Ⓦwww.cowichanlake.ca). Good, cheap **campsites** line the shore, which despite minimal facilities can be quite busy in summer. The best is at Gordon Bay Provincial Park (summer camping $24, winter $10) on the south shore 14km from Lake Cowichan Village on South Shore Road, a popular family place but with a quiet atmosphere and a good sandy **beach**. There are also plenty of hotels, motels and the like in all the lakeside settlements.

Chemainus

CHEMAINUS is the "Little Town That Did", as the billboards for miles around never stop telling you. It created its own tourist attraction after the 1982 closure of the local antiquated sawmill threatened the place with almost overnight extinction, despite the opening of a modern, more efficient mill. In 1983 the town commissioned an artist to paint a huge **mural**, *Steam Donkey at Work*, recording the area's local history. This proved so successful that some 35 panels quickly followed, drawing some 375,000 visitors annually to admire the artwork and tempting them to spend money in local businesses as they did. Ironically, the opening of the modern sawmill has done nothing to deter the welcome influx of resident painters and craftspeople attracted by the murals, a knock-on effect that has done much to enliven the village's pleasant community feel.

As murals go, these are surprisingly good, and if you're driving it's worth the short, well-signed diversion off Hwy 1. You might also want to drop in on the **Chemainus Valley Museum**, 9799 Waterwheel Crescent (daily 10am–4pm, closed mid-Dec to mid-Feb; donation), a community-run museum of local history with displays on logging, mills and pioneer life.

Buses detour here on the run to Nanaimo, and the **train** drops you right next to a mural. There's a **visitor centre** in town at 9796 Willow St (June–Aug daily 9am–5pm; rest of year Mon–Fri 10am–4pm; ⓣ250/246-3944, ⓦwww.chemainus.bc.ca). You can pick up a **ferry** from Chemainus to the small islands of **Kuper** and **Thetis** (both $8.60 for foot passengers, $20.50 for cars).

Practicalities

If you fancy **staying** – the village's cosy waterside setting is nicer than either Duncan or Nanaimo – it's worth booking ahead, as increasing popularity means the local **hotel** and eight B&Bs are in heavy demand in summer. For motel accommodation, try the *Fuller Lake Chemainus Motel*, 9300 Trans-Canada Hwy (ⓣ250/246-3282 or 1-888/246-3255, ⓦwww.chemainus-fullerlakemotel.com; ❹). The best **B&B** is the pretty and whimsically decorated *Bird Song Cottage*, 9909 Maple St (ⓣ250/246-9910, ⓦwww.birdsongcottage.com; ❺). For a **campsite** there is the *Country Maples RV Resort*, 9010 Trans-Canada Hwy (ⓣ250/246-2078, ⓦwww.holidaytrailsresorts.com/countrymaples; $36–47; April–Oct) in sixty acres of open and wooded parkland 16km north of Duncan above the Chemainus River, with showers, laundry and pool. About 5km south of the village on the river is the quiet *Bald Eagle Campground*, 8705 Chemainus Rd (ⓣ250/246-9457 or 1-866/246-9457; $20–25). For **food**, try the cheap, varied snacks at the *Willow Street Café*, 9749 Willow St.

Ladysmith

LADYSMITH's claim to fame is based solely on an accident of geography (although some might know it better as the birthplace of *Baywatch* star Pamela Anderson), as it straddles the 49th Parallel, the latitude that divides mainland Canada and the US. Ladysmith was originally named Oyster Bay, but was rechristened by Robert Dunsmuir (see opposite) at the time of the Boer War battle for Ladysmith (many streets bear the name of Boer War generals). There's little to the place other than the usual motels and garages; its scenic profile would be considerably higher were it not for a huge sawmill and a waterfront that is usually hopelessly jammed with lumber.

The **visitor centre** is at 411 B 1st Ave (mid-June to Aug daily 9am–5pm; Sept–Dec Mon–Fri 8.30am–4.30pm; ⓣ250/245-2112, ⓦwww.ladysmithcofc.com) and has walking maps of the village's "heritage centre". The volunteer-run **Black Nugget Museum**, 12 Gatacre St (irregular hours: call for current opening; ⓣ250/245-4846), is a restored 1881 hotel stuffed with predictable memorabilia of coal mining and pioneers. If you stop off, check out **Transfer Beach Park** on the harbour, where the water's said to be the warmest in the Pacific north of San Francisco.

Nanaimo

With a population of about 75,000, **NANAIMO**, 113km from Victoria, is Vancouver Island's second biggest city, the terminal for **ferries** from Horseshoe Bay and Tsawwassen on the mainland, and a watershed between the island's populated southeastern tip and its wilder, more sparsely peopled countryside to the north and west. In BC, only Vancouver and Kelowna are expanding faster. This said, the town is unexceptional, though the setting, as ever in BC, is eye-catching – particularly around the harbour, which bobs with yachts and rusty fishing boats and, if you've come from Victoria, allows the first views across to the big mountains on the mainland. If you are going to stop here, more than likely it'll be for **Petroglyph Park** or the town's increasingly famous **bungee-jumping** zone. If not, the Nanaimo Parkway provides a 21-kilometre bypass around the town.

Coal first brought white settlers to the region, many of whom made their fortunes here, including the Victorian magnate **Robert Dunsmuir**, who was given £750,000 and almost half the island in return for building the Victoria–Nanaimo railway – an indication of the benefits that could accrue from the British government to those with the pioneering spirit. Five bands of Salish natives originally lived on the site, which they called *Sney-ne-mous*, or "meeting place", from which the present name derives. It was they who innocently showed the local black rock to Hudson's Bay agents in 1852. The old mines are now closed, and the town's pockets are padded today by forestry, deep-sea fishing, tourism and – most notably – by six deep-water docks and a booming port. The town's other minor claim to fame is the **Nanaimo bar**, a glutinous chocolate confection made to varying recipes and on sale everywhere.

Arrival and information

The Nanaimo-Collishaw **airport** is 15km south of downtown on Hwy 19 and is connected by regular shuttle buses to the town centre. Seaplane connections to Vancouver with Harbour Air (see p.808) land close to downtown below Front Sreet on the harbourfront.

Nanaimo's **bus terminal** (Ⓣ250/753-4371) is some way from the harbour on the corner of Comox Road and Terminal Avenue, with six daily buses to Victoria, two to Port Hardy and three or four to Port Alberni, for connections to Tofino and Ucluelet. **BC Ferries** (Ⓣ250/386-3431 or 1-888/223-3779, Ⓦwww.bcferries.com) sail from **Departure Bay** (Ⓣ250/753-1261), 2km north of downtown, to Horseshoe Bay on the mainland (summer hourly 7am–9pm, off-season every 2hr; foot passengers $13.50 one-way, cars $45). The more convenient **Duke Point** terminal (Ⓣ250/722-0181), just south of town, handles ferries from Tsawwassen (same prices). Nanaimo lies on the Victoria–Courtenay **train** line and sees two trains daily; the **train station** is a little west of downtown, at 336 Prideaux St, near the corner of Fitzwilliam Street.

The **visitor centre** is north of the centre off the main hwy in Beban Park at Beban House, 2290 Bowen Rd (daily: early May to early Sept 9am–6pm, early Sept–early Oct 9am–5pm; mid-Oct to Dec Mon–Fri 9am–5pm & Sat 10am–4pm Ⓣ250/756-0106 or 1-800/663-7337, Ⓦwww.tourismnanaimo.com), and can help with accommodation referrals, and provide details of the many **boat rides** and **tours** to local sawmills, canneries, nature reserves and fishing research stations.

Accommodation

Buccaneer Inn 1577 Stewart Ave Ⓣ250/753-1246 or 1-877/282-6337, Ⓦwww.thebuccaneerinn.com. A reliable, if unexciting choice whose main appeal is a convenient location three blocks south of the Departure Bay ferry terminal. Studios, suites and kitchenette rooms available. ③–⑥

Cambie Hostel 63 Victoria Crescent Ⓣ250/754-5323 or 1-877/754-5323, Ⓦwww.cambiehostels.com. A bigger hostel than the one on Nicol St, with fifty beds in small dorm rooms, and some doubles at $44. The hostel also has a very cheap cafe, bakery and bar. Dorm beds $20. ①

Howard Johnson Harbourside Hotel 1 Terminal Ave ⓣ250/753-2241 or 1-800/663-7322, ⓦwww.hojonanaimo.com. Good, reliable rooms in a chain hotel, with the attraction of a pleasant waterfront setting. Also has a heated outdoor pool and restaurant. ❺

Nanaimo International Hostel 65 Nicol St ⓣ250/753-1188, ⓦwww.nanaimohostel.com. Nanaimo's cheapest beds are at this central, private mini-hostel, seven blocks south of the bus terminal and one block south of the Harbour Park Shopping Centre off Hwy 1. Facilities include bike rental, laundry, kitchen and internet access. Dorm beds from $15, and a handful of camping spots ($10) on the lawn (with ocean views) are also available. ❶

Newcastle Island Provincial Park (see p.747; $15 in summer, $10 in winter), has the only pitches (eighteen total, so arrive early) within walking distance of town, apart from the *Nicol Street Hostel*. Other sites are spread along the main road to the north and south. ❶

The town and parks

In downtown Nanaimo, only two sights warrant the considerable amount of energy used to promote them. The **Nanaimo District Museum**, just off the main harbour area at 100 Museum Way, by the Harbour Park Mall (May to early Sept daily 10am–5pm; Oct–April Tues–Sat 10am–5pm; ⓦwww.nanaimomuseum.ca; $2), houses a collection of pioneer, logging, mining, aboriginal peoples and natural history displays. The museum is also responsible for the **Bastion**, two blocks north at the corner of Bastion and Front streets, a wood-planked tower built by the Hudson's Bay Company in 1853 as a store and a stronghold against native attack, though it was never used during such an event; it's the oldest (perhaps the only) such building in the west. It now houses a small **museum** of Hudson's Bay memorabilia (same hours as for the Nanaimo District Museum).

For the wildest of the local parks, head due west of town to **Westwood Lake Park**, good for a couple of hours' lonely hiking and some fine swimming. **Petroglyph Provincial Park**, off Hwy 1, 3km south of downtown, showcases aboriginal peoples' carvings of the sort found all over BC (particularly along coastal waterways), many of them thousands of years old. Often their meaning is vague, but they appear to record important rituals and events. There are plenty of figures – real and mythological – carved into the local sandstone here, though their potential to inspire wonder is somewhat spoilt by more recent graffiti, traffic noise and the first thin edge of Nanaimo's urban sprawl.

Nanaimo is also home to North America's first legal public bungee-jumping site, **Wild Play**, 13km south of the town at 35 Nanaimo River Rd (daily 11.30am–6/8pm; ⓣ250/753-5867 or 1-888/668-7874, ⓦwww.wildplay.com; jumps from $95); look out for the signed turn-off Hwy 1. It's become so popular that variations have been added to the standard 42-metre plunge off the bridge, including ziplining and an aerial tree course.

Eating and drinking

Get your obligatory Nanaimo bar, or other cheap edibles, at the food stands in the **Public Market**, near the ferry terminal on Stewart Avenue (daily 9am–9pm). For bigger meals try *Gina's Mexican Cafe*, perched on the edge of a bluff at 47 Skinner St (ⓣ250/753-5411; ⓦwww.ginasmexicancafe.ca). The town's best **seafood** choice is the *Bluenose Chowder House*, 1340 Stewart Ave (ⓣ250/754-6611; closed Mon), with a nice terrace. Front Street has a choice of places, most with the benefit of terraces or patios looking out to sea. For a **drink** (and/or food), there's the *Longwood Brewpub*, 5775 Turner Rd (ⓣ250/729-8225, ⓦwww.longwoodbrewpub.com).

Excursions from Nanaimo: Newcastle and Gabriola islands

Barely a stone's throw offshore from Nanaimo lies **Newcastle Island**, and beyond it the larger bulk of Gabriola Island, both incongruously graced with palm trees:

they're beneficiaries of what is supposedly Canada's mildest climate. Ferries (Ⓣ250/729-8738, Ⓦwww.nanaimoharbourferry.com) make the ten-minute crossing (foot passengers only) to Newcastle Island on the hour and half hour (April to mid-May daily 10am–5pm; mid-May to early Sept daily 9am–9pm; early Sept to mid-Oct daily 10am–5pm; $4 one-way) from Maffeo Sutton Park (the wharf behind the Civic Arena) to **Newcastle Island Provincial Park**, which has a fine stretch of sand, tame wildlife, no cars, and lots of walking (18km of trails in all) and picnic possibilities. It'll take a couple of hours to walk the 7.5-kilometre trail that encircles the island.

There are about fifteen daily crossings with BC Ferries to **Gabriola Island** (6km, 20min; foot passengers $8.10, cars $19.30), a much quieter place that's home to about two thousand people, many of them artists and writers. Author Malcolm Lowry, he of *Under the Volcano* fame, immortalized the island in a story entitled *October Ferry to Gabriola Island*. Gabriola also offers several **beaches** – the best are Gabriola Sands' Twin Beaches at the island's northwest end and Drumbeg Provincial Park – and lots of scope for scuba diving, birdwatching (eagles and sea birds), beach-combing and easy walking, plus the added curiosity of the **Malaspina Galleries**, a series of caves and bluffs near Gabriola Sands sculpted by wind, frost and surf.

Both islands have numerous **B&Bs** and several **campsites**; if you're thinking of staying the night, check availability with the Nanaimo visitor centre.

From Nanaimo to Port Alberni

North of Nanaimo Hwy 1 is replaced by **Highway 19**, a messy stretch of road spotted with billboards and a rash of motels, marinas and clapboard houses. Almost every last centimetre of the coast is privately owned, this being the chosen site of what appears to be every British Columbian's dream holiday home. Don't expect, therefore, to be able to weave through the houses, wooden huts and boat launches to reach the tempting beaches that flash past below the hwy. For sea and sand you have to hang on for **Parksville**, 37km north of Nanaimo, and its quieter near-neighbour **Qualicum Beach**.

Parksville marks a major parting of the ways: while Hwy 19 continues up the eastern coast to Port Hardy, **Highway 4**, the principal trans-island route, pushes west to **Port Alberni** and on through the tremendously scenic Mackenzie Mountains to the Pacific Rim National Park (see p.835). Greyhound runs up to three **buses** daily from Nanaimo to Port Alberni, where there are connecting services for Ucluelet and Tofino in the national park.

Parksville

The approach to **PARKSVILLE** from the south takes you through lovely wooded dunes, with lanes striking off eastwards to hidden beaches and a half-dozen secluded **campsites**. Four kilometres on is the best of the beaches, stretched along 2km of **Rathtrevor Beach Provincial Park** (the tide goes out a kilometre here to reveal vast swathes of sand). In summer this area is madness and if you want to lay claim to some of the park's **camping** space (summer $24, winter $10) expect to start queuing first thing in the morning or take advantage of the provincial park reservations service (see p.747) The public sand here stretches for 2km and sports all the usual civilized facilities of Canada's tamed outdoors: cooking shelters, picnic spots and walking trails.

The dross starts beyond the bridge into Parksville, and its eight blocks of motels and garages. Yet the worst of the development has been kept off the promenade, which fronts **Parksville Beach**, whose annual **Beach Festival** draws thirty thousand visitors a day in July to watch, among other things, sand sculpting and sandcastle-building competitions. The beach offers lovely views across to the mainland and boasts Canada's warmest sea water – up to 21°C (70°F) in summer.

For **information**, Parksville's Chamber of Commerce is clearly signed off the hwy in downtown at 1275 East Island Hwy (Jan–March & Oct–Nov Mon–Fri 9am–5pm, Sat 10am–4pm; April Mon–Sat 9am–5pm; May–June & first two weeks of Sept daily 9am–5pm; July–Aug daily 9am–6pm; last two weeks of Sept Mon–Fri 9am–5pm, Sat & Sun 10am–4pm; Dec Mon–Fri 9am–5pm; ⓣ250/248-3613, ⓦwww.parksvillechamber.com). Ask for details of the many **hiking** areas and other nearby refuges from the beaches' summer maelstrom, and **fishing**, another of the region's big draws.

If you must **stay**, camping offers the best locations, with good provincial park sites (see p.747) reasonably close at Englishman River Falls and Little Qualicum Falls (see below). There are a multitude of cheapish generic **motels** in town and "resort complexes" out along the beaches, though summer vacancies are few and far between.

Qualicum Beach

QUALICUM BEACH has been dubbed the "Carmel of the North" after the town in California; this pitches things rather high, but compared with Parksville the area has more greenery and charm, and it's infinitely less commercialized (though it probably has just as many summer visitors). More a collection of dispersed houses than a town, at least near the water, Qualicum's seafront is correspondingly wilder and more picturesque, skirted by the road and interrupted only by a **visitor centre** (Jan to mid-May & early Sept to Dec Mon–Sat 9am–4pm; mid-May to early Sept daily 8.30am–6.30pm; ⓣ250/752-9532 or 1-866/887-7106, ⓦwww.qualicum.bc.ca) at 2711 West Island Hwy, the obvious building midway on the strand, and a well-sited **hotel**, the *Sand Pebbles Inn* (ⓣ250/752-6974 or 1-877/556-2326, ⓦwww.spebbles.com; ⑤). A cluster of **motels** sits at its northern end, where the road swings inland. There's plenty of other local accommodation: contact the visitor centre for details. The road becomes quieter to the north and is edged with occasional **campsites**.

Highway 4 to Port Alberni

If you've not yet ventured off the coastal road from Victoria, the short stretch of **Highway 4** to Port Alberni offers the first real taste of the island's beauty. The first worthwhile stop is **Englishman River Falls Provincial Park**, 3km west of Parksville (exit at Errington Rd) and then another 8km south off the hwy. Named after an early immigrant who drowned here, the park wraps around the Englishman River, which tumbles over two main sets of waterfalls. A thirty-minute trail takes in both falls, with plenty of swimming and fishing pools en route. The popular year-round provincial park campsite (summer $19, winter $10) is on the left off the approach road before the river, secreted amongst cedars, dogwoods – BC's official tree – and lush ferns.

Back on the main hwy, another 8km brings you to the **Little Qualicum Hatchery**, given over to chum, trout and chinook salmon, and just beyond it turn right for the **Little Qualicum Falls Provincial Park**, on the north side of Hwy 4, 19km west of Parksville, which is claimed by some to be the island's loveliest small park. A magnificent forest trail follows the river as it drops several hundred metres through a series of gorges and foaming waterfalls. A half-hour stroll gives you views of the main falls, but for a longer hike try the five-hour Wesley Ridge

Trail. There's a sheltered provincial park campsite (summer $19, winter $10) by the river and a recognized swimming area on the river at its southern end.

Midway to Port Alberni, the road passes **Cameron Lake** and then an imperious belt of old-growth forest. At the lake's western end, it's worth walking ten minutes into **McMillan Provincial Park** (no campsite) to reach the famous **Cathedral Grove**, a beautiful group of huge Douglas firs, some of them reaching 70m tall, 2m thick; they are up to a thousand years old. Wandering the grove will take only a few minutes but, just to the east, at the Cameron Lake picnic site, is the start of the area's main **hike**. The well-maintained trail was marked out by railway crews in 1908 and climbs to the summit of **Mount Arrowsmith** (1817m), a long, gentle twenty-kilometre pull through alpine meadows that takes between six and nine hours. The mountain is also one of the island's newer and fast-developing ski areas.

Port Alberni

Self-proclaimed "Gateway to the Pacific" and – along with half of Vancouver Island – "Salmon Capital of the World", **PORT ALBERNI** is a dispersed town more or less dominated by the sights and smells of its huge lumber mills. Despite its relative ugliness, it's also an increasingly popular site for exploring the centre and west coast of the island, and a busy fishing port, situated at the end of the impressive fjord-like Alberni Inlet, Vancouver Island's longest. Various logging and pulp-mill tours are available, but the town's main interest to travellers is as a forward base for the Pacific Rim National Park. Still, if you've ever wanted to hook a salmon, this is probably one of the easier places to do so and there are any number of boats and guides ready to help out.

Arrival and information

Five **buses** daily run from Nanaimo to Port Alberni; the terminal is on Victoria Quay at 5065 Southgate Rd. Connections from here continue to Ucluelet, Bamfield and Tofino.

For help and information on fishing charters, hiking options, minor summer events, or tours of the two local pulp mills, call in at the **visitor centre** (June–Nov Mon–Fri 9am–5pm, Sat & Sun 10am–2pm, 10am–4pm in June; Dec–May Mon–Fri 8am–4pm, Sat & Sun 10am–2pm, 10am–4pm April & May; ⓣ250/724-6535, ⓦwww.avcoc.com), unmissable as you come into town, at 2533 Port Alberni Hwy – look out for the big yellow mural.

Accommodation

Given the early departure of the MV *Lady Rose* (see p.834), there's a good chance you may have to **stay** overnight in Port Alberni. Contact the visitor centre for a list of B&B outlets.

The Best Western Barclay 4277 Stamp Ave ⓣ250/724-7171 or 1-800/563-6590, ⓦwww.bestwesternbarclay.com. A reliable choice with a heated outdoor pool, fitness centre, sauna, on-site liquor store and a café and restaurant. ❻

Bluebird Motel 3755 3rd Ave ⓣ250/723-1153, ⓦwww.bluebirdalberni.ca. The closest to the quay of any of the options in town. It only has twenty simply furnished rooms, some with kitchenettes, so be sure to book in advance. ❸

Edelweiss B&B 2610 12th Ave ⓣ250/723-5940. An excellent B&B choice that's not particularly central, but does have very welcoming hosts. Free wi-fi available. ❸

The Hospitality Inn 3835 Redford St ⓣ250/723-8111, ⓦwww.hospitalityinnportalberni.com. A more memorable central hotel – not terribly cheap, but probably the town's best mid-price bet. Has an outdoor salt water pool, free wi-fi and sells fishing licences. ❺

Somass Motel & RV 5279 River Rd ⓣ250/724-3236 or 1-800/927-2217, ⓦwww.somass-motel.ca. Also a reliable choice, but smaller than the *Best Western*. Has one- and two-bedroom kitchen suites

Boats from Port Alberni

One of the great trips in BC is aboard the **MV Lady Rose**, a small, 73-year-old Scottish-built freighter that plies between Port Alberni, Kildonan, Bamfield, Ucluelet and the Broken Group Islands (see p.846). Primarily a conduit for freight and mail, it also takes up to a hundred passengers, many of whom use it as a drop-off for canoe trips or the West Coast Trail at Bamfield. You could easily ride it simply for the exceptional scenery – huge cliffs and tree-covered mountains – and for the abundant wildlife (sea lions, whales, eagles, depending on the time of year). Another boat – the two hundred-passenger **MV Frances Barkley** – sails a similar route; reservations for trips on both vessels are essential. Remember to take a sweater and jacket and wear sensible shoes: these are still primarily working boats with few creature comforts.

The basic year-round **schedule** is as follows: the boat leaves from the Argyle Pier, 5425 Argyle St at the Alberni Harbour Quay, Port Alberni (Tues, Thurs & Sat 8am). After a stop at **Kildonan** ($25 one-way, $50 return), it arrives in **Bamfield** ($33/66) at 12.30pm. It starts its return journey at 1.30pm, reaching Port Alberni at 5.30pm. From October–May the boat stops on advance request at the Broken Group Islands.

From June to mid-September, there are additional sailings to the **Broken Group Islands** (Mon, Wed & Fri, departs Port Alberni 8am). At 11am, the boat docks at Sechart ($33/66), site of the highly recommended *Sechart Lodge*, the only place to stay on the archipelago if you're not wilderness camping. Cost per night is $140/person, $215 for two sharing a room, including all meals; $15 and $20 less if you stay two or more days. The boat continues to **Ucluelet** ($36/72), arriving at 12.30pm. The return journey starts from Ucluelet at 2pm, calling at Sechart (3.30pm) before arriving back at Port Alberni at 7pm.

From July 2 to September 3 there is an additional sailing (Sun only) on the route from Port Alberni (8am) to Bamfield (1.30pm) and back, with an outbound stop at Sechart at 11am.

For **information** and **reservations on boats and the lodge**, contact Lady Rose Marine Services, 5425 Argyle St, Port Alberni (year-round ⓣ250/723-8313 or April–Sept ⓣ1-800/663-7192, ⓦwww.ladyrosemarine.com). It also offers canoe and kayak **rentals** ($40/day, double kayak $60/day, includes lifejackets, paddles, pumps and spray skirts) as well as transportation of the same to the Broken Group Islands. The Toquart Connector Water Taxi (contact the above numbers or ⓣ250/720-7358) runs between the *Sechart Lodge*, Sechart, Bamfield and the Broken Group Islands for between $45 and $65 per person. Other boats to these destinations can occasionally be picked up from Tofino and Ucluelet.

or standard rooms with fridge and microwave. Guests can also make use of the bbq, the on-site laundry or have staff arrange fishing charters. ④

Campsites

China Creek Marina and Campground
2011 Bamfield Road ⓣ250/723-9812, ⓦwww.portalberniportauthority.ca. A big 250-site campground, 15km south of town on Alberni Inlet, which has a wooded, waterside location and sandy, log-strewn beach. Sites range from $18 in the low season to $23 in the high.

The town and around

From the colourful harbour quay, a small steam train (summer only) runs from the old train station at the corner of Kingsway Avenue and Argyle Street for about half an hour along the waterfront to the **McLean Steam Sawmill** (site open daily year-round; mill building and steam train late June to early Sept Thurs–Mon 10.00–5.15pm; check website for limited and occasional spring, autumn and winter opening and operations; site donation; mill and theatre $15.25; mill, train and theatre $29.95; ⓦwww.alberniheritage.com), an old steam-operated mill at

5633 Smith Rd, which you might also reach by bike or on foot on the twenty-kilometre Log Trail from the visitor centre.

For hot-weather swimming, locals head out to **Sproat Lake Provincial Park**, 8km north of town on Hwy 4. It's hectic in summer, thanks to a fine beach, picnic area and a pair of good campsites (summer $19, winter $10; April–Oct), one on the lake, the other north of the hwy about 1km away; you can take a guided tour of the world's largest fire-fighting planes here or follow the short trails that lead to a few ancient petroglyphs on the park's eastern tip.

Sproat Lake marks the start of the superb scenery that unfolds over the 100km of Hwy 4 west of the town. Only heavily logged areas detract from the grandeur of the Mackenzie Range and the majestic interplay of trees and water. Go prepared, as there's no fuel or shops for about two hours of driving.

Eating and drinking

For coffee, good breakfasts and snacks down by the dock, try the *Blue Door Café* at 5415 Argyle St, an old-fashioned place much-patronized by locals. For fuller meals, including great fish and chips, make for the *Swale Rock Café* 5328 Argyle St (☎250/723-0777).

Pacific Rim National Park

The **Pacific Rim National Park** – the single best reason to visit Vancouver Island – is a stunning amalgam of mountains, coastal rainforest, wild beaches and unkempt marine landscapes that stretches intermittently for 130km between the towns of Tofino in the north and Port Renfrew to the south. It divides into three distinct areas: **Long Beach**, which is the most popular; the **Broken Group**

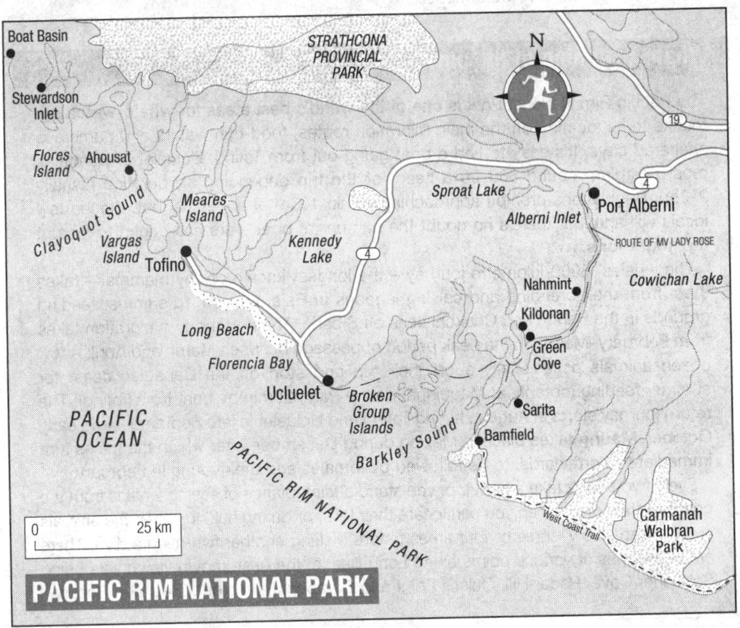

Islands, hundreds of islets only really accessible to sailors and canoeists; and the **West Coast Trail**, a tough but popular long-distance hike. The whole area has also become a magnet for surfing and **whale-watching** enthusiasts, and dozens of small companies run charters out from the main centres to view the migrating mammals. By taking the MV *Lady Rose* from Port Alberni (see box, p.834) to Bamfield or Ucluelet or back, and combining this with shuttle buses or scheduled buses from Victoria, Port Alberni and Nanaimo, a wonderfully varied combination of itineraries is possible around the region.

Lying at the north end of Long Beach, **Tofino**, once a fishing village, has been changed by tourism, but with its natural charm, scenic position and plentiful accommodation, it still makes the best base for general exploration. **Ucluelet** to the south is comparatively less attractive, but almost equally geared to providing tours and accommodating the park's 800,000 or so annual visitors. **Bamfield**, a tiny and picturesque community with a limited amount of in-demand accommodation, lies still farther south and is known mainly as the northern trailhead of the West Coast Trail and a fishing, marine research and whale-watching centre. Unless you fly in, you'll enter the park on Hwy 4 from Port Alberni, which means the first part you'll see is **Long Beach** (see p.841), shadowed along its length to Tofino by Hwy 4. Long Beach is also the site of the park's main information centre and the nearby Wickaninnish Interpretive Centre. There's a **park fee** of $7.80 per person per day, payable at the entrance.

The **weather** on this part of the island has a well-deserved reputation for being appallingly wet, cold and windy – and that's the good days. An average of 300cm of rain falls annually, and in some places it's almost 700cm, well over ten times Victoria's rainfall. So don't count on doing much swimming or sunbathing (though **surfing**'s a possibility): think more in terms of spending your time admiring crashing Pacific breakers, hiking the backcountry and maybe doing some beachcombing. Time your visit to coincide with the worst of the weather off-season – **storm-watching** has become a popular park pastime and rates for accommodation tend to be cheaper.

Whale-watching in the park

The Pacific Rim National Park is one of the world's best areas for **whale-watching**, thanks to its location on the main migration routes, food-rich waters and numerous sheltered bays. It's easy to find a boat going out from Tofino, Ucluelet or Bamfield, most charging around $60–80 a head for the trip depending on duration (usually 2–3hr). Regulations prohibit approaching within 100m of an animal but, though few locals will admit it, there's no doubt the number of boat tours has begun to disrupt the **migrations**.

The whales' 8000-kilometre journey – the longest known of any mammal – takes them from their breeding and calving lagoons in Baja, Mexico, to summer feeding grounds in the Bering and Chukchi seas off Siberia. The northbound migration takes from February–May, with the peak period of passage between March and April. A few dozen animals occasionally abort their trip and stop off the Canadian coast for summer feeding (notably at Maquinna Marine Park, 20min by boat from Tofino). The return journey starts in August, hitting Tofino and Ucluelet in late September and early October. **Mating** takes place in Mexico during December, after which the males turn immediately northwards, to be followed by females and their young in February.

Even if you don't take a boat trip, you stand a faint chance of seeing whales from the coast as they dive, when you can locate their tails, or during fluking, when the animals surface and "blow" three or four times before making another five-minute dive. There are telescopes at various points along Long Beach, the best-known viewpoints being Schooner Cove, Radar Hill, Quistis Point and Combers Beach near Sea Lion Rocks.

Tofino

TOFINO is showing the adverse effects of its ever-increasing tourist influx, but locals are keeping development to a minimum, clearly realizing they have a vested interest in preserving the salty, waterfront charm that brought them – and visitors – here in the first place. Crowning a narrow spit, the fishing village has a location that graces it with magnificent views and plenty of what the tourist literature refers to as "aquaculture". As a service centre it fulfils most functions, offering food, accommodation and a wide variety of boat and sea-plane tours, most of which have a **whale-watching**, surfing (Canada's best surf is close at hand) and fishing angle or provide a means to travel out to **islands and hot springs** close by.

Arrival and information

Tofino is easily reached by **bus** from Port Alberni (2 daily; 3hr) and Nanaimo (1 daily; 4hr 30min), with a single early-morning connection from Victoria, changing at Nanaimo (6hr 30min). The bus depot is on 1st Street near the junction with Neil Street. There is also a mini-bus shuttle (1–2 daily), the Tofino Bus, 564 Campbell St (Ⓣ250/725-2871 or 1-866/986-3466, Ⓦwww.tofinobus.com), from Victoria or Nanaimo at the Departure Bay ferry terminal (connecting with the ferry from Horseshoe Bay). It runs via Port Alberni (4541 Margaret St) and Ucluelet (Murray's Grocery, 1738 Peninsula St). The fare from Victoria is $64 and tickets must be booked by phone or online.

Tofino's **visitor centre** (May–Sept Fri–Mon 9am–5pm, Tues & Wed 10am–6pm; Oct–April daily 9am–5pm; Ⓣ250/725-3414, Ⓦwww.tourismtofino.com) is at 455 Campbell St, and has an exhaustive lowdown on all the logistics of boat and plane tours.

Accommodation

The visitor centre may be able to get you into one of the village's ever-expanding roster of **hotels**, **motels** and **B&Bs**, should you be unwise enough to turn up without reservations in high summer. There are two main concentrations of accommodation options: in Tofino itself or a couple of kilometres east of town on or near Lynn Road, which overlooks Chesterman Beach. Out of town across the water (accessed by water taxi) there are also the desirable self-contained units of the *Hot Springs Cove Lodge* (Ⓣ250/670-1133 or 724-8570; ❻; price includes water-taxi crossing at $60; May–Sept plus period at Christmas and New Year) at Hot Springs Cove (see p.841); book early.

Otherwise, try one of the near-town **campsites** (don't forget there's a park campsite at Long Beach; see pp.841–844) or the **private hostels** that now seem to spring up overnight and disappear just as quickly, though local reports suggest some of these places can be pretty unsalubrious.

Hotels and motels

Cable Cove Inn 201 Main St Ⓣ250/725-4236 or 1-800/663-6449, Ⓦwww.cablecoveinn.com. Stay in high style in one of seven smart rooms at the westernmost edge of town that come complete with jacuzzis, fireplaces and four-poster beds. There's also an on-site spa and a waterside cabin dining room. ❼

Dolphin Motel 1190 Pacific Rim Hwy Ⓣ250/725-3377, Ⓦwww.dolphinmotel.ca. Fourteen rather simply furnished rooms with coffee-maker and fridge or self-catering units 3km south of town; 5-minute walk to Chesterman Beach. ❺

Duffin Cove and Resort 215 Campbell St Ⓣ250/725-3448 or 1-888/629-2903, Ⓦwww.duffin-cove-resort.com. Choose from cabins (for 1–8 people), suites (for 4–8 people) with kitchens and seaview balconies and suites (for 2–3 people) just south of the *Cable Cove Inn* at the western edge of town overlooking Clayoquot Sound. ❽

Maquinna Hotel 120 1st St Ⓣ250/725-3261 or 1-800/665-3199, Ⓦwww.maquinnahotel.com.

Central town location, containing 32 renovated rooms, some overlooking Tofino Harbour and Meares Island. 5

Middle Beach Lodge 400 Mackenzie Beach ⓣ250/725-2900, ⓦwww.middlebeach.com. Extremely nice, secluded 64-room lodge south of town and west of Chesterman Beach with big stone fireplace, deep old chairs and the gentle splash of waves on tiny Templar Beach to lull you to sleep. 6

Ocean Village Beach Resort 555 Hellesen Drive ⓣ250/725-3755, ⓦwww.oceanvillageresort.com. A resort just north of Long Beach, 2km from town on the main road, with accommodation in single or duplex cottages, all with ocean views and kitchen units. Also has a bbq, indoor salt-water pool and free wi-fi. 7

Schooner Motel 315–321 Campbell St ⓣ250/725-3478, ⓦwww.schoonermotel.net. Overlooking Tofino Inlet and Meares Island in the town centre, this eighteen-room motel has some rooms complete with kitchen. 6

Tofino Harbourview Motel 542 Campbell St ⓣ250/725-2055, ⓦwww.tofinomotel.com. A thirteen-room motel on the eastern edge of town; rooms have balconies offering views of the sea and neighbouring islands. Family suites with kitchenettes available. 4

Tofino Swell Lodge 341 Olsen Rd ⓣ250/725-3274, ⓦwww.tofinoswell.com. On the eastern edge of town near Crab Dock, this excellent seven-room lodge on the waterfront looking out to Meares Island has kitchen or plain sleeping units, as well as a jacuzzi, bbq and its own private dock – useful for any fishing charter trips you may be inclined to take. 4

Wickaninnish Inn 500 Osprey Lane at Chesterman Beach ⓣ250/725-3100 or 1-800/333-4604, ⓦwww.wickinn.com. If you're feeling like a splurge (rooms start at $480, less off season), shell out for this superb $8.5–million 45-room inn, situated on a rocky promontory at the western end of Chesterman Beach. All rooms are large and have ocean views, fireplaces and baths big enough for two. As well as the obvious local attractions, storm-watching here is a growing wintertime activity and the spa is one of the best on the continent. 8

Bed and Breakfasts

Brimar 1375 Thornberg Crescent ⓣ250/725-3410 or 1-800/714-9373, ⓦwww.brimarbb.com. At the south end of Chesterman Beach, off Lynn Rd, these three rooms have good Pacific Ocean views and come with a full breakfast. 6

Chesterman Beach B&B 1345 Chesterman Beach Rd ⓣ250/725-3726, ⓦwww.chestermanbeach.net. Three luxurious oceanfront suites on the beach with private entrance and bathrooms, one of which, the Garden Cottage, has a lovely private garden. 8

Gull Cottage 1254 Lynn Rd ⓣ250/725-3177, ⓦwww.gullcottagetofino.com. A few minutes' walk to the beach, at the west end of Lynn Rd, this Victorian-era home has three rooms, all with private bathrooms, and a hot tub in the woods. 6

The Tide's Inn B&B 160 Arnet Rd ⓣ250/725-3765, ⓦwww.tidesinntofino.com. An easy walk south of town (walk down 1st Ave and turn right) on the waterfront with good views of Clayoquot Sound. 6

Wilp Gybuu (Wolf House) 311 Leighton Way ⓣ250/725-2330, ⓦwww.tofinobedandbreakfast.com. Three rooms, all with sea views and en-suite bathroom, in a walkable location south of town close to *The Tide's Inn*. Breakfasts are superb. 6

Hostel

Whalers on the Point Guesthouse (HI) 81 West St ⓣ250/725-3443, ⓦwww.tofinohostel.com. This is the best hostel in town, with fabulous ocean views. Including tax, beds are from $30/person. Private doubles cost $85-145. Facilities include kitchen, games room, sauna, bike rental and storage, surf and wet-suit lockers, and a shuttle service to Long Beach. Reservations are essential. 3

Campsites

Bella Pacifica Campground Pacific Rim Hwy ⓣ250/725-3400, ⓦwww.bellapacifica.com. Sites with hot showers, flush toilets and laundry 2km south of town, with wilderness and oceanfront sites, private nature trails to Templar Beach and walk-on access to Mackenzie Beach. Reservations recommended. Feb to mid-Nov. Sites cost $38–48, depending on the season.

Crystal Cove Beach Resort Mackenzie Beach ⓣ250/725-4213, ⓦwww.crystalcovebeachresort.com. Set in a pretty secluded cove about 3km south of town and 1km from Mackenzie Beach, this 72-site RV park has flush toilets, laundry, showers, offers complimentray coffee in the morning and provides free firewood. If that doesn't appeal, try one of the 34 log cabins (one and two bedroom), all with kitchens and ocean views. Reservations recommended. RV sites $55. Cabins 8

Mackenzie Beach Resort 1101 Pacific Rim Hwy ⓣ250/725-3439, ⓦwww.mackenziebeach.com. Located on a fine sandy beach 2km south of Tofino and 10-minute walk from Long Beach, this place offers cabins, rooms, suites, RV and tent sites; some of the latter are beachside. There's also an indoor pool, jacuzzi, hot showers and kayak rentals. Tents $35–45 low season, $46–56 high; RVs $45/56.

The town and around

Sleepy in the off-season, the place erupts into a commercial frenzy during the summer. Hippies, surfer types and easygoing family groups are the most prevalent – though there's little to do in town other than walk its few streets, enjoy the views and soak up the casual atmosphere.

It's worth visiting the small **Whale Centre** at 411 Campbell St (daily 9am–8pm; free; ⓣ250/725-2132, ⓦwww.tofinowhalecentre.com), one of many places to book whale-watching tours, but also home to exhibits and artefacts devoted to local seafaring and trading history, whales and aboriginal peoples' culture. Another notable place around town is the **Eagle Aerie Gallery**, 350 Campbell St (ⓦwww.royhenryvickers.com), a gallery housed in a traditional long-house-style building with a beautiful cedar interior.

Two fine beaches lie within walking distance to the southeast of the town: **Mackenzie Beach** and **Chesterman's Beach** (for access to the latter take Lynn Rd right just beyond the *Dolphin Motel* as you leave town), the former one of the warmer spots locally, the latter home to a fair number of out-of-town accommodation possibilities (see opposite). Beyond Chesterman lies Frank Island, a tempting proposition at low tide, but private property. The quietest beach around is **Templar**: ask at the visitor centre for directions.

Eating and drinking

Just about everyone in town clusters around the heaving tables of the *Common Loaf Bake Shop* (ⓣ250/725-3915) behind the bank at 180 1st St, deservedly the most popular choice for coffee and snacks; at night, the home-made dough is turned into pizzas instead of bread and rolls. For smoothies, deli food, snacks, wraps and an all-day breakfast, visit *Breakers Delicatessan* at 430 Campbell St (ⓣ250/725-2558, ⓦwww.breakersdeli.com). Best place for a **beer** and **dancing** is the pub downstairs at the *Maquinna Lodge*, 120 Ist St, the place to be on Friday and Saturday nights.

Restaurants

The Pointe Restaurant At the *Wickaninnish Inn* (see opposite), ⓣ250/725-3100. If you fancy a big splurge – and even bigger treat in terms of the quality of food on offer – make your way here, the area's best upmarket restaurant. The views are stunning, but be prepared to pay for them – you'll likley drop over $150 for a full gourmet nine-course special with wine.

Rain Coast Café 101-120 4th St ⓣ250/725-2215, ⓦwww.raincoastcafe.com. Excellent Pacific Rim fusion food is available at this intimate and sleek café, which is open for dinner only from 5.30pm. Mains cost $15–30.

Schooner Restaurant 331 Campbell St ⓣ250/725-3444, ⓦwww.schoonerrestaurant.ca. Equally elevated (mainly fish and seafood) cuisine can be found at breakfast, lunch and dinner at this award-winning, romantic place set in pretty gardens with tremendous views of Tofino Inlet. Mains from $23.

Sea Shanty 300 Main St ⓣ250/725-2902, ⓦwww.himwitsa.com. The decor at this First Nations-owned and operated restaurant won't knock you out, but there's outdoor dining overlooking the harbour – which means tremendous sunsets in good weather. The menu specializes in fresh seafood, but does a range of other dishes, including sandwiches, pizza and steak. Open Feb–Oct.

Sobo 311 Neill St ⓣ250/725-2341, ⓦwww.sobo.ca. This award-winning restaurant, with fun slate floors and driftwood tables, actually started out as a purple catering truck but has now become a hugely popular place to dine, thanks to its superb seasonal Pacific Rim cuisine – try the Killer Fish Tacos. Open for lunch.

Trips from Tofino: Clayoquot Sound

After wandering Tofino's handful of streets, most people head south to explore Long Beach, or put themselves at the mercy of the many boat and plane operators serving the stretch of ocean and landscapes around Tofino known as **Clayoquot Sound**. The name has gained tremendous resonance over the last few years, largely

Tofino activities

Whale-watching

Ucluelet to the south may claim to be the "whale-watching capital of the world", but **whales** are just as easily seen from Tofino. There are plenty of operators, most costing about the same and offering similar **excursions**: all you need do is decide what sort of boat you want to go out on – zodiacs (inflatables), which are bouncier, more thrilling and potentially wetter, or rigid-hull cruisers (covered or uncovered), which are more sedate. See the box on p.836 for more whale-watching tips. If you take tours to Meares Islands, Hot Springs Cove and elsewhere, especially in spring or autumn, you stand a good chance of seeing whales en route anyway – some operators try to combine whale-watching and excursions. Reckon on spending from around $80 for a two- or three-hour trip in a zodiac and $100 on a rigid-hull.

Operators in Tofino include: Clayoquot Connections, 606 Campbell St (ⓣ250/726-8789, ⓦwww.island.net/~dkay), which offers a relatively inexpensive ($25) tour of the harbour and Meares Island; Ocean Outfitters, 368 Main St (ⓣ250/725-2866 or 1-877/90-OCEAN, ⓦwww.oceanoutfitters.bc.ca), which offers a wide range of tours ($79) on rigid or zodiac boats; Jamie's Whaling Station, 606 Campbell St (ⓣ250/725-3919 or 1-800/667-9913, ⓦwww.jamies.com; mid-Feb to Oct), was founded in 1982 and offers a choice of zodiac boats or the twenty-metre *Lady Selkirk*, which comes with heated cabin. If you don't see whales, Jamie's offers vouchers which can be used on another trip. Also long-established (since 1986) is Remote Passages at the bottom end of Wharf Street (ⓣ250/725-3330 or 1-800/666-9833, ⓦwww.remotepassages.com).

Fishing, surfing, kayaking and hiking

Many of the above companies also offer bear-watching, kayaking, hiking, **fishing** charters and other tours; for a more long-established fishing specialist operator contact Smiley Seas Charters, 380 Main St (May–Sept; ⓣ250/725-2557, ⓦwww.smileyseas.com), which is quite happy to have novices aboard. Tofino is quickly becoming the **surfing** capital of Canada, thanks to some enormous Pacific waves, though floating driftwood and big lumps of lumber caught up in the waves can be a hazard. For information, board rental and all other equipment, contact Live to Surf, well east of the town centre at 1180 Pacific Rim Hwy (ⓣ250/725-4464, ⓦwww.livetosurf.com). It rents boards from $25 and many other items, as well as offering lessons (from $55 for 2hr, excluding equipment).

If you want to go out in a **kayak** (no experience required) contact Paddle West Kayaking, 660 Campbell St (ⓣ250/725-3232, ⓦwww.paddlewestkayaking.com), which offers 2½-, 4- and 6-hour trips ($55/68/113). Plenty of other operators offer longer tours with lodge accommodation or wilderness camping. Guided **hikes** and easy nature rambles in the forest and along the seashore are offered by several companies; contact the visitor centre for details.

because it has been the focus for some of the most bitterly fought battles against loggers by environmentalists and aboriginal campaigners.

The Sound stretches for some 65km from Kennedy Lake, to the south of Tofino, to the Hesquiat Peninsula 40km to the north, embracing three major islands – Meares, Vargas and Flores – and numerous smaller islets and coastal inlets. More importantly, it is the largest surviving area of low-altitude temperate **rainforest** in North America. Quite incredibly the BC government in 1993 gave permission to logging companies to fell two-thirds of this irreplaceable and age-old forest. The result was the largest outbreak of **civil disobedience** in Canadian history, resulting in eight hundred arrests, as vast numbers congregated at a peace camp in the area and made daily attempts to stop the logging trucks. The stand-off resulted in partial victory, with the designation of new protected areas and limited recognition of the Nuu-chah-nulth band's moral and literal rights to the land. Yet the region remains in a precarious position, and if it's happened once you can be pretty sure that, where forestry interests are concerned, it'll happen again. There are five main destinations in this region for boat and floatplane trips from Tofino.

Meares and Vargas islands

The nearest journey is to **Meares Island**, easily visible to the east of Tofino and just fifteen minutes away by boat. A beautiful island swathed in lush temperate rainforest, this was one of the areas earmarked for the lumberjack's chainsaw, despite its designation as a Nuu-chah-nulth park in 1985. Currently, its ancient cedars and hemlock are safe and visible on the Meares Island Big Cedar Trail (3km), which meanders among some of the biggest trees you'll ever see, many of them more than a thousand years old and up to 6m across – big enough to put a tunnel through. **Vargas Island**, the next nearest target, lies just 5km north of Tofino and is visited for its beauty, beaches, kayaking and swimming possibilities.

Flores Island

About 20km to the northwest of Tofino is **Flores Island**, which is accessed by boat or plane and, like Vargas Island, is partly protected by partial provincial park status. At the aboriginal peoples' community of Ahousaht you can pick up the Ahousaht Wild Side Heritage Trail ($20), which runs for 16km through idyllic beach and forest scenery to the Mount Flores viewpoint (886m). This is also a chance to encounter aboriginal culture and people at first hand, with **tours** accompanied by local guides available; check with the Tofino visitor centre.

Hot Springs Cove and Hesquiat Peninsula

Perhaps the best, and certainly one of the most popular trips from Tofino, is the 37-kilometre boat or plane ride to **Hot Springs Cove**, site of one of only a handful of hot springs on Vancouver Island. This takes an hour by water-taxi (from $70) or fifteen minutes by floatplane with one of the town's floatplane operators (from $120), though the most cost-effective way of seeing the island is to take a day tour with one of Tofino's many operators, who throw in whale-watching en route (from $95). A thirty-minute trek from the landing stage brings you to the springs, which emerge at a piping 43°C and run, as a creek, to the sea via a small waterfall and four pools, becoming progressively cooler. Be prepared for crowds in summer when swimming costumes can be optional. An expensive hotel, the *Hot Springs Cove Lodge* (see p.837), sits on the cove near the landing stage.

A forty-kilometre trip north takes you to **Hesquiat Peninsula**, where you land at or near Refuge Cove, site of a Hesquiat aboriginal village. Locals offer tours here and some lodgings; ask for details at the Tofino visitor centre.

Long Beach

The most accessible of the park's components, **Long Beach** is just what it says: a long tract of wild, windswept sand and rocky points stretching for about 30km south from Tofino to Ucluelet. Around 19km can be hiked unbroken from Schooner Bay in the west to Half Moon Bay in the east. The snow-covered peaks of the Mackenzie Range provide a scenic backdrop, while behind the beach grows a thick, lush canopy of coastal rainforest. The white-packed sand itself is the sort of primal seascape that is all but extinct in much of the world, scattered with beautiful, sea-sculpted driftwood, smashed by surf, broken by crags and dotted with islets and rock pools oozing with marine life.

▲ Long Beach, Pacific Rim National Park

Long Beach, while a distinct beach in itself, also rather loosely refers to several other beaches to either side, the relative merits of which are outlined opposite. If you haven't done so already, driving or biking Hwy 4 along the beach area is the best time to call in at the Pacific Rim National Park **Visitor Centre** (see p.844), located right off Hwy 4 3km northwest of the Ucluelet–Tofino–Port Alberni road junction; remember, there's a **park fee** of $7.80 per person per day.

Long Beach is noted for its **wildlife**, the BC coastline reputedly having more marine species than any other temperate area in the world. As well as the smaller stuff in tidal pools – starfish, anemones, snails, sponges and suchlike – there are large mammals like whales and sea lions, as well as thousands of migrating birds (especially in Oct & Nov), notably pintails, mallards, black brants and Canada geese. Better weather brings out lots of beachcombers (Japanese glass fishing floats are highly coveted), clam diggers, anglers, surfers, canoeists, windsurfers and divers, though the water is usually too cold to venture in without a wet suit, and rip currents and rogue lumps of driftwood crashed around by the waves can make swimming dangerous. Surf guards patrol the Long Beach day-use area in July and August. And finally, try to resist the temptation to pick up shells as souvenirs – it's against park regulations.

Beaches near Long Beach

As this is a national park, some of Long Beach and its flanking stretches of coastline have been very slightly tamed for human consumption, but in a most discreet and tasteful manner. The best way to get a taste of the area is to walk the beaches or forested shorelines themselves – there are plenty of hidden coves – or to follow any of nine very easy and well-maintained **hiking trails**. If you're driving or biking along Hwy 4, which backs the beaches all the way, there are distinct areas to look out for.

Moving west, the first of these is the five-kilometre **Florencia Beach** (1.5km from the hwy; access by trails 1, 2, 3 and 5; see box below), also known as Wreck Beach and formerly the home of hippie beach dwellers in driftwood shacks before

Long Beach walks

With an eye on the weather and tide, you can **walk** more or less anywhere on and around Long Beach. Various trails and roads drop to the beach from the main Hwy 4 road to Tofino. At the same time there are nine official trails, most of them short and very easy, so you could tackle a few in the course of a leisurely drive or cycle along the road. All the paths are clearly marked from Hwy 4, but it's worth picking up a *Hiker's Guide* from the visitor centre. From east to west you can choose from the following: The linked trails **1** and **2**, the **Willowbrae and Halfmoon Bay trails** (2.8km round-trip), are accessed by turning left at the main Hwy 4 junction and driving or biking 2km towards Ucluelet. A level wooded trail then leads from the trailhead towards the beach. Just before the sea it divides, dropping steeply via steps and ramps, to either the tiny Half Moon Bay or the larger, neighbouring Florencia Bay to the north.

All other walks are accessed off Hwy 4 to Tofino, turning right (north) at the main Hwy 4 junction. The gentle **3 Gold Mine Trail** (3km round-trip, but closed at the time of publication), signed left off the road, leads along Lost Shoe Creek, a former gold-mining area (look out for debris), to Florencia Beach. For walks **4**, **5** and **6**, take the turn left off the hwy for the Wickaninnish Centre. The **4 South Beach Trail** (1.5km round-trip) leaves from behind the centre, leading above forest-fringed shores and coves before climbing to the headlands for a view of the coast and a chance to climb down to South Beach, famous for its big rock-crashing breakers and the sound of the water ripping noisily through the beach pebbles. The **5 Nuu-chah-nulth Trail** (5km) follows the South Beach Trail for a while and then at the top of the first hill is signed left, passing through rainforest before ending at the parking area above Florencia Beach to the east. The **6 Shorepine Bog Trail** (800m) is a wheelchair-accessible boardwalk trail (accessed on the left on the access road to the centre) that wends through the fascinating stunted bog vegetation; trees which are just a metre or so tall here can be hundreds of years old.

Farther west towards Tofino along Hwy 4, the **7 Rainforest Trails** are two small loops (1km each round-trip), one on each side of the road, that follow a boardwalk through virgin temperate rainforest: each has interpretive boards detailing forest life cycle and forest "inhabitants", respectively. Farther down the road on the right at the Combers Beach parking area, a road gives access to the gentle **8 Spruce Fringe Trail** (1.5km loop). This graphically illustrates the effects of the elements on spruce forest, following a log-strewn beach fringe-edged with bent and bowed trees before entering more robust forest farther from the effects of wind and salt spray. It also crosses willow and crab-apple swamps to a glacial terrace, the site of a former shoreline, past the airport turn-off. The **9 Schooner Cove Trail** (1km one-way), leads left off the road through superb tranches of rainforest to an extremely scenic beach at Schooner Cove. Don't fail to climb to the viewpoint on **Radar Hill** off to the right as you get closer to Tofino.

the park's formation. This is something of a local favourite, with relatively few people and good rock pools.

Farther along Hwy 4 you come to a turn-off (Long Beach Rd) for the **Wickaninnish Interpretive Centre** (mid-March to mid-Oct daily 10am–6pm; ⓣ250/726-4701) on a headland at the start of Long Beach, not to be confused with the similarly named well-known hotel and restaurant closer to Tofino (confusingly, the centre also has a restaurant). Wickaninnish was a noted nineteenth-century aboriginal chief, and arbitrator between Europeans and aboriginal fur traders. His name left no doubt as to his number-one status, as it means "having no one in front of him in the canoe".

The centre is the departure point for several trails (see p.843), has telescopes for whale-spotting and a variety of films, displays and exhibits relating to the park and ocean. Around 8km beyond the Long Beach Road turn-off is the entrance to the Green Point park **campsite** (see below) and additional access to Long Beach, while 4km beyond that lies the turn-off on the right to Tofino's small airstrip. Around here the peninsula narrows, with **Grice Bay** coming close to the road on the right (north side), a shallow inlet known in winter for its countless wildfowl. Beyond the airstrip turn-off comes a trail to Schooner Cove and 3.5km beyond that a 1.5-kilometre turn-off to Kap'yong, or **Radar Hill** (96m), the panoramic site of a wartime radar station.

About 4.5km farther on (and a couple of kilometres outside the park boundary) you come to **Cox Bay Beach**, **Chesterman Beach** and **Mackenzie Beach**, all accessed from Hwy 4. Cox and Chesterman are known for their breakers, and Mackenzie for its relative warmth.

Practicalities

Long Beach's **Pacific Rim Visitor Centre** (daily mid-March to late June 9am–5pm; late June to early Sept 9am–7pm; early Sept to mid-Oct 9am–5pm; ⓣ250/726-4212, ⓦwww.pc.gc.ca) is just off Hwy 4, 3km north of the T-junction for Tofino and Ucluelet. It provides a wealth of material on all aspects of the park, and in summer staff offer guided walks and interpretive programmes. For year-round information, call the Park Administration Office (ⓣ250/726-3500). For more Long Beach information, viewing decks with telescopes and lots of well-presented displays, head for the **Wickaninnish Interpretive Centre**, Long Beach Road (see above).

There is one park **campsite**, the *Green Point*, set on a lovely bluff overlooking the beach (from $23.50 for the 94 drive-in sites, with washrooms but no showers; nineteen primitive walk-in sites $17.60). It's likely to be full every day in July and August, and it's first-come, first-served for the walk-in sites (reservations are taken up to three months in advance for the drive-in sites), so you may have to turn up for several days before getting a spot. There's usually a waiting-list system, whereby you're given a number and instructions as to when you should be able to return. The nearest commercial sites and conventional accommodation are in Tofino and Ucluelet.

Ucluelet

UCLUELET, 8km south of the main Hwy 4 Port Alberni junction, means "People of the Sheltered Bay", from the aboriginal word *ucluth* – "wind blowing in from the bay". It was named by the Nuu-chah-nulth, who lived here for centuries before the arrival of whites who came to exploit some of the world's richest fishing grounds immediately offshore. Today the port is still the third largest in BC by volume of fish landed, a trade that gives the town a slightly dispersed appearance and an industrial fringe and makes it a less appealing, if nonetheless popular base for anglers, whale-watchers, water-sports enthusiasts and visitors headed for Long Beach to the north.

Arrival and information

Buses and **boats** call at Ucluelet from Port Alberni and Tofino – a local transit bus generally makes the road trip twice a day en route to and from Tofino and/or Port Alberni, with one connection daily from Port Alberni to Nanaimo and Victoria. Boats from Port Alberni usually dock here three days a week (see p.834). There's plenty of accommodation (though less than Tofino), much of it spread on or just off Peninsula Road, the main approach to and through town from Hwy 4. A car or bike is useful here, as there's relatively little in the small central area, though location isn't vital unless you want to be near the sea. For full details, plus information on the many whale-watching, fishing and other tours, visit the **visitor centre** at 2791 Pacific Rim Hwy near the junction with Hwy 4 (daily: mid-March to June 9am–5pm, July to early Sept 9am–7pm, early Sept to mid-Oct 9am–5pm; rest of the year Tues–Sat 10am–4pm; Ⓣ250/726-4600, Ⓦwww.pacificrimvisitor.com).

Practicalities

There's limited choice for **food** in Ucluelet, but what's there isn't bad. *Blueberries Bakery Café* (Ⓣ250/726-7707), at 1627 Peninsula Rd, serves coffee, snacks, breakfast, lunch and dinner (from $10–20), is licensed and has an outdoor patio with sea views. *Delicado's Surfside Café* (Ⓣ250/726-4246, Ⓦwww.delicados-deli.com; closed Sun), at 2082 Peninsula Rd, is a self-consciously funky café/deli five minutes' north of town, good for eat-in or takeout meals at reasonable prices.

Accommodation

Canadian Princess Resort 1943 Peninsula Rd Ⓣ250/726-7771 or 1-800/663-7090, Ⓦwww.canadianprincess.com (mid-June to Sept). The most unusual is also the most popular. Just west of the centre, with on-shore rooms or good-value one- to six-berth cabins (the smallest rooms share bathrooms) in a former hydrographic survey ship, built in 1932 and moored in the harbour. You can also book upmarket whale-watching and fishing trips here in big, comfortable cabin cruisers and it has a restaurant and bar open to non-residents. ❸–❽

Little Beach Resort 1187 Peninsula Rd Ⓣ250/726-4202, Ⓦwww.littlebeachresort.com. On the prettier outskirts, with eighteen quiet self-contained one- and two-bedroom suites with kitchenettes and just a few steps from Little Beach with great views to the south. ❺

Pacific Rim Motel 1755 Peninsula Rd Ⓣ250/726-7728, Ⓦwww.pacificrimmotel.com. A relatively inexpensive and simple place, located between the harbour and centre near the corner of Bay St. ❹

Surf Junction Campground 2650 Tofino-Ucluelet Hwy Ⓣ250/726-7214, Ⓦwww.surfjunction.com. A kilometre from the park and 500m south of the Tofino-Ucluelet junction, this campsite has 49 sites spread across a wide, wooded area, with lots of room and privacy. $25–35; Jan–Oct.

Ucluelet Public Campground 260 Sea Plane Base Rd (first right off Peninsula Rd after the *Canadian Princess*) Ⓣ250/726-4355, Ⓦwww.ucluelettcampground.com. Tents and RVs are welcome at this site overlooking the harbour to the west of the centre. It has washroom and shower facilities, and all sites have firepits and picnic tables. $22–31/person; March–Sept.

Trails from town and tours

The nearest trails are at **Terrace Beach**, just east of the town off Peninsula Road before the lighthouse. A longer and more coherent trail, the **Wild Pacific Trail**, stretches 14km and links with Halfmoon Bay near Florencia Bay and Long Beach in the national park. The trail starts at the end of Coast Guard Road, passing the nearby Amphirite Point Lighthouse (great views of the ocean and perfect for storm-watching) and the He-Tin-Kis Park, where a boardwalk enables you to complete this first section as a loop.

Many companies here offer whale-watching, fishing and sightseeing **tours**. The longest-established outfit in the region is here, Subtidal Adventures, 1950 Peninsula Rd, at the corner of Norah Road (Ⓣ250/726-7336 or 1-877/444-1134, Ⓦwww.subtidaladventures.com). It runs all the usual boat trips in zodiacs (from $49) or a twelve-metre former coastguard rescue vessel, and offers a nature tour to the Broken Group Islands with a beach stop.

The Broken Group Islands

The only way for the ordinary traveller to approach these hundred or so islands, speckled across Barkley Sound between Ucluelet and Bamfield, is by sea plane, chartered boat or boat tours from Port Alberni or Ucluelet (see p.834 and below); boats dock at Sechart, where you can stay at the former whaling station (see below).

Immensely wild and beautiful, the islands have the reputation for tremendous wildlife (seals, sea lions and whales especially), the best **canoeing** in North America, and some of the continent's finest **diving**. You can hire canoes and gear – contact the *Lady Rose* office in Port Alberni – and then take them on board the *Lady Rose* to be dropped off en route (check current arrangements). You need to know what you're doing, as there's plenty of dangerous water and you should pick up the relevant marine chart (Canadian Hydrographic Service Chart: Broken Group 3670), available locally or from the CHS in Sidney (Ⓣ250/363-6358).

Divers can choose from among fifty shipwrecks claimed by the reefs, rough waters and heavy fogs that beset the aptly named islands. The sheer number of people now visiting the islands, and the state in which they leave some of the campsites, official and otherwise, means measures are being considered to introduce a quota system: contact the park information centre for latest details.

The *Sechart Whaling Station Lodge* (book by calling Ⓣ250/723-8313 or 1-800/663-7192; ❼) is a potentially magical base for exploring and the only place to **stay** if you're not wilderness camping on the archipelago. Access is via the MV *Lady Rose*, which docks nearby (see p.834 for detailed schedule). Seven rough **campsites** also serve the group, but water is hard to come by; pick up the park leaflet on camping and freshwater locations.

Nuu-chah-nulth whale hunts

All the peoples of the northwest coast are famed for their skilfully constructed canoes, but only the **Nuu-chah-nulth** – whose name translates roughly as "all along the mountains" – used these fragile cedar crafts to pursue whales, an activity that was accompanied by elaborate ritual. Before embarking on an expedition the whalers not only were to be trained in the art of capturing these mighty animals but also to be purified through a rigorous programme of fasting, sexual abstinence and bathing. Whalers also visited forest shrines made up of a whale image surrounded by human skulls or corpses and carved wooden representations of deceased whalers – the dead were thought to aid the novice in his task and to bring about the beaching of dead whales near the village.

When the whaler was on the chase, his wife would lie motionless in her bed; it was thought that the whale would become equally docile. His crew propelled the canoe in total silence until the moment of the harpooning, whereupon they frantically back-paddled to escape the animal's violent death throes as it attempted to dive, only to be thwarted by a long line of floats made from inflated sea-lion skins. After exhausting itself, the floating whale was finally killed and boated back to the village, where its meat would be eaten and its blubber processed for its highly prized oil.

Bamfield

BAMFIELD is a quaint spot, half-raised above the ocean on a wooden boardwalk. The village is best known as the northern starting point of the **West Coast Trail** (the trailhead is 5km away at Pachena Bay), but its population jumps to well over two thousand in the summer with the arrival of divers, canoeists, kayakers and fishermen. Plenty of services have sprung up in the more downbeat part of the village away from the boardwalk – tours, fishing charters, stores and galleries – but there's relatively limited accommodation.

Arrival and information

Bamfield is accessible by unpaved road from Port Alberni 102km to the north, by boat – the MV *Lady Rose* – or gravel road from Lake Cowichan 113km to the east. Shuttle **buses** run along the Port Alberni road route if you're without transport and don't want to take the boat: for details, see p.849.

Bamfield's **visitor centre** is in Centennial Park (Ⓣ250/728-3006, Ⓦwww.bamfieldchamber.com), but is open daily (9am–7/8pm) only in July and August.

Accommodation

The village has only limited and mainly expensive **accommodation**, including the modest *McKay Bay Lodge* (Ⓣ250/728-3323, Ⓦwww.bamfield-travel.com; ❺; May–Oct), which overlooks the harbour and is good for families and fishing enthusiasts. Another option is the excellent *Woods End Landing Cottages* (Ⓣ250/728-3383, Ⓦwww.woodsend.travel.bc.ca; ❻), 168 Wild Duck Rd, which has six secluded and high-quality self-contained log cottages sleeping up to four people on a two-acre waterfront site with great opportunities for outdoor activities, bird-watching, scuba diving and kayaking.

If you're **camping**, contact the Ohiaht First Nation Pachena Bay band, which occasionally offers a campsite (Ⓣ250/728-1287, Ⓔroseclif@pachena.net; call for reservations, which are essential, and for latest prices) at Pachena Beach.

The town and around

Despite the influx the village retains its charm, with the boardwalk accessing one side of Bamfield Inlet (the open sea, the other), so that the bay below the boardwalk is a constant hum of activity as boats ply across the water. Trails lead down from the boardwalk to a series of nice small beaches. The village is a good place to join in the activities, birdwatch, walk, beachcomb or sit in cafés. For a short stroll, wander to **Brady's Beach** or the Cape Beale Lighthouse and Keeha and Tapaltos beaches some way beyond. And if you just want to tackle the stage to the trailhead of the West Coast Trail and return to Bamfield in a day, you can walk the 10km (round-trip) to the **Pachena Lighthouse**, starting from the Ross Bible Camp on the Ohiaht First Nation campsite at Pachena Beach. After that, the route becomes the real thing.

The West Coast Trail

One of North America's classic walks, the **West Coast Trail** (WCT) starts 5km south of Bamfield and traverses exceptional coastal scenery for 77km to Port Renfrew. It's no stroll, and though very popular it still requires experience of longer walks, proper equipment and a fair degree of fitness. Still, many people do the first easy stage as a day-trip from Bamfield. Reckon on five to eight days for the full trip; carry all your own food, camp where you can, and be prepared for rain, treacherous stretches, thick soaking forest and almost utter isolation.

Mariners long ago dubbed this area of coastline the "graveyard of the Pacific", and when the SS *Valencia* went down with all hands here in 1906 the government was persuaded that constructing a trail would at least give stranded sailors a chance to walk to safety along the coast. The path followed a basic telegraph route that linked Victoria with outlying towns and lighthouses, and was kept open by linesmen and lighthouse keepers until the 1960s, when it fell into disrepair. Early backpackers reblazed the old trail, which now passes through the land of the Ohiaht First Nation around Bamfield, Ditidaht First Nation country in the trail's middle section and ends in Pacheenaht First Nation land near near Port Renfrew. Wardens from each of these tribes work in association with Parks Canada to oversee the trail's management and the care of traditional native villages and fishing areas.

Weather is a key factor in planning any trip; the trail is really only passable between June and September (July is the driest month), which is also the only period when it's patrolled by wardens and the only time locals are on hand to ferry you (for a fee) across some of the wider rivers en route.

Trail practicalities

Pre-planning is essential, as Parks Canada has a **quota system** and reservation-registration-orientation procedures to protect the environment. Numbers are limited to around eight thousand a year while the path is open (May to end Sept). Sixty people are allowed onto the trail each day: 26 starting at Port Renfrew centre (Gordon River trailhead is 5km north of the town; trailhead information centre ⓣ250/647-5434; daily in season 9am–6pm), 26 at Bamfield (Pachena Bay trailhead is 5km south of Bamfield; information centre ⓣ250/728-3234, daily in season 9am–6pm) and eight from Nitinat Village. These are the *only* allowed entrance and exit points from the trail, except in exceptional circumstances.

Of the 52 places available each day at **Pachena Bay** and **Gordon River**, a minimum of ten (five at each departure point) are available on a first-come, first-served basis. Unless you're very lucky this still doesn't mean you can just turn up and expect to start walking. You must first register in person at either the Port Renfrew or Bamfield centre. Here you'll be given a waiting-list number and told when to come back, which could be in anything between two and ten days.

The quota system doesn't apply in the shoulder season (May to mid-June & last two weeks of Sept), as Parks Canada found the quotas weren't being taken up. Yet it still makes sense to reserve the necessary **WCT Overnight Use Permit** – effectively your passport to the trail and its ferry crossings – in these periods.

Reservations

Reservations can be made from April of the year you wish to walk for June departures, May 1 for July departures, June 1 for August departures and July 1 for September walks. The phones start ringing on the first of the month, so move fast. To make bookings, call ⓣ250/387-1642 or 1-800/435-5622 (Mon–Fri 7am–9pm). Be ready to nominate the location from which you wish to start, the date of departure, two alternative start dates, credit card details and the number in your party. July and August are the most popular months.

Costs

It **costs** $24.50 to make a reservation (payment by Visa or MasterCard). This is nonrefundable, though you may change your date of departure if spaces are available on another day. Another $127.50 per person is payable as a user fee, paid in person at the beginning of the trail. Allow another $16 or so to pay for each of the two ferry crossings (at Gordon River and Nitinat narrows) along the route (paid at the WCT centres at the orientation session – see below: the WCT Overnight Permit is your receipt for these crossings). The total you'll pay is around $180. Standby hikers pay the same rates minus the booking fee. Take cash with you to pay for ferries and nominal fees for camping on native land.

Transport to and from the trail

Several small shuttle-bus companies have sprung up to allow people to **access** the trailheads, mostly from Victoria to Bamfield via Nanaimo (see p.829 or consult the Victoria visitor centre). For the northern trailhead at Bamfield, the most exhilarating and reliable access is via the MV *Lady Rose* or other boats from Port Alberni (see p.834). The West Coast Trail Express, 3954 Bow Rd, Victoria (May to early Oct; ⓣ250/477-8700, ⓦwww.trailbus.com) runs a daily shuttle bus in each direction between Victoria and Pachena Bay/Bamfield via Nanaimo; to Port Renfrew and back from Victoria; and between Bamfield and Port Renfrew. Pick-ups are possible from these points, but reservations are essential to secure a seat from any departure point.

Beginning the hike

You must register in person at the park centre at Bamfield or Port Renfrew between 9am and 12.30pm on the day you have booked to start your walk. (You may want to arrive the night before – if so, book accommodation in Bamfield if you're starting there.) If you miss this deadline your place is forfeited and will be given to someone on the **waiting list**.

You must also attend a compulsory ninety-minute **orientation** session at the trailhead information centre, where you will receive your permit and a briefing on conditions and safety issues. Gordon River sessions are at 9.30am, noon, 1.30pm and 3.30pm; Pachena Bay sessions are at 9.30am, 1.30pm and 3.30pm. Reservations aren't required.

▲ Hikers on the West Coast Trail, Vancouver Island

Further information

Information on the trail, path conditions and preplanning is available from the Parks Canada offices near the trailheads at Pachena Bay (daily May to early Oct 9am–5pm, ⓣ250/728-3234) and Gordon River (same hours; ⓣ250/647-5434), or from the visitor centres in Tofino, Ucluelet, Long Beach or Port Alberni. Updated details are also given at ⓦwww.pc.gc.ca/pacificrim. Literature and **route guides** on the trail are available directly, online or by mail order from most BC bookshops. Two of the best are *The West Coast Trail* by Tim Leaden (Douglas and McIntyre; $12.95) and the more irreverent *Blisters and Bliss: A Trekker's Guide to the West Coast Trail* by Foster, Aiteken and Dewey (B&B Publishing Victoria; $10.95). The recommended **trail map** is the 1:50,000 *West Coast Trail, Port Renfrew–Bamfield*, complete with useful hints for walking the trail, available locally or direct from the Ministry of the Environment, 553 Superior St, Victoria (ⓣ250/387-1441).

Northern Vancouver Island

It's a moot point where the **north of Vancouver Island** starts, but if you're travelling on Hwy 19 the landscape's sudden lurch into more unspoilt wilderness after Qualicum Beach makes as good a watershed as any. The scenery north of Qualicum Beach is uneventful but restful on the eye, and graced with ever-improving views of the mainland. Along Hwy 19 is the hamlet of Buckley Bay, which consists of little more than a ferry terminal to **Denman** and **Hornby islands** (16 sailings daily; 10min; foot passengers $7.90 return; a car $18.50 return).

Few of the towns along Hwy 19 amount to much, and you could bus or drive the length of Vancouver Island to Port Hardy and take the **Inside Passage** ferry up to Prince Rupert – the obvious and most tantalizing itinerary – without missing much. Alternatively, you could follow the main hwy only as far as **Courtenay**, and from there catch a ferry across to the mainland. Yet if you have the means, try to get into the wild, central interior, much of it contained within **Strathcona Provincial Park**.

Denman and Hornby islands

Denman and **Hornby Islands** are two outposts that have been described, with some justification, as the "undiscovered Gulf Islands". The population is made up of artists, craftspeople and a laidback (if wary) mishmash of alternative types. Ferries drop you on the island's west coast a few moments' walk from Denman Village: to get to Hornby you need to head 11km across the island on Denman Road to another terminal at Gravelly Bay, where a fifteen-minute crossing drops you at Hornby's Shingle Spit dock. Most of what happens on Hornby happens at **Tribune Bay** on the far side of the island, 10km away. There's no public transport on either island, so you'll need a car or bike to explore.

Highlights on Denman, the less isolated of the islands, are the beaches of the Sandy Island Provincial Marine Park, an island off the northwest tip (take Northwest Rd from the village), and the 800-metre loop trail of Boyle Point Park at the southernmost tip (just beyond the Gravelly Bay ferry terminal) to the Chrome Island Lighthouse. A left turn off Denman Road after about 4km, or a third of the way to the terminal, brings you to Fillongley Provincial Park, where there's a provincial campsite (see opposite), forest trails and a pretty stretch of coastline.

On sleepy Hornby, **Helliwell Bay Provincial Park** at the island's southern tip (take Helliwell Road from Tribune Bay) and its trails are the highlight; the best is a six-kilometre (1hr–1hr 30min) loop to Helliwell Bluffs, offering plenty of opportunities to see eagles, herons, spring wild flowers and lots of aquatic wildlife. Whaling Station Bay and Tribune Bay Provincial Park have very good beaches (there's a nudist beach at Little Tribune Bay just to the south of the latter), with a campsite (see below) at Tribune Bay.

Practicalities

Accommodation is in short supply on both islands, and it's virtually essential in summer to have prebooked rooms. On Denman the main options are: the *Sea Canary Guesthouse* (Ⓣ250/335-2949 or 1-877/336-2949; ❺), 3305 Kirk Rd, close to the ferry terminal (turn left on Northwest Rd then left again on Kirk) with three guestrooms; and the *Hawthorn House Bed and Breakfast* (Ⓣ250/335-0905; ❹), 3375 Kirk Rd, a restored 1904 heritage building also with three rooms. Try Ⓦwww.denmanisland.com for more B&B options. There's a small (ten-site), rural provincial park **campsite** at Fillongley Provincial Park, close to old-growth forest and pebbly beach, 4km across the island from the ferry on the east shore facing the Lambert Channel (summer $19, winter $10).

Hornby has marginally more **rooms** and **campsites**. *Sea Breeze Lodge* (Ⓣ250/335-2321, Ⓦwww.seabreezelodge.com; ❺), Big Tree 3–2, Fowler Rd, has sixteen waterfront cottages with sea views. You can camp at *Bradsdadsland Waterfront Campsite* (Ⓣ250/335-0757, Ⓦwww.bradsdadsland.com; tents $40–50; May–Oct), 2105 Shingle Spit Rd, 3.3km from the ferry terminal. *Ford's Cove Marina* (Ⓣ250/335-2169, Ⓦwww.fordscove.com; cottages generally let weekly, tents $28–32), at Ford's Cove, 12km from the ferry at Government Wharf, has six fully equipped cottages, grocery store and camp and RV sites. There's also the big *Tribune Bay Campsite* (Ⓣ250/335-2359, Ⓦwww.tribunebay.com; $38–42; June–Sept) on Shields Road, a wooded site close to a sandy beach and with hot showers, restaurant and bike rental.

Eating places on Denman are concentrated near the ferry, notably *The Thatch*, a tourist-oriented restaurant, pub and deli with great views. Across at Tribune Bay the Co-op (no street address) is the hub of island life, with virtually everything you'll need in the way of food and supplies (Ⓣ250/335-1121). For further **information** on Hornby, including accommodation, call Ⓣ250/335-0506 or visit Ⓦwww.hornbyisland.com.

Courtenay

Back along Hwy 19 beyond Buckley Bay is a short stretch of wild, pebbly beach, and then the Comox Valley, open rural country that's not as captivating as the brochures might lead you to expect. Of three settlements here – Comox, Cumberland and **COURTENAY** – only the last is of real interest for all but the most committed Vancouver Island devotee, and only then for its quaint (but tiny) downtown area and as a ferry link to Powell River on the mainland. The terminal is a good twenty minutes' drive from the town down back roads. Courtenay is connected to Nanaimo and Victoria by **bus** (4 daily), and is the terminus for **trains** from Victoria (1 daily).

There are plenty of **motels** along the strip on the southern approach, close to the **visitor centre** (daily 9am–5pm, longer hours in summer; Ⓣ250/334-3234 or 1-888/357-4471, Ⓦwww.comoxvalleychamber.com) at 2040 Cliffe Ave. The best **camping** is 20km north of Courtenay at Miracle Beach Provincial Park – a vast, but very popular, tract of sand ($24 in summer, $10 in winter).

The **Comox Valley** scores higher inland, on the eastern fringes of Strathcona Provincial Park (see p.854) and the **skiing** areas of Forbidden Plateau and Mount Washington, 25km northwest of Comox. There's plenty of **hiking and mountain biking** in summer, when the Forbidden Plateau lifts operate at weekends. A great day-hike on Mount Washington is the five-hour walk on well-marked trails from the ski area across Paradise Meadows to Moat Lake or Circlet Lake. For details of tougher walks (Battleship Lake, Lady Lake), ask at the visitor centre. Access to the trailheads is by minor road from Courtenay.

Campbell River

Of the hundred or so Canadian towns that claim to be "Salmon Capital of the World", **CAMPBELL RIVER**, 46km north of Courtenay, is probably the one that comes closest to justifying the boast. Fish and fishing dominate the place to a ludicrous degree, and you'll soon be heartily sick of pictures of grinning anglers holding impossibly huge chinook salmon. Massive shoals of these monsters are forced into the three-kilometre channel between the town and the mainland, making the job of catching them little more than a formality.

Arrival and information

Campbell River's well-stocked **visitor centre** is at 1235 Shopper's Row (May–June Mon–Sat 9am–5pm & Sun 10am–4pm; July–Aug Mon–Fri 9am–6pm, Sat & Sun 10am–6pm Sept–April Mon–Fri 9am–5pm & Sat 10am–4pm; ⓣ250/287-4636, ⓦwww.visitorcentre.ca). Four **buses** run daily to Victoria, but there's only one, occasionally two, a day north to Port Hardy and towns en route. Airlines big and small also **fly** here. The **bus terminal** is on the corner of Cedar and 13th near the Royal Bank (ⓣ250/287-7151).

The town and around: activities

The town grew to accommodate fishermen from the outset, centred around a hotel built in 1904 after word spread of the colossal fish that local Cape Mudge natives were able to pluck from the sea. Today about sixty percent of all visitors come to dangle a line in the water. Others come for the diving, while for the casual visitor the place serves as the main road access to the wilds of Strathcona Provincial Park or an overnight stop en route for the morning departures of the MV *Uchuck III* from Gold River (see p.855).

If you want to **fish**, hundreds of shops and guides are on hand to help out and hire equipment. It'll cost about $25 a day for the full kit, and about $60 and upwards for a morning's guidance. Huge numbers of people, however, fish for a few dollars from the 182-metre **Discovery Pier**, Canada's first saltwater fishing pier. If you merely want to know something about salmon before they end up on a plate, drop in on the **Quinsam Salmon Hatchery**, 5km west of town on the road to Gold River (daily 8am–4pm).

Practicalities

Campbell River's resort status makes finding **accommodation** easy. Try the carving-stuffed *Campbell River Lodge, Fishing & Adventure Resort* (ⓣ250/287-7446 or 1-800/663-7212, ⓦwww.campbellriverinns.com; ❹), a kilometre north of the town centre at 1760 North Island Hwy. For **camping** try *Parkside Campground* (ⓣ250/830-1428, ⓦwww.parksidecampingrv.com; $20–28; April–Oct), 6301 Gold River Hwy, 5km west of town.

Cheap **places to eat** abound, mainly of the fast-food variety, and in the pricier restaurants there's no prize for spotting the main culinary emphasis.

Quadra Island

Quadra Island and its fine beaches and museum are fifteen minutes away from Campbell River and make a nice respite from the fish – though the famous fishing lodge here has played host over the years to the likes of John Wayne, Kevin Costner and Julie Andrews. Ferries run roughly hourly from the well-signed terminal out of town ($7.90 return for foot passengers, $18.50 return for a car). The main excuse for the crossing is the **Kwagiulth Museum and Cultural Centre**, in Cape Mudge Village south of the terminal near the island's southern tip (take Cape Mudge Rd). The island's other, and main community, Heriot Bay, is on the east coast. The centre is home to one of the country's most noted collections of aboriginal regalia (call for current opening; ⓣ250/285-3733). As elsewhere in Canada, the masks, costumes and ritual objects were confiscated by the government in 1922 in an attempt to stamp out one of the natives' most potent ceremonies, and only came back in the 1980s on condition they would be locked up in a museum. The museum has around three hundred articles; ask for directions to the petroglyphs in the small park across the road.

While on the island you could also laze on its beaches, walk its **trails** – Mortle Lake (5km loop) and Newton Lake from Granite Bay (8km round-trip) – or climb Chinese Mountain (3km round-trip) in its rugged northern reaches for some cracking views. There's swimming in a warm, sheltered bay off a rocky beach at **Rebecca Spit Provincial Park**, a 1.5-kilometre spit near Drew Harbour 8km east of the ferry terminal, but the water's warmer still at the more distant **Village Bay Park**.

For **accommodation**, try the *Heriot Bay Inn & Marina* on Heriot Bay Road (ⓣ250/285-3322, ⓦwww.heriotbayinn.com; ⑤, camping $22–28), which has cottages, thirteen camping and RV sites, or the superb *Tsa-Kwa-Luten Lodge*, 1 Lighthouse Rd (ⓣ250/285-2042 or 1-800/665-7745, ⓦwww.capemudgeresort.com; ⑥; campsites at $30–35), a waterfront lodge by the Cape Mudge Lighthouse. Based on a long house, and with a predominantly aboriginal decorative scheme and design, local aboriginal people built it amid forest on the high bluffs overlooking Discovery Passage. There is a restaurant, cottage and lodge units and many facilities, including sauna, jacuzzi, laundry and access to numerous tours and outdoor activities. The island's only official **campsite** is at the *Heriot Bay Inn & Marina*.

Cortes Island

If you've taken the trouble to see Quadra Island, then you should push on to the still quieter **Cortes Island** (ⓦwww.cortesisland.com), 45 minutes' from Quadra on a second ferry (5 daily; foot passenger $9.20 return, car $21.50), an island with a deeply indented coastline at the neck of Desolation Sound, and among North America's finest sailing and kayaking areas. Life here is very relaxed and the main community is at **Manson's Landing**, 15km from the ferry terminal at Whaletown.

The island is also known for its superlative clams and oysters, exported worldwide, and for one of Canada's leading holistic centres, the Hollyhock Retreat Centre on Highland Road (ⓣ250/935-6576 or 1-800/933-6339, ⓦwww.hollyhock.ca), where you can take all manner of body- and soul-refreshing courses and stay in anything from a tent, dorm or private cottage.

Places to make for around the island include the small **Smelt Bay Provincial Park**, 25km south of the ferry, which has a provincial campsite (summer $15, winter $10) and opportunities to swim, fish, canoe and walk. Nearly adjacent is **Manson's Landing Provincial Park**, with good beaches, and **Hague Lake Provincial Park**, signed from Manson's Landing, with several looped trails such as Sutil Point accessible from different points on the road. If you're in a canoe or boat then you can also make for a couple of marine parks (Von Donop and Mansons Landing) and numerous delightful small bays, lagoons and beaches.

Hiking in Strathcona Provincial Park

Hiking is superb in Strathcona, with a jaw-dropping scenic combination of jagged mountains – including Golden Hinde (2220m) – lakes, rivers, waterfalls and all the trees you could possibly want. There are several shorter, **marked** trails accessible from the hwy (see above). All the longer trails can be tramped in a day, though the most popular, the **Elk River Trail** (10km), which starts from Drum Lake on Hwy 28, lends itself to an overnight stop; popular with backpackers because of its gentle grade, the path ends up at Landslide Lake, an idyllic camping spot. The other highly regarded trail is the **Flower Ridge** walk, a steep 14-kilometre round-trip (extendable by 10km) that starts at the southern end of Buttle Lake and involves a very stiff 1250-metre elevation gain. The same lung-busting ascent is called for on the **Crest Mountain Trail** (10km round-trip), a trail into high mountain country accessed from Hwy 28 at the park's western edge.

In the Forbidden Plateau area, named after a native legend that claimed evil spirits lay in wait to devour women and children who entered its precincts, the most popular trip is the **Forbidden Plateau Skyride** to the summit of Wood Mountain where there's a two-kilometre trail to a viewpoint over Boston Canyon. Backcountry camping is allowed throughout the park, and the backpacking is great once you've hauled up onto the summit ridges above the tree-line. For serious exploration, buy the relevant topographic maps (1:50,000 -92F/11 *Forbidden Plateau* and -92F/12 *Buttle Lake* at MAPS BC, Ministry of Environment and Parks, Parliament Buildings, Victoria.

Strathcona Provincial Park

Vancouver Island's largest protected area, and the oldest park in BC, **Strathcona Provincial Park** (established in 1911) is one of the few places on the island where the scenery approaches the grandeur of the mainland mountains. The island's highest point, Golden Hinde (2220m) is here, and it's also a place where there's a good chance of seeing rare indigenous wildlife (the Roosevelt elk, marmot and black-tailed deer are the most notable examples). Only two areas have any sort of facilities for the visitor – **Forbidden Plateau** on the park's eastern side, approached from Courtenay, and the more popular **Buttle Lake** region, accessible from Campbell River via Hwy 28. The rest of the park is unsullied wilderness, but fully open to backpackers and hardier walkers. Pick up the blue *BC Parks* pamphlet (available from the visitor centre at Campbell River): it has a good general map and gives lots of information.

You'll see numerous pictures of **Della Falls** around Campbell River which, at 440m, are Canada's highest, though unfortunately it'll take a two-day trek and a canoe passage if you're going to see them.

The approach to the park along Hwy 28 is worth taking for the scenery alone; numerous short trails and nature walks are signposted from rest stops, most no more than twenty-minutes' stroll from the car. **Elk Falls Provincial Park**, noted for its gorge and waterfall, is the first stop, ten minutes out of Campbell River. On the access road and lakeshore proper, good **shorter trails** include the 500-metre stroll to impressive Lupin Falls; the Karst Creek Trail (2km loop), which runs through a strange limestone landscape of sinkholes and vanishing streams; Bedwell Lake at the lake's southern end, a steep (600-metre ascent) ten-kilometre round-trip trail to the eponymous lake and high meadows (allow 2hr each way); and Upper Myra Falls (3km each way), which climbs from near the end of the road to a viewpoint over the Myra waterfall. Fifteen **information** shelters around the lake provide some trail and wildlife information.

Park accommodation

Elk Falls Provincial Park has a large **campsite** (summer $14, winter $9; backcountry camping $5), while Buttle Lake has two provincial **campsites** with basic facilities – one alongside the park centre at Buttle Lake, the other at Ralph River (both summer $15, winter $10) on the extreme southern end of Buttle Lake, accessed by the road along the lake's eastern shore. Both have good **swimming** areas nearby.

The park's only commercial accommodation is provided by the *Strathcona Park Lodge* (ⓣ250/286-3122, ⓦwww.strathcona.bc.ca; ❻), just outside the Buttle Lake entrance, a mixture of hotel and outdoor-pursuits centre, where you can **rent canoes, bikes** and other outdoor equipment and sign up for organized tours and activities.

Boats from Gold River

Like the MV *Lady Rose* out of Port Alberni, the **MV Uchuck III** boat trips started as a sideline. The trips are now far more of a commercial enterprise, though it's none the worse for that – just book ahead to make sure of a place. For information and **reservations**, contact Nootka Sound Service Ltd (ⓣ1-877/824-8253, ⓦwww.mvuchuck.com).

There are **four basic routes**, all of them offering wonderful windows onto the wilderness and wildlife (whales, bears, bald eagles and more) of the region's inlets, islands and forested mountains. The dock is at the end of Hwy 28, about 15km southwest of Gold River. There are scheduled halts, but also usually unscheduled calls at logging camps and the like.

The **Tahsis Inlet Day Trip** runs late September to early May, leaving Gold River at 9am and returning at 6pm ($60). The **Friendly Cove Day Trip** ($70 or $35 one-way to Friendly Cove) leaves Gold River every Wednesday and Saturday at 10am mid-June to mid-September. It returns at 4pm on Wednesday and 5.30pm on Saturday, when there is a three-hour stop at Friendly Cove; a $12 landing fee, proceeds from which go to the Mowachaht Band for the redevelopment of the aboriginal site, is included in the ticket price. During the ninety-minute or three-hour halt aboriginal guides offer guided tours around their ancestral home.

The previous stop, at Friendly Cove, is equally historic, for it was here Captain Cook made his first-known landing on the west coast in 1778. Whites named the area and people here "Nootka", though locals today say *nootka* was merely a word of warning to Cook and his crew, meaning "circle around" to avoid hitting offshore rocks. If you're equipped with provisions and wish to stay over, there are **cabins** and a **campsite** here, but call first to confirm arrangements (ⓣ250/283-2054).

The **Kyuquot Adventure** ($335 single, $465 double), is a two-day overnight cruise, departing every Thursday year-round (April–Oct 7am; Nov–March 6am). It takes you much farther north up the coast, returning to Gold River at 4 or 5pm on Friday afternoon: accommodation is included, as is breakfast – though you make it yourself from food supplied – and you can buy Thursday's evening meal on board or onshore at Kyuquot.

The **Esperanza Adventure** (single $240, double $375), is also a two-day trip, departing every Monday at 9am (April–Oct) and returning at 5pm on Tuesday. It combines a stop in Tahsis and Friendly Cove and an overnight stay (with breakfast) in the coastal community of Zeballos. A longer three-day round-trip to Victoria is also available.

A 25 percent deposit is required for these trips, refundable in full up until two weeks before departure. People on all trips should bring warm and waterproof clothing. There's a coffee shop on board for drinks and hot snacks. **Kayakers** should note that they can be deposited by lift into the sea at most points en route by prior arrangement.

Gold River and Tahsis

There's not a lot happening at **GOLD RIVER**, a tiny logging community 89km west of Campbell River – founded in 1965 in the middle of nowhere to service a big pulp mill 12km away at Muchalat Inlet (it closed in 1998). The place only has one hotel and a couple of shops – but the ride over on Hwy 28 is superb, and there's the chance to explore the sublime coastline by boat, the main reason for the settlement's increasing number of visitors. Year-round, the **MV Uchuck III**, a converted World War II US minesweeper, takes mail, cargo and passengers to logging camps and settlements up and down the surrounding coast on a variety of routes (see p.855)

Boat aside, one of the area's two minor attractions is **Quatsino Cave**, the deepest vertical cave in North America, parts of which are open to the public – for details ask at the visitor centre; the other is the **Big Drop**, a stretch of Gold River white water known to kayakers worldwide. The **visitor centre** is at the corner of Hwy 28 and Scout Lake Road (early June to late June Fri–Sun 10am–6pm; late June to early Sept daily 10am–6pm; ⓣ250/283-2418 or 283-2202, ⓦwww.goldriver.ca). **Accommodation** is in short supply: the only large place is the *Ridgeview Motor Inn* (ⓣ250/283-2277 or 1-800/989-3393, ⓦwww.ridgeview-inn.com; ❹), located in a panoramic spot above the village at 395 Donner Court.

There are two beautiful roads north from Gold River, both rough, but worth the jolts for the scenery. One provides an alternative approach to **TAHSIS**, another logging community 70km northwest of Gold River, which has one basic **motel** with a restaurant and pub; advance summer reservations are needed at the twelve-room *Tahsis Motel* (ⓣ250/934-6318, ⓦwww.home.cablerocket.com/~tahsismotel; ❸), at 187 Head Bay Rd; or *Fern's Place B&B* (ⓣ250/934-7851, ⓦwww.home.cablerocket.com/~ferns_place; ❸), at 379 North Maquinna.

North to Port McNeill and beyond

The main hwy north of Campbell River cuts inland and climbs through increasingly rugged and deserted country, particularly after Sayward, the one main community en route. Near Sayward is the marvellously oddball **Valley of a Thousand Faces**: 1400 famous faces painted onto cedar logs, the work of a Dutch artist, and more interesting than it sounds (May–Aug daily 10am–4pm; donation). With a car, you could strike off south from here to **Schoen Lake Provincial Park**, located 12km off Hwy 19 on a rough road south of Woss village and featuring a couple of forest trails and a small, ten-pitch, well-kept campsite ($10). Sayward has one **motel**, the *Fisherboy Park*, 400m off Hwy 19 at 1546 Sayward Rd (ⓣ250/282-3204, ⓦwww.fisherboypark.com; ❸), which also has 36 tent and RV sites ($14-24). **PORT McNEILL**, 180km north of Campbell River and the first real town along Hwy 19, is little more than a motel and logging centre and not somewhere to spend longer than necessary. If you get stuck here, the visitor centre's at 1594 Beach Drive (July–Aug 9am–5pm; rest of year hours variable; ⓣ250/956-3131, ⓦwww.portmcneill.net).

Telegraph Cove

By contrast, tiny **TELEGRAPH COVE**, 8km south of Port McNeill and reached by a rough side road, is a likeable place, though not quite the best of BC's so-called "boardwalk villages", as its growing popularity (and the fact that it is now pretty much owned by a single company) has given it a slightly artificial and commercialized air not evident in somewhere like Bamfield (see p.847). The whole community is raised on wooden stilts over the water, a sight that's made it rather too popular with tourists for its own good.

This is not to take away from its role as one of the island's premier **whale-watching** spots, the main attraction here being the pods of killer whales that calve locally. Some nineteen of these families live or visit Robson Bight, 20km down the Johnstone Strait, which was established as an ecological reserve in 1982 (the whales like the gravel beaches, where they come to rub). This is the world's most accessible and predictable spot to see the creatures – around a ninety percent chance in season.

The best outfit for a trip to see them is Stubbs Island Charters (Ⓣ250/928-3185, 928-3117 or 1-800/665-3066, Ⓦwww.stubbs-island.com), located at the dock at the end of the boardwalk through the old village. The first whale-watching company in BC, it runs 3hr 30min trips (2 daily at 9am & 1pm May to mid-July & late Aug to early Oct; 3 daily at 9am, 1pm & 5.30pm mid-July to late Aug; $89), but they're very popular, so call well in advance to be sure of a place.

Practicalities

In summer you can buy **food** at a café, boardwalk pub and resort (see below), but otherwise the only provision for visitors is an incongruous modern building with shop, ice-cream counter and coffee bar.

The only **accommodation** is the large wooded *Telegraph Cove Resorts* (Ⓣ250/928-3131 or 1-800/200-4665, Ⓦwww.telegraphcoveresort.com; ❻, camping $25–30; May–Oct), a short walk from the village; reservations are essential in summer. It has 24 rooms and 125 RV/tent sites with showers, laundry, restaurant, boat rentals and access to guides, charters and whale-watching tours. The *Hidden Cove Lodge* (Ⓣ250/956-3916, Ⓦwww.hiddencovelodge.com; ❼) at Lewis Point, a secluded cove on Johnstone Strait 7km from Telegraph Cove, has eight superb lodge units, but they go very quickly.

Alert Bay

The breezy fishing village of **ALERT BAY**, on Cormorant Island, is reached by numerous daily ferries from Port McNeill just 8km away (foot passenger $8.45 return, car $19.80). The fifty-minute crossing in the migrating season provides a good chance of seeing whales en route. Despite the predominance of the non-indigenous industries (mainly fish processing), half the population of the island are aboriginal 'Namgis, and a day visit here offers the opportunity to get to grips with something of their history and to meet those who are keeping traditions alive. The **visitor centre** (late June to Aug daily 9am–6pm; rest of year Mon–Fri 9am–5pm; Ⓣ250/974-5024, Ⓦwww.alertbay.ca) is at 116 Fir St to your right as you come off the ferry. Also off to the right from the terminal are the totems of a 'Namgis Burial Ground; you're asked to view from a respectful distance.

Bear left from the terminal out of the main part of the village to reach the excellent **U'Mista Cultural Centre** (mid-May to Sept daily 9am–5pm, rest of the year Tues–Sat 9am–5pm; $8; Ⓣ250/974-5403, Ⓦwww.umista.ca) at 1 Front St, which houses a collection of potlatch items and artefacts. It also shows a couple of award-winning films; you might also come across local kids being taught native languages, songs and dances. More local artefacts are on show in the library and small museum, open most summer afternoons, at 199 Fir St. For years the village also claimed the world's tallest fully carved **totem pole** (other contenders, say knowing villagers, are all pole and no carving), though much to local chagrin Victoria raised a pole in 1994 that the *Guinness Book of Records* has recognized as 2.1m taller. Also worth a look is the wildlife and swamp habitat at the Alert Bay Ecological Park behind the bay, accessible via several trails and boardwalks.

Sointula

SOINTULA village is a wonderful aberration. It's located on Malcolm Island, accessible by ferry en route from Port McNeill to Alert Bay (25min; foot passenger $9.20 return, car $21.50). The fishing village would be a good place to wander at any time, thanks to its briney maritime appeal, but what gives added lustre is the fact that it contains a tiny fossil Finnish settlement. An early cult community, it was founded with Finnish pioneers as a model cooperative settlement in 1901 by Matti Kurrika, a curious mixture of guru, dramatist and philosopher. In 1905 the experiment collapsed, but one hundred Finns from the original settlement stayed on. Their descendants survive to this day, and you'll still hear Finnish being spoken on the streets. You can wander local beaches, explore the island interior by logging road, or spend a few minutes in the **Sointula Finnish Museum**, which is located on 1st Street just to the left after disembarking the ferry; you'll probably need to call someone (Ⓣ250/973-6353 or 973-6764) to come and open up and show you around.

There is one listed **B&B**: the two-room *Sea 4 Miles*, 2km from the ferry at 145 Kaleva Rd (Ⓣ250/973-6486, Ⓦwww.sointulacottages.com; ❺).

Port Hardy

Dominated by copper mining, a large fishing fleet and the usual logging concerns, **PORT HARDY**, a total of 485km from Victoria and 230km from Campbell River, is best known among travellers as the departure point for ships plying one of the more spectacular stretches of the famous **Inside Passage** to Prince Rupert (and on to Alaska) and the **Discovery Coast Passage**.

If you have time to kill waiting for boats, you could visit the modest Port Hardy Museum (year-round Tues–Sat times vary; Ⓣ250/949-8143, Ⓦwww.northislandmuseums.org; donation) at 7110 Market St, or the **Quatse Salmon Stewardship Centre** (May to late Sept Wed–Sun 8.30am–4.30pm; Ⓣ250/902-0336, Ⓦwww.nvisea.org) at 8400 Byng Rd, just off Hwy 19 almost opposite the *Pioneer Inn*.

Arrival and information

If possible, time your arrival in Port Hardy to coincide with one of the Inside Passage **sailings** (see p.860). **Bus** services aren't really scheduled to do this for you, with a bus generally timetabled to meet each *incoming* sailing from Prince Rupert. A bus (Ⓣ250/949-7532 in Port Hardy, Ⓣ250/385-4411 or 388-5248 in Victoria) leaves Victoria daily, sometimes with a change in Nanaimo, arriving at the Port Hardy ferry terminal in the evening to connect with the ferry next morning; in summer an extra service departs from Victoria on the morning before ferry sailings. You can **fly** from Vancouver International Airport to Port Hardy (the airport is 12km south of the town) with Pacific Coastal Airlines (Ⓣ250/273-8666, Ⓦwww.pacific-coastal.com) from around $170 one-way.

The Port Hardy **ferry terminal** is visible from town but is actually 10km away at Bear Cove, where buses stop before terminating opposite the **visitor centre**, at 7250 Market St (mid-May to Aug Mon–Fri 8.30am–6pm, Sat & Sun 9am–5pm; Sept to mid-May Mon–Fri 9am–5pm; Ⓣ250/949-7622, Ⓦwww.ph-chamber.bc.ca). The centre also has details on the immense wilderness of **Cape Scott Provincial Park**, whose interior is accessible only by foot and which is supposed to have some of the most consistently bad weather in the world (and some of the most voracious biting insects). As a short taster you could follow the forty-minute hike from the small campsite and trailhead at San Josef River to some sandy beaches. Increasingly popular, but demanding (allow eight hours plus), is the historic **Cape Scott Trail**, part of a complex web of trails early Danish pioneers hacked from the forest. Around 28km has been reclaimed, opening a trail to the cape itself.

If you stay overnight, leave plenty of time to reach the ferry terminal – sailings in summer are usually around 7.30am. North Island Transportation provides a shuttle service between the ferry and the town's airport, main hotels and the **bus station** at 7210 Market St just south of Hastings Street and the visitor centre; it departs ninety minutes before each sailing (Ⓣ250/949-6300 for information or to arrange a pick-up from hotel or campsite); otherwise call a **taxi** (Ⓣ250/949-8000).

Accommodation

There's a huge amount of pressure on hotel **accommodation** in summer, so it's vital to call ahead if you're not camping or haven't worked your arrival to coincide with one of the ferry sailings. The ferry from Prince Rupert docks around 10.30pm, so you don't want to be hunting out rooms late at night with dozens of others.

There are cheap **rooms** out of town at the *Airport Inn* (Ⓣ250/949-9424 or 1-888-218-2224, Ⓦwww.airportinn-porthardy.com; ❹), 4030 Byng Rd. Five minutes south of town at 4965 Byng Rd, in a park-like setting near the river, is the *Pioneer Inn* (Ⓣ250/949-7271 or 1-800/663-8744, Ⓔpioneer@island.net; ❹), which has 36 rooms and RV sites ($23).

Other hotels include the *Glen Lyon Inn* (Ⓣ250/949-7115, Ⓦwww.glenlyoninn.com; ❹) by the marina at 6435 Hardy Bay Rd, and the large forty-room *Quarterdeck Inn* (Ⓣ250/902-0455 or 1-877/902-0459, Ⓦwww.quarterdeckresort.net; ❻), 6555 Hardy Bay Rd, the town's most comfortable hotel; contact the visitor centre for details on local B&B options.

For **camping**, try the *Quatse River Campground* (Ⓣ250/949-2395, Ⓦwww.quatsecampground.com; $18–25) at 8400 Byng Rd, with 62 spruce-shaded sites almost opposite the *Pioneer Inn*, 5km from the ferry dock. Or go for the larger eighty-site *Sunny Sanctuary Campground* (Ⓣ250/949-8111, Ⓦwww.island.net/~sunnycam; $15–35), 1km north of Ferry Junction and Hwy 19 by the river and ocean at 8080 Goodspeed Rd.

Eating and drinking

You should be able to **eat** well for under $10 in Port Hardy; Granville and Market streets have the main restaurant concentrations. The pub-restaurants of the *Glen Lyon* and *Quarterdeck* (see above), are also both popular; or *Snuggles*, next to the *Pioneer Inn*, which aims at a cosy English pub atmosphere, with live music and steaks, salads and salmon grilled over an open fire. The cafeteria-coffee shop in the *Pioneer* does filling breakfasts and other snacks. For something with more class, *Malone's Oceanside Bistro* (Ⓣ250/949-3050; closed Sun), at 9300 Trustee Rd, is a popular family place with fish, seafood and Greek specialities. Despite the dubious-looking decor, the *Sportsman's*, opposite the visitor centre at the corner of Market and Hastings streets (Ⓣ250/949-7811) offers good steaks and Italian specials.

The Inside and Discovery Coast passages

Taking either the Inside Passage or the Discovery Coast Passage with BC Ferries certainly has to be one of the top experiences of any visit to BC. Both journeys are a great – and cheap – way of getting what people on the big cruise ships get: stunning views of some of the grandest coastal scenery on the continent, including mountains, islands, waterfalls, glaciers, sea lions, whales and eagles.

The Inside Passage

One of Canada's great trips, between Port Hardy and Prince Rupert on the BC mainland, this makes a good leg in any number of convenient itineraries around BC, especially by linking up with the Greyhound bus network or the VIA Rail terminal at Prince Rupert. Some travellers will have come from Washington State, others will want to press on from Prince Rupert to Skagway by boat and then head north into Alaska and the Yukon (see p.875 for Alaska Marine ferries details). Many simply treat it as a cruise, sailing north one day and south the next.

The *Queen of the North* carries 750 passengers, 160 cars and runs every two days, departing at 7.30am on **even-numbered days** in August, **odd-numbered days** in June, July, September and the first half of October. The journey takes around fifteen hours, arriving in Prince Rupert about 10.30pm, sometimes with a stop at Bella Bella. From about October 15–May 25 sailings are less frequent in both directions and are usually predominantly at night (leaving Port Hardy in the late afternoon), which defeats the sightseeing object of the trip.

The cost in the peak mid-June to mid-September season is $150 one-way for foot passengers, $350 for cars; **reservations** are essential throughout the peak season if you're taking a car or want a cabin (ⓣ250/386-3431 or 1-888/223-3779 toll-free in BC , ⓦwww.bcferries.com). Full payment is required up front.

Cabins range from around $65 for two berths with basin, shower and toilet, from October–April, $80 for the same in high season. If you're making the return trip only, you can rent **cabins overnight**, saving the hassle of finding accommodation in Port Hardy. If you do, you're obliged to take the cabin for the following day's return trip. Bigger cabins with two berths, toilets and showers cost $85 in low season, $115 in high season. Luxury cabins are $210 year-round. If you're making a return trip and want to leave your car behind, there are supervised lock-ups in Port Hardy; you can leave vehicles at the ferry terminal, but this isn't recommended. It's vital to book accommodation at your final destination before starting your trip; Port Hardy and Prince Rupert hotels are very busy on days when the boat arrives.

The Discovery Coast Passage

The **Discovery Coast Passage** (summer only) offers many of the scenic rewards of the Inside Passage, but over a shorter and more circuitous route between Port Hardy and **Bella Coola**, where you can pick up the tortuous Hwy 20 through the Coast Mountains to Williams Lake (see p.801) – it goes nowhere else. En route, the boat stops at Bella Bella, Shearwater, Klemtu and Ocean Falls. You can disembark at all of these places, but currently the only places to stay overnight are campsites and a small hotel and B&B at Shearwater (Denny Island). Bella Coola is better equipped, and will probably become more so as the route becomes more popular.

There are **departures** roughly every couple of days between early June and the end of September, currently leaving Port Hardy at 10.15am on Tuesday and Thursday and at 9.30pm on Saturday, and returning from Bella Coola on Monday, Wednesday and Friday. There's a slight catch; while the morning departures offer great scenery, some arrive at Bella Coola at 6.30am, meaning the best bit of the trip – along the inlet to Bella Coola – is in the middle of the night. The Thursday departures are quicker (stopping at Ocean Falls) and make Bella Coola the same day, arriving at 11pm, so the problem is lessened. Alternatively take the 9.30pm departures and wake at 7.30am with a further daylight trip towards Bella Coola, arriving at 6.30am the next morning; read the timetables carefully.

Making the trip southbound from Bella Coola gets round the problem, though there are similar staggered departure and arrival times (services currently leave Monday, Wednesday and Friday at 8am, arriving Port Hardy 9pm on the Monday departure, 7.45am on Wednesday sailing and 9am on the Friday boat), with overnight and same-day journeys and a variety of stopping points depending on the day you travel. There are **no cabins**: you sleep in reclining seats.

Reservations can be made through BC Ferries (same details as Inside Passage). **Prices** for foot passengers are $150 one-way to Bella Coola, $90 to all other destinations; cars cost $305, $180 to all other destinations and $115 for the single-leg options. If you want to camp, stop over or hop on and off, the fares between any two of Bella Bella, Ocean Falls and Klemtu are $32; the price from any of these ports to Bella Coola is $58. Taking a **canoe** or **kayak** costs $10 from Port Hardy to Bella Coola; bicycles cost $5.

Travel details

Trains

Vancouver to: Edmonton via Kamloops (3 weekly; 25hr); Jasper (June–Sept daily except Wed; Oct–May 3 weekly; 19hr).
Victoria to: Courtenay via Nanaimo (1 round-trip daily; 4hr 35min).

Buses

Nanaimo to: Port Alberni (4 daily; 1hr 20min); Port Hardy (1 daily; 6hr 50min); Tofino (1–2 daily; 4hr 30min); Ucluelet (1–2 daily; 3hr 10min); Victoria (7 daily; 2hr 20min).
Port Alberni to: Nanaimo (4 daily; 1hr 20min); Tofino via Ucluelet (1–2 daily; 3hr).
Vancouver to: Banff (4 daily; 14hr 5min); Bellingham (8–10 daily; 1hr 45min); Cache Creek (2 daily; 5hr 40min); Calgary (4 daily; 16hr); Calgary via Kamloops (6 daily; 13hr); Calgary via Penticton, Nelson and Cranbrook (2 daily; 24hr); Calgary via Princeton and Kelowna (2 daily; 18hr); Chilliwack, for Harrison Hot Springs (10 daily; 1hr 45min); Edmonton via Jasper (3 daily; 16hr 30min); Kamloops (8 daily; 5hr); Kelowna (6 daily; 5hr 30min); Nanaimo (8 daily; 5hr); Pemberton (3 daily; 3hr 10min); Penticton (3 daily; 5hr 20min); Powell River (2 daily; 5hr 10min); Prince George via Cache Creek and Williams Lake (2 daily; 13hr); Salmon Arm (6 daily; 7hr 5min); Seattle, US (8–10 daily; 3hr 15min); Sea-Tac Airport, US (8–10 daily; 4hr 10min); Squamish (6 daily; 1hr 15min); Vernon (6 daily; 6hr); Victoria (8 daily; 5hr); Whistler (6 daily; 2hr 30min).
Victoria to: Bamfield (1–3 daily; 6–8hr); Campbell River (5 daily; 5hr); Nanaimo (7 daily; 2hr 20min); Port Hardy (1 daily; 9hr 45min); Port Renfrew (2 daily; 2hr 30min); Vancouver (8–10 daily; 4hr); Vancouver Airport direct (3 daily; 3hr 30min).

Ferries

Bella Coola to: Port Hardy (2–3 weekly; 21hr).
Chemainus to: Thetis Island and Kuper Island (minimum of 10 round-trips daily; 35min).
Courtenay to: Powell River (4 daily; 1hr 15min).
Nanaimo to: Gabriola Island (17 daily; 20min); Vancouver/Horseshoe Bay Terminal (8 daily; 1hr 35min); Vancouver/Tsawwassen Terminal (8 daily; 2hr).
Northern Gulf Islands Denman Island to Hornby Island (minimum 12 round-trips daily; 10min); Quadra Island to Cortes Island (Mon–Sat 6 daily, Sun 5 daily; 45min); Vancouver Island (Buckley Bay) to Denman Island (18 round-trips daily; 10min); Vancouver Island (Campbell River) to Quadra Island (17 round-trips daily; 10min).
Port Hardy to: Bella Coola (1 every two days; 15hr 30min–22hr); Prince Rupert (1 every two days; 15hr).
Powell River to: Courtenay-Comox (4 round-trips daily; 1hr 15min); Texada Island (10 round-trips daily; 35min).
Southern Gulf Islands Vancouver Island (Crofton) to Salt Spring Island/Vesuvius Bay (14 round-trips daily; 20min); Vancouver Island (Swartz Bay) to Salt Spring Island/Fulford Harbour (10 round-trips daily; 35min).
Sunshine Coast to: Horseshoe Bay–Snug Cove (15 round-trips daily; 20 min); Horseshoe Bay–Langdale (8 round-trips daily; 40min); Jervis

Inlet/Earls Cove–Saltery Bay (8–9 round-trips daily; 50min).
Vancouver to: Nanaimo from Horseshoe Bay Terminal (8 daily; 1hr 35min); from Tsawwassen Terminal (8 daily; 2hr); Victoria (Swartz Bay Terminal) from Tsawwassen (hourly summer 7am–9pm; rest of the year minimum 8 daily 7am–9pm; 1hr 35min).
Victoria to: Anacortes and San Juan Islands, US, from Victoria's Inner Harbour (1–2 daily; 2hr 30min); Seattle, US, from Inner Harbour (1–2 daily; 2hr 30min); Vancouver (Tsawwassen) from Swartz Bay (hourly summer 7am–10pm; rest of the year minimum 8 daily; 1hr 35min).

Flights

Vancouver to: Calgary (20 daily; 1hr 15min); Castlegar (1–2 daily; 1hr 20min); Cranbrook (1–2 daily; 2hr 30min); Edmonton (14 daily; 1hr 30min); Kamloops (4–5 daily; 1hr); Kelowna (7–9 daily; 1hr); Montréal (8 daily; 5hr 35min); Ottawa (10 daily; 4hr 40min); Penticton (3–5 daily; 50min); Prince George (5–8 daily; 1hr 10min); Toronto (15 daily; 4hr 55min); Victoria (14 daily; 25min); Winnipeg (8 daily; 2hr 40min).
Victoria to: Calgary (4 daily; 1hr 40min); Vancouver (14 daily; 25min).

11 The North

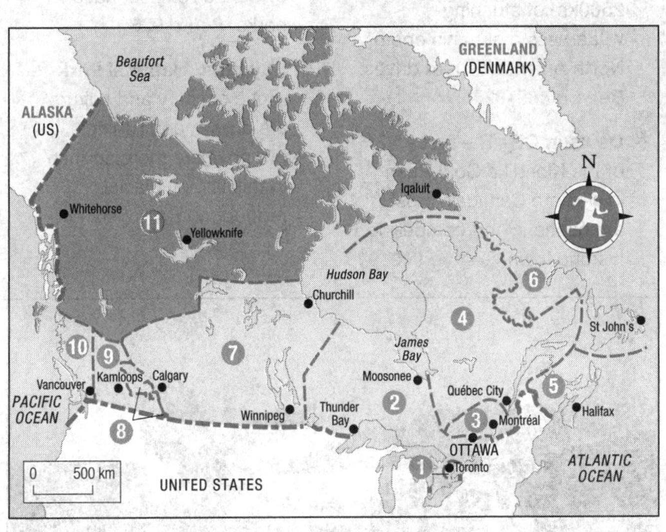
Beaufort Sea
GREENLAND (DENMARK)
ALASKA (US)
Iqaluit
Whitehorse
11
Yellowknife
Hudson Bay
6
Churchill
4
St John's
10
9
7
James Bay
Moosonee
Vancouver
Kamloops
Calgary
Québec City
5
PACIFIC OCEAN
2
Winnipeg
Thunder Bay
3
Montréal
Halifax
8
OTTAWA
1
Toronto
ATLANTIC OCEAN
0 500 km
UNITED STATES

CHAPTER 11 Highlights

* **The Skeena Valley** A glorious wildlife-rich river and estuary flanked by soaring mountains. See p.873

* **Haida Gwaii** A superb archipelago of wild islands whose rich profusion of flora and fauna has earned them the title of "the Canadian Galapagos". See pp.878–886

* **Alaska Highway** Some 2500km of stunning wilderness make this one of North America's great drives. See pp.889–894

* **Dawson City** The focus of the Klondike Gold Rush is western Canada's most atmospheric and compelling historic town. See pp.909–915

* **Dempster Highway** The only public road in North America to cross the Arctic Circle offers a fascinating insight into the tundra and chance encounters with wildlife. See pp.916–918

* **Nahanni National Park** Magnificent gorges, waterfalls and mountain scenery are the chief attractions in one of Canada's finest national parks. See p.926

* **Auyuittuq National Park** Arctic scenery and culture are always compelling, but nowhere more so than in this largely glacial redoubt on Baffin Island. See p.945

▲ Getting into the wild on the South Nahanni River, NWT

11 The North

Although much of Canada still has the flavour of the "last frontier", it's only when you embark north to the Yukon, Northwest Territories or to Nunavut that you know for certain you've left mainstream North American life behind. In the popular imagination, **the north** figures as a perpetually frozen wasteland blasted by ferocious gloomy winters, inhabited – if at all – by hardened characters who make do without civilization. In truth, it's a region where months of summer sunshine offer almost limitless opportunities for outdoor activities and an incredible profusion of flora and fauna; a country within a country, the character of whose settlements has often been forged by the mingling of white settlers and **aboriginal peoples**. The indigenous hunters of the north are as varied as in the south, but two groups predominate: the **Dene**, people of the northern forests who traditionally occupied the Mackenzie River region from the Alberta border to the river's delta at the Beaufort Sea; and the Arctic **Inuit** (literally "the people").

The north is as much a state of mind as a place. People "north of 60" – the 60th Parallel – claim the right to be called **northerners**, and maintain a kinship with Alaskans, but those north of the **Arctic Circle** – the 66th Parallel – look with light-hearted disdain on these "southerners". All mock the inhabitants of the northernmost corners of Alberta and such areas of the so-called Northwest, who, after all, live with the luxury of being able to get around their backcountry by road. Yet to any outsider – in terms of landscape and overall spirit – the north begins well south of the 60th Parallel. Accordingly, this chapter includes not just the territories of the "true north" – **Yukon, Nunavut** and parts of the western Arctic and **Northwest Territories** – but also northern **British Columbia** and **Alberta**, regions of both provinces that are considerably starker and more remote than areas further south.

The two roads into the Yukon strike through northern **British Columbia**: the **Alaska Highway** heads up from the eastern side of the province,

Regional information

Tourism British Columbia ⓣ1-800/663-6000, ⓦwww.hellobc.com.

Haida Gwaii Tourism ⓣ250/559-8316, ⓦwww.haidagwaiitourism.ca.

Tourism Yukon ⓣ867/667-3084, ⓦwww.travelyukon.com.

NWT Tourism ⓣ1-800/661-0788, ⓦwww.spectacularnwt.com.

Travel Alberta ⓣ1-800/252-3782 or 780/427-4321, ⓦwww.travelalberta.com.

Nunavut Tourism ⓣ867/979-6551 or 1-866/686-2888, ⓦwww.nunavuttourism.com.

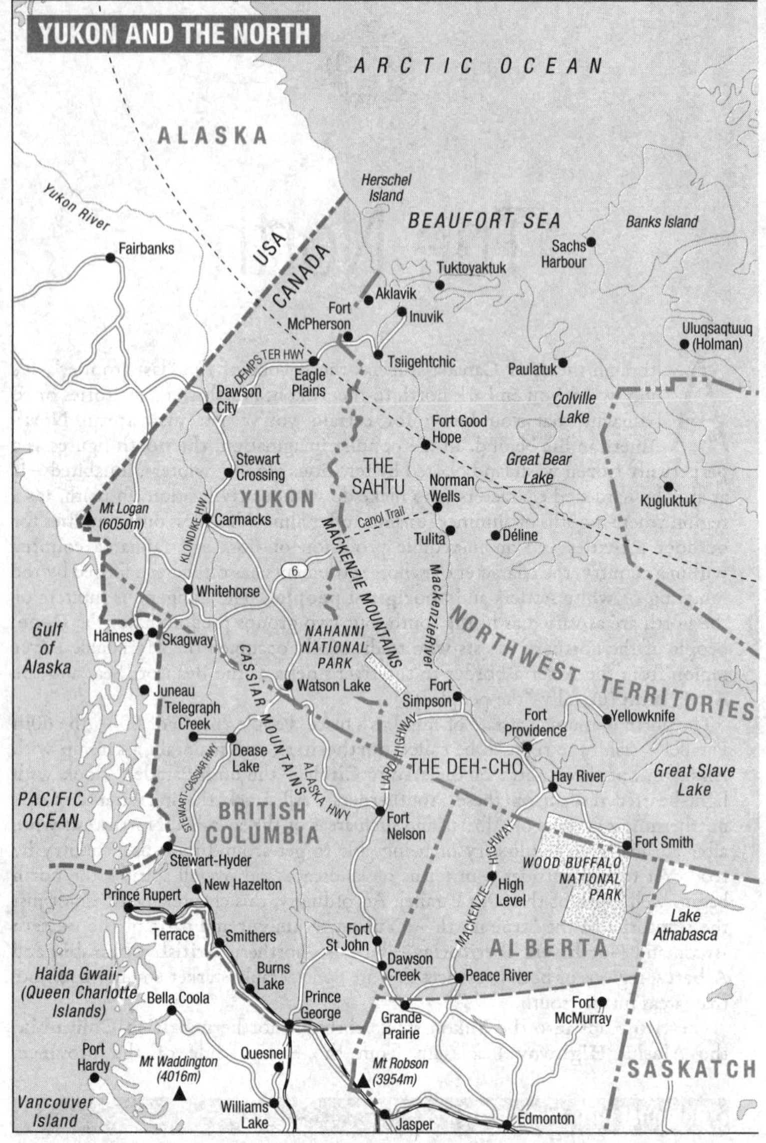

connecting **Dawson Creek** to Fairbanks in Alaska, and to the west is the **Stewart-Cassiar Highway**, from near **Prince Rupert** to **Watson Lake**, on the Yukon border. Though the Stewart-Cassiar's passage through the Coast Mountains offers perhaps the better landscapes, it's the Alaska Hwy – serviced by daily Greyhound **buses** and plentiful motels and campsites – that is more travelled. While the scenery is superb, most towns on both roads are battered and perfunctory places built around lumber mills, oil and gas plants and mining

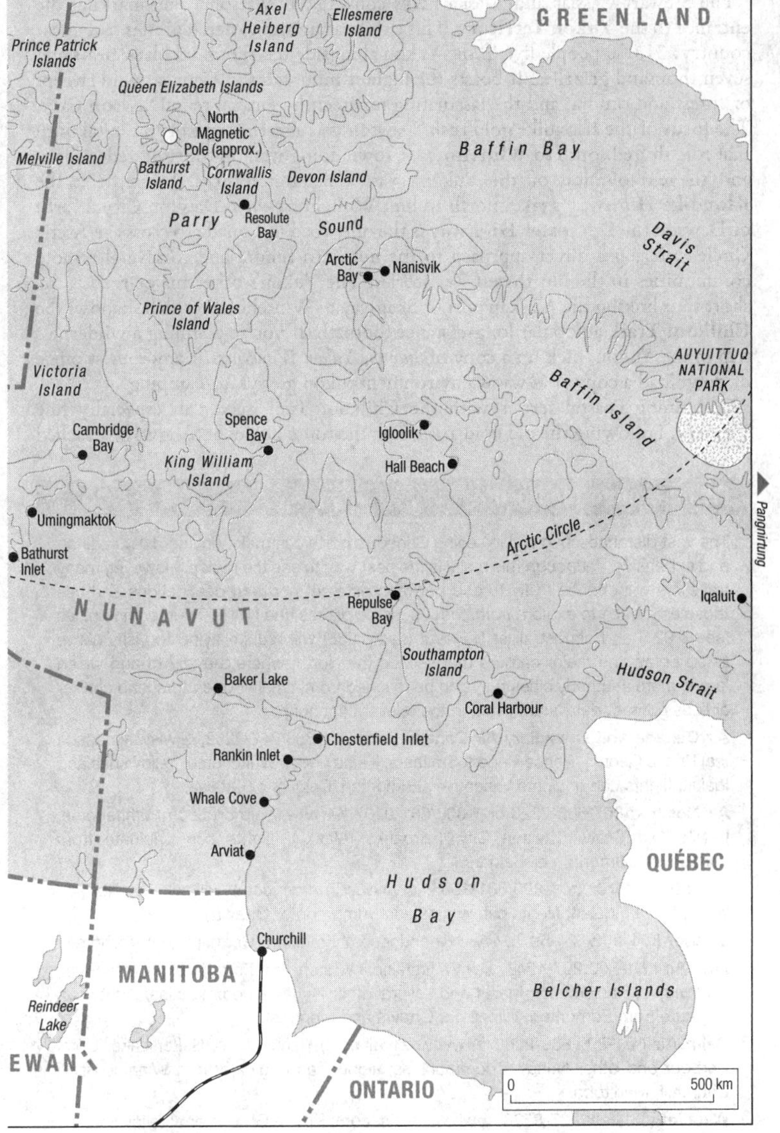

camps, though increasingly they are spawning motels and restaurants to serve the surge of summer visitors out to capture the thrill of driving the frontier hwys. Equally popular are the **sea journeys** offered along northern BC's coast, among the most breathtaking trips in Canada. Prince Rupert, linked by ferry to Vancouver Island, is the springboard for boats to the magnificent **Haida Gwaii** (formerly known as the Queen Charlotte Islands) and a vital way station for boats plying the Inside Passage up to Alaska.

The Stewart-Cassiar and Alaska hwys converge at Watson Lake, marking the entrance to the **Yukon Territory**. This exhilarating and varied region is truly bear country: 31,000 people live in the Yukon alongside ten thousand black bears and seven thousand grizzlies. It boasts the highest mountains in Canada, wild sweeps of forest and tundra, and the fascinating nineteenth-century relic **Dawson City**. The focus of the Klondike gold rush, Dawson was also the territory's capital until that role shifted south to **Whitehorse**, a town doing well on tourism, federal jobs and the exploitation of the Yukon's vast mineral resources. From here, the **Klondike Highway** strikes north to link Whitehorse with Dawson City. North of Dawson the **Dempster Highway** is the only road in Canada to cross the Arctic Circle, offering a direct approach to the northern tundra and to several remote communities in the Northwest Territories. The Yukon's other major road is the short spur linking the Alaskan port of Skagway to Whitehorse, which shadows the **Chilkoot Trail**, a popular long-distance footpath. If you're planning a wilderness trip in the Yukon, pick up a copy of *Into the Yukon Wilderness* at any tourist office or download a copy at Ⓦwww.environmentyukon.gov.yk.ca/camping.

Combining coastal ferries with the Chilkoot Trail makes an especially fine itinerary. Following the old gold-rush trail, the route begins at Skagway – reached

Flying around the North

The vast distances involved in seeing Canada's north can make driving difficult, tiring and expensive – although this really is the best way to see the region. However, many travellers will choose to fly to and between different northern destinations and use those as a base to explore from. Indeed, some places (the NWTs' fly-in communities (see p.921) and almost all of Nunavut (see p.936) will require flying to visit. We've listed below the major carriers that service the North, where they fly to and which larger, more southerly cities they can be reached from; smaller operators' and charter airlines contact details are listed in the relevant account.

Air Canada and subsidiary Air Canada Jazz (Ⓣ1-888/247-2262, Ⓦwww.aircanada.ca) Prince George, Prince Rupert, Smithers, Haida Gwaii, Whitehorse, Yellowknife and Iqaluit; flights can originate Vancouver, Edmonton, Calgary or Ottawa.

Air North (Ⓣ867/668-2228 or 1-800/661-0407, Ⓦwww.flyairnorth.com) Whitehorse, Inuvik, Old Crow, Dawson City, Fairbanks (Alaska); flights can originate from Vancouver, Edmonton or Calgary.

Canadian North (Ⓣ1-800/661-1505, Ⓦwww.cdn-north.com) Yellowknife, Norman Wells, Inuvik, Iqaluit; flights can originate in Edmonton or Ottawa.

Condor (Ⓣ1-800/524-6975, Ⓦwww.condor.com) Frankfurt, Germany to Whitehorse.

First Air (Ⓣ1-800/267-1247, Ⓦwww.firstair.ca) Whitehorse, Fort Simpson, Hay River, Yellowknife, Rankin Inlet, Iqaluit and several other Nunavut communities; flights can originate from Edmonton, Winnipeg, Ottawa and Montréal.

Calm Air (Ⓣ1-800/839-2256, Ⓦwww.calmair.com) Rankin Inlet, Baker Lake, Coral Harbour and other Nunavut communities; flights can originate from Winnipeg and Churchill, Manitoba.

WestJet (Ⓣ1-888/937-8538, Ⓦwww.westjet.com) Prince George and Yellowknife.

One option worth considering is the **Canada's Arctic Circle Airpass**, offered by Air North and Canadian North (Ⓦwww.canadasarcticcircleairpass.com, Ⓣ1-800/661-0407 ext 223), which allows you to fly return from Vancouver, Calgary or Edmonton to five destinations in the Yukon and NWT over 45 days: Whitehorse, Dawson, Inuvik, Norman Wells and Yellowknife. You can "build" various permutations of the pass, but you must overnight in each destination (as you likely would if driving). The cost starts at $879, plus tax.

by ferry from Prince Rupert – then follows the Chilkoot to Whitehorse, before heading north to Dawson City. From there you could continue up the Dempster Highway, or travel on the equally majestic **Top of the World Highway** into the heart of Alaska. Alternatively, many people coming up from Skagway or plying the mainland routes from BC head to Alaska directly on the Alaska Hwy to enjoy views of the extraordinary and largely inaccessible mountain vastness of **Kluane National Park**, which contains Canada's highest peaks and most extensive glacial wilderness.

If the Yukon is the far north at its most accessible, the **Northwest Territories** (NWT) is the region at its most uncompromising. Just three roads nibble at the edges of this almost unimaginably vast area, which occupies a third of Canada's landmass – about the size of India – but contains only sixty thousand people, almost half of whom live in or around **Yellowknife**, the territories' peculiarly overblown capital. Unless you're taking the adventurous and rewarding **Dempster Highway** from Dawson City across the tundra to **Inuvik**, Yellowknife will probably feature on any trip to the NWT, as it's the hub of the (rather expensive) flight network servicing the area's widely dispersed communities.

Otherwise, most visitors come to the NWT to **fish**, **canoe**, hunt, watch **wildlife** or to experience the Inuit aboriginal cultures and ethereal landscapes. After years of negotiations, the Inuit of the eastern NWT finally realized their dream of administering their land with the creation of **Nunavut** on April 1, 1999. This effectively split the former NWT into two distinct regions with the eastern half being renamed Nunavut. One effect has been the **renaming** of most settlements with Inuit names, though in many cases the old English-language names appear in much literature. Nunavut and the "old" western NWT issue their own tourist material; pick up a copy of their respective *Arctic Nunavut Travel Planner* and *Explorers' Guide* brochures, which summarize accommodation options, airline connections, many of the available tours – costing anything from $50 to $5000-plus – and the plethora of outfitters who provide the equipment and backup essential for any but the most superficial trip to the region.

Prince George

Lying 780km north of Vancouver and 380km northwest of Jasper, rough-edged **PRINCE GEORGE** is the general area's services and transport centre and forestry is at the core of its industrial landscape – if you ever wanted the inside story on the lumber business, this is where to find it.

Simon Fraser established a North West Trading Company post here in 1805. As a commercial nexus it quickly altered the lives of the local Carrier Sekani peoples, who abandoned their semi-nomadic migration from winter to summer villages in favour of a permanent settlement alongside the fort. Little changed until 1914 when the arrival of the Grand Trunk Railway spawned an influx of pioneers and loggers. The town was connected by road to Dawson Creek and the north as late as 1951, and saw the arrival of the Pacific Great Eastern Railway in 1958, two developments that give some idea of how recent the opening up of the far north has been.

For the route from Prince George north and east to Dawson Creek, and the Alaska Hwy, see pp.889–894.

Arrival and information

Air Canada Jazz and WestJet fly to Prince George from Vancouver; the airport is 18km east of downtown and linked by regular shuttles.

The aurora borealis

The **aurora borealis**, or **Northern Lights**, is a beautiful and ethereal display of light in the upper atmosphere that can be seen over large areas of northern Canada. The night sky appears to shimmer with dancing curtains of colour, ranging from luminescent monotones – most commonly green or a dark red – to fantastic veils running the full spectrum. The display becomes more animated as it proceeds, twisting and turning in patterns called "rayed bands". As a finale, a corona sometimes appears, in which rays seem to flare in all directions from a central point.

The aurora was long thought to be produced by sunlight reflected from polar snow and ice, or refracted light produced in the manner of a rainbow. Certain Inuit peoples believed the lights were the spirits of animals or ancestors; others thought they represented wicked forces. Old-time gold prospectors thought they might be vapours given off by ore deposits. Research still continues into the phenomenon, and while the earth's geomagnetic field certainly plays some part in the creation of the aurora, its source would appear to lie with the sun – auroras become more distinct and are seen spread over a larger area two days after intense solar activity, the time it takes the "solar wind" to arrive. This wind is composed of fast-moving electrically charged ions. When these hit the earth's atmosphere they respond to the earth's magnetic field and move towards the poles. En route, they strike atoms and molecules of gas in the upper atmosphere, causing them to become temporarily charged or ionized. These molecules then release the charge, or energy, usually in the form of light. Different colours are emitted depending on the gases involved: oxygen produces green hues (or orange at higher altitudes), nitrogen occasionally violet colours.

You should be able to see the Northern Lights as far south as Prince George in BC, over parts of northern Alberta (where on average they're visible some 160 nights a year) and over much of the NWT, Nunavut and northern Manitoba. They are at their most dazzling **from December to March**, when nights are longest and the sky darkest, though they are potentially visible year-round. Look out for a faint glow on the northeastern horizon after dusk, and then – if you're lucky – for the full show as the night deepens

The town is linked three times weekly by VIA Rail **trains** (Ⓣ1-800/561-8630, Ⓦwww.viarail.ca) to Jasper, Edmonton and beyond eastbound, and Prince Rupert westbound (for the Haida Gwaii/Prince Charlotte Islands and Inside Passage ferries); the train station is downtown at 1300 1st Ave (Ⓣ1-888/842-7245). You can get a taxi with either Prince George Taxi (Ⓣ250/564-4444) or Emerald Taxi Ltd (Ⓣ250/563-3333).

Prince George is also a staging post for Greyhound **bus** routes to the north, and integral to the main road routes to Dawson Creek (for the Alaska Hwy) and Prince Rupert (for the Stewart-Cassiar Hwy). The Greyhound **bus station** (Ⓣ250/564-5454 or 1-800/661-1202) is at 1566 12th Ave and close to a handful of the town's many hotels and motels.

The city has two **tourist offices**: one at 1300 1st Ave (May–Sept daily 8am–8pm, Oct–April 8.30am–5pm; Ⓣ250/562-3700 or 1-800/668-7646, Ⓦwww.tourismpg.com); the other at 2800 Hwy 16 (May–Sept daily 8am–8pm).

Accommodation

Prince George has a range of accommodation. A good choice on the Hwy 97 strip is the big *Spruceland Inn* (Ⓣ250/563-0102 or 1-800/663-3295, Ⓦwww.sprucelandinn.com; ❸) at 1391 Central St at the junction of Hwy 97 and 15th Avenue. At *Esther's*

Inn (Ⓣ250/562-4131 or 1-800/663-6844, Ⓦwww.esthersinn.com; ③), one block off the hwy at 1151 Commercial Drive (10th Ave), the price includes a swimming pool, water slides and jacuzzi. Closer to downtown is *Coast Inn of the North*, 770 Brunswick St (Ⓣ250/563-0121 or 1-800/716-6199, Ⓦwww.coasthotels.com; ⑤) with 155 rooms and fine dining facilities. The best options for camping are the *Southpark RV Park*, 8km from town on Hwy 97 South (Ⓣ250/963-7577 or 1-877/963-7275, Ⓦwww.southparkrv.com; $25-32), with hot showers, and the *Blue Spruce RV & Campground* about 5km west at Kimball Road on Hwy 16 (Ⓣ250/964-7272 or 964-4060, Ⓔbluesprucervpark@shaw.ca; $19–25; April to mid-Oct), with heated outdoor pool.

The town and around

Prince George offers a handful of attractions, many of which take in the city's surrounding forests. There are over 1600 lakes within a 150km radius of town, all offering beautiful settings for hiking, fishing and canoeing. A host of **hiking trails** exist through the area, including an easy walk through the Ancient Forest, the world's furthest inland rainforest, while Forests for the World offers 15km of trails and a gorgeous lakeside picnic site. Just north of downtown the Cottonwood Island Nature Park has similar trails with interpretive signs and wood spirit carvings in the trees. The city's central Connaught Hill Park affords a 360 degree view over the city; check with the tourist office for trail details.

The **Railway and Forestry Museum** (May–Aug daily except Tues 10am–5pm; Ⓣ250/563-7351, Ⓦwww.pgrfm.bc.ca; $9), at 850 River Rd, houses the largest vintage rail collection in BC, while the **Exploration Place Museum and Science Centre** (May to mid-Oct Wed–Sun 10am–5pm; Ⓣ250/562-1612, Ⓦwww.theexplorationplace.com; $9), at 333 Becott Place (end of 20th Ave), features exhibits and activities exploring everything from dinosaur fossils to First Nations attractions.

Canfor Tours run free **tours** (June–Aug Mon–Fri; Ⓣ250/561-5700) around some of its mills and processing plants and do a good job explaining the history of the pulp and paper industry; contact the tourist office for reservations.

Eating and drinking

For **food**, try *White Goose Bistro*, 1205 3rd Ave (Ⓣ250/561-1002; closed Sun), specializing in Italian and French cuisine – the duck in cherry red wine sauce ($25) is popular. For no-fuss Italian, *Cimo*, 601 Victoria St (Ⓣ250/564-7975; closed Sun), has an extensive choice of pasta dishes ($12–14). *The Publik* at the junction of hwys 16 & 97 has great food and is a good spot for a **drink**.

Prince George to Prince Rupert

To make the 735-kilometre journey west from Prince George to **Prince Rupert**, you can use either Hwy 16 (the Yellowhead Highway) or the parallel VIA Rail line; neither is terribly scenic by BC standards until you reach the glorious river and mountain landscapes of the **Skeena Valley** 150km before Prince Rupert. Most people make this trip as a link in a much longer journey, either to take **ferries** north to Alaska or south to Port Hardy on Vancouver Island, or to start the Stewart-Cassiar Hwy en route to meet the Alaska Hwy at Watson Lake over the Yukon border. Unless you fly, it's also the only way to reach **Haida Gwaii** (see pp.878–886), accessible by ferry or plane from Prince Rupert. The best place to pause during the journey is near **Hazelton**, approximately 450km from Prince George, where you can visit a little cluster of aboriginal villages.

West of Prince George

Riding out of Prince George you're confronted quickly with the relentless monotony of rolling forests, broken only by the occasional lake and the grey silhouettes of distant low-hilled horizons. The pine beetle, which has infested many of the lodgehole pine trees in the BC interior, has made particular inroads along the stretch heading towards **BURNS LAKE**, 229km to the west. The road travels past vast swaths of red and grey forest, all ravaged by a beetle that has been thriving in increasingly mild winters. Burns Lake is the gateway to the northern end of **Tweedsmuir Provincial Park**, considered to be one of the epicentres of the epidemic. There is a **tourist office** at 540 Hwy 16 West (June–Sept daily 9am–6pm, Jan–May Mon–Fri 9am–4.30pm; ⓣ250/692-3773, ⓦwww.burnslakechamber.ca) which can provide information on the twenty or so **accommodation** options in the area.

Beyond Burns Lake the scenery picks up, though the run of villages continues to offer little but places to fill either the tank or the stomach.

Smithers

SMITHERS, the largest community after Prince George, is a picturesque outdoor adventure hub. The sizeable Swiss population has made their mark on the Alpine-themed downtown, focused on Main Street at the crossroads of Hwy 16.

Smithers is serviced three times weekly by VIA Rail's "Skeena" **train** at 3815 Railway Ave. Greyhound **buses** run twice daily in each direction along Hwy 16 – the station is just west of downtown at 4011 Hwy 16 (ⓣ250/847-2204). There is an **airport** five kilometres west on Hwy 16, with regular Air Canada Jazz flights. The **visitor centre** is at 1411 Court St (mid-May to Aug daily 9am–6pm; Sept to mid-May Mon–Fri 9am–5pm; ⓣ250/847-5072 or 1-800/542-6673, ⓦwww.tourismsmithers.com) and has free internet and information about activities nearby, including fishing, kayaking and riding.

There is mountain biking and hiking in the **Babine Mountains Provincial Park** and downhill and cross-country **skiing** 20km from town on Hudson Bay Mountain (Dec to mid-April; day-pass $45; ⓣ250/665-4299, ⓦwww.skismithers.com; for cross-country skiing contact Bulkley Valley Nordic Centre ⓣ250/847-3828, ⓦwww.bvnordic.ca). For indoor attractions, try the art gallery/museum (Mon–Sat 9am–5pm; ⓔbvmuseum@nucleus.com). at the corner of Main Street and Hwy 16, which has a lovingly-tended exhibit on Smithers' brief brush with notoriety in 1911 – when a local invented the **egg carton**.

Practicalities

Ignore the brace of **motels** on the road and settle for the big white-timbered *Hudson Bay Lodge* (ⓣ250/847-4581 or 1-800/663-5040, ⓦwww.hblodge.com; ⑤) just east of downtown on Hwy 16; it has a great restaurant, *Pepper Jack's*, which has schnitzel and fondue theme nights. The spotless *Smithers Hostel and Guesthouse* at 1766 Main St has kitchen facilities, free internet and dorm beds for $25 (ⓣ250/847-4862, ⓦwww.smithersguesthouse.com; ③). For camping and RVs, the *Riverside Park and Municipal Campground* occupies an idyllic spot northwest of Main Street on the banks of the Bulkley River (ⓣ250/847-3494; $15–25).

For something to eat, *Schimmel's* at 1172 Main St (ⓣ250/847-9044; closed Sun & Mon) packs a European punch, with great coffee, artisan breads, soups, pizzas, tarts and home-made gelato.

The Skeena Valley

Just beyond Smithers, the **Skeena River** carves a beautiful valley through the Coast Mountains, an important trade route for aboriginal peoples and sternwheelers before the coming of the railway in 1912. For a couple of hours the road and railway run past an imposing backdrop of snow-capped peaks half-reflected in the mist-wreathed estuary. Out on the water there's a good chance of seeing the ripples of seals, as well as **bald eagles** perched on the river's immense logjams. Dark valleys peel off the main river's majestic course and delicate threads of waterfalls are repeatedly visible though the trees.

Shortly after Hwy 16 meets the river crashing down from the north near **Hazelton** and **New Hazelton**, a couple of minor roads strike off to four nearby **villages**, where something of the culture of the indigenous **Gitxsan** peoples has been preserved, along with new examples of totem carving and other crafts. The Gitxsan traditionally lived off fish and game rather than agriculture, and were consummate artists and carvers.

'Ksan, Kispiox, Gitwangak and Gitanyow

A few kilometres off Hwy 16, on the High Level Road out of New Hazelton, is **'Ksan**, the most interesting of the four villages and site of an entire reconstructed Gitxsan village. Aboriginal women act as guides around seven cedar longhouses and numerous totem poles, giving a commentary on the carvings, clothes, buildings and masks on show (tours daily April–Sept 9am–5pm; museum same summer hours plus Oct–March Mon–Fri 9.30am–4.30pm; tours $10, museum $5; Ⓣ250/842-5544 or 1-877/842-5518, Ⓦwww.ksan.org).

Kispiox, 13km north of Hazelton, is the ancient Gitxsan home of the Frog, Wolf and Fireweed clans, and was given its name by the old Department for Indian Affairs. It means "place of loud talkers" but locals, not surprisingly, prefer the traditional name, *Anspayaxw*, meaning "the hidden place". The highlights here are fifteen riverside totems.

To the west (500m north of the hwys 16 and 37 junction) is **Gitwangak**, which means "the place of rabbits". It also has some impressive totems, as does **Gitanyow** ("people of a small village"), 21km north on Hwy 37, whose eighteen poles include the 140-year-old "Hole in the Sky" totem. You can sometimes watch poles being repaired at the village's two carving sheds.

The nearest **visitor centre** for the villages is near New Hazelton at the junction of hwys 16 and 62 (mid-May to mid-Sept daily 8am–8pm; Ⓣ250/842-6071 or 842-6571 year-round, Ⓔtourism@newhazelton.ca), but you should also spend a few minutes looking round the evocative old Victorian streets of old **Hazelton** 6km to the northwest on Hwy 62.

Accommodation is limited to a handful of motels in New Hazelton, one of the cheapest being the *Bulkley Valley Motel*, 4444 Hwy 16 (Ⓣ250/842-6817 or 1-888/988-1144, Ⓦwww.bulkleyvalleymotel.com; ❸). Kispiox also has a handful of bed and breakfasts; the closest to the village is the two-room *Trakehnerhof Bed and Breakfast*, Salmon River Road (Ⓣ250/842-5400, Ⓦwww.trakehnerhof.ca; ❹), on the banks of the Skeena River with a spa and sauna. For camping, the *River's Edge Campground*, Kispiox Valley Road (Ⓣ250/842-5822; pitch/RV $15/20), is 7km outside the village on the Kispiox River and attracts many fishing enthusiasts.

Terrace and around

Some 142km before Prince Rupert, Hwy 16 passes through **TERRACE**, the commercial centre of the Skeena Valley. There is a **tourist office** on the hwy at 4511 Keith Ave (June–Aug daily 8am–5pm, rest of year Mon–Fri 8.30am–4.30pm;

©250/635-2063, ⓦ www.terracetourism.bc.ca), but few reasons to stop in the town itself.

You can **ski** 35km west off Hwy 16 at **Shames Mountain** (mid-Dec to mid-April; day-pass $42; ©250/635-3773, ⓦwww.shamesmountain.com), which has 35 trails. Terrace is also a good jumping off point for the 250-year-old lava flows at **Nisga'a Memorial Lava Bed Provincial Park**, 80km to the north. There is a **campsite** here (mid-May to mid-Sept; $10–24) and a visitor centre (mid-June to Sept daily 10am–6pm) that can arrange volcano tours.

Prince Rupert

There's a bracing tang of salt and fish in the air in **PRINCE RUPERT**, a distinctive port on Kaien Island – linked by bridge to the mainland – that comes as an invigorating relief after the run out of Prince George. A stunning place when the mist lifts, it looks out over an archipelago of islands and is ringed by mountains that tumble to the sea along a beautiful fjord-cut coastline. A crowd of cars, backpackers and RVs washes daily through its streets off the Alaska, the Queen Charlotte and Port Hardy **ferries**, complementing the seafront's vibrant activity, and adding to the coffers of a town clearly on the up. In the summer, **cruise ships** make four-hour pit stops here, spewing up to two thousand passengers ashore at a time to gorge on fish and chips and sightsee. There's plenty of outdoor and indoor attractions, and it's an amiable enough spot to while away a day while you're waiting for a boat. Some of the highlights include tours of the world-renowned **Khutzeymateen Grizzly Bear Sanctuary**, whale-watching and a stop at the Museum of Northern British Columbia.

Arrival and information

Many people reach Prince Rupert by **ferry**; for information on ferry trips here from Vancouver or Vancouver Island see p.860.

The Greyhound **bus station** (©250/624-5090), in the centre of town at 815 1st Ave West and 7th St, handles two buses daily for the ten-hour ride to Prince George ($120 one-way). The **train station** is on the waterfront at Fairview Dock; the ticket office is in the BC Ferries building on Hwy 16 (open 2hr either side of departures and arrivals; ©1-888/842-7245, ⓦwww.viarail.ca). Trains to Prince George for connections to Edmonton via Jasper leave on Tuesday, Thursday and Sunday at 8am, arriving in Prince George at 8.30pm. If you're taking the train right through, you'll have to overnight in Prince George, as there are no through-trains to Jasper or Edmonton.

The **airport** is on Digby Island just across the harbour, with ferry connections to the BC and Alaska Marine ferry terminals (see box opposite) and shuttle bus connections to downtown (©250/622-2222), which leave and drop off at the *Highliner Plaza Hotel* at 815 1st Ave West. North Pacific Sea Planes (©250/627-1341 or 1-800/689-4234, ⓦwww.northpacificseaplanes.com) run 45-minute flights to Sandspit, Masset and Queen Charlotte on Haida Gwaii (see pp.878–886) leaving east of town from the Seal Cove seaplane base on Bellis Road.

Prince Rupert's **tourist office** is in the Atlin Terminal on Cow Bay Road (©250/624-5637 or 1-800/667-1994, ⓦwww.tourismprincerupert.com), a little to the north in an older part of town known as Cow Bay; it's a small and funky waterfront enclave boasting attractive cafés, galleries and restaurants.

Accommodation

With more ferry traffic and, consequently, visitors – many of whom, if coming off a later ferry, choose to stay the night before moving on – Prince Rupert's accommodation options have expanded, but it's still a good idea to book ahead.

Ferries from Prince Rupert

Ferry terminals for both BC Ferries (for Port Hardy and the Haida Gwaii) and the Alaska Marine Hwy (for Skagway and Alaska Panhandle ports) are at **Fairview Dock**, 2km southwest of town at the end of Hwy 16. Walk-on tickets for foot passengers are rarely a problem at either terminal, but advance reservations are essential if you're taking a car or want a cabin for any summer crossing. Grab a **taxi** from downtown (ⓣ250/624-2185) to get there.

To Haida Gwaii

BC Ferries operates the MV *Northern Adventure* to **Skidegate Landing** on Haida Gwaii (early-May to late Sept: daily; rest of year: three weekly). The crossing takes between 6hr 30min and 8hr, depending on weather, and costs $39 one-way for foot passengers ($33 low season: late Sept to early-May), plus $140/$115 for cars and $5 for bikes. Two-berth cabins cost $60. Return ferries from Skidegate sometimes provide a connection with the Inside Passage boat to Port Hardy on Vancouver Island (see below). For **reservations** or timetable information, contact BC Ferries on ⓣ250/386-3431 or 1-888/223-3779 anywhere in BC, or in Prince Rupert on ⓣ250/624-9627, ⓦwww.bcferries.com.

To Port Hardy

Ferries to Port Hardy leave every other day in summer for a stunning day-long cruise, aboard the brand new MV *Northern Expedition*, that lasts approximately 17hr, depending on the weather (overnight trip between Oct and mid-Dec, three times every two weeks). One-way fares are $170 for passengers, $390 extra for a car, $5 extra for a bicycle (mid-May to Sept); $125/$285/$5 (Oct); $100/$220/$5 (Nov to mid-Dec). Two-berth cabins cost $70. To take a car on in the summer, you'll need to have booked at least two months in advance (see also Port Hardy, p.858).

To Alaska

Ferries run by **Alaska Marine Highway** (ⓣ250/627-1744 or 1-800/642-0066) go to **Skagway** in Alaska, via (some or all) Ketchikan, Wrangell, Petersburg, Sitka, Hyder, Stewart, Juneau, Haines and Hollis and other minor stops. Frequency is three times a week in the summer and twice a week in winter. Schedules and fares are complicated, given the many possible permutations of route and port, but can be sourced from ⓦwww.alaska.gov/ferry or by calling the central reservations number in Juneau (ⓣ1-800/642-0066) or the Anchorage office (ⓣ907/272-7116). One-way adult fares from Prince Rupert to Skagway start at around US$186, with US$34 extra to bring a bicycle and US$410 for a car. Two- or four-berth cabins can also be booked: reckon on a two-berth cabin from Prince Rupert to Haines or Skagway costing about US$150. Boats stop frequently en route, with the chance to go ashore for a short time, though longer stopovers must be arranged when buying a through-ticket. If you're a foot passenger arrive at least an hour before departure to go through US customs and immigration and three hours early if you have a car. Though the journey takes two days there are various restrictions on the fresh food you can take on board.

Hotels and motels

Crest Hotel 222 1st Ave ⓣ250/624-6771 or 1-800/663-8150, ⓦwww.cresthotel.bc.ca. This is the place to go if you want top of the range accommodation with great views – it's set on a promontory overlooking the harbour.The more expensive suites have two-person jacuzzis (some with views), a fireplace and all the other standard amenities, while cheaper rooms are slightly less plush, but still very nice. ❻

Highliner Plaza Hotel 815 1st Ave ⓣ1-800/668-3115, ⓦwww.highlinerplaza.com. Another good central choice, with 94 spacious rooms, each with a balcony affording views of the harbour and city. ❻

Inn on the Harbour 720 1st Ave ⓣ250/624-9107 or 1-800/663-8155, ⓦwww.innontheharbour.com.

Perhaps the best all-round central choice in town – especially if you can secure a room with a sea view. 5

Parkside Resort 101 11th Ave ⓣ250/624-9131 or 1-888/575-2288, ⓦwww.parksideresortmotel.com. Although it's only 1km east of town, this smart-looking hotel with good rates is likely to have room when the more central options are full. 3

Totem Lodge 1335 Park Ave ⓣ250/624-6761 or 1-800/550-0178, ⓦwww.totemlodge.com. This is the nearest accommodation to the ferry terminals – Park Ave is a continuation of 2nd Ave and runs right to the terminals from downtown. The 31 rooms are very plain and most come with a kitchenette ($7/night fee) and have wi-fi. Continental breakfast included in rate. 4

Hostels and campsites

Black Rooster Roadhouse 501 6th Ave ⓣ250/627-5337 or 1-866/371-5337, ⓦwww.blackrooster.ca. A spacious affair that's half-hostel, half-hotel. Dorm beds are $25, or you can opt for the pricier and better-equipped twin, queen or family rooms (all with in-room phone and TV); groups might want to opt for the ground floor apartments that sleep 4–6. Free wi-fi throughout. 3

Pioneer Backpacker's Inn 167 3rd Ave ⓣ250/624-2334 or 1-888/794-9998, ⓦwww.pioneerhostel.com. You'll have to be quick – or reserve in advance – to get a room here, as it fills up quickly in high season. The rooms are bright but basic, and all with shared bathrooms. The hostel also operates a free shuttle to and from the ferry terminals and train station, has free wi-fi and holds a weekly bbq. Dorms $25, private doubles $60, tent sites $15.

Prince Rupert RV Campground 1750 Park Ave, 1km west of town ⓣ250/627-1000, ⓦwww.princerupertrv.com. This is the only local, big campsite, and so a shame it's rather unattractive. Still, it's only 1km away from the ferry terminals so if you can put up with the RVs you're bound to be one of the first aboard.

The Town

Prince Rupert's port is one of the world's largest deep-water terminals, and handles a huge volume of trade. The region was once the focal point of trade between aboriginal peoples to the north and south, one reason why the Hudson's Bay Company built a post at Fort Simpson, 30km north of the present townsite. For information on how this came to be the terminus of Canada's second transcontinental rail link, visit the **Kwinitsa Station Railway Museum** (June–Aug daily 9am–noon & 1–5pm; donation; ⓣ250/624-3207) near the waterfront on Bill Murray Way.

Prince Rupert's excellent **Museum of Northern British Columbia** (June–Aug Mon–Sat 9am–8pm, Sun 9am–5pm; Sept–May Mon–Sat 9am–5pm; $5;

▲ Grizzly bears near Prince Rupert, BC

The 'spirit' bears of Princess Royal Island

At first glance, you could easily mistake it for a polar or albino black bear. But the elusive **kermode** or 'spirit' bear is actually a white-furred variation of the black bear; a recessive gene passed from both parents gives it its white fur. The kermode is unique to the rugged temperate rainforest along BC's central coast, its habitat concentrated in the fifteen million acres stretching from Bella Coola to Prince Rupert (also known as the Great Bear Rainforest). Despite pressure from conservationists to preserve its habitat, the kermode remains under threat from logging, hunting and mining. The highest number of kermode bears can be found on Princess Royal Island, 200km south of Prince Rupert, where ten percent of black bears are born with white fur. No humans live on the island and access is by boat or floatplane only. One day wildlife-viewing boat tours (ⓣ250/841-2522, ⓦwww.gitgaat.net) operate out of **Hartley Bay**, a remote community of 180 Gitga'at people 140km south of Prince Rupert. The best viewing months are between August and October, when the bears gather around the creeks to feed on spawning salmon. Hartley Bay is accessed by air or water from Prince Rupert: Northco Corp Ferry Service (ⓣ250/624-3337 or 622-8067) runs a twice-weekly service, leaving from the terminal on Cow Bay Road (4hr; $45 one-way), while North Pacific Sea Planes (ⓣ250/627-1341, ⓦwww.northpacificseaplanes.com) operates a Sunday–Friday, one-hour flight ($140 one-way).

For accommodation in Hartley Bay, try the five-room *Squirrel's Den Inn* at 120 Hayimi-isaxaa Way (ⓣ250/841-2727, ⓔchillart@telus.net; ⑤ including meals), or contact *King Pacific Lodge*, a luxury wilderness retreat on a barge moored in **Barnard Harbour** on Princess Royal Island, one hour by boat from Hartley Bay (ⓣ604/987-5452 or 1-888/592-5464, ⓦwww.kingpacificlodge.com; May–Sept; ⑧ including meals). Further down the coast, Klemtu Tourism operates the four- and seven- day Spirit Bear Quest Tour (ⓣ250/839-2346 or 1-877/644-2346, ⓦwww.klemtutourism.com;) and has water-front accommodation (starting at $140) at its newly built *Spirit Bear Lodge* in **Klemtu**. For current information regarding tours, transportation and accommodation in Hartley Bay, contact Gitga'at Tourism at ⓣ250/841-2602.

ⓣ250/624-3207, ⓦwww.museumofnorthernbc.com), 1st Avenue at McBride Street, is housed in an impressive reproduction First Nations cedar longhouse and is particularly strong on the culture and history of the local Tsimshian. The museum also boasts a clutch of wonderful silent archive films on topics ranging from fishing to the building of the railway – ideal ways to whittle away a wet afternoon, of which the city has plenty. There are also a variety of tours and performances throughout the summer, including visiting the town's totem poles, a heritage walking tour of the city and a one-hour tour through the rich history of the Northwest Coast Tsimshian First Nations.

While you're in town, check out some of the local **tours** or **boat trips**, many of which are inexpensive and provide a good way to see the offshore islands and wildlife. Seashore Charters (ⓣ250/624-5645 and 1-800/667-4393, ⓦwww.seashorecharters.com), with an office in the Atlin Terminal, is a good outfit, offering whale-watching tours, canoeing and rainforest excursions as well as half-day archeological and cultural trips to **Pike Island** to view ancient village sites and aboriginal petroglyphs. A very popular trip is the 6hr boat tour to **Khutzeymateen Grizzly Bear Sanctuary** (best time mid-May to early Aug), a remote coastal valley 45km northeast of Prince Rupert created in 1994 to protect BC's largest-known coastal population of **grizzly bears**. In BC, the damage done to grizzly habitats by logging, mining, hunting and other concerns – notably the slaughter of the animals for body parts in dubious Asian remedies – is one of the keenest environmental issues in the province. In the summer, several local tour operators run full-day and multi-day boat tours to view the grizzlies in action; Prince Rupert Adventure Tours (ⓣ250/627-9166 or 1-800/201-8377, ⓦwww.adventuretours.net) runs similar boat tours to the sanctuary while Palmerville (ⓣ250/624-8243, ⓦwww.palmerville.bc.ca) runs a three-hour tour with access via floatplane (from $450), as well as offering rustic accommodation in a floating cabin just outside the sanctuary.

Mount Hays gives a bird's-eye view of the harbour and the chance to spot bald eagles. To reach the steep track providing the only route to the top, take the Wantage Road turn-off on Hwy 16 just out of town. It's three hours to the top but you get fairly good views after clambering a short way up the track. For a less energetic **walk**, take the five-kilometre interpretive loop trail through old growth rainforest to **Butze Rapids** – reversing tidal rapids; the trailhead is about 5km east of town along Hwy 16.

Eating and drinking

Fresh fish is the obvious thing to **eat** locally, preferably at a town institution such as the *Green Apple*, a shack serving a mean halibut and chips for around $10; it's at 301 McBride St (ⓣ250/627-1666; closed Sun) just before Hwy 16 turns into town. For something more upmarket, locals flock to the *Cow Bay Café*, 205 Cow Bay Rd (ⓣ250/627-1212; closed Sun & Mon), which does a roaring trade on the waterfront (mains $15–20). Also in Cow Bay is *Cowpuccinos*, a funky café serving fair-trade coffee, fresh soups, sandwiches and home-made desserts. *Breakers* pub just across the bridge at 117 George Hills Way (ⓣ250/624-5990) is a popular and inexpensive place to sink a beer. For the chicest **bar** north of Vancouver, drop into *Rain Dining Lounge,* at 737 2nd Ave West (ⓣ250/627-8272, ⓦwww.raindl.com), which has an extensive wine and cocktail list and whips up superb and creative food (mains from $15).

Haida Gwaii

Ranged in a gentle arc some 150km off the Prince Rupert coast, **Haida Gwaii**, (until recently known as the **Queen Charlotte Islands**) consists of a triangular-shaped archipelago of two major islands – **Graham** and **Moresby** – and two hundred islets that make an enticing diversion from the heavily travelled sea route up through BC's coast.

The islands are something of a cult destination among travellers and environmentalists – partly for their scenery, flora and fauna and almost legendary remoteness from the mainstream – but also because they've achieved a high profile in the disagreement between the forestry industry and ecology activists. At the forefront of the disagreement were the **Haida**, who have made the islands their home for over ten thousand years (see box opposite). The result of years of negotiations was the creation of the **Gwaii Haannas National Park Reserve and Haida Heritage Site**, which protects large tracts of land, incredible biodiversity, traditional villages and numerous archeological sites. The Haida culture, and in particular the chance to visit their many **deserted villages**, forms an increasing part of the islands' attraction, but many also come here to sample the immensely rich flora and fauna, the profusion of which has earned the islands' the title of the **"Canadian Galapagos"**.

Parts of Haida Gwaii were one of only two areas in western Canada to escape the last Ice Age, which elsewhere altered evolutionary progress; this has resulted in the survival of many so-called **enedmics**, which aren't found anywhere else in the world. Species unique to the islands include a fine yellow daisy, the world's largest subspecies of **black bears**, a subspecies of pine marten, deer mouse, hairy woodpecker, saw-whet owl and Stellar's jay. There are also more **eagles** here than anywhere else in the region, as well as the world's largest population of Peale's peregrine falcons and the elusive **black-footed albatross** – whose wingspan exceeds that of the largest eagles. There's also a good chance of spotting whales, otters, sea lions and other aquatic mammals.

Arrival and information

The islands can be accessed either by **air** or **ferry** from Prince Rupert. Ferries from Prince Rupert (see p.875) dock at tiny Skidegate Landing between Queen Charlotte and Skidegate on **Graham Island**, the northernmost of the group's two main collections of islands.

The Haida

The **Haida** are widely considered to have the most highly developed culture and sophisticated art tradition of BC's aboriginal peoples. Extending from Haida Gwaii to southern Alaska, their lands included major stands of red cedar, the raw material for their huge dugout **canoes**, intricate **carvings** and refined **architecture**. Haida trade links were built on the reputation of their skill; to own a Haida canoe was a major status symbol. The Haida were also feared **warriors**, paddling into rival villages and returning with canoes laden with goods and slaves. Their skill on the open sea made them the "Vikings" of North America.

The Haida divided themselves into two main groups, the **Eagles** and the **Ravens**, which were further divided into hereditary kin groups named after their original village location. Marriage within each major group – or *moiety* – was considered incestuous, so Eagles would always seek Raven mates and vice versa. Descent was **matrilineal**, which meant a chief could not pass his property on to his sons because they would belong to a different *moiety* – instead his inheritance passed to his sister's sons.

Haida **villages** were an impressive sight, their vast cedar-plank houses dominated by fifteen-metre totem poles displaying the kin group's unique animal crest or other mythical creatures, all carved in elegant, fluid lines. Entrance to each house was through the gaping mouth of a massive carved figure; inside, supporting posts were carved into the forms of the crest animals and most household objects were similarly decorative. Equal elaboration attended the many Haida ceremonies, one of the most important being the **memorial potlatch**, which served to mark the end of mourning for a dead chief and the validation of the heir's right to succession. The dead individual was laid out at the top of a carved pole in front of his house, past which visiting chiefs would walk wearing robes of finely woven and patterned mountain-goat wool and immense headdresses fringed with long sea-lion whiskers and ermine skins.

After **European contact** the Haida population was devastated by smallpox and other epidemics. In 1787, there were approximately ten thousand Haida scattered across the archipelago. By 1915, their numbers had been reduced to 588. Consequently, they were forced to leave many of their traditional villages and today live mostly in Old Masset and Skidegate. At other locations, homes and totems fell into disrepair and collectors and museums took artefacts. **SGang Gwaay**, a remote village at the southern tip of Haida Gwaii, remained relatively untouched.

Today, the Haida number around three thousand, and are highly regarded in the North American art world; Bill Reid, Freda Diesing and Robert Davidson are among the best-known figures, and scores of other Haida artists produce a mass of carvings and jewellery for the tourist market. They also play a powerful role in the islands' social, political and cultural life, having been vocal in the formation of sites such as the Gwaii Haanas National Park Reserve and Heritage Site (p.885) and Duu Guusd Tribal Park (p.883).

Flights from Prince Rupert land at **Sandspit** (which has the islands' only airstrip) on Moresby Island. From there, there are regular twenty-minute ferry crossings to Skidegate (7am–10pm, 12 daily; $8 foot passengers, $18.50 cars, $2 kayaks or canoes, bicycles free); check with BC Ferries (Ⓦwww.bcferries.com) for current schedule and fares. Air Canada Jazz flies to Sandspit daily from Vancouver, while Pacific Coastal Airlines (Ⓦwww.pacificcoastal.com) flies to Masset from Vancouver daily in the summer and five times weekly in the winter. You could also go from Prince Rupert with North Pacific Sea Planes (Ⓣ250/627-1341 or 1-800/689-4234, Ⓦwww.northpacificseaplanes.com), which flies to Masset daily, to Sandspit three times a week and to Haida Gwaii on demand. Eagle Transit (Ⓣ250/559-4461 or 1-877/747-4461, Ⓦwww.qcislands.net/eagle) operates a **taxi** service and **airport shuttle** to and from the villages of Queen Charlotte and Skidegate.

Information related to tours, accommodation, attractions and getting around the islands is available from the **tourist office** on 3220 Wharf St (Ⓣ250/559-8316, Ⓦwww.qcinfo.ca) in the village of Queen Charlotte.

Transport on the islands

The easiest and cheapest way to get around the islands is by car – great if you've brought yours over on the ferry, but perhaps prohibitive if you have to rent. Rates run about $50 a day plus mileage. Budget (Ⓣ250/637-5688 or 1-800/557-3228) has offices in Queen Charlotte and at Sandspit airport, as does Thrifty (Ⓣ250/637-2299); in summer you'll need to have booked in advance to secure a vehicle at either. Rates at Rustic Rentals (Ⓣ250/559-4641 or 1-877/559-4557) and Island Auto Rentals (Ⓣ250/559-8415) in Queen Charlotte may be a touch lower than the main companies. If you're planning to drive logging roads (most of the roads are controlled by logging companies) ask at the visitor centres for latest access details.

There's not much for **bicycle** rental – your best bet is to inquire at the Eagles Nest Gallery (Ⓣ250/626-3233), on Main Street in Masset or *Dorothy and Mike's Guest House* (Ⓣ250/559-8439) on 2nd Avenue in Queen Charlotte.

To see the **Haida villages**, virtually all of which are on inaccessible parts of Moresby, you'll need to take a boat, and if you want to see **SGang Gwaay** in a day,

▲ Haida war canoes at a wedding, Haida Gwaii, BC

you'll need to take a pricey tour by seaplane. For flights and tours around Haida Gwaii, contact Inland Air Charters (Ⓣ250/559-8136 or 1-888/624-2577 or in Prince Rupert at 250/624-2577, Ⓦwww.inlandair.bc.ca) in Queen Charlotte, who'll take you out to the deepest backwoods, including Gwaii Haanas National Park Reserve.

Graham Island

Most casual visitors stick to **Graham Island**, where the bulk of the island's roads and accommodation are concentrated along its eastern side, between **Queen Charlotte** in the south and **Masset** some 108km to the north. These settlements and the villages in between – Skidegate, Tlell and Port Clements – lie along Hwy 16, the principal road, and shelter in the lee of the islands, away from a mountainous and indented rocky west coast that boasts the highest combined seismic, wind and tidal energy of any west coast North American coastline. Much of the east coast consists of beautiful half-moon, driftwood-strewn beaches and a provincial park where you can appreciate the milder climes produced by the Pacific's Japanese Current, a warming stream that contributes to the island's lush canopy of thousand-year-old spruce and cedar rainforests. On the downside, though, it drenches both sides of the island with frequent rainstorms, even in summer, so pack a raincoat.

Queen Charlotte

The island's second-largest settlement, **QUEEN CHARLOTTE**, is a picturesque fishing village and administrative centre about 5km west of the Skidegate ferry terminal. The village takes its name from the ship of Captain George Dixon, the British explorer who sailed to Haida Gwaii in 1787, thirteen years after first European contact was probably made by the Spaniard Juan Perez. Until fairly recently, when the logging industry went into steep decline, most of its residents earned a living from the timber companies, whose felling exploits have cleared most of the hills around the port. For a fine overview of the place, try the stroll to the top of **Sleeping Beauty Mountain**, reached by a rough forest road accessible by automobile from Crown Forest Road near Honna Road. Farther afield, you can drive to **Rennell Sound**, a west coast inlet with shingle beaches: take the main logging road north from the town for 22km and then turn left and follow the steep gravel road for 14km. The **Rennell Sound Recreation Site** offers paths through stands of primal rainforest to isolated sandy beaches and a couple of campsites with a number of popular beachfront wilderness pitches (free).

Otherwise, the town is the major place to sign up for any number of outdoor activities; contact the **tourist office**, 3220 Wharf St (May–Sept daily 8:30am–9pm; reduced hours in winter; Ⓣ250/559-8316, Ⓦwww.qcinfo.ca) and be sure to pick up the invaluable and free *Guide to the Queen Charlotte Islands*. The centre is also the place to organize **tours** to the Gwaii Haanas National Park Reserve and Haida Heritage Site (see p.885) as well as fishing, sailing, sightseeing and canoeing trips. They'll also have information on the free, basic campsites on Graham and Moresby islands.

Accommodation

Accommodation is scarce and demand is high in summer; book early or inquire at the tourist office, whose website also has an extensive accommodation list.

The Bunkhouse Campground Resort 921 3rd Ave Ⓣ250/559-8383, 206/259-6013 or 1-888/559-8383, Ⓦwww.islandsretreat.com. This hostel is about 2km out of town and is cheaper than *Premier Creek* but extremely basic. It has twelve dorm beds ($20) as well as 12 tent sites ($15).

Dorothy & Mike's Guest House 3127 2nd Ave Ⓣ250/559-8439, Ⓦwww.qcislands.net/doromike.

An intimate eight-room B&B that has a deck offering good views of the harbour, full cooking facilities and bike rentals. ❸

Kagan Bay Forest Service Campground Honna Forest Service Rd, 4km west of town. This BC Forest Recreation-run site has six lovely first-come, first-served beachfront pitches ($10), with picnic tables. There are pit toilets but no running water.

Premier Creek Lodging 3101 3rd Ave ⓣ250/559-8415 or 1-888/322-3388, ⓦwww.qcislands.net/premier. The first-choice hotel in town is a restored 1910 heritage building overlooking the harbour and Bearskin Bay; it has a small hostel at the back with a kitchen and dorm beds for $25. ❷–❹

Sea Raven Motel 3301 3rd Ave ⓣ250/559-4423 or 1-800/665-9606, ⓦwww.searaven.com. Overlooking Bearskin Bay, the 39 rooms here are rather plain, but perfectly suitable. Kitchenette and family rooms are available. There's also an on-site seafood restaurant. ❸

Eating and drinking

For **food**, locals make for the central *Ocean View Restaurant* (ⓣ250/559-8503) next door to the *Sea Raven Motel*, which serves a wide selection of main courses ($10–25), including plenty of fish and seafood. For great coffee, sandwiches ($6), sweet treats and internet, try the *Purple Onion Deli* at 3207 Wharf St, or cross the road for the equally welcoming *Queen B's*, a fine breakfast and lunch hangout serving savoury snacks ($5–16) and decorated with local art.

Skidegate

Ferries dock at Skidegate Landing, 2km to the south of **SKIDEGATE**. You can browse through the more accessible aspects of Haida culture at the **Haida Heritage Centre at Kaay Llnagaay** (open year-round, call for times; $12, tour extra $6; ⓣ250/559-7885, ⓦwww.haidaheritagecentre.com), located at Second Beach around 500m east of the ferry terminal. The centre – a series of longhouses fronted by totem poles – includes a canoe house, a restaurant, a performance space, an art and carving studio and a museum which, among other things, contains a comprehensive collection of the Haida's treasured argillite carvings. Argillite is a form of black slate-like rock found only on Haida Gwaii, and only in one site, whose location west of Queen Charlotte is kept a closely guarded secret. Also check out the platform here for viewing grey whales during their migrations (April–June). Ask at the museum about the **seafood feasts** held by the Haida Repatriation Committee in July and August and open to everyone for $50. At the canoe house you can view the famous *Loo Taas* ("Wave Eater") canoe, carved by Haida artist Bill Reid. It was made for the Expo '86 world fair in Vancouver and was the first Haida canoe carved since 1909.

About one kilometre up the road in Skidegate village, you can see another of Bill Reid's creations, the Dogfish Totem, that fronts a long house. Further along, you'll see the office of the **Haida Gwaii Watchmen**. Bands of "watchmen" were formed in the 1970s to protect aboriginal sites from vandalism and theft, and still exist today. A popular walk in the area is the **Spirit Lake Trail**, which winds through old growth forest and around two lakes; the trailhead is opposite the George Brown Recreation Centre on Hwy 16.

Tlell and Port Clements

You really can't miss the ranching community of **TLELL**, 36km north of Skidegate, which is spread out over a 5–7km stretch of coastline. Stop here and walk down to the sea, where you can stroll for hours on deserted wind-sculpted dunes; from here it is 90km along the unbroken beach to Rose Point, at the northeast tip of Graham Island. Tlell is a community favoured by craftspeople and alternative types – there's a handful of **galleries** concentrated along Richardson Road. Just north of Richardson Ranch on the main road is the rustic *Cacilia's B&B* (ⓣ250/557-4664,

Ⓦwww.qcislands.net/ceebysea; ❸), a renovated log house set behind the dunes on Hecate Strait. **Bikes** and **kayaks** are usually available for rent here.

Tlell is also at the southern border of the **Naikoon Provincial Park**, an enclave extending over Graham Island's northeast corner and designed to protect fine beach, dune and dwarf-woodland habitats. The park offers numerous trails along the beach and through the forests. **Campers** should head for the *Misty Meadows Campground* ($15; May–Sept) just south of the Tlell River Bridge and 500m north of the **park headquarters** (Ⓣ250/557-4390); backcountry camping is also allowed throughout the park. About 8km beyond, look out for the picnic site and trails at the southern tip of **Mayer Lake**, one of the nicer spots to pull over. The most popular hike is to the **shipwreck of the Pesuta**, which ran aground here in 1927; the trail starts at the picnic site just north of the Tlell River Bridge.

The road cuts inland for **PORT CLEMENTS**, 21km northwest of Tlell. In the past it was famous for the **Golden Spruce** tree, a three hundred-year-old bleached albino sitka spruce, sacred to the Haida; in 1997 a vandal chopped it down. A rare genetic mutation allowed the tree's needles to be bleached by sunlight and geneticists and foresters have produced a few trees now on display at the University of British Columbia and in California. A twenty-minute trail along the banks of the Yakoun River leads to a viewpoint where you can see where the tree once stood; the trailhead is six kilometres south of town along Bayview Drive, and ten kilometres further south – look out for the two hundred-year-old partially carved abandoned **Haida canoe** protruding from the bushes.

The one official **motel** is the twelve-room *Golden Spruce*, 2 Grouse St (Ⓣ250/557-4325 or 1-877/801-4653, Ⓦwww.goldenspruce.ca; ❸). For **camping**, the *Sunset RV and Campground* ($10–15; June–Sept) is at the south end of Bayview Drive. For **food and drink**, the main option is the *Yakoun River Inn* on Bayview Drive (Ⓣ250/557-4440), with meals around $15.

About 20km north of town on the road to Masset, look out for the signed **Pure Lake Provincial Park**, a good place to stop for a picnic along the shores of the lake.

Masset

MASSET, 40km north of Port Clements, is the biggest place on the islands, a scattered, rather ugly town – it's a former military base – of some one thousand people, most of whom are employed in the fishing industry.

The Masset **tourist office**, at 1455 Old Beach Rd (July & Aug daily 9am–5pm; Ⓣ250/626-3982, Ⓦwww.massetbc.com), has full details of wildlife and bird-watching possibilities. The **airport** lies two kilometres east of town.

The Town

Many visitors are here to birdwatch at the **Delkatla Wildlife Sanctuary**, a saltwater marsh north of the village which supports 113 bird species – contact Delkatla Bay Birding Tours (Ⓣ250/626-5015) for guided visits. Others come to wander the neighbouring village of Old Massett – with an extra "t" – 2km to the west, the administrative centre for the Council of the Haida First Nation and where some six hundred aboriginal people still live and work. Visitors should show respect when visiting totem sites, craft houses and community homes. Many locals are involved in producing crafts for tourists, or organizing wilderness tours, but some are restoring and adding to the dozen or so totems still standing locally (it's possible to visit various canoe and carving sheds). For more **information** on where to see carving and on the village in general, visit the Old Massett Council office on Eagle Road (Mon–Fri 9am–5pm; Ⓣ250/626-3337), where you should also enquire about permission to visit the **Duu Guusd Tribal Park**, established by the Haida to protect villages on the coast to the northwest. Two villages here are still active, and the park is used as a base for the Haida Gwaii Rediscovery Centre, which offers courses to children on Haida culture and history.

One of the more popular activities in Masset is to walk the trails around **Tow Hill**, 26km to the east of Old Massett along Tow Hill Road, in Naikoon Provincial Park. Three trails begin by the Hiellen River at the foot of Tow Hill itself. The easiest is the one-kilometre **Blow Hole Trail**, which drops down to striking rock formations and basalt cliffs by the sea. From here you can follow another path to the top of Tow Hill (109m) for superb views of deserted sandy beaches stretching into the hazy distance – on a clear day you can see Alaska approximately 75km away. The third track, the **Cape Fife Trail**, is a longer (10km one-way) hike to the east side of the island where there is a small, basic cabin (free). From here, it's a short jaunt northeast to Rose Spit, the twelve-kilometre finger of land that extends from Graham Island's northeasterly tip. It's an ecological and wildlife reserve of beaches, dunes, marsh and stunted forest, but it's also a sacred Haida site – it was here, according to legend, that the Haida's Raven clan were first tempted from a giant clamshell by a solitary raven.

Practicalities

For **accommodation**, the eighteen-room *Engelhard's Oceanview Lodge*, 1970 Harrison Ave (Ⓣ250/626-3388, Ⓦwww.engelhardsoceanviewlodge.ca; ❻) is a good choice, with a prime position on Masset Inlet. For a true escape, *Rapid Richie's Rustic Rentals* is a collection of off-the-grid beach cabins nestled in rainforest (Ⓣ250/626-5472, Ⓦwww.beachcabins.com; ❸–❹), 16km from Masset along Tow Hill Road. The only nearby **campsite** is the *Hidden Island RV and Resort* (Ⓣ250/626-5286 or 1-866/303-5286, Ⓦwww.hidden-island-resort.ca; $15–25) on Tow Hill Road, 2km north of town alongside the wildlife sanctuary. Further afield there's *Agate Beach* (Ⓔpark@mhtv.ca; $14; May–Sept), a provincial park site near trails and sandy beaches, 26km east of Masset off the secondary road towards Tow Hill.

For a pleasant place to **eat**, join the locals at *Haida Rose*, 415 Frog St (Ⓣ250/626-3310), which does coffee, pastries, soup and sandwiches. *Island Sunrise Café* (Ⓣ250/626-9344) and the nearby *SeaBreeze Restaurant* (Ⓣ250/626-3779), both on Main Street, offer delicious homestyle cooking.

Moresby Island

Moresby Island is all but free from human contact except for deserted Haida villages (one of which contains the world's largest stand of totems), forestry roads and the small logging community of **Sandspit**. The island's biggest draw is the **Gwaii Haanas National Park Reserve and Haida Heritage Site**.

Most locals here and on Graham Island work in Moresby's forests and consequently, the transport system is almost limited to **logging roads**. If you're driving on these, take extreme care and check in with the visitor centre for updated logging activity before setting out. It is highly advisable to rent a 4x4 to access these roads, but many rental agencies will have you sign a waiver stating you will not drive on the logging roads or beaches. Alternatively, if you're determined enough, you can sea kayak, mountain bike or backpack through the interior of northern Moresby Island, but you need to know what you're doing and be prepared to lug plenty of supplies.

Sandspit

Sandspit lies 15km from the **Alliford Bay** terminal for the inter-island ferry link with Skidegate on Graham Island. Seaplanes fly to Alliford Bay from Prince Rupert on demand. Sandspit's **visitor centre** is in the airport terminal building

(May–Sept daily 8am–5pm; ⓣ250/637-5362) and provides information for travel throughout Haida Gwaii.

Accommodation options include the reliable *Moresby Island Guest House* on 385 Beach Rd overlooking the ocean at Shingle Bay, 1km south of the airport (ⓣ250/637-5300; ❸), or the waterfront heritage home *Bayview Garden* (ⓣ250/637-5749 or 1-866/306-6644; ❸), with its three-bedroom cottage and tasty home-cooked breakfasts. For tenting, try the *501 RV/Tent Park* at 501 Beach Rd (ⓣ250/637-5473, ⓔrvpark@island.net; May–Sept; $10–20), but many people choose to sleep on the spit's beaches (not recommended due to the powerful tides): Gray Bay, 21km southeast of Sandspit, has primitive and peaceful **campsites** near gravel and sand beaches; contact the Teal Jones forestry offices on Beach Road (ⓣ250/637-5323) for details.

Gwaii Haanas National Park Reserve and Haida Heritage Site

Gwaii Haanas National Park Reserve and Haida Heritage Site, located on the southern portion of Haida Gwaii, is a 90km-long archipelago of 207 islands, some six hundred Haida archeological sites, five Haida Gwaii Watchmen village sites and 1750km of coastline. A 1993 agreement signed with the federal government gave the Haida joint control of this region and afforded protection to their ancient villages, traditional lands and resources, but some land claims to the region remain unresolved. You'll need money, time and effort to see the park reserve; there are no roads and access is by boat or chartered seaplane only, although experienced sea kayakers and boaters often travel here independently.

Visits to a variety of ancient **Haida village sites** and their totems and ruined dwellings are described here in order of distance (and therefore time and expense) from Sandspit. Closest is **K'uuna Llnagaay (Skedans)**, accessible on day-trips by boat from Moresby Camp on the Cumshewa Inlet, 46km south of Sandspit; access to the camp is by logging road. Farther afield are **T'aanuu Llnagaay, Hlk'yah GaawGa (Windy Bay)** – one of the main battlegrounds in the fight to protect the region in the 1980s – and **Gandll K'in Gwaay.yaay (Hotspring Island)**, whose series of outdoor thermal pools make it one of the most popular destinations. The finest site is the furthest away: **SGang Gwaay (Ninstints)** is close to the southern tip of the archipelago. Residents left around 1880 in the wake of smallpox epidemics and today it contains the most striking of the ruined Haida villages; its longhouses and many mortuary totems are a UNESCO World Heritage Site. In accordance with the wishes of the Haida, little attempt is made to preserve ancient village sites and, within decades, many of these decaying totem poles may have returned to nature.

Park practicalities

The easiest way into the park reserve is with a **tour**; contact the Queen Charlotte visitor centre (ⓣ250/559-8990, ⓦwww.qcinfo.ca or see www.pc.gc.ca/gwaiihaanas for details). Queen Charlotte Adventures (ⓣ250/559-8990, ⓦwww.queencharlotteadventures.com) and Moresby Explorers (ⓣ250/637-2215, ⓦwww.moresbyexplorers.com) offer good one-day and multi-day boat trips into the park. If you want to see SGang Gwaay in one day, the only option is with South Moresby Air Charters (ⓣ250/559-4222 or 1-888/551-4222) whose full-day joint flight and boat tours start from $310.

To visit the reserve as an **independent traveller**, you must make an advance reservation or obtain a stand-by space. Reservations can be made by calling ⓣ1-800/HELLOBC or 250/387-1642, but check ⓦwww.pc.gc.ca/gwaiihaanas for the latest information. There is a $15 per person reservation fee. If you choose not to make a reservation, then six stand-by places daily are available on a first-come, first-served basis from the Parks Canada office at the Haida Heritage Centre at Kaay Llnagaay in Skidegate. The **fee** to visit the park is $20 per person per day and $120 for a season's pass.

An **orientation session** is mandatory for all independent visitors entering Gwaii Haanas (those on guided tours will receive the information as they travel with their guides). Sessions take place at the Haida Heritage Centre at Kaay Llnagaay in Skidegate and at Sandspit airport; contact Parks Canada for updated times and locations (Ⓣ250/559-8818). Sessions last around ninety minutes and cover topics such as public safety, no-trace camping, natural and cultural heritage and the Haida Gwaii Watchmen Programme. Apart from some restricted areas you can **camp** where you wish; fees for camping are included in the park's general entrance fee. There are two **accommodation** options just outside the park's southern boundary: 10km from SGang Gwaay is the *Gwaii Haanas Guest House* (Ⓣ250/559-8689, Ⓦwww.gwaiihaanas.com; ❼), with four rooms in a family homestead (boat or seaplane access only) that lies in ancient rainforest with ocean views, organic food, sea kayak rentals, guided boat tours, birdwatching and other outdoor activity possibilities; or 12km west of SGang Gwaay is the equally delightful and rustic *Rose Harbour Guest House* (Ⓣ250/559-2326, Ⓦwww.roseharbour.com; ❺), at the site of an old whaling station. It offers organized tours.

The Stewart-Cassiar Highway

The 733km stretch of the **Stewart-Cassiar Highway** (Hwy 37) – from the Skeena Valley east of Prince Rupert to Watson Lake just inside the Yukon – is one of the wildest and most beautiful of any road in BC. Though less famous than the Alaska Hwy, the road is increasingly travelled by those who want to capture some of the adventure found on the wilder reaches of its better-known neighbour in the 1950s and 1960s. Some stretches are still gravel and the petrol and repair facilities, let alone food and lodgings, are extremely patchy: don't contemplate the journey unless your vehicle's in top condition, with two spare tyres and spare fuel containers. The road also provides a shorter route from Prince George to the Yukon than the Alaska Hwy.

The hwy has two main side roads worth exploring. The first goes to **Stewart**, with its exceptional sea and mountain scenery, where you can branch off and cross into Alaska at **Hyder**. The second goes to **Telegraph Creek**, a tiny riverside town reminiscent of the early 1900s. There are two additional rough roads midway up the hwy that lead to the wilderness of **Mount Edziza Provincial Park** and the **Spatsizi Plateau Wilderness Park**.

In summer Stewart is added to the itinerary of certain sailings of the Alaska Marine Hwy **ferry** service (see p.875) – albeit infrequently – so with careful planning you could travel overland to Stewart, or ride a boat to Ketchikan and thence to either Skagway or Prince Rupert.

The Stewart-Cassiar Hwy starts near Gitwangak (see p.873), one of several aboriginal villages off Hwy 16. Some hint of the sense of adventure required comes when you hit a section (47km beyond **Cranberry Junction**), where the road doubles up as an airstrip – planes have right of way. Almost immediately after you leave Hwy 16 the road pitches into the mesmerizing high scenery of the Coast Range, a medley of mountain, lake and forest that reaches a crescendo after 156km around **Meziadin Junction**, where Hwy 37A branches off; near here is the first formal place to **stay** – the 62-pitch *Meziadin Lake Provincial Park* **campsite** ($15; May–Oct) 67km east of Stewart and 156km north of Gitwangak.

Stewart

Some 67km west of Meziadin Junction is **STEWART**, Canada's most northerly ice-free port. Here a series of immense glaciers culminates in the dramatic appearance of the unmissable **Bear Glacier**, a vast sky-blue mass of ice that comes down virtually to the hwy and has the strange ability to glow in the dark. Stewart itself, 37km west of the glacier, is a shrivelled mining centre sitting at the end of the Portland Canal, the world's fourth longest fjord, a natural boundary between BC and Alaska that encircles the town with peaks (the ferry ride in from Prince Rupert through some of the west coast's wildest scenery is sensational). Dominating its rocky amphitheatre is **Mount Rainey**, whose cliffs represent one of the greatest vertical rises from sea level in the world.

The most interesting thing to do here would be to take Salmon Glacier Road out 5km beyond Hyder in Alaska to Fish Creek, where from the special viewing platform above the artificial spawning channel you may be lucky enough to see **black bears** catching some of the world's largest chum salmon.

Stewart's **visitor centre** is at 222 5th Ave near Victoria (mid-May to mid-Sept daily 9am–6pm; ⓣ250/636-9224 or 1-888/366-5999, ⓦwww.stewart-hyder.com).

Practicalities

The *King Edward Hotel*, 405 5th Ave (ⓣ250/636-2244 or 1-800/663-3126, ⓦwww.kingedwardhotel.com; ❸–❹) has basic rooms and offers units with kitchenettes in its *King Edward Motel* (❺) on the other side of the street. The nearest **campsite** is the *Rainey Creek Campground* on the edge of town on 8th Avenue (ⓣ250/636-2537 or 1-888/366-5999; May–Sept; $12–20); the tenting area is located across Rainey Creek, a pleasant little stream.

The *King Edward Hotel* is the town's main **pub**, **restaurant** and **coffee shop**; the heaving king crab feast for $40 is enough for two people. Visitors tend to prefer the pleasantly polished *Bitter Creek Café*, part of the *Ripley Creek Inn* complex, which offers an outside deck and a mouthwatering dinner menu that includes pistachio-crusted halibut ($20). For baked snacks, duck into the bakery and deli next door.

Hyder

Most people come to **HYDER**, Stewart's oddball twin, simply to drink in one or both of its two bars. It's a ramshackle place, barely a settlement at all, just 3km from Stewart across the border in Alaska. You'll encounter none of the usual border formalities since there's nothing beyond the end of the road but 800km of wilderness. People use Canadian currency, the police are of the Mountie variety and the phone system (and ⓣ250 area code) are also Canadian. At the *Glacier Inn* the tradition is to pin a dollar to the wall (in case you return broke and need a drink) and then toss back a shot of hard liquor and receive an "I've Been Hyderized" card. The result is many thousands of tacked dollars. It sounds a bit of a tourist trap, but if you arrive out of season there's a genuine amiability about the place that warrants its claims to be "The Friendliest Ghost Town in Alaska".

The community's little **visitor centre** is on the right as you come into town (June to early Sept daily except Wed 9am–1pm).

Practicalities

The town's two bars are often open 23 hours a day and a couple of **motels** are on hand if you literally can't stand any more: the *Sealaska Inn*, Premier Avenue (ⓣ250/636-9006, ⓦwww.sealaskainn.com; ❸) – which has one of the two bars – and the preferable *Grand View Inn* (ⓣ250/636-9174; ❸). They're both cheaper than their Stewart equivalents, and as you're in Alaska there's no room tax to pay.

If you want something to soak up the alcohol, make for the *Sealaska Inn Restaurant* (Ⓣ250/636-2486) for the artery-clogging deep-fried halibut ($14).

Iskut and Dease Lake

For several hundred kilometres beyond the Stewart junction there's nothing along the Stewart-Cassiar other than the odd garage, rest area, campsite, trailhead and patches of burnt or clear-cut forest etched into the Cassiar and Skeena mountains. Yet in places you can still see traces of the incredible 3060km Dominion Telegraph line that used to link the Dawson City goldfields with Vancouver, and glimpse a proposed railway extension out of Prince George that was abandoned in 1977.

ISKUT, an aboriginal village 225km north of Meziadin Junction, arranges tours into the adjacent wilderness parks, which are also accessible by floatplane from Dease Lake. For information, contact the Iskut Band Office (Ⓣ250/234-3331) or local stores and garages. Your best choice for local **accommodation** is the six-room *Red Goat Lodge* (Ⓣ250/234-3261, Ⓦwww.redgoatlodge.com; ④, tents $15.75, RV with hook-ups $26.25; late May to mid-Sept) with a 26-pitch campground 3km south of the village – they also rent kayaks and canoes starting at $15.

DEASE LAKE, 65km north of Iskut, has two **motels** – the *Northway Motor Inn* on Boulder Avenue (Ⓣ250/771-5341 or 1-866/888-2588, Ⓦwww.northwaymotorinn.bcnetwork.com; ③) and the *Arctic Divide Inn & Motel* on the hwy (Ⓣ250/771-3119, Ⓦwww.arcticdivide.ca; ③), still 246km from the junction with the Alaska Hwy to the north. You can **camp** at the *Boya Lake Provincial Park*, a lovely 45-site lakeside campsite 150km north of Dease Lake ($15).

The road from Dease Lake is wild and beautiful, the 240km to the Yukon border passing through some miraculous scenery. Much of this area was swamped with gold-hungry pioneers during the **Cassiar Gold Rush** of 1872–80. In 1877 Alfred Freedman plucked one of the world's largest pure gold nuggets – a 72-ounce monster – from a creek east of present-day **CASSIAR** (133km from the junction with the Alaska Hwy to the north). Today, the mining is of the asbestos variety, 5km from the village.

Telegraph Creek

For a taste of what is possibly a more remarkable landscape than what you see on the Stewart-Cassiar Hwy, it's worth driving the potentially treacherous 113-kilometre side road from Dease Lake to **TELEGRAPH CREEK** (allow 2hr in good conditions). This delightful riverbank town has a look and feel reckoning back to the early twentieth century, when it was a major telegraph station and trading post for the gold-rush towns to the north. The road navigates some incredible gradients and bends, twisting past canyons, old lava beds and touching on several **aboriginal villages**, notably at Tahltan River, where salmon are caught and cured in traditional smokehouses and sold to passing tourists. If you're lucky you might see a Tahltan **bear dog**, a species now virtually extinct; only ankle high, and weighing less than fifteen pounds, these tiny animals were able to keep a bear cornered by barking and darting around until a hunter came to finish it off. Telegraph Creek itself is a lesson in how latter-day pioneers live on the north's last frontiers: it's home to a friendly mixture of city exiles, hunters, trappers and ranchers, but also a cloistered bunch of **religious fundamentalists** who have eschewed the decadent mainstream for wilderness purity. Such groups are

If you're continuing north on the Stewart-Cassiar Hwy to **Watson Lake** and the Alaska Hwy junction, turn to p.893.

growing in BC's outback, a phenomenon that's creating friction with the easygoing types who first settled the backwoods.

Much of the village revolves around the General Delivery – a combined café, grocery and garage – and small adjoining **motel**, the *Stikine River Song Lodge* (Ⓣ250/235-3196, Ⓦwww.stikineriversong.com; ❸), whose rooms include kitchenettes. Enquire at the café for details of rafting and other trips into the backcountry.

The Alaska Highway: Dawson Creek to Whitehorse

Dawson Creek is the launching pad for the Alaska Hwy. While it may not be somewhere you'd otherwise stop, it's almost impossible to avoid a night here whether you're approaching from Edmonton and the east or from Prince George (409km to Dawson Creek) on the scenically more uplifting **John Hart Highway** (Hwy 97). The route from Prince George leads you out of BC's upland interior to the so-called Peace River country, a region that belongs in look and spirit to the Albertan prairies. Greyhound **buses** run two daily services between the two cities (9.15am & 11.30pm departures from Prince George).

The best part of the **Alaska Hwy** – a distance of about 1500km – winds through northern BC from Dawson Creek to Whitehorse, the capital of the Yukon; only 320km of the hwy is actually in Alaska. Don't be fooled by the string of villages emblazoned across the area's maps – only **Fort Nelson** is worth a stop; the rest are no more than a garage, a store and perhaps a motel. **Watson Lake**, on the Yukon border, is the largest of these lesser spots, and also marks the junction of the Alaska and Stewart-Cassiar hwys. Still, it's vital to book ahead for accommodation if travelling this stretch in July or August.

You need to adapt to a different notion of distance on a 2500-kilometre drive: points of interest on the Alaska Hwy are a long way apart, and pleasure comes in broad changes in scenery, the sighting of a solitary moose, or in the passing excitement of a lonely bar.

Highway practicalities

Food, fuel and lodgings are found at between forty- and eighty-kilometre intervals, though cars still need to be in good shape. You should drive with headlights on at all times and take care when passing – or being passed by – heavy trucks. The wilderness – anything up to 800km of it on each side – begins at the hwy's edge and unless you're very experienced, off-road exploration is not suggested. Free guides and pamphlets are available at visitor centres along the route through to Fairbanks, but *The Milepost* (Ⓦwww.themilepost.com), the road's bible, is, for all its mind-numbing detail, the only one you need buy.

From 1201 Alaska Ave in Dawson Creek, Greyhound **buses** depart in the morning and travel to Whitehorse. The twenty-hour trip finishes at around 3am, with only occasional half-hour meal stops, but covers the road's best scenery in daylight; check Ⓦwww.greyhound.ca or Ⓣ1-800/661- 8747 for latest schedules.

Dawson Creek

Except for a small museum next to the town's eye-catching red grain hopper, and taking the obligatory photograph of the cairn marking Mile Zero of the Alaska Hwy, there is one major attraction worth visiting in **DAWSON CREEK**. The

History of the Alaska Highway

The **Alaska Hwy** runs northeast from Mile Zero at Dawson Creek through the Yukon to Mile 1520 in Fairbanks, Alaska. Originally a military road, it's now an all-weather hwy travelled by bus services and thousands of tourists out to recapture the thrill of the days when it was known as the "junkyard of the American automobile". It no longer chews up cars, but the scenery and the sense of pushing through wilderness remain alluring.

In 1940 there was no direct land route to the Yukon or Alaska, other than trappers' trails. But when the Japanese invaded the Aleutian Islands in June 1942 – threatening traditional sea routes north and seemingly ready to attack mainland Alaska – it prompted the US and Canadian governments to build a road north. A proposed coastal route from Hazelton, BC was deemed susceptible to enemy attack, while an inland route bypassing Whitehorse and following the Rockies would have taken five years to build. This left the **Prairie Route**, which followed a line of air bases through Canada into Alaska.

Construction began in **March 1942**, the start of months of misery for the twenty thousand mainly US soldiers who had to ram a road through mountains, mosquito-ridden bogs and over icy rivers during harsh weather. Crews working on the eastern and western sections met at Contact Creek, BC, in September 1942 and completed the last leg to Fairbanks in October; this engineering triumph took less than a year but cost around $140 million.

By 1943 the road needed virtual rebuilding. For seven years workers widened it, raised bridges, reduced gradients, bypassed swampy ground and began removing some of its vast bends – the reason why it's now only **1488 miles** (2394km) to the Mile 1520 post in Fairbanks. All sorts of ideas have been proposed to explain the curves – including that they were to stop Japanese planes using the road as a landing strip. The hwy was opened to civilian use in 1948, but within months so much traffic had broken down and failed to make the trip that it was closed for a year.

The road is now widely celebrated, but there are aspects of its story that are glossed over. Many of the toughest sections were assigned to African-American GIs, few of whom received any credit. Aboriginal peoples on the route were also affected; scores of them died from epidemics brought in by workers. The building of the controversial **Canol pipeline** at the same time left the area littered with poisonous waste and construction junk. Wildlife also suffered, with trigger-happy GIs taking pot shots as they worked; the devastation of game populations was part of the reason for the creation of the Kluane Game Sanctuary, the forerunner of the Yukon's Kluane National Park.

Alaska Highway House (summer daily 9am–5pm; ⓣ250/782-4714; by donation), at 10201 10th St, showcases the history of the Alaska Hwy with interpretive exhibits and audiovisual displays. The **tourist office** (Jan–April Tues–Sat 10am–5pm; May daily 9am–5pm; June to early Sept daily 8am–5.30pm; Sept–Oct Tues–Sat 10am–5pm; Nov–Dec Tues–Sat 10am–5pm; ⓣ250/782-9595 or 1-866/645-3022, ⓦwww.tourismdawsoncreek.com) is at 900 Alaska Ave.

Practicalities

One of the nicer places to **stay** is the romantic *Granaries on Bear Mountain B&B*, 2106 Ski Hill Rd (ⓣ250/782-6302 or 1-888/782-6304, ⓦwww.thegranaries.com; ❼), a luxurious guesthouse with spa. The *Ramada Limited Dawson Creek*, 1748 Alaska Ave (ⓣ250/782-8595 or 1-800/272-6232, ⓦwww.ramada.ca; ❹), is also worthwhile for its countryside views. The nearest **campsite** is the *Mile 0 RV Park and Campground* (ⓣ250/782-2590; $20; May to mid-Sept), 1km west of the centre at the junction of hwys 97 North and 97 South, on the Alaska Hwy.

For something to **eat**, *Caruso's* at 1025 Alaska Ave (☎250/782-4938) has a mix of Asian and Western cuisine (mains $10) and does a popular lunch buffet. Join the locals at 10th Street's *Alaska Pub* for a drink.

Dawson Creek to Prophet River

It takes forty minutes before the benign ridged prairies around Dawson Creek drop suddenly into the broad, flat-bottomed valley of the Peace River, a canyon whose walls are scalloped with creeks, gulches and deep muddy scars. Just across the river is **FORT ST JOHN**, a charmless oil boom town dotted with flare stacks.

PINK MOUNTAIN, 226km from Dawson, with the *Pink Mountain Campsite and RV Park* (☎250/772-5133, ©lory@northwestel.net; $25) and its adjoining service station is a good place to stop for coffee and basic groceries. Thereafter, the road offers immense **views** of utter wilderness in all directions, the trees as dense as ever, but noticeably more stunted than farther south. Look out for the bright "New Forest Planted" signs, more often than not a token riposte from loggers to the ecology lobby, as they are invariably backed by a graveyard of sickly looking trees. If you're **camping**, look out for two provincial sanctuaries over the remaining 236km to Fort Nelson. Around 60km north of Pink Mountain is the *Buckinghorse River Provincial Park* campsite (May–Sept, $10–24); another 69km farther is the *Prophet River Provincial Recreation Area* with a campsite (May–Sept; $9) overlooking the river. This is good birdwatching country, but it's also good bear country, so be careful.

Fort Nelson

One of the hwy's key stops, **FORT NELSON**, is 381km north of Fort St John. This growing industry town exudes the opportunity the North represents, which also means it's a town in transition, with older buildings standing side-by-side with new hotels, restaurants and commercial developments. Much of life here revolves around exploitation of the area's huge natural gas deposits – the town has the world's second-largest gas-processing plant. A small **museum** devoted to the hwy's construction (mid-May to mid-Sept daily 8.30am–7.30pm; ☎250/774-3536, ⓦwww.fortnelsonmuseum.ca; $5) does a good job illustrating the town's frontier past.

The **visitor centre** is at 5500 50th Ave (late May to early Sept daily 8am–8pm; ☎250/774-6400, ⓦwww.tourismnorthernrockies.ca).

Practicalities

Fort Nelson has a large selection of **hotels** and **motels** established to service the burgeoning gas industry and the growing numbers of tourists. On the town's southern approaches the *Bluebell Inn*, 3907 50th Ave South (☎250/774-6961 or 1-800/663-5267, ⓦwww.bluebellinn.ca; ④), is better looking than many of the run-of-the-mill places and offers a full service RV facility.

For somewhere to **eat** and quaff a beer, try *Dan's Neighbourhood Pub* at 4204 50th Ave North.

Fort Nelson to Liard Hot Springs

This stretch is the Alaska Hwy at its best. Landscapes divide markedly around Fort Nelson, where the hwy arches west from the flatter hills of Peace River country to meet the northern Rockies above the plains and plateau of the Liard River. Once the road has picked up the river's headwaters, you're soon in some of BC's most

For details on taking the **Deh Cho Trail** from Fort Nelson along Hwy 77, see p.925.

grandiose scenery. The area either side of the road is some of the world's wildest – twenty million acres of wilderness – and experts say that only parts of Africa surpass the region for the variety of mammals present and the pristine state of its ecosystems. Services and motels become scarcer, but those that exist – though often beaten-up looking places – make atmospheric and often unforgettable stops.

The first worthwhile stop, a kilometre off the hwy on a gravel road, is **Tetsa River Regional Park**, about 77km west of Fort Nelson, which has a nice, secluded campsite ($14; May to mid-Sept) and appealing short hikes through the trees and along the river. Just down the road, *Tetsa River Outfitters* (ⓣ250/774-1005, ⓦwww.campbellriver-fishing.com/tetsa.htm) operates a small lodge and a full service campsite. **Stone Mountain Provincial Park**, 139km west of Fort Nelson, has a campsite (May–Oct; $14) which gives access to a short trail to two hoodoos (rock columns); the longer Flower Springs Lake Trail (6km), leads to a delightful upland mountain lake.

Toad River, 195km from Fort Nelson, has perhaps the best motel on this stretch, the *Toad River Lodge* (ⓣ250/232-5401, ⓦwww.toadriverlodge.com; ❸), with rooms and cabins offering superlative views of thickly forested and deeply cleft mountains on all sides. It also has a gift shop, petrol station and sites for tents ($15) and RVs ($25).

Muncho Lake, 260km from Fort Nelson, sits at the heart of a large provincial park whose ranks of bare mountains provide a foretaste of the barren tundra of the far north. There's a small motel and campsite at the lake's southern end, but it's worth hanging on for the popular *Strawberry Flats* or *McDonald Provincial Park Campgrounds* ($14; May–Sept), midway up the lake's eastern side, or the fine *Northern Rockies Lodge* (ⓣ250/776-3481 or 1-800/663-5269, ⓦwww.northern-rockies-lodge.com; ❺) for a choice of log cabins or camping and RV sites ($30).

Liard Hot Springs

About 70km beyond Muncho Lake is one of the most popular spots on the entire Alaska Hwy, the **Liard Hot Springs**, (ⓣ1-800/776-7000, ⓦwww.env.gov.bc.ca/bcparks; $5) whose **two thermal pools** (Alpha and Beta) are among the best and hottest in BC. They're reached by a short wooden boardwalk across steaming

▲ Liard Hot Springs

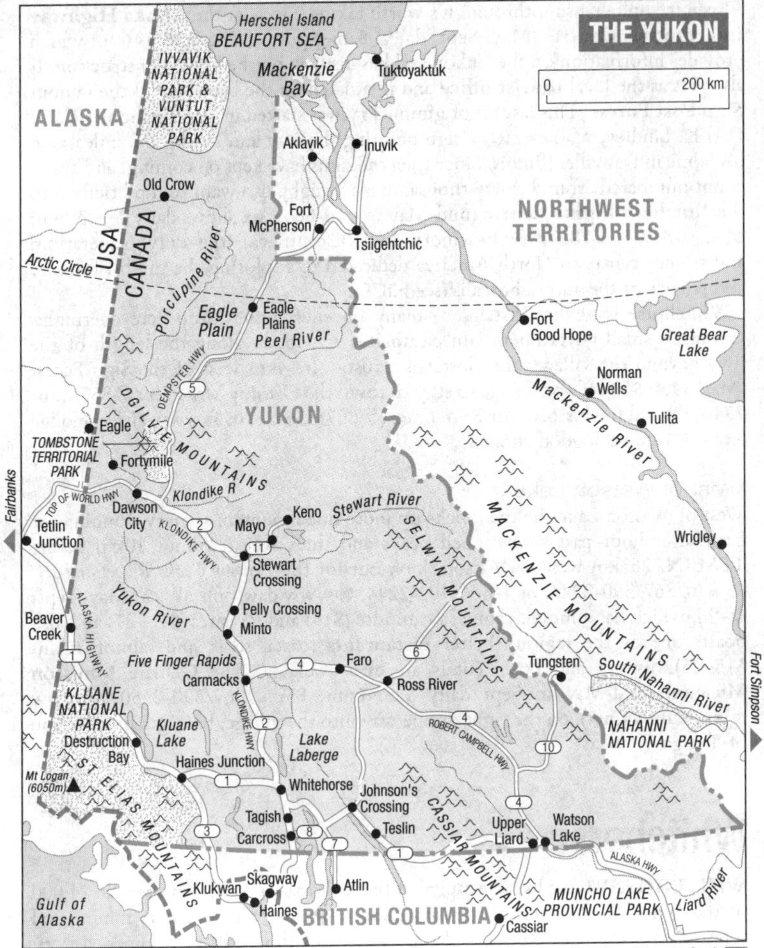

marsh, and are otherwise unspoilt apart from a wooden changing room and the big high-season crowds. As the marsh never freezes, it attracts moose and grizzlies down to drink and graze, and some 250 plant species grow in the mild microhabitat nearby, including fourteen species of orchid. The nearby *Liard River Hotsprings Provincial Park* **campsite** (May to early Oct \$19; early Oct–April \$15) is one of the region's most popular; for bookings see p.747.

Watson Lake

Beyond the Liard Hot Springs the Alaska Hwy follows the Liard River, settling into about 135km of unexceptional scenery before **WATSON LAKE**, just over the Yukon border. The town isn't big, but shops, motels and garages have sprung up here to service the traffic congregating off the Stewart-Cassiar and Robert Campbell hwys to the south and north, respectively. There's also some peaceful hiking trails and plenty of fishing and boating opportunities.

Even if you're passing through it's worth taking a look at the **Alaska Highway Interpretive Centre** (May–Sept daily 8am–8pm; ⓣ250/536-7469), which provides information on the Yukon and has displays on the hwy's construction. It also acts as the local **tourist office** and is situated on the hwy behind the famous **Sign Post Forest**. This last bit of gimmickry was started in 1942 by homesick GI Carl K. Lindley, who erected a sign pointing the way and stating the mileage to his home in Danville, Illinois. Since then the signs have kept on coming, and at last count numbered around thirty thousand. You might also want to dip briefly into the **Northern Lights Centre** (mid-May to mid-Sept, six shows daily 1–8.30pm; $10; ⓣ867/536-7827, ⓦwww.northernlightscentre.ca), the only planetarium and science centre in North America dedicated to exploring the myths, folklore and science of the aurora borealis (see p.870).

Whitehorse is 441km distant, so many travellers wisely stop here overnight. Countless small government-run **campsites** are dotted along the length of the hwy beyond the village; the closest is a rustic site 4km west of the Sign Forest (May–Oct; $12). If you decide to **stay in town** the *Gateway Motor Inn* (ⓣ867/536-7744; ④) and the historic *Air Force Lodge* (ⓣ867/536-2890, ⓦwww.airforcelodge.com; ③) are both good choices.

West of Watson Lake

West of Watson Lake the road picks up more fine mountain scenery, running for hour after hour past snowcapped peaks and thick forest. About 10km before **TESLIN**, 263km west of Watson, look out for the *Dawson Peaks Resort and RV Park* (ⓣ867/390-2244, or 1-866/402-2244, ⓦwww.dawsonpeaks.ca; May–Sept; ④-⑤), which has a motel, cabins, a campsite ($14) and RV sites ($16–27) and also boasts one of the region's better **restaurants** (pasta, steak and salmon mains $15–25); fishing and boat rentals are also available. The **George Johnston Museum** (mid-May to Sept daily 9am–6pm; $5; ⓣ867/390-2550, ⓦwww.gjmuseum.yk.net), on the right on the way into the village, has a good collection of Tlingit artefacts.

Whitehorse

WHITEHORSE is the likeable capital of the **Yukon** and home to more than 24,000 of the region's 33,000 inhabitants. It's also the centre of the Yukon's mining and forestry industries and a busy, welcoming stop for thousands of summer visitors. Although greater Whitehorse spills along the Alaska Hwy for several kilometres, the old **downtown** core is a forty-block grid centred on Main Street and mostly sandwiched between 2nd and 4th avenues. Though now graced only with a handful of pioneer buildings, the place still retains the dour integrity and appealing energy of a frontier town, and at night the baying of timber wolves and coyotes is a reminder of the wilderness immediately beyond the city limits. Nonetheless, the tourist influx provides a fair amount of action in the bars and cafés, and the streets are more appealing and lively than in many northern towns. One can easily spend a day or two here just wandering around, stopping at some of the excellent cafés, restaurants and pubs or taking one of the many short trips into the surrounding hinterland – either way, Whitehorse is an ideal place to recoup after a lengthy road journey.

A brief history of Whitehorse

The town owes its existence to the **Yukon River**, a 3000-kilometre artery that rises in BC's Coast Mountains and flows through the heart of the Yukon and

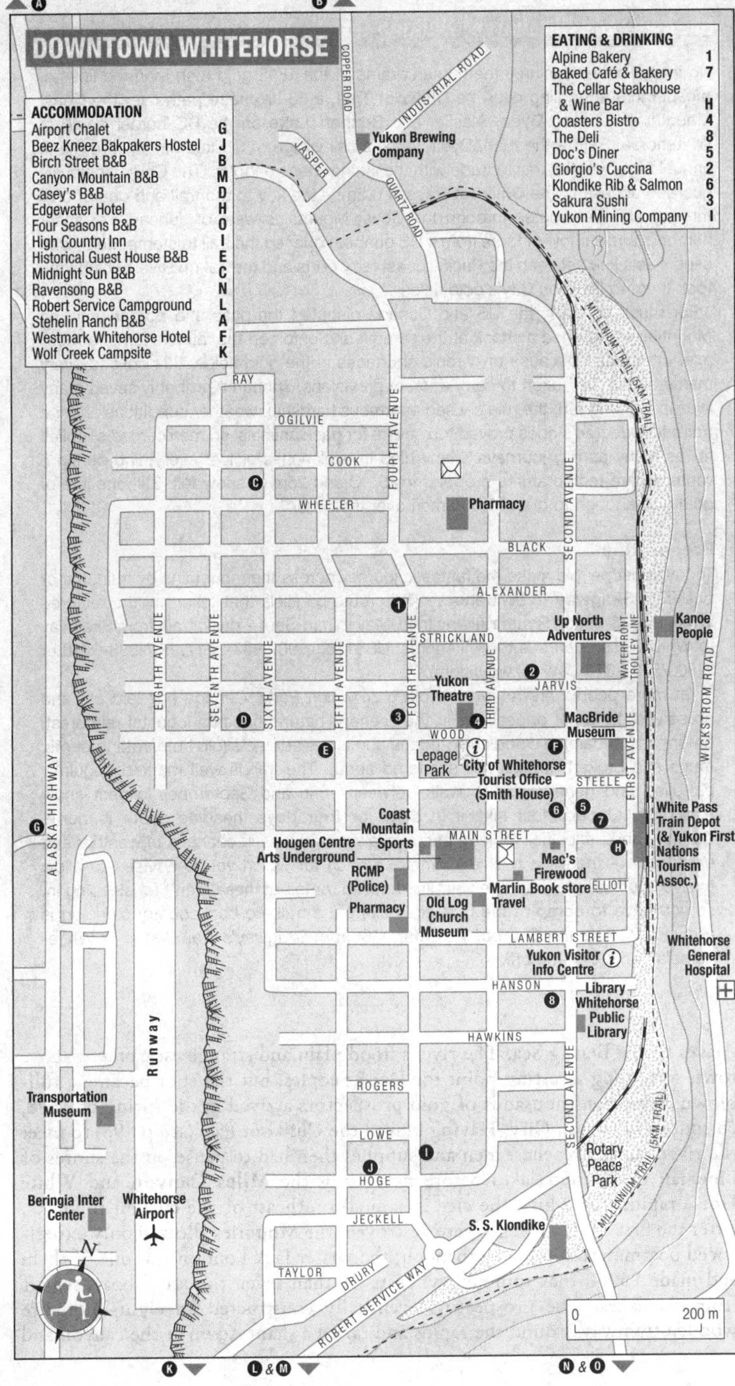

DOWNTOWN WHITEHORSE
ACCOMMODATION
Airport Chalet G
Beez Kneez Bakpakers Hostel J
Birch Street B&B B
Canyon Mountain B&B M
Casey's B&B D
Edgewater Hotel H
Four Seasons B&B O
High Country Inn I
Historical Guest House B&B E
Midnight Sun B&B C
Ravensong B&B N
Robert Service Campground L
Stehelin Ranch B&B A
Westmark Whitehorse Hotel F
Wolf Creek Campsite K
EATING & DRINKING
Alpine Bakery 1
Baked Café & Bakery 7
The Cellar Steakhouse & Wine Bar H
Coasters Bistro 4
The Deli 8
Doc's Diner 5
Giorgio's Cuccina 2
Klondike Rib & Salmon 6
Sakura Sushi 3
Yukon Mining Company I
Yukon Brewing Company
Pharmacy
Up North Adventures
Kanoe People
Yukon Theatre
MacBride Museum
Lepage Park
City of Whitehorse Tourist Office (Smith House)
Coast Mountain Sports
Hougen Centre Arts Underground
RCMP (Police)
Mac's Firewood
Marlin Book store
Travel
Old Log Church Museum
White Pass Train Depot (& Yukon First Nations Tourism Assoc.)
Yukon Visitor Info Centre
Whitehorse General Hospital
Library Whitehorse Public Library
Rotary Peace Park
S. S. Klondike
Transportation Museum
Beringia Inter Center
Whitehorse Airport
Runway
ALASKA HIGHWAY
ROBERT SERVICE WAY
MILLENNIUM TRAIL (5KM TRAIL)
WATERFRONT TROLLEY LINE
WICKSTROM ROAD
COPPER ROAD
INDUSTRIAL ROAD
JASPER
QUARTZ ROAD
RAY
OGILVIE
COOK
WHEELER
BLACK
ALEXANDER
STRICKLAND
JARVIS
WOOD
STEELE
MAIN STREET
ELLIOTT
LAMBERT STREET
HANSON
HAWKINS
ROGERS
LOWE
HOGE
JECKELL
TAYLOR
DRURY
EIGHTH AVENUE
SEVENTH AVENUE
SIXTH AVENUE
FIFTH AVENUE
FOURTH AVENUE
THIRD AVENUE
SECOND AVENUE
FIRST AVENUE
0 200 m

Skagway to Whitehorse: walking the Chilkoot Trail

No image better conjures the human drama of the 1898 gold rush than the lines of prospectors struggling over the **Chilkoot Trail**, a 53-kilometre path over the Coast Mountains between **Dyea**, Alaska, and **Bennett Lake** on the BC border south of Whitehorse. Before the rush, Dyea was a small village of Chilkat Tlingit, who made annual trips over the trail to trade with the interior Dene peoples. The Chilkat jealously guarded access to the **Chilkoot Pass** (1122m) – the key to the trail and one of only three glacier-free routes through the Coast Mountains west of Juneau. Yet sheer numbers and a show of force from a US gunboat opened the trail to stampeders, who used it as a link between the Pacific coast ferry ports and the Yukon River, which then took them to Dawson City's gold fields.

For much of 1897, the US and Canada disputed the pass and border until the Mounties established a shack at the summit and enforced the fateful "ton of goods" rule. Introduced because of chronic shortages in the gold fields, this obliged every man entering the Yukon to carry a ton of provisions. Though it probably saved many lives in the long run, the rule caused enormous hardship: weather conditions and the trail's fifty-degree slopes proved too severe for pack animals, so men carried supplies for as many as fifty journeys. Many died in avalanches or lost everything during a winter where temperatures dropped to -51°C and 25m of snow fell. Still, the lure of gold was enough to drag 22,000 men over the pass.

Preparation

Today, most people make the fantastic journey across the mountains by train, car or bus from **Skagway to Whitehorse**. This route parallels that taken by the restored White Pass & Yukon Route **railway** (mid-May to mid-Sept 2 daily; train from Skagway to White Pass, then bus to Whitehorse; US$116; ⓣ907/983-2217, 867/633-5710 or 1-800/343-7373, ⓦwww.wpyr.com).

Yet more people are **hiking** the old trail, which Parks Canada has laid out and preserved. Its great appeal lies in the scenery, natural habitats (coastal rainforest, tundra and subalpine woodland) and the numerous artefacts (old huts, rotting boots, mugs and broken bottles) still scattered about. The trail is well marked, regularly patrolled and generally fit to walk between June and September (expect snow throughout June); most hike it in **three or four days**, heading south to north. Dangers and difficulties include bears, avalanches, drastic changes in weather and exhaustion – there's a twelve-kilometre stretch for which you're advised to allow twelve hours. There are three warming huts en route but these aren't for sleeping in, so you have to **camp** at the nine sites along the trail: no backcountry camping is allowed. Pick up the *Chilkoot Trail* **map** ($6) from Skagway's Trail Center or Whitehorse's Parks Canada office.

Alaska to the Bering Sea. The river's flood plain and strange escarpment above town were long a resting point for Dene peoples, but the spot became a full-blown city when thousands of gold prospectors arrived in the spring of 1898, en route to Dawson City. Having braved the Chilkoot Pass (see p.896) to meet the river's upper reaches, men and supplies then had to pause on the shores of Lineman or Bennett lakes before navigating the **Miles Canyon** and White Horse rapids (for which the city is named) southeast of the current townsite. After the first boats through were destroyed, the Mounties allowed only experienced boatmen to pilot craft through; the writer Jack London was one of them and made $3000 that summer, when more than seven thousand boats set off from the lakes. The prospectors eventually constructed an eight-kilometre wooden tramway around the rapids and raised a shantytown at the canyon and

Reservations and permits

The number of hikers crossing the Chilkoot Pass into Canada is limited to fifty per day, of which 42 places can be booked in advance ($12) by calling the **reservation system** (℡867/667-3910 or 1-800/661-0486 between 8.30am–4pm;). The remaining eight places are offered on a first-come, first-served basis after 1pm on the day before you plan to start the trail. The busy season is July and the first two weeks of August; outside this time a reservation may not be needed. Order an advance **information pack** by calling the reservation system (see above), or by visiting either Ⓦwww.pc.gc.ca/chilkoot or the government offices in Whitehorse, at 300 Main St 2nd floor, Suite 205 Mon–Fri 8am–noon & 1–4.30pm.

You don't need a **permit** ($51) for day hikes on the US side, but you do for day hikes on the Canadian side, as you do if you're hiking the full length of the trail or even spending one night. Hikers need to go to the Skagway Trail Center on Broadway at 2nd Avenue (late May to early Sept daily 8am–5pm; ℡907/983-9234) to buy a permit and sign a register. Bring **identification** (a passport or enhanced driver's license for North Americans; a passport for everyone else); you may be required to deal with Canadian customs at the Chilkoot Pass ranger station, but you're more likely to do so at the Alaska–Canada border post at Fraser or in Whitehorse.

Transport and supplies

Dyea Dave (℡907/209-5031), Frontier Excursions (℡907/983-2512) and Klondike Tours and Taxis (℡907/983-2400) all run shuttle buses (US$10) from Skagway to the trailhead at **Dyea**, 14km northwest of Skagway. The trail finishes at **Bennett**, where you have a number of options: walk the 12km to the hwy at Log Cabin (there's a marked short cut off the trail which avoids Bennett but there is no signage once you reach the railway tracks) and meet up with Dyea Dave, Frontier Excursions or Klondike Tours and Taxis, who make pick-ups at the end of the trail (call to confirm; US$25); catch the daily service run by Yukon Alaska Tourist Tours (call to confirm; US$14–40; ℡867/668-5944 or 4414, Ⓦwww.yatt.ca) from Log Cabin to either Whitehorse or Skagway; or return to Skagway on the **WP&YR railroad**. In June, July and August the railroad offers the Chilkoot Trail Hikers Service (check for departure days and times ; US$50 one-way to Fraser, US$95 to Skagway, US$95 train and bus combo to Whitehorse), which comprises either a railcar, or one carriage of the Lake Bennett Excursion specially designated for smelly hikers. Buy tickets before the hike or you'll incur a $15 extra fee; for customs reasons the train doesn't stop at Log Cabin.

Besides the usual hiking equipment for a trip like this, also bring **nine metres of rope** to help sling your food and any scented items over the bear poles at each campsite.

tramway's northern head, allowing them to catch their breath before continuing to Dawson City.

The completion of the **White Pass and Yukon Railway** (WP&YR) to Whitehorse put this tentative settlement on a firmer footing and almost at the same time as the gold rush petered out. In the early 1900s the town's population dwindled to four hundred, down from ten thousand. A second boom came in 1942 when thousands of US Army personnel arrived to build the Alaska Hwy, a kick-start that swelled the town's population almost overnight.

Arrival and information

The **airport** (Ⓦwww.gov.yk.ca/yxy) is on the bluff above town, 5km west of downtown; the Whitehorse Shuttle Service ($10) meets all scheduled flights and services most downtown hotels (the service is complimentary for a couple hotels, including the *Westmark*.) Taxis (Ⓣ867/667-4111, 667-4888 or 393-6543) to the centre cost $12–15. The #2 Airport-Hillcrest-Lobird City Bus services downtown from the airport ($2.50).

The Greyhound **bus station** is at 2191 2nd Ave (Ⓣ867/667-2223), at the extreme eastern end of downtown. Buses to and from other destinations, notably those in Alaska, arrive and leave from a variety of destinations. See pp.902–903 for full details of all transport links. Drivers can pick up a three-day free parking **pass** from the City of Whitehorse **tourist office** at Smith House, 3128 3rd Ave (Ⓣ867/668-8687, Ⓦwww.visitwhitehorse.com).

Whitehorse's main downtown **tourist office** is on 2nd Avenue and Hanson Street (mid-May to Sept daily 8am–8pm; rest of year Mon–Fri 9am–5pm; Ⓣ867/667-3084, Ⓦwww.touryukon.com) and has information for the whole territory; pick up copies of the *Yukon Vacation Planner* and the *Visitor Guide* booklets, along with the *City Guides* to Whitehorse, Dawson Creek, Watson Lake, Inuvik and Haines Junction. For information on the Yukon's aboriginal cultures, head to the **Yukon First Nations Tourism Association**, in the White Pass and Yukon Route Train Depot at 1-1109 1st Ave (Mon–Fri 9am–5pm; Ⓣ867/667-7698, Ⓦwww.yfnta.org), and pick up a copy of the *Yukon's First Nations Guide*. For bookshops, see p.901.

For ferry reservations and **tickets** for local events, contact Marlin Travel, 2101A 2nd Ave (Mon–Fri 8.30am–5.30pm; Ⓣ867/668-2867). For information on car, bike, canoe, kayak and outdoor equipment rental, see p.901 & p.902.

Whitehorse tours, walks and boat trips

There are a variety of tours, guided walks and boat trips in and around Whitehorse, and all of them are great ways to get to grips with the city and its surroundings. For some insight into Whitehorse's history, try the 45-minute **downtown walking tour** (June–Aug Mon–Sat 9am, 11am, 1pm & 3pm; $4) offered by the Yukon Historical & Museums Association (Ⓣ867/667-4704, Ⓦwww.heritageyukon.ca), which departs from Donnenworth House at 3126 3rd Ave, next to LePage Park. Alternatively, join one of the free summer strolls organized by the Yukon Conservation Society, 302 Hawkins St (July & Aug daily; Ⓣ867/668-5678, Ⓦwww.yukonconservation.org), who offer two to six-hour walks that delve into the human and natural history of the city and territory.

A good self-guided walk is the route around **Schwatka Lake**, the trail for which begins from the bridge by the SS *Klondike*; the 5km paved, river-hugging Millennium Trail is also pleasant. Both trails take you past the **Whitehorse Fishway** (Mon–Fri June–Aug 9am–5pm; Ⓣ867/633-5965) the world's longest wooden fish ladder, complete with interpretive displays and three underwater windows where you can watch chinook salmon bypass a hydroelectric dam as they swim upstream. Another popular two-kilometre trail goes from the Robert Lowe Bridge (straddling the Miles Canyon, 9km south of Whitehorse) to **Canyon City**, a ghost town from the gold rush era.

Several **river tours** shoot the **Miles Canyon**. The building of the hydroelectric dam has tamed the rapids' violence and replaced them with Schwatka Lake and the two-hour narrated trip on the MV *Schwatka* (May–Sept daily 2pm; June–Aug also 4pm; $30; Ⓣ867/668-4716, Ⓦwww.yukonrivercruises.com) gives a better view of the river's potential ferocity and the canyon's sheer walls than the viewpoints off the road. Board at the dock above the dam about 3km down Canyon Road.

City transport

Whitehorse isn't that big and you'll easily be able to get around to see the central sites on foot. White Horse Transit (ⓣ867/668-7433) operates a bus service connecting the centre with the six suburban neighbourhoods, where you may need to go for some accommodation and restaurants; the fare is $2.50 (exact change only). Another good option is to **rent a bike**; Up North Adventures, 103 Strickland St, (ⓣ867/667-7035, ⓦwww.upnorthadventures.com) does half- and full-day rentals for $15–40, depending on the type of bike. Kanoe People, at Strickland Street and 1st Avenue (ⓣ867/668-4899, ⓦwww.kanoepeople.com), rents bikes starting at $30 per day and $180 weekly.

Accommodation

Whitehorse has a surprising amount of **accommodation**, but in high summer much of it is booked up in advance. If you arrive without a reservation, contact the visitor centre or try the string of **hotels** on Main Street between 1st and 5th avenues; for **B&Bs**, visit ⓦwww.yukonbandb.org. The town has a good private **hostel** and while the Wal-Mart car park is free for RVs, Whitehorse is not bereft of far nicer **RV sites** and **campsites.**

Hotels and B&Bs

Airport Chalet 91634 Alaska Hwy ⓣ867/668-2166 or 1-866/668-2166, ⓦwww.airportchalet.com. Directly opposite the airport and serviceable enough for its purposes. There is internet access in the lobby and a basic restaurant. ④

Birch Street B&B 1501 Birch St, Porter Creek ⓣ867/633-5625, ⓦwww.birchstreet.ca. A 10min drive from downtown this quaint B&B offers cosy, yet spacious rooms with private/shared bathrooms and has easy access to nearby walking or cross-country ski trails. ④

Canyon Mountain B&B 16 Harvey Place, Pineridge ⓣ867/667-7973, ⓦwww.canyonmountainbb.com. Quiet rural setting, 15min from downtown, with spectacular views of Canyon Mountain and friendly hosts. Next door to Meadow Lakes Golf Course. ④

Casey's B&B 608 Wood St ⓣ867/668-7481, ⓦwww.caseybandb.com. Two rooms in a downtown location with hearty breakfasts; kitchen and laundry facilities are available. Free internet access. ⑤

Edgewater Hotel 101 Main St ⓣ867/667-2572 or 1-877/484-3334, ⓦwww.edgewaterhotelwhitehorse.com. Good, high-priced hotel overlooking the Yukon River in the downtown area, with a bar and two popular restaurants. ⑥

Four Seasons B&B 18 Tagish Rd, Riverdale ⓣ867/667-2161, ⓦwww.4seasonsyukon.com. A relaxing and comfortable place to unwind after a lengthy road or river trip. Located less than a 5-minute drive from downtown, with three rooms (shared bathrooms). Dogs accepted. ④

High Country Inn 4051 4th Ave ⓣ867/667-4471 or 1-800/554-4471, ⓦwww.highcountryinn.yk.ca. A pleasant and easygoing hotel at the far western end of 4th Ave, a 10-minute walk from downtown, with a popular bar-patio. There's a wide variety of excellent room deals and weekly rates. Guests have access to free airport shuttle. ⑥

Historical Guest House B&B 505 Wood St ⓣ867/668-3907, ⓦwww.yukongold.com. This two-storey log home two blocks east of Main St was built in 1907 for Sam McGee and his family, the protagonist of a Robert Service poem (see p.912). A newer wing has more modern facilities, two double rooms and a suite, all with private bathrooms. ④

Midnight Sun Bed & Breakfast 6188 6th Ave ⓣ867/667-2255 or 1-866/284-4448, ⓦwww.midnightsunbandbyukon.com. This large home on the northern edge of town has a guest lounge and four comfortable en-suite rooms and serves up delicious breakfasts. Internet access also available. ⑥

Ravensong B&B 11 Donjek Rd, Riverdale ⓣ867/667-4059, ⓦwww.ravensongbb.com. Lovely three-suite setup in quiet residential suburb, 3min drive from downtown. Patio and bbq available as are jacuzzi, laundry and wi-fi. Discounts offered for multi-night stays. ④

Stehelin Ranch B&B 40 Couch Rd, Hidden Valley ⓣ867/633-6482, ⓦwww.stehelinranch.com. Located on the largest privately owned parcel of land in Whitehorse this is a superb place to relax and wind down in an attractive outdoor setting, with four comfortable private rooms. Twenty minutes' drive from downtown, shuttle service to city centre and airport available. ⑤

Westmark Whitehorse Hotel 201 Wood St ⓣ867/393-9700 or 1-800/544-0970, ⓦwww.westmarkhotels.com. If you want to see Whitehorse in style, this is the smartest and most expensive hotel in town. It has 181 rooms, a gift shop and restaurant. Deals are often available in the off-season. 6

Hostels and campsites

Beez Kneez Bakpakers Hostel 408 Hoge St ⓣ867/456-2333, ⓦwww.bzkneez.com. Cosy and friendly place at the western end of downtown (near the junction of 4th Ave and Robert Service Way), with a kitchen, laundry, internet access and free bicycle use. Dorms $26, private doubles $61.

Robert Service campground ⓣ867/668-3721, ⓦwww.robertservicecampground.com. A scenic twenty minutes' walk down South Access Rd, past the SS *Klondike* on the Millennium Trail. Set on the banks of the Yukon River, this site is specifically for tents and backpackers and gets very busy in summer. There are hot showers, clean bathrooms and freshly brewed coffee and baked treats are available daily. When the site is full, you could opt to pitch your tent in the woods above the lake, situated past the dam beyond the campsite or along the bluff above town by the airport. Sites $18, plus $3 for firewood. Mid-May to mid-Sept.

Wolf Creek campsite The nearest government campsite ($12), located off the Alaska Hwy 16km south of town. It has eleven tent sites, forty RV sites and there are no services, but wood and water are available.

The town and around

The main thing to see in town is the **SS Klondike** (May–Sept daily, tours every 30min Mon–Sat 8.30am–6pm, Sun 10am–5pm; $6; ⓣ867/667-4511). It's one of only two surviving paddle steamers in the Yukon, but is now rather sadly beached at the western end of 2nd Avenue at 300 Main St, although it has been beautifully restored to the glory of its 1930s heyday. More than 250 stern-wheelers once plied the river, taking 36 hours to make the 700-kilometre journey to Dawson City, and five days to make the return trip against the current.

The **MacBride Museum** (May–Aug daily 9.30am–5.30pm; call for winter hours; $8; ⓣ867/667-2709, ⓦwww.macbridemuseum.com), housed in a log cabin at 1st Avenue and Wood Street, is packed with stuffed animals, an old WP&YR engine, pioneer and gold-rush memorabilia, as well as hundreds of marvellous archive photos and a display on the Asiatic peoples who crossed the Bering Straits to inhabit the Americas; for an extra $5 you can try your luck at panning for gold. The **Old Log Church Museum** (mid-May to early Sept daily 10am–6pm; $3; ⓣ867/668-2555), 3rd Avenue and Elliott Street, is a modest museum devoted to the pre-contact life of the region's aboriginal peoples, whaling, missionaries, the gold rush and early exploration. For **free beer**, there are tours and tastings at the Yukon Brewing Co (daily tours in summer at 2pm; free; ⓣ867/668-4183, ⓦwww.yukonbeer.com) just north of Wal-Mart at 102 Copper Rd. You may find it easier to resist the widely touted Frantic Follies **stage shows** at the *Westmark Whitehorse Hotel* (late May–early Sept daily 8.30pm; $24; ⓣ867/668-2042, ⓦwww.franticfollies.com). These vaudeville acts of the banjo-plucking and frilly-knickered-dancing variety have been playing in town for around three decades.

Whitehorse has a thriving arts scene and **Arts Underground** (Mon–Fri 9am–5pm, Sat 11am–5pm; ⓣ867/667-6058, ⓦwww.artsunderground.com), 15-305 Main St, on the lower level of the Hougen Centre is a good place to view, buy and get the inside scoop on local artists. Northwest of downtown, the gallery at the **Yukon Arts Centre** (Tues–Fri 10am–5pm; Sat noon–5pm; ⓣ867/667-8485, ⓦwww.yukonartscentre.com), 300 College Drive, exhibits the work of regional and international artists.

Outside downtown, two of the most tempting attractions are up on the bluff above the town on the Alaska Hwy, close to the airport. One is the excellent **Yukon Transportation Museum** (mid-May to Aug daily 10am–6pm; $6, joint ticket with Beringia Interpretive Centre $9; ⓣ867/668-4792, ⓦwww.goytm.ca);

its displays, murals, historical videos, memorabilia and vehicles embrace everything from dog-sledding, early aviation and the construction of the Alaska Hwy to the Canol pipeline, the gold rush and the White Pass and Yukon Railway. Next door is the dynamic **Yukon Beringia Interpretive Centre** (May–Sept daily 9am–6pm; winter Sun 1–5pm; $6; ⓣ867/667-8855, ⓦwww.beringia.com). Beringia was the vast subcontinent that existed 24,000 years ago when the Yukon and Alaska were joined by a land bridge across the Bering Sea to Arctic Russia. The centre's interactive exhibits, films and displays explore the aboriginal history of the time. The flora, fauna and geology of that period are also covered and includes the remains of a 12,000-year-old mammoth.

Eating and drinking

Considering Whitehorse's size – and location – it has a remarkable number of very good cafés and restaurants; a similar sized city south of the 60th parallell might struggle to match the quality of what's on offer here, both in terms of food and the overall geniality you'll encounter on a night out.

Alpine Bakery 411 Alexander St ⓣ867/668-6871. The bread, pizza slices, soups, cakes and freshly squeezed juices are all made from organic ingredients at this popular bakery. Closed Sun & Mon.

Baked Café and Bakery 100 Main St ⓣ867/663-6291. Relaxed atmosphere and a selection of delicious home-baked goods, sandwiches, soups and gelato. It's also one of the best coffee bars in town, brewing locally roasted beans, and has a patio in summer. Free wi-fi. Mon–Sat 7am–6pm, Sun 8.30am–5pm.

The Cellar Steakhouse & Wine Bar At the *Edgewater Hotel* (see p.899). One of the town's best restaurants, serving solid staples such as ribs, steaks, salmon, Arctic char and lobster (mains $30–47). Closed Sun & Mon. The *Edge Bar and Grill* in the same hotel is open daily and has similar food but is less formal (mains $11–26) and serves breakfast.

Coasters Bistro 302 Wood St ⓣ867/456-2788. Quiet place to enjoy a burger, sandwich or soup along with a pint (mains $10–16); sit on the patio in the summer.

The Deli 203 Hanson St ⓣ867/667-7583. Grab a sandwich and a home-made cake or stock up on beef jerky or European meats and cheeses. Closed Mon.

Doc's Diner 2112 2nd Ave ⓣ867/633-6625. One of the few places in town offering an all day breakfast menu. Lunch and dinner meals also served.

Giorgio's Cuccina 206 Jarvis St ⓣ867/668-4050, ⓦwww.giorgioscuccina.com. Italian dishes (mains from $20) served in a setting with ancient Roman decorative flourishes.

Klondike Rib and Salmon 2116 2nd Ave ⓣ867/667-7554. An informal place for excellent fish and chips and northern specialities such as bbq salmon, caribou, bison and muskox (mains $15–30). Extremely popular for dinner. Closed late Sept to mid-May. Reservations recommended.

Sakura Sushi 404 Wood St ⓣ867/668-3298. One of a couple of Japanese restaurants in town serving tempura, teriyaki, sushi and sashimi dishes.

Yukon Mining Company At the *High Country Inn* (see p.899). Popular and lively, this pub has local brews by the Chilkoot Brewing Company and scrumptious bbq food on the deck in summer (mains $10–30).

Listings

Books Mac's Fireweed Books, 203 Main St ⓣ867/668-2434, ⓦwww.macsbooks.ca. Stocks an excellent range of Yukon books, guides, maps, nautical charts and pamphlets.

Car rental Budget, 4178 4th Ave (ⓣ867/667-6200 or 1-800/268-8900, ⓦwww.budgetyukon.com); Norcan, 213 Range Rd (ⓣ867/668-2137, 1-800/661-0445 or 1-800/227-7368, ⓦwww.norcan.yk.ca). Most agencies may have restrictions for taking cars on gravel roads. If you're driving the Dempster Hwy your best option is to rent an RV from Fraserway RV, 9039 Quartz Rd (ⓣ867/668-3438, ⓦwww.fraserway.com).

Currency exchange Marlin Travel 2101A 2nd Ave ⓣ867/668-2867 (Mon–Fri 8.30am–5.30pm).

Directory enquiries ⓣ411.

Emergency services ⓣ911.

Hospital Whitehorse General Hospital, 5 Hospital Road ⓣ867/393-8700, ⓦwww.whitehorsehospital.ca.
Internet Free wi-fi at *Baked Café*. All the hotels have some sort of internet access. The public library, at 2071 2nd Ave downtown, has free public access (Mon–Fri 10am–9pm, Sat 10am–6pm, Sun 1–9pm).
Laundry Norgetown Laundry, 4213 4th Ave.

Outdoor equipment and rental Canoes, kayaks, paddles and life jackets can be rented from Kanoe People or Up North Adventures (see p.899 for both). Canoe and kayak prices start from $35/day, $180/week at both outfits. For other outdoor gear, try Coast Mountain Sports, 208A Main St (ⓣ867/667-4074).
Tour operators/outfitters Kanoe People run multi-day guided canoe trips, as do Up North Adventures. The latter also offers riding and hiking

Transport in the Yukon and NWT

Whitehorse provides the main **transport** links not only to most other points in the Yukon, but also to Alaska and the Northwest Territories. Public transport will get you to surprisingly remote places, but times and schedules change; ask at the tourist office or call providers for the latest. We have arranged the information below alphabetically by destination from Whitehorse, unless stated. Local airlines also service many of the longer routes, such as Whitehorse to Inuvik.

Distances from Whitehorse

Anchorage 1165km
Beaver Creek 457km
Burwash Landing 285km
Carcross 74km
Dawson City 535km
Edmonton 2054km
Fairbanks 980km
Fort Nelson 946km
Haines 415km
Haines Junction 158km
Inuvik 1226km
Prince George 1880km
Seattle 2831km
Tok 639km
Vancouver 2702km
Watson Lake 455km

Transport options from Whitehorse

The best way to explore the Yukon is by renting a car or RV from Whitehorse (see p.901), but a handful of tour operators offer various bus/train combination packages to several locations throughout the territory and into BC and Alaska. All Alaska Direct Bus Lines services (ⓣ867/668-4833 or 1-800/770-6652, ⓦwww.alaskadirectbusline.com) originating in Whitehorse depart from 501 Ogilvie St.
Alaska Highway & Anchorage For westbound journeys, Alaska Direct Bus Lines runs services from Whitehorse (mid-May to Sept Sun, Wed & Fri departs 6am) to reach Haines Junction (2hr; US$75), Burwash Landing (4hr; $80), Beaver Creek (6hr; US$110), Northway Junction (7hr 30min; $120) and Tok (9hr; $135). See Vancouver (opposite) for details of Greyhound buses to Teslin, Watson Lake and points east on the Alaska Hwy. Alaska Direct also runs a service to Anchorage from Whitehorse (US$240) that leaves the Alaska Hwy at Tok.
Atlin (via Tagish and Carcross). The Atlin Express (ⓣ250/651-7617; $28 one-way, $56 return; 3hr 45min) leaves Monday, Wednesday & Friday at noon from the Greyhound bus station.
Carcross See Atlin and Skagway.
Carmacks See Dawson City.
Dawson City Alaska/Yukon Trails (ⓣ1-800/770-7275, ⓦwww.alaskashuttle.com) runs mid-May to mid-September from Whitehorse to Dawson (Sun, Tues & Fri) and from Dawson to Whitehorse (Mon, Wed & Sat), both routes with stops in Stewart Crossing, Carmacks and Braeburn Lodge (US$149/person, minimum 2 passengers); pick up is from the train station and any hotel, B&B or hostel. Up North Adventures (ⓣ867/667-7035, ⓦwww.upnorth.yk.ca) takes passengers from May–September when making weekly runs to pick up canoes and customers ($950 one-way for four), and stops in Carmacks, Pelly Crossing and Mayo.

excursions and winter tours involving dog-sledding, ice-fishing and snowshoeing; check their website or call for pricing details. Guided six-hour mountain bike tours (from $130) of the surrounding hills can be arranged with Boreal Mountain Biking (ⓣ867/332-1722, ⓦwww.borealebiking.ca), across the river at Km6 of the Long Lake Road. A variety of day or multi-day whitewater rafting trips (from $125) on the Tatshenshini River can be arranged at the Tatshenshini Expediting office (ⓣ867/663-2742 or 867/393-3661, ⓦwww.tatshenshiniyukon.com).

Trains White Pass & Yukon Route Railway, Suite 4 1109 1st Ave ⓣ867/633-5710, ⓦwww.wpyr.com.

Pharmacies Shoppers Drugmart, 211 Main St ⓣ867/667-2485;

Police ⓣ867/667-5555 (emergency only).

Post office 211 Main St ⓣ867/667-2485.

Fairbanks Alaska Direct Bus Lines runs three buses per week that connect Fairbanks and Whitehorse, with brief stopovers in Tok on Wednesday, Friday & Sunday. The bus departs Whitehorse at 6am and arrives in Tok at 2pm. You change bus in Tok and leave for Fairbanks at 2.30pm, arriving there at 6.30pm. Cost is US$200.

Haines Junction See Alaska Hwy & Anchorage.

Skagway The best way to reach Skagway and points between is to take a Yukon Alaska Tourist Tours bus, which departs from the old White Pass Railway building at 1109 1st Ave (mid-May to early Sept daily 8.30am ; ⓣ867/633-5710 or 1-866/626-7383 in Whitehorse, 907/983-2115 in Skagway; one-way/return by bus US$60/126; bus-train combination US$125 return; ⓦwww.yatt.ca); pick-ups at Carcross, Log Cabin and Fraser are possible and you arrive in Skagway at 11.20am (Alaska time). The return tours leave Skagway at 2pm (Alaska time), arriving in Whitehorse at 5pm (Yukon time). Gray Lines' Alaskon Express (May–Sept daily; US$50 each way; bus-train combination US$95 each way; ⓣ867/668-3225) run a similar service. The White Pass & Yukon Route rail/bus combination (May–Sept daily; one-way US$116; ⓣ907/983-2217 or 1-800/343-7373, ⓦwww.wpyr.com) departs Whitehorse at 8.30am and 1.30pm and arrives in Skagway four hours later – check website for current departure times.

Tok See Alaska Hwy & Anchorage.

Vancouver via Alaska Hwy, Watson Lake and Dawson Creek. Greyhound buses (ⓣ867/667-2223 or 1-800/661-8747, ⓦwww.greyhound.ca) leave Whitehorse Monday–Saturday at 2pm for Watson Lake and Dawson Creek, where you can pick up connections for Edmonton (29hr from Whitehorse; $285) and Vancouver (40hr from Whitehorse; $270).

Watson Lake See Vancouver.

Airlines in the Yukon

The Yukon has several **airlines** operating scheduled services and several more offering tours and charter flights only. The idea of chartering a small plane may sound expensive, but often the prices are not prohibitive – at least by the standards of land transportation costs in the region -- especially if you can get a group of people together. See p.868 for airline contact details.

Air Canada Daily direct flights from Calgary or Vancouver to Whitehorse.

Air North From Whitehorse: to Vancouver (daily, twice between Tues & Fri); Dawson City and Old Crow (Mon–Fri); Inuvik and Fairbanks (3 weekly); Calgary and Edmonton (3 weekly). Also from Dawson City to: Inuvik and Fairbanks (3 weekly); Old Crow and Whitehorse (6 weekly). Also from Inuvik to Old Crow (1 weekly). All routes also operate in reverse.

First Air From Whitehorse: to Yellowknife (3 weekly).

Charter airlines Alkan Air ⓣ867/668-2107, ⓦwww.alkanair.com; Alpine Aviation ⓣ867/668-7725, ⓦwww.alpineaviationyukon.com; Sifton Air ⓣ867/634-2916 or 1-888/634-2916, ⓦwww.yukonairtours.com.

Condor ⓣ1-800/524-6975, ⓦwww.condor.com. Runs a twice weekly (Tues & Thurs) service from Frankfurt, Germany to Whitehorse in the summer.

Kluane Country

Kluane Country is the pocket of southwest Yukon on and around a scenically stunning 491-kilometre stretch of the Alaska Hwy from Whitehorse to **Beaver Creek** at the border with Alaska. *Kluane* comes from a Southern Tutchone aboriginal word meaning a "place of many fish." Indeed, the area teems with fish, particularly at **Kluane Lake**, the Yukon's highest and largest stretch of water. Today the name is associated more with the all-but-impenetrable wilderness of **Kluane National Park**, a region containing the country's highest mountains, vast ice fields and the greatest diversity of plant and animal species in the far north. The park's main centre is **Haines Junction**, at the intersection of the Alaska Hwy and the Haines Road. Although motels and campsites dot the Alaska Hwy, the only other settlements of any size are **Destruction Bay** and **Burwash Landing** on Kluane Lake. Gray Line's **Alaskon Express** as well as **Alaska Direct** buses (see p.902) ply the length of the Alaska Hwy

Haines Junction

A small, modern village nestled amid some dramatic mountain scenery, **HAINES JUNCTION** is the biggest service centre between Whitehorse (160km away) and Tok in Alaska. There are a handful of overnight possibilities and lots of tour and rental companies for river-rafting, canoeing, fishing, hiking, cycling, riding and glacier flights in Kluane National Park.

It's also the national park's eastern headquarters and the combined **Parks Canada** (Ⓣ867/634-7207, Ⓦwww.parkscanada.gc.ca/kluane) and Yukon **tourist office** is in the Kluane National Park Reserve Building on Logan Street, just off the north side of the Alaska Hwy (mid-May to mid-Sept daily 8am–8pm; Ⓣ867/634-2345).

For cheap and central **accommodation**, local tour operator Paddle Wheel Adventures (Ⓣ867/634-2683, Ⓦwww.paddlewheeladventures.com; ❷), 113 Auriol St, rents two small but delightful cabins, complete with bunk beds and cooking facilities. The *Alcan Motor Inn* (Ⓣ867/634-2371, Ⓦwww.alcanmotorinn.com; ❺), on the junction of Haines Road and the Alaska Hwy, has rooms with kitchenettes. The *Raven Hotel & Gourmet Dining* (Ⓣ867/634-2500, Ⓦwww.ravenhotelyukon.com; ❻), just steps from the tourist office, has a restaurant that includes a German breakfast in its room rate. Foodies will love its elegant evening meals, rated some of the Yukon's best (try the elk), but these will cost around $80 each for three courses. The most central **campsite** is the *Kluane RV Kampground* (Ⓣ867/634-2709; $16.50–27.50; May–Sept), which has wooded RV and tent sites and laundry.

Kluane National Park

KLUANE NATIONAL PARK contains some of the Yukon's greatest but most inaccessible scenery within its 21,980 square kilometres, and for the most part, you'll only see and walk the easterly margins of this UNESCO World Heritage Site from points along the Alaska Hwy (no road runs into the park). Together with the neighbouring Wrangell-St Elias National Park in Alaska, the park protects the **St Elias Mountains**, though from the hwy the peaks you see rearing up to the south are part of the subsidiary Kluane Range. Beyond them, largely invisible from the road, are St Elias's monumental **Icefield Ranges**, which contain Mount St Elias (5488m) and **Mount Logan** (5950m) – Canada's highest point – as well as Mount Denali (Mt McKinley) (6193m), part of the Alaska Range and the highest point in North America; these form the world's second highest coastal range, after the Andes. Below them, and covering more than half the park, is a huge base of mile-deep glaciers and ice fields, the world's second largest non-polar ice field (after Greenland) and just one

Walking in Kluane National Park

Kluane has only fifteen maintained **trails** but experienced walkers will enjoy wilderness routes totalling about 250km, most of which follow old mining roads or creek beds and require overnight rough camping. Several signposted day and multi-day hike trailheads can be accessed from the hwy, each mapped on pamphlets available from Haines Junction visitor centre where staff also organize guided day-walks during the summer.

Six trails start from points along Haines Road, immediately south of Haines Junction. The path nearest town (7km south) and the most popular walk is the fifteen-kilometre round-trip **Auriol Trail**. The trailhead for the classic **King's Throne** walk (5km one-way) lies 27km south of Haines Junction. It's fairly steep, but offers spectacular views of Kathleen Lake; continue past the maintained trail to the summit of the mountain to be rewarded with views of the ice fields. The well maintained **Rock Glacier Trail**, 50km south of Haines Junction, is a twenty-minute jaunt to a view of Dezadeash Lake. For a longer trek, the **Mush Lake Road** route (trailhead 52km south of Haines Junction) is 22km one-way and part of the 85km of the Cottonwood Trail. North of Haines Junction, paths strike out from the Tachal Dhal (Sheep Mountain) visitor centre on Kluane Lake. The **Sheep Mountain Ridge** (11.5km) is a steep, hard slog, but offers good chances of seeing the area's Dall sheep. The longer **Slim's River West Trail** (22.5km one-way) is a difficult hike but lets you see the edges of the park's ice field interior. Backcountry permits ($10/night) are required for those planning **overnight** or multi-day hikes; register at the Haines Junction or Tachal Dhal visitor centres where you can also pick up a mandatory bear-proof food canister.

About 17km north of Haines Junction and just outside the park boundaries on the Alaska Hwy, the **Spruce Beetle Walk** is a two-kilometre interpretive loop trail taking in a patch of forest devastated by the spruce beetle. Thriving in the recent balmier winters, these persistent little borers operate like a slow motion forest fire and have infested and killed an estimated forty percent of the mature spruce trees in Kluane Country since the early 1990s. Look out for red pine needles – a sign of infestation; grey trees without needles have already succumbed.

permanent resident, the legendary **ice worm**. Yet global warming is taking its toll on the ice fields, with levels dropping by approximately 1.8 metres a year.

Unless you're prepared for full-scale expeditions, this interior is off limits, though from around $175 you can take plane and helicopter **tours** over the area; information on these and other guided tours is available from the Whitehorse and Haines Junction visitor centres.

At the edge of the ice fields a drier, warmer range encourages a green belt of meadow, marsh, forest and fen providing sanctuary for a huge variety of **wildlife**, including grizzlies, moose, mountain goats and a four thousand-strong population of white **Dall sheep**. These margins also support the widest spectrum of **birds** in the far north, some 150 species in all, including easily seen raptors such as peregrine falcons, bald and golden eagles, together with smaller birds like arctic terns, mountain bluebirds, tattlers and hawk owls.

Trails (see above) offer the chance to see some of these creatures, but the only **campsite** within the park accessible from the hwy is at *Kathleen Lake*, on the Haines Road 27km south of Haines Junction ($15.70); there is hotel and camping accommodation along the Alaska Hwy.

Kluane Lake

The Kluane region might keep its greatest mountains out of sight, but it makes amends by laying on the stunning **Kluane Lake** along some 60km of the Alaska

Hwy. About 75km northwest of Haines Junction, and hot on the heels of magnificent views of the St Elias Mountains, the huge lake (some four hundred square kilometres) is framed on all sides by snow-covered peaks whose sinister glaciers feed its ice-blue waters. It's not part of the national park, but the **Tachal Dhal** (Sheep Mountain) park visitor kiosk sits at its southern tip (mid-May to early Sept daily 9am–5pm). About 12km before the kiosk is the *Kluane Bed & Breakfast* (Ⓣ867/841-4250, Ⓦwww.kluanecabins.com; ④), with a self-contained chalet and four cabins on the lakeshore.

There are two settlements along the lakeshore, both good places to go boating or fishing and find accommodation. The first is **Destruction Bay**, where you can bed down at the *Talbot Arm Motel* (Ⓣ867/841-4461; ④), which also has a restaurant, café, store, petrol station and RV sites ($12). The best overall local **campsite** is the lovely Yukon government-run *Congdon Creek* ($12) site off the Alaska Hwy, 12km south of Destruction Bay; it's periodically closed during summer due to heavy bear activity. Otherwise, the picturesque *Cottonwood Park Campground* is just outside town and offers more facilities, including a hot tub, store, a log cabin for rent and tent pitches for $16 (Ⓣ867/841-4066, Ⓦwww.yukonweb.com/tourism/cottonwood; mid-May to mid-Oct).

The second town, **Burwash Landing**, is 15km beyond and holds The Kluane Museum (mid-May to early Sept 9am–6.30pm, $4; Ⓣ867/841-5561), with displays on Yukon wildlife and aboriginal history.

Beaver Creek and the US border

BEAVER CREEK, Canada's westernmost settlement, is the last stop before Alaska. The customs post is a couple of kilometres up the road and the border is open 24 hours a day. For full details on crossing the border, and what to expect on the other side, visit the **Yukon tourist office,** 1202 Alaska Hwy (mid-May to early Sept daily 8am–8pm; Ⓣ867/862-7321).

You may wish to **stay** at Beaver Creek, either at the *Westmark Inn* (Ⓣ867/862-7501 or 1-800/544-0970, Ⓦwww.westmarkhotels.com; ⑤; May–Sept), which also offers hostel-type rooms for $59; or the twenty-room *Ida's Motel and Restaurant* (Ⓣ867/862-7223; ④), a distinctive building across the hwy. The *Westmark* has a large, serviced **campsite** (May–Sept; $12), though they're happier to see RVs ($20) than backpackers (try free camping in the woods). There's a good but small government-run site 10km south at the *Snag Junction* (May–Oct; $12).

Those not pushing deeper into Alaska but looping to Dawson City have a great journey ahead: just before Tok, the **Taylor Highway** (Hwy 5) bears northeast off the Alaska Hwy back towards the Yukon border, passing through relatively unexceptional scenery until it hits the US–Canadian border at Little Gold Creek (May–Sept daily 9am–9pm). From here, the 105km road to Dawson City on the **Top of the World Highway** (see p.916) offers sensational views.

Klondike Highway: Whitehorse to Dawson City

Most people approach Dawson City on the Klondike Hwy from Whitehorse, a wonderful, lonely, 536km paved road running through almost utter wilderness. The hwy loosely follows the original winter **overland route** to the gold fields first utilized in 1902; it took five days to compete the chilly journey in horse-drawn stages, with the trip costing an extortionate $125 per person (passengers were also expected to carry enough overproof rum to keep the drivers sufficiently lubricated). Today, the drive takes little more than six hours, but you could easily stretch that out by allowing for frequent stops and a detour along the **Silver Trail** to explore the historic silver mining towns of Mayo and Keno.

Takhini Hot Springs and Lake Laberge

Eight kilometres from Whitehorse, take the turn-off for Hot Springs Road, which brings you ten kilometres later to the topnotch **Takhini Hot Springs** (June to early Sept daily 8am–10pm; rest of year Thurs–Sun only, call for hours; $9.50; ⓣ867/456-8000, ⓦwww.takhinihotsprings.yk.ca). The water in the large pool is a toasty 36°C. You can camp here ($16.50–35) and if you don't want to pay for the privilege of a hot soak, use the public pool at the outflow point in the stream below, which the locals have built.

Back on the hwy, the road carves through a wide, tree-covered valley where you'll catch bursts of purple fireweed flowers. Some 40km north of Whitehorse, the road bypasses the 50km-long **Lake Laberge**, immortalized in Robert Service's poem *The Cremation of Sam McGee*. There is a government campsite ($12) and beach here and the lake is popular for boating. Another 25 km on the road passes through the first of many forest fire-ravaged areas. The unfolding miles of black skeleton trunks from a 1998 blaze reveals how slowly the trees in these parts recover. Twenty-odd kilometres later, **Braeburn Lodge**, opposite the airstrip, is a good place for the massive **cinnamon buns** ($7) that have become de rigueur along this stretch.

Carmacks and Pelly Crosssing

CARMACKS is the first settlement of any note you'll hit. It has two petrol stations, a **visitor centre** on the eastern side of the hwy as you enter town (daily June–Aug 9am–7pm; ⓣ867/863-6271, ⓦwww.carmacks.ca) and a handful of accommodation options. The riverside *Coal Mine Campground* (ⓣ867/863-6363; $12) is at the junction of the Klondike Hwy and the **Robert Campbell Highway**, the latter a scenic gravel road winding 590km east to Watson Lake. Just after the bridge leaving Carmacks, the **Tage Cho Hudan Interpretive Centre** (Mon–Fri 8.30am–4.30pm, Sat 10am–4pm; ⓣ867/863-5830) has exhibits revealing something of the traditional lifestyle of the Northern Tutchone people.

About 25km north of Carmacks, it's worth stopping briefly at the lookout for the formidable **Five Finger Rapids**, formed by five huge pillars that divide the Yukon River into narrow channels. The rapids look benign from above, but many a stampeder lost his belongings and life here. A steep one-kilometre trail leads down from the lookout to the water's edge. Some 80km along the road at **PELLY CROSSING** look out for *Penny's Place*, whose burgers, ice cream and coffee are a favourite among hungry travellers. For camping, try the free *Pelly River Crossing Campground* before the bridge on the riverfront.

Stewart Crossing and the Silver Trail

The village of **STEWART CROSSING**, 60km north of Pelly Crossing, sits at the junction of the **Silver Trail**, a hwy which strikes off northeast for three historic silver mining towns that sprung up following the discovery of silver on Keno Hill in 1919. The first 62km of road is paved and there is a **visitor kiosk** (mid-May to Sept) just after the turn-off for the Silver Trail. The winding drive to Mayo passes through moose habitat and offers scenic views of the Stewart River, which once lured Klondike-area prospectors to the area in the early 1900s.

MAYO, 56km along, has a **tourist office** on the corner of Centre Street and Second Avenue (mid-June to early Sept daily 10am–6pm; ⓣ867/996-2926), in the same building as the **Binet House Interpretive Centre**, which gives a good overview of the area's history and geology. There are two motels here: the central, nine-room *North Star* at 212 4th Ave (ⓣ867/996-2231; ④), and the twelve-room *Bedrock*, 2km north of town (ⓣ867/996-2290, ⓦwww.bedrockmotel.com; ④), with tent ($15) and RV sites ($20).

Push on from here to tiny **KENO CITY**, a weathered collection of wooden buildings whose highlights include a mining museum (June–Sept daily 10am–6pm; ⓣ867/995-2792, ⓦwww.kenocity.info) and the Alpine Interpretive Centre (June–Sept daily 10am–6pm) which houses information and displays on area wildlife. Check out the house constructed with 32,000 beer bottles (the owner thought it would be good insulation). The *Keno City Campground* (ⓣ867/995-3101; $10), has a number of good hiking trails and panoramic views of the Ogilvie and Wernecke mountains from the signpost on Keno Hill.

Stewart Crossing to Dawson City

The scenery picks up considerably after Stewart Crossing for the last stretch of the Klondike Hwy, with wide views of sweeping valleys, rounded mountains and dense forest. Some 40km before Dawson City is the turn-off for the **Dempster Highway** (see pp.916–918). Just before Dawson City, the road wanders through tree-covered hills and then picks up a small, ice-clear river – the **Klondike**. The first small spoil heaps start to appear on the hills to the south, and then suddenly the entire valley bottom turns into a devastated landscape of vast boulders and

The Klondike gold rush

There was nothing quite like the delirium of the 1898 **Klondike gold rush**. Over 100,000 people are estimated to have left home for the region, the largest single one-year mass movement of people that century. About thirty thousand made it, with only four thousand finding some gold. A couple dozen of these made – and lost – huge fortunes.

The first to prospect near the Klondike River was dour Nova Scotian **Robert Henderson**, the very embodiment of the lone pioneer. In early 1896 he panned 8¢ worth of gold from a creek in the hills above present-day Dawson City. Considered an excellent return at the time, Henderson thought the creek would yield more and he panned out another $750 before returning downriver for supplies.

Henderson set about finding a route up the Klondike River to meet the creek he'd prospected. At the river's mouth he met **George Carmack** and two of his aboriginal friends, **Skookum Jim** and **Tagish Charlie**. Henderson told Carmack of his hopes, and then – glancing at the aboriginal pair – uttered the phrase that probably cost him a fortune: "There's a chance for you George, but I don't want any damn Siwashes [aboriginal people] staking on that creek." Henderson wandered off, leaving Carmack to prospect a different set of creeks – the right ones, as it turned out. On August 16, Skookum Jim found $4 of gold on **Bonanza Creek**, an unprecedented amount at the time. The next day Carmack staked the first claim and rushed off to register the find as Henderson prospected almost barren ground over the hills. Two weeks later, all of Bonanza had been staked. Almost all the real fortunes had been secured by that winter, when the weather effectively sealed the region off.

In the spring of 1897, a thousand-odd miners from the West Coast arrived, drawn by vague rumours of a big find. Yet the headlong rush that was to make the Klondike unique followed the July 1897 docking of the *Excelsior* in **San Francisco** and the *Portland* in **Seattle**. Few sights could have been so stirring a proof of the riches up for grabs as that of battered Yukon miners coming down the gangplanks dragging bags, boxes and sacks literally bursting with gold. The press were waiting for the abandoned workings. This continues for several kilometres until the Klondike flows into the much broader **Yukon River** and Dawson City comes suddenly into view.

Dawson City

Few episodes in Canadian history have captured the imagination like the **Klondike gold rush**, and few places have remained as evocative of their past as **DAWSON CITY**, the stampede's tumultuous capital. For a few months in 1898 this former patch of moose pasture became one of the wealthiest and most famous places on earth, as multitudes struggled across huge tracts of wilderness to seek their fortunes in the largest gold deposit of its kind of all time.

An ever-increasing number of tourists and backpackers are drawn here to explore the boardwalks, rutted dirt streets and dozens of false-fronted wooden houses; others come to canoe the Yukon River or travel down the Dempster or Top of the World hwys into Alaska and the Northwest Territories. After decades of decline, Parks Canada is restoring the town and has designated its relics into four **National Historic Sites**: the S.S. *Keno*, Dredge #4, the Dawson Historic Site (comprised of 26 buildings in town) and the Territorial Courthouse. That said, in a spot where permafrost buckles buildings, snow falls in late September and temperatures touch -60°C during winters, there's little real chance of Dawson losing the gritty, weather-worn feel of a true frontier town. Yet recently Dawson City has become somewhat of a cosmopolitan meeting place for the arts set. The Klondike Institute

Portland, which docked carrying two tons of gold – all taken from Klondike creeks by just a few miners. The rush was on.

Whipped up by the media and the Seattle and San Francisco outfitters, thousands embarked on trips that were to claim hundreds of lives. The most common route was to take a boat to **Skagway**, climb the dreaded **Chilkoot Pass**, pick up the Yukon River at Whitehorse and then sail 700km to **Dawson City**. The easiest and most expensive route lay by boat upstream from the mouth of the Yukon River in western Alaska. The most dangerous were the "All Canadian Route" from **Edmonton** and the overland trails through the northern wilderness.

The largest single influx came when the ice melted in **May 1898** and a vast makeshift armada drifted down the Yukon River. Once docked at Dawson City, the boats nestled six deep along a three-kilometre stretch. For most it was to have been a fruitless journey, every inch of the creeks having long been staked – yet in most accounts it's clear this was a rite of passage as much as a quest for wealth.

As for the gold, it's the smaller details that hint at the scale of the rush: the miner's wife who wandered the creek by her cabin picking nuggets from the water; the Great Depression destitutes who panned $40 a day from the dirt under Dawson's boardwalks; the $1000 panned during the Orpheum Theatre's rebuilding in the 1940s – all taken in a morning from under the floorboards where it had drifted fifty years before; or the $200 worth of dust panned nightly from a Dawson saloon's beer mats in 1897.

By about 1899 the rush was over – not because the gold had run out, but because the most easily accessible nuggets had been taken from the creeks. It had been the making of Alaska. Tacoma, Portland, Victoria and San Francisco all felt its impact. Edmonton sprang from almost nothing and Vancouver's population doubled in a year. It was the first of a string of mineral discoveries in the Yukon and the far north, a region whose vast, untapped natural resources are increasingly the subject of attention from multinational corporations as rapacious and determined as their grizzled predecessors.

of Art and Culture has a contemporary **art gallery** and an artist in residence programme that brings over eighteen international artists to town each year. In mid-July, the city hosts its annual Dawson City **Music Festival** (ⓦwww.dcmf.com), attracting scores of local and international musicians.

The city also comes to life in mid-August during the annual **Discovery Days Festival**, which marks the discovery of gold in August 1896. Activities include a parade and arts festival; book accommodation well in advance if visiting at this time. Check the ⓦwww.dawsoncity.ca for more information.

You could easily spend a couple of days here: one to explore the town, the other touring the old Klondike creeks to the east. If possible, prime yourself beforehand with the background to one of the most colourful chapters in Canada's history: Pierre Berton's widely available bestseller *Klondike – The Last Great Gold Rush 1896–1899* is a superbly written introduction to the period and place.

Arrival and information

Dawson City's **airport** is 19km southeast of the town on the Klondike Hwy. It's serviced by Air North, which provides links to Fairbanks, Whitehorse, Inuvik and Old Crow, and Alkan Air charter flights service Inuvik, Old Crow, Mayo and Whitehorse (see p.868 for contact details). Buses to Alaska generally arrive and depart from behind the visitor centre. There are no scheduled airport shuttles, but a handful of companies offer that service for $25 – ask for information at the tourist office.

The city's **tourist office** is at the corner of Front and King streets (second week of May & mid-Sept to late Sept daily 10am–6pm; mid-May to mid-Sept daily 8am–8pm; ⓣ867/993-5566 or 993-7200, ⓦwww.dawsoncity.ca) has a **Parks Canada** desk, shows films and houses historical exhibits. The **Dempster Delta tourist office** (mid-May to mid-Sept daily 9am–8pm; ⓣ867/993-6167 or 1-800/661-0750) is opposite and an essential stop if you're heading north on the Dempster Hwy (see pp.916–918).

Accommodation

In July and August it's pretty much essential to book **accommodation** in advance. Rates are high in the half-dozen or so mid-range establishments, most of which look like old-fashioned wood- and false-fronted hotels. Prices in all drop considerably outside the high summer period and many spots close between September and mid-May.

Hotels and B&Bs

Aurora Inn 5th Ave & Harper ⓣ867/993-6860, ⓦwww.aurorainn.ca. A colourful exterior, cheerful staff and eighteen immaculate rooms make this one of the best picks in town. ❻

Bombay Peggy's 2nd Ave & Princess St ⓣ867/993-6969, ⓦwww.bombaypeggys.com. Nine very comfortable and plush Victorian-style rooms in a central, heritage house of former ill-repute. ❻

Bonanza Gold Motel and RV Park 2km south of Dawson City at the Km 712 marker on the Klondike Hwy ⓣ867/993-6789 or 1-888/993-6789, ⓦwww.bonanzagold.ca. A variety of comfortable rooms and suites all with jacuzzi. Also offers a full-service RV site ($35). Laundromat and wi-fi. ❺

Dawson City B&B 451 Craig St ⓣ867/993-5649 or 1-800/697-6539, ⓦwww.dawsonbb.com. Cosy place in a beautiful setting overlooking the Klondike and Yukon rivers and within walking distance of all major attractions. Wi-fi available and free transport from the airport, bus station and waterfront. ❻

Eldorado 3rd Ave, at Princess ⓣ867/993-5451 or 1-800/764-3536, ⓦwww.eldoradohotel.ca. Much the same as the *Downtown*, with 52 central rooms, some with kitchenettes. ❻

Fifth Ave B&B On 5th Ave near the museum ⓣ867/993-5941 or 1-866/631-5237, ⓦwww.5thavebandb.com. A spacious house with shared kitchen and single, double or triple rooms, all with optional en suite. Look out for the electric-blue exterior. ❺

Klondike Kate's Cabins & Rooms 3rd Ave & King St ⓣ867/993-6527, ⓦwww.klondikekates.ca. Renovated, pretty and popular cabins. April–Sept. ❻

Midnight Sun Hotel 3rd Ave, at Queen ⓣ867/993-5495, ⓦwww.midnightsunhotel.com. Three buildings with a variety of comfortable guest rooms and suites, plus a restaurant. ⑤

Whitehouse Cabins Front St ⓣ867/993-5576, ⓦwww.whitehousecabins.com. Six waterfront cabins with kitchenettes at the northern end of the street beyond the *George Black* ferry. May–Sept. ⑤

Hostels and campsites

Dawson City River Hostel ⓣ867/993-6823, ⓦwww.yukonhostels.com. Across the river from downtown, 200m to the left of the ferry dock. An HI-affiliated collection of bunks in smart log cabins with a good view over town and the river. There are bunk rooms (members $18, nonmembers $22), tent sites ($14/person, $9/person for multiple-occupancy tents) and family and private double rooms (from $46). Amenities include wood-fired showers and stoves, canoe ($250/16 days) and bike rental ($20 /day), bus tours to the Arctic Circle marker and Tombstone Territorial Park and bus transfers to Whitehorse (on demand). No electricity. Cash only. Mid-May to Sept.

Gold Rush Campground 5th Ave, at York ⓣ867/993-5247. A bleak, fully serviced but busy place designed for RVs ($19-35). May–Sept.

Klondike River Campground A government-run site ($12) on the Klondike Hwy 15km east of town. While it's a bit quieter than the *Yukon River Campground* site, it's not as pleasant.

Yukon River Campground Across the river from downtown, 500m to the right of the ferry dock. The main town campsite for tents ($12), but there are no showers – the most central in town are at the *Gold Rush Campground*. Showers also available at the municipal swimming pool by the museum.

The Town

The town's biggest attractions are its **heritage buildings** (see below), but you should start any wander on **Front Street**, the leading edge of a grid running parallel to the Yukon River. Along this stretch and opposite the tourist office is the dramatic-looking **Dänojà Zho**, or "Long Time Ago House", also known as Tr'ondëk Hwëch'in Cultural Centre (June–Sept Mon–Sat 10am–6pm; by appointment rest of year; $5; ⓣ867/993-6768 or 993-7100, ⓦwww.trondekheritage.com), which uses exhibits, guides, videos and live demonstrations to explore the traditional and present-day culture of the Tr'ondëk Hwëch'in, the region's original aboriginal inhabitants. The local **museum** is also good for an hour or two but the atmospheric streets are the most compelling.

The heritage buildings

Fuelled by limitless avarice, between 1898 and 1900 Dawson exploded into a metropolis of thirty thousand people – the largest city in the Canadian West and the equal of Seattle and San Francisco in its opportunities for vice, decadence and good living. There were opera houses, theatres, cinemas (at a time when motion-picture houses were just three years old), steam heating, three hospitals, restaurants with French chefs and bars, brothels and dance halls that generated phenomenal business. Showgirls charged miners $1 – payable in gold or by purchasing an ivory

Distances from Dawson City

Anchorage 828km	**Haines Junction** 671km
Beaver Creek 415km	**Inuvik** 766km
Burwash Landing 587km	**Keno** 285km
Carcross 610km	**Prince George** 2416km
Dawson Creek 2007km	**Skagway** 716km
Destruction Bay 798km	**Tok** 300km
Fairbanks 631km	**Vancouver** 3191km
Fort Nelson 1524km	**Watson Lake** 991km
Haines 927km	**Whitehorse** 536km

▲ The Palace Grand Theatre, Dawson City

token from the bar – for a minute's dance. Cleaners panning the bars' sawdust floors after hours were clearing $50 in gold dust a night. Supply and demand made Dawson an expensive town: a single two-metre frontage fetched as much in rent in a month as a four-bedroom apartment in New York cost for two years.

Remnants of all this can be seen in the town's wealth of heritage buildings, two-dozen of which are under the stewardship of Parks Canada (see opposite for details). The exterior of all the buildings are easily seen on your own, as are the cabins that belonged to two chroniclers of the gold rush, poet **Robert Service** (cabin only open to the public on a limited basis) and the better-known **Jack London**.

The heritage buildings around town date from the earliest days of the rush but many of them have been destroyed by fire or permafrost. Most of these have been deliberately preserved in their tumbledown state. Elsewhere, restoration projects are in full flow, partly financed by profits from the town casino, which also funds the city's many visitor attractions. Permafrost precluded the construction of brick buildings with deep foundations, so restoration engineers have had to work doubly hard to save what are generally all-wood buildings, most notably the **Palace Grand Theatre** (1899) on the corner of 3rd Avenue and King Street. It's rumoured the theatre was originally built from the hulks of two beached paddle steamers.

Nearby, on the corner of King Street and 3rd Avenue, is the 1901 **post office**. On 3rd Avenue and Princess Street, **Harrington's Store** has a "Dawson as They Saw It" exhibition of photos (June–Sept daily 9am–4.30pm; free); near the same junction stands **Billy Bigg's Blacksmith Shop**; at 807 6th Ave is the cream-and-brown clapboard **Anglican Church**, built in 1902 with money collected from the miners. At 4th Avenue and Queen Street is **Diamond Tooth Gertie's Gambling Hall**, named after one of the town's more notorious characters, and still operating as the first legal casino in Canada – it's also the world's northernmost casino (see p.914). The **Firefighters Museum** in City Hall, across from the *George Black* ferry on Front Street, is also worthwhile, with a guided tour of old fire tenders, water pumps and other equipment. In a town built almost entirely of wood, these were once vital to Dawson's survival.

One of the town's more obvious old wooden constructions is the **SS Keno** riverboat, moored on the river just down from the tourist office. It was built in 1922 and ran up and down the Stewart River carrying ore from the mines around Mayo. Not all boats were as lucky as the *Keno*, and a short hike out of town will take you to a **ships' graveyard**. The improvements to transport links made many riverboats redundant and some were beached downstream. Cross the river on the free ferry, walk through the campsite and ten more minutes along the waterfront to reach the ruins of seven boats.

Parks Canada organizes programming for all its National Historic Sites, including a 45-minute walking tour taking in the S.S. *Keno* and the town's heritage buildings (June to mid-Sept several daily; $6.30 each, $13.70 for three; Ⓦwww.pc.gc.ca/dawson). You can enter seven or eight of the latter, usually as part of the tour; check the website for the latest details, as buildings may sometimes be closed for renovation work. Tour tickets are available at the Palace Grand Theatre (June to mid–Sept daily 9:30am–5pm); check there or the tourist office for up-to-date schedules.

The Dawson City Museum

The **Dawson City Museum** (mid-May to Sept daily 10am–6pm; $9; Ⓦwww.dawsonmuseum.ca) at 595 5th Ave is housed in the former Territorial Administration Building and has an excellent historical run-through of the gold rush from the first finds. Fascinating old diaries and newspaper cuttings vividly document the minutiae of pioneer life and events such as the big winter freeze of 1897–98, when temperatures reputedly dropped to -86°C. One of its highlights is the wistful, black-and-white film *City of Gold*, a wonderful award-winning documentary which first drew the attention of the federal government to Dawson's decline in the 1950s. Tours of the museum building are available – check with the visitor centre for times.

The Robert Service and Jack London cabins

The cabins of Dawson's two literary lions, Robert Service and Jack London, are only about 100 metres apart on 8th Avenue, about ten minutes' walk from Front Street.

Most Canadians hold **Robert Service** in high esteem and he has a place in the pantheon of Canadian literature. Verses like *The Shooting of Dan McGrew* and *The Cremation of Sam McGee* (see p.975) combine strong narrative and broad comedy to evoke the myth of the North. Born in Preston, England, in 1874, the poet wrote most of his gold-rush verse before he'd even set foot in the Yukon: he was posted by his bank employers to Whitehorse in 1904 and only made Dawson in 1908. He retired a rich man on the proceeds of his writing – outselling Kipling – spending his last years mainly in France, where he died in 1958. His **cabin**, which is a very accurate restoration, gives an idea of how most people must have lived once Dawson was reasonably established. During the summer people come here to pay homage and join a Parks Canada **tour** which includes a short reading of one or two Service poems (check at the visitor centre for times in July–Sept; $6.30 for cabin and recital).

The unexceptional-looking **Berton House Writers' Retreat** almost opposite the Service cabin was built in 1901 and was the home of another famous Canadian writer, Pierre Berton, until 1932. It now acts as a private retreat for Canadian writers.

Two blocks south is **Jack London's Cabin** ($5), an unpersuasive piece of reconstruction (logs from the original were separated and half of them used to build a cabin in Jack London Square in Oakland, California). London knew far more than Service of the real rigours of northern life, having spent time in 1897 as a

Other Dawson City activities

Dawson City itself has much to offer, but getting outside of town gives you the best idea of just how wild it was – and still is – here. Among the most popular activities are river journeys, including the Gray Line **cruise** on the 110-passenger catamaran *Yukon Queen II*, which in summer runs daily on the Yukon River to Eagle, Alaska, offering a day-long round trip of 170km for around $200 (bring your passport). Gray Line also run tours to the gold fields, rafting trips down the Klondike River and day-long bus tours along the Dempster Hwy to Tombstone National Park; tickets are available from the office at 902 Front St (Ⓣ867/993-5599, Ⓦwww.grayline.com). First Nations-owned Fishwheel Charter Services (Ⓣ867/993-5247) run intimate, two-hour boat tours up the Yukon River that take in a visit to a traditional fish camp; in the winter, dog-sledding and guided camping trips are offered. The *Klondike Spirit* is a side paddler offering afternoon and dinner cruises (June–Sept; $53–83); tickets can be purchased at the *Triple J Hotel*. Trans North Helicopters (Ⓣ867/993-5494, Ⓦwww.tntaheli.com) and Fireweed Helicopters (Ⓣ867/993-5800) run **helicopter trips** over the gold fields.

The *Dawson City River Hostel* and the Trading Post store on Front Street rent **canoes**. Both can give you information on good trips from Dawson City, including the float down the Yukon River to the abandoned gold mining town of Fortymile.

ferryman in Whitehorse before moving north to spend a year holed up on Henderson's Creek above the Klondike River. He returned to California penniless but loaded with material that found expression in *The Call of the Wild*, *White Fang* and *A Daughter of the Snows*. Alongside the hut there's a good little museum of pictures and memorabilia, where talks about London's life and work are given in the summer (hut and museum mid-May to mid-Sept daily 10am–6pm; $2; talks noon & 3pm).

Eating

There are numerous cafés around town, including several good snack places on Front Street. The most popular is *River West Bistro*, with good coffee, soups, sandwiches and cakes. The excellent *Klondike Kate's* (Ⓣ867/993-6527, Ⓦwww.klondikekates.ca; April–Sept), at 3rd Avenue and King Street, is the friendliest, most relaxed place in town for breakfasts and dinners (mains $18–25). The popular *Sourdough Joe's* on Front Street has mouthwatering fish-and-chips. Otherwise, most dining takes place in bigger hotels' restaurants. The *Jack London Grill* (closed Dec) in the *Downtown Hotel* (see p.915) and the *Bonanza Dining Room* in the *Eldorado* (see p.910); all serve seafood, pasta and steak (mains $20), while the *Drunken Goat Taverna* at 950 2nd Ave specializes in Greek food (cash only). The *Aurora Inn Restaurant* (Ⓣ867/993-6860, Ⓦwww.aurorainn.ca; May–Sept) at 5th Avenue and Harper Street serves an eclectic menu of global cuisine (mains $25–35).

Drinking and nightlife

Nightlife revolves around drinking in the main hotel bars, or spending an hour or so at *Diamond Tooth Gertie's Gambling Hall* at 4th Avenue and Queen Street, Canada's oldest legal gambling hall (mid-May to mid-Sept daily 7pm–2am & Fri–Sun opens at 2pm; $6); you need to be over 19 to gamble and all proceeds from here and several other town sights go to the maintenance of the visitor attractions and to the community of Dawson. Three times a night, a singer and can-can girls grace the stage for some over-the-top knicker-flashing, tap-dancing and titillating audience interaction. If you want a taste of a real northern **bar**, try the *Westminster* on 2nd Avenue: it's full of grizzled characters and most certainly not the place for a quiet drink or the faint-hearted. It hosts live music most nights. Other hotel bars provide more sedate alternatives, among which the lounge at *Bombay Peggy's* hotel on 2nd Avenue and Princess Street stands out for its fine atmosphere. The *Sourdough Saloon* at the *Downtown Hotel*, 2nd Avenue and Queen Street is popular with locals and visitors alike, and known for a cocktail that involves a real pickled human toe.

Listings

Books Maximilian's ☎867/993-5486, on the corner of Front & Queen.
Currency exchange and ATM CIBC Queen St, between Front & 2nd ☎867/993-5447.
Internet Free at the public library on 5th Ave and Queen St (June to mid-Aug Tues–Fri 12noon–8pm, Sat 10am–5.30pm; mid-Aug to May Tues–Thurs noon–7.30pm, Fri noon–5.30pm, Sat 10am–5.30pm); Downtown Hotel ($6/hr or $10.50/day); Eldorado Hotel ($6.30/hr) and at Tasty Byte Internet Café on Front St (daily 7.30am–7pm, $3/30min).
Post office 3rd Ave between King and Queen sts (Mon–Fri 8.30am–5.30pm, Sat 11.30am–2.30pm).
Taxi Dee Cee Taxi (☎867/993-3871) $8 in town or $25 to Midnight Dome.

Around Dawson City

Make a point of seeing the two creeks where it all started and where most of the gold was mined – **Bonanza and Eldorado**, both over 20km away from Dawson City along rough roads to the southeast. Today, no big working mine survives in the region, though most of the claims are still owned and definitely out of bounds to amateurs. Another popular local excursion is to **Midnight Dome**, the gouged-out hill behind the town, while farther afield numerous RVs, cyclists and hitchhikers follow the **Top of the World Highway**, which runs on beyond the Alaskan border to link with the Alaska Hwy at Tetlin Junction.

Bonanza and Eldorado creeks

To reach **Bonanza Creek**, follow the Klondike Hwy – the continuation of Front Street – for 4km to the junction with Bonanza Creek Road. The road threads through scenes of apocalyptic piles of boulders and river gravel for some 12km until it comes to a simple cairn marking **Discovery Claim**, the spot staked by George Carmack after pulling out a nugget the size of his thumb. Every 150m along the creek in front of you – the width of a claim – was to yield some 3000kg of gold, about $25 million in 1900 prices.

At Discovery Claim the road forks again, one spur running east up **Eldorado Creek**, the other following Upper Bonanza Road to the summit of **King Solomon's Dome**, where you can look down over smaller scarred rivulets, before returning in a loop to the Klondike Hwy via Hunker Road. As time passed and the easily reached gold was exploited, miners increasingly consolidated claims or sold out to large companies who installed dredges capable of clawing out the bedrock

Dawson City to Alaska or Inuvik

If you're making for Alaska – and Fairbanks in particular – from Dawson City you can take an Alaska/Yukon Trails bus (☎1-800/770-7275, ⓦwww.alaskashuttle.com), which leaves the Dawson City visitor centre at 8am on Sunday, Wednesday & Friday and arrives in Fairbanks at 6.15pm. The cost is US$155.

Inuvik MGM Services (☎867/777-4295, 678-0129 or 678-0139) runs a bus down the Dempster Hwy from Inuvik to Whitehorse ($280 one-way) via Dawson City ($250 one-way) and back. Call for a reservation but note this is an on demand service only and a minimum of eight passengers required.

and gravel. Numerous examples of these industrial dinosaurs litter the creeks, but the largest and most famous is the 1912 **No. 4 Dredge** at Claim 17 BD ("Below Discovery") off Bonanza Creek Road, an extraordinary piece of industrial archeology that from the start of operations in 1913 until 1966 dug up as much as 25kg of gold a day. Modern mines are lucky to produce a quarter of that amount in a week. Tours are available daily on the hour; check at tourist office or Palace Grand for a current schedule.

Without a car or bike you'll have to join up with one of the various **gold-field tours** (from about $40 for a 90min tour) run by either Gray Line or Gold Bottom Mine Tours on Front Street (Ⓣ867/993-5750, Ⓦwww.goldbottom.com). The only place you can pan for free is on Claim 6 in Bonanza Creek, 1km down from Discovery Claim. Gold Bottom Creek at the still-operating Gold Bottom Mine also offers a creek panning experience for $20. Alternatively, nearby at Claim 33 you can pan flakes from a water trough for $11 and guarantee finding gold – because it's been put there; ask the tourist office for directions.

Midnight Dome and Top of the World Highway

The **Midnight Dome** is the distinctive hill rearing up behind Dawson City, half-covered in stunted pines and half-eaten away by landslips. From its summit at midnight on June 21 you can watch the sun dip to the horizon before immediately rising again – Dawson being only 300km south of the Arctic Circle. The Midnight Dome Road runs 8km to the summit (884m) from the Klondike Hwy just outside of town. Without a car it's an extremely steep haul (ask at the tourist office for details of the trail), but more than worth the slog for the massive views over Dawson, the gold fields, the Yukon River's broad meanders and the ranks of mountains stretching away in all directions.

Another popular hike is to **Moosehide**, an aboriginal summer settlement about 7km north of Dawson City, but before entering the village you'll need to obtain a permit from the Tr'ondëk Hwëch'in office (see p.911); access to the settlement is by foot or boat only.

You can snatch further broad vistas from the **Top of the World Highway** (Hwy 9), a summer-only gravel road reached across the Yukon River by the *George Black* **ferry** from Front Street (mid-May to mid-Sept daily 24hr; rest of year 7am–11pm, depending on whether the river is frozen; free; Ⓣ867/993-5441). After 5km the road reaches a great panorama over the area and after 14km another **viewpoint** looks out over the Yukon Valley and the **Ogilvie Mountains** straddling the Arctic Circle; in late summer, many people pile out of their cars around here to pick **wild blueberries**. The road continues above the tree line as a massive belvedere and can be seen switchbacking over barren ridges into the distance. It hits the **Alaska border** 108km from Dawson, where you can cross only when the customs post is open (mid-May to mid-Sept 9am–9pm). Be prepared to do only about 50kph, and ask at the Dawson tourist office about local difficulties and fuel availability.

The Dempster Highway

Begun in 1959 to service northern oilfields, and completed over twenty years later – by which time all the accessible oil had been siphoned off – the 741-kilometre **Dempster Highway** between Dawson City and Inuvik in the Northwest Territories is the only road in Canada to cross the **Arctic Circle**. This route offers a tremendous journey through a superb and ever-changing spectrum of landscapes – mountains, open tundra, rivers, bogs, thousands of

Dempster Highway practicalities

If you're **cycling** or motorbiking – increasingly popular ways of doing the trip – be prepared for rough camping and call at the **Dempster Delta tourist office** (see p.910) in Dawson City for information and pick up a free copy of *The Dempster Highway Travelogue*, which outlines a detailed account of the journey ahead. If you're without your own transport you might pick up a **lift** here, or take the **bus service** run by MGM Services, which only operates on demand (see p.915).

The first **fuel** stop is at the start of the hwy at the *Klondike River Lodge* (daily 6am–10pm; ⓣ867/993-6892; ④); the next is 365km north at the *Eagle Plains Hotel and Service Station* (see p.918). After that it's 193km to Fort McPherson and thereafter there's nothing until Inuvik; take a jerry can (rent them at the *Klondike River Lodge*) and make sure you have two spare tyres and your car is in good condition – the only maintenance facilities are at Eagle Plains. It's worth checking on ⓣ1-800/661-0750 that the two **ferry** services on the route at Peel River (539km; free on demand, spring to late autumn daily 9.30am–12.30am, then ice bridge) and Tsiigehtchic (609km; same details) are running.

wandering caribou and millions of migrating birds. In June the landscape bursts into colour as scores of tiny arctic plants suddenly bloom en masse, while in late August the tundra is ablaze in the most intense hues of red, yellow and orange imaginable. It's also hard to resist the temptation of crossing into the Arctic 445km north of Dawson City, a section that takes you over the most captivating stretch of hwy. Yet the hwy is a hard-packed **gravel road** and the journey to Inuvik (12–15hr) is not a breeze; the road is generally in good condition, but often very slippery when raining, so drive the speed limit and give plenty of room to oncoming traffic. Keep in mind this road is very much about the journey rather than the destination.

The hwy is open year-round except for brief periods during the November freeze and April thaw. All distances given below (unless stated) are from **Kilometre 0** of the hwy, which is at the junction of the North Klondike Hwy, 40km east of Dawson City.

Dawson City to Eagle Plains

About 72km north of Dawson City is **Tombstone Mountain Territorial Park**, the first of the hwy's three rudimentary government-run campsites (31 RV/tent sites; $12). It's a magnificent, 2000-square-kilometre park packed with wildlife and archeological sites and an interpretive centre (mid-May to mid-Sept 9am–9pm) and biologist/botanist on hand to offer guided nature walks.

At **Hart River** (Km80) you may see part of the 1200-strong Hart River Woodland **caribou herd**; unlike the barren-ground herds farther north these caribou have sufficient fodder to graze one area instead of making seasonal migrations. Golden eagles and ptarmigan are also common along the Blackstone River (Km93), as are tundra birds like Lapland longspurs, lesser golden plovers, mew gulls and long-tailed jaegers. This river offers the best chance at **fishing** for arctic grayling – simply pull over on the hwy or by the bridge and spend a few hours casting your line. At Moose Lake (Km105), **moose** can often be seen feeding, along with numerous species of waterfowl such as northern shoveller, American widgeon and the arctic tern, whose Arctic to Antarctic migration is the longest of any bird.

Chapman Lake (Km120) marks the start of the northern **Ogilvie Mountains**, a region that has never been glaciated and so preserves numerous plant and insect species and provides an important early wintering range for the Porcupine

Caribou herd; as many as forty thousand caribou cross the hwy in mid-October – they take four days and have right of way. This rough stretch of road crosses the Ogilvie Mountains at **North Fork Pass** (1289m), the highest elevation on the hwy, at Km139. Unique butterfly species breed at Butterfly Ridge (Km155), close to some obvious caribou trails which cross the region, and it should also be easy to spot Dall sheep, cliff swallows and bald eagles.

Beyond, the hwy goes up to **Eagle Plains** and almost unparalleled access to the subarctic **tundra**, which in summer and autumn is a beautiful medley of colours, the vegetation having been coaxed to riotous life by hours of perpetual daylight. At **Engineer Creek** (Km194) – avoid fishing here, as the river has high iron concentrations – is another government-run campsite (15 RV/tent sites; $12), but the only orthodox accommodation on the hwy within the Yukon is the 32-room *Eagle Plains Hotel and Service Station* at Km369 (Ⓣ867/993-2453, Ⓦwww.eagleplainshotel.com; ❻; camping $10). It has fuel, a garage with mechanic, tyres, lounge, a restaurant and RV park.

The Arctic Circle and beyond

Finally, after travelling 405km you cross the **Arctic Circle**, an imaginary line circumnavigating the globe at 66 ½0N, indicating the point on Earth where the sun will not set for at least one full day. From here on in, the further north you travel, the higher the midnight sun. A sign on the hwy marks the crossover point.

Beyond is a government-run campsite at **Rock River** (Km447; 17 RV and 3 tent sites; $12) and then the road climbs into the **Richardson Mountains** to meet the border of the NWT (Km465) before the less-than-arresting flats of the Peel Plateau and Mackenzie River and the run to Inuvik. The **time changes** at the Yukon–NWT border: NWT time is one hour ahead of Yukon time.

The tiny Gwich'in Dene village of **FORT MCPHERSON** is at Km574, soon after crossing the Peel River. It holds a service station and the *Peel River Inns North* (Ⓣ867/952-2373, Ⓦwww.peelriverinn.com; ❼) with eight rooms and a grocery store next door. The unserviced government-run *Nutuiluie Territorial Campground* is 10km south of Fort McPherson (23 sites; shelter, toilets, showers and water; $15; June–Sept). It has a small **visitor centre** (daily June–early Sept).

At Km609 is the minuscule settlement of **TSIIGEHTCHIC**, 80km south of Inuvik. It was founded as a mission in 1868 and acquired a Hudson's Bay post soon after; a red-roofed 1931 mission church still stands here. On the run to Inuvik (see p.919), there's another campsite at **VADZAIH VAN TSHIK**, at Km692 (11 sites with water, shelter and toilets; $15).

The Western Arctic

The **Western Arctic** region centres on **Inuvik** and encompasses the mighty delta of the **Mackenzie River** – North America's second longest river – and reaches across the Beaufort Sea to the border with Nunavut. The region also includes part of Victoria and Banks islands, the most westerly of Canada's Arctic islands. The delta ranks as one of the continent's great **bird** habitats, with swans, cranes and big raptors among the hundreds of species that either nest in or overfly the region during the spring and autumn. It also offers the chance of seeing pods of **beluga whales** and other big sea mammals, while local **Inuit** guides on Banks Island should be able to lead you to possible sightings of musk ox and white fox.

After Inuvik and the two villages on the short NWT section of the Dempster Hwy – Fort McPherson and Tsiigehtchic – the area's other four settlements are

Tours from Inuvik

Most visitors to Inuvik take a **tour** of some description, and despite the remoteness of the NWT and the isolated nature of its communities, it is remarkably simple – if occasionally rather expensive – to find **tour operators** who offer a wide range of cultural, natural history and other trips. A full list of licensed operators can be found in the *Explorers' Guide to Canada's Northwest Territories* or by visiting ⓦwww.spectacularnwt.com; further information is on ⓣ1-800/661-0788.

Day-trips from Inuvik include tours to the tundra, a traditional bush camp, boat tours on the Mackenzie River, beluga whale-watching, flights over the Mackenzie Delta and trips to the fly-in communities. Arctic Nature Tours (ⓣ867/777-3300 or 1-866/TOUR-TUK, ⓦwww.arcticnaturetours.com) and Up North Tours (ⓣ867/777-2028 or 678-0510, ⓦwww.upnorthtours.ca) are the main operators and have a special bias towards wildlife. Trips include tours to the Babbage River (which, if the timing is right, offers a bird's eye view of the Porcupine caribou herd) and bird and wildlife visits to Hershel Island, a Yukon territorial park in the Beaufort Sea that is still a prime hunting and fishing ground for Inuvialuit (western Arctic Inuit). The companies also offer guided trips to Tuktoyaktuk and can arrange tours with guides based in Aklavik, Paulatuk and Ulukhakok. Midnight Express (ⓣ867/777-4829) offers boat trips on the Mackenzie River, Arctic Chalet (ⓣ867/777-3535, ⓦwww.arcticchalet.com) organizes dog-sledding excursions and Western Arctic Adventures & Equipment (ⓣ867/777-2594) rents canoes and kayaks.

fly-in communities reached from Inuvik. Two of them, **Aklavik** and **Tuktoyaktuk**, are near – by NWT standards – and are the places to fly out to if you want a comparatively accessible taste of aboriginal northern culture. **Sachs Harbour** (on Banks Island), **Holman** (on Victoria Island) and **Paulatuk** (on the coastal mainland) lie much farther afield, and are bases for more arduous tours into the delta and Arctic tundra. Inuvik, along with Yellowknife and Fort Smith, is one of the key centres of the accessible north, and one of the main places from which to take or plan tours farther afield (see box above). It's well worth taking one of the shorter tours to the fly-in communities for a taste of Arctic life, and to enjoy the superb bird's-eye view of the delta.

Inuvik

INUVIK ("the place of man") is the farthest north you can drive on a public hwy in North America – unless you wait for the winter freeze and follow the ice road carved across the Mackenzie River and the Arctic Ocean to the north. Canada's first planned town north of the Arctic Circle, Inuvik is a battered spot begun in 1954 as an administrative centre to replace Aklavik, a settlement to the west wrongly thought to be doomed to envelopment by the Mackenzie River's swirling waters and shifting mud flats. Inuvik is an interesting melting pot of around 3500 people, with Dene, Métis and Inuvialuit living alongside the trappers, pilots, scientists and frontier entrepreneurs drawn here in the 1970s when a boom followed the oil exploration in the delta. Today, the local economy also relies on government jobs, services, tourism and the town's role as a supply and communication centre for much of the western Arctic.

Arrival and information

Flights with Air North from Whitehorse, Dawson City, Old Crow, Fairbanks and other points south service Inuvik's **airport** (ⓣ867/777-2467), 12km south of town. First Air and Canadian North both have numerous northern connections and run weekly and daily flights from Edmonton (Canadian North also runs daily flights from Yellowknife); see p.868 for contact details. A taxi (Ⓣ867/777-5050) from the airport should cost $25–30. Otherwise, you're most likely to arrive in your own vehicle or with the **MGM bus service** (see p.915) along the Dempster Hwy. You can **rent** a car from: Arctic Chalet Car Rental, 25 Carn St (Ⓣ867/777-3535 or 1-800/685-9417, Ⓦwww.arcticchalet.com); Beaufort Delta Rentals, 171 Industrial Rd (Ⓣ867/777-5304, (Ⓔnorthwind@northwestel.net); and Norcan, 60 Franklin Rd (Ⓣ867/777-2346 or 1-877/298-1338, Ⓦwww.norcan.yk.ca). All have phones at the airport. Only Norcan allows for one-way trips, with Whitehorse the only option.

The Western Arctic regional **tourist office** is located near the town's entrance at the eastern end of Mackenzie Road, at the junction with Loucheux Road, a ten-minute walk from the centre (daily: July & Aug 9am–8pm; mid-May or June to early Sept 10am–6pm; Ⓣ867/777-4727, Ⓦwww.spectacularnwt.com). The town's tourist office is at 2 Firth St (Ⓣ867/777-8618, Ⓦwww.inuvik.ca). You can get more background on the area and access the internet at the **Inuvik Centennial Library** (Mon–Thurs 10am–9pm, Fri 10am–6pm, Sat & Sun 1–5pm; Ⓣ867/777-8620), 100 Mackenzie Rd, and pick up **maps**, guides, books and charts at the Boreal Bookstore (Ⓣ867/777-3748), 75 Mackenzie Rd.

The Town

Wandering the town provides an eye-opening introduction to the vagaries of northern life, from the strange stilted buildings designed to prevent their heat melting the **permafrost** (which would have disastrous effects on the piles or gravel pads that serve as foundations), to the street-level "utilidors", which carry water and sewage lines – again, to prevent the permafrost melting.

The influence of Inuvialuit people in local political and economic life has increased, to the extent that the **Western Claims Settlement Act** of 1984 saw the government cede titles to various lands in the area, returning control that had been lost to the fur trade, the church, oil companies and national government. A potent symbol of the church's local role in particular resides in the town's most-photographed building, the **Igloo Church**, or Our Lady of Victory (Ⓣ867/777-2236), a rather incongruous cultural mix. It's on Mackenzie Road, the main street running west to east through town, but isn't always open; ask at the rectory for a glimpse inside and of the paintings by local Inuvialuit artist Mona Thrasher. Behind the church, on the corner of Gwich'in Road and Breynat Street, is the **Inuvik Community Greenhouse** (9am–5pm; Ⓣ867/777-3267, Ⓦwww.inuvikgreenhouse.com), the northernmost greenhouse in North America, blooming with flowers and fruit and vegetables that would otherwise not survive in the harsh climate. It's housed in a converted hockey arena and hosts a small community market on Saturday. The best place in town to pick up unique pieces by Northern artists – including one-off carvings and clothing made from polar bear, wolf or musk ox – is at the not-for-profit **Inuvialuit Regional Corporation Craft Shop**, 3rd Floor 107 Mackenzie Rd (Ⓣ867/777-2737). For 56 days from late June, Inuvik basks in round-the-clock sunshine – it's well worth timing your trip to coincide with the mid-July **Great Northern Arts Festival** (Ⓦwww.gnaf.org), ten fabulous days of exhibitions and performances by local and international artists.

Practicalities

The best **accommodation** option for budget travellers is the cabins (most with kitchenettes) at the excellent lakeside *Arctic Chalet*, 3km from town off the approach road at 25 Carn Rd (Ⓣ867/777-3535 or 1-800/685-9417, Ⓦwww.arcticchalet.com; ③). There are two co-owned **hotels** in town: the big *Eskimo Inn*

(ⓣ867/777-2801, ⓦwww.mackenziehotel.com/eskimo.htm ❻) downtown at 133 Mackenzie Rd, and the *Mackenzie Hotel* (ⓣ867/777-2861; ❼) at 185 Mackenzie Rd. An alternative downtown hotel is the *Capital Suites* at 195 Mackenzie Rd (ⓣ867/678-6300 or 1-877/669-9444, ⓦwww.capitalsuites.ca; ❻). The comfortable *Polar B&B* (ⓣ867/777-2554, ⓦwww.polarbedandbreakfast.com; ❺) at 75 Mackenzie Rd, has four rooms and offers use of the kitchen. *Happy Valley* (ⓣ867/777-3652; $10–30; June–Sept), at the northwest end of town on Franklin Road off Mackenzie Road, is the nearest local **campsite**.

Eating possibilities are largely confined to hotel dining rooms. For coffee, soup and sandwiches, try the *Café Gallery* at 90 Mackenzie St, the *Roost* at 120 Mackenzie St or the *Cloudnine Restaurant* at the airport (closed Sat). *The Mad Trapper Pub*, 124 Mackenzie Rd (Mon–Sat 11am–2am), is a locals place with occasional live music.

The fly-in communities

Accessible only by air except in winter, when incredible snow roads are ploughed across the frozen delta, the region's four **fly-in communities** are close to some fascinating and relatively accessible Arctic landscapes, wildlife and cultures. All are served by Inuvik-based **Aklak Air** (ⓣ867/777-3777 or 1-866/707-4977, ⓦwww.aklakair.ca) or **Daazraii North-Wright Airways** (ⓣ867/777-2220 or 867/678-2749), and have simple grocery stores, though their prices make it wise to bring in some of your own supplies. Some have hotels, but you should be able to camp close to all four; ask permission first at the village head office. The best way to see them is with a tour company from Inuvik (see pp.919–921), but even if you're going under your own steam it's still worth checking with the tour companies for discounted flight-only deals.

Aklavik

AKLAVIK, 50km west of Inuvik on the western bank of the Mackenzie delta, means "Place of the Barren Lands Grizzly Bear". A Hudson's Bay post (which you can still see) aimed at the trade in muskrat fur was established here in 1918, though for generations before the region had been the home of Inuvialuit families who once traded and frequently clashed with the Gwich'in of Alaska and the Yukon. Today both live together in a town that melds modern and traditional, and whose inhabitants are proud not to have jumped ship when they were invited to leave their sinking town for Inuvik in the 1950s. Most are happy to regale you with stories of Albert Johnson, the mysterious "**Mad Trapper of Rat River**", who is buried here. Johnson (supposedly a former Chicago gangster) arrived in Fort McPherson in July 1931, purchased guns and ammunition and later built a cabin-cum-fortress on the delta, not far from Aklavik. After local trappers accused him of tampering with their traps, a constable was sent to question him, but Johnson shot him through the door. A posse of Mounties and local men armed with guns and fistfuls of dynamite then laid siege to Johnson's cabin for fifteen hours but he managed to escape, shooting another Mountie in the process. Johnson grabbed world headlines briefly as he managed to elude capture for a further forty days in the dead of a brutal winter. He was eventually shot on the Eagle River, surrounded by seventeen men and buzzed by a bomb-carrying light plane.

Flights from Inuvik operate daily ($200 return). In town, there are two stores, two restaurants and a two-room boarding house, the *Aklavik Inn* (ⓣ867/978-2461; ❻). You can prepare your own meals here or pay extra for half or full board. For local **information** contact the hamlet office (ⓣ867/978-2351).

Tuktoyaktuk

TUKTOYAKTUK, or simply Tuk, sits on a sandspit on the Beaufort coast about 137km north of Inuvik. It acts as a springboard for oil workers and tourists, both considered outsiders who have diluted the traditional ways of the whale-hunting Karngmalit peoples. The Karngmalit have lived and hunted in small family groups on this fascinating but inhospitable shore for centuries. The settlement's name means "Looks Like Caribou", reflecting its former reputation as a hunting ground for *tuktu*, or caribou. Many locals still hunt, fish and trap, but government, tourism and the oil business now pay most wages.

This is the most popular tour outing from Inuvik, with trips starting at about $280, a sum worth paying just to enjoy the scenic low-altitude flight up here. Most casual visitors come to see pods of beluga and great bowhead whales, or to look at the world's largest concentration of **pingos**, 1400 volcano-like hills, formed by the combination of frost and abundant water, across the delta's otherwise treeless flats; two of the largest have been used as landmarks for centuries.

While in Tuk drop by the **community freezer**, located some thirty feet underground; the rooms are surrounded by permafrost and are used to store caribou meat and fish. The town is also well known for its traditional arts and crafts fashioned from soap stone, caribou antler, whale-bone and musk ox horn. Carvings usually feature polar bears, *inukshuiit* (stone way-markers), hunters and drum dancers.

The best **accommodation** choices are the *Tuktu* (Ⓣ867/977-2280; ❻) and the *Waterfront* (Ⓣ867/977-2487; ❻); both are B&Bs and allow guests use of the kitchens. You should be able to **camp** near the beach, but ask first. Your best option for **food** is the local grocery store.

Flights from Inuvik operate three times daily ($300 return). Inuvik's main tour companies come out here, but if you want a local guide, Arctic Tour Company (Ⓣ867/977-2230, Ⓔrogergruben@netcaster.ca) or Ookpik Tours (Ⓣ867/977-2170, Ⓔookpiktours@yahoo.ca) offer cultural, boat or dog-sledding tours in summer or winter. For more **information** on the settlement, contact the community office (Ⓣ867/977-2286).

Paulatuk and Ikahuk

PAULATUK, 400km east of Inuvik, is one of NWT's smallest permanent communities. Situated on a spur between the Beaufort and an inland lake, the settlement was started by the Roman Catholic Mission in 1935 as a communal focus for the semi-nomadic Karngmalit, who despite such paternalism have fought off the adverse effects of missionaries and trader-introduced alcoholism to hang on to some of their old ways. The village's name means "place of coal", a reference to the coal seams to the northeast, where the (literally) Smoking Hills take their name from the smouldering coal ignited years ago and is still burning.

Hunting, fishing and trapping still provide their economic staples, along with handicrafts aimed at the tourists here mainly for the chance to watch or hunt big game. Key sites for the former activity are the cliffs of the Cape Parry Bird Sanctuary and the **Tuktut Nogait National Park** on the Parry Peninsula to the west, a calving ground for the migrating Bluenose caribou herd. Drop by the Parks Canada interpretive centre (Mon–Fri 9am–5pm; Ⓣ867/580-3233, Ⓔinuvik.info@pc.gc.ca), located in the *Paulatuk Hotel/Visitor Centre*, for information on the park and on licensed guides. Local operators will take you out to both areas, and in spring run trips to look for polar bears on the Amundsen Gulf. Aklak Air **flights** operate three times weekly from Inuvik ($850 return). The only place to **stay** is the aforementioned hotel (Ⓣ867/580-3051, Ⓔpaulatuk_hotel@airware.ca; ❽), which has ten rooms, kitchen facilities and a small store; they will also help you arrange tours. For more **information** on current activities contact the hotel or the hamlet office (Ⓣ867/580-3531).

Ikahuk

The only settlement on Bank's Island, 520km northeast of Inuvik in the Arctic Ocean, is **IKAHUK** ("Place Where One Crosses Over") also known as **Sachs Harbour**.

Ikahuk is the place to see and photograph **musk ox**. Bank's Island is home to the world's largest population of these shaggy beasts (approximately seventy thousand), some of which may be seen grazing close to town. These creatures have managed to carve out an existence since long before the last ice age by surviving on a meagre diet of willows and shrubs. Locals value the animals for their food and underfur (*qiviut*), which is known for its outstanding insulating properties. The *qiviut* is spun and woven into clothes highly sought after the world over. Contact the hamlet office (Ⓣ867/690-4351) for more information on outfitters who will take you to spot these incredible creatures.

R**ooms** are available at the *Kuptana's Guest House* (Ⓣ867/690-3614; ❼ including meals). Ask first and you should be able to **camp** by the beach. There is no restaurant in the town, just a small grocery store. Two Aklak Air **flights** operate from Inuvik twice a week ($1100 return).

Uluqsaqtuuq (Holman)

ULUQSAQTUUQ, or Holman, is one of two communities on Victoria Island and lies on its western shore, just outside Nunavut's borders. Most people are here to **fish** for trout and arctic char or, remarkably, for the novelty of playing one of the world's most northerly nine-hole golf courses (with artificial greens). The settlement developed almost by default, when a Hudson's Bay Company post was moved here from Prince Albert Sound in 1939. Inuit had previously summered here in the search of caribou, but the post encouraged some to settle and sell white-fox furs with the Hudson's Bay traders. Today, the community has become well-known for its **crafts**, notably prints and silk-screened items.

You can buy local crafts and prints around the settlement or at the craft shop. The only **accommodation** is the eight-room *Arctic Char Inn* (Ⓣ867/396-3501, 396-3531 or 1-888/866-6784, Ⓦwww.arcticcharinn.com; ❼), which is also the only place to eat, other than the grocery store. You can **camp** at Okpilik Lake, but should be able to pitch a tent just about anywhere; ask at the hamlet office first.

Scheduled flights arrive on First Air from Yellowknife three times per week.

The Sahtu

The **Sahtu** embraces the Mackenzie River south of its delta as far as Tulita and the great swathe of land across to and including **Great Bear Lake** to the east, the world's eighth largest lake. There's no year-round road access: you either fly in, canoe the Mackenzie – no mean feat – drive on the famed winter access road or sign up with **fishing** and hunting charters that boat or fly you into the backcountry, home to some of North America's finest fishing lodges and lakes. In 1994 a road was built as far as Wrigley, 225km northwest of Fort Simpson (see p.926), but plans to push it through to Inuvik will be a long time in the making. In the meantime, most tours operate out of the area's nominal capital at **Norman Wells**, on the banks of the Mackenzie River in the lee of the Franklin Mountains, which separate the river and Great Bear Lake. The Sahtu has just four other communities: **Fort Good Hope**, north of Norman Wells; **Déline** on Great Bear Lake; **Colville Lake**, north of Great Bear Lake and **Tulita**, south of Norman Wells.

Norman Wells and the Canol Heritage Trail

The region's largest transport hub and community **NORMAN WELLS** overlooks the Mackenzie River. The town owes its economic well-being to **oil**: the local Dene long knew this region as Le Gohlini – "where the oil is" – and explorer Alexander Mackenzie first noticed a yellow liquid seeping from the rocks in 1789. The stuff only began to be fully exploited in 1919 after Dene locals led geologists to the same spot. Drilling and refinement on an industrial scale began in 1932 and increased in World War II when the American government sponsored the building of the **Canol Pipeline** to supply the Alaska Hwy. The pipeline was abandoned in 1945 and its old route is now the **Canol Heritage Trail** (see below).

You can follow the oil and Canol story in the **Norman Wells Historical Centre** (year-round, call for hours; free; Ⓣ867/587-2415), 23 Mackenzie Drive, which is filled with photographs, modest displays and odd memorabilia. Alongside, the settlement's uniquely ecumenical **church** does double duty: Catholics sit on one side, Protestants on the other.

For details of the many fishing-charter companies enquire locally or pick up a copy of the *Explorers' Guide* (Ⓣ1-800-661-0788, Ⓦwww.spectacularnwt.com). Mountain River Outfitters (Ⓣ867/587-2697, Ⓦwww.mountainriver.nt.ca) run **day-trips** up the Mackenzie River to Fort Good Hope and the Arctic Circle (mid-June to mid-Sept) and **rent canoes** and other outdoor equipment. Canoe North Adventures (Ⓣ1-888/941-6654, Ⓦwww.canoenorthadventures.com) supplies logistical support and package tours of the surrounding rivers and lakes.

Practicalities

Canadian North flies daily to Norman Wells from Inuvik, Yellowknife and Edmonton; see p.868 for contact details. North-Wright Air flies to Yellowknife

The Canol Heritage Trail

The **Canol Heritage Trail**, soon to become the **Doi T'oh Territorial Park**, is becoming an increasingly popular **long-distance wilderness trail** stretching 372km from Norman Wells to the Yukon border. The journey can take three to four weeks and ranks among the world's tougher treks, passing through some of the NWT's most spectacular ranges. The route crosses through the Mackenzie Mountains west of Norman Wells, across three challenging rivers (at least one must be crossed by raft) and through **grizzly bear** country. Hikers must be self-sufficient as help can be days away. Unless you sign up for a tour to see this magnificent but utterly wild region, **extensive backcountry experience** is recommended. If you venture on the trail without a guide, inform the local detachment of the RCMP about your itinerary in either Dawson City Ⓣ867/587-2444 or in Ross River, Yukon Ⓣ867/969-5555.

Unfortunately there is currently very little printed information about the trail, although at the time of publication there was talk of reproducing a small handbook to replace the out-of-print *Hiker's Guide to the Canol Trail*, by Tim Hawkings. The NWT government publication contained maps, useful notes about river crossings and the status of trail conditions. Contact the tourist office for more information.

Mountain River Outfitters and Canoe North Adventures (see above for both) provide both package tours and logistical support for individual hikers on the Canol trail.

and Inuvik (Ⓣ867/587-2288 or 587-2333, Ⓦwww.north-wrightairways.com) and offers sightseeing flights. The **airport** is a twenty-minute walk from the centre of the town. The town's **tourist office** is in the Historical Centre and has information on nearby hiking trails.

There are a handful of **hotels** in town, but the best option is the *Mackenzie Valley Hotel* (Ⓣ867/587-2511, Ⓦwww.mackenzievalleyhotel.com; ⑥), which has its own restaurant.

The Deh Cho Trail

Northern Alberta and the adjoining southern portion of the NWT were first opened up to trade courtesy of the mighty rivers that flow through these parts. Traders, particularly the Hudson's Bay Company, used routes along the Peace, Hay, Slave, Liard and Mackenzie rivers to maintain remote outposts and foster commercial relations with aboriginals. Some of these far-flung communities have survived to the present day, and the circuit of roads connecting them has become known as the **Deh Cho Trail,** which local tourism organizations promote extensively (Ⓣ867/873-7200 or 1-800/661-0788, Ⓦwww.dehchotravel.com) in a bid to lure travellers away from the Alaska Hwy.

The southern parts of this 1800-kilometre loop weave their way through an all but uninhabited landscape of rippling hills, rivers, lakes, lonely farms and open prairie. Yet most of the route passes through a monotonous mantle of forest and after hours of motoring through it, the region's very modest communities appear as exceptional highlights. In truth, they offer very few attractions worthy of a stop. The sheer untrammelled wilderness is a boon for adventurers, especially **anglers** or **boaters.** Kayakers and canoers will find extraordinary rapids and waterfalls, and long-distance lake and river systems invite expeditions. But for most outdoor enthusiasts, the main reason to travel the Deh Cho Trail is to reach a trio of attractions off it: the impressive wilderness of **Nahanni National Park**, the bison and crane sanctuary of **Wood Buffalo National Park** and **Yellowknife**, the capital city of the NWT and one of Canada's most accessible and reliable places to enjoy the Northern Lights.

The Deh Cho loop incorporates the initial leg of the **Alaska Highway** (see pp.889–894) before branching off near Fort Nelson onto the **Liard Highway**. This is a long, largely gravel road passing within sight of Nahanni National Park and close to **Fort Simpson**, from where the **Mackenzie Highway** (Hwy 1) pushes its way east and then south beyond the Alberta border (as Hwy 35) to **Peace River.** A number of hwys there allow you to complete the loop back to BC.

Contact Greyhound (Ⓦwww.greyhound.ca) for current schedule information on their long-haul **buses** running up the eastern side of the Deh Cho Trail, connecting Edmonton with Yellowknife, via Peace River and Hay River. These services are supplemented by the Hay River-based Frontier Coachlines, 16 102nd St (Ⓣ867/874-2566 or 873-4892), which run buses to Fort Providence, Yellowknife, Fort Smith and Fort Simpson. Because the roads barely merit travelling for their own sake, **flying** is a tempting time-saving option, though it is expensive unless you organize flights well in advance. If you decide to **drive**, fuel up at virtually every community you pass and, if you are going to camp, prepare for the unwelcome nocturnal attention of **bears**.

The Liard Highway leg: North of Fort Nelson

Beginning 35km north of Fort Nelson, the **Liard Highway** – or BC Hwy 77 which becomes NWT Hwy 7 – pushes north through forested wilderness to the

Nahanni National Park Reserve

With gorges deeper than the Grand Canyon and waterfalls twice the height of Niagara, the vast **Nahanni National Park Reserve** (reserve office ⓣ867/695-3151, ⓦwww.pc.gc.ca/nahanni) ranks as one North America's finest national parks and one of the most rugged wilderness areas anywhere in the world.

Designated a UNESCO World Heritage Site, Nahanni is close to the Yukon border in the heart of the Mackenzie Mountains and surrounds the **South Nahanni River**, a renowned 322-kilometre stretch whose whitewater torrents, pristine mountains and 1200-metre-deep canyons have attracted explorers and thrill-seeking canoeists alike – this is home to one of world's best whitewater runs. Unless you fit one of these categories or can afford to fork out for **guided trips** by boat or sightseeing by air, getting close to the best areas is difficult: the park is totally roadless and wild and there are no formal trails, although heavy use has made some routes well defined. Check the Parks Canada website for full details and descriptions of hiking routes in the park.

A **reservation** and **fee** system is in place for people wishing to use the river: the day-use fee is $24.50, the reservation fee for overnight trips $147.20 and there are strict quotas on visitors, so check the latest details whether you intend to visit independently or with a tour. For full information, contact the reserve office or the tourist office in Fort Simpson.

As for **tours**, the sky's the limit. Operators in Fort Simpson cater to all levels of demand, from day-trippers wanting air tours of the big set-pieces to self-contained canoers and walkers on month-long expeditions who require no more than a drop-off or pick-up by air. Even experienced, self-sufficient explorers should note it saves considerable time, hassle and money to take a three- or four-week tour with a licensed outfitter in Fort Simpson.

The spectacular **Virginia Falls** is the most popular day-trip in the park. Wolverine Air (ⓣ867/695-2263 or 1-888/695-2263 or 1-888/695-2263, ⓦwww.wolverineair.com) will take groups of three for a 5.5hr flight (2hr on the ground) in a floatplane to Nahanni for $1400, with stops at Virginia Falls and at the idyllic Little Doctor Lake at the edge of the mountain range. Simpson Air (ⓣ867/695-2505 or 1-866/995-2505, ⓦwww.simpsonair.ca) offers a slightly cheaper service but very similar trips, as well as a combined flight and cabin rental on Little Doctor Lake ($1650/two days, $2640/week). The day-trip you choose will likely depend on availability, so book well in advance. If you are in a party of less than three and just turn up, contact the airlines and ask to be put on a waiting list – they will contact you if they find others to fill a trip.

For one- to two-week rafting trips ($4880/$5460) contact Canadian River Adventures (ⓣ867/668-3180 or 1-800/297-692, ⓦwww.nahanni.com). Other outfits include Nahanni Wilderness Adventure (ⓣ403/678-3374 or 1-888/897-5223, ⓦwww.nahanniwild.com). North Nahanni Naturalist Lodge (ⓣ1-867/695-2116 or 1-888/880-6665, ⓦwww.nnnlodge.ca) offers other tours of the region and accommodation in a pleasant backcountry lodge.

regional centre **Fort Simpson**. En route it passes the hamlet of **Fort Liard** and offers great views of Nahanni National Park from the roadside **Blackstone Territorial Park** (campsites $15) where there's also a couple of short hiking trails. The road conditions are generally very good even though the hwy's surface is gravel for much of its length. Icy winter conditions pose a threat, as do bison that can wander onto the road at any time of year.

Fort Simpson

All means of access and facilities – including tour operators and outfitters – for the Nahanni National Park are in busy **FORT SIMPSON**, 150km to the park's east,

▲ Virginia Falls, Nahanni National Park Reserve, NWT

at the confluence of the Liard and Mackenzie rivers. This spot has been inhabited for nine thousand years by the Slavey peoples and their ancestors, making it the longest continually inhabited region in the NWT. Most of the town's resources are found along the main drag, **100th Street**, effectively a continuation of the main road through town. At the southern end of the nearly parallell Mackenzie Drive, you'll find the site of the old Hudson's Bay Company post and an area known as the "Flat" or the Papal Grounds, whose tepee and other developments date from the papal visit here on September 20, 1987. A light plane and floatplane airstrip lies just to the northwest of downtown, while the bulk of the outfitters' offices are gathered north of the strip at the top of Mackenzie Drive.

You can get to Fort Simpson by **air** twice a day from Yellowknife using either Air Tindi (Ⓣ867/669-8260 or 1-888/545-6794, Ⓦwww.airtindi.com) or First Air (see p.868 for details). The main **airport** is 12km south of town. The **tourist office** (May–Sept Mon–Fri 9am–8pm, Sat–Sun noon–8pm; Oct–April Mon–Fri 1–5pm; summer Ⓣ867/695-3182, winter Ⓣ867/695-2253, Ⓦwww.fortsimpson.com) is the first building on the left as you come into town.

Practicalities

If you're hoping to **stay** in town, be sure to book ahead. The hotels are on, or just off, 100th Street and include: the 29-room *Nahanni Inn* (Ⓣ867/695-2201; ❻), a standard motel with coffee shop and dining room; the smaller *Maroda Motel* (Ⓣ867/695-2602; ❻), a couple of blocks south, half of whose units have fully equipped kitchenettes; and, 4km southeast of town along the Mackenzie Hwy, the idyllic *Bannockland B&B* (Ⓣ867/695-3337, Ⓦwww.bbcanada.com/1831.html; ❻) with five rooms, all with private bath, and free airport pick-up. The local **campsite**, just southwest of the papal grounds, is operated on a first-come, first-served basis ($15 tents, $20 RVs) but has lots of space, showers and firewood. The dining room of the *Nahanni Inn* or the *Sub-Arctic*, opposite the tourist office, are the places to **eat**.

The Mackenzie Highway leg: Fort Simpson to Hay River

Though it takes its name from the lightly-used leg that runs parallel to the Mackenzie River, the **Mackenzie Hwy** is far more important for the section that hooks south through northern Alberta – providing the vital link for travellers driving between Edmonton, Yellowknife and Wood Buffalo National Park – to its "mile zero" at Grimshaw, Alberta. Though generally in excellent condition this road is about as dull as northern drives get: the hwy ploughs through a tight corridor of seemingly endless evergreens in which views rarely open out and little tempts you to get out and stretch your legs. The notable exceptions are the short and well-marked trails heading to occasional roadside waterfalls that have led local – and optimistic – tourism promoters to dub the hwy the Waterfall Route.

The only stop of interest on the stretch of the Mackenzie Hwy between Fort Simpson and the junction with Hwy 3 to Yellowknife (see p.933) is **Sambaa Deh Falls Territorial Park**; 150km east of Fort Simpson. You can camp (sites $15) here and from the campground, it's a ten-minute hike on an unmarked trail that heads upstream beside the river to a broad-shouldered, pounding waterfall. More impressive is the waterfall further downstream – in view of the hwy and the campground turnoff – where waters plummet dramatically into a narrow gorge.

More waterfalls dot the road beyond the junction with Hwy 3 to Yellowknife, where the Mackenzie Hwy is paved for its remaining 186km journey to the Alberta border. The most impressive of these falls are the 33m-high **Alexandra Falls**, located 72km shy of the Alberta border. In 2003 Ed Lucero plunged his kayak over these falls and, in surviving, made Alexandra the world's highest falls successfully negotiated by kayak.

Practicalities

Services along the NWT stretch of the Mackenzie Hwy are limited. You can **camp** at: Lady Evelyn Falls Territorial Park near Kakiska and the junction to Hwy 3 (tent $15, RV $20); at Louise Falls and Alexandra Falls in **Twin Falls Territorial Park**; and at the **60th Parallel Visitors' Center** (mid-May to mid-Sept 8.30am–8.30pm, ⓣ867/920-1021) on the Alberta border. The only motel is the basic *Twin Falls Inn* (ⓣ867/984-3711; ④) in the village of Enterprise; its restaurant *Winnie's* serves most of the meals in town. A better selection of food and accommodation can be had 43km away at **Hay River** – the gateway to both the **Great Slave Lake**, the third largest in North America, and to **Fort Smith** and **Wood Buffalo National Park** (see p.931).

South of Alberta's provincial border the Mackenzie Hwy becomes **Hwy 35** and a string of campsites provides the only **accommodation** en route to the town of **High Level**. The aboriginal hamlets of Meander River, Steen River and Indian Cabins offer only food and fuel. Located 191km from the NWT border, High Level has a glut of hotels, yet from here south to Manning – the next motel cluster – only a couple of basic campsites and the odd wind-blown store disturb the peace. Official tenting spots are Notikewin Provincial Park (ⓣ780/836-2048; $17; May–Oct), 30km east of Hwy 35 on Hwy 692 – look for the junction 37km north of Manning, and the 49-site *Twin Lakes Provincial Recreation Area* (ⓣ780/836-4046; $20; May–Sept), a total of 65km north of Manning on Hwy 35.

Hay River

HAY RIVER is a typical no-nonsense northern town. Situated on **Great Slave Lake** at the mouth of the Hay River, it's been inhabited for thousands of years by

Dene people. White settlers had put it on the map by 1854, but it wasn't until the 1940s that the town became an important transport centre. It's now also one of the most important **ports** in the north, shipping freight up the Mackenzie River in huge barges to provide a precarious lifeline for High Arctic communities as far away as Inuvik and Tuktoyaktuk. If you're stuck in town, the best way to kill time is to wander down to the wharves for a look.

The town divides into the New Town on the river's west bank – home to most of the motels, restaurants and key buildings – and the somewhat moribund Vale Island across a bridge to the north. Vale Island centres on Mackenzie Drive and is home to the wharves, airport, the remnants of the old town, the campsite and a series of passable and popular **beaches** (the last a total of 7km from the centre of New Town). The best sand is near the campsite on the northeast side of the island at the end of 106th Avenue.

In addition to Greyhound and Frontier Coachlines bus services (see p.934), Hay River is also connected to the outside world via regular flights to Yellowknife with Buffalo Airways, First Air and Canadian North; the latter also provides three flights per week to Edmonton. The **tourist office** (mid-May to mid-Sept daily 9am–9pm; ⓣ867/874-3180, ⓔtourism@northwestel.net) is on Hwy 2 south of the New Town centre on the corner with McBryan Drive. For information on accessing **Wood Buffalo National Park** from Hay River via Fort Simpson on Hwy 5, see p.933.

Practicalities

Much of the ample **accommodation** here is less expensive than elsewhere in the north. An economical but very pleasant choice is the beach-side *Harbour House Bed & Breakfast* (ⓣ867/874-2233; ⑤) on Vale Island. If you'd rather be close to downtown try the *Migrator Motel*, 912 Mackenzie Hwy (ⓣ867/874-6792; ⑤), just north of downtown, between New Town and the Vale Island bridge. For the most comfort after a long haul, try the downtown *Ptarmigan Inn*, 10 J. Gagnier St (ⓣ867/874-6781 or 1-800/661-0842, ⓦwww.ptarmiganinn.com; ⑥), which has a fitness centre, sauna and sports bar. You can **camp** near the beach on Vale Island at the *Hay River Campground* ($20; mid-May to mid-Sept).

For **food** try *Salt 'n' Pepper*, 66 Woodland Drive (ⓣ867/875-4100), which is open until 10pm most nights and specializes in good, inexpensive Cantonese food.

High Level

You're only going to stop in **HIGH LEVEL** – 191km south of the NWT border and 250km north of Peace River – if you want a place to bed down. The huge stock of motel accommodation means room rates are very reasonable, with most motels charging around $80 – yet many of the town's thousand guest rooms are block-booked in advance by seasonal workers. The **tourist office** (summer daily 9am–5pm; rest of year Mon–Fri 9am–5pm; ⓣ780/926-4811) is alongside Hwy 35 at the southern edge of town.

Most of the town's rooms overlook Hwy 35, with the cheapest among them usually at the 75-unit *Four Winds Hotel* (ⓣ780/926-3736; ②), while the *Stardust Motor Inn*, 9704-97th St (ⓣ780/926-4222; ⑤) is a good bit smarter, even if few real extra facilities are offered. Top-flight in town, but with barely more expensive rates, is the *Super 8*, 9502-114 Ave (ⓣ780/841-3448 or 1-866/875-7666; ⑥), with pool, internet access and complimentary breakfast. The best option for **campers** is the forty-site *Aspen Ridge Campground* (April–Oct; ⓣ780/926-4540; sites $20), 3km south of the centre on the main road (Hwy 35).

Most motels have adjoining **restaurants**, with filling pan-North American specials. Among them the *Flamingo Inn*, 9802 97th St, is particularly popular, while the steaks at the *Stardust Motor Inn*'s steakhouse are the best in town.

Peace River

If you're travelling under your own steam you'll probably end up staying overnight in **PEACE RIVER**, 486km from Edmonton. The largest town in the region, it has a handful of standard **motels**: the best choice is the large *Peace Valley Inns*, on the northern edge of downtown at 9609 101st St (ⓣ780/624-2020 or 1-800/661-5897, ⓦwww.peacevalleyinns.com; ❺). Located nearby, the **tourist office** operates out of the old station building at 9309 100th St (summer daily 10am–6pm; ⓣ780/624-2044). For **campers** there's the 84-site *Peace River Lion's Club* campsite with showers (ⓣ780/624-2120; $15; May–Oct) at Lion's Club Park on the west side of the river. For **food**, the *Su Casa Café*, tucked away on 3-9720 94th St, near the river, has Mexican meals; the *Sunflower Cafe*, 4 100th St, serves soups and sandwiches.

From Peace River, the Deh Cho Trail completes its loop by continuing to Grimshaw, where the Mackenzie Hwy officially ends. You can take Hwy 2 from either back into BC.

Fort Smith and Wood Buffalo National Park

Beginning near Hay River, lonely Hwy 5 is the only overland route to **Fort Smith**, which in turn is the only conceivable base for exploring the adjacent **Wood Buffalo National Park**. The drive's an easy 280km haul through forest and swampy muskeg, with the last 150km running within park boundaries on the park's only paved road; traffic along the way is extraordinarily light. It's easy to spend an enjoyable couple of days touring both, investigating the few footpaths and watching bison that are easily seen at the roadside – more often than not wallowing in dust to escape the same ferocious local mosquitoes that force visitors to use liberal amounts of repellent. Even Fort Smith, modest as it is, is a likeable base to soak up some Northern atmosphere, including in its good local history museum.

Fort Smith

Located just over Alberta's northern border in the Northwest Territories, **FORT SMITH** developed along one of the major water routes to the north and is virtually the only settlement for several hundred kilometres east and north. Its site was particularly influenced by the need to avoid a violent set of rapids, an interruption to waterborne transport that required a 25-km portage. In 1872 the Hudson's Bay Company built a post, Fort Fitzgerald, at the rapids' southern end and two years later Fort Smith was established at their northern limit. The settlement eventually became the administrative capital of the NWT, a function passed on to Yellowknife in 1967.

Arrival and Information

The easiest access to Fort Smith and the park is **by plane**, but isn't cheap, with prices of around $300 from Yellowknife and almost twice that from Edmonton. The airport is 5km west of town on McDougal Road. For a taxi from the airport or around town, call Portage Cabs (ⓣ867/872-3333). For **car rental** contact J&M Enterprises, on Portage Avenue (Mon–Sat 8am–6pm; ⓣ867/872-2221). Frontier Coachlines (see p.934) runs three buses per week from Hay River, timed to connect with Greyhound services from Edmonton.

Fort Smith's **tourist office**, at108 King St (daily May–Oct 9am–7pm; Nov–May 1–4pm; ⓣ867/695-3182, ⓦwww.fortsmithtourism.ca), is in the recreation complex, beside the Northern Life Museum. The excellent **National Park Visitor Centre** and headquarters is a short distance west at 149 McDougal Rd (mid-May to early Sept Mon–Fri 9am–noon & 1pm–5pm, Sat & Sun 1–5pm; late Sept to mid-May Mon–Fri 9am–noon & 1–5pm; ⓣ867/872-7960, ⓦwww.parkscanada.gc.ca/buffalo). More **maps and guides** can be found among the cluster of shops at the intersection of McDougal Road and Portage Avenue in the well-stocked North of 60 Books (Ⓣ867/872-2606).

The Town

The disappearance of government jobs has left its mark on the town, as has the opening of the all-weather road between Hay River and Yellowknife, which captured a lot of the freight that used to pass through the region by boat. Still, there are a handful of things to see around town before visiting the park. The **Northern Life Museum**, 110 King St (daily June–Sept 1–5pm and Tues & Thurs 7–9pm; Oct–May Tues–Fri & Sun 1–5pm; free; Ⓣ867/872-2859, Ⓦwww.nwtresearch.com/canoe/museum.htm), is worth a look for its excellent collection of traditional artefacts, crafts, fur-trading memorabilia and archive photographs.

If you fancy a short **hike** or two and a chance to see some of the region's famous white pelicans, try exploring the series of rapids beside town and upstream. All are linked by the Trans Canada Trail, but can be visited from trailheads starting beside the road to Fort Fitzgerald southeast of town. A map is available from the tourist office though the trails themselves are easy enough to follow. **Mountain Rapids** – about 8km southeast of Fort Smith – are of particular interest as the location of a white pelican colony, while **Pelican Rapids** – 12km from Fort Smith and a 45-minute walk through dense vegetation from the road – are most memorable for their thundering bulk. They're readily viewed at close quarters from tongues of granite Canadian shield that jut into the centre of the watercourse.

Practicalities

It's advisable to prebook **accommodation** in summer. The town's hotels are similar in terms of quality, though the larger *Pelican Rapids Inn*, 152 McDougal Rd (Ⓣ867/872-2789; ❻), is fractionally more convenient at the centre of downtown and home to the town's only **restaurant**. The alternative is the *Portage Inn*, 72 Portage Rd (Ⓣ867/872-2276, Ⓔportageinn@auroranet.nt.ca; ❺), where all units have kitchenettes. Lower prices can be found in the *Thebacha B&B River Trails North*, 53 Portage Ave (Ⓣ867/872-2060, Ⓦwww.taigatour.com; ❹), which has two doubles and two singles (no smoking and no alcohol). There's a public **campsite** in *Queen* Elizabeth Territorial Park alongside the Slave River on the northern edge of town (sites $20).

Wood Buffalo National Park

Straddling the border between Alberta and the Northwest Territories, **WOOD BUFFALO NATIONAL PARK** is bigger than Switzerland, making it Canada's largest national park and the world's second-largest protected environment (the largest is in Greenland). Though wild and vast, the park is limited to low hills, lakes, grasslands, boreal forest, salt plains and marsh. These drain into the Peace and Athabasca rivers and then into Lake Claire, forming one of the world's largest freshwater deltas in the process. To the casual visitor the landscape is subtle and unassuming – there are no real "sights" or scenic set pieces to compare with, say, the Rockies – but for dedicated naturalists, or those who are prepared to spend time (and money) letting the landscapes get under their skin, the park holds much of interest, embracing North America's finest limestone scenery, classic swaths of coniferous forest and rare salt-plain habitats.

The park was created in 1922 to protect an estimated 1500 wood bison, but since then it has also become a vital refuge for around fifty other species of mammal, including black bear and lynx. The Peace–Athabasca Delta in the park's southeast corner boasts 227 species of wildfowl – no fewer than four major migration routes cross the area. The world's only river rookery of rare

The Wood Bison of Wood Buffalo

The largest land mammal in North America, the **Wood bison** – commonly called the Wood buffalo – is the longer-legged, darker and more robust relative of the plains bison. Like the plains bison, the wood bison were also mercilessly hunted to the brink of extinction, albeit a couple of decades later in the 1890s which helped prompt the creation of **Wood Buffalo National Park**. Soon after its designation, local herds were bolstered in a dubious way by the introduction of some 6000 plains bison.

As a result, some of the bison in Wood Buffalo National Park today show traits of the Plains Bison, but an even more contentious consequence was the spread of tuberculosis and brucellosis – already rampant in the plains herd – to animals throughout the park. This has created a long-simmering row between conservationists and Alberta's beef lobby, with some (government) scientists asserting the only way to prevent the spread of the diseases (which they claim are highly infectious) to elk and to Alberta's valuable beef herds is to kill all the bison off. Scientists opposed to this plan point out the herd has been infected since the 1920s, yet the disease has survived by internal regulation and natural balance; with animals showing few outward signs of the diseases or of suffering. Furthermore, there has never been an instance of disease transferring itself to humans. Most locals, who are largely opposed to the cull, argue that killing or inoculating every animal would be a daunting task, given the immensity of the animals' range, and that, if even one was missed, the whole cull would be fruitless as disease would presumably erupt afresh when the herd regenerated.

Despite some attempts of small-scale culling and vaccination in the 1950s, there's been little recent action. However, the two disease-free northern herds – that range around the Mackenzie Bison Sanctuary (which surrounds much of Hwy 3 to Yellowknife) and the Liard Hwy near Fort Simpson – are kept that way by constant vigilance in a bison no-go area: any bison found here, disease free or not, are shot. Meanwhile, as a long-term management solution is debated, the park's buffalo – now around five thousand – continue to nibble contentedly.

white pelicans is here and the park is the last refuge of the critically endangered **whooping crane** – discovered nesting in a remote part of the park in 1954 after it was assumed hunters supplying the decorative demands of European aristocrats had made them extinct. Though there were only 21 of the majestic birds in the park in 1954, there are over 230 today – about half the total world population (most of the others being in captivity). Each boasts a 2.4-metre wingspan and nests far from any human contamination on the park's northern fringes. The presence of the cranes, bison and the various rare and unspoiled habitats saw the park declared a UNESCO World Heritage Site in 1983. Another claim to fame for the park is that it's the most northerly breeding site for **red-sided garter snakes**. Able to hibernate in the warm cracks in the limestone bedrock during the winter, in spring these snakes join dozens of others for mating to create an unforgettable writhing mass.

Exploring the park

The best way to absorb the landscape of the park is probably from the air or on a tour (see opposite), or by paddling a canoe around the almost limitless Athabasca, Peace and Slave river systems that were once the main route for trade from the south. The easiest and cheapest way to see some of the park independently is to spend a long day driving a clockwise loop through its northeastern corner from Fort Smith. Completing this loop relies on the use of a sandy dirt road called Parson's Lake Road. Make sure you check on its current condition and suitability for your vehicle at the park tourist office in Fort Smith.

To follow this loop, drive southwest from Fort Smith on Hwy 5, turning off at 8km and following the road to Peace Point. Possible stops along here include the **Salt River Day Use Area** (after 27km), where you can hike the 750m Karstland Loop that acts as an introduction to the local geology and as the start of the straightforward 16.5km day-hike. Stop at a small roadside parking lot about 3km southwest along the road from the Salt River Day Use Area to reach the scenic highlight of this loop: **Grosbeak Lake** – a bleak salt lake flecked with salt-etched rocks; it can be visited in an hour-long round-trip hike. The intersection of the main park road with the **Parson's Lake Road** comes after another 10km. This 42km-long, sandy and often impassable road is the best place to see bison, with good chances of spotting bears along the way also. The road finishes in a junction with a dirt road (close to Hwy 5) you can follow to the **Salt Plains Lookout** for fantastic views of the park and the chance to wander across these remarkable plains. From here the 30km back to Fort Smith on the sealed Hwy 5 quickly completes the loop.

The only licensed operator is Taiga Tour Company (Ⓣ867/872-2060, Ⓦwww.taigatour.com), which offers a full spectrum of paddling and birdwatching tours from $950 per person, including three nights' accommodation; eleven-day expeditions can be arranged by snowmobile, dog sled or canoe. Cheaper and far quicker are the **sightseeing flights** offered by Northwestern Air (Ⓣ1-877/872-2216, Ⓦwww.nwal.ca) and Reliance Airways (Ⓣ867/872-4004, Ⓦwww.relianceairways.ca); prices start at around $80 per person for thirty minutes. Wood Buffalo also offers hiking tours and programs for visitor groups. Phone ahead to the tourist office Ⓣ867/872-7960 to schedule your hike for less than $15 per person.

Staying in the park

If you want to overnight in the park, choose between the only serviced **campsite** (sites $15.70) at Pine Lake, backcountry camping or staying in a cabin at the remote Sweetgrass Station. Camping at Pine Lake is the easiest option and gives you access to its day-use area, pleasant beach and lakeshore hiking trails. Backcountry camping is allowed anywhere in the park if it's at least 1500m from Pine Lake or any road or trail. The park tourist office can advise on good spots and general precautions.

The park's most-visited backcountry destination is the meadowland and delta habitat at **Sweetgrass Station**, 12km south of the Peace River. Built to cull and vaccinate diseased bison, the area is a prime spot from which to watch the animals and admire the other wildlife of the Lake Claire region. You can stay in the cabin (bunks) here free of charge, but must first register with the park tourist office in Fort Smith. Drinking water comes from the river and needs to be boiled and treated. To get here you'll need to canoe or charter a motorboat. For more information on the park's waterways, see the waterway guide at Ⓦwww.pc.gc.ca/buffalo.

Yellowknife

Surrounded by endless expanses of northern lakes, forests and great wilderness lies the NWT's capital city **YELLOWKNIFE** – named after the copper knives of the aboriginal Slavey people. Today, this city of 22,000 attracts adventure seekers who come to experience the city's legendary hospitality, its northern lights, an array of cultural events and a mind-boggling selection of canoe routes and fishing spots. Despite its large-city size, Yellowknife has managed to keep its frontier town atmosphere.

The city's high-rise core of offices and government buildings exists to administer the NWT and support its population in a region whose resources – despite the recent discovery of diamonds to the north – should by all rights support only a small town. Even the Hudson's Bay Company closed its trading post here as early as 1823 on the grounds of economics and, except for traces of gold found by prospectors on the way to the Klondike in 1898, the spot was a forgotten backwater until the advent of commercial gold and uranium mining in the 1930s. This prompted the growth of the **Old Town** on an island and rocky peninsula on Great Slave Lake, and then in 1947 the **New Town** on the sandy plain behind it. In 1967, the year a road to the outside world was completed (Edmonton is 1524km away by car), Yellowknife replaced Ottawa as the seat of government for the NWT. Oiled by bureaucratic profligacy and the odd gold mine, the city has blossomed ever since.

Much of Yellowknife's accessible hinterland is an ideal playground for paddlers and naturalists, or for hunters on the trail of the region's 400,000-strong herd of caribou. Yellowknife itself springs to life during its many **festivals**. One of the most intriguing is the **Caribou Carnival** (Ⓦwww.cariboucarnival.net) in late March, whose attractions include dog-sled racing, Dene hand games, log-sawing competitions, bingo on ice, pond hockey and plenty of music and food. The **Yellowknife Summer Solstice Festival** (Ⓦwww.solsticefestival.ca), a midsummer celebration taking place each June 21, is celebrated with street events, cultural and musical performances. Mid-July brings the annual **Folk on the Rocks** (Ⓦwww.folkontherocks.com) festival, when folk singers from across Canada and the US meet Inuit and Dene folk singers, folk dancers and the famous Inuit "throat singers" in an amazing medley of world music. For information on the city's events and other attractions check Ⓦwww.spectacularnwt.com and Ⓦwww.northernfrontier.com.

Arrival and information

There are regular Canadian North and First Air **flights** to Edmonton, with Canadian North also flying to Calgary. Numerous smaller airlines serve most NWT and many Nunavut destinations. Yellowknife's **airport** is 5km west of the city on Hwy 3. A taxi from there cost around $15; call City Cab (Ⓣ867/873-3034) or Diamond (Ⓣ867/873-6666). **Car rental** companies at or near the airport include Budget, 20 Old Airport Rd (Ⓣ867/920-2776); elsewhere try National, downtown at 5118 50th St and at the airport (Ⓣ867/873-3424 or 920-2970 or 1-866/878-5557) or Hertz Yellowknife (Ⓣ867/920-4070 or 1-800/263-0600), also at the airport. Frontier Coachlines (Ⓣ867/873-4892 or 867/874-2566, Ⓦhttp://frontiercoachlines.yk.tripod.com) run three **buses** weekly from Hay River via Fort Smith (around $90 one-way). The **Northern Frontier regional tourist office** is on the edge of Frame Lake, just north of the Northern Heritage Centre, at 4807 49th St (June–Aug daily 8.30am–6pm; rest of year Mon–Fri 9am–5pm, Sat & Sun noon–4pm; Ⓣ867/873-4262 or 1-877/881-4262, Ⓦwww.northernfrontier.com).

Equipment rentals, outfitters and operators

To rent camping gear, canoes, snowmobiles, fishing tackle and other **outdoor equipment**, or to take part in a guided river trip, contact Narwhal Northern Adventures, 101 5103-51st Ave (Ⓣ867/873-6443, Ⓦwww.ssimicro.com/~narwal). Along with Inuvik, Yellowknife is the headquarters of most of the far north's **outfitters and tour operators**. Many licensed outfits run fishing, wildlife, Arctic sightseeing, canoeing, kayaking, boating and other trips, most ranging from one- or two-day outings up to full-blown three-week mini-expeditions to unimaginably wild areas. You'll find a comprehensive listing in the *Explorers' Guide* booklet, obtainable from national tourist offices before your trip. For more information, check with the tourist office or go to Ⓦwww.northernfrontier.com or Ⓦwww.spectacularnwt.com. If you plan to camp near the city or anywhere else in the territory it is worth visiting Ⓦwww.campingnwt.ca.

Accommodation

Hotel prices in the city are high, so it's worth looking up one of the dozen or so **B&Bs** if you're on a budget. The only **campsite** is the fully serviced *Fred Henne*

Territorial Park (☎867/920-2472; tents $15, RVs $28) by Long Lake off Hwy 3 north of the airport. Trails run to town from here via Frame Lake – allow about an hour, or you can follow the Prospectors' Trail north from the site, a good way to get a taste of the wilderness that encircles Yellowknife.

Bayside B&B 3505 MacDonald Drive ☎867/669-8844 or 867/445-8253, ⓦwww.baysidenorth.com. Located in the heart of Old Town on the shores of Great Slave Lake, this quiet place offers four rooms and a downstairs breakfast café overlooking the waterfront. Floatplane mooring facilities available if you're flying in. ❹

Blue Raven B&B 37 Otto Drive ☎867/873-6328, ⓔtmacfoto@internorth.com. Cosy three-room B&B high on the bluff at the edge of Old Town. There are three simple, modern rooms and grand views from its wonderful sun deck of Great Slave Lake. Excellent cooked breakfasts. ❹

Château Nova 4401 50th Ave ☎867/873-9700 or 1-877/839-1236, ⓦwww.chateaunova.com. Quality mid-range hotel on the fringe of downtown with fairly standard hotel rooms, though the historic photos of Yellowknife's early days dotting their walls are a nice touch. Facilities include in-room internet and a gym, hot tub and sauna. ❻

Embleton House 5203 52nd St ☎867/873-2892 or 1-866/873-2066, ⓦwww.bbcanada.com/embletonhouse. Friendly B&B in a quiet district two blocks from downtown. Rooms range from modest doubles with shared bath to a suite with kitchen and skylight for watching the northern lights. ❹

Island B&B 34 Morrison Drive ☎867/873-4803, ⓦwww.bbcanada.com/island. Located on the waterfront at Latham Island in the Old Town a 5min drive to downtown, this charming place has two non-smoking rooms. Enjoy the northern lights from their living room or deck. ❹

The City

Visitors are steered carefully down the main street, Franklin Avenue (50th Avenue), and down the long hill from the New Town to quaint Old Town cabins such as the **Wildcat Café** (see p.936). Elsewhere, the old town is a shakedown of pitted and buckled roads (the result of permafrost) and a few quaintly battered buildings on the aptly named Ragged Ass Road and Willow Road. These are more or less the only remnants of the old times.

Just west of New Town's core lies the **Prince of Wales Northern Heritage Centre** (June–Aug daily 10.30am–5.30pm; Sept–May Mon–Fri 10.30am–5pm, Sat & Sun noon–5pm; free; ☎867/873-7551, ⓦwww.pwnhc.ca), three blocks from downtown on Frame Lake. Yellowknife's key sight, the modern centre showcases the city's northern history and aboriginal culture with extensive displays of northern artefacts, Inuit carvings and persuasive dioramas of local wildlife and habitats. The Aviation Gallery is devoted to the planes and pilots who for years played (and play) a vital part in keeping the north alive. Just northwest of the centre, also on Frame Lake, stands the $25-million **Northwest Territories Legislative Assembly**, opened in 1993 (there are only 24 members). It's an impressive piece of architecture, much of it open to public view (tours June–Aug Mon–Fri 10.30am, 1.30pm & 3.30pm, Sun 1.30pm; Sept–May Mon–Fri 10.30am; free; ☎867/669-2230 or 1-800/661-0784, ⓦwww.assembly.gov.nt.ca).

Shops around town sell a variety of expensive northern aboriginal crafts, but these are cheaper than you'll find in more southerly cities. Close to town you can walk the trails around Frame Lake and from the campsite on Long Lake (see above). Or, you can drive out on the **Ingraham Trail**, an 81-kilometre hwy that was to be the start of a major NWT "Road to Resources" but which was abandoned in the 1960s. There are plenty of boat launches, picnic sites and campsites en route, as well as short walking trails like the **Cameron River Falls** (48km from Yellowknife) and lakeside beaches where the hardier of the city's population brave the water.

Beginning in late summer and continuing through the long winter months, the evening skies over the city come to life with the northern lights. Numerous outfitters and tour companies cater to Japanese tourists, who arrive here by the hundreds to realize a lifelong dream of experiencing this celestial wonder. Although it's hard to predict the strength of the aurora, any clear night usually brings about a good chance of spotting them. Your best bet is to bundle up and drive a few kilometres out of town where the city lights no longer compete with the evening sky. Simply sit back and wait for the show to begin.

Eating and drinking

Many of Yellowknife's **restaurants** are a little pricey, so if you're on a budget, a couple of ethnic food places offer a good alternative to the grubby diners on 50th Street. Look out for uniquely Northern items like caribou, musk ox and arctic char at some of the city's fancier establishments. Most of the hotels have good dining rooms and much of the **nightlife** revolves around their lounges.

Black Knight Pub 4910 49th St ⓣ867/920-4041. British-themed bar that's become a popular spot for its great range of malts, reasonable bar food and adjoining *Top Knight* nightclub. Closed Sun.

Bullocks Bistro 3534 Weaver Drive ⓣ867/873-3474. Fish and chips meets fine dining in this informal, yet fairly high-end restaurant. You'll only find simply prepared local whitefish, cod, pike and trout on the menu (mains $10–20), along with some delicious chowders. Reservations recommended.

Fuego International 4915 50th St ⓣ867/873-3750, ⓦhttp://fuego.diningon50th.com. Serving a variety of international and northern dishes for lunch and dinner (mains from $15), with an extensive wine list. Live music every night. Closed Sun.

Javaroma 5201 50th Ave ⓣ867/873-4134. Successfully formulaic coffee house with good fresh bagels, pastries and sandwiches and a medley of styles of coffee on offer. The only free wi-fi hot-spot in town.

L'Heritage 5019 49th St ⓣ867/873-9561. The town's premier gourmet restaurant where a French country atmosphere – white linen table cloths, candlelight and polished wood – serves as a backdrop to clever renditions of local foods. Musk ox, bison, deer and elk all appear on the menu (mains $20–37), usually beside unusual sauces: fruit and brandy; bourbon and berries. The game meat fondue is a good way to try a range of what's on offer. Reservations recommended.

Le Frolic 5019 49th St ⓣ867/669-9852. French bistro and watering hole with a giant selection of wines, many tapas-style dishes and buffalo burgers. Mains ($18–25) include panfried pickerel from Great Slave Lake.

Prospectors Bar and Grill 3506 Wiley Rd ⓣ867/920-7639. Great place to try Northern fish and game – tasty mid-priced dishes including musk ox, caribou, white fish and arctic char.

Taste of Saigon 4913 50th Ave ⓣ867/873-9777. Authentic Vietnamese dishes including a hearty *pho* which will warm you up on a cold winter's day.

Trader's Grill in *Explorer Hotel* ⓣ867/873-3531. Another fine dining establishment with a menu offering a wide choice of Northern country food, including musk ox, caribou and lemon butter arctic char (mains from $19). Voted the best Sun brunch in town.

Wildcat Café 3904 Wiley Rd ⓣ867/873-8850. Atmospheric and endlessly busy little café in a log cabin, operating since 1937. Expect to share tables as part of the sociable experience while you enjoy a taste of the region in the form of mid-priced fish dishes – or the excellent caribou medallions in zesty horseradish sauce. Open June–Sept.

Nunavut

Home to only 29,000 people, **Nunavut** (meaning "Our Land" in Inuktitut, the **Inuit** language) covers almost two million square kilometres – a fifth of Canada's land surface and an area five times the size of California, stretching west from Hudson Bay then north through the great "Barrenlands" of the interior to the Arctic islands in the north. From its western edge to the tip of Baffin Island in the east is 2000km (the distance from Washington DC to Denver). From north to south it's even farther – 2500km, the distance from London to Moscow.

Long an amorphous political entity administered not as a semi-autonomous province but by the federal government, the Northwest Territories was formally divided on April 1, 1999 by a land treaty which split the old territories in two and created a new central and eastern Arctic territory termed Nunavut, now firmly established as a political and physical entity. The signing followed fifteen years of low-profile but effective negotiating and campaigning and produced the largest land deal in Canadian history, in which the Inuit got back their homeland (valued at $1.15 billion) in return for renouncing all their claims to the remainder of the NWT. One practical effect of this new political division has been the **renaming** of most of its 28 settlements with Inuit names, though in many cases English-language names have continued to stick; both are given in this book, with the more common appellation given preference.

Nunavut is the land of vast caribou migrations, musk ox, polar bears and endless horizons of fish-filled lakes and rivers. The region is also home to ten thousand year-old glaciers, deep fjords, impressive mountain ranges and open tundra. But besides the **wildlife** and breathtaking **landscapes**, there are a host of activities, including fishing, whale-watching and exotic or high-adventure outdoor pursuits. Add to these the wide spectrum of living **cultural treasures**, from Inuit print-makers and carvers to traditional drummers and "throat" singers.

Most of the region's communities are formed of indigenous Inuit and lie on the arc of Hudson Bay's western coast, from **Arviat** ("place of the bowhead whale") in the south through **Whale Cove** (Tikirarjuaq, "long point"), **Rankin Inlet** (Kangiqtiniq, "deep bay") – the area's main transport and administrative centre – to **Chesterfield Inlet** (Igluligaarjuk, "place with a few igloos") and **Coral Harbour** (Salliq, "large flat island") in the north. In all of these places you will find that the *Nunavummiut*, or Inuit of Nunavut, continue to honour their traditional lifestyle, culture and ancestors. The remainder of Nunavut's population live even further north in the scattered communities dotting Baffin Island and its surrounding archipelago. The capital, at **Iqaluit** on Baffin Island, is home to nearly one-fifth of the territory's population.

Although you'll find an old way of life and stunning Arctic landscapes, don't be alarmed by the physical appearance of most villages; housing here is at a premium

Nunavut practicalities

Exploring Nunavut is hugely rewarding, but far from easy – the entire region has just 21km of hwy. The landscapes are sublime but often inhospitable, so access is invariably by **plane** or helicopter and therefore expensive; we've listed the airlines that service some communities in the relevant account. Whatever your interest or activity, the best way to see the area is with one of the many **tour companies**. For those wishing to trek or canoe the various parks and rivers on their own or in small groups, the best place to purchase topographical and regional maps is at the Ottawa-based World of Maps (Ⓣ1-800/214-8524, Ⓦwww.worldofmaps.com).

Arrival in and **information** on the region's major centres are covered in the following pages. Nunavut publishes its own visitors' guide, the annual *Canada's Arctic Nunavut Travel Planner* (free), which is packed with information, including a full listing of tour operators and outfitters. Information is also available at Ⓣ1-866/686-2888, Ⓦwww.nunavuttourism.com or Ⓦwww.explorenunavut.com. It's also worth exploring Nunavut Parks at Ⓦwww.nunavutparks.com.

Hotel prices in the north are invariably **per person**, not per room, so double all rates if you are two people sharing a double room. Don't be surprised if you are required to share a room with a stranger – this is the north and hotel space is at a premium. Rates sometimes include meals, so are not as steep as they first appear.

Most of the communities in Nunavut have no **banking** facilities – the exception being Iqaluit and Rankin Inlet. If you are short of cash you could withdraw from the ATMs found in many of the smaller communities, usually at the Northern Grocery store or locally run Co-op stores.

and many buildings and infrastructure suffer the effects of the arctic's harsh and changing environment. Houses are built on silts and sit high above the permafrost layer, while some are even cabled down to prevent them from blowing away during the fierce arctic winds. All building supplies, canned grocery goods and supplies must all be shipped in by sealift, which arrive once or twice a year during the brief ice-free months between July and early October. Despite the rundown appearance of these places, it is the warmth and generosity of the Inuit who live there that make staying here the real reward.

Kivalliq region

Nestled along the western shores of Hudson Bay lie a handful of communities that are only accessible by air, boat or snow machine. The region also includes Baker Lake, Nunavut's only inland community, which is renowned for its prints and beautiful soap-stone carvings.

Inland, the land is dominated by gently rolling hills and the vast openness of the tundra. Home to grazing caribou, musk ox, grizzly bears and millions upon millions of migrating songbirds, swans and geese this region is a **naturalist's paradise**. Offshore, in the waters of Hudson Bay, lie one of the world's best spots to observe pods of beluga whale and sea ducks – you may even encounter a polar bear patrolling the shores.

Rankin Inlet (Kangiqtiniq) and around

RANKIN INLET, serves as the business and transportation hub for central Nunavut. The community was founded in 1955 when the North Rankin Nickel Mine opened. Many Inuit families moved from the land to Rankin Inlet to become miners or obtain other industry-related jobs. Although the mine closed in the mid-1960s the community remained, thanks in part to its craft industry, tourism and the entrepreneurial spirit of its residents.

First Air and Canadian North have direct **flights** to Rankin Inlet from Iqaluit and Yellowknife and connecting services from Ottawa and Montréal via Iqaluit. Calm Air (see p.868) has scheduled services from Churchill, Manitoba to Rankin Inlet and most other Kivalliq villages. Chartering a flight to visit the interior can be arranged by contacting Kivalliq Air (Ⓣ867/645-2992 or 1-888/831-8472, Ⓦwww.kivalliqair.com). Rankin Inlet boasts the small regional **Kivalliq Regional Visitor Centre**, housed at the airport, and a post office at the 65-room *Siniktarvik Hotel & Conference Centre* (Ⓣ867/645-2807; ⑧).

The Town

The most prominent attraction is the huge *inukshuk* that sits on the rocks above town. Some of the more popular activities in summer include fishing trips and boat rides to the Marble Island, an important Inuit historical site, with old camps, sunken ships and artefacts from the whaling era. It's also worth hiring Pissuk Outfitting (Ⓣ867/645-4218, Ⓕ645-3322) to take you to **Iqalugaarjuup Nunanga Territorial Park**, some 10km northwest from town on the Meliadine River. Once there, you can walk among the **Thule** sites and see storage caches, ancient fox traps, stone tent rings, kayak cradles and the remains of a sod house. In winter you can experience the traditional skill of igloo building or dog-sledding on the sea ice. If you're in town in mid-May it's worth attending Pakallak Time, an annual **festival** where everyone joins in square dances, games and dogteam races.

For accommodation, try *Tara's Bed & Breakfast* (Ⓣ867/645-3478, Ⓔtarasbb@arctic.ca; ⑦) or the well-equipped and friendly B&B *Nanuq Lodge* (Ⓣ867/645-2650, Ⓦwww.nanuqlodge.com; ⑦), which has internet and a small library of books of local interest. Contact the hamlet (ⓣ867/645-2895) for information on outfitters, tours and other accommodation.

Coral Harbour

CORAL HARBOUR or Salliq ("a large flat island in front of the mainland") is the only settlement on Southampton Island and one of the best places to see **walrus** and **polar bears** (on nearby Coats Island), as well as the beautiful Kirchoffer Falls, 24km of town, and the Thule archeological sites at Native Point, 64km southeast of town. As the English name suggests, Coral Harbour refers to the fossilized coral originally formed some 450 million years ago when the local climate was much more tropical. Outfitters can take you to Fossil Creek Trail to see the best display of **fossils** in Nunavut, or to the East Bay and Harry Gibbons Migratory Bird sanctuaries to see thousands of snow geese, tundra swans, sandhill cranes and scores of other migratory species that gather here each year in spring.

There are **flights** here on Calm Air and on First Air from Iqaluit via Rankin Inlet. **Accommodation** is found at the small *Leonie's Place* (ⓣ867/925-9751 or 925-8810, ⓕ925-8606; ❼ with all meals) or the *Esungark Hotel/Inns North* (ⓣ867/925-9926 or 1-888/866-6784; ❼) run by the Katudgevik Co-op. Contact the hamlet (ⓣ867/925-8867) for information on outfitters, tours and other accommodation options.

Arviat

Arviat, 240km southwest of Rankin Inlet, means the "place of the bowhead whale" and is particularly known for its crafts and the McConnell River Migratory Bird Sanctuary, home to the snowy owl and thousands of nesting waterfowl. In fall, beluga whales congregate in the bays around town and caribou are often spotted foraging nearby. The late autumn months are also the best time to see polar bears feeding along the sea ice's edge. Each year in March the town plays host to the incredible 400km Hudson Bay Quest **dog-sled race** (ⓦwww.wapuskdogsled.com) between Churchill, Manitoba, and Arviat. Residents here are proud of their traditional values and knowledge and welcome the chance to introduce you to throat singing, drum dancing or story telling. Hiking trails and 20km of gravel roads allow you to explore the area outside of town by 4-wheeler, which can be rented from locals (enquire at the hamlet office). The Sivulinut Elders Society hosts cultural events and drum dances throughout town. For more information on the community, tours, outfitters and accommodation call the summer-only Margaret Aniksak **tourist office** (ⓣ867/857-2366) or the hamlet office (ⓣ867/857-2841). There are daily **flights** to Arviat from Rankin Inlet.

Accommodation comprises the *Padlei/Inns North* (ⓣ867/857-2919, ⓦwww.innsnorth.com or www.arviathotel.com; ❼ per person) and *The Bayside B&B* (ⓣ867/857-2653, ⓔbayside2@attcanada.ca; ❼); rates at the latter include three meals a day, though a kitchen facility is available. Head to the well-stocked Northern Store for groceries. Contact the hamlet (ⓣ867/857-2841) for information on outfitters, tours and other accommodation.

Baker Lake (Qamanit'uaq)

Some 260km west of Rankin Inlet at the mouth of the Thelon River is **BAKER LAKE**, or Qamanit'uaq ("far inland" or "huge widening of a river"), the Arctic's only inland Inuit community, which also marks Canada's geographic centre. It has long been a meeting place for members of different Inuit groups and provides a point of access into the **tundra** that characterizes the vastness of the region. This is a subtle landscape that's worth more than its "Barrenland" label suggests, particularly in summer, when the thaw brings to life thousands of tiny streams and lakes, and some three hundred species of wild flowers amid the lichens and grasses that provide fodder for huge herds of musk ox and caribou. Millions of wildfowl can

The Inuit

Distinct from all other Canadian aboriginal peoples by virtue of their culture, language and Asiatic physical features, the **Inuit** are the dominant people of a **territory** extending from northern Alaska to Greenland. They once led a **nomadic** existence in one of the most hostile environments on earth, dwelling in **igloos** during the winter and **skin tents** in the summer, moving around using **kayaks** (*umiaks*) or **dog sleds** (*komatik*). The latter were examples of typical Inuit adaptability – the runners were sometimes made from frozen fish wrapped in sealskin and caribou bones were used for crossbars.

Their prey – caribou, musk ox, seals, walruses, narwhals, beluga whales, polar bears, birds and fish – provided everything: oil for heating and cooking, hides for clothing and tents, harpoon lines and dog harnesses. Using harpoons, bows and arrows and spears, ingenious hunting methods were devised; to catch caribou, for example, huge **inuksuits**, piles of rocks resembling the human form, were used to steer the herd towards hunters.

The Inuit **diet** was composed totally of flesh and every part of the animal was eaten, usually raw, from the eyeballs to the heart. Delicacies included the plaited and dried intestines of seals and whole sealskins stuffed with small birds and left to putrefy until the contents had turned to the consistency of cheese. All food was shared and the successful hunter had to watch his catch being distributed among other families in the group, in accordance with specific relationships, before his own kin were allowed the smallest portion. **Starvation** was common – it was not unusual for whole villages to perish in the winter – and consequently **infanticide**, particularly of females, was employed to keep population sizes down. Elders who could not keep up with the travelling group were abandoned, a fate that also befell some offenders of the social code – though the usual way of resolving conflict was the **song-duel**, whereby the aggrieved would publicly ridicule the behaviour of the offender, who was expected to accept the insults with good grace.

It was a woman who often served as the **shaman,** or *angakok*, maintaining the group's communion with the supernatural. The deity who features most regularly in Inuit myth is a goddess called **Sedna**, whose father mutilated her. Her severed fingers became seals and walruses and her hands became whales, but Sedna lived on as the mother and protector of all sea life, capable of withholding her bounty if strict taboos were not adhered to. These included keeping land and sea products

also be seen, and the huge skies and flat horizons are also one of the best places in Canada to see the **aurora borealis** (see p.870) throughout the fall and winter. Also be sure to take in the **Inuit Camp,** which includes a demonstration by Inuit families of the activities (hunting, trapping and weaving) that might have taken place in a Caribou Inuit camp.

The summer-only Akumalik **tourist office** (hours vary; ⓣ867/793-2456) occupies a reconstructed 1936 Hudson's Bay Company post in the original lakeside building. Staff there can provide information on local tours as well as assist you in organizing a paddling trip on the Thelon or Kazan rivers, both taking you into the heart of the vast tundra. A short walk east along the shore is the **Inuit Heritage Centre** (July & Aug hours vary; ⓣ867/793-2598), which features displays interpreting the culture of the Caribou Inuit. A visit to Baker Lake is not complete until you drop by the Jesse Oonark Centre or the Ookpiktuyuk Art Gallery, both which showcase the beautiful soapstone carvings, wall hangings and fine jewellery the community is renowned for.

Calm Air has daily **flights** here from Rankin Inlet. For **accommodation**, there are the two aircraft-hanger-like structures of *Iglu Hotel* (ⓣ867/793-2801, separate; so seals could never be eaten with caribou and all caribou clothing had to be made before the winter seal hunt.

Sporadic **European contact** dates back to the Norse settlement of Greenland, and early missionaries visited some Inuit. It wasn't until the early 1800s that the two cultures met in earnest. By 1860 commercial **whalers** had begun wintering around the north of Hudson Bay, employing Inuit as crew and hunters for their food in return for European goods. The impact on the Inuit was not really deleterious until the arrival of **American whalers** in 1890, when the liberal dispensing of alcohol and spread of diseases (smallpox and veneral disease) led to a drastic decline in population.

By the early 1900s **fur traders** were encouraging the Inuit to stop hunting off the coast and turn inland, using firearms and traps. The accompanying **missionaries** brought welcome medical help and schools, but put an end to multiple marriages, shamanism and other traditional practices. More changes came when Inuit were employed to build roads, airfields and other military facilities during World War II, and to construct the line of radar installations known as Distant Early Warning system in the Cold War era. As well as bringing new jobs, this also focused government attention on the plight of the Inuit.

The consequent largesse was not wholly beneficial: subsidized housing and welfare payments led many Inuit to abandon their hunting camps and settle in **permanent communities**, usually located in places strategic to Canada's sovereignty in the Arctic. Without knowledge of English and French, these Inuit were left out of all decision-making and often lived in a separate part of towns administered by outsiders. Old values and beliefs were all but eroded by television and radio, and high levels of depression, alcoholism and violence became the norm. The 1982 ban on European imports of sealskins created mass **unemployment**, and although hunting still provides the basics of subsistence, the high cost of ammunition and fuel makes commercial-scale hunting uneconomical.

And yet it's not all gloom. Inuit cooperatives are increasingly successful and the production of **soapstone carvings** – admittedly a commercial adulteration of traditional Inuit ivory art – is very profitable. Having organized themselves into politically active groups and secured **land claims** such as Nunavut, the Inuit are slowly rebuilding an ancient culture that was shattered in under half a century.

Ⓦwww.bakerlakehotel.com; ❼ with all meals) within which there's also the restaurant with its mediocre cafeteria food; alternatives include the small number of rooms and cabins offered by the *Baker Lake Lodge* (Ⓣ867/793-2905 or 867/793-2010; ❺ including pick-up from the airport), and the Inuit-owned *Nunamiut Lodge* (Ⓣ867/793-2127; ❻), which has pretty lake views. There's also a small community **campsite** (free) located on the road to the airport.

Contact the tourist office or the hamlet (Ⓣ867/793-2874) for information on outfitters, tours and other accommodation.

Kitikmeot (The Arctic Coast)

Canada's last frontier, the **Arctic Coast** (or Kitikmeot region) encompasses the country's northern mainland coast from the Mackenzie River to Baffin Island, and – as "coast" is a relative term in a region where the sea is often frozen – numerous islands too, most notably a large part of Victoria Island. It is a barren, ice-carved and wind-scoured landscape of chill lakes and low hills with not a tree to be seen. Braving this setting, which is also nearly completely dark and frozen for nine months of the year, is a permanent population of a few hundred. As recently as sixty years ago, the Inuit (see pp.940–941) here had known little or no contact with the outside world. Few explorers encountered them, and even the most determined of Western agencies – the church and the trading companies – have failed to compromise a people who are still extraordinarily isolated by climate, distance and culture. Yet today, few of the Inuit live according to the ways of popular myth. Except on the odd trapping party, for example, government-built homes have replaced igloos, and rifles, snow bikes, outboard motors and light aircraft have superseded the bone tools, sledges and sealskin kayaks of a generation ago.

You have to be fairly determined to reach any of the region's seven communities, let alone explore the hauntingly beautiful ice fields and tundra. Those that forge their way are usually looking to spot **wildlife**, **fish** or hunt for musk ox, caribou and polar bears. Increasingly, more tourists are visiting this region as part of a cruise through the famed Northwest Passage (see opposite). Most visitors base themselves either at **Kugluktuk** (Coppermine) or at Victoria Island's **Ikaluktutiak** (Cambridge Bay), the transport and service capital. Each main Arctic coast community, remarkably, has **accommodation**, but reservations are vital and prices predictably steep. You need to come prepared: in some cases, even meals must be booked in advance. Basic groceries are usually available at stores, but there are no banks. Various **tour operators** run trips to and from the main centres; for extensive information, send for the *Nunavut Travel Planner* before you go (see p.937).

Cambridge Bay (Ikaluktutiak)

CAMBRIDGE BAY, or Ikaluktutiak ("fair fishing place") lies to the north of the Arctic Circle on the southern shore of **Victoria Island**, Canada's second largest island. You need to be highly motivated to come here, as accommodation, food and flights are all hideously expensive.

Today, it's the regional centre for the Kitikmeot communities and an important staging point for tours or for heading still deeper into the hinterland. It also operates as the administrative focus for the region's western lands, despite being a full 1300km from the capital, Iqaluit. Over the centuries the region was a summer gathering place for the Copper Inuit, attracted here by the abundance of good hunting. Kitikmeot Meats processes caribou and musk ox for export and the Ikaluktutiak Co-op runs a fishery that supplies arctic char nationwide (both concerns are open to the public for direct sales). The Hudson's Bay Company arrived in 1921, late by Canadian standards, and purchased the *Maud*, explorer Roald Amundsen's schooner, for use as a supplies and trading ship. This little piece of Arctic history was used for years before being left to sink into disrepair and, ultimately, then into the harbour, where its hulk can still be seen.

Scheduled flights arrive on Canadian North and First Air from Yellowknife; First Air flies between all the settlements except Bathurst Inlet and Umingmaktok, which can be reached by charter aircraft only.

The region's main **tourist office** (Mon–Fri 9am–5pm, ⓣ867/983-2224) is an attractive modern building overlooking the bay. It has displays on the art, history and culture of the Copper and Netsilik Inuit, as well as exhibits of maps and documents that shed light on the age-old search for the Northwest Passage (see opposite); staff there will provide you with a list of outfitters and any other information.

Practicalities

For **accommodation**, there's the 25-room *Arctic Islands Lodge* (ⓣ867/983-2345 or 1-888/866-6784, ⓦwww.cambridgebayhotel.com; ❼). There are also one- and two-bedroom apartments, a coffee shop and restaurant where meals cost another

The Northwest Passage

Traversed in its entirety fewer than fifty times, the fabled **Northwest Passage** across the top of Canada's Arctic continues to exert a romantic allure – and, in the wake of oil discoveries in the far north, an increasingly economic one. The world's most severe maritime challenge, it involves a 1500-kilometre journey from north of Baffin Island to the Beaufort Sea above Alaska. Some fifty thousand icebergs line the eastern approaches and thick pack ice covers the route for nine months of the year, with temperatures rising above freezing only in July and August. Perpetual darkness reigns for four months of the year and thick fog and blizzards can obscure visibility for the remaining eight. Even with modern technology navigation is extremely difficult: little is known of Arctic tides and currents; sonar is confused by submerged ice; and the featureless tundra of the Arctic islands provides the only few points of visual or radar reference.

John Cabot can hardly have been happy with Henry VII's 1497 order to blaze the northwest trail, the first recorded instance of such an attempt. The passage subsequently excited the imagination of the world's greatest adventurers, men such as Sir Francis Drake, Jacques Cartier, Sir Martin Frobisher, James Cook and **Henry Hudson** – cast adrift by his mutinous crew in 1611 when Hudson Bay turned out to be an icebound trap rather than the actual passage.

Details of a possible route were pieced together over the centuries, though many paid with their lives in the process, most famously **Sir John Franklin**, who vanished into the ice with 129 men in 1845. Many rescue parties set out to find Franklin's vessels, HMS *Erebus* and HMS *Terror*, and it was one searcher, **Robert McClure**, who – in the broadest sense – first transited the route in 1854. Entering from the west, he was trapped for two winters before sledging to meet a rescue boat coming from the east. Norwegian **Roald Amundsen** made the **first sea crossing** in 1906, but only after a three-year voyage. The first single-season traverse was made by a Canadian Mountie, **Henry Larsen**, in 1944 – his schooner, the *St Roch*, is now enshrined in Vancouver's Maritime Museum.

$30–60 per day. The smaller *Green Row Executive Suites* (Ⓣ867/983-3456, Ⓔgreenrow@polarnet.ca; ⑥) has eighteen central, self-contained suites with kitchenettes. You can **camp** 5km away at Freshwater Creek and – if you're self-catering – buy supplies at the Northern store. You should also be able to camp on the shoreline of the bay, but ask at the hamlet office first, and make sure you're well away from and out of sight of any houses. Contact the hamlet office (Ⓣ867/983-4650) for information on outfitters, tours and other accommodation options.

Kugluktuk (Coppermine)

KUGLUKTUK ("place of rapids") lies west of Cambridge Bay on the Canadian "mainland", sitting astride the **Coppermine River** close to the westernmost point of Nunavut. Yellowknife is 600km to the south. The Coronation Gulf, a relatively narrow sea passage, separates the mainland coast from Victoria Island at this point, a vital through-route on the Northwest Passage.

Today, the river provides one of the continent's great **canoe trips**, with most canoeists (or rafters) joining tours or chartering a plane from Yellowknife to the river's headwaters. The 325-kilometre trip downstream takes around ten days. The trip offers sensational opportunities for **watching wildlife**, but you can also strike lucky with wildlife by walking or taking short tours from Kugluktuk itself. The most popular walk (20km one-way) is to the **Bloody Falls**, so called because a party of Inuit were massacred here following an argument with a group of Dene guides accompanying Hearne. If you don't fancy the walk, or only want to go one way – it's tough going in places – you can arrange a boat to take you or pick you up; the tourist office will have full details. In spring, the Nattiq Frolics celebrations feature dancing, a community feast, Inuit games and snowmobile racing.

Access by **air** is provided through Canadian North and First Air from Yellowknife and other local communities. **Information** is available in summer from the Heritage Visitors Centre (July & Aug daily 8.30am–5pm, other times on request; ⓣ867/982-3232) who also organize local walking tours and programmes.

Practicalities

There are two **accommodation** options: the central *Coppermine Inn* (ⓣ867/982-3333, ⓕ982-3340; ❼) has motel rooms or self-contained units and breakfast, lunch and dinner (if you want them) should be reserved in advance; or the smaller *Enokhok Inn* (ⓣ867/982-3197, ⓕ982-4291; ❼ including meals). **Camping** is possible at Kukluktuk Park. As for **eating**, non-residents can use the *Coppermine Inn*, but you need to book meals a day in advance. Contact the tourist office or hamlet office (ⓣ867/982-3126) for information on outfitters, tours and other accommodation.

Baffin Island

Baffin Island comprises half a million square kilometres of Arctic vastness, whose main attraction is **Auyuittuq National Park** on the Cumberland Peninsula, Canada's northernmost accessible national park. With a treeless landscape, mountains towering over 1500m, icy glacial streams and 24-hour daylight from May to July, hiking in the park offers one of the most majestic experiences in Canada. Yet with temperatures rising to a mere 6°C from June to August, it can be a harsh environment that will appeal only to the truly adventurous; expensive though they are, **package tours** are definitely recommended if this is your first venture into such a remote place. Bring all necessary gear with you, as the island supplies are limited.

Iqaluit (Frobisher Bay)

The main gateway to Baffin Island – and capital of Nunavut – is rapidly- growing **Iqaluit** (meaning simply "fish"), whose population of six thousand is predominantly Inuit. Since being selected as Nunavut's capital in December 1995 Iqaluit has seen tremendous change, with the construction of homes, commercial and government buildings continuing apace. Iqaluit has the most to see in terms of culture and in-town attractions of any settlement in Nunavut, but even these activities won't hold your interest for too long – the real sights are to be seen in the surrounding area.

Arrival and information

Getting to Baffin Island is only feasible by **air**. First Air and Canadian North (see p.868 for details) make the round-trip daily from Montréal and Ottawa (3hr). Ticket **prices** can get as low as $800 return, but are usually nearer $1200. Both airlines also link Yellowknife to Iqaluit, via Rankin Inlet (5 weekly; 3hr 50min). Ask about cheap pass deals and other pre-booked flight deals if you're making international flights into Canada: these are often much cheaper bought beforehand in conjunction with the carrier you're using to fly in to the country.

The main Nunavut Tourism office is here (ⓣ867/979-6551 or 1-866/686-2888, ⓦwww.nunavuttourism.com), as is the Unikkaarvik (Baffin Regional) **tourist office** (July & Aug daily 10am–6pm & 1–4pm other times on request; ⓣ867/979-4636), both of which provide information, maps of the town and region, along with information about visiting the rest of Nunavut. **Tour operators** who run trips into the interior abound in Nunavut; consult the *Nunavut Travel Planner* or website (see p.937) or contact the Iqaluit tourist office for more information.

Accommodation

Iqaluit has many **accommodation** options including **B&Bs,** which tend to come and go. The main **hotels** charge more or less similar rates – around $200 per person per night – for similar facilities. They include: *The Navigator Inn* (Ⓣ867/979-6201, Ⓔnavres@nunanet.com; ❼), the *Discovery Lodge* (Ⓣ867/979-4433, Ⓦwww.discoverylodge.com; ❼), the *Frobisher Inn* (Ⓣ867/979-2222 or 1-877/422-9422, Ⓦwww.frobisherinn.com; ❼) and the *Nova Inn* (Ⓣ867/979-6684 or 1-866/497-6933; ❼) with its cosy restaurant. One of the better B&Bs in town is the very comfortable *Accommodations by the Sea* (Ⓣ867/979-6074, Ⓦwww.accommodationsbythesea.ca; ❻), with five bedrooms and a large balcony with a gorgeous view of the surroundings.

The town and around

Things to see in town include a tour of the impressive Legislative Assembly Building (June–Aug daily 1.30pm; winter call for appointment; Ⓣ867/975-5000) housing a fine collection of Inuit art and the ceremonial mace fashioned from an ivory narwhal tusk and adorned with precious minerals mined throughout Nunavut. There's a superb collection of Inuit art and artefacts in the **Nunatta Sunakkutaangit Museum** (call for latest times; Ⓣ867/979-5537), housed in a renovated Hudson's Bay trading post building. Enquire at the tourist office for day tours (by boat in summer, by dog team in winter) to the **Qaummaarviit Territorial Historic Park**, located on an island a short distance from Iqaluit. Artefacts found there indicate the Thule had lived in the region some seven hundred years ago and interpretive signs now explain the significance of tent rings, meat caches and gravesites, some of which can still be seen.

Auyuittuq National Park and Pangnirtung

Straddling the Arctic Circle on the northeast coast of Baffin Island, **Auyuittuq National Park** is one of the most spectacular destinations in the Canadian North. The heart of the park is the massive **Penney Ice Cap**, a remnant of the ice sheet that extended over most of Canada east of the Rockies about eighteen thousand years ago, and the 110km **Pangnirtung/Aksayuk Pass**, a major **hiking route,** which cuts through the mountains between Cumberland Sound and the Davis Strait. *Auyuittuq* is Inuktitut for "the land that never melts" but despite the unrelenting cold in summer the sparse tundra plants bloom and chance encounters with arctic hares and foxes, polar bears, Canada geese, snowy owls and gyrfalcons are a possibility; just offshore you may spot narwhals, walruses, bowhead and beluga whales, as well as harp, ringed and bearded seals. Yet the main attraction is not necessarily the wildlife viewing (sightings are rare) but the shear rugged beauty and raw power of the dramatic landscape.

Arrival and information

There are daily one-hour First Air and/or Canadian North flights from Iqaluit to **PANGNIRTUNG**, or Pang, the gateway to Auyuittuq National Park. Pang's tourist office is in the Angmarlik Interpretive Centre (Ⓣ867/473-8737, various daily hours in summer), which is located next to the Parks Canada office.

The only commercial **place to stay** in Pang is the 25-room *Auyuittuq Lodge* (Ⓣ867/473-8955, Ⓔpanglodge@qiniq.ca; ❼), which also offer tasty meals at an additional cost (you can also order takeaway lunches for when you are out on the land). It is also possible to overnight with local families – inquire at the tourist office for homestay programmes.

Visiting the park

The only transport for the 25km from Pang to Overlord, the south entrance of the park, is by **freighter canoe**, which the Inuit also charter for fishing, whale-watching and sightseeing trips. The rates on these "canoes" – which are like small fishing boats with outboard motors – are set by the Inuit cooperative, and work out at around $130 per person one-way (usually minimum of two passengers). The boats can only pass through the Pangnirtung Fjord after the ice break-up in July and only then during high tides (check at the park office for monthly tide charts). Arrangements for a canoe pick-up should be confirmed by radio from the few emergency shelters in the park. The best choices for transport to the park are Joavie, who runs Alivaktuk Outfitting (Ⓣ867/473-8721), or Charlie, from Komoartok Tours and Outfitting (Ⓣ867/473-8541). Both also arrange sightseeing tours around the region throughout the year.

Services within the park are extremely limited and the **weather** is highly unpredictable. Snowstorms, high wind and rain occur frequently, and deaths from hypothermia have been known even in the height of summer. All-weather hiking gear is essential, and a walking stick is necessary to assist you with the ice-cold stream crossings which occur every 200–300m and can still be waist-high in July. There is no wood for fuel, so a camping stove is essential.

All visitors must participate in a mandatory **safety orientation** briefing held at the Parks Canada office (Ⓣ867/473-2500, Ⓦwww.pc.gc.ca/auyuittuq). Information on this and other parks in the north is available here.

Travel details

Trains

Prince George to: Edmonton via Jasper (3 weekly; 8hr 15min); Prince Rupert (3 weekly; 13hr); Vancouver (mid-June to Oct 1 daily; rest of year 3 weekly; 13hr 30min).
Prince Rupert to: Prince George (3 weekly; 13hr).

Buses

Dawson City to: Inuvik (mid-June to early Sept 2–3 weekly; 12hr); Whitehorse (late June to Sept 3 weekly; Oct & March to early June 2 weekly; rest of year 1 weekly; 7hr 30min).
Dawson Creek to: Edmonton (2 daily; 9hr); Prince George (2 daily; 6hr 30min); Whitehorse (mid-May to mid-Oct 1 daily except Sun; rest of year 3 weekly; 21hr).
Hay River to: Fort Resolution (3 weekly; 6hr); Fort Smith (3 weekly; 7hr); Peace River (daily except Mon; connections for Edmonton and Grande Prairie; 8hr); Yellowknife (3 weekly; 12hr).
Prince George to: Dawson Creek (2 daily; 6hr 30min); Edmonton via Jasper (2 daily; 9hr 45min); Prince Rupert (2 daily; 11hr); Vancouver via Williams Lake and Cache Creek (2 daily; 13hr).
Whitehorse to: Dawson City (June–Sept 3 weekly; Oct & March to early June 2 weekly; rest of year 1 weekly; 7hr 30min); Dawson Creek (mid-May to mid-Oct 1 daily except Sun; rest of year 3 weekly; 21hr); Skagway (mid-May to mid-June 1 daily except Wed & Sun; 4hr).

Flights

Listed below are only the main direct scheduled flights operated by the big carriers; for details on the many small provincial companies operating within the North, turn to each relevant town account.
Inuvik from: Calgary (3 weekly; 5hr); Yellowknife (1 daily; 2hr 35min).
Iqaluit from: Edmonton (2 weekly; 6hr); Montréal (1–2 daily; 3hr); Ottawa (4 weekly; 4hr); Yellowknife (5 weekly; 3hr 50min).
Whitehorse from: Vancouver (3 daily; 2hr 20min).
Yellowknife from: Calgary (1–3 daily; 3hr 20min); Cambridge Bay (3 weekly; 1hr 30min); Edmonton (2–3 daily; 1hr 35min); Fort Smith (1 daily; 1hr 30min); Inuvik (1 daily; 2hr 35min); Norman Wells (1 daily; 1hr 15min); Resolute (2 weekly; 3hr 20min).

Contexts

Contexts

History......949

The natural environment......962

Books......970

History

Fully unified as late as 1949, **Canada** is a country of intertwining histories rather than a single national thread. Not only does each of its provinces maintain a considerable degree of autonomy, but each grouping of aboriginal peoples can claim a heritage that cannot be easily integrated into the story of white, European Canada. Such a complex mosaic militates against generalization, although Canadians themselves continue to grapple with the nature of their own identity. What follows is an attempt to define and clarify key events and themes.

The beginnings

The ancestors of the **aboriginal peoples** of North America first entered the continent around 25,000 years ago, when vast glaciers covered most of the northern continents. It seems likely that North America's first human inhabitants crossed the land bridge linking Asia with present-day Alaska – they were probably Siberian hunter-nomads travelling in pursuit of mammoths, hairy rhinos, bison, wild horses and sloths. These people left very little to mark their passing, apart from some simple graves and the grooved, chipped-stone spearheads that earned them the name **Fluted Point People**. In successive waves the Fluted Point People moved down through North America until they reached the southernmost tip of South America. As they settled, so they slowly developed distinctive cultures and languages, whose degree of elaboration depended on the resources available in their various environments.

Around 3000 BC, another wave of migration passed over from Asia to North America. This wave was made up of the first group of **Inuit** migrants who – because the land bridge was now submerged under today's Bering Strait – made their crossings either in skin-covered boats or on foot over the ice. Within the next thousand years the Inuit occupied the entire northern zone of the continent, moving east as far as Greenland and displacing the earlier occupants. These first Inuit are now called the **Dorset Eskimos** after Cape Dorset, on Baffin Island (see p.944), where archeologists first identified their remains in the 1920s, but they were assimilated or wiped out by the next wave of Inuit. These crossed into the continent three thousand years ago, creating the **Thule** culture – so called after the Greek word for the world's northernmost extremity. The Thule people were the direct ancestors of today's Inuit.

The native peoples

Before the Europeans arrived, the aboriginal peoples of Canada, who numbered around 300,000, were divided into three main language groups: **Algonkian**, **Athapascan** (principally in the north and west) and **Inuktitut** (Inuit). Within these groups existed a multitude of cultures. None of these people had a written language, the wheel was unknown to them and their largest draught animal, prior to the introduction of the horse (via the Spanish), was the dog. Yet over the centuries each of the tribes developed techniques that enabled them to cope and survive.

Immediately prior to European arrival, Canada was divided into a number of cultural zones. In the extreme north lived the nomadic **Inuit** (see pp.940–941), whose basic unit was the family group, small enough to survive in the precarious conditions. The necessarily small-scale nature of Inuit life meant they developed no political structures and gathered together in larger groups only if the supply of food required it – when, for example, the arctic char were running upriver from the sea to spawn, or the caribou were migrating. Immediately to the south of the Inuit, in a zone stretching from the Labrador coast across the Canadian Shield to northern BC, lived the tribes of the **northern forests**. This was also a harsh environment, and consequently these peoples spent most of their time in small nomadic bands following the game on which they depended. Variations between the tribes largely resulted from the type of game they pursued: the **Naskapi** fished and hunted seals on the Labrador coast; the **Chipewyan**, occupying the border country between the tundra and forest to the west of Hudson Bay, mainly hunted caribou; the **Wood Cree**, to the south of the Chipewyan, along the Churchill River, hunted deer and moose; and the **Tahltan** of BC combined hunting with seasonal fishing. Like the Inuit, the political structures of these tribes were rudimentary and, although older men enjoyed a certain respect, there were no "chiefs" in any European sense of the term. Decisions were generally made collectively with the opinions of successful hunters – the guarantors of survival – carrying great weight, as did those of their **shaman**, whose main function was to satisfy the spirits that they believed inhabited every animate and inanimate object around them.

The Iroquois-speakers

The southern zone of Canada, stretching from the St Lawrence River along the northern shores of the Great Lakes to southern BC, was climatically much kinder, and it's in this region that Canada's native peoples developed their most sophisticated cultures. Here, along the banks of the St Lawrence River and the shores of the Great Lakes, lived the **Iroquois-speaking** peoples, who were divided into three tribal confederacies: the **Five Nations**, the **Huron** (see p.153) and the **Neutrals**. All three groups cultivated corn (maize), beans and squash in an agricultural system that enabled them to lead a settled life – often in communities of several hundreds. Iroquois society was divided into matriarchal clans, whose affairs would be governed by a female elder. The clan shared a long house and when a man married (always outside his own clan), he would go to live in the long house of his wife. Tribal chiefs (sachems) were male, but the female elders of the tribe selected them and they also had to belong to a lineage through which the rank of sachem descended. Iroquoian society had its bellicose side, too. An assured winter supply of food enabled the Iroquois to indulge in protracted inter-tribal warfare: in particular, the Five Nations were almost always at war with the Huron.

The Ojibwa and the peoples of the Plains and the West Coast

To the west of the Iroquois, between lakes Superior and Winnipeg, lived the **Ojibwa**, forest hunters who learned to cultivate maize from the Iroquois and also harvested the wild rice that grew on the fringes of the region's lakes. Further west still, on the prairies, lived the peoples of the **Blackfoot Confederation**: the **Piegan**, **Blackfoot** and **Blood** tribes. The economy of this latter grouping was based on the buffalo (or bison): its flesh was eaten; its hide provided clothes and shelter; its bones were made into tools; its sinews were ideal for bow strings; and its hooves were melted down to provide glue. In the late seventeenth century, the hunting techniques of these prairie peoples were transformed by the arrival of the horse, which had made its way – either wild or by trade – from Mexico, where it had been introduced by the Spanish conquistadors. The horse made the bison easy prey and, as with the Iroquois, a ready food supply spawned the development of a militaristic culture centred on the prowess of the tribes' young braves.

On the **Pacific coast**, tribes such as the **Tlingit** and **Salish** were dependent on the ocean, which provided them with a plentiful supply of food. But there was little cohesion within tribes and people from different villages – even though of the same tribe – would at times be in conflict with each other. Yet these tribes had a rich ceremonial and cultural life, as exemplified by the excellence of their woodcarvings, whose most conspicuous manifestations were the **totem poles** (or, more accurately, house posts), which reached colossal sizes in the nineteenth century.

European arrival

The first recorded contact between Europeans and the native peoples of North America occurred around 1000 AD, when a **Norse** expedition sailing from Greenland landed somewhere on the Atlantic seaboard, probably in Newfoundland (see p.482). It was a fairly short-lived stay – according to the Icelandic sagas, the Norse were forced to withdraw from the area they called Vinland because of the hostility of the natives.

More certainty applies to the year 1492, when **Christopher Columbus** set off in search of the westward route to Asia. Columbus bumped into the West Indies instead, but his "discovery" of islands that were presumed to lie off India encouraged other European monarchs to sponsor expeditions of their own. In 1497, **John Cabot**, supported by the English king Henry VII, sailed west and sighted Newfoundland and Cape Breton. On his return, Cabot reported seeing multitudes of cod off Newfoundland, and his much-publicized comments effectively started the **Newfoundland** cod fishery. In less than sixty years, up to four hundred **fishing vessels** from Britain, France and Spain were making annual voyages to the Grand Banks fishing grounds around the island. Some of the fishermen soon established shore bases to cure their catch, and then they started to winter here – which was how settlement of the island began.

By the end of the sixteenth century the cod trade was largely controlled by the British and French, and Newfoundland became an early focus of Anglo–French rivalries, a colonial conflict that continued until England secured control of the island in the 1713 Treaty of Utrecht.

New France

Meanwhile, in 1535, **Jacques Cartier**, on a voyage paid for by the French crown, made his way down the St Lawrence River, also hoping to find Asia. Instead he stumbled upon the Iroquois, first at Stadacona, on the site of Québec City, and later at Hochelaga, today's Montréal. At both places, the Frenchman had a friendly reception, but the Iroquois attitude changed after Cartier seized one of their tribal chiefs and took him back to France. For a time the Iroquois were a barrier to further exploration up the St Lawrence, but subsequently they abandoned their riverside villages, enabling French traders to move up the river buying **furs**, an enterprise pioneered by seasonal fishermen.

The development of this trade aroused the interest of the French king, who in 1603 commissioned **Samuel de Champlain** to chart the St Lawrence. Two years later Champlain founded **Port Royal** (see p.385) in today's Nova Scotia, which became the capital of **Acadie** (Acadia), a colony whose agricultural preoccupations were soon far removed from the main thrust of French colonialism along the St Lawrence. It was here, on a subsequent expedition in 1608, that Champlain established the settlement of Québec City at the heart of **New France**, and, to stimulate the fur trade, allied the French with those tribes he identified as likely to be his principal suppliers. In practice this meant siding with the Huron against the Five Nations, a decision that intensified their traditional hostility. Furthermore, the fur trade destroyed the balance of power between the tribes: first one and then another would receive, in return for their pelts, the latest type of musket as well as iron axes and knives, forcing enemies back to the fur trade to redress the military balance. One terrible consequence of such European intervention was the **extermination of the Huron people** in 1648 by the Five Nations, armed by the Dutch merchants of the Hudson River.

New France settles down

As pandemonium reigned among the aboriginal peoples, the pattern of life in **New France** was becoming well established. On the farmlands of the St Lawrence River a New World feudalism was practised by the land-owning seigneurs and their habitant tenants, while the fur territories – entered at Montréal – were extended deep into the interior. Many of the fur traders adopted native dress, learnt aboriginal languages and took wives from the tribes through which they passed, spawning the mixed-race people known as the **Métis**. The furs they brought back to Montréal were shipped downriver to Québec City and then on to France. But the white population in the French colony remained relatively small – there were only eighteen thousand New French in 1713. In the context of a growing British presence, this represented a dangerous weakness.

The rise of the British

In 1670, Charles II of England had established the **Hudson's Bay Company** and given it control of a million and a half square miles adjacent to its namesake bay, a territory named Rupert's Land, after the king's uncle. Four years later the British captured the Dutch possessions of the Hudson River Valley, thereby trapping New France. Slowly the British closed the net: in 1713, they took control of Acadia, renaming it **Nova Scotia**, and in 1755 they deported its French-speaking farmers. When the Seven Years War broke out in 1756, the French attempted to outflank the British by using the Great Lakes route to occupy the area to the west of the British colonies and then, with the help of their native allies, pin them to the coast. The British won the war by exploiting their naval superiority: a large force under the command of **General James Wolfe** sailed up the St Lawrence in 1759 and, against all expectations, successfully scaled the Heights of Abraham to

The Hudson's Bay Company

In 1661 two Frenchmen, **Medard Chouart des Groseilliers** and **Pierre-Esprit Radisson**, reached the southern tip of Hudson Bay overland and realized it was the same inland sea described by earlier seafaring explorers. They returned to the St Lawrence River laden with furs, where the French governor arrested them for trapping without a licence. Understandably peeved, they turned to England, where Charles II financed them and gave them two ships, the *Eaglet* and the *Nonsuch*. After a mammoth voyage, the *Nonsuch* returned with a fantastic cargo of furs and this led to the incorporation of the **Hudson's Bay Company** by Charles II on May 2, 1670. The Company was granted wide powers, including exclusive trading rights to the entire Hudson Bay watershed, now re-named **Rupert's Land**.

By 1760, HBC **trading posts** had been built at the mouths of all the major rivers flowing into Hudson Bay and these were commanded by **factors**, who took their policy orders from London. The orders were often unrealistic and based on the concept of aboriginal trappers bringing furs to the posts – the direct opposite to the Montréal-based **North West Company**, whose mainly Francophone employees spent months in the wilderness working with the aboriginals. There was intense competition between the HBC and NWC across the north of the continent, occasionally resulting capture Québec City. Montréal fell a few months later – and at that point the French North American empire was effectively finished, though they held onto Louisiana until Napoleon sold it off in 1803.

Native consternation

For the aboriginal peoples, the **ending of the Anglo–French conflict** was a mixed blessing. If the war had turned the tribes into sought-after allies, it had also destroyed the traditional inter-tribal balance of power and subordinated native to European interests. A recognition of the change wrought by the end of the war inspired the uprising of the Ottawas in 1763, when **Pontiac**, their chief, led an unsuccessful assault on Detroit, hoping to restore the French position and halt the progress of the English settlers. Moved largely by a desire for a stable economy, the response of the British was to issue a proclamation which confirmed the legal right of the natives to their lands and set aside the territory to the west of the Appalachian Mountains and the Great Lakes as **Indian Territory**. Although colonial governors were given instructions to remove trespassers on "Indian Land", in reality the proclamation had little practical effect until the twentieth century, when it became a cornerstone of native peoples' attempts to seek compensation for the illegal confiscation of their land.

The Canadiens

The other great problem the British faced in the 1760s was how to deal with the French-speaking **Canadiens** of the defunct New France – the term Canadiens used to distinguish local settlers from those born in France, most of whom left the colony after the British conquest. Initially the British government hoped to anglicize the province, swamping the French-speaking population with English-speaking Protestants. Yet large-scale migration failed to materialize and the second English governor of Québec, **Guy Carleton**, realized – as discontent grew in the American colonies – the loyalty of the Canadiens was of vital importance.

Carleton's plan to secure this loyalty was embodied in the 1774 **Québec Act**, which made a number of concessions to the region's French speakers: Catholics

in violence, but in 1821 the two companies **merged**. They kept the name Hudson's Bay Company and the British parliament granted the new company a commercial monopoly from Hudson Bay to the Pacific.

Local traders fiercely resented these extensive **monopoly** rights and, in a landmark 1849 case, a Manitoban jury found a Métis trader guilty of breaking the monopoly but refused to have him punished. Thereafter, in practice if not by law, the Company's stranglehold on the fur trade ended. Furthermore, the HBC's quasi-governmental powers seemed increasingly anachronistic and when a company official, **James Douglas**, became BC governor in 1858, the British government forced him to resign from the HBC. This marked the beginning of the end of the company's colonial role.

In 1869 the HBC sold Rupert's Land to Canada. In return it received a cash payment, but, more importantly, retained the title to the lands on which trading posts had been built and one-twentieth of the fertile land open to settlement. Given that the trading posts often occupied land that was to be the nucleus of the new cities that were sprouting in the west, this was a remarkably bad deal for Canada – and a great one for the HBC. Subsequently, the HBC became a major real-estate developer and retail chain, a position it maintains today.

were permitted to hold civil appointments, the seigneurial system was maintained and the Roman Catholic Church allowed to collect tithes. Remarkably, all these concessions were made at a time when Catholics in Britain were not politically emancipated.

The migrations

The success of Carleton's policy was seen during the **American War of Independence** (1775–83) – and later during the Anglo-American War of 1812. The Canadiens refused to volunteer for the armed forces of the Crown, but equally they failed to respond to the appeals of the Americans – no doubt calculating that their survival as a distinctive cultural group was more likely under the British than in an English-speaking United States.

In the immediate aftermath of the American War of Independence, the population of what was left of British North America expanded rapidly, both in "Canada" – which then covered the present-day provinces of Québec and Ontario – and in the separate colonies of New Brunswick, Nova Scotia, Prince Edward Island and Newfoundland. The first large wave of migration came from the US as fourty thousand **United Empire Loyalists** (see p.417) made their way north to stay within British jurisdiction. Of these, all but eight thousand moved to Nova Scotia and New Brunswick, the rest going to the western edge of Québec, where they laid the foundations of the future province of Ontario. Between 1783 and 1812 the population of Canada, as defined at the time, trebled to 330,000, with a large part of the increase being the product of the so-called *revanche du berceau* (revenge of the cradle) – an attempt, encouraged by the Catholic clergy, to outbreed the English-speaking population.

War of 1812

However, tensions between Britain and the US still deterred potential colonists, a problem resolved by the **War of 1812**. Neither side was strong enough to win, but by the Treaty of Ghent in 1814 the Americans recognized the legitimacy of British North America, whose border was established along the **49th parallel** west from Lake of the Woods, in what is now northern Ontario, to the Rockies. **Immigration** now boomed, especially in the 1840s, when economic crises and shortages in Britain, as well as the Irish famine, pushed it up to levels that even the fertile Canadiens could not match. Between 1815 and 1850 over 800,000 immigrants poured into British North America. Most headed for **Upper Canada**, later called Ontario, which received 66,000 migrants in 1832 alone.

Faced with this human tide, the surveyors charted new townships as quickly as possible, but they simply couldn't keep pace with demand. One result was that many native peoples were dispossessed in direct contravention of the 1763 proclamation. By 1806 the region's native peoples had lost 4.5 million acres.

The division and union of Canada

Throughout the early and mid-nineteenth century, it was the English-speaking merchants who drove Canada's economic expansion, largely through the Montréal-based fur trade, organized as the **North West Company**. Seeking political changes that would enhance their economic power, they also wanted their own legislative assembly and the universal application of English law, which would not have been acceptable to the French-speakers. In the **Canada Act of 1791**, the British government imposed a compromise, dividing the region into **Upper** and **Lower Canada**, which broadly separated the two linguistic groups along the line of the Ottawa River. In **Lower Canada**, the French-based legal system was retained, as was the right of the Catholic Church to collect tithes, while in **Upper Canada**, English common law was introduced. Both of the new provinces had an elected assembly, though these shared their limited powers with an appointed assembly and executive councils appointed by the provincial governor. This arrangement allowed the assemblies to become the focal points for vocal opposition, but ultimately condemned them to impotence. At the same time, the merchant elite built up chains of influence and power around the appointed provincial governments: in Upper Canada this grouping was called the **Family Compact**, in Lower Canada the **Château Clique**.

Responsible government

By the late 1830s considerable opposition had developed to these cliques. In Upper Canada the **Reform Movement**, led by **William Lyon Mackenzie**, demanded a government accountable to a broad electorate and the expansion of credit facilities for small farmers. In 1837 both Mackenzie and **Louis-Joseph Papineau**, the reform leader in Lower Canada, were sufficiently frustrated to attempt open rebellion. Neither was successful and both were forced into exile in the US, but the rebellions did bring home to the British Government the need for effective reform. This led to the **Act of Union** of 1840, which united Lower and Upper Canada with a single assembly. The rationale for this arrangement was the belief that the French-Canadians were incapable of handling elective government without Anglo-Saxon guidance. Yet the assembly provided equal representation for Canada East and West – in effect the old Lower and Upper Canadas. A few years later, this new assembly achieved **responsible government** almost accidentally. In 1849 the Reform Party, which had a majority of the seats, passed an Act compensating those involved in the 1837 rebellions. The Governor-General, Lord Elgin, disapproved, but he didn't exercise his veto – so, for the first time, a Canadian administration acted on the vote of an elected assembly, rather than imperial sanction.

Foundation of the Liberal and Conservative parties

The **Reform Party**, which pushed through the compensation scheme, included both French- and English-speakers and mainly represented small farmers and businessmen opposed to the power of the cliques. In the 1850s this grouping became the Canadian **Liberal Party**, but attempts to establish a countrywide coalition fell apart in the 1860s with the emergence of "Clear Grit" Liberals in Canada West. The Grits argued for "Representation by Population" – in other words, instead of equal representation for the two halves of Canada, they wanted constituencies based on the total population. As the English-speakers outnumbered the French, the "Rep by Poppers" slogan seemed a direct threat to many of the institutions of French Canada. As a consequence, many French-Canadians transferred their support to the **Conservative Party**, while the radicals of Canada East, the **Rouges**, developed a more nationalist creed.

The **Conservative Party** comprised a number of elements, including the rump of the merchant elite who were so infuriated by their loss of control that they burnt the Montréal parliament building to the ground in 1849. Some of this group campaigned to break the imperial tie and join the US, but, when the party fully emerged in 1854, the old "Compact Tories" were much less influential than a younger generation of moderate conservatives. The lynchpin of this younger group was **John A. Macdonald**, who was to form the first federal government in 1868. Such moderates sought, by overcoming the democratic excesses of the "Grits" and the nationalism of the "Rouges", to weld together an economic and political state that would not be absorbed into the increasingly powerful US.

Confederation

In the mid-1860s Canada had achieved responsible (parliamentary) government, but British North America was still a collection of **self-governing colonies**. In the east, Newfoundland was almost entirely dependent on its cod fishery, Prince Edward Island had a prosperous agricultural economy and both Nova Scotia and New Brunswick had boomed on the backs of their shipbuilding industries. Far to the west, on the Pacific coast, lay fur-trading BC, which had just beaten off American attempts to annex the region during the **Oregon crisis**. The dispute was finally resolved in 1846, when the international frontier was fixed along a westward extension of the original 49th parallel, but this was not the end of BC's problems. In 1858, **gold** was discovered beside the Fraser River and, in response to the influx of American prospectors, BC was hastily designated a Crown Colony – a process repeated in 1895 when gold was discovered in the Yukon's Klondike. Between Canada West and BC stretched thousands of miles of prairie and forest, the old Rupert's Land that was still under the extremely loose authority of the Hudson's Bay Company (see pp.952–953).

Also in the 1860s, the **American Civil War** raised fears of a US invasion of an incoherently structured British North America, at the same time as "Rep by Poppers" agitation was making the status of the French-speaking minority problematic. These issues prompted a series of conferences to discuss the issue of **Confederation**, and after three years of intense debate the British Parliament passed the **British North America Act** of 1867. In effect this was a constitution for the new **Dominion of Canada**, providing for a federal parliament to be established at Ottawa; for Canada East and West to become the provinces of **Québec** and **Ontario** respectively; and for each province to retain a regional government and assembly. All of the existing colonies joined the Confederation except BC, which waited until 1871; Prince Edward Island, till 1873; and Newfoundland, which remained under nominal British control until 1949.

The consolidation of the west

Having settled the question of a constitution, the Dominion turned its attention to the west. In 1869, the territory of the Hudson's Bay Company (see pp.952–953) was bought for £300,000 and the Crown assumed responsibility for the so-called **Northwest Territories** until Canada was considered ready to administer them. Predictably, the wishes of its population – primarily Plains Indians and five thousand **Métis** – were given no heed. The Métis, whose main settlement was near the site of modern-day Winnipeg, were already alarmed by the arrival of Ontario settlers and were even more alarmed when government land surveyors arrived to divide the land into lots that cut right across their holdings. Fearful of their land rights, the Métis formed a provisional government under the leadership of **Louis Riel** and prepared to resist the federal authorities (see opposite).

In the course of the rebellion, Riel executed a troublesome Ontario Orangeman by the name of Thomas Scott, an action that created uproar in Ontario. Despite this, the federal government negotiated with a Métis delegation and appeared to meet all their demands, although Riel was obliged to go into exile in the US. As a result of the negotiations, Ottawa created the new province of **Manitoba** to the west of Ontario in 1870, and set aside 140 acres per person for the Métis – though land speculators and lawyers ensured that fewer than twenty percent of those eligible actually got their land. Dispossession was also the fate of the **Plains Indians**. From 1871 onwards a series of treaties were negotiated, offering native families 160-acre plots and a whole range of goods and services if they signed. By

1877 seven treaties had been agreed (eventually there were eleven), handing over to the government all of the southern prairies. However, the promised aid did not materialize and the native peoples found themselves confined to small, infertile reservations.

The Mounties arrive; the Plains Indians are colonized

In 1874, the federal government's increased interest in the area – spurred by the **Cypress Hills Massacre** of Assiniboine natives the year before (see p.545) – was underlined by the arrival of the first 275 members of the newly formed **Northwest Mounted Police**, the **Mounties** (see p.536), forerunners of today's RCMP. Once the Mounties had brought a semblance of law and order to the Plains, Ottawa passed the **Second Indian Act** of 1880, making a **Minister of Indian Affairs** responsible for the aboriginal peoples. The minister and his superintendents exercised a near dictatorial control with almost any action that a native person might wish to take, from building a house to making a visit off the reservation, subject to approval by a local official and, often, the ministry in Ottawa. The Act decreed that every aboriginal applicant for "enfranchisement" as an ordinary Canadian citizen had to pass through a three-year probation period. They were also to be examined to see if they had attained a sufficient level of "civilization". If "enfranchised," the individual was counted as a so-called **non-status Indian**, as opposed to the **status Indians** of the reservations. These distinctions persist today, with status Indians, of whom there are around 700,000, divided up into around six hundred aboriginal bands. Some bands number fewer than one hundred inhabitants and others more than five thousand, but all now have at least a degree of self-government as well as local fishing, hunting and land rights. Both status and non-status Indians can vote, but the former were only granted this right in 1960.

The revolt of the Métis

During the 1870s, most of the **Métis** had moved west into the territory that was destined to become the province of **Saskatchewan** in 1905. They congregated along the Saskatchewan River in the vicinity of Batoche, but once again federal surveyors caught up with them and, in the 1880s, began to divide the land. In 1885, the Métis rose in **revolt** and, after the return of **Louis Riel**, formed a provisional government. In March they successfully beat off a detachment of Mounties, encouraging the neighbouring Cree to raid a Hudson's Bay Company Store. It seemed that a general aboriginal insurrection might follow, born of the desperation that accompanied the treaty system, the starvation which went with the **disappearance of the buffalo**, and the ravages of smallpox. Ottawa was having none of this: they dispatched a force of seven thousand men plus an armed steamer and after two preliminary skirmishes the Métis and the Cree were crushed. Riel, despite his obvious insanity, was found guilty of treason and hanged in November 1885.

Farmers colonize the Plains

The defeat of the Métis opened a new phase in the development of the west. In 1886 the **first train** ran from Montréal to Vancouver and settlers swarmed onto the prairies, pushing the population to 1,300,000 in 1911, up from 250,000 in 1890. Clifford Sifton, Minister of the Interior, encouraged the large-scale immigration from Eastern Europe of what he called "stalwart peasants in sheepskin coats". These Ukrainian, Polish, Czech and Hungarian **farmers** ploughed up the grasslands and turned central Canada into a vast granary, leading the Dominion into the "wheat boom" of the early twentieth century.

Aboriginal peoples from 1900 to today

For Canada's **aboriginal peoples** the early years of the twentieth century were grim. Herded onto small reservations under the authoritarian control of the ministry, they were subjected to a concerted campaign of **Europeanization** – ceremonies such as the sun dance and the potlatch were banned, and they were obliged to send their children to boarding schools for ten months of the year. Deprived of their traditions and independence, they lapsed into poverty, alcoholism and apathy. In the late 1940s, the academic Frederick Tisdall estimated that no fewer than 65,000 reservation aboriginals were "chronically sick" from starvation. In addition, the Inuit were drawn into increasing dependence on the Hudson's Bay Company (see pp.952–953), who encouraged them to concentrate on hunting for furs rather than food, while the twin agencies of the Christian missions and the RCMP worked to incorporate the Inuit into white culture. Across Canada, a major consequence of the disruption of the traditional way of native life was the spread of disease, especially tuberculosis, which was fifteen to twenty times more prevalent among the aboriginal population than among whites.

In 1951, a new **Indian Act** increased both the autonomy of tribal bands and federal subsidies, but nonetheless aboriginal people remained well behind the rest of Canadian society in all the key economic indicators. In 1969, the average income of a Canadian family was $8874, while 88 percent of aboriginal families earned $3000 or less, with fifty percent earning less than $1000. In that same year, partly as a result of lobbying, all **Indian agents** were withdrawn from reservations, and aboriginal political organizations started receiving government funding. Increasingly, these organizations focused on the need for full recognition of their aboriginal rights and renegotiation of the treaties that had created the reservations.

Political stirrings: the Assembly of First Nations

The early 1980s saw the foundation of the **Assembly of First Nations** (AFN), which championed "Status Indians" in a number of legal actions over treaty rights and opposed federal plans to abolish the whole notion of "Status Indians". Many of these treaty cases were based on breaches of the 1763 proclamation, whose terms stated that native land rights could only be taken away by direct negotiation with the Crown. One Grand Chief of the AFN, **Ovide Mercredi** – a lawyer and former human-rights commissioner – announced his objective was to secure equal status between the AFN and the provincial governments, a stance indicative of the growth in aboriginal self-confidence, despite the continuing impoverishment of the reservations. The political weight of the AFN was made clear in the constitutional talks that took place over the establishment of an **Inuit homeland** in the Northwest Territories, a complex negotiation resulting in an agreement to create two self-governing territories in 1999 (see p.936).

But not all Canada's aboriginals, who comprise around three percent of the country's population, see negotiation as their salvation: the action of armed Mohawks to prevent a golf course being built on tribal burial grounds at **Oka** in Québec (p.234) displayed an almost uncontainable anger against the dominant whites, and divided sympathies across the country. The Oka militants paved the way for more conciliatory voices to hold sway in the AFN, but the balance of power between those committed to negotiation as distinct from those favouring direct action is delicate. As a result, the AFN ploughs on with negotiations that rarely hit the headlines against a backdrop lit by occasional bursts of unrestrained rage.

More positively, there has been a resurgence in **fine and applied art**, and aboriginal ceremonies, like the summer powwows, have started to attract large crowds and more media attention. Aboriginal theatre groups have sprung up across Canada, and there's now a public television channel for indigenous people, the **Aboriginal Peoples Television Network**.

Québec and the future of Canada

Just as Canada's aboriginal peoples drew inspiration from the worldwide national liberation movements of the 1960s, so did the **Québécois**. Ever since the fall of New France (see p.952), the francophones had been deeply concerned about *la survivance*, the continuation of their language and culture. This anxiety had peaks and troughs with two of the most tense periods coming during the world wars: many Québécois opposed conscription on the grounds that it subordinated their interests to those of the English speakers, who in turn regarded them as traitors and cowards or both. Nevertheless, despite these periodic difficulties, the Québécois establishment, comprising both the Catholic clergy and the province's politicians, kept a lid on the discontent, almost always recommending accommodation with the British and later the federal authorities. Characteristically, this elite upheld the traditional values of a very Catholic and a very rural New France and as a consequence Québec's industry and commerce developed under anglophone control. Thus, in early twentieth-century Montréal, a francophone proletariat worked in the factories of anglophone owners, a situation that stirred deep historical resentments. The elite was ill-equipped to deal with its own working class, which in turn helped spur the development of a new generation of Québec **separatists**.

Held in Montréal, **Expo '67** was meant to be a confirmation of Canada's arrival as an industrial power of the first rank. Yet when French president **Charles de Gaulle** used the event as a platform to announce his advocacy of a "free Québec", he ignited a row that has dominated the political agenda ever since. That same year, **René Lévesque** formed the **Parti Québécois** (PQ), with the ultimate goal of full independence, hence the slogan *Maîtres chez nous* ("masters in our own house"). But in 1968 this was offset by the election of a determinedly federalist French-Canadian, **Pierre Trudeau**, as prime minister: the scene was set for a showdown.

The 1980 referendum

The PQ represented the political wing of a social movement that, at its most militant extreme, embraced the activities of the short-lived **Front de la Libération du Québec** (FLQ). In 1970, the FLQ kidnapped and murdered Pierre Laporte, the province's Minister of Labour, an action which provoked Trudeau into putting the troops onto the streets of Montréal. This reaction benefitted the PQ, a modernizing party of the social-democratic left, which came to power in 1976 and set about using state resources to develop economic interests such as the Québec hydroelectric plant on James Bay. It also passed a contentious language law, Bill 101, which made French the province's official language and a compulsory part of the school curriculum. The law also banned English signs on business premises, only allowing them inside establishments – providing the signs are bilingual and the French is printed twice as large as the English. Businesses that fail to comply are at the mercy of the "language police", inspectors of the Office de la Langue Française, who can go to extraordinary lengths – measuring signs, checking business cards – to ensure French is the dominant form of communication. This, for many anglophones, combined with the PQ's ongoing plans for a referendum on secession, prompted an exodus in the tens of thousands from Montréal, chiefly to Toronto. But when the **referendum** came, in 1980, sixty percent of Québec's electorate voted "non" to separation, partly because the 1970s had witnessed a closing of the opportunity gap between the francophone and anglophone communities. But this did not end the affair.

Between referendums: repatriation

Shortly after the first referendum, Prime Minister Trudeau set about **repatriating** the country's constitution. In 1981 he called a late-night meeting on the issue and did not invite Lévesque, literally denying Québec a seat at the table. "The night of the long knives", as the event became known, wound up imposing a constitution on the province that placed its language rights in jeopardy (modifying aspects of Bill 101) and made it unequivocally clear that Québec had no veto power over constitutional amendments (as it maintained it did). Trudeau got his wish and on April 17, 1982, Queen Elizabeth II signed the **Constitution Act**. The Québec provincial government refused to formally sign it – and still hasn't to this day.

The 1995 refererendum

In 1985, **Robert Bourassa**'s Liberals defeated Québec's PQ government, largely on the back of the PQ's poor economic track record. The Liberals held power until 1994, when the PQ bounced back into office, promising to hold another independence referendum. They seemed well set. Polls regularly rated support at around sixty percent, but in 1995 the PQ lost a **second referendum** that rejected independence by just fifty thousand votes. Despite all the subsequent bluster, this was a political disaster for the PQ, and, with the momentum lost, subsequent polls indicated the separatist bubble had well and truly burst. Consequently, although the PQ continued in office for the next few years, they never had the political strength to call another referendum and they were ousted by the province's Liberals in 2003 and kept out of power again in 2007. One of the key reasons for the PQ's failure was its inability to define the precise nature of Québec sovereignty and how future relations with the rest of Canada would be conducted, though this remains a very vexed subject that sets many Canadians frothing at the mouth.

Into the twenty-first century

To say that the rest of Canada has become exasperated with the interminable discussions over the future of Québec would be an understatement – and never more so than during the **Meech Lake** conference of 1990, which conspicuously failed to agree on a new decentralized constitution. The conference was convened by the Conservative **Brian Mulroney**, who had become the country's premier in 1984. Mulroney had other pressing problems, too, though admittedly nothing as fractious as Québec. To begin with, the NAFTA free trade agreement between the US and Canada, which Mulroney pushed through parliament, came into effect in 1989, destroying the country's protective tariffs and thereby exposing its industries to undercutting and causing thousands of redundancies. There was also the collapse of the North Atlantic cod fishery, which brought Nova Scotia and Newfoundland to the brink of economic ruin, while falls in wheat prices hurt the Prairies. Efforts were made to deal with these issues, but few were satisfied and during Mulroney's second term (1988–93), the premier became a byword for incompetence, his party commonly accused of large-scale corruption.

Prime Minister Jean Chrétien

The result of Mulroney's unpopularity was that the Conservatives were almost wiped out in the 1993 federal elections and, equipped with a huge majority, the new **Liberal** administration, under **Jean Chrétien**, once Trudeau's Minister of Finance, set about rebuilding federal prestige. A cautious politician, Chrétien had some success, his pragmatic approach to politics proving sufficiently popular to see him re-elected for a second term in 1997 and a third in 2000, albeit with reduced majorities. However, much of Chrétien's electoral success was down to the **balkanization** of the Canadian political scene. In these years, the Liberals were the only party with any claim to a national presence – with the right-wing Canadian Alliance (formerly the Reform Party), for instance, dominating much of the west, but simply failing to show in the east. Neither were Canadians as a whole politically enthused: in the 2000 federal election, only sixty percent turned out to vote and of these the Liberals only secured the support of 39 percent.

Paul Martin and Stephen Harper

In 2003, Chrétien reluctantly announced his retirement and the Liberals appointed a new leader, **Paul Martin**. Facing the prospect of further electoral defeats, Canada's two rightist parties – the Canadian Alliance and the Progressive Conservatives – belatedly managed to swallow their differences, uniting to form the **Conservative Party**, but were still unable to defeat the Liberals in the federal elections of 2004. The new Liberal administration, with Martin as premier, did not have an overall majority and its political weakness made the government shaky. Still, the Martin regime did manage to pass several progressive measures, including the Civil Marriage Act of 2005 and the Kelowna Accord dedicated to improving the lot of Canada's aboriginal peoples. In the end, it wasn't the politics that did for Martin, but allegations of **corruption**, which swirled round the Prime Minister until the Liberals lost a vote of parliamentary confidence in late 2005. Shortly afterwards the **federal elections of 2006** produced a narrow victory for the Conservatives with **Stephen Harper** becoming the new Prime Minister. Harper's position was strengthened by a good showing for the Conservatives in the federal election of 2008, but the Conservatives still failed to secure an overall parliamentary majority. Since 2008, Harper's minority administration has also ventured into the Québec imbroglio, with Harper suggesting he will recognize that 'the Québécois form a nation within a united Canada' – which has had all the pundits rushing off to the dictionary to define 'nation'. At heart, Harper is a classic rightist, but his proclivities are restrained and constrained by his need for political alliances with other more centrist politicians. What would happen if he secured an overall parliamentary majority is hard to say, but it seems unlikely Canadians want to find out.

The natural environment

Canada has just about every type of **natural habitat** going, from ice-bound polar islands in the far north to sun-drilled pockets of desert along the US border. Between these extremes the country's mountains, forests and grasslands support an incredible variety and profusion of **wildlife** – any brief account can only scratch the surface of what it's possible to see. National and provincial parks offer the best starting places, and we've listed some of the outstanding sites for spotting particular species. Don't expect to see the big attractions like bears and wolves easily; despite the enthusiasm of guides and tourist offices, these are encountered only rarely.

Eastern forests

Canada's **eastern forests** divide into two main groups – the **Carolinian forest** of southwest Ontario, and the **Great Lakes-St Lawrence forest** extending from the edge of the Carolinian forest to Lake Superior and the Gulf of St Lawrence.

The **Carolinian forest** forms a narrow belt of largely deciduous hardwood trees similar to the broad-leaved woodlands found over much of the eastern United States. Trees are often typical of more southerly climes – Kentucky coffee tree, tulip tree, sassafras and sycamore among others, and more ordinary staples like beech, sugar maple and basswood. None of these are rare in the US, but in Canada they grow only here, thanks to the region's rich soils and relatively warm, sheltered climate.

A good deal of the Carolinian flora and fauna is coming under increasing threat from southern Ontario's urban and agricultural sprawl. These days much of the original forest has shrunk to a mosaic of fragments protected by national and provincial parks. The forests are most often visited by tourists for the astounding October colours, but if you're looking for **wildlife** you might also catch Canada's only marsupial, the **opossum**, or other southern species like the **fox squirrel** (introduced on Lake Erie's Pelee Island); the **eastern mole**, which occurs only in Essex County on Lake Erie's north shore; and the **eastern vole**, found only in a narrow band around Lake Erie.

Carolinian birds and reptiles

Naturalists are equally drawn here for the **birds**, many of which are found nowhere else in Canada, especially during seasonal migrations, when up to one hundred species can easily be seen in a day. Most noteworthy of the more unusual species is the **golden swamp warbler**, a bird of almost unnaturally colourful plumage. More common visitors are hooded and Kentucky warblers, blue-winged and golden-winged warblers, gnatcatchers and virtually every species of eastern North American hawk; sharp-shin hawks are common, and during autumn migrations of up to seventy thousand broad-winged hawks might be seen in a single day near Port Stanley on Lake Erie's north shore. In the wetlands bordering the forests, particularly at Long Point on Lake Erie, you can search out **reptiles** found nowhere else in the country. Most impressive is the water-loving **fox snake**, a harmless animal that often reaches well over a metre in length, but is often killed because of its resemblance to the rattlesnake and venomous copperhead – neither of which is found in the region. Also present, but in marked decline, are several **turtle** species, especially Blanding's, wood, spotted and spiny softshell.

Great Lakes-St Lawrence forests

Occurring in one of the most densely populated parts of Canada, the mixed **conifer forests** of the **Great Lakes-St Lawrence** area have been heavily logged

Flora and fauna checklist

This is by no means an exhaustive list of all Canada's **flora and fauna** – simply an indication of the places and the seasons that you are most likely to see certain species and types of wildlife.

Bears Black bears: Glacier National Park, BC and Banff, Jasper and Kananaskis Country, AB. Grizzlies: Glacier National Park, BC and Khutzeymateen Estuary, north of Prince Rupert, BC (*Aug*).

Bison Wood Buffalo National Park, AB.

Butterfly Migrations: Point Pelee and Long Point, Lake Erie, ON. (*Spring and autumn*).

Caribou Dempster Hwy, YT. (*Autumn*).

Cranes and pelicans Last Mountain Lake, SK. (*Late Aug*).

Dall's sheep Sheep Mountain, Kluane National Park, YT. (*Summer*).

Desert species Cacti, sagebrush, rattlesnakes and kangaroo rats: around Osoyoos, BC. (*Summer*).

Eagles and owls Boundary Bay, south of Vancouver, BC. (*Winter*).

Elk Banff, Jasper and Kananaskis Country, AB. (*Summer*).

Orchids Bruce Peninsula National Park, ON. (*Spring and summer*).

Polar bears Near Churchill, MB. (*Autumn*).

Prairie species Hawks, coyotes and rattlesnakes: in the Milk River region, AB. (*May and June*).

Salmon Adams River sockeye salmon run near Salmon Arm, BC. (*Oct*).

Sea birds Gannets, murres and black kittiwakes around Cape St Mary's, NFL. Waterfowl and sea birds in the Haida Gwaii, BC. Northern gannets on Bonaventure Island, Gaspé Peninsula, QC. (*June and July*).

Sea otters and sea lions Off Pacific Rim National Park, Vancouver Island, BC. (*Spring and summer*).

Seals Haida Gwaii, BC. (*Summer*).

Snow Geese Cap-Tourmente, QC. (*Autumn*).

Whales Beluga, fin, humpback, blue and minke whales: near Tadoussac, QC and Bay of Fundy, NB. Killer whales (orcas): Robson Bight in Johnstone Strait, Vancouver Island, BC. All in summer. Grey whales: Pacific Rim National Park, Vancouver Island, BC. (*Spring and summer*).

and severely affected by urbanization. Most of the trees are southern species – beech and sugar maple, red and white pines – but are mixed with the eastern hemlock, spruce, jack pine, paper birch and balsam fir typical of more northerly forests. This region is second only to southern BC in the number of bird species it supports. It also provides for large numbers of **white-tailed deer**, a rare beneficiary of logging as it prefers to browse along clearing edges. In the evergreen stands on the north shore of the St Lawrence River there are also large numbers of Canada's smallest mammal, the **pygmy shrew**. These tiny animals must eat their own weight in food daily and can't rest for more than an hour or so – they'd starve to death if they tried to sleep through the night.

Grassland

Contrary to the popular image of Canada's interior as a huge prairie of waving wheat, true **grassland** covers only ten percent of the country. Most is concentrated in the southernmost reaches of Alberta and Saskatchewan, with tiny spillovers in Manitoba and BC. Two grassland belts once thrived in the region, **tall-grass**

prairie in the north and **shortgrass** in the south. Farming has now not only put large areas of each under crops, but also decimated most of the large mammals that roamed the range – pronghorns, mule and white-tailed deer, elk, wolves, grizzlies, coyotes, foxes and cougars.

The most dramatic loss from the grasslands has been **bison** (or **buffalo**), the continent's largest land mammal. Once numbering an estimated 45 million, Canada's bison are now limited to just a few free-roaming herds. They're extraordinarily impressive animals – the average bull stands six feet at the shoulder and weighs over a ton – and early prairie settlers were so struck with their size that they believed bison, not the climate, had been responsible for clearing the grasslands.

Once almost as prevalent as the bison, but now almost as rare, is the **pronghorn**, a beautiful tawny-gold antelope species. Capable of speeds of over 100kph, it's the continent's swiftest land mammal. Uniquely adapted for speed and stamina, the pronghorn has long legs, a heart twice the size of similar-sized animals, and an astonishingly wide windpipe. It complements its respiratory machinery by running with its mouth open to gulp maximum amounts of air. Though only the size of a large dog, it has larger eyes than those of a horse, a refinement that spots predators several kilometres away. Today, wolves and coyotes are more likely to be after the prairie's new masters – countless small rodents such as **gophers**, **ground squirrels** and **jackrabbits**.

Grassland birds

Birds have had to adapt not only to the prairie's dryness but also to the lack of extensive tree cover, and most species nest on the ground; many are also able to survive on reduced amounts of water and rely on seed-centred diets. Others confine themselves to occasional ponds, lakes and sloughs, which are important breeding grounds for ducks, grebes, herons, pelicans and rails. Other birds typical of the grassland are the marbled godwit, the curlew and raptors such as the **prairie falcon**.

Boreal forest

The **boreal forest** is Canada's largest single ecosystem, bigger than all the others combined. Stretching in a broad belt from Newfoundland to the Yukon, it fills the area between the eastern forests, grasslands and the northern tundra, occupying a good slice of every province except BC. Only certain **trees** thrive in this zone of long, cold winters, short summers and acidic soils: expect to see billions of white and black spruce (plus red spruce in the east), balsam fir, tamarack (larch) and jack pine, as well as such deciduous species as birch, poplar and aspen – all of which are ideal for wood pulp, making the boreal forest the staple resource of the country's **lumber industry**. If you spend any time in the backcountry you'll also come across **muskeg**: neither land nor water, this porridge-like bog is the breeding ground of choice for pestilent hordes of mosquitoes and blackflies – and Canada has 1.3 million square kilometres of it. It also harbours mosses, scrub willow and even the occasional orchid.

The boreal forest supports just about every **animal** recognized as distinctively Canadian: moose, beaver, black bear, wolf and lynx, plus small mammals and creatures such as deer, caribou and coyote from transitional forest-tundra and aspen-parkland habitats to the north and south. **Wolves** are still numerous in Canada, but hunting and harassment has pushed them to the northernmost parts of the boreal forest. Their supposed ferocity is more myth than truth; intelligent and elusive creatures, they rarely harm humans, and it's unlikely you'll see any – though you may well hear their howling if you're out in the sticks. **Lynx** are even more elusive. One of the northern forest's most elegant animals, this big cat requires a 150- to 200-square-kilometre range, making Canada's northern wilderness one of the world's few regions capable of sustaining a viable population.

Beavers and moose

Beavers are commonly seen all over the boreal regions of Canada. You may catch them at dawn or dusk, heads just above the water as they glide across lakes and rivers. Signs of their legendary activity include log jams across streams and ponds, stumps of felled saplings resembling sharpened pencils and dens which look like domed piles of mud and sticks. Lakes, streams and the margins of muskeg are all favoured by **moose**. A lumbering animal with magnificent spreading antlers, it is the largest member of the deer family and is found over most of Canada, but especially near swampy ground. It's also a favourite with hunters, and few northern bars are without their moose head – perhaps the only place you'll see this solitary and reclusive species.

Boreal birds

Forest wetlands also offer refuge for **ducks and geese**, with **loons**, grebes and songbirds attracted to the surrounding undergrowth. Canada's three species of ptarmigan – willow, rock and white-tailed – are also common, and you'll see plenty of big **raptors**, including the great grey owl. Many boreal birds migrate, and even those that don't – hawks, jays, ravens and grouse – tend to move a little way south, sometimes breaking out into southern Canada in mass movements known as "irruptions".

Mountain forests

Mountain forests cover much of western Canada and, depending on location and elevation, divide into four types: West Coast, Columbia, montane and subalpine. The **West Coast**'s torrential rainfall, mild maritime climate, deep soils and long growing season produce Canada's most impressive forests and its biggest trees. Swaths of luxuriant **temperate rainforest** cover much of Vancouver Island and the Pacific coast, dominated by Sitka spruce, western red cedar, Pacific silver fir, western hemlock, western yew and, biggest of all, **Douglas fir**, some of which tower ninety metres high and are 1200 years old. These conifers make valuable timber, and much of this forest is under severe threat from logging. Some of the best stands – a fraction of the original – have been preserved on the Haida Gwaii and in Vancouver Island's Pacific Rim National Park. Below the luxuriant, dripping canopy of the big trees lies an **undergrowth** teeming with life. Shrubs and bushes such as salal, huckleberry and bunchberry thrive alongside mosses, ferns, lichens and orchids. All sorts of animals can be found here, most notably the **cougar** and its main prey, the Columbian **blacktail deer**. **Birds** are legion, and include a wealth of woodland species such as the Townsend's warbler, Wilson's warbler and the orange-crowned warbler. Rarer birds include the rufous hummingbird, which migrates from its Mexican wintering grounds to feed on the forest's numerous nectar-bearing flowers.

Columbia forest

The **Columbia forest** covers the lower slopes (400–1400m) of BC's interior mountains and much of the Rockies. **Trees** here are similar to those of the West Coast's warmer and wetter rainforest with Sitka spruce, which rarely thrives away from the coast, the notable exception. The undercover is also similar, with lots of devil's club (a particularly vicious thorn), azaleas and black and red twinberry. Mountain lily, columbine and bunchberry are among the common flowers. Few mammals live exclusively in the forests with the exception of the **red squirrel**, which in turn is preyed on by hawks, owls, coyotes and weasels. Bigger predators also roam the mountain forest, most notably the **brown bear**, a western variant of the ubiquitous **black bear**. Aside from the coyote, the tough, agile black bear is one of the continent's most successful carnivores and the one you're most likely to see around campsites and rubbish dumps. Black bears have adapted to a wide range of habitats and food sources, and their only natural enemies – save wolves, which may attack young cubs – are hunters. Scarcer but still hunted is the famous **grizzly bear**, a far larger and potentially dangerous creature distinguished by its brownish fur and the ridged hump on its back. The grizzly is largely confined to the remoter slopes of the Rockies and West Coast ranges, where it feeds mainly on berries and salmon. Like other bears, grizzlies are unpredictable and readily provoked – see p.625 for tips on avoiding unpleasant encounters.

Montane forest

Montane forest covers the more southerly and sheltered reaches of the Rockies and the dry plateaux of interior BC, where spindly Douglas fir, western larch, ponderosa pine and the **lodgepole pine** predominate. Like its eastern counterpart, the jack pine, the lodgepole requires intense heat before opening and releasing its seeds, and huge stands of these trees grew in the aftermath of the forest fires which accompanied the building and running of the railways. Plentiful voles and small rodents attract **coyotes**, whose yapping – an announcement of territorial claims – you'll often hear at night close to small towns. Coyotes are spreading northwards into the Yukon and Northwest Territories and eastwards into Ontario and Québec, a proliferation that continues despite massive extermination campaigns, prompted by the coyotes' taste for livestock. Few predators have the speed to keep up with coyotes – only the stealthy **cougar**, or wolves hunting in tandem, can successfully bring them down. Cougars are now severely depleted in Canada, and the BC interior and Vancouver Island are the only regions where they survive in significant numbers. Ponderosa and lodgepole pines provide fine cover for **birds** like goshawks, Swainson's hawks and lesser species such as ruby-crowned kinglets, warblers and pileated woodpeckers. In the forest's lowest reaches both the vegetation and the birdlife are those of the southern prairies – semi-arid regions of sagebrush, prickly pear and bunch grasses, dotted with lakes full of common **ducks** such as the mallard. You might also see the cinnamon teal, a bird whose limited distribution draws birdwatchers to BC on its own account.

Subalpine forest

Subalpine forest covers mountain slopes from 1300m to 2200m throughout the Rockies and much of BC, supporting lodgepole, whitebark and limber pines, alpine fir and Engelmann spruce. It also contains a preponderance of **alpine larch**, a deciduous conifer whose vivid autumnal yellows dot the mountainsides to beautiful effect. One of the more common animals of this zone is the **elk**, a powerful member of the deer family, which can often be seen summering in large herds above the tree line. Elk court and mate during the autumn, making a thin nasal sound called **bugling**; respect their privacy, as rutting elk have notoriously unpredictable temperaments. Small herds of **mule deer** migrate between forests and alpine meadows, using small glands between their hooves to leave a scent for other herd members to follow. Other smaller animals attracted to the subalpine forest include the golden-mantled ground squirrel and birds such as **Clark's nutcracker**, both tame and curious creatures, which often gather around campsites in search of scraps.

Alpine zones

Alpine zones occur in mountains above the tree line, which in Canada means parts of the Rockies, much of BC and large areas of the Yukon. Plant and animal life varies hugely between summer and winter, and according to terrain and exposure to the elements – sometimes it resembles that of the tundra, at others it recalls the profile of lower forest habitats.

In spring, alpine meadows are carpeted with breathtaking displays of **wild flowers**: clumps of Parnassus grass, lilies, Indian paintbrushes and a wealth of yellow flowers such as arnica, cinquefoil and glacier lily. These meadows make excellent pasture, attracting elk and mule deer in summer, as well as full-time residents such as **Dall sheep**, the related **bighorn** and the incredible **mountain goat**, perhaps the hardiest of Canada's bigger mammals. Mountain goats are equipped with short, stolid legs, flexible toes and non-skid soles, all designed for clambering over near-vertical slopes, grazing well out of reach of their less agile predators.

Marmots, resembling hugely overstuffed squirrels, take things easier and hibernate through the worst of the winter and beyond. In a good year they can sleep for eight months, prey only to grizzly bears, which are strong enough and have the claws to dig down into their dens. In their waking periods they can be tame and friendly, often nibbling contentedly in the sunnier corners of campsites. When threatened, however, they produce a piercing and unearthly whistle. The strange little **pika**, a relative of the rabbit, is more elusive but keeps itself busy year-round, living off a miniature haystack of fodder which it builds up during the summer.

Birds are numerous in summer, and include rosy finches, pipits and blue grouse, but few manage to live in the alpine zone year-round. One that does is the **white-tailed ptarmigan**, which, thanks to its heavily feathered feet and legs, is able to snowshoe around deep snow drifts; its white winter plumage provides camouflage.

Coastlines

Canada has three **coastlines**: the **Atlantic**, the **Pacific** and the **Arctic** (dealt with under "Tundra"). Each boasts a profusion of maritime, dunal and intertidal life; the Pacific coast, warmed by the Japanese current, actually has the greatest number of species of any temperate shore. Yet few people are very interested in the small fry – most come for the big mammals, **whales** in particular.

Grey whales are comparatively common in the Pacific, and are often easily spotted from mainland headlands in the February to May and September to October periods as they migrate between the Arctic and their breeding grounds off Mexico. Once hunted close to the point of extinction, they've now returned in large numbers. **Humpback whales** are another favourite, largely because they're curious and follow sightseeing boats, but also because of their surface acrobatics and long, haunting "songs". They too were hunted to near-extinction, and though protected by international agreement since 1966 they still number less than ten percent of their original population. Vancouver Island's inner coast supports one of the world's most concentrated populations of **killer whales** or **orcas**. These are often seen in family groups or "pods" travelling close to shore, usually on the trail of large fish – which on the West Coast means **salmon**. The orca is the only whale whose diet also runs to warm-blooded animals – hence the "killer" tag – and it will gorge on walrus, seal and even minke, grey and beluga whales.

Pacific sea otters, fur seals and sea lions

Another West Coast inhabitant, the **sea otter**, differs from most marine mammals in that it keeps itself warm with a thick soft coat of fur rather than with blubber.

With binoculars, it's often easy to spot these charming creatures lolling on their backs, cracking open sea urchins or mussels with a rock and using their stomachs as anvils; they often lie bobbing asleep, entwined in kelp to stop them floating away. Northern **fur seals** breed on Alaska's Pribilof Islands but are often seen off the BC coast during their migrations. Like their cousin, the northern **sea lion**, a year-round resident, they are "eared seals", who can manage rudimentary shuffling on land thanks to short rear limbs which can be rotated for forward movement. They also swim with strokes from front flippers, as opposed to the slithering, fishlike action of true seals.

The Atlantic coast

The **Atlantic**'s colder waters nurture fewer overall species than the Pacific coast, but many birds and larger mammals – especially **whales** – are common to both. One of the Atlantic region's more distinctive creatures is the **harp seal**, a true seal species that migrates in late winter to breeding grounds off Newfoundland and in the Greenland and White seas. Most pups are born on the pack ice, and for about two weeks sport fluffy white coats that have been highly prized by the fur trade for centuries.

Tundra

Tundra extends over much of northern Yukon, the Northwest Territories and Nunavut, stretching between the boreal forest and the polar seas. Part grassland and part wasteland, it's a region distinguished by high winds, bitter cold and **permafrost**, a layer of perpetually frozen subsoil which covers over thirty percent of Canada. Yet the tundra is not only the domain of ice and emptiness: long hours of summer sunshine and the melting of topsoil nurture a carpet of wild flowers and many species of birds and mammals have adapted to the vagaries of climate and terrain.

Vegetation is uniformly stunted by poor drainage, acidic soils and permafrost, which prevents the formation of deep roots and locks nutrients in the ice. **Trees** like birch and willow can grow, but they spread their branches over a wide area, rarely rising over a metre in height. Over 99 percent of the remaining vegetation consists of perennials like **grasses and sedges**, small flowering annuals, mosses, lichens and shrubs. Most have evolved ingenious ways of protecting themselves against the elements: Arctic cotton grass, for example, grows in large insulated hummocks in which the interior temperature is higher than the air outside. **Wild flowers** during the short, intense spring can be superlative, covering seemingly inert ground in a carpet of purple mountain saxifrage, yellow Arctic poppy and indigo clusters of Arctic forget-me-not.

Tundra mammals and birds

Tundra grasses provide some of the first links in the food chain, nourishing mammals such as white **Arctic ground squirrels**, whose fur the Inuit use to make parka jackets. Vegetation also provides the staple diet of **lemmings**, among the most remarkable of the Arctic fauna. Instead of hibernating these creatures live under the snow, busily tucking away on shoots in order to double their weight daily – the intake they need merely to survive. They also breed almost continuously, which is just as well, for they are the mainstay of a long list of predators. Chief of these are **Arctic white foxes**, ermines and weasels, though birds, bears and Arctic wolves may also hunt them in preference to larger prey. Because they provide a staple diet to so many, lemming populations have a marked effect on the life cycles of numerous creatures.

A notable exception is the **caribou**, a member of the reindeer family and the most populous of the big tundra mammals. Caribou are known for their epic migrations, frequently involving thousands of animals, which start in March when the herds leave their wintering grounds on the fringes of the boreal forest for calving grounds to the north. The exact purpose of these migrations is still debated. They certainly prevent the overgrazing of the tundra's fragile mosses and lichens, and probably also enable the caribou to shake off some of the wolves that would otherwise shadow the herd (wolves have to find southerly dens at this time to bear their own pups). The timing of treks also means calving takes place before the arrival of biting insects, which can claim as many calves as predators – an adult caribou can lose as much as a litre of blood a week to insects.

The tundra's other large mammal is the **musk ox**, a vast, shaggy herbivore and close cousin of the bison. The musk ox's Achilles' heel is a tendency to form lines or circles when threatened – a perfect defence against wolves, but not against hunters, who, until the introduction of conservation measures, threatened to be their undoing. Canada now has some of the world's largest free-roaming herds, although – like the caribou – the Inuit still hunt them for food and fur.

Tundra **birds** number about a hundred species and are mostly migratory. Three-quarters of these are **waterfowl**, which arrive first to take advantage of streams, marshes and small lakes created by surface meltwater: Arctic wetlands provide nesting grounds for numerous swans, geese and ducks, as well as the **loon**, which is immortalized on the back of the Canadian dollar coin. The red-necked **phalarope** is a particularly specialized visitor, able to feed on aquatic insects and plankton, though not as impressive in its abilities as the migratory **Arctic tern**, whose 32,000-kilometre round-trip from the Antarctic is the longest annual migration of any creature on the planet. The handful of non-migratory birds tend to be scavengers like the raven, or predators like the **gyrfalcon**, the world's largest falcon, which preys on Arctic hares and ptarmigan. Jaegers, gulls, hawks and owls largely depend on the lemming.

Fauna on the Arctic **coast** has a food chain that starts with plankton and algae, ranging up through tiny crustaceans, clams and mussels, sea cucumbers and sea urchins, cod, ringed and bearded seals, to beluga whales and **polar bears** – perhaps the most evocative of all tundra creatures. Migrating **birds** are especially common here, notably near Nunaluk Spit on the Yukon coast, which is used as a corridor and stopover by millions of loons, swans, geese and plovers, among others.

Books

Most of the books listed below are **in print and in paperback**, and those that are **out of print** (o/p) may be tracked down either in secondhand bookshops or through Amazon (@www.amazon.co.uk or www.amazon.com). Titles marked with the ★ symbol are especially recommended.

Travelogues

★ **Will Ferguson** *Beauty Tips from Moose Jaw*. Humourist Ferguson spent three years criss-crossing Canada and this finely-observed – and often hilarious – travelogue is the result. Beyond the amusing anecdotes, factual treasures and liberal doses of gentle skepticism though, the book serves to shed some light on Canada's pyschogeography – no small feat in a country so vast. Required reading for not only Canadians, but anyone visiting the country.

John Gimlette *Theatre of Fish: Travels Through Newfoundland and Labrador*. Apparently following in the footsteps of his great-grandfather, Gimlette reaches parts of the province few have travelled in this lively, entertaining journal that is, at times, perhaps a little too colloquial for its own (stylistic) good.

Anna Jameson *Winter Studies and Summer Rambles in Canada*. Originally published in 1839, these tart observations of early Toronto's colonial society are marked by a sense of wonderment at the vastness of Canada's untamed wilderness.

★ **Paul Kane** *Wanderings of an Artist among the Indians of North America*. Kane, one of Canada's better-known landscape artists (see p.87), spent two and a half years travelling from Toronto to the Pacific Coast and back in the 1840s. His witty, racy account of his wanderings makes a delightful read.

Gary and Joanie McGuffin *Quetico: Into the Wild*. The McGuffins love canoeing and have produced several books on their assorted travels – and this is the latest. Remote Quetico Park is in northern Ontario.

Susanna Moodie *Roughing It in the Bush, or Forest Life in Canada*. Intriguing narrative written in 1852, describing an English couple's slow ruin as they attempt to create a new life in southeastern Ontario.

★ **Jan Morris** *O Canada: Travels in an Unknown Country* (o/p). Musings from this well-known travel writer after a coast-to-coast Canadian trip. Comprises a series of finely judged and beautifully written essays on each of Canada's principal cities. Published in 1992, some of Morris's observations are inevitably outmoded, but the book is still an excellent primer.

Grey Owl *The Men of the Last Frontier*; *Tales of an Empty Cabin; Sajo and the Beaver People*. First published in the 1930s, these three books, which are often packaged together in one form or another, give a romantic description of life in the wilds of Canada at the time when exploitation was changing the land forever. Grey Owl's love of animals and the wilderness are inspiring and his forward-thinking, ecological views are surprising. See p.193 for more.

★ **Elizabeth Simcoe** (ed. Mary Innis) *Mrs Simcoe's Diary*. The wife of Upper Canada's first lieutenant governor and an early resident of Toronto, Mrs Simcoe provide detailed observations of the landscape and the fledgling city's way of life, but was also an astute political observer, offering pinprick portraits of major historical figures like the Mohawk chief, Joseph Brant.

Culture, art and society

Kevin Bazzana *Wondrous Strange: the Life and Art of Glenn Gould*. Scholarly, well-researched Gould reader giving the low-down of every facet of the man and his music – in five hundred-odd pages. Gould fans will love it.

Hugh Brody *Maps and Dreams*. Brilliantly written account of the lives and lands of the Beaver aboriginals of northwest Canada. For further acute insights into the ways of the far north see also the same author's *Among the Inuit*.

Stephen Brunt *Gretzky's Tears* and *Searching for Bobby Orr*. Two fascinating looks at the sport that helps define Canada. In *Gretzky's Tears*, Brunt, a sports columnist for the *Globe and Mail* newspaper, tells the story of the trade that sent Wayne Gretzky – considered by most to be the game's best ever player – to Los Angeles from Edmonton; the move helped irrevocably change hockey and had a huge impact on many Canadians. *Searching for Bobby* Orr is more of a character study of another famous Canadian player, whose sheer athletic talent changed the game during an era when hockey was just starting to become more of a "business"; greed, ego, naiveté and disillusionment were to follow.

Lovat Dickson *Wilderness Man: The Strange Story of Grey Owl*. The fascinating story of Archie Belaney, the Englishman who became famous as his adopted persona, Grey Owl (see p.193). Written by his English publisher, who was one of many not to discover the charade until after Grey Owl's death.

Christian F. Feest *Three Centuries of Woodlands Indian Art*. This attractively illustrated book covers every aspect of its subject in revealing detail.

Glenn Gould *The Solitude Trilogy*. These CDs comprise three extraordinary sound documentaries made by Gould for CBC, each dealing with life in the remoter, harsher parts of Canada. A fascinating insight in the words of the people themselves.

Mark Kurlansky *Cod: A Biography of the Fish that Changed the World*. This fascinating book tracks the life and times of the cod and the generations of fishermen who have lived off it. There are sections on over-fishing and the fish's breeding habits along with cod recipes. The Newfoundland cod fishery features prominently and you won't get a more balanced view as to what went wrong – and why the fishery was so decimated.

Barry Lopez *Arctic Dreams*. Extraordinary, award-winning book combining natural history, physics, poetry, earth sciences and philosophy in a dazzling portrait of the far north.

A.B. McKillop *The Spinster and the Prophet: H.G. Wells, Florence Deeks, and the Case of the Plagiarized Text*. In 1925 Toronto teacher and armchair historian Florence Deeks sued the great H.G. Wells for the then-fabulous sum of $500,000 for his supposed literary piracy of her manuscript about the history of the world. Did he do it? Was she simply an overwrought spinster? Read on.

Alan D. McMillan *Native Peoples and Cultures of Canada*. Comprehensive, authoritative account of Canada's native groups from prehistory to current issues of self-government and land claims. Well written, though more an academic textbook than a leisure-time read. Published in 1995, so a little dated.

Dennis Reid *A Concise History of Canadian Painting*. Not especially concise, but a thorough trawl through Canada's leading artists, with bags of biographical detail and lots of black-and-white (and a few colour) illustrations of major works. Goes as far as the early 1980s.

Jonathan Vance *A History of Canadian Culture*. Ambitious, five hundred-page attempt to master its subject with plenty of time to define what exactly culture is – as distinct from/or the same as mass entertainment. Immaculate historical research, including – for example – plays written by sailors ice-bound in the Arctic.

History

Fred Anderson *Crucible of War: The Seven Years' War and the Fate of the British Empire in British North America, 1754–1766*. Lucid and extraordinarily well-researched account of this crucial period in the development of North America. At eight hundred-odd pages, it's perhaps a little too detailed for many tastes, but it's a fascinating read. Included is the story of the fall of Fort William Henry, as celebrated in the film, *The Last of the Mohicans*.

Owen Beattie & John Geiger *Frozen in Time: The Fate of the Franklin Expedition 1845–48*. An account both of the doomed expedition to find the Northwest Passage and the discovery of artefacts and bodies still frozen in the northern ice; worth buying for the extraordinary photos alone.

Carl Benn *The Iroquois in the War of 1812*. In 1812, the US was at war with Canada and one of its armies invaded and briefly occupied Toronto. The role played by the Iroquois peoples in the war was pivotal to Canada's survival and the ramifications of the conflict affected the Iroquois for generations to come.

Pierre Berton *Klondike: the Last Great Goldrush 1896–1899*. Exceptionally readable account from one of Canada's finest and most approachable writers of the characters and epic episodes of the Yukon gold rush. Other Berton titles include *The Arctic Grail*, describing the quest for the North Pole and the Northwest Passage; *The Last Spike: the Great Railway 1881–1885*, an account of the history and building of the transcontinental railway; *Flames across the Border*, a detailed account of the US attack on Canada in 1813–1814; *Vimy*, an account of the World War I battle fought mainly by Canadians which Berton sees as a turning point in the nation's history; and *Niagara*, a wonderful account of everything that has ever gone on there, including details of the assorted lunatics and publicity-seekers who have gone over the falls.

Robert Bothwell *The Penguin History of Canada*. Quite simply the best general history book currently in print. Concise, fair-minded and well-written account and analysis of the country's economic, social and political history.

John English *Citizen of the World: The Life of Pierre Elliott Trudeau Volume One: 1919-1968* and *Just Watch Me: The Life of Pierre Elliott Trudeau: 1968-2000*. Two brilliantly written and researched volumes on Canada's best-known, most flamboyant (an uncommon characteristic in Canadian politicians) and definitely most divisive prime minister.

Will Ferguson *Bastards & Boneheads:* Canada's glorious leaders, past and present. A highly amusing read that examines the country's political leaders and associated scandals, but doesn't shy away from more serious insights and analysis into major incidents such as the Oka crisis (see p.254).

Gerald Friesen *The Canadian Prairies: a History*. Stunningly well-researched and detailed account of the development of Central Canada. A surprisingly entertaining book that's particularly good on the culture of the Métis and Plains Indians.

Peter C. Newman *Empire of the Bay*. Highly acclaimed and readable account of the rise and fall of the Hudson's Bay Company. If this fits the bill, also try Newman's *The Last to Die: Ronald Turpin, Arthur Lucas, and the end of Capital Punishment in Canada*.

George Woodcock *A Social History of Canada*. Erudite and incisive book about the peoples of Canada and the country's development. Woodcock was the most perceptive of Canada's historians and his work has the added advantage of being very readable.

Fiction

Margaret Atwood *Surfacing*. Canada's most eminent novelist is not always easy reading, but her analysis, particularly of women and society, is invariably witty and penetrating. In *Surfacing* the remote landscape of northern Québec plays an instrumental part in an extreme voyage of self-discovery. Other notable works include *Alias Grace*, a dark and sensual tale centred around the true story of one of Canada's most notorious female criminals of the 1840s, and the Booker Prize-winning *The Blind Assassin*. Her latest – *The Year of the Flood* – is less specifically Canadian, but more sci-fi, set in a dystopian, environmentally degraded future.

Lynn Coady *Saints of Big Harbour*. Forceful novel set in rural Nova Scotia dealing with a dysfunctional family – all alcohol and violence. Hardly cheerful, but the characters are immaculately portrayed. Coady's more recent *Strange Heaven* is also set in Nova Scotia and explores themes of motherhood.

Robertson Davies For many years the leading figure of Canada's literary scene, Davies died in 1995 at the age of 82. Among his considerable output are big, dark and complicated webs of familial and social history which include wonderful evocations of the semi-rural Canada of his youth. A good place to start is *What's Bred in the Bone*, part of *The Cornish Trilogy*, whose other titles are *The Rebel Angels* and *The Lyre of Orpheus*. Similarly intriguing is *Fifth Business*, the first part of *The Deptford Trilogy*. *The Cunning Man* is also excellent.

Margaret Laurence *A Jest of God* and *The Stone Angel*. Manitoba-born Laurence epitomized the new vigour that swept through the country's literature during the 1960s – though the best of her fiction was written in England. Most of her books are set in the fictional prairie backwater of Manawaka, and explore the loneliness and frustration of women within an environment of stifling small-town conventionality.

Mary Lawson *The Other Side of the Bridge*. Intricate family/clannish stuff in small-town northern Ontario, on the edge of the lakes, rocks and forests of the Canadian Shield. Deftly written as is Lawson's earlier *Crow Lake*.

Stephen Leacock *Sunshine Sketches of a Little Town*. Whimsical tale of Ontario small-town life; the best of a series based on Leacock's (1869–1944) summertime stays in Orillia (see p.154).

Jack London *Call of the Wild* and *White Fang*. London spent over a year in the Yukon gold fields during the Klondike gold rush. Many of his experiences found their way into his vivid – if sometimes overwrought – tales of the northern wilderness. These are the pick.

Malcolm Lowry *Hear Us O Lord from Heaven thy Dwelling Place*. Lowry spent almost half his writing life (1939–54) in log cabins and beach houses he built for himself around Vancouver. *Hear Us O Lord* is a difficult read to say the least: a fragmentary novella which, amongst other things, describes a disturbing sojourn on Canada's wild Pacific coast.

Ann-Marie MacDonald *Fall on Your Knees*. Entertaining, epic-style family saga from this Toronto-based writer, who has an astute eye for characters and a fine storytelling touch. The novel follows the fortunes of four sisters from Halifax, against a backdrop that sweeps from World War II to the New York jazz scene.

Alistair MacLeod *No Great Mischief*. This forceful, evocative novel tells the tale of a family of Gaelic-speaking Nova Scotians from Cape Breton. Some of the episodes are brilliantly written but it was undoubtedly one of the best Canadian novels of the 1990s.

Anne Michaels *Fugitive Pieces*. This debut novel from an award-winning poet concerns survivors from the Nazis who emigrate to Canada. Their relationship deepens but memory and the past are never far away. A beautiful work.

W.O. Mitchell *Who Has Seen the Wind*. Canada's equivalent of *Huckleberry Finn* is a folksy story of a young boy coming of age in small-town Saskatchewan, with great offbeat characters and fine evocations of prairie life.

L.M. Montgomery *Anne of Green Gables*. Growing pains and bucolic bliss in a children's classic from 1908. Bound to appeal to little girls of all ages; set on Prince Edward Island.

Brian Moore *Black Robe*. Moore emigrated to Canada from Ireland in 1948 and stayed long enough to gain citizenship before moving on to California. *Black Robe* – the story of a missionary's journey into native territory – is typical of the author's preoccupations with Catholicism, repression and redemption.

Alice Munro *Lives of Girls and Women*; *The Progress of Love; The Beggar Maid; Friend of My Youth; Dance of the Happy Shades; Who Do You Think You Are?; Something I've Been Meaning to Tell You; Runaway; The Moons of Jupiter; and Hateship, Friendship, Courtship, Loveship and Marriage*. Among the world's finest living short-story writers, Munro deals primarily with the lives of women in the semi-rural and Protestant backcountry of southwest Ontario. Unsettling emotions are never far beneath the surface crust of everyday life. Among her more recent works, *Open Secrets* focuses on stories set in two small Ontario towns from the days of the early settlers to the present; and *Too Much Happiness* has one of its best stories set at a college in London, Ontario. Otherwise, start with *Who Do You Think You Are?*

Howard Norman *The Haunting of L.* Curious novel of psychosis, deception and sexual shenanigans mostly set in Churchill, Manitoba. The writing is a tad patchy, but the best sections are disconcerting and effecting in equal measure.

Michael Ondaatje *In the Skin of a Lion*. This is the novel that introduces readers to the characters that appear in the more famous *The English Patient*. It's a highly charged work spanning the period between the end of World War I and the Great Depression in Toronto.

E. Annie Proulx *The Shipping News*. The 1994 Pulitzer Prize-winner is a rambling, inconclusive narrative of a social misfit who finds love and happiness of sorts in small-town Newfoundland. Superb descriptions of sea, weather and all things fishy (as distinct from some very average characterization) make it a possible primer for a visit to the province.

Mordecai Richler French-Canadian, working-class and Jewish – Yiddishkeit was Richler's bag. He was the laureate of the minority within a minority within a minority. All his novels explore this relation with broad humour and pathos. In *The Apprenticeship of Duddy Kravitz*, his best-known work, Richler uses his early experiences of Montréal's working-class Jewish ghetto in an acerbic and slick cross-cultural romance built around the ambivalent but tightly drawn figure of Kravitz. Richler's pushy and ironic prose is not to all tastes, but you might also try *Solomon Gursky Was Here* or his later *Barney's Version*, a rip-roaring comic portrait of a reckless artist *manqué*.

Carol Shields *Happenstance*; *The Stone Diaries*; *Larry's Party*. Winner of the Pulitzer Prize, Shields is much lauded for the detail she finds in the everyday. There are moments of great beauty and sensitivity in these books as they chronicle the experiences of bourgeois North American suburbia with unnerving frankness.

Susan Swan *The Wives of Bath*. At a Toronto girls' school in the 1960s, the protagonist, Mouse, struggles with notions of feminine beauty as her best friend struggles with gender identity. A wry novel written in a genre the author described as "sexual gothic".

Miriam Toews *A Complicated Kindness*. Novels set in the Amish/Mennonite communities ('bonnet rippers') are very much in vogue at the moment – and this, set in Manitoba, is one of the best of its type. The protagonist is a 16 year-old girl rebelling against the strictures of her traditional community.

Guy Vanderhaeghe *The Last Crossing*. Set in 1870, a mismatched band of characters set out across the Plains in search of a lost missionary. The account flits between the past and the present – as it does in **Vanderhaeghe**'s comparable *The Englishman's Boy*, set south of the border in the American West.

John Wyndham *The Chrysalids*. A science-fiction classic built around a group of telepathic children and their adventures in post-Holocaust Labrador.

Poetry

Elizabeth Bishop *The Complete Poems, 1927-1979*. Though American by birth, Bishop spent much of her youth in Nova Scotia. Many of her early poems feed off her Canadian childhood and her fascination with the country's rough landscapes.

Leonard Cohen *Stranger Music: Selected Poems & Songs*. A fine collection from a 1960s survivor who enjoyed critical acclaim as a poet before emerging as a husky-throated crooner of bedsit ballads. See also his *Beautiful Losers*, one of the most aggressively experimental Canadian novels of the era.

Robert Service *Special Service: The Best of Robert W. Service*. Service's

Victorian-style ballads of pioneer and gold-rush life have a certain charm and they capture the essence of the gold-rush period. Among them, *The Heart of The Sourdough* is one of the most memorable or you could sample *The Shooting of Dan McGrew*.

Specialist guides

Ben Gadd & Mike Grandmaison *The Canadian Rockies*. Widely available in western Canada's larger bookshops, this is a lovingly produced and pains-takingly detailed handbook of walks, flora, fauna, geology and anything else remotely connected with the Rockies. Latest version published in 2007.

Brian Patton & Bart Robinson The *Canadian Rockies Trail Guide*. An essential guide for anyone wishing to do more than simply scratch the surface of the Rockies' walking possibilities. Latest version published in 2007.

Language

Language

Québécois French..979

Language

Canada has two official **languages** – English and French – plus numerous native tongues. Tensions between the two main language groups play a prominent part in the politics of Canada, but the native languages are more or less ignored except in the country's more remote areas, particularly in the Northwest Territories and Nunavut, where **Inuktitut**, the language of the Inuit, is spoken widely

In a brief glossary such as this there is no space to get to grips with the complexities of aboriginal languages, and very few travellers would have any need of them anyway: most natives (including those in Québec) have a good knowledge of English, especially if they deal with tourists in any capacity.

Québécois French

Québécois French differs from its European source in much the same way as North American English differs from British English. Thus, although Québécois French vocabulary, grammar and syntax are very near European French, speech can pose a few problems. If you plan to be spending much time in French-speaking Canada, consider investing in the *Rough Guide to French* phrasebook.

Tracing its roots back to seventeenth-century vernacular French, Québécois French has preserved features that disappeared long ago in France itself, and it has also been affected by its close contact with English. The end result is a dialect that – frankly – is a source of amusement to many French people and bafflement for those educated in the French language back in Europe, not to mention other parts of Canada. Within Québec itself there are marked regional differences of pronunciation, so much so that Montréalers find it hard to understand northern Québécois.

The Québécois can be extremely sympathetic when visiting English-speakers make the effort to speak French – and most are much more forthcoming with their knowledge of English when talking to a Briton or American than to a Canadian. Similarly easy-going is the attitude towards the formal vous (you), which is used less often in Québec; you may even be corrected when saying "*S'il vous plaît*" with the suggestion that "*S'il te plaît*" is more appropriate. Another popular phrase you are likely to encounter is "*pas de tout*" ("not at all"), which in Québec is pronounced "pan toot", completely different from the French "*pa du too*". The same goes for "*c'est tout?*" ("is that all?"), pronounced "*say toot*"; you're likely to hear this when buying something in a shop.

With **pronunciation** there's little point trying to mimic the local dialect – generally, just stick to the classic French rules.

French pronunciation

French isn't an easy language for English-speakers to **pronounce**, despite the number of words shared with English, but learning the essentials is not difficult. Differentiating words is the initial problem in understanding spoken French; it's very hard to get people to slow down. If, as a last resort, you get them to write it down, you may find you can identify half the words anyway.

Vowels

a as in h**a**t
au as in **o**ver
e as in g**e**t
é between g**e**t and g**a**te
è between g**e**t and g**u**t
eu as in h**ur**t
i as in mach**i**ne
o as in h**o**t
ô as in **o**ver
ou as in f**oo**d
u is a pursed-lip version of tr**ue**

The following are extra-tricky nasal sounds:

an/am and *en/em* like **Don**caster said through your nose
in/im like **an**xious
on/om like **Don**caster said with a heavy cold
un/um like **u**nderstand

Consonants

Consonants are pronounced much as in English, except:

ç is an English **s**
ch is an English **sh**
h is silent
ll as in bayonet
r is growled rather than trilled
th is like an English **t**
w is an English **v**

French words and phrases

The basics

good morning/afternoon/hello	bonjour
good evening	bonsoir
good night	bonne nuit
goodbye	au revoir
yes	oui
no	non
please	s'il vous/te plaît
thank you (very much)	merci (beaucoup)
you're welcome	bienvenue/de rien/je vous en prie
OK	d'accord
How are you?	Comment allez-vous?/ Ça va?
Fine, thanks	Très bien, merci
Do you speak English?	Parlez-vous anglais?
I don't speak French	Je ne parle pas français
I don't understand	Je ne comprends pas
I don't know	Je ne sais pas
Excuse me (in a crowd)	Excusez-moi
Sorry	Pardon/désolé(e)
I'm English	Je suis anglais(e)
Scottish/Welsh	écossais(e)/gallois(e)
Irish/American	irlandais(e)/ américain(e)
Australian	australian(e)
I live in...	Je demeure à...
Wait a minute!	Un instant!
here/there	ici/là
good/bad	bon/mauvais
big/small	grand/petit
cheap/expensive	bon marché/cher
early/late	tôt/tard
hot/cold	chaud/froid
near/far	près (pas loin)/loin

vacant/occupied	libre/occupé	**enough/no more**	assez/ça suffit
quickly/slowly	vite/lentement	**Mr**	Monsieur
loudly/quietly	bruyant/tranquille	**Mrs**	Madame
with/without	avec/sans	**Miss**	Mademoiselle
more/less	plus/moins		

Numbers

1	un/une	**19**	dix-neuf
2	deux	**20**	vingt
3	trois	**21**	vingt-et-un
4	quatre	**22**	vingt-deux
5	cinq	**30**	trente
6	six	**40**	quarante
7	sept	**50**	cinquante
8	huit	**60**	soixante
9	neuf	**70**	soixante-dix
10	dix	**80**	quatre-vingts
11	onze	**90**	quatre-vingt-dix
12	douze	**100**	cent
13	treize	**101**	cent-et-un
14	quatorze	**110**	cent-dix
15	quinze	**200**	deux cents
16	seize	**1000**	mille
17	dix-sept	**2000**	deux milles
18	dix-huit		

Days

Monday	lundi	**afternoon**	l'après-midi
Tuesday	mardi	**evening**	le soir
Wednesday	mercredi	**night**	la nuit
Thursday	jeudi	**yesterday**	hier
Friday	vendredi	**today**	aujourd'hui
Saturday	samedi	**tomorrow**	demain
Sunday	dimanche	**tomorrow morning**	demain matin
morning	le matin		

Months

January	janvier	**July**	juillet
February	février	**August**	août
March	mars	**September**	septembre
April	avril	**October**	octobre
May	mai	**November**	novembre
June	juin	**December**	décembre

Time

minute	minute	**It's 9.00**	Il est neuf heures
hour	heure	**1.05**	une heure cinq
day	jour	**2.15**	deux heures et quart
week	semaine	**5.45**	six heures moins quart
month	mois	**9.40**	dix heures moins vingt
year	année	**10.30**	dix heures et demie
now	maintenant	**noon**	midi
later	plus tard	**midnight**	minuit
What time is it?	Quelle heure est-il?		

Questions and directions

Where?	Où?
When?	Quand?
What?	Quoi?
What is it?	Qu'est-ce que c'est?
How much/many?	Combien?
Why?	Pourquoi?
It is/there is	C'est/Il y a
Is it/is there...?	Est-ce que/Y a-t-il...?
How do I get to...?	Où se trouve...?
How far is it to...?	À quelle distance est-il à...?
Can you give me a lift to...?	Pouvez-vous me conduire jusqu'à...?
Can you tell me when to get off?	Pouvez-vous me dire quand descendre?
What time does it open?	À quelle heure ça ouvre?
How much does it cost?	Combien cela coûte-t-il?
How do you say it in French?	Comment ça se dit en français?

Accommodation

Is there a campsite nearby?	Y a-t-il un camping près d'ici?
tent	tente
cabin	chalet
hostel	auberge de jeunesse
hotel	hôtel
Do you have anything cheaper?	Avez-vous quelque chose de meilleur marché?
full board	tout compris
Can I see the room?	Puis-je peux voir la chambre?
I'll take this one	Je vais prendre celle-ci
I'd like to book a room	J'aimerais réserver une chambre
I have a booking	J'ai une réservation
Can we camp here?	Pouvons-nous camper ici?
How much is it?	C'est combien?
It's expensive	C'est cher
Is breakfast included?	Est-ce que le petit déjeuner est compris?
I'm looking for a nearby hotel	Je cherche un hôtel près d'ici
Do you have a room?	Avez-vous une chambre?
for one/two/three people	pour une/deux/trois personne(s)
for one/two/three nights	pour une/deux/trois nuit(s)
for one week	pour une semaine
with a double bed	avec un lit double
with a shower/bathtub	avec douche/salle de bain
hot/cold water	eau chaude/froide

Travelling

bus	autobus	**What time does it leave?**	Il part à quelle heure?
train	train	**When is the next train to…?**	Quand est le prochain train pour…?
plane	avion	**Do I have to change?**	Dois-je transférer?
car	voiture	**Where does it leave from?**	D'où est-ce qu'il part?
taxi	taxi	**How many kilometres?**	Combien de kilomètres?
bicycle	vélo	**How many hours?**	Combien d'heures?
ferry	traversier	**Which bus do I take to get to...?**	Quel autobus dois-je prendre pour aller à…?
ship	bâteau	**Next stop**	Le prochain arrêt
hitch-hiking	faire du pouce	**Where's the road to…?**	Où est la route pour…?
on foot	à pied		
bus station	terminus d'autobus		
train station	gare centrale		
ferry terminal	quai du traversier		
port	port		
A ticket to…	Un billet pour…		
one-way/return	aller-simple/ aller-retour		
Can I book a seat?	Puis-je réserver un siège?		

Some signs

Entrance/Exit	Entrée/Sortie	**Platform**	Voie
Free admission	Entrée Libre	**Cash desk**	Caisse
Gentlemen/Ladies	Messieurs/Dames	**Go/Walk**	Marchez
WC	Toilette	**Stop**	Arrêtez
Vacant/Engaged	Libre/Occupé	**Customs**	Douanes
Open/Closed	Ouvert/Fermé	**Do not touch!**	Défense de toucher!
Arrivals/Departures	Arrivées/Départs	**Danger!**	Danger!
Closed for holidays	Fermé pour les vacances	**Beware!**	Attention!
Pull/Push	Tirez/Poussez	**First aid**	Premiers soins
Out of order	Hors d'usage/Brisé	**Ring the bell**	Sonnez
To let	À louer	**No smoking**	Défense de fumer

Driving

turn to the left/ right	tournez à gauche/ droite	**tow-away zone**	zone de remorquage
straight ahead	tout droit	**cars towed at owner's expense**	remorquage à vos frais
car park	terrain de stationnement	**one-way street**	sens unique
no parking	défense de stationner/ stationnement interdit	**dead end**	cul-de-sac
		no entry	défense d'entrer
		slow down	ralentir

proceed on flashing green light	attendez le feu vert clignotant	Fill the tank with…	Faîtes le plein avec…
turn on headlights!	allumez vos phares!	…regular	…de l'essence ordinaire
no overtaking	défense de dépasser	…super	…du super
passing lane only	voie réservée au dépassement	…unleaded	…du sans plomb
speed	vitesse	Check the oil	Vérifiez l'huile
self-service	libre-service	battery	la batterie
full service	service complet	radiator	le radiateur
		plugs	bougies d'allumage
		tyre pressure	pression des pneus
		Pump up the tyres	Gonflez les pneus

A French menu reader

Basic terms and ingredients

beurre	butter	pain	bread
chaud	hot	poisson	fish
crème fraiche	sour cream	poivre	pepper
dessert	dessert	salade	salad
frappé	iced	sel	salt
froid	cold	sucre	sugar
fromage	cheese	tourte	tart or pie
hors d'oeuvre	starters	tranche	a slice
legumes	vegetables	viande	meat
oeufs	eggs		

Snacks

un sandwich/une baguette…	a sandwich…	croque-monsieur	grilled cheese and ham sandwich
…de jambon	…with ham	oeufs au plat	fried eggs
…de fromage	…with cheese	oeufs à la coque	boiled eggs
…de saucisson	…with sausage	oeufs durs	hard-boiled eggs
à l'ail	with garlic	oeufs brouillés	scrambled eggs
au poivre	with pepper	omelette nature	plain omelette
		omelette au fromage	cheese omelette

Soups and starters

assiette anglaise	plate of cold meats	crudités with dressing	raw vegetables
bisque	shellfish soup	potage	thick soup, usually vegetable
bouillabaisse	fish soup		
bouillon	broth or stock		
consommé	clear soup		

Meat and poultry

agneau	lamb	**foie**	liver
bifteck	steak	**gibiers**	game
boeuf	beef	**gigot**	leg of venison
canard	duck	**jambon**	ham
cheval	horsemeat	**lard**	bacon
côtelettes	cutlets	**porc**	pork
cuisson	leg of lamb	**poulet**	chicken
dindon	turkey	**saucisse**	sausage
escargots	snails	**veau**	veal

Fish and seafood

anchois	anchovies	**maquereau**	mackerel
anguilles	eels	**morue**	cod
carrelet	plaice	**moules**	mussels
cervettes roses	prawns	**saumon**	salmon
hareng	herring	**sole**	sole
homard	lobster	**truite**	trout
lotte de mer	monkfish		

Cooking methods

saignant	rare (steak)	**fumé**	smoked
a point	medium done (steak)	**grillé**	grilled
bien cuit	well done (steak)	**mijoté**	stewed
au four	baked	**pané**	breaded
bouilli	boiled	**rôti**	roasted
frit/friture	fried/deep fried	**sauté**	lightly cooked in butter

Vegetables and grains

ail	garlic	**oignons**	onions
asperges	asparagus	**petits pois**	peas
carottes	carrots	**poireau**	leek
champignons	mushrooms	**pommes (de terre)**	potatoes
choufleur	cauliflower	**riz**	rice
concombre	cucumber	**tomate**	tomato
laitue	lettuce		

Fruit and nuts

amandes	almonds	**fraises**	strawberries
ananas	pineapple	**framboises**	raspberries
cacahouète	peanut	**marrons**	chestnuts
cérises	cherries	**noisette**	hazelnut
citron	lemon	**pamplemousse**	grapefruit

poire	pear
pomme	apple
prune	plum
pruneau	prune
raisins	grapes

Sweets and desserts

crêpes au sucre	pancakes with sugar
crêpes au citron	pancakes with lemon
crêpes au miel	pancakes with honey
crêpes à la confiture	pancakes with jam/jelly
crêpes suzettes	thin pancakes with orange juice and liqueur
glace	ice cream
madeleine	small, shell-shaped sponge cake
parfait	frozen mousse, sometimes ice cream
petits fours	bite-sized cakes or pastries

Drinks

café	coffee
thé	tea
lait	milk
jus d'orange	orange juice
citron pressé	sweetened lemon juice
bière	beer
vin rouge	red wine
vin blanc	white wine
brut	very dry
sec	dry
demi-sec	sweet
doux	very sweet
eaux de vie	fruit spirit/liquor

Travel store

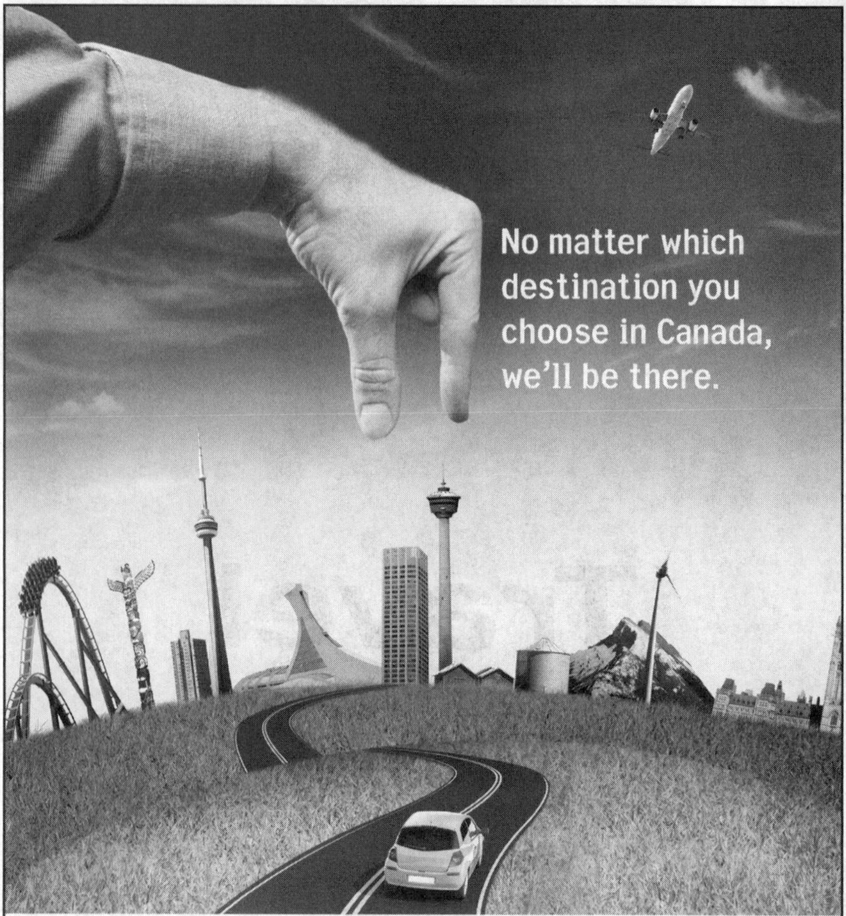
No matter which
destination you
choose in Canada,
we'll be there.

CALL OF THE WILD
Adventure Consultants™
Algonquin Park
Canoe Trips!
Paddle your own canoe & sleep under the stars on
a 3-4 day adventure! Toronto transfers available.
www.CallOfTheWild.ca
www.AlgonquinEcoLodge.com
A unique lodge for those who want the
wilderness without having to "rough it".
905-471-9453

Toronto, Canada
Au Petit Paris Bed and Breakfast

RUBY RANGE ADVENTURE LTD.
SUMMER & WINTER TOURS
HIKING • CANOE • FISHING
HOTEL & CAMPING TOURS
CUSTOM TRIPS
FLY-DRIVES
ALASKA & CANADA
GUIDED ROUND TRIPS
WILDERNESS TOURS
YUKON
LARGER THAN LIFE
Call us today
+1-867-667-2209
www.rubyrange.com/rough

ROUGH GUIDE MAP
France
1:1,000,000 • 1 INCH: 15.8 MILES • 1CM: 10KM
Plastic waterproof map
ideal for planning and touring

ROUGH GUIDES

Small print and

Index

SMALL PRINT

A Rough Guide to Rough Guides

Published in 1982, the first Rough Guide – to Greece – was a student scheme that became a publishing phenomenon. Mark Ellingham, a recent graduate in English from Bristol University, had been travelling in Greece the previous summer and couldn't find the right guidebook. With a small group of friends he wrote his own guide, combining a highly contemporary, journalistic style with a thoroughly practical approach to travellers' needs.

The immediate success of the book spawned a series that rapidly covered dozens of destinations. And, in addition to impecunious backpackers, Rough Guides soon acquired a much broader and older readership that relished the guides' wit and inquisitiveness as much as their enthusiastic, critical approach and value-for-money ethos.

These days, Rough Guides include recommendations from shoestring to luxury and cover more than 200 destinations around the globe, including almost every country in the Americas and Europe, more than half of Africa and most of Asia and Australasia. Our ever-growing team of authors and photographers is spread all over the world, particularly in Europe, the US and Australia.

In the early 1990s, Rough Guides branched out of travel, with the publication of Rough Guides to World Music, Classical Music and the Internet. All three have become benchmark titles in their fields, spearheading the publication of a wide range of books under the Rough Guide name.

Including the travel series, Rough Guides now number more than 350 titles, covering: phrasebooks, waterproof maps, music guides from Opera to Heavy Metal, reference works as diverse as Conspiracy Theories and Shakespeare, and popular culture books from iPods to Poker. Rough Guides also produce a series of more than 120 World Music CDs in partnership with World Music Network.

Visit www.roughguides.com to see our latest publications.

Rough Guide credits

Text editor: Harry Wilson
Layout: Ajay Verma
Cartography: Deshpal Dabas, Rajesh Chhibber
Picture editor: Michelle Bhatia
Production: Rebecca Short
Proofreader: Anita Sach
Cover design: Dan May, Chloë Roberts
Photographers: Tim Draper, Enrique Uranga
Editorial: **London** Ruth Blackmore, Andy Turner, Keith Drew, Edward Aves, Alice Park, Lucy White, Jo Kirby, James Smart, Natasha Foges, Róisín Cameron, James Rice, Lara Kavanagh, Emma Traynor, Emma Gibbs, Kathryn Lane, Monica Woods, Mani Ramaswamy, Lucy Cowie, Alison Roberts, Joe Staines, Peter Buckley, Matthew Milton, Tracy Hopkins, Ruth Tidball; **Delhi** Madhavi Singh, Lubna Shaheen
Design & Pictures: **London** Scott Stickland, Dan May, Diana Jarvis, Mark Thomas, Nicole Newman, Sarah Cummins, Emily Taylor; **Delhi** Umesh Aggarwal, Jessica Subramanian, Ankur Guha, Pradeep Thapliyal, Sachin Tanwar, Anita Singh, Nikhil Agarwal, Sachin Gupta.
Production: Liz Cherry
Cartography: **London** Ed Wright, Katie Lloyd-Jones; **Delhi** Ashutosh Bharti, Rajesh Mishra, Animesh Pathak, Jasbir Sandhu, Karobi Gogoi, Alakananda Roy, Swati Handoo,
Online: **London** Faye Hellon, Jeanette Angell, Fergus Day, Justine Bright, Clare Bryson, Aine Fearon, Adrian Low, Ezgi Celebi; **Delhi** Amit Verma, Rahul Kumar, Narender Kumar, Ravi Yadav, Debojit Borah, Rakesh Kumar, Ganesh Sharma, Shisir Basumatari
Marketing & Publicity: **London** Liz Statham, Jess Carter, Vivienne Watton, Anna Paynton, Rachel Sprackett, Laura Vipond; **New York** Katy Ball, Judi Powers; **Delhi** Ragini Govind
Reference Director: Andrew Lockett
Operations Assistant: Becky Doyle
Operations Manager: Helen Atkinson
Publishing Director (Travel): Clare Currie
Commercial Manager: Gino Magnotta
Managing Director: John Duhigg

SMALL PRINT

Publishing information

This 7th edition published June 2010 by
Rough Guides Ltd,
80 Strand, London WC2R 0RL
11 Community Centre, Panchsheel Park, New Delhi 110017, India
Distributed by the Penguin Group
Penguin Books Ltd,
80 Strand, London WC2R 0RL
Penguin Group (USA)
375 Hudson Street, NY 10014, USA
Penguin Group (Australia)
250 Camberwell Road, Camberwell, Victoria 3124, Australia
Penguin Group (Canada)
195 Harry Walker Parkway N, Newmarket, ON, L3Y 7B3 Canada
Penguin Group (NZ)
67 Apollo Drive, Mairangi Bay, Auckland 1310, New Zealand
Cover concept by Peter Dyer.

Typeset in Bembo and Helvetica to an original design by Henry Iles.
Printed in Italy by L.E.G.O. S.p.A, Lavis (TN)

1016pp includes index
A catalogue record for this book is available from the British Library
ISBN: 978-1-84836-503-2

1 3 5 7 9 8 6 4 2

Help us update

We've gone to a lot of effort to ensure that the seventh edition of **The Rough Guide to Canada** is accurate and up-to-date. However, things change – places get "discovered", opening hours are notoriously fickle, restaurants and rooms raise prices or lower standards. If you feel we've got it wrong or left something out, we'd like to know, and if you can remember the address, the price, the hours, the phone number, so much the better.

Please send your comments with the subject line "**Rough Guide Canada Update**" to ⓔmail @roughguides.com. We'll credit all contributions and send a copy of the next edition (or any other Rough Guide if you prefer) for the very best emails.

Have your questions answered and tell others about your trip at ⓦwww.roughguides.com

Acknowledgements

Steven Horak thanks Harry Wilson for his steady hand at the helm and for diligent editing. A big 'thank you' is also due to the Rough Guides crew in Delhi and London whose hard work made this edition possible.

Tim Jepson thanks his editor; Lucy Hyslop; James and Vicky Ballentyne; Air Canada; Charlotte Fraser and Fairmont Hotels; Claire Griffin and Four Seasons hotels; Kathleen Eccles; Tracy Long and British Airways Holidays; and Anna Whitaker and Virgin Holidays.

Stephen Keeling thanks Randy Brooks at Nova Scotia Tourism, Thresa Burden, Mike Clewer and Laura Walbourne at Western Newfoundland DMO, Kathleen Crotty at Newfoundland & Labrador Tourism, Sheela Curley in PEI, Martin Flynn, Greg Pike and the team at Marble Zip Tours, Bonnie Goudie at Labrador Straits HDC, Rogier Gruys for advice and connections, the incredibly generous Elaine Hann in St John's, Bob Hicks and the team at Gros Morne Adventures, Randy Letto and Monica Surina at Destination Labrador, Elizabeth Ronayne at Marine Atlantic, Diane Roux at Tourism New Brunswick, Pamela Vienneau at Tourism PEI, Todd Wight in Rocky Harbour, Harry Wilson back in London for his superb editing and lastly Tiffany Wu, whose love and support made this possible.

Phil Lee thanks his editor, Harry Wilson, for tackling what must have been a mammoth task with – and in – such good spirits. Special thanks also to Suzanne Morton-Taylor for reaching the furthest parts of Ontario; Diane Helinski of Ontario Tourism for her expert support and advice; Rey Stephen, also of Ontario Tourism, for his efficient attention to detail; Helen Lovekin for her hospitality and the latest news on her home city, Toronto; and the Buers, also of Toronto, for their generous hospitality.

AnneLise Sorensen says merci beaucoup to all who offered their wonderful hospitality and shared travel tips, information, Québécois wine, and lively evenings. A big thank you to the top-notch Tourisme Québec and Montréal, including Yves Gentil and Marie José Pinsonnault; Carole Saint-Laurent; the spirited Signy Stephenson at lovely Auberge Knowlton; wine connoisseur and Domaine Les Brome owner Leon Courville, who was equally generous with his time and his wine; the entire family behind the splendid Manoir Hovey; the dedicated team of the Outaouais region and Mont Tremblant, including Catherine Lacasse. Gracias to Tiet (Uncle) Pere, who has long made Canada his home, and who treated us to a memorable evening followed by a true Canadian breakfast. Thanks to guapo and all my friends in New York, as well as Claire, Mama, and familia for their support and cheery emails. A resounding thanks to the London and Delhi Rough Guides teams, and above all to Harry Wilson, who deftly guided the book to completion. And finally, a big merci and mange tak to Papa Kurt, the best companion a travel writer could ask for.

Christian Williams would like to thank Canadians for being such a friendly and hospitable bunch and to CBC radio for making long journeys feel shorter. Particular gratitude is due to Daryl Demoskoff and Carla Bechard in Saskatchewan; Janice Tober, Jillian Brown and Bill Macdonald in Manitoba; Lindsay Jardine and Vanessa Marmelic in Alberta; and Nancy Dionne in British Columbia. At Rough Guides a big thanks goes to all those involved in the book, particularly Harry Wilson for the smooth editorial ride. Thanks also to my co-authors for their support and teamwork.

Claus Vogel would like to thank Roy Raycroft, Franc Pridoehl, Judith Venaas, Sherry Powney, Yukon Tourism and Parks Canada for their invaluable assistance. A heartfelt thank you to both Sheila Norris and Sheila Dodd for a memorable introduction to the Yukon and more importantly for their endless assistance and generosity throughout this journey. A special thanks to Mom and Dad for looking after Hero during my absence. Finally, I could not complete this project without the wonderful support, encouragement and patience from my editors Mani Ramaswamy and Harry Wilson who entrusted me to introduce readers to Canada's North – a truly remarkable place.

The editor thanks the authors for their hard work; the whole Delhi team for all their efforts, particularly Ajay Verma; Michelle Bhatia for her superb picture research and editing; Anita Sach for her vigilant proofreading; all other Rough Guides editors and colleagues for their overall guidance; and, finally, thanks to Madden, Safruk and Williams – the best men a guy could ever know; this one's for you.

Readers' letters

Thanks to all the readers who have taken the time to write in with comments and suggestions (and apologies if we've inadvertently omitted or misspelt anyone's name):

Mike Banfi, Petra Bishai, CGD Brook, Lee Davis, Dr. Richard & Lucy Delahay, Matthew Dillon, Paulo Dorabela, Gary Elflett, Saskia Geerts, James Glansfield, Kristin Hannahs, Deborah Iredale, Lloyd Jones, Frances Landeryou, M Lodge, Roger Mackin, Louise Mifsud, Ken and Sue Napier, Rachael and Tom Pankhurst, Brian and Mavis Pickard, Claude Perreault, Serge Poulin, Helen Rutter, Rosalie Sadler, Erick Sodhi, Gédéon Verreault, Bryony Webb, Deborah Wehrle, Pam Weir, Tim Yeates

Photo credits

All photos © Rough Guides except the following:

Title page

AGO © Sam Javanrouh, daily dose of imagery

Full page

Alberta Rockies © Gavriel Jecan/SuperStock

Introduction

Inukshuk © ColsQuebec/Alamy
Lighthouse © Russ Heinl, All Canada Photos/Corbis
National Gallery © Miles Ertman/SuperStock
Montreal © Jon Arnold Images/Danita Delimont
Inuit fishing © White Fox/photolibrary
Hoodoos © Danita Delimont/Alamy
Long Beach © Jens Preshaw/SuperStock
Dempster Highway © Henry Georgi/All Canada Photos
Québec City Winter Carnival © Rubens Abboud/Alamy

Things not to miss

01 Just for Laughs Festival © Just for Laughs Festival
02 Snowboarder © Randy Lincks/photolibrary
03 Polar bear © Eric Baccega/SuperStock
04 Parliament © Chris Cheadle/photolibrary
05 Kayaking © Wally Hayes/Nova Scotia Tourism, Culture & Heritage
06 Dawson City © SuperStock
07 Stanley Park © imagebroker/Alamy
08 Calgary Stampede © Christian Williams
09 Live music © Sean Dixon, courtesy of In-Flight Safety
10 Caribou © Alaska Stock LLC/Alamy
11 Ice climbing © Real World People/Alamy
12 Tom Thomson, The West Wind © Courtesy of the AGO
13 Athabasca glacier © Douglas Peoples/SuperStock
15 St John's © Newfoundland and Labrador Tourism
16 Lac Sauvage © Getty Images/First Llght
17 Algonquin Provincial Park © Benjamin Rondel/Corbis
18 Hot Springs Island, Haida Gwaii © David Nunuk/photolibrary
19 Hopewell Rocks, Bay of Fundy © Buddy Mays/Alamy
20 Icefields Parkway © Walter Bibikow/SuperStock
21 Aurora borealis © Edmonton Tourism
22 Niagara Falls © Erik Smits/iStockphoto
23 Lunenburg © Nova Scotia Tourism, Culture & Heritage
24 Pacific Rim National park © Chris Cheadle/photolibrary
25 Montréal smoked meat © Will van Overbeek/National Geographic Society/Corbis
26 Whales © Evgeniya Lazareva/iStockphoto
27 Cavendish Beach © Garry Black/photolibrary
28 Banff backpacker © Jim West/Alamy
29 High tea © Danita Delimont/Alamy
30 Mount Robson © Chris Cheadle/Alamy

Wild Canada colour section

Canoeing © D. Heringa/Creative Media
Lighthouse © Paul A. Souders/Corbis
Gaspésie © Atlantide Phototravel/Corbis
Whale © Sorin Himself/Alamy
Hiker © David Noton Photography/Alamy
Wood bison © Raymond Gehman/Corbis
Caribou © Paul Nicklen/Getty Images

Skiing and snowboarding colour section

Snowboarding © Keith Douglas/photolibrary
Mont Tremblant © Bibikow/photolibrary
Lake Louise © Ryan Creary/photolibrary
Kicking Horse © Ryan Creary/photolibrary
Powder snowboarding © Mike Crane Photography/Alamy
Heli-skiing © Alec Pytlowany/photolibrary
Ski rail © Sean O'Neill/Alamy
Cross-country skiers © First Light/Alamy

Black and whites

p.86 AGO © Tourism Toronto/torontowide.com
p.101 Queen Street West © Tourism Toronto/OTMP
p.119 Maid of the Mist © Adam Booth/iStockphoto
p.185 Canadian War Museum © Harry Foster, CMC/Canadian War Museum
p.195 Moose Factory Cultural Centre © Janusz Wrobel/Alamy
p.203 Skating © All Canada Photos/Alamy
p.258 Bike path © Megapress/Alamy
p.268 Minke whale © Moritz Frei/iStockphoto
p.316 House © SuperStock
p.337 Ice fishing © RENAULT Philippe/hemis.fr
p.350 Rocks © Michel Valiquette/iStockphoto
p.356 Boats © Danita Delimont/Alamy
p.365 Citadel © Nova Scotia Tourism, Culture & Heritage
p.373 Mahone Bay © Bob Rowan/Progressive Image/Corbis
p.383 Vineyard © Alisha Hime/iStockphoto
p.393 Cabot Trail © Nova Scotia Tourism, Culture & Heritage
p.405 Art gallery © Walter Bibikow/SuperStock
p.422 Sign © Arthur Gebuys/Alamy
p.428 Fisherman © Greg Vaughn/Alamy
p.446 Gros Morne National Park © Newfoundland and Labrador Tourism
p.451 Harbourfront © John Sylvester/All Canada Photos
p.473 Iceberg © Thomas Kitchin & Victoria Hurst/photolibrary
p.492 Battle Harbour © Newfoundland and Labrador Tourism
p.502 Canoe © Tourism Saskatchewan/Hans-Gerhard Pfaff
p.513 Boat © All Canada Photos/Alamy
p.532 Mounties © Tourism Saskatchewan/Hans-Gerhard Pfaff
p.542 Grasslands National Park © Tourism Saskatchewan/Greg Huszar Photography
p.577 Cree man © Tim Graham/Corbis

p.598 Polar bear sign © Christian Williams
p.604 Elk © Banff Lake Louise Tourism
p.629 Banff Springs Hotel © Banff Lake Louise Tourism
p.648 Hikers © Banff Lake Louise Tourism
p.665 Kayakers © Philip and Karen Smith/SuperStock
p.680 Hiker © David P. Lewis/iStockphoto
p.698 Helmcken Falls © Chris Wolf/iStockphoto
p.716 River crossing © All Canada Photos/Alamy
p.722 Grape stomping © Gunter Marx/Alamy
p.733 Rafting © All Canada Photos/Alamy
p.812 Whale-watching © JurgaR/istock
p.822 Galiano Island © Botanica/photolibrary
p.864 Floatplane © Blickwinkel/Alamy
p.876 Grizzlies © Kelly Funk/photolibrary
p.880 Haida war canoe © All Canada Photos/Alamy
p.892 Liard Hot Springs © Lucas Payne/Alamy
p.912 Palace Grand © Ron Niebrugge/Alamy
p.927 Virginia Falls © First Light/Alamy

Index

Map entries are in colour.

'Ksan....873
1837 Rebellion....66, 253

A

Abbaye Cistercienne d'Oka....253
Abbaye St-Benoît-du-Lac....262
Aboriginal peoples....10, 214, 949–951, 957, 958
Abram-Village, PEI....443
Acadian Peninsula....427
Acadians, the....387
accommodation....37–40
Adam Lake, MB....529
Agawa Bay....200
Agawa Canyon....198
Ainsworth Hot Springs....711
airlines....30
Akamina Parkway....613, 614, 615
Aklavik....919, 921
Alaska Highway, the....889–894
Alaska Marine Highway....875
Alaskan ferries....875
Alberta....503
Alberta, Manitoba, Saskatchewan &....504–505
Alberta Badlands....548–550
Alert Bay....857
Alexandra Bridge Provincial Park....733
Alexandra Falls....928
Algoma Central Railway....198
Algonquin Provincial Park....161–164
Alliford Bay....884
Alma, NB....421
Alma, QC....342
amethysts....202
Amherstburg....136
Amish....128
Amundsen, Roald....943
Anchorage, Alaska....903
Annapolis Royal....383
Annapolis Valley....382–388
Anne of Green Gables....438, 439
Anticosti, Île d'....352
Anticosti, Parc National d'....352
Arctic Circle....916, 918
Arctic Coast, the....941–944
Arctic Western, the....918–923
Argenta, BC....715
Argentia, NL....463
Arviat....939
Aspen Valley Wildlife Sanctuary....161
Assembly of First Nations....958
Athabasca Falls....657
Athabasca Glacier....656
Athabasca, Lake....595
Atlin....902
ATMs....55
aurora borealis....351, 870, 894
Austin, MB....527
auto rental....34
Auyuittuq National Park....945, *Wild Canada* colour section
Avalon Peninsula, NL....460–464
Awenda Provincial Park....151

B

Babine Mountains Provincial Park....872
Baccalieu Trail, the....462
Baddeck....396
Badlands, Alberta....548–550
Baffin Island....944–946
Baie Sainte-Marie....380
Baie Trinité....346
Baie-Comeau....344
Baie-Johan-Beetz....353
Baie-Ste-Catherine....335
Baie-Ste-Marguerite....335, 339
Baie-St-Paul....328
Bailey's Creek, BC....741
Baker Lake....939
bald eagle....790, 873
Baldy Mountain, MB....570
Balfour....711
Bamfield....847
Banff National Park....622–639
Banff National Park....622
BANFF (town)....623–628
Banff (town)....624
- accommodation....626
- activities, summer....634–635
- activities, winter....636
- arrival....625
- Banff Park Museum....628
- Banff Springs Hotel....629
- biking....634
- boat trips....634
- bookshops....638
- Buffalo Nations Luxton Museum....629
- cafés....637
- Cave & Basin Hot Springs....630
- clubs....638
- drinking....636
- eating....636
- hikes....632
- hikes, winter....636
- hot springs....630
- information....625
- Lake Minnewanka....631
- Mount Norquay....634
- nightlife....638
- park permits....625
- pubs....638
- restaurants....636
- skiing....634
- skiing, cross-country....636
- snowboarding....634
- Sulphur Mountain Gondola....630
- Sunshine Village....635
- transport....625
- Upper Hot Springs....631
- walks....632
- Whyte Museum of the Canadian Rockies....629
- winter sports....634

banks....55
Barkerville Historic Town....803
Bas St-Laurent....305
baseball....50
Basilique de Ste-Anne-de-Beaupré....302
basketball....50
Basque whaling....490
Basse Côte-Nord....353
Basses Laurentides, Les....252
Batoche National Historic Site....578
Battle Creek....545
Battle Harbour, Lab....491
Battle Mountain....741
Battle of the Windmill....173
Battlefords, The....581

Bay Bulls 461
Bay of Fundy 400
Bay of Fundy tidal bore 388
Bayfield 140
BC Forestry Discovery Centre 827
Bear Glacier 887
bears 47, 625, 966
Beaubears Island, NB 426
Beaufort Sea 919
Beausoleil Island 156
Beaver Creek, YT 906
beaver, the 163
Beaverbrook Art Gallery 405
bed and breakfasts 38
beer 43
Bell Homestead 127
Bell Museum, Alexander Graham 396
Bell, Alexander Graham 127, 396
Bella Coola 801
Bellevue, AB 552
Bennett Lake 896, 897
Beothuks, the 456, 475
Bergeronnes, QC 335, 336
Berton, Pierre 913
Bethune, Norman 160
Bic, Parc national du 311
bicycle trail, P'tit Train du Nord 257
Big Beaver, SK 541
Big Chute Marine Railway 155
Big Drop, Gold River, BC 856
Big Hill 675
Big Muddy Badlands 541
Big Tancook 372
Big White Ski Resort 724, *Skiing and snowboarding* colour section
biking *37*
Bird Lake, MB 523
bison 932, 964
Blackcomb Mountain 796–800
blackflies 53
Blackhead, NL 460
Blacks Harbour, NB 412
Blairmore, AB 553
Blanc-Sablon 488
Blomidon Provincial Park 387
Bloody Falls 943
Blue Mountain, ON 148
Blue River, BC 742
Bluenose II 376
Boldt Castle 172
Bonanza Creek 915
Bonaventure 320
Bonavista 470
Bonavista Peninsula 468–471
Bonne Bay 477, 478
books 970–976
Boswell 710
Botanical Beach, BC 825
Botanical Gardens, Royal 113
Bouctouche, NB 425
Bountiful, BC 706
Bow Glacier Falls 654
Bow Lake 654
Bow Valley Parkway 640
Bow Valley Trails 641
Bracebridge 160
Brandon, MB 528
Brant, Joseph 87, 125, 126
Brantford 125
Bras d'Or Lake 392
Bridal Veil Falls 148
Brier Island 382
Brigus 462
Britannia Beach 788
British Columbia Wildlife Park 736
British Columbia, interior 698–742
British Columbia, interior 700
Brockville 172
Broken Group Islands, The 846
Bromont 259
Broom Point, NL 479
Bruce Peninsula National Park 144
Bruce Peninsula, the 142–146
Bruce Trail, the 144
buffalo 932, 964
Burgeo 485
Burgess Shale 677
Burin Peninsula 464
Burns Lake 872
Burwash Landing 906
bus companies 31
buses from the US 29
buses in Canada 35
Butterfly Conservatory, Niagara Falls 120
Buttle Lake 854
Butze Rapids 878

C

Cabot Landing Provincial Park 395
Cabot Trail 392–396, *Wild Canada* colour section
Cabot, John 457, 470
Cache Creek 734
Caddy Lake, MB 522
Cajuns 387
CALGARY 553–565
Calgary 557
accommodation 558
addresses 558
airport 556
arrival 556
ballet 564
bars 564
bookshops 564
Bow River 561
buses to Banff and Lake Louise 556
cafés 563
Calgary Tower 560
Chinese Cultural Centre 561
cinema 564
clubs 564
Deane House 562
Devonian Gardens 560
drinking 563–564
eating 563–564
Eau Claire Market 561
Fort Calgary 561
Glenbow Museum 560
Heritage Park Historical Village 562
history 554
Hunt House 562
information 556
Inglewood Bird Sanctuary 562
Jubilee Auditorium 564
Kensington 561
music venues 564
nightlife 563
opera 564
performing arts 564
Prehistoric Park 562
Prince's Island 561
pubs 564
restaurants 563
Science Centre 561
St George's Island 562
Stampede 555
TELUS World of Science 561
theatre 564
transport, city 556
zoo 562
Cambridge Bay 942
Cameron Lake, BC 833
Cameron River Falls 935
Camp Mercier 304
Campbell River 852
camping 39
Campobello Island 410
campsites in BC 672
Canadian consulates 52
Canadian dollar 55
Canadian embassies 52
Canadian football 49

Canadian high commissions 52
Canadian Rockies, the 604–696
Canadian Rockies 607
Canmore 616–620
Canmore 617
Canmore Nordic Centre ....619, *Skiing and snowboarding* colour section
Canning 387
Cannington Manor........ 530
canoeing........48, 524, 594, *Wild Canada* colour section
Canol Heritage Trail...... 924
Canol pipeline.......890, 924
Canso Causeway 392
Cantons-de-l'Est 259–263
Canyon City.................. 898
Canyon Ste-Anne......... 303
Cap Chat 313
Cap Gaspé 315
Cap-aux-Meules........... 323
Cap-de-Bon-Désir 335, 336
Cape Blomidon 387
Cape Bonavista............ 470
Cape Breton Highlands National Park..... 394, *Wild Canada* colour section
Cape Breton Island 391–400
Cape Breton Island 391
Cape Enrage................. 421
Cape Merry National Historic Site............... 599
Cape North................... 395
Cape Onion 483
Cape Scott Provincial Park 858
Cape Spear 460
Cape Split.................... 387
Cape St Mary's Ecological Reserve..................... 464
Cap-Egmont, PEI 443
Capstick 395
Cap-Tourmente 303
car rental 34
Caraquet, NB................ 427
Carberry....................... 528
Carcross 902
Cardigan, PEI 440
Cardston...................... 552
Cariboo, the 801–804
Caribou, NS.........389, 430
caribou 969
Carleton....................... 321
Carmacks 907
Carr, Emily 89, 762
Cartier, Jacques ...318, 951
Cartwright, Lab............ 492
Cassiar 888
Cassiar, Stewart Highway the 886–889
Castle Hill National Historic Site 463
Castlegar 707
Cathedral Grove, BC 833
Cavendish, PEI 438
CBC 43
Cedar Dunes Provincial Park 443
cell phones 55
Central Ontario ... 158–173
Central Ontario 159
Chalfont Cove 200
Champlain Parkway 186
Champlain, Samuel de 153, 951
Channel-Port aux Basques 485
Chapel of the Mohawks, Her Majesty's Royal... 127
Chapman Lake 917
Charlevoix 327–332
Charlevoix Crater 330
Charlevoix, Traversée de 330
Charlottetown 431–436
Charlottetown 432
Charlottetown, NL 472
Chase, BC 737
Chatham, NB 426
Chemainus 827
Cherryville, BC............. 720
Chester, NS 372
Chesterfield Inlet 937
Chéticamp 393
Chic-Choc Mountains ... 314
Chicoutimi 337, 340
Chief Mountain Highway 613
Chilkoot Pass 896
Chilkoot Trail, the 896–897
China Beach Provincial Park 824
Chippawa 125
Christina Lake, BC 709
Churchill 597–602
Churchill Falls, Lab 498
Churchill River 594
Chute Montmorency..... 301
Chutes Jean-Larouse ... 303
Clayoquot Sound 839
Clear Creek Hot Springs 730
Clearwater Lake Provincial Park 597
Clearwater, BC 739
Clifton Hill 118
climate 12–14
climate change 28
Clinton 801
Cobalt 193
Cochrane 194
Cody Caves 711
Coldstream Valley, BC ... 719
Collingwood 148
Columbia Icefield 655
Columbia River Valley, The 699
Colville Lake 924
Comox Valley 852
Confederation Bridge, NB/PEI 430
Confederation Trail, PEI 431
consulates, Canadian..... 52
conversion table, metric 55
Cook, Captain James ... 749
Coppermine................. 943
Coquihalla Canyon Provincial Park........... 731
Coquihalla Highway 729
Coral Harbour 939
Corner Brook 484
Coronach 541
Cortes Island 853
costs 51
Côte-de-Beaupré 301
Côte-Nord 344–353
Cotes acadiennes......... 380
Coudres, Île aux 330
Cougar Creek 619
cougars 47
Courtenay 851
Cow Head, NL 479
Cowichan Lake 827
Cowichan Valley, The ... 827
Cranberry Junction....... 886
Cranberry Lakes 596
Cranberry Portage 597
Cranbrook, BC 705
Crawford Bay 710
credit cards 55
Creighton 595
Creston, BC 705
crime 52
Crowsnest Pass 552
Cupids 462
currency 55
customs 52
cycling 37
Cypress Hills Interprovincial Park 544–547
Cypress Hills Massacre 545

D

Dalvay, PEI 437
Dartmouth, NS 368
Dauphin, MB 568
Dawson City 909–915
Dawson Creek 592, 786, 889
Dawson Falls 741
Dease Lake 888
Death of General Wolfe 91,183
debit cards 55
Deer Island 411
Deer Lake, NL 475
Deh Cho Trail, the 925
Déline 924
Delkatla Wildlife Sanctuary 883
Della Falls 854
Dempster Highway, **the** 916–918
Dene, the 865
Denman Island 850
Desolation Sound Marine Provincial Park 788
Destruction Bay 906
Digby 381
Digby Gut, the 381
Digby Neck 382
Digby scallops 381
Dinosaur Provincial Park 548
Dinosaur Trail 549
dinosaurs, Royal Tyrrell Museum 549
disabilities, travellers with 58
Discovery Coast Passage 860
Discovery Harbour 151
distance chart 34–35
diving 145
Doaktown 426
Doi T'oh Territorial Park 924
Dolbeau 343
dollar, Canadian 55
Doukhobors ... 570, 707, 708
Dresden 138
drinking 42–43
driveaways 35
driving from the US 28
driving in Canada 32–34
driving laws 33
drugs 52
Drumheller 548
Duck Lake, SK 578, 579
Duck Mountain Provincial Park 569
Duncan 826
Dundurn Castle 113
Durrell 474
Dutch Creek Hoodoos ... 701
duty-free 53
Duu Guusd Tribal Park 883
Dyea, Alaska 896, 897

E

Eagle Plains 918
eagle, bald 790, 873
Earl Grey Pass 715
Earl's Cove 787
East Coast Trail, NL 460
East End, SK 543
East Point, PEI 441
Eastern Townships 259–263
Eastport, Maine 411
Echo Lake, SK 531
Echo Valley Provincial Park 531
EDMONTON 583–590
Edmonton 584
- accommodation 586
- addresses 583
- airport 585
- Alberta Legislative Building 587
- arrival 585
- Art Gallery of Alberta 587
- bars 590
- clubs 590
- Deep Sea Adventure 589
- drinking 589–590
- eating 589–590
- Edmonton Oilers 590
- festivals 585
- Fort Edmonton 588
- Francis Winspear Centre ... 589
- Galaxyland 589
- history 584
- ice hockey 590
- information 586
- Jubilee Auditorium 589
- Margaret Zeidler Star Theatre 589
- music 589
- Muttart Conservatory 587
- nightlife 589
- Old Strathcona 588
- Police Museum 587
- pubs 590
- restaurants 590
- Royal Alberta Museum 588
- TELUS World of Science ... 589
- transport, city 586
- West Edmonton Mall 589
- Whyte Avenue 588
- World Waterpark 589

Edmundston 408
Edson 591
Eldorado Creek 915
electricity 52
Elk Falls Provincial Park 854
Elk Island National Park 582
Elk Lakes Provincial Park 703
Elkford, BC 703
Elkwater, AB 546
Elora 129
embassies, Canadian 52
Emerald Lake (Yoho National Park) 680, 682
emergencies, medical 53
Engineer Creek 918
Englishman River Falls Provincial Park 832
Erie, Lake 133
exchange, currency 55

F

Fairbanks, Alaska 903
Fairmont Hot Springs ... 701
Falcon Lake, MB 522
Falkland, BC 736
farm vacations 39
Fathom Five National Marine Park 145
fauna and flora ..... 962–969, *Wild Canada* colour section
Faunique des Laurentides, Réserve 304
Fauquier 719
Fernie, BC ..... 703, *Skiing and snowboarding* colour section
ferries – to Alaska 875
ferries from the US 30
ferry companies 32
Ferryland 461
festival, Innu Nikamu 347
festivals 44–45
Field, BC 674
Fintry Provincial Park ... 724
fishing 48
Fishing Lakes, SK 530
Five Finger Rapids 907
Fjord du Saguenay 337
flights
- from Australia 27
- from Ireland 27
- from New Zealand 27
- from South Africa 27
- from the UK 27
- from the USA 27
- internal, general 32
- internal, in the NWT 903
- internal, in the Yukon 903
- internal, northern Canada 868

Flin Flon, MB 595

Floe Lake, Kootenay National Park 694
flora, fauna and ...962–969, *Wild Canada* colour section
Florencia Beach 843
Flores Island 841
Flowerpot Island 145
FLQ 214, 959
Flynn, Errol 763
folk music, Newfoundland 458
food 40–42
football, Canadian 49
footpaths, long distance 47
Forbidden Plateau 854
foreign exchange 55
Forestry Discovery Centre, BC 827
Forillon, Parc National de .... 315–317, *Wild Canada* colour section
Fort Battleford 581
Fort Beauséjour 424
Fort Calgary 561
Fort Carlton 579
Fort Dauphin 568
Fort Edmonton Park 588
Fort Erie 125
Fort Frederick, Kingston 169
Fort Garry, Lower 523
Fort George 123
Fort Good Hope 924
Fort Henry, Kingston 169
Fort La Reine, MB 527
Fort Louisbourg 400
Fort Macleod 551
Fort Malden 136
Fort McPherson 918
Fort Nelson 891
Fort Qu'Appelle 531
Fort Simpson 926
Fort Smith 930
Fort St John 891
Fort Steele Heritage Town 704
Fort Walsh 546
Fort Wellington 173
Fort Whoop-Up 550
Fort William 205
Forteau 488
Fortress Mountain 621
Fortune 464
Fox, Terry 201
Frances Lake, MB 522
Frank Slide 553
Franklin, John 943
Fraser Canyon 729
Fraser Valley, the 729–734
Fraser, Simon 732, 750
Fredericton 402–407
Fredericton 403
French Beach Provincial Park 824
French language 979–986
Friendly Cove, BC 855
Frobisher Bay 944
Frobisher, Martin 943
Fulford Harbour 820
Fundy Coast, the 409–423
Fundy National Park 420–421
Fundy Trail Parkway, NB 419
Fundy, Bay of 400
Fundy, Bay of, tidal bore 388

G

Gabriola Island 831
Gaelic Coast, The 396
Gaelic music, Cape Breton Island 392
Gagetown 407
Galena Bay 719
Galiano Island 821
Gallery of Canada, National 181–184
Gambo, NL 472
Gananoque, QC 172
Gander, NL 472
Gandll K'in Gwaay-yaay 885
Ganges 820
Garibaldi Provincial Park 790
gas 32
Gaspé 317
Gaspé Peninsula .... 308–323, *Wild Canada* colour section
Gaspésie, Parc national de la .... 314, *Skiing and snowboarding* colour section
Gatineau 186
Gatineau Park .... 186, *Skiing and snowboarding* colour section
geology, Canadian Rockies 608
Georgian Bay Islands National Park 156
Gibsons 787
Gimli 525
Gitanyow 873
Gîtes du Passant 38
Gitwangak 873
Gitxsan, The 873
Glace Bay 399
Glacier National Park 683–686
Glacier National Park 684
global warming 28
Goat Island 117
Godbout 345
Goderich 140
Gold River, BC 856
Golden, BC 682
Goldstream Provincial Park 826
Good Spirit Lake Provincial Park 571
Goods and Services Tax (GST) 51
Goose Bay 493
Goose Sanctuary, Alf Hole 523
Gordon River 848
Gore Bay 148
Gould, Glenn 84
Graham Island 881
grain elevators 569
Granby 259
Grand Bank 464
Grand Barachois, St-Pierre 468
Grand Beach Provincial Park 525
Grand Bruit 485
Grand Falls, NB 408
Grand Falls–Windsor, NL 475
Grand Forks, BC 709
Grand Harbour, Grand Manan 413
Grand Manan Island 411
Grand Marais, MB 525
Grand Pré National Historic Site 386
Grande Miquelon 467
Grande Prairie 592
Grands-Jardins, Parc national des 329
Grass River Provincial Park 596
Grassi Lakes 619
Grasslands National Park 541
Gravenhurst 160
Gray Creek 710
Great Bear Lake 923
Great Sand Hills, SK 544
Green Gables Heritage Site 438
Green Mountain Lookout 741

Green Park Shipbuilding Museum, PEI 443
Greenwich, PEI 436, 437
Gretzky, Wayne 125
Grey Owl 193, 580
Greyhound buses 31
Grice Bay 844
Grindstone Provincial Park 526
Grizzly Bear Sanctuary, Khuzeymateen 877
grizzly bears 924
Gros Morne National Park .... 476–480, *Wild Canada* colour section
Grosbeak Lake 933
Grosse-Île 326
Grosses-Coques 381
Grotto Canyon 619
Group of Seven 88, 89
GST 51
Gulf Islands Water Taxi 819
Gull Harbour, MB 526
Gwaii Haanas National Park Reserve 885

H

Hagensborg 802
Hague Lake Provincial Park 853
Haida Gwaii 878–886
Haida Heritage Site 885
Haida, the 879
Haines Junction 904
HALIFAX 360–370
Halifax 362
accommodation 363
airport 360
Alexander Keith's Brewery 367
Army Museum 364
arrival 360
Art Gallery of Nova Scotia 365
bars 369
bike rental 370
bookshops 370
cafés 368
Citadel, The 364
clubs 370
Dartmouth 368
drinking 368–370
eating 368–370
Fairview Lawn Cemetery 367
film 370
Grand Parade 365
Halifax Explosion, The 367
Historic Properties 366
information 361
internet access 370
Maritime Museum 366
music, classical 370
music, live 370
nightlife 369
Pier 21, 367
Province House 365
Quaker House 368
restaurants 368
St Paul's Church 365
theatre 370
Titanic, The 367
transport, city 363
waterfront, the 366
Hamilton 112–114
Happy Valley, Lab 493
Happy Valley, Sudbury 196
Harbour Grace 462
Harmonized Sales Tax (HST) 51
Harrington Harbour 351
Harris, Lawren 88, 89
Harrison Hot Springs 729
Hart River 917
Hartland 408
Hartley Bay 877
Hattie Cove 201
Hautes-Gorges, Parc national des 332
Havre-Aubert 326
Havre-St-Pierre 349
Hay River 928
Hazelton 873
Head-Smashed-In Buffalo Jump 551
health 53–54
Hearst, ON 198
Heart Island 172
Heart's Content 463
Hebron, Lab 498
Hecla Provincial Park ... 526
Hecla, MB 526
Hedley 728
Hell's Gate 733
Helliwell Bay Provincial Park 851
Helmcken Falls 741
Hermanville, PEI 441
Hermitage, NL 485
Hershel Island 919
Hesquiat Peninsula 841
high commissions, Canadian 52
High Level, AB 929
hiking .... 46–47, *Wild Canada* colour colour section
Banff 632–633
Bow Valley 641
Canol Heritage Trail 924
Charlevoix 330
Chilkoot Trail, The 896–897
Columbia Icefield 656
Confederation Trail, PEI ... 431
Deh Cho Trail 925
Doi T'oh Territorial Park ... 924
East Coast Trail 460
Georgian Bay Islands National Park 156
Glacier National Park 686
Jasper National Park 666
Kluane National Park 905
Kootenay National Park 692–695
Lake Louise 648
Lake Superior Provincial Park 200
Mount Revelstoke National Park 687
Mount Robson Provincial Park 672
Pukaskwa National Park 201–202
Strathcona Provincial Park854
Waterton Lakes National Park 614–616
Wells Gray Provincial Park 740–741
West Coast Trail, The ... 847–850
Whistler 798
Whitehorse 898
Yoho National Park ... 678–682
Hillcrest, AB 552
Hillside Beach, MB 525
Hinton, AB 591
history 949–961
Hlk'yah GaawGa 885
holidays, public 57
Holman 919, 923
Honey Harbour 155
Hope 731
Hopedale, Lab 497
Hopewell Rocks 422
Hornby Island 850
Horseshoe Bay 787
Horseshoe Falls 117
hostels 39
Hot Springs Cove 841
hotels 38
Hotspring Island 885
houseboating 738
Hudson, Henry 943
Hudson's Bay Company 952–953
Hull, Québec .... see Gatineau
Humber Valley, NL 484
Hunlen Falls 803
Huntsville 160
Huron Tract 141
Huron, Lake 140
Huronia Museum 152
Hutterites, the 544
Hyder 887

I

ice hockey 49

ice wine 124
iceberg-spotting, NL 474
Icefield Ranges 904
Icefields Parkway .... 652–658, *Wild Canada* colour section
Igloo church 920
Igluligaarjuk 937
Ikahuk 923
Ikaluktutiak 942
l'Île-Bonaventure-et-du-Rocher-Percé, Parc national de 319
Île aux Coudres 330
Île aux Marins, St-Pierre 467
Île d' Anticosti 352
Île d'Orléans 299
Île de la Grande-Entrée 326
Île du Cap-aux-Meules 323
Île du Havre-Aubert 326
Île du Havre-aux-Maisons 325
Île-d'Entrée 327
Îles-de-la-Madeleine 323–327
Îles-de-la-Madeleine boat trips 324
Indians, Plains, heritage centre 575
information, tourist 56
Ingalls Head, Grand Manan 413
Inglis 569
Ingonish 395
Ingonish Beach 386
Innu Nikamu festival 347
insect repellent 53
Inside Passage 860
insurance, travel 54
Interlake, MB 526
internet 54
Inuit, the 940–941
Inuvik 919–921
Invermere 700
Iqalugaarjuup Nunanga Territorial Park 938
Iqaluit 944
Iskut 888

J

Jacques-Cartier, Parc national de la 304
Jakeroy Glacier 619
Japanese internment centre 717
Jasper (town) 659–670
Jasper (town) 660
Jasper National Park 658–670
Jasper National Park ... 658
Jasper area 664
Jasper Tramway 663
Jesuits, the 153
John Hart Highway 889
Johnstown, ON 173
Jones Falls 171
Jonquière 341
Jordan River, BC 824
Juan de Fuca Provincial Park 825

K

K'uuna Llnagaay 885
Kagawong 148
Kalamalka Provincial Park 721
Kamloops 734–736
Kamouraska 307
Kananaskis Country 616–621
Kane, Paul 87
Kangiqtiniq 938
Kaslo 714
Kawkawa Lake 731
Kegaska 351
Kejimkujik National Park 377
Kelowna 722
Keno City, YT 908
Kenora 207
Kenosee Lake 530
Keremeos 728
kermode bear 877
Khuzeymateen Grizzly Bear Sanctuary 877
Kiche Manitou Lake 528
Kicking Horse .... 683 & *Skiing and snowboarding* colour section
Kikomun Creek Provincial Park 704
Killbear Provincial Park 158
Kimberley, BC .... 702 & *Skiing and snowboarding* colour section
Kimiwan Lake Bird Sanctuary 593
Kindersley Pass 695
King Solomon's Dome ... 915
King, William Lyon Mackenzie 185
King's Landing, NB 407
Kingston 165–170
Kingston 166
Kingston Mills 171
Kispiox 873
Kitchener 127
Kitikmeot 941–944
Kivalliq region 938
Klemtu 877
Klondike Gold Rush 908–909
Klondike Highway 906
Klondike River 908
Kluane National Park 904–906
Knowlton 260
Knox Mountain 724
Kokanee Creek Provincial Park 711
Kokanee Glacier Provincial Park 711
Kootenay Bay 710
Kootenay Crossing 694
Kootenay Lake 710
Kootenay National Park 689–696
Kootenay National Park 690
Kootenay National Park Hikes 692
Kootenay Pass 706
Kootenays, the 709–720
Kouchibouguac National Park 425
Krieghoff, Cornelius 87
Kugluktuk 943
Kwagiulth Cultural Centre 853

L

L'Anse au Claire 488
L'Anse au Loup 489
L'Anse aux Meadows 482
L'Anse-Amour 488
L'Anse-St-Jean 338
L'Étape 304
La Baleine, QC 330
La Malbaie 331
La Région Évangeline, PEI 442
La Romaine 351
La Ronge 594
Laberge, Lake 907
Labrador 486–500
Labrador 487
Labrador City 499
Labrador Straits, the 488
Lac La Ronge Provincial Park 594
Lac Memphrémagog 260
Lac Saint-Jean 341
lacrosse 50
Lady Franklin Rock 732
Ladysmith 828

Lake Athabasca............595
Lake Cowichan............827
Lake Erie........................133
Lake Huron..................140
Lake Laberge...............907
Lake Louise........642–652, *Skiing and snowboarding* colour section
Lake Louise Vicinity....643
Lake Louise Village.......645
Lake Louise Village 646–647
Lake Minnewanka........631
Lake O'Hara (Yoho National Park)...678–680
Lake O'Hara (Yoho National Park)...........679
Lake Osoyoos.............727
Lake Superior.....199–203
Lake Superior Provincial Park........................199
Lake Winnipeg.............521
Landing Provincial Park 543
Langlade, St-Pierre......468
language.............979–986
Larsen, Henry..............943
Laurentians, the...255–259
Laurentides Wildlife Reserve.....................304
Laurentides, Réserve Faunique des............304
Laval, Monseigneur......284
Le Bic...........................311
Le Massif...........296–297, *Skiing and snowboarding* colour section
Leacock, Stephen........154
Leamington.................136
legal drinking age..........43
Leitch Collieries...........552
Les Éboulements..........329
Les Escoumins.............336
Lesser Slave Lake Provinical Park...........592
Letete..........................411
Lethbridge, AB.............550
Lévis............................298
Lewis, Maud.........366, 382
Liard Highway, The.......925
Liard Hot Springs........892
Liebenthal....................544
Lillooet.........................800
Listuguj........................322
Little Current...............147
Little Manitou Lake, SK 571
Little Qualicum Falls Provincial Park...........832
Liverpool......................377
Lloydminster................582
lobster suppers, PEI....428, 437
Lockeport....................378
London, Jack........912, 913
London................131–133
London.........................132
Long Beach, Tofino, BC 841–844
long distance footpaths 47
Long Harbour, BC........820
Long Island, NS...........382
Long Range Mountains 480
Longue-Pointe-de-Mingan 348
Look-off Provincial Park 387
Lougheed Highway......729
Louisbourg..................399
Lourdes de Blanc-Sablon 488
Lower Fort Garry.........523
Lower Laurentians, The 252
Lower St Lawrence......305
Loyalists, the...............417
Lumby.........................720
Lund...........................788
Lunenburg..........374–377
Lunenburg..................374
Lussier Hot Springs......701
lyme disease.................53
Lytton, BC...................733

M

M'Chigeeng................147
Macdonald, John Alexander.................169
Mackenzie Highway, The 928
Mackenzie River...918, 919
Madeira Park...............787
Madeleine, Îles-de-la- 323–327
Madge Lake, SK...........570
magazines.....................43
Magdalen Islands 323–327
Magnetic Hill, NB........424
Magog........................260
Mahone Bay................373
Maid of the Mist boats 118
mail..............................54
Malaspina Galleries......831
Maligne Lake Road......663
Maligne Canyon...........664
Maligne Lake...............665
Malpeque Bay, PEI.......443
Manicouagan, The........344
Manitoba.....................503
Manitoba, Saskatchewan & Alberta..........504–505
Manitoba Stampede.....521
Manitoba Threshermen's Reunion & Stampede 527
Manitoba wilderness trips 524
Manitou Beach, SK......572
Manitoulin Island 146–148
Manitowaning..............146
Manning......................928
Manning Provincial Park 728
Manoir Papineau..........254
Manson's Landing........853
Maple Creek, SK..........544
maps.............................54
Marble Canyon, Kootenay National Park............693
Marble Mountain ski resort 484
March, Mary...............475
Margaree River Valley...392
Maritime Provinces, the 356–444
Maritime Provinces 358–359
Marten Mountain Lookout 593
Martin, Paul.................961
Martyrs' Shrine............154
Mary's Harbour, Lab.....491
Marystown, NL............464
Mashteuiatsh...............342
Massasauga rattlesnake 157
Masset.........................883
Matane........................313
Matapédia....................322
Mauricie, Parc National de la................................265
Max Lake, MB.............529
Mayer Lake, Haida Gwaii 883
Mayne Island...............823
Mayo, YT....................907
McCrae, John................91
McLean Steam Sawmill, BC..............................834
McLennan....................593
McMillan Provincial Park 833
Meares Island..............841
measurements...............55
Meat Cove...................395
media, the.....................43
medical emergencies.....53
Medicine Hat...............547
Meech Lake.................960

Menihek, Lab 499
Mennonite Heritage Village, MB 521
Mennonite Heritage Village, SK 543
Mennonites 128, 522
menu reader, French 984–986
Mercredi, Ovide 958
Merrickville 171
Metepenagiag Heritage Park, NB 426
Métis 506, 578, 952, 956, 957
metric conversions 55
Meziadin Junction 886
Midland 152
Midnight Dome 916
Miguasha Peninsula 321
Miguasha, Parc national de 321
mileage chart 34–35
Miles Canyon 896, 898
Mingan Archipelago National Park 349, 350, *Wild Canada* colour section
Mingan Coast, the 348
Minister's Island, NB 410
Minnedosa 566
Minnewanka, Lake 631
Miquelon, St-Pierre et 465–468
Miramichi City 426
Miramichi Valley, the 426
Miscouche, PEI 443
Missinipe 594
Mission 730
Mistaken Point Ecological Reserve, NL 461
Mistassini 343
mobile phones 55
Mockbeggar Plantation 471
Mohawks 125, 126, 214, 254, 958
Monashee Provincial Park 720
Moncton 423–424
Monseigneur Laval 284
Mont Albert 314
Mont Tremblant, Parc National du 257
Montague Harbour 821
Montcalm, General 288
Mont-Carmel, PEI 443
Monte Lake, BC 736
Montebello 254
Mont-Edouard 338
Montgomery, Lucy Maud 438, 439
Montmorency Falls 301
Mont-Orford, Parc National du 262
MONTRÉAL 215–251
Montréal 216
Montréal Métro 220
Montréal Downtown 232–233
Montréal Plateau Mont-Royal 238
Montréal Quartier Latin & the Village 246
Montréal Vieux-Montréal 225
accommodation 221–223
airport 218
Alouettes, the 250
arrival 218
Art Contemporain de Montréal, Musée d' 235
Banque de Montréal 226
bars 247–249
Basilique Notre-Dame 224
Basilique-Cathédrale Marie-Reine-du-Monde 233
Beaux Arts, Musée des 236
bike rental 220, 250
Biodôme 240
Biosphère 241
boat trips 230
boulevard St-Laurent 237
cafés 242
Calvet, Maison du 229
Cartier, Sir George-Étienne, Lieu historique national de 228
Cartier, Sir George-Étienne, monument 239
CCA Sculpture Gardens 234
Centaur Theatre 231
Centre Bell 233
Centre Canadien d'Architecture 234
Centre d'Histoire de Montréal 231
Histoire de Montréal, Centre d' 231
Youville Stables 231
Centre de Commerce Mondial 231
Centre des Sciences 230
Champ de Mars 227
Chapelle de Notre-Dame-de-Bonsecours 228
Château Ramezay Museum 228
Christ Church Cathedral 235
classical music 249
Claude Lafitte Art Gallery 236
Golden Square Mile 236
clubs 246–249
Cours Mont-Royal 234
dance 250
drinking 247
eating 242–246
festivals 218
film 250
gay and lesbian 248–249
hostels 222
Hôtel de Ville 227
ice hockey 233, 250
Île Notre-Dame 241
information 219
internet access 251
Jardin Botanique 241
Parc Jean-Drapeau 241
La Ronde 241
Lac aux Castors 239
Maison du Calvet 229
Maison Papineau 229
Maison Smith 239
Marché Bonsecours 229
McCord, Musée 237
McGill University 236
Métro 219
Mont Royal 239
Montréal Canadiens, the 233
Montréal Impact, the 250
Musée d'Archéologie et d'Histoire 230
Musée d'Art Contemporain de Montréal 235
Musée des Beaux Arts 236
Musée McCord 237
Musée Redpath 236
Musée Stewart 241
museum pass 223
Nelson Monument 227
nightlife 246–250
Notre-Dame, Basilique 224
opera 250
Oratoire St-Joseph 239
Palais de Justice 227
Parc Olympique 240
performing arts 249
Place d'Armes 224
Place d'Youville 230
Place de la Grande-Paix 230
Place des Arts 235
Place du Canada 233
Place Jacques-Cartier 227
Place Royale 230
Place Vauquelin 227
Plateau Mont-Royal 237
Quai Jacques-Cartier 230
Quai King-Edward 230
Quartier des Spectacles 235
Quartier Latin 237
Redpath, Musée 236
restaurants 243–246
Ritz-Carlton 236
rue Bonsecours 229
rue Notre-Dame 227
rue Prince-Arthur 237
rue Sherbrooke 235
rue St-Denis 237
rue Ste-Catherine 234
rue St-Jacques 226
rue St-Paul 228
rue St-Sulpice 226
Smith, Maison 239
sports, spectator 250
Square Dorchester 232
Square St-Louis 237
Square Victoria 232

St George's Anglican Church 233
Stade Olympique 240
Stewart, Musée 241
Stock Exchange 232
theatre 249
Tour de l'Horloge 229
transport, city 219, 220
Underground City, The 234
Vieux-Montréal 224
Vieux-Port 229
Mont-Sainte-Anne .... 296–297, 303, *Skiing and snowboarding* colour section
Mont-Saint-Pierre 315
Mont-Tremblant .... 257–259, *Skiing and snowboarding* colour section
Moore, Henry 89
moose 449, 965
Moose Factory Island 194
Moose Jaw 539–541
Moose Mountain Provincial Park 530
Moose Travel Network 36
Moosehide 916
Moosonee 194
Moraine Lake 647, 649–651
Moravian Brethren, Lab 497
Moresby Island 884
Morris, MB 521
mosquitoes 53
motels 38
Motherwell Homestead, SK 530
Mount Armstrong, BC 703
Mount Arrowsmith, BC 833
Mount Assiniboine Provincial Park 694
Mount Dawson 684
Mount Edziza Provincial Park 886
Mount Fernie Provincial Park 704
Mount Fitzwilliam 673
Mount Hays 878
Mount Logan 904
Mount Maxwell Provincial Park 821
Mount Norquay 634, *Skiing and snowboarding* colour section
Mount Rainey 887
Mount Revelstoke National Park 686–689
Mount Revelstoke National Park **687**
Mount Robson Provincial Park 671–673
Mount St Elias 904
Mountain Rapids 931
Mounties, the 536
Moyie 705
Moyie Lake 705
Mulroney, Brian 960
Muncho Lake 892
Murtle River 741
music, Newfoundland 458
muskeg 964
Muskoka Lakes, the 159–161
Muskrat Falls 495

N

Nachvak Fjord 498
Nahanni National Park Reserve 926
Naikoon Provincial Park 883
Nain, Lab 497
Nakiska 621
Nakusp 718
Nakusp Hot Springs 718
Nanaimo 828
Nancy Greene Provincial Park 709
Nancy Island Historic Site 148
Narcisse Wildlife Management Area 526
Natashquan 353
National Gallery of Canada 181–184
National Historic Sites 46
national parks .... 46, *Wild Canada* colour section
Needles, BC 719
Neepawa 565
Nelson, BC 712–714
Nelson, NB 426
New Bonaventure 469
New Brunswick 400–427
New Brunswick **401**
New Denver 717
New Glasgow, PEI 437
New Hazelton 873
New London, PEI 439
Newcastle Island 830
Newcastle, NB 426
Newfoundland .... 448–465 & 468–485
Newfoundland **450**
Newfoundland & Labrador 447–500
Newfoundland & Labrador **448**
Newfoundland folk music 458
Newman Sound 471
newspapers 43
NHL teams 50
Niagara Falls 114–119
Niagara Falls **115**
Niagara Glen Nature Area 120
Niagara Parks Botanical Gardens 120
Niagara Parkway 119
Niagara River Recreation Trail 119
Niagara-on-the-Lake 120–125
Niagara-on-the-Lake **121**
Nikkei Internment Memorial Centre 717
Ninstints 885
Nipigon 202
Nisga's Memorial Lava Bed Provincial Park 874
Nk'Mip Desert Culture Centre 727
Nopiming Provincial Park 523
Nordik Express ship 351
Normandin 343
Norman Wells 924
Norris Point, NL 478
Norstead 483
North Battleford 581
North Bay 192
North Cape, PEI 442
North Fork Pass 918
North Harbour, PEI 441
North Hatley 262
North Head, Grand Manan 412
North Pender Island 822
North Rustico 439
North Sydney, NS 398
North West Company 952
North West Mounted Police 536
North West River, Lab 495
North, the 864–946
North, the **866–867**
Northern Lights 351, 870, 894
Northern Ontario 189–207
Northern Ontario **190–191**
Northern Ranger ferry 497
Northwest Passage, the 943
Northwest Rebellion, the 578
Northwest Territories 865, 869

Nottawasaga Bay...142, 148
Nova Scotia......... 358–400
Nova Scotia................360
Nunavut.............. 936–941
Nuntatsiavut, Lab.........496
Nuu-chah-nulth whale hunts........................846

O

O'Hara, Lake (Yoho National Park)....678–680
O'Keefe Ranch, Historic 721
Oak Hammock Marsh, MB 524
Oak Island, NS 372
Ogilvie Mountains 916, 917
Ogopogo 720
Oil Museum of Canada 139
Oil Springs..................139
Ojibwa 146
Oka......................253, 958
Oka, Parc National d'...254
Okanagan, the 720–727
Okeover Provincial Park 788
Oktoberfest.................128
Old Fort Erie 125
Old Fort William...........206
Ontario................ 106–208
Ontario 108–109
Ontario wines 124
Ontario, Central...158–173
Ontario, Central 159
Ontario, Northern 189–207
Ontario, Northern...190–191
Ontario, Southwest 111–158
Ontario, Southwest......111
Orford 262
Orillia 154
Orwell Corner Historic Village, PEI................440
Osoyoos 727
OTTAWA 174–189
Ottawa................. 176–177
accommodation............. 178
airport............................ 175
arrival............................ 175
Aviation Museum, Canada 185
bars 188
bike rental 189
boat trips........................ 181
bookshops 189
Bytown Museum............. 181
Byward Market............... 187
cafés............................... 187
Canadian War Museum 184
Canadien Civilisations, Musée des.............................. 186
Champlain Parkway......... 186
Changing of the Guard 180
cinema 188
clubs 188
Confederation Square...... 181
dance 188
drinking...................187–189
eating 187–189
festivals 174
Gatineau......................... 186
Gatineau Park 186
history 175
ice hockey...................... 189
information..................... 175
internet access................ 189
Laurier House................. 184
Major's Hill Park 181
Mint, Royal Canadian....... 185
Musée Canadien des Civilisations................ 186
music, classical............... 188
National Arts Centre........ 181
National Gallery.........181–184
Notre Dame Basilica 184
National War Memorial 181
Nepean Point 181
nightlife.......................... 188
opera.............................. 188
Parliament Buildings 179
Parliament Hill 179
Peace Tower 180
performing arts 188
pubs 188
restaurants 188
Rideau Canal................... 181
Rideau Falls 185
Rideau Hall..................... 185
Rockcliffe Parkway 185
Royal Canadian Mint........ 185
Senators, the.................. 189
Sparks Street 181
Sussex Drive 181
theatre 188
transport, city................. 177
Ouimet Canyon Provincial Park 202
Outaouais 251
outdoor activities ....46–49, *Wild Canada* colour section
Owen Sound................ 143

P

P'tit Train du Nord bicycle trail...........................257
Pachena Bay 848
Pacific Rim National Park 835–850
Pacific Rim National Park 835
package holidays 30
Paint Pots....................693
Pangnirtung 945
Panorama Mountain Village ....701, *Skiing and snowboarding* colour section
Panther Falls................655
Papineau, Manoir 254
Paradise Valley 651
parking..........................33
parks, national.......46, *Wild Canada* colour section
parks, provincial ....46, *Wild Canada* colour section
Parksville 831
Parry Sound 157
Parti Québécois...........959
passport control 52
Patriotes 253
Paul Lake Provincial Park 735
Paulatuk..............919, 922
Peace River 930
Peggy's Cove 371
Prince Edward Island 428–444
Prince Edward Island...429
Pelee Island 137
Pelican Rapids 931
Pelly Crossing..............907
Pemberton...................800
Penetanguishene..........149
Penney Ice Cap............945
Penticton 725
Percé 318
Peter Loughead Provincial Park 621
Petite Miquelon, St-Pierre 468
Petroglyph Provincial Park 829, 830
petrol 32
Petrolia 139
Peyto Lake 654
phones...........................55
picnics, bears and 625
Pictou 389
Pike Island 877
Pinery Provincial Park 140
pingos..........................922
Pink Mountain 891
Pinware River Provincial Park 489
pipeline, Canol......890, 924
Placentia Harbour.........463
Plaines d'Abraham 288
Plains Indians 506, 575
Plains of Abraham........288
Plaisance 255

Plaisance, Parc National de 255
Point Pelee National Park .... 137, *Wild Canada* colour section
Point Wolfe, NB 421
Pointe de l'Eglise..........381
Pointe-à-la-Croix 322
Pointe-à-la-Garde.........322
Pointe-au-Père 312
Pointe-au-Pic................331
Pointe-aux-Loups.........325
Pointe-aux-Outardes, Parc Nature de..................345
Pointe-Bleue.................342
Pointe-de-l'Est..............326
Pointe-des-Monts.........346
Pointe-Taillon, Parc de la 344
poison ivy 54
Polar Bear Express.......194
polar-bear watching .....600–601, *Wild Canada* colour section
Porcupine Strand, Lab...493
Port Alberni 833
Port Arthur....................205
Port au Choix 480
Port Carling 160
Port Clements 883
Port Hardy 858
Port Hastings.................392
Port Hope Simpson, Lab 491
Port McNeill...................856
Port Renfrew 824
Port Rexton 470
Port Royal National Historic Site 385
Port Severn 155
Port Stanley...................133
Portage La Prairie..........527
Port-Cartier....................346
Port-Menier 352
Portugal Cove South.....461
post 54
Powell River..................787
Prairie Provinces, the 502–602
Prescott 173
price codes, accommodation...........38
prices..............................51
primitive camping...........40
Prince Albert..................593
Prince Albert National Park................. 579–580
Prince Edward Island National Park.............436
Prince George..... 869–871
Prince of Wales' Fort....599
Prince Rupert...... 874–878
Princess Royal Island 877
provincial parks......46, *Wild Canada* colour section
Provincial Sales Tax (PST) 51
public holidays 57
Pukaskwa National Park 201–202
Purcell Mountains.........699
Purcell Wilderness Conservancy Provincial Park 701
Pure Lake Provincial Park 883

Q

Qamanit'uaq.................939
Qaummaarviit Territorial Historic Park..............945
Qu'Appelle River Valley 530
Quadra Island 853
Qualicum Beach 832
Quatsino Cave...............856
QUÉBEC CITY..... 270–296
Québec City..................272
Québec, Vieux 280
accommodation.............. 275
airport............................ 274
Anglican Cathedral of the Holy Trinity 284
arrival............................. 274
Artillery Park.................. 286
bars 294
Basilique-Cathédrale Notre-Dame de Québec 283
Basse-Ville 277
Battlefields Park............. 288
cafés.............................. 291
Cartier-Brébeuf National Historic Site 290
Cathedral of the Holy Trinity 284
Chalmers-Wesley United Church 286
Chapelle des Jésuites...... 286
Château Frontenac 281
Citadelle 287
classical music................ 295
clubs 294
Couvent des Ursulines..... 285
Discovery Pavilion............ 289
drinking 293–294
eating 291–293
Édifice Price 284
Église Notre-Dame-des-Victoires...........................279
Faubourg St-Jean-Baptiste 287
festivals.......................... 274
funicular 277
Grande-Allée................... 288
Haute-Ville...................... 281
history 273
Hôtel Clarendon 284
Hôtel de Ville................... 284
Hôtel du Parlement.......... 288
information...................... 274
Inuit Art, Brosseau collection of.................................. 290
Jardin des Gouverneurs... 285
Maison Estèbe 279
Maison Hazeur 279
Maison Jacquet 285
Maison Kent.................... 285
Maison Jean-Alfred Moisan 287
Maison Louis-Jolliet......... 277
Maison Maillou................ 281
Martello Tower 289
Musée de l'Amerique Française 283
Musée de la Civilisation... 279
Musée des Ursulines 285
Musée du Fort................. 281
Musée National des Beaux-Arts du Québec 289
music venues.................. 295
nightlife........................... 293
Observatoire.................... 288
Palais de Justice.............. 281
Parc de L'Esplanade 286
Parc des Champs-de-Bataille 288
Parc du Cavalier du Moulin 286
Parc Montmorency 282
parking 274
Parliament Buildings 288
Pavillon Jérôme-Deners... 284
performing arts 294
Place d'Armes................. 281
Place de Paris 279
Place Royale 278
Plains of Abraham............ 288
Porte Prescott.................. 282
Porte St-Jean................... 286
Protestant Burying Ground 287
Quartier du Petit-Champlain 277
Maison Chevalier 278
restaurants 291
rue des Remparts 283
rue du Petit-Champlain.....277
rue du Trésor................... 282
Sanctuaire Notre Dame du Sacré-Coeur 286
Séminaire de Québec 283
St-Jean-Baptiste.............. 287
Terrasse Dufferin 282
theatre 295
cinemas........................... 295
transport, city.................. 275
Vieux-Port 281
Vieux-Québec 277
Québec, history....213, 960
Québec, Northern 304–354
Québec, Northern 270–271

Québec, Southwest 251–266
Québec, Southwest.....212
Québécois French 979–986
Queen Charlotte Islands 878–886
Queen Charlotte (town)...881
Queenston....................120
Queenston Heights Park 120
Quesnel 803
Quidi Vidi, NL 457
Quinsam Salmon Hatchery 852
Quirpon Lighthouse......483
Quw'utsun Cultural Centre 826

R

Rabbit Blanket Lake.....200
radio 43
Radium Hot Springs .... 695, *Wild Canada* colour section
rafting, whitewater........ see whitewater rafting
rail contacts....................31
rail from the US 29
rail in Canada 36
railroads
- Algoma Central Railway... 198
- history 514
- Polar Bear Express 194
- Québec North Shore & Labrador 486
- Rocky Mountaineer.......... 784
- routes, tickets and passes 29, 31, 36
- White Pass & Yukon Railroad 897

Ramea 485
Random Passage, NL 469
Rankin Inlet...................938
Rathtrevor Beach Provincial Park 831
rattlesnake, Massasauga 157
RCMP 536
Rebecca Spit Provincial Park 853
Rebellion of 1837... 66, 253
Red Bay, Lab 490
Red River corridor 521
Red Rock Parkway......613, 614, 615
Redberry Lake World Biosphere Reserve 581
REGINA................ 531–539
Regina..........................533
- accommodation............... 533
- airport............................... 532
- Antique Mall 534
- arrival................................ 532
- bookshops 539
- cafes.................................. 538
- Cathedral Village.............. 534
- drinking 537–538
- Dunlop Art Gallery........... 534
- eating 537–538
- festivals 538
- Government House.......... 537
- history 531
- information 532
- Legislative Building 535
- MacKenzie Art Gallery 535
- Mounties, the 536
- music................................. 537
- nightlife............................. 537
- Plains Museum 534
- RCMP Heritage Centre 536
- restaurants 538
- Royal Saskatchewan Museum 535
- Saskatchewan Science Centre 535
- theatre.............................. 537
- transport, city................... 531
- Wascana Centre Park 534
- Wascana Place 535

Rennell Sound 881
Rennie 523
rentals, vehicle................34
repellent, insect 53
Restigouche, La Bataille-de-la 322
Revelstoke....................688
Revelstoke Dam 689
Reversing Falls Rapids, NB 417
Richardson Mountains...918
Rideau Canal, the.........171
Riding Mountain National Park 566
Riel, Louis....508, 517, 518, 535, 578, 956,957
Rigolet, Lab 497
Rimouski.......................311
Rivière-du-Loup 308–310
Rivière-Éternité.....337, 338
Robert Campbell Highway 907
Roberval 342
Robinson's Island, PEI 437
Rock River....................918
Rockies geology...........608
Rockies, Canadian 604–696
Rockies, Canadian 607
Rockport.......................172
Rocky Harbour, NL 477, 478
rodeo 521, 527, 555
Roderick Haig-Brown Provincial Park...........738
Rogers Pass 685
Rollo Bay, PEI...............441
Roosevelt Campobello International Park 411
Roosevelt, F. D. 409, 410
Rose Blanche 485
Rossland, BC 709
Rossport.......................202
Royal Botanical Gardens 113
Royal Canadian Mounted Police.........................536
Royal Tyrrell Museum...548, 549
Ruckle Provincial Park ...821
Rustico Bay 436
RV rental 34
Ryan Premises National Historic Site 470

S

Sachs Harbour 919, 923
safety, personal 52
Saguenay............ 333–344
Saguenay, Fjord du 337
Saguenay, Parc du 337
Saguenay-St-Laurent, Parc Marin du 337
Sahtu, the.....................923
Saint Ann, PEI 437
Saint John River Valley, NB 407
Saint John, NB.... 414–419
Saint John, NB............415
Saint-Aimé-des-Lacs....332
Sainte-Marie among the Hurons 153
Saint-Félicien................343
Saint-Gédéon 342
Saint-Joseph-de-la-Rive 330
Saint-Prime..................343
Saint-Siméon................331
Salliq............................939
Salmo 706
Salmon Arm, BC 738
Salmon Hatchery, Quinsam 852
Salmon River Interpretive Centre, Big, NB 419
salmon, Atlantic............426
salmon, Pacific 737
Salt Spring Island 820
Saltery Bay Provincial Park 787
Salty Bear Adventure Travel 36

Sambaa Deh Territorial Park 928
Sandon 716
Sandspit 884
Sapp, Allen 582
Sarnia 139
Saskatchewan 503
Manitoba, Saskatchewan & Alberta 504–505
Saskatchewan Crossing 654
Saskatoon 572–577
Saskatoon 573
Saskatoon berry pie 576
Saturna Island 823
Sault Ste Marie 197–199
scallops, Digby 381
Sceptre, SK 544
Schoen Lake Provincial Park 856
Schwatka Lake 898
Scots Bay 387
Sea to Sky Highway 788
Seal Cove, Grand Manan 413
Secord, Laura 120
seigneurial system 306
Seigneurie de Terrebonne 264
Sept-Îles 346
Service, Robert 912, 913
Severn Sound 149–156
Severn Sound 150
SGang Gwaay 879, 885, 889
Shames Mountain 874
Shannon Falls Provincial Park 789
Shaw Festival, the 122
Shediac 425
Sheep Mountain 906
Sheguiandah 147
Shelburne 379
Sherbrooke, NS 390
Sherbrooke, QC 263
Shrewsbury, ON 133
Shuswap Lake 738
Shuswap, the 737–739
Sibley Peninsula 202
Sicamous 738
Sign Post Forest 894
Silver Star Mountain Resort ....721, *Skiing and snowboarding* colour section
Silver Trail, YT 907
Sinclair Pass 695
Sitting Bull, Chief 92, 536, 537
Skagway, Alaska 875, 896, 897
Skedans 885
Skeena Valley, The 873
Skidegate 882
skiing ....48, *Skiing and snowboarding* colour section
ski resorts ....see *Skiing and snowboarding* colour section
Skoki Valley 649
Slave Lake 592
Sleeping Beauty Mountain 881
Sleeping Giant Provincial Park 202
Slocan 717
Slocan Valley 717
Smallwood, Joseph 472
Smelt Bay Provincial Park 853
Smithers 872
Smokey Mountain, Lab 499
snakes 47
snowboarding ....48, *Skiing and snowboarding* colour section
snowfall 14
Sointula 858
Soo, the 197
Sooke 824
Souris, MB 529
Souris, PEI 440
South Gut St Ann's 396
South Pender Island 822
Southern Gulf Islands, the 819–825
Southwest Head, Grand Manan 413
Southwest Ontario 111–158
Southwest Ontario 111
Southwest Québec 251–266
Southwest Québec 212
Spahats Falls 741
Sparwood, BC 703
Spatsizi Plateau Wilderness Park 886
Spiral Tunnels 675
spirit bear 877
sports, spectator 49
Spray Valley Provincial Park 619
Sproat Lake Provincial Park 835
Spruce Woods Provincial Park 528
Squalix 738, 789
Squamish Spit 790
St Andrews 409
St Anthony 481
St Augustine, QC 351
St Bride's 464
St Elias Mountains 904
St Jacobs 128
ST JOHN'S, NL 450–459
St John's, NL 452
accommodation 453
airport 451
Anglican Cathedral 454
arrival 451
bars 459
Basilica, Catholic 455
boat trips 453
bookshops 459
Cabot Tower 457
cafés 458
Cathedral, Anglican 454
Catholic Basilica 455
cinema 459
Colonial Building 455
Commissariat House 455
Courthouse 454
drinking 457–459
eating 457–459
folk music 458
Government House 455
Harbourside Park 454
information 451
Johnson Geo Centre 456
music, live 459
Newfoundland 454
nightlife 459
pubs 459
Quidi Vidi 457
restaurants 458
Rooms, The 455
Signal Hill 456
theatre 459
tours, guided 453
transport, city 451
St Lawrence River, upper 171
St Lawrence Seaway 171
St Martins, NB 419
St Peter's Bay, PEI 437
Stampede, Calgary 555
Stampede, Manitoba 521
Stampede, Manitoba Threshermen's Reunion & 527
Stanhope Beach, PEI 437
Stanley Glacier 693
St-Bernard, QC 330
Steady Brook Falls, NL 484
Ste-Anne-de-Beaupré 302, 335
Ste-Anne-des-Monts 313
Ste-Famille 300
Ste-Flavie 312
Steinbach 521
Ste-Monique 344
Ste-Pétronille 300
Ste-Rose-du-Nord 339

St-Eustache.....252
Stewart.....887
Stewart Crossing.....907
Stewart-Cassiar Highway, the.....886–889
St-François.....300
St-Jean, QC.....300
St-Jean-Port-Joli, QC.....306
St-Jovite.....257
St-Laurent.....300
St-Louis, QC.....330
Stone Mountain Provincial Park.....892
Stoneham.....296–297, *Skiing and snowboarding* colour section
Stowe, Harriet Beecher.....138
St-Pierre et Miquelon.....465–468
St-Pierre, QC.....301
Stratford.....129
Stratford Festival.....130
Strathcona Provincial Park.....854
St-Roch-des-Aulnaies.....307
St-Sauveur-des-Monts.....255
student accommodation.....39
Sturdies Bay.....821
Sudbury.....195–197
Summerside, PEI.....442
Summit Lake.....718
Sun Peaks Resort.....736, *Skiing and snowboarding* colour section
Sunshine Coast, the.....785–788
Sunshine Meadows.....639
Sunshine Village.....635, *Skiing and snowboarding* colour section
Sunwapta Falls.....656
Superior, Lake.....199–203
surfing.....840
Sweetgrass Station.....933
Swift Current, SK.....543
Sydney, NS.....397

T

T'aanuu Llnagaay.....885
Tablelands, NL.....479
Tachal Dhal.....906
Tadoussac.....333–336
Tage Cho Hudan Centre.....907
Tahsis.....855, 856
Takhini Hot Springs.....907
taxes.....51
Taylor Highway.....906
Tecumseh.....136
Telegraph Cove.....856
Telegraph Creek.....888
telephone numbers, useful.....55, 56
Temagami.....192
temperatures, conversion.....55
Terra Nova National Park.....471
Terrace, Skeena Valley.....873
Teslin.....894
Tete-à-la-Beleine.....351
Tetsa River Regional Park.....892
The Pas.....596
Thetis Lake Regional Park.....826
Thirty Thousand Islands.....152, 157
Thompson, MB.....597
Thomson, Tom.....88, 89
Thorsen Creek Petroglyphs.....802
Thousand Faces, Valley of a.....856
Thousand Islands Parkway.....172
Thousand Islands, the.....172
Thunder Bay.....203–207
Thunder Bay.....204
tidal bore, Bay of Fundy.....388
tidal bore, Moncton.....424
Tikirarjuaq.....937
time zones.....55
tipping.....41
Titanic.....366, 367
Tlell.....882
Toad River.....892
Tobermory.....145
Tofino.....837–839
Tok, Alaska.....903
Tombstone Mountain Territorial Park.....917
Top of the World Provincial Park.....701
Top of the World Highway.....916
Torngat Mountains National Park.....498
TORONTO.....63–104
Toronto, Greater.....64–65
Toronto Downtown & Waterfront.....72–73
Toronto Uptown.....74–75
- accommodation.....71
- AGO.....86
- airports.....67, 68
- arrival.....67
- Argonauts, the
- Art Gallery of Ontario.....86
- ballet.....102
- Banking District, The.....79
- bars.....100
- Bata Shoe Museum.....93
- Beach, the.....76
- Blue Jays, the.....102
- bookshops.....103
- Brookfield Place.....82
- Cabbagetown.....76
- cafés.....98
- Campbell House.....85
- Casa Loma.....94
- CBC Centre.....80
- Centre Island.....96
- Chinatown.....76, 90
- cinemas.....102
- City Hall.....83
- classical music.....102
- clubs.....100
- CN Tower.....77
- Dinosaurs, Age of.....92
- Distillery District.....83
- drinking.....98–100
- eating.....98–100
- Eaton Centre.....83
- Elgin Theatre & Winter Garden.....85
- ferries.....96
- festivals.....67
- Fort York.....81
- Gardiner Museum.....93
- Gay Village, The.....76
- Hanlan's Point.....96
- Harbourfront Centre, The.....95
- Hart House.....91
- history.....65
- Hockey Hall of Fame.....81
- ice hockey.....102
- information.....69
- Inuit Art, Toronto Dominion Gallery of.....79
- Kensington Market.....76, 90
- Lake Ontario.....95
- Little Italy.....76
- Little Portugal.....76
- Maple Leafs, the.....102
- markets.....82
- music venues.....100
- music, classical.....102
- Nathan Phillips Square.....83
- neighbourhoods.....76
- nightlife.....100
- Old City Hall.....83
- Ontario Legislative Assembly.....90
- Ontario Science Centre.....97
- opera.....102
- Osgoode Hall.....85
- Power Plant Contemporary Art Gallery.....96
- Queen Street West.....76
- restaurants.....98–100
- Rogers Centre.....78
- Roy Thomson Hall.....80
- Royal Bank Plaza.....79
- Royal Ontario Museum.....91

Sharp Centre for Design 89
SkyDome 78
Spadina House 95
spectator sports 102
St Andrew's Church 80
St James Anglican Cathedral 82
St Lawrence District 82
St Lawrence Hall 82
St Lawrence Market 82
streetcars 70
student rooms 76
subway 70
taxis 70
theatre 102
Toronto Dominion Centre 79
Toronto Dominion Gallery of Inuit Art 79
Toronto International Film Festival 67
Toronto Islands 96
transport, city 69
TTC 69
Union Station 68, 78
University of Toronto 91
vintage fashion 85
Ward's Island 96
waterfront, the 95
West Queen West 76
Winter Garden, Elgin Theatre & 85
Yorkville 76
zoo 97
tourist information 56
Tow Hill, Haida Gwaii 884
Tracadie Bay 437
train companies 31
trains from the US 29
trains in Canada 36
Trans-Canada Highway, Winnipeg to Regina 526–531
Trans-Labrador Highway 489
travel agents 30
travel clinics 53
travel insurance 54
travellers with disabilities 58
Traversée de Charlevoix 330
Trent-Severn Waterway 155
T-Rex Discovery Centre, SK 543
Tribune Bay, BC 850
Trinity 468
Trois-Pistoles 310
Trois-Rivières 264
Trout River Pond 479
Trudeau, Pierre 959
Truro 388
Tsiigehtchic 918
Tuktoyaktuk 919, 922
Tuktut Nogait National Park .... 922, *Wild Canada* colour section
Tulita 924
Turtle Mountain Provincial Park 529
TV 43
Tweedsmuir Provincial Park 802, 803, 872
Twillingate 473
Twin Falls Territorial Park 928
Tyne Valley, PEI 443
Tyrrell Museum, Royal 548, 549

U

U'Mista Cultural Centre 857
Ucluelet 844
Ukrainians in MB 568
Ukranian Cultural Heritage Village 582
Ulukhakok 919
Uluqsaqtuuq 923
Uncle Tom's Cabin Historic Site 138
Underground Railroad .. 138
United Empire Loyalists, the 417
Upper Canada Village ... 173

V

Vadzaih Van Tshik 918
Val Marie 542
Val-David 256
Valemount 742
Valhalla Provincial Park 717
Val-Jalbert 342
Valley of a Thousand Faces 856
VANCOUVER 747–784
Vancouver, central 752–753
Vancouver, greater 748
accommodation 756–760
airport 750
Aquarium 766
arrival 750
Art Gallery 761
bars 780
beach, Kitsilano 769
bike rental 783
Blue Grouse Lake 772
cafés 775
Canada Place 761
Capilano River Regional Park 773
Chinatown 763
cinema 783
clubs 781
Cypress Provincial Park ... 774
dance 783
downtown 761
Dr Sun Yat-Sen Garden ... 764
erinking 775–781
eating 775–781
Ecology Centre 773
Expo site 764
ferries 755
festivals 782
film 783
Gastown 762
gay and lesbian scene 782
Granville Island 767
Grouse Mountain 772
Harbour Centre Building 761
Heritage Harbour 769
history 749
information 751
Kitsilano 769
Lighthouse Park 774
Little Italy 775
Lonsdale Quay 771, 772
Lost Lagoon 765
Lower Seymour Conservation Reserve 774
Lumberman's Arch 766
Lynn Canyon Park 773
Maple Tree Square 762
Maritime Museum 769
Mount Seymour Provincial Park 774
Museum of Anthropology 770
music, live 781
nightlife 781
Nitobe Memorial Garden 771
pubs 780–781
restaurants 775–780
Robson Street 761
Sam Kee building 764
Science World 764
SeaBuses 755
Seymour Conservation Reserve, Lower 774
Siwash Rock 766
SkyTrain 750, 756
Space Centre, H.R. MacMillan 769
Stanley Park 765
Sun Yat-Sen Garden, Dr ... 764
taxis 784
theatre 783
transport, city 754–756
Vancouver Art Gallery 761
Vancouver Lookout 774
Vancouver Museum 768
Vancouver Police Museum 763
Vanier Park 768
Yaletown 766
Vancouver and Vancouver Island 744–862
Vancouver and Vancouver Island 745